GEOGRAPHICAL DISTRIBUTION
OF FINANCIAL FLOWS
TO DEVELOPING COUNTRIES

◆

RÉPARTITION GÉOGRAPHIQUE
DES RESSOURCES FINANCIÈRES
MISES A LA DISPOSITION
DES PAYS EN DÉVELOPPEMENT

DISBURSEMENTS
COMMITMENTS
ECONOMIC INDICATORS

VERSEMENTS
ENGAGEMENTS
INDICATEURS ÉCONOMIQUES

1983/1986

ORGANISATION FOR ECONOMIC CO-OPERATION AND DEVELOPMENT

ORGANISATION DE COOPÉRATION ET DE DÉVELOPPEMENT ÉCONOMIQUES

Pursuant to article 1 of the Convention signed in Paris on 14th December, 1960, and which came into force on 30th September, 1961, the Organisation for Economic Co-operation and Development (OECD) shall promote policies designed:

- to achieve the highest sustainable economic growth and employment and a rising standard of living in Member countries, while maintaining financial stability, and thus to contribute to the development of the world economy;
- to contribute to sound economic expansion in Member as well as non-member countries in the process of economic development; and
- to contribute to the expansion of world trade on a multilateral, non-discriminatory basis in accordance with international obligations.

The original Member countries of the OECD are Austria, Belgium, Canada, Denmark, France, the Federal Republic of Germany, Greece, Iceland, Ireland, Italy, Luxembourg, the Netherlands, Norway, Portugal, Spain, Sweden, Switzerland, Turkey, the United Kingdom and the United States. The following countries became Members subsequently through accession at the dates indicated hereafter: Japan (28th April, 1964), Finland (28th January, 1969), Australia (7th June, 1971) and New Zealand (29th May, 1973).

The Socialist Federal Republic of Yugoslavia takes part in some of the work of the OECD (agreement of 28th October, 1961).

En vertu de l'article 1er de la Convention signée le 14 décembre 1960, à Paris, et entrée en vigueur le 30 septembre 1961, l'Organisation de Coopération et de Développement Économiques (OCDE) a pour objectif de promouvoir des politiques visant :

- à réaliser la plus forte expansion de l'économie et de l'emploi et une progression du niveau de vie dans les pays Membres, tout en maintenant la stabilité financière, et à contribuer ainsi au développement de l'économie mondiale ;
- à contribuer à une saine expansion économique dans les pays Membres, ainsi que non membres, en voie de développement économique ;
- à contribuer à l'expansion du commerce mondial sur une base multilatérale et non discriminatoire conformément aux obligations internationales.

Les Pays membres originaires de l'OCDE sont : la République Fédérale d'Allemagne, l'Autriche, la Belgique, le Canada, le Danemark, l'Espagne, les Etats-Unis, la France, la Grèce, l'Irlande, l'Islande, l'Italie, le Luxembourg, la Norvège, les Pays-Bas, le Portugal, le Royaume-Uni, la Suède, la Suisse et la Turquie. Les pays suivants sont ultérieurement devenus Membres par adhésion aux dates indiquées ci-après : le Japon (28 avril 1964), la Finlande (28 janvier 1969), l'Australie (7 juin 1971) et la Nouvelle-Zélande (29 mai 1973).

La République socialiste fédérative de Yougoslavie prend part à certains travaux de l'OCDE (accord du 28 octobre 1961).

TABLE OF CONTENTS — TABLE DES MATIÈRES

SECTION A

Summary Tables   **Tableaux récapitulatifs**

**Tables for Individual Recipient
Countries and Territories**

**Tableaux par pays
et territoires bénéficiaires**

Developing Countries and Territories Classified as:

Groupes des pays et territoires en développement :

SECTION C

Annex   **Annexe**

Notes: The symbol in the tables:

    —   (or a blank space) means nil, not available or not applicable;

    0.0   less than half the smallest unit shown.

    ..   the sum of the components is not shown because it is incomplete.

Notes :   Signification des signes utilisés dans les tableaux :

    —   (ou un espace blanc) signifie néant, non disponible ou non applicable ;

    0.0   moins de la moitié du plus petit chiffre indiqué ;

    ..   la somme des composantes étant incomplète, aucun chiffre n'est donné.

INTRODUCTION

1. This report, the eighth presenting the volume and sources of the external financial resources provided to individual developing countries and territories contains detailed data on the geographical distribution of:

- Net and gross disbursements,
- Commitments and
- Terms

for over 100 developing countries for 1983, 1984, 1985 and 1986 with background economic data to provide perspective in interpreting the resource flow information for each country. The aim has been to achieve, within the compass of two pages, a comprehensive presentation of the external financing of each country shown.

2. The data show the transactions of each recipient country with[1]:

i) DAC Member countries (individually or as a group);
ii) Multilateral agencies (individually or as a group);
iii) Members of the Organisation of Petroleum Exporting Countries (OPEC) as a group, and of the Members of the Council for Mutual Economic Assistance (CMEA) as a group.

The Member countries of the OECD Development Assistance Committee for which data are presented are: Australia, Austria, Belgium, Canada, Denmark, Finland, France, the Federal Republic of Germany, Italy, Japan, the Netherlands, New Zealand, Norway, Sweden, Switzerland, the United Kingdom and the United States. Data for the Commission of the European Communities, which is also a Member of the DAC, are included under "multilateral agencies". A further separate line (EEC + Members) gives the data for flows from the EEC as an institution and its DAC Member countries combined. The data on financial flows from multilateral sources cover the World Bank, the International Finance Corporation (IFC), the International Development Association (IDA), the Inter-American Development Bank (IDB), the African Development Bank (AfDB), the African Development Fund (AfDF), the Asian Development Bank (AsDB), the Caribbean Development Bank (CarDB), the International Fund for Agricultural Development (IFAD), and the Social Loans programme of the European Resettlement Fund. Financial flows from Arab/OPEC financed multilateral agencies, shown as a group, cover: the Arab Bank for Economic Development in Africa (BADEA), the Arab Fund for Economic and Social Development (AFESD), the Islamic Development Bank, the OPEC Fund for International Development (OFID), the Arab Fund for Technical Assistance to African and Arab Countries (AFTAAAC), and the Islamic Solidarity Fund. The Technical Assistance and Relief Agencies of the United Nations cover mainly the following programmes or agencies: the United Nations regular programme of Technical Assistance (UNTA), the United Nations Development Programme (UNDP), the United Nations High Commissioner for Refugees (UNHCR), the United Nations Relief and Works Agency for Palestine Refugees in the Near East (UNRWA), the United Nations Children's Fund (UNICEF) and the

World Food Programme (WFP). Financial Flows from OPEC Members are shown as a combined total for the following countries: Algeria, Iran, Iraq, Kuwait, Libya, Nigeria, Qatar, Saudi Arabia, the United Arab Emirates and Venezuela[2]. Flows from CMEA countries are shown as a combined total covering Bulgaria, Czechoslavakia, the German Democratic Republic, Hungary, Poland, Romania and the USSR.

3. The data on changes in bank sector claims, given for information are for countries reporting to the Bank for International Settlements[3] and the affiliates in financial centres of banks resident in these countries. They correspond to those in BIS publications, where they are shown adjusted to eliminate the effect of changes in exchange rates between quarters; in the present report, the adjusted quarterly figures have been summed to constitute calendar year estimates. (See Annex, paragraph A16).

Sources of Data

4. DAC bilateral flow figures are based on replies from Member countries to questionnaires issued by the OECD Secretariat. The data on multilateral flows are compiled from published reports of the agencies concerned, supplemented by additional information received directly from them. The bilateral aid figures for OPEC Member countries are based on information provided by the Ministries of Finance of Kuwait, Saudi Arabia, United Arab Emirates, the Abu Dhabi Fund for Arab Economic Development, the Kuwait Fund for Arab Economic Development, the Saudi Fund for Development, the General Board for the South and Arabian Gulf and the Venezuelan Investment Fund. The remaining data are based on secondary sources and OECD Secretariat estimates. The data for OPEC and CMEA countries have been classified and processed as far as possible according to DAC norms and definitions[4].

The data shown for GNP and population in Section C were provided by IBRD specifically for the purpose of inclusion in the present report. The table on balance of payments current account is derived from IMF statistics and those on foreign trade from OECD statistics. They are the latest available at the time of going to press. The figures throughout Section C include some provisional or preliminary estimates, especially for 1986 and, to a limited extent, 1985.

Comprehensiveness

5. The resource flow data shown are based on records that are comprehensive for the majority of the individual categories shown. The omissions are essentially as follows:

i) Flows from countries that are neither developing countries nor members of the DAC (e.g., Luxembourg, South Africa and Spain);
ii) Net flows from CMEA countries;
iii) Private sector flows from OPEC countries;
iv) Only limited data are available on intra-LDC flows.

6.   For developing countries combined, the net balance of payments effect of *iii)* and *iv)* is nil, since inflows to one country are outflows of another. As regards *iv)* it would be misleading, for an individual recipient country, to show the incomplete figure corresponding to the data collected, since it could be treated as if it were the true total. The decision was taken to not show a country's receipts from other developing countries, except for ODA and OOF from OPEC countries, until a satisfactory level of coverage has been achieved.

Unallocated Amounts

7.   A figure that is a comprehensive total reported by a source may include a substantial "geographically unallocated" component. Administrative costs, which are virtually all incurred on the territory of the donor country, are an example. They are excluded from the totals in Section A, and of course from the data for individual recipients in Section B, where, however, they are included under "unallocated" in the table for "all recipients combined". For the amounts involved, see any recent issue of the DAC Chairman's Annual Report. A further portion of the amounts reported to DAC as geographically unallocated is properly classified thus e.g., amounts spent in the donor country on research performed for the benefit of developing countries (e.g., tropical diseases). Another portion reflects defective data collection procedures. The major part however stems from the effect of confidentiality restrictions in preventing a reporting country from disclosing the name of a partner country. For ODA and official sector transactions by DAC Members and multilateral organisations, geographically unallocated amounts are too small in aggregate to cause a substantial understatement of the figure for a given recipient country. However, the large amount of OPEC ODA which is unallocated[5] and the incomplete coverage of bilateral non-concessional flows from OPEC donor countries can involve serious distortion for some recipient countries. For certain categories of private sector flows, in particular private investment, there is a risk that the understatement of a given country's net inflow may be fairly large. This is true of:

a)   Countries hosting investment in the oil sector;

b)   Countries whose investment inflows are derived in large part from source countries whose reporting includes large amounts not allocated by country. These source countries include in particular Canada, Denmark, Finland, New Zealand, Sweden and Switzerland.

PRESENTATION

8.   The report consists of three sections:

Section A

9.   This section contains eight tables covering the period 1980 to 1986. They show the receipts of each developing country or territory, including entities not shown separately in Section B, from DAC countries combined and, all sources combined, respectively, of:

i)   Official Development Assistance: net disbursements;

ii)   Official Development Assistance: commitments;

iii)   Total resource flows: net disbursements.

Two show the receipts of each developing country, from multilateral agencies combined, of net disbursements of Concessional Assistance ("multilateral ODA") and total net disbursements.

Each table in this section contains a recapitulation of the resource receipts of selected developing country groups (see Annex, paragraph A19). These data are also illustrated graphically.

Section B

10.   The tables in this section treat *each developing country individually*[6] showing its resource receipts by type and by donor, with separate sub-totals for DAC Members, multilateral agencies and OPEC donors, with additional data on CMEA countries. These tables are followed by tables of identical format showing the same information for *groups of developing countries* (see Annex, paragraph A19).

Coverage

Detailed Tables for Individual Recipients by Origin of Resources

11.   The layout of each country table in Section B is identical. Two pages are used for each country. They contain three panels of tables showing the following types of flow by origin[7].

—   Total receipts, net;
—   Total ODA, gross and net;
—   ODA commitments;
—   Grants (included in ODA), of which technical cooperation grants;
—   ODA loans, gross and net;
—   Other Official (non-concessional) Flows (OOF), gross and net;
—   Total official flows, gross and net;
—   ODA loan commitments;
—   Grant element of ODA commitments.

12.   In each block within a table, flows from individual DAC Members and multilateral agencies are shown separately along with sub-totals for DAC Members and multilateral agencies, for OPEC donors combined, and for the European Economic Community and its Members combined. The data for OPEC donors are treated as comparable with the figures for DAC Members and multilateral agencies, although there are some differences in the coverage and quality of the data. Omitted from the total reached in this way are financial flows from the IMF (other than loans by the IMF Trust Fund), Member States of the Council for Mutual Economic Assistance (for which commitments and gross disbursements data are however shown separately in the lower right hand blocks: see "Other Aggregates" below), other developing countries, and grants by private voluntary agencies. Loans by banks resident in each DAC Member country are included indistinguishably in the "Total Receipts Net" block. The amount thus included for DAC Members combined falls short of the memorandum figure under "Other Aggregates" shown for "bank sector loans" by the amount of lending out of "financial centres" and certain other adjustments (see Annex, paragraph A16).

13.   In section B, data on commitments are shown in three separate panels: ODA commitments (grants plus loans), ODA loans and the "grant element" of ODA loans. The dollar values of data shown in the first two panels are drawn from Member countries replies to the DAC questionnaire. The percentage data in the grant element panel are derived from the Creditor Reporting System. The grant element may therefore occasionally fail to match the loan record, owing to slight differences in coverage (e.g., equity investment), reported geographical detail, or year of commitment (See Annex, paragraph A.24).

Other Aggregates

14.   Further data for each recipient country are shown for a number of resource flow aggregates, for which detailed information by source is not given in the other blocks of the table. The aggregates have been chosen so as to complete the picture for the country concerned, in terms of the analytical and policy uses of the figures. The additional data cover the main classes of private sector transactions of DAC Member country residents, the commitments by the official sector of (ODA + OOF), the terms of ODA commitments from DAC Members combined and from all sources, and gross disbursements and commitments by CMEA countries as a group.

Section C: Economic Indicators

15.   Data are given for seven indicators:
  — Gross National Product, at current prices and exchange rates;
  — GNP per capita, World Bank Atlas Basis;
  — Population;
  — Real GNP per capita (index 1979 = 100);
  — Current Account Deficit;
  — Exports to OECD, c.i.f;
  — Imports from OECD, f.o.b.

They are given for use in conjunction with the financial flow statistics in Sections A and B. The data relate to the years 1980 to 1986 or the latest year available. The format is identical to that of Section A.

16.   The first four indicators are as defined by IBRD, the source of the figures (see paragraph 4 above), and to whose publications the reader is referred. In certain instances, the totals or indices given for groups of countries include OECD Secretariat estimates up to 1985, although these estimates may not be shown for the individual country or territory concerned. The volume of information for 1986 was too limited to justify presenting data for groups for that year.

17.   The product of the population and GNP per capita figures (IBRD World Atlas Basis) usually differs from the figure for GNP in current prices. The latter is estimated by converting GNP in national currency to US dollars at the current average exchange rate and is, therefore, in the same units as the financial flow data in the body of the table. By contrast, the figures for GNP per capita in US dollars in the World Atlas are estimated by converting national currency GNP to US dollars at the average exchange rate for that year and the preceding two years, adjusted for differences in the rates of inflation between the country and the United States. The result of this computation is divided by the population estimate to obtain GNP per capita. The figure thus reached is the best that can be constructed, given available information, for purposes of ranking countries by per capita income level, but it is not comparable with the ostensibly similar figure derived by converting per capita GNP at current prices to US dollars at the current exchange rate. Population data are mid-year estimates.

18.   The deficit on current account excludes government unrequited transfers; DAC practice is to consider these transfers as part of the capital account. Where totals for regions and income groups are not shown, this is because significant country data are missing. Exports to OECD (c.i.f.) are those presented in other reports as Member countries' imports (c.i.f.) from the countries concerned. Similarly, the figures for imports from OECD (f.o.b.) are actually those for exports (f.o.b.) to a given country.

Concepts and Interpretation of Data

19.   A note on the main concepts used in this report and remarks on specific particularities of the data will be found at the end of the volume.

Timing of Reporting

20.   National data were supplied by Members up to 23rd November 1987.

NOTES AND REFERENCES

1.   Additional aggregate data can be found in the annual report of the Chairman of the DAC "Development Co-operation Efforts and Policies of Members of the Development Assistance Committee, 1987 Review".

2.   Ecuador, Gabon and Indonesia, also OPEC Member countries, provided no bilateral assistance in the period 1980-1986.

3.   All DAC countries except Australia and New Zealand.

4.   See Annex: Definition of Concepts used in this Report.

5.   Up to 42 per cent of OPEC bilateral aid is unallocated, depending on the year.

6.   The reader will find in Section A the main aggregates for countries not shown individually in Section B.

7.   A French translation of certain terms is given in the fold-out at rear.

N.B.   It is recalled that the DAC list of developing countries and territories is designed for statistical purposes, not as guidance for eligibility for aid or other preferential treatment. The names or geographical classification of countries or territories shown in the publication should be construed as having strictly geographical or functional meaning and do not have political implications or imply any expression of view regarding juridical status. The designation "developing countries" is used as a generic term in its own right covering both "countries" and "territories" and does not carry any special meaning as to the political or legal classification of the recipients concerned.

INTRODUCTION

1. Le présent rapport, huitième d'une série consacrée au volume et à l'origine des ressources financières extérieures reçues par les pays et territoires en développement, fournit des données détaillées sur la répartition géographique

— des versements bruts et nets,
— des engagements et
— des conditions de financement

pour chacun de plus d'une centaine de pays et territoires en développement en 1983, 1984, 1985 et 1986. Ces statistiques sont complétées par des données économiques générales permettant d'interpréter les informations sur les apports de ressources à chaque pays dans une perspective plus large. L'objet du rapport est de dépeindre, par le biais d'une présentation synthétique en deux pages, un tableau aussi complet que possible du financement externe de chacun des pays considérés.

2. Les données indiquent les opérations de chaque pays bénéficiaire avec[1] :

    i) Les pays Membres du CAD (séparément ou en groupe) ;

    ii) Les organismes multilatéraux (séparément ou en groupe) ;

    iii) Les pays de l'Organisation des pays exportateurs de pétrole (OPEP) en groupe, et les membres du Conseil d'assistance économique mutuelle (CAEM), également en groupe.

Les pays Membres du Comité d'aide au développement de l'OCDE pour lesquels des données sont présentées sont : l'Australie, l'Autriche, la Belgique, le Canada, le Danemark, les Etats-Unis, la Finlande, la France, l'Italie, le Japon, la Norvège, la Nouvelle-Zélande, les Pays-Bas, la République Fédérale d'Allemagne, le Royaume-Uni, la Suède et la Suisse. Les données relatives à la Commission des Communautés européennes, qui est aussi Membre du CAD, sont comprises sous la rubrique « organismes multilatéraux ». Par ailleurs, une ligne supplémentaire (CEE + Membres) présente des données sur les apports en provenance de la CEE elle-même et de ses pays Membres faisant aussi partie du CAD. Les données relatives aux apports financiers en provenance de sources multilatérales se rapportent aux organismes suivants : Banque mondiale, Société financière internationale (SFI), Association internationale du développement (IDA), Banque interaméricaine de développement (BID), Banque africaine de développement (BAfD), Fonds africain de développement (FAfD), Banque asiatique de développement (BAsD), Banque de développement des Caraïbes (CARIBANK), Fonds international de développement agricole (FIDA) et le programme de prêts sociaux du Fonds de réétablissement européen. Les apports des organismes multilatéraux financés par les pays arabes et les pays de l'OPEP couvrent les organismes et programmes suivants : Banque arabe pour le développement économique en Afrique (BADEA), Fonds arabe pour le développement économique et social (FADES), Banque islamique de développement, Fonds de l'OPEP pour le développement international (FODI), Fonds arabe d'assistance technique aux pays africains et arabes (FATAA), et Fonds de solidarité islamique. Les organismes d'assistance technique et de secours des Nations Unies comprennent essentiellement les programmes ou organismes suivants : programme régulier d'assistance technique de l'Organisation des Nations Unies (ATNU), Programme des Nations Unies pour le développement (PNUD), Haut Commissariat des Nations Unies pour les réfugiés (HCR),

Office de secours et de travaux des Nations Unies pour les réfugiés de Palestine dans le Proche-Orient (UNRWA), Fonds des Nations Unies pour l'enfance (FISE) et Programme alimentaire mondial (PAM). Les apports de ressources financières des Membres de l'OPEP sont indiqués globalement pour les pays suivants : l'Algérie, l'Arabie saoudite, les Emirats arabes unis, l'Irak, l'Iran, le Koweït, la Libye, le Nigéria, le Qatar et le Venezuela[2]. Les apports en provenance des pays Membres du CAEM sont indiqués globalement pour la Bulgarie, la Hongrie, la Pologne, la République démocratique allemande, la Roumanie, la Tchécoslovaquie et l'URSS.

3. Les chiffres relatifs à la variation des créances du secteur bancaire, indiqués pour information concernent les pays faisant des déclarations à la Banque des Règlements internationaux[3] ainsi que les sociétés affiliées, établies dans des centres financiers de banques dont le siège se trouve dans ces pays déclarants. Ils correspondent aux chiffres présentés dans les rapports publiés par la BRI, où les effets des variations des taux de change entre fin de trimestres ont été éliminés. Dans le présent rapport, les chiffres trimestriels ainsi ajustés ont été additionnés afin d'élaborer des estimations portant sur des années entières. (voir l'Annexe, paragraphe A16).

Sources des données

4. Les chiffres concernant les apports bilatéraux du CAD sont fondés sur les réponses fournies par les pays Membres aux questionnaires établis par le Secrétariat de l'OCDE. Les données sur les apports multilatéraux sont extraites des rapports publiés par les organismes intéressés et complétées par des informations supplémentaires communiquées directement par ces organismes. Les chiffres relatifs à l'aide bilatérale des pays Membres de l'OPEP sont fondés sur les renseignements fournis par les ministères des finances du Koweït, de l'Arabie saoudite, des Emirats arabes unis ainsi que par le Fonds d'Abu Dhabi pour le développement économique arabe, le Fonds du Koweït pour le développement économique arabe, le Fonds saoudien pour le développement, l'Administration générale pour l'Arabie du Sud et le Golfe et le Fonds d'investissement vénézuélien. Les autres chiffres ont été établis à partir de sources secondaires et d'estimations du Secrétariat de l'OCDE. Les données présentées pour les pays de l'OPEP et du CAEM ont été, dans la mesure du possible, classées et traitées conformément aux normes et définitions du CAD[4].

Les données présentées pour le PNB ainsi que les indicateurs y afférents figurant dans la section C ont été communiquées par la BIRD expressément en vue de leur inclusion dans le présent rapport et sont les dernières disponibles au moment de l'impression. Ces données contiennent donc des estimations provisoires ou préliminaires, surtout pour 1986 et, dans une moindre mesure, pour 1985.

Les données sur la balance des opérations courantes émanant du FMI. Les données sur les importations en provenance de la zone de l'OCDE et sur les exportations à destination de cette zone, sont compilées tous les ans par l'OCDE à partir des déclarations des pays Membres.

Couverture des données

5. Les données sur les apports de ressources sont tirées de séries qui recouvrent la quasi-totalité des opérations dans

chacune des catégories présentées. Les omissions sont essentiellement les suivantes :

    i) Apports en provenance de pays qui ne sont ni des pays en développement ni des Membres du CAD (par exemple, Luxembourg, Afrique du Sud et l'Espagne) ;

    ii) Apports nets en provenance des pays du CAEM ;

    iii) Apports privés en provenance des pays de l'OPEP ;

    iv) Seules quelques données fragmentaires sont disponibles sur les flux de ressources entre pays en développement.

6.   Pour l'ensemble des pays en développement, les deux dernières catégories *[iii)* et *iv)]* s'annulent au niveau de la balance des paiements, puisque le montant des apports à un pays correspond à des sorties pour le pays partenaire. S'agissant du point *iv)*, aucun chiffre n'est indiqué pour un pays bénéficiaire donné car, les renseignements disponibles étant incomplets, ce chiffre, s'il était présenté, risquerait d'être retenu comme correspondant au vrai total. La décision a donc été prise d'omettre tous les apports de ressources en provenance d'autres pays en développement, à l'exception de l'APD et des AASP en provenance des pays de l'OPEP, jusqu'à ce qu'un niveau satisfaisant de couverture ait été atteint.

Montants non ventilés

7.   Un total notifié par une source peut comprendre une composante parfois importante d'apports « non ventilés sur le plan géographique ». La quasi-totalité des dépenses administratives interviennent, par exemple, sur le territoire du pays donneur. Ces dépenses sont exclues des totaux dans la section A et bien entendu, des données par pays bénéficiaire de la section B où, toutefois, elles sont englobées dans le montant « non ventilé », présenté pour « l'ensemble des bénéficiaires ». Pour plus de précisions sur le montant des dépenses administratives, on peut consulter un des rapports annuels récents du Président du CAD. Une autre partie des montants notifiés au CAD sous la rubrique « non ventilés sur le plan géographique » appartient effectivement à cette catégorie. C'est le cas, notamment, des dépenses encourues dans le pays donneur au titre de la recherche effectuée au profit d'un ensemble de pays en développement (maladies tropicales, par exemple). Une autre partie tient à des méthodes de collecte défectueuses. Cependant, la partie la plus importante des montants inscrits dans la catégorie « non ventilés sur le plan géographique » s'y trouve en raison des règles en matière de confidentialité qui empêchent un pays déclarant de révéler le nom du pays partenaire pour certains types d'opérations. Pour l'APD et les autres opérations entreprises par le secteur public des pays du CAD et par les organismes multilatéraux, les montants qui ne font pas l'objet d'une répartition géographique sont trop peu importants dans l'ensemble pour entraîner une sous-estimation significative du chiffre relatif à un pays bénéficiaire donné. Toutefois, les montants importants non ventilés d'APD des pays de l'OPEP[5] et la couverture variable des apports bilatéraux de ressources assorties de conditions non libérales en provenance de pays donneurs de l'OPEP peuvent se traduire par une distorsion importante pour certains pays bénéficiaires. Pour certaines catégories d'apports du secteur privé, en particulier l'investissement privé, la sous-estimation de l'apport net reçu par un pays donné peut être assez importante. C'est surtout le cas :

    a) Des pays où des investissements sont effectués dans le secteur pétrolier ;

    b) Des pays pour lesquels une partie importante des apports reçus sous forme d'investissements provient

de pays dont les notifications comprennent d'importants montants non ventilés par pays. Dans cette dernière catégorie se trouvent en particulier le Canada, le Danemark, la Finlande, la Nouvelle-Zélande, la Suède et la Suisse.

PRÉSENTATION

8.   Le rapport comprend trois sections :

Section A

9.   Cette section contient huit tableaux couvrant la période 1980 à 1986. Ces tableaux indiquent pour chaque pays ou territoire en développement, y compris ceux qui ne font pas l'objet d'une page à part dans la section B :

    i) L'aide publique au développement : versements nets ;

    ii) L'aide publique au développement : engagements ;

    iii) Les apports totaux de ressources : versements nets,

en provenance, d'une part, de l'ensemble des pays du CAD, et d'autre part de l'ensemble des sources.

    Deux tableaux présentent, pour chaque bénéficiaire, le montant en provenance des organismes multilatéraux des versements nets d'aide à des conditions libérales (« APD multilatérale ») et des versements nets totaux.

    Chaque tableau de cette section présente un état récapitulatif des ressources reçues par différents groupes de pays en développement (voir l'Annexe, paragraphe A19). Ces données font aussi l'objet d'une présentation graphique.

Section B

10.   Les tableaux de cette section concernent *chacun un seul pays en développement*[6] et indiquent les ressources qu'il a reçues, ventilées par types et par donneurs, avec des sous-totaux pour les Membres du CAD, les organismes multilatéraux et les donneurs de l'OPEP, ainsi que des données sur les pays du CAEM. Les tableaux par pays sont complétés par des tableaux de même format présentant les mêmes informations pour certains *groupes de pays en développement* (voir l'Annexe, paragraphe A19).

Couverture

Tableaux détaillés présentant pour les différents pays bénéficiaires les ressources reçues, ventilées par origine

11.   La présentation des tableaux dans la section B est normalisée. Deux pages sont utilisées pour chaque pays. Elles contiennent chacune trois panneaux dans lesquels sont ventilées les catégories suivantes d'apports par origine[7] :

— Recettes totales, nettes ;
— APD totale, montants bruts et nets ;
— Engagements d'APD ;
— Dons (inclus dans l'APD), dont les dons au titre de la coopération technique ;
— Prêts d'APD, montants bruts et nets ;
— Autres apports du secteur public (AASP) (aux conditions du marché), bruts et nets ;
— Apports totaux du secteur public, bruts et nets ;
— Prêts d'APD, engagements ;
— Elément de libéralité des engagements d'APD.

12. Dans chacun des pavés d'un tableau, les apports des différents Membres du CAD et des institutions multilatérales sont indiqués séparément, avec des sous-totaux concernant respectivement l'ensemble des Membres du CAD, l'ensemble des organismes multilatéraux, l'ensemble des Membres de l'OPEP, et la Communauté économique européenne et ses membres en tant que groupe. On a considéré que les données relatives aux donneurs de l'OPEP sont comparables à celles concernant les Membres du CAD et les organismes multilatéraux, bien que leur couverture et leur qualité soient quelque peu différentes. Le montant total obtenu de cette façon ne comprend ni les apports financiers en provenance du FMI (à part les prêts du Fonds fiduciaire), ni ceux des Etats membres du Conseil d'assistance économique mutuelle (pour lesquels, toutefois, les données relatives aux engagements et versements bruts sont présentées dans le pavé du bas à droite : voir « Autres agrégats » ci-dessous), ni les apports d'autres pays en développement, ni les dons des organismes privés bénévoles. Les prêts consentis par les banques ayant leur siège dans chaque pays Membre du CAD sont inclus indistinctement dans les données du pavé « Recettes totales, nettes ». Le montant ainsi inclus pour l'ensemble des Membres du CAD est inférieur aux chiffres présentés pour mémoire dans le pavé « Autres agrégats », concernant les prêts du secteur bancaire ; la différence correspondant aux prêts bancaires consentis à partir des centres financiers et à certains autres ajustements (voir l'Annexe paragraphe A16).

13. Dans la section B, les données relatives aux engagements sont présentées dans trois pavés : engagements d'APD (dons plus prêts), engagements de prêts d'APD, et élément de libéralité (« élément-don ») des prêts d'APD. Les chiffres en dollars dans les deux premiers pavés proviennent des réponses aux questionnaires du CAD. Les pourcentages présentés dans le pavé « élément de libéralité » sont tirés des déclarations reçues dans le cadre du Système de Notification des Pays Créanciers (SNPC), ce qui implique parfois une disparité par rapport aux volumes de prêts indiqués, en raison de divergences mineures de couverture (exemple : prises de participations), le niveau de détail géographique, ou encore de l'année d'engagement (voir l'Annexe, paragraphe A24).

Autres agrégats

14. Sous cette rubrique figurent, pour chaque pays étudié, des renseignements supplémentaires sur certaines catégories d'apports de ressources qui ne sont pas ventilées en détail dans les autres pavés. Les agrégats ont été choisis de manière à compléter les renseignements relatifs aux différents pays, dans la perspective de l'utilisation des données à des fins analytiques ou ayant trait aux mesures à prendre. Les données supplémentaires concernent les principaux types d'opérations entreprises par des résidents des pays Membres du CAD relevant du secteur privé ; les engagements (APD + AASP) souscrits par le secteur public ; les conditions dont sont assortis les engagements d'APD souscrits soit par l'ensemble des Membres du CAD, soit par l'ensemble des sources d'aide, et les versements bruts et engagements des pays du CAEM en tant que groupe.

Section C : Indicateurs économiques

15. Des données sont indiquées pour sept indicateurs :
- Produit national brut, aux prix et taux de change courants ;
- PNB par habitant, sur la base de l'Atlas de la Banque mondiale ;
- Population ;
- PNB réel par habitant (indice 1979 = 100);
- Déficit de la balance des opérations courantes;
- Exportations vers la zone de l'OCDE, c.a.f.;
- Importations en provenance de la zone de l'OCDE, f.o.b.

Elles peuvent être rapprochées des statistiques sur les apports financiers figurant dans les sections A et B. Elles portent sur les années 1980 à 1986, ou la dernière année disponible. La présentation est identique à celle de la section A.

16. Les quatre premiers indicateurs sont calculés conformément aux définitions de la BIRD, qui est la source des données (voir paragraphe 4 ci-dessus), et aux publications de laquelle le lecteur pourra utilement se référer. Dans certains cas, les totaux ou indices présentés pour des groupes de pays pour 1985 et les années antérieures contiennent des estimations du Secrétariat, qui peuvent toutefois ne pas être indiquées pour tous les pays ou territoire dans chaque groupe. Le volume des informations statistiques relatives à 1986 était trop limité pour justifier la présentation de données pour cette dernière année au niveau des groupes.

17. Le chiffre obtenu en multipliant la population par le PNB par habitant, tiré de l'Atlas de la Banque mondiale, diffère généralement du chiffre du PNB aux prix courants. Ce dernier est calculé en convertissant en dollars des Etats-Unis, au taux de change moyen courant, le PNB exprimé en monnaie nationale ; il est donc exprimé dans la même unité que les données sur les apports financiers qui figurent dans les autres pavés du tableau. En revanche, les chiffres du PNB par habitant, en dollars des Etats-Unis, présentés dans l'Atlas sont estimés en convertissant en dollars des Etats-Unis, au taux de change moyen de l'année concernée et les deux années précédentes, et ajustés pour tenir compte de la différence entre le taux d'inflation de la monnaie concernée et le taux d'inflation du dollar des Etats-Unis. Le résultat de ce calcul divisé par le nombre estimé d'habitants, donne ainsi le PNB par tête présenté dans les tableaux. Le chiffre final obtenu est le meilleur que l'on puisse calculer actuellement avec les informations disponibles, si l'on souhaite classer les pays en fonction des niveaux de revenu par habitant. Mais il n'est pas comparable aux chiffres, à première vue analogues, que l'on obtient en convertissant en dollars des Etats-Unis, au taux de change courant, le PNB par habitant aux prix courants. Les données relatives à la population sont des estimations se rapportant à la situation en milieu d'année.

18. Le déficit de la balance des transactions courantes ne comprend pas les transferts gouvernementaux sans contrepartie; le CAD a pour principe de considérer ces transferts comme faisant partie du compte de capital. Certaines données par pays importantes faisant défaut, il n'a pas été possible parfois d'indiquer les totaux par régions et par groupes de pays classés selon le revenu. Les exportations (c.a.f.) à destination de la zone de l'OCDE sont celles qui apparaissent dans d'autres rapports en tant qu'importations (c.a.f.) des pays considérés. De même, les chiffres relatifs aux importations (f.o.b.) en provenance de la zone de l'OCDE correspondent en fait aux exportations (f.o.b.) à destination d'un pays donné.

Concepts et interprétation des données

19. On trouvera en fin de volume une note récapitulant les principaux concepts utilisés, ainsi que des remarques portant sur des aspects particuliers des données contenues dans le rapport.

Date de notification

20. Les données nationales ont été fournies par les Membres jusqu'au 23 novembre 1987.

NOTES ET RÉFÉRENCES

1. On trouvera d'autres données agrégées dans le rapport annuel du Président du CAD « Coopération pour le développement — Efforts et politiques poursuivis par les Membres du Comité d'aide au développement, Examen 1987.

2. L'Equateur, le Gabon et l'Indonésie, qui sont aussi des pays Membres de l'OPEP, n'ont fourni aucune aide bilatérale au cours de la période 1980-1986.

3. Tous les pays du CAD, à l'exception de l'Australie et de la Nouvelle-Zélande.

4. Voir Annexe : Définition des concepts utilisés dans ce rapport.

5. Jusqu'à 42 pour cent de l'aide bilatérale de l'OPEP est « non ventilée », selon les années.

6. Le lecteur trouvera dans la section A les principaux agrégats concernant des pays qui ne font pas l'objet d'une page à part dans la section B.

7. Une traduction française de certains termes est donnée sur le dépliant à la fin de la section B.

N.B.   Il est rappelé que la liste des pays et territoires en développement adoptée par le CAD est destinée à des fins purement statistiques, et n'a pas pour objet d'orienter le choix des pays pouvant bénéficier d'une aide ou d'un autre traitement préférentiel. Les appellations ou le classement géographique des pays ou territoires mentionnés dans cette publication doivent être pris au sens strictement géographique ou fonctionnel ; ils n'ont aucune signification politique et ne reflètent aucune opinion sur le statut juridique desdits pays ou territoires. L'expression « pays en développement » est utilisée comme une appellation générique qui recouvre à la fois des territoires et des pays et à laquelle ne s'attache aucun sens particulier pour le classement politique ou juridique des pays en cause.

EDITOR'S NOTE

1.   For detailed data on debt and debt service, the reader is referred to "Financing and External Debt of Developing Countries" (annual). Claims held by banks and non-bank trade creditors, including short term debt are published jointly by the OECD and the Bank for International Settlements semi-annually with a lag of 6-7 months. The annual OECD report on the "Debt and Other External Liabilities of Developing, CMEA and Certain Other Countries and Territories", is issued in December.

2.   The following is drawn to the attention of users:

   — The disbursements and commitments data for both OPEC and CMEA countries have been revised, in some cases by significant amounts.
   — Significant revisions will be noted for Belgium and the United Kingdom
   — The deflators below (division factors) *for DAC countries combined* will enable the reader to make a rough adjustment of the dollar values shown in this report to correct them for, respectively, exchange rate changes against the dollar, and the combined effect of exchange rate and price changes.

		1983	1984	1985	1986
a)	to correct for exchange rate changes only	109.2	102.7	100.0	118.4
b)	to correct for exchange rate and price changes (i.e. to convert to real terms)	101.0	98.9	100.0	122.6

The following revisions have been made to data shown in earlier editions: Official sector flows — Austria, Belgium, Japan and OPEC countries combined — Private sector flows: significant revisions for the United Kingdom.

The category "Least developed countries" (LLDCs) defined by the United Nations now includes 40 countries. The data for all years shown for this group are for all 40 countries i.e., the historical record has been modified to include countries which were classified as LLDCs after the year concerned.

NOTE DE L'ÉDITEUR

1.   Pour des données détaillés sur l'Endettement Extérieur et le Service de la Dette, le lecteur consultera utilement « Le Financement de l'Endettement Externe des Pays en Développement » (Rapport annuel). Les données sur les créances détenues par les banques et les créanciers non bancaires relatives à leurs opérations commerciales, ainsi que sur la dette à court terme, sont publiées conjointement par l'OCDE et la Banque des Règlements Internationaux semestriellement, avec un décalage de six à sept mois au rapport à la date à laquelle se réfèrent les données. Le lecteur est également renvoyé au rapport de l'OCDE sur l'endettement et les autres obligations extérieures (Statistiques de la Dette Extérieure, Endettement et autres Engagements des pays et territoires en développement, du CAEM et de certains autres pays et territoires), qui paraît en décembre.

2.   L'attention du lecteur est attirée sur les points suivants :

   — Les données concernant les versements et les engagements des pays de l'OPEP et du CAEM ont été révisées, dans certains cas dans des proportions importantes.
   — Des révisions importantes seront notées concernant la Belgique et le Royaume-Uni.
   — Les déflateurs suivants (facteurs de division) concernant l'ensemble des pays du CAD permettront au lecteur d'ajuster approximativement les valeurs en dollars présentées dans ce rapport, pour tenir compte des variations des taux de change par rapport au dollar, et dans l'effet combiné, des variations des taux de change et des prix.

		1983	1984	1985	1986
a)	pour tenir compte des seules variation des taux de change	109.2	102.7	100.0	118.4
b)	pour tenir compte des variations des taux de change et des prix (et obtenir ainsi les données en termes réels)	101.0	98.9	100.0	122.6

Les révisions suivantes ont été apportées aux données présentées dans les numéros antérieurs de cette publication : apports du secteur public : Autriche, Belgique, Japon et ensemble des pays de l'OPEP ; apports du secteur privé : des révisions importantes pour le Royaume-Uni.

La catégorie « Les pays les moins avancés » (PMA) définie par les Nations-Unies comprend désormais 40 pays. Les données présentés dans ce rapport pour ce groupe pour chaque année étudiée, recouvrent l'ensemble de ces 40 pays, c'est-à-dire que la série chronologique pour ce groupe a été modifiée afin d'y inclure des pays qui n'ont été classés comme PMA qu'après l'année à laquelle se réfèrent les données.

BASIC SUMMARY TABLES

TABLEAUX RESUMES DE BASE

	1980	1981	1982	1983	1984	1985	1986
EUROPE							
Cyprus	30.9	25.8	14.0	6.6	4.1	20.7	23.5
Gibraltar	11.2	7.4	3.1	3.4	11.0	28.9	20.8
Greece	19.5	7.1	4.3	5.6	8.1	6.9	15.2
Malta	2.8	39.3	20.1	33.1	4.3	5.6	0.9
Portugal	108.1	79.1	45.6	35.3	80.8	98.9	120.9
Turkey	713.8	511.0	528.1	293.9	188.7	136.7	234.7
Yugoslavia	-19.4	-17.6	-10.5	-0.4	-1.4	6.8	14.4
Europe Unallocated	5.4	7.3	11.1	14.5	6.5	7.5	0.4
TOTAL	*872.3*	*659.5*	*615.8*	*392.0*	*302.0*	*312.0*	*430.9*
NORTH OF SAHARA							
Algeria	117.6	146.1	130.0	86.1	112.1	142.0	119.4
Egypt	1187.0	1105.0	1236.8	1241.0	1650.6	1680.8	1566.2
Libya	9.9	2.0	2.4	2.4	2.2	3.2	8.4
Morocco	187.8	208.9	229.5	189.5	247.7	317.8	292.1
Tunisia	157.7	161.6	150.1	156.7	140.7	121.7	147.1
North of Sahara Unall.	3.0	0.7	11.2	39.6	2.7	13.4	-0.2
TOTAL	*1663.0*	*1624.3*	*1759.9*	*1715.4*	*2156.0*	*2278.9*	*2132.9*
SOUTH OF SAHARA							
Angola	35.8	39.4	40.0	46.4	59.6	59.6	93.8
Benin	35.7	45.0	40.9	41.3	39.7	47.7	72.5
Botswana	83.5	75.9	83.2	74.6	64.9	59.1	82.0
Burkina Faso	151.1	158.1	147.0	128.0	122.2	122.2	175.3
Burundi	59.8	65.0	75.3	69.3	70.4	77.2	89.8
Cameroon	171.4	134.2	155.3	109.3	154.7	126.3	176.5
Cape Verde	39.0	36.3	42.6	45.3	39.3	40.8	76.3
Central African Rep.	75.1	72.8	68.8	64.8	68.3	61.6	84.9
Chad	20.2	31.3	35.3	51.4	58.9	95.8	102.2
Comoros	13.4	17.8	14.2	15.1	18.2	18.0	20.8
Congo	55.4	42.7	59.5	55.0	67.3	46.9	100.7
Cote d'Ivoire	151.9	91.2	102.2	140.7	114.2	110.5	137.7
Djibouti	32.0	36.3	44.5	41.4	48.5	46.4	64.6
Equatorial Guinea	1.2	4.3	5.1	4.0	8.0	6.9	10.5
Ethiopia	91.4	76.2	77.0	93.1	187.2	416.3	401.5
Gabon	49.1	35.9	58.0	56.7	67.4	51.9	58.7
Gambia	16.5	19.3	23.7	21.3	32.3	31.2	59.0
Ghana	107.1	87.4	65.5	60.8	95.3	95.9	120.6
Guinea	32.5	31.2	26.8	26.6	42.2	59.8	97.6
Guinea-Bissau	34.4	41.4	33.7	32.2	30.6	24.3	40.6
Kenya	277.0	362.8	333.5	338.6	294.4	328.9	385.3
Lesotho	63.7	62.3	57.2	64.7	66.0	51.5	56.0
Liberia	60.1	86.4	85.2	88.3	107.5	64.3	69.1
Madagascar	90.8	93.4	159.2	117.0	97.5	99.4	176.2
Malawi	75.6	82.1	65.0	56.2	51.7	52.9	89.5
Mali	131.4	133.0	96.3	96.9	223.7	251.3	203.8
Mauritania	53.5	66.7	61.8	72.1	68.7	100.3	105.1
Mauritius	25.2	47.7	30.8	24.6	24.4	22.2	47.9
Mayotte	22.7	14.7	12.7	14.6	13.8	19.8	26.1
Mozambique	114.8	110.0	160.6	160.4	190.1	216.9	319.2
Namibia	–	–	–	0.0	–	2.8	6.6
Niger	105.0	122.5	123.6	107.0	101.9	206.4	183.8
Nigeria	17.4	16.8	16.7	29.2	14.7	15.9	39.7
Reunion	486.7	633.6	397.3	385.6	328.9	351.9	441.1
Rwanda	96.7	102.7	99.1	94.7	96.0	103.2	123.7
St. Helena	8.8	8.2	10.2	9.9	10.0	12.1	13.5
Sao Tome & Principe	1.2	1.8	3.8	3.4	4.0	3.0	7.0
Senegal	181.9	214.5	189.0	212.4	245.7	196.5	315.7
Seychelles	18.3	13.7	14.7	13.7	13.6	12.2	20.7
Sierra Leone	56.8	33.8	55.7	35.6	22.6	30.3	51.3
Somalia	139.3	139.8	141.6	151.4	193.1	163.2	353.9
Sudan	272.1	295.9	357.7	438.6	309.0	647.2	464.1
Swaziland	32.7	23.8	18.8	20.6	17.6	18.2	24.8
Tanzania	523.7	485.6	485.2	429.4	409.8	372.6	514.2
Togo	52.1	36.9	50.4	48.8	53.1	53.3	91.7
Uganda	42.3	78.6	52.8	43.7	47.2	42.3	77.3
Zaire	316.8	277.1	250.8	193.5	209.4	209.6	296.1
Zambia	234.4	179.2	189.8	180.2	181.8	215.4	349.0
Zimbabwe	112.2	137.0	142.2	185.6	243.6	214.2	191.3
East African Community	5.5	5.0	4.2	5.2	2.5	10.8	1.8
DOM/TOM Unallocated	–	–	–	–	–	–	–
EAMA Unallocated	94.7	2.1	4.6	37.2	59.4	–	–
South of Sahara Unall.	48.3	101.1	236.5	163.0	125.5	262.1	371.4
TOTAL	*5017.7*	*5110.0*	*5105.4*	*4999.1*	*5216.1*	*5949.1*	*7482.1*
Africa Unspecified	142.3	128.7	132.6	132.3	143.8	187.2	162.1
AFRICA TOTAL	*6823.0*	*6863.0*	*6997.8*	*6846.8*	*7515.9*	*8415.3*	*9777.1*
N.& C. AMERICA							
Aruba	–	–	–	–	–	12.0	40.4
Bahamas	0.2	0.1	0.1	0.1	8.0	0.1	0.2
Barbados	2.0	4.0	2.0	11.6	4.7	5.0	2.9

	1980	1981
Belize	11.0	8.4
Bermuda	0.1	0.0
Costa Rica	22.8	29.7
Cuba	11.1	2.6
Dominican Republic	57.2	53.9
El Salvador	49.5	109.1
Guadeloupe	85.0	27.1
Guatemala	33.5	31.4
Haiti	62.8	67.0
Honduras	47.7	57.1
Jamaica	83.6	110.1
Martinique	563.8	448.6
Mexico	55.0	102.4
Netherlands Antilles	86.9	69.2
Nicaragua	116.6	59.2
Panama	18.3	21.5
St. Pierre & Miquelon	27.9	25.2
Trinidad & Tobago	1.4	-5.9
Anguilla	2.3	2.6
Antigua and Barbuda	2.6	6.7
Cayman Islands	1.0	0.4
Dominica	8.4	5.9
Grenada	0.5	0.3
Montserrat	3.1	2.6
St. Kitts-Nevis	2.7	2.2
St. Lucia	2.7	3.8
St. Vincent and Gr.	2.0	3.5
Turks & Caicos Isl.	3.0	6.8
Virgin Islands	2.9	2.6
West Indies Unall.	7.9	7.5
DOM/TOM Unallocated	–	–
N.& C. America Unall.	13.2	33.2
TOTAL	*1388.3*	*1298.7*
SOUTH AMERICA		
Argentina	32.1	28.5
Bolivia	99.0	98.4
Brazil	58.3	206.7
Chile	-13.2	-4.5
Colombia	31.8	43.3
Ecuador	23.3	25.2
Falkland Islands	2.3	2.1
Guiana	109.3	79.2
Guyana	12.5	17.7
Paraguay	25.3	30.9
Peru	176.6	187.0
Suriname	77.1	94.0
Uruguay	5.3	6.6
Venezuela	15.1	13.0
South America Unall.	5.3	7.4
TOTAL	*660.0*	*835.4*
America Unspecified	60.2	73.8
AMERICA TOTAL	*2108.5*	*2207.9*
MIDDLE EAST		
Bahrain	0.4	1.2
Iran	30.8	6.5
Iraq	5.7	5.0
Israel	892.1	772.1
Jordan	96.3	111.9
Kuwait	7.5	6.5
Lebanon	24.9	60.2
Oman	1.8	3.5
Qatar	0.4	0.5
Saudi Arabia	8.9	18.7
Syria	61.7	63.8
United Arab Emirates	1.7	-2.2
Yemen	78.5	77.4
Yemen, Dem.	4.1	4.7
Middle East Unall.	3.0	21.5
TOTAL	*1217.8*	*1151.0*
SOUTH ASIA		
Afghanistan	11.4	-7.9
Bangladesh	850.2	672.0
Bhutan	1.7	2.6
Burma	231.3	203.4
India	633.4	930.6
Maldives	1.9	2.8
Nepal	84.0	88.0
Pakistan	339.2	421.2
Sri Lanka	296.1	286.8

1982	1983	1984	1985	1986
6.8	12.3	12.5	20.3	22.4
0.0	0.1	0.0	0.0	0.0
59.4	217.1	185.7	238.9	164.8
1.5	1.9	6.4	2.5	3.7
93.5	57.0	142.3	162.1	62.9
176.4	239.2	227.6	306.4	316.3
163.4	153.5	118.1	147.6	153.6
31.5	49.6	40.5	62.4	111.3
78.7	78.8	71.0	102.6	126.4
97.5	107.0	170.9	207.7	239.8
152.5	156.2	156.0	158.2	160.5
315.2	270.1	231.8	268.6	341.2
142.1	135.9	75.3	122.6	247.2
61.7	63.1	55.9	62.3	56.3
76.9	73.0	71.7	67.2	104.6
25.7	22.9	56.8	44.5	28.2
26.3	23.9	17.6	17.1	21.1
1.4	1.7	1.5	0.8	16.4
2.0	2.2	1.5	1.5	2.6
2.3	1.4	1.5	2.1	4.4
0.2	0.1	0.0	-0.1	-0.1
6.0	4.8	11.1	9.3	6.9
1.4	1.7	22.8	30.6	16.9
3.3	1.7	1.8	1.7	3.3
1.8	1.5	1.6	2.3	1.8
2.9	4.0	2.9	2.4	2.0
2.6	1.5	1.1	1.7	8.4
10.2	6.4	5.3	4.7	8.0
2.7	1.8	1.1	1.5	1.3
5.5	5.6	8.8	9.0	23.2
–	–	–	–	–
29.0	46.3	61.5	114.1	78.5
1582.3	1753.9	1775.3	2190.0	2377.4
23.9	28.2	25.6	31.0	57.8
89.4	133.5	109.6	126.4	196.6
162.1	93.5	140.0	64.2	132.6
-4.0	6.5	9.7	45.8	-0.4
52.8	36.4	41.6	36.7	36.7
30.3	37.3	61.4	70.8	85.6
7.0	13.7	8.0	13.8	15.0
82.0	73.2	65.9	76.0	106.1
13.8	10.5	6.4	6.0	9.1
61.4	35.7	33.1	28.3	45.6
144.0	235.6	241.6	285.7	250.5
98.4	2.3	1.5	3.0	3.3
3.6	4.0	4.2	5.8	25.3
14.4	15.3	15.0	13.4	17.2
29.0	6.6	10.9	28.5	18.1
807.9	732.0	774.5	835.4	999.1
78.1	107.1	75.9	91.9	109.0
2468.3	2593.0	2625.6	3117.2	3485.5
0.8	0.5	0.6	0.8	1.5
2.4	39.7	2.0	1.0	13.4
5.2	7.1	-0.4	20.6	20.9
857.4	1345.0	1255.9	1978.3	1937.0
65.4	82.2	63.8	70.5	109.5
3.5	3.7	3.4	3.2	3.7
65.2	71.3	54.9	44.7	38.5
4.9	4.5	6.5	14.7	29.4
0.5	0.5	0.5	0.6	1.5
39.1	35.3	26.6	17.2	19.7
64.9	69.5	15.2	13.1	41.4
2.4	2.3	2.4	1.8	32.7
85.1	72.1	82.2	84.3	115.2
9.7	6.6	5.3	10.5	1.6
10.2	7.1	18.1	40.8	7.1
1216.7	1747.2	1537.1	2302.0	2372.9
0.5	5.4	-1.0	6.9	-1.7
822.0	582.6	674.5	621.9	760.9
3.2	2.9	4.8	6.6	13.9
208.0	215.7	148.8	253.2	307.7
471.2	749.9	633.8	515.9	1014.9
0.9	3.2	3.4	6.9	11.4
111.4	109.5	98.4	123.5	170.2
400.4	254.1	302.7	427.9	610.4
305.4	347.0	318.7	334.1	388.2

	1980	1981	1982	1983	1984	1985	1986
South Asia Unall.	-2.0	-0.1	2.0	0.9	0.2	3.6	2.4
TOTAL	2447.2	2599.6	2324.9	2271.2	2184.2	2300.5	3278.3
FAR EAST ASIA							
Brunei	0.0	0.2	0.3	0.4	0.8	1.3	2.5
China	22.2	52.2	458.5	492.5	502.3	573.7	660.7
Hong Kong	3.6	3.6	3.7	4.7	9.3	16.7	14.1
Indonesia	844.2	799.5	751.9	619.2	548.7	502.7	605.2
Kampuchea	48.6	17.9	14.5	8.3	8.4	5.6	5.7
Korea	117.3	325.9	15.4	9.9	-34.9	-8.1	-23.5
Korea, Dem.	–	–	–	–	–	0.4	1.1
Laos	16.7	16.8	21.3	12.6	13.8	15.5	19.2
Macao	0.1	0.0	0.1	0.1	0.1	0.1	0.1
Malaysia	106.2	117.3	103.8	144.3	299.3	202.6	175.3
Mongolia	–	–	–	–	0.1	0.4	0.6
Philippines	205.4	331.0	276.4	358.5	355.8	437.6	886.8
Singapore	9.4	18.4	17.8	12.3	38.7	21.8	27.8
Taiwan	-4.6	-5.8	-8.3	-5.3	-1.4	-2.1	-0.5
Thailand	305.0	315.9	271.5	339.7	357.1	385.5	391.1
Viet Nam	151.9	125.2	101.9	70.9	80.7	54.2	90.0
Far East Asia Unall.	14.7	13.3	17.9	24.4	26.3	21.7	30.7
TOTAL	1840.8	2131.3	2046.7	2092.4	2205.2	2229.4	2886.7
Asia Unspecified	61.2	39.1	53.4	80.5	53.3	57.2	83.6
ASIA TOTAL	5567.0	5921.1	5641.7	6191.3	5979.7	6889.1	8621.5
OCEANIA							
Cook Islands	9.9	9.2	9.5	7.9	7.4	8.8	25.5
Fiji	31.7	30.3	30.0	22.3	23.5	26.3	32.4
Kiribati	18.6	13.7	14.4	14.4	10.4	10.9	11.9
Nauru	0.0	0.0	0.0	0.0	0.0	0.1	0.0
New Caledonia	197.7	147.5	158.2	181.6	129.6	145.2	205.5
Niue	3.4	3.9	4.2	5.5	3.1	3.5	3.9
Pacif. Isl.(Trust Tr.)	108.5	136.0	161.4	132.6	184.7	158.2	230.8
Papua New Guinea	286.9	304.0	276.3	274.4	294.9	240.6	243.0
Polynesia, French	159.5	146.4	172.6	177.6	171.6	170.5	247.2
Solomon Islands	31.0	24.3	22.0	18.2	13.7	13.5	19.4
Tokelau	1.8	1.3	1.8	1.7	1.7	1.6	1.8
Tonga	13.0	14.6	12.4	13.3	12.4	10.6	11.6
Tuvalu	4.5	4.5	5.5	3.8	5.2	3.2	3.8
Vanuatu	43.3	24.4	23.3	24.4	22.2	18.9	20.8
Wallis & Futuna	8.3	8.3	7.1	0.4	0.5	0.0	0.0
Western Samoa	13.7	14.2	15.4	16.6	11.0	13.2	18.1
TOM Unallocated	–	2.8	–	–	–	–	–
Oceania Unallocated	16.4	15.2	23.8	29.4	20.7	26.2	23.2
TOTAL	948.2	900.6	937.8	923.9	912.4	851.0	1098.8
LDCS Unspecified	992.0	857.2	941.8	774.3	1415.4	1353.2	1599.1
TOTAL,ALL LDCS	17310.9	17409.2	17603.2	17721.2	18751.1	20937.8	25013.0
INCOME GROUPS							
LLDCS	3490.7	3332.5	3559.5	3283.6	3478.4	4209.6	4970.4
CHINA AND INDIA	655.6	982.8	929.7	1242.3	1136.1	1089.6	1675.6
OTHER LOW-INCOME	4709.8	4601.2	4711.9	4411.3	4813.2	5079.0	6121.9
LOW MIDDLE-INCOME	3118.9	3086.3	3151.4	3376.6	3467.3	3619.4	4446.2
UPPER MIDDLE-INCOME	3865.0	4090.8	3660.0	3933.6	3824.6	4713.0	5288.6
UNALLOCATED	1471.0	1315.6	1590.7	1473.8	2031.5	2227.1	2510.4

Legend:
○——○ LLDCS
· · · · · CHINA AND INDIA
—·—· OTHER LICS
——— LMICS
— — — UMICS

	1980	1981	1982	1983	1984	1985	1986
EUROPE							
Cyprus	53.2	44.3	31.2	19.0	17.4	37.3	35.3
Gibraltar	11.2	7.4	3.1	3.4	11.0	28.9	20.8
Greece	40.1	13.9	12.1	12.7	12.5	13.4	20.5
Malta	16.0	49.5	25.4	44.0	11.4	18.4	6.9
Portugal	113.1	82.3	49.2	45.4	97.5	102.4	139.1
Turkey	951.7	724.2	644.1	352.4	240.5	176.5	347.2
Yugoslavia	-16.9	-14.8	-7.6	2.6	2.9	10.6	18.6
Europe Unallocated	6.6	17.5	21.0	42.0	20.3	21.8	15.8
TOTAL	*1174.8*	*924.4*	*778.6*	*521.4*	*413.5*	*409.1*	*604.1*
NORTH OF SAHARA							
Algeria	175.9	167.5	136.5	95.0	121.8	173.0	165.1
Egypt	1386.8	1292.3	1416.6	1437.9	1768.7	1766.3	1666.6
Libya	16.7	10.7	12.1	5.7	5.0	5.4	10.9
Morocco	894.2	1033.5	771.1	396.2	352.2	838.2	336.2
Tunisia	232.3	239.5	209.6	205.4	178.2	162.6	199.5
North of Sahara Unall.	3.1	0.7	11.2	39.6	2.7	13.4	-0.2
TOTAL	*2709.1*	*2744.2*	*2557.1*	*2180.0*	*2428.7*	*2958.9*	*2378.1*
SOUTH OF SAHARA							
Angola	52.6	61.0	60.0	75.3	95.0	91.5	131.2
Benin	91.1	81.6	80.6	86.4	77.6	95.8	138.1
Botswana	106.1	96.9	101.5	103.6	102.7	96.5	102.3
Burkina Faso	212.3	216.8	212.8	183.5	188.6	197.4	283.9
Burundi	117.4	122.0	126.8	140.0	141.4	142.6	187.6
Cameroon	265.0	198.7	212.4	129.0	186.5	159.3	225.1
Cape Verde	64.4	50.3	54.9	59.9	63.9	69.7	109.5
Central African Rep.	111.0	101.6	89.7	92.9	113.6	104.3	139.3
Chad	35.3	59.7	64.7	95.3	115.2	181.7	165.0
Comoros	43.3	46.6	38.9	38.2	41.0	47.6	46.3
Congo	92.1	81.0	93.1	108.4	97.9	71.2	110.2
Cote d'Ivoire	210.3	123.7	136.8	155.8	127.9	124.7	186.5
Djibouti	73.1	64.5	58.9	65.6	102.1	81.4	115.1
Equatorial Guinea	9.3	10.2	14.0	11.1	15.0	17.2	21.7
Ethiopia	211.8	245.0	199.7	339.3	363.7	714.8	641.8
Gabon	55.8	43.5	62.3	63.8	75.5	61.1	78.9
Gambia	54.8	68.2	47.6	42.1	53.6	50.1	100.9
Ghana	192.5	147.7	141.2	110.0	216.0	204.4	371.5
Guinea	89.6	106.7	90.1	67.5	123.4	119.2	174.9
Guinea-Bissau	59.5	65.2	65.2	64.2	55.2	57.7	71.0
Kenya	396.6	449.4	485.1	400.5	411.1	438.1	458.0
Lesotho	94.4	104.2	93.4	107.7	100.7	94.2	87.8
Liberia	98.0	108.6	108.9	118.5	133.2	90.6	97.3
Madagascar	230.1	234.3	241.7	183.5	153.4	187.8	316.4
Malawi	143.3	137.6	121.2	116.8	158.5	113.0	202.9
Mali	267.3	230.3	210.3	214.5	320.3	379.9	372.2
Mauritania	175.9	233.7	187.0	175.6	173.6	201.4	186.6
Mauritius	33.1	58.4	47.8	40.7	35.5	28.6	56.3
Mayotte	22.7	14.9	12.7	14.6	14.0	20.8	28.3
Mozambique	169.1	143.6	207.9	210.8	259.1	300.1	421.3
Namibia	–	–	–	0.0	–	6.0	15.6
Niger	170.1	193.4	257.5	174.8	161.0	304.9	307.8
Nigeria	35.7	40.7	36.8	47.6	33.0	32.3	59.8
Reunion	495.1	643.4	400.5	410.7	346.3	383.5	505.7
Rwanda	155.4	153.7	150.7	149.4	164.7	181.2	210.7
St. Helena	8.8	8.3	10.2	9.9	10.0	12.2	13.5
Sao Tome & Principe	3.9	6.1	9.9	11.6	11.3	12.5	12.4
Senegal	262.1	396.7	284.8	322.3	367.9	294.1	567.4
Seychelles	21.7	17.0	18.3	15.6	15.1	22.2	28.6
Sierra Leone	90.9	60.1	82.2	66.0	60.8	65.9	87.1
Somalia	433.3	374.6	462.1	343.0	350.1	353.3	523.3
Sudan	583.4	631.9	740.4	961.9	621.8	1128.6	940.2
Swaziland	50.1	36.7	28.2	33.5	29.7	25.4	34.6
Tanzania	678.7	702.7	684.0	593.9	557.9	486.9	680.9
Togo	91.0	62.9	77.2	112.0	110.0	114.0	174.3
Uganda	113.6	135.8	132.8	137.1	162.6	182.7	197.8
Zaire	427.5	393.6	348.2	314.5	312.2	324.8	448.1
Zambia	318.4	231.6	317.1	216.9	239.5	328.5	464.5
Zimbabwe	164.1	212.3	216.1	208.5	297.8	237.1	224.8
East African Community	5.5	5.0	4.2	5.2	2.5	10.8	1.8
DOM/TOM Unallocated	–	–	–	–	–	–	–
EAMA Unallocated	94.7	2.1	4.5	37.2	59.4	–	–
South of Sahara Unall.	94.8	123.5	241.2	175.6	197.7	486.6	392.3
TOTAL	*8076.6*	*8137.9*	*8174.0*	*7962.3*	*8226.3*	*9536.1*	*11518.8*
Africa Unspecified	171.6	207.3	211.1	221.9	739.9	389.1	408.1
AFRICA TOTAL	*10957.3*	*11089.3*	*10942.2*	*10364.2*	*11394.9*	*12884.1*	*14305.0*
N.& C. AMERICA							
Aruba	–	–	–	–	–	12.0	40.4
Bahamas	2.1	2.0	1.9	0.9	10.9	0.9	5.8
Barbados	13.9	17.2	12.9	19.0	8.8	8.3	3.8

	1980	1981
Belize	14.7	11.4
Bermuda	0.3	0.2
Costa Rica	64.8	54.7
Cuba	32.0	13.7
Dominican Republic	125.0	105.1
El Salvador	96.5	167.4
Guadeloupe	88.9	28.1
Guatemala	72.8	75.4
Haiti	105.2	106.9
Honduras	103.0	109.3
Jamaica	136.0	154.7
Martinique	568.8	449.8
Mexico	56.0	99.6
Netherlands Antilles	96.6	73.6
Nicaragua	222.8	172.2
Panama	45.7	39.3
St. Pierre & Miquelon	27.9	25.2
Trinidad & Tobago	4.7	-1.4
Anguilla	2.3	2.6
Antigua and Barbuda	5.6	9.1
Cayman Islands	1.5	1.0
Dominica	17.7	15.3
Grenada	3.2	6.1
Montserrat	3.6	3.4
St. Kitts-Nevis	6.2	3.8
St. Lucia	8.6	11.5
St. Vincent and Gr.	9.7	9.2
Turks & Caicos Isl.	3.4	7.1
Virgin Islands	4.7	3.8
West Indies Unall.	7.9	7.5
DOM/TOM Unallocated	-1.9	8.3
N.& C. America Unall.	14.5	34.0
TOTAL	*1964.7*	*1826.9*
SOUTH AMERICA		
Argentina	18.5	43.8
Bolivia	169.7	169.0
Brazil	85.4	235.0
Chile	-9.7	-7.0
Colombia	90.1	101.6
Ecuador	46.4	59.1
Falkland Islands	2.3	2.1
Guiana	111.7	81.8
Guyana	41.6	64.7
Paraguay	30.5	54.6
Peru	203.2	233.3
Suriname	82.2	96.8
Uruguay	9.8	7.5
Venezuela	15.3	14.3
South America Unall.	5.3	7.4
TOTAL	*902.3*	*1164.1*
America Unspecified	192.8	136.9
AMERICA TOTAL	*3059.8*	*3127.9*
MIDDLE EAST		
Bahrain	156.0	142.5
Iran	30.9	8.9
Iraq	8.4	8.9
Israel	892.2	772.4
Jordan	1275.1	1064.9
Kuwait	10.2	9.4
Lebanon	237.2	455.1
Oman	167.9	230.7
Qatar	0.9	1.1
Saudi Arabia	15.5	29.6
Syria	1696.5	1500.3
United Arab Emirates	4.2	0.7
Yemen	471.6	410.7
Yemen, Dem.	100.1	86.9
Middle East Unall.	167.5	206.3
TOTAL	*5234.2*	*4928.4*
SOUTH ASIA		
Afghanistan	32.3	23.2
Bangladesh	1282.5	1104.2
Bhutan	8.3	9.8
Burma	308.7	283.4
India	2146.5	1910.1
Maldives	21.4	12.8
Nepal	163.1	180.6
Pakistan	1130.4	763.7
Sri Lanka	389.6	377.3

1982	1983	1984	1985	1986
12.1	15.1	14.0	22.0	24.1
0.1	0.1	0.1	0.9	0.1
80.3	252.1	217.6	280.1	195.7
16.5	13.2	12.0	18.2	18.0
136.5	102.4	197.8	221.8	105.6
223.1	295.0	262.8	345.1	355.3
173.2	188.2	131.2	164.9	205.6
63.7	75.8	65.4	82.8	134.8
127.6	133.7	134.9	152.9	175.3
158.1	191.6	289.6	276.2	288.5
180.3	180.7	170.3	169.2	177.1
325.9	298.6	247.3	293.4	380.4
139.9	131.6	83.4	144.6	251.6
65.0	65.1	63.0	64.8	57.5
120.8	120.4	113.7	102.4	150.3
41.0	47.0	72.1	69.2	52.2
26.4	24.4	17.6	17.1	21.1
5.7	5.6	4.6	6.6	19.1
2.0	2.3	1.7	2.7	3.0
5.0	3.4	2.9	3.0	5.1
0.6	0.4	0.4	0.1	2.0
17.3	10.2	16.6	16.9	11.2
6.7	8.0	27.5	34.8	24.8
4.0	2.2	1.8	2.2	3.8
3.2	2.8	3.6	4.5	5.5
8.2	6.9	5.7	7.0	11.8
7.6	5.3	4.0	5.6	12.4
10.3	6.7	6.9	5.6	8.9
3.8	3.2	1.9	2.1	1.5
5.5	5.6	8.8	9.1	31.5
0.0	–	–	–	–
32.7	47.7	67.7	121.4	84.9
2017.8	*2265.1*	*2266.3*	*2668.4*	*2868.6*
29.9	47.4	49.2	39.4	87.6
147.4	173.6	171.9	202.1	321.4
208.1	100.8	160.8	122.8	178.4
-8.4	0.2	2.5	40.4	-5.1
96.8	86.2	88.1	61.7	63.5
53.0	63.7	136.2	135.8	146.5
7.3	13.7	8.1	13.8	15.0
92.6	75.0	70.4	89.9	137.1
39.0	30.7	23.1	27.0	30.7
85.1	51.3	50.4	50.1	66.4
187.9	297.1	310.1	316.4	271.5
101.5	3.9	5.1	6.0	5.6
3.9	2.7	3.9	4.9	26.7
12.4	10.0	14.1	11.2	16.0
29.0	6.6	10.9	29.0	22.9
1085.4	*962.8*	*1104.7*	*1150.4*	*1384.2*
155.3	203.1	151.8	181.1	168.3
3258.5	*3430.9*	*3522.8*	*3999.9*	*4421.1*
93.1	217.4	199.3	72.4	99.6
2.9	47.8	12.9	16.5	26.9
6.4	12.9	4.0	26.0	33.3
857.4	1345.0	1255.9	1978.4	1937.1
798.6	787.3	685.9	541.0	537.1
5.9	5.2	4.5	4.2	5.0
187.0	126.7	77.4	94.2	62.2
132.4	71.0	66.7	78.0	83.8
1.1	1.3	1.3	1.9	2.3
57.2	43.6	35.7	28.8	31.3
961.5	989.8	852.9	623.0	842.6
5.0	4.3	3.4	3.2	34.2
412.5	327.9	325.2	275.3	233.5
142.9	105.7	102.1	112.5	58.0
260.1	34.1	41.5	66.6	36.0
3924.1	*4120.0*	*3668.5*	*3921.9*	*4022.9*
9.3	13.5	6.7	16.8	2.3
1346.2	1066.7	1200.3	1151.3	1455.7
11.3	13.0	17.9	24.1	40.0
318.9	302.0	274.8	355.7	415.7
1545.1	1740.7	1609.3	1526.8	2059.2
5.4	11.0	5.6	9.2	16.3
200.6	200.8	198.3	236.3	300.9
849.2	668.6	683.0	735.2	951.9
415.5	472.6	466.6	484.6	570.7

	1980	1981	1982	1983	1984	1985	1986
South Asia Unall.	-2.0	-0.1	2.0	0.9	0.2	103.6	128.6
TOTAL	*5480.8*	*4665.0*	*4703.6*	*4489.7*	*4462.6*	*4643.6*	*5941.3*
FAR EAST ASIA							
Brunei	0.0	0.2	0.3	0.4	0.8	1.4	2.5
China	66.1	477.0	524.0	669.6	798.2	940.0	1133.9
Hong Kong	10.9	9.5	7.9	8.8	13.8	20.5	18.5
Indonesia	949.5	975.4	906.3	744.5	672.7	603.2	711.2
Kampuchea	281.2	130.0	43.9	36.7	16.9	12.9	13.2
Korea	139.0	330.6	34.0	8.0	-36.6	-8.6	-17.3
Korea, Dem.	–	–	–	–	–	5.7	5.6
Laos	40.9	35.0	38.3	29.7	34.1	37.0	48.2
Macao	4.4	0.0	0.7	0.6	0.5	0.4	0.4
Malaysia	135.0	143.3	135.3	176.6	326.6	229.2	192.8
Mongolia	–	–	–	–	0.1	3.3	4.6
Philippines	299.8	376.1	333.4	429.0	397.0	486.2	955.8
Singapore	14.0	21.8	20.5	14.6	41.0	23.9	29.7
Taiwan	-3.6	7.8	-6.4	8.2	5.4	-9.7	-10.1
Thailand	418.4	406.7	388.9	431.7	474.1	480.9	496.3
Viet Nam	228.5	242.4	135.5	105.9	109.9	114.0	146.5
Far East Asia Unall.	14.7	13.3	18.3	24.4	26.3	21.8	38.3
TOTAL	*2598.9*	*3169.0*	*2580.9*	*2688.7*	*2880.7*	*2962.0*	*3769.9*
Asia Unspecified	107.5	106.5	110.0	145.9	796.1	142.1	1737.3
ASIA TOTAL	*13421.4*	*12868.8*	*11318.5*	*11444.3*	*11807.8*	*11669.6*	*15471.3*
OCEANIA							
Cook Islands	10.7	10.5	10.4	9.3	8.1	9.7	26.4
Fiji	36.1	40.5	35.4	32.7	31.3	31.9	42.5
Kiribati	19.2	15.3	15.1	16.8	11.9	12.0	13.4
Nauru	0.0	0.0	0.0	0.0	0.0	0.1	0.0
New Caledonia	198.0	150.2	158.7	181.9	130.5	145.4	206.6
Niue	3.7	4.2	4.4	5.6	3.2	3.5	4.2
Pacif. Isl.(Trust Tr.)	109.3	136.4	162.0	134.0	185.5	159.3	232.2
Papua New Guinea	325.9	335.9	310.7	332.8	321.8	258.9	263.6
Polynesia, French	159.5	146.7	173.2	177.8	172.0	172.0	247.6
Solomon Islands	44.5	31.1	28.4	27.5	19.4	20.8	30.2
Tokelau	1.9	1.4	1.9	1.8	1.8	1.8	2.0
Tonga	16.4	18.0	17.4	17.9	15.7	13.6	15.1
Tuvalu	4.9	5.4	6.2	4.2	5.5	3.3	4.4
Vanuatu	44.0	30.4	26.0	26.9	24.5	21.8	24.4
Wallis & Futuna	8.3	8.6	7.3	1.6	1.6	0.2	0.1
Western Samoa	25.7	25.0	22.8	26.7	20.2	19.4	23.3
TOM Unallocated	–	2.8	–	–	–	–	–
Oceania Unallocated	16.4	15.2	23.8	29.4	20.7	26.2	23.3
TOTAL	*1024.4*	*977.7*	*1003.7*	*1027.0*	*973.6*	*899.9*	*1159.1*
LDCS Unspecified	4142.3	3833.2	2294.2	2382.4	2130.1	2459.8	2275.6
TOTAL,ALL LDCS	*33780.0*	*32821.4*	*29595.7*	*29170.2*	*30242.6*	*32322.3*	*38236.2*
INCOME GROUPS							
LLDCS	6599.2	6408.4	6818.1	6530.6	6597.2	7666.4	8676.7
CHINA AND INDIA	2212.6	2387.1	2069.1	2410.3	2407.5	2466.8	3193.0
OTHER LOW-INCOME	7167.2	6578.4	6630.8	6103.9	6623.4	6812.6	8351.1
LOW MIDDLE-INCOME	5058.4	5030.4	4613.1	4391.7	4300.9	4766.6	5299.1
UPPER MIDDLE-INCOME	7701.6	7689.7	6040.0	6332.3	6037.2	6527.4	7351.9
UNALLOCATED	5041.0	4727.3	3423.9	3401.4	4276.5	4082.5	5364.4

Legend:
- ○○○○○ LLDCS
- - - - - CHINA AND INDIA
- —·—·— OTHER LICS
- ——— LMICS
- - - - - UMICS

Chart x-axis: 80 81 82 83 84 85 86; y-axis: 2000, 3000, 4000, 5000, 6000, 7000, 8000, 9000

	1980	1981	1982	1983	1984	1985	1986		1980	1981
EUROPE								Belize	3.6	3.1
Cyprus	21.5	17.4	17.1	10.2	11.1	13.5	11.1	Bermuda	0.2	0.2
Gibraltar	–	–	–	–	–	–	–	Costa Rica	42.1	25.0
Greece	20.6	6.8	7.8	7.0	4.5	6.5	5.3	Cuba	20.9	11.1
Malta	9.7	10.6	1.7	1.3	1.4	0.3	1.6	Dominican Republic	66.8	51.2
Portugal	4.9	3.2	3.6	10.0	16.8	3.4	18.2	El Salvador	47.0	58.2
Turkey	22.5	48.8	22.4	34.3	21.7	12.4	80.3	Guadeloupe	3.8	0.9
Yugoslavia	2.4	2.8	2.9	3.0	4.3	3.8	4.2	Guatemala	39.3	44.0
Europe Unallocated	1.2	10.3	10.0	27.5	13.8	14.3	15.4	Haiti	42.3	39.9
TOTAL	*82.8*	*99.9*	*65.5*	*93.4*	*73.4*	*54.2*	*135.9*	Honduras	55.4	52.2
								Jamaica	32.5	44.6
NORTH OF SAHARA								Martinique	5.0	1.2
Algeria	16.9	19.2	9.4	12.5	9.7	22.0	17.8	Mexico	1.0	-2.8
Egypt	195.7	206.2	222.6	247.9	167.7	135.2	96.3	Netherlands Antilles	9.6	4.5
Libya	6.8	8.7	9.8	3.3	2.8	2.2	2.5	Nicaragua	104.0	86.1
Morocco	66.0	65.5	62.6	86.8	31.2	63.2	41.1	Panama	27.5	17.9
Tunisia	25.5	35.3	27.5	37.2	29.0	35.7	36.5	St. Pierre & Miquelon	–	0.0
North of Sahara Unall.	0.1	–	–	–	–	–	–	Trinidad & Tobago	3.2	4.5
TOTAL	*311.0*	*335.0*	*331.8*	*387.7*	*240.5*	*258.2*	*194.1*	Anguilla	–	–
								Antigua and Barbuda	3.0	2.4
SOUTH OF SAHARA								Cayman Islands	0.5	0.6
Angola	16.2	21.6	19.5	28.7	34.3	31.9	36.5	Dominica	9.4	9.4
Benin	52.9	35.3	39.3	43.0	38.1	45.3	62.9	Grenada	2.7	5.8
Botswana	22.6	21.0	12.2	20.6	27.6	34.2	21.5	Montserrat	0.5	0.8
Burkina Faso	61.2	58.8	62.0	55.1	54.3	71.7	98.0	St. Kitts-Nevis	3.5	1.6
Burundi	53.9	55.0	45.4	64.1	57.8	59.1	89.4	St. Lucia	6.0	7.7
Cameroon	70.9	64.7	60.7	25.8	24.2	29.7	45.2	St. Vincent and Gr.	7.8	5.7
Cape Verde	23.4	14.1	10.7	14.3	23.3	27.1	31.4	Turks & Caicos Isl.	0.4	0.2
Central African Rep.	33.8	28.8	19.8	27.8	45.1	42.4	50.4	Virgin Islands	1.8	1.3
Chad	15.1	28.5	25.6	43.7	56.0	85.9	62.8	West Indies Unall.	–	–
Comoros	13.4	16.2	14.4	16.8	18.3	25.3	23.1	DOM/TOM Unallocated	-1.9	8.3
Congo	21.7	25.7	26.8	26.5	20.2	25.4	10.3	N.& C. America Unall.	1.3	0.7
Cote d'Ivoire	58.5	32.5	34.5	15.0	13.6	14.2	48.7	*TOTAL*	*553.1*	*501.2*
Djibouti	8.6	14.6	12.6	12.8	20.2	22.8	21.5			
Equatorial Guinea	8.1	6.0	8.9	7.1	7.1	10.3	11.1	**SOUTH AMERICA**		
Ethiopia	120.4	150.5	122.7	175.9	175.6	288.5	240.0	Argentina	-13.6	15.3
Gabon	6.7	4.3	3.7	6.0	5.7	9.4	6.2	Bolivia	71.0	71.2
Gambia	30.9	28.0	20.5	19.7	20.4	18.1	42.8	Brazil	21.6	26.7
Ghana	59.3	43.6	72.8	53.6	125.2	113.1	247.5	Chile	3.5	-2.5
Guinea	56.9	50.7	34.8	41.6	51.3	57.3	73.0	Colombia	58.3	58.4
Guinea-Bissau	23.7	23.8	26.7	25.9	22.4	30.5	26.8	Ecuador	23.1	34.0
Kenya	119.6	84.5	146.0	58.0	85.5	87.8	68.0	Falkland Islands	–	0.0
Lesotho	30.6	41.6	36.2	40.4	31.5	39.6	32.2	Guiana	2.4	2.6
Liberia	28.7	19.8	22.5	30.0	25.6	26.3	28.1	Guyana	30.6	48.6
Madagascar	91.4	85.4	79.7	73.4	64.1	93.1	141.7	Paraguay	5.3	23.6
Malawi	67.7	55.5	56.1	60.6	106.8	60.1	113.2	Peru	26.6	46.3
Mali	103.4	90.1	74.2	85.9	87.9	101.9	128.5	Suriname	5.1	2.8
Mauritania	36.0	50.5	48.8	57.8	56.8	48.6	56.8	Uruguay	4.5	0.9
Mauritius	7.9	9.6	15.2	13.5	8.1	4.4	6.7	Venezuela	0.2	1.3
Mayotte	–	0.2	–	–	0.2	1.0	2.2	South America Unall.	–	–
Mozambique	34.1	32.7	40.9	49.2	66.1	76.9	95.4	*TOTAL*	*238.5*	*329.2*
Namibia	–	–	–	–	–	3.2	9.1	America Unspecified	128.6	59.2
Niger	63.6	50.7	43.6	49.8	52.0	96.2	117.9	*AMERICA TOTAL*	*920.3*	*889.5*
Nigeria	18.3	24.0	20.1	18.4	18.3	16.3	20.0			
Reunion	8.4	9.9	3.2	25.1	17.5	31.6	64.6	**MIDDLE EAST**		
Rwanda	57.5	50.5	51.6	53.1	62.8	72.8	80.9	Bahrain	8.1	3.2
St. Helena	–	0.1	0.0	0.0	0.0	0.0	0.0	Iran	0.1	1.4
Sao Tome & Principe	2.7	4.3	6.0	8.2	7.4	9.5	5.4	Iraq	4.8	3.9
Senegal	79.1	129.1	79.6	62.0	63.6	60.2	218.2	Israel	0.2	0.3
Seychelles	3.4	2.0	3.2	1.9	1.5	8.5	6.5	Jordan	46.4	33.3
Sierra Leone	29.8	26.3	26.2	30.4	24.7	35.4	30.0	Kuwait	2.7	3.0
Somalia	166.3	188.2	160.1	152.4	150.1	153.8	166.8	Lebanon	19.1	25.1
Sudan	192.2	222.5	217.1	166.0	195.5	267.2	285.5	Oman	7.5	2.8
Swaziland	17.4	13.0	9.3	13.0	12.1	7.1	9.8	Qatar	0.6	0.6
Tanzania	127.5	173.2	187.5	149.6	140.4	104.3	161.5	Saudi Arabia	6.5	11.0
Togo	38.8	25.6	23.0	60.4	54.9	51.7	74.7	Syria	30.2	54.7
Uganda	69.9	57.1	78.9	89.1	118.1	139.6	117.1	United Arab Emirates	2.5	2.8
Zaire	105.7	102.0	91.8	120.6	102.8	115.2	152.0	Yemen	54.5	69.5
Zambia	61.6	50.4	52.3	33.3	57.7	113.1	115.4	Yemen, Dem.	46.4	50.0
Zimbabwe	47.0	67.4	29.8	22.8	53.3	25.5	35.6	Middle East Unall.	164.5	184.8
East African Community	–	–	–	–	–	–	–	*TOTAL*	*394.0*	*446.2*
DOM/TOM Unallocated	–	–	–	–	–	–	–			
EAMA Unallocated	–	–	0.0	–	–	–	–	**SOUTH ASIA**		
South of Sahara Unall.	42.3	8.6	2.7	7.2	18.1	83.8	20.9	Afghanistan	19.4	10.5
TOTAL	*2409.3*	*2397.8*	*2278.9*	*2255.8*	*2523.9*	*2976.6*	*3614.0*	Bangladesh	362.1	375.6
Africa Unspecified	29.3	75.6	78.5	89.6	105.7	201.9	211.9	Bhutan	6.6	7.2
AFRICA TOTAL	*2749.6*	*2808.3*	*2689.2*	*2733.0*	*2870.1*	*3436.7*	*4020.0*	Burma	77.4	80.0
								India	1521.7	1050.1
N.& C. AMERICA								Maldives	4.4	3.8
Aruba	–	–	–	–	–	–	–	Nepal	72.3	83.8
Bahamas	2.0	1.9	1.8	0.8	2.8	0.8	5.6	Pakistan	418.4	339.4
Barbados	12.0	13.2	11.0	7.4	3.7	2.3	1.0	Sri Lanka	87.5	89.9

1982	1983	1984	1985	1986
5.3	2.8	1.4	1.7	1.7
0.1	0.0	0.1	0.9	0.1
20.9	35.0	31.9	41.2	30.8
15.0	11.3	5.6	15.7	14.3
42.3	42.8	46.0	45.2	29.7
42.3	51.0	33.5	38.7	24.4
9.8	34.7	13.1	17.2	52.0
32.2	26.2	24.9	20.4	23.5
48.9	54.9	63.9	50.3	48.8
60.6	83.2	114.8	64.9	43.7
29.1	24.5	14.3	11.0	16.5
10.7	28.6	15.6	24.8	39.2
-2.2	-4.2	8.1	22.0	4.4
3.3	2.0	7.1	2.6	1.2
43.9	47.5	42.0	35.2	45.8
15.3	24.0	15.2	24.7	24.0
0.0	0.5	–	–	–
4.3	3.8	3.1	5.8	2.7
–	0.1	0.3	1.2	0.4
2.7	2.0	1.4	0.8	0.7
0.4	0.3	0.4	0.1	2.0
11.2	5.5	5.5	7.6	4.0
4.9	5.7	4.8	4.2	7.5
0.7	0.5	0.1	0.5	0.5
1.4	1.4	2.0	2.2	3.7
5.3	2.9	2.8	4.5	9.8
5.0	3.8	2.9	3.9	4.1
0.2	0.3	1.6	0.8	0.9
1.1	1.4	0.8	0.6	0.2
–	–	–	0.1	8.4
0.0	–	–	–	–
3.6	1.4	6.2	7.3	6.5
431.0	501.9	475.6	459.3	457.9
6.0	19.2	23.6	8.4	29.8
59.0	40.2	62.4	75.7	124.8
46.0	8.6	23.4	60.3	47.3
-4.4	-6.3	-7.2	-5.4	-4.7
44.1	49.8	46.5	24.9	26.7
22.7	26.4	74.8	65.1	60.9
0.3	–	0.0	–	–
10.6	1.9	4.5	13.9	31.0
25.3	20.2	16.7	21.0	21.6
23.8	15.7	17.3	21.8	20.8
43.9	61.5	68.5	30.7	21.1
3.1	1.6	3.6	3.1	2.3
0.4	-1.3	-0.3	-0.9	1.4
-2.0	-5.3	-0.9	-2.3	-1.1
–	–	–	0.6	4.8
278.5	232.1	332.7	316.7	386.5
73.2	92.5	75.9	89.2	59.3
782.7	826.5	884.2	865.2	903.6
2.8	1.5	0.6	0.0	-0.1
0.5	8.1	10.9	15.4	13.5
2.7	7.6	6.3	5.7	12.3
–	–	–	0.1	0.1
33.2	21.8	21.2	16.0	20.7
2.4	1.5	1.1	1.0	1.3
39.8	39.5	22.4	26.3	21.1
2.4	2.9	6.2	3.9	1.9
0.6	0.8	0.8	1.3	0.9
18.1	8.0	9.1	11.6	11.6
17.0	40.3	24.1	36.9	55.2
2.6	2.1	0.9	1.3	1.5
75.1	63.5	56.3	60.3	57.8
61.4	67.4	53.0	56.8	47.0
249.9	27.0	23.3	25.8	28.8
508.4	291.8	236.1	262.3	273.6
8.4	10.3	8.3	11.4	7.3
398.2	387.8	512.0	520.1	613.5
8.1	10.0	12.8	14.7	17.8
111.0	86.3	126.1	102.5	108.0
1186.3	1127.4	1015.9	1048.0	1087.4
3.0	4.2	2.8	3.6	5.1
89.2	92.2	100.8	114.3	126.7
428.7	414.6	434.7	389.8	413.2
110.9	124.4	144.5	145.0	160.6

	1980	1981	1982	1983	1984	1985	1986
South Asia Unall.	–	–	–	–	–	–	–
TOTAL	2569.8	2040.4	2343.7	2257.3	2357.8	2349.4	2539.5
FAR EAST ASIA							
Brunei	0.0	–	–	0.0	–	0.1	0.1
China	43.9	424.7	65.5	141.4	246.5	344.3	450.5
Hong Kong	7.3	6.0	4.3	4.1	4.5	3.8	4.4
Indonesia	94.3	156.8	145.5	124.3	108.1	99.3	85.6
Kampuchea	231.6	112.1	29.4	28.4	8.5	7.3	7.5
Korea	10.8	4.9	23.4	2.8	2.9	4.0	4.4
Korea, Dem.	–	–	–	–	–	5.2	4.4
Laos	24.1	18.2	17.0	17.1	20.4	21.5	29.0
Macao	4.4	–	0.7	0.5	0.4	0.3	0.3
Malaysia	19.3	15.7	16.4	15.9	13.3	11.9	8.8
Mongolia	–	–	–	–	–	2.9	3.9
Philippines	90.8	45.1	55.5	71.0	41.6	49.3	69.3
Singapore	4.0	3.4	2.6	2.4	2.2	2.1	1.9
Taiwan	-0.2	-0.2	-0.5	-0.5	-0.5	-0.5	-0.5
Thailand	103.4	81.9	84.9	81.6	99.0	84.2	97.1
Viet Nam	70.1	113.0	30.6	32.4	29.2	44.4	52.5
Far East Asia Unall.	–	–	0.4	–	–	0.2	7.6
TOTAL	703.7	981.6	475.6	521.6	576.1	680.3	826.7
Asia Unspecified	46.3	66.6	56.5	65.4	71.5	84.9	96.4
ASIA TOTAL	3713.8	3534.7	3384.3	3136.1	3241.5	3376.9	3736.1
OCEANIA							
Cook Islands	0.8	1.3	0.9	1.4	0.7	1.0	0.9
Fiji	4.5	10.2	5.4	10.5	7.8	5.6	10.1
Kiribati	0.6	1.6	0.7	2.4	1.6	1.2	1.5
Nauru	–	–	–	–	–	–	–
New Caledonia	0.3	2.7	0.4	0.3	0.9	0.2	1.1
Niue	0.3	0.3	0.2	0.1	0.1	0.0	0.3
Pacif. Isl.(Trust Tr.)	0.8	0.5	0.6	1.4	0.8	1.1	1.4
Papua New Guinea	38.6	31.7	34.4	58.7	27.1	18.6	20.8
Polynesia, French	–	0.3	0.6	0.3	0.5	1.5	0.4
Solomon Islands	13.5	6.8	6.4	9.3	5.5	6.1	8.4
Tokelau	0.1	0.1	0.1	0.1	0.1	0.2	0.2
Tonga	3.5	3.5	5.0	4.7	3.3	3.0	3.5
Tuvalu	0.4	0.9	0.8	0.4	0.3	0.2	0.6
Vanuatu	0.7	6.1	2.7	2.5	2.3	2.9	3.6
Wallis & Futuna	–	0.3	0.2	1.2	1.2	0.2	0.1
Western Samoa	12.0	10.8	7.5	10.1	9.3	5.9	4.5
TOM Unallocated	–	0.1	–	–	–	–	–
Oceania Unallocated	–	–	–	–	–	–	0.1
TOTAL	75.8	76.9	65.8	103.3	61.2	47.5	57.5
LDCS Unspecified	248.0	516.1	537.5	682.9	639.1	688.1	618.4
TOTAL,ALL LDCS	7790.3	7925.4	7525.0	7575.2	7769.5	8468.6	9471.5
INCOME GROUPS							
LLDCS	2156.6	2244.7	2185.7	2295.0	2549.9	2862.0	3188.4
CHINA AND INDIA	1565.6	1474.9	1251.8	1268.9	1262.4	1392.3	1537.9
OTHER LOW-INCOME	1925.6	1824.2	1815.5	1691.7	1810.8	1782.9	2196.0
LOW MIDDLE-INCOME	954.9	920.6	770.0	820.8	679.5	645.3	775.4
UPPER MIDDLE-INCOME	527.9	531.0	489.8	505.5	513.5	589.9	695.4
UNALLOCATED	659.6	930.1	1012.2	993.3	953.5	1196.2	1078.4

Legend:
- LLDCS
- CHINA AND INDIA
- OTHER LICS
- LMICS
- UMICS

	1980	1981	1982	1983	1984	1985	1986
EUROPE							
Cyprus	29.7	26.0	27.4	20.8	18.6	81.0	97.8
Gibraltar	–	–	–	–	–	–	–
Greece	93.9	4.3	46.2	19.0	28.5	63.3	1.3
Malta	9.3	10.3	1.5	0.9	1.0	-0.1	2.2
Portugal	106.8	60.0	125.2	140.0	36.8	125.5	34.0
Turkey	266.2	482.1	545.8	406.2	505.4	636.2	668.1
Yugoslavia	203.1	164.8	240.3	165.4	276.1	216.3	90.4
Europe Unallocated	1.2	10.3	10.0	27.5	13.8	14.3	15.4
TOTAL	*710.3*	*757.6*	*996.3*	*779.6*	*880.2*	*1136.5*	*909.3*
NORTH OF SAHARA							
Algeria	56.4	61.6	-18.8	89.3	56.5	235.4	67.9
Egypt	360.6	351.1	316.7	386.3	355.7	287.6	232.1
Libya	15.9	8.7	7.6	1.4	1.8	30.6	-2.4
Morocco	115.5	181.9	175.4	284.6	242.8	390.1	404.5
Tunisia	82.3	146.8	92.5	109.7	107.1	144.9	135.3
North of Sahara Unall.	0.1	–	–	–	–	–	–
TOTAL	*630.9*	*750.1*	*573.4*	*871.3*	*763.9*	*1088.6*	*837.4*
SOUTH OF SAHARA							
Angola	16.2	21.6	19.5	28.7	34.3	34.8	42.0
Benin	56.3	38.7	38.9	42.6	37.4	44.7	63.3
Botswana	26.4	30.7	28.8	39.1	50.4	74.1	30.9
Burkina Faso	63.0	56.4	61.8	57.9	53.9	73.5	103.8
Burundi	54.2	55.2	46.2	74.0	68.3	65.2	94.5
Cameroon	106.0	85.4	79.6	59.9	64.3	76.0	125.5
Cape Verde	23.4	14.1	17.8	18.4	24.0	28.3	31.4
Central African Rep.	34.0	28.7	19.7	28.6	46.6	45.9	57.0
Chad	15.1	28.5	25.6	43.7	56.0	85.9	62.8
Comoros	13.4	22.0	13.8	16.9	20.1	28.5	23.8
Congo	22.2	29.9	36.8	35.5	38.6	46.4	26.5
Cote d'Ivoire	147.5	66.1	236.2	198.1	207.4	36.9	121.9
Djibouti	8.6	14.6	12.6	12.8	20.2	22.8	21.5
Equatorial Guinea	8.8	7.4	11.5	8.3	7.4	10.0	11.3
Ethiopia	118.3	149.2	120.8	174.6	173.8	285.4	237.6
Gabon	9.2	8.8	12.9	14.7	11.9	11.2	20.4
Gambia	36.6	35.8	19.3	22.5	23.5	19.7	42.8
Ghana	83.2	67.8	81.1	51.2	117.4	117.8	255.1
Guinea	63.7	57.9	25.6	41.4	62.7	57.5	67.1
Guinea-Bissau	28.5	25.4	28.7	29.9	25.8	33.5	27.5
Kenya	163.9	129.5	221.4	149.0	195.4	189.0	77.5
Lesotho	30.6	41.8	38.3	42.8	36.2	50.3	31.6
Liberia	53.0	39.3	29.7	40.7	43.7	47.1	27.9
Madagascar	91.4	86.7	80.3	70.9	63.7	96.5	159.4
Malawi	83.5	82.2	78.1	63.0	108.2	64.3	114.6
Mali	103.7	88.4	75.8	86.8	90.7	101.0	127.2
Mauritania	36.7	66.5	86.5	84.1	55.7	52.8	48.3
Mauritius	22.6	33.4	22.5	20.6	30.5	28.5	9.0
Mayotte	–	0.2	–	–	0.2	1.0	2.2
Mozambique	34.3	40.6	49.8	54.1	68.3	85.3	104.7
Namibia	–	–	–	–	–	3.2	9.1
Niger	81.5	67.1	35.0	57.5	49.1	96.2	118.4
Nigeria	64.4	72.4	141.1	171.8	249.9	255.6	474.3
Reunion	8.4	9.9	3.2	25.1	17.5	31.6	64.6
Rwanda	57.6	50.6	52.9	53.7	62.5	72.5	80.8
St. Helena	–	0.1	0.0	0.0	0.0	0.0	0.0
Sao Tome & Principe	2.7	4.3	6.0	8.2	7.4	9.5	5.4
Senegal	105.2	152.6	91.7	99.5	69.7	63.9	222.7
Seychelles	5.8	3.3	7.2	3.0	2.2	13.0	10.2
Sierra Leone	33.2	27.6	26.5	29.5	21.1	34.8	27.1
Somalia	201.1	190.4	158.6	147.4	150.8	146.2	161.6
Sudan	196.3	255.8	211.2	153.4	179.4	262.4	257.5
Swaziland	34.4	24.5	24.0	27.5	11.8	3.9	16.8
Tanzania	149.1	191.1	194.9	166.9	147.9	138.3	140.6
Togo	70.6	23.0	20.5	59.3	53.9	50.6	72.3
Uganda	71.7	61.9	85.4	98.1	123.3	190.0	121.2
Zaire	129.1	96.2	87.4	118.2	98.7	139.2	196.9
Zambia	91.6	75.8	71.3	36.1	76.7	178.7	142.6
Zimbabwe	40.6	111.0	49.8	67.4	106.2	76.0	73.9
East African Community	–	–	–	–	–	–	–
DOM/TOM Unallocated	–	–	–	–	–	–	–
EAMA Unallocated	–	–	0.0	–	–	–	–
South of Sahara Unall.	42.3	8.6	2.7	-7.5	2.6	-59.0	14.3
TOTAL	*2939.6*	*2878.7*	*2888.6*	*2925.4*	*3267.1*	*3620.1*	*4379.6*
Africa Unspecified	33.9	75.5	78.5	95.6	108.1	211.6	220.5
AFRICA TOTAL	*3604.5*	*3704.4*	*3540.4*	*3892.2*	*4139.1*	*4920.2*	*5437.5*
N.& C. AMERICA							
Aruba	–	–	–	–	–	–	–
Bahamas	4.6	4.1	7.3	3.6	3.3	0.0	13.8
Barbados	14.6	22.1	25.8	18.8	14.2	9.1	8.1

	1980	1981
Belize	4.4	3.1
Bermuda	0.2	0.2
Costa Rica	74.2	48.6
Cuba	20.9	11.1
Dominican Republic	102.6	78.0
El Salvador	61.6	65.5
Guadeloupe	3.8	0.9
Guatemala	67.3	73.9
Haiti	42.3	39.9
Honduras	90.2	74.3
Jamaica	93.2	99.3
Martinique	5.0	1.2
Mexico	656.2	719.8
Netherlands Antilles	9.6	4.5
Nicaragua	111.1	111.3
Panama	67.0	35.6
St. Pierre & Miquelon	–	0.0
Trinidad & Tobago	3.5	5.2
Anguilla		
Antigua and Barbuda	3.9	2.9
Cayman Islands	0.5	2.0
Dominica	9.4	9.4
Grenada	3.2	6.3
Montserrat	0.8	1.1
St. Kitts-Nevis	3.5	2.1
St. Lucia	6.2	8.9
St. Vincent and Gr.	7.8	5.7
Turks & Caicos Isl.	0.4	0.2
Virgin Islands	1.9	1.3
West Indies Unall.	–	–
DOM/TOM Unallocated	-1.9	8.3
N.& C. America Unall.	5.7	4.5
TOTAL	*1473.6*	*1450.9*
SOUTH AMERICA		
Argentina	47.3	236.9
Bolivia	140.3	96.9
Brazil	462.5	506.1
Chile	29.4	57.4
Colombia	243.7	307.1
Ecuador	97.1	118.0
Falkland Islands	–	0.0
Guiana	2.4	2.6
Guyana	41.2	72.6
Paraguay	35.1	62.5
Peru	193.7	168.3
Suriname	5.1	2.8
Uruguay	15.6	5.3
Venezuela	-26.4	-29.7
South America Unall.	–	–
TOTAL	*1287.0*	*1606.7*
America Unspecified	145.4	64.5
AMERICA TOTAL	*2906.0*	*3122.0*
MIDDLE EAST		
Bahrain	8.1	3.2
Iran	-48.1	-48.8
Iraq	1.0	-0.1
Israel	-3.2	28.9
Jordan	102.3	113.4
Kuwait	2.7	3.0
Lebanon	46.1	41.1
Oman	13.2	15.3
Qatar	0.6	0.6
Saudi Arabia	6.5	11.0
Syria	83.1	96.8
United Arab Emirates	7.8	2.8
Yemen	73.3	87.1
Yemen, Dem.	58.7	37.0
Middle East Unall.	164.5	184.8
TOTAL	*516.6*	*575.8*
SOUTH ASIA		
Afghanistan	19.4	10.5
Bangladesh	350.5	375.3
Bhutan	6.6	7.2
Burma	78.1	79.9
India	1611.3	1220.2
Maldives	4.4	11.3
Nepal	71.9	83.4
Pakistan	450.0	348.5
Sri Lanka	90.3	86.5

1982	1983	1984	1985	1986
5.6	4.1	3.5	5.5	2.4
0.1	0.0	0.1	0.9	0.1
35.5	53.8	70.0	140.1	95.5
15.0	11.3	5.6	15.7	14.3
75.5	70.0	70.9	90.3	56.2
56.5	122.8	69.0	73.5	32.4
9.8	34.7	13.1	17.2	52.0
83.1	38.6	59.7	111.7	45.1
48.9	55.6	63.9	50.3	48.7
101.3	135.4	227.1	138.9	67.9
152.7	89.8	62.7	106.4	40.5
10.7	28.6	15.6	24.8	39.2
428.1	197.1	776.3	689.7	888.9
3.3	2.0	7.1	2.6	1.2
54.2	74.8	64.4	39.8	60.7
77.9	110.7	118.2	79.9	100.5
0.0	0.5	–	–	–
0.8	-1.5	-0.1	1.0	101.8
–	0.1	0.3	1.2	0.6
3.1	2.5	2.1	1.1	0.8
2.3	3.1	5.1	0.9	2.0
11.3	5.4	5.5	7.7	4.1
4.9	6.8	5.4	4.1	11.3
0.9	0.5	0.1	0.5	0.9
1.5	1.7	2.0	2.2	3.7
5.5	3.3	3.7	4.8	10.0
5.0	5.4	3.1	4.1	4.1
0.2	0.3	2.6	1.1	0.9
1.1	1.4	1.0	0.6	0.2
–	–	–	0.1	8.1
0.0	–	–	–	–
15.3	3.6	6.2	10.2	7.8
1243.1	*1084.9*	*1681.5*	*1636.0*	*1723.4*
140.9	165.9	200.6	219.4	391.5
67.6	48.1	63.6	81.1	133.3
749.7	1171.6	1183.6	647.5	1092.3
43.2	207.7	344.3	451.6	443.3
292.4	321.6	484.6	600.5	450.2
104.1	83.8	110.3	115.8	283.9
0.3	–	0.0	–	–
10.6	1.9	4.5	13.9	31.0
42.5	35.3	24.5	28.1	32.6
72.9	46.9	71.7	51.4	50.2
221.3	183.1	222.4	152.1	120.3
3.1	1.6	3.6	3.1	2.3
29.3	21.9	55.9	26.9	45.1
-26.3	-24.4	-19.4	-28.0	-15.5
–	–	–	0.6	4.8
1751.7	*2264.9*	*2750.2*	*2363.9*	*3065.4*
91.9	125.4	111.9	118.5	66.1
3086.7	*3475.1*	*4543.6*	*4118.5*	*4854.8*
2.8	1.5	10.5	-1.1	-1.2
-47.0	-41.8	-37.7	-34.0	-40.9
-1.9	19.6	63.2	-24.3	35.3
-29.5	-13.5	0.2	-14.1	-0.7
107.0	51.1	45.4	76.7	78.3
2.4	1.5	1.1	1.0	1.3
45.2	45.5	19.8	26.7	13.4
0.0	7.2	31.2	21.8	18.2
0.6	0.8	0.8	1.3	0.9
18.1	8.0	9.1	11.6	11.6
15.9	77.6	63.9	91.1	71.4
5.3	0.4	1.0	1.3	1.5
60.2	79.4	65.3	65.7	72.5
66.8	47.0	53.0	62.4	45.3
249.9	27.0	23.3	25.8	28.8
495.6	*311.2*	*350.0*	*311.9*	*335.5*
8.4	10.3	8.3	11.4	7.3
367.8	418.0	496.2	511.5	591.7
8.1	10.0	12.8	14.7	17.8
110.8	86.2	125.9	102.3	107.7
1546.8	1434.4	1262.2	1233.7	1473.3
3.0	4.2	2.8	2.8	4.5
88.9	92.2	103.2	116.8	126.5
491.0	479.7	534.9	512.0	443.4
121.5	141.8	158.9	146.1	157.7

	1980	1981	1982	1983	1984	1985	1986
South Asia Unall.	–	–	–	–	–	–	–
TOTAL	*2682.4*	*2222.9*	*2746.3*	*2676.9*	*2705.1*	*2651.2*	*2929.9*

FAR EAST ASIA

	1980	1981	1982	1983	1984	1985	1986
Brunei	0.0	–	–	0.0	–	0.1	0.1
China	37.4	419.7	61.1	141.3	315.2	693.3	771.3
Hong Kong	19.0	10.7	10.9	6.2	1.4	-1.9	-2.0
Indonesia	439.7	517.4	718.7	687.9	918.0	845.3	826.8
Kampuchea	231.6	112.1	29.4	28.4	8.5	7.3	7.5
Korea	240.2	364.2	669.9	478.7	447.9	165.9	-79.1
Korea, Dem.	–	–	–	–	–	5.2	4.4
Laos	24.1	18.2	17.0	17.1	20.4	21.5	29.0
Macao	4.4	–	0.7	0.5	0.4	0.3	0.3
Malaysia	105.5	119.7	150.2	125.4	78.2	32.3	-15.1
Mongolia	–	–	–	–	–	2.9	3.9
Philippines	352.1	547.0	343.1	758.0	370.1	249.6	158.4
Singapore	9.9	-2.5	0.1	-0.6	-8.7	-16.0	-22.7
Taiwan	-18.0	-17.8	-18.4	-17.6	-17.6	-17.4	-21.3
Thailand	322.3	391.8	510.0	543.8	430.5	380.1	248.7
Viet Nam	70.7	113.9	30.6	32.3	29.1	44.3	52.4
Far East Asia Unall.	–	–	0.4	–	–	0.2	7.6
TOTAL	*1838.9*	*2594.2*	*2523.4*	*2801.4*	*2593.3*	*2413.0*	*1970.1*
Asia Unspecified	46.3	66.6	56.5	65.4	72.2	84.9	96.4
ASIA TOTAL	*5084.1*	*5459.5*	*5821.8*	*5854.9*	*5720.6*	*5461.0*	*5331.9*

OCEANIA

	1980	1981	1982	1983	1984	1985	1986
Cook Islands	0.8	1.3	0.9	1.4	0.7	1.0	0.9
Fiji	24.5	20.8	28.4	42.4	16.1	0.4	13.3
Kiribati	0.6	9.5	0.7	2.4	1.6	1.2	1.5
Nauru	–	–	–	–	–	–	–
New Caledonia	0.8	3.8	2.8	0.3	0.9	0.2	0.0
Niue	0.3	0.3	0.2	0.1	0.1	0.0	0.3
Pacif. Isl.(Trust Tr.)	0.8	0.5	0.6	1.4	0.8	1.1	1.4
Papua New Guinea	47.8	36.5	40.9	66.9	37.6	32.3	57.8
Polynesia, French	–	0.3	0.6	0.3	–	1.5	0.4
Solomon Islands	13.5	6.8	6.4	9.3	5.5	6.1	8.4
Tokelau	0.1	0.1	0.1	0.1	0.1	0.2	0.2
Tonga	3.5	3.5	5.0	4.7	3.3	3.0	3.5
Tuvalu	0.4	0.9	0.8	0.4	0.3	0.2	0.6
Vanuatu	0.7	6.1	2.7	2.5	2.3	2.9	3.6
Wallis & Futuna	–	0.3	0.2	1.2	1.2	0.2	0.1
Western Samoa	12.0	10.8	7.5	10.1	9.3	5.9	4.5
TOM Unallocated	–	0.1	–	–	–	–	–
Oceania Unallocated	–	–	–	–	–	–	0.1
TOTAL	*105.4*	*101.6*	*97.7*	*143.5*	*79.6*	*56.0*	*96.5*
LDCS Unspecified	228.9	496.3	608.1	655.5	619.6	688.1	627.1
TOTAL, ALL LDCS	*12639.2*	*13641.4*	*14150.9*	*14800.9*	*15982.6*	*16380.2*	*17257.1*

INCOME GROUPS

	1980	1981	1982	1983	1984	1985	1986
LLDCS	2333.4	2412.3	2221.2	2410.3	2595.3	3010.7	3135.2
CHINA AND INDIA	1648.6	1639.9	1607.9	1575.8	1577.4	1927.0	2244.5
OTHER LOW-INCOME	2758.3	2548.9	2749.3	2690.8	3188.4	3122.8	3264.6
LOW MIDDLE-INCOME	2301.4	2848.9	2975.7	3387.9	3019.1	3069.5	3017.4
UPPER MIDDLE-INCOME	2931.1	3271.9	3483.7	3743.6	4644.7	4154.9	4498.3
UNALLOCATED	666.4	919.4	1113.2	992.4	957.7	1095.3	1097.0

Legend:
- LLDCS
- CHINA AND INDIA
- OTHER LICS
- LMICS
- UMICS

	1980	1981	1982	1983	1984	1985	1986
EUROPE							
Cyprus	37.0	93.9	11.9	19.0	2.4	93.6	75.5
Gibraltar	17.4	35.3	29.4	13.7	19.8	24.4	11.8
Greece	676.9	127.4	32.5	-6.0	586.2	90.7	-152.3
Malta	27.3	90.1	360.8	46.7	4.1	16.6	5.3
Portugal	318.6	903.5	928.2	393.0	503.2	352.6	-550.4
Turkey	1345.3	1316.9	893.0	249.7	554.0	427.6	1138.7
Yugoslavia	972.5	296.5	-51.1	324.3	311.8	36.8	-47.5
Europe Unallocated	1714.7	1156.7	839.9	1648.9	345.8	269.0	-245.3
TOTAL	*5109.7*	*4020.4*	*3044.5*	*2689.4*	*2327.2*	*1311.4*	*235.8*
NORTH OF SAHARA							
Algeria	1457.9	1135.3	-61.4	784.3	500.2	595.4	-261.4
Egypt	1990.4	2073.9	2968.9	2883.1	2814.4	2714.0	2378.0
Libya	1019.5	-74.8	-171.9	-137.5	133.3	16.3	82.7
Morocco	552.9	407.8	822.8	373.2	910.4	653.9	594.5
Tunisia	215.7	333.8	415.2	390.0	271.9	150.7	179.9
North of Sahara Unall.	6.1	28.0	71.9	66.6	-58.7	35.3	-166.8
TOTAL	*5242.6*	*3904.0*	*4045.6*	*4359.6*	*4571.5*	*4165.6*	*2806.7*
SOUTH OF SAHARA							
Angola	184.1	276.6	333.5	146.4	166.3	223.7	233.0
Benin	331.9	78.5	151.8	46.3	132.7	128.0	112.8
Botswana	27.0	80.0	83.7	82.5	121.6	81.3	138.9
Burkina Faso	164.9	158.4	190.9	137.0	120.8	114.0	169.3
Burundi	63.9	79.5	104.8	95.1	75.4	85.9	83.0
Cameroon	604.9	475.5	371.5	305.0	212.0	153.0	161.8
Cape Verde	39.0	36.6	43.2	45.4	39.3	40.5	79.3
Central African Rep.	93.4	77.0	81.1	70.8	68.1	65.7	81.8
Chad	19.5	25.4	33.6	49.8	56.9	96.5	99.9
Comoros	14.3	19.0	13.9	16.2	18.1	18.0	21.0
Congo	46.6	173.3	424.6	236.0	65.6	15.5	310.2
Cote d'Ivoire	771.0	194.6	612.0	288.5	225.9	229.5	346.9
Djibouti	31.9	38.7	44.8	42.8	77.1	68.1	28.5
Equatorial Guinea	1.2	4.1	-2.4	3.9	10.4	7.7	20.0
Ethiopia	93.2	92.3	100.2	112.0	248.1	488.6	452.3
Gabon	-36.4	83.9	161.8	258.5	56.3	202.3	275.2
Gambia	38.3	29.7	19.8	14.7	35.3	38.5	71.4
Ghana	118.1	120.7	71.1	77.8	124.2	114.8	171.2
Guinea	71.7	54.7	48.4	29.4	36.7	64.5	109.1
Guinea-Bissau	37.1	41.6	32.5	30.3	33.6	26.8	40.8
Kenya	393.6	445.9	348.5	323.2	316.4	321.2	602.9
Lesotho	63.7	64.3	59.1	64.4	56.9	66.0	60.9
Liberia	354.9	614.5	448.7	-169.7	-212.6	-158.1	-89.0
Madagascar	284.8	316.9	285.1	123.1	243.5	120.4	162.8
Malawi	105.8	111.0	57.0	42.4	79.9	53.4	114.3
Mali	133.0	141.6	104.7	96.7	217.5	253.2	197.4
Mauritania	42.1	64.7	75.6	89.8	76.3	113.3	102.3
Mauritius	47.0	60.3	50.2	20.9	26.5	-0.3	57.0
Mayotte	22.7	14.7	12.7	14.6	13.8	19.8	26.1
Mozambique	288.2	378.6	290.5	179.8	131.0	239.2	247.1
Namibia	–	–	–	0.0	–	21.8	-92.1
Niger	172.4	276.4	168.8	129.3	79.6	190.7	170.0
Nigeria	1136.8	1587.8	1859.4	1907.3	302.2	-91.5	438.8
Reunion	547.9	704.0	447.7	385.6	430.5	482.8	552.1
Rwanda	96.8	102.5	101.0	104.3	93.8	108.1	130.5
St. Helena	8.8	10.9	13.0	9.9	10.0	12.1	13.5
Sao Tome & Principe	1.2	1.8	3.8	3.4	4.0	3.0	7.0
Senegal	340.9	273.8	383.1	314.7	351.6	230.2	419.2
Seychelles	20.2	27.1	22.4	15.0	22.7	14.4	23.5
Sierra Leone	56.8	40.2	58.1	36.9	43.0	26.4	59.0
Somalia	210.9	131.7	299.8	134.8	205.0	188.6	449.3
Sudan	353.7	303.1	433.4	614.2	395.9	660.3	430.1
Swaziland	44.9	32.7	24.3	25.6	42.5	28.0	27.0
Tanzania	687.5	644.8	542.1	391.4	445.2	395.8	503.6
Togo	110.3	27.2	72.9	49.0	61.0	38.6	54.8
Uganda	64.1	91.9	83.8	49.3	43.9	31.5	74.5
Zaire	622.2	519.5	340.1	-9.5	668.6	351.8	437.7
Zambia	262.1	342.7	276.7	175.3	321.5	332.2	528.0
Zimbabwe	203.1	304.8	373.3	286.1	325.2	238.1	145.1
East African Community	5.5	5.0	4.2	5.2	2.5	10.8	1.8
DOM/TOM Unallocated	–	–	–	–	–	-1.2	–
EAMA Unallocated	94.7	2.1	4.6	37.2	59.4	–	–
South of Sahara Unall.	311.5	529.8	1064.2	674.2	227.7	345.3	26.7
TOTAL	*9803.4*	*10312.3*	*11229.1*	*8212.3*	*7009.3*	*6909.0*	*8888.2*
Africa Unspecified	375.8	920.3	1592.2	1778.9	-29.6	-290.4	-286.9
AFRICA TOTAL	*15421.8*	*15136.6*	*16866.9*	*14350.8*	*11551.2*	*10784.2*	*11408.0*
N.& C. AMERICA							
Aruba	–	–	–	–	–	12.0	40.2
Bahamas	67.0	240.7	243.4	826.7	-79.7	525.3	903.6
Barbados	8.5	15.9	22.8	15.2	-15.9	18.9	34.4

	1980	1981
Belize	13.4	8.9
Bermuda	1075.8	-595.2
Costa Rica	90.1	51.1
Cuba	19.7	39.7
Dominican Republic	52.1	52.2
El Salvador	73.2	122.9
Guadeloupe	167.0	103.1
Guatemala	69.3	148.1
Haiti	78.4	76.4
Honduras	108.0	142.6
Jamaica	93.2	133.9
Martinique	733.6	499.0
Mexico	3806.4	6190.0
Netherlands Antilles	205.1	1300.1
Nicaragua	129.0	96.5
Panama	693.6	1305.6
St. Pierre & Miquelon	27.7	24.9
Trinidad & Tobago	89.4	43.6
Anguilla	2.3	2.6
Antigua and Barbuda	2.6	11.7
Cayman Islands	284.7	349.9
Dominica	8.1	11.8
Grenada	0.5	0.3
Montserrat	3.1	2.6
St. Kitts-Nevis	2.7	2.2
St. Lucia	3.5	4.6
St. Vincent and Gr.	3.0	3.5
Turks & Caicos Isl.	1.3	6.3
Virgin Islands	65.1	1.3
West Indies Unall.	75.0	5.8
DOM/TOM Unallocated	–	–
N.& C. America Unall.	639.0	-284.9
TOTAL	*8691.3*	*10117.6*
SOUTH AMERICA		
Argentina	2726.2	2449.7
Bolivia	16.6	132.1
Brazil	3841.1	7060.8
Chile	379.6	1420.6
Colombia	589.5	942.4
Ecuador	141.9	254.6
Falkland Islands	2.3	2.1
Guiana	116.0	85.7
Guyana	0.7	14.0
Paraguay	39.7	61.5
Peru	431.4	643.0
Suriname	75.0	92.8
Uruguay	65.5	54.9
Venezuela	1329.3	1072.8
South America Unall.	101.9	137.9
TOTAL	*9856.7*	*14424.8*
America Unspecified	2709.4	3706.1
AMERICA TOTAL	*21257.4*	*28248.5*
MIDDLE EAST		
Bahrain	-69.2	41.8
Iran	546.7	-693.7
Iraq	172.9	425.0
Israel	1278.3	1031.6
Jordan	308.1	368.7
Kuwait	71.8	90.5
Lebanon	145.0	104.2
Oman	16.7	-43.0
Qatar	-55.4	-50.9
Saudi Arabia	187.6	514.2
Syria	12.8	103.4
United Arab Emirates	237.9	-741.7
Yemen	142.1	97.8
Yemen, Dem.	124.9	21.2
Middle East Unall.	-3212.0	79.0
TOTAL	*-91.8*	*1348.3*
SOUTH ASIA		
Afghanistan	22.4	-8.3
Bangladesh	858.8	653.4
Bhutan	1.7	2.6
Burma	324.6	248.0
India	804.9	1191.2
Maldives	1.7	4.4
Nepal	82.7	88.4
Pakistan	493.0	473.0
Sri Lanka	334.6	334.6

1982	1983	1984	1985	1986
7.7	16.6	23.0	23.6	16.7
995.1	99.2	337.5	788.0	1048.9
75.0	214.8	232.4	267.7	251.6
-125.7	-87.9	50.4	24.7	-53.5
89.2	49.3	165.1	184.7	295.8
165.5	190.5	224.7	301.8	298.4
215.4	187.9	159.3	229.2	253.6
102.0	165.3	102.0	226.3	81.5
82.6	70.9	71.2	94.7	124.7
78.5	107.0	149.6	237.5	230.1
194.2	221.4	316.4	137.3	60.5
357.0	310.9	265.7	332.5	385.9
4301.3	3646.3	13091.9	-2294.4	398.3
904.1	-343.3	-1736.5	-1204.2	-1444.5
94.6	97.1	81.3	76.7	111.2
1603.8	686.2	1164.3	1648.6	1755.7
22.9	24.0	18.9	17.9	21.7
44.8	68.0	146.4	-318.8	-95.8
2.0	2.2	1.5	1.5	2.6
3.3	1.2	-6.1	21.6	33.8
288.0	204.2	808.8	812.1	1009.5
9.1	4.9	23.5	28.2	14.3
-7.3	11.7	25.3	29.5	17.1
3.3	1.7	1.8	1.7	3.3
1.8	1.5	-4.6	2.5	1.6
4.2	5.0	1.7	2.4	1.5
2.8	-0.3	1.2	3.7	8.4
10.2	9.0	-7.0	4.7	9.3
8.8	18.8	4.9	-60.3	-0.1
-6.9	9.9	-7.7	538.3	393.1
–	–	–	-5.9	–
185.6	266.5	864.0	187.7	111.1
9978.9	*7102.2*	*16475.1*	*2897.4*	*6324.3*
1391.0	308.5	902.0	1856.0	4504.5
75.9	90.8	100.4	125.8	171.1
6836.2	4916.0	6607.6	702.7	-457.6
1019.9	471.3	1898.5	-328.1	-390.9
1258.3	964.8	686.5	-277.1	674.8
187.4	302.9	951.9	-51.3	725.7
22.7	2.7	8.0	13.8	14.7
85.0	80.1	70.9	89.5	132.4
14.4	-1.2	-1.1	7.2	3.6
148.5	128.2	78.6	31.7	62.1
955.0	858.7	462.3	-182.2	-49.9
98.2	-0.5	-1.7	6.4	73.5
172.7	383.7	217.3	-150.7	15.9
1833.2	-749.4	-286.4	-897.7	2812.0
258.6	405.5	68.1	1031.5	3.6
14356.8	*8162.1*	*11762.8*	*1977.5*	*8295.7*
2938.3	*2895.3*	*1873.8*	*-176.0*	*-702.2*
27274.1	*18159.6*	*30111.7*	*4698.9*	*13917.7*
454.9	215.2	79.0	181.2	-20.4
-752.5	-704.3	-328.1	-325.9	-287.2
730.5	628.0	1899.3	849.2	-95.9
1580.6	2181.8	1985.1	2562.6	2296.1
298.1	89.4	182.3	-202.0	111.7
130.4	-53.7	-26.9	-186.0	67.8
71.1	52.2	90.4	33.7	125.6
-9.6	158.4	189.3	116.7	235.4
-73.6	-109.2	-96.2	-12.6	-16.2
470.0	179.6	-308.5	160.1	-396.9
58.0	68.0	70.6	38.0	108.7
303.4	-29.4	88.3	-294.5	-90.5
173.9	208.1	65.4	76.0	100.8
36.5	3.1	1.4	12.9	-12.4
182.5	744.9	319.3	-35.3	650.3
3653.9	*3631.9*	*4210.8*	*2974.2*	*2776.7*
3.5	5.1	-2.0	-15.8	-1.4
862.3	591.9	725.1	598.9	754.6
3.2	2.9	4.8	6.6	14.0
307.2	211.3	200.0	254.5	306.1
735.8	889.7	929.7	1263.2	2332.0
-2.5	1.3	3.3	6.8	12.2
110.5	106.1	99.2	131.0	200.3
619.9	219.4	180.4	399.7	601.9
353.2	393.3	483.8	433.4	368.0

	1980	1981	1982	1983	1984	1985	1986
South Asia Unall.	-5.0	22.7	3.6	152.3	2.4	5.4	7.0
TOTAL	*2919.4*	*3009.9*	*2996.6*	*2573.2*	*2626.6*	*3083.7*	*4594.6*
FAR EAST ASIA							
Brunei	-18.7	-30.3	23.8	7.5	-2.5	-3.6	-4.3
China	286.2	1468.7	617.1	571.0	582.6	1585.3	2693.9
Hong Kong	891.2	1758.4	1172.2	1094.6	1272.7	-1196.9	-1600.4
Indonesia	1329.2	4032.1	2090.4	2449.6	2410.0	998.0	808.2
Kampuchea	49.6	17.9	14.4	8.3	6.4	5.6	6.0
Korea	571.9	1169.5	842.7	842.8	1536.9	1456.8	497.6
Korea, Dem.	–	–	–	–	–	-11.3	-21.1
Laos	15.8	16.8	21.1	12.9	14.8	42.6	19.4
Macao	-0.2	2.8	2.6	19.0	6.8	-7.8	-3.7
Malaysia	573.4	860.7	668.4	1608.2	1327.8	187.2	55.3
Mongolia	–	–	–	–	0.1	0.4	0.8
Philippines	615.7	696.7	612.4	785.1	576.2	386.2	960.3
Singapore	742.0	1387.1	914.2	192.5	1347.1	-176.2	-99.1
Taiwan	455.7	700.7	443.5	-44.5	-63.3	-493.4	-452.6
Thailand	781.0	1162.6	695.8	722.9	1023.6	488.7	294.8
Viet Nam	124.5	184.5	104.2	41.8	81.1	38.7	90.8
Far East Asia Unall.	9.2	9.6	53.8	1039.8	125.2	84.6	220.2
TOTAL	*6426.8*	*13437.8*	*8276.5*	*9351.6*	*10245.6*	*3384.7*	*3465.9*
Asia Unspecified	-1344.0	45.5	-2073.0	-1382.5	1390.5	404.6	1400.6
ASIA TOTAL	*7910.4*	*17841.5*	*12854.0*	*14174.2*	*18473.5*	*9847.1*	*12237.9*
OCEANIA							
Cook Islands	10.7	10.4	11.2	9.9	7.0	9.6	26.4
Fiji	56.1	65.0	47.3	22.8	15.8	22.1	34.0
Kiribati	18.6	13.5	14.5	14.3	9.8	10.8	12.3
Nauru	-2.1	2.7	-4.3	-8.0	-0.2	2.3	45.7
New Caledonia	214.3	151.4	163.1	197.3	131.7	161.5	218.5
Niue	3.4	3.9	4.2	5.5	3.1	3.5	3.9
Pacif. Isl.(Trust Tr.)	109.4	144.5	170.0	158.4	206.9	154.1	373.3
Papua New Guinea	346.1	287.1	559.6	508.2	483.6	299.8	162.4
Polynesia, French	155.6	157.6	176.6	191.0	175.0	212.8	262.7
Solomon Islands	31.1	23.3	22.0	21.5	19.8	14.6	20.9
Tokelau	1.8	1.3	1.8	1.7	1.7	1.6	1.8
Tonga	12.6	14.6	12.4	13.3	12.4	10.6	11.6
Tuvalu	4.5	4.5	5.2	3.8	5.2	3.2	3.8
Vanuatu	41.7	23.4	29.5	32.1	43.0	35.6	-32.3
Wallis & Futuna	8.3	8.3	7.1	0.4	0.5	0.8	0.0
Western Samoa	13.2	13.8	15.2	20.9	4.3	14.2	17.7
TOM Unallocated	–	2.8	–	–	–	–	–
Oceania Unallocated	18.9	10.3	28.7	46.8	28.8	21.9	18.8
TOTAL	*1044.1*	*938.2*	*1264.1*	*1240.0*	*1148.4*	*978.9*	*1181.4*
LDCS Unspecified	10638.1	10810.3	4829.2	1772.8	-1987.5	341.0	7014.5
TOTAL,ALL LDCS	*61381.5*	*76995.5*	*66132.8*	*52386.6*	*61624.5*	*27961.5*	*45995.2*
INCOME GROUPS							
LLDCS	4532.3	3824.5	4361.5	3655.2	3921.6	4470.6	5075.3
CHINA AND INDIA	1091.1	2659.9	1352.8	1460.7	1512.3	2848.4	5025.9
OTHER LOW-INCOME	7504.0	10724.1	9132.4	7476.9	8408.9	6820.8	7518.4
LOW MIDDLE-INCOME	7973.3	8754.6	9727.1	8125.9	6952.1	4308.7	6199.9
UPPER MIDDLE-INCOME	28142.2	33845.3	31581.7	21505.8	37605.5	6746.3	13729.2
UNALLOCATED	12138.6	17187.0	9977.4	10162.1	3224.1	2766.6	8446.5

Legend: ⊶⊶⊶ LLDCS; ------ CHINA AND INDIA; —·—· OTHER LICS; ——— LMICS; - - - UMICS

TOTAL NET DISBURSEMENTS FROM ALL SOURCES COMBINED TO INDIVIDUAL RECIPIENTS

	1980	1981	1982	1983	1984	1985	1986
EUROPE							
Cyprus	67.4	120.9	39.4	42.1	23.2	177.7	174.0
Gibraltar	17.4	35.3	29.4	13.7	19.8	24.4	11.8
Greece	770.9	131.7	183.7	170.6	614.8	125.3	-151.0
Malta	60.3	100.0	366.5	57.7	11.3	29.0	15.8
Portugal	425.4	963.5	1053.4	533.0	540.0	478.1	-516.5
Turkey	1826.9	1963.3	1540.1	703.8	1268.4	1187.2	1869.1
Yugoslavia	1398.8	827.9	140.8	406.9	586.7	243.1	40.6
Europe Unallocated	1715.9	1167.0	849.9	1676.4	359.5	283.3	-229.9
TOTAL	*6283.0*	*5309.6*	*4203.2*	*3604.1*	*3423.7*	*2548.1*	*1213.9*
NORTH OF SAHARA							
Algeria	1545.4	1210.0	-243.6	845.8	502.7	831.3	-152.3
Egypt	2329.1	2404.9	3194.8	3131.6	3094.7	2951.9	2620.5
Libya	1035.4	-66.1	-164.2	-136.1	135.1	46.9	78.9
Morocco	1309.8	1344.5	1540.5	783.3	1229.6	1508.7	1011.9
Tunisia	390.0	528.3	554.9	507.8	427.3	307.4	326.0
North of Sahara Unall.	6.2	28.0	71.9	66.6	-58.7	35.3	-166.8
TOTAL	*6616.0*	*5449.6*	*4954.3*	*5199.0*	*5330.6*	*5681.5*	*3718.2*
SOUTH OF SAHARA							
Angola	200.9	298.2	353.5	175.2	201.7	258.5	275.9
Benin	400.8	119.6	192.2	90.9	169.9	175.5	178.8
Botswana	53.4	110.7	118.6	130.0	182.2	158.6	168.7
Burkina Faso	227.9	214.7	256.5	200.4	187.6	191.9	283.7
Burundi	121.7	136.8	157.1	175.7	156.9	157.4	185.9
Cameroon	733.3	560.4	447.2	358.6	283.7	232.0	290.8
Cape Verde	64.4	50.7	62.5	64.1	64.6	70.6	112.5
Central African Rep.	129.4	105.8	102.0	99.7	115.0	111.9	142.8
Chad	34.7	53.9	63.0	93.7	113.2	182.4	162.7
Comoros	44.2	53.6	37.9	39.5	42.8	50.8	47.1
Congo	83.6	215.8	466.2	298.7	113.1	60.8	335.9
Cote d'Ivoire	918.4	260.6	848.2	486.6	433.3	266.5	468.8
Djibouti	73.0	66.9	59.2	67.1	130.8	103.2	78.9
Equatorial Guinea	10.0	11.5	9.1	12.1	17.8	17.7	31.4
Ethiopia	211.5	259.8	227.2	356.9	416.6	784.0	690.1
Gabon	-30.3	93.0	175.4	272.9	60.7	203.3	309.6
Gambia	82.3	86.5	42.5	38.2	59.6	58.9	113.4
Ghana	227.4	205.2	158.0	124.7	237.1	228.1	429.7
Guinea	133.9	137.3	102.5	70.1	129.3	124.1	180.6
Guinea-Bissau	67.0	67.1	66.0	66.4	61.6	63.3	71.9
Kenya	557.4	577.5	575.5	476.2	543.1	531.6	685.1
Lesotho	94.1	106.2	97.2	109.7	96.2	119.3	92.1
Liberia	417.0	656.2	479.7	-128.9	-168.8	-111.0	-61.1
Madagascar	424.0	459.7	370.1	227.1	283.7	209.4	320.7
Malawi	189.3	193.2	135.2	105.4	188.1	117.7	229.0
Mali	269.2	237.2	220.8	220.2	322.0	380.9	364.5
Mauritania	221.9	258.6	249.7	235.7	185.3	231.4	175.3
Mauritius	69.6	94.7	74.4	44.1	60.0	30.2	67.7
Mayotte	22.7	14.9	12.7	14.6	14.0	20.8	28.3
Mozambique	342.8	420.1	346.6	235.1	202.2	330.7	358.6
Namibia	–	–	–	0.0	–	25.0	-83.1
Niger	258.4	363.8	306.7	207.5	135.7	289.6	294.6
Nigeria	1201.2	1660.1	2400.5	2079.0	552.2	164.2	913.2
Reunion	556.3	713.9	450.9	410.7	448.0	514.4	616.6
Rwanda	155.8	153.6	153.8	159.5	162.1	185.8	217.4
St. Helena	8.8	10.9	13.0	9.9	10.0	12.2	13.5
Sao Tome & Principe	3.9	6.1	9.9	11.6	11.3	12.5	12.4
Senegal	442.9	479.0	588.6	460.2	491.6	340.4	676.0
Seychelles	26.8	32.0	31.6	21.8	24.6	28.0	35.0
Sierra Leone	94.1	67.8	84.9	66.4	77.7	61.4	91.9
Somalia	553.0	368.8	618.9	345.9	362.6	371.0	613.5
Sudan	898.5	776.9	834.5	1209.1	697.8	1139.8	884.4
Swaziland	79.3	57.1	48.2	53.0	54.3	31.8	43.8
Tanzania	864.0	879.9	748.3	664.6	654.8	564.7	649.4
Togo	180.9	50.6	97.2	111.1	116.9	98.2	135.0
Uganda	137.2	153.9	170.2	151.7	164.6	222.2	199.1
Zaire	742.0	623.1	425.6	100.9	758.3	491.0	634.7
Zambia	376.2	420.5	475.1	214.8	398.2	510.9	670.6
Zimbabwe	248.7	423.8	467.1	353.6	432.3	311.6	217.0
East African Community	5.5	5.0	4.2	5.2	2.5	10.8	1.8
DOM/TOM Unallocated	–	–	–	–	–	-1.2	–
EAMA Unallocated	94.7	2.1	4.5	37.2	59.4	–	–
South of Sahara Unall.	358.4	552.2	1069.0	674.0	286.3	427.8	41.0
TOTAL	*13681.7*	*13927.4*	*15509.2*	*12108.1*	*10804.3*	*11172.7*	*13697.1*
Africa Unspecified	409.7	998.9	1670.6	1874.5	568.9	-78.8	-32.4
AFRICA TOTAL	*20707.4*	*20375.9*	*22134.0*	*19181.6*	*16703.8*	*16775.4*	*17382.9*
N.& C. AMERICA							
Aruba	–	–	–	–	–	12.0	40.2
Bahamas	71.6	244.8	250.7	830.3	-76.4	525.2	917.4
Barbados	23.1	41.4	52.3	37.2	-0.4	28.6	41.6

	1980	1981
Belize	17.9	11.9
Bermuda	1076.0	-595.0
Costa Rica	174.3	123.7
Cuba	40.6	50.8
Dominican Republic	216.9	152.2
El Salvador	149.3	215.0
Guadeloupe	170.8	104.1
Guatemala	154.1	248.7
Haiti	120.7	116.3
Honduras	209.7	237.5
Jamaica	277.1	294.3
Martinique	738.6	500.2
Mexico	4462.5	6909.8
Netherlands Antilles	214.8	1304.5
Nicaragua	250.4	359.2
Panama	773.5	1407.0
St. Pierre & Miquelon	27.7	25.0
Trinidad & Tobago	92.8	48.9
Anguilla	2.3	2.6
Antigua and Barbuda	6.5	14.5
Cayman Islands	285.2	351.9
Dominica	17.4	21.3
Grenada	3.7	6.6
Montserrat	3.8	3.7
St. Kitts-Nevis	6.2	4.2
St. Lucia	9.7	14.0
St. Vincent and Gr.	10.7	9.2
Turks & Caicos Isl.	1.8	6.5
Virgin Islands	67.0	2.6
West Indies Unall.	75.0	5.8
DOM/TOM Unallocated	-1.9	8.3
N.& C. America Unall.	644.7	-280.5
TOTAL	*10394.4*	*11970.7*
SOUTH AMERICA		
Argentina	2773.4	2686.6
Bolivia	156.2	227.9
Brazil	4484.2	7801.5
Chile	409.0	1477.3
Colombia	832.8	1249.1
Ecuador	237.5	369.8
Falkland Islands	2.3	2.1
Guiana	118.4	88.3
Guyana	39.3	85.0
Paraguay	74.8	124.0
Peru	628.4	807.6
Suriname	80.1	95.6
Uruguay	81.0	60.2
Venezuela	1302.9	1043.1
South America Unall.	101.9	137.9
TOTAL	*11322.3*	*16256.0*
America Unspecified	2858.8	3774.6
AMERICA TOTAL	*24575.6*	*32001.4*
MIDDLE EAST		
Bahrain	88.9	186.1
Iran	498.6	-741.5
Iraq	171.8	424.8
Israel	1275.1	1060.5
Jordan	1554.4	1502.3
Kuwait	74.5	93.5
Lebanon	384.3	515.3
Oman	282.3	185.3
Qatar	-54.9	-50.3
Saudi Arabia	194.9	525.1
Syria	1671.5	1542.4
United Arab Emirates	250.5	-733.7
Yemen	554.0	451.8
Yemen, Dem.	233.2	90.4
Middle East Unall.	-3047.5	263.8
TOTAL	*4131.5*	*5315.8*
SOUTH ASIA		
Afghanistan	43.3	22.7
Bangladesh	1279.5	1223.5
Bhutan	8.3	9.8
Burma	402.7	327.9
India	2407.5	2340.8
Maldives	21.2	21.8
Nepal	161.4	180.6
Pakistan	1378.6	971.1
Sri Lanka	426.9	420.0

1982	1983	1984	1985	1986
13.3	20.7	26.5	29.1	19.1
995.2	99.2	337.5	788.9	1048.9
134.7	288.5	305.5	413.4	320.3
-110.7	-76.6	56.0	40.3	-39.2
205.6	120.0	262.2	311.3	377.6
259.4	337.3	303.0	379.0	327.5
225.1	222.6	172.4	246.4	305.5
203.6	215.8	174.3	337.7	132.7
131.5	126.4	135.1	145.0	173.4
179.2	259.5	391.5	386.1	299.7
398.0	337.9	369.8	265.4	105.3
367.8	339.5	281.3	357.3	425.2
4775.7	3795.4	13868.2	-1604.6	1287.1
907.4	-341.3	-1729.4	-1201.6	-1443.3
176.9	171.0	189.9	116.5	171.9
1745.4	828.2	1293.9	1718.1	1844.2
22.9	24.5	18.9	17.9	21.7
45.6	66.5	146.3	-317.8	6.0
2.0	2.3	1.7	2.7	3.2
6.9	3.7	-3.9	22.7	34.5
290.3	207.4	813.9	813.0	1011.4
20.4	10.3	29.0	35.9	18.6
-0.7	19.0	30.7	33.6	28.6
4.2	2.2	1.8	2.2	4.2
3.4	3.2	-2.6	4.7	5.3
9.7	8.3	5.4	7.1	11.5
7.8	5.1	4.2	7.8	12.5
10.3	9.4	-4.4	5.8	10.3
9.9	20.1	5.9	-59.8	0.1
-6.9	9.9	-7.7	538.4	401.2
0.0	–	–	-5.9	–
200.9	270.6	873.8	207.4	118.9
11537.5	*8274.0*	*18273.7*	*4609.8*	*8042.9*
1531.9	475.0	1102.6	2075.3	4896.0
142.2	138.8	163.7	206.9	304.4
7628.1	6119.9	7786.6	1348.7	634.7
1062.4	678.6	2242.8	123.5	52.4
1550.3	1286.2	1171.0	323.4	1125.0
288.3	383.7	1059.0	64.4	1009.6
23.0	2.7	8.0	13.8	14.7
95.6	81.9	75.4	103.3	163.4
56.9	34.1	23.4	35.3	47.0
221.4	175.1	150.3	83.2	112.3
1179.9	1015.8	681.9	-30.1	70.5
101.3	1.1	1.9	9.4	75.8
202.0	405.6	273.3	-123.7	61.0
1810.9	-773.7	-305.8	-925.7	2796.5
258.6	405.5	68.1	1032.1	8.4
16152.8	*10430.3*	*14502.3*	*4339.9*	*11371.7*
3034.3	3024.1	1985.7	-57.5	-627.7
30724.6	*21728.4*	*34761.7*	*8892.2*	*18786.8*
554.0	464.7	287.7	261.7	119.9
-799.5	-746.1	-365.9	-359.7	-328.2
1027.1	650.3	1960.7	924.6	-61.9
1551.0	2168.3	1985.3	2548.5	2295.4
1104.4	833.1	825.3	326.1	593.7
132.8	-52.3	-25.8	-185.0	69.1
198.4	113.6	110.3	83.6	141.7
79.4	207.7	262.4	182.9	291.1
-73.0	-108.4	-95.4	-11.3	-15.3
488.0	188.0	-299.4	171.6	-385.3
912.2	1036.0	948.0	702.1	926.0
313.7	-28.2	89.3	-293.2	-89.0
486.4	479.7	317.4	272.4	233.7
175.9	82.6	98.2	120.5	42.3
432.4	771.9	342.7	-9.5	679.1
6583.1	*6060.9*	*6440.8*	*4735.4*	*4512.2*
12.3	13.2	5.6	-5.9	2.5
1356.0	1106.2	1250.1	1119.7	1429.6
11.3	13.0	17.9	24.1	40.1
418.0	297.5	325.9	356.7	413.8
2170.2	2248.0	2151.5	2459.8	3762.1
9.0	9.0	5.5	8.4	16.6
199.4	197.4	201.5	246.3	330.8
1131.0	696.4	664.6	860.7	973.7
471.9	530.4	642.4	585.0	547.6

	1980	1981	1982	1983	1984	1985	1986
South Asia Unall.	-5.0	22.7	3.6	152.3	2.4	105.4	133.2
TOTAL	*6124.4*	*5540.8*	*5782.5*	*5263.3*	*5267.4*	*5760.2*	*7650.0*
FAR EAST ASIA							
Brunei	-18.7	-30.3	23.8	7.5	-2.5	-3.5	-4.2
China	323.6	1888.4	678.1	748.1	947.2	2308.7	3487.8
Hong Kong	910.3	1769.1	1183.1	1100.8	1274.0	-1198.9	-1602.5
Indonesia	1757.5	4547.1	2870.6	3116.2	3322.8	1823.4	1655.3
Kampuchea	282.2	130.0	43.7	36.7	14.8	12.9	13.5
Korea	817.6	1515.1	1516.0	1306.9	1978.1	1616.2	419.9
Korea, Dem.	–	–	–	–	–	-6.0	-16.7
Laos	39.9	35.0	38.1	30.1	35.2	64.1	48.4
Macao	4.2	2.8	3.2	19.5	7.2	-7.5	-3.4
Malaysia	688.5	990.7	833.8	1750.0	1420.0	234.2	49.0
Mongolia	–	–	–	–	0.1	3.3	4.7
Philippines	971.4	1243.7	944.8	1542.6	945.9	635.2	1118.4
Singapore	752.4	1384.6	914.3	191.9	1338.5	-192.2	-121.8
Taiwan	438.9	696.7	427.6	-48.1	-73.7	-518.0	-483.0
Thailand	1113.6	1563.2	1238.2	1277.0	1472.1	880.0	551.6
Viet Nam	201.7	302.6	137.8	76.7	110.2	98.4	147.2
Far East Asia Unall.	9.2	9.6	54.1	1039.8	125.2	84.8	227.9
TOTAL	*8292.1*	*16048.3*	*10907.3*	*12195.7*	*12915.2*	*5835.1*	*5492.2*
Asia Unspecified	-1297.7	112.9	-2016.4	-1317.2	2134.0	489.5	3054.3
ASIA TOTAL	**17250.3**	**27017.8**	**21256.4**	**22202.8**	**26757.4**	**16820.2**	**20708.7**
OCEANIA							
Cook Islands	11.4	11.7	12.1	11.3	7.6	10.6	27.3
Fiji	80.6	85.9	75.6	65.3	31.9	22.5	47.2
Kiribati	19.2	23.1	15.2	16.7	11.4	12.0	13.8
Nauru	-2.1	2.7	-4.3	-8.0	-0.2	2.3	45.7
New Caledonia	215.0	155.2	165.9	197.6	132.6	161.7	218.5
Niue	3.7	4.2	4.4	5.6	3.2	3.5	4.2
Pacif. Isl.(Trust Tr.)	110.2	144.9	170.6	159.7	207.7	155.2	374.7
Papua New Guinea	394.3	323.8	600.6	574.8	521.0	331.8	220.0
Polynesia, French	155.6	157.8	177.3	191.3	175.0	214.3	263.1
Solomon Islands	44.6	30.1	28.5	30.9	25.5	22.0	31.7
Tokelau	1.9	1.4	1.9	1.8	1.8	1.8	2.0
Tonga	16.1	18.0	17.4	17.9	15.7	13.6	15.1
Tuvalu	4.9	5.4	5.9	4.2	5.5	3.3	4.4
Vanuatu	42.4	29.5	33.1	35.6	45.3	38.5	-28.7
Wallis & Futuna	8.3	8.6	7.3	1.6	1.6	1.0	0.1
Western Samoa	25.1	24.6	22.6	31.0	13.6	20.4	22.9
TOM Unallocated	–	2.8	–	–	–	–	–
Oceania Unallocated	18.9	10.3	28.7	46.8	28.8	21.9	18.9
TOTAL	*1150.0*	*1040.0*	*1362.9*	*1384.2*	*1228.0*	*1036.2*	*1280.7*
LDCS Unspecified	13769.2	13766.6	6252.1	3353.6	-1292.3	1447.6	7699.7
TOTAL,ALL LDCS	**83735.5**	**99511.3**	**85933.2**	**71454.7**	**81582.4**	**47519.8**	**67072.7**
INCOME GROUPS							
LLDCS	8127.6	7325.6	7720.1	7248.3	7165.1	8113.7	8736.7
CHINA AND INDIA	2731.1	4229.2	2848.3	2996.0	3098.7	4768.5	7250.0
OTHER LOW-INCOME	10795.6	13561.6	12133.7	10096.7	11548.0	9917.1	10830.5
LOW MIDDLE-INCOME	11427.0	12887.2	14027.4	11785.0	10401.2	8020.6	9295.1
UPPER MIDDLE-INCOME	34938.5	40919.7	37292.3	27237.6	43890.7	12168.6	19632.9
UNALLOCATED	15715.8	20588.0	11911.5	12091.1	5478.8	4531.3	11327.6

Legend: ○—○—○ LLDCS · · · · · CHINA AND INDIA —·—·— OTHER LICS ——— LMICS – – – – UMICS

	1980	1981	1982	1983	1984	1985	1986
EUROPE							
Cyprus	30.4	45.9	20.5	21.7	25.2	21.7	18.1
Gibraltar	1.1	0.9	3.3	46.0	8.5	5.8	13.2
Greece	9.9	10.4	11.3	15.9	18.5	17.8	22.4
Malta	3.4	65.2	10.6	28.0	8.9	8.5	5.6
Portugal	140.4	85.7	46.3	52.6	140.5	96.5	134.1
Turkey	771.9	849.8	439.2	349.2	529.0	295.7	314.5
Yugoslavia	8.1	4.9	14.2	12.7	38.3	10.3	81.6
Europe Unallocated	7.4	4.0	8.3	12.7	4.4	4.8	5.2
TOTAL	*972.7*	*1066.7*	*553.6*	*538.9*	*773.2*	*461.1*	*594.8*
NORTH OF SAHARA							
Algeria	121.3	154.8	301.5	145.0	58.1	75.1	94.3
Egypt	1370.5	1529.8	1583.3	1422.0	1735.6	1853.5	1575.7
Libya	9.9	2.2	2.6	3.2	2.4	3.4	3.5
Morocco	232.2	326.7	267.5	422.6	449.7	301.2	379.3
Tunisia	474.2	161.8	213.2	108.5	160.9	202.5	326.4
North of Sahara Unall.	0.4	0.5	11.1	39.2	5.3	13.4	0.4
TOTAL	*2208.5*	*2175.9*	*2379.1*	*2140.6*	*2412.1*	*2449.1*	*2379.6*
SOUTH OF SAHARA							
Angola	57.7	40.5	66.2	43.0	67.6	76.4	86.9
Benin	57.8	60.3	58.5	41.6	74.4	41.7	72.2
Botswana	112.8	74.4	86.8	83.5	88.1	68.5	117.9
Burkina Faso	170.4	189.4	146.3	135.0	159.1	127.4	201.2
Burundi	89.9	93.0	69.0	70.4	73.6	77.3	78.1
Cameroon	134.2	145.4	182.7	153.7	260.0	141.3	213.4
Cape Verde	39.8	45.7	46.7	53.6	47.6	42.5	60.5
Central African Rep.	99.2	72.6	78.8	79.9	77.3	75.0	101.6
Chad	21.4	49.7	42.8	56.2	76.7	133.7	137.2
Comoros	15.2	27.1	17.9	18.6	24.6	12.7	22.7
Congo	64.0	61.8	64.9	76.1	65.2	47.8	114.6
Cote d'Ivoire	172.1	156.5	130.8	153.6	156.1	106.0	147.0
Djibouti	35.5	45.1	51.5	51.3	54.4	44.7	88.8
Equatorial Guinea	5.7	6.7	6.7	6.0	9.0	7.2	15.9
Ethiopia	79.9	92.0	96.0	106.9	285.4	372.5	454.5
Gabon	58.7	38.4	59.3	65.7	85.1	60.9	57.9
Gambia	36.2	35.6	23.9	29.3	44.6	23.4	56.2
Ghana	133.4	90.1	60.9	128.4	79.1	149.3	141.0
Guinea	57.3	49.5	46.4	64.8	62.7	108.4	153.6
Guinea-Bissau	43.0	41.2	29.1	36.8	30.2	32.4	41.9
Kenya	325.2	260.2	469.6	317.6	479.5	315.5	452.5
Lesotho	82.6	65.3	41.5	61.8	60.2	53.3	71.0
Liberia	52.8	82.6	106.8	82.3	92.4	60.1	90.0
Madagascar	95.7	121.1	135.0	120.2	135.8	140.8	173.9
Malawi	84.4	91.0	62.7	69.9	71.3	67.8	192.6
Mali	109.2	167.1	82.2	151.8	296.7	242.2	209.5
Mauritania	64.0	75.9	60.1	60.9	106.6	90.9	111.7
Mauritius	44.7	42.6	50.4	30.9	28.0	24.5	60.8
Mayotte	58.7	12.7	9.4	14.6	10.0	19.9	26.1
Mozambique	123.9	154.0	155.0	214.8	224.7	239.1	444.3
Namibia	–	–	–	0.0	–	10.2	7.3
Niger	123.8	169.4	130.7	188.9	196.6	169.4	248.8
Nigeria	38.0	132.5	26.7	29.8	30.9	28.8	46.8
Reunion	754.4	640.7	610.7	651.6	492.1	356.7	446.5
Rwanda	145.2	113.5	104.9	79.6	110.2	110.0	110.3
St. Helena	8.1	7.3	10.2	9.9	10.0	12.1	13.5
Sao Tome & Principe	2.5	6.0	2.6	3.7	4.3	1.9	7.7
Senegal	205.9	243.0	218.6	280.1	258.8	246.4	396.4
Seychelles	14.2	17.0	9.4	18.6	12.7	11.4	18.1
Sierra Leone	57.1	54.9	38.4	24.7	27.6	90.9	58.9
Somalia	234.4	271.7	184.0	197.7	185.9	207.9	564.6
Sudan	624.7	349.6	356.8	430.3	396.3	636.9	534.3
Swaziland	21.4	28.4	35.0	29.8	22.7	24.2	45.1
Tanzania	674.9	457.0	533.9	385.2	384.3	367.9	637.7
Togo	104.1	40.3	44.5	81.5	75.7	159.0	108.7
Uganda	80.0	90.0	40.6	93.3	88.4	48.6	122.2
Zaire	377.8	273.2	222.2	222.5	236.0	189.1	304.8
Zambia	276.6	218.6	182.7	219.2	252.7	265.8	307.3
Zimbabwe	196.4	218.0	287.8	221.6	269.0	145.8	226.3
East African Community	4.7	5.5	7.5	5.3	6.7	11.6	2.8
DOM/TOM Unallocated	–	–	–	–	–	–	–
EAMA Unallocated	140.0	–	2.4	–	73.6	–	–
South of Sahara Unall.	33.4	128.5	284.2	194.3	127.6	277.0	418.3
TOTAL	*6642.3*	*5952.3*	*5871.6*	*5946.2*	*6587.9*	*6374.7*	*8821.6*
Africa Unspecified	97.9	122.4	144.5	165.0	144.5	254.8	182.0
AFRICA TOTAL	*8948.7*	*8250.6*	*8395.1*	*8251.8*	*9144.5*	*9078.5*	*11383.2*
N.& C. AMERICA							
Aruba	–	–	–	–	–	30.1	16.2
Bahamas	0.2	0.1	0.1	0.1	0.1	0.1	0.1
Barbados	1.7	6.8	3.8	11.8	8.9	5.8	5.4

	1980	1981
Belize	6.3	3.3
Bermuda	0.1	0.0
Costa Rica	25.0	34.1
Cuba	2.5	2.5
Dominican Republic	83.1	52.3
El Salvador	81.7	108.5
Guadeloupe	478.2	396.7
Guatemala	24.4	29.6
Haiti	46.9	83.3
Honduras	114.0	80.0
Jamaica	84.8	171.5
Martinique	593.9	463.5
Mexico	51.0	162.1
Netherlands Antilles	92.6	73.1
Nicaragua	165.2	78.3
Panama	7.5	18.9
St. Pierre & Miquelon	32.4	28.3
Trinidad & Tobago	1.8	1.7
Anguilla	2.4	3.1
Antigua and Barbuda	2.5	2.4
Cayman Islands	0.4	0.5
Dominica	6.0	6.6
Grenada	0.3	7.9
Montserrat	2.0	1.6
St. Kitts-Nevis	2.5	2.0
St. Lucia	1.7	3.4
St. Vincent and Gr.	1.3	2.5
Turks & Caicos Isl.	12.3	4.5
Virgin Islands	3.8	2.3
West Indies Unall.	2.5	11.8
DOM/TOM Unallocated	–	6.7
N.& C. America Unall.	45.6	23.4
TOTAL	*1976.6*	*1872.8*
SOUTH AMERICA		
Argentina	25.8	29.0
Bolivia	67.7	53.4
Brazil	221.5	332.6
Chile	42.9	39.5
Colombia	128.6	43.2
Ecuador	51.2	41.1
Falkland Islands	1.0	1.5
Guiana	155.1	127.2
Guyana	14.3	10.7
Paraguay	82.3	50.2
Peru	206.5	199.1
Suriname	269.1	111.7
Uruguay	7.3	11.2
Venezuela	16.3	15.3
South America Unall.	16.9	7.0
TOTAL	*1306.5*	*1072.7*
America Unspecified	30.5	65.5
AMERICA TOTAL	*3313.5*	*3011.1*
MIDDLE EAST		
Bahrain	0.7	0.9
Iran	39.3	14.9
Iraq	5.8	5.7
Israel	528.9	825.7
Jordan	161.0	65.9
Kuwait	7.5	6.6
Lebanon	20.6	49.0
Oman	7.3	3.1
Qatar	0.4	0.5
Saudi Arabia	8.9	9.4
Syria	70.9	28.1
United Arab Emirates	1.9	2.6
Yemen	201.2	66.2
Yemen, Dem.	5.2	5.2
Middle East Unall.	9.7	20.6
TOTAL	*1069.4*	*1104.2*
SOUTH ASIA		
Afghanistan	7.9	4.4
Bangladesh	1301.7	840.4
Bhutan	1.1	4.9
Burma	129.1	317.3
India	1296.5	1417.9
Maldives	3.7	1.5
Nepal	112.9	115.1
Pakistan	377.0	476.7
Sri Lanka	383.9	458.7

1982	1983	1984	1985	1986
10.9	38.9	14.7	34.6	12.6
0.0	0.1	0.0	0.0	0.0
142.2	191.3	229.4	316.7	196.6
0.9	1.2	6.4	3.6	4.7
119.2	111.1	179.6	173.1	162.0
209.4	254.9	336.7	389.6	367.5
371.5	329.6	142.6	151.1	159.7
36.9	43.7	94.4	114.1	154.1
86.3	90.9	100.3	110.6	136.4
116.4	202.6	120.1	312.7	185.9
174.9	210.0	247.9	163.9	154.5
419.9	457.2	482.2	271.9	344.9
193.0	79.0	130.5	218.7	193.1
64.9	79.9	61.5	67.7	64.3
75.2	89.5	69.4	120.2	82.0
20.0	16.5	52.6	53.8	44.3
18.3	25.6	12.8	18.8	21.5
1.2	2.5	1.7	13.1	27.1
2.0	2.2	2.8	1.5	2.4
1.0	17.2	2.8	2.7	0.8
0.2	0.0	–	–	0.1
9.0	10.1	3.8	2.0	7.3
2.3	1.8	57.0	18.8	2.3
3.3	1.7	3.3	1.7	3.1
2.0	9.0	5.4	0.6	1.4
3.8	1.9	7.2	4.9	2.0
1.1	1.1	18.4	0.9	4.0
10.2	6.5	6.9	4.7	8.0
2.7	1.8	1.1	1.6	1.3
13.1	6.6	48.6	55.6	51.0
0.0	–	–	–	–
52.3	72.6	51.4	198.9	93.7
2167.7	2368.7	2500.4	2864.0	2510.3
23.8	32.2	28.4	35.7	88.1
54.9	204.5	129.7	108.9	190.1
193.8	93.9	182.5	368.8	171.0
38.6	40.6	48.3	54.7	56.9
89.6	78.2	113.3	61.4	208.2
49.0	59.6	63.9	130.9	109.6
28.1	2.4	3.8	13.2	18.5
105.2	107.2	63.9	86.6	107.0
10.7	19.0	10.7	5.7	4.8
46.9	29.0	33.9	77.1	51.0
198.5	293.5	269.2	207.3	190.9
2.8	3.2	0.8	2.2	4.5
10.8	7.2	16.5	9.3	34.8
12.5	18.3	17.7	12.6	19.0
23.8	5.6	9.8	9.4	10.8
888.9	994.1	992.3	1183.6	1265.0
66.9	106.8	68.1	58.7	82.8
3123.5	3469.6	3560.8	4106.3	3858.1
0.9	0.5	0.6	0.8	1.5
12.4	52.5	17.3	16.0	13.8
5.7	12.2	28.5	66.9	7.3
930.8	1361.8	1317.9	2035.9	2008.8
106.4	80.8	85.9	150.4	132.8
3.6	3.7	3.4	3.3	3.7
84.3	77.5	61.1	38.2	53.9
19.5	18.6	17.7	23.8	22.9
0.5	0.5	0.5	0.6	1.5
31.8	34.1	25.9	15.3	19.8
22.0	20.5	17.2	14.9	29.7
2.3	2.3	2.5	45.9	3.4
92.3	93.0	76.4	80.0	117.1
50.6	8.0	23.3	26.9	3.2
21.4	18.8	24.4	64.1	5.3
1384.3	1784.7	1702.5	2582.8	2424.8
5.3	6.1	4.7	7.6	8.1
694.3	700.9	782.7	698.6	866.7
1.4	8.0	3.8	15.4	14.7
401.7	149.3	384.3	275.5	364.6
1191.2	1008.3	1772.6	721.3	1307.3
3.1	8.0	7.6	6.2	8.7
138.7	109.7	106.0	198.1	159.2
567.1	701.4	659.2	807.4	594.0
276.3	346.8	374.8	294.3	524.7

	1980	1981	1982	1983	1984	1985	1986
South Asia Unall.	0.5	1.4	2.3	2.7	2.0	18.7	24.0
TOTAL	3614.1	3638.3	3281.5	3041.2	4097.5	3043.1	3872.0
FAR EAST ASIA							
Brunei	0.0	0.2	0.3	0.4	0.9	1.3	2.7
China	489.5	403.4	606.1	634.8	503.4	549.2	871.8
Hong Kong	4.9	4.6	4.5	5.2	15.7	14.1	13.5
Indonesia	1483.3	838.5	865.5	861.0	998.6	1153.8	626.5
Kampuchea	47.3	15.6	9.1	11.7	8.4	3.2	3.8
Korea	309.2	388.3	50.8	231.0	249.7	272.3	42.7
Korea, Dem.	–	–	–	–	–	0.3	1.2
Laos	45.3	20.6	11.3	18.3	18.5	10.6	31.3
Macao	2.5	0.0	0.1	0.1	0.1	0.1	0.1
Malaysia	193.2	166.1	276.2	138.6	333.4	190.9	313.2
Mongolia	–	–	–	–	0.1	0.4	0.7
Philippines	400.5	411.4	431.5	507.9	423.3	338.7	1008.9
Singapore	29.0	29.0	20.7	19.1	46.1	28.4	25.3
Taiwan	2.7	1.2	1.8	2.7	7.6	2.4	2.5
Thailand	382.8	396.2	542.6	530.9	468.8	491.2	459.1
Viet Nam	223.8	92.4	81.7	78.7	55.6	64.6	85.7
Far East Asia Unall.	21.2	13.6	41.9	22.2	66.8	25.7	44.5
TOTAL	3635.2	2781.2	2943.9	3062.6	3197.0	3147.2	3533.5
Asia Unspecified	43.2	40.9	35.9	67.8	38.2	34.7	63.4
ASIA TOTAL	8361.8	7564.6	7645.6	7956.3	9035.2	8807.8	9893.7
OCEANIA							
Cook Islands	8.7	8.0	11.2	7.2	7.5	7.3	10.2
Fiji	25.5	35.1	19.3	18.5	30.1	27.2	47.3
Kiribati	11.5	9.5	12.9	14.2	8.7	10.8	6.4
Nauru	–	0.0	0.0	0.1	0.1	0.1	0.0
New Caledonia	172.8	138.0	120.0	153.7	111.5	155.9	213.6
Niue	1.7	3.5	5.0	5.4	3.4	3.6	2.5
Pacif. Isl.(Trust Tr.)	124.9	110.7	140.7	155.7	162.4	119.2	215.6
Papua New Guinea	308.1	303.4	284.4	310.3	300.5	246.7	231.3
Polynesia, French	175.1	149.1	141.3	153.2	135.9	178.3	253.0
Solomon Islands	18.8	18.8	37.6	12.0	12.8	7.9	24.2
Tokelau	0.2	2.3	1.6	1.9	1.7	1.3	1.7
Tonga	13.8	20.9	11.5	12.7	10.3	7.6	15.2
Tuvalu	2.4	5.5	3.7	3.0	3.8	3.1	12.5
Vanuatu	70.7	24.7	26.1	25.0	21.7	21.2	19.0
Wallis & Futuna	9.7	9.6	6.5	7.2	8.1	11.4	–
Western Samoa	14.7	26.6	10.4	12.3	15.2	21.6	12.4
TOM Unallocated	–	1.3	–	–	77.2	–	–
Oceania Unallocated	13.7	16.6	21.2	32.0	47.1	22.0	22.9
TOTAL	972.4	883.5	853.4	924.5	958.1	845.1	1087.8
LDCS Unspecified	1916.1	1967.6	2443.0	2200.4	2842.2	2510.5	3308.6
TOTAL,ALL LDCS	24485.2	22744.2	23014.2	23341.5	26313.9	25809.3	30126.2
INCOME GROUPS							
LLDCS	5076.1	4041.7	3619.6	3760.2	4284.1	4624.8	5975.8
CHINA AND INDIA	1786.0	1821.3	1797.3	1643.1	2275.9	1270.5	2179.0
OTHER LOW-INCOME	5902.2	5364.5	5588.3	5629.0	6280.2	6533.4	6542.3
LOW MIDDLE-INCOME	4063.4	4073.4	4059.7	4297.5	4780.0	3993.6	5082.4
UPPER MIDDLE-INCOME	5273.9	5006.0	4769.5	5059.7	5055.8	5827.3	6030.8
UNALLOCATED	2383.6	2437.2	3179.7	2952.0	3637.9	3559.8	4315.9

Legend: LLDCS · CHINA AND INDIA · OTHER LICS · LMICS · UMICS

	1980	1981	1982	1983	1984	1985	1986		1980	1981
EUROPE								Belize	9.8	4.4
Cyprus	60.6	63.3	44.9	37.7	48.4	35.3	43.7	Bermuda	0.3	0.2
Gibraltar	1.1	0.9	3.3	46.0	8.5	5.8	13.2	Costa Rica	64.3	54.1
Greece	33.5	12.4	13.0	17.7	20.8	22.8	26.9	Cuba	37.5	12.2
Malta	14.0	76.5	23.5	28.5	9.1	8.9	9.0	Dominican Republic	125.7	159.3
Portugal	144.4	88.9	99.2	63.3	150.6	107.5	178.6	El Salvador	143.8	161.3
Turkey	1268.0	1163.9	487.3	467.0	567.9	364.2	373.5	Guadeloupe	498.9	401.2
Yugoslavia	10.5	7.7	17.1	15.7	43.8	13.9	85.8	Guatemala	105.6	76.3
Europe Unallocated	8.7	14.2	18.3	40.2	18.1	24.3	20.6	Haiti	80.0	136.8
TOTAL	*1540.8*	*1427.9*	*706.5*	*716.1*	*867.1*	*582.7*	*751.4*	Honduras	225.3	99.3
								Jamaica	138.5	187.5
NORTH OF SAHARA								Martinique	612.7	471.2
Algeria	225.2	187.0	313.2	207.4	213.4	153.8	121.9	Mexico	116.4	179.3
Egypt	1817.9	1748.7	1739.9	1523.5	1840.4	1949.3	1708.3	Netherlands Antilles	104.3	74.8
Libya	16.7	11.0	12.3	6.5	5.2	5.6	6.0	Nicaragua	264.4	141.4
Morocco	635.8	1094.3	637.5	541.6	539.6	860.1	615.8	Panama	46.5	84.4
Tunisia	570.6	292.8	352.3	214.9	290.2	296.1	551.4	St. Pierre & Miquelon	32.4	29.1
North of Sahara Unall.	0.5	0.5	11.1	39.2	5.3	13.4	0.4	Trinidad & Tobago	4.4	4.3
TOTAL	*3266.7*	*3334.2*	*3066.3*	*2533.1*	*2894.1*	*3278.3*	*3003.7*	Anguilla	2.4	3.1
								Antigua and Barbuda	5.1	3.2
SOUTH OF SAHARA								Cayman Islands	0.7	0.6
Angola	86.9	62.9	103.0	92.2	104.3	113.9	132.7	Dominica	15.0	20.9
Benin	103.5	132.6	154.5	71.1	165.1	95.5	126.3	Grenada	2.6	24.3
Botswana	152.1	117.1	125.2	101.7	110.1	113.1	144.9	Montserrat	3.0	1.7
Burkina Faso	250.8	334.1	289.0	252.7	246.2	249.5	253.3	St. Kitts-Nevis	3.7	4.0
Burundi	180.5	252.5	121.3	172.3	123.5	199.7	160.1	St. Lucia	11.5	10.4
Cameroon	213.4	231.1	234.3	198.8	304.3	167.3	266.1	St. Vincent and Gr.	8.7	12.4
Cape Verde	76.1	73.6	62.0	96.3	94.1	61.6	89.1	Turks & Caicos Isl.	12.7	5.3
Central African Rep.	131.5	88.0	155.9	147.8	96.8	117.5	172.9	Virgin Islands	5.6	3.3
Chad	35.2	98.2	67.9	109.8	144.5	210.0	256.7	West Indies Unall.	2.5	11.8
Comoros	39.9	80.6	76.9	39.3	50.5	26.3	34.1	DOM/TOM Unallocated	-6.3	6.9
Congo	145.3	130.5	73.6	112.1	71.2	58.1	134.9	N.& C. America Unall.	45.6	23.4
Cote d'Ivoire	183.4	209.1	169.9	172.9	169.4	115.7	210.2	*TOTAL*	*2731.4*	*2424.1*
Djibouti	109.3	96.1	123.9	89.5	111.0	76.1	151.7			
Equatorial Guinea	19.7	19.5	13.6	21.9	26.9	41.0	41.9	**SOUTH AMERICA**		
Ethiopia	227.2	315.3	295.8	498.4	603.6	626.8	808.4	Argentina	36.9	87.3
Gabon	65.7	42.7	99.8	76.6	92.1	67.0	59.4	Bolivia	115.3	76.2
Gambia	104.9	79.0	50.8	66.5	82.1	33.2	118.7	Brazil	353.6	391.9
Ghana	251.1	156.9	109.5	291.9	287.2	420.9	351.1	Chile	49.8	45.4
Guinea	179.5	121.3	130.4	141.9	237.4	176.7	242.7	Colombia	243.3	96.0
Guinea-Bissau	68.8	63.4	62.4	122.6	76.1	62.1	62.9	Ecuador	146.7	115.7
Kenya	453.3	399.1	715.7	398.4	659.8	399.3	644.1	Falkland Islands	1.0	1.5
Lesotho	140.0	115.4	71.6	101.8	125.2	91.9	134.4	Guiana	163.4	131.3
Liberia	72.4	98.0	174.3	91.0	145.2	86.3	100.3	Guyana	23.4	47.5
Madagascar	237.7	271.9	218.2	248.1	235.0	263.2	330.6	Paraguay	114.6	101.4
Malawi	150.1	211.8	84.1	270.3	143.9	222.0	265.4	Peru	292.8	281.3
Mali	219.4	303.0	354.1	300.5	411.4	438.1	351.5	Suriname	273.5	113.8
Mauritania	351.1	276.0	224.6	163.2	191.5	231.3	180.6	Uruguay	11.0	14.7
Mauritius	77.8	58.7	86.0	36.5	40.9	30.0	68.1	Venezuela	20.8	20.2
Mayotte	58.7	12.8	9.4	14.6	13.5	19.9	26.1	South America Unall.	16.9	7.0
Mozambique	184.2	188.4	254.9	262.2	308.1	357.1	525.5	*TOTAL*	*1862.7*	*1530.9*
Namibia	–	–	–	0.0	–	13.7	11.3	America Unspecified	156.2	121.6
Niger	201.5	345.9	250.3	254.3	346.0	261.0	443.0	*AMERICA TOTAL*	*4750.3*	*4076.6*
Nigeria	61.7	156.9	47.6	63.1	55.3	59.4	65.5	**MIDDLE EAST**		
Reunion	780.7	670.2	648.7	708.8	528.9	387.1	483.8	Bahrain	199.0	124.4
Rwanda	210.2	217.1	204.8	197.0	161.0	199.1	217.3	Iran	39.4	17.3
St. Helena	8.1	7.3	10.2	9.9	10.0	12.2	13.5	Iraq	10.5	9.6
Sao Tome & Principe	4.4	8.9	7.4	10.7	15.2	13.9	40.9	Israel	529.1	826.0
Senegal	377.1	381.3	481.5	428.2	445.8	312.9	641.2	Jordan	1418.0	1209.6
Seychelles	29.1	33.0	11.8	22.5	14.0	23.1	19.3	Kuwait	10.3	9.5
Sierra Leone	81.3	121.9	81.6	59.5	84.9	110.9	90.7	Lebanon	304.5	542.6
Somalia	501.8	562.4	513.2	352.4	417.2	389.5	778.1	Oman	80.9	20.6
Sudan	1222.1	655.9	620.3	1245.2	720.4	1301.9	1304.5	Qatar	1.0	1.1
Swaziland	35.8	36.2	45.8	54.7	39.3	28.0	54.6	Saudi Arabia	15.5	20.3
Tanzania	947.7	703.5	729.8	516.3	516.7	464.9	884.3	Syria	2130.9	1321.6
Togo	145.5	87.8	111.7	169.5	125.8	234.2	174.9	United Arab Emirates	4.3	5.5
Uganda	216.2	206.1	215.7	295.5	308.8	150.3	216.1	Yemen	573.1	360.3
Zaire	574.3	367.3	445.1	378.4	376.1	386.6	580.4	Yemen, Dem.	154.3	127.0
Zambia	323.1	343.7	406.3	256.9	343.3	450.4	452.0	Middle East Unall.	174.1	208.0
Zimbabwe	275.7	346.7	402.2	294.9	315.0	161.5	260.5	*TOTAL*	*5644.8*	*4803.4*
East African Community	4.7	5.5	7.5	5.3	7.1	11.6	2.8			
DOM/TOM Unallocated	–	–	–	–	–	–	–	**SOUTH ASIA**		
EAMA Unallocated	140.0	2.0	18.1	–	73.6	–	–	Afghanistan	17.3	14.9
South of Sahara Unall.	119.5	179.4	312.7	257.0	399.7	365.8	423.4	Bangladesh	2182.9	1661.2
TOTAL	*10829.6*	*10078.6*	*10284.9*	*10343.2*	*10774.6*	*10508.9*	*13602.7*	Bhutan	15.4	11.8
Africa Unspecified	127.3	201.1	230.1	260.8	888.7	358.9	453.5	Burma	300.4	452.6
AFRICA TOTAL	*14223.6*	*13613.9*	*13581.3*	*13137.1*	*14557.4*	*14146.1*	*17059.9*	India	2823.1	3495.0
								Maldives	30.1	12.6
N.& C. AMERICA								Nepal	271.4	260.6
Aruba	–	–	–	–	–	30.1	16.2	Pakistan	1209.9	1174.1
Bahamas	2.0	1.5	2.1	1.5	1.2	1.4	3.6	Sri Lanka	689.2	746.6
Barbados	6.1	14.7	8.1	24.8	13.3	15.8	6.1			

1982	1983	1984	1985	1986
13.2	41.5	15.5	38.9	23.3
0.1	0.1	0.1	0.1	0.1
206.0	199.1	283.4	355.8	226.0
15.7	8.7	10.3	18.1	18.2
268.8	143.2	249.2	216.1	166.1
262.3	282.7	352.2	429.2	402.7
420.2	350.8	156.9	160.9	187.1
89.8	95.3	107.7	142.3	178.3
195.9	155.4	135.1	155.0	211.3
176.2	271.6	177.1	384.0	312.0
206.7	247.8	263.2	194.4	176.4
468.0	477.9	501.8	293.6	366.3
247.0	102.9	150.8	257.4	232.3
68.3	84.9	64.1	69.5	64.5
111.6	114.4	92.5	141.7	116.6
28.8	37.0	64.8	83.1	49.6
18.3	25.6	12.8	18.8	21.5
4.5	9.2	6.5	18.9	38.8
2.0	4.2	3.3	3.2	4.7
1.7	17.6	3.5	4.6	3.4
0.6	0.7	1.9	0.6	1.0
19.5	15.0	7.1	9.5	16.9
10.3	7.6	62.2	33.7	7.7
3.5	1.7	3.4	2.4	3.7
2.3	10.9	10.7	3.9	4.8
8.0	6.9	25.4	6.6	10.8
6.5	2.3	32.5	3.0	16.0
10.3	7.9	7.5	5.0	8.7
3.9	3.0	1.2	1.7	4.8
13.1	6.6	48.6	55.7	52.0
0.1	–	–	–	–
56.3	80.2	95.3	199.3	99.9
2949.4	*2839.1*	*2961.0*	*3354.2*	*3051.4*
92.7	63.9	103.2	44.1	106.3
179.6	294.1	188.9	138.9	308.7
290.2	174.6	226.9	434.7	205.2
43.5	43.8	51.4	60.0	62.6
120.4	96.4	136.8	83.5	232.8
129.3	126.3	126.7	178.3	172.2
28.3	2.5	3.8	13.3	18.8
120.2	116.4	77.9	102.5	129.2
21.2	26.2	18.7	38.2	23.3
110.0	83.3	47.1	81.7	54.9
291.8	326.2	293.3	226.5	234.8
6.0	13.3	7.3	11.2	5.4
14.0	9.0	55.5	18.7	37.6
16.7	21.4	20.2	15.6	22.5
26.4	5.6	15.3	9.4	21.5
1490.4	*1402.8*	*1372.9*	*1456.8*	*1635.9*
125.1	171.7	133.4	125.2	156.3
4564.9	*4413.5*	*4467.4*	*4936.2*	*4843.6*
130.0	240.5	148.4	59.2	103.3
12.9	60.6	28.1	31.5	27.3
8.4	26.4	40.0	68.6	12.5
930.8	1361.8	1317.9	2035.9	2009.5
981.0	799.9	690.5	617.8	772.7
5.9	5.2	4.5	4.2	5.0
428.5	151.1	86.3	104.7	79.0
58.5	103.8	73.9	84.6	67.1
1.1	1.3	1.3	1.9	2.4
49.8	42.5	34.9	26.8	31.4
1274.3	1120.5	900.7	885.9	1000.0
4.9	4.3	3.4	48.2	4.8
525.5	404.5	498.3	252.5	322.7
240.6	96.5	131.9	213.3	60.3
271.8	46.7	48.3	89.8	34.1
4923.9	*4465.6*	*4008.6*	*4525.1*	*4532.2*
14.5	17.0	13.8	19.4	17.6
1752.2	1664.7	1655.8	1530.4	1539.7
12.4	35.0	35.3	54.1	41.0
610.0	360.7	434.8	343.0	469.1
2133.9	2190.7	2810.7	2017.4	1913.5
10.7	16.6	18.9	9.7	13.4
210.0	282.5	418.7	372.8	304.7
1230.6	1349.9	1403.0	1393.7	1291.7
503.9	467.4	541.5	452.5	794.3

	1980	1981	1982	1983	1984	1985	1986
South Asia Unall.	0.5	1.4	3.3	2.7	2.0	118.7	155.2
TOTAL	*7540.2*	*7830.8*	*6481.6*	*6387.2*	*7334.4*	*6311.8*	*6540.2*

FAR EAST ASIA

	1980	1981	1982	1983	1984	1985	1986
Brunei	0.0	0.2	0.3	0.5	0.9	1.4	2.8
China	533.4	590.9	963.1	931.6	897.9	1210.1	1449.6
Hong Kong	12.2	10.5	8.8	9.3	20.1	17.8	18.0
Indonesia	1733.5	1052.5	959.0	982.0	1060.9	1249.3	719.1
Kampuchea	261.1	128.7	38.4	40.2	17.1	10.3	11.3
Korea	320.6	394.2	75.0	235.3	303.4	277.6	49.0
Korea, Dem.	–	–	–	–	–	5.4	5.6
Laos	82.5	50.6	19.4	53.9	40.8	25.4	61.0
Macao	6.9	0.0	0.7	0.6	0.5	0.4	0.4
Malaysia	234.6	193.8	289.2	155.6	361.1	210.5	325.7
Mongolia	–	–	–	–	0.1	3.3	4.6
Philippines	450.2	475.0	495.5	534.9	458.9	365.9	1103.5
Singapore	33.5	32.6	23.5	21.7	48.6	33.4	27.3
Taiwan	49.6	1.2	1.8	2.7	85.5	2.4	2.5
Thailand	493.4	554.5	628.0	615.4	519.3	562.0	497.7
Viet Nam	283.3	147.5	106.2	106.1	98.7	101.2	132.4
Far East Asia Unall.	21.2	13.6	43.1	22.2	66.8	26.0	51.4
TOTAL	*4516.2*	*3645.8*	*3652.0*	*3711.9*	*3980.5*	*4102.3*	*4461.9*
Asia Unspecified	90.3	107.5	87.8	133.1	735.6	111.2	1907.6
ASIA TOTAL	*17791.4*	*16387.4*	*15145.4*	*14697.9*	*16059.0*	*15050.4*	*17441.9*

OCEANIA

	1980	1981	1982	1983	1984	1985	1986
Cook Islands	10.4	8.8	13.4	7.8	8.1	7.9	10.9
Fiji	29.3	40.8	26.1	30.1	34.5	42.4	53.5
Kiribati	12.6	10.9	16.3	16.6	9.9	13.7	7.6
Nauru		0.0	0.0	0.1	0.1	0.1	0.0
New Caledonia	172.8	139.2	121.4	155.5	111.6	155.9	214.7
Niue	2.1	3.8	5.2	5.5	3.5	3.6	2.7
Pacif. Isl.(Trust Tr.)	125.6	111.2	141.3	157.1	163.2	120.3	217.1
Papua New Guinea	348.5	346.0	338.0	357.4	320.9	269.4	274.9
Polynesia, French	177.8	149.2	141.3	155.1	137.1	178.5	253.5
Solomon Islands	32.5	24.8	47.5	28.1	25.9	11.8	44.0
Tokelau	0.2	2.4	1.7	2.0	1.8	1.5	1.9
Tonga	14.6	26.4	15.1	19.7	15.2	9.1	19.8
Tuvalu	3.5	6.3	4.4	3.3	4.5	3.3	12.7
Vanuatu	72.9	30.8	32.5	30.7	22.7	29.0	22.1
Wallis & Futuna	10.6	9.7	8.7	7.2	8.1	11.4	0.1
Western Samoa	25.7	46.7	16.1	18.2	26.1	30.9	29.4
TOM Unallocated	–	1.4	–	–	77.2	–	–
Oceania Unallocated	13.7	16.6	27.2	32.0	47.9	22.0	22.9
TOTAL	*1052.8*	*974.9*	*956.3*	*1026.3*	*1018.2*	*910.6*	*1187.7*
LDCS Unspecified	5028.1	4986.2	3855.0	3799.4	3546.6	3567.2	4020.6
TOTAL,ALL LDCS	*44387.0*	*41466.9*	*38809.5*	*37790.2*	*40515.8*	*39193.2*	*45305.1*

INCOME GROUPS

	1980	1981	1982	1983	1984	1985	1986
LLDCS	9592.0	8417.2	8249.4	8663.3	8747.5	8907.6	10388.8
CHINA AND INDIA	3356.5	4085.9	3097.1	3122.3	3708.5	3227.5	3363.1
OTHER LOW-INCOME	9247.0	7936.0	8451.5	7843.3	8643.7	8794.1	9498.9
LOW MIDDLE-INCOME	6105.7	6304.7	5523.3	5306.7	5546.8	5209.3	6295.3
UPPER MIDDLE-INCOME	10142.5	8815.0	8381.5	7952.1	7659.8	7956.3	8336.8
UNALLOCATED	5943.3	5908.0	5106.9	4902.6	6209.6	5098.4	7422.1

Chart legend:
⊙—⊙—⊙—⊙ LLDCS
------ CHINA AND INDIA
—·—·— OTHER LICS
—— LMICS
---- UMICS

Chart y-axis: 11000, 10000, 9000, 8000, 7000, 6000, 5000, 4000, 3000
Chart x-axis: 80 81 82 83 84 85 86

INDIVIDUAL COUNTRY TABLES

TABLEAUX PAR PAYS

TOTAL RECEIPTS NET | TOTAL ODA NET | TOTAL ODA GROSS

	1983	1984	1985	1986	1983	1984	1985	1986		1983
DAC COUNTRIES										
Australia	–	–	0.0	–	–	–	0.0	–	Australia	–
Austria	0.7	0.1	0.2	0.1	0.7	0.1	0.2	0.1	Austria	0.7
Belgium	–	0.0	0.0	–	–	0.0	0.0	–	Belgium	–
Canada	-0.1	-0.2	-0.7	–	–	–	–	–	Canada	–
Denmark	0.1	0.2	0.0	-0.3	0.1	0.2	0.0	-0.3	Denmark	0.2
Finland	–	0.0	0.0	–	–	0.0	0.0	–	Finland	–
France	0.8	0.7	3.2	0.5	0.8	0.7	3.2	0.5	France	0.8
Germany, Fed. Rep.	-1.0	-0.5	1.3	-2.4	-0.9	-0.6	1.3	-2.6	Germany, Fed. Rep.	3.3
Ireland	–	–	–	–	–	–	–	–	Ireland	–
Italy	0.2	–	–	0.7	0.2	–	–	0.7	Italy	0.2
Japan	-0.1	-0.3	–	–	-0.1	-0.3	–	–	Japan	0.1
Netherlands	0.7	–	–	0.4	0.7	–	–	0.4	Netherlands	0.7
New Zealand	–	–	0.0	0.0	–	–	0.0	0.0	New Zealand	–
Norway	5.1	–	0.7	1.1	5.1	–	0.7	1.1	Norway	5.1
Sweden	0.5	1.5	1.0	2.8	0.5	1.5	1.0	2.8	Sweden	0.5
Switzerland	–	–	–	–	–	–	–	–	Switzerland	–
United Kingdom	0.2	0.4	0.5	0.6	0.3	0.4	0.5	0.6	United Kingdom	0.3
United States	-2.0	-4.0	-22.0	-5.0	-2.0	-3.0	–	-5.0	United States	–
TOTAL	*5.1*	*-2.0*	*-15.8*	*-1.4*	*5.4*	*-1.0*	*6.9*	*-1.7*	*TOTAL*	*11.9*
MULTILATERAL										
AF.D.F.	–	–	–	–	–	–	–	–	AF.D.F.	–
AF.D.B.	–	–	–	–	–	–	–	–	AF.D.B.	–
AS.D.B	-0.2	-0.2	–	-0.7	-0.2	-0.2	–	-0.7	AS.D.B	–
CAR.D.B.	–	–	–	–	–	–	–	–	CAR.D.B.	–
E.E.C.	–	–	–	–	–	–	–	–	E.E.C.	–
IBRD	–	–	–	–	–	–	–	–	IBRD	–
IDA	-0.3	-0.4	-0.3	-1.0	-0.3	-0.4	-0.3	-1.0	IDA	–
I.D.B.	–	–	–	–	–	–	–	–	I.D.B.	–
IFAD	–	–	–	–	–	–	–	–	IFAD	–
I.F.C.	–	–	–	–	–	–	–	–	I.F.C.	–
IMF TRUST FUND	–	–	–	–	–	–	–	–	IMF TRUST FUND	–
U.N. AGENCIES	–	–	–	–	–	–	–	–	U.N. AGENCIES	–
UNDP	5.5	5.9	7.0	5.8	5.5	5.9	7.0	5.8	UNDP	5.5
UNTA	1.8	1.0	2.0	1.5	1.8	1.0	2.0	1.5	UNTA	1.8
UNICEF	2.5	1.5	1.8	1.4	2.5	1.5	1.8	1.4	UNICEF	2.5
UNRWA	–	–	–	–	–	–	–	–	UNRWA	–
WFP	0.2	0.2	0.1	0.0	0.2	0.2	0.1	0.0	WFP	0.2
UNHCR	–	–	0.0	0.0	–	–	0.0	0.0	UNHCR	–
Other Multilateral	1.0	0.5	0.9	0.6	1.0	0.5	0.9	0.6	Other Multilateral	1.0
Arab OPEC Agencies	-0.2	-0.2	–	-0.4	-0.2	-0.2	–	-0.4	Arab OPEC Agencies	–
TOTAL	*10.3*	*8.3*	*11.4*	*7.3*	*10.3*	*8.3*	*11.4*	*7.3*	*TOTAL*	*11.0*
OPEC COUNTRIES	*-2.1*	*-0.7*	*-1.5*	*-3.3*	*-2.1*	*-0.7*	*-1.5*	*-3.3*	*OPEC COUNTRIES*	*0.3*
E.E.C.+ MEMBERS	*1.1*	*0.9*	*5.1*	*-0.5*	*1.2*	*0.7*	*5.0*	*-0.7*	*E.E.C.+ MEMBERS*	*5.5*
TOTAL	*13.2*	*5.6*	*-5.9*	*2.6*	*13.5*	*6.7*	*16.8*	*2.3*	*TOTAL*	*23.1*

ODA LOANS GROSS | ODA LOANS NET | GRANTS

	1983	1984	1985	1986	1983	1984	1985	1986		1983
DAC COUNTRIES										
Australia	–	–	–	–	–	–	–	–	Australia	–
Austria	–	–	–	–	–	–	–	–	Austria	0.7
Belgium	–	–	–	–	–	–	–	–	Belgium	–
Canada	–	–	–	–	–	–	–	–	Canada	–
Denmark	–	–	–	–	-0.1	-0.1	–	-0.3	Denmark	0.2
Finland	–	–	–	–	–	–	–	–	Finland	–
France	–	–	–	–	–	–	–	–	France	0.8
Germany, Fed. Rep.	0.1	–	–	0.0	-4.0	-2.9	-1.5	-5.5	Germany, Fed. Rep.	3.1
Ireland	–	–	–	–	–	–	–	–	Ireland	–
Italy	–	–	–	–	–	–	–	–	Italy	0.2
Japan	–	–	–	–	-0.2	-0.3	–	–	Japan	0.1
Netherlands	–	–	–	–	–	–	–	–	Netherlands	0.7
New Zealand	–	–	–	–	–	–	–	–	New Zealand	–
Norway	–	–	–	–	–	–	–	–	Norway	5.1
Sweden	–	–	–	–	–	–	–	–	Sweden	0.5
Switzerland	–	–	–	–	–	–	–	–	Switzerland	–
United Kingdom	–	–	–	–	0.0	-0.1	-0.1	-0.1	United Kingdom	0.3
United States	–	–	–	–	-2.0	-3.0	–	-5.0	United States	–
TOTAL	*0.1*	*–*	*–*	*0.0*	*-6.4*	*-6.4*	*-1.5*	*-10.8*	*TOTAL*	*11.8*
MULTILATERAL	*–*	*-0.2*	*–*	*–*	*-0.7*	*-0.8*	*-0.3*	*-2.1*	*MULTILATERAL*	*11.0*
OPEC COUNTRIES	*0.3*	*1.4*	*–*	*–*	*-2.1*	*-0.9*	*-1.5*	*-3.3*	*OPEC COUNTRIES*	*–*
E.E.C.+ MEMBERS	*0.1*	*–*	*–*	*0.0*	*-4.2*	*-3.1*	*-1.5*	*-5.8*	*E.E.C.+ MEMBERS*	*5.4*
TOTAL	*0.4*	*1.2*	*–*	*0.0*	*-9.2*	*-8.1*	*-3.3*	*-16.3*	*TOTAL*	*22.7*

TOTAL OFFICIAL GROSS | TOTAL OFFICIAL NET | TOTAL OOF GROSS

	1983	1984	1985	1986	1983	1984	1985	1986		1983
DAC COUNTRIES										
Australia	–	–	0.0	–	–	–	0.0	–	Australia	–
Austria	0.7	0.1	0.2	0.1	0.7	0.1	0.2	0.1	Austria	–
Belgium	–	0.0	0.0	–	–	0.0	0.0	–	Belgium	–
Canada	–	–	–	–	-0.1	-0.2	-0.7	–	Canada	–
Denmark	0.2	0.3	0.0	-0.3	0.1	0.2	0.0	-0.3	Denmark	–
Finland	–	0.0	0.0	–	–	0.0	0.0	–	Finland	–
France	0.8	0.7	3.2	0.5	0.8	0.7	3.2	0.5	France	–
Germany, Fed. Rep.	3.3	2.3	2.8	2.9	-0.9	-0.6	1.3	-2.6	Germany, Fed. Rep.	–
Ireland	–	–	–	–	–	–	–	–	Ireland	–
Italy	0.2	–	–	0.7	0.2	–	–	0.7	Italy	–
Japan	0.1	–	–	–	-0.1	-0.3	–	–	Japan	–
Netherlands	0.7	–	–	0.4	0.7	–	–	0.4	Netherlands	–
New Zealand	–	–	0.0	0.0	–	–	0.0	0.0	New Zealand	–
Norway	5.1	–	0.7	1.1	5.1	–	0.7	1.1	Norway	–
Sweden	0.5	1.5	1.0	2.8	0.5	1.5	1.0	2.8	Sweden	–
Switzerland	–	–	–	–	–	–	–	–	Switzerland	–
United Kingdom	0.3	0.5	0.6	0.6	0.3	0.4	0.5	0.6	United Kingdom	–
United States	–	–	–	–	-2.0	-4.0	-22.0	-5.0	United States	–
TOTAL	*11.9*	*5.4*	*8.4*	*9.1*	*5.2*	*-2.2*	*-15.8*	*-1.7*	*TOTAL*	*–*
MULTILATERAL	*11.0*	*9.0*	*11.7*	*9.4*	*10.3*	*8.3*	*11.4*	*7.3*	*MULTILATERAL*	*–*
OPEC COUNTRIES	*0.3*	*1.6*	*–*	*–*	*-2.1*	*-0.7*	*-1.5*	*-3.3*	*OPEC COUNTRIES*	*–*
E.E.C.+ MEMBERS	*5.5*	*3.8*	*6.5*	*5.1*	*1.2*	*0.7*	*5.0*	*-0.7*	*E.E.C.+ MEMBERS*	*–*
TOTAL	*23.1*	*15.9*	*20.1*	*18.6*	*13.4*	*5.5*	*-5.9*	*2.3*	*TOTAL*	*–*

ODA COMMITMENTS

1984	1985	1986	1983	1984	1985	1986
–	0.0	–	–	–	–	–
0.1	0.2	0.1	0.7	0.1	0.2	–
0.0	0.0	–	–	–	–	–
–	–	–	–	0.3	–	–
0.3	0.0	–	–	–	–	–
0.0	0.0	–	–	0.0	–	–
0.7	3.2	0.5	0.8	0.7	2.4	0.5
2.3	2.8	2.9	2.6	2.2	2.9	3.0
–	–	–	–	–	–	–
–	–	0.7	0.2	–	–	0.7
–	–	–	0.1	–	–	–
–	–	0.4	0.8	–	–	0.4
–	0.0	0.0	–	0.0	0.0	–
–	0.7	1.1	–	–	0.0	–
1.5	1.0	2.8	0.5	0.8	1.5	2.8
–	–	–	–	–	–	–
0.5	0.6	0.6	0.3	0.5	0.6	0.6
–	–	–	0.1	0.1	0.1	0.1
5.4	*8.4*	*9.1*	*6.1*	*4.7*	*7.6*	*8.1*
–	–	–	–	–	–	–
–	–	–	–	–	–	–
–	–	–	–	–	0.0	0.0
–	–	–	–	–	–	–
–	–	–	–	–	–	–
–	–	–	–	–	–	–
–	–	–	11.0	9.2	11.7	9.4
5.9	7.0	5.8	–	–	–	–
1.0	2.0	1.5	–	–	–	–
1.5	1.8	1.4	–	–	–	–
0.2	0.1	0.0	–	–	–	–
–	0.0	0.0	–	–	–	–
0.5	0.9	0.6	–	–	–	–
-0.2	–	–	–	–	–	–
9.0	*11.7*	*9.4*	*11.0*	*9.2*	*11.7*	*9.5*
1.6	–	–	–	–	–	–
3.8	*6.5*	*5.1*	*4.7*	*3.4*	*5.8*	*5.2*
15.9	*20.1*	*18.6*	*17.0*	*13.8*	*19.4*	*17.6*

TECH. COOP. GRANTS

1984	1985	1986	1983	1984	1985	1986
–	0.0	–	–	–	–	–
0.1	0.2	0.1	0.1	–	–	–
0.0	0.0	–	–	–	–	–
–	–	–	–	–	–	–
0.3	0.0	–	–	–	–	–
0.0	0.0	–	–	0.0	0.0	–
0.7	3.2	0.5	0.8	0.7	0.9	0.5
2.3	2.8	2.9	3.1	2.3	2.4	2.6
–	–	–	–	–	–	–
–	–	0.7	0.0	–	–	–
–	–	–	0.1	–	–	–
–	–	0.4	–	–	–	–
–	0.0	0.0	–	–	–	–
–	0.7	1.1	–	–	0.0	–
1.5	1.0	2.8	–	–	–	–
–	–	–	–	–	–	–
0.5	0.6	0.6	0.3	0.4	0.5	0.5
–	–	–	–	–	–	–
5.4	*8.4*	*9.2*	*4.4*	*3.4*	*3.8*	*3.6*
9.2	*11.7*	*9.4*	*10.8*	*9.0*	*11.6*	*9.4*
0.2	–	–	–	–	–	–
3.8	*6.5*	*5.1*	*4.2*	*3.4*	*3.8*	*3.6*
15.2	*20.1*	*18.6*	*15.2*	*12.4*	*15.4*	*13.0*

(column 1 totals: 14.8 20.1 18.6)

TOTAL OOF NET

1984	1985	1986	1983	1984	1985	1986
–	–	–	–	–	–	–
–	–	–	–	–	–	–
–	–	–	-0.1	-0.2	-0.7	–
–	–	–	–	–	–	–
–	–	–	–	–	–	–
–	–	–	–	–	–	–
–	–	–	–	–	–	–
–	–	–	–	–	–	–
–	–	–	–	–	–	–
–	–	–	–	–	–	–
–	–	–	–	–	–	–
–	–	–	–	-1.0	-22.0	–
–	–	–	-0.1	-1.2	-22.7	–
–	–	–	–	–	–	–
–	–	–	–	–	–	–
–	–	–	*-0.1*	*-1.2*	*-22.7*	–

ODA COMMITMENTS : LOANS

DAC COUNTRIES

	1983	1984	1985	1986
Australia	–	–	–	–
Austria	–	–	–	–
Belgium	–	–	–	–
Canada	–	–	–	–
Denmark	–	–	–	–
Finland	–	–	–	–
France	–	–	–	–
Germany, Fed. Rep.	–	–	–	–
Ireland	–	–	–	–
Italy	–	–	–	–
Japan	–	–	–	–
Netherlands	–	–	–	–
New Zealand	–	–	–	–
Norway	–	–	–	–
Sweden	–	–	–	–
Switzerland	–	–	–	–
United Kingdom	–	–	–	–
United States	0.1	0.1	0.1	0.1
TOTAL	*0.1*	*0.1*	*0.1*	*0.1*
MULTILATERAL	–	–	–	–
OPEC COUNTRIES				
E.E.C.+ MEMBERS	–	–	–	–
TOTAL	*0.1*	*0.1*	*0.1*	*0.1*

GRANT ELEMENT OF ODA

DAC COUNTRIES

	1983	1984	1985	1986
Australia	–	–	–	–
Austria	100.0	100.0	100.0	–
Belgium	–	–	–	–
Canada	–	100.0	–	–
Denmark	–	–	–	–
Finland	–	100.0	–	–
France	100.0	100.0	100.0	100.0
Germany, Fed. Rep.	100.0	100.0	100.0	100.0
Ireland	–	–	–	–
Italy	100.0	–	–	100.0
Japan	100.0	–	–	–
Netherlands	100.0	–	–	100.0
New Zealand	–	100.0	100.0	–
Norway	–	–	100.0	–
Sweden	100.0	100.0	100.0	100.0
Switzerland	–	–	–	–
United Kingdom	100.0	100.0	100.0	100.0
United States	67.1	67.1	67.1	67.1
TOTAL	*99.5*	*99.3*	*99.6*	*99.6*
MULTILATERAL	*100.0*	*100.0*	*100.0*	*100.0*
OPEC COUNTRIES	–	–	–	–
E.E.C.+ MEMBERS	*100.0*	*100.0*	*100.0*	*100.0*
TOTAL	*99.8*	*99.8*	*99.8*	*99.8*

OTHER AGGREGATES

COMMITMENTS: ALL SOURCES

	1983	1984	1985	1986
TOTAL BILATERAL	312.4	286.2	233.3	230.9
of which				
OPEC	–	–	–	–
CMEA	306.3	281.5	225.7	222.8
TOTAL MULTILATERAL	11.0	9.2	11.7	9.5
TOTAL BIL.& MULTIL.	323.4	295.3	245.0	240.4
of which				
ODA Grants	291.6	125.6	26.3	139.3
ODA Loans	31.8	169.7	218.7	101.1

DISBURSEMENTS:

DAC COUNTRIES COMBINED

	1983	1984	1985	1986
OFFICIAL & PRIVATE				
GROSS:				
Contractual Lending	0.1	–	–	0.1
Export Credits Total	–	–	–	0.1
Export Credits Private	–	–	–	0.1
NET:				
Contractual Lending	-6.6	-7.7	-24.3	-10.7
Export Credits Total	-0.2	-1.3	-22.7	0.1
PRIVATE SECTOR NET	-0.1	0.2	0.1	0.3
Direct Investment	–	–	–	–
Portfolio Investment	-0.1	0.3	0.1	0.1
Export Credits	0.0	-0.1	–	0.1

MARKET BORROWING:

CHANGE IN CLAIMS

	1983	1984	1985	1986
Banks	–	-4.0	4.0	2.0

MEMORANDUM ITEM:

	1983	1984	1985	1986
CMEA Countr.(Gross)	348.9	229.3	238.1	265.0

TOTAL RECEIPTS NET / TOTAL ODA NET / TOTAL ODA GROSS

	1983	1984	1985	1986	1983	1984	1985	1986	1983
	TOTAL RECEIPTS NET				TOTAL ODA NET				TOTAL ODA GROSS
DAC COUNTRIES									
Australia	-0.2	–	0.1	–	0.0	–	0.1	–	0.0
Austria	20.8	34.6	69.0	62.5	21.0	63.0	96.5	63.4	21.0
Belgium	250.0	142.8	62.1	-161.8	2.3	1.9	1.4	1.5	2.3
Canada	72.9	101.6	5.4	-55.2	18.9	5.3	4.8	1.7	18.9
Denmark	535.5	92.1	21.3	-71.0	-0.1	-0.1	-0.1	0.2	–
Finland	–	0.8	-0.1	0.3	–	–	–	0.3	–
France	378.9	449.5	680.8	192.5	39.0	39.0	36.8	45.9	48.8
Germany, Fed. Rep.	-141.5	-8.1	-72.9	-136.0	1.6	1.1	-1.7	-2.9	3.3
Ireland	–	–	–	–	–	–	–	–	–
Italy	49.9	-165.8	-11.7	116.0	0.9	1.1	1.3	1.3	0.9
Japan	-262.5	-50.7	13.3	-77.3	0.7	0.9	-0.7	-2.5	1.7
Netherlands	-37.1	-39.2	-21.7	-62.5	0.8	0.1	0.0	–	0.8
New Zealand	–	–	–	–	–	–	–	–	–
Norway	0.0	0.1	1.2	–	–	0.0	1.2	–	–
Sweden	22.1	72.4	13.9	7.2	1.9	0.4	1.9	10.5	1.9
Switzerland	-10.9	-45.0	-37.2	-0.1	0.1	0.5	0.4	-0.1	0.1
United Kingdom	-9.5	23.3	2.7	52.2	0.1	0.0	0.1	0.3	0.1
United States	-84.0	-108.0	-131.0	-128.0	-1.0	-1.0	–	–	–
TOTAL	*784.3*	*500.2*	*595.4*	*-261.4*	*86.1*	*112.1*	*142.0*	*119.4*	*99.8*
MULTILATERAL									
AF.D.F.	–	–	–	–	–	–	–	–	–
AF.D.B.	-1.5	-1.8	-1.9	-1.1	–	–	–	–	–
AS.D.B	–	–	–	–	–	–	–	–	–
CAR.D.B.	–	–	–	–	–	–	–	–	–
E.E.C.	8.0	2.2	16.3	14.9	2.4	2.9	7.0	3.2	2.4
IBRD	43.4	26.0	106.1	87.4	–	–	–	–	–
IDA	–	–	–	–	–	–	–	–	–
I.D.B.	–	–	–	–	–	–	–	–	–
IFAD	–	–	–	–	–	–	–	–	–
I.F.C.	–	–	–	–	–	–	–	–	–
IMF TRUST FUND	–	–	–	–	–	–	–	–	–
U.N. AGENCIES	–	–	–	–	–	–	–	–	–
UNDP	3.9	3.8	3.3	3.6	3.9	3.8	3.3	3.6	3.9
UNTA	0.4	0.2	0.6	0.9	0.4	0.2	0.6	0.9	0.4
UNICEF	0.1	0.1	0.2	0.4	0.1	0.1	0.2	0.4	0.1
UNRWA	–	–	–	–	–	–	–	–	–
WFP	1.7	0.1	4.9	2.3	1.7	0.1	4.9	2.3	1.7
UNHCR	3.2	3.5	3.3	3.8	3.2	3.5	3.3	3.8	3.2
Other Multilateral	0.1	0.0	0.3	0.2	0.1	0.0	0.3	0.2	0.1
Arab OPEC Agencies	30.0	22.3	102.4	-44.3	0.8	-1.0	2.5	3.5	2.2
TOTAL	*89.3*	*56.5*	*235.4*	*67.9*	*12.5*	*9.7*	*22.0*	*17.8*	*13.9*
OPEC COUNTRIES	*-27.7*	*-54.0*	*0.6*	*41.2*	*-3.6*	*0.0*	*9.1*	*27.9*	*0.0*
E.E.C.+ MEMBERS	*1034.2*	*496.7*	*677.0*	*-55.7*	*46.9*	*46.0*	*44.8*	*49.4*	*58.6*
TOTAL	*845.8*	*502.7*	*831.3*	*-152.3*	*95.0*	*121.8*	*173.0*	*165.1*	*113.7*

ODA LOANS GROSS / ODA LOANS NET / GRANTS

	1983	1984	1985	1986	1983	1984	1985	1986	1983
	ODA LOANS GROSS				ODA LOANS NET				GRANTS
DAC COUNTRIES									
Australia	–	–	–	–	–	–	–	–	0.0
Austria	20.5	62.9	96.4	63.2	20.5	62.9	96.4	63.2	0.5
Belgium	–	–	–	–	–	–	–	–	2.3
Canada	18.6	5.1	4.5	0.8	18.6	4.7	4.2	-0.4	0.3
Denmark	–	–	–	–	-0.1	-0.1	-0.1	-0.1	–
Finland	–	–	–	–	–	–	–	–	–
France	2.1	–	–	–	-7.7	-7.6	-6.7	-10.5	46.7
Germany, Fed. Rep.	–	–	–	–	-1.7	-2.5	-5.1	-8.0	3.3
Ireland	–	–	–	–	–	–	–	–	–
Italy	–	–	–	–	–	–	–	–	0.9
Japan	–	1.2	0.6	–	-0.9	-0.7	-1.7	-3.4	1.7
Netherlands	–	–	–	–	–	–	–	–	0.8
New Zealand	–	–	–	–	–	–	–	–	–
Norway	–	–	–	–	–	–	–	–	–
Sweden	–	–	–	–	–	–	–	–	1.9
Switzerland	–	–	–	–	–	–	–	–	0.1
United Kingdom	–	–	–	–	–	–	–	–	0.1
United States	–	–	–	–	-1.0	-1.0	-1.0	–	–
TOTAL	*41.2*	*69.2*	*101.5*	*64.0*	*27.5*	*55.7*	*86.0*	*40.5*	*58.6*
MULTILATERAL	*3.3*	*–*	*3.7*	*4.7*	*1.9*	*-1.0*	*2.5*	*3.5*	*10.6*
OPEC COUNTRIES	*–*	*–*	*–*	*14.2*	*-3.6*	*–*	*–*	*14.2*	*0.0*
E.E.C.+ MEMBERS	*3.2*	*–*	*–*	*–*	*-8.5*	*-10.2*	*-12.0*	*-18.6*	*55.4*
TOTAL	*44.5*	*69.2*	*105.2*	*82.9*	*25.8*	*54.7*	*88.4*	*58.3*	*69.3*

TOTAL OFFICIAL GROSS / TOTAL OFFICIAL NET / TOTAL OOF GROSS

	1983	1984	1985	1986	1983	1984	1985	1986	1983
	TOTAL OFFICIAL GROSS				TOTAL OFFICIAL NET				TOTAL OOF GROSS
DAC COUNTRIES									
Australia	0.0	–	0.1	–	0.0	–	0.1	–	–
Austria	21.0	63.0	96.5	63.4	20.8	62.3	95.9	62.5	–
Belgium	2.3	12.1	13.4	1.5	2.3	12.1	13.4	1.5	–
Canada	144.7	153.6	99.8	47.7	88.9	116.0	12.0	-50.0	125.8
Denmark	87.6	113.1	99.3	29.9	75.9	93.9	65.9	-10.1	87.6
Finland	–	–	–	0.3	–	–	–	0.3	–
France	48.8	50.8	46.9	56.4	39.0	43.2	40.2	45.9	–
Germany, Fed. Rep.	32.9	42.2	21.4	27.2	-2.7	4.9	-16.4	-24.7	29.6
Ireland	–	–	–	–	–	–	–	–	–
Italy	0.9	1.1	1.3	1.3	-12.3	-12.7	-13.2	-14.4	–
Japan	166.4	139.9	90.3	79.5	83.3	9.0	-49.2	-145.9	164.8
Netherlands	0.8	0.1	0.0	–	0.8	0.1	0.0	–	–
New Zealand	–	–	–	–	–	–	–	–	–
Norway	–	0.0	1.2	–	–	0.0	1.2	–	–
Sweden	37.5	90.7	28.9	43.4	28.0	82.4	6.9	18.8	35.6
Switzerland	0.1	0.5	0.4	0.1	0.1	0.5	0.4	-0.1	–
United Kingdom	0.1	0.0	0.1	0.3	0.1	0.0	0.1	0.3	–
United States	1.0	2.0	4.0	–	-84.0	-108.0	-131.0	-128.0	1.0
TOTAL	*544.1*	*669.2*	*503.6*	*350.8*	*240.1*	*303.7*	*26.2*	*-244.0*	*444.3*
MULTILATERAL	*161.5*	*176.4*	*324.2*	*283.7*	*89.3*	*56.5*	*235.4*	*67.9*	*147.6*
OPEC COUNTRIES	*53.1*	*0.0*	*9.1*	*41.2*	*-27.7*	*-54.0*	*0.6*	*41.2*	*53.1*
E.E.C.+ MEMBERS	*181.8*	*222.3*	*199.4*	*132.5*	*111.1*	*143.7*	*106.2*	*13.4*	*123.2*
TOTAL	*758.6*	*845.6*	*836.8*	*675.7*	*301.7*	*306.2*	*262.1*	*-134.9*	*644.9*

ODA COMMITMENTS

Country	1984	1985	1986	1983	1984	1985	1986
Australia	–	0.1	–	0.0	–	–	–
Austria	63.0	96.5	63.4	85.2	0.1	12.2	–
Belgium	1.9	1.4	1.5	1.3	1.2	0.7	1.5
Canada	5.6	5.0	2.9	0.5	0.4	9.2	0.5
Denmark	–	–	0.3	–	–	–	–
Finland	–	–	0.3	–	–	–	–
France	46.6	43.5	56.4	46.7	46.6	42.2	56.4
Germany, Fed. Rep.	3.6	3.4	5.1	3.5	4.8	5.1	21.7
Ireland	–	–	–	–	–	–	–
Italy	1.1	1.3	1.3	4.6	1.5	1.9	2.4
Japan	2.8	1.6	0.9	1.8	1.6	1.1	1.0
Netherlands	0.1	0.0	–	0.1	0.1	0.0	–
New Zealand	–	–	–	–	–	–	–
Norway	0.0	1.2	–	–	0.0	–	–
Sweden	0.4	1.9	10.5	1.1	1.4	1.9	10.5
Switzerland	0.5	0.4	0.1	0.1	0.5	0.4	0.1
United Kingdom	0.0	0.1	0.3	0.1	0.0	0.1	0.3
United States	–	1.0	–	–	–	–	0.4
TOTAL	125.6	157.5	142.9	145.0	58.1	75.1	94.3
	–	–	–	–	–	–	–
	–	–	–	–	–	–	–
	–	–	–	–	–	–	–
	2.9	7.0	3.2	2.0	5.6	9.0	6.1
	–	–	–	–	–	–	–
	–	–	–	–	–	–	–
	–	–	–	–	–	–	10.3
	–	–	–	–	–	–	–
	–	–	–	9.3	7.9	12.5	11.1
	3.8	3.3	3.6	–	–	–	–
	0.2	0.6	0.9	–	–	–	–
	0.1	0.2	0.4	–	–	–	–
	–	–	–	–	–	–	–
	0.1	4.9	2.3	–	–	–	–
	3.5	3.3	3.8	–	–	–	–
	0.0	0.3	0.2	–	–	–	–
	–	3.7	4.7	–	–	–	–
	10.8	23.2	18.9	11.3	13.4	21.5	27.5
	0.0	9.1	27.9	51.1	141.9	57.1	–
	56.2	56.8	68.0	58.2	59.8	59.1	88.4
	136.4	189.8	189.7	207.4	213.4	153.8	121.9

TECH. COOP. GRANTS

Country	1984	1985	1986	1983	1984	1985	1986
Australia	–	0.1	–	0.0	–	0.1	–
Austria	0.1	0.1	0.1	0.5	–	–	–
Belgium	1.9	1.4	1.5	1.4	1.3	1.1	1.0
Canada	0.5	0.6	2.2	–	–	1.0	–
Denmark	–	–	0.3	–	–	–	0.3
Finland	–	–	0.3	–	–	–	–
France	46.6	43.5	56.4	36.0	34.9	28.2	38.2
Germany, Fed. Rep.	3.6	3.4	5.1	3.3	3.5	3.4	4.6
Ireland	–	–	–	–	–	–	–
Italy	1.1	1.3	1.3	0.8	0.9	0.8	1.0
Japan	1.6	1.0	0.9	1.7	1.6	1.0	0.9
Netherlands	0.1	0.0	–	0.1	0.0	0.0	–
New Zealand	–	–	–	–	–	–	–
Norway	0.0	1.2	–	–	0.0	–	–
Sweden	0.4	1.9	10.5	0.0	–	1.0	0.2
Switzerland	0.5	0.4	0.1	0.0	–	–	–
United Kingdom	0.0	0.1	0.3	0.1	0.0	0.1	0.2
United States	–	1.0	–	–	–	–	–
TOTAL	56.4	56.0	78.9	43.9	42.3	36.5	46.4
	10.8	19.5	14.3	7.7	7.7	7.6	8.8
	0.0	9.1	13.6	–	–	–	–
	56.2	56.8	68.0	41.7	40.7	33.5	45.3
	67.1	84.6	106.8	51.6	50.0	44.1	55.2

TOTAL OOF NET

Country	1984	1985	1986	1983	1984	1985	1986
Australia	–	–	–	–	–	–	–
Austria	–	–	–	-0.2	-0.7	-0.6	-0.9
Belgium	10.3	11.9	0.0	–	10.3	11.9	0.0
Canada	148.0	94.8	44.8	69.9	110.8	7.3	-51.7
Denmark	113.1	99.3	29.5	76.0	94.0	66.0	-10.2
Finland	–	–	–	–	–	–	–
France	4.3	3.4	–	–	4.3	3.4	–
Germany, Fed. Rep.	38.6	18.0	22.2	-4.3	3.7	-14.7	-21.8
Ireland	–	–	–	–	–	–	–
Italy	–	–	–	-13.2	-13.8	-14.5	-15.7
Japan	137.1	88.7	78.6	82.6	8.1	-48.5	-143.4
Netherlands	–	–	–	–	–	–	–
New Zealand	–	–	–	–	–	–	–
Norway	–	–	–	–	–	–	–
Sweden	90.3	27.0	32.9	26.1	82.0	5.0	8.3
Switzerland	–	–	–	–	–	–	–
United Kingdom	2.0	3.0	–	-83.0	-107.0	-131.0	-128.0
United States	543.6	346.0	207.9	153.9	191.6	-115.8	-363.4
TOTAL	165.6	301.0	264.8	76.8	46.8	213.4	50.1
	–	–	13.4	-24.1	-54.0	-8.5	13.4
	166.2	142.6	64.5	64.2	97.7	61.4	-36.0
	709.2	647.0	486.0	206.6	184.4	89.1	-300.0

ODA COMMITMENTS : LOANS

DAC COUNTRIES

	1983	1984	1985	1986
Australia	–	–	–	–
Austria	85.1	–	12.1	–
Belgium	–	–	–	–
Canada	–	–	–	–
Denmark	–	–	–	–
Finland	–	–	–	–
France	–	–	–	–
Germany, Fed. Rep.	–	–	–	12.8
Ireland	–	–	–	–
Italy	–	–	–	–
Japan	–	–	–	–
Netherlands	–	–	–	–
New Zealand	–	–	–	–
Norway	–	–	–	–
Sweden	–	–	–	–
Switzerland	–	–	–	–
United Kingdom	–	–	–	–
United States	–	–	–	–
TOTAL	85.1	–	12.1	12.8
MULTILATERAL	–	2.1	–	10.3
OPEC COUNTRIES	51.1	–	57.1	–
E.E.C.+ MEMBERS	–	2.1	–	12.8
TOTAL	136.2	2.1	69.2	23.1

GRANT ELEMENT OF ODA

DAC COUNTRIES

	1983	1984	1985	1986
Australia	100.0	–	–	–
Austria	30.2	100.0	28.1	–
Belgium	100.0	100.0	100.0	100.0
Canada	100.0	100.0	100.0	100.0
Denmark	–	–	–	–
Finland	–	–	–	–
France	100.0	100.0	100.0	100.0
Germany, Fed. Rep.	100.0	100.0	100.0	79.7
Ireland	–	–	–	–
Italy	100.0	100.0	100.0	100.0
Japan	100.0	100.0	100.0	100.0
Netherlands	100.0	100.0	100.0	–
New Zealand	–	–	–	–
Norway	–	100.0	–	–
Sweden	100.0	100.0	100.0	100.0
Switzerland	100.0	100.0	100.0	100.0
United Kingdom	100.0	100.0	100.0	100.0
United States	–	–	100.0	–
TOTAL	59.0	100.0	88.3	95.3
MULTILATERAL	100.0	100.0	100.0	85.0
OPEC COUNTRIES	40.0	100.0	46.2	–
E.E.C.+ MEMBERS	100.0	100.0	100.0	95.0
TOTAL	56.5	100.0	74.3	93.0

OTHER AGGREGATES

COMMITMENTS: ALL SOURCES

	1983	1984	1985	1986
TOTAL BILATERAL	890.7	499.0	259.6	501.2
of which				
OPEC	95.7	151.9	57.1	12.5
CMEA	307.6	–	–	350.0
TOTAL MULTILATERAL	252.4	423.7	433.3	337.2
TOTAL BIL.& MULTIL.	1143.1	922.7	693.0	838.4
of which				
ODA Grants	71.2	211.3	84.6	98.8
ODA Loans	386.2	2.1	69.2	23.1

DISBURSEMENTS:

DAC COUNTRIES COMBINED

	1983	1984	1985	1986
OFFICIAL & PRIVATE				
GROSS:				
Contractual Lending	2791.9	1987.8	2144.5	1033.9
Export Credits Total	2750.6	1913.9	2039.5	967.3
Export Credits Private	2306.4	1385.3	1708.9	762.1
NET:				
Contractual Lending	824.0	231.6	257.8	-682.0
Export Credits Total	796.4	171.2	168.5	-724.9
PRIVATE SECTOR NET	544.2	196.5	569.2	-17.4
Direct Investment	4.7	-108.5	-5.8	-7.4
Portfolio Investment	-103.0	310.4	275.4	349.1
Export Credits	642.6	-5.5	299.6	-359.1

MARKET BORROWING:

CHANGE IN CLAIMS

	1983	1984	1985	1986
Banks	–	549.0	710.0	1469.0

MEMORANDUM ITEM:

	1983	1984	1985	1986
CMEA Countr.(Gross)	5.3	–	–	–

DISBURSEMENTS, UNLESS OTHERWISE STATED

TOTAL RECEIPTS NET | TOTAL ODA NET | TOTAL ODA GROSS

	1983	1984	1985	1986	1983	1984	1985	1986		1983
TOTAL RECEIPTS NET					**TOTAL ODA NET**				**TOTAL ODA GROSS**	
DAC COUNTRIES										
Australia	0.0	—	—	1.2	0.0	—	—	—	Australia	0.0
Austria	0.1	0.8	1.4	1.2	0.1	0.8	1.4	1.2	Austria	0.1
Belgium	1.3	33.8	1.1	37.3	0.1	1.9	0.1	0.2	Belgium	0.1
Canada	0.2	0.7	1.8	3.8	0.2	0.7	1.8	3.8	Canada	0.2
Denmark	7.5	-0.5	-2.3	-0.7	2.2	1.3	0.9	4.5	Denmark	2.2
Finland	—	0.0	0.2	1.1	—	0.0	0.2	1.1	Finland	—
France	110.7	79.0	106.2	91.7	1.1	1.1	1.4	6.3	France	1.1
Germany, Fed. Rep.	2.0	3.0	4.5	-0.6	1.5	2.5	2.5	4.1	Germany, Fed. Rep.	1.5
Ireland	—	—	—	—	—	—	—	—	Ireland	—
Italy	13.1	-1.4	21.7	27.0	17.5	11.2	16.3	31.6	Italy	17.5
Japan	-4.0	-4.6	3.2	-4.8	0.0	—	—	0.5	Japan	0.0
Netherlands	15.2	16.4	15.9	24.9	8.9	16.7	8.1	16.8	Netherlands	9.3
New Zealand	—	—	—	—	—	—	—	—	New Zealand	—
Norway	0.5	0.2	0.3	—	0.5	0.2	0.3	0.3	Norway	0.5
Sweden	9.3	14.6	18.7	25.5	12.1	14.6	18.7	14.8	Sweden	12.1
Switzerland	-2.2	1.7	6.9	1.3	0.2	1.5	0.8	1.3	Switzerland	0.2
United Kingdom	0.6	28.8	5.2	-1.6	0.1	0.2	0.2	0.5	United Kingdom	0.1
United States	-8.0	-6.0	39.0	27.0	2.0	7.0	7.0	7.0	United States	2.0
TOTAL	*146.4*	*166.3*	*223.7*	*233.0*	*46.4*	*59.6*	*59.6*	*93.8*	*TOTAL*	*46.9*
MULTILATERAL										
AF.D.F.	—	—	—	—	—	—	—	—	AF.D.F.	—
AF.D.B.	—	—	2.8	5.5	—	—	—	—	AF.D.B.	—
AS.D.B	—	—	—	—	—	—	—	—	AS.D.B	—
CAR.D.B.	—	—	—	—	—	—	—	—	CAR.D.B.	—
E.E.C.	2.5	8.7	7.2	9.8	2.5	8.7	7.2	9.8	E.E.C.	2.5
IBRD	—	—	—	—	—	—	—	—	IBRD	—
IDA	—	—	—	—	—	—	—	—	IDA	—
I.D.B.	—	—	—	—	—	—	—	—	I.D.B.	—
IFAD	—	—	—	—	—	—	—	—	IFAD	—
I.F.C.	—	—	—	—	—	—	—	—	I.F.C.	—
IMF TRUST FUND	—	—	—	—	—	—	—	—	IMF TRUST FUND	—
U.N. AGENCIES	—	—	—	—	—	—	—	—	U.N. AGENCIES	—
UNDP	5.3	3.4	4.3	6.1	5.3	3.4	4.3	6.1	UNDP	5.3
UNTA	0.9	0.5	1.0	0.9	0.9	0.5	1.0	0.9	UNTA	0.9
UNICEF	3.0	3.3	4.1	3.3	3.0	3.3	4.1	3.3	UNICEF	3.0
UNRWA	—	—	—	—	—	—	—	—	UNRWA	—
WFP	8.5	9.5	7.1	6.5	8.5	9.5	7.1	6.5	WFP	8.5
UNHCR	5.0	6.0	4.9	2.6	5.0	6.0	4.9	2.6	UNHCR	5.0
Other Multilateral	1.7	1.8	1.3	1.3	1.7	1.8	1.3	1.3	Other Multilateral	1.7
Arab OPEC Agencies	1.8	1.1	2.1	5.9	1.8	1.1	2.1	5.9	Arab OPEC Agencies	1.8
TOTAL	*28.7*	*34.3*	*34.8*	*42.0*	*28.7*	*34.3*	*31.9*	*36.5*	*TOTAL*	*28.7*
OPEC COUNTRIES	*0.2*	*1.2*	*—*	*0.8*	*0.2*	*1.2*	*—*	*0.8*	*OPEC COUNTRIES*	*0.2*
E.E.C.+ MEMBERS	*153.0*	*167.6*	*159.4*	*187.8*	*33.8*	*43.5*	*36.6*	*73.6*	*E.E.C.+ MEMBERS*	*34.3*
TOTAL	*175.2*	*201.7*	*258.5*	*275.9*	*75.3*	*95.0*	*91.5*	*131.2*	*TOTAL*	*75.7*

ODA LOANS GROSS | ODA LOANS NET | GRANTS

	1983	1984	1985	1986	1983	1984	1985	1986		1983
ODA LOANS GROSS					**ODA LOANS NET**				**GRANTS**	
DAC COUNTRIES										
Australia	—	—	—	—	—	—	—	—	Australia	0.0
Austria	—	0.8	1.3	0.7	—	0.8	1.3	0.7	Austria	0.1
Belgium	—	—	0.1	—	—	—	0.1	—	Belgium	0.1
Canada	—	—	—	—	—	—	—	—	Canada	0.2
Denmark	—	—	—	4.2	—	—	—	4.2	Denmark	2.2
Finland	—	—	—	—	—	—	—	—	Finland	—
France	—	—	0.6	5.1	—	—	0.6	5.1	France	1.1
Germany, Fed. Rep.	—	—	—	—	—	—	—	—	Germany, Fed. Rep.	1.5
Ireland	—	—	—	—	—	—	—	—	Ireland	—
Italy	10.2	3.2	10.6	16.0	10.2	3.2	10.6	16.0	Italy	7.3
Japan	—	—	—	0.5	—	—	—	0.5	Japan	0.0
Netherlands	5.2	12.8	7.2	12.1	4.8	12.7	7.2	12.1	Netherlands	4.1
New Zealand	—	—	—	—	—	—	—	—	New Zealand	—
Norway	—	—	—	—	—	—	—	—	Norway	0.5
Sweden	—	—	—	—	—	—	—	—	Sweden	12.1
Switzerland	—	—	—	—	—	—	—	—	Switzerland	0.2
United Kingdom	—	—	—	—	—	—	—	—	United Kingdom	0.1
United States	—	—	—	—	—	—	—	—	United States	2.0
TOTAL	*15.4*	*16.8*	*19.8*	*38.6*	*15.0*	*16.7*	*19.8*	*38.6*	*TOTAL*	*31.4*
MULTILATERAL	*1.8*	*1.1*	*2.1*	*6.8*	*1.8*	*1.1*	*2.1*	*5.9*	*MULTILATERAL*	*26.9*
OPEC COUNTRIES	*—*	*—*	*—*	*0.8*	*—*	*—*	*—*	*0.8*	*OPEC COUNTRIES*	*0.2*
E.E.C.+ MEMBERS	*15.4*	*16.0*	*18.4*	*37.4*	*15.0*	*15.9*	*18.4*	*37.4*	*E.E.C.+ MEMBERS*	*18.8*
TOTAL	*17.2*	*17.9*	*21.9*	*46.1*	*16.8*	*17.8*	*21.9*	*45.3*	*TOTAL*	*58.5*

TOTAL OFFICIAL GROSS | TOTAL OFFICIAL NET | TOTAL OOF GROSS

	1983	1984	1985	1986	1983	1984	1985	1986		1983
TOTAL OFFICIAL GROSS					**TOTAL OFFICIAL NET**				**TOTAL OOF GROSS**	
DAC COUNTRIES										
Australia	0.0	—	—	—	0.0	—	—	—	Australia	—
Austria	0.1	0.8	1.4	1.2	0.1	0.8	1.4	1.2	Austria	—
Belgium	0.1	2.4	0.6	0.2	0.1	2.4	0.6	0.2	Belgium	—
Canada	0.2	0.7	1.8	3.8	0.2	0.7	1.8	3.8	Canada	—
Denmark	8.0	3.6	0.9	4.5	8.0	1.7	-0.2	1.7	Denmark	5.8
Finland	—	0.0	0.2	1.1	—	0.0	0.2	1.1	Finland	—
France	1.1	1.1	1.4	6.3	1.1	1.1	1.4	6.3	France	—
Germany, Fed. Rep.	1.3	2.5	2.5	4.1	1.3	2.5	2.5	4.1	Germany, Fed. Rep.	-0.1
Ireland	—	—	—	—	—	—	—	—	Ireland	—
Italy	17.5	11.2	28.0	34.8	17.5	11.2	27.8	34.7	Italy	—
Japan	0.0	—	—	0.5	0.0	—	—	0.5	Japan	—
Netherlands	9.3	16.7	8.1	16.8	8.9	16.7	8.1	16.8	Netherlands	—
New Zealand	—	—	—	—	—	—	—	—	New Zealand	—
Norway	0.5	0.2	0.3	0.3	0.5	0.2	0.3	0.3	Norway	—
Sweden	22.9	14.6	18.7	27.6	12.3	14.6	18.7	21.7	Sweden	10.8
Switzerland	0.2	1.5	0.8	1.3	0.2	1.5	0.8	1.3	Switzerland	—
United Kingdom	0.1	0.2	0.2	0.5	0.1	0.2	0.2	0.5	United Kingdom	—
United States	5.0	7.0	51.0	39.0	-8.0	-6.0	39.0	27.0	United States	3.0
TOTAL	*66.4*	*62.5*	*115.8*	*141.8*	*42.3*	*47.5*	*102.5*	*121.0*	*TOTAL*	*19.5*
MULTILATERAL	*28.7*	*34.3*	*34.8*	*42.9*	*28.7*	*34.3*	*34.8*	*42.0*	*MULTILATERAL*	*—*
OPEC COUNTRIES	*0.2*	*1.2*	*—*	*0.8*	*0.2*	*1.2*	*—*	*0.8*	*OPEC COUNTRIES*	*—*
E.E.C.+ MEMBERS	*40.0*	*46.4*	*48.8*	*76.9*	*39.5*	*44.5*	*47.5*	*74.0*	*E.E.C.+ MEMBERS*	*5.7*
TOTAL	*95.3*	*97.9*	*150.6*	*185.5*	*71.1*	*83.0*	*137.3*	*163.9*	*TOTAL*	*19.5*

ODA COMMITMENTS

1984	1985	1986	1983	1984	1985	1986
–	–	–	0.0	–	–	–
0.8	1.4	1.2	3.7	–	0.1	–
1.9	0.1	0.2	–	1.2	–	0.2
0.7	1.8	3.8	0.2	0.7	1.7	3.8
1.3	0.9	4.5	–	0.9	0.1	12.6
0.0	0.2	1.1	–	0.0	0.2	0.5
1.1	1.4	6.3	7.2	8.6	0.8	6.3
2.5	2.5	4.1	1.9	2.4	2.8	4.8
–	–	–	–	–	–	–
11.2	16.3	31.6	3.1	11.9	50.9	16.7
–	–	0.5	0.0	–	–	1.6
16.7	8.1	16.8	12.3	16.8	0.5	17.6
–	–	–	–	–	–	–
0.2	0.3	0.3	–	0.3	0.2	0.2
14.6	18.7	14.8	13.7	17.4	13.8	14.8
1.5	0.8	1.3	0.1	1.4	0.8	1.2
0.2	0.2	0.5	0.1	0.2	0.2	0.5
7.0	7.0	7.0	0.8	5.8	4.5	6.2
59.6	59.6	93.8	43.0	67.6	76.4	86.9
–	–	–	14.5	–	1.0	18.1
–	–	–	–	–	–	–
–	–	–	–	–	–	–
8.7	7.2	9.8	10.3	12.3	13.6	6.9
–	–	–	–	–	–	–
–	–	–	–	–	–	–
–	–	–	–	–	–	–
–	–	–	–	–	–	–
–	–	–	24.4	24.4	22.6	20.8
3.4	4.3	6.1	–	–	–	–
0.5	1.0	0.9	–	–	–	–
3.3	4.1	3.3	–	–	–	–
–	–	–	–	–	–	–
9.5	7.1	6.5	–	–	–	–
6.0	4.9	2.6	–	–	–	–
1.8	1.3	1.3	–	–	–	–
1.1	2.1	6.8	–	–	0.2	–
34.3	31.9	37.3	49.2	36.7	37.4	45.8
1.2	–	0.8	–	–	–	–
43.5	36.6	73.6	34.8	54.3	68.8	65.5
95.1	91.5	132.0	92.2	104.3	113.9	132.7

TECH. COOP. GRANTS

1984	1985	1986	1983	1984	1985	1986
–	–	–	0.0	–	–	–
0.1	0.1	0.5	0.1	–	–	–
1.9	0.0	0.2	–	–	–	–
0.7	1.8	3.8	–	–	–	–
1.3	0.9	0.3	1.9	0.6	0.4	2.3
0.0	0.2	1.1	–	0.0	0.1	0.0
1.1	0.8	1.2	0.6	1.1	0.8	1.2
2.5	2.5	4.1	1.2	1.6	1.3	1.5
–	–	–	–	–	–	–
7.9	5.7	15.5	0.6	1.3	2.1	3.5
–	–	0.0	0.0	–	–	0.0
4.0	0.9	4.6	0.3	0.3	0.0	1.1
–	–	–	–	–	–	–
0.2	0.3	0.3	–	0.0	0.0	0.1
14.6	18.7	14.8	4.7	3.7	4.9	4.1
1.5	0.8	1.3	0.1	0.1	–	0.1
0.2	0.2	0.5	0.1	0.1	0.2	0.2
7.0	7.0	7.0	–	–	–	–
42.9	39.9	55.3	9.6	8.7	9.8	14.0
33.2	29.8	30.6	15.8	14.9	15.6	14.3
1.2	–	–	–	–	–	–
27.6	18.2	36.2	4.7	4.9	4.8	9.8
77.2	69.7	85.8	25.5	23.6	25.3	28.4

TOTAL OOF NET

1984	1985	1986	1983	1984	1985	1986
–	–	–	–	–	–	–
0.5	0.5	–	–	0.5	0.5	–
–	–	–	–	–	–	–
2.3	–	–	5.8	0.4	-1.1	-2.8
–	–	–	–	–	–	–
–	–	–	-0.1	–	–	0.0
–	11.7	3.2	–	–	11.5	3.2
–	–	–	–	–	–	–
–	–	–	–	–	–	–
–	–	12.8	0.1	–	–	6.9
–	–	–	–	–	–	–
–	44.0	32.0	-10.0	-13.0	32.0	20.0
2.8	56.2	48.0	-4.2	-12.0	42.9	27.2
–	2.8	5.5	–	–	2.8	5.5
–	–	–	–	–	–	–
2.8	12.2	3.2	5.7	1.0	10.9	0.3
2.8	59.0	53.5	-4.2	-12.0	45.7	32.7

ODA COMMITMENTS : LOANS

DAC COUNTRIES	1983	1984	1985	1986
Australia	–	–	–	–
Austria	3.6	–	–	–
Belgium	–	–	–	–
Canada	–	–	–	–
Denmark	–	–	–	12.4
Finland	–	–	–	–
France	6.2	7.6	–	5.1
Germany, Fed. Rep.	–	–	–	–
Ireland	–	–	–	–
Italy	–	–	38.6	–
Japan	–	–	–	1.6
Netherlands	8.2	12.8	–	13.9
New Zealand	–	–	–	–
Norway	–	–	–	–
Sweden	–	–	–	–
Switzerland	–	–	–	–
United Kingdom	–	–	–	–
United States	–	–	–	–
TOTAL	17.9	20.4	38.6	32.9
MULTILATERAL	14.5	–	1.0	18.1
OPEC COUNTRIES	–	–	–	–
E.E.C.+ MEMBERS	14.3	20.4	38.6	31.3
TOTAL	32.4	20.4	39.7	51.1

GRANT ELEMENT OF ODA

DAC COUNTRIES	1983	1984	1985	1986
Australia	100.0	–	–	–
Austria	37.5	–	100.0	–
Belgium	–	100.0	84.6	100.0
Canada	100.0	100.0	100.0	100.0
Denmark	–	100.0	100.0	75.5
Finland	–	100.0	100.0	100.0
France	100.0	40.1	100.0	40.2
Germany, Fed. Rep.	100.0	100.0	100.0	100.0
Ireland	–	–	–	–
Italy	100.0	100.0	57.1	100.0
Japan	100.0	–	–	100.0
Netherlands	73.4	69.5	100.0	68.6
New Zealand	–	–	–	–
Norway	–	100.0	100.0	100.0
Sweden	100.0	100.0	100.0	100.0
Switzerland	100.0	100.0	100.0	100.0
United Kingdom	100.0	100.0	100.0	100.0
United States	100.0	100.0	100.0	100.0
TOTAL	84.9	84.8	71.5	83.0
MULTILATERAL	95.0	100.0	99.5	92.9
OPEC COUNTRIES	–	–	–	–
E.E.C.+ MEMBERS	88.6	81.0	68.3	78.2
TOTAL	90.7	90.1	80.7	86.3

OTHER AGGREGATES

COMMITMENTS: ALL SOURCES

	1983	1984	1985	1986
TOTAL BILATERAL	133.1	203.8	81.4	200.8
of which				
OPEC	–	–	–	–
CMEA	–	51.4	5.0	107.0
TOTAL MULTILATERAL	96.0	36.7	37.4	79.5
TOTAL BIL.& MULTIL.	229.1	240.5	118.9	280.3
of which				
ODA Grants	59.8	85.3	79.2	188.6
ODA Loans	32.4	70.4	39.7	51.1

DISBURSEMENTS:
DAC COUNTRIES COMBINED

OFFICIAL & PRIVATE	1983	1984	1985	1986
GROSS:				
Contractual Lending	140.1	159.5	274.8	175.6
Export Credits Total	124.8	142.8	255.0	137.1
Export Credits Private	105.2	140.5	199.3	89.1
NET:				
Contractual Lending	30.0	43.5	149.4	95.4
Export Credits Total	15.1	26.8	129.6	56.9
PRIVATE SECTOR NET	104.1	118.7	121.2	112.0
Direct Investment	104.3	67.1	19.9	113.7
Portfolio Investment	-19.3	12.2	14.1	-31.4
Export Credits	19.1	39.4	87.2	29.7

MARKET BORROWING:
CHANGE IN CLAIMS

	1983	1984	1985	1986
Banks	–	60.0	296.0	97.0

MEMORANDUM ITEM:

	1983	1984	1985	1986
CMEA Countr.(Gross)	5.0	6.4	10.0	31.0

TOTAL RECEIPTS NET

DAC COUNTRIES	1983	1984	1985	1986
Australia	-0.7	-0.7	-0.3	—
Austria	-1.4	-1.8	-1.1	-0.7
Belgium	-46.4	132.6	69.6	15.3
Canada	-0.5	1.3	1.8	-8.6
Denmark	-2.5	-1.1	-2.0	-0.3
Finland	-2.4	-8.3	0.0	0.6
France	59.4	191.3	312.4	423.6
Germany, Fed. Rep.	171.7	113.0	424.0	536.4
Ireland	—	—	—	—
Italy	-40.8	-30.8	19.3	241.1
Japan	-20.0	121.1	348.2	200.7
Netherlands	71.9	-21.1	0.9	30.3
New Zealand	—	—	—	—
Norway	-0.1	0.1	-0.4	0.2
Sweden	0.3	-6.0	—	1.3
Switzerland	-28.1	-23.5	-15.7	0.1
United Kingdom	-84.8	26.9	18.4	-23.4
United States	233.0	409.0	681.0	3088.0
TOTAL	308.5	902.0	1856.0	4504.5
MULTILATERAL				
AF.D.F.	—	—	—	—
AF.D.B.	—	—	—	—
AS.D.B	—	—	—	—
CAR.D.B.	—	—	—	—
E.E.C.	0.2	—	0.3	0.1
IBRD	29.8	15.0	75.1	273.6
IDA	—	—	—	—
I.D.B.	121.4	165.5	136.4	96.5
IFAD	—	—	—	—
I.F.C.	8.1	12.3	-0.5	3.8
IMF TRUST FUND	—	—	—	—
U.N. AGENCIES				
UNDP	3.3	2.9	4.4	14.3
UNTA	0.5	0.4	0.8	0.4
UNICEF	—	0.1	0.5	0.8
UNRWA	—	—	—	—
WFP	—	—	—	—
UNHCR	2.5	3.9	1.9	1.4
Other Multilateral	0.1	0.5	0.4	0.6
Arab OPEC Agencies	—	—	—	—
TOTAL	165.9	200.6	219.4	391.5
OPEC COUNTRIES	0.6	—	—	—
E.E.C.+ MEMBERS	128.7	410.8	842.9	1223.1
TOTAL	475.0	1102.6	2075.3	4896.0

TOTAL ODA NET

DAC COUNTRIES	1983	1984	1985	1986
Australia	0.1	0.1	0.0	0.2
Austria	0.4	0.2	0.3	0.5
Belgium	0.7	1.3	1.5	1.5
Canada	0.0	—	—	—
Denmark	—	—	0.0	0.0
Finland	—	—	—	—
France	3.4	3.5	2.9	4.6
Germany, Fed. Rep.	16.8	9.9	12.6	26.0
Ireland	—	—	—	—
Italy	1.5	3.0	4.4	9.4
Japan	5.6	8.7	8.4	16.2
Netherlands	1.5	0.8	0.9	0.9
New Zealand	—	—	—	—
Norway	—	0.0	0.1	0.2
Sweden	0.3	0.1	—	0.3
Switzerland	0.0	0.1	0.0	0.1
United Kingdom	—	—	—	—
United States	-2.0	-2.0	—	-2.0
TOTAL	28.2	25.6	31.0	57.8
MULTILATERAL				
AF.D.F.	—	—	—	—
AF.D.B.	—	—	—	—
AS.D.B	—	—	—	—
CAR.D.B.	—	—	—	—
E.E.C.	0.2	—	0.3	0.1
IBRD	—	—	—	—
IDA	—	—	—	—
I.D.B.	12.6	15.8	-0.1	12.2
IFAD	—	—	—	—
I.F.C.	—	—	—	—
IMF TRUST FUND	—	—	—	—
U.N. AGENCIES				
UNDP	3.3	2.9	4.4	14.3
UNTA	0.5	0.4	0.8	0.4
UNICEF	—	0.1	0.5	0.8
UNRWA	—	—	—	—
WFP	—	—	—	—
UNHCR	2.5	3.9	1.9	1.4
Other Multilateral	0.1	0.5	0.4	0.6
Arab OPEC Agencies	—	—	—	—
TOTAL	19.2	23.6	8.4	29.8
OPEC COUNTRIES	—	—	—	—
E.E.C.+ MEMBERS	23.7	17.4	21.4	41.5
TOTAL	47.4	49.2	39.4	87.6

TOTAL ODA GROSS

	1983
Australia	—
Austria	0.1
Belgium	0.4
Canada	0.7
Denmark	0.0
Finland	—
France	3.4
Germany, Fed. Rep.	19.7
Ireland	—
Italy	1.5
Japan	5.6
Netherlands	1.5
New Zealand	—
Norway	—
Sweden	0.3
Switzerland	0.0
United Kingdom	—
United States	—
TOTAL	33.2
AF.D.F.	—
AF.D.B.	—
AS.D.B	—
CAR.D.B.	—
E.E.C.	0.2
IBRD	—
IDA	—
I.D.B.	24.9
IFAD	—
I.F.C.	—
IMF TRUST FUND	—
U.N. AGENCIES	—
UNDP	3.3
UNTA	0.5
UNICEF	—
UNRWA	—
WFP	—
UNHCR	2.5
Other Multilateral	0.1
Arab OPEC Agencies	—
TOTAL	31.5
OPEC COUNTRIES	—
E.E.C.+ MEMBERS	26.7
TOTAL	64.6

ODA LOANS GROSS

DAC COUNTRIES	1983	1984	1985	1986
Australia	—	—	—	—
Austria	—	—	—	—
Belgium	—	—	—	—
Canada	—	—	—	—
Denmark	—	—	—	—
Finland	—	—	—	—
France	—	—	—	—
Germany, Fed. Rep.	7.9	0.0	0.1	20.8
Ireland	—	—	—	—
Italy	—	—	—	—
Japan	1.7	2.1	1.8	4.9
Netherlands	—	—	—	—
New Zealand	—	—	—	—
Norway	—	—	—	—
Sweden	—	—	—	—
Switzerland	—	—	—	—
United Kingdom	—	—	—	—
United States	—	—	—	—
TOTAL	9.6	2.1	1.9	25.7
MULTILATERAL	24.8	28.9	12.4	28.7
OPEC COUNTRIES	—	—	—	—
E.E.C.+ MEMBERS	7.9	0.0	0.1	20.8
TOTAL	34.4	31.0	14.3	54.4

ODA LOANS NET

DAC COUNTRIES	1983	1984	1985	1986
Australia	—	—	—	—
Austria	—	—	—	—
Belgium	—	—	—	—
Canada	0.0	0.0	0.0	0.0
Denmark	—	—	—	—
Finland	—	—	—	—
France	—	—	—	—
Germany, Fed. Rep.	5.0	0.0	0.0	6.6
Ireland	—	—	—	—
Italy	—	—	—	—
Japan	1.7	1.6	1.8	4.3
Netherlands	—	—	—	—
New Zealand	—	—	—	—
Norway	—	—	—	—
Sweden	—	—	—	—
Switzerland	—	—	—	—
United Kingdom	—	—	—	—
United States	-2.0	-2.0	—	-2.0
TOTAL	4.7	-0.5	1.7	8.9
MULTILATERAL	12.5	15.8	-0.1	12.2
OPEC COUNTRIES	—	—	—	—
E.E.C.+ MEMBERS	5.0	0.0	0.0	6.6
TOTAL	17.2	15.3	1.7	21.1

GRANTS

	1983
Australia	—
Austria	0.1
Belgium	0.4
Canada	0.7
Denmark	0.0
Finland	—
France	3.4
Germany, Fed. Rep.	11.8
Ireland	—
Italy	1.5
Japan	3.9
Netherlands	1.5
New Zealand	—
Norway	—
Sweden	0.3
Switzerland	0.0
United Kingdom	—
United States	—
TOTAL	23.6
MULTILATERAL	6.7
OPEC COUNTRIES	—
E.E.C.+ MEMBERS	18.7
TOTAL	30.2

TOTAL OFFICIAL GROSS

DAC COUNTRIES	1983	1984	1985	1986
Australia	—	—	—	—
Austria	0.1	0.1	0.0	0.2
Belgium	0.4	0.4	0.4	0.5
Canada	0.7	1.3	1.5	12.9
Denmark	0.0	—	0.0	0.2
Finland	—	—	0.0	0.0
France	3.4	3.5	63.4	49.4
Germany, Fed. Rep.	83.9	66.1	107.7	445.2
Ireland	—	—	—	—
Italy	5.4	10.0	11.0	152.1
Japan	23.1	32.1	28.5	35.4
Netherlands	1.5	0.8	0.9	0.9
New Zealand	—	—	—	—
Norway	—	0.0	0.1	0.2
Sweden	2.4	1.6	1.0	2.1
Switzerland	0.0	0.1	0.0	0.1
United Kingdom	—	—	—	—
United States	58.0	21.0	20.0	210.0
TOTAL	178.9	137.1	234.5	909.1
MULTILATERAL	235.9	330.0	367.8	641.4
OPEC COUNTRIES	0.6	—	—	—
E.E.C.+ MEMBERS	94.8	80.9	183.7	648.4
TOTAL	415.5	467.2	602.4	1550.6

TOTAL OFFICIAL NET

DAC COUNTRIES	1983	1984	1985	1986
Australia	—	—	—	—
Austria	-1.4	-1.2	-0.6	-0.7
Belgium	0.4	0.4	0.4	0.5
Canada	0.0	1.3	1.8	-8.6
Denmark	0.0	—	0.0	0.2
Finland	—	—	0.0	0.0
France	3.4	3.5	63.4	44.1
Germany, Fed. Rep.	71.2	65.6	106.1	364.9
Ireland	—	—	—	—
Italy	-0.5	5.8	10.9	152.1
Japan	20.9	30.6	24.8	26.2
Netherlands	1.5	0.8	0.9	0.9
New Zealand	—	—	—	—
Norway	—	0.0	0.1	0.2
Sweden	0.2	0.2	-2.0	-1.7
Switzerland	0.0	0.1	0.0	0.1
United Kingdom	—	—	—	—
United States	33.0	19.0	20.0	69.0
TOTAL	128.7	126.1	225.8	647.1
MULTILATERAL	165.9	200.6	219.4	391.5
OPEC COUNTRIES	0.6	—	—	—
E.E.C.+ MEMBERS	76.2	76.2	182.0	562.7
TOTAL	295.2	326.7	445.1	1038.6

TOTAL OOF GROSS

	1983
Australia	—
Austria	—
Belgium	—
Canada	—
Denmark	—
Finland	—
France	—
Germany, Fed. Rep.	64.2
Ireland	—
Italy	3.9
Japan	17.5
Netherlands	—
New Zealand	—
Norway	—
Sweden	2.1
Switzerland	—
United Kingdom	—
United States	58.0
TOTAL	145.8
MULTILATERAL	204.4
OPEC COUNTRIES	0.6
E.E.C.+ MEMBERS	68.2
TOTAL	350.8

ODA COMMITMENTS

1984	1985	1986	1983	1984	1985	1986
–	–	–	–	–	–	–
0.1	0.0	0.2	0.1	0.1	0.0	–
0.2	0.3	0.5	–	–	–	0.5
1.3	1.5	1.5	1.0	1.2	1.5	2.7
–	–	–	–	–	–	–
–	0.0	0.0	–	–	–	–
3.5	2.9	4.6	3.4	3.5	2.9	4.6
9.9	12.7	40.2	12.2	10.6	16.4	43.2
–	–	–	–	–	–	–
3.0	4.4	9.4	3.6	4.2	6.0	18.0
9.2	8.4	16.7	10.5	6.4	7.4	17.9
0.8	0.9	0.9	1.4	1.0	0.6	0.8
–	–	–	–	–	–	–
0.0	0.1	0.2	–	0.0	0.0	0.1
0.1	–	0.3	0.1	1.3	0.9	0.3
0.1	0.0	0.1	–	0.1	0.0	0.0
–	–	–	–	–	–	–
–	–	–	0.0	–	–	–
28.2	*31.1*	*74.6*	*32.2*	*28.4*	*35.7*	*88.1*
–	–	–	–	–	–	–
–	–	–	–	–	–	–
–	–	–	–	–	–	–
–	0.3	0.1	0.2	0.4	0.4	0.7
–	–	–	–	–	–	–
28.9	12.4	28.7	25.1	66.6	–	–
–	–	–	–	–	–	–
–	–	–	–	–	–	–
–	–	–	6.4	7.9	8.1	17.6
2.9	4.4	14.3	–	–	–	–
0.4	0.8	0.4	–	–	–	–
0.1	0.5	0.8	–	–	–	–
–	–	–	–	–	–	–
3.9	1.9	1.4	–	–	–	–
0.5	0.4	0.6	–	–	–	–
–	–	–	–	–	–	–
36.8	*20.8*	*46.3*	*31.7*	*74.9*	*8.5*	*18.3*
–	–	–	–	–	–	–
17.4	*21.5*	*55.7*	*20.8*	*19.7*	*26.3*	*67.8*
65.0	**52.0**	**120.9**	**63.9**	**103.2**	**44.1**	**106.3**

TECH. COOP. GRANTS

1984	1985	1986	1983	1984	1985	1986
–	–	–	–	–	–	–
0.1	0.0	0.2	0.1	–	–	–
0.2	0.3	0.5	0.0	0.0	0.1	0.0
1.3	1.5	1.5	0.5	–	0.0	–
–	–	–	0.0	–	–	–
–	0.0	0.0	–	–	0.0	0.0
3.5	2.9	4.6	3.4	3.5	2.9	4.6
9.9	12.7	19.4	11.4	9.8	12.1	19.2
–	–	–	–	–	–	–
3.0	4.4	9.4	0.8	3.0	3.5	9.4
7.1	6.7	11.9	3.9	3.9	4.8	11.6
0.8	0.9	0.9	1.3	0.7	0.5	0.8
–	–	–	–	–	–	–
0.0	0.1	0.2	–	0.0	0.0	0.1
0.1	–	0.3	–	–	–	0.2
0.1	0.0	0.1	0.0	–	0.0	0.0
–	–	–	–	–	–	–
–	–	–	–	–	–	–
26.1	*29.3*	*48.9*	*21.6*	*20.8*	*24.0*	*45.9*
7.9	*8.4*	*17.6*	*6.4*	*7.9*	*8.1*	*17.6*
–	–	–	–	–	–	–
17.4	*21.4*	*34.9*	*17.0*	*16.9*	*19.2*	*34.0*
34.0	**37.7**	**66.5**	**27.9**	**28.7**	**32.1**	**63.4**

TOTAL OOF NET

1984	1985	1986	1983	1984	1985	1986
–	–	–	–	–	–	–
–	–	–	-1.5	-1.3	-0.6	-0.9
0.2	0.1	–	–	0.2	0.1	–
–	–	11.4	-0.7	0.0	0.4	-10.1
–	0.0	0.2	–	–	0.0	0.2
–	60.5	44.8	–	–	60.5	39.4
56.1	95.0	405.0	54.5	55.8	93.5	338.8
–	–	–	–	–	–	–
7.1	6.6	142.7	-2.0	2.8	6.6	142.7
22.9	20.1	18.7	15.3	21.9	16.3	10.0
–	–	–	–	–	–	–
–	–	–	–	–	–	–
1.6	1.0	1.8	-0.1	0.1	-2.0	-2.0
–	–	–	–	–	–	–
21.0	20.0	210.0	35.0	21.0	20.0	71.0
108.9	*203.4*	*834.6*	*100.5*	*100.5*	*194.8*	*589.2*
293.3	*347.0*	*595.1*	*146.7*	*177.0*	*211.0*	*361.7*
–	–	–	0.6	–	–	–
63.4	*162.3*	*592.6*	*52.5*	*58.8*	*160.7*	*521.2*
402.2	**550.4**	**1429.7**	**247.8**	**277.5**	**405.8**	**950.9**

ODA COMMITMENTS : LOANS

	1983	1984	1985	1986
DAC COUNTRIES				
Australia	–	–	–	–
Austria	–	–	–	–
Belgium	–	–	–	0.5
Canada	–	–	–	–
Denmark	–	–	–	–
Finland	–	–	–	–
France	–	–	–	–
Germany, Fed. Rep.	–	–	–	20.8
Ireland	–	–	–	–
Italy	–	–	–	–
Japan	1.7	2.1	1.8	4.9
Netherlands	–	–	–	–
New Zealand	–	–	–	–
Norway	–	–	–	–
Sweden	–	–	–	–
Switzerland	–	–	–	–
United Kingdom	–	–	–	–
United States	–	–	–	–
TOTAL	*1.7*	*2.1*	*1.8*	*25.7*
MULTILATERAL	*25.1*	*66.6*	*–*	*–*
OPEC COUNTRIES	*–*	*–*	*–*	*–*
E.E.C.+ MEMBERS	*–*	*–*	*–*	*20.8*
TOTAL	*26.8*	*68.7*	*1.8*	*25.7*

GRANT ELEMENT OF ODA

	1983	1984	1985	1986
DAC COUNTRIES				
Australia	–	–	–	–
Austria	100.0	100.0	100.0	–
Belgium	–	–	–	100.0
Canada	100.0	100.0	100.0	100.0
Denmark	–	–	–	–
Finland	–	–	–	–
France	100.0	100.0	100.0	100.0
Germany, Fed. Rep.	100.0	100.0	100.0	60.6
Ireland	–	–	–	–
Italy	100.0	100.0	100.0	100.0
Japan	89.5	78.6	54.1	81.8
Netherlands	100.0	100.0	100.0	100.0
New Zealand	–	–	–	–
Norway	–	100.0	100.0	100.0
Sweden	100.0	100.0	100.0	100.0
Switzerland	–	100.0	100.0	100.0
United Kingdom	–	–	–	–
United States	100.0	–	–	–
TOTAL	*96.6*	*95.2*	*82.3*	*77.0*
MULTILATERAL	*100.0*	*50.7*	*100.0*	*100.0*
OPEC COUNTRIES	*–*	*–*	*–*	*–*
E.E.C.+ MEMBERS	*100.0*	*100.0*	*100.0*	*74.9*
TOTAL	*97.2*	*57.5*	*85.0*	*81.0*

OTHER AGGREGATES

COMMITMENTS: ALL SOURCES

	1983	1984	1985	1986
TOTAL BILATERAL	67.7	69.9	235.5	958.5
of which				
OPEC	1.9	–	4.8	–
CMEA	–	–	30.0	100.0
TOTAL MULTILATERAL	185.1	518.5	363.4	1067.7
TOTAL BIL.& MULTIL.	252.8	588.4	598.8	2026.1
of which				
ODA Grants	37.2	34.6	42.4	80.6
ODA Loans	26.8	68.7	1.8	25.7

DISBURSEMENTS:

DAC COUNTRIES COMBINED

	1983	1984	1985	1986
OFFICIAL & PRIVATE				
GROSS:				
Contractual Lending	382.8	350.0	340.3	1162.4
Export Credits Total	367.7	292.6	196.4	445.4
Export Credits Private	227.4	239.2	135.2	302.1
NET:				
Contractual Lending	-24.6	130.9	100.5	660.2
Export Credits Total	-33.7	76.3	-41.8	-4.1
PRIVATE SECTOR NET	179.8	775.9	1630.2	3857.5
Direct Investment	104.7	134.6	171.5	283.4
Portfolio Investment	204.8	610.1	1554.6	3512.0
Export Credits	-129.7	31.2	-95.8	62.1

MARKET BORROWING:

CHANGE IN CLAIMS

	1983	1984	1985	1986
Banks	–	-957.0	2165.0	1946.0

MEMORANDUM ITEM:

	1983	1984	1985	1986
CMEA Countr.(Gross)	0.5	–	–	–

TOTAL RECEIPTS NET / TOTAL ODA NET / TOTAL ODA GROSS

	1983	1984	1985	1986	1983	1984	1985	1986		1983
TOTAL RECEIPTS NET					**TOTAL ODA NET**				**TOTAL ODA GROSS**	
DAC COUNTRIES										
Australia	10.4	0.1	0.0	0.0	0.1	0.1	0.0	0.0	Australia	0.1
Austria	–	–	–	–	–	–	–	–	Austria	–
Belgium	9.9	-0.9	29.7	78.8	–	–	–	–	Belgium	–
Canada	-0.1	7.7	-0.1	-2.2	0.0	7.9	–	–	Canada	0.0
Denmark	0.0	0.0			–	–	–	–	Denmark	–
Finland	–	–	–	–	–	–	–	–	Finland	–
France	-44.6	-33.8	21.5	-32.0	–	0.0	–	–	France	–
Germany, Fed. Rep.	220.7	5.2	-0.4	16.6	–	–	–	–	Germany, Fed. Rep.	–
Ireland	–	–			–	–	–	–	Ireland	–
Italy	–	–	–	-0.2	–	–	–	–	Italy	–
Japan	-2.6	58.7	114.5	811.0	0.0	0.0	0.0	0.1	Japan	0.0
Netherlands	–	-20.9	0.1	-1.5	–	–	0.1	0.1	Netherlands	–
New Zealand	–	–			–	–	–	–	New Zealand	–
Norway	0.1	26.4	4.1		–	–	–	–	Norway	–
Sweden	–	27.8	92.0	84.0	–	–	–	–	Sweden	–
Switzerland	2.2	–			–	–	–	–	Switzerland	–
United Kingdom	-15.1	16.2	43.9	-0.7	0.0	0.0	0.0	0.0	United Kingdom	0.0
United States	646.0	-166.0	220.0	-50.0	–	–	–	–	United States	–
TOTAL	*826.7*	*-79.7*	*525.3*	*903.6*	*0.1*	*8.0*	*0.1*	*0.2*	*TOTAL*	*0.1*
MULTILATERAL										
AF.D.F.	–	–	–	–	–	–	–	–	AF.D.F.	–
AF.D.B.	–	–	–	–	–	–	–	–	AF.D.B.	–
AS.D.B	–	–	–	–	–	–	–	–	AS.D.B	–
CAR.D.B.	0.2	0.2	–	0.9	0.1	0.2	–	0.2	CAR.D.B.	0.1
E.E.C.	0.1	0.9	–	0.7	0.1	0.9	–	0.7	E.E.C.	0.1
IBRD	1.4	0.4	1.2	0.5	–	–	–	–	IBRD	–
IDA	–	–	–	–	–	–	–	–	IDA	–
I.D.B.	1.3	0.7	-2.0	10.9	–	0.7	–	4.0	I.D.B.	–
IFAD	–	–	–	–	–	–	–	–	IFAD	–
I.F.C.	–	–	–	–	–	–	–	–	I.F.C.	–
IMF TRUST FUND	–	–	–	–	–	–	–	–	IMF TRUST FUND	–
U.N. AGENCIES	–	–	–	–	–	–	–	–	U.N. AGENCIES	–
UNDP	0.5	0.3	0.3	0.3	0.5	0.3	0.3	0.3	UNDP	0.5
UNTA	0.1	0.1	0.2	0.3	0.1	0.1	0.2	0.3	UNTA	0.1
UNICEF	–	0.5	–	–	–	0.5	–	–	UNICEF	–
UNRWA	–	–	–	–	–	–	–	–	UNRWA	–
WFP	–	–	–	–	–	–	–	–	WFP	–
UNHCR	–	–	–	–	–	–	–	–	UNHCR	–
Other Multilateral	0.1	0.2	0.2	0.2	0.1	0.2	0.2	0.2	Other Multilateral	0.1
Arab OPEC Agencies	–	–	–	–	–	–	–	–	Arab OPEC Agencies	–
TOTAL	*3.6*	*3.3*	*0.0*	*13.8*	*0.8*	*2.8*	*0.8*	*5.6*	*TOTAL*	*0.8*
OPEC COUNTRIES	–	–	–	–	–	–	–	–	**OPEC COUNTRIES**	–
E.E.C.+ MEMBERS	*171.0*	*-33.4*	*94.8*	*61.6*	*0.1*	*0.9*	*0.1*	*0.8*	*E.E.C.+ MEMBERS*	*0.1*
TOTAL	*830.4*	*-76.4*	*525.2*	*917.4*	*0.9*	*10.9*	*0.9*	*5.8*	*TOTAL*	*0.9*

ODA LOANS GROSS / ODA LOANS NET / GRANTS

	1983	1984	1985	1986	1983	1984	1985	1986		1983
ODA LOANS GROSS					**ODA LOANS NET**				**GRANTS**	
DAC COUNTRIES										
Australia	–				–				Australia	0.1
Austria	–	–	–	–	–	–	–	–	Austria	–
Belgium	–	–	–	–	–	–	–	–	Belgium	–
Canada	–	3.6	–	–	–	3.0	–	–	Canada	0.0
Denmark	–	–	–	–	–	–	–	–	Denmark	–
Finland	–	–	–	–	–	–	–	–	Finland	–
France	–	–	–	–	–	–	–	–	France	–
Germany, Fed. Rep.	–	–	–	–	–	–	–	–	Germany, Fed. Rep.	–
Ireland	–	–	–	–	–	–	–	–	Ireland	–
Italy	–	–	–	–	–	–	–	–	Italy	–
Japan	–	–	–	–	–	–	–	–	Japan	0.0
Netherlands	–	–	–	–	–	–	–	–	Netherlands	–
New Zealand	–	–	–	–	–	–	–	–	New Zealand	–
Norway	–	–	–	–	–	–	–	–	Norway	–
Sweden	–	–	–	–	–	–	–	–	Sweden	–
Switzerland	–	–	–	–	–	–	–	–	Switzerland	–
United Kingdom	–	–	–	–	–	–	–	–	United Kingdom	0.0
United States	–	–	–	–	–	–	–	–	United States	–
TOTAL	*–*	*3.6*	*–*	*–*	*–*	*3.0*	*–*	*–*	*TOTAL*	*0.1*
MULTILATERAL	*0.2*	*0.5*	*–*	*3.8*	*0.2*	*0.5*	*–*	*3.8*	*MULTILATERAL*	*0.6*
OPEC COUNTRIES	–	–	–	–	–	–	–	–	**OPEC COUNTRIES**	–
E.E.C.+ MEMBERS	*0.1*	*0.4*	*–*	*–*	*0.1*	*0.4*	*–*	*–*	*E.E.C.+ MEMBERS*	*0.0*
TOTAL	*0.2*	*4.1*	*–*	*3.8*	*0.2*	*3.5*	*–*	*3.8*	*TOTAL*	*0.7*

TOTAL OFFICIAL GROSS / TOTAL OFFICIAL NET / TOTAL OOF GROSS

	1983	1984	1985	1986	1983	1984	1985	1986		1983
TOTAL OFFICIAL GROSS					**TOTAL OFFICIAL NET**				**TOTAL OOF GROSS**	
DAC COUNTRIES										
Australia	0.1	0.1	0.0	0.0	0.1	0.1	0.0	0.0	Australia	–
Austria	–	–	–	–	–	–	–	–	Austria	–
Belgium	–	0.0	0.1	–	–	0.0	0.1	–	Belgium	–
Canada	0.0	8.6	–	0.7	-0.1	7.7	-0.1	-2.2	Canada	–
Denmark	–	–	–	–	–	–	–	–	Denmark	–
Finland	–	–	–	–	–	–	–	–	Finland	–
France	–	0.0	–	–	–	0.0	–	–	France	–
Germany, Fed. Rep.	–	–	–	3.5	–	–	–	3.5	Germany, Fed. Rep.	–
Ireland	–	–	–	–	–	–	–	–	Ireland	–
Italy	–	–	–	–	–	–	–	–	Italy	–
Japan	0.0	0.0	0.0	0.1	0.0	0.0	0.0	0.1	Japan	–
Netherlands	–	–	0.1	0.1	–	–	0.1	0.1	Netherlands	–
New Zealand	–	–	–	–	–	–	–	–	New Zealand	–
Norway	–	–	–	–	–	–	–	–	Norway	–
Sweden	–	27.8	92.0	84.0	–	27.8	92.0	84.0	Sweden	–
Switzerland	–	–	–	–	–	–	–	–	Switzerland	–
United Kingdom	0.0	0.0	0.0	0.0	0.0	0.0	0.0	0.0	United Kingdom	–
United States	–	–	–	1.0	–	–	–	1.0	United States	–
TOTAL	*0.1*	*36.5*	*92.2*	*89.3*	*0.0*	*35.7*	*92.0*	*86.4*	*TOTAL*	*–*
MULTILATERAL	*4.2*	*4.2*	*3.3*	*15.9*	*3.6*	*3.3*	*0.0*	*13.8*	*MULTILATERAL*	*3.4*
OPEC COUNTRIES	–	–	–	–	–	–	–	–	**OPEC COUNTRIES**	–
E.E.C.+ MEMBERS	*0.1*	*1.0*	*0.2*	*4.3*	*0.1*	*1.0*	*0.2*	*4.3*	*E.E.C.+ MEMBERS*	*–*
TOTAL	*4.3*	*40.7*	*95.5*	*105.2*	*3.6*	*38.9*	*92.0*	*100.1*	*TOTAL*	*3.4*

ODA COMMITMENTS

1984	1985	1986	1983	1984	1985	1986
0.1	0.0	0.0	0.0	–	0.0	–
–	–	–	–	–	–	–
8.6	–	–	0.0	–	–	–
–	–	–	–	–	–	–
0.0	–	–	–	0.0	–	–
–	–	–	–	–	–	–
–	–	–	–	–	–	–
0.0	0.0	0.1	0.0	0.0	0.0	0.1
–	0.1	0.1	–	–	0.1	0.1
–	–	–	–	–	–	–
–	–	–	–	–	–	–
–	–	–	–	–	–	–
0.0	0.0	0.0	0.0	0.0	0.0	0.0
–	–	–	–	–	–	–
8.7	*0.1*	*0.2*	*0.1*	*0.1*	*0.1*	*0.1*
–	–	–	–	–	–	–
–	–	–	–	–	–	–
0.2	–	0.2	–	–	–	0.9
0.9	–	0.7	0.8	0.1	0.4	1.8
–	–	–	–	–	–	–
0.7	–	4.0	–	–	–	–
–	–	–	–	–	–	–
–	–	–	–	–	–	–
0.3	0.3	0.3	0.6	1.1	0.8	0.8
0.1	0.2	0.3	–	–	–	–
0.5	–	–	–	–	–	–
–	–	–	–	–	–	–
0.2	0.2	0.2	–	–	–	–
–	–	–	–	–	–	–
2.8	*0.8*	*5.6*	*1.5*	*1.2*	*1.2*	*3.4*
–	–	–	–	–	–	–
0.9	*0.1*	*0.8*	*0.8*	*0.1*	*0.6*	*1.8*
11.5	*0.9*	*5.8*	*1.5*	*1.2*	*1.4*	*3.6*

TECH. COOP. GRANTS

1984	1985	1986	1983	1984	1985	1986
0.1	0.0	0.0	0.1	0.1	0.0	0.0
–	–	–	–	–	–	–
4.9	–	–	0.0	–	0.1	–
–	–	–	–	–	–	–
0.0	–	–	–	0.0	–	–
–	–	–	–	–	–	–
–	–	–	–	–	–	–
0.0	0.0	0.1	0.0	0.0	0.0	0.1
–	0.1	0.1	–	–	0.1	0.1
–	–	–	–	–	–	–
–	–	–	–	–	–	–
–	–	–	–	–	–	–
0.0	0.0	0.0	0.0	0.0	0.0	0.0
–	–	–	–	–	–	–
5.0	*0.1*	*0.2*	*0.1*	*0.1*	*0.2*	*0.2*
2.3	*0.8*	*1.9*	*0.6*	*1.1*	*0.8*	*0.9*
–	–	–	–	–	–	–
0.6	*0.1*	*0.8*	*0.0*	*0.0*	*0.1*	*0.2*
7.4	*0.9*	*2.0*	*0.8*	*1.2*	*1.0*	*1.1*

TOTAL OOF NET

1984	1985	1986	1983	1984	1985	1986
–	–	–	–	–	–	–
0.0	0.1	–	–	0.0	0.1	–
–	–	0.7	-0.1	-0.2	-0.1	-2.2
–	–	–	–	–	–	–
–	–	–	–	–	–	–
–	–	3.5	–	–	–	3.5
–	–	–	–	–	–	–
–	–	–	–	–	–	–
–	–	–	–	–	–	–
–	–	–	–	–	–	–
27.8	92.0	84.0	–	27.8	92.0	84.0
–	–	–	–	–	–	–
–	–	1.0	–	–	–	1.0
27.9	*92.1*	*89.1*	*-0.1*	*27.6*	*91.9*	*86.2*
1.3	*2.5*	*10.3*	*2.8*	*0.4*	*-0.8*	*8.2*
–	–	–	–	–	–	–
0.0	*0.1*	*3.5*	*–*	*0.0*	*0.1*	*3.5*
29.2	*94.6*	*99.4*	*2.7*	*28.1*	*91.1*	*94.4*

ODA COMMITMENTS : LOANS

	1983	1984	1985	1986
DAC COUNTRIES				
Australia	–	–	–	–
Austria	–	–	–	–
Belgium	–	–	–	–
Canada	–	–	–	–
Denmark	–	–	–	–
Finland	–	–	–	–
France	–	–	–	–
Germany, Fed. Rep.	–	–	–	–
Ireland	–	–	–	–
Italy	–	–	–	–
Japan	–	–	–	–
Netherlands	–	–	–	–
New Zealand	–	–	–	–
Norway	–	–	–	–
Sweden	–	–	–	–
Switzerland	–	–	–	–
United Kingdom	–	–	–	–
United States	–	–	–	–
TOTAL	–	–	–	–
MULTILATERAL	–	–	–	0.8
OPEC COUNTRIES	–	–	–	–
E.E.C.+ MEMBERS	–	–	–	–
TOTAL	–	–	–	*0.8*

GRANT ELEMENT OF ODA

	1983	1984	1985	1986
DAC COUNTRIES				
Australia	100.0	–	100.0	–
Austria	–	–	–	–
Belgium	–	–	–	–
Canada	100.0	–	–	–
Denmark	–	–	–	–
Finland	–	–	–	–
France	–	100.0	–	–
Germany, Fed. Rep.	–	–	–	–
Ireland	–	–	–	–
Italy	–	–	–	–
Japan	100.0	100.0	100.0	100.0
Netherlands	–	–	100.0	100.0
New Zealand	–	–	–	–
Norway	–	–	–	–
Sweden	–	–	–	–
Switzerland	–	–	–	–
United Kingdom	100.0	100.0	100.0	100.0
United States	–	–	–	–
TOTAL	*100.0*	*100.0*	*100.0*	*100.0*
MULTILATERAL	*100.0*	*100.0*	*100.0*	*100.0*
OPEC COUNTRIES	–	–	–	–
E.E.C.+ MEMBERS	*100.0*	*100.0*	*100.0*	*100.0*
TOTAL	*100.0*	*100.0*	*100.0*	*100.0*

OTHER AGGREGATES

COMMITMENTS: ALL SOURCES

	1983	1984	1985	1986
TOTAL BILATERAL	0.1	27.9	93.0	84.1
of which				
OPEC	–	–	–	–
CMEA	–	–	–	–
TOTAL MULTILATERAL	1.5	1.2	10.2	25.2
TOTAL BIL.& MULTIL.	1.5	29.1	103.2	109.3
of which				
ODA Grants	1.5	1.2	1.4	2.7
ODA Loans	–	–	–	0.8

DISBURSEMENTS:

DAC COUNTRIES COMBINED

OFFICIAL & PRIVATE

	1983	1984	1985	1986
GROSS:				
Contractual Lending	24.8	45.6	97.0	161.4
Export Credits Total	24.8	42.0	97.0	160.4
Export Credits Private	24.8	14.2	5.0	72.3
NET:				
Contractual Lending	-26.3	17.5	44.9	150.0
Export Credits Total	-26.3	14.4	44.9	149.0
PRIVATE SECTOR NET	826.8	-115.3	433.2	817.3
Direct Investment	704.8	65.1	130.3	556.9
Portfolio Investment	148.1	-167.3	349.8	196.5
Export Credits	-26.2	-13.1	-46.9	63.8

MARKET BORROWING:

CHANGE IN CLAIMS

	1983	1984	1985	1986
Banks	–	–	–	–

MEMORANDUM ITEM:

	1983	1984	1985	1986
CMEA Countr.(Gross)	–	–	–	–

TOTAL RECEIPTS NET | TOTAL ODA NET | TOTAL ODA GROSS

	1983	1984	1985	1986	1983	1984	1985	1986	1983
DAC COUNTRIES									
Australia	9.8	71.7	-13.6	0.0	9.8	31.3	3.9	9.3	9.8
Austria	-0.2	-0.3	0.1	0.1	0.1	0.1	0.1	0.1	0.1
Belgium	0.7	-3.9	10.0	1.0	0.7	0.4	10.0	0.9	0.7
Canada	87.5	84.5	78.4	71.1	87.5	84.5	78.4	71.1	87.5
Denmark	20.6	22.3	40.6	30.1	20.6	22.3	40.6	30.0	20.6
Finland	0.6	3.1	4.2	2.3	0.6	3.1	4.2	2.3	0.6
France	15.7	15.0	19.1	15.8	10.0	12.6	14.4	13.7	10.0
Germany, Fed. Rep.	34.6	45.9	47.5	69.0	35.3	46.1	46.6	70.9	35.3
Ireland	0.1	0.1	0.1	0.1	0.1	0.1	0.1	0.1	0.1
Italy	0.1	0.4	0.6	0.4	0.1	0.3	0.6	0.4	0.1
Japan	104.3	122.7	123.6	257.7	104.2	123.3	121.5	248.5	104.7
Netherlands	30.5	60.6	42.4	42.8	30.9	61.0	41.8	40.9	30.9
New Zealand	0.1	0.0	0.1	0.2	0.1	0.0	0.1	0.2	0.1
Norway	25.6	21.9	22.4	43.0	25.6	21.9	22.4	43.0	25.6
Sweden	17.8	10.9	16.7	22.5	17.8	10.9	16.7	22.5	17.8
Switzerland	3.2	4.1	3.3	6.2	3.2	4.1	3.3	6.2	3.2
United Kingdom	37.0	47.1	44.6	53.3	36.3	46.5	52.2	54.9	37.5
United States	204.0	219.0	159.0	139.0	200.0	206.0	165.0	146.0	205.0
TOTAL	*591.9*	*725.1*	*598.9*	*754.6*	*582.6*	*674.5*	*621.9*	*760.9*	*589.4*
MULTILATERAL									
AF.D.F.	–	–	–	–	–	–	–	–	–
AF.D.B.	–	–	–	–	–	–	–	–	–
AS.D.B	48.5	77.1	143.2	139.4	49.2	77.8	143.8	140.1	49.5
CAR.D.B.	–	–	–	–	–	–	–	–	–
E.E.C.	40.8	49.4	6.8	20.1	40.8	49.4	6.8	20.1	40.8
IBRD	–	–	-0.9	-1.4	–	–	–	–	–
IDA	199.2	246.8	272.9	334.5	199.2	246.8	272.9	334.5	201.1
I.D.B.	–	–	–	–	–	–	–	–	–
IFAD	4.6	6.3	16.2	23.0	4.6	6.3	16.2	23.0	4.6
I.F.C.	–	–	0.7	4.0	–	–	–	–	–
IMF TRUST FUND	–	–	–	–	–	–	–	–	–
U.N. AGENCIES	–	–	–	–	–	–	–	–	–
UNDP	24.5	26.0	28.5	33.6	24.5	26.0	28.5	33.6	24.5
UNTA	3.4	2.4	4.9	2.5	3.4	2.4	4.9	2.5	3.4
UNICEF	12.6	13.1	12.6	14.6	12.6	13.1	12.6	14.6	12.6
UNRWA	–	–	–	–	–	–	–	–	–
WFP	35.4	71.8	26.2	40.0	35.4	71.8	26.2	40.0	35.4
UNHCR	0.1	0.1	0.0	0.1	0.1	0.1	0.0	0.1	0.1
Other Multilateral	5.4	6.4	5.9	4.0	5.4	6.4	5.9	4.0	5.4
Arab OPEC Agencies	43.7	-3.2	-5.4	-22.8	12.7	11.9	2.3	1.0	14.0
TOTAL	*418.0*	*496.2*	*511.5*	*591.7*	*387.8*	*512.0*	*520.1*	*613.4*	*391.2*
OPEC COUNTRIES	*96.3*	*28.8*	*9.2*	*83.3*	*96.3*	*13.8*	*9.2*	*81.3*	*109.1*
E.E.C.+ MEMBERS	*180.0*	*237.0*	*211.6*	*232.6*	*174.5*	*238.7*	*213.1*	*231.9*	*175.8*
TOTAL	*1106.2*	*1250.1*	*1119.7*	*1429.6*	*1066.7*	*1200.3*	*1151.3*	*1455.7*	*1089.8*

ODA LOANS GROSS | ODA LOANS NET | GRANTS

	1983	1984	1985	1986	1983	1984	1985	1986	1983
DAC COUNTRIES									
Australia	–	–	–	–	–	–	–	–	9.8
Austria	–	–	–	–	–	–	–	–	0.1
Belgium	–	–	7.6	–	–	-0.1	7.6	-0.7	0.7
Canada	–	–	–	–	–	–	–	–	87.5
Denmark	1.6	4.4	–	–	1.6	4.4	–	-27.8	18.9
Finland	0.4	–	–	–	0.4	–	–	–	0.3
France	4.2	4.9	4.6	5.9	4.2	4.9	4.6	5.9	5.8
Germany, Fed. Rep.	–	–	–	–	–	–	–	–	35.3
Ireland	–	–	–	–	–	–	–	–	0.1
Italy	–	–	–	–	–	–	–	–	0.1
Japan	61.8	79.7	67.0	204.8	61.4	75.1	59.3	189.8	42.8
Netherlands	0.8	1.8	0.4	0.2	0.7	0.5	0.4	0.2	30.1
New Zealand	–	–	–	–	–	–	–	–	0.1
Norway	–	–	–	–	–	–	–	–	25.6
Sweden	–	–	–	–	–	–	0.0	–	17.8
Switzerland	–	–	–	–	–	–	0.0	0.0	3.2
United Kingdom	–	–	–	–	-1.2	-1.2	-1.1	-1.3	37.5
United States	40.0	26.0	11.0	21.0	35.0	18.0	8.0	3.0	165.0
TOTAL	*108.8*	*116.7*	*90.6*	*231.9*	*102.1*	*101.5*	*78.8*	*169.1*	*480.6*
MULTILATERAL	*268.2*	*349.4*	*444.8*	*509.6*	*264.7*	*342.4*	*434.8*	*498.4*	*123.0*
OPEC COUNTRIES	*29.1*	*18.6*	*14.6*	*91.9*	*16.3*	*3.7*	*-3.3*	*77.6*	*80.0*
E.E.C.+ MEMBERS	*6.7*	*11.0*	*12.6*	*6.1*	*5.4*	*8.4*	*11.4*	*-23.7*	*169.2*
TOTAL	*406.1*	*484.7*	*550.0*	*833.4*	*383.1*	*447.7*	*510.2*	*745.1*	*683.6*

TOTAL OFFICIAL GROSS | TOTAL OFFICIAL NET | TOTAL OOF GROSS

	1983	1984	1985	1986	1983	1984	1985	1986	1983
DAC COUNTRIES									
Australia	9.8	31.3	3.9	9.3	9.8	31.3	3.9	9.3	–
Austria	0.1	0.1	0.1	0.1	-0.2	-0.3	0.1	0.1	–
Belgium	0.7	0.5	10.0	1.6	0.7	0.4	10.0	0.9	–
Canada	87.5	84.5	78.4	71.1	87.5	84.5	78.4	71.1	–
Denmark	20.6	22.3	40.6	57.9	20.6	22.3	40.6	30.1	–
Finland	0.6	3.1	4.2	2.3	0.6	3.1	4.2	2.3	–
France	10.0	12.6	14.4	13.7	10.0	12.6	14.4	13.7	–
Germany, Fed. Rep.	35.3	46.1	46.6	70.9	34.5	45.8	46.1	70.9	–
Ireland	0.1	0.1	0.1	0.1	0.1	0.1	0.1	0.1	–
Italy	0.1	0.3	0.6	0.4	0.1	0.3	0.6	0.4	–
Japan	104.7	127.9	129.2	263.4	104.2	123.3	121.5	248.5	–
Netherlands	31.1	62.9	42.1	42.0	30.9	61.5	42.1	42.0	0.2
New Zealand	0.1	0.0	0.1	0.2	0.1	0.0	0.1	0.2	–
Norway	25.6	21.9	22.4	43.0	25.6	21.9	22.4	43.0	–
Sweden	17.8	10.9	16.7	22.5	17.8	10.9	16.7	22.5	–
Switzerland	3.2	4.1	3.3	6.3	3.2	4.1	3.3	6.2	–
United Kingdom	37.5	47.7	53.4	56.2	36.3	46.5	52.2	54.9	–
United States	209.0	229.0	168.0	164.0	204.0	219.0	159.0	139.0	4.0
TOTAL	*593.6*	*705.2*	*634.1*	*824.9*	*585.6*	*687.2*	*615.7*	*755.1*	*4.2*
MULTILATERAL	*467.4*	*579.7*	*604.8*	*679.6*	*418.0*	*496.2*	*511.5*	*591.7*	*76.1*
OPEC COUNTRIES	*109.1*	*43.7*	*27.1*	*97.6*	*96.3*	*28.8*	*9.2*	*83.3*	*–*
E.E.C.+ MEMBERS	*176.0*	*241.9*	*214.6*	*262.9*	*173.8*	*238.9*	*212.9*	*233.1*	*0.2*
TOTAL	*1170.0*	*1328.6*	*1266.0*	*1602.1*	*1099.9*	*1212.2*	*1136.4*	*1430.1*	*80.3*

ODA COMMITMENTS

1984	1985	1986	1983	1984	1985	1986
31.3	3.9	9.3	10.7	10.6	14.1	9.0
0.1	0.1	0.1	0.1	0.1	0.1	–
0.5	10.0	1.6	–	–	3.9	1.6
84.5	78.4	71.1	131.1	63.0	110.5	137.6
22.3	40.6	57.8	33.9	79.3	17.6	9.5
3.1	4.2	2.3	0.3	5.8	0.1	7.8
12.6	14.4	13.7	12.7	14.8	22.2	13.7
46.1	46.6	70.9	92.4	56.4	43.5	54.6
0.1	0.1	0.1	0.1	0.1	0.1	0.1
0.3	0.6	0.4	0.1	0.3	0.8	0.4
127.9	129.2	263.4	96.2	207.0	184.2	266.1
62.3	41.8	40.9	43.4	36.6	50.9	68.5
0.0	0.1	0.2	0.1	0.0	0.1	0.1
21.9	22.4	43.0	10.2	7.8	22.3	53.6
10.9	16.7	22.5	19.4	17.8	17.3	22.5
4.1	3.3	6.3	4.9	6.4	3.2	6.9
47.7	53.4	56.2	25.5	78.4	28.4	92.5
214.0	168.0	164.0	220.1	198.5	179.4	122.5
689.7	*633.8*	*823.7*	*700.9*	*782.7*	*698.6*	*866.7*
–	–	–	–	–	–	–
–	–	–	–	–	–	–
78.2	145.9	142.4	273.5	306.8	279.7	85.7
–	–	–	–	–	–	–
49.4	6.8	20.1	53.6	43.1	41.9	43.6
–	–	–	–	–	–	–
249.4	277.9	340.9	234.4	342.0	373.0	433.0
–	–	–	–	–	–	–
9.8	18.3	23.7	10.9	23.1	0.2	11.0
–	–	–	–	–	–	–
–	–	–	81.3	119.7	78.1	94.7
26.0	28.5	33.6	–	–	–	–
2.4	4.9	2.5	–	–	–	–
13.1	12.6	14.6	–	–	–	–
–	–	–	–	–	–	–
71.8	26.2	40.0	–	–	–	–
0.1	0.0	0.1	–	–	–	–
6.4	5.9	4.0	–	–	–	–
12.4	3.1	2.8	15.0	11.5	20.2	5.0
519.0	*530.1*	*624.7*	*668.7*	*846.2*	*793.1*	*673.0*
28.7	*27.1*	*95.6*	*295.1*	*26.9*	*38.8*	–
241.3	*214.3*	*261.7*	*261.6*	*309.0*	*209.2*	*284.3*
1237.3	*1191.0*	*1544.0*	*1664.7*	*1655.8*	*1530.4*	*1539.7*

TECH. COOP. GRANTS

1984	1985	1986	1983	1984	1985	1986
31.3	3.9	9.3	1.5	2.5	1.3	0.9
0.1	0.1	0.1	0.1	–	–	–
0.5	2.4	1.6	0.2	0.2	0.5	0.1
84.5	78.4	71.1	1.0	–	3.6	–
17.9	40.6	57.8	6.6	4.5	5.3	9.2
3.1	4.2	2.3	0.3	0.3	0.8	1.1
7.8	9.8	7.8	0.4	1.0	0.4	0.7
46.1	46.6	70.9	9.5	12.7	10.7	12.3
0.1	0.1	0.1	0.1	0.1	0.1	0.1
0.3	0.6	0.4	0.1	0.3	0.1	0.0
48.2	62.2	58.7	6.1	5.2	6.3	9.3
60.5	41.4	40.7	7.5	7.1	6.2	7.4
0.0	0.1	0.2	0.1	0.0	0.0	0.1
21.9	22.4	43.0	0.9	0.9	0.4	0.6
10.9	16.7	22.5	3.0	1.7	2.5	–
4.1	3.3	6.3	0.5	0.4	0.3	0.4
47.7	53.4	56.2	7.4	11.8	14.0	16.0
188.0	157.0	143.0	85.0	61.0	77.0	45.0
572.9	*543.2*	*591.8*	*130.2*	*109.7*	*129.5*	*103.3*
169.6	*85.3*	*115.1*	*45.9*	*47.9*	*39.3*	*54.7*
10.1	*12.5*	*3.7*	–	–	–	–
230.3	*201.7*	*255.6*	*31.8*	*37.8*	*37.3*	*45.8*
752.6	*641.0*	*710.6*	*176.1*	*157.6*	*168.8*	*158.1*

TOTAL OOF NET

1984	1985	1986	1983	1984	1985	1986
–	–	–	–	–	–	–
–	–	–	-0.4	-0.4	0.0	–
–	–	–	–	–	–	–
–	–	0.1	–	–	–	0.1
–	–	–	–	–	–	–
–	–	–	-0.8	-0.3	-0.5	–
–	–	–	–	–	–	–
–	–	–	–	–	–	–
0.5	0.3	1.1	0.1	0.5	0.3	1.1
–	–	–	–	–	–	–
–	–	–	–	–	–	–
–	–	–	–	–	–	–
15.0	–	–	4.0	13.0	-6.0	-7.0
15.5	*0.3*	*1.2*	*2.9*	*12.7*	*-6.2*	*-5.8*
60.7	*74.7*	*54.9*	*30.3*	*-15.8*	*-8.6*	*-21.8*
15.0	–	*2.0*	–	*15.0*	–	*2.0*
0.5	*0.3*	*1.2*	*-0.7*	*0.1*	*-0.2*	*1.2*
91.2	*75.1*	*58.1*	*33.2*	*12.0*	*-14.8*	*-25.6*

ODA COMMITMENTS : LOANS

DAC COUNTRIES

	1983	1984	1985	1986
Australia	–	–	–	–
Austria	–	–	–	–
Belgium	–	–	2.7	–
Canada	–	–	–	–
Denmark	–	–	–	–
Finland	–	–	–	–
France	7.4	6.3	8.9	5.9
Germany, Fed. Rep.	–	–	–	–
Ireland	–	–	–	–
Italy	–	–	–	–
Japan	45.7	155.8	113.2	163.2
Netherlands	–	0.2	7.8	–
New Zealand	–	–	–	–
Norway	–	–	–	–
Sweden	–	–	–	–
Switzerland	–	–	–	–
United Kingdom	–	–	–	–
United States	14.1	24.1	7.8	19.5
TOTAL	*67.3*	*186.4*	*140.4*	*188.6*
MULTILATERAL	*533.8*	*681.9*	*672.8*	*534.7*
OPEC COUNTRIES	*65.1*	*8.8*	*29.0*	–
E.E.C.+ MEMBERS	*7.4*	*6.5*	*19.3*	*5.9*
TOTAL	*666.1*	*877.1*	*842.1*	*723.2*

GRANT ELEMENT OF ODA

DAC COUNTRIES

	1983	1984	1985	1986
Australia	100.0	100.0	100.0	100.0
Austria	100.0	100.0	100.0	–
Belgium	–	–	86.5	100.0
Canada	100.0	100.0	100.0	100.0
Denmark	100.0	100.0	100.0	100.0
Finland	100.0	100.0	100.0	100.0
France	82.8	87.8	88.6	88.0
Germany, Fed. Rep.	100.0	100.0	100.0	100.0
Ireland	100.0	100.0	100.0	100.0
Italy	100.0	100.0	100.0	100.0
Japan	89.2	78.3	82.8	83.1
Netherlands	100.0	100.0	95.7	100.0
New Zealand	100.0	100.0	100.0	100.0
Norway	100.0	100.0	100.0	100.0
Sweden	100.0	100.0	100.0	100.0
Switzerland	100.0	100.0	100.0	100.0
United Kingdom	100.0	100.0	100.0	100.0
United States	97.9	96.3	98.6	94.8
TOTAL	*97.7*	*93.4*	*94.3*	*93.9*
MULTILATERAL	*83.5*	*84.2*	*83.7*	*85.3*
OPEC COUNTRIES	*88.3*	*79.6*	*73.8*	–
E.E.C.+ MEMBERS	*99.2*	*99.4*	*97.2*	*99.4*
TOTAL	*90.3*	*88.4*	*88.4*	*90.1*

OTHER AGGREGATES

COMMITMENTS: ALL SOURCES

	1983	1984	1985	1986
TOTAL BILATERAL	1107.0	824.9	823.3	875.0
of which				
OPEC	325.1	26.9	38.8	7.5
CMEA	75.0	–	82.0	–
TOTAL MULTILATERAL	717.4	896.2	881.9	714.6
TOTAL BIL.& MULTIL.	1824.4	1721.1	1705.2	1589.6
of which				
ODA Grants	998.6	778.7	688.3	816.5
ODA Loans	741.1	877.1	924.1	723.2

DISBURSEMENTS:

DAC COUNTRIES COMBINED

OFFICIAL & PRIVATE

	1983	1984	1985	1986
GROSS:				
Contractual Lending	147.4	197.0	150.4	259.5
Export Credits Total	38.4	79.7	59.5	26.5
Export Credits Private	34.4	64.7	59.5	26.5
NET:				
Contractual Lending	132.6	154.6	79.8	145.0
Export Credits Total	31.2	53.0	1.2	-25.3
PRIVATE SECTOR NET	6.3	37.9	-16.8	-0.5
Direct Investment	1.1	3.8	-6.7	-1.1
Portfolio Investment	-22.4	-6.2	-17.3	18.9
Export Credits	27.6	40.3	7.3	-18.3

MARKET BORROWING:

CHANGE IN CLAIMS

	1983	1984	1985	1986
Banks	–	90.0	34.0	20.0

MEMORANDUM ITEM:

	1983	1984	1985	1986
CMEA Countr.(Gross)	38.2	29.2	24.5	46.0

TOTAL RECEIPTS NET

	1983	1984	1985	1986
DAC COUNTRIES				
Australia	–	–	0.0	0.0
Austria	–	–	–	0.0
Belgium	–	0.3	2.3	-2.8
Canada	8.1	2.9	0.1	1.2
Denmark	–	–	–	–
Finland	0.0	–	–	0.9
France	0.0	0.1	4.1	1.5
Germany, Fed. Rep.	0.1	0.0	0.2	0.1
Ireland	–	–	–	–
Italy	–	–	–	0.0
Japan	0.1	0.1	22.7	25.7
Netherlands	0.2	0.2	0.4	0.6
New Zealand	0.0	–	–	–
Norway	–	–	–	0.0
Sweden	-2.6	-2.7	-3.0	5.1
Switzerland	–	–	-13.1	–
United Kingdom	1.3	-17.9	4.3	2.2
United States	8.0	1.0	1.0	–
TOTAL	15.2	-15.9	18.9	34.4
MULTILATERAL				
AF.D.F.	–	–	–	–
AF.D.B.	–	–	–	–
AS.D.B	–	–	–	–
CAR.D.B.	4.7	1.4	0.5	7.0
E.E.C.	1.5	3.0	1.0	2.2
IBRD	5.3	5.1	6.1	0.5
IDA	–	–	–	–
I.D.B.	5.1	4.0	1.6	-1.8
IFAD	–	–	–	–
I.F.C.	–	0.3	–	–
IMF TRUST FUND	–	–	–	–
U.N. AGENCIES	–	–	–	–
UNDP	0.5	0.4	0.3	0.3
UNTA	0.2	0.2	0.1	0.2
UNICEF	–	–	–	–
UNRWA	–	–	–	–
WFP	0.2	0.1	0.1	0.0
UNHCR	–	–	–	–
Other Multilateral	0.5	0.3	0.1	0.1
Arab OPEC Agencies	0.9	-0.4	-0.7	-0.6
TOTAL	18.8	14.2	9.1	8.1
OPEC COUNTRIES	3.2	1.3	0.6	-0.9
E.E.C.+ MEMBERS	3.1	-14.3	12.2	3.8
TOTAL	37.2	-0.4	28.6	41.6

TOTAL ODA NET

	1983	1984	1985	1986
DAC COUNTRIES				
Australia	–	–	0.0	0.0
Austria	–	–	–	0.0
Belgium	–	–	–	–
Canada	4.0	3.1	4.3	1.2
Denmark	–	–	–	–
Finland	0.0	–	–	0.9
France	0.0	0.1	0.1	0.1
Germany, Fed. Rep.	–	0.1	0.2	0.1
Ireland	–	–	–	–
Italy	–	–	–	0.0
Japan	0.1	0.1	0.0	0.0
Netherlands	0.2	0.2	0.4	0.2
New Zealand	0.0	–	–	–
Norway	–	–	–	0.0
Sweden	–	–	–	–
Switzerland	–	–	–	–
United Kingdom	0.2	0.1	0.1	0.3
United States	7.0	1.0	–	–
TOTAL	11.6	4.7	5.0	2.9
MULTILATERAL				
AF.D.F.	–	–	–	–
AF.D.B.	–	–	–	–
AS.D.B	–	–	–	–
CAR.D.B.	3.6	0.2	0.1	0.0
E.E.C.	0.2	0.4	0.7	1.5
IBRD	–	–	–	–
IDA	–	–	–	–
I.D.B.	2.3	2.5	1.2	-0.8
IFAD	–	–	–	–
I.F.C.	–	–	–	–
IMF TRUST FUND	–	–	–	–
U.N. AGENCIES	–	–	–	–
UNDP	0.5	0.4	0.3	0.3
UNTA	0.2	0.2	0.1	0.2
UNICEF	–	–	–	–
UNRWA	–	–	–	–
WFP	0.2	0.1	0.1	0.0
UNHCR	–	–	–	–
Other Multilateral	0.5	0.3	0.1	0.1
Arab OPEC Agencies	–	-0.3	-0.4	-0.3
TOTAL	7.4	3.7	2.3	1.0
OPEC COUNTRIES	–	0.4	1.0	–
E.E.C.+ MEMBERS	0.7	0.9	1.4	2.2
TOTAL	19.0	8.7	8.3	3.8

TOTAL ODA GROSS

	1983
Australia	–
Austria	–
Belgium	–
Canada	4.6
Denmark	–
Finland	0.0
France	0.0
Germany, Fed. Rep.	–
Ireland	–
Italy	–
Japan	0.1
Netherlands	0.2
New Zealand	0.0
Norway	–
Sweden	–
Switzerland	–
United Kingdom	0.6
United States	7.0
TOTAL	12.6
AF.D.F.	–
AF.D.B.	–
AS.D.B	–
CAR.D.B.	3.6
E.E.C.	0.2
IBRD	–
IDA	–
I.D.B.	2.5
IFAD	–
I.F.C.	–
IMF TRUST FUND	–
U.N. AGENCIES	–
UNDP	0.5
UNTA	0.2
UNICEF	–
UNRWA	–
WFP	0.2
UNHCR	–
Other Multilateral	0.5
Arab OPEC Agencies	–
TOTAL	7.6
OPEC COUNTRIES	–
E.E.C.+ MEMBERS	1.1
TOTAL	20.2

ODA LOANS GROSS

	1983	1984	1985	1986
DAC COUNTRIES				
Australia	–	–	–	–
Austria	–	–	–	–
Belgium	–	–	–	–
Canada	1.0	–	1.8	0.8
Denmark	–	–	–	–
Finland	–	–	–	0.9
France	–	–	–	–
Germany, Fed. Rep.	–	–	–	–
Ireland	–	–	–	–
Italy	–	–	–	–
Japan	–	–	–	–
Netherlands	–	–	–	–
New Zealand	–	–	–	–
Norway	–	–	–	–
Sweden	–	–	–	–
Switzerland	–	–	–	–
United Kingdom	–	–	–	–
United States	7.0	–	–	–
TOTAL	8.0	–	1.8	1.7
MULTILATERAL	5.7	1.9	2.0	0.0
OPEC COUNTRIES	–	0.4	1.0	–
E.E.C.+ MEMBERS	0.1	–	–	–
TOTAL	13.6	2.4	4.8	1.7

ODA LOANS NET

	1983	1984	1985	1986
DAC COUNTRIES				
Canada	0.4	–	1.3	0.3
Finland	–	–	–	0.9
United Kingdom	-0.4	-0.3	-0.3	-0.3
United States	7.0	–	–	–
TOTAL	7.0	-0.3	0.9	0.8
MULTILATERAL	5.4	1.6	1.0	-1.1
OPEC COUNTRIES	–	0.4	1.0	–
E.E.C.+ MEMBERS	-0.3	-0.3	-0.3	-0.3
TOTAL	12.4	1.7	2.9	-0.3

GRANTS

	1983
Australia	–
Austria	–
Belgium	–
Canada	3.6
Denmark	–
Finland	0.0
France	0.0
Germany, Fed. Rep.	–
Ireland	–
Italy	–
Japan	0.1
Netherlands	0.2
New Zealand	0.0
Norway	–
Sweden	–
Switzerland	–
United Kingdom	0.6
United States	–
TOTAL	4.6
MULTILATERAL	1.9
OPEC COUNTRIES	–
E.E.C.+ MEMBERS	1.0
TOTAL	6.5

TOTAL OFFICIAL GROSS

	1983	1984	1985	1986
DAC COUNTRIES				
Australia	–	–	0.0	0.0
Austria	–	–	–	0.0
Belgium	–	–	–	–
Canada	10.5	6.5	6.2	1.8
Denmark	–	–	–	–
Finland	0.0	–	–	0.9
France	0.0	0.1	0.1	0.1
Germany, Fed. Rep.	–	0.1	0.2	0.1
Ireland	–	–	–	–
Italy	–	–	–	0.0
Japan	0.1	0.1	0.0	0.0
Netherlands	0.2	0.2	0.4	0.2
New Zealand	0.0	–	–	–
Norway	–	–	–	0.0
Sweden	–	–	–	–
Switzerland	–	–	–	–
United Kingdom	0.6	0.5	0.4	0.7
United States	8.0	1.0	1.0	1.0
TOTAL	19.4	8.4	8.3	4.7
MULTILATERAL	21.6	18.1	14.2	15.0
OPEC COUNTRIES	3.5	1.9	1.5	–
E.E.C.+ MEMBERS	2.5	4.2	2.4	3.9
TOTAL	44.5	28.5	23.9	19.7

TOTAL OFFICIAL NET

	1983	1984	1985	1986
DAC COUNTRIES				
Australia	–	–	0.0	0.0
Austria	–	–	–	0.0
Belgium	–	–	–	–
Canada	8.1	2.9	0.1	1.2
Denmark	–	–	–	–
Finland	0.0	–	–	0.9
France	0.0	0.1	0.1	0.1
Germany, Fed. Rep.	–	0.1	0.2	0.1
Ireland	–	–	–	–
Italy	–	–	–	0.0
Japan	0.1	0.1	0.0	0.0
Netherlands	0.2	0.2	0.4	0.2
New Zealand	0.0	–	–	–
Norway	–	–	–	0.0
Sweden	–	–	–	–
Switzerland	–	–	–	–
United Kingdom	0.2	0.1	-0.5	-0.5
United States	8.0	1.0	1.0	–
TOTAL	16.6	4.5	1.2	2.1
MULTILATERAL	18.8	14.2	9.1	8.1
OPEC COUNTRIES	3.2	1.3	0.6	-0.9
E.E.C.+ MEMBERS	1.9	3.5	1.1	2.1
TOTAL	38.5	20.0	10.9	9.2

TOTAL OOF GROSS

	1983
Australia	–
Austria	–
Belgium	–
Canada	5.9
Denmark	–
Finland	–
France	–
Germany, Fed. Rep.	–
Ireland	–
Italy	–
Japan	–
Netherlands	–
New Zealand	–
Norway	–
Sweden	–
Switzerland	–
United Kingdom	–
United States	1.0
TOTAL	6.9
MULTILATERAL	14.0
OPEC COUNTRIES	3.5
E.E.C.+ MEMBERS	1.4
TOTAL	24.4

ODA COMMITMENTS

1984	1985	1986	1983	1984	1985	1986
–	0.0	0.0	–	–	–	–
–	–	0.0	–	–	–	–
3.1	4.8	1.8	3.9	7.7	3.6	4.3
–	–	0.9	–	–	1.5	–
0.1	0.1	0.1	0.0	0.1	0.1	0.1
0.1	0.2	0.1	–	0.4	0.1	0.1
–	–	–	–	–	–	–
–	0.0	0.0	–	–	–	0.0
0.1	0.0	0.0	0.1	0.1	0.0	0.0
0.2	0.4	0.2	0.0	0.2	0.1	0.2
–	–	0.0	–	–	–	–
–	–	–	–	–	–	0.0
–	–	–	–	–	–	–
0.5	0.4	0.7	0.6	0.5	0.4	0.7
1.0	–	–	7.0	–	–	–
5.0	5.9	3.7	11.8	8.9	5.8	5.4
–	–	–	–	–	–	–
–	–	–	–	–	–	–
–	–	–	–	–	–	–
0.2	0.1	0.0	0.5	0.1	–	0.1
0.4	0.7	1.5	0.3	0.3	2.3	–
–	–	–	–	–	–	–
2.8	1.9	–	2.0	3.0	7.0	–
–	–	–	–	–	–	–
–	–	–	–	–	–	–
–	–	–	1.3	0.9	0.6	0.7
0.4	0.3	0.3	–	–	–	–
0.2	0.1	0.2	–	–	–	–
–	–	–	–	–	–	–
0.1	0.1	0.0	–	–	–	–
–	–	–	–	–	–	–
0.3	0.1	0.1	–	–	–	–
-0.3	–	–	–	–	–	–
4.0	3.3	2.2	4.0	4.3	10.0	0.7
0.4	1.0	–	9.0	–	–	–
1.3	1.7	2.5	1.0	1.5	3.0	1.0
9.4	10.2	5.9	24.8	13.3	15.7	6.1

TECH. COOP. GRANTS

1984	1985	1986	1983	1984	1985	1986
–	0.0	0.0	–	–	0.0	–
–	–	0.0	–	–	–	–
3.1	3.0	1.0	0.4	–	1.3	–
–	–	–	0.0	–	–	–
0.1	0.1	0.1	0.0	0.1	0.1	0.1
0.1	0.2	0.1	–	0.1	0.2	0.1
–	–	0.0	–	–	–	0.0
0.1	0.0	0.0	0.1	0.1	0.0	0.0
0.2	0.4	0.2	0.2	0.2	0.4	0.2
–	–	–	0.0	–	–	–
–	–	0.0	–	–	–	0.0
–	–	–	–	–	–	–
0.5	0.4	0.7	0.6	0.5	0.4	0.7
1.0	–	–	–	–	–	–
5.0	4.1	2.0	1.3	0.9	2.4	1.1
2.1	1.3	2.1	1.1	0.8	0.6	0.7
–	–	–	–	–	–	–
1.3	1.7	2.5	0.8	0.8	1.0	1.1
7.1	5.4	4.2	2.5	1.7	2.9	1.8

TOTAL OOF NET

1984	1985	1986	1983	1984	1985	1986
–	–	–	–	–	–	–
–	–	–	–	–	–	–
3.5	1.4	–	4.1	-0.1	-4.2	–
–	–	–	–	–	–	–
–	–	–	–	–	–	–
–	–	–	–	–	–	–
–	–	–	–	–	–	–
–	–	–	–	–	–	–
–	–	–	–	–	–	–
–	–	–	–	–	–	–
–	–	–	–	–	–	–
–	–	–	–	–	–	–
–	1.0	1.0	0.0	0.0	-0.6	-0.8
–	–	–	1.0	–	1.0	–
3.5	2.4	1.0	5.0	-0.2	-3.8	-0.8
14.1	10.9	12.8	11.4	10.6	6.8	7.1
1.5	0.5	–	3.2	0.9	-0.4	-0.9
2.9	0.8	1.4	1.2	2.5	-0.2	0.0
19.0	13.7	13.8	19.6	11.3	2.6	5.4

ODA COMMITMENTS : LOANS

DAC COUNTRIES

	1983	1984	1985	1986
Australia	–	–	–	–
Austria	–	–	–	–
Belgium	–	–	–	–
Canada	–	4.6	–	–
Denmark	–	–	–	–
Finland	–	–	1.5	–
France	–	–	–	–
Germany, Fed. Rep.	–	–	–	–
Ireland	–	–	–	–
Italy	–	–	–	–
Japan	–	–	–	–
Netherlands	–	–	–	–
New Zealand	–	–	–	–
Norway	–	–	–	–
Sweden	–	–	–	–
Switzerland	–	–	–	–
United Kingdom	–	–	–	–
United States	7.0	–	–	–
TOTAL	7.0	4.6	1.5	–
MULTILATERAL	2.5	3.0	7.0	–
OPEC COUNTRIES	9.0	–	–	–
E.E.C.+ MEMBERS	–	–	–	–
TOTAL	18.5	7.6	8.5	–

GRANT ELEMENT OF ODA

DAC COUNTRIES

	1983	1984	1985	1986
Australia	–	–	–	–
Austria	–	–	–	–
Belgium	–	–	–	–
Canada	100.0	94.0	100.0	100.0
Denmark	–	–	–	–
Finland	–	–	–	–
France	100.0	100.0	100.0	100.0
Germany, Fed. Rep.	–	100.0	100.0	100.0
Ireland	–	–	–	–
Italy	–	–	–	100.0
Japan	100.0	100.0	100.0	100.0
Netherlands	100.0	100.0	100.0	100.0
New Zealand	–	–	–	–
Norway	–	–	–	100.0
Sweden	–	–	–	–
Switzerland	–	–	–	–
United Kingdom	100.0	100.0	100.0	100.0
United States	44.0	–	–	–
TOTAL	66.7	94.8	100.0	100.0
MULTILATERAL	100.0	75.3	78.3	100.0
OPEC COUNTRIES	50.2	–	–	–
E.E.C.+ MEMBERS	100.0	100.0	100.0	100.0
TOTAL	62.3	86.7	84.9	100.0

OTHER AGGREGATES

COMMITMENTS: ALL SOURCES

	1983	1984	1985	1986
TOTAL BILATERAL	22.5	20.8	5.8	5.4
of which				
OPEC	10.4	0.5	–	–
CMEA	–	–	–	–
TOTAL MULTILATERAL	19.4	50.7	31.9	31.0
TOTAL BIL.& MULTIL.	41.9	71.5	37.7	36.4
of which				
ODA Grants	6.3	5.6	7.3	6.1
ODA Loans	18.5	7.6	8.5	–

DISBURSEMENTS:

DAC COUNTRIES COMBINED

	1983	1984	1985	1986
OFFICIAL & PRIVATE				
GROSS:				
Contractual Lending	18.0	6.9	9.5	17.6
Export Credits Total	10.0	6.9	7.7	16.0
Export Credits Private	3.2	3.5	5.3	15.0
NET:				
Contractual Lending	10.6	-2.0	-16.4	8.0
Export Credits Total	3.6	-1.7	-16.7	7.9
PRIVATE SECTOR NET	-1.4	-20.4	17.7	32.4
Direct Investment	0.0	-18.8	3.9	-0.1
Portfolio Investment	0.0	-0.1	27.3	24.5
Export Credits	-1.4	-1.5	-13.5	7.9

MARKET BORROWING:

CHANGE IN CLAIMS

	1983	1984	1985	1986
Banks	–	–	–	–

MEMORANDUM ITEM:

	1983	1984	1985	1986
CMEA Countr.(Gross)	–	–	–	–

TOTAL RECEIPTS NET

DAC COUNTRIES	1983	1984	1985	1986
Australia	–	0.0	0.0	0.0
Austria	–	–	–	–
Belgium	–	0.0	2.7	-3.5
Canada	2.2	–	2.7	5.5
Denmark	–	–	–	–
Finland	–	–	–	–
France	0.0	-0.1	0.1	-0.3
Germany, Fed. Rep.	–	0.1	0.1	0.0
Ireland	–	–	–	–
Italy	–	0.1	–	0.1
Japan	–	0.0	0.0	0.3
Netherlands	0.2	0.0	0.1	0.0
New Zealand	–	–	–	–
Norway	–	0.3	–	–
Sweden	–	9.0	–	–
Switzerland	0.0	–	–	–
United Kingdom	8.2	8.6	5.0	1.5
United States	6.0	5.0	13.0	13.0
TOTAL	16.6	23.0	23.6	16.7
MULTILATERAL				
AF.D.F.	–	–	–	–
AF.D.B.	–	–	–	–
AS.D.B	–	–	–	–
CAR.D.B.	2.1	1.1	1.3	0.7
E.E.C.	0.2	0.4	0.7	0.5
IBRD	0.9	1.3	2.4	0.4
IDA	–	–	–	–
I.D.B.	–	–	–	–
IFAD	–	–	–	–
I.F.C.	–	–	–	–
IMF TRUST FUND	–	–	–	–
U.N. AGENCIES	–	–	–	–
UNDP	0.4	0.2	0.3	0.3
UNTA	0.2	0.3	0.3	0.2
UNICEF	0.1	0.1	0.5	0.3
UNRWA	–	–	–	–
WFP	0.1	–	–	–
UNHCR	–	–	–	–
Other Multilateral	0.1	0.2	0.1	0.1
Arab OPEC Agencies	–	–	–	–
TOTAL	4.1	3.5	5.5	2.4
OPEC COUNTRIES	–	–	–	–
E.E.C.+ MEMBERS	8.6	9.1	8.6	-1.7
TOTAL	20.7	26.5	29.1	19.1

TOTAL ODA NET

DAC COUNTRIES	1983	1984	1985	1986
Australia	–	0.0	0.0	0.0
Austria	–	–	–	–
Belgium	–	–	–	–
Canada	2.2	–	2.7	5.5
Denmark	–	–	–	–
Finland	–	–	–	–
France	0.0	–	–	–
Germany, Fed. Rep.	–	0.0	0.0	0.0
Ireland	–	–	–	–
Italy	–	0.1	–	0.1
Japan	–	0.0	0.0	0.3
Netherlands	0.2	0.0	0.1	0.0
New Zealand	–	–	–	–
Norway	–	0.3	–	–
Sweden	–	–	–	–
Switzerland	0.0	–	–	–
United Kingdom	3.9	7.1	5.4	4.4
United States	6.0	5.0	12.0	12.0
TOTAL	12.3	12.5	20.3	22.4
AF.D.F.	–	–	–	–
AF.D.B.	–	–	–	–
AS.D.B	–	–	–	–
CAR.D.B.	1.8	0.7	0.9	0.7
E.E.C.	0.2	0.0	-0.2	0.2
IBRD	–	–	–	–
IDA	–	–	–	–
I.D.B.	–	–	–	–
IFAD	–	–	–	–
I.F.C.	–	–	–	–
IMF TRUST FUND	–	–	–	–
U.N. AGENCIES	–	–	–	–
UNDP	0.4	0.2	0.3	0.3
UNTA	0.2	0.3	0.3	0.2
UNICEF	0.1	0.1	0.5	0.3
UNRWA	–	–	–	–
WFP	0.1	–	–	–
UNHCR	–	–	–	–
Other Multilateral	0.1	0.2	0.1	0.1
Arab OPEC Agencies	–	–	–	–
TOTAL	2.8	1.4	1.7	1.7
OPEC COUNTRIES	–	–	–	–
E.E.C.+ MEMBERS	4.3	7.2	5.3	4.8
TOTAL	15.1	14.0	22.0	24.1

TOTAL ODA GROSS

	1983
Australia	–
Austria	–
Belgium	–
Canada	2.2
Denmark	–
Finland	–
France	0.0
Germany, Fed. Rep.	–
Ireland	–
Italy	–
Japan	–
Netherlands	0.2
New Zealand	–
Norway	–
Sweden	–
Switzerland	0.0
United Kingdom	4.1
United States	6.0
TOTAL	12.5
AF.D.F.	–
AF.D.B.	–
AS.D.B	–
CAR.D.B.	1.8
E.E.C.	0.2
IBRD	–
IDA	–
I.D.B.	–
IFAD	–
I.F.C.	–
IMF TRUST FUND	–
U.N. AGENCIES	–
UNDP	0.4
UNTA	0.2
UNICEF	0.1
UNRWA	–
WFP	0.1
UNHCR	–
Other Multilateral	0.1
Arab OPEC Agencies	–
TOTAL	2.8
OPEC COUNTRIES	–
E.E.C.+ MEMBERS	4.5
TOTAL	15.3

ODA LOANS GROSS

DAC COUNTRIES	1983	1984	1985	1986
Australia	–	–	–	–
Austria	–	–	–	–
Belgium	–	–	–	–
Canada	–	–	–	–
Denmark	–	–	–	–
Finland	–	–	–	–
France	–	–	–	–
Germany, Fed. Rep.	–	–	–	–
Ireland	–	–	–	–
Italy	–	–	–	–
Japan	–	–	–	–
Netherlands	–	–	–	–
New Zealand	–	–	–	–
Norway	–	–	–	–
Sweden	–	–	–	–
Switzerland	–	–	–	–
United Kingdom	–	2.3	4.8	3.3
United States	5.0	–	8.0	6.0
TOTAL	5.0	2.3	12.8	9.3
MULTILATERAL	2.0	0.7	0.9	0.7
OPEC COUNTRIES	–	–	–	–
E.E.C.+ MEMBERS	0.2	2.3	4.8	3.3
TOTAL	7.0	3.0	13.7	10.0

ODA LOANS NET

DAC COUNTRIES	1983	1984	1985	1986
Australia	–	–	–	–
Austria	–	–	–	–
Belgium	–	–	–	–
Canada	–	–	-0.2	-0.1
Denmark	–	–	–	–
Finland	–	–	–	–
France	–	–	–	–
Germany, Fed. Rep.	–	–	–	–
Ireland	–	–	–	–
Italy	–	–	–	–
Japan	–	–	–	–
Netherlands	–	–	–	–
New Zealand	–	–	–	–
Norway	–	–	–	–
Sweden	–	–	–	–
Switzerland	–	–	–	–
United Kingdom	-0.2	2.2	4.6	3.1
United States	5.0	–	8.0	6.0
TOTAL	4.8	2.2	12.4	9.0
MULTILATERAL	2.0	0.7	0.9	0.7
OPEC COUNTRIES	–	–	–	–
E.E.C.+ MEMBERS	–	2.2	4.6	3.1
TOTAL	6.8	2.9	13.3	9.7

GRANTS

	1983
Australia	–
Austria	–
Belgium	–
Canada	2.2
Denmark	–
Finland	–
France	0.0
Germany, Fed. Rep.	–
Ireland	–
Italy	–
Japan	–
Netherlands	0.2
New Zealand	–
Norway	–
Sweden	–
Switzerland	0.0
United Kingdom	4.1
United States	1.0
TOTAL	7.5
MULTILATERAL	0.8
OPEC COUNTRIES	–
E.E.C.+ MEMBERS	4.3
TOTAL	8.3

TOTAL OFFICIAL GROSS

DAC COUNTRIES	1983	1984	1985	1986
Australia	–	0.0	0.0	0.0
Austria	–	–	–	–
Belgium	–	–	–	–
Canada	2.2	–	2.9	5.7
Denmark	–	–	–	–
Finland	–	–	–	–
France	0.0	–	–	–
Germany, Fed. Rep.	–	0.1	0.0	0.0
Ireland	–	–	–	–
Italy	–	0.1	–	0.1
Japan	–	0.0	0.0	0.3
Netherlands	0.2	0.0	0.1	0.0
New Zealand	–	–	–	–
Norway	–	0.3	–	–
Sweden	–	–	–	–
Switzerland	0.0	–	–	–
United Kingdom	9.3	8.0	7.4	4.7
United States	6.0	5.0	13.0	14.0
TOTAL	17.7	13.5	23.4	24.8
MULTILATERAL	4.1	3.5	5.5	2.4
OPEC COUNTRIES	–	–	–	–
E.E.C.+ MEMBERS	9.7	8.5	8.1	5.3
TOTAL	21.7	17.0	28.9	27.2

TOTAL OFFICIAL NET

DAC COUNTRIES	1983	1984	1985	1986
Australia	–	0.0	0.0	0.0
Austria	–	–	–	–
Belgium	–	–	–	–
Canada	2.2	–	2.7	5.5
Denmark	–	–	–	–
Finland	–	–	–	–
France	0.0	–	–	–
Germany, Fed. Rep.	–	0.1	–	–
Ireland	–	–	–	–
Italy	–	0.1	–	0.1
Japan	–	0.0	0.0	0.3
Netherlands	0.2	0.0	0.1	0.0
New Zealand	–	–	–	–
Norway	–	0.3	–	–
Sweden	–	–	–	–
Switzerland	0.0	–	–	–
United Kingdom	9.1	7.9	6.3	3.2
United States	6.0	5.0	13.0	13.0
TOTAL	17.5	13.4	22.1	22.2
MULTILATERAL	4.1	3.5	5.5	2.4
OPEC COUNTRIES	–	–	–	–
E.E.C.+ MEMBERS	9.5	8.4	7.0	3.8
TOTAL	21.6	16.9	27.6	24.6

TOTAL OOF GROSS

	1983
Australia	–
Austria	–
Belgium	–
Canada	–
Denmark	–
Finland	–
France	–
Germany, Fed. Rep.	0.0
Ireland	–
Italy	0.1
Japan	0.3
Netherlands	0.0
New Zealand	–
Norway	–
Sweden	–
Switzerland	–
United Kingdom	5.
United States	–
TOTAL	5.
MULTILATERAL	1.
OPEC COUNTRIES	–
E.E.C.+ MEMBERS	5.
TOTAL	6.

ODA COMMITMENTS

1984	1985	1986	1983	1984	1985	1986
0.0	0.0	0.0	–	0.0	0.0	–
–	–	–	–	–	–	–
–	–	–	–	–	–	–
–	2.9	5.7	24.1	0.9	0.6	0.2
–	–	–	–	–	–	–
–	–	–	0.0	–	–	–
–	–	–	0.0	–	–	–
0.0	0.0	0.0	0.0	0.0	0.0	0.0
–	–	–	–	–	–	–
0.1	–	0.1	–	0.1	–	0.1
0.0	0.0	0.3	–	0.0	0.0	0.3
0.0	0.1	0.0	0.2	0.0	0.1	0.0
–	–	–	–	–	–	–
0.3	–	–	0.3	–	–	–
–	–	–	–	–	–	–
–	–	–	–	–	–	–
7.2	5.7	4.6	1.4	8.9	10.6	1.3
5.0	12.0	12.0	12.8	4.8	23.3	10.7
12.7	20.7	22.7	38.9	14.7	34.6	12.6
–	–	–	–	–	–	–
–	–	–	–	–	–	–
0.7	0.9	0.7	0.9	0.1	0.9	9.3
0.0	-0.2	0.2	0.7	–	0.0	0.5
–	–	–	–	–	–	–
–	–	–	–	–	–	–
–	–	–	0.2	–	2.3	–
–	–	–	–	–	–	–
–	–	–	0.8	0.7	1.1	0.8
0.2	0.3	0.3	–	–	–	–
0.3	0.3	0.2	–	–	–	–
0.1	0.5	0.3	–	–	–	–
–	–	–	–	–	–	–
–	–	–	–	–	–	–
0.2	0.1	0.1	–	–	–	–
–	–	–	–	–	–	–
1.4	1.7	1.7	2.6	0.8	4.3	10.7
–	–	–	–	–	–	–
7.3	5.5	5.0	2.3	9.0	10.7	2.0
14.1	22.4	24.4	41.5	15.5	38.9	23.3

TECH. COOP. GRANTS

1984	1985	1986	1983	1984	1985	1986
0.0	0.0	0.0	–	0.0	0.0	0.0
–	–	–	–	–	–	–
–	2.9	5.7	0.3	–	0.8	–
–	–	–	–	–	–	–
–	–	–	0.0	–	–	–
0.0	0.0	0.0	–	0.0	0.0	0.0
0.1	–	0.1	–	0.1	–	0.1
0.0	0.0	0.3	–	0.0	0.0	0.3
0.0	0.1	0.0	0.2	0.0	0.1	0.0
0.3	–	–	–	–	–	–
–	–	–	–	–	–	–
4.9	0.9	1.3	1.4	0.9	0.9	1.3
5.0	4.0	6.0	1.0	5.0	4.0	6.0
10.4	7.8	13.4	2.9	6.1	5.8	7.8
0.7	0.9	1.0	0.7	0.7	1.1	1.1
–	–	–	–	–	–	–
5.0	0.7	1.7	1.6	1.0	0.9	1.7
11.1	8.7	14.4	3.6	6.8	6.9	8.8

TOTAL OOF NET

1984	1985	1986	1983	1984	1985	1986
–	–	–	–	–	–	–
–	–	–	–	–	–	–
–	–	–	–	–	–	–
–	–	–	–	–	–	–
–	–	–	–	–	–	–
0.0	–	–	–	0.0	0.0	–
–	–	–	–	–	–	–
–	–	–	–	–	–	–
–	–	–	–	–	–	–
–	–	–	–	–	–	–
–	–	–	–	–	–	–
0.8	1.7	0.1	5.2	0.8	0.9	-1.2
–	1.0	2.0	–	–	1.0	1.0
0.8	2.7	2.1	5.2	0.8	1.9	-0.2
2.1	3.8	0.7	1.3	2.1	3.8	0.7
–	–	–	–	–	–	–
1.2	2.7	0.3	5.2	1.2	1.8	-0.9
2.9	6.5	2.7	6.5	2.9	5.7	0.5

ODA COMMITMENTS : LOANS

DAC COUNTRIES

	1983	1984	1985	1986
Australia	–	–	–	–
Austria	–	–	–	–
Belgium	–	–	–	–
Canada	–	–	–	–
Denmark	–	–	–	–
Finland	–	–	–	–
France	–	–	–	–
Germany, Fed. Rep.	–	–	–	–
Ireland	–	–	–	–
Italy	–	–	–	–
Japan	–	–	–	–
Netherlands	–	–	–	–
New Zealand	–	–	–	–
Norway	–	–	–	–
Sweden	–	–	–	–
Switzerland	–	–	–	–
United Kingdom	–	8.0	9.7	–
United States	6.0	0.9	13.0	1.5
TOTAL	6.0	8.9	22.7	1.5
MULTILATERAL	1.5	–	2.3	8.3
OPEC COUNTRIES	–	–	–	–
E.E.C.+ MEMBERS	0.6	8.0	9.7	–
TOTAL	7.5	8.9	25.0	9.8

GRANT ELEMENT OF ODA

DAC COUNTRIES

	1983	1984	1985	1986
Australia	–	100.0	100.0	–
Austria	–	–	–	–
Belgium	–	–	–	–
Canada	100.0	100.0	100.0	100.0
Denmark	–	–	–	–
Finland	–	–	–	–
France	100.0	–	–	–
Germany, Fed. Rep.	100.0	100.0	100.0	100.0
Ireland	–	–	–	–
Italy	–	100.0	–	100.0
Japan	–	100.0	100.0	100.0
Netherlands	100.0	100.0	100.0	100.0
New Zealand	–	–	–	–
Norway	100.0	–	–	–
Sweden	–	–	–	–
Switzerland	–	–	–	–
United Kingdom	100.0	69.3	68.1	100.0
United States	83.9	93.5	80.7	95.2
TOTAL	94.7	79.3	77.3	95.9
MULTILATERAL	100.0	100.0	100.0	100.0
OPEC COUNTRIES	–	–	–	–
E.E.C.+ MEMBERS	100.0	69.6	68.5	100.0
TOTAL	94.8	80.4	78.5	96.5

OTHER AGGREGATES

COMMITMENTS: ALL SOURCES

	1983	1984	1985	1986
TOTAL BILATERAL	45.0	14.7	36.1	15.4
of which				
OPEC	–	–	–	–
CMEA	–	–	–	–
TOTAL MULTILATERAL	10.1	0.8	4.3	18.3
TOTAL BIL.& MULTIL.	55.1	15.5	40.5	33.6
of which				
ODA Grants	34.0	6.6	13.9	13.5
ODA Loans	7.5	8.9	25.0	9.8

DISBURSEMENTS:

DAC COUNTRIES COMBINED

	1983	1984	1985	1986
OFFICIAL & PRIVATE				
GROSS:				
Contractual Lending	18.9	20.4	17.2	11.1
Export Credits Total	8.7	17.3	1.7	-0.3
Export Credits Private	8.7	17.3	1.7	-0.3
NET:				
Contractual Lending	9.1	12.7	13.1	6.8
Export Credits Total	-0.9	9.7	-1.1	-2.0
PRIVATE SECTOR NET	-0.9	9.7	1.5	-5.5
Direct Investment	–	–	0.0	–
Portfolio Investment	–	-0.1	2.7	-3.5
Export Credits	-0.9	9.7	-1.1	-2.0

MARKET BORROWING:

CHANGE IN CLAIMS

	1983	1984	1985	1986
Banks	–	-1.0	-7.0	20.0

MEMORANDUM ITEM:

	1983	1984	1985	1986
CMEA Countr.(Gross)	–	–	–	–

DISBURSEMENTS, UNLESS OTHERWISE STATED

	1983	1984	1985	1986		1983	1984	1985	1986		1983
TOTAL RECEIPTS NET					**TOTAL ODA NET**					**TOTAL ODA GROSS**	
DAC COUNTRIES											
Australia	–	–	–	–		–	–	–	–	Australia	–
Austria	0.0	–	0.0	0.0		0.0	–	0.0	0.0	Austria	0.0
Belgium	4.4	23.4	13.0	-5.7		2.3	0.5	0.7	1.2	Belgium	2.3
Canada	0.8	2.3	0.4	0.3		1.8	1.2	0.7	0.5	Canada	1.8
Denmark	1.4	0.3	4.7	–		1.4	0.3	4.7	–	Denmark	1.4
Finland	–	–	–	–		–	–	–	–	Finland	–
France	18.2	9.1	6.1	23.8		14.0	16.4	13.4	25.6	France	14.1
Germany, Fed. Rep.	11.4	11.7	17.5	26.8		11.7	11.9	15.5	26.8	Germany, Fed. Rep.	11.7
Ireland	–	–	–	–		–	–	–	–	Ireland	–
Italy	0.3	0.4	0.5	2.6		0.3	0.4	0.6	2.6	Italy	0.3
Japan	2.2	1.0	1.5	2.7		2.2	1.0	1.5	2.7	Japan	2.2
Netherlands	2.0	1.4	6.9	-5.9		2.7	1.4	2.1	3.4	Netherlands	2.7
New Zealand	–	–	–	–		–	–	–	–	New Zealand	–
Norway	0.6	81.9	73.9	67.8		0.6	0.4	2.9	0.3	Norway	0.6
Sweden	–	–	–	–		–	–	–	–	Sweden	–
Switzerland	2.2	3.0	2.3	6.2		2.2	3.0	2.3	6.2	Switzerland	2.2
United Kingdom	0.8	-4.8	-1.8	-8.6		0.1	0.2	0.2	0.2	United Kingdom	0.1
United States	2.0	3.0	3.0	3.0		2.0	3.0	3.0	3.0	United States	2.0
TOTAL	46.3	132.7	128.0	112.8		41.3	39.7	47.7	72.5	TOTAL	41.4
MULTILATERAL											
AF.D.F.	6.2	3.7	3.6	10.4		6.2	3.7	3.6	10.4	AF.D.F.	6.3
AF.D.B.	0.1	-0.4	-1.4	-1.6		–	–	–	–	AF.D.B.	–
AS.D.B	–	–	–	–		–	–	–	–	AS.D.B	–
CAR.D.B.	–	–	–	–		–	–	–	–	CAR.D.B.	–
E.E.C.	7.8	6.5	5.1	10.5		7.8	6.5	5.1	10.5	E.E.C.	7.9
IBRD	–	–	–	–		–	–	–	–	IBRD	–
IDA	15.6	12.7	18.7	26.5		15.6	12.7	18.7	26.5	IDA	16.7
I.D.B.	–	–	–	–		–	–	–	–	I.D.B.	–
IFAD	1.5	3.2	4.4	4.8		1.5	3.2	4.4	4.8	IFAD	1.5
I.F.C.	–	–	–	–		–	–	–	–	I.F.C.	–
IMF TRUST FUND	–	–	–	–		–	–	–	–	IMF TRUST FUND	–
U.N. AGENCIES	–	–	–	–		–	–	–	–	U.N. AGENCIES	–
UNDP	3.7	5.0	5.4	4.6		3.7	5.0	5.4	4.6	UNDP	3.7
UNTA	1.0	0.6	0.7	0.9		1.0	0.6	0.7	0.9	UNTA	1.0
UNICEF	0.9	0.9	1.0	0.7		0.9	0.9	1.0	0.7	UNICEF	0.9
UNRWA	–	–	–	–		–	–	–	–	UNRWA	–
WFP	0.3	3.1	3.4	2.8		0.3	3.1	3.4	2.8	WFP	0.3
UNHCR	0.1	0.1	0.4	0.7		0.1	0.1	0.4	0.7	UNHCR	0.1
Other Multilateral	1.6	1.8	1.3	0.9		1.6	1.8	1.3	0.9	Other Multilateral	1.6
Arab OPEC Agencies	3.6	0.3	2.1	2.1		4.2	0.5	1.3	0.2	Arab OPEC Agencies	5.0
TOTAL	42.6	37.4	44.7	63.3		43.0	38.1	45.3	62.9	TOTAL	45.0
OPEC COUNTRIES	2.0	-0.2	2.9	2.7		2.0	-0.2	2.9	2.7	OPEC COUNTRIES	2.4
E.E.C.+ MEMBERS	46.3	48.0	52.0	43.4		40.3	37.6	42.3	70.4	E.E.C.+ MEMBERS	40.4
TOTAL	90.9	169.9	175.5	178.8		86.4	77.6	95.8	138.1	TOTAL	88.7
ODA LOANS GROSS					**ODA LOANS NET**					**GRANTS**	
DAC COUNTRIES											
Australia	–	–	–	–		–	–	–	–	Australia	–
Austria	–	–	–	–		–	–	–	–	Austria	0.0
Belgium	2.0	–	–	0.3		2.0	–	–	0.3	Belgium	0.3
Canada	–	–	–	–		–	–	–	–	Canada	1.8
Denmark	1.4	0.3	4.7	–		1.4	0.3	4.7	–	Denmark	–
Finland	–	–	–	–		–	–	–	–	Finland	–
France	4.6	2.5	4.1	14.6		4.5	2.3	3.8	13.8	France	9.5
Germany, Fed. Rep.	–	–	–	–		–	–	–	–	Germany, Fed. Rep.	11.7
Ireland	–	–	–	–		–	–	–	–	Ireland	–
Italy	–	–	–	–		–	–	–	–	Italy	0.3
Japan	–	–	–	–		–	–	–	–	Japan	2.2
Netherlands	–	–	0.1	–		–	–	0.1	–	Netherlands	2.7
New Zealand	–	–	–	–		–	–	–	–	New Zealand	–
Norway	–	–	–	–		–	–	–	–	Norway	0.6
Sweden	–	–	–	–		–	–	–	–	Sweden	–
Switzerland	–	–	–	–		–	–	–	–	Switzerland	2.2
United Kingdom	–	–	–	–		–	–	–	–	United Kingdom	0.1
United States	–	–	–	–		–	–	–	–	United States	2.0
TOTAL	7.9	2.8	8.9	15.0		7.9	2.5	8.7	14.2	TOTAL	33.4
MULTILATERAL	29.3	21.8	28.5	43.0		27.3	20.0	27.6	41.7	MULTILATERAL	15.7
OPEC COUNTRIES	2.3	–	3.4	3.0		2.0	-0.4	2.8	2.6	OPEC COUNTRIES	0.1
E.E.C.+ MEMBERS	7.9	3.1	8.9	15.0		7.8	2.8	8.7	14.0	E.E.C.+ MEMBERS	32.5
TOTAL	39.5	24.6	40.8	60.9		37.1	22.2	39.0	58.5	TOTAL	49.2
TOTAL OFFICIAL GROSS					**TOTAL OFFICIAL NET**					**TOTAL OOF GROSS**	
DAC COUNTRIES											
Australia	–	–	0.0	0.0		0.0	–	0.0	0.0	Australia	–
Austria	0.0	–	0.0	0.0		0.0	–	0.0	0.0	Austria	–
Belgium	2.3	1.7	1.6	1.4		2.3	1.7	1.6	1.4	Belgium	–
Canada	1.8	2.3	0.7	0.5		0.8	2.3	0.4	0.3	Canada	–
Denmark	1.4	0.3	4.7	–		1.4	0.3	4.7	–	Denmark	–
Finland	–	–	–	–		–	–	–	–	Finland	–
France	14.1	16.7	13.7	26.4		13.9	16.3	13.3	25.6	France	–
Germany, Fed. Rep.	11.7	11.9	17.3	27.1		11.7	11.9	17.3	26.9	Germany, Fed. Rep.	–
Ireland	–	–	–	–		–	–	–	–	Ireland	–
Italy	0.3	0.4	0.6	2.6		0.3	0.4	0.6	2.6	Italy	–
Japan	2.2	1.0	1.5	2.7		2.2	1.0	1.5	2.7	Japan	–
Netherlands	2.7	1.4	2.1	3.4		2.7	1.4	2.1	3.4	Netherlands	–
New Zealand	–	–	–	–		–	–	–	–	New Zealand	–
Norway	0.6	0.4	2.9	0.3		0.6	0.4	2.9	0.3	Norway	–
Sweden	–	–	–	–		–	–	–	–	Sweden	–
Switzerland	2.2	3.0	2.3	6.2		2.2	3.0	2.3	6.2	Switzerland	–
United Kingdom	0.1	0.2	0.2	0.2		0.1	0.2	0.2	0.2	United Kingdom	–
United States	2.0	3.0	3.0	3.0		2.0	3.0	3.0	3.0	United States	–
TOTAL	41.4	42.2	50.7	73.8		40.1	41.8	50.0	72.6	TOTAL	–
MULTILATERAL	46.5	40.2	48.0	72.4		42.6	37.4	44.7	63.3	MULTILATERAL	1.5
OPEC COUNTRIES	2.4	0.2	3.4	3.0		2.0	-0.2	2.9	2.7	OPEC COUNTRIES	–
E.E.C.+ MEMBERS	40.4	39.2	45.4	71.8		40.1	38.7	45.0	70.7	E.E.C.+ MEMBERS	–
TOTAL	90.2	82.6	102.1	149.2		84.7	79.1	97.6	138.5	TOTAL	1.5

ODA COMMITMENTS

1984	1985	1986	1983	1984	1985	1986
–	0.0	0.0	–	–	0.0	–
0.5	0.7	1.2	2.0	–	–	1.2
1.2	0.7	0.5	1.7	0.5	0.3	0.5
0.3	4.7	–	–	–	–	–
–	–	–	–	–	–	–
16.6	13.7	26.4	24.1	28.6	17.2	26.4
11.9	15.5	26.8	4.9	34.1	6.7	32.5
–	–	–	–	–	–	–
0.4	0.6	2.6	0.3	0.6	0.7	4.6
1.0	1.5	2.7	0.0	2.0	2.4	1.2
1.4	2.1	3.4	2.8	3.5	1.0	2.7
–	–	–	–	–	–	–
0.4	2.9	0.3	0.8	0.4	2.8	–
–	–	–	–	–	–	–
3.0	2.3	6.2	3.5	0.9	8.6	0.4
0.2	0.2	0.2	0.1	0.2	0.2	0.2
3.0	3.0	3.0	1.4	3.6	1.8	2.4
39.9	48.0	73.3	41.6	74.4	41.7	72.2
3.8	3.6	10.5	–	0.9	18.2	–
–	–	–	–	–	–	–
–	–	–	–	–	–	–
6.6	5.1	10.7	12.5	8.7	16.4	12.6
–	–	–	–	–	–	–
13.9	19.2	26.9	–	55.4	–	26.9
–	–	–	–	–	–	–
3.2	4.4	4.8	–	–	–	–
–	–	–	–	–	–	–
–	–	–	7.7	11.5	12.2	10.6
5.0	5.4	4.6	–	–	–	–
0.6	0.7	0.9	–	–	–	–
0.9	1.0	0.7	–	–	–	–
–	–	–	–	–	–	–
3.1	3.4	2.8	–	–	–	–
0.1	0.4	0.7	–	–	–	–
1.8	1.3	0.9	–	–	–	–
0.9	1.7	0.8	9.4	4.0	7.0	4.1
39.9	46.2	64.2	29.5	80.5	53.8	54.1
0.2	3.4	3.0	0.1	10.3	0.0	–
38.0	42.6	71.3	46.6	75.6	42.1	80.3
80.0	97.6	140.6	71.1	165.1	95.5	126.3

TECH. COOP. GRANTS

1984	1985	1986	1983	1984	1985	1986
–	–	–	–	–	–	–
–	0.0	0.0	0.0	–	–	–
0.5	0.7	0.8	0.2	0.2	0.2	0.3
1.2	0.7	0.5	0.0	–	0.4	–
–	–	–	–	0.3	–	–
14.1	9.6	11.8	7.0	7.1	7.5	8.8
11.9	15.5	26.8	8.1	8.5	9.4	13.7
–	–	–	–	–	–	–
0.4	0.6	2.6	0.3	0.4	0.6	2.0
1.0	1.5	2.7	0.0	0.1	0.1	0.0
1.4	2.0	3.4	0.8	1.2	1.4	2.7
–	–	–	–	–	–	–
0.4	2.9	0.3	–	0.0	–	–
–	–	–	–	–	–	–
3.0	2.3	6.2	0.7	0.7	0.7	1.4
0.2	0.2	0.2	0.1	0.1	0.2	0.2
3.0	3.0	3.0	1.0	1.0	1.0	1.0
37.1	39.0	58.4	18.2	19.6	21.5	30.2
18.1	17.7	21.2	7.3	8.5	8.8	8.2
0.2	0.1	0.0	–	–	–	–
34.9	33.7	56.4	16.5	17.8	19.2	28.2
55.4	56.8	79.7	25.5	28.1	30.3	38.4

TOTAL OOF NET

1984	1985	1986	1983	1984	1985	1986
–	–	–	–	–	–	–
–	–	–	–	–	–	–
1.2	0.9	0.2	–	1.2	0.9	0.2
1.1	–	–	-1.0	1.1	-0.3	-0.2
–	–	–	–	–	–	–
–	–	–	–	–	–	–
0.0	–	–	-0.1	-0.1	0.0	–
–	1.8	0.3	–	–	1.8	0.1
–	–	–	–	–	–	–
–	–	–	–	–	–	–
–	–	–	–	–	–	–
–	–	–	–	–	–	–
–	–	–	–	–	–	–
–	–	–	–	–	–	–
–	–	–	–	–	–	–
2.3	2.7	0.5	-1.2	2.1	2.4	0.1
0.3	1.9	8.2	-0.4	-0.6	-0.6	0.3
–	–	–	–	–	–	–
1.2	2.7	0.5	-0.1	1.1	2.7	0.3
2.6	4.6	8.6	-1.6	1.5	1.8	0.4

ODA COMMITMENTS : LOANS

DAC COUNTRIES

	1983	1984	1985	1986
Australia	–	–	–	–
Austria	–	–	–	–
Belgium	2.0	–	–	0.3
Canada	–	–	–	–
Denmark	–	–	–	–
Finland	–	–	–	–
France	13.1	13.6	8.3	14.6
Germany, Fed. Rep.	–	–	–	–
Ireland	–	–	–	–
Italy	–	–	–	–
Japan	–	–	–	–
Netherlands	–	0.2	–	–
New Zealand	–	–	–	–
Norway	–	–	–	–
Sweden	–	–	· –	–
Switzerland	–	–	–	–
United Kingdom	–	–	–	–
United States	–	–	–	–
TOTAL	*15.1*	*13.8*	*8.3*	*15.0*
MULTILATERAL	*6.5*	*63.8*	*24.9*	*30.8*
OPEC COUNTRIES	*–*	*10.1*	*–*	*–*
E.E.C.+ MEMBERS	*15.1*	*17.3*	*8.3*	*15.0*
TOTAL	*21.6*	*87.7*	*33.2*	*45.8*

GRANT ELEMENT OF ODA

DAC COUNTRIES

	1983	1984	1985	1986
Australia	–	–	–	–
Austria	–	–	100.0	–
Belgium	84.7	–	–	95.2
Canada	100.0	100.0	100.0	100.0
Denmark	–	–	–	–
Finland	–	–	–	–
France	86.2	71.1	65.5	99.2
Germany, Fed. Rep.	100.0	100.0	100.0	100.0
Ireland	–	–	–	–
Italy	100.0	100.0	100.0	100.0
Japan	100.0	100.0	100.0	100.0
Netherlands	100.0	98.3	100.0	100.0
New Zealand	–	–	–	–
Norway	100.0	100.0	100.0	–
Sweden	–	–	–	–
Switzerland	100.0	100.0	100.0	100.0
United Kingdom	100.0	100.0	100.0	100.0
United States	100.0	100.0	100.0	100.0
TOTAL	*92.2*	*88.8*	*85.8*	*99.7*
MULTILATERAL	*87.8*	*85.6*	*88.1*	*87.6*
OPEC COUNTRIES	*100.0*	*42.9*	*100.0*	*–*
E.E.C.+ MEMBERS	*93.2*	*88.5*	*85.9*	*99.8*
TOTAL	*89.6*	*84.3*	*87.1*	*93.9*

OTHER AGGREGATES

COMMITMENTS: ALL SOURCES

	1983	1984	1985	1986
TOTAL BILATERAL	41.6	87.7	41.8	72.2
of which				
OPEC	0.1	10.3	0.0	–
CMEA	–	–	0.0	–
TOTAL MULTILATERAL	29.5	96.1	74.0	62.1
TOTAL BIL.& MULTIL.	71.1	183.8	115.8	134.3
of which				
ODA Grants	49.5	77.4	62.4	80.5
ODA Loans	21.6	87.7	33.2	45.8

DISBURSEMENTS:

DAC COUNTRIES COMBINED

	1983	1984	1985	1986
OFFICIAL & PRIVATE				
GROSS:				
Contractual Lending	26.2	107.1	92.2	93.3
Export Credits Total	18.3	104.3	83.2	78.1
Export Credits Private	18.3	103.2	81.4	78.1
NET:				
Contractual Lending	14.0	72.0	70.5	62.5
Export Credits Total	6.3	69.6	61.9	48.1
PRIVATE SECTOR NET	6.1	90.9	77.9	40.2
Direct Investment	-0.1	0.0	-0.1	1.1
Portfolio Investment	-1.1	22.3	17.6	-9.3
Export Credits	7.4	68.5	60.5	48.5

MARKET BORROWING:

CHANGE IN CLAIMS

	1983	1984	1985	1986
Banks	–	-28.0	-2.0	-47.0

MEMORANDUM ITEM:

	1983	1984	1985	1986
CMEA Countr.(Gross)	1.0	–	0.0	–

TOTAL RECEIPTS NET / TOTAL ODA NET / TOTAL ODA GROSS

	TRN 1983	TRN 1984	TRN 1985	TRN 1986	ODAN 1983	ODAN 1984	ODAN 1985	ODAN 1986	ODAG 1983
DAC COUNTRIES									
Australia	24.3	11.3	3.0	3.3	–	–	–	–	–
Austria	–	–	–	–	–	–	–	–	–
Belgium	7.5	-12.5	6.2	23.6	–	–	–	–	–
Canada	31.5	-8.6	-35.2	-27.6	–	–	–	–	–
Denmark	4.6	-0.4	-1.7	-2.3	–	–	–	–	–
Finland	–	–	–	–	–	–	–	–	–
France	-6.8	-43.1	46.9	18.1	–	0.0	–	–	–
Germany, Fed. Rep.	1.1	-9.6	30.2	56.2	–	–	–	–	–
Ireland	–	–	–	–	–	–	–	–	–
Italy	-2.1	-2.4	-1.3	-1.6	–	–	–	–	–
Japan	-38.2	-1.9	38.7	77.1	–	–	0.0	–	–
Netherlands	12.2	-11.2	–	-128.2	–	–	–	–	–
New Zealand	–	–	–	–	–	–	–	–	–
Norway	0.0	8.6	2.4	-1.3	–	–	–	–	–
Sweden	12.0	–	-9.0	-1.3	–	–	–	–	–
Switzerland	–	–	–	–	–	–	–	–	–
United Kingdom	-6.9	504.4	-97.1	-8.4	0.1	0.0	0.0	0.0	0.1
United States	60.0	-97.0	805.0	1040.0	–	–	–	–	–
TOTAL	99.2	337.5	788.0	1048.9	0.1	0.0	0.0	0.0	0.1
MULTILATERAL									
AF.D.F.	–	–	–	–	–	–	–	–	–
AF.D.B.	–	–	–	–	–	–	–	–	–
AS.D.B	–	–	–	–	–	–	–	–	–
CAR.D.B.	–	–	–	–	–	–	–	–	–
E.E.C.	–	–	0.9	–	–	–	0.9	–	–
IBRD	–	–	–	–	–	–	–	–	–
IDA	–	–	–	–	–	–	–	–	–
I.D.B.	–	–	–	–	–	–	–	–	–
IFAD	–	–	–	–	–	–	–	–	–
I.F.C.	–	–	–	–	–	–	–	–	–
IMF TRUST FUND	–	–	–	–	–	–	–	–	–
U.N. AGENCIES	–	–	–	–	–	–	–	–	–
UNDP	0.0	0.0	0.0	0.1	0.0	0.0	0.0	0.1	0.0
UNTA	–	0.0	–	–	–	0.0	–	–	–
UNICEF	–	–	–	–	–	–	–	–	–
UNRWA	–	–	–	–	–	–	–	–	–
WFP	–	–	–	–	–	–	–	–	–
UNHCR	–	–	–	–	–	–	–	–	–
Other Multilateral	–	–	0.0	–	–	–	0.0	–	–
Arab OPEC Agencies	–	–	–	–	–	–	–	–	–
TOTAL	0.0	0.1	0.9	0.1	0.0	0.1	0.9	0.1	0.0
OPEC COUNTRIES	–	–	–	–	–	–	–	–	–
E.E.C.+ MEMBERS	9.6	425.1	-15.9	-42.6	0.1	0.0	0.9	0.0	0.1
TOTAL	99.2	337.5	788.9	1048.9	0.1	0.1	0.9	0.1	0.1

ODA LOANS GROSS / ODA LOANS NET / GRANTS

	LG 1983	LG 1984	LG 1985	LG 1986	LN 1983	LN 1984	LN 1985	LN 1986	GRANTS 1983
DAC COUNTRIES									
Australia	–	–	–	–	–	–	–	–	–
Austria	–	–	–	–	–	–	–	–	–
Belgium	–	–	–	–	–	–	–	–	–
Canada	–	–	–	–	–	–	–	–	–
Denmark	–	–	–	–	–	–	–	–	–
Finland	–	–	–	–	–	–	–	–	–
France	–	–	–	–	–	–	–	–	–
Germany, Fed. Rep.	–	–	–	–	–	–	–	–	–
Ireland	–	–	–	–	–	–	–	–	–
Italy	–	–	–	–	–	–	–	–	–
Japan	–	–	–	–	–	–	–	–	–
Netherlands	–	–	–	–	–	–	–	–	–
New Zealand	–	–	–	–	–	–	–	–	–
Norway	–	–	–	–	–	–	–	–	–
Sweden	–	–	–	–	–	–	–	–	–
Switzerland	–	–	–	–	–	–	–	–	–
United Kingdom	–	–	–	–	–	–	–	–	0.1
United States	–	–	–	–	–	–	–	–	–
TOTAL	–	–	–	–	–	–	–	–	0.1
MULTILATERAL	–	–	–	–	–	–	–	–	0.0
OPEC COUNTRIES	–	–	–	–	–	–	–	–	–
E.E.C.+ MEMBERS	–	–	–	–	–	–	–	–	0.1
TOTAL	–	–	–	–	–	–	–	–	0.1

TOTAL OFFICIAL GROSS / TOTAL OFFICIAL NET / TOTAL OOF GROSS

	OG 1983	OG 1984	OG 1985	OG 1986	ON 1983	ON 1984	ON 1985	ON 1986	OOF 1983
DAC COUNTRIES									
Australia	–	–	–	3.5	–	–	–	3.3	–
Austria	–	–	–	–	–	–	–	–	–
Belgium	–	0.0	0.0	0.0	–	0.0	0.0	0.0	–
Canada	47.8	22.4	–	–	31.5	-8.6	-35.2	-27.6	47.8
Denmark	4.6	0.6	–	–	4.6	0.6	-0.4	-0.9	4.6
Finland	–	–	–	–	–	–	–	–	–
France	–	0.0	–	–	–	0.0	–	–	–
Germany, Fed. Rep.	–	–	–	–	-1.0	-2.2	-2.7	–	–
Ireland	–	–	–	–	–	–	–	–	–
Italy	–	–	–	–	–	–	–	–	–
Japan	–	–	0.0	–	–	–	0.0	–	–
Netherlands	–	–	–	–	–	–	–	–	–
New Zealand	–	–	–	–	–	–	–	–	–
Norway	–	–	–	–	–	–	–	–	–
Sweden	10.8	2.1	–	–	9.9	–	-3.0	-2.5	10.8
Switzerland	–	–	–	–	–	–	–	–	–
United Kingdom	0.1	0.0	0.0	0.0	0.1	0.0	0.0	0.0	–
United States	–	–	–	–	–	–	–	–	–
TOTAL	63.3	25.1	0.1	3.5	45.1	-10.1	-41.4	-27.8	63.2
MULTILATERAL	0.0	0.1	0.9	0.1	0.0	0.1	0.9	0.1	–
OPEC COUNTRIES	–	–	–	–	–	–	–	–	–
E.E.C.+ MEMBERS	4.6	0.6	0.9	0.1	3.7	-1.5	-2.3	-0.9	4.6
TOTAL	63.3	25.2	1.0	3.6	45.1	-10.1	-40.5	-27.7	63.2

BERMUDA

ODA COMMITMENTS

1984	1985	1986	1983	1984	1985	1986
–	–	–	–	–	–	–
–	–	–	–	–	–	–
–	–	–	–	–	–	–
–	–	–	–	–	–	–
–	–	–	–	–	–	–
0.0	–	–	–	0.0	–	–
–	–	–	–	–	–	–
–	–	–	–	–	–	–
–	0.0	–	0.0	–	0.0	–
–	–	–	–	–	–	–
–	–	–	–	–	–	–
–	–	–	–	–	–	–
–	–	–	–	–	–	–
–	–	–	–	–	–	–
0.0	0.0	0.0	0.1	0.0	0.0	0.0
–	–	–	–	–	–	–
0.0	0.0	0.0	0.1	0.0	0.0	0.0
–	–	–	–	–	–	–
–	–	–	–	–	–	–
–	–	–	–	–	–	–
–	0.9	–	–	–	–	–
–	–	–	–	–	–	–
–	–	–	–	–	–	–
–	–	–	–	–	–	–
–	–	–	0.0	0.1	0.0	0.1
0.0	0.0	0.1	–	–	–	–
0.0	–	–	–	–	–	–
–	–	–	–	–	–	–
–	–	–	–	–	–	–
–	0.0	–	–	–	–	–
–	–	–	–	–	–	–
0.1	0.9	0.1	0.0	0.1	0.0	0.1
–	–	–	–	–	–	–
0.0	0.9	0.0	0.1	0.0	0.0	0.0
0.1	0.9	0.1	0.1	0.1	0.1	0.1

TECH. COOP. GRANTS

1984	1985	1986	1983	1984	1985	1986
–	–	–	–	–	–	–
–	–	–	–	–	–	–
–	–	–	–	–	0.0	–
–	–	–	–	–	–	–
0.0	–	–	–	0.0	–	–
–	–	–	–	–	–	–
–	–	–	–	–	–	–
–	0.0	–	–	–	0.0	–
–	–	–	–	–	–	–
–	–	–	–	–	–	–
–	–	–	–	–	–	–
–	–	–	–	–	–	–
0.0	0.0	0.0	0.1	0.0	0.0	0.0
–	–	–	–	–	–	–
0.0	0.0	0.0	0.1	0.0	0.1	0.0
0.1	0.9	0.1	0.0	0.1	0.0	0.1
–	–	–	–	–	–	–
0.0	0.9	0.0	0.1	0.0	0.0	0.0
0.1	0.9	0.1	0.1	0.1	0.1	0.1

TOTAL OOF NET

1984	1985	1986	1983	1984	1985	1986
–	–	3.5	–	–	–	3.3
0.0	0.0	0.0	–	0.0	0.0	0.0
22.4	–	–	31.5	-8.6	-35.2	-27.6
0.6	–	–	4.6	0.6	-0.4	-0.9
–	–	–	–	–	–	–
–	–	–	-1.0	-2.2	-2.7	–
–	–	–	–	–	–	–
–	–	–	–	–	–	–
–	–	–	–	–	–	–
2.1	–	–	9.9	–	-3.0	-2.5
–	–	–	–	–	–	–
–	–	–	–	–	–	–
25.1	0.0	3.5	45.0	-10.2	-41.4	-27.8
–	–	–	–	–	–	–
0.6	0.0	0.0	3.6	-1.6	-3.2	-0.9
25.1	0.0	3.5	45.0	-10.2	-41.4	-27.8

ODA COMMITMENTS : LOANS

DAC COUNTRIES	1983	1984	1985	1986
Australia	–	–	–	–
Austria	–	–	–	–
Belgium	–	–	–	–
Canada	–	–	–	–
Denmark	–	–	–	–
Finland	–	–	–	–
France	–	–	–	–
Germany, Fed. Rep.	–	–	–	–
Ireland	–	–	–	–
Italy	–	–	–	–
Japan	–	–	–	–
Netherlands	–	–	–	–
New Zealand	–	–	–	–
Norway	–	–	–	–
Sweden	–	–	–	–
Switzerland	–	–	–	–
United Kingdom	–	–	–	–
United States	–	–	–	–
TOTAL	–	–	–	–
MULTILATERAL	–	–	–	–
OPEC COUNTRIES	–	–	–	–
E.E.C.+ MEMBERS	–	–	–	–
TOTAL	–	–	–	–

GRANT ELEMENT OF ODA

DAC COUNTRIES	1983	1984	1985	1986
Australia	–	–	–	–
Austria	–	–	–	–
Belgium	–	–	–	–
Canada	–	–	–	–
Denmark	–	–	–	–
Finland	–	–	–	–
France	–	100.0	–	–
Germany, Fed. Rep.	–	–	–	–
Ireland	–	–	–	–
Italy	–	–	–	–
Japan	100.0	–	100.0	–
Netherlands	–	–	–	–
New Zealand	–	–	–	–
Norway	–	–	–	–
Sweden	–	–	–	–
Switzerland	–	–	–	–
United Kingdom	100.0	100.0	100.0	100.0
United States	–	–	–	–
TOTAL	100.0	100.0	100.0	100.0
MULTILATERAL	100.0	100.0	100.0	100.0
OPEC COUNTRIES	–	–	–	–
E.E.C.+ MEMBERS	100.0	100.0	100.0	100.0
TOTAL	100.0	100.0	100.0	100.0

OTHER AGGREGATES

COMMITMENTS: ALL SOURCES

	1983	1984	1985	1986
TOTAL BILATERAL	10.9	2.1	3.7	-2.5
of which				
OPEC	–	–	–	–
CMEA	–	–	–	–
TOTAL MULTILATERAL	0.0	0.1	0.0	0.1
TOTAL BIL.& MULTIL.	10.9	2.1	3.7	-2.4
of which				
ODA Grants	0.1	0.1	0.1	0.1
ODA Loans	–	–	–	–

DISBURSEMENTS:
DAC COUNTRIES COMBINED

	1983	1984	1985	1986
OFFICIAL & PRIVATE				
GROSS:				
Contractual Lending	90.5	38.5	14.4	6.3
Export Credits Total	90.5	38.5	14.4	6.3
Export Credits Private	27.3	13.4	14.4	2.8
NET:				
Contractual Lending	19.4	-48.8	-70.7	-54.5
Export Credits Total	19.4	-48.8	-70.7	-54.5
PRIVATE SECTOR NET	54.1	347.6	829.4	1076.6
Direct Investment	388.9	808.7	1126.7	1525.9
Portfolio Investment	-309.1	-422.5	-268.0	-422.6
Export Credits	-25.6	-38.6	-29.3	-26.7

MARKET BORROWING:
CHANGE IN CLAIMS

	1983	1984	1985	1986
Banks	–	–	–	–

MEMORANDUM ITEM:

	1983	1984	1985	1986
CMEA Countr.(Gross)	–	–	–	–

TOTAL RECEIPTS NET / TOTAL ODA NET / TOTAL ODA GROSS

	TOTAL RECEIPTS NET				TOTAL ODA NET				TOTAL ODA GROSS
	1983	1984	1985	1986	1983	1984	1985	1986	1983
DAC COUNTRIES									
Australia	—	0.0	—	—	—	0.0	—	—	—
Austria	0.2	0.1	0.1	0.1	0.2	0.1	0.1	0.1	0.2
Belgium	-5.1	20.8	23.7	-6.3	2.8	1.6	1.6	2.4	2.8
Canada	4.2	9.7	2.2	3.8	4.3	9.7	2.2	3.8	4.4
Denmark	2.0	0.9	4.8	0.8	2.5	1.1	4.8	0.8	2.7
Finland	0.0	0.1	0.1	0.1	0.1	0.1	0.1	0.1	0.1
France	-1.6	-2.0	4.5	-4.5	2.8	2.8	2.8	3.8	2.8
Germany, Fed. Rep.	7.4	7.8	15.0	22.8	10.6	9.7	11.3	19.6	10.7
Ireland	—	—	—	—	—	—	—	—	—
Italy	-1.5	1.7	2.3	11.2	0.7	2.5	2.8	11.7	0.7
Japan	24.4	24.6	17.5	20.6	34.7	29.6	22.6	23.8	35.6
Netherlands	9.4	7.8	6.3	11.5	9.0	7.5	4.8	11.5	9.0
New Zealand	—	—	—	—	—	—	—	—	—
Norway	1.4	2.0	1.4	2.2	1.4	2.0	1.4	2.2	1.4
Sweden	0.8	-0.8	0.3	0.1	1.2	1.0	1.3	0.5	1.2
Switzerland	3.0	-2.0	-16.8	10.5	2.4	4.2	3.7	10.5	2.4
United Kingdom	-8.7	-5.4	0.4	-1.9	1.7	1.5	1.8	2.9	1.8
United States	55.0	35.0	64.0	100.0	59.0	36.0	65.0	103.0	68.0
TOTAL	*90.8*	*100.4*	*125.8*	*171.1*	*133.5*	*109.6*	*126.4*	*196.6*	*143.9*
MULTILATERAL									
AF.D.F.	—	—	—	—	—	—	—	—	—
AF.D.B.	—	—	—	—	—	—	—	—	—
AS.D.B	—	—	—	—	—	—	—	—	—
CAR.D.B.	—	—	—	—	—	—	—	—	—
E.E.C.	5.1	12.3	15.1	22.0	5.1	12.3	15.1	22.0	5.1
IBRD	0.5	-2.0	-1.2	-14.6	0.3	0.2	—	—	0.3
IDA	2.8	1.3	0.7	3.0	2.8	1.3	0.7	3.0	3.3
I.D.B.	28.3	41.1	43.8	106.0	20.4	37.6	37.2	82.5	23.2
IFAD	0.7	0.6	3.4	2.3	0.7	0.6	3.4	2.3	0.7
I.F.C.	-0.3	-0.1	—	-0.4	—	—	—	—	—
IMF TRUST FUND	—	—	—	—	—	—	—	—	—
U.N. AGENCIES	—	—	—	—	—	—	—	—	—
UNDP	2.9	2.7	7.6	7.0	2.9	2.7	7.6	7.0	2.9
UNTA	1.0	0.6	0.8	0.9	1.0	0.6	0.8	0.9	1.0
UNICEF	1.6	2.3	3.3	1.9	1.6	2.3	3.3	1.9	1.6
UNRWA	—	—	—	—	—	—	—	—	—
WFP	3.5	3.6	5.3	5.2	3.5	3.6	5.3	5.2	3.5
UNHCR	0.2	—	—	—	0.2	—	—	—	0.2
Other Multilateral	0.8	0.8	1.0	0.5	0.8	0.8	1.0	0.5	0.8
Arab OPEC Agencies	1.1	0.5	1.2	-0.4	1.1	0.5	1.2	-0.4	1.2
TOTAL	*48.0*	*63.6*	*81.1*	*133.3*	*40.2*	*62.4*	*75.7*	*124.8*	*43.7*
OPEC COUNTRIES	—	*-0.2*	—	—	—	—	—	—	—
E.E.C.+ MEMBERS	*7.0*	*43.8*	*72.1*	*55.7*	*35.1*	*39.0*	*45.1*	*74.6*	*35.6*
TOTAL	**138.8**	**163.7**	**206.9**	**304.4**	**173.6**	**171.9**	**202.1**	**321.4**	**187.5**

ODA LOANS GROSS / ODA LOANS NET / GRANTS

	ODA LOANS GROSS				ODA LOANS NET				GRANTS
	1983	1984	1985	1986	1983	1984	1985	1986	1983
DAC COUNTRIES									
Australia	—	—	—	—	—	—	—	—	—
Austria	—	—	—	—	—	—	—	—	0.2
Belgium	1.5	—	—	—	1.5	—	—	—	1.3
Canada	—	—	—	—	0.0	0.0	0.0	0.0	4.4
Denmark	1.7	0.7	4.6	0.0	1.5	0.6	4.5	-5.4	1.0
Finland	—	—	—	—	—	—	—	—	0.1
France	1.0	0.6	1.9	—	1.0	0.6	1.8	0.0	1.8
Germany, Fed. Rep.	2.4	1.4	0.7	1.9	2.3	1.1	0.1	1.7	8.3
Ireland	—	—	—	—	—	—	—	—	—
Italy	—	—	—	—	—	—	—	—	0.7
Japan	26.2	15.2	8.5	8.5	25.2	14.3	7.6	7.9	9.5
Netherlands	—	—	—	—	—	—	—	—	9.0
New Zealand	—	—	—	—	—	—	—	—	—
Norway	—	—	—	—	—	—	—	—	1.4
Sweden	—	—	—	—	—	—	—	—	1.2
Switzerland	—	—	—	—	—	—	—	—	2.4
United Kingdom	—	—	—	—	-0.1	0.0	—	—	1.8
United States	1.0	3.0	39.0	32.0	-8.0	-2.0	31.0	25.0	67.0
TOTAL	*33.8*	*20.9*	*54.7*	*42.4*	*23.3*	*14.5*	*45.0*	*29.0*	*110.1*
MULTILATERAL	*24.3*	*43.1*	*48.1*	*94.0*	*20.8*	*39.3*	*42.5*	*86.7*	*19.4*
OPEC COUNTRIES	—	—	—	—	—	—	—	—	—
E.E.C.+ MEMBERS	*6.6*	*2.7*	*7.1*	*1.9*	*6.2*	*2.3*	*6.4*	*-3.8*	*29.0*
TOTAL	**58.1**	**64.0**	**102.7**	**136.4**	**44.1**	**53.9**	**87.5**	**115.7**	**129.5**

TOTAL OFFICIAL GROSS / TOTAL OFFICIAL NET / TOTAL OOF GROSS

	TOTAL OFFICIAL GROSS				TOTAL OFFICIAL NET				TOTAL OOF GROSS
	1983	1984	1985	1986	1983	1984	1985	1986	1983
DAC COUNTRIES									
Australia	—	0.0	—	—	—	0.0	—	—	—
Austria	0.2	0.1	0.1	0.1	0.2	0.1	0.1	0.1	—
Belgium	2.8	2.1	2.0	2.4	2.8	2.1	2.0	2.4	—
Canada	4.4	9.8	2.2	3.8	4.2	9.7	2.2	3.8	—
Denmark	2.7	1.2	4.8	6.2	2.5	1.1	4.8	0.8	—
Finland	0.1	0.1	0.1	0.1	0.1	0.1	0.1	0.1	—
France	2.8	2.8	2.9	3.8	2.8	2.8	2.8	3.8	—
Germany, Fed. Rep.	10.7	10.8	14.2	26.1	9.4	9.4	13.0	25.8	—
Ireland	—	—	—	—	—	—	—	—	—
Italy	0.7	2.5	2.8	11.7	0.7	2.5	2.8	11.7	—
Japan	35.6	30.6	23.6	24.5	34.7	29.6	22.6	23.8	—
Netherlands	9.0	7.5	4.8	11.5	9.0	7.5	4.8	11.5	—
New Zealand	—	—	—	—	—	—	—	—	—
Norway	1.4	2.0	1.4	2.2	1.4	2.0	1.4	2.2	—
Sweden	1.2	1.0	1.3	0.5	1.2	1.0	1.3	0.1	—
Switzerland	2.4	4.2	3.7	10.5	2.4	4.2	3.7	10.5	—
United Kingdom	1.8	1.6	1.8	2.9	1.7	1.5	1.8	2.9	—
United States	68.0	41.0	73.0	113.0	55.0	35.0	64.0	100.0	—
TOTAL	*143.9*	*117.3*	*138.8*	*219.3*	*128.1*	*108.7*	*127.6*	*199.4*	*—*
MULTILATERAL	*61.2*	*84.5*	*102.7*	*164.2*	*48.0*	*63.6*	*81.1*	*133.3*	*17.6*
OPEC COUNTRIES	—	—	—	—	—	*-0.2*	—	—	—
E.E.C.+ MEMBERS	*35.6*	*40.8*	*48.5*	*86.6*	*34.0*	*39.2*	*47.3*	*80.8*	*—*
TOTAL	**205.1**	**201.8**	**241.5**	**383.5**	**176.1**	**172.1**	**208.7**	**332.8**	**17.6**

ODA COMMITMENTS

1984	1985	1986	1983	1984	1985	1986
0.0	–	–	–	0.0	–	–
0.1	0.1	0.1	0.1	0.1	0.1	–
1.6	1.6	2.4	2.2	1.0	0.8	2.4
9.8	2.2	3.8	3.9	9.3	1.7	2.7
1.2	4.8	6.2	1.5	6.7	0.1	0.1
0.1	0.1	0.1	0.1	0.1	0.1	0.1
2.8	2.9	3.8	6.3	2.2	0.9	3.8
9.9	11.9	19.8	9.2	11.6	14.1	38.0
–	–	–	–	–	–	–
2.5	2.8	11.7	0.8	2.4	8.9	13.6
30.6	23.6	24.5	63.6	17.1	18.5	21.4
7.5	4.8	11.5	10.7	10.4	2.8	19.4
–	–	–	–	–	–	–
2.0	1.4	2.2	4.1	2.2	2.8	1.8
1.0	1.3	0.5	2.8	0.4	0.6	0.5
4.2	3.7	10.5	2.6	3.8	4.6	8.3
1.6	1.8	2.9	1.8	1.6	1.8	2.9
41.0	73.0	110.0	94.8	60.9	51.1	75.1
115.9	*136.1*	*210.0*	*204.4*	*129.7*	*108.9*	*190.1*
–	–	–	–	–	–	–
–	–	–	–	–	–	–
–	–	–	–	–	–	–
12.3	15.1	22.0	20.6	27.0	8.7	21.5
0.2	–	–	–	–	–	–
2.1	1.7	4.0	–	–	–	70.0
40.5	41.5	88.0	58.9	9.2	–	11.6
0.7	3.7	2.6	0.2	11.1	0.3	–
–	–	–	–	–	–	–
–	–	–	9.9	10.0	18.1	15.5
2.7	7.6	7.0	–	–	–	–
0.6	0.8	0.9	–	–	–	–
2.3	3.3	1.9	–	–	–	–
–	–	–	–	–	–	–
3.6	5.3	5.2	–	–	–	–
0.8	1.0	0.5	–	–	–	–
0.5	1.2	–	–	2.0	3.0	–
66.2	*81.3*	*132.1*	*89.6*	*59.3*	*30.1*	*118.6*
–	–	–	–	–	–	–
39.4	*45.8*	*80.2*	*53.1*	*62.8*	*38.1*	*101.6*
182.1	*217.3*	*342.1*	*294.1*	*188.9*	*138.9*	*308.7*

TECH. COOP. GRANTS

1984	1985	1986	1983	1984	1985	1986
0.0	–	–	–	–	–	–
0.1	0.1	0.1	0.2	–	–	–
1.6	1.6	2.4	0.3	0.3	0.2	0.3
9.8	2.2	3.8	1.2	–	1.7	–
0.5	0.3	6.2	0.4	0.1	0.1	0.2
0.1	0.1	0.1	0.0	0.1	0.1	–
2.2	1.0	3.8	1.4	2.0	0.9	3.8
8.5	11.2	17.9	7.2	8.1	11.0	17.1
–	–	–	–	–	–	–
2.5	2.8	11.7	0.2	1.6	2.8	5.8
15.4	15.0	15.9	5.4	5.6	5.3	8.7
7.5	4.8	11.5	1.4	1.3	1.9	1.7
–	–	–	–	–	–	–
2.0	1.4	2.2	–	0.0	0.0	0.1
1.0	1.3	0.5	–	0.1	0.2	0.3
4.2	3.7	10.5	0.7	0.6	0.5	1.7
1.6	1.8	2.9	1.6	1.4	1.7	2.6
38.0	34.0	78.0	2.0	2.0	4.0	6.0
95.0	*81.4*	*167.6*	*22.0*	*23.0*	*30.4*	*48.2*
23.1	*33.2*	*38.1*	*6.4*	*6.4*	*12.8*	*10.4*
–	–	–	–	–	–	–
36.8	*38.6*	*78.3*	*12.5*	*14.7*	*18.6*	*31.5*
118.1	*114.6*	*205.7*	*28.4*	*29.5*	*43.1*	*58.6*

TOTAL OOF NET

1984	1985	1986	1983	1984	1985	1986
–	–	–	–	–	–	–
0.5	0.5	0.0	–	0.5	0.5	0.0
–	0.0	–	-0.2	–	–	–
–	–	–	–	–	0.0	–
–	–	–	–	–	–	–
0.9	2.3	6.3	-1.2	-0.3	1.7	6.3
–	–	–	–	–	–	–
–	–	–	–	–	–	–
–	–	–	–	–	–	–
–	–	–	–	–	–	–
–	–	–	–	–	–	-0.4
–	–	–	–	–	–	–
–	–	3.0	-4.0	-1.0	-1.0	-3.0
1.4	*2.7*	*9.3*	*-5.4*	*-0.9*	*1.2*	*2.8*
18.3	*21.4*	*32.1*	*7.9*	*1.2*	*5.4*	*8.5*
–	–	–	–	-0.2	–	–
1.4	*2.7*	*6.3*	*-1.2*	*0.1*	*2.2*	*6.3*
19.7	*24.2*	*41.5*	*2.5*	*0.1*	*6.6*	*11.3*

ODA COMMITMENTS : LOANS

DAC COUNTRIES

	1983	1984	1985	1986
Australia	–	–	–	–
Austria	–	–	–	–
Belgium	1.5	–	–	–
Canada	–	–	–	–
Denmark	–	6.3	–	–
Finland	–	–	–	–
France	3.9	–	–	–
Germany, Fed. Rep.	–	1.6	3.4	17.7
Ireland	–	–	–	–
Italy	–	–	–	–
Japan	53.4	1.9	1.9	2.6
Netherlands	–	–	–	–
New Zealand	–	–	–	–
Norway	–	–	–	–
Sweden	–	–	–	–
Switzerland	–	–	–	–
United Kingdom	–	–	–	–
United States	16.0	31.5	31.5	6.3
TOTAL	*74.8*	*41.2*	*36.8*	*26.6*
MULTILATERAL	*58.9*	*22.3*	*3.0*	*81.6*
OPEC COUNTRIES	–	–	–	–
E.E.C.+ MEMBERS	*5.4*	*7.9*	*3.4*	*17.7*
TOTAL	*133.7*	*63.5*	*39.8*	*108.2*

GRANT ELEMENT OF ODA

DAC COUNTRIES

	1983	1984	1985	1986
Australia	–	100.0	–	–
Austria	100.0	100.0	100.0	–
Belgium	89.6	100.0	100.0	100.0
Canada	100.0	100.0	100.0	100.0
Denmark	100.0	77.6	100.0	100.0
Finland	100.0	100.0	100.0	100.0
France	79.5	100.0	100.0	100.0
Germany, Fed. Rep.	100.0	95.4	91.8	84.2
Ireland	–	–	–	–
Italy	100.0	100.0	100.0	100.0
Japan	59.8	91.9	96.1	95.2
Netherlands	100.0	100.0	100.0	100.0
New Zealand	–	–	–	–
Norway	100.0	100.0	100.0	100.0
Sweden	100.0	100.0	100.0	100.0
Switzerland	100.0	100.0	100.0	100.0
United Kingdom	100.0	100.0	100.0	100.0
United States	95.1	85.1	80.8	97.6
TOTAL	*84.5*	*90.4*	*89.2*	*95.3*
MULTILATERAL	*79.8*	*89.5*	*89.0*	*87.1*
OPEC COUNTRIES	–	–	–	–
E.E.C.+ MEMBERS	*97.1*	*96.8*	*97.0*	*94.1*
TOTAL	*82.2*	*90.1*	*89.1*	*92.2*

OTHER AGGREGATES

COMMITMENTS: ALL SOURCES

	1983	1984	1985	1986
TOTAL BILATERAL	209.5	129.7	108.9	194.5
of which				
OPEC	3.0	–	–	–
CMEA	–	–	–	–
TOTAL MULTILATERAL	89.6	128.1	30.1	250.7
TOTAL BIL.& MULTIL.	299.1	257.7	138.9	445.3
of which				
ODA Grants	160.4	125.4	99.2	200.5
ODA Loans	133.7	63.5	39.8	108.2

DISBURSEMENTS:

DAC COUNTRIES COMBINED

	1983	1984	1985	1986
OFFICIAL & PRIVATE				
GROSS:				
Contractual Lending	38.1	32.5	63.5	46.4
Export Credits Total	4.4	10.7	6.5	-5.4
Export Credits Private	4.4	10.7	6.5	-5.4
NET:				
Contractual Lending	-15.2	-9.4	21.2	11.3
Export Credits Total	-38.6	-24.7	-25.5	-27.1
PRIVATE SECTOR NET	-37.3	-8.3	-1.7	-28.4
Direct Investment	0.2	0.2	0.9	1.2
Portfolio Investment	-4.3	14.1	21.8	-8.9
Export Credits	-33.2	-22.6	-24.5	-20.6

MARKET BORROWING:

CHANGE IN CLAIMS

	1983	1984	1985	1986
Banks	–	-45.0	-83.0	-20.0

MEMORANDUM ITEM:

	1983	1984	1985	1986
CMEA Countr.(Gross)	1.0	0.3	–	–

TOTAL RECEIPTS NET / TOTAL ODA NET / TOTAL ODA GROSS

	TOTAL RECEIPTS NET 1983	1984	1985	1986	TOTAL ODA NET 1983	1984	1985	1986	TOTAL ODA GROSS 1983
DAC COUNTRIES									
Australia	0.5	0.5	0.5	0.4	0.5	0.5	0.5	0.4	0.5
Austria	0.0	0.0	–	0.0	0.0	0.0	–	0.0	0.0
Belgium	–	0.1	0.1	0.5	–	0.1	0.0	0.2	–
Canada	3.6	4.9	4.8	23.5	3.6	4.9	4.9	7.6	3.6
Denmark	0.3	1.0	2.2	6.7	0.3	1.0	2.2	6.7	0.3
Finland	0.2	0.0	0.0	0.4	0.2	0.0	0.0	0.4	0.2
France	1.3	1.0	0.8	2.0	0.2	0.3	0.3	1.5	0.2
Germany, Fed. Rep.	23.1	39.5	23.7	43.2	20.1	13.0	13.2	12.5	20.1
Ireland	0.0	–	–	0.1	0.0	–	–	0.1	0.0
Italy	0.6	0.2	0.0	0.3	–	0.2	0.0	0.3	–
Japan	0.1	0.3	-0.1	1.2	0.1	0.1	0.0	1.2	0.1
Netherlands	3.3	1.9	2.8	5.0	3.3	1.9	2.1	4.6	3.3
New Zealand	0.0	–	0.0	0.1	0.0	–	0.0	0.1	0.0
Norway	8.0	7.8	11.1	11.7	8.0	7.8	11.1	11.7	8.0
Sweden	11.9	11.0	7.3	21.8	11.6	11.0	7.3	16.3	11.6
Switzerland	0.0	0.7	-0.6	0.2	0.0	0.0	0.0	0.2	0.0
United Kingdom	16.7	39.6	17.6	12.0	13.7	11.0	6.3	8.2	15.1
United States	13.0	13.0	11.0	10.0	13.0	13.0	11.0	10.0	13.0
TOTAL	*82.5*	*121.6*	*81.3*	*138.9*	*74.6*	*64.9*	*59.1*	*82.0*	*76.0*
MULTILATERAL									
AF.D.F.	0.6	4.2	2.3	0.4	0.6	4.2	2.3	0.4	0.6
AF.D.B.	0.9	1.9	18.9	9.9	–	–	–	–	–
AS.D.B	–	–	–	–	–	–	–	–	–
CAR.D.B.	–	–	–	–	–	–	–	–	–
E.E.C.	5.2	11.2	7.1	7.2	2.1	6.8	2.8	7.2	2.1
IBRD	14.5	16.6	14.5	-1.2	–	–	–	–	–
IDA	-0.1	-0.1	-0.2	-0.2	-0.1	-0.1	-0.2	-0.2	–
I.D.B.	–	–	–	–	–	–	–	–	–
IFAD	0.1	0.3	0.8	0.4	0.1	0.3	0.8	0.4	0.1
I.F.C.	–	–	–	0.2	–	–	–	–	–
IMF TRUST FUND	–	–	–	–	–	–	–	–	–
U.N. AGENCIES	–	–	–	–	–	–	–	–	–
UNDP	1.7	2.2	2.4	2.1	1.7	2.2	2.4	2.1	1.7
UNTA	0.3	0.4	0.6	0.7	0.3	0.4	0.6	0.7	0.3
UNICEF	0.2	0.3	0.2	0.6	0.2	0.3	0.2	0.6	0.2
UNRWA	–	–	–	–	–	–	–	–	–
WFP	9.9	10.3	22.1	9.3	9.9	10.3	22.1	9.3	9.9
UNHCR	0.9	1.2	1.1	1.0	0.9	1.2	1.1	1.0	0.9
Other Multilateral	0.9	1.2	1.1	1.9	0.9	1.2	1.1	1.9	0.9
Arab OPEC Agencies	3.9	0.6	3.3	-1.4	4.0	0.7	1.0	-1.9	4.3
TOTAL	*39.1*	*50.4*	*74.1*	*30.9*	*20.6*	*27.6*	*34.2*	*21.5*	*21.1*
OPEC COUNTRIES	*8.5*	*10.1*	*3.2*	*-1.1*	*8.5*	*10.1*	*3.2*	*-1.1*	*8.5*
E.E.C.+ MEMBERS	*50.4*	*94.6*	*54.4*	*76.8*	*39.7*	*34.3*	*27.0*	*41.2*	*41.1*
TOTAL	*130.0*	*182.2*	*158.6*	*168.7*	*103.6*	*102.7*	*96.5*	*102.3*	*105.5*

ODA LOANS GROSS / ODA LOANS NET / GRANTS

	ODA LOANS GROSS 1983	1984	1985	1986	ODA LOANS NET 1983	1984	1985	1986	GRANTS 1983
DAC COUNTRIES									
Australia	–	–	–	–	–	–	–	–	0.5
Austria	–	–	–	–	–	–	–	–	0.0
Belgium	–	–	–	–	–	–	–	–	–
Canada	–	–	–	–	–	–	–	–	3.6
Denmark	–	–	–	–	–	–	–	–	0.3
Finland	–	–	–	–	–	–	–	–	0.2
France	–	0.1	0.2	0.8	–	0.1	0.2	0.8	0.2
Germany, Fed. Rep.	–	–	–	–	–	–	–	–	20.1
Ireland	–	–	–	–	–	–	–	–	0.0
Italy	–	–	–	–	–	–	–	–	–
Japan	–	–	–	1.2	–	–	–	1.2	0.1
Netherlands	–	–	0.1	0.6	–	–	0.1	0.6	3.3
New Zealand	–	–	–	–	–	–	–	–	0.0
Norway	–	–	–	–	–	–	–	–	8.0
Sweden	–	–	–	–	–	–	–	–	11.6
Switzerland	–	–	–	–	–	–	–	–	0.0
United Kingdom	0.1	0.0	0.1	–	-1.3	-1.5	-1.5	-1.7	15.0
United States	–	–	–	–	–	–	–	-1.0	13.0
TOTAL	*0.1*	*0.1*	*0.3*	*2.6*	*-1.3*	*-1.5*	*-1.2*	*-0.2*	*75.9*
MULTILATERAL	*5.0*	*7.0*	*5.1*	*1.0*	*4.5*	*6.2*	*3.8*	*-1.5*	*16.1*
OPEC COUNTRIES	*8.5*	*10.5*	*4.7*	*0.2*	*8.5*	*10.1*	*3.2*	*-1.1*	*–*
E.E.C.+ MEMBERS	*0.1*	*1.2*	*0.3*	*1.4*	*-1.3*	*-0.3*	*-1.2*	*-0.5*	*41.0*
TOTAL	*13.6*	*17.6*	*10.2*	*3.7*	*11.7*	*14.9*	*5.9*	*-2.8*	*92.0*

TOTAL OFFICIAL GROSS / TOTAL OFFICIAL NET / TOTAL OOF GROSS

	TOTAL OFFICIAL GROSS 1983	1984	1985	1986	TOTAL OFFICIAL NET 1983	1984	1985	1986	TOTAL OOF GROSS 1983
DAC COUNTRIES									
Australia	0.5	0.5	0.5	0.4	0.5	0.5	0.5	0.4	–
Austria	0.0	0.0	–	0.0	0.0	0.0	–	0.0	–
Belgium	–	0.1	0.1	0.2	–	0.1	0.1	0.2	–
Canada	3.6	4.9	4.9	24.2	3.6	4.9	4.8	23.5	–
Denmark	0.3	1.0	2.2	6.7	0.3	1.0	2.2	6.7	–
Finland	0.2	0.0	0.0	0.4	0.2	0.0	0.0	0.4	–
France	0.2	0.3	0.3	1.5	0.2	0.3	0.3	1.5	–
Germany, Fed. Rep.	22.8	46.0	33.9	43.3	22.8	46.0	26.8	43.3	2.6
Ireland	0.0	–	–	0.1	0.0	–	–	0.1	–
Italy	–	0.2	0.0	0.3	–	0.2	0.0	0.3	–
Japan	0.1	0.1	0.0	1.2	0.1	0.1	0.0	1.2	–
Netherlands	3.3	1.9	2.8	5.0	3.3	1.9	2.8	5.0	–
New Zealand	0.0	–	0.0	0.1	0.0	–	0.0	0.1	–
Norway	8.0	7.8	11.1	11.7	8.0	7.8	11.1	11.7	–
Sweden	11.6	11.0	7.3	21.6	11.6	11.0	7.3	21.6	–
Switzerland	0.0	0.0	0.0	0.2	0.0	0.0	0.0	0.2	–
United Kingdom	20.2	21.4	11.4	18.8	17.4	18.5	8.3	16.1	5.1
United States	13.0	13.0	11.0	11.0	13.0	13.0	11.0	10.0	–
TOTAL	*83.6*	*108.3*	*85.5*	*146.7*	*80.9*	*105.5*	*75.3*	*142.2*	*7.7*
MULTILATERAL	*43.6*	*56.5*	*82.0*	*42.8*	*39.1*	*50.4*	*74.1*	*30.9*	*22.4*
OPEC COUNTRIES	*8.5*	*10.5*	*4.7*	*0.2*	*8.5*	*10.1*	*3.2*	*-1.1*	*–*
E.E.C.+ MEMBERS	*52.0*	*82.5*	*58.2*	*83.8*	*49.1*	*79.3*	*47.6*	*80.3*	*10.9*
TOTAL	*135.6*	*175.3*	*172.3*	*189.8*	*128.4*	*166.1*	*152.7*	*172.0*	*30.1*

MILLION US DOLLARS, UNLESS OTHERWISE STATED

ODA COMMITMENTS

1984	1985	1986	1983	1984	1985	1986
0.5	0.5	0.4	0.3	0.5	0.4	0.3
0.0	–	0.0	–	–	–	–
0.1	0.0	0.2	–	–	–	1.3
4.9	4.9	7.6	5.0	5.8	6.8	8.6
1.0	2.2	6.7	0.5	0.5	7.3	15.3
0.0	0.0	0.4	0.1	0.0	–	0.5
0.3	0.3	1.5	6.6	5.8	0.2	1.5
13.0	13.2	12.5	18.0	23.8	4.9	15.1
–	–	0.1	0.0	–	–	0.1
0.2	0.0	0.3	–	0.2	0.0	0.3
0.1	0.0	1.2	0.2	0.0	0.0	12.5
1.9	2.1	4.6	2.5	3.2	2.1	4.9
–	0.0	0.1	–	–	–	–
7.8	11.1	11.7	9.9	11.5	16.1	15.6
11.0	7.3	16.3	12.6	10.9	10.6	16.3
0.0	0.0	0.2	–	0.0	0.5	0.1
12.6	7.9	9.9	16.6	10.0	7.0	9.3
13.0	11.0	11.0	11.3	15.9	12.6	16.1
66.5	60.6	84.7	83.5	88.1	68.5	117.9
4.2	2.4	0.5	–	–	8.6	–
–	–	–	–	–	–	–
6.8	2.8	7.3	4.2	4.2	8.4	11.4
–	–	–	–	–	–	–
0.3	0.8	0.4	–	–	–	–
–	–	–	–	–	–	–
–	–	–	14.0	15.7	27.5	15.6
2.2	2.4	2.1	–	–	–	–
0.4	0.6	0.7	–	–	–	–
0.3	0.2	0.6	–	–	–	–
–	–	–	–	–	–	–
10.3	22.1	9.3	–	–	–	–
1.2	1.1	1.0	–	–	–	–
1.2	1.1	1.9	–	–	–	–
1.3	2.0	–	–	2.0	–	–
28.4	35.5	23.9	18.2	22.0	44.5	27.0
10.5	4.7	0.2	–	–	–	–
35.9	28.5	43.1	48.3	47.8	29.9	59.4
105.4	100.7	108.8	101.7	110.1	113.1	144.9

TECH. COOP. GRANTS

1984	1985	1986	1983	1984	1985	1986
0.5	0.5	0.4	0.3	0.3	0.4	0.3
0.0	–	0.0	0.0	–	–	–
0.1	0.0	0.2	–	–	–	–
4.9	4.9	7.6	3.1	–	3.1	–
1.0	2.2	6.7	0.3	0.4	1.2	1.6
0.0	0.0	0.4	0.1	0.0	0.0	0.1
0.3	0.2	0.7	0.2	0.3	0.2	0.7
13.0	13.2	12.5	6.4	6.4	5.9	8.2
–	–	0.1	0.0	–	–	0.1
0.2	0.0	0.3	–	–	0.0	0.0
0.1	0.0	0.0	0.1	0.0	0.0	0.0
1.9	2.0	4.1	2.0	1.9	1.7	2.4
–	0.0	0.1	0.0	–	0.0	0.1
7.8	11.1	11.7	2.8	3.4	3.4	4.2
11.0	7.3	16.3	2.7	2.3	2.4	3.5
0.0	0.0	0.2	0.0	–	–	0.0
12.6	7.8	9.9	8.4	6.4	5.3	7.0
13.0	11.0	11.0	10.0	8.0	8.0	8.0
66.4	60.3	82.1	36.4	29.4	31.5	36.2
21.4	30.3	22.9	4.1	5.4	5.4	7.2
–	–	–	–	–	–	–
34.7	28.2	41.7	17.3	15.3	14.2	21.0
87.8	90.6	105.1	40.5	34.8	36.9	43.4

TOTAL OOF NET

1984	1985	1986	1983	1984	1985	1986
–	–	–	–	–	–	–
0.0	0.0	–	–	0.0	0.0	–
–	–	16.6	–	–	-0.1	15.9
0.0	0.0	–	–	0.0	0.0	–
–	–	–	–	–	–	–
33.0	20.7	30.9	2.6	33.0	13.7	30.8
–	–	–	–	–	–	–
–	0.7	0.4	–	–	0.7	0.4
–	–	–	–	–	–	–
–	–	5.3	–	–	–	5.3
–	–	–	–	–	–	–
8.8	3.5	8.8	3.7	7.5	1.9	7.8
–	–	–	–	–	–	–
41.8	24.9	62.0	6.3	40.6	16.3	60.3
28.1	46.6	18.9	18.4	22.8	39.9	9.4
–	–	–	–	–	–	–
46.6	29.6	40.7	9.4	45.0	20.6	39.1
69.9	71.5	81.0	24.8	63.4	56.2	69.7

ODA COMMITMENTS : LOANS

DAC COUNTRIES

	1983	1984	1985	1986
Australia	–	–	–	–
Austria	–	–	–	–
Belgium	–	–	–	1.2
Canada	–	–	–	–
Denmark	–	–	–	–
Finland	–	–	–	–
France	6.4	5.6	–	0.8
Germany, Fed. Rep.	–	–	–	–
Ireland	–	–	–	–
Italy	–	–	–	–
Japan	–	–	–	12.5
Netherlands	–	–	0.1	–
New Zealand	–	–	–	–
Norway	–	–	–	–
Sweden	–	–	–	–
Switzerland	–	–	–	–
United Kingdom	–	–	–	–
United States	–	–	–	–
TOTAL	6.4	5.6	0.1	14.4
MULTILATERAL	–	2.6	8.6	–
OPEC COUNTRIES	–	–	–	–
E.E.C.+ MEMBERS	6.4	6.2	0.1	2.0
TOTAL	6.4	8.2	8.7	14.4

GRANT ELEMENT OF ODA

DAC COUNTRIES

	1983	1984	1985	1986
Australia	100.0	100.0	100.0	100.0
Austria	–	–	–	–
Belgium	–	–	–	81.7
Canada	100.0	100.0	100.0	100.0
Denmark	100.0	100.0	100.0	100.0
Finland	100.0	100.0	–	100.0
France	100.0	60.8	100.0	100.0
Germany, Fed. Rep.	100.0	100.0	100.0	100.0
Ireland	100.0	–	–	100.0
Italy	–	100.0	100.0	100.0
Japan	100.0	100.0	100.0	51.1
Netherlands	100.0	100.0	100.0	100.0
New Zealand	–	–	–	–
Norway	100.0	100.0	100.0	100.0
Sweden	100.0	100.0	100.0	100.0
Switzerland	–	100.0	100.0	100.0
United Kingdom	100.0	100.0	100.0	100.0
United States	100.0	100.0	100.0	100.0
TOTAL	100.0	97.4	100.0	94.6
MULTILATERAL	100.0	93.2	96.7	100.0
OPEC COUNTRIES	–	–	–	–
E.E.C.+ MEMBERS	100.0	95.2	100.0	99.6
TOTAL	100.0	96.6	98.7	95.6

OTHER AGGREGATES

COMMITMENTS: ALL SOURCES

	1983	1984	1985	1986
TOTAL BILATERAL	109.6	104.6	93.9	149.4
of which				
OPEC	–	–	–	–
CMEA	–	–	–	–
TOTAL MULTILATERAL	78.2	67.9	106.8	34.6
TOTAL BIL.& MULTIL.	187.9	172.4	200.7	184.1
of which				
ODA Grants	95.3	101.9	104.3	130.5
ODA Loans	6.4	8.2	8.7	14.4

DISBURSEMENTS:

DAC COUNTRIES COMBINED

	1983	1984	1985	1986
OFFICIAL & PRIVATE				
GROSS:				
Contractual Lending	11.2	67.1	37.4	75.7
Export Credits Total	3.4	25.6	12.2	33.1
Export Credits Private	3.4	25.2	12.1	11.1
NET:				
Contractual Lending	5.2	59.8	23.5	56.5
Export Credits Total	0.2	21.2	8.3	17.6
PRIVATE SECTOR NET	1.6	16.1	6.0	-3.3
Direct Investment	1.1	1.7	0.4	0.8
Portfolio Investment	0.4	-6.4	-2.9	-0.5
Export Credits	0.2	20.8	8.4	-3.6

MARKET BORROWING:

CHANGE IN CLAIMS

	1983	1984	1985	1986
Banks	–	–	–	–

MEMORANDUM ITEM:

	1983	1984	1985	1986
CMEA Countr.(Gross)	–	–	–	–

DISBURSEMENTS, UNLESS OTHERWISE STATED

	1983	1984	1985	1986	1983	1984	1985	1986		1983
TOTAL RECEIPTS NET					**TOTAL ODA NET**				**TOTAL ODA GROSS**	
DAC COUNTRIES										
Australia	0.0	0.0	0.7	-0.1	0.0	0.0	0.0	0.0	Australia	0.0
Austria	0.3	-3.0	-2.0	0.1	0.3	0.2	0.1	0.1	Austria	0.5
Belgium	-96.1	453.3	-325.7	-474.9	1.4	1.1	1.5	1.3	Belgium	1.4
Canada	36.8	26.4	1.5	11.4	2.1	7.1	5.8	4.4	Canada	2.8
Denmark	-3.1	0.9	-0.2	-2.3	–	–	–	–	Denmark	–
Finland	-0.9	-0.1	-0.1	0.4	0.0	0.0	0.0	0.2	Finland	0.0
France	649.8	877.3	167.9	17.7	18.7	30.2	21.1	16.8	France	19.7
Germany, Fed. Rep.	666.0	702.0	720.6	338.9	41.3	35.1	35.7	52.0	Germany, Fed. Rep.	45.3
Ireland	0.0	0.0	0.0	0.0	0.0	0.0	0.0	0.0	Ireland	0.0
Italy	172.5	279.3	273.3	-48.0	2.6	3.8	3.8	7.4	Italy	2.6
Japan	223.0	1040.4	123.3	112.1	27.1	35.6	40.6	32.3	Japan	29.0
Netherlands	192.3	75.1	-14.3	48.1	3.9	6.6	5.7	4.3	Netherlands	4.1
New Zealand	–	–	–	–	–	–	–	–	New Zealand	–
Norway	0.0	4.7	1.6	1.7	–	0.3	0.3	0.3	Norway	–
Sweden	15.4	72.4	9.1	16.1	0.4	0.1	0.1	–	Sweden	0.4
Switzerland	77.4	0.5	14.1	1.1	0.6	0.7	0.4	1.1	Switzerland	0.6
United Kingdom	90.7	383.4	66.0	-29.9	8.1	8.2	5.2	1.3	United Kingdom	8.5
United States	2892.0	2695.0	-333.0	-450.0	-13.0	11.0	-56.0	11.0	United States	2.0
TOTAL	4916.0	6607.6	702.7	-457.6	93.5	139.9	64.2	132.6	TOTAL	116.7
MULTILATERAL										
AF.D.F.	–	–	–	–	–	–	–	–	AF.D.F.	–
AF.D.B.	–	–	–	–	–	–	–	–	AF.D.B.	–
AS.D.B	–	–	–	–	–	–	–	–	AS.D.B	–
CAR.D.B.	–	–	–	–	–	–	–	–	CAR.D.B.	–
E.E.C.	0.7	0.4	0.9	1.4	0.7	0.4	0.9	1.4	E.E.C.	0.7
IBRD	931.0	938.9	350.7	993.6	–	–	–	–	IBRD	–
IDA	–	–	–	–	–	–	–	–	IDA	–
I.D.B.	148.5	216.6	284.5	163.4	-6.2	6.7	37.4	30.3	I.D.B.	36.2
IFAD	1.0	-0.3	1.3	0.5	1.0	-0.3	1.3	0.5	IFAD	1.0
I.F.C.	77.4	11.5	-10.5	-81.7	–	–	–	–	I.F.C.	–
IMF TRUST FUND	–	–	–	–	–	–	–	–	IMF TRUST FUND	–
U.N. AGENCIES	–	–	–	–	–	–	–	–	U.N. AGENCIES	–
UNDP	8.8	6.9	5.9	6.9	8.8	6.9	5.9	6.9	UNDP	8.8
UNTA	1.3	1.3	2.0	2.2	1.3	1.3	2.0	2.2	UNTA	1.3
UNICEF	1.1	1.1	1.1	1.4	1.1	1.1	1.1	1.4	UNICEF	1.1
UNRWA	–	–	–	–	–	–	–	–	UNRWA	–
WFP	1.4	6.4	9.2	2.7	1.4	6.4	9.2	2.7	WFP	1.4
UNHCR	–	0.0	–	–	–	0.0	–	–	UNHCR	–
Other Multilateral	0.5	0.8	2.5	1.8	0.5	0.8	2.5	1.8	Other Multilateral	0.5
Arab OPEC Agencies	–	–	–	–	–	–	–	–	Arab OPEC Agencies	–
TOTAL	1171.6	1183.6	647.5	1092.3	8.6	23.4	60.3	47.3	TOTAL	51.0
OPEC COUNTRIES	32.2	-4.5	-1.5	-0.1	-1.3	-2.5	-1.7	-1.4	OPEC COUNTRIES	0.6
E.E.C.+ MEMBERS	1672.7	2771.7	888.5	-149.0	76.7	85.4	73.7	84.4	E.E.C.+ MEMBERS	82.2
TOTAL	6119.9	7786.6	1348.7	634.6	100.8	160.8	122.8	178.4	TOTAL	168.4

	1983	1984	1985	1986	1983	1984	1985	1986		1983
ODA LOANS GROSS					**ODA LOANS NET**				**GRANTS**	
DAC COUNTRIES										
Australia	–	–	–	–	–	–	–	–	Australia	0.0
Austria	–	–	–	–	-0.1	-0.1	-0.2	-0.3	Austria	0.5
Belgium	–	–	–	–	–	–	–	–	Belgium	1.4
Canada	0.3	1.0	0.3	0.2	-0.4	0.4	-0.1	-0.2	Canada	2.5
Denmark	–	–	–	–	–	–	–	–	Denmark	–
Finland	–	–	–	–	–	–	–	–	Finland	0.0
France	12.7	23.1	17.5	4.4	11.7	20.7	14.9	3.5	France	7.0
Germany, Fed. Rep.	13.8	7.7	11.6	43.4	9.8	7.0	7.9	12.4	Germany, Fed. Rep.	31.6
Ireland	–	–	–	–	–	–	–	–	Ireland	0.0
Italy	–	–	–	–	–	–	–	–	Italy	2.6
Japan	14.3	22.2	37.8	23.6	12.5	19.9	24.9	8.4	Japan	14.6
Netherlands	–	–	–	–	-0.2	-0.1	-0.1	-0.2	Netherlands	4.1
New Zealand	–	–	–	–	–	–	–	–	New Zealand	–
Norway	–	–	–	–	–	–	–	–	Norway	–
Sweden	–	–	–	–	–	0.0	–	–	Sweden	0.4
Switzerland	–	–	–	–	–	–	–	–	Switzerland	0.6
United Kingdom	–	–	–	–	-0.4	-0.9	–	–	United Kingdom	8.5
United States	1.0	–	–	–	-14.0	-2.0	-69.0	-3.0	United States	1.0
TOTAL	42.0	54.0	67.3	71.5	18.8	44.7	-21.7	20.5	TOTAL	74.7
MULTILATERAL	37.2	49.0	83.4	77.7	-5.2	6.4	38.6	30.8	MULTILATERAL	13.8
OPEC COUNTRIES	0.6	3.0	1.9	2.1	-1.3	-2.6	-1.7	-1.4	OPEC COUNTRIES	–
E.E.C.+ MEMBERS	26.4	30.8	29.1	47.8	20.9	26.6	22.6	15.7	E.E.C.+ MEMBERS	55.8
TOTAL	79.8	106.0	152.5	151.3	12.3	48.6	15.2	49.9	TOTAL	88.5

	1983	1984	1985	1986	1983	1984	1985	1986		1983
TOTAL OFFICIAL GROSS					**TOTAL OFFICIAL NET**				**TOTAL OOF GROSS**	
DAC COUNTRIES										
Australia	0.0	0.0	0.7	0.0	0.0	0.0	0.7	-0.1	Australia	–
Austria	0.5	0.3	0.3	0.5	0.3	0.2	0.1	0.1	Austria	–
Belgium	1.4	9.3	4.3	1.3	1.4	8.3	3.7	1.0	Belgium	–
Canada	54.4	35.2	20.6	20.0	44.7	30.7	8.7	11.4	Canada	51.6
Denmark	0.2	1.2	0.1	0.2	-0.3	1.0	-0.2	-2.7	Denmark	0.2
Finland	0.0	0.0	0.0	0.2	0.0	0.0	0.0	0.2	Finland	–
France	19.7	135.0	201.9	26.2	18.7	132.6	172.6	13.5	France	–
Germany, Fed. Rep.	208.1	369.3	672.0	567.8	182.4	354.5	561.5	431.4	Germany, Fed. Rep.	162.7
Ireland	0.0	0.0	0.0	0.0	0.0	0.0	0.0	0.0	Ireland	0.0
Italy	6.6	15.7	256.1	36.7	-12.7	14.5	254.9	34.3	Italy	4.0
Japan	41.9	42.0	78.4	114.6	10.0	35.9	64.9	92.4	Japan	12.9
Netherlands	4.3	6.9	5.8	4.5	4.1	6.8	5.6	4.1	Netherlands	0.2
New Zealand	–	–	–	–	–	–	–	–	New Zealand	–
Norway	–	0.3	0.3	0.3	–	0.3	0.3	0.3	Norway	–
Sweden	0.4	0.3	0.1	–	0.4	0.2	0.1	–	Sweden	–
Switzerland	0.6	0.7	0.4	1.1	0.6	0.7	0.4	1.1	Switzerland	–
United Kingdom	8.5	10.4	5.2	1.3	8.1	9.4	5.1	1.3	United Kingdom	–
United States	160.0	127.0	717.0	53.0	55.0	101.0	371.0	-12.0	United States	158.0
TOTAL	506.5	753.8	1963.2	827.7	312.7	696.1	1449.3	576.3	TOTAL	389.7
MULTILATERAL	1578.2	1706.8	1267.6	2001.4	1171.6	1183.6	647.5	1092.3	MULTILATERAL	1527.3
OPEC COUNTRIES	53.6	13.1	4.9	3.4	32.2	-4.5	-1.5	-0.1	OPEC COUNTRIES	53.0
E.E.C.+ MEMBERS	249.4	548.4	1146.4	639.4	202.3	527.5	1004.1	484.2	E.E.C.+ MEMBERS	167.2
TOTAL	2138.3	2473.7	3235.7	2832.5	1516.5	1875.1	2095.3	1668.5	TOTAL	1970.0

ODA COMMITMENTS

1984	1985	1986	1983	1984	1985	1986
0.0	0.0	0.0	0.0	0.0	0.0	0.0
0.3	0.3	0.5	0.4	0.3	0.3	–
1.1	1.5	1.3	0.8	0.7	0.7	1.3
7.7	6.2	4.9	2.8	11.3	8.1	4.0
–	–	–	–	–	–	–
0.0	0.0	0.2	–	0.0	–	0.5
32.7	23.7	17.8	7.0	43.6	27.4	17.8
35.8	39.3	82.9	48.4	43.1	92.3	76.7
0.0	0.0	0.0	0.0	0.0	0.0	0.0
3.8	3.8	7.4	4.4	5.1	5.4	11.7
38.0	53.5	47.4	24.2	34.4	206.0	36.3
6.8	5.8	4.5	4.2	6.9	6.0	4.2
–	–	–	–	–	–	–
0.3	0.3	0.3	–	0.2	0.2	0.4
0.1	0.1	–	0.1	0.1	–	–
0.7	0.4	1.1	0.5	0.6	0.3	0.9
9.1	5.2	1.3	0.9	0.7	0.8	1.0
13.0	13.0	14.0	0.3	35.6	21.2	16.3
149.3	*153.2*	*183.6*	*93.9*	*182.5*	*368.8*	*171.0*
–	–	–	–	–	–	–
–	–	–	–	–	–	–
–	–	–	–	–	–	–
0.4	0.9	1.4	1.0	1.8	1.7	1.2
–	–	–	–	–	–	–
48.1	80.6	75.3	66.5	26.0	43.5	18.0
1.0	2.9	2.4	–	–	–	–
–	–	–	–	–	–	–
–	–	–	13.1	16.6	20.7	15.1
6.9	5.9	6.9	–	–	–	–
1.3	2.0	2.2	–	–	–	–
1.1	1.1	1.4	–	–	–	–
–	–	–	–	–	–	–
6.4	9.2	2.7	–	–	–	–
0.0	–	–	–	–	–	–
0.8	2.5	1.8	–	–	–	–
–	–	–	–	–	–	–
66.0	*105.0*	*94.2*	*80.7*	*44.4*	*65.9*	*34.3*
3.0	*1.9*	*2.1*	–	–	–	–
89.6	*80.2*	*116.6*	*66.7*	*101.9*	*134.3*	*113.7*
218.2	*260.2*	*279.8*	*174.6*	*226.9*	*434.7*	*205.2*

TECH. COOP. GRANTS

1984	1985	1986	1983	1984	1985	1986
0.0	0.0	0.0	–	–	0.0	0.0
0.3	0.3	0.5	0.5	–	–	–
1.1	1.5	1.3	0.0	0.0	0.1	0.0
6.6	5.9	4.7	0.8	–	2.8	–
–	–	–	–	–	–	–
0.0	0.0	0.2	0.0	0.0	0.0	0.0
9.5	6.2	13.3	7.0	9.4	6.2	13.3
28.1	27.7	39.6	31.0	26.9	27.0	37.3
0.0	0.0	0.0	0.0	0.0	0.0	0.0
3.8	3.8	7.4	2.5	3.7	3.8	6.1
15.8	15.7	23.9	14.6	15.8	15.7	23.9
6.8	5.8	4.5	3.7	4.6	5.3	4.2
–	–	–	–	–	–	–
0.3	0.3	0.3	–	0.0	0.2	0.1
0.1	0.1	–	–	–	–	–
0.7	0.4	1.1	0.1	0.1	0.1	0.1
9.1	5.2	1.3	0.8	0.4	0.7	1.0
13.0	13.0	14.0	–	–	–	–
95.2	*85.9*	*112.0*	*61.1*	*60.9*	*61.8*	*86.1*
17.0	*21.7*	*16.5*	*11.7*	*10.1*	*11.5*	*12.6*
0.0	–	–	–	–	–	–
58.8	*51.1*	*68.8*	*45.1*	*45.1*	*43.0*	*62.2*
112.2	*107.6*	*128.5*	*72.8*	*71.1*	*73.3*	*98.8*

TOTAL OOF NET

1984	1985	1986	1983	1984	1985	1986
–	0.6	–	–	–	0.6	-0.1
–	–	–	–	–	–	–
8.2	2.9	–	–	7.2	2.2	-0.3
27.6	14.4	15.2	42.6	23.6	2.9	7.0
1.2	0.1	0.2	-0.3	1.0	-0.2	-2.7
–	–	–	–	–	–	–
102.4	178.2	8.4	–	102.4	151.6	-3.3
333.6	632.7	484.8	141.1	319.5	525.8	379.4
11.9	252.3	29.3	-15.3	10.7	251.1	26.9
4.0	24.8	67.2	-17.1	0.3	24.2	60.1
0.2	–	–	0.2	0.2	-0.1	-0.2
–	–	–	–	–	–	–
0.1	–	–	–	0.1	–	–
1.3	–	–	–	1.3	-0.1	0.0
114.0	704.0	39.0	68.0	90.0	427.0	-23.0
604.5	*1810.0*	*644.2*	*219.2*	*556.2*	*1385.1*	*443.7*
1640.8	*1162.6*	*1907.2*	*1163.1*	*1160.2*	*587.2*	*1045.0*
10.2	*3.0*	*1.4*	*33.5*	*-2.0*	*0.1*	*1.4*
458.8	*1066.2*	*522.8*	*125.7*	*442.2*	*930.4*	*399.7*
2255.5	*2975.6*	*2552.7*	*1415.7*	*1714.4*	*1972.5*	*1490.1*

ODA COMMITMENTS : LOANS

DAC COUNTRIES

	1983	1984	1985	1986
Australia	–	–	–	–
Austria	–	–	–	–
Belgium	–	–	–	–
Canada	–	0.2	–	–
Denmark	–	–	–	–
Finland	–	–	–	–
France	–	34.1	21.2	4.4
Germany, Fed. Rep.	12.1	15.8	60.4	31.8
Ireland	–	–	–	–
Italy	–	–	–	–
Japan	8.4	18.4	189.0	10.0
Netherlands	–	–	–	–
New Zealand	–	–	–	–
Norway	–	–	–	–
Sweden	–	–	–	–
Switzerland	–	–	–	–
United Kingdom	–	–	–	–
United States	–	–	–	–
TOTAL	*20.5*	*68.5*	*270.6*	*46.3*
MULTILATERAL	*66.5*	*26.0*	*43.5*	*18.0*
OPEC COUNTRIES	–	–	–	–
E.E.C.+ MEMBERS	*12.1*	*49.9*	*81.6*	*36.3*
TOTAL	*87.0*	*94.5*	*314.1*	*64.3*

GRANT ELEMENT OF ODA

DAC COUNTRIES

	1983	1984	1985	1986
Australia	100.0	100.0	100.0	100.0
Austria	100.0	100.0	100.0	–
Belgium	100.0	100.0	100.0	100.0
Canada	100.0	100.0	100.0	100.0
Denmark	–	–	–	–
Finland	–	100.0	–	100.0
France	100.0	62.2	75.9	100.0
Germany, Fed. Rep.	84.2	76.7	53.8	63.9
Ireland	100.0	100.0	100.0	100.0
Italy	100.0	100.0	100.0	100.0
Japan	87.4	84.8	40.1	94.1
Netherlands	100.0	100.0	100.0	100.0
New Zealand	–	–	–	–
Norway	–	100.0	100.0	100.0
Sweden	100.0	100.0	–	–
Switzerland	100.0	100.0	100.0	100.0
United Kingdom	100.0	46.0	100.0	100.0
United States	100.0	100.0	100.0	100.0
TOTAL	*88.6*	*82.2*	*53.7*	*81.6*
MULTILATERAL	*56.0*	*63.1*	*68.3*	*84.8*
OPEC COUNTRIES	–	–	–	–
E.E.C.+ MEMBERS	*88.5*	*73.6*	*63.3*	*74.7*
TOTAL	*73.1*	*76.0*	*56.0*	*82.1*

OTHER AGGREGATES

COMMITMENTS: ALL SOURCES

	1983	1984	1985	1986
TOTAL BILATERAL	302.0	844.2	1716.2	509.1
of which				
OPEC	69.7	20.0	5.9	–
CMEA	–	–	–	50.0
TOTAL MULTILATERAL	2560.6	731.9	2049.4	2299.3
TOTAL BIL.& MULTIL.	2862.5	1576.0	3765.6	2808.4
of which				
ODA Grants	87.6	132.4	120.6	140.9
ODA Loans	87.0	94.5	314.1	64.3

DISBURSEMENTS:

DAC COUNTRIES COMBINED

OFFICIAL & PRIVATE	1983	1984	1985	1986
GROSS:				
Contractual Lending	2064.8	2185.9	3075.0	1299.0
Export Credits Total	1994.0	1772.5	1470.0	977.4
Export Credits Private	1633.1	1528.0	1198.2	583.3
NET:				
Contractual Lending	905.6	1131.3	1249.0	83.2
Export Credits Total	867.3	738.9	-210.0	-104.5
PRIVATE SECTOR NET	4603.3	5911.5	-746.6	-1033.9
Direct Investment	674.0	1478.5	549.2	195.5
Portfolio Investment	3261.7	3901.9	-1181.9	-848.3
Export Credits	667.7	531.0	-113.8	-381.0

MARKET BORROWING:

CHANGE IN CLAIMS

	1983	1984	1985	1986
Banks	–	6603.0	-1648.0	467.0

MEMORANDUM ITEM:

	1983	1984	1985	1986
CMEA Countr.(Gross)	–	–	–	–

	1983	1984	1985	1986	1983	1984	1985	1986		1983
	TOTAL RECEIPTS NET				**TOTAL ODA NET**				**TOTAL ODA GROSS**	
DAC COUNTRIES										
Australia	–	0.0	–	0.0	–	0.0	–	0.0	Australia	–
Austria	0.3	-0.2	-0.1	0.4	0.3	0.2	0.2	0.4	Austria	0.3
Belgium	0.6	1.6	0.9	2.1	0.9	1.7	1.1	2.3	Belgium	0.9
Canada	7.3	7.4	9.1	12.1	7.3	7.4	9.1	12.1	Canada	7.3
Denmark	0.5	1.0	2.8	8.9	0.5	1.0	2.8	8.9	Denmark	0.5
Finland	0.1	0.0	–	0.2	0.1	0.0	–	0.2	Finland	0.1
France	53.2	35.4	19.3	33.9	43.5	35.3	26.5	40.0	France	43.5
Germany, Fed. Rep.	14.9	11.5	12.2	22.5	14.9	11.5	11.9	22.9	Germany, Fed. Rep.	14.9
Ireland	–	–	–	–	–	–	–	–	Ireland	–
Italy	0.5	2.1	5.4	35.2	0.5	2.1	5.4	35.2	Italy	0.5
Japan	2.2	4.4	5.3	4.3	3.2	4.6	5.3	4.3	Japan	3.2
Netherlands	29.1	17.7	13.7	17.7	25.6	17.7	13.7	16.4	Netherlands	25.6
New Zealand	–	–	–	–	–	–	–	–	New Zealand	–
Norway	1.0	0.0	0.0	3.6	1.0	0.0	0.0	3.6	Norway	1.0
Sweden	0.3	1.0	0.0	–	0.3	1.0	0.0	–	Sweden	0.3
Switzerland	2.9	2.5	1.9	2.7	2.9	2.5	1.9	2.7	Switzerland	2.9
United Kingdom	-2.7	-0.8	-0.5	-0.3	0.1	0.2	0.4	0.2	United Kingdom	0.1
United States	27.0	37.0	44.0	26.0	27.0	37.0	44.0	26.0	United States	27.0
TOTAL	*137.0*	*120.8*	*114.0*	*169.3*	*128.0*	*122.2*	*122.2*	*175.3*	*TOTAL*	*128.0*
MULTILATERAL										
AF.D.F.	0.6	1.6	5.5	12.2	0.6	1.6	5.5	12.2	AF.D.F.	0.6
AF.D.B.	-0.2	-0.5	1.3	6.4	–	–	–	–	AF.D.B.	–
AS.D.B	–	–	–	–	–	–	–	–	AS.D.B	–
CAR.D.B.	–	–	–	–	–	–	–	–	CAR.D.B.	–
E.E.C.	18.2	19.3	14.8	8.1	15.5	17.0	13.8	8.7	E.E.C.	15.7
IBRD	–	–	–	–	–	–	–	–	IBRD	–
IDA	18.4	12.8	20.8	31.3	18.4	12.8	20.8	31.3	IDA	18.6
I.D.B.	–	–	–	–	–	–	–	–	I.D.B.	–
IFAD	1.0	0.8	1.0	1.8	1.0	0.8	1.0	1.8	IFAD	1.0
I.F.C.	–	–	–	–	–	–	–	–	I.F.C.	–
IMF TRUST FUND	–	–	–	–	–	–	–	–	IMF TRUST FUND	–
U.N. AGENCIES	–	–	–	–	–	–	–	–	U.N. AGENCIES	–
UNDP	7.6	8.2	7.8	11.2	7.6	8.2	7.8	11.2	UNDP	7.6
UNTA	1.2	0.7	1.0	2.3	1.2	0.7	1.0	2.3	UNTA	1.2
UNICEF	1.7	2.4	3.3	2.9	1.7	2.4	3.3	2.9	UNICEF	1.7
UNRWA	–	–	–	–	–	–	–	–	UNRWA	–
WFP	4.3	7.3	7.1	5.6	4.3	7.3	7.1	5.6	WFP	4.3
UNHCR	0.2	0.2	0.2	0.3	0.2	0.2	0.2	0.3	UNHCR	0.2
Other Multilateral	2.8	5.4	8.1	12.6	2.8	5.4	8.1	12.6	Other Multilateral	2.8
Arab OPEC Agencies	2.1	-4.3	2.7	9.3	1.8	-2.1	3.2	9.3	Arab OPEC Agencies	2.7
TOTAL	*57.9*	*53.9*	*73.5*	*103.8*	*55.1*	*54.3*	*71.7*	*98.0*	*TOTAL*	*56.5*
OPEC COUNTRIES	*5.5*	*13.0*	*4.4*	*10.6*	*0.5*	*12.1*	*3.5*	*10.6*	*OPEC COUNTRIES*	*0.5*
E.E.C.+ MEMBERS	*114.2*	*87.8*	*68.6*	*128.1*	*101.5*	*86.4*	*75.5*	*134.6*	*E.E.C.+ MEMBERS*	*101.7*
TOTAL	**200.4**	**187.6**	**191.9**	**283.7**	**183.5**	**188.6**	**197.4**	**283.9**	**TOTAL**	**185.0**

	1983	1984	1985	1986	1983	1984	1985	1986		1983
	ODA LOANS GROSS				**ODA LOANS NET**				**GRANTS**	
DAC COUNTRIES										
Australia	–	–	–	–	–	–	–	–	Australia	–
Austria	–	–	–	–	–	–	–	–	Austria	0.3
Belgium	–	–	–	–	–	–	–	–	Belgium	0.9
Canada	–	–	–	–	–	–	–	–	Canada	7.3
Denmark	0.5	1.0	0.2	0.1	0.5	1.0	0.2	0.1	Denmark	0.0
Finland	–	–	–	–	–	–	–	–	Finland	0.1
France	16.5	10.8	8.1	15.0	16.5	10.7	7.8	14.2	France	27.0
Germany, Fed. Rep.	–	–	–	–	–	–	–	–	Germany, Fed. Rep.	14.9
Ireland	–	–	–	–	–	–	–	–	Ireland	–
Italy	–	–	–	–	–	–	–	–	Italy	0.5
Japan	–	–	–	–	–	–	–	–	Japan	3.2
Netherlands	5.3	–	–	0.3	5.3	–	–	0.3	Netherlands	20.3
New Zealand	–	–	–	–	–	–	–	–	New Zealand	–
Norway	–	–	–	–	–	–	–	–	Norway	1.0
Sweden	–	–	–	–	–	–	–	–	Sweden	0.3
Switzerland	–	–	–	–	–	–	–	–	Switzerland	2.9
United Kingdom	–	–	–	–	–	–	–	–	United Kingdom	0.1
United States	–	–	–	–	–	–	–	–	United States	27.0
TOTAL	*22.3*	*11.8*	*8.3*	*15.3*	*22.3*	*11.8*	*8.0*	*14.6*	*TOTAL*	*105.7*
MULTILATERAL	*24.2*	*13.7*	*30.1*	*57.8*	*22.9*	*12.9*	*29.3*	*53.1*	*MULTILATERAL*	*32.2*
OPEC COUNTRIES	*–*	*11.4*	*3.5*	*7.9*	*-0.1*	*11.4*	*3.4*	*7.9*	*OPEC COUNTRIES*	*0.5*
E.E.C.+ MEMBERS	*23.6*	*11.9*	*8.3*	*17.5*	*23.3*	*11.5*	*8.0*	*15.3*	*E.E.C.+ MEMBERS*	*78.1*
TOTAL	**46.6**	**37.0**	**41.8**	**81.0**	**45.1**	**36.1**	**40.7**	**75.6**	**TOTAL**	**138.4**

	1983	1984	1985	1986	1983	1984	1985	1986		1983
	TOTAL OFFICIAL GROSS				**TOTAL OFFICIAL NET**				**TOTAL OOF GROSS**	
DAC COUNTRIES										
Australia	–	0.0	–	0.0	–	0.0	–	0.0	Australia	–
Austria	0.3	0.2	0.2	0.4	0.3	0.2	0.2	0.4	Austria	–
Belgium	0.9	1.7	1.1	2.3	0.9	1.7	1.1	2.3	Belgium	–
Canada	7.3	7.4	9.1	12.1	7.3	7.4	9.1	12.1	Canada	–
Denmark	0.5	1.0	2.8	8.9	0.5	1.0	2.8	8.9	Denmark	–
Finland	0.1	0.0	–	0.2	0.1	0.0	–	0.2	Finland	–
France	52.7	35.9	27.1	40.8	52.6	35.8	26.3	39.6	France	9.2
Germany, Fed. Rep.	14.9	11.5	11.9	22.9	14.9	11.5	11.9	22.9	Germany, Fed. Rep.	–
Ireland	–	–	–	–	–	–	–	–	Ireland	–
Italy	0.5	2.1	5.4	35.2	0.5	2.1	5.4	35.2	Italy	–
Japan	3.2	4.6	5.3	4.3	3.2	4.6	5.3	4.3	Japan	–
Netherlands	25.6	17.7	13.7	16.9	25.6	17.7	13.7	16.9	Netherlands	–
New Zealand	–	–	–	–	–	–	–	–	New Zealand	–
Norway	1.0	0.0	0.0	3.6	1.0	0.0	0.0	3.6	Norway	–
Sweden	0.3	1.0	0.0	–	0.3	1.0	0.0	–	Sweden	–
Switzerland	2.9	2.5	1.9	2.7	2.9	2.5	1.9	2.7	Switzerland	–
United Kingdom	0.1	0.2	0.4	0.2	0.1	0.2	0.4	0.2	United Kingdom	–
United States	27.0	37.0	44.0	26.0	27.0	37.0	44.0	26.0	United States	–
TOTAL	*137.2*	*122.8*	*122.9*	*176.5*	*137.1*	*122.7*	*122.1*	*175.4*	*TOTAL*	*9.2*
MULTILATERAL	*61.9*	*57.4*	*75.6*	*109.7*	*57.9*	*53.9*	*73.5*	*103.8*	*MULTILATERAL*	*5.5*
OPEC COUNTRIES	*5.5*	*13.0*	*4.5*	*10.6*	*5.5*	*13.0*	*4.4*	*10.6*	*OPEC COUNTRIES*	*5.0*
E.E.C.+ MEMBERS	*113.7*	*89.7*	*77.6*	*137.3*	*113.3*	*89.2*	*76.3*	*134.2*	*E.E.C.+ MEMBERS*	*11.9*
TOTAL	**204.6**	**193.2**	**203.0**	**296.8**	**200.5**	**189.5**	**200.0**	**289.8**	**TOTAL**	**19.6**

ODA COMMITMENTS

1984	1985	1986	1983	1984	1985	1986
0.0	–	0.0	–	0.0	0.0	–
0.2	0.2	0.4	0.2	0.3	0.2	–
1.7	1.1	2.3	–	1.1	0.5	2.3
7.4	9.1	12.1	16.1	31.8	5.0	8.6
1.0	2.8	8.9	–	10.6	0.1	0.1
0.0	–	0.2	0.0	0.0	–	–
35.3	26.8	40.8	39.2	38.6	27.3	40.8
11.5	11.9	22.9	17.9	9.8	43.2	19.9
–	–	–	–	–	–	–
2.1	5.4	35.2	6.7	6.4	13.1	72.6
4.6	5.3	4.3	4.7	6.6	4.2	4.6
17.7	13.7	16.4	25.6	12.2	13.0	20.7
–	–	–	–	–	–	–
0.0	0.0	3.6	–	2.5	–	1.3
1.0	0.0	–	0.3	–	0.3	–
2.5	1.9	2.7	3.4	0.5	0.3	5.9
0.2	0.4	0.2	0.1	0.2	0.4	0.2
37.0	44.0	26.0	20.8	38.6	20.0	24.3
122.2	*122.5*	*176.0*	*135.0*	*159.1*	*127.4*	*201.2*
1.6	5.6	12.3	13.8	4.5	14.6	8.7
–	–	–	–	–	–	–
–	–	–	–	–	–	–
17.3	13.8	10.1	28.7	6.7	18.0	2.6
–	–	–	–	–	–	–
13.1	21.3	32.2	–	7.4	61.9	–
–	–	–	–	–	–	–
0.8	1.0	1.8	–	–	–	–
–	–	–	–	–	–	–
–	–	–	–	–	–	–
–	–	–	17.8	24.2	27.5	34.8
8.2	7.8	11.2	–	–	–	–
0.7	1.0	2.3	–	–	–	–
2.4	3.3	2.9	–	–	–	–
–	–	–	–	–	–	–
7.3	7.1	5.6	–	–	–	–
0.2	0.2	0.3	–	–	–	–
5.4	8.1	12.6	–	–	–	–
-1.9	3.4	11.5	2.6	14.9	0.1	6.0
55.1	*72.5*	*102.7*	*62.8*	*57.7*	*122.1*	*52.2*
12.1	*3.6*	*10.6*	*54.9*	*29.4*	*0.0*	–
86.8	*75.8*	*136.8*	*118.1*	*85.6*	*115.6*	*159.1*
189.5	*198.6*	*289.3*	*252.7*	*246.2*	*249.5*	*253.3*

TECH. COOP. GRANTS

1984	1985	1986	1983	1984	1985	1986
0.0	–	0.0	–	–	–	–
0.2	0.2	0.4	0.3	–	–	–
1.7	1.1	2.3	0.2	0.4	0.3	0.5
7.4	9.1	12.1	1.5	–	2.4	–
0.0	2.6	8.9	0.0	0.5	1.0	0.4
0.0	–	0.2	0.0	0.0	–	–
24.6	18.7	25.8	17.9	18.2	13.2	20.3
11.5	11.9	22.9	10.1	7.5	7.9	11.0
–	–	–	–	–	–	–
2.1	5.4	35.2	0.5	1.9	2.9	7.0
4.6	5.3	4.3	0.1	0.1	0.0	0.2
17.7	13.7	16.2	8.1	8.0	7.6	11.5
–	–	–	–	–	–	–
0.0	0.0	3.6	–	–	–	–
1.0	0.0	–	–	1.0	0.0	–
2.5	1.9	2.7	0.8	0.8	0.9	0.9
0.2	0.4	0.2	0.1	0.2	0.2	0.2
37.0	44.0	26.0	12.0	16.0	13.0	14.0
110.4	*114.3*	*160.7*	*51.7*	*54.5*	*49.3*	*65.9*
41.4	*42.4*	*44.9*	*13.5*	*16.9*	*20.4*	*30.3*
0.7	*0.1*	*2.7*	–	–	–	–
74.9	*67.6*	*119.3*	*37.0*	*36.7*	*33.0*	*51.9*
152.5	*156.7*	*208.3*	*65.2*	*71.4*	*69.7*	*96.2*

TOTAL OOF NET

1984	1985	1986	1983	1984	1985	1986
–	–	–	–	–	–	–
–	–	–	–	–	–	–
–	0.0	–	–	–	0.0	–
–	–	–	–	–	–	–
–	–	–	–	–	–	–
–	–	–	–	–	–	–
0.5	0.3	–	9.1	0.5	-0.2	-0.3
–	–	–	–	–	–	–
–	–	–	–	–	–	–
–	–	0.5	–	–	–	0.5
–	–	–	–	–	–	–
–	–	–	–	–	–	–
–	–	–	–	–	–	–
–	–	–	–	–	–	–
–	–	–	–	–	–	–
0.5	*0.4*	*0.5*	*9.1*	*0.5*	*-0.2*	*0.2*
2.3	*3.1*	*7.0*	*2.8*	*-0.4*	*1.8*	*5.8*
0.9	*0.9*	–	*5.0*	*0.9*	*0.9*	–
2.8	*1.8*	*0.5*	*11.9*	*2.8*	*0.8*	*-0.5*
3.8	*4.4*	*7.5*	*16.9*	*1.0*	*2.5*	*6.0*

ODA COMMITMENTS : LOANS

DAC COUNTRIES

	1983	1984	1985	1986
Australia	–	–	–	–
Austria	–	–	–	–
Belgium	–	–	–	–
Canada	–	–	–	–
Denmark	–	–	–	–
Finland	–	–	–	–
France	13.1	13.7	11.8	15.0
Germany, Fed. Rep.	–	–	–	–
Ireland	–	–	–	–
Italy	–	–	–	–
Japan	–	–	–	–
Netherlands	5.3	–	–	0.3
New Zealand	–	–	–	–
Norway	–	–	–	–
Sweden	–	–	–	–
Switzerland	–	–	–	–
United Kingdom	–	–	–	–
United States	–	–	–	–
TOTAL	*18.3*	*13.7*	*11.8*	*15.3*
MULTILATERAL	*22.4*	*24.0*	*81.8*	*14.7*
OPEC COUNTRIES	*13.7*	*21.4*	–	–
E.E.C.+ MEMBERS	*24.5*	*13.7*	*17.1*	*15.3*
TOTAL	*54.4*	*59.0*	*93.6*	*30.0*

GRANT ELEMENT OF ODA

DAC COUNTRIES

	1983	1984	1985	1986
Australia	–	100.0	100.0	–
Austria	100.0	100.0	100.0	–
Belgium	–	100.0	100.0	100.0
Canada	100.0	100.0	100.0	100.0
Denmark	–	100.0	100.0	100.0
Finland	100.0	100.0	–	–
France	84.7	77.3	82.7	77.7
Germany, Fed. Rep.	100.0	100.0	100.0	100.0
Ireland	–	–	–	–
Italy	100.0	100.0	100.0	100.0
Japan	100.0	100.0	100.0	100.0
Netherlands	91.8	100.0	100.0	100.0
New Zealand	–	–	–	–
Norway	–	100.0	–	100.0
Sweden	100.0	–	100.0	–
Switzerland	100.0	100.0	100.0	100.0
United Kingdom	100.0	100.0	100.0	100.0
United States	100.0	100.0	100.0	100.0
TOTAL	*94.1*	*94.5*	*96.3*	*94.7*
MULTILATERAL	*90.8*	*87.2*	*88.9*	*92.0*
OPEC COUNTRIES	*88.4*	*61.3*	*100.0*	–
E.E.C.+ MEMBERS	*92.8*	*89.8*	*95.7*	*93.4*
TOTAL	*92.0*	*88.8*	*92.8*	*94.1*

OTHER AGGREGATES

COMMITMENTS: ALL SOURCES

	1983	1984	1985	1986
TOTAL BILATERAL	204.1	190.5	135.8	202.2
of which				
OPEC	59.9	31.2	4.1	–
CMEA	–	0.2	–	0.2
TOTAL MULTILATERAL	62.8	80.3	122.1	56.2
TOTAL BIL.& MULTIL.	266.9	270.7	257.8	258.4
of which				
ODA Grants	198.3	187.3	155.9	223.5
ODA Loans	54.4	59.0	93.6	30.0

DISBURSEMENTS:

DAC COUNTRIES COMBINED

	1983	1984	1985	1986
OFFICIAL & PRIVATE				
GROSS:				
Contractual Lending	40.2	16.0	9.7	11.5
Export Credits Total	8.7	3.7	1.1	-4.3
Export Credits Private	8.7	3.7	1.1	-4.3
NET:				
Contractual Lending	33.4	9.9	2.9	9.6
Export Credits Total	2.0	-2.3	-4.9	-5.1
PRIVATE SECTOR NET	-0.1	-1.9	-8.1	-6.1
Direct Investment	-0.9	-0.1	-1.2	1.0
Portfolio Investment	-1.2	0.5	-2.0	-2.0
Export Credits	2.0	-2.3	-4.9	-5.1

MARKET BORROWING:

CHANGE IN CLAIMS

	1983	1984	1985	1986
Banks	–	-4.0	-6.0	-7.0

MEMORANDUM ITEM:

	1983	1984	1985	1986
CMEA Countr.(Gross)	–	0.2	–	0.2

TOTAL RECEIPTS NET

DAC COUNTRIES	1983	1984	1985	1986
Australia	5.4	6.9	6.7	7.0
Austria	–	-3.0	-2.9	0.1
Belgium	-2.0	1.8	-0.6	-2.0
Canada	1.8	1.5	2.3	1.1
Denmark	0.7	3.0	4.7	2.8
Finland	2.4	1.1	1.4	4.1
France	13.1	-2.4	5.2	8.2
Germany, Fed. Rep.	76.3	29.7	64.0	17.2
Ireland	–	–	–	–
Italy	2.2	5.9	-0.8	2.4
Japan	100.6	114.5	141.6	225.8
Netherlands	2.3	0.4	-2.1	16.3
New Zealand	–	0.0	–	0.0
Norway	-2.7	39.0	33.1	33.5
Sweden	-0.3	-0.2	–	–
Switzerland	-2.0	-2.3	-0.9	1.6
United Kingdom	9.6	-2.9	-5.2	-20.7
United States	4.0	7.0	8.0	9.0
TOTAL	*211.3*	*200.0*	*254.5*	*306.1*
MULTILATERAL				
AF.D.F.	–	–	–	–
AF.D.B.	–	–	–	–
AS.D.B	16.6	24.7	32.4	26.6
CAR.D.B.	–	–	–	–
E.E.C.	1.8	1.9	2.1	14.6
IBRD	–	–	–	–
IDA	43.0	79.4	42.9	43.8
I.D.B.	–	–	–	–
IFAD	–	–	–	–
I.F.C.	–	–	–	–
IMF TRUST FUND	–	–	–	–
U.N. AGENCIES	–	–	–	–
UNDP	8.8	7.7	12.4	11.8
UNTA	2.2	1.0	2.6	0.7
UNICEF	7.0	5.3	8.7	8.1
UNRWA	–	–	–	–
WFP	0.1	–	–	–
UNHCR	–	–	–	–
Other Multilateral	1.8	1.6	1.7	2.6
Arab OPEC Agencies	4.9	4.4	-0.5	-0.4
TOTAL	*86.2*	*125.9*	*102.3*	*107.7*
OPEC COUNTRIES	–	*0.0*	–	–
E.E.C.+ MEMBERS	*103.9*	*37.4*	*67.2*	*38.6*
TOTAL	*297.5*	*325.8*	*356.7*	*413.8*

TOTAL ODA NET

DAC COUNTRIES	1983	1984	1985	1986
Australia	6.7	8.2	7.7	7.9
Austria	–	0.0	0.0	0.1
Belgium	0.0	–	–	–
Canada	1.8	1.5	2.3	1.1
Denmark	0.7	3.0	4.7	2.8
Finland	2.4	1.1	1.4	4.1
France	2.3	2.1	6.9	5.1
Germany, Fed. Rep.	75.3	25.1	65.0	22.4
Ireland	–	–	–	–
Italy	2.6	1.8	-0.2	2.4
Japan	113.4	95.4	154.0	244.1
Netherlands	2.3	0.4	1.2	2.4
New Zealand	–	0.0	–	0.0
Norway	1.4	1.1	0.9	0.5
Sweden	–	–	–	–
Switzerland	0.1	0.9	0.1	1.6
United Kingdom	2.7	1.1	1.3	4.3
United States	4.0	7.0	8.0	9.0
TOTAL	*215.7*	*148.7*	*253.2*	*307.7*
MULTILATERAL				
AF.D.F.	–	–	–	–
AF.D.B.	–	–	–	–
AS.D.B	16.8	24.9	32.6	26.8
CAR.D.B.	–	–	–	–
E.E.C.	1.8	1.9	2.1	14.6
IBRD	–	–	–	–
IDA	43.0	79.4	42.9	43.8
I.D.B.	–	–	–	–
IFAD	–	–	–	–
I.F.C.	–	–	–	–
IMF TRUST FUND	–	–	–	–
U.N. AGENCIES	–	–	–	–
UNDP	8.8	7.7	12.4	11.8
UNTA	2.2	1.0	2.6	0.7
UNICEF	7.0	5.3	8.7	8.1
UNRWA	–	–	–	–
WFP	0.1	–	–	–
UNHCR	–	–	–	–
Other Multilateral	1.8	1.6	1.7	2.6
Arab OPEC Agencies	4.9	4.4	-0.5	-0.4
TOTAL	*86.3*	*126.1*	*102.5*	*108.0*
OPEC COUNTRIES	–	*0.0*	–	–
E.E.C.+ MEMBERS	*87.7*	*35.4*	*80.9*	*53.9*
TOTAL	*302.0*	*274.8*	*355.7*	*415.7*

TOTAL ODA GROSS

	1983
Australia	6.7
Austria	–
Belgium	0.0
Canada	1.8
Denmark	0.7
Finland	2.4
France	2.7
Germany, Fed. Rep.	79.0
Ireland	–
Italy	2.6
Japan	120.8
Netherlands	2.3
New Zealand	–
Norway	1.4
Sweden	–
Switzerland	0.1
United Kingdom	2.7
United States	4.0
TOTAL	*227.1*
AF.D.F.	–
AF.D.B.	–
AS.D.B	16.8
CAR.D.B.	–
E.E.C.	1.8
IBRD	–
IDA	43.2
I.D.B.	–
IFAD	–
I.F.C.	–
IMF TRUST FUND	–
U.N. AGENCIES	–
UNDP	8.8
UNTA	2.2
UNICEF	7.0
UNRWA	–
WFP	0.1
UNHCR	–
Other Multilateral	1.8
Arab OPEC Agencies	5.0
TOTAL	*86.6*
OPEC COUNTRIES	–
E.E.C.+ MEMBERS	*91.7*
TOTAL	*313.8*

ODA LOANS GROSS

DAC COUNTRIES	1983	1984	1985	1986
Australia	–	–	–	–
Austria	–	–	–	–
Belgium	–	–	–	–
Canada	0.0	0.0	–	–
Denmark	–	2.9	4.5	2.7
Finland	1.6	0.2	–	3.0
France	2.5	2.0	7.1	5.2
Germany, Fed. Rep.	73.3	23.7	65.0	25.9
Ireland	–	–	–	–
Italy	1.3	–	–	–
Japan	72.4	61.6	119.7	197.2
Netherlands	1.5	–	1.0	1.7
New Zealand	–	–	–	–
Norway	–	–	–	–
Sweden	–	–	–	–
Switzerland	–	–	–	–
United Kingdom	–	–	–	–
United States	–	–	–	–
TOTAL	*152.7*	*90.5*	*197.3*	*235.7*
MULTILATERAL	*64.9*	*109.4*	*76.8*	*73.0*
OPEC COUNTRIES	–	–	–	–
E.E.C.+ MEMBERS	*78.6*	*28.7*	*77.6*	*35.6*
TOTAL	*217.6*	*199.9*	*274.1*	*308.7*

ODA LOANS NET

DAC COUNTRIES	1983	1984	1985	1986
Australia	–	–	–	–
Austria	–	–	–	–
Belgium	–	–	–	–
Canada	0.0	0.0	–	0.0
Denmark	–	2.9	4.5	2.7
Finland	1.6	0.2	–	3.0
France	2.1	1.7	6.8	4.8
Germany, Fed. Rep.	69.6	18.3	57.4	14.6
Ireland	–	–	–	–
Italy	1.3	–	-0.3	-0.4
Japan	65.0	47.3	104.9	175.2
Netherlands	1.5	–	0.8	1.5
New Zealand	–	–	–	–
Norway	–	–	–	–
Sweden	–	–	–	–
Switzerland	–	–	–	–
United Kingdom	–	–	–	–
United States	–	–	–	–
TOTAL	*141.2*	*70.5*	*174.0*	*201.4*
MULTILATERAL	*64.6*	*108.5*	*74.9*	*70.1*
OPEC COUNTRIES	–	–	–	–
E.E.C.+ MEMBERS	*74.5*	*23.0*	*69.1*	*23.2*
TOTAL	*205.9*	*179.0*	*248.9*	*271.5*

GRANTS

	1983
Australia	6.7
Austria	–
Belgium	0.0
Canada	1.7
Denmark	0.7
Finland	0.8
France	0.2
Germany, Fed. Rep.	5.7
Ireland	–
Italy	1.3
Japan	48.4
Netherlands	0.8
New Zealand	–
Norway	1.4
Sweden	–
Switzerland	0.1
United Kingdom	2.7
United States	4.0
TOTAL	*74.5*
MULTILATERAL	*21.7*
OPEC COUNTRIES	–
E.E.C.+ MEMBERS	*13.2*
TOTAL	*96.1*

TOTAL OFFICIAL GROSS

DAC COUNTRIES	1983	1984	1985	1986
Australia	6.7	8.2	7.7	7.9
Austria	–	0.0	0.0	0.1
Belgium	0.0	0.2	0.2	–
Canada	1.8	1.5	2.3	1.1
Denmark	0.7	3.0	4.7	2.8
Finland	2.4	1.1	1.4	4.1
France	2.7	2.4	7.2	5.5
Germany, Fed. Rep.	79.0	37.6	74.3	33.7
Ireland	–	–	–	–
Italy	2.6	1.8	0.1	2.8
Japan	120.8	109.7	168.9	266.1
Netherlands	2.3	0.4	1.3	2.6
New Zealand	–	0.0	–	0.0
Norway	1.4	1.1	0.9	0.5
Sweden	–	–	–	–
Switzerland	0.1	0.9	0.1	1.6
United Kingdom	2.7	1.1	1.3	4.3
United States	4.0	7.0	8.0	9.0
TOTAL	*227.1*	*176.0*	*278.4*	*342.0*
MULTILATERAL	*86.7*	*127.0*	*104.4*	*110.8*
OPEC COUNTRIES	–	*0.0*	–	–
E.E.C.+ MEMBERS	*91.7*	*48.4*	*91.2*	*66.3*
TOTAL	*313.8*	*303.0*	*382.8*	*452.9*

TOTAL OFFICIAL NET

DAC COUNTRIES	1983	1984	1985	1986
Australia	5.4	6.9	6.7	7.0
Austria	–	0.0	0.0	0.1
Belgium	0.0	0.2	0.2	–
Canada	1.8	1.5	2.3	1.1
Denmark	0.7	3.0	4.7	2.8
Finland	2.4	1.1	1.4	4.1
France	2.3	2.1	6.9	5.1
Germany, Fed. Rep.	75.3	32.2	66.3	21.3
Ireland	–	–	–	–
Italy	2.6	1.8	-0.2	2.4
Japan	113.4	95.4	154.0	244.1
Netherlands	2.3	0.4	1.2	2.4
New Zealand	–	0.0	–	0.0
Norway	1.4	1.1	0.9	0.5
Sweden	-0.3	-0.2	–	–
Switzerland	0.1	0.9	0.1	1.6
United Kingdom	2.7	1.1	1.3	4.3
United States	4.0	7.0	8.0	9.0
TOTAL	*214.1*	*154.5*	*253.7*	*305.6*
MULTILATERAL	*86.2*	*125.9*	*102.2*	*107.7*
OPEC COUNTRIES	–	*0.0*	–	–
E.E.C.+ MEMBERS	*87.7*	*42.7*	*82.4*	*52.8*
TOTAL	*300.3*	*280.4*	*356.0*	*413.3*

TOTAL OOF GROSS

	1983
Australia	–
Austria	–
Belgium	–
Canada	–
Denmark	–
Finland	–
France	–
Germany, Fed. Rep.	–
Ireland	–
Italy	–
Japan	–
Netherlands	–
New Zealand	–
Norway	–
Sweden	–
Switzerland	–
United Kingdom	–
United States	–
TOTAL	–
MULTILATERAL	*0.1*
OPEC COUNTRIES	–
E.E.C.+ MEMBERS	–
TOTAL	*0.1*

ODA COMMITMENTS

	1984	1985	1986	1983	1984	1985	1986
Australia	8.2	7.7	7.9	3.4	12.2	4.9	6.2
Austria	0.0	0.0	0.1	–	–	0.0	–
Belgium	–	–	–	–	–	–	–
Canada	1.5	2.3	1.1	3.3	0.2	2.7	2.7
Denmark	3.0	4.7	2.8	–	–	–	–
Finland	1.1	1.4	4.1	0.3	8.2	0.2	8.7
France	2.4	7.2	5.5	0.2	4.7	25.8	5.5
Germany, Fed. Rep.	30.5	72.6	33.7	41.5	60.8	15.9	14.7
Ireland	–	–	–	–	–	–	–
Italy	1.8	0.1	2.8	1.4	5.7	0.2	1.9
Japan	109.7	168.9	266.1	76.5	272.0	204.0	280.4
Netherlands	0.4	1.3	2.6	0.6	0.4	2.3	2.5
New Zealand	0.0	–	0.0	–	0.0	–	0.3
Norway	1.1	0.9	0.5	0.2	1.0	0.5	8.0
Sweden	–	–	–	–	–	–	–
Switzerland	0.9	0.1	1.6	0.1	0.1	1.4	6.7
United Kingdom	1.1	1.3	4.3	2.9	0.8	0.9	10.7
United States	7.0	8.0	9.0	18.9	18.4	16.8	16.2
TOTAL	*168.7*	*276.5*	*342.0*	*149.3*	*384.3*	*275.5*	*364.6*
	–	–	–	–	–	–	–
	25.2	33.2	28.2	79.6	10.0	10.0	35.0
	–	–	–	–	–	–	–
	1.9	2.1	14.6	2.2	–	–	0.2
	–	–	–	–	–	–	–
	80.0	43.8	44.9	102.7	25.0	32.3	44.0
	–	–	–	–	–	–	–
	–	–	–	–	–	–	–
	–	–	–	19.9	15.5	25.3	23.2
	7.7	12.4	11.8	–	–	–	–
	1.0	2.6	0.7	–	–	–	–
	5.3	8.7	8.1	–	–	–	–
	–	–	–	–	–	–	–
	–	–	–	–	–	–	–
	1.6	1.7	2.6	–	–	–	–
	4.4	–	–	7.0	–	–	2.2
TOTAL	*127.0*	*104.4*	*110.8*	*211.4*	*50.5*	*67.5*	*104.5*
	0.0	–	–	–	–	–	–
	41.1	89.3	66.3	48.8	72.3	44.9	35.5
TOTAL	*295.7*	*380.9*	*452.9*	*360.7*	*434.8*	*343.0*	*469.1*

TECH. COOP. GRANTS

	1984	1985	1986	1983	1984	1985	1986
Australia	8.2	7.7	7.9	1.1	0.3	1.3	1.9
Austria	0.0	0.0	0.1	–	–	–	–
Belgium	–	–	–	0.1	–	0.0	–
Canada	1.5	2.3	1.1	0.7	0.0	0.4	0.1
Denmark	0.0	0.2	0.1	0.8	0.5	0.5	0.9
Finland	0.9	1.4	1.1	0.2	0.4	0.2	0.3
France	0.4	0.2	0.3	–	–	–	–
Germany, Fed. Rep.	6.8	7.6	7.8	5.5	6.6	7.2	7.3
Ireland	–	–	–	–	–	–	–
Italy	1.8	0.1	2.8	0.0	0.1	0.1	1.9
Japan	48.1	49.2	69.0	6.2	6.2	5.8	7.6
Netherlands	0.4	0.3	0.9	0.4	0.4	0.0	0.7
New Zealand	0.0	–	0.0	–	–	–	–
Norway	1.1	0.9	0.5	–	0.1	0.1	0.1
Sweden	–	–	–	–	–	–	–
Switzerland	0.9	0.1	1.6	0.0	0.0	–	0.1
United Kingdom	1.1	1.3	4.3	0.9	0.8	0.9	1.3
United States	7.0	8.0	9.0	1.0	7.0	5.0	9.0
TOTAL	*78.3*	*79.2*	*106.3*	*16.7*	*22.3*	*21.5*	*30.9*
MULTILATERAL	17.6	27.6	37.9	19.8	15.5	25.3	23.2
OPEC	0.0	–	–	–	–	–	–
E.E.C.+ MEMBERS	12.5	11.8	30.7	7.7	8.2	8.8	11.5
TOTAL	*95.9*	*106.8*	*144.2*	*36.5*	*37.8*	*46.8*	*54.1*

TOTAL OOF NET

	1984	1985	1986	1983	1984	1985	1986
Australia	–	–	–	-1.3	-1.3	-1.0	-0.9
Austria	–	–	–	–	–	–	–
Belgium	–	–	–	–	–	–	–
Canada	0.2	0.2	–	–	0.2	0.2	–
Denmark	–	–	–	–	–	–	–
Finland	–	–	–	–	–	–	–
France	–	–	–	–	–	–	–
Germany, Fed. Rep.	7.0	1.7	–	–	7.0	1.3	-1.1
Ireland	–	–	–	–	–	–	–
Italy	–	–	–	–	–	–	–
Japan	–	–	–	–	–	–	–
Netherlands	–	–	–	-0.3	-0.2	–	–
New Zealand	–	–	–	–	–	–	–
Norway	–	–	–	–	–	–	–
Sweden	–	–	–	–	–	–	–
Switzerland	–	–	–	–	–	–	–
United Kingdom	–	–	–	–	–	–	–
United States	7.3	1.9	–	-1.5	5.8	0.5	-2.1
TOTAL	*7.3*	*1.9*	*–*	*-1.5*	*5.8*	*0.5*	*-2.1*
MULTILATERAL	0.0	–	–	-0.1	-0.2	-0.2	-0.3
OPEC	–	–	–	–	–	–	–
E.E.C.+ MEMBERS	7.3	1.9	–	–	7.3	1.5	-1.1
TOTAL	*7.3*	*1.9*	*–*	*-1.7*	*5.6*	*0.2*	*-2.4*

ODA COMMITMENTS : LOANS

DAC COUNTRIES	1983	1984	1985	1986
Australia	–	–	–	–
Austria	–	–	–	–
Belgium	–	–	–	–
Canada	–	–	–	–
Denmark	–	–	–	–
Finland	–	–	–	–
France	–	4.4	25.6	5.2
Germany, Fed. Rep.	38.8	50.2	11.6	6.9
Ireland	–	–	–	–
Italy	–	–	–	–
Japan	30.7	225.3	149.4	214.5
Netherlands	–	–	2.3	–
New Zealand	–	–	–	–
Norway	–	–	–	–
Sweden	–	–	–	–
Switzerland	–	–	–	–
United Kingdom	–	–	–	–
United States	–	–	–	–
TOTAL	*69.5*	*279.8*	*188.8*	*226.6*
MULTILATERAL	*189.3*	*35.0*	*42.2*	*81.2*
OPEC COUNTRIES	*–*	*–*	*–*	*–*
E.E.C.+ MEMBERS	*38.8*	*54.5*	*39.4*	*12.1*
TOTAL	*258.8*	*314.8*	*231.0*	*307.8*

GRANT ELEMENT OF ODA

DAC COUNTRIES	1983	1984	1985	1986
Australia	100.0	100.0	100.0	100.0
Austria	–	–	100.0	100.0
Belgium	–	–	–	–
Canada	100.0	100.0	100.0	100.0
Denmark	–	–	–	–
Finland	100.0	100.0	100.0	100.0
France	100.0	66.0	65.1	100.0
Germany, Fed. Rep.	75.7	51.1	68.0	92.2
Ireland	–	–	–	–
Italy	100.0	100.0	100.0	100.0
Japan	85.4	64.7	70.2	67.7
Netherlands	100.0	100.0	60.2	100.0
New Zealand	–	100.0	–	100.0
Norway	100.0	100.0	100.0	100.0
Sweden	–	–	–	–
Switzerland	100.0	100.0	100.0	100.0
United Kingdom	100.0	100.0	100.0	100.0
United States	100.0	100.0	100.0	100.0
TOTAL	*85.8*	*66.8*	*72.5*	*74.5*
MULTILATERAL	*81.7*	*85.7*	*90.5*	*84.3*
OPEC COUNTRIES	*–*	*–*	*–*	*–*
E.E.C.+ MEMBERS	*79.4*	*56.7*	*66.7*	*96.2*
TOTAL	*83.4*	*70.1*	*75.6*	*76.7*

OTHER AGGREGATES

COMMITMENTS: ALL SOURCES

	1983	1984	1985	1986
TOTAL BILATERAL	149.3	384.3	275.5	364.6
of which				
OPEC	–	–	–	–
CMEA	–	–	–	–
TOTAL MULTILATERAL	211.4	50.5	67.5	104.5
TOTAL BIL.& MULTIL.	360.7	434.8	343.0	469.1
of which				
ODA Grants	101.9	120.0	112.0	161.3
ODA Loans	258.8	314.8	231.0	307.8

DISBURSEMENTS:

DAC COUNTRIES COMBINED

OFFICIAL & PRIVATE	1983	1984	1985	1986
GROSS:				
Contractual Lending	206.0	177.8	253.5	293.0
Export Credits Total	53.4	87.3	56.2	57.3
Export Credits Private	53.4	80.3	54.5	57.3
NET:				
Contractual Lending	136.6	122.0	178.7	202.7
Export Credits Total	-4.6	51.5	4.6	1.3
PRIVATE SECTOR NET	-2.8	45.5	0.8	0.5
Direct Investment	-0.4	0.8	–	0.1
Portfolio Investment	0.7	-1.3	-3.6	-3.1
Export Credits	-3.1	46.0	4.3	3.4

MARKET BORROWING:

CHANGE IN CLAIMS	1983	1984	1985	1986
Banks	–	-10.0	27.0	-44.0

MEMORANDUM ITEM:

	1983	1984	1985	1986
CMEA Countr.(Gross)	16.0	11.0	0.6	6.0

	1983	1984	1985	1986	1983	1984	1985	1986		1983
TOTAL RECEIPTS NET					**TOTAL ODA NET**				**TOTAL ODA GROSS**	
DAC COUNTRIES										
Australia	–	–	–	–	–	–	–	–	Australia	–
Austria	0.0	0.1	0.2	0.3	0.0	0.1	0.2	0.3	Austria	0.0
Belgium	14.8	18.5	18.4	19.2	14.7	16.3	19.2	19.2	Belgium	14.7
Canada	0.8	1.8	1.2	1.0	0.8	1.8	1.2	1.0	Canada	0.8
Denmark	0.1	0.1	0.0	–	0.1	0.1	0.0	–	Denmark	0.1
Finland	0.7	0.3	0.3	0.0	0.7	0.3	0.3	0.0	Finland	0.7
France	46.7	21.1	19.4	12.3	21.2	17.7	22.6	20.7	France	21.2
Germany, Fed. Rep.	19.9	14.1	12.6	14.1	19.8	14.2	12.6	14.2	Germany, Fed. Rep.	19.8
Ireland	0.1	0.2	0.3	0.2	0.1	0.2	0.3	0.2	Ireland	0.1
Italy	0.9	1.7	16.7	6.2	0.9	1.6	3.8	6.2	Italy	0.9
Japan	1.2	4.1	1.7	6.0	1.2	4.1	1.7	6.0	Japan	1.2
Netherlands	0.7	0.6	1.8	4.4	0.7	0.6	1.8	2.8	Netherlands	0.7
New Zealand	–	–	–	–	–	–	–	–	New Zealand	–
Norway	1.3	0.1	1.2	3.2	1.3	0.1	1.2	3.2	Norway	1.3
Sweden	–	–	–	–	–	–	–	–	Sweden	–
Switzerland	0.9	0.7	3.3	10.7	0.9	1.3	3.3	10.7	Switzerland	0.9
United Kingdom	0.1	0.1	0.1	0.1	0.1	0.1	0.1	0.1	United Kingdom	0.1
United States	7.0	12.0	9.0	5.0	7.0	12.0	9.0	5.0	United States	7.0
TOTAL	*95.1*	*75.4*	*85.9*	*83.0*	*69.3*	*70.4*	*77.2*	*89.8*	*TOTAL*	*69.3*
MULTILATERAL										
AF.D.F.	6.6	5.4	10.3	14.6	6.6	5.4	10.3	14.6	AF.D.F.	6.6
AF.D.B.	6.4	10.5	4.9	4.0	–	–	–	–	AF.D.B.	–
AS.D.B	–	–	–	–	–	–	–	–	AS.D.B	–
CAR.D.B.	–	–	–	–	–	–	–	–	CAR.D.B.	–
E.E.C.	12.5	10.0	9.5	11.2	12.5	10.0	9.5	11.2	E.E.C.	12.5
IBRD	–	–	–	–	–	–	–	–	IBRD	–
IDA	27.2	26.5	17.7	43.1	27.2	26.5	17.7	43.1	IDA	28.2
I.D.B.	–	–	–	–	–	–	–	–	I.D.B.	–
IFAD	0.5	1.5	5.6	2.4	0.5	1.5	5.6	2.4	IFAD	0.5
I.F.C.	3.5	–	–	-0.7	–	–	–	–	I.F.C.	–
IMF TRUST FUND	–	–	–	–	–	–	–	–	IMF TRUST FUND	–
U.N. AGENCIES	–	–	–	–	–	–	–	–	U.N. AGENCIES	–
UNDP	7.8	6.2	6.5	7.6	7.8	6.2	6.5	7.6	UNDP	7.8
UNTA	1.0	0.9	0.8	1.0	1.0	0.9	0.8	1.0	UNTA	1.0
UNICEF	1.2	1.1	2.7	2.7	1.2	1.1	2.7	2.7	UNICEF	1.2
UNRWA	–	–	–	–	–	–	–	–	UNRWA	–
WFP	2.5	2.8	1.5	1.5	2.5	2.8	1.5	1.5	WFP	2.5
UNHCR	1.0	1.0	0.7	0.8	1.0	1.0	0.7	0.8	UNHCR	1.0
Other Multilateral	2.4	2.6	3.0	2.5	2.4	2.6	3.0	2.5	Other Multilateral	2.4
Arab OPEC Agencies	1.4	0.0	1.9	3.9	1.4	0.0	0.7	2.1	Arab OPEC Agencies	1.9
TOTAL	*74.0*	*68.3*	*65.2*	*94.5*	*64.1*	*57.8*	*59.1*	*89.4*	*TOTAL*	*65.6*
OPEC COUNTRIES	*6.6*	*13.2*	*6.3*	*8.4*	*6.6*	*13.2*	*6.3*	*8.4*	*OPEC COUNTRIES*	*7.1*
E.E.C.+ MEMBERS	*95.7*	*66.3*	*78.7*	*67.9*	*70.0*	*60.7*	*70.0*	*74.7*	*E.E.C.+ MEMBERS*	*70.0*
TOTAL	*175.7*	*156.9*	*157.4*	*185.9*	*140.0*	*141.4*	*142.6*	*187.6*	*TOTAL*	*142.0*
ODA LOANS GROSS					**ODA LOANS NET**				**GRANTS**	
DAC COUNTRIES										
Australia	–	–	–	–	–	–	–	–	Australia	–
Austria	–	–	–	–	–	–	–	–	Austria	0.0
Belgium	–	1.7	3.4	–	–	1.7	3.4	–	Belgium	14.7
Canada	–	–	–	–	–	–	–	–	Canada	0.8
Denmark	–	–	–	–	–	–	–	–	Denmark	0.1
Finland	–	–	–	–	–	–	–	–	Finland	0.7
France	10.1	6.7	13.1	9.2	10.1	6.7	13.1	8.6	France	11.1
Germany, Fed. Rep.	–	–	–	0.0	–	–	–	0.0	Germany, Fed. Rep.	19.8
Ireland	–	–	–	–	–	–	–	–	Ireland	0.1
Italy	–	–	0.2	1.6	–	–	0.2	1.6	Italy	0.9
Japan	–	–	–	–	–	–	–	–	Japan	1.2
Netherlands	–	–	0.8	1.9	–	–	0.8	1.9	Netherlands	0.7
New Zealand	–	–	–	–	–	–	–	–	New Zealand	–
Norway	–	–	–	–	–	–	–	–	Norway	1.3
Sweden	–	–	–	–	–	–	–	–	Sweden	–
Switzerland	–	–	–	–	–	–	–	–	Switzerland	0.9
United Kingdom	–	–	–	–	–	–	–	–	United Kingdom	0.1
United States	–	–	–	–	–	–	–	–	United States	7.0
TOTAL	*10.1*	*8.5*	*17.4*	*12.7*	*10.1*	*8.5*	*17.4*	*12.1*	*TOTAL*	*59.2*
MULTILATERAL	*39.7*	*36.2*	*36.7*	*65.4*	*38.2*	*35.1*	*34.4*	*62.9*	*MULTILATERAL*	*25.9*
OPEC COUNTRIES	*3.4*	*9.9*	*3.4*	*8.2*	*2.9*	*9.4*	*2.2*	*7.4*	*OPEC COUNTRIES*	*3.7*
E.E.C.+ MEMBERS	*12.6*	*10.3*	*17.4*	*13.3*	*12.6*	*10.2*	*17.4*	*12.7*	*E.E.C.+ MEMBERS*	*57.4*
TOTAL	*53.2*	*54.5*	*57.6*	*86.3*	*51.2*	*53.0*	*54.1*	*82.3*	*TOTAL*	*88.8*
TOTAL OFFICIAL GROSS					**TOTAL OFFICIAL NET**				**TOTAL OOF GROSS**	
DAC COUNTRIES										
Australia	–	–	–	–	–	–	–	–	Australia	–
Austria	0.0	0.1	0.2	0.3	0.0	0.1	0.2	0.3	Austria	–
Belgium	14.7	16.6	19.6	19.4	14.7	16.6	19.6	19.4	Belgium	–
Canada	0.8	1.8	1.2	1.0	0.8	1.8	1.2	1.0	Canada	–
Denmark	0.1	0.1	0.0	–	0.1	0.1	0.0	–	Denmark	–
Finland	0.7	0.3	0.3	0.0	0.7	0.3	0.3	0.0	Finland	–
France	21.2	17.9	22.8	21.3	21.1	17.8	22.7	20.7	France	–
Germany, Fed. Rep.	19.8	14.2	12.6	14.2	19.8	14.2	12.6	14.2	Germany, Fed. Rep.	–
Ireland	0.1	0.2	0.3	0.2	0.1	0.2	0.3	0.2	Ireland	–
Italy	0.9	1.6	3.8	6.2	0.9	1.6	3.8	6.2	Italy	–
Japan	1.2	4.1	1.7	6.0	1.2	4.1	1.7	6.0	Japan	–
Netherlands	0.7	0.6	1.8	2.8	0.7	0.6	1.8	2.8	Netherlands	–
New Zealand	–	–	–	–	–	–	–	–	New Zealand	–
Norway	1.3	0.1	1.2	3.2	1.3	0.1	1.2	3.2	Norway	–
Sweden	–	–	–	–	–	–	–	–	Sweden	–
Switzerland	0.9	1.3	3.3	10.7	0.9	1.3	3.3	10.7	Switzerland	–
United Kingdom	0.1	0.1	0.1	0.1	0.1	0.1	0.1	0.1	United Kingdom	–
United States	7.0	12.0	9.0	5.0	7.0	12.0	9.0	5.0	United States	–
TOTAL	*69.3*	*70.8*	*77.7*	*90.5*	*69.2*	*70.8*	*77.7*	*90.0*	*TOTAL*	*–*
MULTILATERAL	*75.6*	*69.8*	*68.2*	*98.9*	*74.0*	*68.3*	*65.2*	*94.5*	*MULTILATERAL*	*10.0*
OPEC COUNTRIES	*7.1*	*13.7*	*7.4*	*9.2*	*6.6*	*13.2*	*6.3*	*8.4*	*OPEC COUNTRIES*	*–*
E.E.C.+ MEMBERS	*70.0*	*61.2*	*70.5*	*75.4*	*69.9*	*61.1*	*70.4*	*74.9*	*E.E.C.+ MEMBERS*	*–*
TOTAL	*152.0*	*154.3*	*153.4*	*198.6*	*149.8*	*152.2*	*149.2*	*192.8*	*TOTAL*	*10.0*

ODA COMMITMENTS

1984	1985	1986	1983	1984	1985	1986
0.1	0.2	0.3	0.2	0.0	0.2	–
16.3	19.2	19.2	8.1	11.0	9.0	20.3
1.8	1.2	1.0	1.2	2.3	1.1	0.3
0.1	0.0	–	–	–	0.0	–
0.3	0.3	0.0	-0.7	0.4	0.2	-0.2
17.7	22.6	21.3	21.6	19.5	27.4	21.3
14.2	12.6	14.2	21.9	17.7	14.2	8.9
0.2	0.3	0.2	0.1	0.2	0.3	0.2
1.6	3.8	6.2	0.9	5.3	3.7	7.2
4.1	1.7	6.0	4.2	1.4	4.9	4.1
0.6	1.8	2.8	1.1	1.3	3.5	0.8
–	–	–	–	–	–	–
0.1	1.2	3.2	–	0.2	–	–
–	–	–	–	–	–	–
1.3	3.3	10.7	1.8	2.2	4.3	9.4
0.1	0.1	0.1	0.1	0.1	0.1	0.1
12.0	9.0	5.0	9.9	12.1	8.6	5.7
70.4	77.2	90.4	70.4	73.6	77.3	78.1
5.4	10.4	14.7	12.2	0.7	32.9	13.7
–	–	–	–	–	–	–
10.0	9.5	11.2	28.5	15.6	13.3	15.6
–	–	–	–	–	–	–
26.9	19.2	44.4	30.8	5.1	52.7	31.2
–	–	–	–	–	–	–
1.5	5.6	2.9	–	–	–	–
–	–	–	–	–	–	–
–	–	–	15.8	14.5	15.2	16.0
6.2	6.5	7.6	–	–	–	–
0.9	0.8	1.0	–	–	–	–
1.1	2.7	2.7	–	–	–	–
–	–	–	–	–	–	–
2.8	1.5	1.5	–	–	–	–
1.0	0.7	0.8	–	–	–	–
2.6	3.0	2.5	–	–	–	–
0.5	1.4	2.8	–	5.0	1.6	3.0
58.9	61.5	91.9	87.3	41.0	115.7	79.5
13.7	7.4	9.2	14.6	8.9	6.7	2.6
60.7	70.0	75.3	82.2	70.7	71.4	74.4
143.0	146.1	191.6	172.3	123.5	199.7	160.1

TECH. COOP. GRANTS

1984	1985	1986	1983	1984	1985	1986
–	–	–	–	–	–	–
0.1	0.2	0.3	0.0	–	–	–
14.6	15.8	19.2	10.2	10.0	10.5	13.1
1.8	1.2	1.0	0.2	–	0.6	–
0.1	0.0	–	0.1	0.1	–	–
0.3	0.3	0.0	0.7	0.3	0.3	0.0
11.0	9.5	12.1	7.8	7.6	6.8	9.5
14.2	12.6	14.2	6.9	5.6	5.5	7.0
0.2	0.3	0.2	0.1	0.2	0.3	0.1
1.6	3.7	4.6	0.9	1.6	2.3	4.0
4.1	1.7	6.0	–	0.1	0.3	0.3
0.6	1.0	0.9	0.5	0.5	0.7	0.3
–	–	–	–	–	–	–
0.1	1.2	3.2	–	–	–	–
–	–	–	–	–	–	–
1.3	3.3	10.7	0.6	0.8	0.8	0.7
0.1	0.1	0.1	0.1	0.1	0.1	0.1
12.0	9.0	5.0	2.0	4.0	4.0	4.0
61.9	59.7	77.7	30.0	30.9	32.0	39.2
22.7	24.8	26.5	13.3	11.8	13.7	14.7
3.8	4.0	1.0	–	–	–	–
50.4	52.5	62.0	26.5	25.7	26.1	34.2
88.4	88.5	105.3	43.3	42.7	45.7	53.8

TOTAL OOF NET

1984	1985	1986	1983	1984	1985	1986
–	–	–	–	–	–	–
–	–	–	–	–	–	–
0.3	0.4	0.2	–	0.3	0.4	0.2
–	–	–	–	–	–	–
–	–	–	–	–	–	–
0.1	0.2	–	0.0	0.1	0.1	–
–	–	–	–	–	–	–
–	–	–	–	–	–	–
–	–	–	–	–	–	–
–	–	–	–	–	–	–
–	–	–	–	–	–	–
–	–	–	–	–	–	–
–	–	–	–	–	–	–
–	–	–	–	–	–	–
0.4	0.6	0.2	0.0	0.4	0.5	0.2
10.9	6.7	6.9	9.9	10.5	6.1	5.1
–	–	–	–	–	–	–
0.4	0.6	0.2	0.0	0.4	0.5	0.2
11.4	7.3	7.1	9.8	10.9	6.6	5.3

ODA COMMITMENTS : LOANS

DAC COUNTRIES	1983	1984	1985	1986
Australia	–	–	–	–
Austria	–	–	–	–
Belgium	–	1.7	1.2	1.1
Canada	–	–	–	–
Denmark	–	–	–	–
Finland	–	–	–	–
France	8.6	9.2	19.6	9.2
Germany, Fed. Rep.	–	–	–	–
Ireland	–	–	–	–
Italy	–	2.6	–	–
Japan	–	–	–	–
Netherlands	–	–	2.7	–
New Zealand	–	–	–	–
Norway	–	–	–	–
Sweden	–	–	–	–
Switzerland	–	–	–	–
United Kingdom	–	–	–	–
United States	–	–	–	–
TOTAL	8.6	13.5	23.5	10.3
MULTILATERAL	55.2	13.2	87.2	50.8
OPEC COUNTRIES	14.6	8.9	6.7	2.6
E.E.C.+ MEMBERS	20.7	15.9	23.5	13.3
TOTAL	78.3	35.6	117.3	63.7

GRANT ELEMENT OF ODA

DAC COUNTRIES	1983	1984	1985	1986
Australia	–	–	–	–
Austria	100.0	100.0	100.0	–
Belgium	100.0	97.5	95.2	97.4
Canada	100.0	100.0	100.0	100.0
Denmark	–	–	100.0	–
Finland	100.0	100.0	100.0	100.0
France	59.2	68.2	62.9	79.1
Germany, Fed. Rep.	100.0	100.0	100.0	100.0
Ireland	100.0	100.0	100.0	100.0
Italy	100.0	75.7	100.0	100.0
Japan	100.0	100.0	100.0	100.0
Netherlands	100.0	100.0	69.0	100.0
New Zealand	–	–	–	–
Norway	–	100.0	–	–
Sweden	–	–	–	–
Switzerland	100.0	100.0	100.0	100.0
United Kingdom	100.0	100.0	100.0	100.0
United States	100.0	100.0	100.0	100.0
TOTAL	82.6	89.4	85.3	93.9
MULTILATERAL	92.1	89.3	85.5	87.7
OPEC COUNTRIES	45.9	53.2	49.5	52.8
E.E.C.+ MEMBERS	82.6	88.6	84.1	93.3
TOTAL	82.8	87.0	84.2	90.1

OTHER AGGREGATES

COMMITMENTS: ALL SOURCES

	1983	1984	1985	1986
TOTAL BILATERAL	85.0	82.6	84.0	80.7
of which				
OPEC	14.6	8.9	6.7	2.6
CMEA	–	–	–	–
TOTAL MULTILATERAL	87.3	49.0	116.0	79.5
TOTAL BIL.& MULTIL.	172.3	131.5	200.0	160.1
of which				
ODA Grants	94.1	87.9	82.4	96.4
ODA Loans	78.3	35.6	117.3	63.7

DISBURSEMENTS:
DAC COUNTRIES COMBINED

OFFICIAL & PRIVATE	1983	1984	1985	1986
GROSS:				
Contractual Lending	23.8	14.0	32.1	5.4
Export Credits Total	13.7	5.4	14.5	-7.2
Export Credits Private	13.7	5.4	14.5	-7.2
NET:				
Contractual Lending	19.4	9.9	27.7	3.9
Export Credits Total	9.4	1.4	10.2	-8.2
PRIVATE SECTOR NET	25.8	4.6	8.3	-7.0
Direct Investment	3.0	1.2	0.2	0.3
Portfolio Investment	13.4	2.1	-2.2	0.9
Export Credits	9.4	1.4	10.2	-8.2

MARKET BORROWING:
CHANGE IN CLAIMS

	1983	1984	1985	1986
Banks	–	2.0	6.0	-5.0

MEMORANDUM ITEM:

	1983	1984	1985	1986
CMEA Countr.(Gross)	–	–	–	–

TOTAL RECEIPTS NET | TOTAL ODA NET | TOTAL ODA GROSS

	TOTAL RECEIPTS NET 1983	1984	1985	1986	TOTAL ODA NET 1983	1984	1985	1986	TOTAL ODA GROSS 1983
DAC COUNTRIES									
Australia	–	–	–	0.0	–	–	–	0.0	–
Austria	0.0	0.0	0.0	0.0	0.0	0.0	0.0	0.0	0.0
Belgium	43.1	19.9	62.1	15.9	8.3	9.4	2.9	8.2	8.3
Canada	17.3	18.0	16.9	-3.5	13.7	23.6	15.0	13.4	13.7
Denmark	6.2	22.1	3.2	15.5	0.0	12.0	0.0	17.9	0.0
Finland	–	0.0	–	0.1	–	0.0	–	0.1	–
France	201.8	94.1	11.1	11.6	55.6	69.2	57.0	65.6	59.9
Germany, Fed. Rep.	-1.0	27.8	29.9	34.3	9.9	12.1	11.3	22.2	12.4
Ireland	0.0	0.0	0.0	0.0	0.0	0.0	0.0	0.0	0.0
Italy	-0.7	-0.4	10.0	42.1	0.7	2.3	10.6	11.9	0.7
Japan	0.8	1.7	1.6	4.9	0.1	2.0	1.2	4.9	0.1
Netherlands	24.0	-9.1	-2.4	-4.3	2.9	3.1	2.9	3.8	3.1
New Zealand	–	–	–	–	–	–	–	–	–
Norway	–	–	0.1	0.1	–	–	0.1	0.1	–
Sweden	0.7	-0.1	–	-0.1	–	–	–	–	–
Switzerland	5.5	5.7	12.2	8.2	2.6	3.9	5.1	8.2	2.5
United Kingdom	2.4	12.2	2.4	34.1	4.5	7.2	5.1	2.1	4.6
United States	5.0	20.0	6.0	3.0	11.0	10.0	15.0	18.0	12.0
TOTAL	*305.0*	*212.0*	*153.0*	*161.8*	*109.3*	*154.7*	*126.3*	*176.5*	*117.4*
MULTILATERAL									
AF.D.F.	–	0.0	–	–	–	0.0	–	–	–
AF.D.B.	1.3	6.6	8.9	14.6	–	–	–	–	–
AS.D.B	–	–	–	–	–	–	–	–	–
CAR.D.B.	–	–	–	–	–	–	–	–	–
E.E.C.	3.8	7.6	22.0	46.3	5.2	7.1	12.5	26.8	6.5
IBRD	35.8	35.3	31.2	45.3	2.1	1.2	2.5	–	2.1
IDA	12.0	6.7	3.0	3.0	12.0	6.7	3.0	3.0	12.6
I.D.B.	–	–	–	–	–	–	–	–	–
IFAD	0.4	0.7	0.9	4.9	0.4	0.7	0.9	4.9	0.4
I.F.C.	0.5	-1.1	-0.6	1.9	–	–	–	–	–
IMF TRUST FUND	–	–	–	–	–	–	–	–	–
U.N. AGENCIES	–	–	–	–	–	–	–	–	–
UNDP	4.2	2.7	4.6	4.8	4.2	2.7	4.6	4.8	4.2
UNTA	0.9	0.4	0.9	0.9	0.9	0.4	0.9	0.9	0.9
UNICEF	0.4	0.7	0.4	1.0	0.4	0.7	0.4	1.0	0.4
UNRWA	–	–	–	–	–	–	–	–	–
WFP	1.0	1.1	4.8	2.4	1.0	1.1	4.8	2.4	1.0
UNHCR	0.6	0.7	1.6	2.3	0.6	0.7	1.6	2.3	0.6
Other Multilateral	1.2	0.9	0.9	0.9	1.2	0.9	0.9	0.9	1.2
Arab OPEC Agencies	-2.1	2.0	-2.5	-2.8	-2.1	2.0	-2.2	-1.8	0.3
TOTAL	*59.9*	*64.3*	*76.0*	*125.5*	*25.8*	*24.2*	*29.7*	*45.2*	*30.1*
OPEC COUNTRIES	*-6.4*	*7.4*	*3.0*	*3.5*	*-6.1*	*7.6*	*3.3*	*3.5*	*0.2*
E.E.C.+ MEMBERS	*279.6*	*174.3*	*138.2*	*195.5*	*87.1*	*122.4*	*102.4*	*158.6*	*95.5*
TOTAL	*358.6*	*283.7*	*232.0*	*290.8*	*129.0*	*186.5*	*159.3*	*225.1*	*147.7*

ODA LOANS GROSS | ODA LOANS NET | GRANTS

	ODA LOANS GROSS 1983	1984	1985	1986	ODA LOANS NET 1983	1984	1985	1986	GRANTS 1983
DAC COUNTRIES									
Australia	–	–	–	–	0.0	0.0	0.0	0.0	–
Austria	–	–	–	–	–	–	–	–	0.0
Belgium	–	4.8	–	3.4	–	4.8	–	3.4	8.3
Canada	9.0	18.1	9.2	3.5	9.0	18.0	8.8	3.0	4.8
Denmark	–	12.0	0.1	18.0	–	12.0	0.0	17.9	0.0
Finland	–	–	–	–	–	–	–	–	–
France	21.8	19.0	25.4	25.3	17.5	15.9	21.2	19.3	38.1
Germany, Fed. Rep.	3.9	5.5	5.7	13.2	1.5	3.5	2.8	8.7	8.5
Ireland	–	–	–	–	–	–	–	–	0.0
Italy	–	–	8.7	9.3	–	–	8.7	9.3	0.7
Japan	–	–	–	–	–	–	–	–	0.1
Netherlands	0.7	1.2	0.1	–	0.5	1.2	-0.2	–	2.4
New Zealand	–	–	–	–	–	–	–	–	–
Norway	–	–	–	–	–	–	–	–	–
Sweden	–	–	–	–	–	–	–	–	–
Switzerland	0.6	2.2	3.2	5.4	0.6	2.2	3.2	5.4	2.0
United Kingdom	4.1	6.9	4.8	–	4.0	6.8	3.9	-0.4	0.5
United States	–	–	–	1.0	-1.0	-1.0	-1.0	–	12.0
TOTAL	*40.0*	*69.6*	*57.2*	*79.0*	*31.9*	*63.3*	*47.5*	*66.4*	*77.4*
MULTILATERAL	*17.0*	*16.0*	*7.4*	*9.0*	*12.7*	*11.2*	*2.6*	*4.3*	*13.1*
OPEC COUNTRIES	*–*	*12.1*	*7.1*	*6.9*	*-6.3*	*7.6*	*3.3*	*3.5*	*0.2*
E.E.C.+ MEMBERS	*32.4*	*51.3*	*44.8*	*69.1*	*24.0*	*44.7*	*35.0*	*56.2*	*63.1*
TOTAL	*57.0*	*97.7*	*71.7*	*94.9*	*38.2*	*82.1*	*53.4*	*74.2*	*90.7*

TOTAL OFFICIAL GROSS | TOTAL OFFICIAL NET | TOTAL OOF GROSS

	TOTAL OFFICIAL GROSS 1983	1984	1985	1986	TOTAL OFFICIAL NET 1983	1984	1985	1986	TOTAL OOF GROSS 1983
DAC COUNTRIES									
Australia	–	–	–	0.0	–	–	–	0.0	–
Austria	0.0	0.0	0.0	0.1	0.0	0.0	0.0	0.0	0.0
Belgium	8.3	9.8	3.7	8.3	8.3	9.8	3.7	8.3	–
Canada	25.7	30.1	37.1	21.9	17.3	18.0	16.9	-3.5	11.9
Denmark	2.1	15.2	4.2	20.5	2.1	15.0	3.6	18.3	2.1
Finland	–	0.0	–	0.1	–	0.0	–	0.1	–
France	68.1	79.1	75.2	89.2	56.5	69.1	61.8	71.4	8.3
Germany, Fed. Rep.	12.4	27.3	28.1	46.5	9.7	25.2	24.9	36.9	–
Ireland	0.0	0.0	0.0	0.0	0.0	0.0	0.0	0.0	–
Italy	0.7	2.3	10.6	11.9	0.2	1.3	9.8	11.3	–
Japan	0.1	2.0	1.2	4.9	0.1	2.0	1.2	4.9	–
Netherlands	3.2	3.1	3.2	3.8	3.0	3.1	2.4	3.8	0.1
New Zealand	–	–	–	–	–	–	–	–	–
Norway	–	–	0.1	0.1	–	–	0.1	0.1	–
Sweden	0.8	–	–	–	0.7	-0.1	–	-0.1	0.8
Switzerland	2.5	3.9	5.1	8.2	2.6	3.9	5.1	8.2	–
United Kingdom	4.8	7.5	9.7	5.5	4.6	7.4	8.8	5.0	0.1
United States	13.0	29.0	16.0	19.0	13.0	20.0	6.0	3.0	1.0
TOTAL	*141.8*	*209.3*	*194.2*	*239.8*	*110.0*	*174.6*	*144.2*	*167.7*	*24.4*
MULTILATERAL	*78.9*	*86.1*	*104.4*	*161.6*	*59.9*	*64.3*	*76.0*	*125.5*	*48.8*
OPEC COUNTRIES	*0.2*	*12.1*	*7.2*	*6.9*	*-6.4*	*7.4*	*3.0*	*3.5*	*–*
E.E.C.+ MEMBERS	*108.4*	*156.6*	*161.8*	*239.1*	*88.2*	*138.4*	*137.0*	*201.3*	*12.9*
TOTAL	*220.9*	*307.6*	*305.7*	*408.3*	*163.5*	*246.3*	*223.3*	*296.6*	*73.2*

CAMEROON

ODA COMMITMENTS

1984	1985	1986	1983	1984	1985	1986
–	–	0.0	–	–	–	–
0.0	0.0	0.1	0.0	0.0	0.0	–
9.4	2.9	8.2	4.5	7.7	1.5	8.2
23.7	15.3	13.9	8.4	65.1	26.0	45.1
12.0	0.1	18.0	–	13.0	–	18.5
0.0	–	0.1	–	–	–	–
72.3	61.2	71.6	72.1	79.0	62.6	71.6
14.0	14.2	26.7	48.5	19.2	5.0	27.1
0.0	0.0	0.0	0.0	0.0	0.0	0.0
2.3	10.6	11.9	1.9	22.0	4.2	5.2
2.0	1.2	4.9	0.1	17.6	3.3	1.8
3.1	3.2	3.8	2.5	2.0	3.0	4.0
–	–	–	–	–	–	–
–	0.1	0.1	–	–	0.0	0.1
–	–	–	–	–	–	–
3.9	5.1	8.2	1.6	0.9	12.3	2.2
7.4	5.9	2.6	0.5	0.4	1.0	1.8
11.0	16.0	19.0	13.6	33.1	22.4	27.6
161.0	*135.9*	*189.1*	*153.7*	*260.0*	*141.2*	*213.4*
0.0	–	–	–	0.8	1.8	20.8
–	–	–	–	–	–	–
–	–	–	–	–	–	–
8.5	14.0	28.7	22.3	11.9	3.8	15.8
1.2	2.5	–	–	–	–	–
7.6	4.0	4.1	–	–	–	–
–	–	–	–	–	–	–
0.7	0.9	4.9	14.4	–	–	–
–	–	–	–	–	–	–
–	–	–	8.3	6.5	13.1	12.2
2.7	4.6	4.8	–	–	–	–
0.4	0.9	0.9	–	–	–	–
0.7	0.4	1.0	–	–	–	–
–	–	–	–	–	–	–
1.1	4.8	2.4	–	–	–	–
0.7	1.6	2.3	–	–	–	–
0.9	0.9	0.9	–	–	–	–
4.4	0.0	–	–	6.1	–	3.9
28.9	*34.5*	*49.9*	*44.9*	*25.2*	*18.8*	*52.7*
12.1	*7.2*	*6.9*	*0.2*	*19.1*	*7.3*	–
129.0	*112.2*	*171.5*	*152.2*	*155.3*	*81.1*	*152.4*
202.1	*177.6*	*245.8*	*198.8*	*304.3*	*167.3*	*266.1*

TECH. COOP. GRANTS

1984	1985	1986	1983	1984	1985	1986
–	–	0.0	–	–	–	–
0.0	0.0	0.1	0.0	–	–	–
4.7	2.9	4.9	0.7	0.7	0.8	1.1
5.5	6.1	10.4	0.8	–	3.1	–
0.0	–	–	0.0	0.4	0.1	0.7
0.0	–	0.1	–	0.0	–	0.0
53.2	35.8	46.3	30.6	35.0	27.4	41.0
8.6	8.6	13.5	8.5	8.5	8.4	13.4
0.0	0.0	0.0	0.0	0.0	0.0	0.0
2.3	1.9	2.6	0.7	2.3	1.9	2.6
2.0	1.2	4.9	0.1	0.2	0.7	1.3
2.0	3.1	3.8	2.1	2.0	1.9	3.5
–	–	–	–	–	–	–
–	0.1	0.1	–	–	–	0.1
–	–	–	–	–	–	–
1.7	1.9	2.9	0.9	0.8	0.7	1.3
0.4	1.2	2.6	0.5	0.4	1.0	1.6
11.0	16.0	18.0	7.0	9.0	8.0	15.0
91.4	*78.8*	*110.1*	*52.0*	*59.3*	*54.2*	*81.6*
13.0	*27.1*	*40.9*	*7.3*	*5.4*	*8.4*	*10.1*
0.0	*0.0*	*0.0*	–	–	–	–
77.7	*67.4*	*102.4*	*43.1*	*49.3*	*41.6*	*64.2*
104.4	*105.9*	*151.0*	*59.2*	*64.7*	*62.5*	*91.7*

TOTAL OOF NET

1984	1985	1986	1983	1984	1985	1986
–	–	–	–	–	–	–
–	–	–	–	–	–	–
0.4	0.7	0.1	–	0.4	0.7	0.1
6.5	21.8	7.9	3.6	-5.5	1.9	-16.9
3.2	4.1	2.5	2.1	3.0	3.6	0.5
–	–	–	–	–	–	–
6.8	14.0	17.6	0.9	-0.1	4.8	5.8
13.3	13.8	19.8	-0.3	13.0	13.6	14.6
–	–	–	-0.5	-0.9	-0.9	-0.5
–	–	–	–	–	–	–
–	–	–	0.1	–	-0.5	–
–	–	–	–	–	–	–
–	–	–	–	–	–	–
–	–	–	0.7	-0.1	–	-0.1
0.2	3.7	2.9	0.1	0.1	3.7	2.9
18.0	–	–	-6.0	10.0	-9.0	-15.0
48.3	*58.2*	*50.8*	*0.7*	*19.9*	*18.0*	*-8.8*
57.2	*69.9*	*111.7*	*34.1*	*40.1*	*46.3*	*80.3*
–	–	–	*-0.2*	*-0.2*	*-0.2*	–
27.6	*49.6*	*67.6*	*1.1*	*16.1*	*34.6*	*42.7*
105.5	*128.1*	*162.4*	*34.6*	*59.7*	*64.0*	*71.5*

ODA COMMITMENTS : LOANS

DAC COUNTRIES

	1983	1984	1985	1986
Australia	–	–	–	–
Austria	–	–	–	–
Belgium	–	4.8	–	3.4
Canada	5.7	56.9	–	–
Denmark	–	13.0	–	18.5
Finland	–	–	–	–
France	32.5	25.7	28.0	25.3
Germany, Fed. Rep.	42.7	4.4	–	8.3
Ireland	–	–	–	–
Italy	–	17.7	–	–
Japan	–	15.1	–	–
Netherlands	0.1	–	–	–
New Zealand	–	–	–	–
Norway	–	–	–	–
Sweden	–	–	–	–
Switzerland	–	–	9.8	–
United Kingdom	–	–	–	–
United States	4.0	17.9	–	8.5
TOTAL	*85.0*	*155.5*	*37.8*	*63.9*
MULTILATERAL	*34.7*	*6.9*	*1.8*	*24.8*
OPEC COUNTRIES	–	*19.1*	*7.3*	–
E.E.C.+ MEMBERS	*95.7*	*65.6*	*28.0*	*55.5*
TOTAL	*119.8*	*181.4*	*46.9*	*88.7*

GRANT ELEMENT OF ODA

DAC COUNTRIES

	1983	1984	1985	1986
Australia	–	–	–	–
Austria	100.0	100.0	100.0	–
Belgium	100.0	90.0	100.0	93.7
Canada	93.1	90.7	100.0	100.0
Denmark	–	76.0	–	74.5
Finland	–	–	–	–
France	68.7	79.2	70.7	73.8
Germany, Fed. Rep.	85.3	96.2	100.0	82.3
Ireland	100.0	100.0	100.0	100.0
Italy	100.0	54.7	100.0	100.0
Japan	100.0	59.6	100.0	100.0
Netherlands	100.0	100.0	100.0	100.0
New Zealand	–	–	–	–
Norway	–	–	100.0	100.0
Sweden	–	–	–	–
Switzerland	100.0	100.0	86.7	100.0
United Kingdom	100.0	100.0	100.0	100.0
United States	91.5	84.4	100.0	91.2
TOTAL	*79.6*	*81.1*	*85.8*	*85.2*
MULTILATERAL	*100.0*	*69.3*	*98.4*	*89.1*
OPEC COUNTRIES	*100.0*	*52.8*	*40.1*	–
E.E.C.+ MEMBERS	*77.5*	*80.0*	*77.4*	*80.9*
TOTAL	*80.8*	*77.9*	*85.2*	*85.9*

OTHER AGGREGATES

COMMITMENTS: ALL SOURCES

	1983	1984	1985	1986
TOTAL BILATERAL	213.4	358.4	199.2	258.9
of which				
OPEC	0.2	19.1	7.3	–
CMEA	–	–	–	6.4
TOTAL MULTILATERAL	134.5	68.8	207.3	188.2
TOTAL BIL.& MULTIL.	348.0	427.1	406.6	447.0
of which				
ODA Grants	79.0	122.9	120.4	177.4
ODA Loans	119.8	181.4	46.9	88.7

DISBURSEMENTS:

DAC COUNTRIES COMBINED

	1983	1984	1985	1986
OFFICIAL & PRIVATE				
GROSS:				
Contractual Lending	344.5	283.9	286.6	200.5
Export Credits Total	295.9	207.0	211.3	98.5
Export Credits Private	280.1	166.4	172.0	70.8
NET:				
Contractual Lending	172.2	106.5	101.3	88.2
Export Credits Total	139.1	42.8	45.5	11.1
PRIVATE SECTOR NET	195.0	37.4	8.8	-5.9
Direct Investment	9.7	14.8	-0.5	32.0
Portfolio Investment	45.8	-1.1	-27.3	-68.5
Export Credits	139.6	23.8	36.5	30.7

MARKET BORROWING:

CHANGE IN CLAIMS

	1983	1984	1985	1986
Banks	–	34.0	-1.0	10.0

MEMORANDUM ITEM:

	1983	1984	1985	1986
CMEA Countr.(Gross)	–	–	–	–

DISBURSEMENTS, UNLESS OTHERWISE STATED

TOTAL RECEIPTS NET

DAC COUNTRIES	1983	1984	1985	1986
Australia	—	—	—	—
Austria	0.1	0.1	0.1	0.1
Belgium	0.1	0.1	-0.5	0.0
Canada	0.2	0.2	0.4	0.1
Denmark	0.1	—	1.2	0.5
Finland	—	—	—	—
France	53.9	53.8	50.9	56.4
Germany, Fed. Rep.	4.4	8.3	6.7	9.0
Ireland	—	—	—	—
Italy	1.6	0.8	1.4	6.0
Japan	4.2	2.4	2.2	7.3
Netherlands	0.1	0.3	0.0	0.3
New Zealand	—	—	—	—
Norway	—	—	—	—
Sweden	—	—	—	—
Switzerland	0.1	0.3	0.3	0.1
United Kingdom	0.0	0.0	0.1	0.1
United States	6.0	2.0	3.0	2.0
TOTAL	70.8	68.1	65.7	81.8
MULTILATERAL				
AF.D.F.	5.5	5.0	8.9	6.1
AF.D.B.	0.8	1.6	3.1	6.2
AS.D.B	—	—	—	—
CAR.D.B.	—	—	—	—
E.E.C.	11.8	12.0	10.1	7.3
IBRD	—	—	—	—
IDA	3.8	11.8	10.5	19.1
I.D.B.	—	—	—	—
IFAD	0.4	0.3	1.1	1.1
I.F.C.	—	—	—	—
IMF TRUST FUND	—	—	—	—
U.N. AGENCIES				
UNDP	2.3	4.4	4.1	5.0
UNTA	0.8	0.7	0.7	1.0
UNICEF	0.8	1.7	0.9	1.2
UNRWA	—	—	—	—
WFP	1.0	1.2	1.7	1.9
UNHCR	1.2	5.8	2.9	3.7
Other Multilateral	0.5	0.5	0.6	0.7
Arab OPEC Agencies	-0.1	1.7	1.4	3.7
TOTAL	28.6	46.6	45.9	57.0
OPEC COUNTRIES	0.3	0.2	0.4	4.0
E.E.C.+ MEMBERS	72.0	75.2	69.8	79.5
TOTAL	99.7	115.0	111.9	142.8

TOTAL ODA NET

	1983	1984	1985	1986
Australia	—	—	—	—
Austria	0.1	0.1	0.1	0.1
Belgium	0.1	0.2	0.1	0.1
Canada	0.2	0.2	0.4	0.1
Denmark	0.1	—	0.1	0.5
Finland	—	—	—	—
France	54.1	54.4	47.2	59.8
Germany, Fed. Rep.	4.6	8.3	6.8	8.9
Ireland	—	—	—	—
Italy	0.2	0.2	1.4	5.6
Japan	4.2	2.4	2.2	7.3
Netherlands	0.1	0.3	0.0	0.3
New Zealand	—	—	—	—
Norway	—	—	—	—
Sweden	—	—	—	—
Switzerland	0.1	0.3	0.3	0.1
United Kingdom	0.0	0.0	0.1	0.1
United States	1.0	2.0	3.0	2.0
TOTAL	64.8	68.3	61.6	84.9
AF.D.F.	5.5	5.0	8.9	6.1
AF.D.B.	—	—	—	—
AS.D.B	—	—	—	—
CAR.D.B.	—	—	—	—
E.E.C.	11.8	12.0	10.1	7.3
IBRD	—	—	—	—
IDA	3.8	11.8	10.5	19.1
I.D.B.	—	—	—	—
IFAD	0.4	0.3	1.1	1.1
I.F.C.	—	—	—	—
IMF TRUST FUND	—	—	—	—
U.N. AGENCIES				
UNDP	2.3	4.4	4.1	5.0
UNTA	0.8	0.7	0.7	1.0
UNICEF	0.8	1.7	0.9	1.2
UNRWA	—	—	—	—
WFP	1.0	1.2	1.7	1.9
UNHCR	1.2	5.8	2.9	3.7
Other Multilateral	0.5	0.5	0.6	0.7
Arab OPEC Agencies	-0.1	1.7	0.9	3.3
TOTAL	27.8	45.1	42.4	50.4
OPEC COUNTRIES	0.3	0.2	0.4	4.0
E.E.C.+ MEMBERS	71.0	75.4	65.7	82.6
TOTAL	92.9	113.6	104.3	139.3

TOTAL ODA GROSS

	1983
Australia	—
Austria	0.1
Belgium	0.1
Canada	0.2
Denmark	0.1
Finland	—
France	54.1
Germany, Fed. Rep.	4.7
Ireland	—
Italy	0.2
Japan	4.2
Netherlands	0.1
New Zealand	—
Norway	—
Sweden	—
Switzerland	0.1
United Kingdom	0.0
United States	1.0
TOTAL	64.9
AF.D.F.	5.5
AF.D.B.	—
AS.D.B	—
CAR.D.B.	—
E.E.C.	11.8
IBRD	—
IDA	3.9
I.D.B.	—
IFAD	0.4
I.F.C.	—
IMF TRUST FUND	—
U.N. AGENCIES	
UNDP	2.3
UNTA	0.8
UNICEF	0.8
UNRWA	—
WFP	1.0
UNHCR	1.2
Other Multilateral	0.5
Arab OPEC Agencies	—
TOTAL	28.0
OPEC COUNTRIES	0.3
E.E.C.+ MEMBERS	71.0
TOTAL	93.2

ODA LOANS GROSS

DAC COUNTRIES	1983	1984	1985	1986
Australia	—	—	—	—
Austria	—	—	—	—
Belgium	—	—	—	—
Canada	—	—	—	—
Denmark	—	—	—	—
Finland	—	—	—	—
France	13.6	18.2	17.7	22.4
Germany, Fed. Rep.	0.5	—	—	0.2
Ireland	—	—	—	—
Italy	—	—	—	—
Japan	—	—	—	—
Netherlands	—	—	—	—
New Zealand	—	—	—	—
Norway	—	—	—	—
Sweden	—	—	—	—
Switzerland	—	—	—	—
United Kingdom	—	—	—	—
United States	—	—	—	—
TOTAL	14.1	18.2	17.7	22.6
MULTILATERAL	9.8	20.9	23.5	30.9
OPEC COUNTRIES	0.3	0.5	1.0	4.3
E.E.C.+ MEMBERS	14.1	20.3	19.2	23.1
TOTAL	24.2	39.7	42.3	57.8

ODA LOANS NET

DAC COUNTRIES	1983	1984	1985	1986
Australia	—	—	—	—
Austria	—	—	—	—
Belgium	—	—	—	—
Canada	—	—	—	—
Denmark	—	—	—	—
Finland	—	—	—	—
France	13.6	13.9	14.1	17.1
Germany, Fed. Rep.	0.4	-10.6	0.0	—
Ireland	—	—	—	—
Italy	—	—	—	—
Japan	—	—	—	—
Netherlands	—	—	—	—
New Zealand	—	—	—	—
Norway	—	—	—	—
Sweden	—	—	—	—
Switzerland	—	—	—	—
United Kingdom	—	—	—	—
United States	—	—	—	—
TOTAL	14.0	3.2	14.0	17.1
MULTILATERAL	9.5	20.8	22.9	30.1
OPEC COUNTRIES	0.3	0.2	0.4	4.0
E.E.C.+ MEMBERS	14.0	5.3	15.5	17.6
TOTAL	23.9	24.2	37.3	51.2

GRANTS

	1983
Australia	0.1
Austria	0.1
Belgium	0.2
Canada	0.1
Denmark	—
Finland	
France	40.5
Germany, Fed. Rep.	4.2
Ireland	
Italy	0.2
Japan	4.2
Netherlands	0.1
New Zealand	
Norway	
Sweden	
Switzerland	0.1
United Kingdom	0.6
United States	1.0
TOTAL	50.8
MULTILATERAL	18.
E.E.C.+ MEMBERS	57.
TOTAL	69.

TOTAL OFFICIAL GROSS

DAC COUNTRIES	1983	1984	1985	1986
Australia	—	—	—	—
Austria	0.1	0.1	0.1	0.1
Belgium	0.1	0.2	0.1	0.1
Canada	0.2	0.2	0.4	0.1
Denmark	0.1	—	1.2	0.5
Finland	—	—	—	—
France	55.6	59.0	54.7	65.2
Germany, Fed. Rep.	4.7	18.9	6.9	10.1
Ireland	—	—	—	—
Italy	1.6	0.8	1.4	6.2
Japan	4.2	2.4	2.2	7.3
Netherlands	0.1	0.3	0.0	0.3
New Zealand	—	—	—	—
Norway	—	—	—	—
Sweden	—	—	—	—
Switzerland	0.1	0.3	0.3	0.1
United Kingdom	0.0	0.0	0.1	0.1
United States	8.0	3.0	3.0	3.0
TOTAL	74.7	85.1	70.2	93.0
MULTILATERAL	29.0	46.8	46.7	57.9
OPEC COUNTRIES	0.3	0.5	1.0	4.3
E.E.C.+ MEMBERS	73.9	91.2	74.4	89.7
TOTAL	104.0	132.5	117.9	155.2

TOTAL OFFICIAL NET

DAC COUNTRIES	1983	1984	1985	1986
Australia	—	—	—	—
Austria	0.1	0.1	0.1	0.1
Belgium	0.1	0.2	0.1	0.1
Canada	0.2	0.2	0.4	0.1
Denmark	0.1	—	1.2	0.5
Finland	—	—	—	—
France	55.3	54.6	50.8	59.8
Germany, Fed. Rep.	4.5	8.2	6.8	8.9
Ireland	—	—	—	—
Italy	1.6	0.8	1.4	6.2
Japan	4.2	2.4	2.2	7.3
Netherlands	0.1	0.3	0.0	0.3
New Zealand	—	—	—	—
Norway	—	—	—	—
Sweden	—	—	—	—
Switzerland	0.1	0.3	0.3	0.1
United Kingdom	0.0	0.0	0.1	0.1
United States	6.0	2.0	3.0	2.0
TOTAL	72.3	69.1	66.1	85.5
MULTILATERAL	28.6	46.6	45.9	57.0
OPEC COUNTRIES	0.3	0.2	0.4	4.0
E.E.C.+ MEMBERS	73.5	76.1	70.3	83.3
TOTAL	101.2	115.9	112.4	146.6

TOTAL OOF GROSS

	1983
Australia	
Austria	
Belgium	
Canada	
Denmark	
Finland	
France	1.
Germany, Fed. Rep.	
Ireland	
Italy	1.
Japan	
Netherlands	
New Zealand	
Norway	
Sweden	
Switzerland	
United Kingdom	
United States	7
TOTAL	9.
MULTILATERAL	1.
OPEC COUNTRIES	
E.E.C.+ MEMBERS	2.
TOTAL	10.

ODA COMMITMENTS

1984	1985	1986		1983	1984	1985	1986
–	–	–		–	–	0.1	–
0.1	0.1	0.1		–	–	–	0.1
0.2	0.1	0.1		0.2	0.4	0.3	0.2
0.2	0.4	0.1		–	–	–	9.9
–	0.1	0.5		–	–	–	–
58.8	50.9	65.2		67.1	54.3	52.5	65.2
18.9	6.9	9.1		6.5	17.2	12.7	11.7
–	–	–		–	–	–	–
0.2	1.4	5.6		0.2	0.3	1.5	5.7
2.4	2.2	7.3		4.3	1.3	4.0	4.0
0.3	0.0	0.3		0.1	0.3	0.1	0.3
–	–	–		–	–	–	–
–	–	–		–	–	–	–
0.3	0.3	0.1		0.1	0.2	0.2	–
0.0	0.1	0.1		0.0	0.0	0.1	0.1
2.0	3.0	2.0		1.4	3.5	3.7	4.6
83.3	*65.3*	*90.5*		*79.9*	*77.3*	*75.0*	*101.6*
5.0	9.0	6.1		15.3	0.3	7.9	–
–	–	–		–	–	–	–
–	–	–		–	–	–	–
12.0	10.1	7.3		18.8	1.7	3.2	2.5
–	–	–		–	–	–	–
11.9	10.6	19.2		21.4	–	8.0	41.9
–	–	–		–	–	–	–
0.3	1.1	1.1		–	3.1	–	4.0
–	–	–		–	–	–	–
–	–	–		6.5	14.4	10.9	13.5
4.4	4.1	5.0		–	–	–	–
0.7	0.7	1.0		–	–	–	–
1.7	0.9	1.2		–	–	–	–
–	–	–		–	–	–	–
1.2	1.7	1.9		–	–	–	–
5.8	2.9	3.7		–	–	–	–
0.5	0.6	0.7		–	–	–	–
1.7	1.4	3.9		–	–	7.7	4.0
45.2	*43.0*	*51.2*		*62.1*	*19.5*	*37.7*	*65.9*
0.5	*1.0*	*4.3*		*5.8*	*–*	*4.8*	*5.4*
90.4	*69.4*	*88.2*		*92.8*	*73.8*	*69.9*	*95.4*
129.1	***109.3***	***145.9***		***147.8***	***96.8***	***117.5***	***172.9***

TECH. COOP. GRANTS

1984	1985	1986		1983	1984	1985	1986
–	–	–		0.1	–	–	–
0.1	0.1	0.1		–	–	–	–
0.2	0.1	0.1		–	–	0.1	–
0.2	0.4	0.1		0.1	–	0.1	0.1
–	0.1	0.5		–	–	–	–
40.5	33.2	42.8		18.9	19.2	18.0	24.6
18.9	6.9	8.9		3.8	3.3	3.0	5.3
–	–	–		–	–	–	–
0.2	1.4	5.6		0.2	0.2	0.3	0.3
2.4	2.2	7.3		0.1	0.2	0.2	0.4
0.3	0.0	0.3		0.1	0.3	0.0	0.3
–	–	–		–	–	–	–
–	–	–		–	–	–	–
0.3	0.3	0.1		0.1	0.1	0.1	0.1
0.0	0.1	0.1		0.0	0.0	0.1	0.1
2.0	3.0	2.0		–	2.0	3.0	2.0
65.1	*47.5*	*67.9*		*23.4*	*25.3*	*24.7*	*33.1*
24.3	*19.5*	*20.3*		*5.5*	*13.1*	*9.2*	*12.7*
–	–	–		–	–	–	–
70.1	*50.2*	*65.0*		*23.1*	*23.0*	*21.4*	*31.7*
89.4	***67.0***	***88.1***		***28.9***	***38.5***	***34.0***	***45.8***

TOTAL OOF NET

1984	1985	1986		1983	1984	1985	1986
–	–	–		–	–	–	–
–	–	–		–	–	–	–
–	–	–		–	–	–	–
–	1.1	–		–	–	1.1	–
–	–	–		–	–	–	–
0.2	3.8	–		1.3	0.2	3.5	–
–	–	1.0		-0.1	0.0	-0.1	0.0
–	–	–		–	–	–	–
0.6	–	0.6		1.4	0.6	–	0.6
–	–	–		–	–	–	–
–	–	–		–	–	–	–
–	–	–		–	–	–	–
–	–	–		–	–	–	–
–	–	–		–	–	–	–
1.0	–	1.0		5.0	–	–	–
1.8	*5.0*	*2.6*		*7.5*	*0.7*	*4.6*	*0.6*
1.6	*3.7*	*6.7*		*0.8*	*1.6*	*3.5*	*6.6*
–	–	–		–	–	–	–
0.8	*5.0*	*1.6*		*2.5*	*0.7*	*4.6*	*0.6*
3.4	***8.6***	***9.3***		***8.3***	***2.3***	***8.1***	***7.3***

ODA COMMITMENTS : LOANS

DAC COUNTRIES	1983	1984	1985	1986
Australia	–	–	–	–
Austria	–	–	–	–
Belgium	–	–	–	–
Canada	–	–	–	–
Denmark	–	–	–	–
Finland	–	–	–	–
France	26.7	13.0	20.9	22.4
Germany, Fed. Rep.	–	–	–	0.2
Ireland	–	–	–	–
Italy	–	–	–	–
Japan	–	–	–	–
Netherlands	–	–	–	–
New Zealand	–	–	–	–
Norway	–	–	–	–
Sweden	–	–	–	–
Switzerland	–	–	–	–
United Kingdom	–	–	–	–
United States	–	–	–	–
TOTAL	*26.7*	*13.0*	*20.9*	*22.6*
MULTILATERAL	*41.3*	*3.4*	*23.6*	*49.9*
OPEC COUNTRIES	*5.8*	*–*	*4.4*	*5.4*
E.E.C.+ MEMBERS	*31.2*	*13.0*	*20.9*	*22.6*
TOTAL	*73.8*	*16.3*	*48.9*	*78.0*

GRANT ELEMENT OF ODA

DAC COUNTRIES	1983	1984	1985	1986
Australia	–	–	–	–
Austria	–	–	100.0	–
Belgium	–	–	–	100.0
Canada	100.0	100.0	100.0	100.0
Denmark	–	–	–	100.0
Finland	–	–	–	–
France	83.0	84.7	77.7	81.9
Germany, Fed. Rep.	100.0	100.0	100.0	98.8
Ireland	–	–	–	–
Italy	100.0	100.0	100.0	100.0
Japan	100.0	100.0	100.0	100.0
Netherlands	100.0	100.0	100.0	100.0
New Zealand	–	–	–	–
Norway	–	–	–	–
Sweden	–	–	–	–
Switzerland	100.0	100.0	100.0	–
United Kingdom	100.0	100.0	100.0	100.0
United States	100.0	100.0	100.0	100.0
TOTAL	*85.9*	*89.2*	*84.4*	*88.6*
MULTILATERAL	*89.2*	*96.7*	*80.5*	*84.1*
OPEC COUNTRIES	*48.6*	*–*	*40.0*	*43.0*
E.E.C.+ MEMBERS	*87.3*	*88.7*	*83.3*	*87.8*
TOTAL	*85.7*	*90.7*	*81.3*	*85.4*

OTHER AGGREGATES

COMMITMENTS: ALL SOURCES

	1983	1984	1985	1986
TOTAL BILATERAL	94.2	107.5	82.3	110.4
of which				
OPEC	5.8	–	4.8	5.4
CMEA	–	–	–	–
TOTAL MULTILATERAL	63.5	19.5	37.7	65.9
TOTAL BIL.& MULTIL.	157.7	127.0	120.0	176.3
of which				
ODA Grants	74.0	80.5	68.5	95.0
ODA Loans	73.8	16.3	48.9	78.0

DISBURSEMENTS:

DAC COUNTRIES COMBINED

OFFICIAL & PRIVATE	1983	1984	1985	1986
GROSS:				
Contractual Lending	29.1	22.8	25.2	25.3
Export Credits Total	5.1	2.8	2.6	0.1
Export Credits Private	5.1	2.8	2.6	0.1
NET:				
Contractual Lending	20.2	3.6	18.5	17.8
Export Credits Total	-3.4	-1.4	-0.1	-0.9
PRIVATE SECTOR NET	-1.5	-0.9	-0.5	-3.8
Direct Investment	0.4	-0.2	–	0.1
Portfolio Investment	-0.5	-0.3	-0.4	-4.0
Export Credits	-1.4	-0.4	-0.1	0.1

MARKET BORROWING:

CHANGE IN CLAIMS

	1983	1984	1985	1986
Banks	–	-2.0	3.0	3.0

MEMORANDUM ITEM:

	1983	1984	1985	1986
CMEA Countr.(Gross)	–	–	–	–

DISBURSEMENTS, UNLESS OTHERWISE STATED

TOTAL RECEIPTS NET

DAC COUNTRIES	1983	1984	1985	1986
Australia	–	0.2	–	–
Austria	–	–	–	0.0
Belgium	0.1	0.1	1.3	0.3
Canada	0.8	1.8	2.6	0.4
Denmark	0.1	–	–	–
Finland	–	0.1	0.1	0.8
France	24.4	33.4	33.5	46.7
Germany, Fed. Rep.	4.6	2.3	7.8	9.9
Ireland	–	–	–	–
Italy	9.2	4.6	25.1	24.3
Japan	–	–	–	–
Netherlands	1.0	1.0	2.4	4.3
New Zealand	–	–	–	–
Norway	0.2	–	0.2	0.5
Sweden	0.1	0.6	0.4	0.1
Switzerland	2.2	1.9	2.3	2.5
United Kingdom	0.2	0.0	1.9	0.1
United States	7.0	11.0	19.0	10.0
TOTAL	*49.8*	*56.9*	*96.5*	*99.9*
MULTILATERAL				
AF.D.F.	0.8	5.2	5.9	2.3
AF.D.B.	–	–	–	–
AS.D.B	–	–	–	–
CAR.D.B.	–	–	–	–
E.E.C.	15.8	22.0	19.1	18.2
IBRD	–	–	–	–
IDA	0.3	0.9	2.6	8.0
I.D.B.	–	–	–	–
IFAD	–	–	–	–
I.F.C.	–	–	–	–
IMF TRUST FUND	–	–	–	–
U.N. AGENCIES	–	–	–	–
UNDP	3.5	5.1	10.7	16.2
UNTA	1.3	0.6	0.9	1.3
UNICEF	1.9	1.8	3.4	3.0
UNRWA	–	–	–	–
WFP	11.3	17.5	40.6	8.0
UNHCR	1.3	0.1	0.0	0.0
Other Multilateral	7.6	2.7	1.6	3.6
Arab OPEC Agencies	-0.2	0.3	0.9	2.1
TOTAL	*43.6*	*56.0*	*85.9*	*62.8*
OPEC COUNTRIES	*0.3*	*0.3*	*–*	*–*
E.E.C.+ MEMBERS	*55.3*	*63.3*	*91.1*	*103.8*
TOTAL	**93.7**	**113.2**	**182.4**	**162.7**

TOTAL ODA NET

DAC COUNTRIES	1983	1984	1985	1986
Australia	–	0.2	–	–
Austria	–	–	–	0.0
Belgium	0.1	0.1	1.3	0.3
Canada	0.8	1.8	2.6	0.4
Denmark	0.1	–	–	–
Finland	–	0.1	0.1	0.8
France	25.9	35.3	32.9	48.7
Germany, Fed. Rep.	4.6	2.3	7.7	10.2
Ireland	–	–	–	–
Italy	9.2	4.6	25.1	24.3
Japan	–	–	–	–
Netherlands	1.0	1.0	2.4	4.3
New Zealand	–	–	–	–
Norway	0.2	–	0.2	0.5
Sweden	0.1	0.6	0.4	0.1
Switzerland	2.2	1.9	2.3	2.5
United Kingdom	0.2	0.0	1.9	0.1
United States	7.0	11.0	19.0	10.0
TOTAL	*51.4*	*58.9*	*95.8*	*102.2*
MULTILATERAL				
AF.D.F.	0.8	5.2	5.9	2.3
AF.D.B.	–	–	–	–
AS.D.B	–	–	–	–
CAR.D.B.	–	–	–	–
E.E.C.	15.8	22.0	19.1	18.2
IBRD	–	–	–	–
IDA	0.3	0.9	2.6	8.0
I.D.B.	–	–	–	–
IFAD	–	–	–	–
I.F.C.	–	–	–	–
IMF TRUST FUND	–	–	–	–
U.N. AGENCIES	–	–	–	–
UNDP	3.5	5.1	10.7	16.2
UNTA	1.3	0.6	0.9	1.3
UNICEF	1.9	1.8	3.4	3.0
UNRWA	–	–	–	–
WFP	11.3	17.5	40.6	8.0
UNHCR	1.3	0.1	0.0	0.0
Other Multilateral	7.6	2.7	1.6	3.6
Arab OPEC Agencies	-0.2	0.3	0.9	2.1
TOTAL	*43.6*	*56.0*	*85.9*	*62.8*
OPEC COUNTRIES	*0.3*	*0.3*	*–*	*–*
E.E.C.+ MEMBERS	*56.9*	*65.2*	*90.4*	*106.1*
TOTAL	**95.3**	**115.2**	**181.7**	**165.0**

TOTAL ODA GROSS

	1983
Australia	–
Austria	–
Belgium	0.1
Canada	0.8
Denmark	0.1
Finland	–
France	25.9
Germany, Fed. Rep.	4.6
Ireland	–
Italy	9.2
Japan	–
Netherlands	1.0
New Zealand	–
Norway	0.2
Sweden	0.1
Switzerland	2.2
United Kingdom	0.2
United States	7.0
TOTAL	*51.4*
AF.D.F.	0.9
AF.D.B.	–
AS.D.B	–
CAR.D.B.	–
E.E.C.	15.8
IBRD	–
IDA	0.4
I.D.B.	–
IFAD	–
I.F.C.	–
IMF TRUST FUND	–
U.N. AGENCIES	–
UNDP	3.5
UNTA	1.3
UNICEF	1.9
UNRWA	–
WFP	11.3
UNHCR	1.3
Other Multilateral	7.6
Arab OPEC Agencies	0.0
TOTAL	*44.1*
OPEC COUNTRIES	*0.3*
E.E.C.+ MEMBERS	*57.0*
TOTAL	**95.7**

ODA LOANS GROSS

DAC COUNTRIES	1983	1984	1985	1986
Australia	–	–	–	–
Austria	–	–	–	–
Belgium	–	–	–	–
Canada	–	–	–	–
Denmark	–	–	–	–
Finland	–	–	–	–
France	1.3	3.5	4.8	6.0
Germany, Fed. Rep.	0.1	–	–	–
Ireland	–	–	–	–
Italy	–	–	–	–
Japan	–	–	–	–
Netherlands	–	–	–	–
New Zealand	–	–	–	–
Norway	–	–	–	–
Sweden	–	–	–	–
Switzerland	–	–	–	–
United Kingdom	–	–	–	–
United States	–	–	–	–
TOTAL	*1.4*	*3.5*	*4.8*	*6.0*
MULTILATERAL	*1.3*	*6.3*	*10.3*	*15.1*
OPEC COUNTRIES	*–*	*–*	*–*	*–*
E.E.C.+ MEMBERS	*1.4*	*3.5*	*4.8*	*6.0*
TOTAL	**2.7**	**9.8**	**15.1**	**21.1**

ODA LOANS NET

	1983	1984	1985	1986
	–	–	–	–
	–	–	–	–
	–	–	–	–
	–	–	–	–
	–	–	–	–
	–	–	–	–
France	1.3	3.5	4.8	6.0
Germany	0.1	-4.3	–	–
	–	–	–	–
	–	–	–	–
	–	–	–	–
	–	–	–	–
	–	–	–	–
	–	–	–	–
	–	–	–	–
	–	–	–	–
	–	–	–	–
	–	–	–	–
TOTAL	*1.4*	*-0.9*	*4.8*	*6.0*
MULTILATERAL	*0.9*	*6.0*	*8.6*	*11.8*
OPEC COUNTRIES	*–*	*–*	*–*	*–*
E.E.C.+ MEMBERS	*1.3*	*-0.9*	*4.8*	*5.4*
TOTAL	**2.3**	**5.1**	**13.4**	**17.8**

GRANTS

	1983
Australia	–
Austria	–
Belgium	0.1
Canada	0.8
Denmark	0.1
Finland	–
France	24.6
Germany, Fed. Rep.	4.6
Ireland	–
Italy	9.2
Japan	–
Netherlands	1.0
New Zealand	–
Norway	0.2
Sweden	0.1
Switzerland	2.2
United Kingdom	0.2
United States	7.0
TOTAL	*50.0*
MULTILATERAL	*42.8*
OPEC COUNTRIES	*0.3*
E.E.C.+ MEMBERS	*55.6*
TOTAL	**93.0**

TOTAL OFFICIAL GROSS

DAC COUNTRIES	1983	1984	1985	1986
Australia	–	0.2	–	–
Austria	–	–	–	0.0
Belgium	0.1	0.1	1.3	0.3
Canada	0.8	1.8	2.6	0.4
Denmark	0.1	–	–	–
Finland	–	0.1	0.1	0.8
France	25.9	35.6	32.9	48.8
Germany, Fed. Rep.	4.6	6.6	7.7	10.2
Ireland	–	–	–	–
Italy	9.2	4.6	25.1	24.3
Japan	–	–	–	–
Netherlands	1.0	1.0	2.4	4.3
New Zealand	–	–	–	–
Norway	0.2	–	0.2	0.5
Sweden	0.1	0.6	0.4	0.1
Switzerland	2.2	1.9	2.3	2.5
United Kingdom	0.2	0.0	1.9	0.1
United States	7.0	11.0	19.0	10.0
TOTAL	*51.4*	*63.6*	*95.8*	*102.2*
MULTILATERAL	*44.1*	*56.3*	*87.6*	*66.0*
OPEC COUNTRIES	*0.3*	*0.3*	*–*	*–*
E.E.C.+ MEMBERS	*57.0*	*69.9*	*90.4*	*106.7*
TOTAL	**95.7**	**120.2**	**183.3**	**168.3**

TOTAL OFFICIAL NET

DAC COUNTRIES	1983	1984	1985	1986
Australia	–	0.2	–	–
Austria	–	–	–	0.0
Belgium	0.1	0.1	1.3	0.3
Canada	0.8	1.8	2.6	0.4
Denmark	0.1	–	–	–
Finland	–	0.1	0.1	0.8
France	25.8	35.6	32.8	48.7
Germany, Fed. Rep.	4.6	2.3	7.7	10.2
Ireland	–	–	–	–
Italy	9.2	4.6	25.1	24.3
Japan	–	–	–	–
Netherlands	1.0	1.0	2.4	4.3
New Zealand	–	–	–	–
Norway	0.2	–	0.2	0.5
Sweden	0.1	0.6	0.4	0.1
Switzerland	2.2	1.9	2.3	2.5
United Kingdom	0.2	0.0	1.9	0.1
United States	7.0	11.0	19.0	10.0
TOTAL	*51.3*	*59.2*	*95.7*	*102.2*
MULTILATERAL	*43.6*	*56.0*	*85.9*	*62.8*
OPEC COUNTRIES	*0.3*	*0.3*	*–*	*–*
E.E.C.+ MEMBERS	*56.8*	*65.5*	*90.3*	*106.1*
TOTAL	**95.2**	**115.5**	**181.6**	**165.0**

TOTAL OOF GROSS

	1983
Australia	–
Austria	–
Belgium	–
Canada	–
Denmark	–
Finland	–
France	–
Germany, Fed. Rep.	–
Ireland	–
Italy	–
Japan	–
Netherlands	–
New Zealand	–
Norway	–
Sweden	–
Switzerland	–
United Kingdom	–
United States	–
TOTAL	*–*
MULTILATERAL	*–*
OPEC COUNTRIES	*–*
E.E.C.+ MEMBERS	*–*
TOTAL	**–**

CHAD

ODA COMMITMENTS

1984	1985	1986	1983	1984	1985	1986
0.2	—	—	—	—	—	—
—	—	0.0	—	—	—	—
0.1	1.3	0.3	—	—	0.6	0.3
1.8	2.6	0.4	0.9	1.9	2.7	0.6
—	—	—	—	—	—	—
0.1	0.1	0.8	—	0.1	0.1	—
35.3	32.9	48.8	35.3	39.2	37.2	48.8
6.6	7.7	10.2	1.8	7.5	15.0	12.1
—	—	—	—	—	—	—
4.6	25.1	24.3	9.2	4.6	40.7	48.3
—	—	—	—	—	—	—
1.0	2.4	4.3	1.1	0.9	3.8	10.5
—	—	—	—	—	—	—
—	0.2	0.5	—	—	—	—
0.6	0.4	0.1	0.0	0.4	0.2	0.1
1.9	2.3	2.5	3.1	1.3	3.3	2.4
0.0	1.9	0.1	0.2	0.0	1.9	0.1
11.0	19.0	10.0	4.5	20.8	28.2	14.2
63.2	*95.8*	*102.2*	*56.2*	*76.7*	*133.7*	*137.2*
5.2	6.2	2.5	—	—	—	35.1
—	—	—	—	—	—	—
—	—	—	—	—	—	—
22.0	19.1	18.8	16.2	32.0	19.1	17.3
—	—	—	—	—	—	—
1.1	4.0	9.9	—	—	—	35.0
—	—	—	—	—	—	—
—	—	—	—	—	—	—
—	—	—	—	—	—	—
—	—	—	26.9	27.7	57.3	32.1
5.1	10.7	16.2	—	—	—	—
0.6	0.9	1.3	—	—	—	—
1.8	3.4	3.0	—	—	—	—
—	—	—	—	—	—	—
17.5	40.6	8.0	—	—	—	—
0.1	0.0	0.0	—	—	—	—
2.7	1.6	3.6	—	—	—	—
0.3	0.9	2.7	0.1	8.1	—	—
56.3	*87.6*	*66.0*	*43.2*	*67.8*	*76.3*	*119.5*
0.3	—	—	10.5	0.0	—	—
69.6	*90.4*	*106.7*	*63.8*	*84.2*	*118.3*	*137.3*
119.8	***183.3***	***168.3***	***109.8***	***144.5***	***210.0***	***256.7***

TECH. COOP. GRANTS

1984	1985	1986	1983	1984	1985	1986
0.2	—	—	—	0.2	—	—
—	—	0.0	—	—	—	—
0.1	1.3	0.3	—	—	0.2	—
1.8	2.6	0.4	0.2	—	—	—
—	—	—	0.0	—	—	—
0.1	0.1	0.8	—	—	—	—
31.8	28.1	42.8	3.0	5.1	5.4	10.0
6.6	7.7	10.2	0.2	0.3	0.7	3.1
—	—	—	—	—	—	—
4.6	25.1	24.3	0.1	0.2	16.8	1.9
—	—	—	—	—	—	—
1.0	2.4	4.3	0.1	0.2	0.2	1.7
—	—	—	—	—	—	—
—	0.2	0.5	—	—	—	—
0.6	0.4	0.1	—	—	—	—
1.9	2.3	2.5	0.3	0.5	0.6	0.9
0.0	1.9	0.1	0.0	0.0	0.1	0.1
11.0	19.0	10.0	2.0	2.0	2.0	4.0
59.7	*91.0*	*96.2*	*6.1*	*8.6*	*25.9*	*21.6*
50.0	77.3	51.0	15.6	10.2	16.7	24.4
0.3	—	—	—	—	—	—
66.1	*85.6*	*100.7*	*3.5*	*5.9*	*23.2*	*17.0*
110.0	***168.3***	***147.2***	***21.7***	***18.8***	***42.6***	***46.0***

TOTAL OOF NET

1984	1985	1986	1983	1984	1985	1986
—	—	—	—	—	—	—
—	—	—	—	—	—	—
—	—	—	—	—	—	—
—	—	—	—	—	—	—
—	—	—	—	—	—	—
0.4	—	—	-0.1	0.3	-0.1	—
—	—	—	—	—	—	—
—	—	—	—	—	—	—
—	—	—	—	—	—	—
—	—	—	—	—	—	—
—	—	—	—	—	—	—
—	—	—	—	—	—	—
—	—	—	—	—	—	—
—	—	—	—	—	—	—
—	—	—	—	—	—	—
0.4	—	—	-0.1	0.3	-0.1	—
—	—	—	—	—	—	—
—	—	—	—	—	—	—
0.4	—	—	-0.1	0.3	-0.1	—
0.4	*—*	*—*	*-0.1*	*0.3*	*-0.1*	*—*

ODA COMMITMENTS : LOANS

DAC COUNTRIES

	1983	1984	1985	1986
Australia	—	—	—	—
Austria	—	—	—	—
Belgium	—	—	—	—
Canada	—	—	—	—
Denmark	—	—	—	—
Finland	—	—	—	—
France	9.8	6.4	11.9	6.0
Germany, Fed. Rep.	—	—	—	—
Ireland	—	—	—	—
Italy	—	—	—	—
Japan	—	—	—	—
Netherlands	—	—	—	—
New Zealand	—	—	—	—
Norway	—	—	—	—
Sweden	—	—	—	—
Switzerland	—	—	—	—
United Kingdom	—	—	—	—
United States	—	—	—	—
TOTAL	*9.8*	*6.4*	*11.9*	*6.0*
MULTILATERAL	*—*	*4.0*	*1.5*	*70.1*
OPEC COUNTRIES	*—*	*—*	*—*	*—*
E.E.C.+ MEMBERS	*9.8*	*6.4*	*13.4*	*6.0*
TOTAL	*9.8*	*10.4*	*13.4*	*76.1*

GRANT ELEMENT OF ODA

DAC COUNTRIES

	1983	1984	1985	1986
Australia	—	—	—	—
Austria	—	—	—	—
Belgium	—	—	100.0	100.0
Canada	100.0	100.0	100.0	100.0
Denmark	—	—	—	—
Finland	—	100.0	100.0	—
France	90.4	93.2	78.0	96.3
Germany, Fed. Rep.	100.0	100.0	100.0	100.0
Ireland	—	—	—	—
Italy	100.0	100.0	100.0	100.0
Japan	—	—	—	—
Netherlands	100.0	100.0	100.0	100.0
New Zealand	—	—	—	—
Norway	—	—	—	—
Sweden	100.0	100.0	100.0	100.0
Switzerland	100.0	100.0	100.0	100.0
United Kingdom	100.0	100.0	100.0	100.0
United States	100.0	100.0	100.0	100.0
TOTAL	*94.2*	*96.5*	*93.9*	*98.7*
MULTILATERAL	*100.0*	*98.6*	*100.0*	*89.7*
OPEC COUNTRIES	*100.0*	*100.0*	*—*	*—*
E.E.C.+ MEMBERS	*94.9*	*96.8*	*93.0*	*98.7*
TOTAL	*97.1*	*97.5*	*96.1*	*94.5*

OTHER AGGREGATES

COMMITMENTS: ALL SOURCES

	1983	1984	1985	1986
TOTAL BILATERAL	66.7	76.7	133.7	137.2
of which				
OPEC	10.5	0.0	—	—
CMEA	—	—	—	—
TOTAL MULTILATERAL	43.2	67.8	76.3	119.5
TOTAL BIL.& MULTIL.	109.8	144.5	210.0	256.7
of which				
ODA Grants	100.1	134.1	196.6	180.6
ODA Loans	9.8	10.4	13.4	76.1

DISBURSEMENTS:

DAC COUNTRIES COMBINED

	1983	1984	1985	1986
OFFICIAL & PRIVATE				
GROSS:				
Contractual Lending	2.4	3.9	6.5	4.0
Export Credits Total	1.0	0.0	1.7	-2.0
Export Credits Private	1.0	0.0	1.7	-2.0
NET:				
Contractual Lending	-0.8	-2.4	4.9	3.7
Export Credits Total	-2.1	-1.9	0.2	-2.2
PRIVATE SECTOR NET	-1.5	-2.2	0.8	-2.3
Direct Investment	0.1	—	0.2	0.4
Portfolio Investment	0.5	-0.4	0.4	-0.5
Export Credits	-2.1	-1.9	0.2	-2.2

MARKET BORROWING:

CHANGE IN CLAIMS

	1983	1984	1985	1986
Banks	—	-3.0	-1.0	—

MEMORANDUM ITEM:

	1983	1984	1985	1986
CMEA Countr.(Gross)	—	—	—	—

DISBURSEMENTS, UNLESS OTHERWISE STATED

TOTAL RECEIPTS NET / TOTAL ODA NET / TOTAL ODA GROSS

	TOTAL RECEIPTS NET 1983	1984	1985	1986	TOTAL ODA NET 1983	1984	1985	1986	TOTAL ODA GROSS 1983
DAC COUNTRIES									
Australia	-0.3	-0.4	-0.3	-0.3	0.0	0.0	0.0	0.0	0.0
Austria	0.1	-1.2	-1.2	0.1	0.1	0.1	0.1	0.1	0.1
Belgium	-14.4	77.9	-21.1	-33.8	0.6	0.9	1.1	1.4	0.6
Canada	-0.3	0.9	-1.1	1.1	2.1	3.6	3.8	2.2	2.4
Denmark	-1.8	0.2	-1.3	-2.2	0.2	–	–	–	0.2
Finland	0.0	0.0	0.1	6.5	0.0	0.0	0.1	0.1	0.0
France	35.4	23.4	82.1	-38.6	1.6	1.1	2.2	3.4	3.2
Germany, Fed. Rep.	35.3	49.6	68.1	-9.9	11.5	11.0	15.2	16.2	14.5
Ireland	–	–	–	–	–	–	–	–	–
Italy	-1.3	-30.9	-0.8	-1.8	0.3	0.3	1.3	0.5	0.3
Japan	81.4	320.5	167.2	-18.8	4.1	1.7	6.7	5.4	6.0
Netherlands	3.1	6.7	3.2	0.7	4.0	3.1	4.7	4.5	4.6
New Zealand	–	0.0	0.0	–	–	0.0	0.0	–	–
Norway	-0.6	0.0	0.9	1.0	–	0.0	0.8	0.7	–
Sweden	-0.4	-1.8	-1.9	-1.8	0.0	0.2	0.1	–	–
Switzerland	-7.5	1.6	1.4	0.6	0.4	0.4	1.2	0.6	0.4
United Kingdom	2.4	52.1	47.8	1.2	0.6	0.3	0.4	0.6	0.7
United States	340.0	1400.0	-671.0	-295.0	-19.0	-13.0	8.0	-36.0	9.0
TOTAL	*471.3*	*1898.5*	*-328.1*	*-390.9*	*6.5*	*9.7*	*45.8*	*-0.4*	*42.0*
MULTILATERAL									
AF.D.F.	–	–	–	–	–	–	–	–	–
AF.D.B.	–	–	–	–	–	–	–	–	–
AS.D.B	–	–	–	–	–	–	–	–	–
CAR.D.B.	–	–	–	–	–	–	–	–	–
E.E.C.	–	–	1.0	0.8	–	–	1.0	0.8	–
IBRD	12.7	18.0	212.0	340.5	–	–	–	–	–
IDA	-0.7	-0.7	-0.7	-0.7	-0.7	-0.7	-0.7	-0.7	–
I.D.B.	192.9	315.6	227.7	93.8	-8.4	-9.3	-9.4	-8.9	–
IFAD	–	–	–	–	–	–	–	–	–
I.F.C.	–	8.7	8.0	4.9	–	–	–	–	–
IMF TRUST FUND	–	–	–	–	–	–	–	–	–
U.N. AGENCIES	–	–	–	–	–	–	–	–	–
UNDP	2.1	2.0	2.4	3.0	2.1	2.0	2.4	3.0	2.1
UNTA	0.6	0.5	0.7	0.8	0.6	0.5	0.7	0.8	0.6
UNICEF	0.1	0.1	0.2	0.1	0.1	0.1	0.2	0.1	0.1
UNRWA	–	–	–	–	–	–	–	–	–
WFP	–	–	–	–	–	–	–	–	–
UNHCR	–	–	–	–	–	–	–	–	–
Other Multilateral	0.1	0.2	0.4	0.1	0.1	0.2	0.4	0.1	0.1
Arab OPEC Agencies	–	–	–	–	–	–	–	–	–
TOTAL	*207.7*	*344.3*	*451.6*	*443.3*	*-6.3*	*-7.2*	*-5.4*	*-4.7*	*2.8*
OPEC COUNTRIES	*-0.3*	–	–	–	–	–	–	–	–
E.E.C.+ MEMBERS	*58.8*	*178.9*	*178.7*	*-83.5*	*18.8*	*16.6*	*25.8*	*27.4*	*24.0*
TOTAL	*678.6*	*2242.8*	*123.5*	*52.4*	*0.2*	*2.5*	*40.4*	*-5.1*	*44.8*

ODA LOANS GROSS / ODA LOANS NET / GRANTS

	ODA LOANS GROSS 1983	1984	1985	1986	ODA LOANS NET 1983	1984	1985	1986	GRANTS 1983
DAC COUNTRIES									
Australia	–	–	–	–	–	–	–	–	0.0
Austria	–	–	–	–	–	–	–	–	0.1
Belgium	–	–	–	–	–	–	–	–	0.6
Canada	0.0	–	–	–	-0.4	-0.2	-0.2	-0.2	2.5
Denmark	–	–	–	–	–	–	–	–	0.2
Finland	–	–	–	–	–	–	–	–	0.0
France	–	–	–	0.8	-1.6	-1.6	-0.4	-0.4	3.2
Germany, Fed. Rep.	–	–	–	4.0	-3.0	-1.8	-1.0	-1.4	14.5
Ireland	–	–	–	–	–	–	–	–	–
Italy	–	–	–	–	–	–	–	–	0.3
Japan	2.0	–	–	1.9	0.1	-1.9	-2.2	-2.3	4.0
Netherlands	–	–	–	–	-0.6	-0.5	-0.5	-2.5	4.6
New Zealand	–	–	–	–	–	–	–	–	–
Norway	–	–	–	–	–	–	–	–	–
Sweden	–	–	–	–	0.0	–	0.0	–	–
Switzerland	–	–	–	–	–	–	–	–	0.4
United Kingdom	–	–	–	–	-0.1	–	–	–	0.7
United States	–	–	–	–	-28.0	-23.0	-8.0	-43.0	9.0
TOTAL	*2.0*	–	–	*6.6*	*-33.5*	*-29.0*	*-12.3*	*-49.8*	*40.0*
MULTILATERAL	–	–	–	–	*-9.1*	*-10.0*	*-10.1*	*-9.7*	*2.8*
OPEC COUNTRIES	–	–	–	–	–	–	–	–	–
E.E.C.+ MEMBERS	–	–	–	*4.8*	*-5.2*	*-3.9*	*-1.9*	*-4.3*	*24.0*
TOTAL	*2.0*	–	–	*6.6*	*-42.7*	*-39.0*	*-22.5*	*-59.4*	*42.9*

TOTAL OFFICIAL GROSS / TOTAL OFFICIAL NET / TOTAL OOF GROSS

	TOTAL OFFICIAL GROSS 1983	1984	1985	1986	TOTAL OFFICIAL NET 1983	1984	1985	1986	TOTAL OOF GROSS 1983
DAC COUNTRIES									
Australia	0.0	0.0	0.0	0.0	-0.4	-0.4	-0.3	-0.3	–
Austria	0.1	0.1	0.1	0.1	0.1	0.1	0.1	0.1	–
Belgium	0.6	0.9	1.1	1.4	0.1	0.9	1.1	1.4	–
Canada	3.9	4.9	4.4	5.7	-0.2	0.6	-1.0	1.2	1.5
Denmark	0.2	–	–	–	0.2	–	–	–	–
Finland	0.0	0.0	0.1	0.1	0.0	0.0	0.1	0.1	–
France	3.2	2.7	2.6	11.8	-2.3	1.1	2.2	10.6	–
Germany, Fed. Rep.	14.5	12.8	16.3	21.9	7.2	10.6	15.2	16.0	–
Ireland	–	–	–	–	–	–	–	–	–
Italy	0.3	0.3	1.3	0.5	0.3	0.3	1.3	0.5	–
Japan	6.0	3.6	9.0	9.6	4.1	1.7	6.7	5.4	–
Netherlands	4.6	3.6	5.2	7.0	3.9	2.9	4.7	3.6	–
New Zealand	–	0.0	0.0	–	–	0.0	0.0	–	–
Norway	–	0.0	0.8	0.7	–	0.0	0.8	0.7	–
Sweden	0.3	0.2	0.2	–	0.0	-0.2	0.1	-0.3	0.3
Switzerland	0.4	0.4	1.2	0.6	-0.3	0.4	1.2	0.6	–
United Kingdom	0.7	0.3	0.4	0.6	0.5	0.3	0.4	0.6	–
United States	15.0	10.0	17.0	157.0	-47.0	-28.0	-7.0	58.0	6.0
TOTAL	*49.7*	*39.8*	*59.6*	*216.9*	*-33.9*	*-9.6*	*25.5*	*98.2*	*7.7*
MULTILATERAL	*235.4*	*387.1*	*491.5*	*499.3*	*207.7*	*344.3*	*451.6*	*443.3*	*232.6*
OPEC COUNTRIES	–	–	–	–	*-0.3*	–	–	–	–
E.E.C.+ MEMBERS	*24.0*	*20.5*	*27.8*	*43.9*	*9.9*	*16.1*	*25.7*	*33.5*	*24.0*
TOTAL	*285.1*	*426.9*	*551.1*	*716.2*	*173.5*	*334.7*	*477.2*	*541.5*	*240.3*

ODA COMMITMENTS

1984	1985	1986	1983	1984	1985	1986
0.0	0.0	0.0	0.0	0.0	0.0	0.0
0.1	0.1	0.1	0.1	0.1	0.1	–
0.9	1.1	1.4	–	–	0.5	1.4
3.8	4.0	2.4	3.0	4.6	4.2	2.0
–	–	–	–	–	0.2	–
0.0	0.1	0.1	0.0	0.1	–	0.1
2.7	2.6	4.6	3.2	2.7	2.6	4.6
12.8	16.2	21.6	12.2	13.5	18.9	20.2
–	–	–	–	–	–	–
0.3	1.3	0.5	0.3	0.3	1.3	0.5
3.6	9.0	9.6	5.7	8.5	5.0	9.5
3.6	5.2	7.0	4.4	4.3	5.2	6.0
0.0	0.0	–	–	0.0	0.0	–
0.0	0.8	0.7	–	0.0	0.2	0.5
0.2	0.2	–	0.2	2.5	2.1	–
0.4	1.2	0.6	0.3	0.4	1.2	0.5
0.3	0.4	0.6	0.7	0.3	0.4	0.6
10.0	16.0	7.0	10.5	11.1	12.8	11.1
38.7	*58.1*	*56.0*	*40.6*	*48.3*	*54.7*	*56.9*
–	–	–	–	–	–	–
–	–	–	–	–	–	–
–	–	–	–	–	–	–
–	1.0	0.8	0.4	0.4	1.6	1.6
–	–	–	–	–	–	–
–	0.1	0.1	–	–	–	–
–	–	–	–	–	–	–
–	–	–	–	–	–	–
–	–	–	2.8	2.7	3.7	4.0
2.0	2.4	3.0	–	–	–	–
0.5	0.7	0.8	–	–	–	–
0.1	0.2	0.1	–	–	–	–
–	–	–	–	–	–	–
–	–	–	–	–	–	–
0.2	0.4	0.1	–	–	–	–
–	–	–	–	–	–	–
2.7	4.8	4.9	3.2	3.1	5.3	5.6
–	–	–	–	–	–	–
20.5	*27.7*	*36.4*	*21.1*	*21.4*	*30.7*	*34.8*
41.4	*62.9*	*61.0*	*43.8*	*51.4*	*60.0*	*62.6*

TECH. COOP. GRANTS

1984	1985	1986	1983	1984	1985	1986
0.0	0.0	0.0	–	–	–	–
0.1	0.1	0.1	0.1	–	–	–
0.9	1.1	1.4	0.1	0.2	0.1	0.1
3.8	4.0	2.4	1.6	–	0.3	–
–	–	–	0.2	–	–	–
0.0	0.1	0.1	0.0	0.0	0.1	–
2.7	2.6	3.8	3.2	2.7	2.6	3.8
12.8	16.2	17.6	13.7	11.5	15.2	17.2
–	–	–	–	–	–	–
0.3	1.3	0.5	0.3	0.3	0.7	0.5
3.6	9.0	7.7	3.4	3.4	4.5	6.7
3.6	5.2	7.0	3.2	2.2	3.6	4.1
0.0	0.0	–	–	–	–	–
0.0	0.8	0.7	–	0.0	0.1	0.1
0.2	0.2	–	–	–	–	–
0.4	1.2	0.6	0.0	0.0	0.0	0.0
0.3	0.4	0.6	0.7	0.3	0.3	0.3
10.0	16.0	7.0	–	–	–	–
38.7	*58.1*	*49.4*	*26.4*	*20.6*	*27.4*	*33.0*
2.7	4.8	4.9	2.8	2.7	3.7	4.0
–	–	–	–	–	–	–
20.5	*27.7*	*31.7*	*21.3*	*17.1*	*22.5*	*26.2*
41.4	*62.9*	*54.4*	*29.3*	*23.3*	*31.1*	*37.0*

TOTAL OOF NET

1984	1985	1986	1983	1984	1985	1986
–	–	–	-0.4	-0.4	-0.3	-0.3
0.0	–	–	-0.5	0.0	–	–
1.1	0.4	3.4	-2.3	-3.0	-4.8	-1.0
–	–	–	–	–	–	–
–	–	7.2	-3.9	–	–	7.2
–	0.2	0.3	-4.3	-0.4	0.0	-0.2
–	–	–	–	–	–	–
–	–	–	–	–	–	–
–	–	–	-0.1	-0.2	0.0	-0.9
–	–	–	–	–	–	–
–	–	–	–	-0.4	–	-0.3
–	–	–	-0.6	–	–	–
–	–	–	-0.1	–	–	–
–	1.0	150.0	-28.0	-15.0	-15.0	94.0
1.1	*1.5*	*160.8*	*-40.4*	*-19.3*	*-20.2*	*98.6*
384.3	*486.8*	*494.4*	*214.0*	*351.6*	*457.0*	*448.0*
–	–	–	-0.3	–	–	–
0.0	0.2	7.5	-9.0	-0.6	-0.1	6.1
385.5	*488.3*	*655.2*	*173.2*	*332.2*	*436.8*	*546.6*

ODA COMMITMENTS : LOANS

DAC COUNTRIES

	1983	1984	1985	1986
Australia	–	–	–	–
Austria	–	–	–	–
Belgium	–	–	–	–
Canada	–	–	–	–
Denmark	–	–	–	–
Finland	–	–	–	–
France	–	–	–	0.8
Germany, Fed. Rep.	–	–	–	4.0
Ireland	–	–	–	–
Italy	–	–	–	–
Japan	2.0	–	–	1.9
Netherlands	–	–	–	–
New Zealand	–	–	–	–
Norway	–	–	–	–
Sweden	–	–	–	–
Switzerland	–	–	–	–
United Kingdom	–	–	–	–
United States	–	–	–	–
TOTAL	*2.0*	*–*	*–*	*6.6*
MULTILATERAL	–	–	–	–
OPEC COUNTRIES				
E.E.C.+ MEMBERS	–	–	–	4.8
TOTAL	*2.0*	*–*	*–*	*6.6*

GRANT ELEMENT OF ODA

DAC COUNTRIES

	1983	1984	1985	1986
Australia	100.0	100.0	100.0	100.0
Austria	100.0	100.0	100.0	–
Belgium	–	–	100.0	100.0
Canada	100.0	100.0	100.0	100.0
Denmark	–	–	100.0	–
Finland	100.0	100.0	–	100.0
France	100.0	100.0	100.0	100.0
Germany, Fed. Rep.	100.0	100.0	100.0	82.5
Ireland	–	–	–	–
Italy	100.0	100.0	100.0	100.0
Japan	74.8	100.0	100.0	82.4
Netherlands	100.0	100.0	100.0	100.0
New Zealand	–	100.0	100.0	–
Norway	–	100.0	100.0	100.0
Sweden	100.0	100.0	100.0	–
Switzerland	100.0	100.0	100.0	100.0
United Kingdom	100.0	100.0	100.0	100.0
United States	100.0	100.0	100.0	100.0
TOTAL	*96.5*	*100.0*	*100.0*	*90.7*
MULTILATERAL	*100.0*	*100.0*	*100.0*	*100.0*
OPEC COUNTRIES	–	–	–	–
E.E.C.+ MEMBERS	*100.0*	*100.0*	*100.0*	*89.6*
TOTAL	*96.7*	*100.0*	*100.0*	*91.6*

OTHER AGGREGATES

COMMITMENTS: ALL SOURCES

	1983	1984	1985	1986
TOTAL BILATERAL	47.5	50.4	61.1	258.3
of which				
OPEC	–	–	1.1	–
CMEA	–	–	–	–
TOTAL MULTILATERAL	714.2	432.4	1142.5	681.4
TOTAL BIL.& MULTIL.	761.7	482.8	1203.6	939.7
of which				
ODA Grants	41.8	51.4	60.0	56.0
ODA Loans	2.0	–	–	6.6

DISBURSEMENTS:

DAC COUNTRIES COMBINED

OFFICIAL & PRIVATE

	1983	1984	1985	1986
GROSS:				
Contractual Lending	162.2	231.6	281.3	267.5
Export Credits Total	160.2	231.6	280.3	103.4
Export Credits Private	152.5	230.4	279.8	100.1
NET:				
Contractual Lending	-47.7	22.4	61.3	-5.7
Export Credits Total	7.3	58.5	83.6	-104.3
PRIVATE SECTOR NET	505.1	1908.1	-353.7	-489.0
Direct Investment	25.3	22.8	106.4	103.7
Portfolio Investment	453.6	1814.6	-553.9	-538.3
Export Credits	26.2	70.7	93.8	-54.5

MARKET BORROWING:

CHANGE IN CLAIMS

	1983	1984	1985	1986
Banks	–	684.0	438.0	-682.0

MEMORANDUM ITEM:

	1983	1984	1985	1986
CMEA Countr.(Gross)	–	–	–	–

TOTAL RECEIPTS NET | TOTAL ODA NET | TOTAL ODA GROSS

	TOTAL RECEIPTS NET				TOTAL ODA NET				TOTAL ODA GROSS
	1983	1984	1985	1986	1983	1984	1985	1986	1983
DAC COUNTRIES									
Australia	4.1	7.5	32.0	23.4	6.5	10.8	17.3	14.4	6.5
Austria	0.3	0.2	0.4	0.5	0.3	0.2	0.3	0.5	0.3
Belgium	-0.9	-25.2	-2.2	-19.7	6.0	6.2	6.9	1.8	6.0
Canada	3.7	5.4	23.8	29.8	5.0	6.7	15.5	18.0	5.0
Denmark	8.7	11.8	31.2	14.7	5.2	2.2	8.3	19.2	5.2
Finland	0.0	0.0	2.2	0.2	0.0	0.0	2.2	0.2	0.0
France	10.0	32.1	8.2	51.4	4.7	6.0	6.3	9.9	4.7
Germany, Fed. Rep.	133.6	13.4	16.5	62.0	96.7	57.5	97.6	51.2	104.8
Ireland	0.0	0.0	0.1	0.1	0.0	0.0	0.1	0.1	0.0
Italy	-15.0	37.5	41.8	102.8	11.1	9.9	14.4	31.9	11.1
Japan	383.9	595.9	1182.4	2086.4	350.2	389.4	387.9	497.0	350.2
Netherlands	–	–	0.4	7.7	–	–	0.4	2.4	–
New Zealand	–	–	–	–	–	–	–	–	–
Norway	7.1	26.4	12.6	12.2	5.8	11.9	3.6	4.5	5.8
Sweden	5.0	7.1	13.4	32.0	0.6	0.8	11.4	6.3	0.6
Switzerland	0.1	-16.6	44.6	0.3	0.1	0.1	0.1	0.3	0.1
United Kingdom	-3.4	76.1	9.0	-1.8	0.3	0.8	1.6	3.2	0.3
United States	34.0	-189.0	169.0	292.0	–	–	–	–	–
TOTAL	*571.0*	*582.6*	*1585.3*	*2693.9*	*492.5*	*502.3*	*573.7*	*660.7*	*500.5*
MULTILATERAL									
AF.D.F.	–	–	–	–	–	–	–	–	–
AF.D.B.	–	–	–	–	–	–	–	–	–
AS.D.B	-4.1	-4.2	-4.6	-4.8	–	–	–	0.1	–
CAR.D.B.	–	–	–	–	–	–	–	–	–
E.E.C.	–	–	0.9	7.5	–	–	0.9	7.5	–
IBRD	4.0	72.9	353.6	324.3	–	–	–	–	–
IDA	67.2	123.9	213.7	282.0	67.2	123.9	213.7	282.0	67.2
I.D.B.	–	–	–	–	–	–	–	–	–
IFAD	3.0	10.3	19.7	23.0	3.0	10.3	19.7	23.0	3.0
I.F.C.	–	–	–	1.4	–	–	–	–	–
IMF TRUST FUND	–	–	–	–	–	–	–	–	–
U.N. AGENCIES	–	–	–	–	–	–	–	–	–
UNDP	20.7	15.4	14.4	17.3	20.7	15.4	14.4	17.3	20.7
UNTA	3.0	1.6	4.5	3.2	3.0	1.6	4.5	3.2	3.0
UNICEF	6.1	5.2	6.7	16.7	6.1	5.2	6.7	16.7	6.1
UNRWA	–	–	–	–	–	–	–	–	–
WFP	25.0	79.7	67.9	84.5	25.0	79.7	67.9	84.5	25.0
UNHCR	6.5	4.1	3.6	4.8	6.5	4.1	3.6	4.8	6.5
Other Multilateral	10.0	6.4	12.9	11.4	10.0	6.4	12.9	11.4	10.0
Arab OPEC Agencies	–	–	–	–	–	–	–	–	–
TOTAL	*141.3*	*315.2*	*693.3*	*771.3*	*141.4*	*246.5*	*344.3*	*450.5*	*141.4*
OPEC COUNTRIES	*35.7*	*49.4*	*30.2*	*22.7*	*35.7*	*49.4*	*21.9*	*22.7*	*35.7*
E.E.C.+ MEMBERS	*132.9*	*145.8*	*105.8*	*224.7*	*124.1*	*82.5*	*136.4*	*127.2*	*132.1*
TOTAL	*748.1*	*947.2*	*2308.7*	*3487.8*	*669.6*	*798.2*	*940.0*	*1133.9*	*677.6*

ODA LOANS GROSS | ODA LOANS NET | GRANTS

	ODA LOANS GROSS				ODA LOANS NET				GRANTS
	1983	1984	1985	1986	1983	1984	1985	1986	1983
DAC COUNTRIES									
Australia	–	–	–	–	–	–	–	–	6.5
Austria	–	–	–	–	–	–	–	–	0.3
Belgium	5.9	5.8	6.1	0.4	5.9	5.8	6.1	0.4	0.2
Canada	–	–	–	–	–	–	–	–	5.0
Denmark	4.3	1.5	6.7	17.9	4.3	1.5	6.7	17.9	0.9
Finland	–	–	2.1	–	–	–	2.1	–	0.0
France	–	–	–	–	–	–	–	–	4.7
Germany, Fed. Rep.	92.2	53.9	97.2	56.4	84.1	41.5	77.0	19.2	12.6
Ireland	–	–	–	–	–	–	–	–	0.0
Italy	1.0	3.9	3.2	17.6	1.0	3.9	3.2	17.5	10.2
Japan	299.1	347.9	345.2	410.1	299.1	347.9	345.2	410.1	51.1
Netherlands	–	–	–	–	–	–	–	–	–
New Zealand	–	–	–	–	–	–	–	–	–
Norway	–	–	–	–	–	–	–	–	5.8
Sweden	–	–	–	–	–	–	–	–	0.6
Switzerland	–	–	–	–	–	–	–	–	0.1
United Kingdom	–	–	–	–	–	–	–	–	0.3
United States	–	–	–	–	–	–	–	–	–
TOTAL	*402.4*	*412.9*	*460.5*	*502.4*	*394.3*	*400.6*	*440.2*	*465.1*	*98.2*
MULTILATERAL	*70.2*	*134.2*	*233.5*	*305.0*	*70.2*	*134.2*	*233.5*	*305.0*	*71.2*
OPEC COUNTRIES	*35.7*	*49.4*	*25.1*	*25.7*	*35.7*	*49.4*	*21.9*	*22.7*	*0.0*
E.E.C.+ MEMBERS	*103.3*	*65.1*	*113.2*	*92.3*	*95.3*	*52.7*	*92.9*	*55.0*	*28.8*
TOTAL	*508.2*	*596.5*	*719.1*	*833.0*	*500.2*	*584.1*	*695.6*	*792.7*	*169.4*

TOTAL OFFICIAL GROSS | TOTAL OFFICIAL NET | TOTAL OOF GROSS

	TOTAL OFFICIAL GROSS				TOTAL OFFICIAL NET				TOTAL OOF GROSS
	1983	1984	1985	1986	1983	1984	1985	1986	1983
DAC COUNTRIES									
Australia	7.7	11.0	20.8	36.0	4.1	7.5	20.8	34.9	1.2
Austria	0.3	0.2	0.3	0.5	0.3	0.2	0.3	0.5	–
Belgium	6.0	9.8	9.5	1.8	6.0	9.8	9.5	1.8	–
Canada	5.0	6.7	25.1	32.4	3.7	5.4	23.8	29.8	–
Denmark	8.7	23.4	12.9	25.3	8.7	23.4	12.9	20.3	3.5
Finland	0.0	0.0	2.2	0.2	0.0	0.0	2.2	0.2	–
France	4.7	6.0	6.3	9.9	4.7	6.0	6.3	9.9	–
Germany, Fed. Rep.	114.0	70.5	133.1	112.7	106.0	52.9	102.7	61.8	9.3
Ireland	0.0	0.0	0.1	0.1	0.0	0.0	0.1	0.1	–
Italy	21.8	40.0	27.5	32.5	20.1	37.3	20.2	23.7	10.7
Japan	561.0	531.2	442.5	889.4	457.1	530.2	441.0	651.6	210.8
Netherlands	–	–	0.4	2.4	–	–	0.4	2.4	–
New Zealand	–	–	–	–	–	–	–	–	–
Norway	5.8	11.9	3.6	4.5	5.8	11.9	3.6	4.5	–
Sweden	9.3	12.9	19.4	38.6	5.0	7.1	13.4	32.0	8.7
Switzerland	0.1	0.1	0.1	0.3	0.1	0.1	0.1	0.3	–
United Kingdom	0.3	0.8	1.6	3.2	0.3	0.8	1.6	3.2	–
United States	9.0	20.0	6.0	2.0	9.0	20.0	6.0	-8.0	9.0
TOTAL	*753.7*	*744.3*	*711.4*	*1191.7*	*631.0*	*712.3*	*664.8*	*868.8*	*253.2*
MULTILATERAL	*145.4*	*319.5*	*697.9*	*776.2*	*141.3*	*315.2*	*693.3*	*771.2*	*4.0*
OPEC COUNTRIES	*35.7*	*49.4*	*33.4*	*25.7*	*35.7*	*49.4*	*30.2*	*22.7*	*–*
E.E.C.+ MEMBERS	*155.6*	*150.4*	*192.2*	*195.4*	*145.9*	*130.0*	*154.5*	*130.6*	*23.4*
TOTAL	*934.9*	*1113.1*	*1442.6*	*1993.5*	*808.0*	*1076.9*	*1388.3*	*1662.7*	*257.2*

ODA COMMITMENTS

1984	1985	1986	1983	1984	1985	1986
10.8	17.3	14.4	11.5	18.4	17.1	16.3
0.2	0.3	0.5	0.3	0.2	0.3	–
6.2	6.9	1.8	5.9	5.2	2.1	11.0
6.7	15.5	18.0	31.0	33.0	15.0	24.8
2.2	8.3	19.2	–	14.5	24.5	34.2
0.0	2.2	0.2	–	2.1	–	10.1
6.0	6.3	9.9	4.7	6.0	6.3	9.9
69.9	117.9	88.4	199.4	37.5	27.6	69.1
0.0	0.1	0.1	0.0	0.0	0.1	0.1
9.9	14.4	32.0	24.3	18.3	66.3	64.0
389.4	387.9	497.0	343.6	352.5	357.7	616.9
–	0.4	2.4	–	–	1.2	1.6
–	–	–	–	–	0.0	–
11.9	3.6	4.5	11.1	14.0	2.4	4.1
0.8	11.4	6.3	2.7	1.1	10.7	6.4
0.1	0.1	0.3	–	–	16.3	0.1
0.8	1.6	3.2	0.3	0.8	1.6	3.2
514.7	*594.1*	*698.0*	*634.8*	*503.4*	*549.2*	*871.8*
–	–	–	–	–	–	–
–	–	–	–	–	–	–
–	–	0.1	–	–	–	–
–	–	–	–	–	–	–
–	0.9	7.5	–	4.7	0.4	13.8
123.9	213.7	282.0	180.0	253.5	507.3	400.0
–	–	–	–	–	–	–
10.3	19.7	23.0	–	24.0	–	12.4
–	–	–	–	–	–	–
–	–	–	–	–	–	–
–	–	–	71.2	112.3	110.0	137.9
15.4	14.4	17.3	–	–	–	–
1.6	4.5	3.2	–	–	–	–
5.2	6.7	16.7	–	–	–	–
–	–	–	–	–	–	–
79.7	67.9	84.5	–	–	–	–
4.1	3.6	4.8	–	–	–	–
6.4	12.9	11.4	–	–	–	–
246.5	*344.3*	*450.5*	*251.2*	*394.5*	*617.7*	*564.2*
49.4	*25.1*	*25.7*	*45.6*	*–*	*43.2*	*13.7*
94.9	*156.7*	*164.5*	*234.6*	*87.0*	*130.1*	*206.9*
810.6	*963.5*	*1174.2*	*931.6*	*897.9*	*1210.1*	*1449.6*

TECH. COOP. GRANTS

1984	1985	1986	1983	1984	1985	1986
10.8	17.3	14.4	6.0	10.8	9.1	12.1
0.2	0.3	0.5	0.3	–	–	–
0.4	0.8	1.4	0.1	0.3	0.4	0.9
6.7	15.5	18.0	0.9	–	6.4	–
0.6	1.6	1.3	0.9	0.6	0.7	1.8
0.0	0.0	0.2	0.0	0.0	0.0	0.1
6.0	6.3	9.9	4.7	6.0	6.3	9.9
16.0	20.6	32.0	12.6	16.0	20.6	28.0
0.0	0.1	0.1	0.0	0.0	0.1	0.1
6.1	11.2	14.4	3.0	6.1	6.0	10.0
41.5	42.7	86.9	20.5	27.3	31.2	61.2
–	0.4	2.4	–	–	0.4	1.4
–	–	–	–	–	–	–
11.9	3.6	4.5	0.9	0.7	0.6	2.3
0.8	11.4	6.3	0.2	0.8	1.5	1.9
0.1	0.1	0.3	0.1	0.1	0.1	0.2
0.8	1.6	3.2	0.3	0.8	1.6	3.2
–	–	–	–	–	–	–
101.8	*133.5*	*195.6*	*50.3*	*69.4*	*85.0*	*133.0*
112.3	*110.9*	*145.5*	*46.3*	*32.7*	*42.1*	*53.4*
–	*0.0*	*–*	*–*	*–*	*–*	*–*
29.8	*43.5*	*72.2*	*21.6*	*29.7*	*36.1*	*55.2*
214.1	*244.4*	*341.1*	*96.6*	*102.0*	*127.1*	*186.4*

TOTAL OOF NET

1984	1985	1986	1983	1984	1985	1986
0.2	3.5	21.6	-2.3	-3.3	3.5	20.5
–	–	–	–	–	–	–
3.6	2.7	0.0	–	3.6	2.7	0.0
–	9.6	14.4	-1.3	-1.3	8.3	11.8
21.2	4.6	6.1	3.5	21.2	4.6	1.0
–	–	–	–	–	–	–
0.7	15.2	24.3	9.3	-4.6	5.1	10.6
30.1	13.1	0.5	9.0	27.3	5.8	-8.2
141.8	54.6	392.4	106.9	140.9	53.1	154.6
–	–	–	–	–	–	–
12.1	8.0	32.3	4.4	6.3	2.0	25.7
–	–	–	–	–	–	–
20.0	6.0	2.0	9.0	20.0	6.0	-8.0
229.6	*117.3*	*493.7*	*138.5*	*210.0*	*91.1*	*208.1*
72.9	*353.6*	*325.7*	*-0.1*	*68.7*	*349.0*	*320.8*
–	*8.3*	*–*	*–*	*–*	*8.3*	*–*
55.5	*35.6*	*30.9*	*21.8*	*47.5*	*18.1*	*3.4*
302.5	*479.1*	*819.4*	*138.4*	*278.7*	*448.3*	*528.9*

ODA COMMITMENTS : LOANS

DAC COUNTRIES

	1983	1984	1985	1986
Australia	–	–	–	–
Austria	–	–	–	–
Belgium	5.9	5.2	2.1	9.6
Canada	–	–	–	–
Denmark	–	14.5	22.7	32.8
Finland	–	1.2	–	9.9
France	–	–	–	–
Germany, Fed. Rep.	180.4	14.4	–	27.5
Ireland	–	–	–	–
Italy	3.5	4.2	53.7	47.0
Japan	290.5	301.7	318.8	483.2
Netherlands	–	–	–	–
New Zealand	–	–	–	–
Norway	–	–	–	–
Sweden	–	–	–	–
Switzerland	–	–	16.3	–
United Kingdom	–	–	–	–
United States	–	–	–	–
TOTAL	*480.2*	*341.2*	*413.5*	*609.9*
MULTILATERAL	*180.0*	*277.3*	*507.3*	*412.4*
OPEC COUNTRIES	*45.6*	*–*	*43.2*	*13.7*
E.E.C.+ MEMBERS	*189.7*	*38.3*	*78.5*	*116.9*
TOTAL	*705.8*	*618.5*	*964.1*	*1036.1*

GRANT ELEMENT OF ODA

DAC COUNTRIES

	1983	1984	1985	1986
Australia	100.0	100.0	100.0	100.0
Austria	100.0	100.0	100.0	–
Belgium	84.2	84.7	84.6	85.8
Canada	100.0	100.0	100.0	100.0
Denmark	–	85.3	86.9	86.1
Finland	–	61.6	–	70.2
France	100.0	100.0	100.0	67.6
Germany, Fed. Rep.	36.5	72.0	100.0	70.9
Ireland	100.0	100.0	100.0	100.0
Italy	91.9	86.7	61.2	64.5
Japan	63.9	62.4	57.9	63.3
Netherlands	–	–	100.0	100.0
New Zealand	–	–	100.0	–
Norway	100.0	100.0	100.0	100.0
Sweden	100.0	100.0	100.0	100.0
Switzerland	–	–	–	100.0
United Kingdom	100.0	100.0	100.0	100.0
United States	–	–	–	–
TOTAL	*60.0*	*70.3*	*66.4*	*67.7*
MULTILATERAL	*88.8*	*87.0*	*86.7*	*87.1*
OPEC COUNTRIES	*37.1*	*–*	*35.6*	*25.9*
E.E.C.+ MEMBERS	*44.8*	*81.7*	*77.7*	*72.8*
TOTAL	*65.7*	*78.6*	*74.9*	*74.5*

OTHER AGGREGATES

COMMITMENTS: ALL SOURCES

	1983	1984	1985	1986
TOTAL BILATERAL	947.1	537.1	1268.4	1748.9
of which				
OPEC	45.6	–	59.7	13.7
CMEA	–	–	–	–
TOTAL MULTILATERAL	549.7	1010.5	1294.8	1251.6
TOTAL BIL.& MULTIL.	1496.9	1547.7	2563.2	3000.4
of which				
ODA Grants	225.8	279.4	246.0	413.6
ODA Loans	705.8	618.5	964.1	1036.1

DISBURSEMENTS:

DAC COUNTRIES COMBINED

	1983	1984	1985	1986
OFFICIAL & PRIVATE				
GROSS:				
Contractual Lending	1376.4	1073.3	997.4	1632.5
Export Credits Total	766.1	522.2	482.0	738.1
Export Credits Private	720.8	434.3	422.3	636.4
NET:				
Contractual Lending	337.3	339.5	306.6	601.5
Export Credits Total	-161.5	-199.2	-188.5	-19.5
PRIVATE SECTOR NET	-60.0	-129.7	920.5	1825.1
Direct Investment	-3.1	65.7	221.6	198.1
Portfolio Investment	138.7	72.1	920.8	1698.7
Export Credits	-195.5	-267.5	-222.0	-71.6

MARKET BORROWING:

CHANGE IN CLAIMS

	1983	1984	1985	1986
Banks	–	1427.0	4878.0	779.0

MEMORANDUM ITEM:

	1983	1984	1985	1986
CMEA Countr.(Gross)	–	–	–	–

COLOMBIA

TOTAL RECEIPTS NET

DAC COUNTRIES	1983	1984	1985	1986
Australia	0.0	0.0	6.8	-6.3
Austria	0.3	0.4	0.5	0.6
Belgium	-5.9	13.4	-12.5	-9.4
Canada	70.3	47.7	27.1	7.8
Denmark	-0.1	-1.9	37.6	0.3
Finland	-0.4	-0.4	1.2	1.9
France	149.2	47.6	-16.5	45.9
Germany, Fed. Rep.	19.3	-12.0	139.2	151.5
Ireland	–	–	–	–
Italy	-0.3	6.5	9.1	3.8
Japan	88.4	66.9	15.8	278.7
Netherlands	12.8	43.0	4.4	20.0
New Zealand	–	0.0	0.0	0.1
Norway	–	0.0	1.3	1.6
Sweden	16.4	8.0	45.0	33.7
Switzerland	48.6	3.7	2.6	1.2
United Kingdom	4.1	26.7	2.3	26.4
United States	562.0	437.0	-541.0	117.0
TOTAL	964.8	686.5	-277.1	674.8
MULTILATERAL				
AF.D.F.	–	–	–	–
AF.D.B.	–	–	–	–
AS.D.B	–	–	–	–
CAR.D.B.	–	–	–	–
E.E.C.	0.2	–	0.9	2.2
IBRD	164.5	305.1	421.0	277.4
IDA	-0.7	-0.7	-0.3	-1.1
I.D.B.	148.7	166.3	156.3	155.9
IFAD	–	–	1.0	0.2
I.F.C.	0.3	4.4	6.9	2.9
IMF TRUST FUND	–	–	–	–
U.N. AGENCIES	–	–	–	–
UNDP	2.8	4.6	5.0	5.2
UNTA	0.9	0.9	1.4	1.1
UNICEF	2.1	1.8	2.2	2.6
UNRWA	–	–	–	–
WFP	1.9	1.2	5.3	2.8
UNHCR	–	–	–	–
Other Multilateral	1.0	1.1	0.9	1.0
Arab OPEC Agencies	–	–	–	–
TOTAL	321.6	484.6	600.5	450.2
OPEC COUNTRIES	-0.2	-0.1	–	–
E.E.C.+ MEMBERS	179.3	123.2	164.5	240.8
TOTAL	1286.2	1171.0	323.4	1125.0

TOTAL ODA NET

DAC COUNTRIES	1983	1984	1985	1986
Australia	–	–	0.1	1.1
Austria	0.3	0.4	0.5	0.6
Belgium	1.0	0.7	0.7	1.1
Canada	7.0	7.7	5.5	8.1
Denmark	-0.1	0.0	0.0	-0.1
Finland	0.1	0.0	0.2	0.1
France	7.0	4.1	3.7	3.6
Germany, Fed. Rep.	14.3	11.9	16.2	17.3
Ireland	–	–	–	–
Italy	2.6	3.1	4.3	10.2
Japan	15.2	24.6	13.9	7.2
Netherlands	9.4	10.0	8.5	11.4
New Zealand	–	0.0	0.0	0.1
Norway	–	0.0	0.6	0.2
Sweden	–	–	–	0.5
Switzerland	1.0	0.8	1.0	1.2
United Kingdom	0.5	0.3	0.8	1.2
United States	-22.0	-22.0	-19.0	-27.0
TOTAL	36.4	41.6	36.7	36.7
AF.D.F.	–	–	–	–
AF.D.B.	–	–	–	–
AS.D.B	–	–	–	–
CAR.D.B.	–	–	–	–
E.E.C.	0.2	–	0.9	2.2
IBRD	–	–	–	–
IDA	-0.7	-0.7	-0.3	-1.1
I.D.B.	41.7	37.7	8.6	12.7
IFAD	–	–	1.0	0.2
I.F.C.	–	–	–	–
IMF TRUST FUND	–	–	–	–
U.N. AGENCIES	–	–	–	–
UNDP	2.8	4.6	5.0	5.2
UNTA	0.9	0.9	1.4	1.1
UNICEF	2.1	1.8	2.2	2.6
UNRWA	–	–	–	–
WFP	1.9	1.2	5.3	2.8
UNHCR	–	–	–	–
Other Multilateral	1.0	1.1	0.9	1.0
Arab OPEC Agencies	–	–	–	–
TOTAL	49.8	46.5	24.9	26.7
OPEC COUNTRIES	–	–	–	–
E.E.C.+ MEMBERS	34.9	30.0	35.0	47.0
TOTAL	86.2	88.1	61.7	63.5

TOTAL ODA GROSS

	1983
Australia	–
Austria	0.3
Belgium	1.1
Canada	7.5
Denmark	
Finland	0.1
France	7.8
Germany, Fed. Rep.	18.7
Ireland	–
Italy	2.6
Japan	15.2
Netherlands	9.9
New Zealand	–
Norway	–
Sweden	–
Switzerland	1.0
United Kingdom	1.0
United States	1.0
TOTAL	66.3
AF.D.F.	–
AF.D.B.	–
AS.D.B	–
CAR.D.B.	–
E.E.C.	0.2
IBRD	–
IDA	–
I.D.B.	56.7
IFAD	–
I.F.C.	–
IMF TRUST FUND	–
U.N. AGENCIES	–
UNDP	2.8
UNTA	0.9
UNICEF	2.1
UNRWA	–
WFP	1.9
UNHCR	–
Other Multilateral	1.0
Arab OPEC Agencies	–
TOTAL	65.5
OPEC COUNTRIES	–
E.E.C.+ MEMBERS	41.2
TOTAL	131.8

ODA LOANS GROSS

DAC COUNTRIES	1983	1984	1985	1986
Australia	–	–	–	–
Austria	–	–	–	–
Belgium	–	–	–	–
Canada	1.9	2.1	0.1	–
Denmark	–	–	–	–
Finland	–	–	–	–
France	3.6	0.2	0.7	0.0
Germany, Fed. Rep.	4.4	2.6	8.7	6.7
Ireland	–	–	–	–
Italy	–	–	1.2	6.5
Japan	11.9	18.4	8.5	–
Netherlands	0.9	1.9	1.4	0.3
New Zealand	–	–	–	–
Norway	–	–	–	–
Sweden	–	–	–	–
Switzerland	–	–	–	–
United Kingdom	0.2	0.0	0.2	0.0
United States	–	–	–	–
TOTAL	22.9	25.2	20.7	13.6
MULTILATERAL	56.5	53.2	26.8	31.2
OPEC COUNTRIES	–	–	–	–
E.E.C.+ MEMBERS	9.1	4.7	12.1	13.6
TOTAL	79.4	78.4	47.5	44.7

ODA LOANS NET

DAC COUNTRIES	1983	1984	1985	1986
Australia	–	–	–	–
Austria	–	–	–	–
Belgium	0.0	-0.1	–	-0.2
Canada	1.3	1.1	-0.7	-1.2
Denmark	-0.1	0.0	0.0	-0.1
Finland	–	–	–	–
France	2.8	-0.5	-0.2	-1.0
Germany, Fed. Rep.	-0.1	-0.8	4.4	-0.4
Ireland	–	–	–	–
Italy	–	–	1.2	6.5
Japan	11.9	18.4	8.5	–
Netherlands	0.4	1.3	0.6	-1.1
New Zealand	–	–	–	–
Norway	–	–	–	–
Sweden	–	–	–	–
Switzerland	–	–	–	–
United Kingdom	-0.2	-0.3	-0.1	-0.3
United States	-23.0	-24.0	-22.0	-31.0
TOTAL	-7.0	-5.1	-8.3	-28.8
MULTILATERAL	40.8	36.9	9.1	11.8
OPEC COUNTRIES	–	–	–	–
E.E.C.+ MEMBERS	2.8	-0.5	5.9	3.4
TOTAL	33.8	31.9	0.8	-17.0

GRANTS

	1983
Australia	–
Austria	0.3
Belgium	1.1
Canada	5.7
Denmark	0.1
Finland	
France	4.2
Germany, Fed. Rep.	14.4
Ireland	–
Italy	2.6
Japan	3.4
Netherlands	9.0
New Zealand	–
Norway	–
Sweden	–
Switzerland	1.0
United Kingdom	0.8
United States	1.0
TOTAL	43.5
MULTILATERAL	9.0
OPEC COUNTRIES	–
E.E.C.+ MEMBERS	32.1
TOTAL	52.4

TOTAL OFFICIAL GROSS

DAC COUNTRIES	1983	1984	1985	1986
Australia	–	–	0.1	1.1
Austria	0.3	0.4	0.5	0.6
Belgium	1.1	1.2	1.0	1.3
Canada	75.9	53.1	46.3	25.6
Denmark	–	0.6	0.4	0.4
Finland	0.1	0.0	0.2	0.1
France	7.8	4.8	4.5	4.7
Germany, Fed. Rep.	24.2	17.1	66.5	38.7
Ireland	–	–	–	–
Italy	2.6	5.3	6.1	10.2
Japan	94.6	70.7	65.0	130.4
Netherlands	9.9	10.6	9.2	12.8
New Zealand	–	0.0	0.0	0.1
Norway	–	0.0	0.6	0.2
Sweden	14.3	6.3	7.0	40.8
Switzerland	1.0	0.8	1.0	1.2
United Kingdom	1.0	0.6	1.1	1.5
United States	129.0	156.0	132.0	101.0
TOTAL	361.9	327.6	341.3	370.7
MULTILATERAL	485.2	673.0	814.4	764.8
OPEC COUNTRIES	–	–	–	–
E.E.C.+ MEMBERS	46.7	40.3	89.7	71.9
TOTAL	847.1	1000.6	1155.8	1135.5

TOTAL OFFICIAL NET

DAC COUNTRIES	1983	1984	1985	1986
Australia	–	–	0.1	1.1
Austria	0.3	0.4	0.5	0.6
Belgium	1.0	1.0	1.0	1.1
Canada	70.3	47.7	27.1	7.8
Denmark	-0.1	0.5	0.3	0.4
Finland	0.1	0.0	0.2	0.1
France	7.0	4.1	3.7	3.6
Germany, Fed. Rep.	11.9	3.0	54.3	18.2
Ireland	–	–	–	–
Italy	2.5	5.1	5.2	9.3
Japan	82.4	54.1	39.6	81.3
Netherlands	9.2	9.9	8.3	11.1
New Zealand	–	0.0	0.0	0.1
Norway	–	0.0	0.6	0.2
Sweden	12.1	1.0	–	35.1
Switzerland	1.0	0.8	1.0	1.2
United Kingdom	0.5	0.3	0.8	1.2
United States	96.0	116.0	94.0	54.0
TOTAL	294.4	243.9	236.4	226.2
MULTILATERAL	321.6	484.6	600.5	450.2
OPEC COUNTRIES	-0.2	-0.1	–	–
E.E.C.+ MEMBERS	32.3	23.9	74.4	47.0
TOTAL	615.8	728.4	836.9	676.5

TOTAL OOF GROSS

	1983
Australia	–
Austria	–
Belgium	–
Canada	68.4
Denmark	–
Finland	–
France	–
Germany, Fed. Rep.	5.5
Ireland	–
Italy	–
Japan	79.4
Netherlands	–
New Zealand	–
Norway	–
Sweden	14.3
Switzerland	–
United Kingdom	–
United States	128.0
TOTAL	295.6
MULTILATERAL	419.7
OPEC COUNTRIES	–
E.E.C.+ MEMBERS	5.5
TOTAL	715.3

ODA COMMITMENTS

1984	1985	1986	1983	1984	1985	1986
–	0.1	1.1	–	–	0.1	–
0.4	0.5	0.6	0.3	0.3	0.5	–
0.8	0.7	1.3	0.6	–	–	1.3
8.7	6.3	9.3	8.2	6.6	9.5	3.0
–	–	–	–	–	–	–
0.0	0.2	0.1	0.1	0.0	0.2	0.0
4.8	4.5	4.7	20.7	4.7	3.9	4.7
15.3	20.5	24.4	22.3	65.4	10.1	40.3
–	–	–	–	–	–	–
3.1	4.3	10.2	6.3	18.3	10.2	9.6
24.6	13.9	7.2	3.5	3.7	5.6	117.9
10.6	9.2	12.8	10.5	5.9	8.1	12.3
0.0	0.0	0.1	–	0.1	0.1	–
0.0	0.6	0.2	–	0.0	0.1	0.1
–	–	0.5	–	–	0.1	0.5
0.8	1.0	1.2	0.6	1.0	0.9	4.8
0.6	1.1	1.5	0.8	0.8	0.9	1.5
2.0	3.0	4.0	4.3	6.8	11.5	12.2
71.8	65.7	79.1	78.2	113.3	61.4	208.2
–	–	–	–	–	–	–
–	–	–	–	–	–	–
–	–	–	–	–	–	–
–	0.9	2.2	0.2	3.9	3.3	5.0
–	–	–	–	–	–	–
53.2	25.9	31.0	9.3	10.0	4.0	7.0
–	1.0	0.2	–	–	–	–
–	–	–	–	–	–	–
–	–	–	8.7	9.6	14.9	12.7
4.6	5.0	5.2	–	–	–	–
0.9	1.4	1.1	–	–	–	–
1.8	2.2	2.6	–	–	–	–
–	–	–	–	–	–	–
1.2	5.3	2.8	–	–	–	–
–	–	–	–	–	–	–
1.1	0.9	1.0	–	–	–	–
–	–	–	–	–	–	–
62.8	42.6	46.1	18.2	23.4	22.1	24.7
–	–	–	–	–	–	–
35.3	41.2	57.1	61.5	98.8	36.4	74.6
134.6	108.3	125.2	96.4	136.7	83.5	232.8

TECH. COOP. GRANTS

1984	1985	1986	1983	1984	1985	1986
–	0.1	1.1	–	–	0.0	–
0.4	0.5	0.6	0.3	–	–	–
0.8	0.7	1.3	0.1	0.0	0.1	0.1
6.6	6.2	9.3	2.4	–	1.4	–
–	–	–	–	–	–	–
0.0	0.2	0.1	–	–	–	0.0
4.7	3.9	4.6	4.2	4.7	3.9	4.6
12.7	11.8	17.7	14.4	12.7	11.6	17.6
–	–	–	–	–	–	–
3.1	3.2	3.7	1.7	3.0	3.2	3.0
6.3	5.4	7.2	2.7	3.4	3.8	6.4
8.7	7.8	12.5	8.4	8.3	6.7	11.1
0.0	0.0	0.1	–	0.0	0.0	0.0
0.0	0.6	0.2	–	0.0	0.0	0.0
–	–	0.5	–	–	–	–
0.8	1.0	1.2	0.3	0.3	0.2	0.5
0.6	0.9	1.5	0.7	0.6	0.9	1.2
2.0	3.0	4.0	–	–	–	–
46.6	45.0	65.5	35.2	33.0	31.7	44.6
9.6	15.9	14.9	6.7	8.3	9.5	9.9
–	–	–	–	–	–	–
30.5	29.1	43.5	29.4	29.3	26.2	37.6
56.2	60.9	80.4	41.9	41.3	41.2	54.5

TOTAL OOF NET

1984	1985	1986	1983	1984	1985	1986
–	–	–	–	–	–	–
0.3	0.3	–	–	0.3	0.3	–
44.4	40.0	16.3	63.4	40.0	21.6	-0.3
0.6	0.4	0.4	–	0.6	0.3	0.4
–	–	–	–	–	–	–
1.8	46.0	14.3	-2.4	-8.9	38.1	0.9
–	–	–	–	–	–	–
2.3	1.8	–	0.0	2.1	0.9	-1.0
46.1	51.1	123.3	67.2	29.4	25.7	74.1
–	–	–	-0.2	-0.2	-0.2	-0.2
–	–	–	–	–	–	–
6.3	7.0	40.3	12.1	1.0	–	34.7
–	–	–	–	–	–	–
–	–	–	–	–	–	–
154.0	129.0	97.0	118.0	138.0	113.0	81.0
255.8	275.6	291.6	258.0	202.3	199.7	189.5
610.2	771.8	718.8	271.8	438.1	575.6	423.5
–	–	–	-0.2	-0.1	–	–
5.0	48.5	14.8	-2.7	-6.1	39.4	0.1
866.0	1047.4	1010.4	529.6	640.3	775.3	613.0

ODA COMMITMENTS : LOANS

DAC COUNTRIES

	1983	1984	1985	1986
Australia	–	–	–	–
Austria	–	–	–	–
Belgium	–	–	–	–
Canada	–	–	–	–
Denmark	–	–	–	–
Finland	–	–	–	–
France	16.5	–	–	0.0
Germany, Fed. Rep.	12.3	49.7	–	10.1
Ireland	–	–	–	–
Italy	–	8.6	–	–
Japan	–	–	–	108.5
Netherlands	–	–	–	–
New Zealand	–	–	–	–
Norway	–	–	–	–
Sweden	–	–	–	–
Switzerland	–	–	–	4.1
United Kingdom	–	0.2	–	–
United States	–	–	–	–
TOTAL	*28.9*	*58.5*	*–*	*122.8*
MULTILATERAL	*9.3*	*10.0*	*4.0*	*7.0*
OPEC COUNTRIES	*–*	*–*	*–*	*–*
E.E.C.+ MEMBERS	*28.9*	*58.5*	*–*	*10.2*
TOTAL	*38.2*	*68.5*	*4.0*	*129.8*

GRANT ELEMENT OF ODA

DAC COUNTRIES

	1983	1984	1985	1986
Australia	–	–	100.0	–
Austria	100.0	100.0	100.0	–
Belgium	100.0	–	–	100.0
Canada	100.0	100.0	100.0	100.0
Denmark	–	–	–	–
Finland	100.0	100.0	100.0	100.0
France	59.4	100.0	100.0	75.7
Germany, Fed. Rep.	81.3	54.8	100.0	91.5
Ireland	–	–	–	–
Italy	100.0	73.7	100.0	100.0
Japan	100.0	100.0	100.0	43.5
Netherlands	100.0	100.0	100.0	100.0
New Zealand	–	100.0	100.0	–
Norway	–	100.0	100.0	100.0
Sweden	–	–	100.0	100.0
Switzerland	100.0	100.0	100.0	88.0
United Kingdom	100.0	91.9	100.0	100.0
United States	100.0	100.0	100.0	100.0
TOTAL	*83.9*	*69.6*	*100.0*	*66.3*
MULTILATERAL	*67.1*	*81.1*	*86.1*	*91.8*
OPEC COUNTRIES	*–*	*–*	*–*	*–*
E.E.C.+ MEMBERS	*79.5*	*65.2*	*100.0*	*90.6*
TOTAL	*78.8*	*71.9*	*95.8*	*68.8*

OTHER AGGREGATES

COMMITMENTS: ALL SOURCES

	1983	1984	1985	1986
TOTAL BILATERAL	111.7	338.1	241.5	460.7
of which				
OPEC	–	–	–	–
CMEA	–	–	0.6	25.0
TOTAL MULTILATERAL	526.2	1173.9	1140.1	530.7
TOTAL BIL.& MULTIL.	637.9	1512.1	1381.6	991.4
of which				
ODA Grants	58.2	68.2	80.1	103.0
ODA Loans	38.2	68.5	4.0	154.8

DISBURSEMENTS:

DAC COUNTRIES COMBINED

OFFICIAL & PRIVATE

	1983	1984	1985	1986
GROSS:				
Contractual Lending	532.7	510.1	645.2	493.0
Export Credits Total	509.8	484.3	624.1	479.0
Export Credits Private	214.2	229.4	349.2	187.8
NET:				
Contractual Lending	335.0	249.3	371.9	222.6
Export Credits Total	342.3	254.0	380.0	251.2
PRIVATE SECTOR NET	670.4	442.6	-513.5	448.6
Direct Investment	256.4	249.0	-618.0	-67.0
Portfolio Investment	329.9	141.2	-76.2	453.7
Export Credits	84.1	52.4	180.8	61.9

MARKET BORROWING:

CHANGE IN CLAIMS

	1983	1984	1985	1986
Banks	–	-421.0	-738.0	-26.0

MEMORANDUM ITEM:

	1983	1984	1985	1986
CMEA Countr.(Gross)	–	–	–	–

DISBURSEMENTS, UNLESS OTHERWISE STATED

TOTAL RECEIPTS NET

DAC COUNTRIES

	1983	1984	1985	1986
Australia	1.0	0.5	0.1	0.4
Austria	–	–	0.0	–
Belgium	0.1	0.8	0.7	1.9
Canada	0.8	0.3	0.3	0.1
Denmark	–	–	–	–
Finland	–	–	–	–
France	11.7	13.0	14.0	17.2
Germany, Fed. Rep.	0.8	1.2	0.5	0.4
Ireland	–	–	–	–
Italy	0.1	0.1	–	–
Japan	1.7	2.2	1.2	0.9
Netherlands	–	–	0.1	0.2
New Zealand	–	–	–	–
Norway	–	–	–	–
Sweden	–	–	–	–
Switzerland	0.1	0.0	–	0.1
United Kingdom	–	–	–	–
United States	..	–	1.0	–
TOTAL	16.2	18.1	18.0	21.0

MULTILATERAL

	1983	1984	1985	1986
AF.D.F.	2.1	4.9	3.9	2.9
AF.D.B.	2.6	2.6	3.4	0.6
AS.D.B	–	–	–	–
CAR.D.B.	–	–	–	–
E.E.C.	2.3	2.8	6.1	5.5
IBRD	–	–	–	–
IDA	2.1	3.8	5.5	4.7
I.D.B.	–	–	–	–
IFAD	–	–	0.3	0.6
I.F.C.	–	–	–	–
IMF TRUST FUND	–	–	–	–
U.N. AGENCIES	–	–	–	–
UNDP	2.5	1.6	2.0	2.6
UNTA	0.8	0.7	0.8	0.8
UNICEF	0.2	0.1	0.1	0.3
UNRWA	–	–	–	–
WFP	3.2	1.5	1.3	1.7
UNHCR	–	–	–	–
Other Multilateral	0.7	0.4	0.5	0.5
Arab OPEC Agencies	0.5	1.9	4.6	3.7
TOTAL	16.9	20.1	28.5	23.8
OPEC COUNTRIES	6.4	4.5	4.3	2.4
E.E.C.+ MEMBERS	14.9	17.9	21.4	25.1
TOTAL	39.5	42.8	50.8	47.1

TOTAL ODA NET

DAC COUNTRIES

	1983	1984	1985	1986
Australia	1.0	0.5	0.1	0.4
Austria	–	–	0.0	–
Belgium	0.1	0.8	0.7	1.7
Canada	0.8	0.3	0.3	0.1
Denmark	–	–	–	–
Finland	–	–	–	–
France	10.5	13.2	14.0	17.2
Germany, Fed. Rep.	0.8	1.2	0.5	0.4
Ireland	–	–	–	–
Italy	0.1	0.1	–	–
Japan	1.7	2.2	1.2	0.9
Netherlands	–	–	0.1	0.2
New Zealand	–	–	–	–
Norway	–	–	–	–
Sweden	–	–	–	–
Switzerland	0.1	0.0	–	0.1
United Kingdom	–	–	–	–
United States	–	–	1.0	–
TOTAL	15.1	18.2	18.0	20.8

MULTILATERAL

	1983	1984	1985	1986
AF.D.F.	2.1	4.9	3.9	2.9
AF.D.B.	–	–	–	–
AS.D.B	–	–	–	–
CAR.D.B.	–	–	–	–
E.E.C.	2.3	2.8	6.1	5.5
IBRD	–	–	–	–
IDA	2.1	3.8	5.5	4.7
I.D.B.	–	–	–	–
IFAD	–	–	0.3	0.6
I.F.C.	–	–	–	–
IMF TRUST FUND	–	–	–	–
U.N. AGENCIES	–	–	–	–
UNDP	2.5	1.6	2.0	2.6
UNTA	0.8	0.7	0.8	0.8
UNICEF	0.2	0.1	0.1	0.3
UNRWA	–	–	–	–
WFP	3.2	1.5	1.3	1.7
UNHCR	–	–	–	–
Other Multilateral	0.7	0.4	0.5	0.5
Arab OPEC Agencies	2.9	2.6	4.7	3.7
TOTAL	16.8	18.3	25.3	23.1
OPEC COUNTRIES	6.4	4.5	4.3	2.4
E.E.C.+ MEMBERS	13.7	18.0	21.4	24.9
TOTAL	38.2	41.0	47.6	46.3

TOTAL ODA GROSS

	1983
Australia	1.0
Austria	–
Belgium	0.1
Canada	0.8
Denmark	–
Finland	–
France	10.5
Germany, Fed. Rep.	0.8
Ireland	–
Italy	0.1
Japan	1.7
Netherlands	–
New Zealand	–
Norway	–
Sweden	–
Switzerland	0.1
United Kingdom	–
United States	–
TOTAL	15.1
AF.D.F.	2.1
AF.D.B.	–
AS.D.B	–
CAR.D.B.	–
E.E.C.	2.3
IBRD	–
IDA	2.1
I.D.B.	–
IFAD	–
I.F.C.	–
IMF TRUST FUND	–
U.N. AGENCIES	–
UNDP	2.5
UNTA	0.8
UNICEF	0.2
UNRWA	–
WFP	3.2
UNHCR	–
Other Multilateral	0.7
Arab OPEC Agencies	3.6
TOTAL	17.4
OPEC COUNTRIES	6.4
E.E.C.+ MEMBERS	13.7
TOTAL	38.9

ODA LOANS GROSS

DAC COUNTRIES

	1983	1984	1985	1986
Australia	–	–	–	–
Austria	–	–	–	–
Belgium	–	–	–	–
Canada	–	–	–	–
Denmark	–	–	–	–
Finland	–	–	–	–
France	1.4	3.5	3.8	3.6
Germany, Fed. Rep.	–	–	–	–
Ireland	–	–	–	–
Italy	–	–	–	–
Japan	–	–	–	–
Netherlands	–	–	–	–
New Zealand	–	–	–	–
Norway	–	–	–	–
Sweden	–	–	–	–
Switzerland	–	–	–	–
United Kingdom	–	–	–	–
United States	–	–	–	–
TOTAL	1.4	3.5	3.8	3.6
MULTILATERAL	7.7	11.4	14.6	11.4
OPEC COUNTRIES	4.5	4.3	4.1	2.5
E.E.C.+ MEMBERS	1.4	3.5	3.8	3.6
TOTAL	13.7	19.2	22.5	17.5

ODA LOANS NET

	1983	1984	1985	1986
Australia	–	–	–	–
Austria	–	–	–	–
Belgium	–	–	–	–
Canada	–	–	–	–
Denmark	–	–	–	–
Finland	–	–	–	–
France	1.4	3.5	3.8	3.6
Germany, Fed. Rep.	–	–	–	–
Ireland	–	–	–	–
Italy	–	–	–	–
Japan	–	–	–	–
Netherlands	–	–	–	–
New Zealand	–	–	–	–
Norway	–	–	–	–
Sweden	–	–	–	–
Switzerland	–	–	–	–
United Kingdom	–	–	–	–
United States	–	–	–	–
TOTAL	1.4	3.5	3.8	3.6
MULTILATERAL	7.1	11.1	14.5	11.1
OPEC COUNTRIES	4.4	3.8	3.9	2.2
E.E.C.+ MEMBERS	1.4	3.5	3.8	3.6
TOTAL	13.0	18.4	22.2	16.9

GRANTS

	1983
Australia	1.0
Austria	–
Belgium	0.1
Canada	0.8
Denmark	–
Finland	–
France	9.1
Germany, Fed. Rep.	0.8
Ireland	–
Italy	0.1
Japan	1.7
Netherlands	–
New Zealand	–
Norway	–
Sweden	–
Switzerland	0.1
United Kingdom	–
United States	–
TOTAL	13.6
MULTILATERAL	9.6
OPEC COUNTRIES	1.9
E.E.C.+ MEMBERS	12.3
TOTAL	25.2

TOTAL OFFICIAL GROSS

DAC COUNTRIES

	1983	1984	1985	1986
Australia	1.0	0.5	0.1	0.4
Austria	–	–	0.0	–
Belgium	0.1	0.8	0.7	1.7
Canada	0.8	0.3	0.3	0.1
Denmark	–	–	–	–
Finland	–	–	–	–
France	10.5	13.2	14.0	17.2
Germany, Fed. Rep.	0.8	1.2	0.5	0.4
Ireland	–	–	–	–
Italy	0.1	0.1	–	–
Japan	1.7	2.2	1.2	0.9
Netherlands	–	–	0.1	0.2
New Zealand	–	–	–	–
Norway	–	–	–	–
Sweden	–	–	–	–
Switzerland	0.1	0.0	–	0.1
United Kingdom	–	–	–	–
United States	–	–	1.0	–
TOTAL	15.1	18.2	18.0	20.8
MULTILATERAL	19.9	21.1	28.8	24.0
OPEC COUNTRIES	6.4	5.0	4.5	2.7
E.E.C.+ MEMBERS	13.7	18.0	21.4	25.0
TOTAL	41.4	44.4	51.4	47.5

TOTAL OFFICIAL NET

	1983	1984	1985	1986
Australia	1.0	0.5	0.1	0.4
Austria	–	–	0.0	–
Belgium	0.1	0.8	0.7	1.7
Canada	0.8	0.3	0.3	0.1
Denmark	–	–	–	–
Finland	–	–	–	–
France	10.5	13.2	14.0	17.2
Germany, Fed. Rep.	0.8	1.2	0.5	0.4
Ireland	–	–	–	–
Italy	0.1	0.1	–	–
Japan	1.7	2.2	1.2	0.9
Netherlands	–	–	0.1	0.2
New Zealand	–	–	–	–
Norway	–	–	–	–
Sweden	–	–	–	–
Switzerland	0.1	0.0	–	0.1
United Kingdom	–	–	–	–
United States	–	–	1.0	–
TOTAL	15.1	18.2	18.0	20.8
MULTILATERAL	16.9	20.1	28.5	23.8
OPEC COUNTRIES	6.4	4.5	4.3	2.4
E.E.C.+ MEMBERS	13.7	18.0	21.4	24.9
TOTAL	38.3	42.9	50.8	46.9

TOTAL OOF GROSS

	1983
Australia	–
Austria	–
Belgium	–
Canada	–
Denmark	–
Finland	–
France	–
Germany, Fed. Rep.	–
Ireland	–
Italy	–
Japan	–
Netherlands	–
New Zealand	–
Norway	–
Sweden	–
Switzerland	–
United Kingdom	–
United States	–
TOTAL	–
MULTILATERAL	2.0
OPEC COUNTRIES	–
E.E.C.+ MEMBERS	–
TOTAL	2.0

ODA COMMITMENTS

1984	1985	1986	1983	1984	1985	1986
0.5	0.1	0.4	–	0.6	0.4	0.4
–	0.0	–	–	–	0.0	–
0.8	0.7	1.7	–	–	–	1.7
0.3	0.3	0.1	0.7	0.3	0.3	0.1
–	–	–	–	–	–	–
–	–	–	–	–	–	–
13.2	14.0	17.2	16.5	18.7	10.8	17.2
1.2	0.5	0.4	0.8	0.7	0.4	0.3
–	–	–	–	–	–	–
0.1	–	–	0.1	0.1	–	–
2.2	1.2	0.9	0.5	2.9	0.6	2.1
–	0.1	0.2	–	–	0.1	0.2
–	–	–	–	–	–	–
–	–	–	–	–	–	–
0.0	–	0.1	0.1	0.0	–	0.1
–	–	–	–	–	–	–
–	1.0	–	0.0	1.3	0.0	0.8
18.2	*18.0*	*20.8*	*18.6*	*24.6*	*12.7*	*22.7*
4.9	3.9	2.9	–	5.0	–	–
–	–	–	–	–	–	–
–	–	–	–	–	–	–
2.8	6.1	5.5	2.2	7.3	8.8	4.4
–	–	–	–	–	–	–
3.8	5.5	4.7	5.2	5.0	–	–
–	–	–	–	–	–	–
–	0.3	0.6	–	3.1	–	–
–	–	–	–	–	–	–
–	–	–	7.4	4.3	4.7	5.9
1.6	2.0	2.6	–	–	–	–
0.7	0.8	0.8	–	–	–	–
0.1	0.1	0.3	–	–	–	–
–	–	–	–	–	–	–
1.5	1.3	1.7	–	–	–	–
–	–	–	–	–	–	–
0.4	0.5	0.5	–	–	–	–
2.9	4.9	3.9	–	0.7	–	1.1
18.6	*25.4*	*23.4*	*14.7*	*25.3*	*13.5*	*11.4*
5.0	*4.5*	*2.7*	*5.9*	*0.7*	*0.2*	–
18.0	*21.4*	*25.0*	*19.5*	*26.7*	*20.1*	*23.8*
41.8	*47.9*	*46.9*	*39.3*	*50.5*	*26.3*	*34.1*

TECH. COOP. GRANTS

1984	1985	1986	1983	1984	1985	1986
0.5	0.1	0.4	–	0.0	0.0	0.0
–	0.0	–	–	–	–	–
0.8	0.7	1.7	0.0	0.6	0.6	1.5
0.3	0.3	0.1	0.2	–	0.5	–
–	–	–	–	–	–	–
9.6	10.2	13.6	4.6	5.2	5.7	6.7
1.2	0.5	0.4	0.8	0.6	0.5	0.4
–	–	–	–	–	–	–
0.1	–	–	–	0.1	–	–
2.2	1.2	0.9	0.2	0.1	0.2	0.3
–	0.1	0.2	–	–	0.1	0.2
–	–	–	–	–	–	–
–	–	–	–	–	–	–
0.0	–	0.1	–	–	–	0.0
–	1.0	–	–	–	–	–
14.7	*14.2*	*17.2*	*5.8*	*6.6*	*7.7*	*9.0*
7.2	*10.8*	*12.0*	*4.2*	*2.8*	*3.4*	*4.5*
0.8	*0.4*	*0.2*	–	–	–	–
14.5	*17.6*	*21.4*	*5.4*	*6.4*	*7.0*	*9.1*
22.6	*25.4*	*29.4*	*9.9*	*9.4*	*11.1*	*13.6*

TOTAL OOF NET

1984	1985	1986	1983	1984	1985	1986
–	–	–	–	–	–	–
–	–	–	–	–	–	–
–	–	–	–	–	–	–
–	–	–	–	–	–	–
–	–	–	–	–	–	–
–	–	–	–	–	–	–
–	–	–	–	–	–	–
–	–	–	–	–	–	–
–	–	–	–	–	–	–
–	–	–	–	–	–	–
2.6	*3.4*	*0.6*	*0.1*	*1.9*	*3.3*	*0.6*
–	–	–	–	–	–	–
–	–	–	–	–	–	–
2.6	*3.4*	*0.6*	*0.1*	*1.9*	*3.3*	*0.6*

ODA COMMITMENTS : LOANS

DAC COUNTRIES	1983	1984	1985	1986
Australia	–	–	–	–
Austria	–	–	–	–
Belgium	–	–	–	–
Canada	–	–	–	–
Denmark	–	–	–	–
Finland	–	–	–	–
France	7.5	7.5	0.8	3.6
Germany, Fed. Rep.	–	–	–	–
Ireland	–	–	–	–
Italy	–	–	–	–
Japan	–	–	–	–
Netherlands	–	–	–	–
New Zealand	–	–	–	–
Norway	–	–	–	–
Sweden	–	–	–	–
Switzerland	–	–	–	–
United Kingdom	–	–	–	–
United States	–	–	–	–
TOTAL	*7.5*	*7.5*	*0.8*	*3.6*
MULTILATERAL	*5.2*	*13.1*	–	*1.0*
OPEC COUNTRIES	*5.8*	–	–	–
E.E.C.+ MEMBERS	*7.5*	*7.5*	*0.8*	*3.6*
TOTAL	*18.4*	*20.5*	*0.8*	*4.6*

GRANT ELEMENT OF ODA

DAC COUNTRIES	1983	1984	1985	1986
Australia	–	100.0	100.0	100.0
Austria	–	–	100.0	–
Belgium	–	–	–	100.0
Canada	100.0	100.0	100.0	100.0
Denmark	–	–	–	–
Finland	–	–	–	–
France	92.3	79.1	95.8	93.7
Germany, Fed. Rep.	100.0	100.0	100.0	100.0
Ireland	–	–	–	–
Italy	100.0	100.0	–	–
Japan	100.0	100.0	100.0	100.0
Netherlands	–	–	100.0	100.0
New Zealand	–	–	–	–
Norway	–	–	–	–
Sweden	–	–	–	–
Switzerland	100.0	100.0	–	100.0
United Kingdom	–	–	–	–
United States	100.0	100.0	100.0	100.0
TOTAL	*93.5*	*84.1*	*96.4*	*95.2*
MULTILATERAL	*94.1*	*91.0*	*100.0*	*94.4*
OPEC COUNTRIES	*60.9*	*100.0*	*100.0*	–
E.E.C.+ MEMBERS	*93.9*	*85.4*	*97.7*	*95.4*
TOTAL	*88.2*	*87.7*	*98.3*	*95.0*

OTHER AGGREGATES

COMMITMENTS: ALL SOURCES	1983	1984	1985	1986
TOTAL BILATERAL	24.6	25.2	12.8	22.7
of which				
OPEC	5.9	0.7	0.2	–
CMEA	–	–	–	–
TOTAL MULTILATERAL	14.7	25.3	13.5	11.4
TOTAL BIL.& MULTIL.	39.3	50.5	26.3	34.1
of which				
ODA Grants	20.9	30.0	25.5	29.5
ODA Loans	18.4	20.5	0.8	4.6

DISBURSEMENTS:

DAC COUNTRIES COMBINED	1983	1984	1985	1986
OFFICIAL & PRIVATE				
GROSS:				
Contractual Lending	1.4	3.5	3.8	3.3
Export Credits Total	–	–	–	-0.3
Export Credits Private	–	–	–	-0.3
NET:				
Contractual Lending	1.3	3.4	3.8	3.3
Export Credits Total	-0.1	-0.1	–	-0.3
PRIVATE SECTOR NET	1.2	-0.1	-0.1	0.2
Direct Investment	–	–	–	–
Portfolio Investment	1.3	0.0	-0.1	0.5
Export Credits	-0.1	-0.1	–	-0.3

MARKET BORROWING:

CHANGE IN CLAIMS

	1983	1984	1985	1986
Banks	–	1.0	–	1.0

MEMORANDUM ITEM:

	1983	1984	1985	1986
CMEA Countr.(Gross)	–	–	–	–

DISBURSEMENTS, UNLESS OTHERWISE STATED

TOTAL RECEIPTS NET

DAC COUNTRIES	1983	1984	1985	1986
Australia	–	–	–	–
Austria	0.0	0.0	0.0	–
Belgium	2.3	9.9	1.2	-6.5
Canada	1.8	1.0	8.7	4.5
Denmark	-0.1	0.0	0.0	0.3
Finland	0.0	0.0	–	–
France	260.9	57.8	-26.4	211.9
Germany, Fed. Rep.	-25.6	4.1	7.7	52.9
Ireland	–	–	–	–
Italy	-6.7	-4.9	0.6	20.8
Japan	2.0	-3.4	0.9	-0.4
Netherlands	-0.6	0.8	0.9	1.6
New Zealand	–	–	–	–
Norway	–	0.1	0.1	0.1
Sweden	–	–	–	–
Switzerland	-3.7	-5.2	-0.7	0.1
United Kingdom	3.5	3.4	20.6	23.9
United States	2.0	2.0	2.0	1.0
TOTAL	236.0	65.6	15.5	310.2
MULTILATERAL				
AF.D.F.	0.5	0.9	1.9	1.4
AF.D.B.	7.9	12.5	6.6	2.3
AS.D.B	–	–	–	–
CAR.D.B.	–	–	–	–
E.E.C.	6.4	7.7	17.0	4.5
IBRD	1.1	4.9	10.1	8.9
IDA	9.2	4.6	3.3	2.2
I.D.B.	–	–	–	–
IFAD	–	0.0	0.5	0.1
I.F.C.	–	0.7	0.6	0.9
IMF TRUST FUND	–	–	–	–
U.N. AGENCIES	–	–	–	–
UNDP	3.2	2.3	2.1	2.9
UNTA	0.6	0.7	0.7	0.8
UNICEF	0.1	0.2	0.1	0.3
UNRWA	–	–	–	–
WFP	0.3	0.9	1.2	0.7
UNHCR	0.4	0.4	0.5	0.5
Other Multilateral	1.2	0.6	0.4	0.4
Arab OPEC Agencies	4.8	2.2	1.5	0.7
TOTAL	35.5	38.6	46.4	26.6
OPEC COUNTRIES	27.2	8.9	-1.2	-0.8
E.E.C.+ MEMBERS	240.2	78.8	21.6	309.4
TOTAL	298.7	113.1	60.8	335.9

TOTAL ODA NET

DAC COUNTRIES	1983	1984	1985	1986
Australia	–	–	–	–
Austria	0.0	0.0	0.0	–
Belgium	0.1	1.5	0.1	2.4
Canada	1.5	1.2	0.7	0.6
Denmark	-0.1	0.0	0.0	–
Finland	0.0	0.0	–	–
France	44.0	45.4	33.9	88.7
Germany, Fed. Rep.	6.4	6.6	5.4	5.3
Ireland	–	–	–	–
Italy	0.1	10.2	4.3	1.8
Japan	0.1	0.0	0.1	0.3
Netherlands	0.6	0.1	0.0	0.4
New Zealand	–	–	–	–
Norway	–	0.1	0.1	0.1
Sweden	–	–	–	–
Switzerland	0.2	0.1	0.2	0.1
United Kingdom	0.1	0.1	0.2	0.2
United States	2.0	2.0	2.0	1.0
TOTAL	55.0	67.3	46.9	100.7
MULTILATERAL				
AF.D.F.	0.5	0.9	1.9	1.4
AF.D.B.	–	–	–	–
AS.D.B	–	–	–	–
CAR.D.B.	–	–	–	–
E.E.C.	6.4	7.4	16.1	1.2
IBRD	–	–	–	–
IDA	9.2	4.6	3.3	2.2
I.D.B.	–	–	–	–
IFAD	–	0.0	0.5	0.1
I.F.C.	–	–	–	–
IMF TRUST FUND	–	–	–	–
U.N. AGENCIES	–	–	–	–
UNDP	3.2	2.3	2.1	2.9
UNTA	0.6	0.7	0.7	0.8
UNICEF	0.1	0.2	0.1	0.3
UNRWA	–	–	–	–
WFP	0.3	0.9	1.2	0.7
UNHCR	0.4	0.4	0.5	0.5
Other Multilateral	1.2	0.6	0.4	0.4
Arab OPEC Agencies	4.8	2.2	-1.3	-0.2
TOTAL	26.5	20.2	25.4	10.3
OPEC COUNTRIES	26.9	10.4	-1.1	-0.8
E.E.C.+ MEMBERS	57.7	71.2	60.0	99.9
TOTAL	108.4	97.9	71.2	110.2

TOTAL ODA GROSS

	1983
Australia	–
Austria	0.0
Belgium	0.1
Canada	1.5
Denmark	–
Finland	0.0
France	47.2
Germany, Fed. Rep.	6.8
Ireland	–
Italy	0.1
Japan	0.1
Netherlands	0.6
New Zealand	–
Norway	–
Sweden	–
Switzerland	0.2
United Kingdom	0.1
United States	2.0
TOTAL	58.6
AF.D.F.	0.5
AF.D.B.	–
AS.D.B	–
CAR.D.B.	–
E.E.C.	6.6
IBRD	–
IDA	9.3
I.D.B.	–
IFAD	–
I.F.C.	–
IMF TRUST FUND	–
U.N. AGENCIES	–
UNDP	3.2
UNTA	0.6
UNICEF	0.1
UNRWA	–
WFP	0.3
UNHCR	0.4
Other Multilateral	1.2
Arab OPEC Agencies	4.9
TOTAL	27.0
OPEC COUNTRIES	27.7
E.E.C.+ MEMBERS	61.5
TOTAL	113.3

ODA LOANS GROSS

DAC COUNTRIES	1983	1984	1985	1986
Australia	–	–	–	–
Austria	–	–	–	–
Belgium	–	1.3	–	2.2
Canada	1.1	0.8	0.2	0.3
Denmark	–	–	–	–
Finland	–	–	–	–
France	12.7	13.8	9.2	61.9
Germany, Fed. Rep.	4.0	2.7	2.5	2.6
Ireland	–	–	–	–
Italy	–	9.5	3.5	1.0
Japan	–	–	–	–
Netherlands	0.1	–	–	0.9
New Zealand	–	–	–	–
Norway	–	–	–	–
Sweden	–	–	–	–
Switzerland	–	–	–	–
United Kingdom	–	–	–	–
United States	–	–	–	–
TOTAL	17.8	28.2	15.2	68.9
MULTILATERAL	14.8	8.6	6.0	4.6
OPEC COUNTRIES	27.7	13.0	1.8	0.0
E.E.C.+ MEMBERS	16.8	27.4	15.1	68.9
TOTAL	60.3	49.7	22.9	73.5

ODA LOANS NET

DAC COUNTRIES	1983	1984	1985	1986
Australia	–	–	–	–
Austria	–	–	–	–
Belgium	–	1.3	–	2.2
Canada	1.1	0.8	0.2	0.3
Denmark	-0.1	0.0	0.0	–
Finland	–	–	–	–
France	9.5	11.6	7.7	58.4
Germany, Fed. Rep.	3.7	2.2	1.9	0.6
Ireland	–	–	–	–
Italy	–	9.5	3.5	1.0
Japan	–	–	–	–
Netherlands	0.1	–	-0.1	0.2
New Zealand	–	–	–	–
Norway	–	–	–	–
Sweden	–	–	–	–
Switzerland	–	–	–	–
United Kingdom	–	–	–	–
United States	–	–	–	–
TOTAL	14.3	25.3	13.0	62.8
MULTILATERAL	14.3	7.5	4.3	3.3
OPEC COUNTRIES	26.9	10.4	-1.1	-0.8
E.E.C.+ MEMBERS	13.0	24.4	12.8	62.4
TOTAL	55.4	43.2	16.3	65.3

GRANTS

	1983
Australia	–
Austria	0.0
Belgium	0.1
Canada	0.4
Denmark	–
Finland	0.0
France	34.5
Germany, Fed. Rep.	2.8
Ireland	–
Italy	0.1
Japan	0.1
Netherlands	0.5
New Zealand	–
Norway	–
Sweden	–
Switzerland	0.2
United Kingdom	0.1
United States	2.0
TOTAL	40.7
MULTILATERAL	12.3
OPEC COUNTRIES	–
E.E.C.+ MEMBERS	44.7
TOTAL	53.0

TOTAL OFFICIAL GROSS

DAC COUNTRIES	1983	1984	1985	1986
Australia	–	–	–	–
Austria	0.0	0.0	0.0	–
Belgium	0.1	1.8	0.4	3.0
Canada	2.1	1.4	10.0	5.5
Denmark	–	–	–	–
Finland	0.0	0.0	–	–
France	55.1	59.8	48.6	243.2
Germany, Fed. Rep.	6.8	7.1	7.1	7.4
Ireland	–	–	–	–
Italy	1.7	10.2	4.3	19.3
Japan	0.1	0.0	0.1	0.3
Netherlands	0.6	0.8	0.7	1.1
New Zealand	–	–	–	–
Norway	–	0.1	0.1	0.1
Sweden	–	–	–	–
Switzerland	0.2	0.1	0.2	0.1
United Kingdom	0.1	0.1	0.2	0.2
United States	2.0	2.0	2.0	1.0
TOTAL	68.7	83.4	73.7	281.1
MULTILATERAL	39.0	42.4	54.4	34.3
OPEC COUNTRIES	29.1	13.0	3.2	0.0
E.E.C.+ MEMBERS	71.0	87.7	78.5	279.0
TOTAL	136.8	138.8	131.3	315.4

TOTAL OFFICIAL NET

DAC COUNTRIES	1983	1984	1985	1986
Australia	–	–	–	–
Austria	0.0	0.0	0.0	–
Belgium	0.1	1.8	0.4	3.0
Canada	1.8	1.0	8.7	4.5
Denmark	-0.1	0.0	0.0	–
Finland	0.0	0.0	–	–
France	51.8	57.5	46.7	239.7
Germany, Fed. Rep.	6.4	6.3	6.5	5.4
Ireland	–	–	–	–
Italy	-5.8	3.2	0.0	16.4
Japan	0.1	0.0	0.1	0.3
Netherlands	-0.6	0.8	0.6	0.4
New Zealand	–	–	–	–
Norway	–	0.1	0.1	0.1
Sweden	–	–	–	–
Switzerland	0.2	0.1	0.2	0.1
United Kingdom	0.1	0.1	0.2	0.2
United States	2.0	2.0	2.0	1.0
TOTAL	56.1	72.9	65.4	271.0
MULTILATERAL	35.5	38.6	46.4	26.6
OPEC COUNTRIES	27.2	8.9	-1.2	-0.8
E.E.C.+ MEMBERS	58.5	77.3	71.4	269.6
TOTAL	118.9	120.3	110.6	296.7

TOTAL OOF GROSS

	1983
Australia	–
Austria	–
Belgium	–
Canada	0.6
Denmark	–
Finland	–
France	8.0
Germany, Fed. Rep.	–
Ireland	–
Italy	1.6
Japan	–
Netherlands	–
New Zealand	–
Norway	–
Sweden	–
Switzerland	–
United Kingdom	–
United States	–
TOTAL	10.2
MULTILATERAL	12.0
OPEC COUNTRIES	1.4
E.E.C.+ MEMBERS	9.6
TOTAL	23.5

ODA COMMITMENTS

1984	1985	1986	1983	1984	1985	1986
–	–	–	–	–	–	–
0.0	0.0	–	0.0	–	0.0	–
1.5	0.1	2.4	–	1.3	–	2.4
1.2	0.7	0.6	0.4	0.4	0.4	0.4
–	–	–	–	–	–	–
0.0	–	–	0.0	0.0	–	–
47.6	35.4	92.1	51.2	55.0	37.1	92.1
7.1	6.0	7.3	8.4	4.5	6.0	8.9
–	–	–	–	–	–	–
10.2	4.3	1.8	13.8	1.0	3.2	8.5
0.0	0.1	0.3	0.1	0.0	0.2	0.0
0.1	0.1	1.1	0.7	0.1	0.1	1.1
–	–	–	–	–	–	–
0.1	0.1	0.1	0.2	0.1	0.1	0.1
–	–	–	–	–	–	–
0.1	0.2	0.1	0.1	0.1	0.1	0.1
0.1	0.2	0.2	0.1	0.1	0.2	0.2
2.0	2.0	1.0	1.1	2.6	0.4	1.0
70.2	*49.1*	*106.8*	*76.1*	*65.2*	*47.8*	*114.6*
0.9	1.9	1.4	–	–	–	–
–	–	–	–	–	–	–
–	–	–	25.8	0.9	5.3	10.2
7.5	16.3	1.6	–	–	–	–
4.8	3.5	2.4	4.5	–	–	4.4
0.0	0.5	0.1	–	–	–	–
–	–	–	5.7	5.1	4.9	5.7
–	–	–	–	–	–	–
2.3	2.1	2.9	–	–	–	–
0.7	0.7	0.8	–	–	–	–
0.2	0.1	0.3	–	–	–	–
–	–	–	–	–	–	–
0.9	1.2	0.7	–	–	–	–
0.4	0.5	0.5	–	–	–	–
0.6	0.4	0.4	–	–	–	–
2.8	–	0.4	–	–	–	–
21.2	*27.1*	*11.6*	*36.0*	*6.0*	*10.2*	*20.3*
13.0	*1.8*	*0.0*	–	–	–	–
74.3	*62.3*	*106.4*	*99.9*	*62.9*	*51.9*	*123.3*
104.4	*77.9*	*118.4*	*112.1*	*71.2*	*58.1*	*134.9*

TECH. COOP. GRANTS

1984	1985	1986	1983	1984	1985	1986
0.0	0.0	–	0.0	–	–	–
0.3	0.1	0.2	–	0.0	0.0	0.0
0.4	0.6	0.3	0.1	–	0.7	–
–	–	–	–	–	–	–
0.0	–	–	0.0	0.0	–	–
33.8	26.2	30.2	22.1	23.4	20.2	27.1
4.4	3.5	4.7	2.1	3.7	3.1	4.3
–	–	–	–	–	–	–
0.7	0.9	0.7	0.1	0.7	0.9	0.7
0.0	0.1	0.3	0.1	0.0	0.1	0.0
0.1	0.1	0.2	0.1	0.1	0.1	0.2
–	–	–	–	–	–	–
0.1	0.1	0.1	–	0.1	0.1	0.1
–	–	–	–	–	–	–
0.1	0.2	0.1	0.1	0.1	0.1	0.1
0.1	0.2	0.2	0.1	0.1	0.2	0.2
2.0	2.0	1.0	2.0	2.0	2.0	1.0
42.0	*33.9*	*37.9*	*26.8*	*30.2*	*27.4*	*33.5*
12.6	*21.1*	*7.0*	*5.4*	*4.2*	*3.8*	*5.0*
46.9	*47.2*	*37.5*	*24.5*	*28.0*	*24.5*	*32.5*
54.7	*55.0*	*44.9*	*32.2*	*34.4*	*31.1*	*38.5*

TOTAL OOF NET

1984	1985	1986	1983	1984	1985	1986
–	–	–	–	–	–	–
–	–	–	–	–	–	–
0.3	0.3	0.6	–	0.3	0.3	0.6
0.2	9.3	4.9	0.4	-0.2	8.0	3.9
–	–	–	–	–	–	–
12.2	13.3	151.1	7.8	12.1	12.8	151.1
–	1.1	0.1	–	-0.3	1.1	0.1
–	–	–	–	–	–	–
–	–	17.6	-5.9	-7.0	-4.3	14.6
0.6	0.6	–	-1.2	0.6	0.6	–
–	–	–	–	–	–	–
–	–	–	–	–	–	–
–	–	–	–	–	–	–
–	–	–	–	–	–	–
–	–	–	–	–	–	–
13.3	*24.6*	*174.2*	*1.1*	*5.5*	*18.4*	*170.3*
21.2	*27.4*	*22.8*	*9.0*	*18.4*	*21.0*	*16.2*
–	*1.4*	–	*0.4*	*-1.5*	*-0.1*	–
13.5	*16.2*	*172.6*	*0.8*	*6.1*	*11.4*	*169.7*
34.4	*53.4*	*197.0*	*10.5*	*22.4*	*39.4*	*186.5*

ODA COMMITMENTS : LOANS

DAC COUNTRIES	1983	1984	1985	1986
Australia	–	–	–	–
Austria	–	–	–	–
Belgium	–	1.3	–	2.2
Canada	–	–	–	–
Denmark	–	–	–	–
Finland	–	–	–	–
France	16.4	21.0	11.9	61.9
Germany, Fed. Rep.	3.7	1.2	3.3	2.7
Ireland	–	–	–	–
Italy	13.5	–	–	7.0
Japan	–	–	–	–
Netherlands	0.1	–	–	0.9
New Zealand	–	–	–	–
Norway	–	–	–	–
Sweden	–	–	–	–
Switzerland	–	–	–	–
United Kingdom	–	–	–	–
United States	–	–	0.0	0.1
TOTAL	*33.7*	*23.5*	*15.2*	*74.7*
MULTILATERAL	*13.2*	*0.6*	–	*14.2*
OPEC COUNTRIES	–	–	–	–
E.E.C.+ MEMBERS	*42.4*	*24.1*	*15.2*	*84.5*
TOTAL	*46.8*	*24.1*	*15.2*	*88.9*

GRANT ELEMENT OF ODA

DAC COUNTRIES	1983	1984	1985	1986
Australia	–	–	–	–
Austria	100.0	–	100.0	–
Belgium	–	79.8	–	82.0
Canada	100.0	100.0	100.0	100.0
Denmark	–	–	–	–
Finland	100.0	100.0	–	–
France	78.6	73.2	87.4	51.6
Germany, Fed. Rep.	79.8	90.5	64.8	79.2
Ireland	–	–	–	–
Italy	44.9	100.0	100.0	64.2
Japan	100.0	100.0	100.0	100.0
Netherlands	100.0	100.0	100.0	100.0
New Zealand	–	–	–	–
Norway	100.0	100.0	100.0	100.0
Sweden	–	–	–	–
Switzerland	100.0	100.0	100.0	100.0
United Kingdom	100.0	100.0	100.0	100.0
United States	100.0	100.0	95.4	97.4
TOTAL	*73.4*	*76.4*	*85.5*	*55.8*
MULTILATERAL	*90.1*	*100.0*	*100.0*	*83.2*
OPEC COUNTRIES	–	–	–	–
E.E.C.+ MEMBERS	*77.8*	*75.3*	*86.9*	*55.4*
TOTAL	*77.8*	*78.2*	*88.4*	*58.0*

OTHER AGGREGATES

COMMITMENTS: ALL SOURCES

	1983	1984	1985	1986
TOTAL BILATERAL	92.5	164.3	84.2	153.0
of which				
OPEC	4.0	–	–	–
CMEA	–	25.0	–	7.2
TOTAL MULTILATERAL	62.5	14.6	61.0	55.1
TOTAL BIL.& MULTIL.	155.1	178.9	145.1	208.0
of which				
ODA Grants	65.2	47.1	42.9	46.0
ODA Loans	46.9	24.1	15.2	96.1

DISBURSEMENTS:

DAC COUNTRIES COMBINED

OFFICIAL & PRIVATE	1983	1984	1985	1986
GROSS:				
Contractual Lending	256.6	202.9	173.3	256.0
Export Credits Total	230.8	161.9	144.2	19.6
Export Credits Private	228.6	161.8	133.9	12.8
NET:				
Contractual Lending	154.5	65.8	44.6	234.4
Export Credits Total	133.7	28.1	18.1	4.2
PRIVATE SECTOR NET	179.9	-7.3	-49.8	39.2
Direct Investment	2.6	-40.0	-6.4	-0.5
Portfolio Investment	38.2	-2.5	-56.9	38.4
Export Credits	139.1	35.3	13.4	1.3

MARKET BORROWING:

CHANGE IN CLAIMS

	1983	1984	1985	1986
Banks	–	30.0	78.0	187.0

MEMORANDUM ITEM:

	1983	1984	1985	1986
CMEA Countr.(Gross)	3.3	1.8	4.9	2.0

DISBURSEMENTS, UNLESS OTHERWISE STATED

	TOTAL RECEIPTS NET 1983	1984	1985	1986	TOTAL ODA NET 1983	1984	1985	1986	TOTAL ODA GROSS 1983
DAC COUNTRIES									
Australia	-0.1	-0.1	0.0	–	–	0.0	0.0	–	–
Austria	–	-0.8	-0.8	0.1	–	0.0	0.0	0.1	0.0
Belgium	-3.2	5.2	0.5	6.2	0.0	0.3	0.1	0.1	0.0
Canada	7.2	5.3	4.7	6.6	7.2	5.3	5.3	7.4	7.2
Denmark	-0.3	-0.3	-0.3	-0.4	0.1	–	–	–	0.1
Finland	0.0	–	0.0	0.0	0.0	–	0.0	0.0	0.0
France	-1.1	0.7	1.0	26.7	0.7	1.1	1.0	1.9	0.7
Germany, Fed. Rep.	6.4	4.2	6.6	13.0	5.8	5.4	6.8	12.5	5.8
Ireland	–	–	–	–	–	–	–	–	–
Italy	-1.5	0.6	10.2	5.0	0.4	4.2	13.5	5.4	0.4
Japan	-4.8	33.1	8.5	19.9	0.8	0.9	0.6	2.8	1.0
Netherlands	7.8	-0.7	11.7	11.4	1.1	1.8	10.9	3.9	1.1
New Zealand	–	–	–	–	–	–	–	–	–
Norway	–	11.8	10.9	5.2	–	0.6	0.2	0.3	–
Sweden	-0.2	-2.2	-0.7	0.1	0.0	0.1	0.3	0.6	0.0
Switzerland	-0.2	0.3	0.8	1.1	0.3	0.5	0.8	1.1	0.3
United Kingdom	1.8	0.4	15.8	16.6	0.7	-0.2	0.4	0.8	0.7
United States	203.0	175.0	199.0	140.0	200.0	166.0	199.0	128.0	201.0
TOTAL	*214.8*	*232.4*	*267.7*	*251.6*	*217.1*	*185.7*	*238.9*	*164.8*	*218.4*
MULTILATERAL									
AF.D.F.	–	–	–	–	–	–	–	–	–
AF.D.B.	–	–	–	–	–	–	–	–	–
AS.D.B	–	–	–	–	–	–	–	–	–
CAR.D.B.	–	–	–	–	–	–	–	–	–
E.E.C.	0.5	2.7	0.9	4.0	0.5	2.7	0.9	4.0	0.5
IBRD	6.0	17.0	63.3	26.7	–	–	–	–	–
IDA	-0.2	-0.2	-0.2	-0.2	-0.2	-0.2	-0.2	-0.2	–
I.D.B.	39.2	39.1	60.9	51.3	27.1	17.6	27.5	13.0	28.7
IFAD	0.5	0.7	1.7	2.4	0.5	0.7	1.7	2.4	0.5
I.F.C.	0.7	-0.4	-0.6	-0.4	–	–	–	–	–
IMF TRUST FUND	–	–	–	–	–	–	–	–	–
U.N. AGENCIES	–	–	–	–	–	–	–	–	–
UNDP	1.2	1.6	1.6	1.2	1.2	1.6	1.6	1.2	1.2
UNTA	0.6	0.5	0.6	0.7	0.6	0.5	0.6	0.7	0.6
UNICEF	0.1	0.0	0.1	0.2	0.1	0.0	0.1	0.2	0.1
UNRWA	–	–	–	–	–	–	–	–	–
WFP	0.4	0.5	0.8	1.3	0.4	0.5	0.8	1.3	0.4
UNHCR	4.3	7.5	7.4	7.3	4.3	7.5	7.4	7.3	4.3
Other Multilateral	0.9	1.1	1.0	1.2	0.9	1.1	1.0	1.2	0.9
Arab OPEC Agencies	-0.2	-0.1	2.6	-0.2	-0.2	-0.1	-0.2	-0.2	–
TOTAL	*53.8*	*70.0*	*140.1*	*95.5*	*35.0*	*31.9*	*41.2*	*30.8*	*37.1*
OPEC COUNTRIES	*19.9*	*3.1*	*5.6*	*-26.8*	–	–	–	–	–
E.E.C.+ MEMBERS	*10.5*	*12.7*	*46.2*	*82.6*	*9.3*	*15.0*	*33.5*	*28.7*	*9.3*
TOTAL	**288.5**	**305.5**	**413.4**	**320.3**	**252.1**	**217.6**	**280.1**	**195.7**	**255.4**

	ODA LOANS GROSS 1983	1984	1985	1986	ODA LOANS NET 1983	1984	1985	1986	GRANTS 1983
DAC COUNTRIES									
Australia	–	–	–	–	–	–	–	–	–
Austria	–	–	–	–	0.0	0.0	–	–	0.0
Belgium	–	–	–	–	–	–	–	–	0.0
Canada	5.9	3.6	3.5	3.7	5.9	3.6	3.5	3.7	1.4
Denmark	–	–	–	–	–	–	–	–	0.1
Finland	–	–	–	–	–	–	–	–	0.0
France	–	–	–	–	–	–	–	–	0.7
Germany, Fed. Rep.	2.5	1.0	2.0	7.5	2.5	0.8	2.0	5.5	3.3
Ireland	–	–	–	–	–	–	–	–	–
Italy	–	–	11.4	0.6	–	–	11.4	0.6	0.4
Japan	–	–	–	–	-0.2	-0.2	-1.0	-0.2	1.0
Netherlands	–	–	9.5	0.4	–	–	9.5	0.4	1.1
New Zealand	–	–	–	–	–	–	–	–	–
Norway	–	–	–	–	–	–	–	–	–
Sweden	–	–	–	–	–	–	–	–	0.0
Switzerland	–	–	–	–	–	–	–	–	0.3
United Kingdom	0.0	–	–	–	–	-0.6	–	–	0.7
United States	154.0	68.0	33.0	41.0	153.0	64.0	33.0	37.0	47.0
TOTAL	*162.3*	*72.6*	*59.4*	*53.2*	*161.1*	*67.5*	*58.3*	*47.0*	*56.0*
MULTILATERAL	*28.4*	*20.9*	*35.2*	*23.6*	*26.3*	*16.3*	*28.8*	*14.9*	*8.7*
OPEC COUNTRIES	–	–	–	–	–	–	–	–	–
E.E.C.+ MEMBERS	*2.5*	*1.0*	*22.9*	*8.5*	*2.5*	*0.1*	*22.9*	*6.5*	*6.8*
TOTAL	**190.7**	**93.6**	**94.6**	**76.8**	**187.4**	**83.8**	**87.1**	**61.9**	**64.7**

	TOTAL OFFICIAL GROSS 1983	1984	1985	1986	TOTAL OFFICIAL NET 1983	1984	1985	1986	TOTAL OOF GROSS 1983
DAC COUNTRIES									
Australia	–	0.0	0.0	–	–	0.0	0.0	–	–
Austria	0.0	0.0	0.0	0.1	–	0.0	0.0	0.1	–
Belgium	0.0	0.3	0.1	0.1	0.0	0.3	0.1	0.1	–
Canada	7.2	5.3	5.3	7.6	7.2	5.3	4.7	6.6	–
Denmark	0.1	–	0.1	–	0.1	–	0.0	–	–
Finland	0.0	–	0.0	0.0	0.0	–	0.0	0.0	0.0
France	0.7	1.1	1.0	8.8	0.7	1.1	1.0	8.0	–
Germany, Fed. Rep.	5.8	5.6	6.9	15.0	5.8	5.4	6.9	12.9	0.0
Ireland	–	–	–	–	–	–	–	–	–
Italy	2.4	4.2	13.5	5.4	2.4	4.2	13.5	5.4	2.0
Japan	1.0	1.1	1.6	3.0	0.8	0.9	0.6	2.8	–
Netherlands	1.1	1.8	11.1	4.1	1.1	1.8	11.1	4.1	–
New Zealand	–	–	–	–	–	–	–	–	–
Norway	–	0.6	0.2	0.3	–	0.6	0.2	0.3	–
Sweden	0.0	0.1	0.3	0.6	-0.9	-0.9	-0.7	-0.7	–
Switzerland	0.3	0.5	0.8	1.1	0.3	0.5	0.8	1.1	–
United Kingdom	2.8	2.2	16.4	16.9	2.2	1.6	16.2	16.6	2.1
United States	204.0	183.0	201.0	148.0	203.0	175.0	199.0	140.0	3.0
TOTAL	*225.5*	*205.7*	*258.3*	*210.9*	*222.7*	*195.6*	*253.4*	*197.3*	*7.1*
MULTILATERAL	*75.3*	*95.2*	*169.3*	*136.1*	*53.8*	*70.0*	*140.1*	*95.5*	*38.2*
OPEC COUNTRIES	*23.3*	*12.2*	*12.8*	*10.0*	*19.9*	*3.1*	*5.6*	*-26.8*	*23.3*
E.E.C.+ MEMBERS	*13.4*	*17.8*	*49.9*	*54.3*	*12.8*	*16.9*	*49.6*	*51.2*	*4.1*
TOTAL	**324.1**	**313.0**	**440.4**	**357.0**	**296.4**	**268.7**	**399.0**	**265.9**	**68.7**

MILLION US DOLLARS, UNLESS OTHERWISE STATED

COSTA RICA

ODA COMMITMENTS

1984	1985	1986	1983	1984	1985	1986
0.0	0.0	–	–	0.0	0.0	–
0.0	0.0	0.1	0.0	0.0	0.0	–
0.3	0.1	0.1	–	–	–	0.1
5.3	5.3	7.4	13.9	1.8	14.9	3.8
–	–	–	–	–	–	–
–	0.0	0.0	–	–	0.0	–
1.1	1.0	1.9	2.4	4.4	0.9	1.9
5.6	6.8	14.5	8.2	7.7	6.4	16.3
–	–	–	–	–	–	–
4.2	13.5	5.4	2.2	18.8	17.5	24.5
1.1	1.6	3.0	7.3	1.3	66.4	3.0
1.8	10.9	3.9	0.7	11.9	1.9	4.3
–	–	–	–	–	–	–
0.6	0.2	0.3	–	0.6	1.5	0.4
0.1	0.3	0.6	–	0.5	0.5	0.6
0.5	0.8	1.1	0.9	0.5	0.2	1.4
0.4	0.4	0.8	0.7	0.4	0.4	0.8
170.0	199.0	132.0	155.1	181.4	206.0	139.5
190.9	239.9	171.0	191.3	229.4	316.7	196.6
–	–	–	–	–	–	–
–	–	–	–	–	–	–
2.7	0.9	4.0	0.4	0.0	10.5	2.0
–	–	–	–	–	–	–
22.0	33.6	21.3	–	28.3	–	–
0.7	1.7	2.4	–	–	–	5.9
–	–	–	–	–	–	–
–	–	–	7.3	11.2	11.4	11.8
1.6	1.6	1.2	–	–	–	–
0.5	0.6	0.7	–	–	–	–
0.0	0.1	0.2	–	–	–	–
–	–	–	–	–	–	–
0.5	0.8	1.3	–	–	–	–
7.5	7.4	7.3	–	–	–	–
1.1	1.0	1.2	–	–	–	–
-0.1	–	–	–	–	–	–
36.5	47.6	39.5	7.8	39.5	21.9	19.8
–	–	–	–	14.5	17.2	9.6
15.9	33.5	30.7	14.6	43.2	37.5	49.9
227.4	287.5	210.5	199.1	283.4	355.8	226.0

TECH. COOP. GRANTS

1984	1985	1986	1983	1984	1985	1986
0.0	0.0	–	–	–	0.0	–
0.0	0.0	0.1	0.0	–	–	–
0.3	0.1	0.1	0.0	0.0	–	0.0
1.7	1.8	3.7	1.1	–	0.7	–
–	–	–	0.1	–	–	–
–	0.0	0.0	0.0	–	–	–
1.1	1.0	1.9	0.7	1.0	0.9	1.9
4.6	4.9	7.0	3.3	4.6	4.8	6.7
–	–	–	–	–	–	–
4.2	2.1	4.8	0.4	1.9	2.1	1.5
1.1	1.6	3.0	1.0	1.1	1.4	2.7
1.8	1.4	3.6	1.0	0.9	1.2	3.1
–	–	–	–	–	–	–
0.6	0.2	0.3	–	0.0	0.0	0.2
0.1	0.3	0.6	0.0	0.1	0.3	–
0.5	0.8	1.1	0.0	0.2	0.1	0.2
0.4	0.4	0.8	0.7	0.4	0.4	0.8
102.0	166.0	91.0	3.0	5.0	5.0	9.0
118.3	180.5	117.8	11.2	15.2	16.8	26.0
15.6	12.4	15.9	7.0	10.7	10.6	10.5
–	–	–	–	–	–	–
14.9	10.6	22.2	6.1	8.8	9.3	14.0
133.9	193.0	133.7	18.2	25.9	27.5	36.5

TOTAL OOF NET

1984	1985	1986	1983	1984	1985	1986
–	–	–	–	–	–	–
–	–	–	–	–	–	–
–	–	0.2	–	–	-0.6	-0.8
–	0.1	–	–	–	0.0	–
–	–	–	–	–	–	–
–	–	6.9	–	–	–	6.1
–	0.1	0.5	–	–	0.1	0.4
–	–	–	2.0	–	–	–
–	–	–	–	–	–	–
–	0.2	0.1	–	–	0.2	0.1
–	–	–	–	–	–	–
–	–	–	-0.9	-1.0	-1.0	-1.3
1.8	16.1	16.2	1.5	1.8	15.8	15.9
13.0	2.0	16.0	3.0	9.0	–	12.0
14.8	18.4	39.9	5.6	9.9	14.5	32.4
58.6	121.7	96.6	18.8	38.1	98.9	64.6
12.2	12.8	10.0	19.9	3.1	5.6	-26.8
1.8	16.4	23.7	3.5	1.8	16.1	22.5
85.6	152.9	146.5	44.3	51.1	119.0	70.3

ODA COMMITMENTS : LOANS

DAC COUNTRIES

	1983	1984	1985	1986
Australia	–	–	–	–
Austria	–	–	–	–
Belgium	–	–	–	0.1
Canada	12.2	–	10.6	–
Denmark	–	–	–	–
Finland	–	–	–	–
France	1.7	3.4	–	1.9
Germany, Fed. Rep.	3.3	1.6	–	4.1
Ireland	–	–	–	–
Italy	–	13.0	15.0	19.5
Japan	6.2	–	64.6	3.0
Netherlands	–	10.1	–	0.7
New Zealand	–	–	–	–
Norway	–	–	–	–
Sweden	–	–	–	–
Switzerland	–	–	–	–
United Kingdom	–	–	–	–
United States	108.2	81.2	20.8	5.0
TOTAL	131.6	109.2	111.0	29.2
MULTILATERAL	–	28.3	–	5.9
OPEC COUNTRIES	–	14.5	17.2	9.6
E.E.C.+ MEMBERS	5.0	28.0	15.0	24.2
TOTAL	131.6	152.0	128.2	44.8

GRANT ELEMENT OF ODA

DAC COUNTRIES

	1983	1984	1985	1986
Australia	–	100.0	100.0	–
Austria	100.0	100.0	100.0	–
Belgium	–	–	–	100.0
Canada	91.6	100.0	92.5	100.0
Denmark	–	–	–	–
Finland	–	–	100.0	–
France	100.0	64.1	100.0	100.0
Germany, Fed. Rep.	74.3	83.3	100.0	81.5
Ireland	–	–	–	–
Italy	100.0	60.2	51.1	65.7
Japan	100.0	100.0	40.4	100.0
Netherlands	100.0	66.2	100.0	93.8
New Zealand	–	–	–	–
Norway	–	100.0	100.0	100.0
Sweden	–	100.0	100.0	100.0
Switzerland	100.0	100.0	100.0	100.0
United Kingdom	100.0	25.3	100.0	100.0
United States	73.0	82.9	94.8	99.0
TOTAL	75.4	79.8	82.1	93.3
MULTILATERAL	100.0	100.0	82.5	88.0
OPEC COUNTRIES	–	42.7	48.8	37.0
E.E.C.+ MEMBERS	83.7	64.9	77.2	76.6
TOTAL	76.4	78.6	80.6	90.4

OTHER AGGREGATES

COMMITMENTS: ALL SOURCES

	1983	1984	1985	1986
TOTAL BILATERAL	233.3	281.5	348.3	244.6
of which				
OPEC	11.8	27.3	27.7	9.6
CMEA	–	–	–	–
TOTAL MULTILATERAL	68.9	97.8	105.4	221.2
TOTAL BIL.& MULTIL.	302.2	379.3	453.7	465.7
of which				
ODA Grants	67.5	131.4	227.6	181.2
ODA Loans	131.6	152.0	128.2	44.8

DISBURSEMENTS:

DAC COUNTRIES COMBINED

OFFICIAL & PRIVATE

	1983	1984	1985	1986
GROSS:				
Contractual Lending	175.3	102.0	92.8	115.0
Export Credits Total	5.8	14.6	15.1	22.2
Export Credits Private	5.8	14.6	15.1	22.0
NET:				
Contractual Lending	142.4	73.9	79.6	89.1
Export Credits Total	-25.2	-8.5	4.4	6.6
PRIVATE SECTOR NET	-7.9	36.8	14.4	54.3
Direct Investment	3.1	-14.0	-3.4	0.2
Portfolio Investment	13.3	54.3	10.9	44.5
Export Credits	-24.2	-3.5	6.8	9.7

MARKET BORROWING:

CHANGE IN CLAIMS

	1983	1984	1985	1986
Banks	–	-213.0	-32.0	32.0

MEMORANDUM ITEM:

	1983	1984	1985	1986
CMEA Countr.(Gross)	–	–	–	–

TOTAL RECEIPTS NET / TOTAL ODA NET / TOTAL ODA GROSS

DAC COUNTRIES

	TOTAL RECEIPTS NET 1983	1984	1985	1986	TOTAL ODA NET 1983	1984	1985	1986	TOTAL ODA GROSS 1983
Australia	-0.2	—	—	—	—	—	—	—	—
Austria	0.0	-3.8	-3.7	0.1	0.0	0.0	0.0	0.1	0.0
Belgium	-0.4	44.6	-20.7	-18.9	3.1	3.2	2.9	2.9	3.1
Canada	25.1	24.5	13.0	6.0	4.5	10.1	10.5	10.8	4.7
Denmark	-0.1	-0.2	-0.2	-0.2	0.0	0.2	0.0	0.0	0.1
Finland	—	—	0.0	0.0	—	—	0.0	0.0	—
France	213.3	131.5	184.7	280.4	105.9	79.9	72.8	90.3	110.4
Germany, Fed. Rep.	31.2	43.6	11.7	17.8	19.8	17.4	14.0	13.8	21.3
Ireland	—	—	—	—	—	—	—	—	—
Italy	44.0	35.4	3.0	18.8	0.8	0.7	0.7	1.0	0.8
Japan	-2.2	1.0	12.1	16.5	0.8	0.7	7.9	16.2	0.8
Netherlands	-0.6	-3.1	-4.6	-9.3	3.8	0.5	0.4	0.5	3.9
New Zealand	—	—	—	—	—	—	—	—	—
Norway	1.7	27.3	25.9	30.0	0.3	0.2	0.2	0.1	0.3
Sweden	—	—	—	—	—	—	—	—	—
Switzerland	-29.1	-91.2	-1.6	0.2	0.3	0.2	0.2	0.2	0.3
United Kingdom	9.0	15.3	-1.2	1.6	1.4	1.0	0.8	1.6	1.5
United States	-3.0	1.0	11.0	4.0	—	—	—	—	—
TOTAL	288.5	225.9	229.5	346.9	140.7	114.2	110.5	137.7	147.3

MULTILATERAL

	TOTAL RECEIPTS NET 1983	1984	1985	1986	TOTAL ODA NET 1983	1984	1985	1986	TOTAL ODA GROSS 1983
AF.D.F.	—	—	—	—	—	—	—	—	—
AF.D.B.	5.4	4.9	0.3	18.4	—	—	—	—	—
AS.D.B	—	—	—	—	—	—	—	—	—
CAR.D.B.	—	—	—	—	—	—	—	—	—
E.E.C.	9.0	13.2	4.0	37.4	10.0	9.8	9.3	42.5	11.3
IBRD	180.1	185.7	27.8	60.2	1.1	0.2	0.0	—	1.1
IDA	0.0	-0.1	-0.1	-0.1	0.0	-0.1	-0.1	-0.1	—
I.D.B.	—	—	—	—	—	—	—	—	—
IFAD	—	—	0.1	0.1	—	—	0.1	0.1	—
I.F.C.	-0.3	—	—	-0.3	—	—	—	—	—
IMF TRUST FUND	—	—	—	—	—	—	—	—	—
U.N. AGENCIES									—
UNDP	2.1	1.9	2.2	3.1	2.1	1.9	2.2	3.1	2.1
UNTA	0.7	0.6	0.6	0.9	0.7	0.6	0.6	0.9	0.7
UNICEF	0.5	0.3	0.7	0.7	0.5	0.3	0.7	0.7	0.5
UNRWA	—	—	—	—	—	—	—	—	—
WFP	—	—	0.4	0.4	—	—	0.4	0.4	—
UNHCR	0.2	0.3	0.3	0.3	0.2	0.3	0.3	0.3	0.2
Other Multilateral	0.5	0.7	0.6	0.7	0.5	0.7	0.6	0.7	0.5
Arab OPEC Agencies	—	—	—	—	—	—	—	—	—
TOTAL	198.1	207.4	36.9	121.9	15.0	13.6	14.2	48.7	16.4
OPEC COUNTRIES	0.0	0.1	0.1	0.0	0.0	0.1	0.1	0.0	0.0
E.E.C.+ MEMBERS	305.3	280.4	176.7	327.5	144.8	112.7	100.9	152.8	152.5
TOTAL	486.6	433.3	266.5	468.8	155.8	127.8	124.7	186.4	163.7

ODA LOANS GROSS / ODA LOANS NET / GRANTS

DAC COUNTRIES

	ODA LOANS GROSS 1983	1984	1985	1986	ODA LOANS NET 1983	1984	1985	1986	GRANTS 1983
Australia	—	—	—	—	—	—	—	—	—
Austria	—	—	—	—	—	—	—	—	0.0
Belgium	—	—	—	—	—	—	—	—	3.1
Canada	1.5	6.7	6.4	8.3	1.2	6.5	6.3	8.2	3.2
Denmark	—	—	—	—	-0.1	—	-0.2	-0.1	0.1
Finland	—	—	—	—	—	—	—	—	—
France	38.2	37.8	51.0	31.7	33.7	32.8	44.5	21.1	72.2
Germany, Fed. Rep.	15.7	12.9	12.6	24.1	14.1	11.7	8.3	5.1	5.7
Ireland	—	—	—	—	—	—	—	—	—
Italy	—	—	—	—	—	—	—	—	0.8
Japan	—	—	6.3	9.5	—	—	6.3	9.5	0.8
Netherlands	3.5	0.3	—	—	3.4	0.2	—	-0.1	0.4
New Zealand	—	—	—	—	—	—	—	—	—
Norway	—	—	—	—	—	—	—	—	0.3
Sweden	—	—	—	—	—	—	—	—	—
Switzerland	—	—	—	—	—	—	—	—	0.3
United Kingdom	1.3	0.8	0.8	1.2	1.2	0.8	0.4	1.2	0.3
United States	—	—	—	—	—	—	—	-1.0	—
TOTAL	60.1	58.4	77.1	74.7	53.5	52.0	65.6	43.8	87.2
MULTILATERAL	6.4	7.9	0.1	0.1	5.0	6.3	0.0	-2.0	10.0
OPEC COUNTRIES									0.0
E.E.C.+ MEMBERS	63.9	59.4	64.4	57.0	56.3	51.7	53.0	25.1	88.6
TOTAL	66.5	66.4	77.2	74.9	58.6	58.3	65.7	41.9	97.2

TOTAL OFFICIAL GROSS / TOTAL OFFICIAL NET / TOTAL OOF GROSS

DAC COUNTRIES

	TOTAL OFFICIAL GROSS 1983	1984	1985	1986	TOTAL OFFICIAL NET 1983	1984	1985	1986	TOTAL OOF GROSS 1983
Australia	—	—	—	—	—	—	—	—	—
Austria	0.0	0.0	0.0	0.1	0.0	0.0	0.0	0.1	—
Belgium	3.1	16.0	16.8	19.0	3.1	16.0	16.8	19.0	—
Canada	32.6	27.9	18.8	14.3	25.1	24.5	13.0	6.0	27.9
Denmark	0.1	0.2	0.2	0.2	-0.1	-0.2	-0.2	-0.1	—
Finland	—	—	0.0	0.0	—	—	0.0	0.0	—
France	158.5	196.3	156.7	178.6	146.7	183.3	139.2	158.3	48.1
Germany, Fed. Rep.	29.0	39.5	19.2	52.4	24.4	33.5	10.4	23.2	7.7
Ireland	—	—	—	—	—	—	—	—	—
Italy	0.8	9.1	6.9	1.0	0.1	9.1	6.9	0.9	—
Japan	0.8	0.7	7.9	16.2	0.8	0.7	7.9	16.2	—
Netherlands	3.9	0.6	0.4	2.1	3.6	0.3	0.2	1.7	—
New Zealand	—	—	—	—	—	—	—	—	—
Norway	0.3	0.2	0.2	0.1	0.3	0.2	0.2	0.1	—
Sweden	—	—	—	—	—	—	—	—	—
Switzerland	0.3	0.2	0.2	0.2	0.3	0.2	0.2	0.2	—
United Kingdom	2.7	2.2	3.4	9.5	2.6	2.2	3.0	9.1	1.2
United States	5.0	3.0	24.0	19.0	-3.0	1.0	11.0	4.0	5.0
TOTAL	237.1	295.8	254.8	312.8	203.8	270.7	208.7	238.5	89.9
MULTILATERAL	228.5	250.4	90.6	194.9	198.1	207.4	36.9	121.9	212.1
OPEC COUNTRIES	0.0	0.1	0.1	0.0	0.0	0.1	0.1	0.0	0.0
E.E.C.+ MEMBERS	217.3	286.6	216.2	312.7	189.4	257.3	180.3	249.3	64.8
TOTAL	465.7	546.2	345.4	507.8	402.0	478.1	245.7	360.4	302.0

MILLION US DOLLARS, UNLESS OTHERWISE STATED

COTE D'IVOIRE

ODA COMMITMENTS

1984	1985	1986	1983	1984	1985	1986
—	—	—	—	—	—	—
0.0	0.0	0.1	0.0	0.0	0.0	—
3.2	2.9	2.9	1.7	2.1	1.4	2.9
10.4	10.6	10.9	2.5	23.8	2.2	4.2
0.2	0.2	0.2	—	0.2	0.2	0.1
—	0.0	0.0	—	—	—	—
84.9	79.3	100.9	116.8	111.3	83.1	100.9
18.6	18.3	32.8	5.3	13.2	11.8	32.2
—	—	—	—	—	—	—
0.7	0.7	1.0	0.8	0.7	0.9	2.3
0.7	7.9	16.2	21.7	3.5	3.7	0.7
0.6	0.4	0.6	4.0	0.6	0.4	0.6
—	—	—	—	—	—	—
0.2	0.2	0.1	0.2	0.1	0.2	0.3
—	—	—	—	—	—	—
0.2	0.2	0.2	0.2	0.1	0.1	0.4
1.0	1.2	1.7	0.3	0.3	0.4	0.4
—	—	1.0	0.1	0.4	1.6	2.0
120.7	*121.9*	*168.6*	*153.6*	*156.1*	*106.0*	*147.0*
—	—	—	—	—	—	—
—	—	—	—	—	—	—
11.3	9.3	44.6	15.4	6.9	4.9	50.2
0.2	0.0	—	—	—	—	—
—	—	—	—	—	—	—
—	0.1	0.1	—	2.7	—	6.9
—	—	—	—	—	—	—
—	—	—	4.0	3.7	4.8	6.1
1.9	2.2	3.1	—	—	—	—
0.6	0.6	0.9	—	—	—	—
0.3	0.7	0.7	—	—	—	—
—	—	—	—	—	—	—
—	0.4	0.4	—	—	—	—
0.3	0.3	0.3	—	—	—	—
0.7	0.6	0.7	—	—	—	—
—	—	—	—	—	—	—
15.2	*14.2*	*50.8*	*19.3*	*13.3*	*9.7*	*63.3*
0.1	*0.1*	*0.0*	*0.0*	—	—	—
120.5	*112.3*	*184.7*	*144.2*	*135.1*	*102.9*	*189.7*
135.9	**136.2**	**219.5**	**172.9**	**169.4**	**115.7**	**210.2**

TECH. COOP. GRANTS

1984	1985	1986	1983	1984	1985	1986
—	—	—	—	—	—	—
0.0	0.0	0.1	0.0	—	—	—
3.2	2.9	2.9	2.5	2.5	2.0	2.0
3.7	4.2	2.6	0.7	—	1.9	—
0.2	0.2	0.2	0.1	0.2	0.2	0.2
—	0.0	0.0	—	—	0.0	0.0
47.2	28.3	69.2	69.9	45.3	27.2	67.3
5.7	5.7	8.7	5.6	5.6	5.5	8.3
—	—	—	—	—	—	—
0.7	0.7	1.0	0.8	0.7	0.7	1.0
0.7	1.7	6.8	0.4	0.4	0.7	0.6
0.3	0.4	0.6	0.4	0.3	0.4	0.4
—	—	—	—	—	—	—
0.2	0.2	0.1	0.1	0.1	0.0	0.1
—	—	—	—	—	—	—
0.2	0.2	0.2	0.1	0.1	0.1	0.1
0.3	0.4	0.4	0.3	0.3	0.4	0.4
—	—	1.0	—	—	—	1.0
62.2	*44.8*	*93.9*	*80.8*	*55.4*	*39.1*	*81.4*
7.3	*14.1*	*50.7*	*4.0*	*3.7*	*4.5*	*5.7*
0.1	*0.1*	*0.0*	—	—	—	—
61.1	*47.9*	*127.7*	*79.5*	*54.8*	*36.3*	*79.7*
69.6	**59.0**	**144.6**	**84.8**	**59.1**	**43.5**	**87.1**

TOTAL OOF NET

1984	1985	1986	1983	1984	1985	1986
—	—	—	—	—	—	—
12.8	13.9	16.0	—	12.8	13.9	16.0
17.5	8.2	3.4	20.6	14.4	2.5	-4.9
—	—	—	-0.1	-0.4	-0.2	-0.4
111.4	77.4	77.8	40.8	103.4	66.4	68.0
20.9	0.9	19.6	4.6	16.0	-3.5	9.4
—	—	—	—	—	—	—
8.4	6.2	—	-0.7	8.4	6.2	-0.1
—	—	1.6	-0.2	-0.2	-0.2	1.3
—	—	—	—	—	—	—
—	—	—	—	—	—	—
—	—	—	—	—	—	—
1.1	2.2	7.8	1.2	1.1	2.2	7.5
3.0	24.0	18.0	-3.0	1.0	11.0	4.0
175.1	*132.9*	*144.2*	*63.1*	*156.5*	*98.2*	*100.8*
235.2	*76.3*	*144.1*	*183.1*	*193.8*	*22.8*	*73.2*
—	—	—	—	—	—	—
166.1	*103.9*	*128.1*	*44.6*	*144.5*	*79.4*	*96.5*
410.3	**209.2**	**288.3**	**246.2**	**350.3**	**121.0**	**174.0**

ODA COMMITMENTS : LOANS

DAC COUNTRIES

	1983	1984	1985	1986
Australia	—	—	—	—
Austria	—	—	—	—
Belgium	—	—	—	—
Canada	—	19.3	0.1	—
Denmark	—	—	—	—
Finland	—	—	—	—
France	44.8	64.1	54.6	31.7
Germany, Fed. Rep.	2.9	5.0	7.1	21.8
Ireland	—	—	—	—
Italy	—	—	—	—
Japan	21.1	—	—	—
Netherlands	3.5	0.3	—	—
New Zealand	—	—	—	—
Norway	—	—	—	—
Sweden	—	—	—	—
Switzerland	—	—	—	—
United Kingdom	—	—	—	—
United States	—	—	—	—
TOTAL	*72.2*	*88.6*	*61.7*	*53.5*
MULTILATERAL	*11.3*	*2.7*	—	*6.9*
OPEC COUNTRIES	—	—	—	—
E.E.C.+ MEMBERS	*62.5*	*69.3*	*61.7*	*53.5*
TOTAL	**83.6**	**91.3**	**61.7**	**60.4**

GRANT ELEMENT OF ODA

DAC COUNTRIES

	1983	1984	1985	1986
Australia	—	—	—	—
Austria	100.0	100.0	100.0	—
Belgium	100.0	100.0	100.0	100.0
Canada	100.0	91.4	98.4	100.0
Denmark	—	100.0	100.0	100.0
Finland	—	—	—	—
France	71.4	56.7	80.6	71.2
Germany, Fed. Rep.	87.7	85.4	83.4	56.7
Ireland	—	—	—	—
Italy	100.0	100.0	100.0	100.0
Japan	44.2	100.0	100.0	100.0
Netherlands	66.8	81.6	100.0	100.0
New Zealand	—	—	—	—
Norway	100.0	100.0	100.0	100.0
Sweden	—	—	—	—
Switzerland	100.0	100.0	100.0	100.0
United Kingdom	100.0	100.0	100.0	100.0
United States	100.0	100.0	100.0	100.0
TOTAL	*69.1*	*66.5*	*84.6*	*70.8*
MULTILATERAL	*100.0*	*87.9*	*100.0*	*95.6*
OPEC COUNTRIES	*100.0*	—	—	—
E.E.C.+ MEMBERS	*73.3*	*62.9*	*83.8*	*76.8*
TOTAL	**70.6**	**68.2**	**86.6**	**77.7**

OTHER AGGREGATES

COMMITMENTS: ALL SOURCES

	1983	1984	1985	1986
TOTAL BILATERAL	275.4	310.0	232.5	200.9
of which				
OPEC	0.0	—	—	—
CMEA	—	—	—	—
TOTAL MULTILATERAL	316.0	29.1	295.1	404.3
TOTAL BIL.& MULTIL.	591.4	339.1	527.6	605.2
of which				
ODA Grants	89.3	78.2	53.9	149.8
ODA Loans	83.6	91.3	61.7	60.4

DISBURSEMENTS:

DAC COUNTRIES COMBINED

OFFICIAL & PRIVATE

	1983	1984	1985	1986
GROSS:				
Contractual Lending	302.3	405.1	267.3	188.9
Export Credits Total	192.9	201.2	66.6	-26.6
Export Credits Private	152.3	172.7	58.4	-30.0
NET:				
Contractual Lending	81.6	173.6	77.4	64.6
Export Credits Total	-13.6	-15.2	-100.4	-107.7
PRIVATE SECTOR NET	84.6	-44.8	20.8	108.3
Direct Investment	71.3	-0.5	28.4	15.0
Portfolio Investment	48.4	-10.6	77.9	173.4
Export Credits	-35.1	-33.7	-85.5	-80.0

MARKET BORROWING:

CHANGE IN CLAIMS

	1983	1984	1985	1986
Banks	—	-245.0	-53.0	41.0

MEMORANDUM ITEM:

	1983	1984	1985	1986
CMEA Countr.(Gross)	—	—	—	—

TOTAL RECEIPTS NET

DAC COUNTRIES	1983	1984	1985	1986
Australia	–	4.9	5.3	-1.9
Austria	-2.6	1.0	-1.8	-0.7
Belgium	-3.1	16.2	-0.2	-5.2
Canada	7.2	0.1	-1.9	1.5
Denmark	-2.9	-5.7	-1.9	-0.4
Finland	-0.7	2.2	-1.2	-0.1
France	-8.5	60.4	34.0	-38.3
Germany, Fed. Rep.	4.8	3.6	1.9	-0.1
Ireland	–	–	–	–
Italy	2.0	20.6	29.2	13.9
Japan	-95.8	-42.9	-36.0	-25.2
Netherlands	-0.4	11.6	1.8	0.6
New Zealand	–	–	–	–
Norway	0.0	0.1	0.0	0.6
Sweden	3.2	2.3	1.8	5.4
Switzerland	13.2	-9.2	-0.8	0.0
United Kingdom	-4.5	-14.7	-5.6	-3.4
United States	..	–	–	–
TOTAL	**-87.9**	**50.4**	**24.7**	**-53.5**
MULTILATERAL				
AF.D.F.	–	–	–	–
AF.D.B.	–	–	–	–
AS.D.B	–	–	–	–
CAR.D.B.	–	–	–	–
E.E.C.	–	–	–	–
IBRD	–	–	–	–
IDA	–	–	–	–
I.D.B.	–	–	–	–
IFAD	3.9	1.7	1.2	0.8
I.F.C.	–	–	–	–
IMF TRUST FUND	–	–	–	–
U.N. AGENCIES	–	–	–	–
UNDP	3.1	1.7	2.9	3.2
UNTA	1.0	0.9	0.7	1.1
UNICEF	0.1	0.0	0.1	0.1
UNRWA	–	–	–	–
WFP	1.8	–	9.7	7.6
UNHCR	–	–	–	–
Other Multilateral	1.4	1.2	1.1	1.4
Arab OPEC Agencies	–	–	–	–
TOTAL	**11.3**	**5.6**	**15.7**	**14.3**
OPEC COUNTRIES	–	–	–	–
E.E.C.+ MEMBERS	-12.5	92.0	59.3	-33.0
TOTAL	**-76.6**	**56.0**	**40.3**	**-39.2**

TOTAL ODA NET

DAC COUNTRIES	1983	1984	1985	1986
Australia	–	–	–	–
Austria	0.0	2.9	–	0.0
Belgium	0.0	0.0	–	–
Canada	-0.1	0.1	0.1	0.1
Denmark	–	–	–	–
Finland	-0.2	-0.2	-0.1	-0.2
France	0.3	0.6	0.5	0.7
Germany, Fed. Rep.	0.0	0.1	0.0	0.1
Ireland	–	–	–	–
Italy	0.1	0.2	0.1	0.1
Japan	0.1	0.1	0.1	0.2
Netherlands	0.0	0.4	0.0	-0.2
New Zealand	–	–	–	–
Norway	–	–	–	0.6
Sweden	1.5	2.3	1.8	2.3
Switzerland	0.1	–	–	0.0
United Kingdom	–	–	–	–
United States	–	–	–	–
TOTAL	**1.9**	**6.4**	**2.5**	**3.7**
MULTILATERAL				
AF.D.F.	–	–	–	–
AF.D.B.	–	–	–	–
AS.D.B	–	–	–	–
CAR.D.B.	–	–	–	–
E.E.C.	–	–	–	–
IBRD	–	–	–	–
IDA	–	–	–	–
I.D.B.	–	–	–	–
IFAD	3.9	1.7	1.2	0.8
I.F.C.	–	–	–	–
IMF TRUST FUND	–	–	–	–
U.N. AGENCIES	–	–	–	–
UNDP	3.1	1.7	2.9	3.2
UNTA	1.0	0.9	0.7	1.1
UNICEF	0.1	0.0	0.1	0.1
UNRWA	–	–	–	–
WFP	1.8	–	9.7	7.6
UNHCR	–	–	–	–
Other Multilateral	1.4	1.2	1.1	1.4
Arab OPEC Agencies	–	–	–	–
TOTAL	**11.3**	**5.6**	**15.7**	**14.3**
OPEC COUNTRIES	–	–	–	–
E.E.C.+ MEMBERS	0.5	1.3	0.7	0.6
TOTAL	**13.2**	**12.0**	**18.2**	**18.0**

TOTAL ODA GROSS

	1983
Australia	–
Austria	0.0
Belgium	0.0
Canada	0.3
Denmark	–
Finland	0.0
France	0.3
Germany, Fed. Rep.	0.0
Ireland	–
Italy	0.1
Japan	0.1
Netherlands	0.0
New Zealand	–
Norway	–
Sweden	1.5
Switzerland	0.1
United Kingdom	–
United States	–
TOTAL	**2.5**
AF.D.F.	–
AF.D.B.	–
AS.D.B	–
CAR.D.B.	–
E.E.C.	–
IBRD	–
IDA	–
I.D.B.	–
IFAD	3.9
I.F.C.	–
IMF TRUST FUND	–
U.N. AGENCIES	–
UNDP	3.1
UNTA	1.0
UNICEF	0.1
UNRWA	–
WFP	1.8
UNHCR	–
Other Multilateral	1.4
Arab OPEC Agencies	–
TOTAL	**11.3**
OPEC COUNTRIES	–
E.E.C.+ MEMBERS	0.5
TOTAL	**13.8**

ODA LOANS GROSS

DAC COUNTRIES	1983	1984	1985	1986
Australia	–	–	–	–
Austria	–	2.8	–	–
Belgium	–	–	–	–
Canada	0.2	–	0.5	–
Denmark	–	–	–	–
Finland	–	–	–	–
France	–	–	–	–
Germany, Fed. Rep.	–	–	–	–
Ireland	–	–	–	–
Italy	–	–	–	–
Japan	–	–	–	–
Netherlands	0.0	0.2	0.3	0.0
New Zealand	–	–	–	–
Norway	–	–	–	–
Sweden	–	–	–	–
Switzerland	–	–	–	–
United Kingdom	–	–	–	–
United States	–	–	–	–
TOTAL	**0.2**	**3.0**	**0.8**	**0.0**
MULTILATERAL	3.9	1.7	1.2	1.3
OPEC COUNTRIES	–	–	–	–
E.E.C.+ MEMBERS	0.0	0.2	0.3	0.0
TOTAL	**4.1**	**4.7**	**2.0**	**1.3**

ODA LOANS NET

DAC COUNTRIES	1983	1984	1985	1986
Australia	–	–	–	–
Austria	–	2.8	–	–
Belgium	–	–	–	–
Canada	-0.2	–	–	–
Denmark	–	–	–	–
Finland	-0.2	-0.2	-0.2	-0.2
France	–	–	–	–
Germany, Fed. Rep.	–	–	–	–
Ireland	–	–	–	–
Italy	–	–	–	–
Japan	–	–	–	–
Netherlands	0.0	0.1	-0.3	-0.5
New Zealand	–	–	–	–
Norway	–	–	0.0	0.0
Sweden	–	–	–	–
Switzerland	–	–	–	–
United Kingdom	–	–	–	–
United States	–	–	–	–
TOTAL	**-0.4**	**2.8**	**-0.5**	**-0.7**
MULTILATERAL	3.9	1.7	1.2	0.8
OPEC COUNTRIES	–	–	–	–
E.E.C.+ MEMBERS	0.0	0.1	-0.3	-0.5
TOTAL	**3.6**	**4.5**	**0.7**	**0.1**

GRANTS

	1983
Australia	–
Austria	0.0
Belgium	0.0
Canada	0.1
Denmark	–
Finland	0.0
France	0.3
Germany, Fed. Rep.	0.0
Ireland	–
Italy	0.1
Japan	0.1
Netherlands	0.0
New Zealand	–
Norway	–
Sweden	1.5
Switzerland	0.1
United Kingdom	–
United States	–
TOTAL	**2.3**
MULTILATERAL	7.4
OPEC COUNTRIES	–
E.E.C.+ MEMBERS	0.5
TOTAL	**9.7**

TOTAL OFFICIAL GROSS

DAC COUNTRIES	1983	1984	1985	1986
Australia	–	5.1	6.2	0.1
Austria	0.6	2.9	–	0.0
Belgium	7.3	3.3	10.8	0.0
Canada	7.7	0.1	0.5	2.5
Denmark	–	–	–	–
Finland	0.0	–	0.0	0.0
France	23.5	26.1	1.0	15.8
Germany, Fed. Rep.	0.1	2.3	1.6	1.9
Ireland	–	–	–	–
Italy	5.3	22.3	6.4	0.1
Japan	0.1	0.1	0.1	0.2
Netherlands	0.0	0.5	0.7	0.3
New Zealand	–	–	–	–
Norway	–	–	–	0.6
Sweden	3.8	2.3	1.8	2.3
Switzerland	0.1	–	–	0.0
United Kingdom	–	–	–	–
United States	–	–	–	–
TOTAL	**48.5**	**65.0**	**29.1**	**23.8**
MULTILATERAL	11.3	5.6	15.7	14.8
OPEC COUNTRIES	–	–	–	–
E.E.C.+ MEMBERS	36.3	54.5	20.5	18.1
TOTAL	**59.8**	**70.6**	**44.8**	**38.6**

TOTAL OFFICIAL NET

DAC COUNTRIES	1983	1984	1985	1986
Australia	–	4.9	5.3	-1.9
Austria	-2.6	1.0	-1.8	-0.7
Belgium	7.3	3.1	10.6	0.0
Canada	7.2	0.1	-1.9	1.5
Denmark	–	–	–	–
Finland	-0.2	-0.2	-0.1	-0.2
France	23.5	26.1	-0.3	15.8
Germany, Fed. Rep.	0.1	2.3	1.6	1.9
Ireland	–	–	–	–
Italy	4.5	21.3	6.0	-0.2
Japan	0.1	0.1	0.1	-0.2
Netherlands	0.0	0.4	0.0	-0.2
New Zealand	–	–	–	–
Norway	–	–	–	0.6
Sweden	-1.7	2.3	1.8	2.3
Switzerland	0.1	–	–	–
United Kingdom	–	–	–	–
United States	–	–	–	–
TOTAL	**38.4**	**61.5**	**21.2**	**17.4**
MULTILATERAL	11.3	5.6	15.7	14.3
OPEC COUNTRIES	–	–	–	–
E.E.C.+ MEMBERS	35.5	53.3	17.9	17.3
TOTAL	**49.7**	**67.1**	**36.9**	**31.7**

TOTAL OOF GROSS

	1983
Australia	–
Austria	0.6
Belgium	7.3
Canada	7.4
Denmark	–
Finland	–
France	23.2
Germany, Fed. Rep.	0.1
Ireland	–
Italy	5.3
Japan	–
Netherlands	–
New Zealand	–
Norway	–
Sweden	2.2
Switzerland	–
United Kingdom	–
United States	–
TOTAL	**46.1**
MULTILATERAL	
OPEC COUNTRIES	–
E.E.C.+ MEMBERS	35.9
TOTAL	**46.1**

ODA COMMITMENTS

1984	1985	1986	1983	1984	1985	1986
2.9	–	0.0	0.0	2.8	–	–
0.0	–	–	–	–	–	–
0.1	0.5	0.1	0.2	–	0.5	0.2
–	0.0	0.0	–	0.0	–	–
0.6	0.5	0.7	0.3	0.6	0.5	0.7
0.1	0.0	0.1	0.0	0.1	0.0	0.1
–	–	–	–	–	–	–
0.2	0.1	0.1	0.1	0.2	0.3	0.2
0.1	0.1	0.2	0.1	0.1	0.1	0.3
0.5	0.7	0.3	0.0	0.4	0.7	0.2
–	–	0.6	–	–	1.0	0.8
2.3	1.8	2.3	0.4	2.2	0.5	2.3
–	–	0.0	–	–	–	–
–	–	–	–	–	–	–
–	–	–	–	–	–	–
6.7	3.7	4.4	1.2	6.4	3.6	4.7
–	–	–	–	–	–	–
–	–	–	–	–	–	–
–	–	–	–	–	–	–
–	–	–	–	–	0.0	0.0
–	–	–	–	–	–	–
–	–	–	–	–	–	–
1.7	1.2	1.3	0.2	–	–	–
–	–	–	–	–	–	–
–	–	–	7.4	3.8	14.5	13.5
1.7	2.9	3.2	–	–	–	–
0.9	0.7	1.1	–	–	–	–
0.0	0.1	0.1	–	–	–	–
–	–	–	–	–	–	–
–	9.7	7.6	–	–	–	–
–	–	–	–	–	–	–
1.2	1.1	1.4	–	–	–	–
5.6	15.7	14.8	7.6	3.8	14.5	13.5
–	–	–	–	–	–	–
1.3	1.3	1.1	0.5	1.3	1.5	1.2
12.2	19.4	19.2	8.7	10.3	18.1	18.2

TECH. COOP. GRANTS

1984	1985	1986	1983	1984	1985	1986
–	–	–	–	–	–	–
0.0	–	0.0	0.0	–	–	–
0.0	–	–	–	–	–	–
0.1	0.1	0.1	0.1	–	–	–
–	–	–	–	–	–	–
–	0.0	0.0	0.0	–	–	0.0
0.6	0.5	0.7	0.3	0.6	0.5	0.7
0.1	0.0	0.1	0.0	0.1	0.0	0.1
–	–	–	–	–	–	–
0.2	0.1	0.1	0.1	0.2	0.1	0.1
0.1	0.1	0.2	0.1	0.1	0.1	0.2
0.3	0.3	0.2	0.0	0.3	0.3	0.2
–	–	0.6	–	–	–	0.0
2.3	1.8	2.3	1.1	1.8	1.8	1.7
–	–	0.0	0.0	–	–	0.0
–	–	–	–	–	–	–
–	–	–	–	–	–	–
3.7	3.0	4.4	1.7	3.1	2.9	3.1
3.8	14.5	13.5	5.6	3.8	4.8	5.9
–	–	–	–	–	–	–
1.2	1.0	1.1	0.5	1.2	1.0	1.1
7.5	17.4	17.9	7.3	6.9	7.7	8.9

TOTAL OOF NET

1984	1985	1986	1983	1984	1985	1986
5.1	6.2	0.1	–	4.9	5.3	-1.9
–	–	–	-2.6	-1.9	-1.8	-0.8
3.3	10.8	0.0	7.3	3.1	10.6	0.0
–	–	2.3	7.3	–	-2.0	1.4
–	–	–	–	–	–	–
25.6	0.5	15.2	23.2	25.6	-0.8	15.2
2.2	1.6	1.8	0.1	2.2	1.6	1.8
–	–	–	–	–	–	–
22.1	6.3	–	4.4	21.2	5.8	-0.3
–	–	–	–	–	–	–
–	–	–	–	–	–	–
–	–	–	–	–	–	–
–	–	–	-3.3	–	0.0	-1.7
–	–	–	–	–	–	–
–	–	–	–	–	–	–
58.3	25.4	19.4	36.5	55.1	18.7	13.7
–	–	–	–	–	–	–
53.2	19.1	17.0	35.0	52.1	17.2	16.7
58.3	25.4	19.4	36.5	55.1	18.7	13.7

ODA COMMITMENTS : LOANS

DAC COUNTRIES

	1983	1984	1985	1986
Australia	–	–	–	–
Austria	–	2.8	–	–
Belgium	–	–	–	–
Canada	0.2	–	0.5	–
Denmark	–	–	–	–
Finland	–	–	–	–
France	–	–	–	–
Germany, Fed. Rep.	–	–	–	–
Ireland	–	–	–	–
Italy	–	–	–	–
Japan	–	–	–	–
Netherlands	–	0.1	0.2	–
New Zealand	–	–	–	–
Norway	–	–	–	–
Sweden	–	–	–	–
Switzerland	–	–	–	–
United Kingdom	–	–	–	–
United States	–	–	–	–
TOTAL	0.2	2.9	0.7	–
MULTILATERAL	–	–	–	–
OPEC COUNTRIES	–	–	–	–
E.E.C.+ MEMBERS	–	0.1	0.2	–
TOTAL	0.2	2.9	0.7	–

GRANT ELEMENT OF ODA

DAC COUNTRIES

	1983	1984	1985	1986
Australia	–	–	–	–
Austria	100.0	66.2	–	–
Belgium	–	–	–	–
Canada	100.0	–	33.1	100.0
Denmark	–	–	–	–
Finland	–	100.0	–	–
France	100.0	100.0	100.0	100.0
Germany, Fed. Rep.	100.0	100.0	100.0	100.0
Ireland	–	–	–	–
Italy	100.0	100.0	100.0	100.0
Japan	100.0	100.0	100.0	100.0
Netherlands	100.0	91.8	87.7	100.0
New Zealand	–	–	–	–
Norway	–	–	100.0	100.0
Sweden	100.0	100.0	100.0	100.0
Switzerland	–	–	–	–
United Kingdom	–	–	–	–
United States	–	–	–	–
TOTAL	100.0	84.6	88.6	100.0
MULTILATERAL	100.0	100.0	100.0	100.0
OPEC COUNTRIES	–	–	–	–
E.E.C.+ MEMBERS	100.0	97.5	94.3	100.0
TOTAL	100.0	90.3	97.7	100.0

OTHER AGGREGATES

COMMITMENTS: ALL SOURCES

	1983	1984	1985	1986
TOTAL BILATERAL	737.3	731.3	716.3	883.5
of which				
OPEC	–	–	–	–
CMEA	696.0	672.0	680.0	870.4
TOTAL MULTILATERAL	7.6	3.8	14.5	13.5
TOTAL BIL.& MULTIL.	744.9	735.1	730.8	897.0
of which				
ODA Grants	8.6	7.3	17.4	18.2
ODA Loans	696.2	674.9	680.7	870.4

DISBURSEMENTS:

DAC COUNTRIES COMBINED

	1983	1984	1985	1986
OFFICIAL & PRIVATE				
GROSS:				
Contractual Lending	90.7	124.8	131.6	8.9
Export Credits Total	52.5	69.7	112.0	-8.1
Export Credits Private	44.4	63.9	105.8	-10.5
NET:				
Contractual Lending	-84.8	1.6	16.7	-38.2
Export Credits Total	-122.5	-53.0	-0.1	-54.5
PRIVATE SECTOR NET	-126.3	-11.1	3.5	-70.9
Direct Investment	0.1	0.2	0.2	0.2
Portfolio Investment	-5.5	44.5	4.4	-19.9
Export Credits	-120.9	-55.8	-1.1	-51.2

MARKET BORROWING:

CHANGE IN CLAIMS

	1983	1984	1985	1986
Banks	–	49.0	196.0	117.0

MEMORANDUM ITEM:

	1983	1984	1985	1986
CMEA Countr.(Gross)	696.0	672.0	680.0	870.5

DISBURSEMENTS, UNLESS OTHERWISE STATED

	1983	1984	1985	1986	1983	1984	1985	1986		1983
TOTAL RECEIPTS NET					**TOTAL ODA NET**				**TOTAL ODA GROSS**	
DAC COUNTRIES									Australia	0.1
Australia	1.3	-0.2	-0.2	-0.1	0.1	0.1	0.0	0.0	Austria	0.8
Austria	-0.3	-1.2	-0.6	-0.8	-0.3	-1.2	-0.6	-0.8	Belgium	—
Belgium	-3.2	-1.4	-1.6	0.1	—	—	—	—	Canada	0.1
Canada	—	0.1	0.0	-0.1	0.1	0.2	—	0.0	Denmark	—
Denmark	0.3	0.0	0.0	—	—	—	—	—	Finland	—
Finland	-0.4	-0.4	-0.3	—	—	—	—	—	France	2.2
France	-3.5	-26.6	33.9	33.0	2.2	1.9	2.1	2.1	Germany, Fed. Rep.	4.0
Germany, Fed. Rep.	21.4	42.7	40.1	-6.4	3.0	0.4	0.0	-0.5	Ireland	—
Ireland	—	—	—	—	—	—	—	—	Italy	0.0
Italy	-2.0	-2.1	0.6	0.1	0.0	0.3	0.3	0.1	Japan	0.0
Japan	0.0	1.8	5.9	6.5	0.0	0.0	0.1	—	Netherlands	0.0
Netherlands	2.1	1.9	4.2	3.3	0.0	0.0	0.0	0.0	New Zealand	—
New Zealand	—	—	—	—	—	—	—	—	Norway	—
Norway	—	—	-3.4	2.5	—	—	—	—	Sweden	—
Sweden	—	0.0	0.0	—	—	0.0	0.0	0.0	Switzerland	—
Switzerland	0.1	-0.5	1.0	0.0	—	—	—	0.6	United Kingdom	0.6
United Kingdom	3.2	-8.8	-2.9	20.6	0.5	0.4	0.8	0.6	United States	1.0
United States	..	-3.0	17.0	17.0	1.0	2.0	18.0	22.0	**TOTAL**	8.8
TOTAL	19.1	2.4	93.6	75.5	6.6	4.1	20.7	23.5		
MULTILATERAL										
AF.D.F.	—	—	—	—	—	—	—	—	AF.D.F.	—
AF.D.B.	—	—	—	—	—	—	—	—	AF.D.B.	—
AS.D.B	—	—	—	—	—	—	—	—	AS.D.B	—
CAR.D.B.	—	—	—	—	—	—	—	—	CAR.D.B.	—
E.E.C.	4.0	6.1	3.9	7.9	0.8	2.4	2.9	4.2	E.E.C.	0.8
IBRD	6.3	3.6	5.7	-5.3	—	—	—	—	IBRD	—
IDA	—	—	—	—	—	—	—	—	IDA	—
I.D.B.	—	—	—	—	—	—	—	—	I.D.B.	—
IFAD	—	—	—	0.2	—	—	—	0.2	IFAD	—
I.F.C.	1.2	0.2	-0.1	-0.3	—	—	—	—	I.F.C.	—
IMF TRUST FUND	—	—	—	—	—	—	—	—	IMF TRUST FUND	—
U.N. AGENCIES									U.N. AGENCIES	
UNDP	0.5	0.3	0.4	0.4	0.5	0.3	0.4	0.4	UNDP	0.5
UNTA	0.4	0.2	0.4	0.4	0.4	0.2	0.4	0.4	UNTA	0.4
UNICEF	—	—	—	—	—	—	—	—	UNICEF	—
UNRWA	—	—	—	—	—	—	—	—	UNRWA	—
WFP	1.3	0.2	0.7	1.6	1.3	0.2	0.7	1.6	WFP	1.3
UNHCR	5.3	7.4	5.9	2.9	5.3	7.4	5.9	2.9	UNHCR	5.3
Other Multilateral	1.6	0.6	63.9	90.0	1.6	0.6	3.1	1.5	Other Multilateral	1.6
Arab OPEC Agencies	0.4	0.0	0.0	—	0.4	0.0	0.0	—	Arab OPEC Agencies	0.4
TOTAL	20.8	18.6	81.0	97.8	10.2	11.1	13.5	11.1	**TOTAL**	10.2
OPEC COUNTRIES	2.2	2.2	3.1	0.7	2.2	2.2	3.1	0.7	**OPEC COUNTRIES**	2.6
E.E.C.+ MEMBERS	22.4	11.9	78.1	58.5	6.6	5.4	6.0	6.4	**E.E.C.+ MEMBERS**	7.7
TOTAL	42.1	23.2	177.7	174.0	19.0	17.4	37.3	35.3	**TOTAL**	21.6
ODA LOANS GROSS					**ODA LOANS NET**				**GRANTS**	
DAC COUNTRIES										
Australia	—	—	—	—	—	—	—	—	Australia	0.1
Austria	0.5	—	—	—	-0.6	-1.5	-1.0	-1.3	Austria	0.3
Belgium	—	—	—	—	—	—	—	—	Belgium	—
Canada	—	—	—	—	—	—	—	—	Canada	0.1
Denmark	—	—	—	—	—	—	—	—	Denmark	—
Finland	—	—	—	—	—	—	—	—	Finland	—
France	1.4	1.1	1.7	1.2	1.4	1.0	1.5	1.1	France	0.8
Germany, Fed. Rep.	2.4	0.1	—	—	1.4	-1.0	-1.1	-1.8	Germany, Fed. Rep.	1.6
Ireland	—	—	—	—	—	—	—	—	Ireland	—
Italy	—	—	—	—	—	—	—	—	Italy	0.0
Japan	—	—	—	—	—	—	—	—	Japan	0.0
Netherlands	—	—	—	—	—	—	—	—	Netherlands	0.0
New Zealand	—	—	—	—	—	—	—	—	New Zealand	—
Norway	—	—	—	—	—	—	—	—	Norway	—
Sweden	—	—	—	—	—	—	—	—	Sweden	—
Switzerland	—	—	—	—	—	—	—	—	Switzerland	—
United Kingdom	—	—	—	—	-0.1	-0.1	0.0	0.0	United Kingdom	0.6
United States	—	—	—	—	—	—	—	—	United States	1.0
TOTAL	4.3	1.2	1.7	1.2	2.0	-1.6	-0.6	-2.1	TOTAL	4.5
MULTILATERAL	2.0	1.6	3.2	2.4	2.0	1.6	3.1	2.0	MULTILATERAL	8.2
OPEC COUNTRIES	2.6	2.5	3.8	2.4	2.2	2.2	3.1	0.7	**OPEC COUNTRIES**	0.0
E.E.C.+ MEMBERS	4.6	2.8	2.2	1.9	3.5	1.5	0.9	0.0	**E.E.C.+ MEMBERS**	3.1
TOTAL	8.9	5.3	8.7	5.9	6.3	2.2	5.6	0.6	**TOTAL**	12.7
TOTAL OFFICIAL GROSS					**TOTAL OFFICIAL NET**				**TOTAL OOF GROSS**	
DAC COUNTRIES										
Australia	1.3	0.1	0.0	0.0	1.2	-0.2	-0.2	-0.1	Australia	1.3
Austria	0.8	0.3	0.4	0.5	-0.3	-1.2	-0.6	-0.8	Austria	—
Belgium	—	0.0	—	—	—	0.0	—	—	Belgium	—
Canada	0.1	0.2	—	0.0	—	0.1	0.0	-0.1	Canada	—
Denmark	—	—	—	—	—	—	—	—	Denmark	—
Finland	—	—	—	—	—	—	—	—	Finland	—
France	2.2	2.0	2.3	2.2	2.2	1.9	2.1	2.1	France	—
Germany, Fed. Rep.	4.8	11.1	4.5	1.3	3.8	9.5	2.2	-2.3	Germany, Fed. Rep.	0.8
Ireland	—	—	—	—	—	—	—	—	Ireland	—
Italy	0.0	0.3	0.3	0.1	0.0	0.3	0.3	0.1	Italy	—
Japan	0.0	0.0	0.1	—	0.0	0.0	0.1	—	Japan	—
Netherlands	0.0	0.0	0.0	0.0	0.0	0.0	0.0	0.0	Netherlands	—
New Zealand	—	—	—	—	—	—	—	—	New Zealand	—
Norway	—	—	—	—	—	—	—	—	Norway	—
Sweden	—	0.0	0.0	—	—	0.0	0.0	—	Sweden	—
Switzerland	—	—	—	0.0	—	—	—	0.0	Switzerland	0.0
United Kingdom	0.6	0.5	0.8	0.6	0.5	0.4	0.8	0.6	United Kingdom	—
United States	1.0	2.0	18.0	22.0	—	1.0	17.0	21.0	United States	—
TOTAL	10.8	16.5	26.3	26.8	7.4	11.9	21.7	20.4	TOTAL	2.0
MULTILATERAL	29.0	27.8	91.1	115.8	20.8	18.6	81.0	97.8	MULTILATERAL	18.8
OPEC COUNTRIES	2.6	2.5	3.8	2.4	2.2	2.2	3.1	0.7	**OPEC COUNTRIES**	—
E.E.C.+ MEMBERS	11.6	20.2	12.1	12.7	10.4	18.2	9.3	8.3	**E.E.C.+ MEMBERS**	3.9
TOTAL	42.4	46.9	121.2	144.9	30.4	32.7	105.7	118.9	**TOTAL**	20.8

MILLION US DOLLARS, UNLESS OTHERWISE STATED

ODA COMMITMENTS

	1984	1985	1986	1983	1984	1985	1986
	0.1	0.0	0.0	0.0	0.1	0.0	0.0
	0.3	0.4	0.5	0.3	0.3	0.4	—
	—	—	—	—	—	—	—
	0.2	—	0.0	0.3	—	—	0.1
	—	—	—	—	—	—	—
	—	—	—	—	—	—	—
	2.0	2.3	2.2	4.8	4.4	4.3	2.2
	1.4	1.1	1.3	0.6	0.9	0.6	0.7
	—	—	—	—	—	—	—
	0.3	0.3	0.1	0.0	4.0	0.4	0.2
	0.0	0.1	—	0.0	0.0	0.1	—
	0.0	0.0	0.0	0.0	0.0	0.0	0.0
	—	—	—	—	—	—	—
	—	—	—	—	—	—	—
	0.0	0.0	—	—	—	—	—
	—	—	0.0	—	—	—	—
	0.5	0.8	0.6	0.6	0.5	0.8	0.6
	2.0	18.0	22.0	15.0	15.0	15.0	14.4
	6.9	23.0	26.8	21.7	25.2	21.7	18.1
	—	—	—	—	—	—	—
	—	—	—	—	—	—	—
	—	—	—	—	—	—	—
	2.4	2.9	4.2	—	—	2.9	4.7
	—	—	—	—	—	—	—
	—	—	—	—	—	—	—
	—	—	0.2	—	4.6	—	—
	—	—	—	—	—	—	—
	—	—	—	7.8	8.7	8.0	5.6
	0.3	0.4	0.4	—	—	—	—
	0.2	0.4	0.4	—	—	—	—
	—	—	—	—	—	—	—
	0.2	0.7	1.6	—	—	—	—
	7.4	5.9	2.9	—	—	—	—
	0.6	3.2	1.9	—	—	2.7	1.5
	0.0	0.0	—	—	—	—	—
	11.1	13.6	11.4	7.8	13.3	13.7	11.8
	2.5	3.8	2.4	8.2	9.9	0.0	13.7
	6.6	7.4	8.3	6.0	9.7	9.1	8.4
	20.5	40.4	40.6	37.7	48.4	35.3	43.7

TECH. COOP. GRANTS

	1984	1985	1986	1983	1984	1985	1986
	0.1	0.0	0.0	0.1	0.1	0.0	0.0
	0.3	0.4	0.5	0.3	—	—	—
	—	—	—	—	—	—	—
	0.2	—	0.0	0.1	—	—	—
	—	—	—	—	—	—	—
	0.9	0.6	1.0	0.8	0.9	0.6	1.0
	1.4	1.1	1.3	1.6	1.4	1.1	1.3
	—	—	—	—	—	—	—
	0.3	0.3	0.1	0.0	0.3	0.3	0.1
	0.0	0.1	—	0.0	0.0	0.1	—
	0.0	0.0	0.0	0.0	0.0	0.0	0.0
	—	—	—	—	—	—	—
	—	—	—	—	—	—	—
	0.0	0.0	—	—	—	—	—
	—	—	0.0	—	—	—	—
	0.5	0.8	0.6	0.6	0.5	0.8	0.6
	2.0	18.0	22.0	—	—	—	—
	5.7	21.3	25.6	3.5	3.2	2.9	3.0
	9.5	10.4	9.1	6.6	8.5	7.2	4.0
	—	0.0	—	—	—	—	—
	3.9	5.2	6.4	3.1	3.1	2.8	3.0
	15.2	31.7	34.7	10.1	11.6	10.1	7.0

TOTAL OOF NET

	1984	1985	1986	1983	1984	1985	1986
	—	—	—	1.1	-0.2	-0.2	-0.2
	—	—	—	—	—	—	—
	0.0	—	—	-0.1	-0.1	0.0	-0.1
	—	—	—	—	—	—	—
	—	—	—	—	—	—	—
	9.6	3.4	—	0.8	9.1	2.2	-1.8
	—	—	—	—	—	—	—
	—	—	—	—	—	—	—
	—	—	—	—	—	—	—
	—	—	—	—	—	—	—
	—	—	—	—	—	—	—
	—	—	—	-1.0	-1.0	-1.0	-1.0
	9.7	3.4	—	0.8	7.8	1.0	-3.1
	16.8	77.4	104.3	10.6	7.5	67.4	86.7
	—	—	—	—	—	—	—
	13.6	4.7	4.4	3.9	12.8	3.2	1.9
	26.4	80.8	104.3	11.5	15.3	68.4	83.6

ODA COMMITMENTS : LOANS

DAC COUNTRIES	1983	1984	1985	1986
Australia	—	—	—	—
Austria	—	—	—	—
Belgium	—	—	—	—
Canada	—	—	—	0.1
Denmark	—	—	—	—
Finland	—	—	—	—
France	4.0	3.5	3.7	1.2
Germany, Fed. Rep.	—	—	—	—
Ireland	—	—	—	—
Italy	—	3.7	—	—
Japan	—	—	—	—
Netherlands	—	—	—	—
New Zealand	—	—	—	—
Norway	—	—	—	—
Sweden	—	—	—	—
Switzerland	—	—	—	—
United Kingdom	—	—	—	—
United States	—	—	—	—
TOTAL	4.0	7.2	3.7	1.2
MULTILATERAL	—	4.6	5.6	2.7
OPEC COUNTRIES	8.2	9.9	—	13.7
E.E.C.+ MEMBERS	4.0	7.2	6.5	2.4
TOTAL	12.2	21.7	9.3	17.6

GRANT ELEMENT OF ODA

DAC COUNTRIES	1983	1984	1985	1986
Australia	100.0	100.0	100.0	100.0
Austria	100.0	100.0	100.0	—
Belgium	—	—	—	—
Canada	100.0	—	—	100.0
Denmark	—	—	—	—
Finland	—	—	—	—
France	100.0	74.8	72.7	100.0
Germany, Fed. Rep.	100.0	100.0	100.0	100.0
Ireland	—	—	—	—
Italy	100.0	47.9	100.0	100.0
Japan	100.0	100.0	100.0	—
Netherlands	100.0	100.0	100.0	100.0
New Zealand	—	—	—	—
Norway	—	—	—	—
Sweden	—	—	—	—
Switzerland	—	—	—	—
United Kingdom	100.0	100.0	100.0	100.0
United States	100.0	100.0	100.0	100.0
TOTAL	100.0	87.6	94.6	100.0
MULTILATERAL	100.0	100.0	100.0	100.0
OPEC COUNTRIES	26.0	27.5	100.0	26.2
E.E.C.+ MEMBERS	100.0	67.5	81.3	100.0
TOTAL	81.9	76.4	96.1	74.6

OTHER AGGREGATES

COMMITMENTS: ALL SOURCES

	1983	1984	1985	1986
TOTAL BILATERAL	32.0	38.1	22.2	44.4
of which				
OPEC	8.2	9.9	0.0	13.7
CMEA	—	—	—	—
TOTAL MULTILATERAL	34.3	57.1	102.9	124.6
TOTAL BIL.& MULTIL.	66.3	95.1	125.1	169.0
of which				
ODA Grants	25.5	26.7	26.0	26.1
ODA Loans	12.2	21.7	9.3	17.6

DISBURSEMENTS:

DAC COUNTRIES COMBINED

OFFICIAL & PRIVATE	1983	1984	1985	1986
GROSS:				
Contractual Lending	35.9	27.1	57.9	76.0
Export Credits Total	31.6	25.9	56.2	74.8
Export Credits Private	29.6	16.3	52.8	74.8
NET:				
Contractual Lending	5.7	-41.5	24.3	50.5
Export Credits Total	3.6	-39.9	24.9	52.6
PRIVATE SECTOR NET	11.7	-9.5	72.0	55.1
Direct Investment	1.2	3.0	4.7	4.7
Portfolio Investment	7.7	35.2	43.3	-5.2
Export Credits	2.8	-47.6	23.9	55.7

MARKET BORROWING:

CHANGE IN CLAIMS

	1983	1984	1985	1986
Banks	—	120.0	155.0	106.0

MEMORANDUM ITEM:

	1983	1984	1985	1986
CMEA Countr.(Gross)	—	—	—	—

TOTAL RECEIPTS NET / TOTAL ODA NET / TOTAL ODA GROSS

	1983	1984	1985	1986	1983	1984	1985	1986		1983
TOTAL RECEIPTS NET					**TOTAL ODA NET**				**TOTAL ODA GROSS**	
DAC COUNTRIES										
Australia	–	–	–	–	–	–	–	–	Australia	–
Austria	0.0	0.3	–	–	0.0	0.3	–	–	Austria	0.0
Belgium	–	0.0	0.0	1.4	–	–	0.1	0.2	Belgium	–
Canada	0.2	0.4	0.1	0.1	0.2	0.4	0.1	0.1	Canada	0.2
Denmark	0.1	0.0	–	–	0.1	–	–	–	Denmark	0.1
Finland	–	–	–	–	–	–	–	–	Finland	–
France	36.6	56.5	46.0	4.0	34.8	37.1	36.5	40.6	France	36.2
Germany, Fed. Rep.	2.5	2.5	3.9	2.9	2.8	2.5	3.9	2.9	Germany, Fed. Rep.	2.8
Ireland	0.2	0.1	0.1	0.1	0.2	0.1	0.1	0.1	Ireland	0.2
Italy	–	0.5	1.2	15.4	–	0.5	1.2	15.3	Italy	–
Japan	0.3	1.3	0.0	1.3	0.3	1.3	0.0	1.3	Japan	0.3
Netherlands	–	0.0	–	–	–	0.0	–	–	Netherlands	–
New Zealand	–	–	–	–	–	–	–	–	New Zealand	–
Norway	–	0.0	–	–	–	0.0	–	–	Norway	–
Sweden	–	–	–	–	–	–	–	–	Sweden	–
Switzerland	0.1	1.3	0.4	0.2	0.1	1.3	0.4	0.2	Switzerland	0.1
United Kingdom	–	9.2	12.4	-0.7	–	0.0	–	–	United Kingdom	–
United States	3.0	5.0	4.0	4.0	3.0	5.0	4.0	4.0	United States	3.0
TOTAL	42.8	77.1	68.2	28.5	41.4	48.5	46.4	64.6	TOTAL	42.8
MULTILATERAL										
AF.D.F.	0.1	–	0.8	2.8	0.1	–	0.8	2.8	AF.D.F.	0.1
AF.D.B.	–	–	–	–	–	–	–	–	AF.D.B.	–
AS.D.B	–	–	–	–	–	–	–	–	AS.D.B	–
CAR.D.B.	–	–	–	–	–	–	–	–	CAR.D.B.	–
E.E.C.	1.5	2.5	1.4	1.3	1.5	2.5	1.4	1.3	E.E.C.	1.5
IBRD	–	–	–	–	–	–	–	–	IBRD	–
IDA	0.6	0.8	5.1	3.6	0.6	0.8	5.1	3.6	IDA	0.6
I.D.B.	–	–	–	–	–	–	–	–	I.D.B.	–
IFAD	0.4	0.3	0.3	0.1	0.4	0.3	0.3	0.1	IFAD	0.4
I.F.C.	–	–	–	–	–	–	–	–	I.F.C.	–
IMF TRUST FUND	–	–	–	–	–	–	–	–	IMF TRUST FUND	–
U.N. AGENCIES	–	–	–	–	–	–	–	–	U.N. AGENCIES	–
UNDP	1.5	1.4	1.4	1.3	1.5	1.4	1.4	1.3	UNDP	1.5
UNTA	0.4	0.6	0.5	1.0	0.4	0.6	0.5	1.0	UNTA	0.4
UNICEF	1.0	0.6	1.0	0.2	1.0	0.6	1.0	0.2	UNICEF	1.0
UNRWA	–	–	–	–	–	–	–	–	UNRWA	–
WFP	1.3	0.9	2.8	1.9	1.3	0.9	2.8	1.9	WFP	1.3
UNHCR	3.8	3.3	2.6	2.3	3.8	3.3	2.6	2.3	UNHCR	3.8
Other Multilateral	0.4	0.2	0.1	0.1	0.4	0.2	0.1	0.1	Other Multilateral	0.4
Arab OPEC Agencies	2.0	9.7	6.8	6.9	2.0	9.7	6.8	6.9	Arab OPEC Agencies	2.2
TOTAL	12.8	20.2	22.8	21.5	12.8	20.2	22.8	21.5	TOTAL	13.1
OPEC COUNTRIES	11.4	33.5	12.3	28.9	11.4	33.5	12.3	28.9	OPEC COUNTRIES	11.4
E.E.C.+ MEMBERS	40.8	71.3	65.0	24.3	39.3	42.7	43.3	60.4	E.E.C.+ MEMBERS	40.7
TOTAL	67.1	130.8	103.2	78.9	65.6	102.2	81.4	115.1	TOTAL	67.3

ODA LOANS GROSS / ODA LOANS NET / GRANTS

	1983	1984	1985	1986	1983	1984	1985	1986		1983
ODA LOANS GROSS					**ODA LOANS NET**				**GRANTS**	
DAC COUNTRIES										
Australia	–	–	–	–	–	–	–	–	Australia	–
Austria	–	–	–	–	–	–	–	–	Austria	0.0
Belgium	–	–	–	–	–	–	–	–	Belgium	–
Canada	–	–	–	–	–	–	–	–	Canada	0.2
Denmark	–	–	–	–	–	–	–	–	Denmark	0.1
Finland	–	–	–	–	–	–	–	–	Finland	–
France	3.6	6.8	4.9	2.3	2.2	5.6	-6.2	2.2	France	32.6
Germany, Fed. Rep.	1.4	1.1	0.5	–	1.4	1.1	0.5	-3.7	Germany, Fed. Rep.	1.4
Ireland	–	–	–	–	–	–	–	–	Ireland	0.2
Italy	–	–	–	–	–	–	–	–	Italy	–
Japan	–	–	–	–	–	–	–	–	Japan	0.3
Netherlands	–	–	–	–	–	–	–	–	Netherlands	–
New Zealand	–	–	–	–	–	–	–	–	New Zealand	–
Norway	–	–	–	–	–	–	–	–	Norway	–
Sweden	–	–	–	–	–	–	–	–	Sweden	–
Switzerland	–	–	–	–	–	–	–	–	Switzerland	0.1
United Kingdom	–	–	–	–	–	–	–	–	United Kingdom	–
United States	–	–	–	–	–	–	–	–	United States	3.0
TOTAL	5.0	7.9	5.4	2.3	3.6	6.7	-5.7	-1.5	TOTAL	37.8
MULTILATERAL	3.5	10.5	13.5	14.2	3.2	10.4	13.0	13.0	MULTILATERAL	9.6
OPEC COUNTRIES	5.8	13.5	12.5	7.7	5.8	13.5	11.8	6.9	OPEC COUNTRIES	5.7
E.E.C.+ MEMBERS	5.3	7.9	5.5	2.3	3.9	6.7	-5.6	-1.6	E.E.C.+ MEMBERS	35.5
TOTAL	14.2	31.8	31.4	24.1	12.6	30.6	19.1	18.4	TOTAL	53.1

TOTAL OFFICIAL GROSS / TOTAL OFFICIAL NET / TOTAL OOF GROSS

	1983	1984	1985	1986	1983	1984	1985	1986		1983
TOTAL OFFICIAL GROSS					**TOTAL OFFICIAL NET**				**TOTAL OOF GROSS**	
DAC COUNTRIES										
Australia	–	–	–	–	–	–	–	–	Australia	–
Austria	0.0	0.3	–	–	0.0	0.3	–	–	Austria	–
Belgium	–	–	0.1	0.2	–	–	0.1	0.2	Belgium	–
Canada	0.2	0.4	0.1	0.1	0.2	0.4	0.1	0.1	Canada	–
Denmark	0.1	–	–	–	0.1	–	–	–	Denmark	–
Finland	–	–	–	–	–	–	–	–	Finland	–
France	36.2	38.3	47.7	40.7	34.6	36.9	36.5	40.6	France	–
Germany, Fed. Rep.	2.8	2.5	3.9	6.6	2.8	2.5	3.9	2.9	Germany, Fed. Rep.	–
Ireland	0.2	0.1	0.1	0.1	0.2	0.1	0.1	0.1	Ireland	–
Italy	–	0.5	1.2	15.3	–	0.5	1.2	15.3	Italy	–
Japan	0.3	1.3	0.0	1.3	0.3	1.3	0.0	1.3	Japan	–
Netherlands	–	0.0	–	–	–	0.0	–	–	Netherlands	–
New Zealand	–	–	–	–	–	–	–	–	New Zealand	–
Norway	–	0.0	–	–	–	0.0	–	–	Norway	–
Sweden	–	–	–	–	–	–	–	–	Sweden	–
Switzerland	0.1	1.3	0.4	0.2	0.1	1.3	0.4	0.2	Switzerland	–
United Kingdom	–	0.0	–	–	–	0.0	–	–	United Kingdom	–
United States	3.0	5.0	4.0	4.0	3.0	5.0	4.0	4.0	United States	–
TOTAL	42.8	49.7	57.5	68.4	41.2	48.3	46.3	64.6	TOTAL	–
MULTILATERAL	13.1	20.3	23.2	22.7	12.8	20.2	22.8	21.5	MULTILATERAL	–
OPEC COUNTRIES	11.4	33.5	12.9	29.7	11.4	33.5	12.3	28.9	OPEC COUNTRIES	–
E.E.C.+ MEMBERS	40.7	43.9	54.4	64.3	39.1	42.6	43.2	60.4	E.E.C.+ MEMBERS	–
TOTAL	67.3	103.5	93.7	120.8	65.4	102.0	81.4	115.1	TOTAL	–

ODA COMMITMENTS

1984	1985	1986	1983	1984	1985	1986
–	–	–	–	–	–	–
0.3	–	–	0.1	0.4	–	–
–	0.1	0.2	–	–	–	0.2
0.4	0.1	0.1	0.2	0.3	0.1	0.1
–	–	–	–	–	–	–
–	–	–	–	–	–	–
38.2	47.7	40.7	43.1	38.1	34.6	40.7
2.5	3.9	6.6	2.1	2.0	2.9	6.2
0.1	0.1	0.1	0.2	0.1	0.1	0.1
0.5	1.2	15.3	0.2	5.4	2.6	36.6
1.3	0.0	1.3	1.5	0.0	0.0	1.3
0.0	–	–	–	0.0	0.0	–
–	–	–	–	–	–	–
0.0	–	–	–	–	–	–
–	–	–	–	–	–	–
1.3	0.4	0.2	0.1	1.3	0.4	0.2
0.0	–	–	–	0.0	–	–
5.0	4.0	4.0	3.8	6.7	3.9	3.4
49.7	*57.5*	*68.4*	*51.3*	*54.4*	*44.7*	*88.7*
–	0.8	2.8	12.6	2.3	–	17.2
–	–	–	–	–	–	–
–	–	–	–	–	–	–
–	–	–	–	–	–	–
2.5	1.4	1.3	2.6	1.7	1.5	2.7
–	–	–	–	–	–	–
0.8	5.1	3.6	–	11.0	5.0	–
–	–	–	–	–	–	–
0.3	0.3	0.1	–	0.1	1.3	–
–	–	–	–	–	–	–
–	–	–	–	–	–	–
–	–	–	8.3	6.9	8.4	6.8
1.4	1.4	1.3	–	–	–	–
0.6	0.5	1.0	–	–	–	–
0.6	1.0	0.2	–	–	–	–
–	–	–	–	–	–	–
0.9	2.8	1.9	–	–	–	–
3.3	2.6	2.3	–	–	–	–
0.2	0.1	0.1	–	–	–	–
9.7	7.2	8.0	13.6	9.5	6.3	2.8
20.3	*23.2*	*22.7*	*37.1*	*31.5*	*22.5*	*29.5*
33.5	*12.9*	*29.7*	*1.2*	*25.1*	*9.0*	*33.4*
43.9	*54.4*	*64.3*	*48.1*	*47.3*	*41.8*	*86.6*
103.4	***93.7***	***120.8***	***89.5***	***111.0***	***76.1***	***151.7***

TECH. COOP. GRANTS

1984	1985	1986	1983	1984	1985	1986
–	–	–	–	–	–	–
0.3	–	–	–	–	–	–
–	0.1	0.2	–	–	–	–
0.4	0.1	0.1	0.1	–	0.1	–
–	–	–	0.1	–	–	–
–	–	–	–	–	–	–
31.4	42.8	38.5	19.7	19.4	19.6	28.1
1.4	3.4	6.6	1.3	0.8	0.7	1.3
0.1	0.1	0.1	0.2	0.1	0.1	0.1
0.5	1.2	15.3	–	0.4	0.5	7.0
1.3	0.0	1.3	0.0	0.0	0.0	0.1
0.0	–	–	–	0.0	–	–
–	–	–	–	–	–	–
0.0	–	–	–	–	–	–
–	–	–	–	–	–	–
1.3	0.4	0.2	–	–	–	–
0.0	–	–	–	0.0	–	–
5.0	4.0	4.0	1.0	3.0	3.0	4.0
41.8	*52.1*	*66.1*	*22.3*	*23.8*	*24.0*	*40.5*
9.8	*9.7*	*8.6*	*7.1*	*6.0*	*5.7*	*5.0*
20.0	*0.5*	*22.0*	–	–	–	–
36.0	*48.9*	*62.0*	*21.2*	*20.8*	*20.8*	*36.5*
71.6	***62.3***	***96.7***	***29.3***	***29.8***	***29.7***	***45.5***

TOTAL OOF NET

1984	1985	1986	1983	1984	1985	1986
–	–	–	–	–	–	–
–	–	–	–	–	–	–
–	–	–	–	–	–	–
–	–	–	–	–	–	–
–	–	–	–	–	–	–
–	–	–	–	–	–	–
0.1	–	–	-0.2	-0.1	0.0	–
–	–	–	–	–	–	–
–	–	–	–	–	–	–
–	–	–	–	–	–	–
–	–	–	–	–	–	–
–	–	–	–	–	–	–
–	–	–	–	–	–	–
–	–	–	–	–	–	–
–	–	–	–	–	–	–
–	–	–	–	–	–	–
–	–	–	–	–	–	–
–	–	–	–	–	–	–
0.1	–	–	*-0.2*	*-0.1*	*0.0*	–
–	–	–	–	–	–	–
–	–	–	–	–	–	–
0.1	–	–	*-0.2*	*-0.1*	*0.0*	–
0.1	–	–	***-0.2***	***-0.1***	***0.0***	–

ODA COMMITMENTS : LOANS

	1983	1984	1985	1986
DAC COUNTRIES				
Australia	–	–	–	–
Austria	–	–	–	–
Belgium	–	–	–	–
Canada	–	–	–	–
Denmark	–	–	–	–
Finland	–	–	–	–
France	11.4	7.4	2.5	2.3
Germany, Fed. Rep.	–	–	–	–
Ireland	–	–	–	–
Italy	–	–	–	–
Japan	–	–	–	–
Netherlands	–	–	–	–
New Zealand	–	–	–	–
Norway	–	–	–	–
Sweden	–	–	–	–
Switzerland	–	–	–	–
United Kingdom	–	–	–	–
United States	–	–	–	–
TOTAL	*11.4*	*7.4*	*2.5*	*2.3*
MULTILATERAL	*26.2*	*22.7*	*12.6*	*19.9*
OPEC COUNTRIES	–	*25.1*	*9.0*	*12.0*
E.E.C.+ MEMBERS	*11.4*	*7.4*	*2.5*	*2.3*
TOTAL	***37.6***	***55.2***	***24.1***	***34.2***

GRANT ELEMENT OF ODA

	1983	1984	1985	1986
DAC COUNTRIES				
Australia	–	–	–	–
Austria	100.0	100.0	–	–
Belgium	–	–	–	100.0
Canada	100.0	100.0	100.0	100.0
Denmark	–	–	–	–
Finland	–	–	–	–
France	88.8	86.5	96.7	94.3
Germany, Fed. Rep.	100.0	100.0	100.0	100.0
Ireland	100.0	100.0	100.0	100.0
Italy	100.0	100.0	100.0	100.0
Japan	100.0	100.0	100.0	100.0
Netherlands	–	100.0	100.0	–
New Zealand	–	–	–	–
Norway	–	–	–	–
Sweden	–	–	–	–
Switzerland	100.0	100.0	100.0	100.0
United Kingdom	–	100.0	–	–
United States	100.0	100.0	100.0	100.0
TOTAL	*90.7*	*90.5*	*97.4*	*97.3*
MULTILATERAL	*73.6*	*73.5*	*76.7*	*84.1*
OPEC COUNTRIES	*100.0*	*59.6*	*52.4*	*80.3*
E.E.C.+ MEMBERS	*90.0*	*89.1*	*97.2*	*97.3*
TOTAL	***82.7***	***78.9***	***85.4***	***91.1***

OTHER AGGREGATES

	1983	1984	1985	1986
COMMITMENTS: ALL SOURCES				
TOTAL BILATERAL	52.4	79.5	53.6	122.1
of which				
OPEC	1.2	25.1	9.0	33.4
CMEA	–	–	–	–
TOTAL MULTILATERAL	37.1	31.5	22.5	29.5
TOTAL BIL.& MULTIL.	89.5	111.0	76.1	151.7
of which				
ODA Grants	51.9	55.7	52.1	117.5
ODA Loans	37.6	55.2	24.1	34.2
DISBURSEMENTS:				
DAC COUNTRIES COMBINED				
OFFICIAL & PRIVATE				
GROSS:				
Contractual Lending	7.6	37.8	26.1	-31.7
Export Credits Total	2.6	29.9	20.7	-34.0
Export Credits Private	2.6	29.9	20.7	-34.0
NET:				
Contractual Lending	5.2	35.2	13.7	-36.5
Export Credits Total	1.8	28.6	19.4	-34.9
PRIVATE SECTOR NET	1.7	28.7	21.8	-36.1
Direct Investment	0.0	0.2	0.2	1.2
Portfolio Investment	-0.1	-0.1	2.1	-2.4
Export Credits	1.8	28.6	19.4	-34.9
MARKET BORROWING:				
CHANGE IN CLAIMS				
Banks	–	35.0	81.0	-66.0
MEMORANDUM ITEM:				
CMEA Countr.(Gross)	–	–	–	–

	1983	1984	1985	1986		1983	1984	1985	1986		1983
TOTAL RECEIPTS NET					**TOTAL ODA NET**					**TOTAL ODA GROSS**	
DAC COUNTRIES											
Australia	0.0	0.0	–	–		–	–	–	–	Australia	–
Austria	0.0	0.0	–	0.0		0.0	0.0	–	0.0	Austria	0.0
Belgium	0.6	0.5	1.2	-1.7		0.2	0.1	0.1	0.2	Belgium	0.2
Canada	1.5	2.6	2.3	-1.4		1.5	2.6	2.3	0.5	Canada	1.7
Denmark	–	–	–	–		–	–	–	–	Denmark	–
Finland	–	–	–	–		–	–	–	–	Finland	–
France	1.0	-3.0	-0.4	4.3		0.7	0.4	0.5	1.9	France	0.7
Germany, Fed. Rep.	12.0	9.6	7.4	7.6		10.3	4.0	5.7	5.6	Germany, Fed. Rep.	10.3
Ireland	–	–	–	–		–	–	–	–	Ireland	–
Italy	0.1	2.3	2.0	11.9		0.1	2.3	2.3	11.9	Italy	0.1
Japan	-1.1	6.1	10.0	29.8		3.3	3.5	10.0	12.4	Japan	3.3
Netherlands	1.9	2.4	2.9	2.6		1.9	1.6	1.3	1.4	Netherlands	1.9
New Zealand	–	–	–	–		–	–	–	–	New Zealand	–
Norway	0.0	10.5	9.8	10.8		0.6	0.0	0.4	0.1	Norway	0.6
Sweden	1.3	0.5	0.5	0.8		1.3	0.5	0.5	0.8	Sweden	1.3
Switzerland	0.0	-0.5	–	0.0		0.0	0.0	–	0.0	Switzerland	0.0
United Kingdom	0.3	0.1	0.0	0.1		0.3	0.3	0.0	0.1	United Kingdom	0.3
United States	32.0	134.0	149.0	231.0		37.0	127.0	139.0	28.0	United States	47.0
TOTAL	*49.3*	*165.1*	*184.7*	*295.8*		*57.0*	*142.3*	*162.1*	*62.9*	*TOTAL*	*67.2*
MULTILATERAL											
AF.D.F.	–	–	–	–		–	–	–	–	AF.D.F.	–
AF.D.B.	–	–	–	–		–	–	–	–	AF.D.B.	–
AS.D.B	–	–	–	–		–	–	–	–	AS.D.B	–
CAR.D.B.	–	–	–	–		–	–	–	–	CAR.D.B.	–
E.E.C.	0.0	0.3	0.1	3.3		0.0	0.3	0.1	3.3	E.E.C.	0.0
IBRD	23.4	11.5	6.7	-5.4		–	–	–	–	IBRD	–
IDA	-0.2	-0.2	-0.2	-0.3		-0.2	-0.2	-0.2	-0.3	IDA	–
I.D.B.	42.1	52.4	77.4	52.0		38.0	40.5	39.9	21.6	I.D.B.	41.0
IFAD	1.3	1.8	2.0	2.0		1.3	1.8	2.0	2.0	IFAD	1.3
I.F.C.	-0.3	1.6	0.9	1.5		–	–	–	–	I.F.C.	–
IMF TRUST FUND	–	–	–	–		–	–	–	–	IMF TRUST FUND	–
U.N. AGENCIES										U.N. AGENCIES	
UNDP	1.9	1.9	1.4	1.1		1.9	1.9	1.4	1.1	UNDP	1.9
UNTA	0.5	0.4	0.7	0.5		0.5	0.4	0.7	0.5	UNTA	0.5
UNICEF	0.4	0.3	0.5	0.4		0.4	0.3	0.5	0.4	UNICEF	0.4
UNRWA	–	–	–	–		–	–	–	–	UNRWA	–
WFP	–	–	–	–		–	–	–	–	WFP	–
UNHCR	–	–	–	–		–	–	–	–	UNHCR	–
Other Multilateral	1.1	1.3	0.9	1.1		1.1	1.3	0.9	1.1	Other Multilateral	1.1
Arab OPEC Agencies	-0.2	-0.2	0.0	–		-0.2	-0.2	–	–	Arab OPEC Agencies	–
TOTAL	*70.0*	*70.9*	*90.3*	*56.2*		*42.8*	*46.0*	*45.2*	*29.7*	*TOTAL*	*46.2*
OPEC COUNTRIES	*0.6*	*26.1*	*36.3*	*25.6*		*2.6*	*9.6*	*14.5*	*13.1*	**OPEC COUNTRIES**	*2.6*
E.E.C.+ MEMBERS	*15.8*	*12.1*	*13.2*	*28.1*		*13.4*	*8.8*	*10.0*	*24.4*	*E.E.C.+ MEMBERS*	*13.4*
TOTAL	*120.0*	*262.2*	*311.3*	*377.6*		*102.4*	*197.8*	*221.8*	*105.6*	*TOTAL*	*116.0*

	1983	1984	1985	1986		1983	1984	1985	1986		1983
ODA LOANS GROSS					**ODA LOANS NET**					**GRANTS**	
DAC COUNTRIES											
Australia	–	–	–	–		–	–	–	–	Australia	–
Austria	–	–	–	–		–	–	–	–	Austria	0.0
Belgium	–	–	–	–		–	–	–	–	Belgium	0.2
Canada	0.1	0.3	0.2	–		-0.1	0.1	0.1	-0.1	Canada	1.6
Denmark	–	–	–	–		–	–	–	–	Denmark	–
Finland	–	–	–	–		–	–	–	–	Finland	–
France	–	–	–	1.2		–	–	–	1.1	France	0.7
Germany, Fed. Rep.	7.2	1.1	1.5	1.3		7.2	1.1	1.5	-0.2	Germany, Fed. Rep.	3.1
Ireland	–	–	–	–		–	–	–	–	Ireland	–
Italy	–	–	–	–		–	–	–	–	Italy	0.1
Japan	1.4	3.5	7.9	7.4		1.4	3.5	7.9	7.2	Japan	1.9
Netherlands	–	–	–	–		–	–	–	–	Netherlands	1.9
New Zealand	–	–	–	–		–	–	–	–	New Zealand	–
Norway	–	–	–	–		–	–	–	–	Norway	0.6
Sweden	–	–	–	–		–	–	–	–	Sweden	1.3
Switzerland	–	–	–	–		–	–	–	–	Switzerland	0.0
United Kingdom	–	–	–	–		–	–	–	–	United Kingdom	0.3
United States	37.0	69.0	45.0	37.0		27.0	64.0	40.0	16.0	United States	10.0
TOTAL	*45.7*	*73.8*	*54.6*	*46.9*		*35.5*	*68.7*	*49.5*	*23.9*	*TOTAL*	*21.5*
MULTILATERAL	*40.2*	*43.6*	*47.0*	*29.9*		*36.9*	*39.6*	*40.5*	*22.5*	*MULTILATERAL*	*5.9*
OPEC COUNTRIES	*2.6*	*9.6*	*14.5*	*13.1*		*2.6*	*9.6*	*14.5*	*13.1*	**OPEC COUNTRIES**	*–*
E.E.C.+ MEMBERS	*7.2*	*1.1*	*1.5*	*2.5*		*7.2*	*1.1*	*1.5*	*0.8*	*E.E.C.+ MEMBERS*	*6.2*
TOTAL	*88.5*	*126.9*	*116.1*	*89.8*		*74.9*	*117.9*	*104.5*	*59.4*	*TOTAL*	*27.5*

	1983	1984	1985	1986		1983	1984	1985	1986		1983
TOTAL OFFICIAL GROSS					**TOTAL OFFICIAL NET**					**TOTAL OOF GROSS**	
DAC COUNTRIES											
Australia	–	–	–	–		–	–	–	–	Australia	–
Austria	0.0	0.0	–	0.0		0.0	0.0	–	0.0	Austria	–
Belgium	0.2	0.1	0.1	0.2		0.2	0.1	0.1	0.2	Belgium	–
Canada	1.7	2.7	2.4	0.6		1.5	2.6	2.3	-1.4	Canada	–
Denmark	–	–	–	–		–	–	–	–	Denmark	–
Finland	–	–	–	–		–	–	–	–	Finland	–
France	0.7	0.4	0.5	2.1		0.7	0.4	0.5	1.9	France	–
Germany, Fed. Rep.	11.0	4.6	6.0	7.5		10.8	4.6	5.9	4.3	Germany, Fed. Rep.	0.7
Ireland	–	–	–	–		–	–	–	–	Ireland	–
Italy	0.1	2.3	2.3	11.9		0.1	2.3	2.3	11.9	Italy	–
Japan	3.3	3.5	10.0	12.6		3.3	3.5	10.0	12.4	Japan	–
Netherlands	1.9	2.4	2.6	1.4		1.9	2.4	2.6	1.4	Netherlands	–
New Zealand	–	–	–	–		–	–	–	–	New Zealand	–
Norway	0.6	0.0	0.4	0.1		0.6	0.0	0.4	0.1	Norway	–
Sweden	1.3	0.5	0.5	0.8		1.3	0.5	0.5	0.8	Sweden	–
Switzerland	0.0	0.0	–	0.0		0.0	0.0	–	0.0	Switzerland	–
United Kingdom	0.3	0.1	0.0	0.1		0.3	0.1	0.0	0.1	United Kingdom	–
United States	47.0	140.0	160.0	270.0		32.0	134.0	149.0	231.0	United States	–
TOTAL	*67.9*	*156.8*	*184.9*	*307.3*		*52.5*	*150.6*	*173.7*	*262.8*	*TOTAL*	*0.7*
MULTILATERAL	*77.9*	*85.0*	*106.7*	*81.6*		*70.0*	*70.9*	*90.3*	*56.2*	*MULTILATERAL*	*31.7*
OPEC COUNTRIES	*27.0*	*41.0*	*40.3*	*34.5*		*0.6*	*26.1*	*36.3*	*25.6*	**OPEC COUNTRIES**	*24.4*
E.E.C.+ MEMBERS	*14.1*	*10.2*	*11.7*	*26.5*		*13.9*	*10.2*	*11.5*	*23.2*	*E.E.C.+ MEMBERS*	*0.7*
TOTAL	*172.7*	*282.8*	*331.9*	*423.4*		*123.1*	*247.7*	*300.3*	*344.5*	*TOTAL*	*56.8*

1984	1985	1986	1983	1984	1985	1986

ODA COMMITMENTS

1984	1985	1986	1983	1984	1985	1986
–	–	–	–	–	–	–
0.0	–	0.0	0.0	0.0	–	–
0.1	0.1	0.2	–	–	–	0.2
2.7	2.4	0.6	1.6	9.4	1.7	0.7
–	–	–	–	–	–	–
–	–	–	–	–	–	–
0.4	0.5	2.1	3.5	3.0	0.5	2.1
4.0	5.7	7.1	7.9	3.9	8.0	16.2
–	–	–	–	–	–	–
2.3	2.3	11.9	2.5	5.4	5.4	8.1
3.5	10.0	12.6	39.5	2.6	4.1	70.0
1.6	1.3	1.4	1.7	1.7	1.2	1.1
–	–	–	–	–	–	–
0.0	0.4	0.1	–	0.2	0.3	0.0
0.5	0.5	0.8	–	0.5	1.0	0.8
0.0	–	0.0	–	–	–	–
0.1	0.0	0.1	0.3	0.1	0.0	0.1
132.0	144.0	49.0	54.2	153.0	151.0	62.8
147.4	*167.2*	*85.9*	*111.1*	*179.6*	*173.1*	*162.0*
–	–	–	–	–	–	–
–	–	–	–	–	–	–
–	–	–	–	–	–	–
0.3	0.1	3.3	0.1	4.8	0.7	0.6
–	–	–	–	–	–	–
44.2	46.1	28.7	28.2	18.5	–	–
1.8	2.0	2.0	–	0.2	–	–
–	–	–	–	–	–	–
–	–	–	3.8	3.8	3.5	3.1
1.9	1.4	1.1	–	–	–	–
0.4	0.7	0.5	–	–	–	–
0.3	0.5	0.4	–	–	–	–
–	–	–	–	–	–	–
–	–	–	–	–	–	–
1.3	0.9	1.1	–	–	–	–
-0.2						0.4
49.9	*51.7*	*37.1*	*32.2*	*27.2*	*4.1*	*4.1*
9.6	*14.5*	*13.1*	*–*	*42.4*	*38.8*	*–*
8.8	*10.0*	*26.1*	*15.9*	*18.7*	*15.8*	*28.2*
206.9	***233.4***	***136.0***	***143.2***	***249.2***	***216.1***	***166.1***

TECH. COOP. GRANTS

1984	1985	1986	1983	1984	1985	1986
–	–	–	–	–	–	–
0.0	–	0.0	0.0	–	–	–
0.1	0.1	0.2	–	0.0	–	–
2.5	2.2	0.6	0.4	–	0.5	–
–	–	–	–	–	–	–
0.4	0.5	0.9	0.5	0.4	0.5	0.6
2.9	4.2	5.8	3.1	2.9	4.2	5.7
–	–	–	–	–	–	–
2.3	2.3	11.9	0.1	0.4	0.4	4.6
0.1	2.1	5.2	1.7	0.1	2.1	3.3
1.6	1.3	1.4	1.4	1.0	1.1	1.0
–	–	–	–	–	–	–
0.0	0.4	0.1	–	0.0	0.3	0.0
0.5	0.5	0.8	1.3	0.5	0.5	–
0.0	–	0.0	0.0	0.0	–	0.0
0.1	0.0	0.1	0.3	0.1	0.0	0.1
63.0	99.0	12.0	4.0	5.0	7.0	7.0
73.6	*112.6*	*39.0*	*12.8*	*10.5*	*16.5*	*22.3*
6.3	*4.7*	*7.2*	*3.8*	*3.8*	*3.5*	*3.1*
–	–	–	–	–	–	–
7.8	*8.5*	*23.6*	*5.3*	*4.8*	*6.2*	*12.0*
79.9	***117.3***	***46.2***	***16.7***	***14.2***	***20.0***	***25.4***

TOTAL OOF NET

1984	1985	1986	1983	1984	1985	1986
–	–	–	–	–	–	–
–	–	–	–	–	–	–
–	–	–	–	–	–	-1.9
–	–	–	–	–	–	–
–	–	–	–	–	–	–
–	–	–	–	–	–	–
0.6	0.3	0.4	0.5	0.6	0.2	-1.2
–	–	–	–	–	–	–
–	–	–	–	–	–	–
0.8	1.4	–	–	0.8	1.4	–
–	–	–	–	–	–	–
–	–	–	–	–	–	–
–	–	–	–	–	–	–
–	–	–	–	–	–	–
8.0	16.0	221.0	-5.0	7.0	10.0	203.0
9.4	*17.7*	*221.4*	*-4.5*	*8.4*	*11.6*	*199.9*
35.1	*55.0*	*44.5*	*27.2*	*25.0*	*45.1*	*26.5*
31.5	*25.8*	*21.4*	*-1.9*	*16.6*	*21.8*	*12.5*
1.4	*1.7*	*0.4*	*0.5*	*1.4*	*1.6*	*-1.2*
75.9	***98.5***	***287.3***	***20.7***	***49.9***	***78.5***	***238.9***

ODA COMMITMENTS : LOANS

DAC COUNTRIES	1983	1984	1985	1986
Australia	–	–	–	–
Austria	–	–	–	–
Belgium	–	–	–	–
Canada	–	7.3	–	–
Denmark	–	–	–	–
Finland	–	–	–	–
France	3.0	2.6	–	1.2
Germany, Fed. Rep.	–	–	–	11.0
Ireland	–	–	–	–
Italy	–	–	–	–
Japan	37.4	0.3	0.4	64.4
Netherlands	–	–	–	–
New Zealand	–	–	–	–
Norway	–	–	–	–
Sweden	–	–	–	–
Switzerland	–	–	–	–
United Kingdom	–	–	–	–
United States	40.4	83.8	49.0	41.2
TOTAL	*80.8*	*93.9*	*49.5*	*117.9*
MULTILATERAL	*28.2*	*18.5*	*–*	*–*
OPEC COUNTRIES	*–*	*42.4*	*38.8*	*–*
E.E.C.+ MEMBERS	*3.0*	*2.6*	*–*	*12.2*
TOTAL	***109.0***	***154.9***	***88.3***	***117.9***

GRANT ELEMENT OF ODA

DAC COUNTRIES	1983	1984	1985	1986
Australia	–	–	–	–
Austria	100.0	100.0	–	–
Belgium	–	–	–	100.0
Canada	100.0	92.3	100.0	100.0
Denmark	–	–	–	–
Finland	–	–	–	–
France	100.0	72.9	100.0	100.0
Germany, Fed. Rep.	100.0	100.0	100.0	56.0
Ireland	–	–	–	–
Italy	100.0	100.0	100.0	100.0
Japan	45.3	91.8	92.0	42.8
Netherlands	100.0	100.0	100.0	100.0
New Zealand	–	–	–	–
Norway	–	100.0	100.0	100.0
Sweden	–	100.0	100.0	100.0
Switzerland	–	–	–	–
United Kingdom	100.0	100.0	100.0	100.0
United States	72.1	77.6	84.0	68.0
TOTAL	*66.1*	*79.9*	*85.8*	*58.2*
MULTILATERAL	*76.9*	*79.8*	*100.0*	*100.0*
OPEC COUNTRIES	*–*	*41.8*	*29.1*	*–*
E.E.C.+ MEMBERS	*100.0*	*95.7*	*100.0*	*73.6*
TOTAL	***71.4***	***74.1***	***75.9***	***59.2***

OTHER AGGREGATES

COMMITMENTS: ALL SOURCES

	1983	1984	1985	1986
TOTAL BILATERAL	141.5	258.6	249.5	385.0
of which				
OPEC	30.4	66.4	61.0	–
CMEA	–	–	–	–
TOTAL MULTILATERAL	123.3	214.2	191.2	153.1
TOTAL BIL.& MULTIL.	264.8	472.8	440.8	538.0
of which				
ODA Grants	34.2	94.4	127.8	48.2
ODA Loans	109.0	154.9	88.3	117.9

DISBURSEMENTS:

DAC COUNTRIES COMBINED

OFFICIAL & PRIVATE	1983	1984	1985	1986
GROSS:				
Contractual Lending	59.9	169.0	87.2	300.9
Export Credits Total	13.5	85.9	14.9	32.6
Export Credits Private	13.5	85.9	14.9	32.6
NET:				
Contractual Lending	-15.1	109.0	43.6	195.2
Export Credits Total	-50.1	30.9	-23.5	-47.5
PRIVATE SECTOR NET	-3.2	14.5	11.1	33.0
Direct Investment	0.0	–	0.2	3.5
Portfolio Investment	42.9	-17.4	28.4	58.1
Export Credits	-46.1	31.9	-17.5	-28.6

MARKET BORROWING:

CHANGE IN CLAIMS

	1983	1984	1985	1986
Banks	–	-104.0	10.0	-4.0

MEMORANDUM ITEM:

	1983	1984	1985	1986
CMEA Countr.(Gross)	–	–	–	–

DISBURSEMENTS, UNLESS OTHERWISE STATED

	1983	1984	1985	1986	1983	1984	1985	1986		1983
TOTAL RECEIPTS NET					**TOTAL ODA NET**				**TOTAL ODA GROSS**	
DAC COUNTRIES										
Australia	0.5	–	0.1	–	0.6	–	0.1	–	Australia	0.6
Austria	0.2	0.1	0.2	0.2	0.2	0.1	0.2	0.2	Austria	0.2
Belgium	2.9	45.1	-12.1	-14.2	1.7	5.9	1.7	2.5	Belgium	1.7
Canada	-2.1	1.1	6.0	3.7	1.3	1.2	1.2	0.5	Canada	1.7
Denmark	-0.2	-0.5	-2.4	-1.9	0.1	0.1	0.0	-0.1	Denmark	0.1
Finland	1.0	0.1	0.3	0.1	1.0	0.1	0.3	0.1	Finland	1.0
France	15.0	39.1	21.5	32.1	1.2	2.5	1.5	5.0	France	1.2
Germany, Fed. Rep.	25.2	10.2	21.8	17.0	9.0	7.4	8.7	13.7	Germany, Fed. Rep.	9.4
Ireland	0.0	0.0	0.0	0.0	0.0	0.0	0.0	0.0	Ireland	0.0
Italy	-3.3	10.6	-21.1	43.1	5.7	10.5	6.5	5.1	Italy	5.7
Japan	-12.0	198.5	93.0	115.5	2.6	2.0	1.9	2.9	Japan	3.1
Netherlands	7.1	-4.7	-0.3	17.6	1.5	1.6	1.8	2.6	Netherlands	1.5
New Zealand	–		0.0	0.0	–	–	0.0	0.0	New Zealand	–
Norway	-0.1	41.2	39.1	31.5	0.4	0.2	0.2	0.5	Norway	0.4
Sweden	24.3	11.8	13.2	20.0	1.0	0.2	0.2	0.2	Sweden	1.0
Switzerland	-5.0	2.0	-5.6	1.5	1.2	0.9	1.5	1.5	Switzerland	1.2
United Kingdom	3.4	-13.6	-7.0	-9.5	0.7	0.7	0.8	1.1	United Kingdom	1.1
United States	246.0	611.0	-198.0	469.0	9.0	28.0	44.0	50.0	United States	11.0
TOTAL	302.9	951.9	-51.3	725.7	37.3	61.4	70.8	85.6	TOTAL	41.0
MULTILATERAL										
AF.D.F.	–	–	–	–	–	–	–	–	AF.D.F.	–
AF.D.B.	–	–	–	–	–	–	–	–	AF.D.B.	–
AS.D.B	–	–	–	–	–	–	–	–	AS.D.B	–
CAR.D.B.	–	–	–	–	–	–	–	–	CAR.D.B.	–
E.E.C.	3.4	1.0	1.4	0.5	3.4	1.0	1.4	0.5	E.E.C.	3.4
IBRD	27.0	46.3	15.5	125.7	–	–	–	–	IBRD	–
IDA	-0.3	-0.5	-0.6	-0.6	-0.3	-0.5	-0.6	-0.6	IDA	–
I.D.B.	44.9	58.5	94.9	149.6	13.6	66.5	55.7	49.6	I.D.B.	17.6
IFAD		-0.2	0.3	–		-0.2	0.3	–	IFAD	–
I.F.C.	-0.9	-2.8	-4.1	-2.7	–	–	–	–	I.F.C.	–
IMF TRUST FUND	–	–	–	–	–	–	–	–	IMF TRUST FUND	–
U.N. AGENCIES	–	–	–	–	–	–	–	–	U.N. AGENCIES	
UNDP	2.5	2.9	2.5	5.5	2.5	2.9	2.5	5.5	UNDP	2.5
UNTA	1.2	1.2	1.0	1.0	1.2	1.2	1.0	1.0	UNTA	1.2
UNICEF	0.5	0.6	0.5	0.4	0.5	0.6	0.5	0.4	UNICEF	0.5
UNRWA	–	–	–	–	–	–	–	–	UNRWA	–
WFP	2.8	1.6	2.8	3.1	2.8	1.6	2.8	3.1	WFP	2.8
UNHCR	–	–	–	–	–	–	–	–	UNHCR	–
Other Multilateral	2.8	1.8	1.6	1.4	2.8	1.8	1.6	1.4	Other Multilateral	2.8
Arab OPEC Agencies		0.0				0.0			Arab OPEC Agencies	
TOTAL	83.8	110.3	115.8	283.9	26.4	74.8	65.1	60.9	TOTAL	30.8
OPEC COUNTRIES	-3.0	-3.1	–	–	–	–	–	–	OPEC COUNTRIES	–
E.E.C.+ MEMBERS	53.5	87.1	1.7	84.8	23.3	29.7	22.4	30.2	E.E.C.+ MEMBERS	24.2
TOTAL	383.7	1059.0	64.4	1009.6	63.7	136.2	135.8	146.5	TOTAL	71.8
ODA LOANS GROSS					**ODA LOANS NET**				**GRANTS**	
DAC COUNTRIES										
Australia	–	–	–	–	–	–	–	–	Australia	0.6
Austria	–	–	–	–	–	–	–	–	Austria	0.2
Belgium	–	3.5	–	–	–	3.5	–	–	Belgium	1.7
Canada	–	–	–	–	-0.4	-0.2	-0.2	-0.2	Canada	1.7
Denmark	–	–	–	–	0.0	0.0	0.0	-0.1	Denmark	0.1
Finland	0.9	–	0.3	–	0.9	–	0.3	–	Finland	0.1
France	–	–	0.1	1.8	–	–	0.1	1.8	France	1.2
Germany, Fed. Rep.	0.6	1.3	1.2	8.3	0.2	0.3	0.9	0.6	Germany, Fed. Rep.	8.8
Ireland	–	–	–	–	–	–	–	–	Ireland	0.0
Italy	–	–	–	–	–	–	–	–	Italy	5.7
Japan	–	0.8	3.4	7.2	-0.5	0.4	-0.1	-0.4	Japan	3.1
Netherlands	–	–	–	0.0	–	–	–	0.0	Netherlands	1.5
New Zealand	–	–	–	–	–	–	–	–	New Zealand	–
Norway	–	–	–	–	–	–	–	–	Norway	0.4
Sweden	–	–	–	–	–	–	–	–	Sweden	1.0
Switzerland	–	–	–	–	–	–	–	0.0	Switzerland	1.2
United Kingdom	–	–	–	–	-0.4	-0.1	0.0	-0.1	United Kingdom	1.1
United States	3.0	8.0	26.0	15.0	1.0	4.0	22.0	10.0	United States	8.0
TOTAL	4.5	13.6	31.0	32.3	0.8	7.9	22.9	11.6	TOTAL	36.5
MULTILATERAL	17.5	71.5	61.6	56.8	13.1	65.3	53.9	49.0	MULTILATERAL	13.4
OPEC COUNTRIES	–	–	–	–	–	–	–	–	OPEC COUNTRIES	–
E.E.C.+ MEMBERS	0.6	4.7	1.3	10.1	-0.2	3.7	1.0	2.3	E.E.C.+ MEMBERS	23.6
TOTAL	21.9	85.1	92.6	89.1	13.9	73.2	76.8	60.6	TOTAL	49.8
TOTAL OFFICIAL GROSS					**TOTAL OFFICIAL NET**				**TOTAL OOF GROSS**	
DAC COUNTRIES										
Australia	0.6	–	0.1	–	0.6	–	0.1	–	Australia	–
Austria	0.2	0.1	0.2	0.2	0.2	0.1	0.2	0.2	Austria	–
Belgium	1.7	7.3	1.8	3.5	1.7	7.3	1.8	3.5	Belgium	–
Canada	1.7	1.5	6.9	16.6	-2.1	1.1	6.0	3.3	Canada	–
Denmark	0.9	1.1	1.3	2.1	0.8	0.0	0.1	-0.9	Denmark	0.8
Finland	1.0	0.1	0.3	0.1	1.0	0.1	0.3	0.1	Finland	–
France	1.2	9.1	1.6	39.1	1.2	9.1	1.3	39.1	France	–
Germany, Fed. Rep.	11.0	15.0	10.9	26.2	10.3	12.4	8.7	14.5	Germany, Fed. Rep.	1.6
Ireland	0.0	0.0	0.0	0.0	0.0	0.0	0.0	0.0	Ireland	–
Italy	5.7	36.8	6.5	89.1	4.9	36.7	6.3	89.1	Italy	–
Japan	3.7	4.0	6.3	29.2	1.8	3.4	2.8	21.5	Japan	0.6
Netherlands	1.5	1.6	1.8	4.9	1.5	1.5	1.8	4.6	Netherlands	–
New Zealand	–	–	0.0	0.0	–	–	0.0	0.0	New Zealand	–
Norway	0.4	0.2	0.2	0.5	0.4	0.2	0.2	0.5	Norway	–
Sweden	11.3	11.5	14.2	24.5	11.3	11.5	14.2	22.3	Sweden	10.3
Switzerland	1.2	0.9	1.5	1.5	1.2	0.9	1.5	1.5	Switzerland	–
United Kingdom	1.2	1.2	1.2	1.2	0.8	1.2	1.2	1.1	United Kingdom	0.1
United States	13.0	49.0	57.0	71.0	7.0	42.0	53.0	61.0	United States	2.0
TOTAL	56.3	139.3	111.9	309.6	42.8	127.6	99.5	261.2	TOTAL	15.4
MULTILATERAL	109.4	148.0	173.1	358.3	83.8	110.3	115.8	283.9	MULTILATERAL	78.6
OPEC COUNTRIES	0.1	–	–	–	-3.0	-3.1	–	–	OPEC COUNTRIES	0.1
E.E.C.+ MEMBERS	26.6	73.0	26.5	166.5	24.8	69.2	22.5	151.4	E.E.C.+ MEMBERS	2.5
TOTAL	165.8	287.4	285.0	667.9	123.6	234.7	215.3	545.1	TOTAL	94.1

ECUADOR

ODA COMMITMENTS

1984	1985	1986	1983	1984	1985	1986
–	0.1	–	0.9	–	0.1	–
0.1	0.2	0.2	0.1	0.1	0.2	–
5.9	1.7	2.5	4.9	1.6	0.9	2.5
1.5	1.4	0.7	1.9	1.5	1.2	0.8
0.1			–	–	–	–
0.1	0.3	0.1	0.0	0.1	0.5	0.1
2.5	1.5	5.0	1.2	2.5	3.7	5.0
8.4	9.0	21.4	12.1	9.4	13.6	23.9
0.0	0.0	0.0	0.0	0.0	0.0	0.0
10.5	6.5	5.1	10.4	12.5	7.7	8.6
2.3	5.4	10.5	3.9	2.3	50.2	7.1
1.6	1.8	2.6	1.3	1.5	2.1	2.6
–	0.0	0.0	–	0.0	0.1	–
0.2	0.2	0.5	0.8	0.1	0.2	0.2
0.2	0.2	0.2	0.1	0.3	0.2	0.2
0.9	1.5	1.5	1.0	2.4	0.6	1.4
0.7	0.8	1.2	1.1	0.7	0.8	1.2
32.0	48.0	55.0	20.0	29.0	48.8	56.0
67.1	*78.8*	*106.3*	*59.6*	*63.9*	*130.9*	*109.6*
–	–	–	–	–	–	–
–	–	–	–	–	–	–
1.0	1.4	0.5	6.6	0.3	0.8	0.8
–	–	–	–	–	–	–
72.0	62.8	56.8	44.9	54.4	38.4	50.4
–	0.4	–	5.4	–	–	–
–	–	–	–	–	–	–
–	–	–	9.8	8.0	8.2	11.4
2.9	2.5	5.5	–	–	–	–
1.2	1.0	1.0	–	–	–	–
0.6	0.5	0.4	–	–	–	–
1.6	2.8	3.1	–	–	–	–
1.8	1.6	1.4	–	–	–	–
0.0	–	–	–	–	–	–
81.0	*72.8*	*68.7*	*66.7*	*62.7*	*47.5*	*62.6*
–	–	–	–	–	–	–
30.7	22.8	38.1	37.5	28.5	29.6	44.5
148.1	*151.6*	*175.0*	*126.3*	*126.7*	*178.3*	*172.2*

TECH. COOP. GRANTS

1984	1985	1986	1983	1984	1985	1986
–	0.1	–	0.1	–	–	–
0.1	0.2	0.2	0.1	–	–	–
2.5	1.7	2.5	1.1	0.8	0.9	1.5
1.5	1.4	0.7	0.7	–	0.3	–
0.1	–	–	0.1	0.1	–	–
0.1	0.0	0.1	0.0	0.0	0.0	–
2.5	1.5	3.2	1.2	2.5	1.5	3.2
7.1	7.8	13.1	8.3	7.2	7.7	12.7
0.0	0.0	0.0	0.0	0.0	0.0	0.0
10.5	6.5	5.1	2.3	9.5	4.9	4.9
1.5	2.0	3.3	1.2	0.8	1.8	3.3
1.6	1.8	2.5	1.2	1.4	1.7	2.4
–	0.0	0.0	–	–	0.0	0.0
0.2	0.2	0.5	0.0	0.1	0.0	0.0
0.2	0.2	0.2	0.1	0.2	0.2	0.2
0.9	1.5	1.5	0.4	0.4	0.3	0.2
0.7	0.8	1.2	1.0	0.7	0.8	1.2
24.0	22.0	40.0	4.0	8.0	8.0	14.0
53.5	*47.9*	*74.0*	*21.9*	*31.8*	*28.2*	*43.6*
9.5	*11.2*	*11.9*	*7.0*	*6.4*	*5.5*	*8.3*
–	–	–	–	–	–	–
26.0	*21.5*	*27.9*	*15.2*	*22.4*	*17.5*	*25.8*
63.1	*59.1*	*85.9*	*28.8*	*38.2*	*33.6*	*51.9*

TOTAL OOF NET

1984	1985	1986	1983	1984	1985	1986
–	–	–	–	–	–	–
1.4	0.1	1.0	–	1.4	0.1	1.0
–	5.5	15.9	-3.4	-0.1	4.8	2.8
1.0	1.3	2.1	0.8	-0.1	0.1	-0.8
6.6	0.1	34.2	–	6.6	-0.3	34.2
6.5	1.9	4.8	1.4	5.0	–	0.8
26.3	–	84.0	-0.8	26.1	-0.2	84.0
1.6	0.9	18.7	-0.7	1.5	0.9	18.5
–	–	2.3	–	0.0	0.0	2.0
–	–	–	–	–	–	–
11.4	14.0	24.3	10.3	11.4	14.0	22.0
0.5	0.3	0.1	0.1	0.5	0.3	0.1
17.0	9.0	16.0	-2.0	14.0	9.0	11.0
72.3	33.1	203.3	5.6	66.2	28.8	175.6
67.0	100.3	289.7	57.4	35.5	50.7	223.1
–	–	–	-3.0	-3.1	–	–
42.3	3.8	128.4	1.4	39.5	0.1	121.2
139.3	*133.4*	*493.0*	*59.9*	*98.5*	*79.5*	*398.6*

ODA COMMITMENTS : LOANS

DAC COUNTRIES	1983	1984	1985	1986
Australia	–	–	–	–
Austria	–	–	–	–
Belgium	3.9	–	–	–
Canada	–	–	–	–
Denmark	–	–	–	–
Finland	–	–	0.5	–
France	–	–	2.2	1.8
Germany, Fed. Rep.	–	1.7	3.4	7.4
Ireland	–	–	–	–
Italy	–	–	–	–
Japan	–	1.5	48.0	3.5
Netherlands	–	–	–	0.0
New Zealand	–	–	–	–
Norway	–	–	–	–
Sweden	–	–	–	–
Switzerland	–	–	–	–
United Kingdom	–	–	–	–
United States	6.0	14.0	21.3	13.8
TOTAL	*9.9*	*17.2*	*75.4*	*26.6*
MULTILATERAL	*50.3*	*54.4*	*38.4*	*50.4*
OPEC COUNTRIES	–	–	–	–
E.E.C.+ MEMBERS	*3.9*	*1.7*	*5.6*	*9.3*
TOTAL	*60.2*	*71.6*	*113.8*	*77.0*

GRANT ELEMENT OF ODA

DAC COUNTRIES	1983	1984	1985	1986
Australia	100.0	–	100.0	–
Austria	100.0	100.0	100.0	–
Belgium	84.8	100.0	100.0	100.0
Canada	100.0	100.0	100.0	100.0
Denmark	–	–	–	–
Finland	100.0	100.0	–	100.0
France	100.0	100.0	80.6	85.4
Germany, Fed. Rep.	100.0	85.5	84.2	75.4
Ireland	100.0	100.0	100.0	100.0
Italy	100.0	100.0	100.0	100.0
Japan	100.0	100.0	39.3	56.1
Netherlands	100.0	100.0	100.0	100.0
New Zealand	–	100.0	100.0	–
Norway	100.0	100.0	100.0	100.0
Sweden	100.0	100.0	100.0	100.0
Switzerland	100.0	100.0	100.0	100.0
United Kingdom	100.0	100.0	100.0	100.0
United States	89.7	83.3	77.4	89.0
TOTAL	*95.3*	*90.1*	*66.0*	*85.5*
MULTILATERAL	*79.2*	*76.0*	*100.0*	*76.7*
OPEC COUNTRIES	–	–	–	–
E.E.C.+ MEMBERS	*98.0*	*95.2*	*90.3*	*85.2*
TOTAL	*84.3*	*82.5*	*68.2*	*82.3*

OTHER AGGREGATES

COMMITMENTS: ALL SOURCES

	1983	1984	1985	1986
TOTAL BILATERAL	72.7	151.3	165.7	266.8
of which				
OPEC	0.2	–	0.1	–
CMEA	–	–	–	–
TOTAL MULTILATERAL	105.1	314.7	389.5	517.4
TOTAL BIL.& MULTIL.	177.8	466.0	555.2	784.2
of which				
ODA Grants	66.1	55.0	64.5	95.2
ODA Loans	60.2	71.6	113.8	77.0

DISBURSEMENTS:

DAC COUNTRIES COMBINED

	1983	1984	1985	1986
OFFICIAL & PRIVATE				
GROSS:				
Contractual Lending	113.6	269.3	311.7	465.5
Export Credits Total	106.4	198.8	268.1	289.3
Export Credits Private	93.8	183.6	247.7	230.0
NET:				
Contractual Lending	-16.0	152.3	161.4	196.0
Export Credits Total	-19.5	88.2	127.6	42.8
PRIVATE SECTOR NET	260.1	824.3	-150.8	464.5
Direct Investment	37.6	-75.7	44.5	165.9
Portfolio Investment	244.9	821.7	-305.1	289.7
Export Credits	-22.4	78.4	109.8	8.9

MARKET BORROWING:

CHANGE IN CLAIMS

	1983	1984	1985	1986
Banks	–	-129.0	204.0	119.0

MEMORANDUM ITEM:

	1983	1984	1985	1986
CMEA Countr.(Gross)	–	–	–	–

	1983	1984	1985	1986	1983	1984	1985	1986	1983
TOTAL RECEIPTS NET					**TOTAL ODA NET**				**TOTAL ODA GROSS**
DAC COUNTRIES									
Australia	-170.7	9.7	130.0	82.8	12.5	6.7	0.4	6.6	Australia 12.5
Austria	35.3	20.3	27.6	15.2	15.8	17.6	19.2	15.8	Austria 17.0
Belgium	-4.3	39.3	61.3	-2.9	0.1	3.4	0.5	0.8	Belgium 0.1
Canada	-9.0	17.7	-12.0	-37.8	6.2	11.0	8.4	5.4	Canada 6.2
Denmark	23.8	0.1	6.9	-5.6	1.0	4.6	1.7	0.1	Denmark 1.8
Finland	3.2	11.2	5.6	13.0	2.2	7.4	5.0	7.6	Finland 2.2
France	410.7	772.3	358.8	676.6	20.3	49.3	38.0	91.3	France 21.9
Germany, Fed. Rep.	282.8	246.7	129.4	140.2	97.0	138.9	131.5	92.2	Germany, Fed. Rep. 98.7
Ireland	–	0.1	0.0	0.0	–	0.1	0.0	0.0	Ireland –
Italy	665.5	73.8	76.8	2.5	10.3	38.5	11.5	24.2	Italy 11.9
Japan	43.6	109.9	60.4	255.9	50.4	81.5	73.0	125.7	Japan 60.0
Netherlands	32.9	19.8	24.1	26.7	12.6	18.3	11.1	26.7	Netherlands 12.8
New Zealand	–	–	–	0.0	–	–	–	0.0	New Zealand –
Norway	-3.9	64.5	59.4	68.4	1.2	0.5	0.4	0.3	Norway 1.2
Sweden	29.4	9.4	-13.9	4.7	2.0	1.3	2.1	0.5	Sweden 2.0
Switzerland	76.6	32.4	-32.6	0.2	1.8	0.2	0.4	0.2	Switzerland 1.8
United Kingdom	23.2	12.1	85.1	77.1	14.8	19.5	23.7	21.9	United Kingdom 16.0
United States	1444.0	1375.0	1747.0	1061.0	993.0	1252.0	1354.0	1147.0	United States 1040.0
TOTAL	**2883.1**	**2814.4**	**2714.0**	**2378.0**	**1241.0**	**1650.6**	**1680.8**	**1566.2**	**TOTAL 1305.9**
MULTILATERAL									
AF.D.F.	11.5	3.9	0.7	7.2	11.5	3.9	0.7	7.2	AF.D.F. 11.5
AF.D.B.	8.6	8.8	8.5	19.3	–	–	–	–	AF.D.B. –
AS.D.B	–	–	–	–	–	–	–	–	AS.D.B –
CAR.D.B.	–	–	–	–	–	–	–	–	CAR.D.B. –
E.E.C.	60.8	60.7	40.0	57.0	35.5	38.0	34.3	22.6	E.E.C. 35.5
IBRD	112.1	161.1	148.3	71.1	5.6	4.7	12.8	1.6	IBRD 5.6
IDA	141.6	97.7	50.3	33.9	141.6	97.7	50.3	33.9	IDA 142.6
I.D.B.	–	–	–	–	–	–	–	–	I.D.B. –
IFAD	0.7	1.7	7.1	8.4	0.7	1.7	7.1	8.4	IFAD 0.7
I.F.C.	-1.9	0.1	2.7	12.6	–	–	–	–	I.F.C. –
IMF TRUST FUND	–	–	–	–	–	–	–	–	IMF TRUST FUND –
U.N. AGENCIES									U.N. AGENCIES
UNDP	7.6	5.0	5.1	8.4	7.6	5.0	5.1	8.4	UNDP 7.6
UNTA	1.9	2.0	1.8	1.7	1.9	2.0	1.8	1.7	UNTA 1.9
UNICEF	6.2	4.0	5.3	4.8	6.2	4.0	5.3	4.8	UNICEF 6.2
UNRWA	–	–	–	–	–	–	–	–	UNRWA –
WFP	38.2	10.6	19.0	7.3	38.2	10.6	19.0	7.3	WFP 38.2
UNHCR	2.6	2.3	1.8	1.3	2.6	2.3	1.8	1.3	UNHCR 2.6
Other Multilateral	4.1	5.9	4.7	4.5	4.1	5.9	4.7	4.5	Other Multilateral 4.1
Arab OPEC Agencies	-7.5	-8.2	-7.7	-5.4	-7.5	-8.2	-7.7	-5.4	Arab OPEC Agencies –
TOTAL	**386.3**	**355.7**	**287.6**	**232.1**	**247.9**	**167.7**	**135.2**	**96.3**	**TOTAL 256.4**
OPEC COUNTRIES	**-137.8**	**-75.4**	**-49.7**	**10.4**	**-51.0**	**-49.6**	**-49.7**	**4.2**	**OPEC COUNTRIES 7.1**
E.E.C.+ MEMBERS	**1495.4**	**1225.0**	**782.5**	**971.6**	**191.7**	**310.6**	**252.2**	**279.8**	**E.E.C.+ MEMBERS 198.8**
TOTAL	**3131.6**	**3094.7**	**2951.9**	**2620.5**	**1437.9**	**1768.7**	**1766.3**	**1666.6**	**TOTAL 1569.5**
ODA LOANS GROSS					**ODA LOANS NET**				**GRANTS**
DAC COUNTRIES									
Australia	–	–	–	–	–	–	–	–	Australia 12.5
Austria	15.7	21.4	19.8	14.7	14.5	16.4	17.7	13.3	Austria 1.3
Belgium	–	3.0	–	0.4	–	3.0	–	0.4	Belgium 0.1
Canada	4.1	6.5	3.7	1.1	4.1	6.5	3.7	0.3	Canada 2.1
Denmark	1.7	5.2	2.5	1.2	0.9	4.4	1.5	-0.1	Denmark 0.2
Finland	–	4.0	1.1	1.2	–	4.0	1.1	1.2	Finland 2.2
France	13.5	32.6	26.0	62.1	11.9	31.5	22.8	60.4	France 8.4
Germany, Fed. Rep.	80.4	124.7	119.6	65.4	78.7	120.1	112.9	44.7	Germany, Fed. Rep. 18.3
Ireland	–	–	–	–	–	–	–	–	Ireland –
Italy	–	26.0	1.3	9.6	-1.6	24.6	0.0	7.9	Italy 11.9
Japan	41.5	73.7	64.8	111.1	31.9	54.3	42.3	79.3	Japan 18.5
Netherlands	5.5	12.2	5.2	6.2	5.3	11.4	4.1	5.0	Netherlands 7.3
New Zealand	–	–	–	–	–	–	–	–	New Zealand –
Norway	0.8	–	–	–	0.8	–	–	–	Norway 0.3
Sweden	–	–	–	–	–	–	–	–	Sweden 2.0
Switzerland	1.6	–	0.6	–	1.6	0.0	0.4	–	Switzerland 0.1
United Kingdom	0.9	3.2	2.9	1.5	-0.3	2.1	1.8	0.3	United Kingdom 15.1
United States	352.0	286.0	267.0	228.0	305.0	244.0	220.0	186.0	United States 688.0
TOTAL	**517.6**	**598.5**	**514.4**	**502.4**	**452.7**	**522.4**	**428.2**	**398.6**	**TOTAL 788.3**
MULTILATERAL	**160.4**	**108.1**	**72.9**	**53.6**	**151.8**	**99.9**	**63.1**	**44.7**	**MULTILATERAL 96.0**
OPEC COUNTRIES	**7.0**	**3.1**	**3.0**	**6.9**	**-51.0**	**-49.7**	**-49.9**	**-44.5**	**OPEC COUNTRIES 0.1**
E.E.C.+ MEMBERS	**102.0**	**206.9**	**157.4**	**146.4**	**94.9**	**197.1**	**143.1**	**118.5**	**E.E.C.+ MEMBERS 96.8**
TOTAL	**685.1**	**709.7**	**590.3**	**562.9**	**553.5**	**572.6**	**441.4**	**398.7**	**TOTAL 884.4**
TOTAL OFFICIAL GROSS					**TOTAL OFFICIAL NET**				**TOTAL OOF GROSS**
DAC COUNTRIES									
Australia	12.5	6.7	0.4	6.6	12.0	6.2	0.0	6.2	Australia –
Austria	18.6	22.6	21.2	17.2	17.4	17.3	18.7	15.2	Austria 1.6
Belgium	0.1	7.3	5.1	0.8	0.1	7.3	5.1	0.8	Belgium –
Canada	8.1	66.0	26.1	11.8	-8.7	18.0	-11.9	-37.7	Canada 1.9
Denmark	23.1	8.1	8.3	3.4	20.3	5.4	5.4	-2.6	Denmark 21.2
Finland	2.2	7.4	5.0	7.6	2.2	7.4	5.0	7.6	Finland –
France	21.9	50.5	41.2	93.0	20.3	49.3	38.0	91.3	France –
Germany, Fed. Rep.	135.9	148.8	175.2	155.2	118.5	123.9	148.4	105.6	Germany, Fed. Rep. 37.2
Ireland	–	0.1	0.0	0.0	–	0.1	0.0	0.0	Ireland –
Italy	11.9	72.1	34.8	27.0	5.5	65.8	25.4	12.2	Italy –
Japan	60.0	100.8	95.6	157.5	50.4	81.5	73.0	125.7	Japan –
Netherlands	12.8	19.1	12.2	28.0	12.6	18.3	11.1	26.7	Netherlands –
New Zealand	–	–	–	0.0	–	–	–	0.0	New Zealand –
Norway	1.2	0.5	0.4	0.3	1.2	0.5	0.4	0.3	Norway –
Sweden	40.4	8.1	19.1	13.9	31.2	2.9	-13.9	4.7	Sweden 38.4
Switzerland	1.8	0.2	0.7	0.2	1.8	0.2	0.4	0.2	Switzerland –
United Kingdom	16.0	20.6	24.8	23.1	14.8	19.5	23.7	21.9	United Kingdom –
United States	1083.0	1358.0	1511.0	1191.0	1032.0	1297.0	1441.0	1114.0	United States 43.0
TOTAL	**1449.3**	**1896.8**	**1980.9**	**1736.5**	**1331.6**	**1720.6**	**1769.8**	**1492.0**	**TOTAL 143.4**
MULTILATERAL	**435.6**	**417.9**	**375.9**	**357.9**	**386.3**	**355.7**	**287.6**	**232.0**	**MULTILATERAL 179.2**
OPEC COUNTRIES	**13.4**	**9.4**	**9.4**	**61.9**	**-137.8**	**-75.4**	**-49.7**	**10.4**	**OPEC COUNTRIES 6.3**
E.E.C.+ MEMBERS	**284.2**	**389.8**	**346.7**	**394.1**	**252.9**	**350.3**	**297.1**	**312.9**	**E.E.C.+ MEMBERS 85.4**
TOTAL	**1898.3**	**2324.1**	**2366.2**	**2156.2**	**1580.0**	**2000.9**	**2007.7**	**1734.5**	**TOTAL 328.8**

ODA COMMITMENTS

1984	1985	1986	1983	1984	1985	1986
6.7	0.4	6.6	8.1	6.3	9.4	6.6
22.6	21.2	17.2	36.3	35.2	1.6	–
3.4	0.5	0.8	3.4	–	–	0.4
11.0	8.4	6.1	9.6	20.3	24.0	2.8
5.4	2.7	1.4	16.4	–	0.1	27.8
7.4	5.0	7.6	1.1	33.4	8.3	2.9
50.5	41.2	93.0	59.8	17.8	86.1	93.0
143.5	138.2	112.9	78.3	142.5	128.5	143.7
0.1	0.0	0.0	–	0.1	0.0	0.0
39.9	12.8	25.8	21.4	26.2	29.0	42.9
100.8	95.6	157.5	238.9	79.1	90.5	88.6
19.1	12.2	28.0	22.0	17.8	6.2	23.7
–	–	0.0	–	–	–	–
0.5	0.4	0.3	–	0.3	0.2	0.4
1.3	2.1	0.5	0.8	1.3	1.9	0.5
0.2	0.7	0.2	0.0	12.9	0.0	0.1
20.6	24.8	23.1	14.3	45.8	23.6	12.3
1294.0	1401.0	1189.0	911.7	1296.7	1444.0	1130.1
1726.7	*1767.0*	*1670.0*	*1422.0*	*1735.6*	*1853.5*	*1575.7*
3.9	0.7	7.2	–	13.6	20.2	–
–	–	–	–	–	–	–
–	–	–	–	–	–	–
38.0	34.3	22.6	40.9	51.5	37.6	49.7
4.7	12.8	1.6	–	–	–	–
99.1	52.4	36.3	–	–	–	–
1.7	7.1	8.4	–	9.9	–	–
–	–	–	–	–	–	–
–	–	–	60.5	29.9	37.8	27.9
5.0	5.1	8.4	–	–	–	–
2.0	1.8	1.7	–	–	–	–
4.0	5.3	4.8	–	–	–	–
–	–	–	–	–	–	–
10.6	19.0	7.3	–	–	–	–
2.3	1.8	1.3	–	–	–	–
5.9	4.7	4.5	–	–	–	–
-1.3	–	1.0	–	–	–	–
176.0	*145.0*	*105.1*	*101.4*	*104.8*	*95.6*	*77.6*
3.2	*3.2*	*55.6*	*0.1*	–	*0.2*	*55.0*
320.3	*266.6*	*307.7*	*256.4*	*301.7*	*311.2*	*393.4*
1905.8	*1915.1*	*1830.8*	*1523.5*	*1840.4*	*1949.3*	*1708.3*

TECH. COOP. GRANTS

1984	1985	1986	1983	1984	1985	1986
6.7	0.4	6.6	0.2	0.0	0.2	0.0
1.2	1.4	2.5	1.1	–	–	–
0.4	0.5	0.4	0.0	0.1	0.1	–
4.4	4.7	5.1	1.0	–	0.9	–
0.2	0.2	0.3	0.2	0.7	0.3	0.3
3.4	3.9	6.4	1.3	1.5	1.7	5.0
17.8	15.2	30.9	8.4	8.6	7.6	12.0
18.8	18.6	47.5	18.1	16.2	17.4	22.8
0.1	0.0	0.0	–	0.1	0.0	0.0
13.9	11.5	16.3	8.5	9.0	5.1	10.4
27.2	30.8	46.4	8.3	10.4	10.0	11.6
6.9	7.1	21.8	3.4	3.8	4.0	5.0
–	–	0.0	–	–	–	–
0.5	0.4	0.3	0.1	0.2	0.2	0.1
1.3	2.1	0.5	0.0	–	0.5	0.5
0.2	0.1	0.2	0.1	0.1	0.0	0.1
17.4	21.9	21.6	9.7	8.3	6.0	8.0
1008.0	1134.0	961.0	419.0	568.0	518.0	421.0
1128.3	*1252.6*	*1167.6*	*479.4*	*626.7*	*572.0*	*496.8*
67.9	*72.1*	*51.6*	*22.4*	*19.2*	*18.8*	*20.6*
0.1	*0.2*	*48.7*	–	–	–	–
113.4	*109.2*	*161.3*	*48.2*	*46.5*	*40.5*	*58.5*
1196.2	*1324.9*	*1267.9*	*501.7*	*645.9*	*590.8*	*517.4*

TOTAL OOF NET

1984	1985	1986	1983	1984	1985	1986
–	–	–	-0.5	-0.5	-0.4	-0.3
			1.6	-0.4	-0.5	-0.7
3.9	4.6	–	–	3.9	4.6	–
55.0	17.7	5.7	-14.8	7.0	-20.3	-43.1
2.7	5.6	2.0	19.3	0.8	3.7	-2.7
–	–	–	–	–	–	–
5.3	37.0	42.3	21.5	-14.9	16.9	13.4
32.2	22.0	1.1	-4.8	27.3	13.9	-12.0
–	–	–	–	–	–	–
–	–	–	–	–	–	–
–	–	–	–	–	–	–
6.9	17.0	13.3	29.2	1.7	-16.0	4.2
–	–	–	–	–	–	–
64.0	110.0	2.0	39.0	45.0	87.0	-33.0
170.0	*213.9*	*66.4*	*90.5*	*69.9*	*89.0*	*-74.2*
242.0	*230.9*	*252.8*	*138.5*	*188.0*	*152.4*	*135.8*
6.3	*6.3*	*6.3*	*-86.9*	*-25.8*	–	*6.3*
69.5	*80.1*	*86.5*	*61.3*	*39.7*	*44.9*	*33.1*
418.2	*451.1*	*325.5*	*142.1*	*232.1*	*241.4*	*67.9*

ODA COMMITMENTS : LOANS

DAC COUNTRIES

	1983	1984	1985	1986
Australia	–	–	–	–
Austria	32.9	34.4	0.2	–
Belgium	3.4	–	–	–
Canada	5.1	–	2.1	–
Denmark	16.4	–	–	27.8
Finland	–	29.1	–	–
France	45.8	–	71.9	62.1
Germany, Fed. Rep.	54.9	123.2	100.9	86.3
Ireland	–	–	–	–
Italy	–	–	6.0	14.2
Japan	209.3	55.1	56.4	52.0
Netherlands	13.5	12.6	–	4.4
New Zealand	–	–	–	–
Norway	–	–	–	–
Sweden	–	–	–	–
Switzerland	–	12.8	–	–
United Kingdom	–	–	–	–
United States	9.5	457.1	213.2	191.5
TOTAL	*390.8*	*724.3*	*450.6*	*438.3*
MULTILATERAL	–	*25.8*	*20.2*	–
OPEC COUNTRIES	–	–	–	–
E.E.C.+ MEMBERS	*134.1*	*138.2*	*178.8*	*194.8*
TOTAL	*390.8*	*750.1*	*470.9*	*438.3*

GRANT ELEMENT OF ODA

DAC COUNTRIES

	1983	1984	1985	1986
Australia	100.0	100.0	100.0	100.0
Austria	36.6	32.2	93.9	30.0
Belgium	84.4	–	84.5	100.0
Canada	94.8	100.0	99.1	100.0
Denmark	75.7	–	100.0	75.3
Finland	100.0	73.1	100.0	100.0
France	69.8	100.0	71.4	78.0
Germany, Fed. Rep.	68.6	66.1	75.6	66.4
Ireland	–	100.0	100.0	100.0
Italy	100.0	100.0	88.9	82.1
Japan	60.0	67.3	63.3	72.4
Netherlands	75.4	71.5	100.0	92.7
New Zealand	–	–	–	–
Norway	–	100.0	100.0	100.0
Sweden	100.0	100.0	100.0	100.0
Switzerland	100.0	81.8	100.0	100.0
United Kingdom	100.0	100.0	100.0	100.0
United States	99.7	88.7	95.3	94.6
TOTAL	*87.7*	*85.0*	*91.3*	*88.5*
MULTILATERAL	*100.0*	*91.9*	*96.4*	*100.0*
OPEC COUNTRIES	*100.0*	–	*100.0*	*100.0*
E.E.C.+ MEMBERS	*79.5*	*82.2*	*81.0*	*78.4*
TOTAL	*88.5*	*85.4*	*91.6*	*89.4*

OTHER AGGREGATES

COMMITMENTS: ALL SOURCES

	1983	1984	1985	1986
TOTAL BILATERAL	1693.6	2339.6	1998.1	1769.9
of which				
OPEC	0.1	–	0.2	55.0
CMEA	100.0	329.0	100.0	100.0
TOTAL MULTILATERAL	596.3	676.8	462.2	374.8
TOTAL BIL.& MULTIL.	2289.9	3016.3	2460.3	2144.6
of which				
ODA Grants	1132.7	1090.2	1478.5	1270.0
ODA Loans	390.8	900.1	570.9	438.3

DISBURSEMENTS:

DAC COUNTRIES COMBINED

	1983	1984	1985	1986
OFFICIAL & PRIVATE				
GROSS:				
Contractual Lending	2667.7	2427.0	2097.8	2251.1
Export Credits Total	2147.0	1828.3	1582.2	1747.5
Export Credits Private	2006.8	1662.4	1374.1	1682.3
NET:				
Contractual Lending	1582.2	1407.7	1106.5	1240.9
Export Credits Total	1137.1	895.4	687.7	856.0
PRIVATE SECTOR NET	1551.6	1093.8	944.2	886.0
Direct Investment	383.6	208.3	475.5	-73.3
Portfolio Investment	129.1	66.2	-125.2	42.8
Export Credits	1038.9	819.3	593.9	916.5

MARKET BORROWING:

CHANGE IN CLAIMS

	1983	1984	1985	1986
Banks	–	599.0	-63.0	-484.0

MEMORANDUM ITEM:

	1983	1984	1985	1986
CMEA Countr.(Gross)	2.6	13.3	36.2	14.0

EL SALVADOR

TOTAL RECEIPTS NET

DAC COUNTRIES	1983	1984	1985	1986
Australia	–	0.1	0.1	0.1
Austria	0.1	0.0	0.0	0.2
Belgium	0.0	0.1	0.2	0.4
Canada	1.7	2.0	1.2	3.3
Denmark	0.3	0.2	–	–
Finland	0.1	0.1	–	0.6
France	-2.2	-1.0	-1.4	-14.6
Germany, Fed. Rep.	3.4	1.9	7.9	22.7
Ireland	–	–	–	0.0
Italy	-2.3	-1.0	9.2	10.7
Japan	-0.4	-1.4	-2.4	-1.7
Netherlands	0.9	3.9	1.4	2.7
New Zealand	–	–	–	0.0
Norway	0.3	0.5	0.3	1.0
Sweden	–	0.0	0.0	0.8
Switzerland	-40.5	0.2	0.7	0.9
United Kingdom	0.0	0.1	-0.5	0.4
United States	229.0	219.0	285.0	271.0
TOTAL	*190.5*	*224.7*	*301.8*	*298.4*
MULTILATERAL				
AF.D.F.	–	–	–	–
AF.D.B.	–	–	–	–
AS.D.B	–	–	–	–
CAR.D.B.	–	–	–	–
E.E.C.	0.3	0.8	0.3	1.0
IBRD	0.9	5.9	6.4	-4.0
IDA	-0.3	-0.3	-0.3	-0.6
I.D.B.	111.0	52.8	47.9	19.3
IFAD	–	–	0.5	4.1
I.F.C.	–	–	–	–
IMF TRUST FUND	–	–	–	–
U.N. AGENCIES	–	–	–	–
UNDP	1.7	1.5	1.5	2.2
UNTA	0.8	0.5	0.5	0.6
UNICEF	0.3	0.4	0.2	0.5
UNRWA	–	–	–	–
WFP	7.3	6.9	15.9	9.2
UNHCR	–	–	–	0.1
Other Multilateral	1.0	0.7	0.6	0.3
Arab OPEC Agencies	-0.1	-0.1	–	-0.1
TOTAL	*122.8*	*69.0*	*73.5*	*32.4*
OPEC COUNTRIES	*24.0*	*9.4*	*3.8*	*-3.4*
E.E.C.+ MEMBERS	*0.6*	*5.0*	*17.1*	*23.2*
TOTAL	**337.3**	**303.0**	**379.0**	**327.5**

TOTAL ODA NET

DAC COUNTRIES	1983	1984	1985	1986
Australia	–	0.1	0.1	0.1
Austria	0.1	0.0	0.0	0.2
Belgium	0.1	0.1	0.2	0.4
Canada	1.7	2.0	1.2	3.3
Denmark	0.3	0.2	–	–
Finland	0.1	0.1	–	0.6
France	0.1	0.0	0.1	0.0
Germany, Fed. Rep.	3.3	2.2	8.2	22.6
Ireland	–	–	–	0.0
Italy	0.1	0.1	10.3	10.7
Japan	0.5	-0.8	-3.5	-1.0
Netherlands	1.7	1.7	1.7	4.3
New Zealand	–	–	–	0.0
Norway	0.3	0.5	0.3	1.0
Sweden	–	0.0	0.0	0.8
Switzerland	0.1	0.1	0.7	0.9
United Kingdom	–	–	0.3	0.4
United States	231.0	221.0	287.0	272.0
TOTAL	*239.2*	*227.6*	*306.4*	*316.3*
AF.D.F.	–	–	–	–
AF.D.B.	–	–	–	–
AS.D.B	–	–	–	–
CAR.D.B.	–	–	–	–
E.E.C.	0.3	0.8	0.3	1.0
IBRD	–	–	–	–
IDA	-0.3	-0.3	-0.3	-0.6
I.D.B.	40.1	23.2	19.6	7.3
IFAD	–	–	0.5	4.1
I.F.C.	–	–	–	–
IMF TRUST FUND	–	–	–	–
U.N. AGENCIES	–	–	–	–
UNDP	1.7	1.5	1.5	2.2
UNTA	0.8	0.5	0.5	0.6
UNICEF	0.3	0.4	0.2	0.5
UNRWA	–	–	–	–
WFP	7.3	6.9	15.9	9.2
UNHCR	–	–	–	0.1
Other Multilateral	1.0	0.7	0.6	0.3
Arab OPEC Agencies	-0.1	-0.1	–	-0.1
TOTAL	*51.0*	*33.5*	*38.7*	*24.4*
OPEC COUNTRIES	*4.7*	*1.7*	*–*	*14.6*
E.E.C.+ MEMBERS	*5.9*	*5.4*	*20.9*	*39.3*
TOTAL	**295.0**	**262.8**	**345.1**	**355.3**

TOTAL ODA GROSS

	1983
Australia	–
Austria	0.1
Belgium	0.1
Canada	1.9
Denmark	0.3
Finland	0.1
France	0.2
Germany, Fed. Rep.	3.6
Ireland	–
Italy	0.1
Japan	1.4
Netherlands	1.7
New Zealand	–
Norway	0.3
Sweden	–
Switzerland	0.1
United Kingdom	–
United States	233.0
TOTAL	*242.7*
AF.D.F.	–
AF.D.B.	–
AS.D.B	–
CAR.D.B.	–
E.E.C.	0.3
IBRD	–
IDA	–
I.D.B.	42.6
IFAD	–
I.F.C.	–
IMF TRUST FUND	–
U.N. AGENCIES	–
UNDP	1.7
UNTA	0.8
UNICEF	0.3
UNRWA	–
WFP	7.3
UNHCR	–
Other Multilateral	1.0
Arab OPEC Agencies	–
TOTAL	*54.0*
OPEC COUNTRIES	*4.7*
E.E.C.+ MEMBERS	*6.3*
TOTAL	**301.4**

ODA LOANS GROSS

DAC COUNTRIES	1983	1984	1985	1986
Australia	–	–	–	–
Austria	–	–	–	–
Belgium	–	–	–	–
Canada	0.3	0.2	–	–
Denmark	–	–	–	–
Finland	–	–	–	–
France	–	–	–	–
Germany, Fed. Rep.	–	–	5.5	15.6
Ireland	–	–	–	–
Italy	–	–	–	–
Japan	–	–	–	–
Netherlands	–	–	–	–
New Zealand	–	–	–	–
Norway	–	–	–	–
Sweden	–	–	–	–
Switzerland	–	–	–	–
United Kingdom				
United States	81.0	61.0	87.0	64.0
TOTAL	*81.3*	*61.2*	*92.5*	*79.6*
MULTILATERAL	*41.9*	*24.9*	*24.0*	*15.3*
OPEC COUNTRIES	*4.7*	*1.7*	*–*	*14.6*
E.E.C.+ MEMBERS	*–*	*–*	*5.5*	*15.6*
TOTAL	**127.9**	**87.8**	**116.5**	**109.5**

ODA LOANS NET

DAC COUNTRIES	1983	1984	1985	1986
Australia	–	–	–	–
Austria	–	–	–	–
Belgium	–	–	–	–
Canada	0.1	0.1	-0.1	-0.1
Denmark	–	–	–	–
Finland	–	–	–	–
France	-0.1	-0.2	-0.1	-0.4
Germany, Fed. Rep.	-0.2	-0.2	5.3	15.3
Ireland	–	–	–	–
Italy	–	–	–	–
Japan	-0.9	-0.9	-3.7	-2.5
Netherlands	–	–	–	–
New Zealand	–	–	–	–
Norway	–	–	–	–
Sweden	–	–	–	–
Switzerland	–	–	–	–
United Kingdom				
United States	79.0	59.0	86.0	61.0
TOTAL	*77.9*	*57.8*	*87.4*	*73.3*
MULTILATERAL	*39.0*	*22.1*	*19.8*	*10.0*
OPEC COUNTRIES	*4.7*	*1.7*	*–*	*14.6*
E.E.C.+ MEMBERS	*-0.4*	*-0.4*	*5.2*	*14.9*
TOTAL	**121.5**	**81.5**	**107.1**	**97.9**

GRANTS

	1983
Australia	–
Austria	0.1
Belgium	0.1
Canada	1.5
Denmark	0.3
Finland	0.1
France	0.2
Germany, Fed. Rep.	3.6
Ireland	–
Italy	0.1
Japan	1.4
Netherlands	1.7
New Zealand	–
Norway	0.3
Sweden	–
Switzerland	0.1
United Kingdom	–
United States	152.0
TOTAL	*161.4*
MULTILATERAL	*12.1*
OPEC COUNTRIES	*–*
E.E.C.+ MEMBERS	*6.3*
TOTAL	**173.5**

TOTAL OFFICIAL GROSS

DAC COUNTRIES	1983	1984	1985	1986
Australia	–	0.1	0.1	0.1
Austria	0.1	0.0	0.0	0.2
Belgium	0.1	0.1	0.2	0.4
Canada	1.9	2.1	1.4	3.4
Denmark	0.3	0.2	–	–
Finland	0.1	0.1	–	0.6
France	0.2	0.2	0.3	0.4
Germany, Fed. Rep.	3.7	2.5	8.4	22.9
Ireland	–	–	–	0.0
Italy	0.1	0.1	10.3	10.7
Japan	1.4	0.1	0.1	1.5
Netherlands	1.7	1.7	1.7	4.3
New Zealand	–	–	–	0.0
Norway	0.3	0.5	0.3	1.0
Sweden	–	0.0	0.0	0.8
Switzerland	0.1	0.1	0.7	0.9
United Kingdom	–	0.3	0.1	0.4
United States	233.0	223.0	288.0	275.0
TOTAL	*242.9*	*231.1*	*311.5*	*322.6*
MULTILATERAL	*133.2*	*78.1*	*90.8*	*57.7*
OPEC COUNTRIES	*28.8*	*16.4*	*13.8*	*25.0*
E.E.C.+ MEMBERS	*6.4*	*5.9*	*21.2*	*40.0*
TOTAL	**404.9**	**325.7**	**416.1**	**405.3**

TOTAL OFFICIAL NET

DAC COUNTRIES	1983	1984	1985	1986
Australia	–	0.1	0.1	0.1
Austria	0.1	0.0	0.0	0.2
Belgium	0.1	0.1	0.2	0.4
Canada	1.7	2.0	1.2	3.3
Denmark	0.3	0.2	–	–
Finland	0.1	0.1	–	0.6
France	0.1	0.0	0.1	0.0
Germany, Fed. Rep.	3.4	2.2	8.1	22.6
Ireland	–	–	–	0.0
Italy	0.1	0.1	10.3	10.7
Japan	0.5	-0.8	-3.5	-1.0
Netherlands	1.7	1.7	1.7	4.3
New Zealand	–	–	–	0.0
Norway	0.3	0.5	0.3	1.0
Sweden	–	0.0	0.0	0.8
Switzerland	0.1	0.1	0.7	0.9
United Kingdom	–	0.3	0.1	0.4
United States	229.3	219.0	285.0	271.0
TOTAL	*237.3*	*225.6*	*304.3*	*315.3*
MULTILATERAL	*122.8*	*69.0*	*73.5*	*32.4*
OPEC COUNTRIES	*24.0*	*9.4*	*3.8*	*-3.4*
E.E.C.+ MEMBERS	*6.0*	*5.4*	*20.8*	*39.3*
TOTAL	**384.1**	**304.0**	**381.5**	**344.4**

TOTAL OOF GROSS

	1983
Australia	–
Austria	–
Belgium	–
Canada	–
Denmark	–
Finland	–
France	–
Germany, Fed. Rep.	0.1
Ireland	–
Italy	–
Japan	–
Netherlands	–
New Zealand	–
Norway	–
Sweden	–
Switzerland	–
United Kingdom	–
United States	–
TOTAL	*0.1*
MULTILATERAL	*79.3*
OPEC COUNTRIES	*24.1*
E.E.C.+ MEMBERS	*0.1*
TOTAL	**103.5**

Left section

ODA COMMITMENTS

1984	1985	1986	1983	1984	1985	1986
0.1	0.1	0.1	–	0.1	–	–
0.0	0.0	0.2	0.0	0.0	0.0	–
0.1	0.2	0.4	–	–	–	0.4
2.1	1.4	3.4	1.6	1.8	1.3	0.6
0.2	–	–	–	–	–	–
0.1	–	0.6	0.1	0.1	–	–
0.2	0.3	0.4	0.2	0.2	0.3	0.4
2.4	8.4	22.9	3.6	13.7	6.5	32.6
–	–	0.0	–	–	–	0.0
0.1	10.3	10.7	0.1	5.1	10.6	9.8
0.1	0.1	1.5	1.4	0.1	0.8	5.4
1.7	1.7	4.3	1.0	1.8	2.0	3.8
–	–	0.0	–	–	0.0	–
0.5	0.3	1.0	–	0.0	0.0	0.1
0.0	0.0	0.8	–	3.7	5.5	0.8
0.1	0.7	0.9	0.1	0.1	0.7	0.9
0.3	0.1	0.4	–	0.3	0.1	0.4
223.0	288.0	275.0	246.7	309.7	361.9	312.4
231.1	*311.5*	*322.6*	*254.9*	*336.7*	*389.6*	*367.5*
–	–	–	–	–	–	–
–	–	–	–	–	–	–
–	–	–	–	–	–	–
0.8	0.3	1.0	–	0.7	–	5.1
–	–	–	–	–	–	–
25.7	23.5	11.8	7.5	–	21.0	17.4
–	0.5	4.1	–	5.0	–	–
–	–	–	–	–	–	–
–	–	–	11.0	9.9	18.7	12.8
1.5	1.5	2.2	–	–	–	–
0.5	0.5	0.6	–	–	–	–
0.4	0.2	0.5	–	–	–	–
6.9	15.9	9.2	–	–	–	–
–	–	0.1	–	–	–	–
0.7	0.6	0.3	–	–	–	–
-0.1	–	–	–	–	–	–
36.3	*43.0*	*29.6*	*18.5*	*15.5*	*39.7*	*35.3*
1.7	–	*14.6*	*9.3*	–	–	–
5.8	*21.2*	*40.0*	*4.9*	*21.7*	*19.4*	*52.4*
269.1	*354.5*	*366.9*	*282.7*	*352.2*	*429.2*	*402.7*

TECH. COOP. GRANTS

1984	1985	1986	1983	1984	1985	1986
0.1	0.1	0.1	–	0.0	–	0.0
0.0	0.0	0.2	0.0	–	–	–
0.1	0.2	0.4	–	–	–	–
1.9	1.4	3.4	0.1	–	0.0	–
0.2	–	–	–	–	–	–
0.1	–	0.6	0.0	0.0	–	–
0.2	0.3	0.4	0.2	0.2	0.3	0.4
2.4	2.9	7.3	1.9	1.8	2.5	6.4
–	–	0.0	–	–	–	0.0
0.1	10.3	10.7	0.1	0.1	0.3	2.0
0.1	0.1	1.5	0.1	0.1	0.1	0.3
1.7	1.7	4.3	0.4	0.7	0.8	2.6
–	–	0.0	–	–	–	–
0.5	0.3	1.0	–	0.0	0.0	–
0.0	0.0	0.8	–	–	–	0.8
0.1	0.7	0.9	–	–	–	–
0.3	0.1	0.4	–	0.0	–	0.1
162.0	201.0	211.0	9.0	26.0	28.0	57.0
169.8	*219.0*	*243.0*	*11.9*	*29.1*	*32.0*	*69.7*
11.4	*19.0*	*14.4*	*3.7*	*3.0*	*2.8*	*3.6*
–	–	–	–	–	–	–
5.8	*15.7*	*24.4*	*2.6*	*2.9*	*3.9*	*11.5*
181.3	*238.0*	*257.4*	*15.6*	*32.1*	*34.8*	*73.3*

TOTAL OOF NET

1984	1985	1986	1983	1984	1985	1986
–	–	–	–	–	–	–
–	–	–	–	–	–	–
–	–	–	–	–	–	–
–	–	–	–	–	–	–
–	–	–	–	–	–	–
–	–	–	–	–	–	–
0.1	–	–	0.1	–	-0.1	–
–	–	–	–	–	–	–
–	–	–	–	–	–	–
–	–	–	–	–	–	–
–	–	–	–	–	–	–
–	–	–	–	–	–	–
–	–	–	-2.0	-2.0	-2.0	-1.0
0.1	–	–	*-1.9*	*-2.0*	*-2.1*	*-1.0*
41.8	*47.8*	*28.1*	*71.8*	*35.5*	*34.7*	*8.0*
14.8	*13.8*	*10.4*	*19.3*	*7.7*	*3.8*	*-18.0*
0.1	–	–	*0.1*	–	*-0.1*	–
56.6	*61.6*	*38.4*	*89.2*	*41.2*	*36.4*	*-11.0*

Right section

ODA COMMITMENTS : LOANS

DAC COUNTRIES	1983	1984	1985	1986
Australia	–	–	–	–
Austria	–	–	–	–
Belgium	–	–	–	–
Canada	–	–	–	–
Denmark	–	–	–	–
Finland	–	–	–	–
France	–	–	–	–
Germany, Fed. Rep.	–	10.5	–	21.1
Ireland	–	–	–	–
Italy	–	–	–	–
Japan	–	–	–	–
Netherlands	–	–	–	–
New Zealand	–	–	–	–
Norway	–	–	–	–
Sweden	–	–	–	–
Switzerland	–	–	–	–
United Kingdom	–	–	–	–
United States	88.6	93.1	70.2	8.0
TOTAL	*88.6*	*103.6*	*70.2*	*29.1*
MULTILATERAL	*7.5*	*5.0*	*21.0*	*17.4*
OPEC COUNTRIES	*9.3*	–	–	–
E.E.C.+ MEMBERS	–	*10.5*	–	*21.1*
TOTAL	*105.4*	*108.6*	*91.2*	*46.5*

GRANT ELEMENT OF ODA

DAC COUNTRIES	1983	1984	1985	1986
Australia	–	100.0	–	–
Austria	100.0	100.0	100.0	–
Belgium	–	–	–	100.0
Canada	100.0	100.0	100.0	100.0
Denmark	–	–	–	–
Finland	100.0	100.0	–	–
France	100.0	100.0	100.0	100.0
Germany, Fed. Rep.	100.0	80.6	100.0	89.3
Ireland	–	–	–	100.0
Italy	100.0	100.0	100.0	100.0
Japan	100.0	100.0	100.0	100.0
Netherlands	100.0	100.0	100.0	100.0
New Zealand	–	–	100.0	–
Norway	–	100.0	100.0	100.0
Sweden	–	100.0	100.0	100.0
Switzerland	100.0	100.0	100.0	100.0
United Kingdom	–	100.0	100.0	100.0
United States	89.1	90.8	93.8	99.2
TOTAL	*89.4*	*90.8*	*94.2*	*98.3*
MULTILATERAL	*87.0*	*90.0*	*88.8*	*85.7*
OPEC COUNTRIES	*50.2*	–	–	–
E.E.C.+ MEMBERS	*100.0*	*87.7*	*100.0*	*93.4*
TOTAL	*88.0*	*90.7*	*93.7*	*97.2*

OTHER AGGREGATES

COMMITMENTS: ALL SOURCES

	1983	1984	1985	1986
TOTAL BILATERAL	278.5	349.4	400.3	367.5
of which				
OPEC	23.6	12.8	10.8	–
CMEA	–	–	–	–
TOTAL MULTILATERAL	24.5	116.0	39.7	40.9
TOTAL BIL.& MULTIL.	303.0	465.4	440.0	408.3
of which				
ODA Grants	177.3	243.6	338.1	356.3
ODA Loans	105.4	108.6	91.2	46.5

DISBURSEMENTS:

DAC COUNTRIES COMBINED

	1983	1984	1985	1986
OFFICIAL & PRIVATE				
GROSS:				
Contractual Lending	101.7	95.5	116.8	78.7
Export Credits Total	20.2	34.2	24.3	-0.9
Export Credits Private	20.2	34.2	24.3	-0.9
NET:				
Contractual Lending	29.1	66.8	81.9	48.6
Export Credits Total	-48.9	9.0	-5.4	-24.7
PRIVATE SECTOR NET	-46.8	-0.9	-2.5	-16.9
Direct Investment	–	–	1.9	0.7
Portfolio Investment	0.0	-11.9	-1.1	6.1
Export Credits	-46.9	11.0	-3.4	-23.7

MARKET BORROWING:

CHANGE IN CLAIMS

	1983	1984	1985	1986
Banks	–	10.0	-7.0	-1.0

MEMORANDUM ITEM:

	1983	1984	1985	1986
CMEA Countr.(Gross)	–	–	–	–

DISBURSEMENTS, UNLESS OTHERWISE STATED

	1983	1984	1985	1986		1983	1984	1985	1986		1983
TOTAL RECEIPTS NET					**TOTAL ODA NET**					**TOTAL ODA GROSS**	
DAC COUNTRIES											
Australia	3.6	11.9	16.5	24.2		3.6	11.9	8.6	8.3	Australia	3.6
Austria	1.2	0.9	2.0	0.9		1.2	0.9	2.0	0.9	Austria	1.2
Belgium	0.5	0.3	9.8	12.4		0.4	0.2	8.2	5.5	Belgium	0.4
Canada	14.9	18.6	46.5	15.7		16.7	20.8	34.7	19.1	Canada	16.7
Denmark	4.1	0.5	2.2	0.0		4.1	0.5	2.2	0.0	Denmark	4.1
Finland	2.7	2.7	10.6	9.0		2.7	2.7	10.6	9.0	Finland	2.7
France	3.6	9.0	21.1	7.1		5.0	5.2	6.5	10.3	France	5.0
Germany, Fed. Rep.	9.5	28.5	27.0	28.2		9.3	28.3	25.4	25.1	Germany, Fed. Rep.	11.3
Ireland	0.0	0.1	0.0	0.3		0.0	0.1	0.0	0.3	Ireland	0.0
Italy	22.0	71.2	112.2	174.7		15.3	44.9	81.6	151.6	Italy	16.1
Japan	-0.8	2.3	6.5	18.0		1.4	2.5	6.6	5.3	Japan	2.6
Netherlands	0.4	9.2	8.0	6.4		2.5	9.2	8.0	8.4	Netherlands	2.5
New Zealand	—	—	—	—		—	—	—	—	New Zealand	—
Norway	2.3	9.0	12.0	9.4		2.3	9.0	12.0	9.4	Norway	2.3
Sweden	16.0	18.3	24.6	36.9		15.5	17.9	24.6	35.2	Sweden	15.5
Switzerland	2.0	5.8	6.0	3.7		2.0	5.8	6.0	3.7	Switzerland	2.0
United Kingdom	24.1	41.9	41.5	16.6		5.1	8.4	36.1	18.4	United Kingdom	5.2
United States	6.0	18.0	142.0	89.0		6.0	19.0	143.0	91.0	United States	8.0
TOTAL	*112.0*	*248.1*	*488.6*	*452.3*		*93.1*	*187.2*	*416.3*	*401.5*	*TOTAL*	*99.1*
MULTILATERAL											
AF.D.F.	11.6	4.9	17.1	15.2		11.6	4.9	17.1	15.2	AF.D.F.	11.6
AF.D.B.	2.8	2.6	1.4	3.9		—	—	—	—	AF.D.B.	—
AS.D.B	—	—	—	—		—	—	—	—	AS.D.B	—
CAR.D.B	—	—	—	—		—	—	—	—	CAR.D.B.	—
E.E.C.	47.4	57.9	103.3	85.7		47.4	57.9	103.3	85.7	E.E.C.	47.4
IBRD	-4.1	-4.4	-4.5	-6.3		—	—	—	—	IBRD	—
IDA	41.1	39.3	48.0	35.3		41.1	39.3	48.0	35.3	IDA	42.3
I.D.B.	—	—	—	—		—	—	—	—	I.D.B.	—
IFAD	6.0	3.6	8.4	9.0		6.0	3.6	8.4	9.0	IFAD	6.0
I.F.C.	—	—	—	—		—	—	—	—	I.F.C.	—
IMF TRUST FUND	—	—	—	—		—	—	—	—	IMF TRUST FUND	—
U.N. AGENCIES	—	—	—	—		—	—	—	—	U.N. AGENCIES	—
UNDP	8.3	10.6	19.4	23.2		8.3	10.6	19.4	23.2	UNDP	8.3
UNTA	2.3	1.8	2.7	2.6		2.3	1.8	2.7	2.6	UNTA	2.3
UNICEF	12.6	12.6	20.4	15.1		12.6	12.6	20.4	15.1	UNICEF	12.6
UNRWA	—	—	—	—		—	—	—	—	UNRWA	—
WFP	33.1	27.8	47.1	30.3		33.1	27.8	47.1	30.3	WFP	33.1
UNHCR	10.7	13.4	20.7	21.8		10.7	13.4	20.7	21.8	UNHCR	10.7
Other Multilateral	3.1	4.0	2.5	3.1		3.1	4.0	2.5	3.1	Other Multilateral	3.1
Arab OPEC Agencies	-0.2	-0.2	-1.2	-1.1		-0.2	-0.2	-1.2	-1.1	Arab OPEC Agencies	—
TOTAL	*174.6*	*173.8*	*285.4*	*237.6*		*175.9*	*175.6*	*288.5*	*240.0*	*TOTAL*	*177.4*
OPEC COUNTRIES	*70.3*	*-5.3*	*10.0*	*0.2*		*70.3*	*0.8*	*10.0*	*0.2*	*OPEC COUNTRIES*	*70.3*
E.E.C. + MEMBERS	*111.5*	*218.6*	*325.2*	*331.3*		*89.1*	*154.7*	*271.5*	*305.3*	*E.E.C. + MEMBERS*	*91.9*
TOTAL	*356.9*	*416.6*	*784.0*	*690.1*		*339.3*	*363.7*	*714.8*	*641.8*	*TOTAL*	*346.8*
ODA LOANS GROSS					**ODA LOANS NET**					**GRANTS**	
DAC COUNTRIES											
Australia	—	—	—	—		—	—	—	—	Australia	3.6
Austria	—	—	—	—		—	—	—	—	Austria	1.2
Belgium	—	—	—	0.7		—	—	—	0.7	Belgium	0.4
Canada	—	—	—	—		—	—	—	—	Canada	16.7
Denmark	—	—	—	—		—	—	—	—	Denmark	4.1
Finland	—	—	—	—		—	—	—	—	Finland	2.7
France	—	1.1	0.9	0.9		—	1.1	0.9	0.9	France	5.0
Germany, Fed. Rep.	1.2	0.5	0.2	3.3		-0.7	-0.7	-1.0	1.2	Germany, Fed. Rep.	10.0
Ireland	—	—	—	—		—	—	—	—	Ireland	0.0
Italy	2.5	34.2	20.0	19.4		1.8	33.2	18.6	18.1	Italy	13.6
Japan	—	—	—	—		-1.1	-1.1	-0.9	-1.9	Japan	2.6
Netherlands	—	—	—	—		—	—	—	—	Netherlands	2.5
New Zealand	—	—	—	—		—	—	—	—	New Zealand	—
Norway	—	—	—	—		—	—	—	—	Norway	2.3
Sweden	—	—	—	—		—	—	—	—	Sweden	15.5
Switzerland	—	—	—	—		—	—	—	—	Switzerland	2.0
United Kingdom	0.0	0.0	—	—		-0.1	-0.9	-0.3	-0.3	United Kingdom	5.2
United States	—	—	—	—		-2.0	-2.0	-3.0	-3.0	United States	8.0
TOTAL	*3.8*	*35.8*	*21.1*	*24.3*		*-2.2*	*29.5*	*14.3*	*15.6*	*TOTAL*	*95.3*
MULTILATERAL	*59.9*	*49.7*	*76.2*	*63.2*		*58.5*	*47.9*	*72.7*	*58.9*	*MULTILATERAL*	*117.5*
OPEC COUNTRIES	*70.0*	*1.3*	*10.0*	*—*		*70.0*	*0.3*	*9.0*	*—*	*OPEC COUNTRIES*	*0.3*
E.E.C. + MEMBERS	*3.8*	*36.1*	*21.5*	*24.8*		*1.0*	*33.0*	*18.6*	*21.1*	*E.E.C. + MEMBERS*	*88.1*
TOTAL	*133.7*	*86.7*	*107.2*	*87.4*		*126.3*	*77.6*	*96.0*	*74.5*	*TOTAL*	*213.1*
TOTAL OFFICIAL GROSS					**TOTAL OFFICIAL NET**					**TOTAL OOF GROSS**	
DAC COUNTRIES											
Australia	3.6	11.9	8.8	8.3		3.6	11.9	8.7	8.3	Australia	—
Austria	1.2	0.9	2.0	0.9		1.2	0.9	2.0	0.9	Austria	—
Belgium	0.4	0.4	8.5	5.6		0.4	0.4	8.5	5.6	Belgium	—
Canada	16.7	20.8	48.2	19.3		14.9	18.6	46.5	15.7	Canada	—
Denmark	4.1	0.5	2.2	0.0		4.1	0.5	2.2	0.0	Denmark	—
Finland	2.7	2.7	10.6	9.0		2.7	2.7	10.6	9.0	Finland	—
France	5.0	5.2	6.5	10.3		5.0	5.2	6.5	10.3	France	—
Germany, Fed. Rep.	11.3	29.5	26.6	27.2		9.3	28.3	25.4	25.1	Germany, Fed. Rep.	—
Ireland	0.0	0.1	0.0	0.3		0.0	0.1	0.0	0.3	Ireland	—
Italy	18.1	56.5	95.9	162.9		17.3	55.0	94.5	161.6	Italy	2.0
Japan	2.6	3.6	7.5	7.3		1.4	2.5	6.6	5.3	Japan	—
Netherlands	2.5	9.2	8.0	8.4		2.5	9.2	8.0	8.4	Netherlands	—
New Zealand	—	—	—	—		—	—	—	—	New Zealand	—
Norway	2.3	9.0	12.0	9.4		2.3	9.0	12.0	9.4	Norway	—
Sweden	16.5	17.9	24.6	38.1		16.3	17.7	24.6	37.4	Sweden	1.1
Switzerland	2.0	5.8	6.0	3.7		2.0	5.8	6.0	3.7	Switzerland	—
United Kingdom	5.2	9.4	36.4	18.7		5.1	8.4	36.1	18.4	United Kingdom	—
United States	8.0	21.0	148.0	95.0		6.0	18.0	142.0	89.0	United States	—
TOTAL	*102.1*	*204.2*	*451.8*	*424.4*		*94.1*	*194.1*	*440.3*	*408.4*	*TOTAL*	*3.1*
MULTILATERAL	*180.9*	*180.6*	*294.0*	*249.4*		*174.6*	*173.8*	*285.4*	*237.6*	*MULTILATERAL*	*3.5*
OPEC COUNTRIES	*70.3*	*-4.3*	*11.0*	*0.2*		*70.3*	*-5.3*	*10.0*	*0.2*	*OPEC COUNTRIES*	*—*
E.E.C. + MEMBERS	*93.9*	*168.5*	*287.5*	*319.1*		*91.1*	*165.0*	*284.6*	*315.4*	*E.E.C. + MEMBERS*	*2.0*
TOTAL	*353.3*	*380.5*	*756.7*	*673.9*		*339.0*	*362.6*	*735.7*	*646.2*	*TOTAL*	*6.6*

ODA COMMITMENTS

1984	1985	1986	1983	1984	1985	1986
11.9	8.6	8.3	4.7	8.9	10.1	8.0
0.9	2.0	0.9	1.2	0.9	2.2	–
0.2	8.2	5.5	–	–	4.0	4.8
20.8	34.7	19.1	15.0	21.9	43.8	19.4
0.5	2.2	0.0	5.9	0.2	8.5	6.1
2.7	10.6	9.0	5.0	1.4	14.2	9.3
5.2	6.5	10.3	8.7	4.2	5.4	10.3
29.5	26.6	27.2	8.3	30.8	29.5	25.8
0.1	0.0	0.3	0.0	0.1	0.0	0.3
45.9	83.0	152.9	18.0	96.9	92.8	160.7
3.6	7.5	7.3	2.6	6.4	6.8	11.7
9.2	8.0	8.4	2.4	10.8	6.1	8.9
–	–	–	–	–	–	0.0
9.0	12.0	9.4	3.7	1.6	0.3	0.9
17.9	24.6	35.2	19.2	21.4	21.1	35.2
5.8	6.0	3.7	2.7	5.7	5.7	3.7
9.4	36.4	18.7	5.2	9.3	36.4	18.7
21.0	146.0	94.0	4.2	65.1	85.5	130.9
193.5	*423.0*	*410.2*	*106.9*	*285.4*	*372.5*	*454.5*
4.9	17.1	15.3	55.3	21.4	40.2	55.7
–	–	–	–	–	–	–
57.9	103.3	85.7	52.7	84.2	45.5	70.6
–	–	–	–	–	–	–
41.1	50.3	38.4	132.0	136.0	30.0	112.5
–	–	–	–	–	–	–
3.6	8.4	9.0	11.1	–	14.6	11.4
–	–	–	–	–	–	–
–	–	–	70.2	70.2	112.9	95.9
10.6	19.4	23.2	–	–	–	–
1.8	2.7	2.6	–	–	–	–
12.6	20.4	15.1	–	–	–	–
–	–	–	–	–	–	–
27.8	47.1	30.3	–	–	–	–
13.4	20.7	21.8	–	–	–	–
4.0	2.5	3.1	–	–	–	–
-0.2	–	–	–	5.0	–	7.8
177.5	*292.0*	*244.3*	*321.2*	*316.7*	*243.2*	*353.9*
1.8	*11.0*	*0.2*	*70.3*	*1.5*	*11.0*	–
157.8	*274.4*	*309.0*	*101.2*	*236.4*	*228.4*	*306.1*
372.7	*726.0*	*654.7*	*498.4*	*603.6*	*626.8*	*808.4*

TECH. COOP. GRANTS

1984	1985	1986	1983	1984	1985	1986
11.9	8.6	8.3	0.2	0.4	0.5	0.4
0.9	2.0	0.9	0.3	–	–	–
0.2	8.2	4.8	0.0	0.0	0.1	0.0
20.8	34.7	19.1	0.9	–	0.6	–
0.5	2.2	0.0	2.4	0.3	0.1	–
2.7	10.6	9.0	0.7	1.5	2.8	2.8
4.1	5.7	9.4	3.4	3.9	3.2	6.1
29.0	26.5	23.9	7.4	14.5	12.4	9.9
0.1	0.0	0.3	0.0	0.0	0.0	0.3
11.7	63.0	133.5	5.2	9.8	7.6	20.3
3.6	7.5	7.3	0.9	1.6	3.2	2.7
9.2	8.0	8.4	1.1	1.8	2.3	2.2
–	–	–	–	–	–	–
9.0	12.0	9.4	0.1	0.1	0.1	0.2
17.9	24.6	35.2	2.9	3.9	4.7	3.5
5.8	6.0	3.7	0.3	0.1	0.2	0.0
9.3	36.4	18.7	0.6	0.6	0.8	1.5
21.0	146.0	94.0	–	–	–	–
157.7	*401.9*	*385.9*	*26.5*	*38.5*	*38.4*	*49.8*
127.8	*215.8*	*181.1*	*37.1*	*42.4*	*65.8*	*65.7*
0.5	*1.0*	*0.2*	–	–	–	–
121.7	*252.9*	*284.2*	*20.2*	*30.8*	*26.4*	*40.3*
286.0	*618.7*	*567.3*	*63.6*	*80.9*	*104.2*	*115.5*

TOTAL OOF NET

1984	1985	1986	1983	1984	1985	1986
–	0.1	–	–	–	0.1	-0.1
–	–	–	–	–	–	–
0.2	0.3	0.1	–	0.2	0.3	0.1
–	13.5	0.2	-1.8	-2.2	11.8	-3.5
–	–	–	–	–	–	–
–	–	–	–	–	–	–
–	–	–	–	–	–	–
10.6	12.9	10.0	2.0	10.2	12.9	10.0
–	–	–	–	–	–	–
–	–	–	–	–	–	–
–	–	3.0	0.8	-0.2	–	2.3
–	–	–	–	–	–	–
–	2.0	1.0	–	-1.0	-1.0	-2.0
10.7	*28.7*	*14.2*	*1.0*	*6.9*	*24.0*	*6.8*
3.2	*2.0*	*5.0*	*-1.3*	*-1.8*	*-3.1*	*-2.4*
-6.1	–	–	–	*-6.1*	–	–
10.7	*13.1*	*10.1*	*2.0*	*10.3*	*13.1*	*10.1*
7.7	*30.7*	*19.2*	*-0.4*	*-1.1*	*20.9*	*4.4*

ODA COMMITMENTS : LOANS

DAC COUNTRIES	1983	1984	1985	1986
Australia	–	–	–	–
Austria	–	–	–	–
Belgium	–	–	–	–
Canada	–	–	–	–
Denmark	–	–	–	–
Finland	–	–	–	–
France	2.4	–	0.3	0.9
Germany, Fed. Rep.	–	–	3.4	–
Ireland	–	–	–	–
Italy	–	71.6	25.0	1.8
Japan	–	–	–	–
Netherlands	–	–	–	–
New Zealand	–	–	–	–
Norway	–	–	–	–
Sweden	–	–	–	–
Switzerland	–	–	–	–
United Kingdom	–	–	–	–
United States	–	–	–	–
TOTAL	*2.4*	*71.6*	*28.7*	*2.6*
MULTILATERAL	*212.4*	*177.6*	*84.6*	*184.1*
OPEC COUNTRIES	*70.0*	*1.3*	*10.0*	–
E.E.C.+ MEMBERS	*16.6*	*86.8*	*28.7*	*3.1*
TOTAL	*284.8*	*250.5*	*123.2*	*186.7*

GRANT ELEMENT OF ODA

DAC COUNTRIES	1983	1984	1985	1986
Australia	100.0	100.0	100.0	100.0
Austria	100.0	100.0	100.0	–
Belgium	–	–	98.2	100.0
Canada	100.0	100.0	100.0	100.0
Denmark	100.0	100.0	100.0	100.0
Finland	100.0	100.0	100.0	100.0
France	90.2	100.0	95.7	100.0
Germany, Fed. Rep.	100.0	100.0	98.1	100.0
Ireland	100.0	100.0	100.0	100.0
Italy	100.0	63.4	87.1	99.6
Japan	100.0	100.0	100.0	100.0
Netherlands	100.0	100.0	100.0	100.0
New Zealand	–	–	100.0	–
Norway	100.0	100.0	100.0	100.0
Sweden	100.0	100.0	100.0	100.0
Switzerland	100.0	100.0	100.0	100.0
United Kingdom	100.0	100.0	100.0	100.0
United States	100.0	100.0	100.0	100.0
TOTAL	*99.2*	*87.6*	*96.5*	*99.9*
MULTILATERAL	*89.8*	*89.7*	*94.0*	*90.0*
OPEC COUNTRIES	*31.6*	*54.7*	*40.9*	–
E.E.C.+ MEMBERS	*99.0*	*84.0*	*94.4*	*99.8*
TOTAL	*82.9*	*88.6*	*94.6*	*95.5*

OTHER AGGREGATES

COMMITMENTS: ALL SOURCES

	1983	1984	1985	1986
TOTAL BILATERAL	463.0	439.6	694.8	625.6
of which				
OPEC	70.3	1.5	11.0	–
CMEA	279.6	112.1	298.3	158.9
TOTAL MULTILATERAL	321.2	340.3	243.2	375.4
TOTAL BIL.& MULTIL.	784.3	779.9	938.1	1001.0
of which				
ODA Grants	273.0	403.7	537.5	625.2
ODA Loans	504.9	312.0	387.5	342.1

DISBURSEMENTS:

DAC COUNTRIES COMBINED

OFFICIAL & PRIVATE	1983	1984	1985	1986
GROSS:				
Contractual Lending	44.0	109.3	117.6	117.3
Export Credits Total	38.2	63.0	83.6	83.1
Export Credits Private	37.2	63.0	68.0	79.0
NET:				
Contractual Lending	21.0	84.2	87.3	66.0
Export Credits Total	21.2	44.0	60.1	40.4
PRIVATE SECTOR NET	17.9	54.1	48.3	44.0
Direct Investment	-2.6	5.1	0.2	0.4
Portfolio Investment	-1.7	1.1	-1.1	-0.1
Export Credits	22.2	47.9	49.2	43.7

MARKET BORROWING:

CHANGE IN CLAIMS

	1983	1984	1985	1986
Banks	–	46.0	-10.0	-11.0

MEMORANDUM ITEM:

	1983	1984	1985	1986
CMEA Countr.(Gross)	130.2	162.0	122.1	77.5

	1983	1984	1985	1986	1983	1984	1985	1986		1983

TOTAL RECEIPTS NET / **TOTAL ODA NET** / **TOTAL ODA GROSS**

	1983	1984	1985	1986	1983	1984	1985	1986		1983
DAC COUNTRIES										
Australia	6.4	2.0	12.8	11.1	9.6	9.9	10.0	13.8	Australia	9.6
Austria	—	—	—	—	—	—	—	0.1	Austria	—
Belgium	0.0	0.0	0.0	0.1	—	—	—	0.1	Belgium	—
Canada	0.5	0.2	0.4	0.3	0.5	0.2	0.4	0.3	Canada	0.5
Denmark	—	—	—	—	—	—	—	—	Denmark	—
Finland	0.1	0.3	—	0.0	0.1	0.3	—	0.0	Finland	0.1
France	0.2	0.5	—	0.6	0.2	0.5	—	0.6	France	0.2
Germany, Fed. Rep.	1.3	0.9	1.0	1.4	1.2	0.9	1.0	1.4	Germany, Fed. Rep.	1.2
Ireland	—	—	—	—	—	—	—	—	Ireland	—
Italy	—	—	—	—	—	—	—	—	Italy	—
Japan	3.9	1.7	4.7	10.6	2.1	3.4	8.2	11.0	Japan	2.1
Netherlands	-0.1	1.2	0.5	0.4	0.3	1.2	0.5	0.4	Netherlands	0.3
New Zealand	3.5	3.4	3.4	2.3	3.5	3.4	3.4	2.3	New Zealand	3.5
Norway	—	0.0	0.0	0.1	—	0.0	0.0	0.1	Norway	—
Sweden	—	—	—	—	—	—	—	—	Sweden	—
Switzerland	—	—	—	—	—	—	—	—	Switzerland	—
United Kingdom	6.2	4.8	-0.7	7.2	2.9	1.7	1.8	1.6	United Kingdom	4.2
United States	1.0	1.0	—	—	2.0	2.0	1.0	1.0	United States	2.0
TOTAL	22.8	15.8	22.1	34.0	22.3	23.5	26.3	32.4	**TOTAL**	23.6
MULTILATERAL										
AF.D.F.	—	—	—	—	—	—	—	—	AF.D.F.	—
AF.D.B.	—	—	—	—	—	—	—	—	AF.D.B.	—
AS.D.B	6.0	7.1	0.2	1.8	0.8	0.5	0.2	0.4	AS.D.B	0.8
CAR.D.B.	—	—	—	—	—	—	—	—	CAR.D.B.	—
E.E.C.	10.4	7.3	4.2	10.2	6.4	4.3	3.6	6.8	E.E.C.	6.4
IBRD	16.8	-1.3	-5.5	-5.6	—	—	—	—	IBRD	—
IDA	—	—	—	—	—	—	—	—	IDA	—
I.D.B.	—	—	—	—	—	—	—	—	I.D.B.	—
IFAD	—	—	—	—	—	—	—	—	IFAD	—
I.F.C.	6.0	—	-0.4	4.0	—	—	—	—	I.F.C.	—
IMF TRUST FUND	—	—	—	—	—	—	—	—	IMF TRUST FUND	—
U.N. AGENCIES									U.N. AGENCIES	
UNDP	0.8	0.8	0.3	1.2	0.8	0.8	0.3	1.2	UNDP	0.8
UNTA	1.0	0.7	0.3	0.8	1.0	0.7	0.3	0.8	UNTA	1.0
UNICEF	—	—	—	—	—	—	—	—	UNICEF	—
UNRWA	—	—	—	—	—	—	—	—	UNRWA	—
WFP	0.4	0.5	0.1	—	0.4	0.5	0.1	—	WFP	0.4
UNHCR	—	—	—	—	—	—	—	—	UNHCR	—
Other Multilateral	1.0	1.0	1.1	0.9	1.0	1.0	1.1	0.9	Other Multilateral	1.0
Arab OPEC Agencies	—	—	—	—	—	—	—	—	Arab OPEC Agencies	—
TOTAL	42.4	16.1	0.4	13.3	10.5	7.8	5.6	10.1	**TOTAL**	10.5
OPEC COUNTRIES	—	—	—	—	—	—	—	—	**OPEC COUNTRIES**	
E.E.C.+ MEMBERS	17.9	14.5	5.0	19.9	11.0	8.6	6.9	10.8	E.E.C.+ MEMBERS	12.3
TOTAL	65.3	31.9	22.5	47.2	32.7	31.3	31.9	42.5	**TOTAL**	34.0

ODA LOANS GROSS / **ODA LOANS NET** / **GRANTS**

	1983	1984	1985	1986	1983	1984	1985	1986		1983
DAC COUNTRIES										
Australia	—	—	—	—	—	—	—	—	Australia	9.6
Austria	—	—	—	—	—	—	—	—	Austria	—
Belgium	—	—	—	—	—	—	—	—	Belgium	—
Canada	—	—	—	—	—	—	—	—	Canada	0.5
Denmark	—	—	—	—	—	—	—	—	Denmark	—
Finland	—	—	—	—	—	—	—	—	Finland	0.1
France	—	—	—	—	—	—	—	—	France	0.2
Germany, Fed. Rep.	—	—	—	—	—	—	—	—	Germany, Fed. Rep.	1.2
Ireland	—	—	—	—	—	—	—	—	Ireland	—
Italy	—	—	—	—	—	—	—	—	Italy	—
Japan	—	—	—	—	—	—	—	—	Japan	2.1
Netherlands	—	0.9	—	—	—	0.9	—	—	Netherlands	0.3
New Zealand	—	—	—	—	—	—	—	—	New Zealand	3.5
Norway	—	—	—	—	—	—	—	—	Norway	—
Sweden	—	—	—	—	—	—	—	—	Sweden	—
Switzerland	—	—	—	—	—	—	—	—	Switzerland	—
United Kingdom	—	—	—	—	-1.3	-1.1	-1.1	-1.3	United Kingdom	4.2
United States	—	—	—	—	—	—	—	—	United States	2.0
TOTAL	—	0.9	—	—	-1.3	-0.2	-1.1	-1.3	**TOTAL**	23.6
MULTILATERAL	2.8	0.9	0.1	2.7	2.8	0.9	0.1	2.7	**MULTILATERAL**	7.7
OPEC COUNTRIES	—	—	—	—	—	—	—	—	**OPEC COUNTRIES**	
E.E.C.+ MEMBERS	2.8	1.8	0.1	2.7	1.5	0.7	-1.1	1.3	E.E.C.+ MEMBERS	9.8
TOTAL	2.8	1.8	0.1	2.7	1.5	0.7	-1.1	1.3	**TOTAL**	31.4

TOTAL OFFICIAL GROSS / **TOTAL OFFICIAL NET** / **TOTAL OOF GROSS**

	1983	1984	1985	1986	1983	1984	1985	1986		1983
DAC COUNTRIES										
Australia	9.6	9.9	10.0	13.8	8.7	6.2	6.9	11.1	Australia	—
Austria	—	—	—	—	—	—	—	—	Austria	—
Belgium	—	—	—	0.1	—	—	—	0.1	Belgium	—
Canada	0.5	0.2	0.4	0.3	0.5	0.2	0.4	0.3	Canada	—
Denmark	—	—	—	—	—	—	—	—	Denmark	—
Finland	0.1	0.3	—	0.0	0.1	0.3	—	0.0	Finland	—
France	0.2	0.5	—	0.6	0.2	0.5	—	0.6	France	—
Germany, Fed. Rep.	1.2	0.9	1.0	1.4	1.2	0.9	1.0	1.4	Germany, Fed. Rep.	—
Ireland	—	—	—	—	—	—	—	—	Ireland	—
Italy	—	—	—	—	—	—	—	—	Italy	—
Japan	2.1	3.4	8.2	11.0	2.1	3.4	8.2	11.0	Japan	—
Netherlands	0.3	1.2	0.5	0.4	0.3	1.2	0.5	0.4	Netherlands	—
New Zealand	3.5	3.4	3.4	2.3	3.5	3.4	3.4	2.3	New Zealand	—
Norway	—	0.0	0.0	0.1	—	0.0	0.0	0.1	Norway	—
Sweden	—	—	—	—	—	—	—	—	Sweden	—
Switzerland	—	—	—	—	—	—	—	—	Switzerland	—
United Kingdom	6.0	6.2	5.1	10.5	3.8	4.3	2.9	7.4	United Kingdom	1.
United States	2.0	2.0	1.0	1.0	1.0	1.0	—	—	United States	—
TOTAL	25.4	28.1	29.6	41.3	21.3	21.4	23.3	34.5	**TOTAL**	1.
MULTILATERAL	47.6	23.4	9.4	24.6	42.4	16.1	0.4	13.3	**MULTILATERAL**	37.
OPEC COUNTRIES	—	—	—	—	—	—	—	—	**OPEC COUNTRIES**	
E.E.C.+ MEMBERS	19.0	17.2	12.5	25.8	15.9	14.2	8.6	20.1	E.E.C.+ MEMBERS	6.
TOTAL	73.0	51.4	39.0	65.8	63.8	37.5	23.7	47.8	**TOTAL**	39.

MILLION US DOLLARS, UNLESS OTHERWISE STATED

ODA COMMITMENTS

1984	1985	1986	1983	1984	1985	1986
9.9	10.0	13.8	5.1	11.2	9.6	24.7
–	–	0.1	–	–	–	0.1
0.2	0.4	0.3	0.7	0.2	0.6	0.3
0.3	–	0.0	–	0.0	–	–
0.5	–	0.6	0.2	0.5	–	0.6
0.9	1.0	1.4	1.8	0.5	1.7	1.9
–	–	–	–	–	–	–
3.4	8.2	11.0	2.3	9.2	7.4	13.0
1.2	0.5	0.4	0.2	1.0	0.4	0.4
3.4	3.4	2.3	3.7	3.7	3.5	1.1
0.0	0.0	0.1	–	–	–	–
–	–	–	–	–	–	–
2.8	2.9	2.9	3.4	2.4	2.8	2.9
2.0	1.0	1.0	1.2	1.4	1.1	2.4
24.6	27.4	33.7	18.5	30.1	27.2	47.3
–	–	–	–	–	–	–
0.5	0.2	0.4	–	–	–	–
–	–	–	–	–	–	–
4.3	3.6	6.8	8.4	1.3	13.4	3.3
–	–	–	–	–	–	–
–	–	–	–	–	–	–
–	–	–	–	–	–	–
–	–	–	3.2	3.0	1.9	2.9
0.8	0.3	1.2	–	–	–	–
0.7	0.3	0.8	–	–	–	–
–	–	–	–	–	–	–
0.5	0.1	–	–	–	–	–
–	–	–	–	–	–	–
1.0	1.1	0.9	–	–	–	–
–	–	–	–	–	–	–
7.8	5.6	10.1	11.6	4.3	15.2	6.2
–	–	–	–	–	–	–
9.7	8.0	12.1	13.9	5.7	18.3	9.1
32.4	33.0	43.8	30.1	34.5	42.4	53.5

TECH. COOP. GRANTS

1984	1985	1986	1983	1984	1985	1986
9.9	10.0	13.8	3.7	6.0	5.1	8.8
–	–	0.1	–	–	–	–
0.2	0.4	0.3	0.2	–	0.1	–
0.3	–	0.0	0.1	0.3	–	0.0
0.5	–	0.6	0.2	0.5	–	0.6
0.9	1.0	1.4	1.2	0.9	1.0	1.4
–	–	–	–	–	–	–
3.4	8.2	11.0	2.0	3.1	3.5	4.7
0.2	0.5	0.4	0.3	0.2	0.5	0.4
3.4	3.4	2.3	1.0	0.8	0.9	1.3
0.0	0.0	0.1	–	–	–	–
–	–	–	–	–	–	–
2.8	2.9	2.9	3.1	2.4	2.4	1.6
2.0	1.0	1.0	2.0	2.0	1.0	1.0
23.7	27.4	33.7	13.7	16.3	14.6	19.7
6.9	5.6	7.5	2.8	2.5	1.8	3.1
–	–	–	–	–	–	–
7.9	7.9	9.5	4.8	4.1	3.9	4.0
30.6	33.0	41.2	16.5	18.8	16.3	22.8

TOTAL OOF NET

1984	1985	1986	1983	1984	1985	1986
–	–	–	-0.9	-3.7	-3.1	-2.7
–	–	–	–	–	–	–
–	–	–	–	–	–	–
–	–	–	–	–	–	–
–	–	–	–	–	–	–
–	–	–	–	–	–	–
–	–	–	–	–	–	–
–	–	–	–	–	–	–
–	–	–	–	–	–	–
–	–	–	–	–	–	–
–	–	–	–	–	–	–
–	–	–	–	–	–	–
3.4	2.2	7.6	0.9	2.7	1.1	5.9
–	–	–	-1.0	-1.0	-1.0	-1.0
3.4	2.2	7.6	-1.0	-2.1	-3.0	2.2
15.6	3.8	14.4	32.0	8.3	-5.2	3.1
–	–	–	–	–	–	–
7.5	4.5	13.7	4.9	5.6	1.7	9.3
19.0	6.0	22.0	31.0	6.2	-8.2	5.3

ODA COMMITMENTS : LOANS

DAC COUNTRIES	1983	1984	1985	1986
Australia	–	–	–	–
Austria	–	–	–	–
Belgium	–	–	–	–
Canada	–	–	–	–
Denmark	–	–	–	–
Finland	–	–	–	–
France	–	–	–	–
Germany, Fed. Rep.	–	–	–	–
Ireland	–	–	–	–
Italy	–	–	–	–
Japan	–	–	–	–
Netherlands	–	0.9	–	–
New Zealand	–	–	–	–
Norway	–	–	–	–
Sweden	–	–	–	–
Switzerland	–	–	–	–
United Kingdom	–	–	–	–
United States	–	–	–	–
TOTAL	–	0.9	–	–
MULTILATERAL	0.7	–	2.8	1.0
OPEC COUNTRIES	–	–	–	–
E.E.C.+ MEMBERS	0.7	0.9	2.8	1.0
TOTAL	0.7	0.9	2.8	1.0

GRANT ELEMENT OF ODA

DAC COUNTRIES	1983	1984	1985	1986
Australia	100.0	100.0	100.0	100.0
Austria	–	–	–	–
Belgium	–	–	–	100.0
Canada	100.0	100.0	100.0	100.0
Denmark	–	–	–	–
Finland	–	100.0	–	–
France	100.0	100.0	–	100.0
Germany, Fed. Rep.	100.0	100.0	100.0	100.0
Ireland	–	–	–	–
Italy	–	–	–	–
Japan	100.0	100.0	100.0	100.0
Netherlands	100.0	64.0	100.0	100.0
New Zealand	100.0	100.0	100.0	100.0
Norway	–	–	–	–
Sweden	–	–	–	–
Switzerland	–	–	–	–
United Kingdom	100.0	100.0	100.0	100.0
United States	100.0	100.0	100.0	100.0
TOTAL	100.0	98.8	100.0	100.0
MULTILATERAL	100.0	100.0	100.0	100.0
OPEC COUNTRIES	–	–	–	–
E.E.C.+ MEMBERS	100.0	93.4	100.0	100.0
TOTAL	100.0	98.9	100.0	100.0

OTHER AGGREGATES

COMMITMENTS: ALL SOURCES

	1983	1984	1985	1986
TOTAL BILATERAL	18.5	35.9	27.2	51.0
of which				
OPEC	–	–	–	–
CMEA	–	–	–	–
TOTAL MULTILATERAL	17.6	7.5	48.6	21.2
TOTAL BIL.& MULTIL.	36.1	43.4	75.8	72.3
of which				
ODA Grants	29.4	33.5	39.7	52.5
ODA Loans	0.7	0.9	2.8	1.0

DISBURSEMENTS:

DAC COUNTRIES COMBINED

	1983	1984	1985	1986
OFFICIAL & PRIVATE				
GROSS:				
Contractual Lending	11.3	4.9	3.5	9.7
Export Credits Total	9.4	0.5	1.3	2.1
Export Credits Private	9.4	0.5	1.3	2.1
NET:				
Contractual Lending	0.4	-3.5	-9.4	1.0
Export Credits Total	0.9	-6.0	-9.1	-3.4
PRIVATE SECTOR NET	1.5	-5.6	-1.3	-0.6
Direct Investment	-1.6	-4.3	3.7	-0.8
Portfolio Investment	0.5	-0.1	0.3	0.1
Export Credits	2.6	-1.2	-5.3	0.1

MARKET BORROWING:

CHANGE IN CLAIMS

	1983	1984	1985	1986
Banks	–	-10.0	5.0	44.0

MEMORANDUM ITEM:

	1983	1984	1985	1986
CMEA Countr.(Gross)	–	–	–	–

TOTAL RECEIPTS NET | TOTAL ODA NET | TOTAL ODA GROSS

DAC COUNTRIES	1983	1984	1985	1986	1983	1984	1985	1986	1983
Australia	—	—	—	—	—	—	—	—	—
Austria	—	—	—	—	—	—	—	—	—
Belgium	57.5	31.2	25.5	-24.9	1.4	2.0	2.4	1.7	1.4
Canada	2.3	4.6	5.3	6.5	0.6	1.1	1.7	3.4	0.6
Denmark	—	—	—	—	—	—	—	—	—
Finland	-0.1	-0.1	0.8	—	—	—	—	—	—
France	202.6	44.0	140.7	205.4	53.0	62.6	45.7	50.7	54.2
Germany, Fed. Rep.	-3.2	16.2	16.2	44.1	0.4	0.1	0.3	0.7	0.8
Ireland	—	—	—	—	—	—	—	—	—
Italy	-0.4	-12.3	1.1	0.8	0.9	0.6	0.7	0.3	0.9
Japan	-6.3	-28.4	-27.1	-1.4	-0.6	-0.9	-0.9	-0.5	0.4
Netherlands	0.0	6.5	0.5	4.1	0.0	0.0	—	1.4	0.1
New Zealand	—	—	—	—	—	—	—	—	—
Norway	6.0	—	—	—	—	—	—	—	—
Sweden	—	—	—	—	—	—	—	—	—
Switzerland	-6.3	0.1	0.1	0.1	0.1	0.1	0.1	0.1	0.1
United Kingdom	7.5	-6.5	30.3	35.6	0.0	0.0	0.0	0.0	0.0
United States	-1.0	1.0	9.0	5.0	1.0	2.0	2.0	1.0	1.0
TOTAL	258.5	56.3	202.3	275.2	56.7	67.4	51.9	58.7	59.4

MULTILATERAL	1983	1984	1985	1986	1983	1984	1985	1986	1983
AF.D.F.	—	—	—	—	—	—	—	—	—
AF.D.B.	5.9	5.6	2.3	12.7	—	—	—	—	—
AS.D.B	—	—	—	—	—	—	—	—	—
CAR.D.B.	—	—	—	—	—	—	—	—	—
E.E.C.	6.6	5.4	5.8	4.5	3.3	2.6	5.0	1.7	3.5
IBRD	-0.6	-2.2	-1.4	-1.2	—	—	—	—	—
IDA	—	—	—	—	—	—	—	—	—
I.D.B.	—	—	—	—	—	—	—	—	—
IFAD	—	—	—	—	—	—	—	—	—
I.F.C.	—	—	—	—	—	—	—	—	—
IMF TRUST FUND	—	—	—	—	—	—	—	—	—
U.N. AGENCIES	—	—	—	—	—	—	—	—	—
UNDP	2.1	2.5	3.1	2.8	2.1	2.5	3.1	2.8	2.1
UNTA	0.4	0.4	0.5	0.6	0.4	0.4	0.5	0.6	0.4
UNICEF	—	—	—	—	—	—	—	—	—
UNRWA	—	—	—	—	—	—	—	—	—
WFP	—	—	—	—	—	—	—	—	—
UNHCR	0.1	0.1	0.1	0.1	0.1	0.1	0.1	0.1	0.1
Other Multilateral	0.3	0.3	0.4	0.3	0.3	0.3	0.4	0.3	0.3
Arab OPEC Agencies	-0.2	-0.1	0.4	0.7	-0.2	-0.1	0.4	0.7	—
TOTAL	14.7	11.9	11.2	20.4	6.0	5.7	9.4	6.2	6.4
OPEC COUNTRIES	-0.3	-7.5	-10.1	14.0	1.0	2.4	-0.2	14.0	2.4
E.E.C.+ MEMBERS	270.5	84.4	220.1	269.6	59.0	67.8	54.1	56.5	60.9
TOTAL	272.8	60.7	203.3	309.6	63.8	75.6	61.1	78.8	68.2

ODA LOANS GROSS | ODA LOANS NET | GRANTS

DAC COUNTRIES	1983	1984	1985	1986	1983	1984	1985	1986	1983
Australia	—	—	—	—	—	—	—	—	—
Austria	—	—	—	—	—	—	—	—	—
Belgium	1.0	1.1	1.4	—	1.0	1.1	1.4	—	0.4
Canada	0.4	0.6	1.2	2.8	0.4	0.6	1.2	2.8	0.2
Denmark	—	—	—	—	—	—	—	—	—
Finland	—	—	—	—	—	—	—	—	—
France	8.5	10.2	13.4	22.5	7.3	9.3	12.6	22.0	45.7
Germany, Fed. Rep.	—	—	—	0.5	-0.5	-0.4	-0.5	0.2	0.8
Ireland	—	—	—	—	—	—	—	—	—
Italy	—	—	—	—	—	—	—	0.0	0.9
Japan	—	—	—	—	-1.0	-1.0	-1.0	-1.4	0.4
Netherlands	—	—	—	1.3	0.0	0.0	0.0	1.3	0.1
New Zealand	—	—	—	—	—	—	—	—	—
Norway	—	—	—	—	—	—	—	—	—
Sweden	—	—	—	—	—	—	—	—	—
Switzerland	—	—	—	—	—	—	—	—	0.1
United Kingdom	—	—	—	—	—	—	—	—	0.0
United States	—	—	—	—	—	—	—	—	1.0
TOTAL	9.9	12.0	16.0	27.1	7.2	9.6	13.8	24.8	49.5
MULTILATERAL	0.5	0.5	2.0	1.2	0.1	0.1	1.7	0.7	5.9
OPEC COUNTRIES	2.4	3.7	6.1	14.7	1.0	2.4	-0.2	14.0	—
E.E.C.+ MEMBERS	10.0	11.8	16.3	24.6	8.1	10.3	14.8	23.4	50.9
TOTAL	12.8	16.2	24.1	43.0	8.4	12.2	15.2	39.5	55.4

TOTAL OFFICIAL GROSS | TOTAL OFFICIAL NET | TOTAL OOF GROSS

DAC COUNTRIES	1983	1984	1985	1986	1983	1984	1985	1986	1983
Australia	—	—	—	—	—	—	—	—	—
Austria	—	—	—	—	—	—	—	—	—
Belgium	1.4	2.4	3.4	1.7	1.0	2.0	3.0	1.2	—
Canada	2.4	4.8	6.6	8.7	2.3	4.6	5.3	6.5	1.8
Denmark	—	—	—	—	—	—	—	—	—
Finland	—	—	—	—	—	—	—	—	—
France	63.2	73.1	56.8	70.4	54.6	67.6	47.7	66.1	9.0
Germany, Fed. Rep.	1.4	1.6	6.0	4.0	-1.2	-0.6	3.0	2.0	0.6
Ireland	—	—	—	—	—	—	—	—	—
Italy	2.1	0.6	0.7	0.3	1.0	0.0	-0.2	-0.7	1.2
Japan	0.4	0.1	0.1	0.8	-0.6	-0.9	-0.9	-0.5	—
Netherlands	0.1	—	0.0	1.4	0.0	-0.1	-0.1	1.3	—
New Zealand	—	—	—	—	—	—	—	—	—
Norway	—	—	—	—	—	—	—	—	—
Sweden	—	—	—	—	—	—	—	—	—
Switzerland	0.1	0.1	0.1	0.1	0.1	0.1	0.1	0.1	—
United Kingdom	0.0	0.0	0.0	0.0	0.0	0.0	0.0	0.0	—
United States	2.0	3.0	11.0	6.0	-1.0	1.0	9.0	5.0	1.0
TOTAL	73.0	85.6	84.6	93.4	56.1	73.6	66.8	80.9	13.6
MULTILATERAL	18.5	17.4	16.4	26.5	14.7	11.9	11.1	20.4	12.1
OPEC COUNTRIES	2.4	3.7	6.1	14.7	-0.3	-7.5	-10.1	14.0	—
E.E.C.+ MEMBERS	75.5	84.1	74.0	84.2	61.9	74.2	59.2	74.4	14.6
TOTAL	93.9	106.8	107.0	134.6	70.4	78.0	67.8	115.4	25.7

ODA COMMITMENTS

1984	1985	1986	1983	1984	1985	1986
–	–	–	–	–	–	–
2.0	2.4	1.7	2.0	0.3	1.0	1.7
1.1	1.7	3.4	4.3	0.4	9.3	0.3
–	–	–	–	–	–	–
						--
63.5	46.5	51.3	55.6	73.8	47.8	51.3
0.5	0.8	1.0	0.7	0.1	0.6	0.4
–	–	–	–	–	–	–
0.6	0.7	0.3	1.8	9.2	0.8	0.6
0.1	0.1	0.8	0.2	0.1	0.2	0.7
–	0.0	1.4	0.0	–	0.0	1.4
–	–	–	–	–	–	–
0.1	0.1	0.1	0.0	0.0	0.0	–
0.0	0.0	0.0	0.0	0.0	0.0	0.0
2.0	2.0	1.0	1.0	1.2	1.1	1.5
69.8	54.2	60.9	65.7	85.1	60.9	57.9
–	–	–	–	–	–	–
–	–	–	–	–	–	–
–	–	–	–	–	–	–
2.8	5.2	2.1	2.4	2.8	2.0	-2.2
–	–	–	–	–	–	–
–	–	–	–	–	–	–
–	–	–	–	–	–	–
			2.9	3.3	4.1	3.7
2.5	3.1	2.8	–	–	–	–
0.4	0.5	0.6	–	–	–	–
–	–	–	–	–	–	–
0.1	0.1	0.1	–	–	–	–
0.3	0.4	0.3	–	–	–	–
–	0.5	0.9	5.6	1.0	–	–
6.0	9.8	6.7	10.9	7.0	6.1	1.5
3.7	6.1	14.7	–	–	–	–
69.4	55.5	57.7	62.6	86.2	52.3	53.2
79.6	70.0	82.4	76.6	92.1	67.0	59.4

TECH. COOP. GRANTS

1984	1985	1986	1983	1984	1985	1986
–	–	–	–	–	–	–
0.9	1.1	1.7	0.4	0.7	0.8	0.9
0.4	0.5	0.6	0.6	–	0.9	–
–	–	–	–	–	–	–
53.3	33.1	28.7	17.2	22.7	20.9	25.7
0.5	0.8	0.5	0.8	0.5	0.8	0.5
–	–	–	–	–	–	–
0.6	0.7	0.3	0.9	0.6	0.7	0.3
0.1	0.1	0.8	0.2	0.1	0.1	0.6
–	0.0	0.1	0.1	–	0.0	0.1
–	–	–	–	–	–	–
–	–	–	–	–	–	–
0.1	0.1	0.1	0.1	0.0	0.1	0.1
0.0	0.0	0.0	0.0	0.0	0.0	0.0
2.0	2.0	1.0	1.0	2.0	2.0	1.0
57.8	38.2	33.8	21.2	26.6	26.1	29.2
5.6	7.7	5.5	2.9	3.3	4.1	3.9
–	–	–	–	–	–	–
57.6	39.2	33.1	19.4	24.5	23.1	27.8
63.4	45.9	39.3	24.1	29.9	30.2	33.1

TOTAL OOF NET

1984	1985	1986	1983	1984	1985	1986
–	–	–	–	–	–	–
0.4	1.0	–	-0.4	0.0	0.6	-0.5
3.7	4.9	5.3	1.7	3.6	3.6	3.1
–	–	–	–	–	–	–
9.7	10.3	19.2	1.6	5.0	2.0	15.4
1.1	5.2	3.0	-1.5	-0.6	2.6	1.3
–	–	–	0.1	-0.6	-0.9	-1.0
–	–	–	-0.1	-0.1	-0.1	-0.1
–	–	–	–	–	–	–
–	–	–	–	–	–	–
–	–	–	–	–	–	–
1.0	9.0	5.0	-2.0	-1.0	7.0	4.0
15.9	30.4	32.5	-0.7	6.2	14.9	22.2
11.4	6.6	19.8	8.7	6.2	1.8	14.3
–	–	–	-1.3	-10.0	-10.0	–
14.7	18.4	26.5	3.0	6.4	5.1	17.9
27.2	37.0	52.2	6.7	2.5	6.7	36.5

ODA COMMITMENTS : LOANS

DAC COUNTRIES

	1983	1984	1985	1986
Australia	–	–	–	–
Austria	–	–	–	–
Belgium	2.0	0.3	0.5	–
Canada	4.0	–	9.1	–
Denmark	–	–	–	–
Finland	–	–	–	–
France	9.4	20.3	15.0	22.5
Germany, Fed. Rep.	–	–	–	–
Ireland	–	–	–	–
Italy	–	8.1	–	–
Japan	–	–	–	–
Netherlands	–	–	–	1.3
New Zealand	–	–	–	–
Norway	–	–	–	–
Sweden	–	–	–	–
Switzerland	–	–	–	–
United Kingdom	–	–	–	–
United States	–	–	–	–
TOTAL	15.3	28.6	24.6	23.8
MULTILATERAL	7.8	3.6	–	–
OPEC COUNTRIES	–	–	–	–
E.E.C.+ MEMBERS	13.5	31.2	15.5	23.8
TOTAL	23.1	32.2	24.6	23.8

GRANT ELEMENT OF ODA

DAC COUNTRIES

	1983	1984	1985	1986
Australia	–	–	–	–
Austria	–	–	–	–
Belgium	79.9	80.9	85.4	100.0
Canada	90.5	100.0	89.9	100.0
Denmark	–	–	–	–
Finland	–	–	–	–
France	87.9	80.6	78.5	77.0
Germany, Fed. Rep.	100.0	100.0	100.0	100.0
Ireland	–	–	–	–
Italy	100.0	50.2	100.0	100.0
Japan	100.0	100.0	100.0	100.0
Netherlands	100.0	–	100.0	100.0
New Zealand	–	–	–	–
Norway	–	–	–	–
Sweden	–	–	–	–
Switzerland	100.0	100.0	100.0	–
United Kingdom	100.0	100.0	100.0	100.0
United States	100.0	100.0	100.0	100.0
TOTAL	88.5	77.7	81.4	79.4
MULTILATERAL	61.1	94.8	100.0	100.0
OPEC COUNTRIES	–	–	–	–
E.E.C.+ MEMBERS	88.2	77.3	80.1	77.3
TOTAL	85.3	78.6	83.1	80.0

OTHER AGGREGATES

COMMITMENTS: ALL SOURCES

	1983	1984	1985	1986
TOTAL BILATERAL	115.9	140.8	75.9	83.9
of which				
OPEC	–	–	–	–
CMEA	–	–	–	–
TOTAL MULTILATERAL	30.4	14.9	50.2	1.5
TOTAL BIL.& MULTIL.	146.3	155.7	126.1	85.5
of which				
ODA Grants	53.5	59.9	42.4	35.6
ODA Loans	23.1	32.2	24.6	23.8

DISBURSEMENTS:

DAC COUNTRIES COMBINED

	1983	1984	1985	1986
OFFICIAL & PRIVATE				
GROSS:				
Contractual Lending	253.7	267.5	340.2	215.2
Export Credits Total	234.8	245.9	313.9	169.0
Export Credits Private	230.2	240.1	294.7	155.7
NET:				
Contractual Lending	95.9	49.4	137.0	143.2
Export Credits Total	87.6	35.2	121.7	103.6
PRIVATE SECTOR NET	202.5	-17.3	135.5	194.3
Direct Investment	79.4	9.9	35.9	84.0
Portfolio Investment	33.7	-61.1	-9.7	14.2
Export Credits	89.3	33.9	109.4	96.1

MARKET BORROWING:

CHANGE IN CLAIMS

	1983	1984	1985	1986
Banks	–	23.0	224.0	237.0

MEMORANDUM ITEM:

	1983	1984	1985	1986
CMEA Countr.(Gross)	–	–	–	–

DISBURSEMENTS, UNLESS OTHERWISE STATED

TOTAL RECEIPTS NET / TOTAL ODA NET / TOTAL ODA GROSS

	1983	1984	1985	1986	1983	1984	1985	1986		1983
DAC COUNTRIES										
Australia	0.0	0.0	0.0	0.0	0.0	0.0	0.0	0.0	Australia	0.0
Austria	0.0	-0.6	-0.3	0.0	0.0	0.0	0.0	0.0	Austria	0.0
Belgium	0.3	0.2	0.0	-0.1	0.0	0.1	–	–	Belgium	0.0
Canada	1.2	0.6	0.9	0.2	1.2	0.6	0.9	0.2	Canada	1.2
Denmark	0.3	0.1	0.3	0.1	0.4	0.2	0.4	0.1	Denmark	0.4
Finland	0.0	–	–	–	0.0	–	–	–	Finland	0.0
France	0.2	2.7	3.6	11.3	0.5	2.9	3.6	5.8	France	0.5
Germany, Fed. Rep.	8.1	8.2	5.2	6.0	8.2	7.7	5.1	5.5	Germany, Fed. Rep.	8.3
Ireland	0.1	0.0	0.0	0.2	0.1	0.0	0.0	0.2	Ireland	0.1
Italy	0.0	0.0	1.7	15.3	–	0.0	1.8	15.3	Italy	–
Japan	0.1	3.4	1.2	1.6	0.1	3.4	1.2	1.6	Japan	0.1
Netherlands	0.7	2.4	3.0	6.0	0.7	2.4	3.0	6.0	Netherlands	0.7
New Zealand	–	–	–	–	–	–	–	–	New Zealand	–
Norway	0.5	10.9	10.1	9.1	0.9	0.4	0.8	1.1	Norway	0.9
Sweden	–	0.5	0.2	0.0	–	0.1	0.2	0.1	Sweden	–
Switzerland	0.0	0.0	0.1	0.1	0.0	0.0	0.1	0.1	Switzerland	0.0
United Kingdom	-2.8	-3.2	2.5	12.6	3.1	4.4	4.1	13.9	United Kingdom	3.6
United States	6.0	10.0	10.0	9.0	6.0	10.0	10.0	9.0	United States	6.0
TOTAL	14.7	35.3	38.5	71.4	21.3	32.3	31.2	59.0	TOTAL	21.9
MULTILATERAL										
AF.D.F.	3.6	1.6	2.8	9.1	3.6	1.6	2.8	9.1	AF.D.F.	3.6
AF.D.B.	1.2	1.3	1.5	0.0	–	–	–	–	AF.D.B.	–
AS.D.B	–	–	–	–	–	–	–	–	AS.D.B	–
CAR.D.B.	–	–	–	–	–	–	–	–	CAR.D.B.	–
E.E.C.	2.0	4.0	2.2	10.4	2.0	4.0	2.2	10.4	E.E.C.	2.0
IBRD	–	–	–	–	–	–	–	–	IBRD	–
IDA	4.9	2.4	3.8	13.9	4.9	2.4	3.8	13.9	IDA	5.0
I.D.B.	–	–	–	–	–	–	–	–	I.D.B.	–
IFAD	0.9	1.1	0.5	1.4	0.9	1.1	0.5	1.4	IFAD	0.9
I.F.C.	–	2.8	–	–	–	–	–	–	I.F.C.	–
IMF TRUST FUND	–	–	–	–	–	–	–	–	IMF TRUST FUND	–
U.N. AGENCIES	–	–	–	–	–	–	–	–	U.N. AGENCIES	–
UNDP	3.1	3.0	2.0	3.0	3.1	3.0	2.0	3.0	UNDP	3.1
UNTA	0.7	0.5	0.7	0.6	0.7	0.5	0.7	0.6	UNTA	0.7
UNICEF	0.1	0.2	0.4	0.4	0.1	0.2	0.4	0.4	UNICEF	0.1
UNRWA	–	–	–	–	–	–	–	–	UNRWA	–
WFP	2.5	5.0	3.6	2.5	2.5	5.0	3.6	2.5	WFP	2.5
UNHCR	–	–	–	–	–	–	–	–	UNHCR	–
Other Multilateral	1.7	1.4	1.8	1.5	1.7	1.4	1.8	1.5	Other Multilateral	1.7
Arab OPEC Agencies	1.8	0.1	0.2	–	0.2	1.2	0.2	–	Arab OPEC Agencies	0.6
TOTAL	22.5	23.5	19.7	42.8	19.7	20.4	18.1	42.8	TOTAL	20.2
OPEC COUNTRIES	1.1	0.9	0.8	-0.9	1.1	0.9	0.8	-0.9	OPEC COUNTRIES	1.9
E.E.C.+ MEMBERS	8.8	14.5	18.5	61.9	15.0	21.7	20.1	57.3	E.E.C.+ MEMBERS	15.6
TOTAL	38.2	59.6	58.9	113.4	42.1	53.6	50.1	100.9	TOTAL	44.0

ODA LOANS GROSS / ODA LOANS NET / GRANTS

	1983	1984	1985	1986	1983	1984	1985	1986		1983
DAC COUNTRIES										
Australia	–	–	–	–	–	–	–	–	Australia	0.0
Austria	–	–	–	–	–	–	–	–	Austria	0.0
Belgium	–	–	–	–	–	–	–	–	Belgium	0.0
Canada	–	–	–	–	–	–	–	–	Canada	1.2
Denmark	–	–	0.0	–	–	–	0.0	–	Denmark	0.4
Finland	–	–	–	–	–	–	–	–	Finland	0.0
France	0.1	2.5	3.3	5.2	0.1	2.5	3.3	5.2	France	0.4
Germany, Fed. Rep.	–	0.0	–	–	-0.1	-0.1	-0.1	-0.1	Germany, Fed. Rep.	8.3
Ireland	–	–	–	–	–	–	–	–	Ireland	0.1
Italy	–	–	–	–	–	–	–	–	Italy	–
Japan	–	–	–	–	–	–	–	–	Japan	0.1
Netherlands	–	–	–	–	–	–	–	–	Netherlands	0.7
New Zealand	–	–	–	–	–	–	–	–	New Zealand	–
Norway	–	–	–	–	–	–	–	–	Norway	0.9
Sweden	–	–	–	–	–	–	–	–	Sweden	–
Switzerland	–	–	–	–	–	–	–	–	Switzerland	0.0
United Kingdom	0.0	–	–	–	-0.5	-0.5	-0.4	-0.6	United Kingdom	3.6
United States	–	–	–	–	–	–	–	–	United States	6.0
TOTAL	0.1	2.6	3.3	5.2	-0.5	2.0	2.8	4.5	TOTAL	21.8
MULTILATERAL	10.1	7.1	8.3	24.6	9.6	6.9	8.2	24.3	MULTILATERAL	10.2
OPEC COUNTRIES	1.3	2.4	0.7	0.6	0.5	0.4	0.7	-0.9	OPEC COUNTRIES	0.6
E.E.C.+ MEMBERS	0.1	3.1	4.3	5.2	-0.5	2.6	3.7	4.4	E.E.C.+ MEMBERS	15.5
TOTAL	11.5	12.1	12.3	30.4	9.5	9.3	11.6	27.9	TOTAL	32.6

TOTAL OFFICIAL GROSS / TOTAL OFFICIAL NET / TOTAL OOF GROSS

	1983	1984	1985	1986	1983	1984	1985	1986		1983
DAC COUNTRIES										
Australia	0.0	0.0	0.0	0.0	0.0	0.0	0.0	0.0	Australia	–
Austria	0.0	0.0	0.0	0.0	0.0	0.0	0.0	0.0	Austria	–
Belgium	0.0	0.1	–	–	0.0	0.1	–	–	Belgium	–
Canada	1.2	0.6	0.9	0.2	1.2	0.6	0.9	0.2	Canada	–
Denmark	0.4	0.2	0.4	0.1	0.4	0.2	0.4	0.1	Denmark	–
Finland	0.0	–	–	–	0.0	–	–	–	Finland	–
France	0.5	3.0	3.6	11.0	0.5	3.0	3.6	11.0	France	–
Germany, Fed. Rep.	8.4	8.1	5.3	6.1	8.2	8.0	5.2	5.9	Germany, Fed. Rep.	0.1
Ireland	0.1	0.0	0.0	0.2	0.1	0.0	0.0	0.2	Ireland	–
Italy	–	0.0	1.8	15.3	–	0.0	1.8	15.3	Italy	–
Japan	0.1	3.4	1.2	1.6	0.1	3.4	1.2	1.6	Japan	–
Netherlands	0.7	2.4	3.0	6.0	0.7	2.4	3.0	6.0	Netherlands	–
New Zealand	–	–	–	–	–	–	–	–	New Zealand	–
Norway	0.9	0.4	0.8	1.1	0.9	0.4	0.8	1.1	Norway	–
Sweden	–	0.5	0.2	0.2	–	0.5	0.2	0.0	Sweden	–
Switzerland	0.0	0.0	0.1	0.1	0.0	0.0	0.1	0.1	Switzerland	–
United Kingdom	3.6	4.9	4.7	14.5	3.1	4.4	4.1	13.9	United Kingdom	–
United States	6.0	10.0	10.0	9.0	6.0	10.0	10.0	9.0	United States	–
TOTAL	22.0	33.7	32.0	65.3	21.4	33.1	31.3	64.5	TOTAL	0.1
MULTILATERAL	24.0	26.8	19.9	44.9	22.5	23.5	19.7	42.8	MULTILATERAL	3.8
OPEC COUNTRIES	1.9	2.9	0.8	0.6	1.1	0.9	0.8	-0.9	OPEC COUNTRIES	–
E.E.C.+ MEMBERS	15.7	22.7	21.1	63.7	15.0	22.2	20.2	62.9	E.E.C.+ MEMBERS	0.1
TOTAL	47.9	63.4	52.7	110.9	44.9	57.5	51.8	106.4	TOTAL	3.8

ODA COMMITMENTS

1984	1985	1986	1983	1984	1985	1986
0.0	0.0	0.0	0.0	0.0	0.0	–
0.0	0.0	0.0	0.0	0.0	0.0	–
0.1	–	–	–	–	–	–
0.6	0.9	0.2	1.7	0.8	0.6	0.3
0.2	0.4	0.1	–	0.1	0.7	–
–	–	–	–	–	–	–
2.9	3.6	5.8	10.2	14.8	0.3	5.8
7.8	5.2	5.7	3.8	4.4	1.9	5.9
0.0	0.0	0.2	0.1	0.0	0.0	0.2
0.0	1.8	15.3	–	0.0	1.8	20.3
3.4	1.2	1.6	2.4	2.0	1.1	2.2
2.4	3.0	6.0	0.5	3.9	1.9	4.3
–	–	–	–	–	–	–
0.4	0.8	1.1	0.1	6.9	0.2	0.3
0.1	0.2	0.2	–	–	–	0.2
0.0	0.1	0.1	0.0	0.0	0.1	0.1
4.9	4.6	14.5	2.6	2.5	2.5	10.5
10.0	10.0	9.0	7.8	8.9	12.5	6.2
32.9	*31.7*	*59.7*	*29.3*	*44.6*	*23.4*	*56.2*
1.6	2.8	9.1	17.4	–	–	16.3
–	–	–	–	–	–	–
–	–	–	–	–	–	–
4.1	2.3	10.6	5.1	0.7	1.1	8.9
–	–	–	–	–	–	–
2.5	3.8	14.1	–	20.9	–	29.3
–	–	–	–	–	–	–
1.1	0.5	1.4	–	4.7	–	–
–	–	–	–	–	–	–
–	–	–	8.1	10.1	8.7	8.0
3.0	2.0	3.0	–	–	–	–
0.5	0.7	0.6	–	–	–	–
0.2	0.4	0.4	–	–	–	–
–	–	–	–	–	–	–
5.0	3.6	2.5	–	–	–	–
–	–	–	–	–	–	–
1.4	1.8	1.5	–	–	–	–
1.3	0.2	–	1.0	1.1	–	–
20.6	*18.3*	*43.1*	*31.6*	*37.4*	*9.8*	*62.5*
2.9	*0.8*	*0.6*	*5.7*	*0.0*	*0.0*	*–*
22.3	*20.7*	*58.1*	*22.3*	*26.5*	*10.1*	*55.9*
56.4	**50.8**	**103.4**	**66.5**	**82.1**	**33.2**	**118.7**

TECH. COOP. GRANTS

1984	1985	1986	1983	1984	1985	1986
0.0	0.0	0.0	0.0	0.0	0.0	0.0
0.0	0.0	0.0	0.0	–	–	–
0.1	–	–	0.0	–	–	–
0.6	0.9	0.2	0.5	–	0.7	–
0.2	0.4	0.1	0.4	0.2	0.2	–
–	–	–	0.0	–	–	–
0.4	0.3	0.6	0.2	0.3	0.3	0.6
7.8	5.2	5.7	2.3	2.7	2.3	2.5
0.0	0.0	0.2	0.1	0.0	0.0	0.2
0.0	1.8	15.3	–	0.0	1.8	14.3
3.4	1.2	1.6	0.1	0.1	0.3	0.4
2.4	3.0	6.0	0.4	0.4	0.4	0.8
–	–	–	–	–	–	–
0.4	0.8	1.1	–	0.0	0.1	0.0
0.1	0.2	0.2	–	0.0	–	–
0.0	0.1	0.1	–	–	–	0.0
4.9	4.6	14.5	2.1	2.0	2.0	3.1
10.0	10.0	9.0	4.0	4.0	5.0	5.0
30.3	*28.4*	*54.5*	*10.2*	*9.8*	*12.9*	*26.9*
13.5	*10.0*	*18.5*	*5.6*	*5.0*	*5.0*	*5.6*
0.5	*0.1*	*0.0*	*–*	*–*	*–*	*–*
19.2	*16.4*	*52.9*	*5.6*	*5.6*	*6.9*	*21.5*
44.3	**38.4**	**73.1**	**15.8**	**14.8**	**17.9**	**32.5**

TOTAL OOF NET

1984	1985	1986	1983	1984	1985	1986
–	–	–	–	–	–	–
–	–	–	–	–	–	–
–	–	–	–	–	–	–
–	–	–	–	–	–	–
0.1	–	5.2	–	0.1	–	5.2
0.3	0.2	0.4	0.1	0.3	0.1	0.4
–	–	–	–	–	–	–
0.1	0.1	–	–	0.1	0.1	–
–	–	–	–	–	–	–
0.4	–	–	–	0.4	–	-0.1
–	–	–	–	–	–	–
–	0.1	–	–	–	0.0	–
0.8	*0.4*	*5.6*	*0.1*	*0.8*	*0.2*	*5.5*
6.2	*1.5*	*1.8*	*2.7*	*3.1*	*1.5*	*0.0*
–	–	–	–	–	–	–
0.4	*0.4*	*5.6*	*0.1*	*0.4*	*0.2*	*5.6*
7.0	**1.9**	**7.5**	**2.8**	**3.9**	**1.7**	**5.5**

ODA COMMITMENTS : LOANS

DAC COUNTRIES

	1983	1984	1985	1986
Australia	–	–	–	–
Austria	–	–	–	–
Belgium	–	–	–	–
Canada	–	–	–	–
Denmark	–	–	–	–
Finland	–	–	–	–
France	9.9	14.5	–	5.2
Germany, Fed. Rep.	–	–	–	–
Ireland	–	–	–	–
Italy	–	–	–	–
Japan	–	–	–	–
Netherlands	–	–	–	–
New Zealand	–	–	–	–
Norway	–	–	–	–
Sweden	–	–	–	–
Switzerland	–	–	–	–
United Kingdom	–	–	–	–
United States	–	–	–	–
TOTAL	*9.9*	*14.5*	*–*	*5.2*
MULTILATERAL	*18.4*	*26.3*	*–*	*45.6*
OPEC COUNTRIES	*–*	*–*	*–*	*–*
E.E.C.+ MEMBERS	*9.9*	*14.5*	*–*	*5.2*
TOTAL	**28.2**	**40.8**	**–**	**50.9**

GRANT ELEMENT OF ODA

DAC COUNTRIES

	1983	1984	1985	1986
Australia	100.0	100.0	100.0	–
Austria	100.0	100.0	100.0	–
Belgium	–	–	–	–
Canada	100.0	100.0	100.0	100.0
Denmark	–	100.0	100.0	–
Finland	–	–	–	–
France	100.0	37.5	100.0	100.0
Germany, Fed. Rep.	100.0	100.0	100.0	100.0
Ireland	100.0	100.0	100.0	100.0
Italy	–	100.0	100.0	100.0
Japan	100.0	100.0	100.0	100.0
Netherlands	100.0	100.0	100.0	100.0
New Zealand	–	–	–	–
Norway	100.0	100.0	100.0	100.0
Sweden	–	–	–	100.0
Switzerland	100.0	100.0	100.0	100.0
United Kingdom	100.0	100.0	100.0	100.0
United States	100.0	100.0	100.0	100.0
TOTAL	*100.0*	*79.3*	*100.0*	*100.0*
MULTILATERAL	*88.7*	*87.1*	*100.0*	*87.3*
OPEC COUNTRIES	*100.0*	*100.0*	*100.0*	*–*
E.E.C.+ MEMBERS	*100.0*	*65.1*	*100.0*	*100.0*
TOTAL	**93.7**	**82.8**	**100.0**	**93.0**

OTHER AGGREGATES

COMMITMENTS: ALL SOURCES

	1983	1984	1985	1986
TOTAL BILATERAL	35.0	45.1	23.6	56.1
of which				
OPEC	5.7	0.0	0.0	–
CMEA	–	–	–	–
TOTAL MULTILATERAL	40.0	38.6	10.0	62.5
TOTAL BIL.& MULTIL.	74.9	83.8	33.6	118.6
of which				
ODA Grants	38.3	41.3	33.2	67.9
ODA Loans	28.2	40.8	–	50.9

DISBURSEMENTS:

DAC COUNTRIES COMBINED

OFFICIAL & PRIVATE

	1983	1984	1985	1986
GROSS:				
Contractual Lending	9.3	17.9	14.2	21.8
Export Credits Total	9.2	14.9	10.5	10.9
Export Credits Private	9.2	14.5	10.5	10.9
NET:				
Contractual Lending	-6.7	6.6	10.7	16.7
Export Credits Total	-6.3	4.1	7.8	6.6
PRIVATE SECTOR NET	-6.7	2.2	7.2	7.0
Direct Investment	-0.4	-1.7	-0.5	0.0
Portfolio Investment	0.0	0.1	-0.1	0.2
Export Credits	-6.3	3.8	7.8	6.7

MARKET BORROWING:

CHANGE IN CLAIMS

	1983	1984	1985	1986
Banks	–	14.0	-5.0	1.0

MEMORANDUM ITEM:

	1983	1984	1985	1986
CMEA Countr.(Gross)	–	–	–	–

	1983	1984	1985	1986		1983	1984	1985	1986		1983
TOTAL RECEIPTS NET					**TOTAL ODA NET**					**TOTAL ODA GROSS**	
DAC COUNTRIES											
Australia	1.8	1.9	0.3	0.4		1.8	1.9	0.3	0.4	Australia	1.8
Austria	0.1	-0.4	-0.3	0.2		0.1	0.1	0.1	0.2	Austria	0.1
Belgium	0.0	0.0	-0.1	0.1		0.0	0.1	0.1	0.2	Belgium	0.0
Canada	4.6	35.8	17.4	20.2		5.9	36.7	17.5	16.5	Canada	6.2
Denmark	0.0	-0.2	-0.1	-0.2		0.0	-0.2	-0.1	-0.2	Denmark	0.3
Finland	0.2	0.1	0.0	0.1		0.2	0.1	0.0	0.1	Finland	0.2
France	3.0	-0.8	-0.1	14.8		1.6	1.2	1.3	1.8	France	1.9
Germany, Fed. Rep.	19.1	11.0	16.2	21.5		19.1	10.8	16.6	21.9	Germany, Fed. Rep.	25.4
Ireland	0.0	0.0	0.0	0.1		0.0	0.0	0.0	0.1	Ireland	0.0
Italy	-1.9	0.8	-2.5	-2.7		1.9	0.8	0.6	4.8	Italy	1.9
Japan	6.2	8.7	20.4	24.9		7.4	12.7	24.0	29.4	Japan	7.4
Netherlands	5.6	2.4	0.8	16.1		5.4	4.2	2.7	9.4	Netherlands	5.4
New Zealand	0.0	–	–	–		0.0	–	–	–	New Zealand	0.0
Norway	1.4	28.5	27.1	26.5		1.4	0.4	0.5	0.5	Norway	1.4
Sweden	–	0.0	–	–		–	0.0	–	–	Sweden	–
Switzerland	0.7	4.7	9.7	3.1		0.6	4.8	9.7	3.1	Switzerland	0.6
United Kingdom	30.1	14.6	15.9	39.2		8.2	3.8	11.5	24.4	United Kingdom	10.1
United States	7.0	17.0	10.0	7.0		7.0	18.0	11.0	8.0	United States	12.0
TOTAL	77.8	124.2	114.8	171.2		60.8	95.3	95.9	120.6	TOTAL	74.9
MULTILATERAL											
AF.D.F.	4.0	5.2	19.2	13.0		4.0	5.2	19.2	13.0	AF.D.F.	4.0
AF.D.B.	1.0	0.4	1.9	8.8		–	–	–	–	AF.D.B.	–
AS.D.B	–	–	–	–		–	–	–	–	AS.D.B	–
CAR.D.B.	–	–	–	–		–	–	–	–	CAR.D.B.	–
E.E.C.	14.8	45.2	11.5	37.8		13.7	46.4	11.5	39.4	E.E.C.	13.8
IBRD	-3.4	-2.7	-1.8	-8.8		1.0	4.2	0.4	–	IBRD	1.0
IDA	16.3	48.9	62.8	169.6		16.3	48.9	62.8	169.6	IDA	16.9
I.D.B.	–	–	–	–		–	–	–	–	I.D.B.	–
IFAD	0.4	0.3	1.8	2.4		0.4	0.3	1.8	2.4	IFAD	0.4
I.F.C.	–	–	5.0	10.0		–	–	–	–	I.F.C.	–
IMF TRUST FUND	–	–	–	–		–	–	–	–	IMF TRUST FUND	–
U.N. AGENCIES	–	–	–	–		–	–	–	–	U.N. AGENCIES	–
UNDP	3.0	3.0	3.4	3.7		3.0	3.0	3.4	3.7	UNDP	3.0
UNTA	0.9	0.6	0.9	1.1		0.9	0.6	0.9	1.1	UNTA	0.9
UNICEF	1.3	1.5	1.9	2.1		1.3	1.5	1.9	2.1	UNICEF	1.3
UNRWA	–	–	–	–		–	–	–	–	UNRWA	–
WFP	9.9	14.2	10.5	17.0		9.9	14.2	10.5	17.0	WFP	9.9
UNHCR	0.2	0.1	0.2	0.2		0.2	0.1	0.2	0.2	UNHCR	0.2
Other Multilateral	1.4	1.7	1.5	1.0		1.4	1.7	1.5	1.0	Other Multilateral	1.4
Arab OPEC Agencies	1.6	-0.9	-1.0	-2.6		1.6	-0.9	-1.0	-1.9	Arab OPEC Agencies	2.6
TOTAL	51.2	117.4	117.8	255.1		53.6	125.2	113.1	247.5	TOTAL	55.2
OPEC COUNTRIES	-4.4	-4.5	-4.6	3.4		-4.4	-4.5	-4.6	3.4	OPEC COUNTRIES	0.3
E.E.C.+ MEMBERS	70.6	72.9	41.6	126.7		50.0	67.1	44.1	101.8	E.E.C.+ MEMBERS	58.9
TOTAL	124.7	237.1	228.1	429.7		110.0	216.0	204.4	371.5	TOTAL	130.4
ODA LOANS GROSS					**ODA LOANS NET**					**GRANTS**	
DAC COUNTRIES											
Australia	–	–	–	–		–	–	–	–	Australia	1.8
Austria	–	–	–	–		–	–	–	–	Austria	0.1
Belgium	–	–	–	–		–	–	–	–	Belgium	0.0
Canada	1.3	0.5	0.2	0.2		1.0	0.2	-0.7	-0.8	Canada	5.0
Denmark	0.1	–	–	–		-0.2	-0.2	-0.2	-0.3	Denmark	0.2
Finland	–	–	–	–		–	–	–	–	Finland	0.2
France	–	–	–	–		-0.3	-0.1	-0.1	-0.1	France	1.9
Germany, Fed. Rep.	16.2	7.3	13.7	18.5		9.8	2.1	8.6	11.5	Germany, Fed. Rep.	9.3
Ireland	–	–	–	–		–	–	–	–	Ireland	0.0
Italy	–	–	–	–		–	–	–	–	Italy	1.9
Japan	0.5	3.4	12.5	10.9		0.5	3.4	12.5	10.9	Japan	6.9
Netherlands	0.0	1.1	1.5	0.6		0.0	1.1	0.4	-0.8	Netherlands	5.3
New Zealand	–	–	–	–		–	–	–	–	New Zealand	0.0
Norway	–	–	–	–		–	–	–	–	Norway	1.4
Sweden	–	–	–	–		–	–	–	–	Sweden	–
Switzerland	–	–	–	–		–	–	–	–	Switzerland	0.6
United Kingdom	6.3	2.1	2.6	0.9		4.4	0.8	-0.8	-3.2	United Kingdom	3.8
United States	2.0	1.0	7.0	6.0		-3.0	-5.0	–	–	United States	10.0
TOTAL	26.3	15.4	37.5	37.1		12.2	2.3	19.6	17.1	TOTAL	48.6
MULTILATERAL	28.5	88.5	86.2	189.6		26.9	87.1	84.2	186.5	MULTILATERAL	26.7
OPEC COUNTRIES	–	–	–	–		-4.6	-4.6	-5.9	-4.5	OPEC COUNTRIES	0.3
E.E.C.+ MEMBERS	26.3	39.9	18.8	23.6		17.4	33.1	8.8	10.6	E.E.C.+ MEMBERS	32.6
TOTAL	54.9	103.9	123.7	226.7		34.5	84.8	97.9	199.1	TOTAL	75.5
TOTAL OFFICIAL GROSS					**TOTAL OFFICIAL NET**					**TOTAL OOF GROSS**	
DAC COUNTRIES											
Australia	1.8	1.9	0.3	0.4		1.8	1.9	0.3	0.4	Australia	–
Austria	0.1	0.1	0.1	0.2		0.1	0.1	0.1	0.2	Austria	–
Belgium	0.0	0.1	0.1	0.2		0.0	0.1	0.1	0.2	Belgium	–
Canada	6.2	37.0	18.4	21.5		4.6	35.8	17.4	20.2	Canada	–
Denmark	0.3	–	0.1	0.1		0.0	-0.2	-0.1	-0.2	Denmark	–
Finland	0.2	0.1	0.0	0.1		0.2	0.1	0.0	0.1	Finland	–
France	1.9	1.3	1.4	1.9		1.5	0.9	1.2	1.5	France	–
Germany, Fed. Rep.	25.4	16.0	21.7	28.9		19.1	10.8	16.6	21.9	Germany, Fed. Rep.	–
Ireland	0.0	0.0	0.0	0.1		0.0	0.0	0.0	0.1	Ireland	–
Italy	1.9	0.8	0.6	4.8		1.9	0.8	0.6	4.8	Italy	–
Japan	7.4	12.7	24.0	29.4		7.4	12.7	24.0	29.4	Japan	–
Netherlands	5.6	4.3	3.7	15.0		5.6	4.3	2.6	13.6	Netherlands	0.2
New Zealand	0.0	–	–	–		0.0	–	–	–	New Zealand	–
Norway	1.4	0.4	0.5	0.5		1.4	0.4	0.5	0.5	Norway	–
Sweden	–	0.0	–	–		–	0.0	–	–	Sweden	–
Switzerland	0.6	4.8	9.7	3.1		0.6	4.8	9.7	3.1	Switzerland	–
United Kingdom	10.1	5.1	15.0	28.5		8.2	3.8	11.5	24.4	United Kingdom	–
United States	12.0	24.0	18.0	14.0		6.0	17.0	11.0	8.0	United States	–
TOTAL	75.1	108.4	113.7	148.8		58.6	93.3	95.6	128.2	TOTAL	0.2
MULTILATERAL	67.0	130.4	131.8	273.0		51.2	117.4	117.8	255.1	MULTILATERAL	11.8
OPEC COUNTRIES	0.3	0.1	1.4	7.9		-4.4	-4.5	-4.6	3.4	OPEC COUNTRIES	–
E.E.C.+ MEMBERS	61.3	74.0	54.1	119.0		51.1	65.7	44.0	104.1	E.E.C.+ MEMBERS	2.5
TOTAL	142.3	238.9	246.9	429.7		105.4	206.2	208.9	386.8	TOTAL	12.0

GHANA

ODA COMMITMENTS

1984	1985	1986	1983	1984	1985	1986
1.9	0.3	0.4	0.1	1.7	0.1	0.1
0.1	0.1	0.2	0.1	0.1	0.1	–
0.1	0.1	0.2	–	–	–	0.2
37.0	18.4	17.5	32.8	11.4	38.0	14.2
–	0.1	0.1	0.0	–	0.1	–
0.1	0.0	0.1	0.2	0.0	0.0	–
1.3	1.4	1.9	1.9	1.2	12.5	1.9
16.0	21.7	28.9	35.1	7.2	8.0	32.9
0.0	0.0	0.1	0.0	0.0	0.0	0.1
0.8	0.6	4.8	1.9	0.8	0.9	5.1
12.7	24.0	29.4	37.3	7.1	41.8	12.0
4.2	3.7	10.8	4.5	7.2	2.1	12.1
–	–	–	0.0	–	–	–
0.4	0.5	0.5	2.4	0.4	0.1	0.3
0.0	–	–	0.2	–	–	–
4.8	9.7	3.1	0.6	6.1	8.4	5.8
5.1	15.0	28.5	3.8	7.3	18.4	36.3
24.0	18.0	14.0	7.6	28.5	18.8	20.0
108.3	*113.7*	*140.6*	*128.4*	*79.1*	*149.3*	*141.0*
5.2	19.2	13.3	31.0	28.0	29.1	–
–	–	–	–	–	–	–
–	–	–	–	–	–	–
46.5	11.5	39.5	42.5	34.0	13.2	31.9
4.2	0.4	–	–	–	–	–
49.5	63.8	170.4	73.3	125.0	187.0	127.5
0.3	1.8	2.4	–	–	–	12.6
–	–	–	–	–	–	–
–	–	–	16.6	21.1	18.4	25.1
3.0	3.4	3.7	–	–	–	–
0.6	0.9	1.1	–	–	–	–
1.5	1.9	2.1	–	–	–	–
–	–	–	–	–	–	–
14.2	10.5	17.0	–	–	–	–
0.1	0.2	0.2	–	–	–	–
1.7	1.5	1.0	–	–	–	–
0.0	–	0.0	–	–	6.0	–
126.6	*115.1*	*250.6*	*163.3*	*208.1*	*253.6*	*197.1*
0.1	*1.4*	*7.9*	*0.3*	–	*17.9*	*13.0*
73.9	*54.1*	*114.8*	*89.7*	*57.7*	*55.2*	*120.5*
235.0	**230.1**	**399.1**	**291.9**	**287.2**	**420.9**	**351.1**

TECH. COOP. GRANTS

1984	1985	1986	1983	1984	1985	1986
1.9	0.3	0.4	0.4	0.4	0.3	0.4
0.1	0.1	0.2	0.1	–	–	–
0.1	0.1	0.2	–	0.0	0.0	0.0
36.5	18.2	17.3	0.9	–	3.7	–
–	0.1	0.1	0.1	–	0.0	0.1
0.1	0.0	0.1	0.2	0.1	0.0	0.1
1.3	1.4	1.9	1.4	1.2	1.2	1.9
8.8	8.0	10.4	8.4	7.5	7.1	9.3
0.0	0.0	0.1	0.0	0.0	0.0	0.1
0.8	0.6	4.8	0.1	0.5	0.5	4.8
9.3	11.6	18.6	3.1	2.9	3.2	4.6
3.1	2.3	10.2	1.1	0.9	1.3	2.1
–	–	–	–	–	–	–
0.4	0.5	0.5	–	0.1	0.1	0.1
0.0	–	–	–	–	–	–
4.8	9.7	3.1	0.1	0.0	0.0	0.1
3.0	12.3	27.6	3.6	2.8	3.2	4.6
23.0	11.0	8.0	3.0	2.0	2.0	2.0
93.0	*76.2*	*103.5*	*22.5*	*18.4*	*22.7*	*30.1*
38.2	*28.9*	*61.0*	*6.7*	*6.9*	*7.9*	*8.9*
0.1	*1.4*	*7.9*	–	–	–	–
34.0	*35.3*	*91.3*	*14.7*	*12.9*	*13.4*	*23.8*
131.2	**106.5**	**172.4**	**29.1**	**25.3**	**30.6**	**39.0**

TOTAL OOF NET

1984	1985	1986	1983	1984	1985	1986
–	–	–	–	–	–	–
0.0	0.0	–	–	0.0	0.0	–
–	–	4.0	-1.3	-0.8	-0.1	3.7
–	0.0	0.0	–	–	0.0	–
–	–	–	–	–	–	–
–	–	–	-0.1	-0.2	-0.1	-0.3
–	0.0	–	–	–	0.0	–
–	–	–	–	–	–	–
–	–	–	–	–	–	–
0.1	–	4.2	0.2	0.1	-0.1	4.2
–	–	–	–	–	–	–
–	–	–	–	–	–	–
–	–	–	-1.0	-1.0	–	–
0.1	*0.0*	*8.2*	*-2.2*	*-2.0*	*-0.2*	*7.7*
3.8	*16.7*	*22.4*	*-2.3*	*-7.8*	*4.7*	*7.6*
–	–	–	–	–	–	–
0.1	*0.0*	*4.2*	*1.1*	*-1.4*	*-0.1*	*2.3*
3.9	**16.7**	**30.6**	**-4.6**	**-9.8**	**4.5**	**15.3**

ODA COMMITMENTS : LOANS

DAC COUNTRIES

	1983	1984	1985	1986
Australia	–	–	–	–
Austria	–	–	–	–
Belgium	–	–	–	–
Canada	–	–	–	–
Denmark	–	–	–	–
Finland	–	–	–	–
France	–	–	11.1	–
Germany, Fed. Rep.	28.5	–	–	21.9
Ireland	–	–	–	–
Italy	–	–	–	–
Japan	24.8	–	24.8	–
Netherlands	0.0	3.1	–	–
New Zealand	–	–	–	–
Norway	–	–	–	–
Sweden	–	–	–	–
Switzerland	–	–	–	–
United Kingdom	–	–	–	–
United States	1.0	0.6	9.9	6.4
TOTAL	*54.3*	*3.8*	*45.8*	*28.3*
MULTILATERAL	*138.4*	*165.5*	*222.1*	*140.1*
OPEC COUNTRIES	–	–	*8.7*	*13.0*
E.E.C.+ MEMBERS	*62.7*	*15.6*	*11.1*	*21.9*
TOTAL	**192.7**	**169.2**	**276.5**	**181.3**

GRANT ELEMENT OF ODA

DAC COUNTRIES

	1983	1984	1985	1986
Australia	100.0	100.0	100.0	100.0
Austria	100.0	100.0	100.0	–
Belgium	–	–	–	100.0
Canada	100.0	100.0	100.0	100.0
Denmark	100.0	–	100.0	–
Finland	100.0	100.0	100.0	–
France	100.0	100.0	37.7	40.7
Germany, Fed. Rep.	86.5	100.0	100.0	88.8
Ireland	100.0	100.0	100.0	100.0
Italy	100.0	100.0	100.0	100.0
Japan	68.8	100.0	72.2	100.0
Netherlands	100.0	82.7	100.0	100.0
New Zealand	100.0	–	–	–
Norway	100.0	100.0	100.0	100.0
Sweden	100.0	–	–	–
Switzerland	100.0	100.0	100.0	100.0
United Kingdom	100.0	100.0	100.0	100.0
United States	95.5	99.3	82.8	89.6
TOTAL	*87.0*	*98.2*	*84.8*	*91.4*
MULTILATERAL	*86.3*	*85.3*	*84.7*	*86.4*
OPEC COUNTRIES	*100.0*	–	*71.5*	*36.9*
E.E.C.+ MEMBERS	*91.4*	*97.3*	*85.9*	*91.6*
TOTAL	**86.7**	**89.0**	**84.2**	**86.7**

OTHER AGGREGATES

COMMITMENTS: ALL SOURCES

	1983	1984	1985	1986
TOTAL BILATERAL	142.3	82.3	183.4	154.9
of which				
OPEC	0.3	–	17.9	13.0
CMEA	13.7	0.3	12.0	–
TOTAL MULTILATERAL	163.3	232.6	317.7	266.0
TOTAL BIL.& MULTIL.	305.6	314.9	501.1	420.9
of which				
ODA Grants	99.9	118.2	144.3	169.8
ODA Loans	192.8	169.2	276.5	181.3

DISBURSEMENTS:

DAC COUNTRIES COMBINED

	1983	1984	1985	1986
OFFICIAL & PRIVATE				
GROSS:				
Contractual Lending	62.5	65.1	94.1	124.1
Export Credits Total	36.0	49.7	56.7	82.8
Export Credits Private	36.0	49.7	56.7	78.8
NET:				
Contractual Lending	26.3	25.1	38.8	65.7
Export Credits Total	13.9	23.0	19.3	44.7
PRIVATE SECTOR NET	19.3	30.9	19.2	43.0
Direct Investment	0.4	10.0	2.8	-0.2
Portfolio Investment	2.7	-3.9	-3.0	2.2
Export Credits	16.3	24.8	19.4	40.9

MARKET BORROWING:

CHANGE IN CLAIMS

	1983	1984	1985	1986
Banks	–	63.0	172.0	-11.0

MEMORANDUM ITEM:

	1983	1984	1985	1986
CMEA Countr.(Gross)	0.7	0.3	2.5	1.0

GREECE

TOTAL RECEIPTS NET · TOTAL ODA NET · TOTAL ODA GROSS

	TOTAL RECEIPTS NET 1983	1984	1985	1986	TOTAL ODA NET 1983	1984	1985	1986	TOTAL ODA GROSS 1983
DAC COUNTRIES									
Australia	2.1	—	—	0.0	—	—	—	0.0	—
Austria	2.5	-12.5	-12.1	2.6	2.4	1.9	1.8	2.6	2.5
Belgium	6.2	222.0	-11.1	-63.7	—	—	—	—	—
Canada	-4.1	-6.0	-2.8	-1.6	—	—	—	0.1	—
Denmark	-1.3	-3.0	-2.9	-3.9	—	—	—	—	—
Finland	-1.6	-2.5	-2.5	—	—	—	—	—	—
France	48.2	-81.5	114.5	161.7	4.2	4.5	3.2	4.9	5.0
Germany, Fed. Rep.	3.3	1.9	111.4	-2.5	5.4	7.0	6.8	10.3	7.9
Ireland	—	—	—	—	—	—	—	—	—
Italy	-29.3	-18.8	-9.9	-14.7	0.7	0.8	0.9	1.6	0.7
Japan	-43.3	416.4	51.6	-39.7	0.1	—	0.2	0.4	0.1
Netherlands	-0.1	-0.1	-0.1	-55.6	-0.1	-0.1	-0.1	-0.1	—
New Zealand	—	—	—	—	—	—	—	—	—
Norway	—	—	0.7	0.2	—	—	—	0.2	—
Sweden	-0.3	-0.5	—	-0.6	—	—	—	—	—
Switzerland	-2.6	-2.5	-3.4	0.3	—	0.0	—	0.3	—
United Kingdom	-15.8	30.3	-37.8	-36.8	—	—	—	—	—
United States	30.0	43.0	-105.0	-98.0	-7.0	-6.0	-6.0	-5.0	-3.0
TOTAL	*-6.0*	*586.2*	*90.7*	*-152.3*	*5.6*	*8.1*	*6.9*	*15.2*	*13.2*
MULTILATERAL									
AF.D.F.	—	—	—	—	—	—	—	—	—
AF.D.B.	—	—	—	—	—	—	—	—	—
AS.D.B	—	—	—	—	—	—	—	—	—
CAR.D.B.	—	—	—	—	—	—	—	—	—
E.E.C.	14.0	10.9	1.6	0.9	5.3	2.2	1.6	0.9	5.3
IBRD	9.7	22.0	0.8	-23.8	—	—	—	—	—
IDA	—	—	—	—	—	—	—	—	—
I.D.B.	—	—	—	—	—	—	—	—	—
IFAD	—	—	—	—	—	—	—	—	—
I.F.C.	-6.5	-6.6	-1.2	-0.4	—	—	—	—	—
IMF TRUST FUND	—	—	—	—	—	—	—	—	—
U.N. AGENCIES	—	—	—	—	—	—	—	—	—
UNDP	0.4	0.7	0.5	1.2	0.4	0.7	0.5	1.2	0.4
UNTA	0.4	0.2	0.1	0.2	0.4	0.2	0.1	0.2	0.4
UNICEF	—	—	—	0.0	—	—	—	0.0	—
UNRWA	—	—	—	—	—	—	—	—	—
WFP	—	—	—	—	—	—	—	—	—
UNHCR	0.6	1.2	1.4	1.2	0.6	1.2	1.4	1.2	0.6
Other Multilateral	0.3	0.2	60.2	22.1	0.3	0.2	2.9	1.8	0.4
Arab OPEC Agencies	—	—	—	—	—	—	—	—	—
TOTAL	*19.0*	*28.5*	*63.3*	*1.3*	*7.0*	*4.5*	*6.5*	*5.3*	*7.1*
OPEC COUNTRIES	157.6	—	-28.8	—	—	—	—	—	—
E.E.C.+ MEMBERS	*25.3*	*161.7*	*165.8*	*-14.6*	*15.5*	*14.3*	*12.5*	*17.6*	*18.9*
TOTAL	**170.6**	**614.8**	**125.3**	**-150.9**	**12.7**	**12.5**	**13.4**	**20.5**	**20.3**

ODA LOANS GROSS · ODA LOANS NET · GRANTS

	ODA LOANS GROSS 1983	1984	1985	1986	ODA LOANS NET 1983	1984	1985	1986	GRANTS 1983
DAC COUNTRIES									
Australia	—	—	—	—	—	—	—	—	—
Austria	—	—	—	—	-0.1	-0.1	-0.1	-0.1	2.5
Belgium	—	—	—	—	—	—	—	—	—
Canada	—	—	—	—	—	—	—	—	—
Denmark	—	—	—	—	—	—	—	—	—
Finland	—	—	—	—	—	—	—	—	—
France	—	—	—	—	-0.8	-0.2	-1.1	-0.8	5.0
Germany, Fed. Rep.	0.3	3.0	1.6	3.3	-2.3	-3.9	-3.8	-4.3	7.7
Ireland	—	—	—	—	—	—	—	—	—
Italy	—	—	—	—	—	—	—	—	0.7
Japan	—	—	—	—	—	—	—	—	0.1
Netherlands	—	—	—	—	-0.1	-0.1	-0.1	-0.1	—
New Zealand	—	—	—	—	—	—	—	—	—
Norway	—	—	—	—	—	—	—	—	—
Sweden	—	—	—	—	—	—	—	—	—
Switzerland	—	—	—	—	—	—	—	—	—
United Kingdom	—	—	—	—	—	—	—	—	—
United States	—	—	—	—	-4.0	-4.0	-3.0	-3.0	-3.0
TOTAL	*0.3*	*3.0*	*1.6*	*3.3*	*-7.3*	*-8.3*	*-8.1*	*-8.3*	*13.0*
MULTILATERAL	*2.6*	*—*	*2.9*	*1.9*	*2.5*	*0.0*	*2.8*	*1.7*	*4.5*
OPEC COUNTRIES	—	—	—	—	—	—	—	—	
E.E.C.+ MEMBERS	*2.8*	*3.0*	*1.6*	*3.3*	*-0.6*	*-4.2*	*-5.0*	*-5.2*	*16.1*
TOTAL	**2.8**	**3.0**	**4.5**	**5.1**	**-4.8**	**-8.3**	**-5.3**	**-6.5**	**17.5**

TOTAL OFFICIAL GROSS · TOTAL OFFICIAL NET · TOTAL OOF GROSS

	TOTAL OFFICIAL GROSS 1983	1984	1985	1986	TOTAL OFFICIAL NET 1983	1984	1985	1986	TOTAL OOF GROSS 1983
DAC COUNTRIES									
Australia	—	—	—	0.0	—	—	—	0.0	—
Austria	2.5	2.0	1.9	2.6	2.4	1.9	1.8	2.6	—
Belgium	—	—	—	—	—	—	—	—	—
Canada	—	—	—	0.1	-4.1	-6.0	-2.8	-1.6	—
Denmark	—	—	—	—	—	—	—	—	—
Finland	—	—	—	—	—	—	—	—	—
France	5.0	4.7	4.3	5.7	4.2	4.5	3.2	4.9	—
Germany, Fed. Rep.	24.4	23.6	16.4	19.3	1.1	1.9	-2.2	-6.5	16.5
Ireland	—	—	—	—	—	—	—	—	—
Italy	0.7	0.8	2.6	2.2	0.7	0.8	2.5	0.9	—
Japan	0.1	—	0.2	0.4	0.1	—	0.2	0.4	—
Netherlands	—	—	—	—	-0.1	-0.1	-0.1	-0.1	—
New Zealand	—	—	—	—	—	—	—	—	—
Norway	—	—	—	0.2	—	—	—	0.2	—
Sweden	—	—	—	—	—	-0.4	—	-0.4	—
Switzerland	—	0.0	—	0.3	—	0.0	—	0.3	—
United Kingdom	—	—	—	—	—	—	—	—	—
United States	-3.0	10.0	-3.0	-2.0	-20.0	2.0	-11.0	-15.0	—
TOTAL	*29.7*	*41.1*	*22.4*	*28.9*	*-15.8*	*4.6*	*-8.3*	*-14.3*	*16.5*
MULTILATERAL	*72.6*	*87.6*	*95.0*	*34.5*	*19.0*	*28.6*	*63.3*	*1.3*	*65.5*
OPEC COUNTRIES	157.6	—	—	—	157.6	—	-28.8	—	157.6
E.E.C.+ MEMBERS	*58.4*	*57.6*	*24.9*	*28.1*	*19.9*	*17.9*	*5.0*	*0.1*	*39.5*
TOTAL	**259.9**	**128.7**	**117.5**	**63.4**	**160.8**	**33.2**	**26.2**	**-13.0**	**239.5**

ODA COMMITMENTS

1984	1985	1986	1983	1984	1985	1986
—	—	0.0	—	—	—	0.0
2.0	1.9	2.6	2.5	2.0	1.9	—
—	—	—	—	—	—	—
—	—	0.1	—	—	—	0.1
—	—	—	—	—	—	—
—	—	—	—	—	—	—
4.7	4.3	5.7	5.0	4.7	4.3	5.7
13.9	12.3	17.8	7.6	10.8	10.5	14.3
—	—	—	—	—	—	—
0.8	0.9	1.6	0.7	0.8	0.9	1.6
—	0.2	0.4	0.1	0.2	0.2	0.4
—	—	—	—	—	—	—
—	—	0.2	—	—	—	—
—	—	—	—	—	—	—
0.0	—	0.3	—	—	—	0.3
—	—	—	—	—	—	—
-2.0	-3.0	-2.0	—	—	—	—
19.4	*16.6*	*26.8*	*15.9*	*18.5*	*17.8*	*22.4*
—	—	—	—	—	—	—
—	—	—	—	—	—	—
—	—	—	—	—	—	—
2.2	1.6	0.9	—	—	—	—
—	—	—	—	—	—	—
—	—	—	—	—	—	—
—	—	—	—	—	—	—
—	—	—	—	—	—	—
—	—	—	1.8	2.3	2.1	2.6
0.7	0.5	1.2	—	—	—	—
0.2	0.1	0.2	—	—	—	—
—	—	0.0	—	—	—	—
—	—	—	—	—	—	—
1.2	1.4	1.2	—	—	—	—
0.2	3.0	2.0	—	—	2.9	1.9
—	—	—	—	—	—	—
4.5	*6.6*	*5.4*	*1.8*	*2.3*	*5.0*	*4.5*
—	—	—	—	—	—	—
21.5	*19.1*	*26.0*	*13.3*	*16.3*	*15.7*	*21.6*
23.9	***23.2***	***32.2***	***17.7***	***20.8***	***22.8***	***26.9***

TECH. COOP. GRANTS

1984	1985	1986	1983	1984	1985	1986
—	—	0.0	—	—	—	0.0
2.0	1.9	2.6	2.5	—	—	—
—	—	0.1	—	—	—	—
—	—	—	—	—	—	—
4.7	4.3	5.7	5.0	4.7	4.3	5.7
10.8	10.7	14.6	7.6	9.4	10.3	14.0
—	—	—	—	—	—	—
0.8	0.9	1.6	0.7	0.8	0.9	1.6
—	0.2	0.4	0.1	—	0.2	0.4
—	—	—	—	—	—	—
—	—	0.2	—	—	—	—
—	—	—	—	—	—	—
0.0	—	0.3	—	0.0	—	0.0
—	—	—	—	—	—	—
-2.0	-3.0	-2.0	—	—	—	—
16.3	*15.0*	*23.5*	*15.9*	*14.9*	*15.7*	*21.7*
4.5	*3.7*	*3.5*	*1.8*	*2.3*	*2.1*	*2.6*
—	—	—	—	—	—	—
18.5	*17.5*	*22.8*	*13.3*	*14.9*	*15.5*	*21.3*
20.8	***18.7***	***27.0***	***17.7***	***17.2***	***17.8***	***24.3***

TOTAL OOF NET

1984	1985	1986	1983	1984	1985	1986
—	—	—	—	—	—	—
—	—	—	—	—	—	—
—	—	—	-4.1	-6.0	-2.8	-1.7
—	—	—	—	—	—	—
—	—	—	—	—	—	—
—	—	—	—	—	—	—
9.7	4.2	1.5	-4.3	-5.1	-9.0	-16.7
—	1.7	0.6	—	—	1.6	-0.7
—	—	—	—	—	—	—
—	—	—	—	—	—	—
—	—	—	—	—	—	—
—	—	—	—	-0.4	—	-0.4
—	—	—	—	—	—	—
12.0	—	—	-13.0	8.0	-5.0	-10.0
21.7	*5.8*	*2.1*	*-21.4*	*-3.4*	*-15.2*	*-29.6*
83.1	*88.5*	*29.1*	*11.9*	*24.1*	*56.9*	*-3.9*
—	—	—	*157.6*	—	*-28.8*	—
36.1	*5.8*	*2.1*	*4.4*	*3.6*	*-7.5*	*-17.4*
104.9	***94.3***	***31.2***	***148.1***	***20.7***	***12.9***	***-33.5***

ODA COMMITMENTS : LOANS

DAC COUNTRIES

	1983	1984	1985	1986
Australia	—	—	—	—
Austria	—	—	—	—
Belgium	—	—	—	—
Canada	—	—	—	—
Denmark	—	—	—	—
Finland	—	—	—	—
France	—	—	—	—
Germany, Fed. Rep.	—	—	—	—
Ireland	—	—	—	—
Italy	—	—	—	—
Japan	—	—	—	—
Netherlands	—	—	—	—
New Zealand	—	—	—	—
Norway	—	—	—	—
Sweden	—	—	—	—
Switzerland	—	—	—	—
United Kingdom	—	—	—	—
United States	—	—	—	—
TOTAL	—	—	—	—
MULTILATERAL	—	—	2.9	1.9
OPEC COUNTRIES	—	—	—	—
E.E.C.+ MEMBERS	—	—	—	—
TOTAL	—	—	*2.9*	*1.9*

GRANT ELEMENT OF ODA

DAC COUNTRIES

	1983	1984	1985	1986
Australia	—	—	—	100.0
Austria	100.0	100.0	100.0	—
Belgium	—	—	—	—
Canada	—	—	—	100.0
Denmark	—	—	—	—
Finland	—	—	—	—
France	100.0	100.0	100.0	100.0
Germany, Fed. Rep.	100.0	100.0	100.0	100.0
Ireland	—	—	—	—
Italy	100.0	100.0	100.0	100.0
Japan	100.0	100.0	100.0	100.0
Netherlands	—	—	—	—
New Zealand	—	—	—	—
Norway	—	—	—	—
Sweden	—	—	—	—
Switzerland	—	—	—	100.0
United Kingdom	—	—	—	—
United States	—	—	—	—
TOTAL	*100.0*	*100.0*	*100.0*	*100.0*
MULTILATERAL	*100.0*	*100.0*	*100.0*	*100.0*
OPEC COUNTRIES	—	—	—	—
E.E.C.+ MEMBERS	*100.0*	*100.0*	*100.0*	*100.0*
TOTAL	*100.0*	*100.0*	*100.0*	*100.0*

OTHER AGGREGATES

COMMITMENTS: ALL SOURCES

	1983	1984	1985	1986
TOTAL BILATERAL	206.0	18.5	35.6	22.4
of which				
OPEC	190.1	—	17.8	—
CMEA	—	—	—	—
TOTAL MULTILATERAL	1.8	2.3	67.1	31.1
TOTAL BIL.& MULTIL.	207.8	20.8	102.7	53.5
of which				
ODA Grants	17.7	20.8	19.9	25.1
ODA Loans	—	—	2.9	1.9

DISBURSEMENTS:

DAC COUNTRIES COMBINED

	1983	1984	1985	1986
OFFICIAL & PRIVATE				
GROSS:				
Contractual Lending	256.5	197.2	87.8	8.8
Export Credits Total	256.2	194.2	86.2	5.5
Export Credits Private	239.8	172.4	80.4	3.4
NET:				
Contractual Lending	-199.9	-87.9	-200.0	-243.8
Export Credits Total	-192.6	-79.6	-192.0	-235.5
PRIVATE SECTOR NET	9.8	581.6	99.0	-137.9
Direct Investment	-34.7	-23.8	54.6	66.8
Portfolio Investment	215.7	681.6	221.1	1.2
Export Credits	-171.2	-76.2	-176.7	-206.0

MARKET BORROWING:

CHANGE IN CLAIMS

	1983	1984	1985	1986
Banks	—	1195.0	1151.0	-1278.0

MEMORANDUM ITEM:

	1983	1984	1985	1986
CMEA Countr.(Gross)	—	—	—	—

GUATEMALA

	1983	1984	1985	1986		1983	1984	1985	1986		1983
TOTAL RECEIPTS NET					**TOTAL ODA NET**					**TOTAL ODA GROSS**	
DAC COUNTRIES											
Australia	–	0.0	–	0.0		–	0.0	–	0.0	Australia	–
Austria	1.4	1.2	1.2	1.5		1.4	1.2	1.2	1.5	Austria	1.4
Belgium	-0.1	-0.4	-0.6	0.1		0.3	0.2	0.2	0.2	Belgium	0.3
Canada	0.9	-0.8	-0.2	-0.9		2.9	1.5	1.6	0.9	Canada	2.9
Denmark	–	-0.1	–	–		0.1	–	–	–	Denmark	0.1
Finland	–	–	–	–		–	–	–	–	Finland	–
France	43.3	16.0	137.6	4.1		0.4	0.5	0.5	3.5	France	0.4
Germany, Fed. Rep.	17.7	11.9	8.7	29.1		5.2	4.2	4.4	11.2	Germany, Fed. Rep.	5.3
Ireland	–	–	–	–		–	–	–	–	Ireland	–
Italy	-27.9	0.4	-8.9	8.7		0.5	0.3	0.6	2.8	Italy	0.5
Japan	1.5	-0.3	1.3	4.7		1.5	1.5	1.3	2.6	Japan	1.5
Netherlands	0.9	1.2	1.9	2.0		0.9	1.2	1.9	2.0	Netherlands	0.9
New Zealand	–	–	–	–		–	–	–	–	New Zealand	–
Norway	0.2	0.6	1.1	0.8		0.4	0.6	0.6	0.5	Norway	0.4
Sweden	–	0.4	0.0	–		–	0.4	0.0	–	Sweden	–
Switzerland	-0.9	35.6	0.0	0.2		0.1	0.1	0.1	0.2	Switzerland	0.1
United Kingdom	-2.6	-0.8	-0.8	-0.8		–	–	0.0	0.0	United Kingdom	–
United States	131.0	37.0	85.0	32.0		36.0	29.0	50.0	86.0	United States	38.0
TOTAL	*165.3*	*102.0*	*226.3*	*81.5*		*49.6*	*40.5*	*62.4*	*111.3*	*TOTAL*	*51.6*
MULTILATERAL											
AF.D.F.	–	–	–	–		–	–	–	–	AF.D.F.	–
AF.D.B.	–	–	–	–		–	–	–	–	AF.D.B.	–
AS.D.B	–	–	–	–		–	–	–	–	AS.D.B	–
CAR.D.B.	–	–	–	–		–	–	–	–	CAR.D.B.	–
E.E.C.	–	–	0.3	0.2		–	–	0.3	0.2	E.E.C.	–
IBRD	6.5	-6.6	35.5	-0.4		2.4	–	–	–	IBRD	2.4
IDA	–	–	–	–		–	–	–	–	IDA	–
I.D.B.	29.3	60.4	63.8	34.7		18.6	16.7	6.7	12.4	I.D.B.	21.7
IFAD	–	–	–	0.4		–	–	–	0.4	IFAD	–
I.F.C.	-2.3	-2.2	-1.3	-0.2		–	–	–	–	I.F.C.	–
IMF TRUST FUND	–	–	–	–		–	–	–	–	IMF TRUST FUND	–
U.N. AGENCIES	–	–	–	–		–	–	–	–	U.N. AGENCIES	–
UNDP	1.7	1.0	1.4	1.9		1.7	1.0	1.4	1.9	UNDP	1.7
UNTA	0.4	0.6	0.5	0.5		0.4	0.6	0.5	0.5	UNTA	0.4
UNICEF	0.6	0.5	0.7	0.6		0.6	0.5	0.7	0.6	UNICEF	0.6
UNRWA	–	–	–	–		–	–	–	–	UNRWA	–
WFP	1.7	5.4	10.3	7.0		1.7	5.4	10.3	7.0	WFP	1.7
UNHCR	–	–	–	0.1		–	–	–	0.1	UNHCR	–
Other Multilateral	0.8	0.8	0.6	0.5		0.8	0.8	0.6	0.5	Other Multilateral	0.8
Arab OPEC Agencies	-0.1	-0.1	-0.1	-0.1		-0.1	-0.1	-0.1	-0.1	Arab OPEC Agencies	–
TOTAL	*38.6*	*59.7*	*111.7*	*45.1*		*26.2*	*24.9*	*20.4*	*23.5*	*TOTAL*	*29.3*
OPEC COUNTRIES	*11.8*	*12.5*	*-0.3*	*6.1*		–	–	–	–	**OPEC COUNTRIES**	–
E.E.C.+ MEMBERS	*31.3*	*28.3*	*138.1*	*43.4*		*7.4*	*6.2*	*7.8*	*19.9*	*E.E.C.+ MEMBERS*	*7.4*
TOTAL	**215.7**	**174.3**	**337.7**	**132.7**		**75.8**	**65.4**	**82.8**	**134.8**	**TOTAL**	**80.9**

	1983	1984	1985	1986		1983	1984	1985	1986		1983
ODA LOANS GROSS					**ODA LOANS NET**					**GRANTS**	
DAC COUNTRIES											
Australia	–	–	–	–		–	–	–	–	Australia	–
Austria	–	–	–	–		–	–	–	–	Austria	1.4
Belgium	–	–	–	–		–	–	–	–	Belgium	0.3
Canada	1.4	0.2	0.1	–		1.4	0.2	0.1	–	Canada	1.5
Denmark	–	–	–	–		–	–	–	–	Denmark	0.1
Finland	–	–	–	–		–	–	–	–	Finland	–
France	–	–	–	2.5		–	–	–	2.5	France	0.4
Germany, Fed. Rep.	0.1	0.1	–	–		0.1	0.0	0.0	0.0	Germany, Fed. Rep.	5.1
Ireland	–	–	–	–		–	–	–	–	Ireland	–
Italy	–	–	–	0.0		–	–	–	–	Italy	0.5
Japan	–	–	–	–		–	–	–	–	Japan	1.5
Netherlands	–	–	–	–		–	–	–	–	Netherlands	0.9
New Zealand	–	–	–	–		–	–	–	–	New Zealand	–
Norway	–	–	–	–		–	–	–	–	Norway	0.4
Sweden	–	–	–	–		–	–	–	–	Sweden	–
Switzerland	–	–	–	–		–	–	–	–	Switzerland	0.1
United Kingdom	–	–	–	–		–	–	–	–	United Kingdom	–
United States	20.0	14.0	28.0	45.0		18.0	12.0	26.0	42.0	United States	18.0
TOTAL	*21.5*	*14.3*	*28.1*	*47.6*		*19.5*	*12.3*	*26.1*	*44.5*	*TOTAL*	*30.1*
MULTILATERAL	*22.0*	*20.1*	*9.7*	*18.3*		*18.9*	*16.7*	*5.7*	*12.7*	*MULTILATERAL*	*7.3*
OPEC COUNTRIES	–	–	–	–		–	–	–	–	**OPEC COUNTRIES**	–
E.E.C.+ MEMBERS	*0.1*	*0.1*	–	*2.6*		*0.1*	*0.0*	*0.0*	*2.5*	*E.E.C.+ MEMBERS*	*7.3*
TOTAL	**43.5**	**34.4**	**37.8**	**65.8**		**38.4**	**28.9**	**31.8**	**57.2**	**TOTAL**	**37.4**

	1983	1984	1985	1986		1983	1984	1985	1986		1983
TOTAL OFFICIAL GROSS					**TOTAL OFFICIAL NET**					**TOTAL OOF GROSS**	
DAC COUNTRIES											
Australia	–	0.0	–	0.0		–	0.0	–	0.0	Australia	–
Austria	1.4	1.2	1.2	1.5		1.4	1.2	1.2	1.5	Austria	–
Belgium	0.3	0.2	0.2	0.2		0.3	0.2	0.2	0.2	Belgium	–
Canada	2.9	1.5	1.6	0.9		0.9	-0.7	-0.2	-0.9	Canada	–
Denmark	0.1	–	–	–		0.1	–	–	–	Denmark	–
Finland	–	–	–	–		–	–	–	–	Finland	–
France	0.4	0.5	0.5	3.5		0.4	0.5	0.5	3.5	France	–
Germany, Fed. Rep.	20.5	15.2	9.0	20.7		20.4	11.3	6.7	17.4	Germany, Fed. Rep.	15.3
Ireland	–	–	–	–		–	–	–	–	Ireland	–
Italy	0.5	0.3	0.6	2.8		0.5	0.3	0.6	2.8	Italy	–
Japan	1.5	1.5	1.3	2.6		1.5	1.5	1.3	2.6	Japan	–
Netherlands	0.9	1.2	1.9	2.0		0.9	1.2	1.9	2.0	Netherlands	–
New Zealand	–	–	–	–		–	–	–	–	New Zealand	–
Norway	0.4	0.6	0.6	0.5		0.4	0.6	0.6	0.5	Norway	–
Sweden	–	0.4	0.0	–		–	0.4	0.0	–	Sweden	–
Switzerland	0.1	0.1	0.1	0.2		0.1	0.1	0.1	0.2	Switzerland	–
United Kingdom	–	–	0.0	0.0		–	–	0.0	0.0	United Kingdom	–
United States	38.0	31.0	52.0	89.0		33.0	21.0	47.0	83.0	United States	–
TOTAL	*66.9*	*53.4*	*69.0*	*123.9*		*59.8*	*37.3*	*59.9*	*112.8*	*TOTAL*	*15.3*
MULTILATERAL	*58.8*	*80.5*	*136.5*	*74.0*		*38.6*	*59.7*	*111.7*	*45.1*	*MULTILATERAL*	*29.5*
OPEC COUNTRIES	*20.0*	*19.5*	*14.3*	*9.8*		*11.8*	*12.5*	*-0.3*	*6.1*	**OPEC COUNTRIES**	*20.0*
E.E.C.+ MEMBERS	*22.7*	*17.2*	*12.4*	*29.4*		*22.5*	*13.3*	*10.1*	*26.1*	*E.E.C.+ MEMBERS*	*15.3*
TOTAL	**145.6**	**153.5**	**219.7**	**207.6**		**110.2**	**109.5**	**171.2**	**164.0**	**TOTAL**	**64.7**

ODA COMMITMENTS

1984	1985	1986	1983	1984	1985	1986
0.0	–	0.0	–	0.0	–	–
1.2	1.2	1.5	1.3	1.2	1.2	–
0.2	0.2	0.2	–	–	–	0.2
1.5	1.6	0.9	1.0	1.4	1.7	0.9
–	–	–	–	–	–	–
0.5	0.5	3.5	0.4	0.5	7.2	3.5
4.2	4.5	11.2	4.2	5.4	8.1	27.1
–	–	–	–	–	–	–
0.3	0.6	2.8	0.6	30.4	17.8	2.8
1.5	1.3	2.6	1.6	1.5	1.6	2.6
1.2	1.9	2.0	0.8	1.4	2.2	2.2
–	–	–	–	–	–	–
0.6	0.6	0.5	–	0.2	0.3	0.1
0.4	0.0	–	0.4	2.1	0.9	–
0.1	0.1	0.2	0.1	–	0.1	0.3
–	0.0	0.0	–	–	0.0	0.0
31.0	52.0	89.0	33.3	50.4	73.1	114.5
42.5	64.5	114.3	43.7	94.4	114.1	154.1
–	–	–	–	–	–	–
–	–	–	–	–	–	–
–	–	–	–	–	–	–
–	0.3	0.2	0.0	0.2	0.8	0.2
–	–	–	–	–	–	–
20.2	10.6	17.9	45.3	–	–	13.4
–	–	0.4	–	4.9	–	–
–	–	–	–	–	–	–
–	–	–	5.2	8.2	13.5	10.6
1.0	1.4	1.9	–	–	–	–
0.6	0.5	0.5	–	–	–	–
0.5	0.7	0.6	–	–	–	–
–	–	–	–	–	–	–
5.4	10.3	7.0	–	–	–	–
–	–	0.1	–	–	–	–
0.8	0.6	0.5	–	–	–	–
-0.1	–	–	1.1	–	–	–
28.3	24.4	29.1	51.6	13.3	14.3	24.2
–	–	–	–	–	14.0	–
6.3	7.9	19.9	6.0	37.9	36.0	36.0
70.8	88.8	143.4	95.3	107.7	142.3	178.3

TECH. COOP. GRANTS

1984	1985	1986	1983	1984	1985	1986
0.0	–	0.0	–	0.0	–	–
1.2	1.2	1.5	1.4	–	–	–
0.2	0.2	0.2	0.0	0.0	–	0.0
1.2	1.5	0.9	0.2	–	0.2	–
–	–	–	–	–	–	–
0.5	0.5	1.0	0.4	0.5	0.5	1.0
4.2	4.5	11.2	3.7	2.7	2.7	9.4
–	–	–	–	–	–	–
0.3	0.6	2.8	0.3	0.3	0.3	2.5
1.5	1.3	2.6	1.5	1.5	1.3	2.3
1.2	1.9	2.0	0.8	0.7	1.1	1.5
–	–	–	–	–	–	–
0.6	0.6	0.5	–	–	–	–
0.4	0.0	–	–	–	–	–
0.1	0.1	0.2	0.0	0.0	0.0	0.1
–	0.0	0.0	–	–	0.0	–
17.0	24.0	44.0	4.0	6.0	15.0	9.0
28.2	36.3	66.8	12.2	11.6	21.0	25.8
8.2	14.7	10.8	3.5	2.9	3.2	3.6
–	–	–	–	–	–	–
6.2	7.9	17.4	5.2	4.1	4.5	14.4
36.4	51.0	77.6	15.7	14.5	24.2	29.3

TOTAL OOF NET

1984	1985	1986	1983	1984	1985	1986
–	–	–	–	–	–	–
–	–	–	–	–	–	–
–	–	–	-2.0	-2.2	-1.8	-1.8
–	–	–	–	–	–	–
–	–	–	–	–	–	–
11.0	4.5	9.5	15.2	7.0	2.2	6.2
–	–	–	–	–	–	–
–	–	–	–	–	–	–
–	–	–	–	–	–	–
11.0	4.5	9.5	–	–	–	–
–	–	–	–	–	–	–
–	–	–	–	–	–	–
–	–	–	–	–	–	–
–	–	–	–	–	–	–
–	–	–	-3.0	-8.0	-3.0	-3.0
11.0	4.5	9.5	10.2	-3.2	-2.6	1.4
52.2	112.1	44.9	12.4	34.8	91.3	21.6
19.5	14.3	9.8	11.8	12.5	-0.3	6.1
11.0	4.5	9.5	15.2	7.0	2.2	6.2
82.6	130.9	64.2	34.4	44.1	88.4	29.2

ODA COMMITMENTS : LOANS

DAC COUNTRIES

	1983	1984	1985	1986
Australia	–	–	–	–
Austria	–	–	–	–
Belgium	–	–	–	–
Canada	–	–	–	–
Denmark	–	–	–	–
Finland	–	–	–	–
France	–	–	6.7	2.5
Germany, Fed. Rep.	–	–	–	9.2
Ireland	–	–	–	–
Italy	–	30.0	14.7	–
Japan	–	–	–	–
Netherlands	–	–	–	–
New Zealand	–	–	–	–
Norway	–	–	–	–
Sweden	–	–	–	–
Switzerland	–	–	–	–
United Kingdom	–	–	–	–
United States	17.5	32.9	33.5	47.9
TOTAL	17.5	62.9	54.8	59.6
MULTILATERAL	46.4	4.9	–	13.4
OPEC COUNTRIES	–	–	14.0	–
E.E.C.+ MEMBERS	–	30.0	21.4	11.7
TOTAL	63.9	67.7	68.8	73.0

GRANT ELEMENT OF ODA

DAC COUNTRIES

	1983	1984	1985	1986
Australia	–	100.0	–	–
Austria	100.0	100.0	100.0	–
Belgium	–	–	–	100.0
Canada	100.0	100.0	100.0	100.0
Denmark	–	–	–	–
Finland	–	–	–	–
France	100.0	100.0	70.1	100.0
Germany, Fed. Rep.	100.0	100.0	100.0	94.3
Ireland	–	–	–	–
Italy	100.0	45.8	55.2	100.0
Japan	100.0	100.0	100.0	100.0
Netherlands	100.0	100.0	100.0	100.0
New Zealand	–	–	–	–
Norway	–	100.0	100.0	100.0
Sweden	100.0	100.0	100.0	–
Switzerland	)100.0	–	100.0	100.0
United Kingdom	–	–	100.0	100.0
United States	82.4	74.9	79.0	81.4
TOTAL	86.6	69.2	77.7	84.9
MULTILATERAL	77.1	76.8	100.0	83.9
OPEC COUNTRIES	–	–	45.2	–
E.E.C.+ MEMBERS	100.0	56.6	71.9	95.4
TOTAL	80.7	71.5	76.7	84.8

OTHER AGGREGATES

COMMITMENTS: ALL SOURCES

	1983	1984	1985	1986
TOTAL BILATERAL	86.3	120.7	153.0	155.1
of which				
OPEC	18.9	14.3	24.1	–
CMEA	–	–	–	–
TOTAL MULTILATERAL	192.7	77.2	249.9	180.6
TOTAL BIL.& MULTIL.	279.0	197.9	402.8	335.7
of which				
ODA Grants	31.4	40.0	73.5	105.3
ODA Loans	63.9	67.7	68.8	73.0

DISBURSEMENTS:

DAC COUNTRIES COMBINED

	1983	1984	1985	1986
OFFICIAL & PRIVATE				
GROSS:				
Contractual Lending	76.7	116.1	85.5	83.3
Export Credits Total	54.9	95.0	52.8	26.3
Export Credits Private	39.9	90.9	52.8	26.3
NET:				
Contractual Lending	15.9	72.1	26.8	33.0
Export Credits Total	-3.7	54.4	-2.8	-18.2
PRIVATE SECTOR NET	105.5	64.7	166.5	-31.3
Direct Investment	26.0	19.7	140.4	3.4
Portfolio Investment	93.3	-18.0	22.9	-21.6
Export Credits	-13.7	63.0	3.2	-13.0

MARKET BORROWING:

CHANGE IN CLAIMS

	1983	1984	1985	1986
Banks	–	-88.0	111.0	-105.0

MEMORANDUM ITEM:

	1983	1984	1985	1986
CMEA Countr.(Gross)	–	–	–	–

TOTAL RECEIPTS NET

DAC COUNTRIES	1983	1984	1985	1986
Australia	–	–	–	–
Austria	–	0.0	0.0	0.0
Belgium	0.2	0.6	1.5	9.3
Canada	0.6	9.8	11.2	2.8
Denmark	0.5	3.4	0.7	3.6
Finland	–	0.1	0.0	–
France	5.3	3.9	20.0	35.9
Germany, Fed. Rep.	9.9	6.1	6.7	11.6
Ireland	–	–	–	–
Italy	0.4	2.2	3.2	7.0
Japan	3.2	2.7	5.0	3.2
Netherlands	0.1	0.1	1.2	0.8
New Zealand	–	–	–	–
Norway	–	12.8	12.2	16.6
Sweden	–	–	–	–
Switzerland	7.2	-7.1	-5.6	5.9
United Kingdom	0.1	0.1	0.4	0.4
United States	2.0	2.0	8.0	12.0
TOTAL	*29.4*	*36.7*	*64.5*	*109.1*
MULTILATERAL				
AF.D.F.	3.0	1.1	7.6	12.0
AF.D.B.	2.6	4.7	3.5	2.4
AS.D.B	–	–	–	–
CAR.D.B.	–	–	–	–
E.E.C.	13.0	13.5	10.4	15.0
IBRD	-3.6	-3.8	-5.0	-7.8
IDA	16.0	19.8	21.5	35.5
I.D.B.	–	–	–	–
IFAD	0.2	0.3	3.3	4.4
I.F.C.	2.4	12.4	-1.0	-2.4
IMF TRUST FUND	–	–	–	–
U.N. AGENCIES	–	–	–	–
UNDP	5.3	5.2	4.4	5.8
UNTA	0.9	0.8	2.5	0.8
UNICEF	0.7	1.0	0.9	1.0
UNRWA	–	–	–	–
WFP	1.6	2.1	0.9	1.4
UNHCR	–	1.1	–	–
Other Multilateral	0.8	1.3	2.9	1.7
Arab OPEC Agencies	-1.6	3.2	5.6	-2.6
TOTAL	*41.4*	*62.7*	*57.5*	*67.1*
OPEC COUNTRIES	*-0.6*	*29.8*	*2.1*	*4.4*
E.E.C.+ MEMBERS	*29.5*	*29.9*	*44.1*	*83.5*
TOTAL	*70.1*	*129.3*	*124.1*	*180.6*

TOTAL ODA NET

	1983	1984	1985	1986
Australia	–	–	–	–
Austria	–	0.0	0.0	0.0
Belgium	0.0	0.2	1.1	0.5
Canada	0.6	9.8	11.2	2.8
Denmark	0.5	3.4	0.7	3.6
Finland	–	0.1	0.0	–
France	9.4	9.4	21.8	46.1
Germany, Fed. Rep.	6.7	8.5	8.0	13.0
Ireland	–	–	–	–
Italy	0.7	3.3	3.2	6.8
Japan	3.2	2.7	5.7	3.5
Netherlands	0.1	0.1	1.2	0.4
New Zealand	–	–	–	–
Norway	–	0.1	0.2	2.6
Sweden	–	–	–	–
Switzerland	0.3	0.3	0.3	5.9
United Kingdom	0.1	0.1	0.4	0.4
United States	5.0	4.0	6.0	12.0
TOTAL	*26.6*	*42.2*	*59.8*	*97.6*
AF.D.F.	3.0	1.1	7.6	12.0
AF.D.B.	–	–	–	–
AS.D.B	–	–	–	–
CAR.D.B.	–	–	–	–
E.E.C.	12.3	13.9	8.2	12.9
IBRD	–	–	–	–
IDA	16.0	19.8	21.5	35.5
I.D.B.	–	–	–	–
IFAD	0.2	0.3	3.3	4.4
I.F.C.	–	–	–	–
IMF TRUST FUND	–	–	–	–
U.N. AGENCIES	–	–	–	–
UNDP	5.3	5.2	4.4	5.8
UNTA	0.9	0.8	2.5	0.8
UNICEF	0.7	1.0	0.9	1.0
UNRWA	–	–	–	–
WFP	1.6	2.1	0.9	1.4
UNHCR	–	1.1	–	–
Other Multilateral	0.8	1.3	2.9	1.7
Arab OPEC Agencies	0.8	4.8	5.1	-2.4
TOTAL	*41.6*	*51.3*	*57.3*	*73.0*
OPEC COUNTRIES	*-0.6*	*29.8*	*2.1*	*4.4*
E.E.C.+ MEMBERS	*29.9*	*38.9*	*44.5*	*83.6*
TOTAL	*67.5*	*123.4*	*119.2*	*174.9*

TOTAL ODA GROSS

	1983
Australia	–
Austria	–
Belgium	0.0
Canada	0.6
Denmark	0.5
Finland	–
France	9.5
Germany, Fed. Rep.	6.7
Ireland	–
Italy	1.0
Japan	3.3
Netherlands	0.1
New Zealand	–
Norway	–
Sweden	–
Switzerland	0.3
United Kingdom	0.1
United States	6.0
TOTAL	*28.0*
AF.D.F.	3.0
AF.D.B.	–
AS.D.B	–
CAR.D.B.	–
E.E.C.	12.4
IBRD	–
IDA	16.0
I.D.B.	–
IFAD	0.2
I.F.C.	–
IMF TRUST FUND	–
U.N. AGENCIES	–
UNDP	5.3
UNTA	0.9
UNICEF	0.7
UNRWA	–
WFP	1.6
UNHCR	–
Other Multilateral	0.8
Arab OPEC Agencies	1.9
TOTAL	*42.7*
OPEC COUNTRIES	*0.8*
E.E.C.+ MEMBERS	*30.2*
TOTAL	*71.5*

ODA LOANS GROSS

DAC COUNTRIES	1983	1984	1985	1986
Australia	–	–	–	–
Austria	–	–	–	–
Belgium	–	–	–	–
Canada	–	–	–	–
Denmark	0.5	3.4	–	-0.8
Finland	–	–	–	–
France	8.2	6.6	13.1	38.2
Germany, Fed. Rep.	–	–	–	–
Ireland	–	–	–	–
Italy	–	–	–	–
Japan	–	–	0.3	0.1
Netherlands	–	–	–	–
New Zealand	–	–	–	–
Norway	–	–	–	2.4
Sweden	–	–	–	–
Switzerland	–	–	–	–
United Kingdom	–	–	–	–
United States	5.0	5.0	6.0	6.0
TOTAL	*13.7*	*15.0*	*19.4*	*45.9*
MULTILATERAL	*25.8*	*28.5*	*38.6*	*53.0*
OPEC COUNTRIES	*–*	*4.8*	*3.4*	*5.1*
E.E.C.+ MEMBERS	*13.3*	*12.4*	*13.7*	*37.4*
TOTAL	*39.4*	*48.3*	*61.4*	*104.0*

ODA LOANS NET

	1983	1984	1985	1986
Australia	–	–	–	–
Austria	–	–	–	–
Belgium	–	–	–	–
Canada	–	–	–	–
Denmark	0.5	3.4	–	-0.8
Finland	–	–	–	–
France	8.1	6.6	13.1	38.2
Germany, Fed. Rep.	–	–	–	–
Ireland	–	–	–	–
Italy	-0.2	-0.2	–	–
Japan	-0.1	-0.1	0.2	-0.2
Netherlands	–	–	-1.8	–
New Zealand	–	–	–	–
Norway	–	–	–	2.4
Sweden	–	–	–	–
Switzerland	–	–	–	–
United Kingdom	–	–	–	–
United States	4.0	3.0	4.0	6.0
TOTAL	*12.2*	*12.6*	*15.5*	*45.7*
MULTILATERAL	*24.7*	*28.4*	*37.0*	*49.4*
OPEC COUNTRIES	*-1.4*	*4.5*	*2.1*	*4.4*
E.E.C.+ MEMBERS	*13.0*	*12.2*	*11.9*	*37.4*
TOTAL	*35.5*	*45.5*	*54.6*	*99.5*

GRANTS

	1983
Australia	–
Austria	–
Belgium	0.0
Canada	0.6
Denmark	–
Finland	–
France	1.3
Germany, Fed. Rep.	6.7
Ireland	–
Italy	1.0
Japan	3.3
Netherlands	0.1
New Zealand	–
Norway	–
Sweden	–
Switzerland	0.3
United Kingdom	0.1
United States	1.0
TOTAL	*14.3*
MULTILATERAL	*16.9*
OPEC COUNTRIES	*0.8*
E.E.C.+ MEMBERS	*16.9*
TOTAL	*32.1*

TOTAL OFFICIAL GROSS

DAC COUNTRIES	1983	1984	1985	1986
Australia	–	–	–	–
Austria	–	0.0	0.0	0.0
Belgium	0.0	0.2	1.1	8.3
Canada	0.6	9.8	11.2	2.8
Denmark	0.5	3.5	0.7	3.6
Finland	–	0.1	0.0	–
France	11.9	9.4	24.6	48.8
Germany, Fed. Rep.	7.4	9.0	8.3	13.4
Ireland	–	–	–	–
Italy	1.0	3.5	3.2	6.8
Japan	3.3	2.9	5.8	3.7
Netherlands	0.1	0.1	3.0	0.4
New Zealand	–	–	–	–
Norway	–	0.1	0.2	2.6
Sweden	–	–	–	–
Switzerland	0.3	0.3	0.3	5.9
United Kingdom	0.1	0.1	0.4	0.4
United States	6.0	6.0	10.0	12.0
TOTAL	*31.0*	*45.1*	*68.8*	*108.7*
MULTILATERAL	*49.9*	*71.4*	*65.9*	*85.4*
OPEC COUNTRIES	*0.8*	*30.1*	*3.4*	*5.1*
E.E.C.+ MEMBERS	*34.1*	*39.7*	*52.1*	*97.3*
TOTAL	*81.7*	*146.6*	*138.1*	*199.2*

TOTAL OFFICIAL NET

	1983	1984	1985	1986
Australia	–	–	–	–
Austria	–	0.0	0.0	0.0
Belgium	0.0	0.2	1.1	8.3
Canada	0.6	9.8	11.2	2.8
Denmark	0.5	3.4	0.7	3.6
Finland	–	0.1	0.0	–
France	11.0	8.8	23.9	48.1
Germany, Fed. Rep.	5.7	6.6	7.2	12.4
Ireland	–	–	–	–
Italy	0.4	3.0	3.2	6.8
Japan	3.2	2.7	5.7	3.5
Netherlands	0.1	0.1	1.2	0.4
New Zealand	–	–	–	–
Norway	–	0.1	0.2	2.6
Sweden	–	–	–	–
Switzerland	0.3	0.3	0.3	5.9
United Kingdom	0.1	0.1	0.4	0.4
United States	2.0	2.0	8.0	12.0
TOTAL	*23.9*	*37.5*	*63.1*	*106.7*
MULTILATERAL	*41.4*	*62.7*	*57.5*	*67.0*
OPEC COUNTRIES	*-0.6*	*29.8*	*2.1*	*4.4*
E.E.C.+ MEMBERS	*30.9*	*35.8*	*48.1*	*94.8*
TOTAL	*64.6*	*130.0*	*122.8*	*178.2*

TOTAL OOF GROSS

	1983
Australia	–
Austria	–
Belgium	–
Canada	–
Denmark	–
Finland	–
France	2.4
Germany, Fed. Rep.	0.6
Ireland	–
Italy	–
Japan	–
Netherlands	–
New Zealand	–
Norway	–
Sweden	–
Switzerland	–
United Kingdom	–
United States	–
TOTAL	*3.0*
MULTILATERAL	*7.2*
OPEC COUNTRIES	*–*
E.E.C.+ MEMBERS	*3.9*
TOTAL	*10.2*

ODA COMMITMENTS

	1984	1985	1986	1983	1984	1985	1986
Australia	–	–	–	–	0.0	0.0	–
Austria	0.0	0.0	0.0	–	–	0.6	0.5
Belgium	0.2	1.1	0.5	4.5	22.5	5.5	0.5
Canada	9.8	11.2	2.8	–	–	–	7.1
Denmark	3.4	0.7	3.6	–	0.2	–	–
Finland	0.1	0.0	–	–	–	–	–
France	9.4	21.8	46.1	11.4	10.8	71.0	46.1
Germany, Fed. Rep.	8.5	8.0	13.0	10.9	11.2	4.2	21.5
Ireland	–	–	–	–	–	–	–
Italy	3.5	3.2	6.8	1.0	3.7	5.1	11.5
Japan	2.9	5.8	3.7	29.9	6.6	1.1	34.4
Netherlands	0.1	3.0	0.4	0.1	0.1	3.0	0.4
New Zealand	–	–	–	–	–	–	–
Norway	0.1	0.2	2.6	–	0.0	0.2	2.6
Sweden	–	–	–	–	–	–	–
Switzerland	0.3	0.3	5.9	0.1	0.1	–	5.8
United Kingdom	0.1	0.4	0.4	0.1	0.1	0.4	0.4
United States	6.0	8.0	12.0	6.9	7.4	10.3	30.0
TOTAL	**44.5**	**63.7**	**97.8**	**64.8**	**62.7**	**108.4**	**153.6**
	1.2	7.8	12.2	15.4	27.5	2.3	7.5
	–	–	–	–	–	–	–
	13.9	8.2	12.9	7.6	26.8	13.4	7.4
	–	–	–	–	–	–	–
	19.8	21.6	35.7	24.0	46.7	35.5	51.8
	0.3	3.3	4.4	–	–	5.6	–
	–	–	–	9.2	11.5	11.6	10.6
	5.2	4.4	5.8	–	–	–	–
	0.8	2.5	0.8	–	–	–	–
	1.0	0.9	1.0	–	–	–	–
	–	–	–	–	–	–	–
	2.1	0.9	1.4	–	–	–	–
	1.1	–	–	–	–	–	–
	1.3	2.9	1.7	–	–	–	–
	4.8	6.4	0.7	–	7.0	–	11.8
MULTILATERAL	*51.5*	*58.9*	*76.5*	*56.2*	*119.5*	*68.3*	*89.1*
OPEC COUNTRIES	*30.1*	*3.4*	*5.1*	*20.9*	*55.2*	*–*	*–*
E.E.C.+ MEMBERS	*39.1*	*46.4*	*83.6*	*31.1*	*52.7*	*104.8*	*87.8*
TOTAL	**126.1**	**126.0**	**179.4**	**141.9**	**237.4**	**176.7**	**242.7**

TECH. COOP. GRANTS

	1984	1985	1986	1983	1984	1985	1986
Australia	–	–	–	–	–	–	–
Austria	0.0	0.0	0.0	–	–	–	–
Belgium	0.2	1.1	0.5	–	–	–	–
Canada	9.8	11.2	2.8	0.2	–	1.0	–
Denmark	–	0.7	4.4	–	0.0	0.0	0.2
Finland	0.1	0.0	–	–	–	–	–
France	2.9	8.7	7.8	1.3	1.9	1.8	4.4
Germany, Fed. Rep.	8.5	8.0	13.0	3.1	2.8	2.5	3.8
Ireland	–	–	–	–	–	–	–
Italy	3.5	3.2	6.8	0.3	2.1	1.5	3.7
Japan	2.9	5.5	3.7	0.4	0.5	0.2	0.4
Netherlands	0.1	3.0	0.4	0.1	0.1	0.2	0.4
New Zealand	–	–	–	–	–	–	–
Norway	0.1	0.2	0.2	–	0.0	0.2	0.2
Sweden	–	–	–	–	–	–	–
Switzerland	0.3	0.3	5.9	0.2	0.2	0.3	0.3
United Kingdom	0.1	0.4	0.4	0.1	0.1	0.4	0.4
United States	1.0	2.0	6.0	1.0	1.0	1.0	3.0
TOTAL	**29.5**	**44.3**	**51.9**	**6.7**	**8.5**	**9.2**	**16.7**
MULTILATERAL	*23.0*	*20.3*	*23.6*	*7.7*	*9.4*	*10.7*	*9.9*
	25.3	*–*	*–*	*–*	*–*	*–*	*–*
E.E.C.+ MEMBERS	*26.7*	*32.7*	*46.2*	*4.9*	*6.9*	*6.5*	*13.4*
TOTAL	**77.8**	**64.6**	**75.4**	**14.4**	**17.9**	**19.9**	**26.5**

TOTAL OOF NET

	1984	1985	1986	1983	1984	1985	1986
Australia	–	–	–	–	–	–	–
Austria	–	–	–	–	–	–	–
Belgium	–	–	7.8	–	–	–	7.8
Canada	–	–	–	–	–	–	–
Denmark	0.0	–	–	–	0.0	–	–
Finland	–	–	–	–	–	–	–
France	–	2.8	2.7	1.6	-0.6	2.1	2.0
Germany, Fed. Rep.	0.5	0.3	0.4	-1.0	-1.9	-0.8	-0.6
Ireland	–	–	–	-0.3	-0.3	–	–
Italy	–	–	–	–	–	–	–
Japan	–	–	–	–	–	–	–
Netherlands	–	–	–	–	–	–	–
New Zealand	–	–	–	–	–	–	–
Norway	–	2.0	–	-3.0	-2.0	2.0	–
Sweden	0.6	5.1	11.0	-2.7	-4.7	3.3	9.2
Switzerland	19.9	7.0	8.9	-0.2	11.3	0.2	-5.9
United Kingdom	–	–	–	–	–	–	–
United States	0.6	5.7	13.6	1.0	-3.1	3.5	11.3
TOTAL	**20.5**	**12.1**	**19.8**	**-2.9**	**6.7**	**3.6**	**3.3**

ODA COMMITMENTS : LOANS

DAC COUNTRIES

	1983	1984	1985	1986
Australia	–	–	–	–
Austria	–	–	–	–
Belgium	–	–	–	–
Canada	–	–	–	–
Denmark	–	–	–	–
Finland	–	–	–	–
France	10.1	5.3	60.4	38.2
Germany, Fed. Rep.	–	–	–	–
Ireland	–	–	–	–
Italy	–	–	–	–
Japan	25.9	–	–	29.7
Netherlands	–	–	–	–
New Zealand	–	–	–	–
Norway	–	–	–	2.4
Sweden	–	–	–	–
Switzerland	–	–	–	–
United Kingdom	–	–	–	–
United States	4.8	4.8	5.7	6.0
TOTAL	*40.7*	*10.1*	*66.1*	*76.3*
MULTILATERAL	*43.1*	*81.8*	*44.9*	*70.9*
OPEC COUNTRIES	**11.3**	**29.9**	**–**	**–**
E.E.C.+ MEMBERS	*13.8*	*7.5*	*62.0*	*38.2*
TOTAL	**95.0**	**121.7**	**111.0**	**147.3**

GRANT ELEMENT OF ODA

DAC COUNTRIES

	1983	1984	1985	1986
Australia	–	–	–	–
Austria	–	100.0	100.0	–
Belgium	–	–	100.0	100.0
Canada	100.0	100.0	100.0	100.0
Denmark	–	–	100.0	–
Finland	–	100.0	–	–
France	49.7	67.5	44.5	55.5
Germany, Fed. Rep.	100.0	100.0	100.0	100.0
Ireland	–	–	–	–
Italy	100.0	100.0	100.0	100.0
Japan	62.4	100.0	100.0	75.9
Netherlands	100.0	100.0	100.0	100.0
New Zealand	–	–	–	–
Norway	–	100.0	100.0	34.4
Sweden	–	–	–	–
Switzerland	100.0	100.0	–	100.0
United Kingdom	100.0	100.0	100.0	100.0
United States	70.8	72.7	76.7	91.7
TOTAL	*72.8*	*91.2*	*61.6*	*77.7*
MULTILATERAL	*86.9*	*87.4*	*89.1*	*81.3*
OPEC COUNTRIES	**74.4**	**74.8**	**–**	**–**
E.E.C.+ MEMBERS	*86.8*	*93.1*	*61.9*	*75.4*
TOTAL	**78.9**	**85.5**	**71.8**	**79.0**

OTHER AGGREGATES

COMMITMENTS: ALL SOURCES

	1983	1984	1985	1986
TOTAL BILATERAL	88.2	234.9	123.3	153.9
of which				
OPEC	23.3	55.2	–	–
CMEA	–	116.9	7.0	–
TOTAL MULTILATERAL	99.9	144.6	78.6	89.1
TOTAL BIL.& MULTIL.	188.0	379.5	201.8	243.1
of which				
ODA Grants	46.8	115.7	65.7	95.5
ODA Loans	95.0	238.6	118.0	147.3

DISBURSEMENTS:

DAC COUNTRIES COMBINED

	1983	1984	1985	1986
OFFICIAL & PRIVATE				
GROSS:				
Contractual Lending	33.6	31.2	41.8	58.9
Export Credits Total	17.6	16.0	17.3	2.0
Export Credits Private	16.9	15.6	17.3	2.0
NET:				
Contractual Lending	13.2	1.8	19.6	55.4
Export Credits Total	0.5	-8.1	0.4	0.3
PRIVATE SECTOR NET	5.5	-0.7	1.4	2.4
Direct Investment	0.4	0.7	1.1	4.0
Portfolio Investment	1.4	4.7	-0.5	-2.1
Export Credits	3.7	-6.2	0.8	0.5

MARKET BORROWING:

CHANGE IN CLAIMS

	1983	1984	1985	1986
Banks	–	-11.0	22.0	-29.0

MEMORANDUM ITEM:

	1983	1984	1985	1986
CMEA Countr.(Gross)	6.0	4.8	11.3	7.0

	1983	1984	1985	1986		1983	1984	1985	1986		1983
TOTAL RECEIPTS NET					**TOTAL ODA NET**					**TOTAL ODA GROSS**	
DAC COUNTRIES											
Australia	–	–	–	–		–	–	–	–	Australia	–
Austria	0.1	0.1	0.0	0.1		0.1	0.1	0.0	0.1	Austria	0.1
Belgium	-1.4	-0.3	-0.1	0.3		0.1	0.2	0.5	0.2	Belgium	0.1
Canada	0.3	0.3	0.6	0.1		0.3	0.3	0.6	0.1	Canada	0.3
Denmark	1.5	0.4	0.2	0.3		1.5	0.4	0.2	0.3	Denmark	1.5
Finland	–	0.2	–	–		–	0.2	–	–	Finland	–
France	2.7	5.0	6.8	5.6		2.7	2.7	2.7	3.7	France	2.8
Germany, Fed. Rep.	0.6	0.8	0.5	1.1		0.6	0.7	0.6	1.2	Germany, Fed. Rep.	0.6
Ireland	–	–	–	–		–	–	–	–	Ireland	–
Italy	6.6	3.8	2.1	10.5		6.6	2.7	2.5	10.9	Italy	6.6
Japan	1.2	1.3	1.3	1.5		1.2	1.3	1.3	1.5	Japan	1.2
Netherlands	7.2	9.6	4.3	6.3		7.2	9.6	4.3	7.5	Netherlands	7.2
New Zealand	–	–	–	–		–	–	–	–	New Zealand	–
Norway	0.2	–	0.0	0.1		0.2	–	0.0	0.1	Norway	0.2
Sweden	9.0	7.1	8.8	11.1		8.9	7.1	8.8	11.1	Sweden	8.9
Switzerland	0.2	2.3	0.3	0.8		0.6	2.3	0.8	0.8	Switzerland	0.6
United Kingdom	0.1	0.0	–	0.1		0.2	0.0	–	0.1	United Kingdom	0.2
United States	2.0	3.0	2.0	3.0		2.0	3.0	2.0	3.0	United States	2.0
TOTAL	*30.3*	*33.5*	*26.8*	*40.8*		*32.1*	*30.5*	*24.3*	*40.6*	*TOTAL*	*32.2*
MULTILATERAL											
AF.D.F.	3.7	2.1	0.6	1.0		3.7	2.1	0.6	1.0	AF.D.F.	3.8
AF.D.B.	4.0	2.8	1.2	–		–	–	–	–	AF.D.B.	–
AS.D.B	–	–	–	–		–	–	–	–	AS.D.B	–
CAR.D.B.	–	–	–	–		–	–	–	–	CAR.D.B.	–
E.E.C.	4.4	8.9	6.5	6.1		4.4	8.9	6.5	6.1	E.E.C.	4.4
IBRD	–	–	–	–		–	–	–	–	IBRD	–
IDA	10.7	4.6	14.6	10.1		10.7	4.6	14.6	10.1	IDA	10.7
I.D.B.	–	–	–	–		–	–	–	–	I.D.B.	–
IFAD	–	–	–	0.4		–	–	–	0.4	IFAD	–
I.F.C.	–	–	–	–		–	–	–	–	I.F.C.	–
IMF TRUST FUND	–	–	–	–		–	–	–	–	IMF TRUST FUND	–
U.N. AGENCIES										U.N. AGENCIES	
UNDP	2.6	2.6	4.1	4.3		2.6	2.6	4.1	4.3	UNDP	2.6
UNTA	0.8	0.5	0.7	0.8		0.8	0.5	0.7	0.8	UNTA	0.8
UNICEF	0.3	0.6	0.7	0.5		0.3	0.6	0.7	0.5	UNICEF	0.3
UNRWA	–	–	–	–		–	–	–	–	UNRWA	–
WFP	1.7	2.3	2.1	1.8		1.7	2.3	2.1	1.8	WFP	1.7
UNHCR	–	–	–	–		–	–	–	–	UNHCR	–
Other Multilateral	1.3	0.8	1.3	1.9		1.3	0.8	1.3	1.9	Other Multilateral	1.3
Arab OPEC Agencies	0.3	0.6	1.7	0.6		0.3	–	0.0	0.0	Arab OPEC Agencies	0.8
TOTAL	*29.9*	*25.8*	*33.5*	*27.5*		*25.9*	*22.4*	*30.5*	*26.8*	*TOTAL*	*26.4*
OPEC COUNTRIES	*6.2*	*2.3*	*3.0*	*3.6*		*6.2*	*2.3*	*3.0*	*3.6*	*OPEC COUNTRIES*	*6.2*
E.E.C.+ MEMBERS	*21.7*	*28.2*	*20.2*	*30.3*		*23.3*	*25.2*	*17.3*	*30.1*	*E.E.C.+ MEMBERS*	*23.3*
TOTAL	**66.4**	**61.6**	**63.3**	**71.9**		**64.2**	**55.2**	**57.7**	**71.0**	**TOTAL**	**64.7**
ODA LOANS GROSS					**ODA LOANS NET**					**GRANTS**	
DAC COUNTRIES											
Australia	–	–	–	–		–	–	–	–	Australia	–
Austria	–	–	–	–		–	–	–	–	Austria	0.1
Belgium	–	–	–	–		–	–	–	–	Belgium	0.1
Canada	–	–	–	–		–	–	–	–	Canada	0.3
Denmark	–	–	–	–		–	–	–	–	Denmark	1.5
Finland	–	–	–	–		–	–	–	–	Finland	–
France	0.3	–	0.0	0.2		0.2	–	0.0	0.2	France	2.5
Germany, Fed. Rep.	–	–	–	0.1		–	–	–	0.1	Germany, Fed. Rep.	0.6
Ireland	–	–	–	–		–	–	–	–	Ireland	–
Italy	–	–	–	–		–	–	–	–	Italy	6.6
Japan	–	–	–	–		–	–	–	–	Japan	1.2
Netherlands	0.0	1.1	0.6	0.7		0.0	1.1	-5.6	–	Netherlands	7.2
New Zealand	–	–	–	–		–	–	–	–	New Zealand	–
Norway	–	–	–	–		–	–	–	–	Norway	0.2
Sweden	–	–	–	–		–	–	–	–	Sweden	8.9
Switzerland	–	–	–	–		–	–	–	–	Switzerland	0.6
United Kingdom	–	–	–	–		–	–	–	–	United Kingdom	0.2
United States	–	–	–	–		–	–	–	–	United States	2.0
TOTAL	*0.3*	*1.1*	*0.6*	*0.9*		*0.3*	*1.1*	*-5.5*	*0.2*	*TOTAL*	*31.9*
MULTILATERAL	*15.2*	*6.8*	*16.8*	*11.7*		*14.7*	*6.8*	*16.3*	*11.4*	*MULTILATERAL*	*11.2*
OPEC COUNTRIES	*5.6*	*2.3*	*3.6*	*1.8*		*5.6*	*2.3*	*2.5*	*1.5*	*OPEC COUNTRIES*	*0.6*
E.E.C.+ MEMBERS	*0.3*	*1.1*	*1.7*	*0.9*		*0.3*	*1.1*	*-4.4*	*0.2*	*E.E.C.+ MEMBERS*	*23.0*
TOTAL	**21.1**	**10.2**	**20.9**	**14.3**		**20.6**	**10.2**	**13.2**	**13.1**	**TOTAL**	**43.6**
TOTAL OFFICIAL GROSS					**TOTAL OFFICIAL NET**					**TOTAL OOF GROSS**	
DAC COUNTRIES											
Australia	–	–	–	–		–	–	–	–	Australia	–
Austria	0.1	0.1	0.0	0.1		0.1	0.1	0.0	0.1	Austria	–
Belgium	0.1	0.2	0.5	0.2		0.1	0.2	0.5	0.2	Belgium	–
Canada	0.3	0.3	0.6	0.1		0.3	0.3	0.6	0.1	Canada	–
Denmark	1.5	0.4	0.2	0.3		1.5	0.4	0.2	0.3	Denmark	–
Finland	–	0.2	–	–		–	0.2	–	–	Finland	–
France	2.8	2.7	2.9	3.7		2.7	2.7	2.9	3.7	France	–
Germany, Fed. Rep.	0.6	0.7	0.6	1.2		0.6	0.7	0.6	1.2	Germany, Fed. Rep.	–
Ireland	–	–	–	–		–	–	–	–	Ireland	–
Italy	6.6	2.7	2.5	10.9		6.6	2.7	2.5	10.9	Italy	–
Japan	1.2	1.3	1.3	1.5		1.2	1.3	1.3	1.5	Japan	–
Netherlands	7.2	9.5	10.4	8.2		7.2	9.6	4.3	7.5	Netherlands	–
New Zealand	–	–	–	–		–	–	–	–	New Zealand	–
Norway	0.2	–	0.0	0.1		0.2	–	0.0	0.1	Norway	–
Sweden	9.2	7.1	8.8	11.1		9.0	7.1	8.8	11.1	Sweden	0.3
Switzerland	0.6	2.3	0.8	0.8		0.6	2.3	0.8	0.8	Switzerland	–
United Kingdom	0.2	0.0	–	0.1		0.2	0.0	–	0.1	United Kingdom	–
United States	2.0	3.0	2.0	3.0		2.0	3.0	2.0	3.0	United States	–
TOTAL	*32.4*	*30.6*	*30.6*	*41.3*		*32.3*	*30.6*	*24.5*	*40.6*	*TOTAL*	*0.3*
MULTILATERAL	*30.3*	*26.3*	*34.0*	*27.7*		*29.9*	*25.8*	*33.5*	*27.5*	*MULTILATERAL*	*4.0*
OPEC COUNTRIES	*6.2*	*2.3*	*4.0*	*3.9*		*6.2*	*2.3*	*3.0*	*3.6*	*OPEC COUNTRIES*	*–*
E.E.C.+ MEMBERS	*23.3*	*25.2*	*23.6*	*30.8*		*23.3*	*25.2*	*17.5*	*30.1*	*E.E.C.+ MEMBERS*	*–*
TOTAL	**69.0**	**59.2**	**68.6**	**72.9**		**68.4**	**58.6**	**60.9**	**71.6**	**TOTAL**	**4.2**

GUINEA-BISSAU

ODA COMMITMENTS

1984	1985	1986	1983	1984	1985	1986
–	–	–	–	–	–	–
0.1	0.0	0.1	–	–	0.0	–
0.2	0.5	0.2	–	–	–	0.2
0.3	0.6	0.1	0.3	0.3	0.4	0.3
0.4	0.2	0.3	0.6	0.6	–	–
0.2	–	–	–	0.2	–	–
2.7	2.7	3.7	3.8	2.9	2.3	3.7
0.7	0.6	1.2	1.0	1.3	2.3	2.7
–	–	–	–	–	–	–
2.7	2.5	10.9	8.7	2.2	2.6	13.4
1.3	1.3	1.5	1.3	2.7	1.1	–
9.5	10.4	8.2	9.4	4.4	10.3	7.6
–	–	–	–	–	0.0	–
–	0.0	0.1	–	–	–	–
7.1	8.8	11.1	8.5	9.5	8.2	11.1
2.3	0.8	0.8	1.0	2.2	1.1	0.5
0.0	–	0.1	0.3	0.0	–	0.1
3.0	2.0	3.0	2.0	4.0	4.2	2.4
30.5	*30.4*	*41.3*	*36.8*	*30.2*	*32.4*	*41.9*
2.1	1.1	1.3	6.4	3.1	–	–
–	–	–	–	–	–	–
–	–	–	–	–	–	–
8.9	6.5	6.1	4.4	11.0	8.4	6.2
–	–	–	–	–	–	–
4.6	14.6	10.1	29.1	24.0	–	5.0
–	–	0.4	7.7	–	–	–
–	–	–	–	–	–	–
–	–	–	6.8	6.7	8.9	9.3
2.6	4.1	4.3	–	–	–	–
0.5	0.7	0.8	–	–	–	–
0.6	0.7	0.5	–	–	–	–
–	–	–	–	–	–	–
2.3	2.1	1.8	–	–	–	–
–	–	–	–	–	–	–
0.8	1.3	1.9	1.5	0.5	1.0	0.5
22.4	*31.0*	*27.1*	*55.9*	*45.3*	*18.2*	*21.0*
2.3	*4.0*	*3.9*	*29.9*	*0.5*	*11.6*	–
25.2	*23.4*	*30.8*	*28.2*	*22.4*	*25.8*	*34.0*
55.2	**65.4**	**72.2**	**122.6**	**76.1**	**62.1**	**62.9**

TECH. COOP. GRANTS

1984	1985	1986	1983	1984	1985	1986
–	–	–	0.1	–	–	–
0.1	0.0	0.1	–	–	–	–
0.2	0.5	0.2	0.5	–	0.2	–
0.3	0.6	0.1	1.4	0.2	–	0.0
0.4	0.2	0.3	–	–	–	–
0.2	–	–	–	–	–	–
2.7	2.7	3.6	1.2	1.2	1.2	1.3
0.7	0.6	1.1	0.4	0.8	0.6	0.8
–	–	–	–	–	–	–
2.7	2.5	10.9	0.3	0.9	0.7	3.9
1.3	1.3	1.5	–	0.0	–	–
8.5	9.9	7.5	1.3	1.1	1.5	2.1
–	–	–	–	–	–	–
–	0.0	0.1	–	–	–	–
7.1	8.8	11.1	4.6	2.1	2.8	3.4
2.3	0.8	0.8	0.3	0.1	0.1	0.2
0.0	–	0.1	0.0	0.0	–	0.1
3.0	2.0	3.0	1.0	1.0	1.0	2.0
29.5	*29.8*	*40.4*	*11.1*	*7.4*	*8.1*	*13.7*
15.6	*14.2*	*15.4*	*5.0*	*4.4*	*6.8*	*8.7*
–	*0.5*	*2.1*	–	–	–	–
24.1	*21.7*	*29.9*	*4.6*	*4.2*	*4.0*	*9.4*
45.1	**44.5**	**57.9**	**16.1**	**11.8**	**14.9**	**22.5**

TOTAL OOF NET

1984	1985	1986	1983	1984	1985	1986
–	–	–	–	–	–	–
0.0	–	–	–	0.0	–	–
–	–	–	–	–	–	–
–	–	–	–	–	–	–
–	0.2	–	–	–	0.2	–
–	–	–	–	–	–	–
–	–	–	–	–	–	–
–	–	–	–	–	–	–
–	–	–	–	–	–	–
–	–	–	0.1	–	–	–
–	–	–	–	–	–	–
–	–	–	–	–	–	–
0.0	0.2	–	0.1	0.0	0.2	–
4.0	3.0	0.7	4.0	3.4	3.0	0.7
–	–	–	–	–	–	–
0.0	0.2	–	–	0.0	0.2	–
4.0	**3.2**	**0.7**	**4.1**	**3.4**	**3.2**	**0.7**

ODA COMMITMENTS : LOANS

DAC COUNTRIES

	1983	1984	1985	1986
Australia	–	–	–	–
Austria	–	–	–	–
Belgium	–	–	–	–
Canada	–	–	–	–
Denmark	–	–	–	–
Finland	–	–	–	–
France	–	–	0.5	0.2
Germany, Fed. Rep.	–	–	–	–
Ireland	–	–	–	–
Italy	–	–	–	–
Japan	–	–	–	–
Netherlands	–	–	–	–
New Zealand	–	–	–	–
Norway	–	–	–	–
Sweden	–	–	–	–
Switzerland	–	–	–	–
United Kingdom	–	–	–	–
United States	–	–	–	–
TOTAL	–	–	*0.5*	*0.2*
MULTILATERAL	*43.8*	*30.6*	*0.1*	*5.3*
OPEC COUNTRIES	*23.1*	–	*7.1*	–
E.E.C.+ MEMBERS	–	*3.0*	*0.5*	*0.2*
TOTAL	**66.9**	**30.6**	**7.7**	**5.5**

GRANT ELEMENT OF ODA

DAC COUNTRIES

	1983	1984	1985	1986
Australia	–	–	–	–
Austria	–	–	100.0	–
Belgium	–	–	–	100.0
Canada	100.0	100.0	100.0	100.0
Denmark	100.0	100.0	–	–
Finland	–	100.0	–	–
France	100.0	100.0	93.2	100.0
Germany, Fed. Rep.	100.0	100.0	100.0	100.0
Ireland	–	–	–	–
Italy	100.0	100.0	100.0	100.0
Japan	100.0	100.0	100.0	–
Netherlands	100.0	100.0	100.0	100.0
New Zealand	–	–	100.0	–
Norway	–	–	–	–
Sweden	100.0	100.0	100.0	100.0
Switzerland	100.0	100.0	100.0	100.0
United Kingdom	100.0	100.0	–	100.0
United States	100.0	100.0	100.0	100.0
TOTAL	*100.0*	*100.0*	*99.5*	*100.0*
MULTILATERAL	*86.4*	*87.3*	*99.9*	*95.2*
OPEC COUNTRIES	*67.4*	*100.0*	*74.1*	–
E.E.C.+ MEMBERS	*100.0*	*100.0*	*99.4*	*100.0*
TOTAL	**85.8**	**92.2**	**94.9**	**98.4**

OTHER AGGREGATES

COMMITMENTS: ALL SOURCES

	1983	1984	1985	1986
TOTAL BILATERAL	68.8	30.7	45.4	46.6
of which				
OPEC	29.9	0.5	13.1	–
CMEA	1.8	–	–	4.7
TOTAL MULTILATERAL	65.9	45.3	18.2	25.7
TOTAL BIL.& MULTIL.	134.7	76.1	63.7	72.3
of which				
ODA Grants	55.8	45.5	54.5	57.4
ODA Loans	68.7	30.6	7.7	9.8

DISBURSEMENTS:

DAC COUNTRIES COMBINED

	1983	1984	1985	1986
OFFICIAL & PRIVATE				
GROSS:				
Contractual Lending	1.1	2.4	1.7	1.3
Export Credits Total	0.8	1.3	0.9	0.4
Export Credits Private	0.5	1.3	0.9	0.4
NET:				
Contractual Lending	-0.3	0.8	-6.5	0.2
Export Credits Total	-0.6	-0.3	-1.2	–
PRIVATE SECTOR NET	-2.0	3.0	2.3	0.2
Direct Investment	–	2.3	1.4	0.8
Portfolio Investment	-1.3	1.0	2.1	-0.6
Export Credits	-0.7	-0.3	-1.2	–

MARKET BORROWING:

CHANGE IN CLAIMS

	1983	1984	1985	1986
Banks	–	-2.0	4.0	-2.0

MEMORANDUM ITEM:

	1983	1984	1985	1986
CMEA Countr.(Gross)	0.5	5.8	3.5	0.4

	TOTAL RECEIPTS NET				TOTAL ODA NET				TOTAL ODA GROSS
	1983	1984	1985	1986	1983	1984	1985	1986	1983
DAC COUNTRIES									
Australia	0.0	0.1	0.1	0.1	0.0	0.1	0.1	0.1	0.0
Austria	–	–	–	–	–	–	–	–	–
Belgium	–	–	–	0.1	–	–	–	–	–
Canada	2.4	0.8	0.2	0.6	3.2	1.6	1.1	1.1	3.2
Denmark	-0.1	-0.2	-0.3	-0.3	0.0	–	–	–	0.0
Finland	–	–	–	0.1	–	–	–	–	–
France	–	–	–	0.1	–	–	–	–	–
Germany, Fed. Rep.	-1.1	-0.5	-0.5	0.0	0.2	0.0	-0.1	0.0	0.2
Ireland	0.0	–	–	–	0.0	–	–	–	0.0
Italy	–	–	–	–	–	–	–	–	–
Japan	0.3	2.3	3.6	3.1	–	2.2	3.4	3.1	0.3
Netherlands	-0.6	0.1	0.4	-0.8	0.8	1.0	0.1	0.0	0.8
New Zealand	–	–	–	–	–	–	–	–	–
Norway	–	–	–	0.0	–	–	–	0.0	–
Sweden	–	–	–	–	–	–	–	–	–
Switzerland	0.0	–	0.0	0.0	0.0	–	0.0	0.0	0.0
United Kingdom	-2.2	-1.7	3.9	-2.4	2.2	0.5	0.5	0.7	2.4
United States	..	-2.0	–	3.0	4.0	1.0	1.0	4.0	4.0
TOTAL	*-1.2*	*-1.1*	*7.2*	*3.6*	*10.5*	*6.4*	*6.0*	*9.1*	*11.0*
MULTILATERAL									
AF.D.F.	–	–	–	–	–	–	–	–	–
AF.D.B.	–	–	–	–	–	–	–	–	–
AS.D.B	–	–	–	–	–	–	–	–	–
CAR.D.B.	0.5	0.3	0.4	–	0.0	–	–	–	0.0
E.E.C.	3.5	1.8	2.3	8.3	3.5	1.8	2.3	8.3	3.5
IBRD	7.3	2.7	-0.4	-1.2	–	–	–	–	–
IDA	-0.1	0.2	1.1	5.6	-0.1	0.2	1.1	5.6	–
I.D.B.	23.7	19.2	23.8	18.0	15.4	13.3	16.2	5.8	15.4
IFAD	–	–	–	–	–	–	–	–	–
I.F.C.	-0.2	–	-0.1	–	–	–	–	–	–
IMF TRUST FUND	–	–	–	–	–	–	–	–	–
U.N. AGENCIES									
UNDP	0.7	1.2	0.7	1.1	0.7	1.2	0.7	1.1	0.7
UNTA	0.6	0.4	0.4	0.3	0.6	0.4	0.4	0.3	0.6
UNICEF	0.1	0.1	0.1	0.3	0.1	0.1	0.1	0.3	0.1
UNRWA	–	–	–	–	–	–	–	–	–
WFP	0.2	0.1	–	0.1	0.2	0.1	–	0.1	0.2
UNHCR	–	–	–	–	–	–	–	–	–
Other Multilateral	0.1	0.1	0.2	0.2	0.1	0.1	0.2	0.2	0.1
Arab OPEC Agencies	-1.1	-1.5	-0.4	-0.4	-0.3	-0.4	–	–	–
TOTAL	*35.3*	*24.5*	*28.1*	*32.6*	*20.2*	*16.7*	*21.0*	*21.6*	*20.6*
OPEC COUNTRIES	–	–	–	*10.8*	–	–	–	–	–
E.E.C.+ MEMBERS	*-0.5*	*-0.5*	*5.8*	*5.1*	*6.7*	*3.4*	*2.7*	*9.1*	*6.9*
TOTAL	*34.1*	*23.4*	*35.3*	*47.0*	*30.7*	*23.1*	*27.0*	*30.7*	*31.6*

	ODA LOANS GROSS				ODA LOANS NET				GRANTS
	1983	1984	1985	1986	1983	1984	1985	1986	1983
DAC COUNTRIES									
Australia	–	–	–	–	–	–	–	–	0.0
Austria	–	–	–	–	–	–	–	–	–
Belgium	–	–	–	–	–	–	–	–	–
Canada	2.3	0.9	0.1	0.1	2.3	0.9	0.1	0.1	0.9
Denmark	–	–	–	–	–	–	–	–	0.0
Finland	–	–	–	–	–	–	–	–	–
France	–	–	–	–	–	–	–	–	–
Germany, Fed. Rep.	0.2	–	–	–	0.2	–	-0.2	–	0.0
Ireland	–	–	–	–	–	–	–	–	0.0
Italy	–	–	–	–	–	–	–	–	–
Japan	0.3	–	–	–	-0.1	–	0.0	0.0	0.1
Netherlands	0.3	–	–	–	0.3	–	–	–	0.5
New Zealand	–	–	–	–	–	–	–	–	–
Norway	–	–	–	–	–	–	–	–	–
Sweden	–	–	–	–	–	–	–	–	–
Switzerland	–	–	–	–	–	–	–	–	0.0
United Kingdom	1.6	0.1	–	–	1.5	–	–	–	0.7
United States	2.0	–	–	3.0	2.0	–	–	3.0	2.0
TOTAL	*6.7*	*0.9*	*0.1*	*3.1*	*6.2*	*0.9*	*-0.1*	*3.1*	*4.3*
MULTILATERAL	*17.2*	*10.6*	*15.3*	*12.3*	*16.8*	*10.4*	*15.1*	*12.0*	*3.4*
OPEC COUNTRIES	–	–	–	–	–	–	–	–	–
E.E.C.+ MEMBERS	*4.0*	*0.2*	–	*1.3*	*3.9*	*0.0*	*-0.2*	*1.1*	*2.8*
TOTAL	*23.9*	*11.5*	*15.3*	*15.5*	*23.0*	*11.2*	*15.0*	*15.1*	*7.7*

	TOTAL OFFICIAL GROSS				TOTAL OFFICIAL NET				TOTAL OOF GROSS
	1983	1984	1985	1986	1983	1984	1985	1986	1983
DAC COUNTRIES									
Australia	0.0	0.1	0.1	0.1	0.0	0.1	0.1	0.1	–
Austria	–	–	–	–	–	–	–	–	–
Belgium	–	–	–	–	–	–	–	–	–
Canada	3.2	1.6	1.1	1.1	2.4	0.8	0.2	0.6	–
Denmark	0.0	–	–	–	0.0	–	–	–	–
Finland	–	–	–	–	–	–	–	–	–
France	–	–	–	–	–	–	–	–	–
Germany, Fed. Rep.	0.3	0.1	0.0	0.0	-0.4	-0.5	-0.7	0.0	0.1
Ireland	0.0	–	–	–	0.0	–	–	–	–
Italy	–	–	–	–	–	–	–	–	–
Japan	0.3	2.2	3.4	3.2	–	2.2	3.4	3.1	–
Netherlands	0.8	1.0	0.1	0.0	0.8	1.0	0.1	0.0	–
New Zealand	–	–	–	–	–	–	–	–	–
Norway	–	–	–	0.0	–	–	–	–	–
Sweden	–	–	–	–	–	–	–	–	–
Switzerland	0.0	–	0.0	0.0	0.0	–	0.0	0.0	–
United Kingdom	2.4	0.6	0.5	0.7	2.2	0.5	0.5	0.7	–
United States	4.0	1.0	1.0	4.0	–	-2.0	–	3.0	–
TOTAL	*11.0*	*6.4*	*6.2*	*9.2*	*5.2*	*2.0*	*3.5*	*7.6*	*0.1*
MULTILATERAL	*37.6*	*27.9*	*31.0*	*35.4*	*35.3*	*24.5*	*28.1*	*32.6*	*16.9*
OPEC COUNTRIES	–	–	–	*11.0*	–	–	–	*10.8*	–
E.E.C.+ MEMBERS	*6.9*	*3.6*	*2.9*	*9.2*	*6.1*	*2.8*	*2.2*	*9.1*	*0.1*
TOTAL	*48.6*	*34.3*	*37.2*	*55.6*	*40.4*	*26.5*	*31.5*	*51.0*	*17.0*

ODA COMMITMENTS

1984	1985	1986	1983	1984	1985	1986
0.1	0.1	0.1	0.0	0.1	0.0	0.0
–	–	–	–	–	–	–
1.6	1.1	1.1	15.9	6.3	0.9	0.6
–	–	–	–	–	–	–
–	–	–	–	–	–	–
0.0	0.0	0.0	0.0	0.0	0.0	0.0
–	–	–	0.0	–	–	–
–	–	–	–	0.0	0.0	–
2.2	3.4	3.2	1.6	2.8	4.1	0.1
1.0	0.1	0.0	0.4	0.9	0.1	0.0
–	–	0.0	–	–	–	–
–	–	–	–	–	–	0.0
–	0.0	0.0	–	–	–	–
0.6	0.5	0.7	0.7	0.5	0.5	0.7
1.0	1.0	4.0	0.3	–	0.1	3.2
6.4	6.2	9.2	19.0	10.7	5.7	4.8
–	–	–	–	–	–	–
–	–	–	–	–	–	–
–	–	–	–	–	–	0.0
2.0	2.3	8.5	5.5	3.2	4.9	2.3
–	–	–	–	–	–	–
0.3	1.3	5.6	–	–	8.8	7.0
13.3	16.2	5.8	–	–	14.4	–
–	–	–	–	0.1	–	6.1
–	–	–	–	–	–	–
–	–	–	–	–	–	–
–	–	–	1.7	1.8	1.4	2.0
1.2	0.7	1.1	–	–	–	–
0.4	0.4	0.3	–	–	–	–
0.1	0.1	0.3	–	–	–	–
0.1	–	0.1	–	–	–	–
0.1	0.2	0.2	–	–	–	–
-0.4	–	–	–	3.0	3.0	1.1
16.9	21.1	21.9	7.2	8.1	32.5	18.5
–	–	–	–	–	–	–
3.6	2.9	9.2	6.6	4.6	5.5	3.1
23.3	27.3	31.0	26.2	18.7	38.2	23.3

TECH. COOP. GRANTS

1984	1985	1986	1983	1984	1985	1986
0.1	0.1	0.1	0.0	0.1	0.1	0.1
–	–	–	–	–	–	–
0.7	1.1	1.0	0.2	–	0.4	–
–	–	–	0.0	–	–	–
–	–	–	–	–	–	–
0.0	0.0	0.0	0.0	0.0	0.0	0.0
–	–	–	0.0	–	–	–
2.2	3.4	3.2	0.1	0.2	0.1	0.1
1.0	0.1	0.0	0.3	0.1	0.0	0.0
–	–	0.0	–	–	–	–
–	–	–	–	–	–	0.0
–	0.0	0.0	–	–	0.0	0.0
0.5	0.5	0.7	0.7	0.5	0.5	0.7
1.0	1.0	1.0	1.0	2.0	1.0	1.0
5.5	6.1	6.0	2.4	2.9	2.2	2.0
6.3	5.9	9.5	1.6	1.7	1.4	2.1
–	–	–	–	–	–	–
3.4	2.9	8.0	1.1	0.6	0.5	1.0
11.8	12.0	15.6	3.9	4.6	3.6	4.1

TOTAL OOF NET

1984	1985	1986	1983	1984	1985	1986
–	–	–	–	–	–	–
–	–	–	-0.7	-0.8	-1.0	-0.6
–	–	–	–	–	–	–
–	–	–	–	–	–	–
0.0	–	–	-0.6	-0.6	-0.6	–
–	–	–	–	–	–	–
–	–	–	–	–	–	–
–	–	–	–	–	–	–
–	–	–	–	–	–	–
–	–	–	–	–	–	–
–	–	–	-4.0	-3.0	-1.0	-1.0
0.0	–	–	-5.3	-4.3	-2.5	-1.6
10.9	9.8	13.6	15.1	7.8	7.1	11.1
–	–	11.0	–	–	–	10.8
0.0	–	–	-0.6	-0.6	-0.6	–
10.9	9.8	24.6	9.7	3.4	4.5	20.2

ODA COMMITMENTS : LOANS

DAC COUNTRIES	1983	1984	1985	1986
Australia	–	–	–	–
Austria	–	–	–	–
Belgium	–	–	–	–
Canada	11.4	–	–	–
Denmark	–	–	–	–
Finland	–	–	–	–
France	–	–	–	–
Germany, Fed. Rep.	–	–	–	–
Ireland	–	–	–	–
Italy	–	–	–	–
Japan	0.3	–	–	–
Netherlands	–	–	–	–
New Zealand	–	–	–	–
Norway	–	–	–	0.0
Sweden	–	–	–	–
Switzerland	–	–	–	–
United Kingdom	–	–	–	–
United States	0.2	–	–	3.0
TOTAL	11.8	–	–	3.0
MULTILATERAL	–	5.4	29.3	14.1
OPEC COUNTRIES	–	–	–	–
E.E.C.+ MEMBERS	–	2.4	3.1	–
TOTAL	11.8	5.4	29.3	17.1

GRANT ELEMENT OF ODA

DAC COUNTRIES	1983	1984	1985	1986
Australia	100.0	100.0	100.0	100.0
Austria	–	–	–	–
Belgium	–	–	–	–
Canada	92.7	100.0	100.0	100.0
Denmark	–	–	–	–
Finland	–	–	–	–
France	–	–	–	–
Germany, Fed. Rep.	100.0	100.0	100.0	100.0
Ireland	100.0	–	–	–
Italy	–	100.0	100.0	–
Japan	88.7	100.0	100.0	100.0
Netherlands	100.0	100.0	100.0	100.0
New Zealand	–	–	–	–
Norway	–	–	–	100.0
Sweden	–	–	–	–
Switzerland	–	–	–	–
United Kingdom	100.0	100.0	100.0	100.0
United States	71.9	–	100.0	62.5
TOTAL	92.5	100.0	100.0	74.4
MULTILATERAL	100.0	64.7	81.3	77.1
OPEC COUNTRIES	–	–	–	–
E.E.C.+ MEMBERS	100.0	100.0	100.0	100.0
TOTAL	94.6	87.7	86.4	76.5

OTHER AGGREGATES

COMMITMENTS: ALL SOURCES	1983	1984	1985	1986
TOTAL BILATERAL	25.4	16.8	10.8	4.8
of which				
OPEC	–	–	–	–
CMEA	–	–	5.0	–
TOTAL MULTILATERAL	7.2	48.8	76.6	18.5
TOTAL BIL.& MULTIL.	32.6	65.6	87.4	23.3
of which				
ODA Grants	14.4	13.4	9.0	6.2
ODA Loans	11.8	5.4	29.3	17.1

DISBURSEMENTS:
DAC COUNTRIES COMBINED

OFFICIAL & PRIVATE	1983	1984	1985	1986
GROSS:				
Contractual Lending	8.3	1.7	1.0	3.5
Export Credits Total	1.5	0.8	1.0	0.4
Export Credits Private	1.5	0.8	1.0	0.4
NET:				
Contractual Lending	-8.5	-14.1	-7.6	-4.1
Export Credits Total	-11.8	-12.0	-6.4	-6.2
PRIVATE SECTOR NET	-6.4	-3.1	3.8	-4.0
Direct Investment	0.1	5.5	5.7	0.0
Portfolio Investment	3.0	2.0	3.0	1.7
Export Credits	-9.4	-10.7	-4.9	-5.6

MARKET BORROWING:
CHANGE IN CLAIMS

	1983	1984	1985	1986
Banks	–	-5.0	-14.0	-4.0

MEMORANDUM ITEM:

	1983	1984	1985	1986
CMEA Countr.(Gross)	–	–	1.9	–

DISBURSEMENTS, UNLESS OTHERWISE STATED

TOTAL RECEIPTS NET / TOTAL ODA NET / TOTAL ODA GROSS

	TOTAL RECEIPTS NET 1983	1984	1985	1986	TOTAL ODA NET 1983	1984	1985	1986	TOTAL ODA GROSS 1983
DAC COUNTRIES									
Australia	–	0.0	0.0	0.0	–	0.0	0.0	0.0	–
Austria	0.0	-0.3	-0.3	–	0.0	–	–	–	0.0
Belgium	1.0	5.6	-2.4	-0.6	1.7	1.5	1.5	2.6	1.7
Canada	11.4	8.0	6.0	4.7	11.4	8.0	6.0	4.7	11.4
Denmark	–	–	–	–	–	–	–	–	–
Finland	–	–	–	–	–	–	–	–	–
France	-1.0	4.8	20.2	17.2	6.2	6.7	20.6	14.4	6.2
Germany, Fed. Rep.	12.8	8.0	7.7	10.0	12.4	8.4	7.6	10.5	12.4
Ireland	–	–	–	–	–	–	–	–	–
Italy	1.8	-0.7	-0.3	1.7	0.0	0.4	0.1	1.7	0.0
Japan	1.6	2.4	6.3	4.3	1.6	1.4	6.3	4.3	1.6
Netherlands	1.1	1.9	1.3	0.3	1.5	1.6	1.6	1.1	1.5
New Zealand	–	–	–	–	–	–	–	–	–
Norway	–	–	–	0.0	–	–	–	0.0	–
Sweden	–	–	–	0.1	–	–	–	0.1	–
Switzerland	1.0	0.4	2.4	2.5	2.0	0.9	2.8	2.5	2.0
United Kingdom	0.2	0.0	-0.1	0.5	0.0	0.0	–	0.5	0.0
United States	41.0	41.0	54.0	84.0	42.0	42.0	56.0	84.0	43.0
TOTAL	*70.9*	*71.2*	*94.7*	*124.7*	*78.8*	*71.0*	*102.6*	*126.4*	*79.8*
MULTILATERAL									
AF.D.F.	–	–	–	–	–	–	–	–	–
AF.D.B.	–	–	–	–	–	–	–	–	–
AS.D.B	–	–	–	–	–	–	–	–	–
CAR.D.B.	–	–	–	–	–	–	–	–	–
E.E.C.	2.1	5.1	4.1	4.3	2.1	5.1	4.1	4.3	2.1
IBRD	–	–	–	–	–	–	–	–	–
IDA	25.6	28.9	21.8	25.9	25.6	28.9	21.8	25.9	25.7
I.D.B.	14.9	16.2	10.7	3.1	14.9	16.2	10.7	3.1	15.6
IFAD	0.8	2.3	3.6	2.6	0.8	2.3	3.6	2.6	0.8
I.F.C.	0.7	–	–	-0.1	–	–	–	–	–
IMF TRUST FUND	–	–	–	–	–	–	–	–	–
U.N. AGENCIES	–	–	–	–	–	–	–	–	–
UNDP	5.3	4.8	4.1	5.7	5.3	4.8	4.1	5.7	5.3
UNTA	0.7	0.7	0.8	0.5	0.7	0.7	0.8	0.5	0.7
UNICEF	1.4	1.2	1.6	1.7	1.4	1.2	1.6	1.7	1.4
UNRWA	–	–	–	–	–	–	–	–	–
WFP	1.2	2.4	0.9	2.4	1.2	2.4	0.9	2.4	1.2
UNHCR	–	–	–	–	–	–	–	–	–
Other Multilateral	1.5	2.0	1.8	1.2	1.5	2.0	1.8	1.2	1.5
Arab OPEC Agencies	1.4	0.4	1.0	1.4	1.4	0.4	1.0	1.4	1.6
TOTAL	*55.6*	*63.9*	*50.3*	*48.7*	*54.9*	*63.9*	*50.3*	*48.8*	*55.8*
OPEC COUNTRIES	–	–	–	–	–	–	–	–	–
E.E.C.+ MEMBERS	*17.9*	*24.9*	*30.3*	*33.3*	*23.9*	*23.7*	*35.5*	*35.1*	*23.9*
TOTAL	**126.4**	**135.1**	**145.0**	**173.4**	**133.7**	**134.9**	**152.9**	**175.3**	**135.6**

ODA LOANS GROSS / ODA LOANS NET / GRANTS

	ODA LOANS GROSS 1983	1984	1985	1986	ODA LOANS NET 1983	1984	1985	1986	GRANTS 1983
DAC COUNTRIES									
Australia	–	–	–	–	–	–	–	–	–
Austria	–	–	–	–	–	–	–	–	0.0
Belgium	–	–	–	–	–	–	–	–	1.7
Canada	–	–	–	–	–	–	–	–	11.4
Denmark	–	–	–	–	–	–	–	–	–
Finland	–	–	–	–	–	–	–	–	–
France	1.0	2.2	14.7	6.5	1.0	2.2	14.7	6.5	5.3
Germany, Fed. Rep.	–	0.2	–	–	–	0.2	-0.1	-12.0	12.4
Ireland	–	–	–	–	–	–	–	–	–
Italy	–	–	–	–	–	–	–	–	0.0
Japan	–	–	–	–	–	–	–	–	1.6
Netherlands	–	–	–	–	–	–	–	–	1.5
New Zealand	–	–	–	–	–	–	–	–	–
Norway	–	–	–	–	–	–	–	–	–
Sweden	–	–	–	–	–	–	–	–	–
Switzerland	–	–	–	–	–	–	–	–	2.0
United Kingdom	–	–	–	–	–	–	–	–	0.0
United States	12.0	12.0	1.0	1.0	11.0	11.0	1.0	1.0	31.0
TOTAL	*13.0*	*14.4*	*15.7*	*7.5*	*12.0*	*13.4*	*15.7*	*-4.5*	*66.8*
MULTILATERAL	*42.7*	*45.8*	*36.1*	*35.9*	*41.8*	*44.4*	*34.5*	*32.9*	*13.1*
OPEC COUNTRIES	–	–	–	–	–	–	–	–	–
E.E.C.+ MEMBERS	*1.0*	*2.4*	*14.7*	*6.5*	*1.0*	*2.4*	*14.7*	*-5.5*	*22.9*
TOTAL	**55.7**	**60.2**	**51.9**	**43.4**	**53.8**	**57.8**	**50.2**	**28.4**	**79.9**

TOTAL OFFICIAL GROSS / TOTAL OFFICIAL NET / TOTAL OOF GROSS

	TOTAL OFFICIAL GROSS 1983	1984	1985	1986	TOTAL OFFICIAL NET 1983	1984	1985	1986	TOTAL OOF GROSS 1983
DAC COUNTRIES									
Australia	–	0.0	0.0	0.0	–	0.0	0.0	0.0	–
Austria	0.0	–	–	–	0.0	–	–	–	–
Belgium	1.7	1.5	1.5	2.6	1.7	1.5	1.5	2.6	–
Canada	11.4	8.0	6.0	4.7	11.4	8.0	6.0	4.7	–
Denmark	–	–	–	–	–	–	–	–	–
Finland	–	–	–	–	–	–	–	–	–
France	6.2	6.7	20.6	14.4	6.2	6.7	20.6	14.4	–
Germany, Fed. Rep.	12.5	8.4	7.6	22.5	12.3	8.3	7.6	10.5	0.1
Ireland	–	–	–	–	–	–	–	–	–
Italy	0.0	0.4	0.1	1.7	0.0	0.4	0.1	1.7	–
Japan	1.6	1.4	6.3	4.3	1.6	1.4	6.3	4.3	–
Netherlands	1.5	1.6	1.6	1.1	1.5	1.6	1.6	1.1	–
New Zealand	–	–	–	–	–	–	–	–	–
Norway	–	–	–	0.0	–	–	–	0.0	–
Sweden	–	–	–	0.1	–	–	–	0.1	–
Switzerland	2.0	0.9	2.8	2.5	2.0	0.9	2.8	2.5	–
United Kingdom	0.0	0.0	–	0.5	0.0	0.0	–	0.5	–
United States	43.0	44.0	56.0	84.0	41.0	41.0	54.0	84.0	–
TOTAL	*79.9*	*73.0*	*102.7*	*138.5*	*77.8*	*70.0*	*100.6*	*126.4*	*0.1*
MULTILATERAL	*56.5*	*65.2*	*52.0*	*51.8*	*55.6*	*63.9*	*50.3*	*48.7*	*0.7*
OPEC COUNTRIES	–	–	–	–	–	–	–	–	–
E.E.C.+ MEMBERS	*23.9*	*23.8*	*35.6*	*47.1*	*23.8*	*23.7*	*35.5*	*35.1*	*0.1*
TOTAL	**136.4**	**138.3**	**154.7**	**190.2**	**133.3**	**133.8**	**150.9**	**175.2**	**0.8**

ODA COMMITMENTS

1984	1985	1986	1983	1984	1985	1986
0.0	0.0	0.0	–	0.0	0.0	0.0
–	–	–	–	–	–	–
1.5	1.5	2.6	0.9	1.0	0.8	2.6
8.0	6.0	4.7	14.0	4.0	12.9	2.7
–	–	–	–	–	–	–
6.7	20.6	14.4	16.3	26.6	15.6	14.4
8.4	7.6	22.5	8.6	10.5	9.0	24.7
–	–	–	–	–	–	–
0.4	0.1	1.7	0.0	0.4	0.1	1.7
1.4	6.3	4.3	0.0	6.9	4.7	5.2
1.6	1.6	1.1	1.4	1.1	1.9	0.5
–	–	0.0	–	–	0.0	–
–	–	0.1	–	–	–	0.1
0.9	2.8	2.5	3.7	0.1	7.2	1.4
0.0	–	0.5	0.0	0.0	–	0.5
43.0	56.0	84.0	45.9	49.6	58.3	82.5
72.0	*102.7*	*138.5*	*90.9*	*100.3*	*110.6*	*136.4*
–	–	–	–	–	–	–
–	–	–	–	–	–	–
–	–	–	–	–	–	–
5.1	4.1	4.3	2.3	0.6	0.5	7.4
–	–	–	–	–	–	–
29.0	22.0	26.4	27.1	22.1	10.0	–
17.5	12.1	5.5	17.4	–	24.7	56.0
2.3	3.6	2.6	4.9	–	0.1	–
–	–	–	–	–	–	–
–	–	–	10.1	11.0	9.2	11.6
4.8	4.1	5.7	–	–	–	–
0.7	0.8	0.5	–	–	–	–
1.2	1.6	1.7	–	–	–	–
–	–	–	–	–	–	–
2.4	0.9	2.4	–	–	–	–
–	–	–	–	–	–	–
2.0	1.8	1.2	–	–	–	–
0.4	1.0	1.4	2.9	1.2	–	–
65.2	*52.0*	*51.8*	*64.5*	*34.8*	*44.4*	*74.9*
–	–	–	–	–	–	–
23.8	*35.5*	*47.1*	*29.5*	*40.2*	*27.9*	*51.8*
137.3	*154.6*	*190.2*	*155.4*	*135.1*	*155.0*	*211.3*

TECH. COOP. GRANTS

1984	1985	1986	1983	1984	1985	1986
0.0	0.0	0.0	–	0.0	–	0.0
–	–	–	0.0	–	–	–
1.5	1.5	2.6	–	–	–	–
8.0	6.0	4.7	0.6	–	2.1	–
–	–	–	–	–	–	–
4.4	5.9	7.9	3.4	3.2	3.9	5.8
8.2	7.6	22.5	2.3	2.1	2.9	5.6
–	–	–	–	–	–	–
0.4	0.1	1.7	0.0	0.4	0.1	1.0
1.4	6.3	4.3	0.0	0.1	0.1	0.3
1.6	1.6	1.1	0.4	1.2	1.0	0.3
–	–	–	–	–	–	–
–	–	0.0	–	–	–	–
–	–	0.1	–	–	–	–
0.9	2.8	2.5	0.4	0.3	0.4	0.2
0.0	0.0	0.5	0.0	0.0	–	0.0
31.0	55.0	83.0	15.0	17.0	23.0	29.0
57.6	*87.0*	*131.0*	*22.2*	*24.4*	*33.4*	*42.3*
19.5	*15.8*	*15.9*	*8.9*	*8.6*	*8.3*	*9.2*
–	–	–	–	–	–	–
21.4	*20.8*	*40.6*	*6.1*	*7.0*	*7.9*	*12.8*
77.1	*102.8*	*146.8*	*31.0*	*33.0*	*41.7*	*51.5*

TOTAL OOF NET

1984	1985	1986	1983	1984	1985	1986
–	–	–	–	–	–	–
–	–	–	–	–	–	–
–	–	–	–	–	–	–
–	–	–	–	–	–	–
–	–	–	–	–	–	–
–	–	–	–	–	–	–
–	–	–	–	–	–	–
–	0.0	0.0	0.0	0.0	–	0.0
–	–	–	–	–	–	–
–	–	–	–	–	–	–
–	–	–	–	–	–	–
–	–	–	–	–	–	–
–	–	–	–	–	–	–
1.0	–	–	-1.0	-1.0	-2.0	–
1.0	*0.0*	*0.0*	*-1.0*	*-1.0*	*-2.0*	*0.0*
–	–	–	0.7	–	–	-0.1
–	–	–	–	–	–	–
–	0.0	0.0	0.0	0.0	–	0.0
1.0	*0.0*	*0.0*	*-0.3*	*-1.0*	*-2.0*	*-0.1*

ODA COMMITMENTS : LOANS

	1983	1984	1985	1986
DAC COUNTRIES				
Australia	–	–	–	–
Austria	–	–	–	–
Belgium	–	–	–	–
Canada	–	–	–	–
Denmark	–	–	–	–
Finland	–	–	–	–
France	11.0	21.6	9.1	6.5
Germany, Fed. Rep.	–	–	–	–
Ireland	–	–	–	–
Italy	–	–	–	–
Japan	–	–	–	–
Netherlands	–	–	–	–
New Zealand	–	–	–	–
Norway	–	–	–	–
Sweden	–	–	–	–
Switzerland	–	–	–	–
United Kingdom	–	–	–	–
United States	11.9	12.4	–	0.3
TOTAL	*22.9*	*34.0*	*9.1*	*6.8*
MULTILATERAL	*51.2*	*23.3*	*34.7*	*56.0*
OPEC COUNTRIES	–	–	–	–
E.E.C.+ MEMBERS	*11.0*	*21.6*	*9.1*	*6.5*
TOTAL	*74.1*	*57.2*	*43.8*	*62.8*

GRANT ELEMENT OF ODA

	1983	1984	1985	1986
DAC COUNTRIES				
Australia	–	100.0	100.0	100.0
Austria	–	–	–	–
Belgium	100.0	100.0	100.0	100.0
Canada	100.0	100.0	100.0	100.0
Denmark	–	–	–	–
Finland	–	–	–	–
France	100.0	43.3	86.0	65.7
Germany, Fed. Rep.	100.0	100.0	100.0	100.0
Ireland	–	–	–	–
Italy	100.0	100.0	100.0	100.0
Japan	100.0	100.0	100.0	100.0
Netherlands	100.0	100.0	100.0	100.0
New Zealand	–	–	100.0	–
Norway	–	–	–	–
Sweden	–	–	–	100.0
Switzerland	100.0	100.0	100.0	100.0
United Kingdom	100.0	100.0	–	100.0
United States	91.5	91.9	100.0	99.9
TOTAL	*95.1*	*80.9*	*98.6*	*93.9*
MULTILATERAL	*82.4*	*83.0*	*86.9*	*78.3*
OPEC COUNTRIES	–	–	–	–
E.E.C.+ MEMBERS	*100.0*	*62.5*	*93.4*	*85.9*
TOTAL	*88.0*	*81.7*	*95.6*	*88.7*

OTHER AGGREGATES

COMMITMENTS: ALL SOURCES	1983	1984	1985	1986
TOTAL BILATERAL	92.2	100.3	110.9	136.9
of which				
OPEC	–	–	–	–
CMEA	–	–	–	–
TOTAL MULTILATERAL	66.0	34.8	44.4	74.9
TOTAL BIL.& MULTIL.	158.2	135.1	155.4	211.8
of which				
ODA Grants	81.4	77.9	111.2	148.5
ODA Loans	74.1	57.2	43.8	62.8

DISBURSEMENTS:	1983	1984	1985	1986
DAC COUNTRIES COMBINED				
OFFICIAL & PRIVATE				
GROSS:				
Contractual Lending	15.9	15.4	15.8	7.0
Export Credits Total	2.8	0.0	0.0	-0.5
Export Credits Private	2.8	0.0	0.0	-0.5
NET:				
Contractual Lending	11.0	9.1	11.7	-5.2
Export Credits Total	0.1	-5.2	-4.0	-0.6
PRIVATE SECTOR NET	-6.9	1.2	-5.9	-1.7
Direct Investment	-1.8	0.6	0.2	0.1
Portfolio Investment	-5.3	3.9	-4.1	-1.2
Export Credits	0.1	-3.2	-2.0	-0.6

MARKET BORROWING:	1983	1984	1985	1986
CHANGE IN CLAIMS				
Banks	–	-10.0	-1.0	2.0

MEMORANDUM ITEM:	1983	1984	1985	1986
CMEA Countr.(Gross)	–	–	–	–

TOTAL RECEIPTS NET / TOTAL ODA NET / TOTAL ODA GROSS

	TOTAL RECEIPTS NET				TOTAL ODA NET				TOTAL ODA GROSS
	1983	1984	1985	1986	1983	1984	1985	1986	1983
DAC COUNTRIES									
Australia	–	–	0.0	0.1	–	–	0.0	0.1	–
Austria	0.0	0.0	0.0	0.1	0.0	0.0	0.0	0.1	0.0
Belgium	-1.5	-3.2	-1.9	3.2	0.0	0.2	0.2	0.1	0.0
Canada	2.0	6.9	3.9	0.5	5.2	10.2	9.6	1.0	5.2
Denmark	-0.7	-0.4	–	–	–	–	–	–	–
Finland	0.2	0.0	0.0	0.1	0.2	0.0	0.0	0.1	0.2
France	15.4	3.5	10.9	7.3	3.7	1.0	2.4	2.9	3.7
Germany, Fed. Rep.	4.6	5.5	12.0	12.4	4.0	8.7	5.9	12.4	4.0
Ireland	–	–	–	–	–	–	–	–	–
Italy	-1.4	0.3	19.0	-7.6	1.7	0.2	0.7	2.4	1.7
Japan	9.6	0.9	10.7	28.4	17.1	13.7	18.9	36.2	17.3
Netherlands	0.9	7.5	4.7	3.4	3.0	5.6	3.6	1.9	3.0
New Zealand	–	–	–	–	–	–	–	–	–
Norway	0.3	0.4	0.2	0.1	0.3	0.4	0.2	0.1	0.3
Sweden	–	–	–	–	–	–	–	–	–
Switzerland	3.7	4.8	13.0	6.6	5.2	6.9	4.4	6.6	5.2
United Kingdom	10.0	4.5	4.7	0.7	2.6	1.1	0.9	1.1	2.6
United States	64.0	119.0	160.0	175.0	64.0	123.0	161.0	175.0	66.0
TOTAL	*107.0*	*149.6*	*237.5*	*230.1*	*107.0*	*170.9*	*207.7*	*239.8*	*109.2*
MULTILATERAL									
AF.D.F.	–	–	–	–	–	–	–	–	–
AF.D.B.	–	–	–	–	–	–	–	–	–
AS.D.B	–	–	–	–	–	–	–	–	–
CAR.D.B.	–	–	–	–	–	–	–	–	–
E.E.C.	6.4	10.9	2.9	3.9	6.4	10.9	2.9	3.9	6.4
IBRD	50.4	48.4	32.2	11.8	0.8	0.7	–	–	0.8
IDA	1.5	0.6	0.1	-0.7	1.5	0.6	0.1	-0.7	1.9
I.D.B.	46.2	135.0	73.6	24.3	43.4	70.4	31.8	11.9	47.2
IFAD	2.5	2.5	2.1	1.8	2.5	2.5	2.1	1.8	2.5
I.F.C.	-0.2	–	–	–	–	–	–	–	–
IMF TRUST FUND	–	–	–	–	–	–	–	–	–
U.N. AGENCIES	–	–	–	–	–	–	–	–	–
UNDP	5.9	4.0	4.1	4.0	5.9	4.0	4.1	4.0	5.9
UNTA	0.5	0.4	0.6	0.5	0.5	0.4	0.6	0.5	0.5
UNICEF	0.4	0.3	0.6	0.3	0.4	0.3	0.6	0.3	0.4
UNRWA	–	–	–	–	–	–	–	–	–
WFP	5.0	6.5	5.8	6.1	5.0	6.5	5.8	6.1	5.0
UNHCR	11.7	12.0	11.0	13.8	11.7	12.0	11.0	13.8	11.7
Other Multilateral	0.9	0.9	1.5	1.3	0.9	0.9	1.5	1.3	0.9
Arab OPEC Agencies	4.3	5.7	4.4	0.6	4.3	5.7	4.4	0.6	4.5
TOTAL	*135.4*	*227.1*	*138.9*	*67.9*	*83.2*	*114.8*	*64.9*	*43.7*	*87.6*
OPEC COUNTRIES	*17.2*	*14.8*	*9.8*	*1.7*	*1.4*	*3.9*	*3.7*	*5.0*	*1.4*
E.E.C.+ MEMBERS	*33.7*	*28.5*	*52.4*	*23.2*	*21.5*	*27.6*	*16.5*	*24.7*	*21.5*
TOTAL	**259.5**	**391.5**	**386.1**	**299.7**	**191.6**	**289.6**	**276.2**	**288.5**	*198.2*

ODA LOANS GROSS / ODA LOANS NET / GRANTS

	ODA LOANS GROSS				ODA LOANS NET				GRANTS
	1983	1984	1985	1986	1983	1984	1985	1986	1983
DAC COUNTRIES									
Australia	–	–	–	–	–	–	–	–	–
Austria	–	–	–	–	–	–	–	–	0.0
Belgium	–	–	–	–	–	–	–	–	0.0
Canada	0.3	6.4	7.1	0.1	0.3	6.4	7.1	0.1	4.9
Denmark	–	–	–	–	–	–	–	–	–
Finland	–	–	–	–	–	–	–	–	0.2
France	3.4	0.6	1.9	2.3	3.4	0.6	1.9	2.3	0.3
Germany, Fed. Rep.	–	4.2	0.6	5.6	–	4.2	0.6	5.6	4.0
Ireland	–	–	–	–	–	–	–	–	–
Italy	–	–	–	–	–	–	–	–	1.7
Japan	6.3	10.4	6.9	24.3	6.1	6.3	6.9	24.3	11.0
Netherlands	–	4.0	2.0	0.0	–	4.0	2.0	0.0	3.0
New Zealand	–	–	–	–	–	–	–	–	–
Norway	–	–	–	–	–	–	–	–	0.3
Sweden	–	–	–	–	–	–	–	–	–
Switzerland	0.3	3.4	1.2	1.3	0.3	3.4	1.2	1.3	4.9
United Kingdom	2.1	0.7	0.2	0.4	2.1	0.7	0.2	0.4	0.5
United States	29.0	43.0	45.0	34.0	27.0	41.0	45.0	30.0	37.0
TOTAL	*41.4*	*72.5*	*64.9*	*68.0*	*39.2*	*66.5*	*64.9*	*64.0*	*67.8*
MULTILATERAL	*56.3*	*81.0*	*42.0*	*19.1*	*51.9*	*77.4*	*37.1*	*13.6*	*31.3*
OPEC COUNTRIES	*1.4*	*3.9*	*3.7*	*5.0*	*1.4*	*3.9*	*3.7*	*5.0*	
E.E.C.+ MEMBERS	*5.5*	*9.4*	*4.7*	*8.4*	*5.5*	*9.4*	*4.7*	*8.4*	*16.0*
TOTAL	**99.1**	**157.4**	**110.5**	**92.1**	**92.5**	**147.7**	**105.6**	**82.6**	*99.1*

TOTAL OFFICIAL GROSS / TOTAL OFFICIAL NET / TOTAL OOF GROSS

	TOTAL OFFICIAL GROSS				TOTAL OFFICIAL NET				TOTAL OOF GROSS
	1983	1984	1985	1986	1983	1984	1985	1986	1983
DAC COUNTRIES									
Australia	–	–	0.0	0.1	–	–	0.0	0.1	–
Austria	0.0	0.0	0.0	0.1	0.0	0.0	0.0	0.1	–
Belgium	0.0	0.2	0.2	0.1	0.0	0.2	0.2	0.1	–
Canada	5.2	10.2	9.6	1.0	2.0	6.9	3.9	0.5	–
Denmark	–	–	–	–	–	–	–	–	–
Finland	0.2	0.0	0.0	0.1	0.2	0.0	0.0	0.1	–
France	3.7	1.0	2.3	2.9	3.7	1.0	2.4	2.9	–
Germany, Fed. Rep.	4.0	8.7	5.9	12.4	4.0	8.7	5.9	12.4	–
Ireland	–	–	–	–	–	–	–	–	–
Italy	1.7	0.2	0.7	2.4	1.7	0.2	0.7	2.4	–
Japan	19.2	21.1	18.9	36.2	19.0	17.0	18.9	36.2	1.9
Netherlands	4.1	7.8	3.6	1.9	4.1	7.5	3.2	1.8	1.1
New Zealand	–	–	–	–	–	–	–	–	–
Norway	0.3	0.4	0.2	0.1	0.3	0.4	0.2	0.1	–
Sweden	–	–	–	–	–	–	–	–	–
Switzerland	5.2	6.9	4.4	6.6	5.2	6.9	4.4	6.6	–
United Kingdom	10.1	4.6	4.7	1.8	10.1	4.6	4.7	0.7	7.6
United States	67.0	125.0	161.0	179.0	64.0	119.0	160.0	175.0	1.0
TOTAL	*120.7*	*186.0*	*211.6*	*244.6*	*114.4*	*172.3*	*204.4*	*238.8*	*11.5*
MULTILATERAL	*147.9*	*242.2*	*160.3*	*98.3*	*135.4*	*227.1*	*138.9*	*67.9*	*60.3*
OPEC COUNTRIES	*19.5*	*17.9*	*15.9*	*9.3*	*17.2*	*14.8*	*9.8*	*1.7*	*18.1*
E.E.C.+ MEMBERS	*30.2*	*33.3*	*20.3*	*25.4*	*30.2*	*33.0*	*19.9*	*24.2*	*8.7*
TOTAL	**288.2**	**446.1**	**387.8**	**352.1**	**266.9**	**414.1**	**353.1**	**308.4**	*90.0*

Left section

1984	1985	1986	1983	1984	1985	1986

ODA COMMITMENTS

1984	1985	1986	1983	1984	1985	1986
—	0.0	0.1	—	—	0.0	—
0.0	0.0	0.1	0.0	—	0.0	—
0.2	0.2	0.1	—	—	—	0.1
10.2	9.6	1.0	29.1	2.4	1.6	9.4
—	—	—	—	—	—	—
0.0	0.0	0.1	0.1	—	0.0	—
1.0	2.3	2.9	4.4	5.0	0.6	2.9
8.7	5.9	12.4	9.1	4.2	23.1	9.0
—	—	—	—	—	—	—
0.2	0.7	2.4	0.0	0.2	0.7	3.0
17.8	18.9	36.2	48.9	8.8	52.8	16.1
5.6	3.6	1.9	1.7	5.8	3.4	1.7
—	—	—	—	—	—	—
0.4	0.2	0.1	0.3	0.5	—	0.0
—	—	—	—	—	0.0	—
6.9	4.4	6.6	4.9	2.6	8.9	9.5
1.1	0.9	1.1	0.5	0.5	0.7	0.7
125.0	161.0	179.0	103.7	90.2	220.8	133.4
177.0	*207.7*	*243.8*	*202.6*	*120.1*	*312.7*	*185.9*
—	—	—	—	—	—	—
—	—	—	—	—	—	—
—	—	—	—	—	—	—
10.9	2.9	3.9	5.6	7.9	1.9	4.1
0.7	—	—	—	—	—	—
1.1	0.7	—	—	—	—	—
73.4	36.0	16.8	9.2	25.0	39.6	96.0
2.5	2.1	1.8	—	—	—	—
—	—	—	—	—	—	—
—	—	—	24.3	24.1	23.7	26.0
4.0	4.1	4.0	—	—	—	—
0.4	0.6	0.5	—	—	—	—
0.3	0.6	0.3	—	—	—	—
—	—	—	—	—	—	—
6.5	5.8	6.1	—	—	—	—
12.0	11.0	13.8	—	—	—	—
0.9	1.5	1.3	—	—	—	—
5.7	4.4	0.6	14.3	—	—	—
118.4	*69.8*	*49.2*	*53.4*	*57.0*	*65.2*	*126.1*
3.9	3.7	5.0	15.6	—	6.1	—
27.6	16.5	24.7	21.2	23.5	30.5	21.6
299.3	*281.1*	*298.0*	*271.6*	*177.1*	*384.0*	*312.0*

TECH. COOP. GRANTS

1984	1985	1986	1983	1984	1985	1986
—	0.0	0.1	—	—	0.0	0.0
0.0	0.0	0.1	0.0	—	—	—
0.2	0.2	0.1	—	—	0.0	0.0
3.8	2.5	0.8	0.5	—	0.6	—
—	—	—	—	—	—	—
0.0	0.0	0.1	0.2	0.0	—	0.0
0.4	0.5	0.5	0.3	0.4	0.3	0.3
4.5	5.3	6.8	1.9	2.7	3.0	2.7
—	—	—	—	—	—	—
0.2	0.7	2.4	0.0	0.2	0.5	2.4
7.4	12.0	11.9	2.3	3.8	4.1	4.5
1.7	1.6	1.9	1.0	1.1	0.9	1.7
—	—	—	—	—	—	—
0.4	0.2	0.1	—	0.0	—	—
—	—	—	—	—	—	—
3.6	3.2	5.3	0.9	1.2	1.1	1.4
0.5	0.7	0.7	0.5	0.5	0.7	0.7
82.0	116.0	145.0	10.0	17.0	15.0	26.0
104.5	*142.9*	*175.8*	*17.7*	*26.8*	*26.3*	*39.7*
37.4	*27.7*	*30.1*	*19.3*	*17.6*	*17.9*	*20.1*
—	—	—	—	—	—	—
18.2	*11.8*	*16.3*	*3.7*	*4.8*	*5.4*	*8.0*
141.9	*170.6*	*205.9*	*37.0*	*44.3*	*44.2*	*59.8*

TOTAL OOF NET

1984	1985	1986	1983	1984	1985	1986
—	—	—	—	—	—	—
—	—	—	—	—	—	—
—	—	—	-3.1	-3.3	-5.7	-0.5
—	—	—	—	—	—	—
—	—	—	—	—	—	—
—	—	—	—	—	—	—
—	—	—	—	—	—	—
—	—	—	—	—	—	—
3.3	—	—	1.9	3.3	—	—
2.2	—	—	1.1	1.9	-0.4	-0.1
—	—	—	—	—	—	—
—	—	—	—	—	—	—
3.5	3.9	0.7	7.6	3.5	3.9	-0.4
—	—	—	—	-4.0	-1.0	—
9.0	*3.9*	*0.7*	*7.4*	*1.3*	*-3.3*	*-1.0*
123.8	*90.5*	*49.2*	*52.2*	*112.3*	*74.0*	*24.2*
14.0	*12.2*	*4.3*	*15.7*	*10.9*	*6.1*	*-3.3*
5.7	*3.9*	*0.7*	*8.7*	*5.3*	*3.5*	*-0.5*
146.8	*106.6*	*54.2*	*75.4*	*124.5*	*76.8*	*20.0*

Right section

	1983	1984	1985	1986

ODA COMMITMENTS : LOANS

DAC COUNTRIES	1983	1984	1985	1986
Australia	—	—	—	—
Austria	—	—	—	—
Belgium	—	—	—	—
Canada	26.2	—	—	—
Denmark	—	—	—	—
Finland	—	—	—	—
France	4.1	4.7	—	2.3
Germany, Fed. Rep.	2.1	—	16.3	3.7
Ireland	—	—	—	—
Italy	—	—	—	—
Japan	41.0	—	40.3	—
Netherlands	—	4.3	1.7	—
New Zealand	—	—	—	—
Norway	—	—	—	—
Sweden	—	—	—	—
Switzerland	—	—	—	—
United Kingdom	—	—	—	—
United States	43.0	35.3	29.0	30.4
TOTAL	*116.3*	*44.2*	*87.4*	*36.4*
MULTILATERAL	*23.5*	*25.0*	*39.6*	*96.0*
OPEC COUNTRIES	*15.6*	—	*6.1*	—
E.E.C.+ MEMBERS	*6.2*	*8.9*	*18.0*	*6.0*
TOTAL	*155.3*	*69.2*	*133.1*	*132.4*

GRANT ELEMENT OF ODA

DAC COUNTRIES	1983	1984	1985	1986
Australia	—	—	100.0	—
Austria	100.0	—	100.0	—
Belgium	—	—	—	100.0
Canada	90.6	100.0	100.0	100.0
Denmark	—	—	—	—
Finland	100.0	—	100.0	—
France	100.0	71.1	100.0	71.5
Germany, Fed. Rep.	96.1	100.0	84.7	93.2
Ireland	—	—	—	—
Italy	100.0	100.0	100.0	100.0
Japan	58.4	100.0	60.8	100.0
Netherlands	100.0	67.1	80.1	100.0
New Zealand	—	—	—	—
Norway	100.0	100.0	—	100.0
Sweden	—	—	100.0	—
Switzerland	100.0	100.0	100.0	100.0
United Kingdom	100.0	100.0	100.0	100.0
United States	87.8	88.3	96.0	93.1
TOTAL	*81.8*	*88.4*	*89.2*	*94.0*
MULTILATERAL	*79.4*	*99.3*	*89.8*	*77.9*
OPEC COUNTRIES	*50.2*	—	*42.9*	—
E.E.C.+ MEMBERS	*97.9*	*85.8*	*86.2*	*91.5*
TOTAL	*79.5*	*90.7*	*88.6*	*87.5*

OTHER AGGREGATES

COMMITMENTS: ALL SOURCES

	1983	1984	1985	1986
TOTAL BILATERAL	232.5	138.0	337.0	186.3
of which				
OPEC	29.2	12.2	10.5	—
CMEA	—	—	—	—
TOTAL MULTILATERAL	218.4	91.7	101.0	190.5
TOTAL BIL.& MULTIL.	450.9	229.7	438.0	376.8
of which				
ODA Grants	116.3	107.8	250.9	179.6
ODA Loans	155.3	69.2	133.1	132.4

DISBURSEMENTS:

DAC COUNTRIES COMBINED

OFFICIAL & PRIVATE	1983	1984	1985	1986
GROSS:				
Contractual Lending	74.7	93.5	111.0	88.4
Export Credits Total	23.6	15.3	42.3	19.7
Export Credits Private	21.7	12.0	42.3	19.7
NET:				
Contractual Lending	47.3	57.3	88.6	51.0
Export Credits Total	-1.6	-14.5	20.2	-12.5
PRIVATE SECTOR NET	-7.4	-22.6	33.0	-8.8
Direct Investment	-8.1	-4.2	-1.2	0.2
Portfolio Investment	0.1	-7.9	7.2	3.1
Export Credits	0.7	-10.5	27.0	-12.0

MARKET BORROWING:

CHANGE IN CLAIMS

	1983	1984	1985	1986
Banks	—	3.0	-34.0	-24.0

MEMORANDUM ITEM:

	1983	1984	1985	1986
CMEA Countr.(Gross)	—	—	—	—

	1983	1984	1985	1986	1983	1984	1985	1986	1983
	TOTAL RECEIPTS NET				**TOTAL ODA NET**				**TOTAL ODA GROSS**
DAC COUNTRIES									
Australia	56.8	43.8	12.3	77.8	0.1	5.2	11.3	7.3	0.1
Austria	0.0	0.1	0.7	0.0	0.0	–	0.4	0.0	0.0
Belgium	20.6	75.0	171.5	-44.5	0.0	0.0	0.0	0.0	0.0
Canada	0.0	0.0	0.1	1.0	0.0	0.1	0.1	0.0	0.0
Denmark	1.2	-0.4	-0.5	-0.5	–	–	–	–	–
Finland	–	–	–	0.0	–	–	–	0.0	
France	129.9	58.6	75.6	196.6	1.3	1.4	1.4	2.0	1.3
Germany, Fed. Rep.	77.3	1.7	106.2	422.7	1.8	1.6	1.8	2.6	1.8
Ireland	–	–	–	–	–	–	–	–	–
Italy	0.7	4.5	15.1	3.5	0.0	0.0	0.0	0.1	0.0
Japan	307.1	403.3	29.1	778.7	1.4	1.2	1.3	1.6	1.5
Netherlands	45.0	-32.3	0.0	66.2	0.1	0.0	0.0	0.1	0.1
New Zealand	–	–	–	–	–	–	–	–	–
Norway	1.9	19.6	7.7	25.2	–	–	0.0	0.1	–
Sweden	-3.7	-6.4	-6.0	-3.1	–	–	–	–	–
Switzerland	-2.6	-2.7	-1.8	–	0.0	–	–	–	0.0
United Kingdom	203.3	159.9	114.9	-98.1	-0.1	-0.3	0.4	0.3	0.3
United States	257.0	548.0	-1722.0	-3026.0	–	–	–	–	–
TOTAL	*1094.6*	*1272.7*	*-1196.9*	*-1600.4*	*4.7*	*9.3*	*16.7*	*14.1*	*5.2*
MULTILATERAL									
AF.D.F.	–	–	–	–	–	–	–	–	–
AF.D.B.	–	–	–	–	–	–	–	–	–
AS.D.B	2.1	-3.1	-5.7	-6.5	–	–	–	–	–
CAR.D.B.	–	–	–	–	–	–	–	–	–
E.E.C.	–	–	–	–	–	–	–	–	–
IBRD	–	–	–	–	–	–	–	–	–
IDA	–	–	–	–	–	–	–	–	–
I.D.B.	–	–	–	–	–	–	–	–	–
IFAD	–	–	–	–	–	–	–	–	–
I.F.C.	–	–	–	–	–	–	–	–	–
IMF TRUST FUND	–	–	–	–	–	–	–	–	–
U.N. AGENCIES									
UNDP	0.1	0.1	0.1	0.1	0.1	0.1	0.1	0.1	0.1
UNTA	0.1	0.1	0.0	0.1	0.1	0.1	0.0	0.1	0.1
UNICEF	–	–	–	–	–	–	–	–	–
UNRWA	–	–	–	–	–	–	–	–	–
WFP	–	–	–	–	–	–	–	–	–
UNHCR	4.0	4.3	3.7	4.2	4.0	4.3	3.7	4.2	4.0
Other Multilateral	0.0	0.1	0.0	0.1	0.0	0.1	0.0	0.1	0.0
Arab OPEC Agencies	–	–	–	–	–	–	–	–	–
TOTAL	*6.2*	*1.4*	*-1.9*	*-2.0*	*4.1*	*4.5*	*3.8*	*4.4*	*4.1*
OPEC COUNTRIES	–	–	–	–	–	–	–	–	–
E.E.C.+ MEMBERS	*478.0*	*267.0*	*482.9*	*545.9*	*3.1*	*2.8*	*3.6*	*5.1*	*3.5*
TOTAL	*1100.8*	*1274.0*	*-1198.9*	*-1602.5*	*8.8*	*13.8*	*20.5*	*18.5*	*9.4*

	1983	1984	1985	1986	1983	1984	1985	1986	1983
	ODA LOANS GROSS				**ODA LOANS NET**				**GRANTS**
DAC COUNTRIES									
Australia	–	–	–	–	–	–	–	–	0.1
Austria	–	–	0.4	–	–	–	0.4	–	0.0
Belgium	–	–	–	–	–	–	–	–	0.0
Canada	–	–	–	–	–	–	–	–	0.0
Denmark	–	–	–	–	–	–	–	–	–
Finland	–	–	–	–	–	–	–	–	–
France	–	–	–	–	–	–	–	–	1.3
Germany, Fed. Rep.	–	–	–	–	–	–	–	–	1.8
Ireland	–	–	–	–	–	–	–	–	–
Italy	–	–	–	–	–	–	–	–	0.0
Japan	–	0.1	–	–	-0.2	-0.1	-0.3	-0.4	1.5
Netherlands	–	–	–	–	–	–	–	–	0.1
New Zealand	–	–	–	–	–	–	–	–	–
Norway	–	–	–	–	–	–	–	–	–
Sweden	–	–	–	–	–	–	–	–	–
Switzerland	–	–	–	–	–	–	–	–	0.0
United Kingdom	–	–	–	–	-0.4	-0.4	–	–	0.3
United States	–	–	–	–	–	–	–	–	–
TOTAL	*–*	*0.1*	*0.4*	*–*	*-0.6*	*-0.5*	*0.1*	*-0.4*	*5.2*
MULTILATERAL	*–*	*–*	*–*	*–*	*–*	*–*	*–*	*–*	*4.1*
OPEC COUNTRIES	–	–	–	–	–	–	–	–	
E.E.C.+ MEMBERS	*–*	*–*	*–*	*–*	*-0.4*	*-0.4*	*–*	*–*	*3.5*
TOTAL	*–*	*0.1*	*0.4*	*–*	*-0.6*	*-0.5*	*0.1*	*-0.4*	*9.4*

	1983	1984	1985	1986	1983	1984	1985	1986	1983
	TOTAL OFFICIAL GROSS				**TOTAL OFFICIAL NET**				**TOTAL OOF GROSS**
DAC COUNTRIES									
Australia	0.1	5.2	11.3	7.3	-0.1	5.0	11.2	7.1	–
Austria	0.0	–	0.4	0.0	0.0	–	0.4	0.0	–
Belgium	0.0	1.3	0.9	0.0	0.0	1.3	0.9	0.0	–
Canada	0.0	0.1	0.1	0.0	0.0	0.0	0.1	0.0	–
Denmark	1.4	0.0	–	0.0	1.4	-0.3	-0.3	-0.3	1.4
Finland	–	–	–	0.0	–	–	–	0.0	–
France	1.3	1.4	1.4	2.0	1.3	1.4	1.4	2.0	–
Germany, Fed. Rep.	1.8	1.6	1.8	2.6	1.8	1.6	1.8	2.6	–
Ireland	–	–	–	–	–	–	–	–	–
Italy	0.3	0.0	0.0	0.1	0.2	-0.1	0.0	0.1	0.3
Japan	1.5	1.3	1.6	1.9	1.4	1.2	1.3	1.6	–
Netherlands	0.1	0.0	0.0	0.1	0.1	0.0	0.0	0.1	–
New Zealand	–	–	–	–	–	–	–	–	–
Norway	–	–	0.0	0.1	–	–	0.0	0.1	–
Sweden	1.8	–	–	–	1.3	-1.9	-2.0	-1.4	1.8
Switzerland	0.0	–	–	–	0.0	–	–	–	–
United Kingdom	0.3	0.2	0.4	0.3	-0.1	-0.3	0.4	0.3	–
United States	5.0	–	–	–	-10.0	-14.0	-14.0	-11.0	5.0
TOTAL	*13.7*	*11.2*	*17.9*	*14.4*	*-2.8*	*-6.1*	*1.2*	*1.2*	*8.5*
MULTILATERAL	*12.0*	*7.6*	*4.9*	*4.8*	*6.2*	*1.4*	*-1.9*	*-2.0*	*7.8*
OPEC COUNTRIES	–	–	–	–	–	–	–	–	–
E.E.C.+ MEMBERS	*5.2*	*4.5*	*4.5*	*5.1*	*4.7*	*3.8*	*4.2*	*4.7*	*1.7*
TOTAL	*25.7*	*18.8*	*22.8*	*19.2*	*3.4*	*-4.7*	*-0.7*	*-0.8*	*16.3*

ODA COMMITMENTS

1984	1985	1986	1983	1984	1985	1986
5.2	11.3	7.3	0.0	10.4	8.8	6.3
–	0.4	0.0	0.0	0.3	0.2	–
0.0	0.0	0.0	–	–	–	0.0
0.1	0.1	0.0	0.0	0.1	0.1	0.0
–	–	–	–	–	–	⊥
–	–	0.0	–	–	–	–
1.4	1.4	2.0	1.3	1.4	1.4	2.0
1.6	1.8	2.6	1.5	1.8	1.4	2.5
–	–	–	–	–	–	–
0.0	0.0	0.1	0.0	0.0	0.0	0.1
1.3	1.6	1.9	1.7	1.4	1.7	2.1
0.0	0.0	0.1	0.1	0.0	0.0	0.1
–	0.0	0.1	–	–	–	–
–	–	–	0.0	–	–	–
–	–	–	–	–	–	–
0.2	0.4	0.3	0.3	0.2	0.4	0.3
–	–	–	0.2	0.1	0.1	0.1
9.9	17.0	14.4	5.2	15.7	14.1	13.5
–	–	–	–	–	–	–
–	–	–	–	–	–	–
–	–	–	–	–	–	–
–	–	–	–	–	–	–
–	–	–	–	–	–	–
–	–	–	–	–	–	–
–	–	–	–	–	–	–
–	–	–	–	–	–	–
–	–	–	4.1	4.5	3.8	4.4
0.1	0.1	0.1	–	–	–	–
0.1	0.0	0.1	–	–	–	–
–	–	–	–	–	–	–
4.3	3.7	4.2	–	–	–	–
0.1	0.0	0.1	–	–	–	–
–	–	–	–	–	–	–
4.5	3.8	4.4	4.1	4.5	3.8	4.4
–	–	–	–	–	–	–
3.2	3.6	5.1	3.3	3.4	3.2	5.0
14.4	20.8	18.9	9.3	20.1	17.8	18.0

TECH. COOP. GRANTS

1984	1985	1986	1983	1984	1985	1986
5.2	11.3	7.3	0.1	5.2	11.3	7.3
–	0.0	0.0	0.0	–	–	–
0.0	0.0	0.0	–	–	–	–
0.1	0.1	0.0	0.1	–	0.2	–
–	–	0.0	–	–	–	0.0
1.4	1.4	2.0	1.3	1.4	1.4	2.0
1.6	1.8	2.6	1.8	1.6	1.8	2.4
0.0	0.0	0.1	0.0	0.0	0.0	0.1
1.3	1.6	1.9	1.5	1.3	1.6	1.9
0.0	0.0	0.1	0.1	0.0	0.0	0.1
–	0.0	0.1	–	–	–	–
–	–	–	–	–	–	–
0.2	0.4	0.3	0.3	0.2	0.4	0.3
–	–	–	–	–	–	–
9.8	16.6	14.4	5.2	9.7	16.6	14.0
4.5	3.8	4.4	4.1	4.5	3.8	4.4
–	–	–	–	–	–	–
3.2	3.6	5.1	3.5	3.2	3.6	4.8
14.3	20.4	18.9	9.3	14.2	20.4	18.4

TOTAL OOF NET

1984	1985	1986	1983	1984	1985	1986
			-0.2	-0.2	-0.1	-0.1
			–	–	–	–
1.3	0.9	0.0	–	1.3	0.9	0.0
–	–	–	-0.1	-0.1	–	–
0.0	–	–	1.4	-0.3	-0.3	-0.3
–	–	–	–	–	–	–
–	–	–	–	–	–	–
–	–	–	0.1	-0.1	–	–
–	–	–	–	–	–	–
–	–	–	–	–	–	–
–	–	–	–	–	–	–
–	–	–	1.3	-1.9	-2.0	-1.4
–	–	–	–	–	–	–
–	–	–	-10.0	-14.0	-14.0	-11.0
1.3	0.9	0.0	-7.5	-15.3	-15.5	-12.9
3.1	1.1	0.4	2.1	-3.1	-5.7	-6.5
–	–	–	–	–	–	–
1.3	0.9	0.0	1.5	1.0	0.6	-0.3
4.4	2.0	0.4	-5.4	-18.5	-21.2	-19.3

ODA COMMITMENTS : LOANS

DAC COUNTRIES

	1983	1984	1985	1986
Australia	–	–	–	–
Austria	–	0.3	0.1	–
Belgium	–	–	–	–
Canada	–	–	–	–
Denmark	–	–	–	–
Finland	–	–	–	–
France	–	–	–	–
Germany, Fed. Rep.	–	–	–	–
Ireland	–	–	–	–
Italy	–	–	–	–
Japan	–	0.1	–	–
Netherlands	–	–	–	–
New Zealand	–	–	–	–
Norway	–	–	–	–
Sweden	–	–	–	–
Switzerland	–	–	–	–
United Kingdom	–	–	–	–
United States	–	–	–	–
TOTAL	–	0.4	0.1	–
MULTILATERAL	–	–	.	–
OPEC COUNTRIES	–	–	–	–
E.E.C.+ MEMBERS	–	–	–	–
TOTAL	–	0.4	0.1	–

GRANT ELEMENT OF ODA

DAC COUNTRIES

	1983	1984	1985	1986
Australia	100.0	100.0	100.0	100.0
Austria	100.0	38.6	100.0	–
Belgium	–	–	–	100.0
Canada	100.0	100.0	100.0	100.0
Denmark	–	–	–	–
Finland	–	–	–	–
France	100.0	100.0	100.0	100.0
Germany, Fed. Rep.	100.0	100.0	100.0	100.0
Ireland	–	–	–	–
Italy	100.0	100.0	100.0	100.0
Japan	100.0	97.5	100.0	100.0
Netherlands	100.0	100.0	100.0	100.0
New Zealand	–	–	–	–
Norway	–	–	–	–
Sweden	–	–	–	–
Switzerland	100.0	–	–	–
United Kingdom	100.0	100.0	100.0	100.0
United States	100.0	100.0	100.0	100.0
TOTAL	100.0	98.7	100.0	100.0
MULTILATERAL	100.0	100.0	100.0	100.0
OPEC COUNTRIES	–	–	–	–
E.E.C.+ MEMBERS	100.0	100.0	100.0	100.0
TOTAL	100.0	99.0	100.0	100.0

OTHER AGGREGATES

COMMITMENTS: ALL SOURCES

	1983	1984	1985	1986
TOTAL BILATERAL	7.0	15.7	14.1	12.1
of which				
OPEC	–	–	–	–
CMEA	–	–	–	–
TOTAL MULTILATERAL	4.1	4.5	3.8	4.4
TOTAL BIL.& MULTIL.	11.2	20.1	17.8	16.6
of which				
ODA Grants	9.3	19.8	17.7	18.0
ODA Loans	–	0.4	0.1	–

DISBURSEMENTS:

DAC COUNTRIES COMBINED

	1983	1984	1985	1986
OFFICIAL & PRIVATE				
GROSS:				
Contractual Lending	719.3	586.8	331.4	394.3
Export Credits Total	719.3	586.7	331.0	394.3
Export Credits Private	710.8	586.7	331.0	394.3
NET:				
Contractual Lending	275.8	277.2	4.5	-21.0
Export Credits Total	276.4	277.7	4.4	-20.6
PRIVATE SECTOR NET	1097.4	1278.7	-1198.1	-1601.6
Direct Investment	603.0	698.4	-134.5	778.7
Portfolio Investment	210.6	286.0	-1084.4	-2372.5
Export Credits	283.9	294.4	20.8	-7.8

MARKET BORROWING:

CHANGE IN CLAIMS

	1983	1984	1985	1986
Banks	–	–	–	–

MEMORANDUM ITEM:

	1983	1984	1985	1986
CMEA Countr.(Gross)	–	–	–	–

	TOTAL RECEIPTS NET				TOTAL ODA NET				TOTAL ODA GROSS
	1983	1984	1985	1986	1983	1984	1985	1986	1983
DAC COUNTRIES									
Australia	2.0	3.3	2.8	2.0	1.8	2.2	2.6	1.8	1.8
Austria	5.2	-3.8	-4.1	1.0	5.3	-1.0	-0.8	5.1	7.2
Belgium	7.4	85.2	63.3	39.8	6.2	5.4	-0.8	-1.7	7.6
Canada	35.1	66.9	52.9	73.7	40.6	64.9	42.3	46.5	48.7
Denmark	42.9	30.1	23.9	38.1	44.1	31.0	24.2	38.7	45.1
Finland	4.7	0.7	7.7	0.7	0.2	0.6	0.4	0.7	0.2
France	137.5	154.6	457.4	847.8	20.9	43.6	65.2	72.3	27.0
Germany, Fed. Rep.	127.9	121.9	159.9	268.7	140.1	95.2	86.5	166.5	186.3
Ireland	0.1	0.1	0.1	0.1	0.1	0.1	0.1	0.1	0.1
Italy	-1.5	48.3	35.1	21.8	-2.0	10.3	13.3	30.3	0.2
Japan	199.2	123.9	67.6	457.3	129.5	21.6	21.9	226.7	178.9
Netherlands	81.9	64.2	66.7	104.3	70.3	60.8	60.1	101.1	80.3
New Zealand	0.0	0.0	0.0	0.1	0.0	0.0	0.0	0.1	0.0
Norway	48.1	37.6	51.6	54.6	20.4	19.4	23.4	24.8	20.4
Sweden	51.1	53.3	75.1	225.4	47.8	50.3	41.1	80.8	47.8
Switzerland	29.9	28.3	14.7	10.2	21.8	20.5	14.1	10.2	21.8
United Kingdom	7.5	75.2	58.4	296.8	144.8	144.1	93.3	162.1	193.6
United States	111.0	40.0	130.0	-110.0	58.0	65.0	29.0	49.0	159.0
TOTAL	889.7	929.7	1263.2	2332.0	749.9	633.8	515.9	1014.9	1025.8
MULTILATERAL									
AF.D.F.	–	–	–	–	–	–	–	–	–
AF.D.B.	–	–	–	–	–	–	–	–	–
AS.D.B	–	–	–	–	–	–	–	–	–
CAR.D.B.	–	–	–	–	–	–	–	–	–
E.E.C.	80.2	91.6	72.1	58.7	80.2	91.6	72.1	58.7	80.2
IBRD	308.3	264.4	169.8	397.5	14.7	21.2	14.0	0.2	14.7
IDA	899.4	782.1	819.9	888.2	899.4	782.1	819.9	888.2	931.0
I.D.B.	–	–	–	–	–	–	–	–	–
IFAD	14.8	13.0	34.9	26.3	14.8	13.0	34.9	26.3	14.8
I.F.C.	13.4	3.1	29.9	-11.4	–	–	–	–	–
IMF TRUST FUND	–	–	–	–	–	–	–	–	–
U.N. AGENCIES	–	–	–	–	–	–	–	–	–
UNDP	19.5	26.1	23.7	32.4	19.5	26.1	23.7	32.4	19.5
UNTA	4.7	1.7	5.6	2.2	4.7	1.7	5.6	2.2	4.7
UNICEF	33.2	31.0	31.9	46.3	33.2	31.0	31.9	46.3	33.2
UNRWA	–	–	–	–	–	–	–	–	–
WFP	28.5	17.6	23.4	17.2	28.5	17.6	23.4	17.2	28.5
UNHCR	3.0	3.9	3.5	4.0	3.0	3.9	3.5	4.0	3.0
Other Multilateral	20.7	27.5	16.2	14.1	20.7	27.5	16.2	14.1	20.7
Arab OPEC Agencies	8.9	0.2	2.8	-2.1	8.9	0.2	2.8	-2.1	10.9
TOTAL	1434.4	1262.2	1233.7	1473.3	1127.4	1015.9	1048.0	1087.4	1161.1
OPEC COUNTRIES	-76.2	-40.4	-37.1	-43.2	-136.6	-40.4	-37.1	-43.2	16.4
E.E.C.+ MEMBERS	483.7	671.2	937.0	1675.9	504.6	481.9	414.0	628.1	620.2
TOTAL	2248.0	2151.5	2459.8	3762.1	1740.7	1609.3	1526.8	2059.2	2203.2

	ODA LOANS GROSS				ODA LOANS NET				GRANTS
	1983	1984	1985	1986	1983	1984	1985	1986	1983
DAC COUNTRIES									
Australia	–	–	–	–	–	–	–	–	1.8
Austria	6.8	0.0	0.2	6.6	4.9	-1.3	-1.1	4.7	0.4
Belgium	6.8	6.1	–	–	5.5	4.6	-1.7	-2.6	0.7
Canada	30.8	47.2	33.1	23.4	22.7	43.2	21.6	15.5	17.9
Denmark	27.9	13.8	11.2	13.8	26.9	13.0	10.4	12.8	17.2
Finland	–	–	0.2	0.3	–	–	0.2	0.3	0.2
France	21.3	43.0	64.1	71.9	15.1	37.7	58.7	64.5	5.7
Germany, Fed. Rep.	155.9	112.0	102.9	199.4	109.7	68.8	59.0	130.5	30.4
Ireland	–	–	–	–	–	–	–	–	0.1
Italy	–	7.7	8.5	26.2	-2.1	6.1	7.4	24.7	0.2
Japan	165.5	54.2	59.3	268.7	116.1	4.0	7.8	197.2	13.4
Netherlands	39.8	14.2	33.6	38.9	29.7	2.2	20.4	18.7	40.6
New Zealand	–	–	–	–	–	–	–	–	0.0
Norway	–	–	–	–	–	–	–	–	20.4
Sweden	–	–	–	–	–	–	–	–	47.8
Switzerland	–	–	1.1	1.2	–	–	1.1	1.2	21.8
United Kingdom	–	–	–	–	-48.7	-51.7	-44.7	-48.3	193.6
United States	33.0	62.0	29.0	70.0	-68.0	-48.0	-74.0	-51.0	126.0
TOTAL	487.7	360.2	343.3	720.3	211.8	78.5	64.9	368.2	538.1
MULTILATERAL	971.3	854.6	920.7	972.7	937.8	816.4	871.6	912.5	189.7
OPEC COUNTRIES	16.2	52.3	52.1	39.5	-136.7	-40.6	-39.6	-43.4	0.1
E.E.C.+ MEMBERS	251.7	196.8	220.4	350.2	136.1	80.6	109.5	200.3	368.6
TOTAL	1475.3	1267.0	1316.1	1732.5	1012.8	854.3	896.9	1237.3	727.9

	TOTAL OFFICIAL GROSS				TOTAL OFFICIAL NET				TOTAL OOF GROSS
	1983	1984	1985	1986	1983	1984	1985	1986	1983
DAC COUNTRIES									
Australia	1.8	3.4	2.9	1.8	1.8	3.4	2.8	1.6	–
Austria	7.2	0.3	0.6	6.9	5.2	-3.8	-3.8	1.0	–
Belgium	7.6	6.9	1.0	1.0	6.2	5.5	-0.7	-1.7	–
Canada	48.7	76.9	67.0	85.9	32.6	66.9	52.9	73.7	–
Denmark	45.1	31.8	25.1	39.8	44.2	31.0	24.2	38.7	0.1
Finland	0.2	0.6	0.4	0.7	0.2	0.6	0.4	0.7	–
France	27.0	49.0	70.6	79.8	20.9	43.6	65.2	72.3	–
Germany, Fed. Rep.	188.1	157.9	192.9	295.7	137.1	109.6	143.6	209.0	1.8
Ireland	0.1	0.1	0.1	0.1	0.1	0.1	0.1	0.1	–
Italy	0.2	11.9	14.4	31.8	-2.0	10.3	13.3	30.3	–
Japan	184.3	73.4	73.5	298.1	134.5	13.6	20.4	224.6	5.4
Netherlands	80.3	72.8	76.9	124.4	70.3	60.8	63.7	104.2	–
New Zealand	0.0	0.0	0.0	0.1	0.0	0.0	0.0	0.1	–
Norway	20.4	19.4	23.4	24.8	20.4	19.4	23.4	24.8	–
Sweden	48.0	54.1	74.1	226.8	47.8	54.0	74.1	225.8	0.1
Switzerland	21.8	20.5	14.1	10.1	21.8	20.5	14.1	10.2	–
United Kingdom	193.6	195.8	138.0	210.4	144.8	144.1	93.3	162.1	–
United States	163.0	183.0	134.0	170.0	50.0	63.0	23.0	22.0	4.0
TOTAL	1037.2	958.0	908.9	1608.0	735.8	642.6	609.9	1199.4	11.4
MULTILATERAL	1550.5	1409.4	1380.4	1711.8	1434.4	1262.2	1233.7	1473.3	389.5
OPEC COUNTRIES	93.9	52.5	54.7	39.8	-76.2	-40.4	-37.1	-43.2	77.5
E.E.C.+ MEMBERS	622.1	617.8	591.1	841.5	501.7	496.4	474.7	673.7	1.9
TOTAL	2681.6	2419.9	2344.0	3359.5	2094.1	1864.4	1806.5	2629.6	478.4

ODA COMMITMENTS

1984	1985	1986	1983	1984	1985	1986
2.2	2.6	1.8	2.3	2.6	2.3	1.1
0.3	0.6	6.9	5.8	0.3	0.3	—
6.8	0.9	0.9	13.7	—	—	0.9
68.8	53.8	54.4	46.9	229.7	18.2	64.4
31.8	25.1	39.7	24.0	36.2	28.1	43.5
0.6	0.4	0.7	1.3	0.3	0.2	0.2
49.0	70.6	79.8	43.4	74.9	44.4	79.8
138.4	130.4	235.4	146.3	247.4	90.8	213.0
0.1	0.1	0.1	0.1	0.1	0.1	0.1
11.9	14.4	31.8	10.1	52.3	47.6	20.7
71.8	73.5	298.1	56.0	403.3	183.9	316.5
72.8	73.3	121.3	103.9	69.5	34.8	156.1
0.0	0.0	0.1	0.0	0.0	0.1	0.1
19.4	23.4	24.8	17.7	25.1	21.2	2.6
50.3	41.1	80.8	47.1	43.1	57.9	80.8
20.5	14.1	10.1	38.5	22.4	13.3	9.9
195.8	138.0	210.4	224.0	284.7	21.8	116.0
175.0	132.0	170.0	227.4	280.8	156.4	201.7
915.5	*794.3*	*1367.0*	*1008.3*	*1772.6*	*721.3*	*1307.3*
—	—	—	—	—	—	—
—	—	—	—	—	—	—
—	—	—	—	—	—	—
91.6	72.1	58.7	103.7	104.6	41.5	112.9
21.2	14.0	0.2	—	—	—	—
820.3	869.1	946.2	833.0	825.7	1100.3	353.0
—	—	—	—	—	—	—
13.0	34.9	26.3	33.5	—	—	0.2
—	—	—	—	—	—	—
—	—	—	109.6	107.8	104.3	116.3
26.1	23.7	32.4	—	—	—	—
1.7	5.6	2.2	—	—	—	—
31.0	31.9	46.3	—	—	—	—
—	—	—	—	—	—	—
17.6	23.4	17.2	—	—	—	—
3.9	3.5	4.0	—	—	—	—
27.5	16.2	14.1	—	—	—	—
0.2	2.8	—	22.5	—	—	—
1054.1	*1097.1*	*1147.6*	*1102.3*	*1038.1*	*1246.1*	*582.3*
52.5	*54.7*	*39.8*	*80.1*	—	*50.0*	*24.0*
598.2	*524.9*	*778.0*	*669.1*	*869.5*	*309.0*	*743.0*
2022.1	**1946.0**	**2554.4**	**2190.7**	**2810.7**	**2017.4**	**1913.5**

TECH. COOP. GRANTS

1984	1985	1986	1983	1984	1985	1986
2.2	2.6	1.8	0.5	1.5	2.1	1.2
0.2	0.3	0.4	0.3	—	—	—
0.8	0.9	0.9	0.0	0.0	0.0	0.2
21.7	20.8	31.0	1.5	—	3.2	—
18.0	13.9	25.9	12.8	7.6	5.5	11.2
0.6	0.3	0.4	0.2	0.3	0.1	0.0
6.0	6.5	7.8	5.7	6.0	6.5	7.8
26.4	27.5	36.0	30.1	26.0	25.1	35.7
0.1	0.1	0.1	0.1	0.1	0.0	0.1
4.2	5.9	5.6	0.2	0.6	0.7	1.9
17.6	14.1	29.5	3.0	3.2	4.5	6.9
58.6	39.7	82.5	8.9	10.2	11.1	22.2
0.0	0.0	0.1	0.0	0.0	—	0.0
19.4	23.4	24.8	0.9	0.9	0.7	0.8
50.3	41.1	80.8	17.8	2.1	2.4	1.7
20.5	13.0	9.0	2.3	1.1	0.7	1.1
195.8	138.0	210.4	15.7	18.0	21.6	20.5
113.0	103.0	100.0	2.0	5.0	13.0	16.0
555.3	*451.0*	*646.7*	*101.7*	*82.4*	*97.2*	*127.4*
199.5	*176.4*	*174.9*	*81.0*	*90.2*	*80.9*	*99.1*
0.3	*2.5*	*0.2*	—	—	—	—
401.3	*304.5*	*427.8*	*73.4*	*68.3*	*70.5*	*99.6*
755.1	**629.9**	**821.9**	**182.8**	**172.5**	**178.1**	**226.4**

TOTAL OOF NET

1984	1985	1986	1983	1984	1985	1986
1.2	0.3	—	—	1.2	0.2	-0.2
—	—	—	-0.1	-2.8	-3.0	-4.1
0.1	0.1	0.0	—	0.1	0.1	0.0
8.1	13.1	31.5	-8.0	2.1	10.6	27.2
—	0.0	0.1	0.1	0.0	0.0	0.0
—	—	—	—	—	—	—
19.5	62.5	60.3	-3.0	14.4	57.0	42.5
—	—	—	—	—	—	—
1.7	—	—	5.0	-8.0	-1.5	-2.1
—	3.6	3.1	—	—	3.6	3.1
—	—	—	—	—	—	—
3.9	33.0	146.0	—	3.8	33.0	145.0
—	—	—	—	—	—	—
8.0	2.0	—	-8.0	-2.0	-6.0	-27.0
42.5	*114.7*	*241.0*	*-14.1*	*8.8*	*94.0*	*184.5*
355.3	*283.3*	*564.2*	*307.0*	*246.3*	*185.7*	*385.9*
—	—	—	*60.4*	—	—	—
19.6	*66.2*	*63.4*	*-2.9*	*14.5*	*60.7*	*45.6*
397.8	**398.0**	**805.2**	**353.4**	**255.1**	**279.7**	**570.4**

ODA COMMITMENTS : LOANS

DAC COUNTRIES

	1983	1984	1985	1986
Australia	—	—	—	—
Austria	5.5	—	—	—
Belgium	13.7	—	—	—
Canada	—	205.4	—	—
Denmark	21.9	23.2	—	22.3
Finland	0.4	—	—	—
France	37.7	68.7	37.9	71.9
Germany, Fed. Rep.	115.2	210.7	58.9	165.7
Ireland	—	—	—	—
Italy	9.9	35.8	46.7	17.2
Japan	37.5	387.7	164.5	287.5
Netherlands	64.8	17.8	3.6	26.9
New Zealand	—	—	—	—
Norway	—	—	—	—
Sweden	—	—	—	—
Switzerland	19.1	—	—	—
United Kingdom	—	—	—	—
United States	64.4	100.6	20.2	45.0
TOTAL	*390.0*	*1049.8*	*331.7*	*636.5*
MULTILATERAL	*889.0*	*825.7*	*1100.3*	*353.0*
OPEC COUNTRIES	*80.0*	—	*47.5*	*24.0*
E.E.C.+ MEMBERS	*263.2*	*356.1*	*147.0*	*304.0*
TOTAL	**1358.9**	**1875.5**	**1479.5**	**1013.4**

GRANT ELEMENT OF ODA

DAC COUNTRIES

	1983	1984	1985	1986
Australia	100.0	100.0	100.0	100.0
Austria	62.0	100.0	100.0	65.7
Belgium	84.3	—	—	100.0
Canada	100.0	91.0	100.0	100.0
Denmark	86.9	90.7	100.0	92.3
Finland	80.0	100.0	100.0	100.0
France	63.6	63.6	66.3	44.8
Germany, Fed. Rep.	86.7	67.5	88.4	74.1
Ireland	100.0	100.0	100.0	100.0
Italy	45.6	60.9	54.1	63.0
Japan	72.8	57.8	59.9	59.3
Netherlands	75.2	89.8	95.9	93.1
New Zealand	100.0	100.0	100.0	100.0
Norway	100.0	100.0	100.0	100.0
Sweden	100.0	100.0	100.0	100.0
Switzerland	90.1	100.0	100.0	100.0
United Kingdom	100.0	100.0	100.0	100.0
United States	91.8	89.7	96.3	93.6
TOTAL	*88.9*	*79.8*	*82.2*	*79.0*
MULTILATERAL	*85.5*	*86.5*	*85.4*	*89.7*
OPEC COUNTRIES	*40.3*	—	*49.2*	*33.8*
E.E.C.+ MEMBERS	*89.3*	*84.1*	*84.2*	*82.1*
TOTAL	**85.4**	**82.3**	**83.1**	**81.6**

OTHER AGGREGATES

COMMITMENTS: ALL SOURCES

	1983	1984	1985	1986
TOTAL BILATERAL	1467.3	2144.8	2012.4	3649.5
of which				
OPEC	100.1	—	50.0	24.0
CMEA	211.9	—	1203.0	2119.9
TOTAL MULTILATERAL	1824.7	2761.7	3199.3	2455.7
TOTAL BIL.& MULTIL.	3292.0	4906.5	5211.7	6105.2
of which				
ODA Grants	831.8	935.2	537.9	900.0
ODA Loans	1547.9	1875.5	2682.5	2718.3

DISBURSEMENTS:

DAC COUNTRIES COMBINED

OFFICIAL & PRIVATE	1983	1984	1985	1986
GROSS:				
Contractual Lending	973.7	712.8	1169.0	2148.6
Export Credits Total	485.9	352.5	822.1	1425.1
Export Credits Private	474.6	310.2	711.1	1187.3
NET:				
Contractual Lending	186.6	58.6	470.8	1485.2
Export Credits Total	-25.3	-11.5	402.3	1113.9
PRIVATE SECTOR NET	153.9	287.1	653.3	1132.6
Direct Investment	5.6	19.2	107.1	89.5
Portfolio Investment	159.4	296.4	234.2	110.6
Export Credits	-11.1	-28.6	312.0	932.5

MARKET BORROWING:

CHANGE IN CLAIMS

	1983	1984	1985	1986
Banks	—	1130.0	1751.0	787.0

MEMORANDUM ITEM:

	1983	1984	1985	1986
CMEA Countr.(Gross)	72.6	91.0	132.0	224.0

TOTAL RECEIPTS NET

DAC COUNTRIES	1983	1984	1985	1986
Australia	32.5	73.3	8.2	45.5
Austria	3.0	3.3	-1.4	5.3
Belgium	31.5	90.5	42.4	23.6
Canada	-2.4	72.4	-27.1	39.1
Denmark	-4.6	-6.4	-15.8	-20.6
Finland	0.9	0.0	1.0	1.4
France	338.7	237.2	189.3	96.4
Germany, Fed. Rep.	188.4	245.4	25.5	82.8
Ireland	–	–	–	–
Italy	18.4	14.7	1.0	9.0
Japan	450.0	561.3	524.0	110.7
Netherlands	159.8	108.5	22.9	253.6
New Zealand	4.1	2.9	1.5	2.4
Norway	-1.7	32.8	25.9	27.0
Sweden	–	30.6	26.0	34.0
Switzerland	-3.0	-7.4	64.3	9.7
United Kingdom	245.2	202.9	23.5	61.3
United States	989.0	748.0	87.0	27.0
TOTAL	2449.6	2410.0	998.0	808.1
MULTILATERAL				
AF.D.F.	–	–	–	–
AF.D.B.	–	–	–	–
AS.D.B	148.3	140.9	142.4	174.2
CAR.D.B.	–	–	–	–
E.E.C.	6.5	3.7	8.6	7.3
IBRD	401.8	656.6	611.4	579.5
IDA	55.3	49.0	32.7	12.4
I.D.B.	–	–	–	–
IFAD	3.6	3.5	12.1	13.2
I.F.C.	16.4	14.9	-1.7	-8.2
IMF TRUST FUND	–	–	–	–
U.N. AGENCIES	–	–	–	–
UNDP	16.9	16.3	14.3	15.6
UNTA	4.0	2.7	4.6	3.6
UNICEF	9.6	11.4	7.6	9.3
UNRWA	–	–	–	–
WFP	16.0	10.1	4.4	9.0
UNHCR	4.5	3.6	3.2	2.5
Other Multilateral	4.8	4.3	5.9	4.0
Arab OPEC Agencies	0.1	1.0	0.0	4.3
TOTAL	687.9	918.0	845.3	826.8
OPEC COUNTRIES	-21.3	-5.2	-19.8	20.4
E.E.C.+ MEMBERS	983.8	896.5	297.3	513.4
TOTAL	3116.2	3322.8	1823.4	1655.3

TOTAL ODA NET

DAC COUNTRIES	1983	1984	1985	1986
Australia	38.7	56.5	46.8	42.0
Austria	3.0	3.3	0.5	0.2
Belgium	12.1	3.2	3.4	11.3
Canada	10.6	26.0	34.1	52.1
Denmark	0.1	0.1	-0.2	-0.2
Finland	0.9	0.5	1.4	1.4
France	66.3	34.8	20.6	39.2
Germany, Fed. Rep.	85.5	92.9	86.9	126.1
Ireland	–	–	–	–
Italy	4.4	1.7	1.2	11.8
Japan	235.5	167.7	161.3	160.8
Netherlands	61.8	78.0	56.6	90.5
New Zealand	4.1	2.9	1.5	2.4
Norway	1.1	1.9	1.6	4.2
Sweden	–	–	–	–
Switzerland	4.2	4.3	6.0	9.7
United Kingdom	11.0	13.9	38.0	7.6
United States	80.0	61.0	43.0	46.0
TOTAL	619.2	548.7	502.7	605.2
MULTILATERAL				
AF.D.F.	–	–	–	–
AF.D.B.	–	–	–	–
AS.D.B	3.0	2.6	6.0	4.3
CAR.D.B.	–	–	–	–
E.E.C.	6.5	3.7	8.6	7.3
IBRD	–	–	–	–
IDA	55.3	49.0	32.7	12.4
I.D.B.	–	–	–	–
IFAD	3.6	3.5	12.1	13.2
I.F.C.	–	–	–	–
IMF TRUST FUND	–	–	–	–
U.N. AGENCIES	–	–	–	–
UNDP	16.9	16.3	14.3	15.6
UNTA	4.0	2.7	4.6	3.6
UNICEF	9.6	11.4	7.6	9.3
UNRWA	–	–	–	–
WFP	16.0	10.1	4.4	9.0
UNHCR	4.5	3.6	3.2	2.5
Other Multilateral	4.8	4.3	5.9	4.0
Arab OPEC Agencies	0.1	0.9	0.0	4.3
TOTAL	124.3	108.1	99.3	85.6
OPEC COUNTRIES	1.0	15.9	1.2	20.4
E.E.C.+ MEMBERS	247.7	228.3	215.1	293.7
TOTAL	744.5	672.7	603.2	711.1

TOTAL ODA GROSS

	1983
Australia	38.7
Austria	4.3
Belgium	13.0
Canada	10.9
Denmark	0.5
Finland	0.9
France	70.4
Germany, Fed. Rep.	107.2
Ireland	–
Italy	4.6
Japan	353.2
Netherlands	71.8
New Zealand	4.1
Norway	1.1
Sweden	–
Switzerland	4.2
United Kingdom	14.4
United States	126.0
TOTAL	825.1
AF.D.F.	–
AF.D.B.	–
AS.D.B	6.3
CAR.D.B.	–
E.E.C.	6.5
IBRD	–
IDA	59.6
I.D.B.	–
IFAD	3.6
I.F.C.	–
IMF TRUST FUND	–
U.N. AGENCIES	–
UNDP	16.9
UNTA	4.0
UNICEF	9.6
UNRWA	–
WFP	16.0
UNHCR	4.5
Other Multilateral	4.8
Arab OPEC Agencies	0.4
TOTAL	132.2
OPEC COUNTRIES	11.5
E.E.C.+ MEMBERS	288.4
TOTAL	968.8

ODA LOANS GROSS

DAC COUNTRIES	1983	1984	1985	1986
Australia	–	–	–	–
Austria	4.0	3.2	0.3	–
Belgium	6.8	–	–	7.8
Canada	4.3	14.8	22.6	44.5
Denmark	–	–	–	–
Finland	–	–	–	–
France	65.3	30.3	23.3	37.7
Germany, Fed. Rep.	76.0	90.2	94.2	148.8
Ireland	–	–	–	–
Italy	4.0	–	–	7.6
Japan	293.1	212.7	206.4	227.5
Netherlands	34.9	59.8	36.1	54.3
New Zealand	–	–	–	–
Norway	–	1.4	1.3	1.7
Sweden	–	–	–	–
Switzerland	–	–	–	–
United Kingdom	–	1.1	1.7	–
United States	87.0	79.0	70.0	75.0
TOTAL	575.4	492.5	455.8	605.0
MULTILATERAL	66.9	66.0	60.8	47.1
OPEC COUNTRIES	10.4	27.2	13.4	33.2
E.E.C.+ MEMBERS	187.0	181.4	155.2	256.2
TOTAL	652.7	585.6	530.0	685.2

ODA LOANS NET

DAC COUNTRIES	1983	1984	1985	1986
Australia	–	–	–	–
Austria	2.7	3.2	0.3	–
Belgium	5.9	-1.1	-1.3	5.7
Canada	4.0	14.2	20.9	42.3
Denmark	-0.3	-0.3	-0.3	-0.3
Finland	–	–	–	–
France	61.2	28.4	16.2	31.0
Germany, Fed. Rep.	54.2	64.7	60.4	91.9
Ireland	–	–	–	–
Italy	3.7	-0.2	-0.2	7.1
Japan	175.4	94.0	85.0	51.0
Netherlands	25.0	48.1	21.9	36.0
New Zealand	–	–	–	–
Norway	–	1.4	1.1	1.7
Sweden	–	–	–	–
Switzerland	–	–	–	–
United Kingdom	-3.4	-2.1	-1.5	-3.3
United States	41.0	26.0	12.0	17.0
TOTAL	369.5	276.2	214.5	280.1
MULTILATERAL	59.0	54.3	49.4	31.8
OPEC COUNTRIES	-0.2	15.7	1.2	20.1
E.E.C.+ MEMBERS	146.3	137.5	95.2	168.0
TOTAL	428.3	346.1	265.0	331.9

GRANTS

	1983
Australia	38.7
Austria	0.2
Belgium	6.2
Canada	6.6
Denmark	0.5
Finland	0.9
France	5.1
Germany, Fed. Rep.	31.3
Ireland	–
Italy	0.6
Japan	60.0
Netherlands	36.9
New Zealand	4.1
Norway	1.1
Sweden	–
Switzerland	4.2
United Kingdom	14.4
United States	39.0
TOTAL	249.7
MULTILATERAL	65.3
OPEC COUNTRIES	1.1
E.E.C.+ MEMBERS	101.4
TOTAL	316.1

TOTAL OFFICIAL GROSS

DAC COUNTRIES	1983	1984	1985	1986
Australia	42.3	67.5	60.0	51.0
Austria	4.3	3.3	0.7	5.3
Belgium	13.0	7.6	8.3	13.4
Canada	25.9	93.4	37.4	69.5
Denmark	6.7	3.3	0.1	0.3
Finland	0.9	0.5	1.4	1.4
France	70.4	36.7	27.7	45.9
Germany, Fed. Rep.	190.6	240.6	185.7	230.5
Ireland	–	–	–	–
Italy	4.6	1.9	1.4	12.4
Japan	362.7	288.4	282.8	360.8
Netherlands	72.3	89.8	78.6	114.3
New Zealand	4.1	2.9	1.5	2.4
Norway	1.1	1.9	1.7	4.2
Sweden	3.9	34.8	30.0	37.5
Switzerland	4.2	4.3	6.0	9.7
United Kingdom	18.7	37.8	43.6	13.0
United States	377.0	338.0	164.0	149.0
TOTAL	1202.7	1252.7	930.8	1120.6
MULTILATERAL	801.5	1064.4	1008.1	1111.7
OPEC COUNTRIES	11.5	27.3	13.5	33.5
E.E.C.+ MEMBERS	382.9	421.4	353.9	437.2
TOTAL	2015.7	2344.5	1952.4	2265.8

TOTAL OFFICIAL NET

DAC COUNTRIES	1983	1984	1985	1986
Australia	35.2	64.3	52.5	45.4
Austria	3.0	3.3	0.7	5.3
Belgium	12.1	6.5	6.9	11.3
Canada	-2.4	72.4	-27.1	39.1
Denmark	2.6	-3.9	-7.0	-11.4
Finland	0.9	0.5	1.4	1.4
France	66.3	34.8	20.6	39.2
Germany, Fed. Rep.	153.1	190.4	113.4	116.3
Ireland	–	–	–	–
Italy	4.4	1.7	1.2	11.8
Japan	245.0	165.5	152.9	172.3
Netherlands	60.0	77.7	62.9	95.2
New Zealand	4.1	2.9	1.5	2.4
Norway	1.1	1.9	1.6	4.2
Sweden	–	30.6	26.0	33.4
Switzerland	4.2	4.3	6.0	9.7
United Kingdom	13.4	34.2	39.9	9.0
United States	250.0	218.0	46.0	26.0
TOTAL	852.9	905.1	499.4	610.6
MULTILATERAL	687.9	918.0	845.3	826.8
OPEC COUNTRIES	-21.3	-5.2	-19.8	20.4
E.E.C.+ MEMBERS	318.4	345.1	246.5	278.8
TOTAL	1519.5	1817.9	1324.8	1457.8

TOTAL OOF GROSS

	1983
Australia	3.6
Austria	–
Belgium	–
Canada	15.0
Denmark	6.3
Finland	–
France	–
Germany, Fed. Rep.	83.4
Ireland	–
Italy	–
Japan	9.5
Netherlands	0.5
New Zealand	–
Norway	–
Sweden	3.9
Switzerland	–
United Kingdom	4.3
United States	251.0
TOTAL	377.5
MULTILATERAL	669.3
OPEC COUNTRIES	–
E.E.C.+ MEMBERS	94.5
TOTAL	1046.9

ODA COMMITMENTS

1984	1985	1986	1983	1984	1985	1986
56.5	46.8	42.0	59.9	54.4	56.6	42.1
3.3	0.5	0.2	0.2	0.1	0.5	–
4.3	4.7	13.4	10.3	2.8	2.3	5.6
26.6	35.9	54.2	30.7	26.8	12.3	54.2
0.4	0.0	0.2	0.3	–	11.3	0.1
0.5	1.4	1.4	1.7	0.1	4.5	5.3
36.7	27.7	45.9	64.6	39.6	26.0	45.9
118.5	120.6	183.0	104.2	163.9	136.7	44.8
–	–	–	–	–	–	–
1.9	1.4	12.4	2.0	4.4	19.0	15.7
286.3	282.8	337.4	370.1	474.2	698.9	165.6
89.8	70.8	108.8	43.2	116.2	43.2	102.3
2.9	1.5	2.4	1.0	1.3	1.4	1.2
1.9	1.7	4.2	2.7	1.6	1.5	4.6
–	–	–	–	–	–	–
4.3	6.0	9.7	4.9	4.2	5.5	20.0
17.1	41.2	10.9	16.0	16.3	25.5	9.4
114.0	101.0	104.0	149.3	92.7	108.7	109.7
765.0	744.1	930.1	861.0	998.6	1153.8	626.4
–	–	–	–	–	–	–
–	–	–	–	–	–	–
6.6	10.2	8.6	–	–	–	–
–	–	–	–	–	–	–
3.7	8.6	7.3	14.3	13.7	0.3	24.0
–	–	–	–	–	–	–
54.4	38.4	18.1	–	–	–	–
–	–	–	–	–	–	–
5.6	13.3	17.6	–	0.2	12.8	0.2
–	–	–	–	–	–	–
–	–	–	–	–	–	–
–	–	–	55.9	48.4	39.9	43.9
16.3	14.3	15.6	–	–	–	–
2.7	4.6	3.6	–	–	–	–
11.4	7.6	9.3	–	–	–	–
–	–	–	–	–	–	–
10.1	4.4	9.0	–	–	–	–
3.6	3.2	2.5	–	–	–	–
4.3	5.9	4.0	–	–	–	–
1.1	0.3	5.3	–	–	7.4	–
119.8	110.7	100.9	70.1	62.3	60.3	68.0
27.3	13.5	33.5	50.9	–	35.2	24.7
272.3	275.1	381.9	254.7	356.9	264.3	247.8
912.1	868.2	1064.4	982.0	1060.9	1249.3	719.1

TECH. COOP. GRANTS

1984	1985	1986	1983	1984	1985	1986
56.5	46.8	42.0	23.8	29.4	27.0	29.6
0.2	0.2	0.2	0.2	–	–	–
4.3	4.7	5.6	1.8	1.9	3.0	3.6
11.8	13.2	9.7	1.9	–	4.8	–
0.4	0.0	0.2	0.5	0.4	0.0	0.2
0.5	1.4	1.4	0.6	0.5	1.0	0.2
6.4	4.5	8.3	4.5	6.4	4.5	8.3
28.3	26.5	34.2	30.0	28.3	25.7	30.7
–	–	–	–	–	–	–
1.9	1.4	4.8	0.4	0.9	1.4	3.5
73.7	76.3	109.8	40.0	43.7	45.3	63.1
29.9	34.7	54.4	23.8	19.1	22.4	39.2
2.9	1.5	2.4	1.3	1.2	0.9	1.3
0.5	0.5	2.5	–	0.2	0.1	0.7
–	–	–	–	–	–	–
4.3	6.0	9.7	0.9	1.0	1.2	2.2
16.0	39.5	10.9	5.8	5.1	6.0	6.1
35.0	31.0	29.0	37.0	27.0	23.0	20.0
272.5	288.3	325.1	172.4	165.0	166.2	208.5
53.8	49.9	53.8	39.9	38.4	35.5	35.0
0.2	0.1	0.3	–	–	–	–
90.9	119.9	125.7	66.8	62.1	62.9	91.5
326.5	338.2	379.2	212.2	203.4	201.6	243.5

TOTAL OOF NET

1984	1985	1986	1983	1984	1985	1986
11.0	13.2	9.0	-3.5	7.8	5.7	3.4
–	0.2	5.1	–	–	0.2	5.1
3.3	3.6	–	–	3.3	3.6	–
66.8	1.6	15.2	-13.0	46.5	-61.2	-13.0
3.0	0.0	0.1	2.5	-4.0	-6.8	-11.3
–	–	–	–	–	–	–
–	–	–	–	–	–	–
122.1	65.0	47.5	67.6	97.5	26.5	-9.8
–	–	–	–	–	–	–
2.1	–	23.4	9.5	-2.2	-8.5	11.5
–	7.8	5.6	-1.8	-0.3	6.3	4.7
–	–	–	–	–	–	–
34.8	30.0	37.5	–	30.6	26.0	33.4
–	–	–	–	–	–	–
20.7	2.4	2.1	2.4	20.3	1.9	1.4
224.0	63.0	45.0	170.0	157.0	3.0	-20.0
487.7	186.8	190.6	233.7	356.4	-3.3	5.5
944.6	897.5	1010.8	563.5	809.9	746.0	741.2
–	–	–	-22.2	-21.1	-21.1	–
149.1	78.8	55.3	70.7	116.8	31.4	-14.9
1432.4	1084.2	1201.4	775.0	1145.3	721.6	746.7

ODA COMMITMENTS : LOANS

DAC COUNTRIES

	1983	1984	1985	1986
Australia	–	–	–	–
Austria	–	–	0.3	–
Belgium	6.9	–	–	–
Canada	12.2	22.1	–	21.6
Denmark	–	–	11.3	–
Finland	–	–	–	–
France	59.4	33.2	21.6	37.7
Germany, Fed. Rep.	71.3	138.1	108.4	3.3
Ireland	–	–	–	–
Italy	–	–	14.5	7.5
Japan	292.7	400.7	619.8	31.7
Netherlands	4.6	82.6	8.5	30.4
New Zealand	–	–	–	–
Norway	2.5	1.4	1.3	1.7
Sweden	–	–	–	–
Switzerland	–	–	–	–
United Kingdom	–	–	–	–
United States	113.6	66.6	67.8	66.7
TOTAL	563.2	744.6	853.4	200.7
MULTILATERAL	–	–	20.2	–
OPEC COUNTRIES	49.8	–	35.1	24.7
E.E.C.+ MEMBERS	142.2	253.9	164.2	78.9
TOTAL	613.0	744.6	908.6	225.3

GRANT ELEMENT OF ODA

DAC COUNTRIES

	1983	1984	1985	1986
Australia	100.0	100.0	100.0	100.0
Austria	100.0	100.0	65.5	–
Belgium	88.9	100.0	85.8	100.0
Canada	95.9	91.6	100.0	96.2
Denmark	100.0	–	74.7	100.0
Finland	100.0	100.0	100.0	100.0
France	70.4	79.3	79.4	71.4
Germany, Fed. Rep.	69.0	49.4	47.8	97.5
Ireland	–	–	–	–
Italy	100.0	100.0	55.6	83.3
Japan	68.8	61.6	58.4	91.0
Netherlands	95.2	69.8	93.7	88.2
New Zealand	100.0	100.0	100.0	100.0
Norway	29.4	38.0	35.8	72.3
Sweden	–	–	–	–
Switzerland	100.0	100.0	92.5	100.0
United Kingdom	100.0	100.0	100.0	100.0
United States	72.6	76.9	77.2	78.0
TOTAL	75.8	66.9	65.2	87.9
MULTILATERAL	100.0	100.0	92.5	100.0
OPEC COUNTRIES	47.6	–	45.0	46.7
E.E.C.+ MEMBERS	78.5	64.6	65.8	86.6
TOTAL	76.1	68.9	65.7	87.6

OTHER AGGREGATES

COMMITMENTS: ALL SOURCES

	1983	1984	1985	1986
TOTAL BILATERAL	1162.2	1284.7	1335.2	863.2
of which				
OPEC	50.9	–	35.2	24.7
CMEA	–	–	–	–
TOTAL MULTILATERAL	1727.3	1637.0	1629.1	1393.7
TOTAL BIL.& MULTIL.	2889.4	2921.7	2964.3	2256.9
of which				
ODA Grants	369.0	316.3	340.7	493.8
ODA Loans	613.0	744.6	908.6	225.3

DISBURSEMENTS:

DAC COUNTRIES COMBINED

	1983	1984	1985	1986
OFFICIAL & PRIVATE				
GROSS:				
Contractual Lending	2207.9	2721.4	1757.1	1621.2
Export Credits Total	1627.6	2208.2	1297.7	1007.4
Export Credits Private	1254.9	1744.5	1124.7	825.6
NET:				
Contractual Lending	1204.9	1592.7	635.2	441.0
Export Credits Total	834.8	1300.1	421.3	160.4
PRIVATE SECTOR NET	1596.7	1504.9	498.6	197.5
Direct Investment	302.7	494.6	-311.3	-508.6
Portfolio Investment	692.4	46.9	375.6	550.7
Export Credits	601.7	963.4	434.3	155.5

MARKET BORROWING:

CHANGE IN CLAIMS

	1983	1984	1985	1986
Banks	–	935.0	29.0	591.0

MEMORANDUM ITEM:

	1983	1984	1985	1986
CMEA Countr.(Gross)	–	–	–	–

TOTAL RECEIPTS NET

	1983	1984	1985	1986
DAC COUNTRIES				
Australia	1.4	0.0	-0.2	0.4
Austria	5.0	4.5	4.6	6.3
Belgium	-7.5	-11.9	-5.9	-7.8
Canada	-12.8	-12.7	-14.7	-13.5
Denmark	-3.5	3.8	1.4	-5.9
Finland	0.1	0.1	0.1	0.1
France	-374.9	-56.5	-40.3	-16.9
Germany, Fed. Rep.	-196.8	-161.4	-89.1	-17.0
Ireland	–	–	–	–
Italy	204.8	6.6	-40.7	50.3
Japan	-183.5	-119.5	-140.0	-238.9
Netherlands	-2.1	-5.4	–	-0.4
New Zealand	–	–	–	–
Norway	0.0	–	–	–
Sweden	-0.5	-1.1	0.6	0.9
Switzerland	15.9	-9.5	-14.4	0.7
United Kingdom	-16.8	34.8	13.0	-45.4
United States	-133.0	–	–	–
TOTAL	*-704.3*	*-328.1*	*-325.9*	*-287.2*
MULTILATERAL				
AF.D.F.	–	–	–	–
AF.D.B.	–	–	–	–
AS.D.B	–	–	–	–
CAR.D.B.	–	–	–	–
E.E.C.	–	–	–	–
IBRD	-49.8	-48.6	-49.4	-54.4
IDA	–	–	–	–
I.D.B.	–	–	–	–
IFAD	–	–	–	–
I.F.C.	–	–	–	–
IMF TRUST FUND	–	–	–	–
U.N. AGENCIES				
UNDP	4.0	2.9	2.6	4.6
UNTA	0.4	0.2	0.8	0.6
UNICEF	0.1	0.0	–	–
UNRWA	–	–	–	–
WFP	–	–	–	–
UNHCR	3.6	7.7	11.9	8.2
Other Multilateral	0.0	0.1	0.2	0.2
Arab OPEC Agencies	–	–	–	–
TOTAL	*-41.8*	*-37.7*	*-34.0*	*-40.9*
OPEC COUNTRIES	–	–	0.1	–
E.E.C.+ MEMBERS	*-396.7*	*-190.0*	*-161.7*	*-43.1*
TOTAL	*-746.1*	*-365.9*	*-359.7*	*-328.2*

TOTAL ODA NET

	1983	1984	1985	1986
Australia	–	–	–	–
Austria	5.4	4.9	4.9	6.5
Belgium	0.1	0.1	0.1	0.5
Canada	–	0.3	–	–
Denmark	0.1	-0.1	-0.1	-0.1
Finland	0.1	0.1	0.1	0.1
France	3.8	2.2	1.2	3.3
Germany, Fed. Rep.	38.0	1.1	1.7	0.3
Ireland	–	–	–	–
Italy	0.2	0.3	0.6	0.8
Japan	-8.6	-7.6	-8.0	1.3
Netherlands	–	0.2	–	–
New Zealand	–	–	–	–
Norway	–	–	–	–
Sweden	1.0	0.6	0.6	0.1
Switzerland	0.0	0.1	0.0	0.7
United Kingdom	-0.4	-0.1	–	–
United States	–	–	–	–
TOTAL	*39.7*	*2.0*	*1.0*	*13.4*
UNDP	4.0	2.9	2.6	4.6
UNTA	0.4	0.2	0.8	0.6
UNICEF	0.1	0.0	–	–
UNHCR	3.6	7.7	11.9	8.2
Other Multilateral	0.0	0.1	0.2	0.2
TOTAL	*8.1*	*10.9*	*15.4*	*13.5*
OPEC COUNTRIES	–	–	0.1	–
E.E.C.+ MEMBERS	*41.8*	*3.7*	*3.4*	*4.8*
TOTAL	*47.8*	*12.9*	*16.5*	*26.9*

TOTAL ODA GROSS

	1983
Australia	–
Austria	5.4
Belgium	0.1
Canada	–
Denmark	0.2
Finland	0.1
France	4.7
Germany, Fed. Rep.	39.9
Ireland	–
Italy	0.2
Japan	1.2
Netherlands	–
New Zealand	–
Norway	–
Sweden	1.0
Switzerland	0.0
United Kingdom	–
United States	–
TOTAL	*52.8*
AF.D.F.	–
AF.D.B.	–
AS.D.B	–
CAR.D.B.	–
E.E.C.	–
IBRD	–
IDA	–
I.D.B.	–
IFAD	–
I.F.C.	–
IMF TRUST FUND	–
U.N. AGENCIES	–
UNDP	4.0
UNTA	0.4
UNICEF	0.1
UNRWA	–
WFP	–
UNHCR	3.6
Other Multilateral	0.0
Arab OPEC Agencies	–
TOTAL	*8.1*
OPEC COUNTRIES	–
E.E.C.+ MEMBERS	*45.1*
TOTAL	*60.9*

ODA LOANS GROSS

	1983	1984	1985	1986
DAC COUNTRIES				
Australia	–	–	–	–
Austria	–	–	–	–
Belgium	–	–	–	–
Canada	–	–	–	–
Denmark	–	–	–	–
Finland	–	–	–	–
France	–	–	–	–
Germany, Fed. Rep.	–	–	–	–
Ireland	–	–	–	–
Italy	–	–	–	–
Japan	–	–	–	–
Netherlands	–	–	–	–
New Zealand	–	–	–	–
Norway	–	–	–	–
Sweden	–	–	–	–
Switzerland	–	–	–	–
United Kingdom	–	–	–	–
United States	–	–	–	–
TOTAL	–	–	–	–
MULTILATERAL	–	–	–	–
OPEC COUNTRIES	–	–	–	–
E.E.C.+ MEMBERS	–	–	–	–
TOTAL	–	–	–	–

ODA LOANS NET

	1983	1984	1985	1986
Australia	0.0	0.0	0.0	0.0
Austria	–	–	–	–
Belgium	–	–	–	–
Canada	–	–	–	–
Denmark	-0.1	-0.1	-0.1	-0.1
Finland	–	–	–	–
France	-0.9	-1.7	-2.2	-1.2
Germany, Fed. Rep.	-1.9	-4.3	-2.3	-3.9
Ireland	–	–	–	–
Italy	–	–	–	–
Japan	-9.8	-9.8	-9.7	-1.2
Netherlands	–	–	–	–
New Zealand	–	–	–	–
Norway	–	–	–	–
Sweden	–	–	–	–
Switzerland	–	–	–	–
United Kingdom	-0.4	-0.1	–	–
United States	–	–	–	–
TOTAL	*-13.1*	*-16.0*	*-14.4*	*-6.4*
MULTILATERAL	–	–	–	–
OPEC COUNTRIES	–	–	–	–
E.E.C.+ MEMBERS	*-3.3*	*-6.2*	*-4.7*	*-5.2*
TOTAL	*-13.1*	*-16.0*	*-14.4*	*-6.4*

GRANTS

	1983
Australia	–
Austria	5.4
Belgium	0.1
Canada	–
Denmark	0.2
Finland	0.1
France	4.7
Germany, Fed. Rep.	39.9
Ireland	–
Italy	0.2
Japan	1.2
Netherlands	–
New Zealand	–
Norway	–
Sweden	1.0
Switzerland	0.0
United Kingdom	–
United States	–
TOTAL	*52.8*
MULTILATERAL	*8.1*
OPEC COUNTRIES	–
E.E.C.+ MEMBERS	*45.1*
TOTAL	*60.9*

TOTAL OFFICIAL GROSS

	1983	1984	1985	1986
DAC COUNTRIES				
Australia	–	–	–	–
Austria	5.4	4.9	4.9	6.5
Belgium	0.1	0.3	0.2	0.5
Canada	0.3	0.3	–	-1.5
Denmark	0.2	–	–	–
Finland	0.1	0.1	0.1	0.1
France	4.7	3.9	3.5	4.5
Germany, Fed. Rep.	39.9	5.8	5.3	9.5
Ireland	–	–	–	–
Italy	0.2	0.3	0.6	0.8
Japan	1.2	2.1	1.8	2.4
Netherlands	–	0.2	–	–
New Zealand	–	–	–	–
Norway	–	–	–	–
Sweden	1.0	0.6	0.6	0.9
Switzerland	0.0	0.1	0.0	0.7
United Kingdom	–	–	–	–
United States	–	–	–	–
TOTAL	*53.1*	*18.5*	*16.8*	*24.4*
MULTILATERAL	*8.1*	*10.9*	*15.4*	*13.5*
OPEC COUNTRIES	–	–	0.1	–
E.E.C.+ MEMBERS	*45.1*	*10.4*	*9.5*	*15.3*
TOTAL	*61.2*	*29.4*	*32.3*	*37.9*

TOTAL OFFICIAL NET

	1983	1984	1985	1986
Australia	–	–	–	–
Austria	5.0	4.5	4.6	6.3
Belgium	0.1	0.3	0.2	0.5
Canada	-13.5	-12.7	-14.7	-13.5
Denmark	0.1	-0.1	-0.1	-0.1
Finland	0.1	0.1	0.1	0.1
France	3.8	2.2	1.2	3.3
Germany, Fed. Rep.	3.8	-0.1	0.9	4.1
Ireland	–	–	–	–
Italy	-1.0	-0.1	0.5	0.8
Japan	-50.7	-49.7	-49.9	1.3
Netherlands	–	0.2	–	–
New Zealand	–	–	–	–
Norway	–	–	–	–
Sweden	1.0	0.6	0.6	0.9
Switzerland	0.0	0.1	0.0	0.7
United Kingdom	-0.4	-0.1	–	–
United States	-133.0	–	–	–
TOTAL	*-184.7*	*-54.9*	*-56.7*	*4.2*
MULTILATERAL	*-41.8*	*-37.7*	*-34.0*	*-40.9*
OPEC COUNTRIES	–	–	0.1	–
E.E.C.+ MEMBERS	*6.4*	*2.2*	*2.7*	*8.6*
TOTAL	*-226.4*	*-92.7*	*-90.6*	*-36.7*

TOTAL OOF GROSS

	1983
Australia	–
Austria	–
Belgium	–
Canada	0.3
Denmark	–
Finland	–
France	–
Germany, Fed. Rep.	–
Ireland	–
Italy	–
Japan	–
Netherlands	–
New Zealand	–
Norway	–
Sweden	–
Switzerland	–
United Kingdom	–
United States	–
TOTAL	*0.3*
MULTILATERAL	–
OPEC COUNTRIES	–
E.E.C.+ MEMBERS	–
TOTAL	*0.3*

ODA COMMITMENTS

	1984	1985	1986	1983	1984	1985	1986
Australia	–	–	–	–	–	–	–
Austria	4.9	4.9	6.5	5.4	4.8	4.9	–
Belgium	0.1	0.1	0.5	–	–	–	0.5
Canada	0.3	–	–	–	0.3	–	–
Denmark	–	–	–	–	–	–	–
Finland	0.1	0.1	0.1	0.0	0.1	0.0	–
France	3.9	3.5	4.5	4.7	3.9	3.5	4.5
Germany, Fed. Rep.	5.4	4.0	4.2	39.9	5.4	4.3	4.2
Ireland	–	–	–	–	–	–	–
Italy	0.3	0.6	0.8	0.2	0.3	0.7	0.8
Japan	2.1	1.8	2.4	1.3	2.2	1.9	3.0
Netherlands	0.2	–	–	–	0.2	–	–
New Zealand	–	–	–	–	–	–	–
Norway	–	–	–	–	–	–	–
Sweden	0.6	0.6	0.1	1.0	–	0.6	0.1
Switzerland	0.1	0.0	0.7	–	0.1	0.0	0.7
United Kingdom	–	–	–	–	–	–	–
United States	–	–	–	–	–	–	–
TOTAL	18.0	15.4	19.8	52.5	17.3	16.0	13.8
	–	–	–	8.1	10.9	15.4	13.5
	2.9	2.6	4.6	–	–	–	–
	0.2	0.8	0.6	–	–	–	–
	0.0	–	–	–	–	–	–
	7.7	11.9	8.2	–	–	–	–
	0.1	0.2	0.2	–	–	–	–
MULTILATERAL	10.9	15.4	13.5	8.1	10.9	15.4	13.5
OPEC COUNTRIES	–	0.1	–	–	–	0.1	–
E.E.C.+ MEMBERS	9.9	8.0	10.0	44.8	9.8	8.5	10.1
TOTAL	28.9	30.9	33.3	60.6	28.1	31.5	27.3

TECH. COOP. GRANTS

	1984	1985	1986	1983	1984	1985	1986
Australia	–	–	–	–	–	–	–
Austria	4.9	4.9	6.5	4.7	–	–	–
Belgium	0.1	0.1	0.5	–	–	–	–
Canada	0.3	–	–	–	–	–	–
Denmark	–	–	–	–	–	–	–
Finland	0.1	0.1	0.1	0.0	0.0	0.0	–
France	3.9	3.5	4.5	4.7	3.9	3.5	4.5
Germany, Fed. Rep.	5.4	4.0	4.2	2.3	1.9	1.8	2.5
Ireland	–	–	–	–	–	–	–
Italy	0.3	0.6	0.8	0.2	0.3	0.6	0.4
Japan	2.1	1.8	2.4	1.2	2.1	1.8	2.4
Netherlands	0.2	–	–	–	–	–	–
New Zealand	–	–	–	–	–	–	–
Norway	–	–	–	–	–	–	–
Sweden	0.6	0.6	0.1	–	–	–	–
Switzerland	0.1	0.0	0.7	0.0	0.0	–	–
United Kingdom	–	–	–	–	–	–	–
United States	–	–	–	–	–	–	–
TOTAL	18.0	15.4	19.8	13.0	8.4	7.5	9.8
MULTILATERAL	10.9	15.4	13.5	8.1	10.9	15.4	13.5
OPEC	–	0.1	–	–	–	–	–
E.E.C.+ MEMBERS	9.9	8.0	10.0	7.2	6.2	5.8	7.3
TOTAL	28.9	30.9	33.3	21.1	19.2	23.0	23.3

TOTAL OOF NET

1984	1985	1986	1983	1984	1985	1986
–	–	–	-0.4	-0.3	-0.3	-0.2
0.2	0.1	–	–	0.2	0.1	–
–	–	-1.5	-13.5	-13.0	-14.7	-13.5
–	–	–	–	–	–	–
–	–	–	–	–	–	–
0.4	1.3	5.3	-34.2	-1.2	-0.7	3.8
–	–	–	-1.2	-0.5	-0.1	–
–	–	–	-42.1	-42.1	-41.9	–
–	–	–	–	–	–	–
–	–	–	–	–	–	–
–	–	0.8	–	–	–	0.8
–	–	–	–	–	–	–
–	–	–	-133.0	–	–	–
0.6	1.4	4.6	-224.4	-56.9	-57.7	-9.1
–	–	–	-49.8	-48.6	-49.4	-54.4
–	–	–	–	–	–	–
0.6	1.4	5.3	-35.4	-1.5	-0.7	3.8
0.6	1.4	4.6	-274.2	-105.5	-107.1	-63.5

ODA COMMITMENTS : LOANS

	1983	1984	1985	1986
DAC COUNTRIES				
Australia	–	–	–	–
Austria	–	–	–	–
Belgium	–	–	–	–
Canada	–	–	–	–
Denmark	–	–	–	–
Finland	–	–	–	–
France	–	–	–	–
Germany, Fed. Rep.	–	–	–	–
Ireland	–	–	–	–
Italy	–	–	–	–
Japan	–	–	–	–
Netherlands	–	–	–	–
New Zealand	–	–	–	–
Norway	–	–	–	–
Sweden	–	–	–	–
Switzerland	–	–	–	–
United Kingdom	–	–	–	–
United States	–	–	–	–
TOTAL	–	–	–	–
MULTILATERAL	–	–	–	–
OPEC COUNTRIES	–	–	–	–
E.E.C.+ MEMBERS	–	–	–	–
TOTAL	–	–	–	–

GRANT ELEMENT OF ODA

	1983	1984	1985	1986
DAC COUNTRIES				
Australia	–	–	–	–
Austria	100.0	100.0	100.0	–
Belgium	–	–	–	100.0
Canada	–	100.0	–	–
Denmark	–	–	–	–
Finland	100.0	100.0	100.0	–
France	100.0	100.0	100.0	100.0
Germany, Fed. Rep.	100.0	100.0	100.0	100.0
Ireland	–	–	–	–
Italy	100.0	100.0	100.0	100.0
Japan	100.0	100.0	100.0	100.0
Netherlands	–	100.0	–	–
New Zealand	–	–	–	–
Norway	–	–	–	–
Sweden	100.0	–	100.0	100.0
Switzerland	–	100.0	100.0	100.0
United Kingdom	–	–	–	–
United States	–	–	–	–
TOTAL	100.0	100.0	100.0	100.0
MULTILATERAL	100.0	100.0	100.0	100.0
OPEC COUNTRIES	–	–	100.0	–
E.E.C.+ MEMBERS	100.0	100.0	100.0	100.0
TOTAL	100.0	100.0	100.0	100.0

OTHER AGGREGATES

COMMITMENTS: ALL SOURCES

	1983	1984	1985	1986
TOTAL BILATERAL	52.8	17.3	16.1	14.7
of which OPEC	–	–	0.1	–
CMEA	–	–	–	–
TOTAL MULTILATERAL	8.1	10.9	15.4	13.5
TOTAL BIL.& MULTIL.	60.9	28.1	31.5	28.2
of which ODA Grants	60.6	28.1	31.5	27.3
ODA Loans	–	–	–	–

DISBURSEMENTS:

DAC COUNTRIES COMBINED

OFFICIAL & PRIVATE

	1983	1984	1985	1986
GROSS:				
Contractual Lending	743.1	79.9	89.8	105.7
Export Credits Total	743.1	79.5	88.5	100.4
Export Credits Private	742.8	79.5	88.5	101.1
NET:				
Contractual Lending	-518.9	-198.8	-202.2	-129.3
Export Credits Total	-471.6	-181.6	-187.0	-126.7
PRIVATE SECTOR NET	-519.6	-273.2	-269.2	-291.5
Direct Investment	-78.5	42.7	-38.1	-107.4
Portfolio Investment	-159.7	-190.2	-101.0	-70.3
Export Credits	-281.4	-125.7	-130.0	-113.8

MARKET BORROWING:

CHANGE IN CLAIMS

	1983	1984	1985	1986
Banks	–	-656.0	284.0	-557.0

MEMORANDUM ITEM:

	1983	1984	1985	1986
CMEA Countr.(Gross)	7.0	0.8	0.7	0.4

TOTAL RECEIPTS NET / TOTAL ODA NET / TOTAL ODA GROSS

	1983	1984	1985	1986	1983	1984	1985	1986	1983
TOTAL RECEIPTS NET					**TOTAL ODA NET**				**TOTAL ODA GROSS**
DAC COUNTRIES									
Australia	50.8	159.3	11.9	-48.6	–	–	–	–	–
Austria	0.6	0.5	0.8	0.6	0.6	0.5	0.8	0.6	0.6
Belgium	0.2	179.2	159.4	-137.6	0.3	0.1	0.0	0.0	0.3
Canada	0.3	0.0	–	–	0.3	0.0	–	–	0.3
Denmark	-1.4	–	–	–	–	–	–	–	–
Finland	0.1	0.1	0.1	0.1	0.1	0.1	0.1	0.1	0.1
France	404.9	323.5	202.4	93.9	2.5	2.7	2.6	3.2	2.5
Germany, Fed. Rep.	278.2	541.3	138.7	173.2	0.5	0.5	0.6	1.1	0.5
Ireland	–	–	–	–	–	–	–	–	–
Italy	8.9	725.7	294.7	-503.2	0.2	0.3	1.8	0.6	0.2
Japan	-365.2	-192.3	42.2	95.6	2.6	-4.6	14.7	15.2	7.7
Netherlands	22.1	10.6	-7.7	0.1	0.0	0.0	0.1	0.1	0.0
New Zealand	–	–	–	–	–	–	–	–	–
Norway	–	0.0	0.1	–	–	0.0	–	–	–
Sweden	22.8	120.8	-17.0	4.1	0.0	0.0	–	–	0.0
Switzerland	-24.8	-28.6	-19.3	–	–	–	–	–	–
United Kingdom	200.4	66.3	55.2	231.0	–	–	–	–	–
United States	30.0	-7.0	-12.0	-5.0	–	–	–	–	–
TOTAL	628.0	1899.3	849.3	-95.9	7.1	-0.4	20.6	20.9	12.3
MULTILATERAL									
AF.D.F.	–	–	–	–	–	–	–	–	–
AF.D.B.	–	–	–	–	–	–	–	–	–
AS.D.B	–	–	–	–	–	–	–	–	–
CAR.D.B.	–	–	–	–	–	–	–	–	–
E.E.C.	–	–	–	–	–	–	–	–	–
IBRD	-5.2	-5.5	-6.0	-7.3	–	–	–	–	–
IDA	–	–	–	–	–	–	–	–	–
I.D.B.	–	–	–	–	–	–	–	–	–
IFAD	–	–	–	–	–	–	–	–	–
I.F.C.	–	–	–	–	–	–	–	–	–
IMF TRUST FUND	–	–	–	–	–	–	–	–	–
U.N. AGENCIES	–	–	–	–	–	–	–	–	–
UNDP	2.0	1.4	1.1	3.7	2.0	1.4	1.1	3.7	2.0
UNTA	0.2	0.1	0.6	0.6	0.2	0.1	0.6	0.6	0.2
UNICEF	–	–	–	–	–	–	–	–	–
UNRWA	–	–	–	–	–	–	–	–	–
WFP	0.0	–	–	–	0.0	–	–	–	0.0
UNHCR	–	–	–	–	–	–	–	–	–
Other Multilateral	0.2	0.0	0.1	0.1	0.2	0.0	0.1	0.1	0.2
Arab OPEC Agencies	22.4	67.3	-20.0	38.2	5.3	4.8	3.9	7.9	5.3
TOTAL	19.6	63.2	-24.3	35.3	7.6	6.3	5.7	12.3	7.6
OPEC COUNTRIES	2.8	-1.9	99.7	-1.3	-1.8	-1.9	-0.3	0.2	0.1
E.E.C.+ MEMBERS	913.4	1846.6	842.6	-142.7	3.5	3.7	5.1	5.0	3.5
TOTAL	650.3	1960.7	924.6	-61.9	12.9	4.0	26.0	33.3	20.0

ODA LOANS GROSS / ODA LOANS NET / GRANTS

	1983	1984	1985	1986	1983	1984	1985	1986	1983
ODA LOANS GROSS					**ODA LOANS NET**				**GRANTS**
DAC COUNTRIES									
Australia	–	–	–	–	–	–	–	–	–
Austria	–	–	0.3	–	–	–	0.3	0.0	0.6
Belgium	–	–	–	–	–	–	–	–	0.3
Canada	–	–	–	–	–	–	–	–	0.3
Denmark	–	–	–	–	–	–	–	–	–
Finland	–	–	–	–	–	–	–	–	0.1
France	–	–	–	–	–	–	–	–	2.5
Germany, Fed. Rep.	–	–	–	–	–	–	–	–	0.5
Ireland	–	–	–	–	–	–	–	–	–
Italy	–	–	–	–	–	–	–	–	0.2
Japan	6.7	–	21.9	21.9	1.5	-6.8	13.4	13.5	1.1
Netherlands	–	–	–	–	–	–	–	–	0.0
New Zealand	–	–	–	–	–	–	–	–	–
Norway	–	–	–	–	–	–	–	–	–
Sweden	–	–	–	–	–	–	–	–	0.0
Switzerland	–	–	–	–	–	–	–	–	–
United Kingdom	–	–	–	–	–	–	–	–	–
United States	–	–	–	–	–	–	–	–	–
TOTAL	6.7	–	22.2	21.9	1.5	-6.8	13.7	13.5	5.6
MULTILATERAL	5.3	5.1	3.2	7.4	5.3	4.8	2.8	6.7	2.3
OPEC COUNTRIES	–	–	–	–	-1.9	-1.9	-0.4	–	0.1
E.E.C.+ MEMBERS	–	–	–	–	–	–	–	–	3.5
TOTAL	11.9	5.1	25.4	29.2	4.9	-3.9	16.1	20.2	8.1

TOTAL OFFICIAL GROSS / TOTAL OFFICIAL NET / TOTAL OOF GROSS

	1983	1984	1985	1986	1983	1984	1985	1986	1983
TOTAL OFFICIAL GROSS					**TOTAL OFFICIAL NET**				**TOTAL OOF GROSS**
DAC COUNTRIES									
Australia	–	–	–	–	–	–	–	–	–
Austria	0.6	0.5	0.8	0.6	0.6	0.5	0.8	0.6	–
Belgium	0.3	0.1	0.0	0.0	0.3	0.1	0.0	0.0	–
Canada	0.3	0.0	–	–	0.3	0.0	–	–	–
Denmark	–	–	–	–	–	–	–	–	–
Finland	0.1	0.1	0.1	0.1	0.1	0.1	0.1	0.1	–
France	2.5	2.7	2.6	3.2	2.5	2.7	2.6	3.2	–
Germany, Fed. Rep.	0.9	0.5	1.5	3.8	0.9	0.3	1.5	3.8	0.3
Ireland	–	–	–	–	–	–	–	–	–
Italy	0.2	0.3	1.8	0.6	0.2	0.3	1.8	0.6	–
Japan	7.7	2.2	23.2	23.6	2.6	-4.6	14.7	15.2	–
Netherlands	0.0	0.0	0.1	0.1	0.0	0.0	0.1	0.1	–
New Zealand	–	–	–	–	–	–	–	–	–
Norway	–	0.0	–	–	–	0.0	–	–	–
Sweden	0.0	0.0	11.0	–	0.0	0.0	11.0	–	–
Switzerland	–	–	–	–	–	–	–	–	–
United Kingdom	–	–	–	–	–	–	–	–	–
United States	30.0	4.0	–	7.0	30.0	-7.0	-12.0	-5.0	30.0
TOTAL	42.6	10.4	41.0	38.9	37.5	-7.6	20.5	18.5	30.3
MULTILATERAL	24.7	77.5	53.4	71.7	19.6	63.2	-24.3	35.3	17.1
OPEC COUNTRIES	4.7	0.0	100.0	0.2	2.8	-1.9	99.7	-1.3	4.6
E.E.C.+ MEMBERS	3.8	3.7	6.0	7.7	3.8	3.4	6.0	7.7	0.3
TOTAL	72.0	87.9	194.4	110.8	59.8	53.7	95.9	52.5	52.1

ODA COMMITMENTS

	1984	1985	1986	1983	1984	1985	1986
Australia	–	–	–	–	–	–	–
Austria	0.5	0.8	0.6	0.6	0.5	0.8	–
Belgium	0.1	0.0	0.0	–	–	–	0.0
Canada	0.0	–	–	0.4	0.1	–	–
Denmark	–	–	–	–	–	–	–
Finland	0.1	0.1	0.1	0.1	0.1	0.0	–
France	2.7	2.6	3.2	2.5	2.7	2.6	3.2
Germany, Fed. Rep.	0.5	0.6	1.1	0.5	0.5	0.6	1.1
Ireland	–	–	–	–	–	–	–
Italy	0.3	1.8	0.6	0.3	0.4	2.1	1.0
Japan	2.2	23.2	23.6	7.8	24.2	60.7	2.0
Netherlands	0.0	0.1	0.1	0.0	0.0	0.1	0.1
New Zealand	0.0	–	–	–	–	–	–
Norway	0.0	–	–	–	0.0	–	–
Sweden	–	–	–	–	–	–	–
Switzerland	–	–	–	–	–	–	–
TOTAL	6.4	29.1	29.3	12.2	28.5	66.9	7.3
	–	–	–	–	–	–	–
	–	–	–	–	–	–	–
	–	–	–	–	–	–	–
	–	–	–	–	–	–	–
	–	–	–	–	–	–	–
	–	–	–	–	–	–	–
	–	–	–	2.3	1.5	1.8	4.4
	1.4	1.1	3.7	–	–	–	–
	0.1	0.6	0.6	–	–	–	–
	–	–	–	–	–	–	–
	0.0	0.1	0.1	–	–	–	–
	5.1	4.4	8.6	11.7	10.0	–	0.7
	6.6	6.1	13.0	14.0	11.5	1.8	5.1
	0.0	0.0	0.2	0.1	–	–	0.2
	3.7	5.1	5.0	3.3	3.7	5.3	5.4
TOTAL	**13.1**	**35.2**	**42.4**	**26.4**	**40.0**	**68.6**	**12.5**

TECH. COOP. GRANTS

	1984	1985	1986	1983	1984	1985	1986
Australia	–	–	–	–	–	–	–
Austria	0.5	0.5	0.6	0.5	–	–	–
Belgium	0.1	0.0	0.0	0.0	0.0	0.0	–
Canada	0.0	–	–	–	–	–	–
Denmark	–	–	–	–	–	–	–
Finland	0.1	0.1	0.1	0.0	0.0	0.0	0.0
France	2.7	2.6	3.2	2.5	2.7	2.6	3.2
Germany, Fed. Rep.	0.5	0.6	1.1	0.5	0.5	0.5	0.9
Ireland	–	–	–	–	–	–	–
Italy	0.3	1.8	0.6	0.2	0.3	0.5	0.4
Japan	2.2	1.3	1.8	1.1	2.2	1.3	1.8
Netherlands	0.0	0.1	0.1	0.0	0.0	0.0	0.1
New Zealand	0.0	–	–	–	–	–	–
Norway	0.0	–	–	0.0	0.0	–	–
Sweden	–	–	–	–	–	–	–
Switzerland	–	–	–	–	–	–	–
TOTAL	6.4	6.9	7.4	4.8	5.8	5.0	6.4
	1.5	2.9	5.6	2.3	1.5	1.8	4.4
	0.0	0.0	0.2	–	–	–	–
	3.7	5.1	5.0	3.3	3.6	3.7	4.6
TOTAL	**7.9**	**9.9**	**13.2**	**7.2**	**7.3**	**6.7**	**10.8**

TOTAL OOF NET

	1984	1985	1986	1983	1984	1985	1986
	–	–	–	–	–	–	–
	–	–	–	–	–	–	–
	–	–	–	–	–	–	–
	–	–	–	–	–	–	–
	–	–	–	–	–	–	–
	–	–	–	–	–	–	–
	–	0.9	2.7	0.3	-0.3	0.9	2.7
	–	–	–	–	–	–	–
	–	–	–	–	–	–	–
	–	–	–	–	–	–	–
	–	–	–	–	–	–	–
	–	–	–	–	–	–	–
	–	11.0	–	–	–	11.0	–
	–	–	–	–	–	–	–
	4.0	–	7.0	30.0	-7.0	-12.0	-5.0
	4.0	11.9	9.7	30.3	-7.3	-0.1	-2.3
	70.9	47.3	58.7	12.0	56.9	-30.0	23.0
	–	100.0	–	4.6	–	100.0	-1.4
	–	0.9	2.7	0.3	-0.3	0.9	2.7
TOTAL	**74.9**	**159.2**	**68.4**	**46.9**	**49.7**	**69.9**	**19.2**

ODA COMMITMENTS : LOANS

DAC COUNTRIES

	1983	1984	1985	1986
Australia	–	–	–	–
Austria	–	–	0.3	–
Belgium	–	–	–	–
Canada	–	–	–	–
Denmark	–	–	–	–
Finland	–	–	–	–
France	–	–	–	–
Germany, Fed. Rep.	–	–	–	–
Ireland	–	–	–	–
Italy	–	–	–	–
Japan	6.7	22.0	59.3	–
Netherlands	–	–	–	–
New Zealand	–	–	–	–
Norway	–	–	–	–
Sweden	–	–	–	–
Switzerland	–	–	–	–
United Kingdom	–	–	–	–
United States	–	–	–	–
TOTAL	*6.7*	*22.0*	*59.6*	*–*
MULTILATERAL	*10.5*	*10.0*	*–*	*–*
OPEC COUNTRIES	*–*	*–*	*–*	*–*
E.E.C.+ MEMBERS	*–*	*–*	*–*	*–*
TOTAL	**17.2**	**32.0**	**59.6**	**–**

GRANT ELEMENT OF ODA

DAC COUNTRIES

	1983	1984	1985	1986
Australia	–	–	–	–
Austria	100.0	100.0	72.5	–
Belgium	–	–	–	100.0
Canada	100.0	100.0	–	–
Denmark	–	–	–	–
Finland	100.0	100.0	100.0	–
France	100.0	100.0	100.0	100.0
Germany, Fed. Rep.	100.0	100.0	100.0	100.0
Ireland	–	–	–	–
Italy	100.0	100.0	100.0	100.0
Japan	100.0	49.9	46.2	100.0
Netherlands	100.0	100.0	100.0	100.0
New Zealand	–	–	–	–
Norway	–	–	–	–
Sweden	–	100.0	–	–
Switzerland	–	–	–	–
United Kingdom	–	–	–	–
United States	–	–	–	–
TOTAL	*100.0*	*57.5*	*50.8*	*100.0*
MULTILATERAL	*53.7*	*46.1*	*100.0*	*100.0*
OPEC COUNTRIES	*100.0*	*–*	*–*	*100.0*
E.E.C.+ MEMBERS	*100.0*	*100.0*	*100.0*	*100.0*
TOTAL	**67.0**	**54.2**	**52.0**	**100.0**

OTHER AGGREGATES

COMMITMENTS: ALL SOURCES

	1983	1984	1985	1986
TOTAL BILATERAL	872.8	2144.7	389.9	7.5
of which				
OPEC	405.1	100.0	100.0	0.2
CMEA	405.0	2016.0	200.0	–
TOTAL MULTILATERAL	88.4	82.5	36.1	80.5
TOTAL BIL.& MULTIL.	961.2	2227.2	425.9	88.0
of which				
ODA Grants	9.2	8.0	9.0	12.5
ODA Loans	17.2	2032.0	59.6	–

DISBURSEMENTS:

DAC COUNTRIES COMBINED

	1983	1984	1985	1986
OFFICIAL & PRIVATE				
GROSS:				
Contractual Lending	1593.4	2417.9	1930.2	1202.8
Export Credits Total	1586.4	2417.9	1907.2	1178.3
Export Credits Private	1556.4	2413.9	1896.2	1171.3
NET:				
Contractual Lending	475.5	1532.0	671.7	-295.7
Export Credits Total	473.6	1539.1	657.1	-311.8
PRIVATE SECTOR NET	590.5	1907.0	828.8	-114.5
Direct Investment	1.5	-4.7	0.4	2.0
Portfolio Investment	145.4	365.6	170.2	190.4
Export Credits	443.6	1546.1	658.1	-306.8

MARKET BORROWING:

CHANGE IN CLAIMS

	1983	1984	1985	1986
Banks	–	1771.0	1236.0	1321.0

MEMORANDUM ITEM:

	1983	1984	1985	1986
CMEA Countr.(Gross)	22.0	18.0	15.0	19.0

TOTAL RECEIPTS NET

DAC COUNTRIES	1983	1984	1985	1986
Australia	1.0	–	0.0	0.0
Austria	0.1	-0.8	0.1	0.1
Belgium	10.7	34.3	13.9	6.2
Canada	-7.0	-18.5	-18.8	-17.4
Denmark	-1.7	-0.4	3.8	0.9
Finland	-0.1	-0.1	-0.1	0.0
France	30.2	-6.5	3.7	7.1
Germany, Fed. Rep.	80.6	90.8	72.2	61.3
Ireland	–	–	–	–
Italy	22.0	-4.0	4.0	16.6
Japan	0.1	7.2	-0.8	-2.4
Netherlands	-22.4	-1.9	-22.3	-6.9
New Zealand	–	–	–	–
Norway		0.1		0.1
Sweden	22.6	0.2	-3.0	-4.9
Switzerland	13.6	13.0	26.1	0.6
United Kingdom	13.0	23.7	13.9	2.6
United States	2019.0	1848.0	2470.0	2232.0
TOTAL	2181.8	1985.1	2562.6	2296.1
MULTILATERAL				
AF.D.F.	–	–	–	–
AF.D.B.	–	–	–	–
AS.D.B	–	–	–	–
CAR.D.B.	–	–	–	–
E.E.C.	-1.8	12.3	0.1	13.2
IBRD	-10.7	-11.1	-13.3	-13.1
IDA	–	–	–	–
I.D.B.	–	–	–	–
IFAD	–	–	–	–
I.F.C.	-1.0	-1.0	-0.9	-0.8
IMF TRUST FUND	–	–	–	–
U.N. AGENCIES	–	–	–	–
UNDP	–	–	–	–
UNTA	–	–	–	–
UNICEF	–	–	–	–
UNRWA	–	–	–	–
WFP	–	–	–	–
UNHCR	–	–	–	–
Other Multilateral	–	–	–	–
Arab OPEC Agencies	–	–	–	–
TOTAL	-13.5	0.2	-14.1	-0.7
OPEC COUNTRIES	–	–	–	–
E.E.C.+ MEMBERS	130.5	148.2	89.2	101.1
TOTAL	2168.3	1985.3	2548.5	2295.4

TOTAL ODA NET

DAC COUNTRIES	1983	1984	1985	1986
Australia	–	–	0.0	0.0
Austria	0.1	0.1	0.1	0.1
Belgium	0.1	0.0	0.1	0.0
Canada	–	0.0	0.1	0.2
Denmark	–	–	–	–
Finland	–	–	–	0.0
France	2.1	2.0	2.1	3.1
Germany, Fed. Rep.	49.2	53.8	25.8	34.5
Ireland	–	–	–	–
Italy	0.2	0.1	1.3	0.3
Japan	0.1	0.2	0.2	0.3
Netherlands	0.7	1.2	0.2	3.8
New Zealand	–	–	–	–
Norway	–	0.0	–	–
Sweden	0.1	0.1	0.0	–
Switzerland	0.4	0.4	0.4	0.6
United Kingdom	–	–	–	–
United States	1292.0	1198.0	1948.0	1894.0
TOTAL	1345.0	1255.9	1978.3	1937.0
MULTILATERAL				
AF.D.F.	–	–	–	–
AF.D.B.	–	–	–	–
AS.D.B	–	–	–	–
CAR.D.B.	–	–	–	–
E.E.C.	–	–	0.1	0.1
IBRD	–	–	–	–
IDA	–	–	–	–
I.D.B.	–	–	–	–
IFAD	–	–	–	–
I.F.C.	–	–	–	–
IMF TRUST FUND	–	–	–	–
U.N. AGENCIES	–	–	–	–
UNDP	–	–	–	–
UNTA	–	–	–	–
UNICEF	–	–	–	–
UNRWA	–	–	–	–
WFP	–	–	–	–
UNHCR	–	–	–	–
Other Multilateral	–	–	–	–
Arab OPEC Agencies	–	–	–	–
TOTAL	–	–	0.1	0.1
OPEC COUNTRIES	–	–	–	–
E.E.C.+ MEMBERS	52.3	57.1	29.6	41.8
TOTAL	1345.0	1255.9	1978.4	1937.1

TOTAL ODA GROSS

	1983
Australia	–
Austria	0.1
Belgium	0.1
Canada	–
Denmark	–
Finland	–
France	2.1
Germany, Fed. Rep.	81.0
Ireland	–
Italy	0.2
Japan	0.1
Netherlands	0.7
New Zealand	–
Norway	–
Sweden	0.1
Switzerland	0.4
United Kingdom	–
United States	1314.0
TOTAL	1398.8
AF.D.F.	–
AF.D.B.	–
AS.D.B	–
CAR.D.B.	–
E.E.C.	–
IBRD	–
IDA	–
I.D.B.	–
IFAD	–
I.F.C.	–
IMF TRUST FUND	–
U.N. AGENCIES	–
UNDP	–
UNTA	–
UNICEF	–
UNRWA	–
WFP	–
UNHCR	–
Other Multilateral	–
Arab OPEC Agencies	–
TOTAL	–
OPEC COUNTRIES	–
E.E.C.+ MEMBERS	84.1
TOTAL	1398.8

ODA LOANS GROSS

DAC COUNTRIES	1983	1984	1985	1986
Australia	–	–	–	–
Austria	–	–	–	–
Belgium	–	–	–	–
Canada	–	–	–	–
Denmark	–	–	–	–
Finland	–	–	–	–
France	–	–	–	–
Germany, Fed. Rep.	72.8	79.7	55.7	78.5
Ireland	–	–	–	–
Italy	–	–	–	–
Japan	–	–	–	–
Netherlands	–	–	–	–
New Zealand	–	–	–	–
Norway	–	–	–	–
Sweden	–	–	–	–
Switzerland	–	–	–	–
United Kingdom	–	–	–	–
United States	–	–	–	–
TOTAL	72.8	79.7	55.7	78.5
MULTILATERAL	–	–	–	–
OPEC COUNTRIES				
E.E.C.+ MEMBERS	72.8	79.7	55.7	78.5
TOTAL	72.8	79.7	55.7	78.5

ODA LOANS NET

DAC COUNTRIES	1983	1984	1985	1986
Australia	–	–	–	–
Austria	–	–	–	–
Belgium	–	–	–	–
Canada	–	–	–	–
Denmark	–	–	–	–
Finland	–	–	–	–
France	–	–	–	–
Germany, Fed. Rep.	41.0	44.5	16.1	17.8
Ireland	–	–	–	–
Italy	–	–	–	–
Japan	–	–	–	–
Netherlands	–	–	–	–
New Zealand	–	–	–	–
Norway	–	–	–	–
Sweden	–	–	–	–
Switzerland	–	–	–	–
United Kingdom	–	–	–	–
United States	-22.0	-20.0	-24.0	-16.0
TOTAL	19.0	24.5	-7.9	1.8
MULTILATERAL	–	–	–	–
OPEC COUNTRIES				
E.E.C.+ MEMBERS	41.0	44.5	16.1	17.8
TOTAL	19.0	24.5	-7.9	1.8

GRANTS

	1983
Australia	–
Austria	0.1
Belgium	0.1
Canada	–
Denmark	–
Finland	–
France	2.1
Germany, Fed. Rep.	8.2
Ireland	–
Italy	0.2
Japan	0.1
Netherlands	0.7
New Zealand	–
Norway	–
Sweden	0.1
Switzerland	0.4
United Kingdom	–
United States	1314.0
TOTAL	1326.0
MULTILATERAL	–
OPEC COUNTRIES	–
E.E.C.+ MEMBERS	11.3
TOTAL	1326.0

TOTAL OFFICIAL GROSS

DAC COUNTRIES	1983	1984	1985	1986
Australia	–	–	0.0	0.0
Austria	0.1	0.1	0.1	0.1
Belgium	0.1	0.6	0.6	0.0
Canada	12.8	5.5	6.1	4.8
Denmark	–	–	–	–
Finland	–	–	–	0.0
France	2.1	2.0	2.1	3.1
Germany, Fed. Rep.	84.3	93.7	72.3	102.8
Ireland	–	–	–	–
Italy	36.0	14.7	23.1	27.6
Japan	0.1	0.2	0.2	0.3
Netherlands	0.7	1.2	0.2	3.8
New Zealand	–	–	–	–
Norway		0.0	–	–
Sweden	27.5	9.1	8.0	5.2
Switzerland	0.4	0.4	0.4	0.6
United Kingdom	–	–	–	–
United States	1395.0	1280.0	1983.0	1917.0
TOTAL	1559.1	1407.6	2096.2	2065.4
MULTILATERAL	–	15.9	0.1	19.8
OPEC COUNTRIES	–	–	–	–
E.E.C.+ MEMBERS	123.2	128.1	98.4	157.1
TOTAL	1559.1	1423.5	2096.2	2085.1

TOTAL OFFICIAL NET

DAC COUNTRIES	1983	1984	1985	1986
Australia	–	–	0.0	0.0
Austria	0.1	0.1	0.1	0.1
Belgium	0.1	0.6	0.6	0.0
Canada	-7.0	-18.5	-18.8	-17.4
Denmark	–	–	–	–
Finland	–	–	–	0.0
France	2.1	2.0	2.1	3.1
Germany, Fed. Rep.	51.0	56.1	29.5	36.1
Ireland	–	–	–	–
Italy	16.7	-11.1	0.0	0.7
Japan	0.1	0.2	0.2	0.3
Netherlands	0.7	1.2	0.2	3.8
New Zealand	–	–	–	–
Norway		0.0	–	–
Sweden	23.5	1.5	-1.0	-7.2
Switzerland	0.4	0.4	0.4	0.6
United Kingdom	–	–	–	–
United States	1336.0	1219.0	1918.0	1863.0
TOTAL	1423.8	1251.5	1931.3	1883.2
MULTILATERAL	-13.5	0.2	-14.1	-0.7
OPEC COUNTRIES	–	–	–	–
E.E.C.+ MEMBERS	68.8	61.0	32.6	56.8
TOTAL	1410.3	1251.7	1917.2	1882.5

TOTAL OOF GROSS

	1983
Australia	–
Austria	–
Belgium	–
Canada	12.8
Denmark	–
Finland	–
France	–
Germany, Fed. Rep.	3.3
Ireland	–
Italy	35.8
Japan	–
Netherlands	–
New Zealand	–
Norway	–
Sweden	27.4
Switzerland	–
United Kingdom	–
United States	81.0
TOTAL	160.3
MULTILATERAL	–
OPEC COUNTRIES	–
E.E.C.+ MEMBERS	39.1
TOTAL	160.3

1984	1985	1986	1983	1984	1985	1986

ODA COMMITMENTS

1984	1985	1986	1983	1984	1985	1986
–	0.0	0.0	–	–	0.0	0.0
0.1	0.1	0.1	0.1	0.1	0.1	–
0.0	0.1	0.0	–	–	–	0.0
0.0	0.1	0.2	–	0.0	0.5	0.3
–	–	0.0	–	–	–	–
–	–	0.0	–	–	–	0.0
2.0	2.1	3.1	2.1	2.0	2.1	3.1
88.9	65.3	95.2	41.1	100.0	53.5	89.1
–	–	–	–	–	–	–
0.1	1.3	0.3	0.2	0.1	1.3	0.3
0.2	0.2	0.3	0.2	0.2	0.2	0.4
1.2	0.2	3.8	0.5	1.1	0.3	3.8
0.0	–	–	–	0.1	–	–
0.1	0.0	–	–	–	–	–
0.4	0.4	0.6	0.3	0.4	0.3	0.5
–	–	–	–	–	–	–
1218.0	1972.0	1910.0	1317.3	1214.0	1977.6	1911.2
1311.0	*2041.9*	*2013.8*	*1361.8*	*1317.9*	*2035.9*	*2008.8*
–	–	–	–	–	–	–
–	–	–	–	–	–	–
–	–	–	–	–	–	–
–	0.1	0.1	–	–	–	0.7
–	–	–	–	–	–	–
–	–	–	–	–	–	–
–	–	–	–	–	–	–
–	–	–	–	–	–	–
–	–	–	–	–	–	–
–	–	–	–	–	–	–
–	–	–	–	–	–	–
–	–	–	–	–	–	–
–	0.1	0.1	–	–	–	0.7
–	–	–	–	–	–	–
92.3	69.1	102.6	43.9	103.2	57.3	97.1
1311.0	*2041.9*	*2013.9*	*1361.8*	*1317.9*	*2035.9*	*2009.5*

TECH. COOP. GRANTS

1984	1985	1986	1983	1984	1985	1986
–	0.0	0.0	–	–	0.0	–
0.1	0.1	0.1	0.1	–	0.1	–
0.0	0.1	0.0	0.0	–	0.0	–
0.0	0.1	0.2	–	–	–	–
–	–	0.0	–	–	–	–
2.0	2.1	3.1	2.1	2.0	2.1	3.1
9.2	9.7	16.7	8.2	9.2	9.7	16.3
–	–	–	–	–	–	–
0.1	1.3	0.3	0.2	0.1	1.3	0.2
0.2	0.2	0.3	0.1	0.2	0.2	0.3
1.2	0.2	3.8	0.7	1.1	0.2	3.8
0.0	–	–	–	–	–	–
0.1	0.0	–	–	0.0	–	–
0.4	0.4	0.6	0.0	0.0	0.0	0.0
–	–	–	–	–	–	–
1218.0	1972.0	1910.0	–	–	–	–
1231.4	*1986.2*	*1935.2*	*11.6*	*12.7*	*13.6*	*23.8*
–	0.1	0.1	–	–	–	–
–	–	–	–	–	–	–
12.6	13.5	24.1	11.2	12.5	13.4	23.5
1231.4	*1986.3*	*1935.3*	*11.6*	*12.7*	*13.6*	*23.8*

TOTAL OOF NET

1984	1985	1986	1983	1984	1985	1986
–	–	–	–	–	–	–
0.6	0.6	–	–	0.6	0.6	–
5.5	6.0	4.6	-7.0	-18.5	-19.0	-17.6
–	–	–	–	–	–	–
–	–	–	–	–	–	–
4.8	7.0	7.6	1.8	2.3	3.7	1.6
–	–	–	–	–	–	–
14.6	21.8	27.3	16.5	-11.2	-1.3	0.3
–	–	–	–	–	–	–
–	–	–	–	–	–	–
–	–	–	–	–	–	–
9.1	8.0	5.2	23.5	1.4	-1.0	-7.2
62.0	11.0	7.0	44.0	21.0	-30.0	-31.0
96.5	*54.3*	*51.6*	*78.8*	*-4.4*	*-47.0*	*-53.8*
15.9	–	*19.7*	*-13.5*	*0.2*	*-14.2*	*-0.8*
–	–	–	–	–	–	–
35.9	*29.3*	*54.5*	*16.5*	*3.9*	*3.0*	*15.0*
112.4	**54.3**	**71.3**	**65.3**	**-4.2**	**-61.2**	**-54.6**

ODA COMMITMENTS : LOANS

DAC COUNTRIES

	1983	1984	1985	1986
Australia	–	–	–	–
Austria	–	–	–	–
Belgium	–	–	–	–
Canada	–	–	–	–
Denmark	–	–	–	–
Finland	–	–	–	–
France	–	–	–	–
Germany, Fed. Rep.	31.3	91.4	42.5	71.4
Ireland	–	–	–	–
Italy	–	–	–	–
Japan	–	–	–	–
Netherlands	–	–	–	–
New Zealand	–	–	–	–
Norway	–	–	–	–
Sweden	–	–	–	–
Switzerland	–	–	–	–
United Kingdom	–	–	–	–
United States	–	–	–	–
TOTAL	*31.3*	*91.4*	*42.5*	*71.4*
MULTILATERAL	–	–	–	–
OPEC COUNTRIES				
E.E.C.+ MEMBERS	*31.3*	*91.4*	*42.5*	*71.4*
TOTAL	**31.3**	**91.4**	**42.5**	**71.4**

GRANT ELEMENT OF ODA

DAC COUNTRIES

	1983	1984	1985	1986
Australia	–	–	100.0	100.0
Austria	100.0	100.0	100.0	–
Belgium	–	–	–	100.0
Canada	–	100.0	100.0	100.0
Denmark	–	–	–	100.0
Finland	–	–	–	100.0
France	100.0	100.0	100.0	100.0
Germany, Fed. Rep.	51.7	42.0	49.8	49.3
Ireland	–	–	–	–
Italy	100.0	100.0	100.0	100.0
Japan	100.0	100.0	100.0	100.0
Netherlands	100.0	100.0	100.0	100.0
New Zealand	–	–	–	–
Norway	–	100.0	–	–
Sweden	–	–	–	–
Switzerland	100.0	100.0	100.0	100.0
United Kingdom	–	–	–	–
United States	100.0	100.0	100.0	100.0
TOTAL	*98.5*	*95.6*	*98.7*	*97.7*
MULTILATERAL	–	–	–	100.0
OPEC COUNTRIES	–	–	–	–
E.E.C.+ MEMBERS	*54.7*	*43.8*	*53.1*	*53.4*
TOTAL	**98.5**	**95.6**	**98.7**	**97.7**

OTHER AGGREGATES

COMMITMENTS: ALL SOURCES

	1983	1984	1985	1986
TOTAL BILATERAL	1393.6	1351.9	2065.6	2033.6
of which				
OPEC	–	–	–	–
CMEA	–	–	–	–
TOTAL MULTILATERAL	–	15.8	–	20.4
TOTAL BIL.& MULTIL.	1393.6	1367.7	2065.6	2054.0
of which				
ODA Grants	1330.5	1226.5	1993.5	1938.1
ODA Loans	31.3	91.4	42.5	71.4

DISBURSEMENTS:
DAC COUNTRIES COMBINED

	1983	1984	1985	1986
OFFICIAL & PRIVATE				
GROSS:				
Contractual Lending	421.2	387.7	312.3	234.8
Export Credits Total	348.5	308.1	256.6	156.3
Export Credits Private	188.2	212.1	202.9	104.7
NET:				
Contractual Lending	164.6	105.2	-12.0	-63.0
Export Credits Total	145.6	80.6	-4.1	-64.8
PRIVATE SECTOR NET	758.0	733.6	631.3	412.9
Direct Investment	-73.4	164.9	134.8	-61.5
Portfolio Investment	764.6	483.1	453.0	485.3
Export Credits	66.8	85.6	43.5	-11.0

MARKET BORROWING:
CHANGE IN CLAIMS

	1983	1984	1985	1986
Banks	–	-676.0	85.0	-593.0

MEMORANDUM ITEM:

	1983	1984	1985	1986
CMEA Countr.(Gross)	–	–	–	–

TOTAL RECEIPTS NET / TOTAL ODA NET / TOTAL ODA GROSS

	TOTAL RECEIPTS NET 1983	1984	1985	1986	TOTAL ODA NET 1983	1984	1985	1986	TOTAL ODA GROSS 1983
DAC COUNTRIES									
Australia	0.4	0.4	0.1	0.2	0.4	0.4	0.1	0.2	0.4
Austria	0.0	–	–	0.0	0.0	–	–	0.0	0.0
Belgium	2.7	1.7	-0.4	-0.8	1.0	0.2	0.1	0.2	1.0
Canada	13.1	18.2	16.7	23.5	16.1	18.2	15.2	25.5	16.5
Denmark	–	0.0	–	0.0	–	–	–	–	–
Finland	0.1	0.2	1.1	2.4	0.1	0.2	0.2	0.1	0.1
France	10.9	6.7	5.8	-1.3	0.3	2.8	0.9	0.6	0.3
Germany, Fed. Rep.	4.5	5.7	3.7	7.0	4.1	5.6	3.7	7.0	4.1
Ireland	–	–	–	–	–	–	–	–	–
Italy	2.7	20.2	3.9	2.6	2.7	5.9	3.3	4.3	2.7
Japan	7.3	15.8	25.5	14.2	6.2	14.1	24.7	10.5	6.2
Netherlands	6.8	7.1	1.7	3.9	7.9	7.1	2.7	3.4	7.9
New Zealand	0.0	0.0	–	0.0	0.0	0.0	–	0.0	0.0
Norway	3.0	20.5	17.9	18.8	2.9	1.7	2.3	2.3	2.9
Sweden	-0.1	0.2	-0.7	-0.9	0.9	0.2	0.3	0.0	0.9
Switzerland	0.9	0.0	0.0	0.0	0.0	0.0	0.0	0.0	0.0
United Kingdom	18.3	20.6	4.1	-3.1	4.5	0.6	3.9	2.5	6.9
United States	151.0	199.0	58.0	-6.0	109.0	99.0	101.0	104.0	111.0
TOTAL	*221.4*	*316.4*	*137.3*	*60.5*	*156.2*	*156.0*	*158.2*	*160.5*	*161.0*
MULTILATERAL									
AF.D.F.	–	–	–	–	–	–	–	–	–
AF.D.B.	–	–	–	–	–	–	–	–	–
AS.D.B	–	–	–	–	–	–	–	–	–
CAR.D.B.	9.4	4.2	9.7	4.8	7.0	0.0	0.1	0.6	7.0
E.E.C.	3.1	5.1	4.6	6.2	3.1	5.1	3.3	5.8	3.1
IBRD	46.5	30.4	56.9	-7.0	–	–	–	–	–
IDA	–	–	–	–	–	–	–	–	–
I.D.B.	25.4	18.8	34.9	31.7	9.2	4.7	2.7	2.7	10.8
IFAD	0.0	1.7	1.0	3.0	0.0	1.7	1.0	3.0	0.0
I.F.C.	1.3	-0.2	-0.7	-0.7	–	–	–	–	–
IMF TRUST FUND	–	–	–	–	–	–	–	–	–
U.N. AGENCIES	–	–	–	–	–	–	–	–	–
UNDP	3.9	1.5	2.2	2.5	3.9	1.5	2.2	2.5	3.9
UNTA	0.6	0.5	0.8	0.6	0.6	0.5	0.8	0.6	0.6
UNICEF	0.3	0.1	0.1	0.2	0.3	0.1	0.1	0.2	0.3
UNRWA	–	–	–	–	–	–	–	–	–
WFP	0.2	0.2	1.5	0.6	0.2	0.2	1.5	0.6	0.2
UNHCR	0.1	0.0	0.0	–	0.1	0.0	0.0	–	0.1
Other Multilateral	0.7	0.5	1.1	0.9	0.7	0.5	1.1	0.9	0.7
Arab OPEC Agencies	-1.6	-0.1	-5.6	-2.3	-0.5	-0.1	-1.7	-0.4	0.0
TOTAL	*89.8*	*62.7*	*106.4*	*40.5*	*24.5*	*14.3*	*11.0*	*16.5*	*26.7*
OPEC COUNTRIES	26.7	-9.2	21.7	4.3	–	–	–	0.1	–
E.E.C.+ MEMBERS	*48.9*	*67.1*	*23.3*	*14.6*	*23.6*	*27.2*	*17.8*	*23.8*	*26.1*
TOTAL	**337.9**	**369.8**	**265.4**	**105.3**	**180.7**	**170.3**	**169.2**	**177.1**	**187.7**

ODA LOANS GROSS / ODA LOANS NET / GRANTS

	ODA LOANS GROSS 1983	1984	1985	1986	ODA LOANS NET 1983	1984	1985	1986	GRANTS 1983
DAC COUNTRIES									
Australia	–	–	–	–	–	–	–	–	0.4
Austria	–	–	–	–	–	–	–	–	0.0
Belgium	1.0	0.1	–	–	1.0	0.1	–	–	0.1
Canada	10.9	6.6	7.0	0.3	10.6	6.5	5.6	0.2	5.5
Denmark	–	–	–	–	–	–	–	–	–
Finland	–	–	–	–	–	–	–	–	0.1
France	0.1	2.6	0.8	0.3	0.1	2.6	0.8	0.3	0.2
Germany, Fed. Rep.	2.5	4.5	1.9	4.7	2.5	4.5	1.9	3.4	1.6
Ireland	–	–	–	–	–	–	–	–	–
Italy	2.0	5.6	1.2	0.0	2.0	5.6	1.2	-0.1	0.7
Japan	6.0	13.4	24.2	9.1	6.0	13.4	24.0	8.9	0.2
Netherlands	4.8	3.4	0.6	2.3	4.8	3.2	0.5	1.4	3.1
New Zealand	–	–	–	–	–	–	–	–	0.0
Norway	–	–	–	–	–	–	–	–	2.9
Sweden	–	–	–	–	–	–	–	–	0.9
Switzerland	–	–	–	–	–	–	–	–	0.0
United Kingdom	5.7	3.7	5.9	2.6	3.2	-0.5	3.0	1.1	1.3
United States	104.0	96.0	66.0	47.0	102.0	86.0	55.0	43.0	7.0
TOTAL	*136.9*	*136.0*	*107.5*	*66.2*	*132.1*	*121.5*	*91.9*	*58.2*	*24.1*
MULTILATERAL	*19.3*	*9.6*	*5.2*	*9.3*	*17.1*	*7.3*	*0.8*	*5.8*	*7.4*
OPEC COUNTRIES	–	–	–	0.1	–	–	–	0.1	–
E.E.C.+ MEMBERS	*18.0*	*21.1*	*10.3*	*9.9*	*15.5*	*16.6*	*7.3*	*6.0*	*8.1*
TOTAL	**156.2**	**145.6**	**112.7**	**75.6**	**149.2**	**128.8**	**92.7**	**64.0**	**31.5**

TOTAL OFFICIAL GROSS / TOTAL OFFICIAL NET / TOTAL OOF GROSS

	TOTAL OFFICIAL GROSS 1983	1984	1985	1986	TOTAL OFFICIAL NET 1983	1984	1985	1986	TOTAL OOF GROSS 1983
DAC COUNTRIES									
Australia	0.4	0.4	0.1	0.2	0.4	0.4	0.1	0.2	–
Austria	0.0	–	–	0.0	0.0	–	–	0.0	–
Belgium	1.0	0.2	0.2	0.2	1.0	0.2	0.2	0.2	–
Canada	16.5	18.3	21.6	25.8	13.1	18.2	16.7	23.5	–
Denmark	–	0.0	–	–	–	0.0	–	0.0	–
Finland	0.1	0.2	0.2	0.1	0.1	0.2	0.2	0.1	–
France	0.3	2.8	3.8	0.6	0.3	2.8	3.6	0.5	–
Germany, Fed. Rep.	4.1	5.6	3.7	8.3	4.1	5.6	3.7	7.0	–
Ireland	–	–	–	–	–	–	–	–	–
Italy	2.7	20.7	3.3	4.5	2.7	20.2	2.7	2.6	–
Japan	6.2	14.1	24.9	10.6	5.6	14.1	24.7	10.3	–
Netherlands	7.9	7.4	2.7	4.3	7.9	7.1	2.3	3.1	–
New Zealand	0.0	0.0	–	0.0	0.0	0.0	–	0.0	–
Norway	2.9	1.7	2.3	2.3	2.9	1.7	2.3	2.3	–
Sweden	0.9	0.2	0.3	0.0	0.9	0.2	0.3	0.0	–
Switzerland	0.0	0.0	0.0	0.0	0.0	0.0	0.0	0.0	–
United Kingdom	13.5	20.4	10.4	5.5	10.6	15.2	4.1	2.0	6.6
United States	115.0	173.0	170.0	121.0	109.0	146.0	141.0	114.0	4.0
TOTAL	*171.6*	*265.0*	*243.4*	*183.3*	*158.8*	*232.0*	*201.8*	*165.7*	*10.6*
MULTILATERAL	*108.8*	*86.4*	*137.1*	*82.5*	*89.8*	*62.7*	*106.4*	*40.5*	*82.2*
OPEC COUNTRIES	36.4	–	38.2	17.2	26.7	-9.2	21.7	4.3	36.4
E.E.C.+ MEMBERS	*32.7*	*62.2*	*28.6*	*29.5*	*29.7*	*56.3*	*21.2*	*21.6*	*6.6*
TOTAL	**316.8**	**351.4**	**418.7**	**283.0**	**275.3**	**285.5**	**330.0**	**210.6**	**129.1**

Left panel

1984	1985	1986	1983	1984	1985	1986
ODA COMMITMENTS						
0.4	0.1	0.2	0.2	0.3	0.2	0.0
–	–	0.0	0.0	–	–	–
0.2	0.1	0.2	1.0	0.1	–	0.2
18.3	16.6	25.6	25.9	20.4	57.9	27.4
–	–	–	–	–	–	–
0.2	0.2	0.1	0.0	0.3	–	–
2.8	1.0	0.6	4.2	3.8	0.3	0.6
5.6	3.7	8.3	7.9	3.8	10.9	4.1
–	–	–	–	–	–	–
5.9	3.3	4.5	11.4	2.4	5.0	7.2
14.1	24.9	10.6	43.8	26.0	1.3	1.6
7.4	2.7	4.3	2.6	2.9	0.8	4.8
0.0	–	0.0	–	–	–	–
1.7	2.3	2.3	1.5	2.0	2.0	1.6
0.2	0.3	0.0	–	0.3	–	0.0
0.0	0.0	0.0	0.0	0.0	–	0.0
4.8	6.7	4.0	6.4	4.4	8.1	1.5
109.0	112.0	108.0	105.1	181.1	77.6	105.6
170.6	*173.8*	*168.5*	*210.0*	*247.9*	*163.9*	*154.5*
–	–	–	–	–	–	–
–	–	–	–	–	–	–
0.0	0.1	0.6	3.6	–	4.1	–
5.1	3.3	5.8	7.7	7.5	6.2	10.3
–	–	–	–	–	–	–
6.9	5.4	5.8	20.8	–	14.6	6.7
1.7	1.0	3.0	–	–	–	–
–	–	–	–	–	–	–
–	–	–	5.7	2.9	5.7	4.8
1.5	2.2	2.5	–	–	–	–
0.5	0.8	0.6	–	–	–	–
0.1	0.1	0.2	–	–	–	–
–	–	–	–	–	–	–
0.2	1.5	0.6	–	–	–	–
0.0	0.0	–	–	–	–	–
0.5	1.1	0.9	–	–	–	–
–	–	–	–	–	–	–
16.6	*15.4*	*20.0*	*37.8*	*10.4*	*30.5*	*21.8*
–	–	0.1	–	4.9	–	–
31.7	*20.8*	*27.7*	*41.3*	*24.9*	*31.1*	*28.6*
187.1	**189.2**	**188.7**	**247.8**	**263.2**	**194.4**	**176.4**
TECH. COOP. GRANTS						
0.4	0.1	0.2	0.4	0.4	0.1	0.1
–	–	0.0	0.0	–	–	–
0.0	0.1	0.2	–	–	–	–
11.7	9.6	25.3	0.9	–	1.4	–
–	–	–	–	–	–	–
0.2	0.2	0.1	0.1	0.2	0.1	–
0.2	0.2	0.3	0.2	0.2	0.2	0.2
1.1	1.8	3.6	1.6	1.0	1.8	3.6
–	–	–	–	–	–	–
0.2	2.1	4.5	0.7	0.2	0.9	4.0
0.7	0.7	1.5	0.2	0.7	0.7	1.1
3.9	2.1	1.9	1.5	0.9	1.1	0.8
0.0	–	0.0	0.0	0.0	–	–
1.7	2.3	2.3	0.1	0.1	0.0	0.1
0.2	0.3	0.0	0.2	0.2	0.2	0.0
0.0	0.0	0.0	–	–	–	–
1.1	0.9	1.5	1.3	1.1	0.9	1.1
13.0	46.0	61.0	6.0	7.0	10.0	14.0
34.5	*66.3*	*102.3*	*13.1*	*11.9*	*17.3*	*25.0*
7.0	10.2	10.8	5.5	2.7	4.2	5.5
–	–	–	–	–	–	–
10.6	*10.5*	*17.8*	*5.3*	*3.4*	*4.8*	*11.0*
41.5	**76.5**	**113.1**	**18.6**	**14.6**	**21.4**	**30.5**
TOTAL OOF NET						
–	–	–	–	–	–	–
0.0	0.0	0.0	–	0.0	0.0	0.0
–	5.0	0.2	-3.0	–	1.5	-2.0
0.0	–	–	–	0.0	–	0.0
–	–	–	–	–	–	–
–	2.9	–	–	–	2.7	-0.1
–	–	–	–	–	–	–
14.9	–	–	–	14.3	-0.6	-1.7
–	–	–	-0.5	–	–	-0.1
–	–	–	–	–	-0.4	-0.2
–	–	–	–	–	–	–
–	–	–	–	–	–	–
15.6	3.6	1.5	6.1	14.6	0.3	-0.5
64.0	58.0	13.0	–	47.0	40.0	10.0
94.5	*69.5*	*14.7*	*2.6*	*76.0*	*43.6*	*5.3*
69.8	*121.7*	*62.5*	*65.3*	*48.4*	*95.4*	*24.0*
–	*38.2*	*17.1*	*26.7*	*-9.2*	*21.7*	*4.2*
30.5	*7.8*	*1.9*	*6.1*	*29.0*	*3.4*	*-2.2*
164.3	**229.4**	**94.3**	**94.6**	**115.2**	**160.8**	**33.4**

Right panel

ODA COMMITMENTS : LOANS

DAC COUNTRIES	1983	1984	1985	1986
Australia	–	–	–	–
Austria	–	–	–	–
Belgium	1.0	0.1	–	–
Canada	23.5	–	2.3	–
Denmark	–	–	–	–
Finland	–	–	–	–
France	4.0	3.6	0.1	0.3
Germany, Fed. Rep.	5.9	1.8	6.1	1.0
Ireland	–	–	–	–
Italy	8.8	–	–	1.9
Japan	43.6	25.3	0.4	0.3
Netherlands	–	–	–	2.3
New Zealand	–	–	–	–
Norway	–	–	–	–
Sweden	–	–	–	–
Switzerland	–	–	–	–
United Kingdom	5.2	3.3	7.2	–
United States	93.0	169.3	14.4	43.0
TOTAL	*184.9*	*203.5*	*30.5*	*48.8*
MULTILATERAL	*26.7*	*4.8*	*18.6*	*6.7*
OPEC COUNTRIES	–	*4.9*	–	–
E.E.C.+ MEMBERS	*27.1*	*13.6*	*13.4*	*5.5*
TOTAL	*211.7*	*213.2*	*49.1*	*55.5*

GRANT ELEMENT OF ODA

DAC COUNTRIES	1983	1984	1985	1986
Australia	100.0	100.0	100.0	100.0
Austria	100.0	–	–	–
Belgium	78.8	79.7	–	100.0
Canada	91.0	100.0	97.3	100.0
Denmark	–	–	–	–
Finland	100.0	100.0	–	–
France	100.0	68.6	100.0	100.0
Germany, Fed. Rep.	52.9	70.2	85.9	81.9
Ireland	–	–	–	–
Italy	55.0	100.0	100.0	92.4
Japan	31.6	44.2	76.8	87.5
Netherlands	100.0	100.0	100.0	82.6
New Zealand	–	–	–	–
Norway	100.0	100.0	100.0	100.0
Sweden	–	100.0	–	100.0
Switzerland	100.0	100.0	–	100.0
United Kingdom	41.9	22.0	46.8	100.0
United States	64.5	60.3	91.8	80.2
TOTAL	*60.0*	*61.5*	*91.6*	*84.9*
MULTILATERAL	*82.4*	*79.7*	*82.9*	*91.1*
OPEC COUNTRIES	–	*46.4*	–	–
E.E.C.+ MEMBERS	*63.4*	*57.4*	*80.3*	*92.7*
TOTAL	*62.3*	*62.2*	*90.4*	*85.7*

OTHER AGGREGATES

COMMITMENTS: ALL SOURCES	1983	1984	1985	1986
TOTAL BILATERAL	259.9	392.9	217.4	187.6
of which				
OPEC	19.9	23.3	12.1	–
CMEA	–	–	–	22.0
TOTAL MULTILATERAL	270.9	114.1	49.5	82.4
TOTAL BIL.& MULTIL.	530.9	507.1	266.9	270.0
of which				
ODA Grants	36.2	50.0	145.3	120.9
ODA Loans	211.7	213.2	49.1	55.5

DISBURSEMENTS:

DAC COUNTRIES COMBINED

OFFICIAL & PRIVATE	1983	1984	1985	1986
GROSS:				
Contractual Lending	210.5	345.3	278.6	122.1
Export Credits Total	67.0	135.7	101.6	41.4
Export Credits Private	63.0	114.8	101.6	41.2
NET:				
Contractual Lending	160.6	258.0	164.3	34.0
Export Credits Total	22.4	64.9	11.3	-35.3
PRIVATE SECTOR NET	62.6	84.4	-64.5	-105.2
Direct Investment	0.9	0.7	-105.2	-22.9
Portfolio Investment	35.8	23.2	11.8	-52.9
Export Credits	25.9	60.5	28.8	-29.4

MARKET BORROWING:

CHANGE IN CLAIMS

	1983	1984	1985	1986
Banks	–	39.0	49.0	-86.0

MEMORANDUM ITEM:

	1983	1984	1985	1986
CMEA Countr.(Gross)	–	–	–	–

DISBURSEMENTS, UNLESS OTHERWISE STATED

TOTAL RECEIPTS NET

DAC COUNTRIES	1983	1984	1985	1986
Australia	0.3	0.7	0.1	0.6
Austria	0.2	0.2	0.3	0.2
Belgium	0.4	2.3	3.6	-4.3
Canada	0.5	0.3	0.7	0.7
Denmark	-0.7	0.0	4.5	-1.9
Finland	–	0.2	–	–
France	16.1	9.2	-3.1	38.7
Germany, Fed. Rep.	21.6	8.0	15.0	16.6
Ireland	–	–	–	–
Italy	35.9	-6.1	25.9	7.6
Japan	27.7	115.4	-4.7	29.5
Netherlands	-0.1	0.2	-0.5	1.2
New Zealand	–	–	–	–
Norway	4.5	0.1	-0.2	0.0
Sweden	-0.3	-0.9	-0.4	-0.6
Switzerland	2.7	-5.0	-3.9	0.8
United Kingdom	-9.3	61.8	-238.3	17.7
United States	-10.0	-4.0	-1.0	5.0
TOTAL	89.4	182.3	-202.0	111.7
MULTILATERAL				
AF.D.F.	–	–	–	–
AF.D.B.	–	–	–	–
AS.D.B	–	–	–	–
CAR.D.B.	–	–	–	–
E.E.C.	11.5	6.6	9.4	7.9
IBRD	26.9	23.1	54.6	67.8
IDA	1.9	-0.8	-0.9	-0.9
I.D.B.	–	–	–	–
IFAD	2.3	2.6	2.9	3.8
I.F.C.	-1.9	-9.3	-12.3	-13.5
IMF TRUST FUND	–	–	–	–
U.N. AGENCIES	–	–	–	–
UNDP	2.4	1.9	1.7	1.9
UNTA	0.8	0.4	0.8	0.8
UNICEF	0.1	0.4	0.2	0.1
UNRWA	–	–	–	–
WFP	4.3	9.1	5.2	7.5
UNHCR	–	–	–	–
Other Multilateral	1.3	1.1	0.9	1.0
Arab OPEC Agencies	1.5	10.3	14.1	1.9
TOTAL	51.1	45.4	76.7	78.3
OPEC COUNTRIES	692.6	597.7	451.4	403.7
E.E.C.+ MEMBERS	75.3	81.9	-183.5	83.4
TOTAL	833.1	825.3	326.1	593.7

TOTAL ODA NET

DAC COUNTRIES	1983	1984	1985	1986
Australia	0.3	0.2	0.5	0.6
Austria	0.2	0.2	0.1	0.2
Belgium	0.0	0.1	0.1	0.1
Canada	0.5	0.3	0.7	0.7
Denmark	-0.2	-0.2	-0.5	-0.5
Finland	–	0.2	–	–
France	10.2	4.3	2.2	3.2
Germany, Fed. Rep.	14.4	9.4	19.2	17.6
Ireland	–	–	–	–
Italy	9.6	2.8	16.6	7.0
Japan	19.4	19.8	13.2	37.5
Netherlands	0.3	0.8	0.1	0.4
New Zealand	–	–	–	–
Norway	4.5	0.1	-0.2	0.0
Sweden	–	0.0	0.6	0.0
Switzerland	0.2	0.1	0.5	0.8
United Kingdom	1.0	4.8	-0.6	4.1
United States	22.0	21.0	18.0	38.0
TOTAL	82.2	63.8	70.5	109.5
AF.D.F.	–	–	–	–
AF.D.B.	–	–	–	–
AS.D.B	–	–	–	–
CAR.D.B.	–	–	–	–
E.E.C.	6.1	3.7	5.4	5.6
IBRD	–	–	–	–
IDA	1.9	-0.8	-0.9	-0.9
I.D.B.	–	–	–	–
IFAD	2.3	2.6	2.9	3.8
I.F.C.	–	–	–	–
IMF TRUST FUND	–	–	–	–
U.N. AGENCIES	–	–	–	–
UNDP	2.4	1.9	1.7	1.9
UNTA	0.8	0.4	0.8	0.8
UNICEF	0.1	0.4	0.2	0.1
UNRWA	–	–	–	–
WFP	4.3	9.1	5.2	7.5
UNHCR	–	–	–	–
Other Multilateral	1.3	1.1	0.9	1.0
Arab OPEC Agencies	2.6	2.9	-0.3	1.0
TOTAL	21.8	21.2	16.0	20.7
OPEC COUNTRIES	683.3	600.9	454.6	406.9
E.E.C.+ MEMBERS	41.2	25.6	42.5	37.4
TOTAL	787.3	685.9	541.0	537.1

TOTAL ODA GROSS

	1983
Australia	0.3
Austria	0.2
Belgium	0.0
Canada	0.5
Denmark	–
Finland	–
France	10.5
Germany, Fed. Rep.	18.6
Ireland	–
Italy	9.6
Japan	20.0
Netherlands	0.3
New Zealand	–
Norway	4.5
Sweden	–
Switzerland	0.2
United Kingdom	4.2
United States	24.0
TOTAL	92.9
AF.D.F.	–
AF.D.B.	–
AS.D.B	–
CAR.D.B.	–
E.E.C.	6.1
IBRD	–
IDA	2.4
I.D.B.	–
IFAD	2.3
I.F.C.	–
IMF TRUST FUND	–
U.N. AGENCIES	–
UNDP	2.4
UNTA	0.8
UNICEF	0.1
UNRWA	–
WFP	4.3
UNHCR	–
Other Multilateral	1.3
Arab OPEC Agencies	5.8
TOTAL	25.5
OPEC COUNTRIES	697.8
E.E.C.+ MEMBERS	49.2
TOTAL	816.2

ODA LOANS GROSS

DAC COUNTRIES	1983	1984	1985	1986
Australia	–	–	–	–
Austria	0.0	–	–	–
Belgium	–	–	–	–
Canada	–	–	–	–
Denmark	–	–	–	–
Finland	–	–	–	–
France	8.2	2.3	0.1	–
Germany, Fed. Rep.	9.1	4.8	15.1	13.5
Ireland	–	–	–	–
Italy	8.4	0.9	15.1	3.9
Japan	19.4	21.7	13.9	37.3
Netherlands	–	–	–	–
New Zealand	–	–	–	–
Norway	4.0	–	–	–
Sweden	–	–	–	–
Switzerland	–	–	–	–
United Kingdom	0.8	0.6	0.6	4.6
United States	14.0	16.0	11.0	17.0
TOTAL	63.9	46.2	55.8	76.2
MULTILATERAL	12.3	10.0	7.2	10.9
OPEC COUNTRIES	86.5	88.2	73.1	31.8
E.E.C.+ MEMBERS	28.2	9.6	31.8	23.4
TOTAL	162.6	144.4	136.1	118.8

ODA LOANS NET

DAC COUNTRIES	1983	1984	1985	1986
Australia	–	–	–	–
Austria	0.0	–	–	–
Belgium	–	–	–	–
Canada	–	–	–	–
Denmark	-0.2	-0.2	-0.5	-0.5
Finland	–	–	–	–
France	7.9	2.1	0.0	-0.3
Germany, Fed. Rep.	4.8	1.4	11.5	7.8
Ireland	–	–	–	–
Italy	8.4	0.9	15.1	3.2
Japan	18.7	19.3	11.5	33.9
Netherlands	–	–	–	–
New Zealand	–	–	–	–
Norway	4.0	–	-0.5	-0.6
Sweden	–	–	–	–
Switzerland	–	–	–	–
United Kingdom	-2.3	-2.8	-3.1	0.4
United States	12.0	12.0	7.0	13.0
TOTAL	53.2	32.6	41.1	56.9
MULTILATERAL	8.6	5.7	2.5	5.4
OPEC COUNTRIES	72.0	33.9	17.7	-6.3
E.E.C.+ MEMBERS	20.2	2.4	23.9	12.1
TOTAL	133.8	72.1	61.4	56.0

GRANTS

	1983
Australia	0.3
Austria	0.2
Belgium	0.0
Canada	0.5
Denmark	–
Finland	–
France	2.3
Germany, Fed. Rep.	9.5
Ireland	–
Italy	1.2
Japan	0.6
Netherlands	0.3
New Zealand	–
Norway	0.6
Sweden	–
Switzerland	0.2
United Kingdom	3.3
United States	10.0
TOTAL	29.0
MULTILATERAL	13.3
OPEC COUNTRIES	611.3
E.E.C.+ MEMBERS	21.0
TOTAL	653.6

TOTAL OFFICIAL GROSS

DAC COUNTRIES	1983	1984	1985	1986
Australia	0.3	0.2	0.5	0.6
Austria	0.2	0.2	0.1	0.2
Belgium	0.0	0.1	0.1	0.1
Canada	0.5	0.3	0.7	0.7
Denmark	–	0.6	0.6	–
Finland	–	0.2	–	–
France	10.5	4.5	2.3	3.5
Germany, Fed. Rep.	18.6	12.8	22.8	23.2
Ireland	–	–	–	–
Italy	18.0	2.8	16.6	7.7
Japan	20.0	22.2	15.6	40.9
Netherlands	0.3	0.8	0.1	0.4
New Zealand	–	–	–	–
Norway	4.5	0.1	0.3	0.5
Sweden	–	0.0	0.6	0.7
Switzerland	0.2	0.1	0.5	0.8
United Kingdom	4.2	8.2	3.0	8.3
United States	27.0	35.0	46.0	42.0
TOTAL	104.2	88.0	109.8	129.4
MULTILATERAL	115.1	149.2	159.0	199.5
OPEC COUNTRIES	709.8	655.2	509.9	445.0
E.E.C.+ MEMBERS	63.6	37.2	56.0	53.0
TOTAL	929.2	892.4	778.7	773.9

TOTAL OFFICIAL NET

DAC COUNTRIES	1983	1984	1985	1986
Australia	0.3	0.2	0.5	0.6
Austria	0.2	0.2	0.1	0.2
Belgium	0.0	0.1	0.1	0.1
Canada	0.5	0.3	0.7	0.7
Denmark	-0.2	0.4	-0.2	-0.5
Finland	–	0.2	–	–
France	10.2	4.3	2.2	3.2
Germany, Fed. Rep.	14.4	9.4	19.2	17.6
Ireland	–	–	–	–
Italy	18.0	1.9	16.6	7.0
Japan	19.4	19.8	13.2	37.5
Netherlands	0.3	0.8	0.1	0.4
New Zealand	–	–	–	–
Norway	4.5	0.1	-0.2	0.0
Sweden	-0.3	-0.9	-0.4	-0.6
Switzerland	0.2	0.1	0.5	0.8
United Kingdom	1.0	4.8	-0.6	4.1
United States	-10.0	-4.0	-1.0	5.0
TOTAL	58.3	37.5	50.7	76.0
MULTILATERAL	51.1	45.4	76.7	78.3
OPEC COUNTRIES	692.6	597.7	451.4	403.7
E.E.C.+ MEMBERS	55.1	28.1	46.7	39.7
TOTAL	802.1	680.4	578.8	558.0

TOTAL OOF GROSS

	1983
Australia	–
Austria	–
Belgium	–
Canada	–
Denmark	–
Finland	–
France	–
Germany, Fed. Rep.	–
Ireland	–
Italy	8.4
Japan	–
Netherlands	–
New Zealand	–
Norway	–
Sweden	–
Switzerland	–
United Kingdom	–
United States	3.0
TOTAL	11.4
MULTILATERAL	89.6
OPEC COUNTRIES	12.0
E.E.C.+ MEMBERS	14.4
TOTAL	113.0

ODA COMMITMENTS

1984	1985	1986	1983	1984	1985	1986
0.2	0.5	0.6	0.1	1.9	1.6	0.2
0.2	0.1	0.2	0.2	0.2	0.1	—
0.1	0.1	0.1	—	—	—	0.1
0.3	0.7	0.7	—	0.6	0.3	0.7
—	0.0	—	—	—	—	—
0.2	—	—	—	0.2	—	—
4.5	2.3	3.5	2.3	2.2	24.8	3.5
12.8	22.8	23.2	12.5	53.8	8.0	18.8
—	—	—	—	—	—	—
2.8	16.6	7.7	27.1	7.5	10.4	2.0
22.2	15.6	40.9	0.6	0.7	1.7	7.7
0.8	0.1	0.4	0.0	0.8	0.0	0.1
—	—	—	—	—	—	—
0.1	0.3	0.5	4.6	—	0.0	0.0
0.0	0.6	0.0	—	—	0.6	0.0
0.1	0.5	0.8	0.0	0.0	0.5	0.8
8.2	3.0	8.3	3.3	7.8	2.5	3.7
25.0	22.0	42.0	30.2	10.2	100.0	95.3
77.4	85.2	128.7	80.8	85.9	150.4	132.8
—	—	—	—	—	—	—
—	—	—	—	—	—	—
—	—	—	—	—	—	—
3.7	5.4	5.6	7.7	1.9	4.5	7.4
—	—	—	—	—	—	—
—	—	—	—	—	—	—
2.6	2.9	3.8	—	—	—	—
—	—	—	—	—	—	—
—	—	—	8.9	13.0	8.8	11.3
1.9	1.7	1.9	—	—	—	—
0.4	0.8	0.8	—	—	—	—
0.4	0.2	0.1	—	—	—	—
—	—	—	—	—	—	—
9.1	5.2	7.5	—	—	—	—
—	—	—	—	—	—	—
1.1	0.9	1.0	—	—	—	—
6.4	3.5	5.7	21.5	—	17.1	24.3
25.6	20.6	26.3	38.1	14.9	30.4	43.0
655.2	509.9	445.0	680.9	589.8	437.0	596.9
32.8	50.4	48.7	52.8	74.0	50.1	35.5
758.2	615.8	600.0	799.9	690.5	617.8	772.7

TECH. COOP. GRANTS

1984	1985	1986	1983	1984	1985	1986
0.2	0.5	0.6	0.0	0.1	0.4	0.5
0.2	0.1	0.2	0.2	—	—	—
0.1	0.1	0.1	0.0	0.0	0.0	—
0.3	0.7	0.7	0.2	—	0.0	—
—	0.0	—	—	0.1	0.0	—
0.2	—	—	—	0.0	—	—
2.2	2.3	3.5	2.3	2.2	2.2	3.5
8.0	7.7	9.8	8.7	7.9	7.6	9.7
—	—	—	—	—	—	—
1.9	1.4	3.8	0.6	1.9	0.6	1.2
0.5	1.7	3.6	0.5	0.5	1.6	3.6
0.8	0.1	0.4	0.2	0.7	0.1	0.1
—	—	—	—	—	—	—
0.1	0.3	0.5	—	—	0.0	0.0
0.0	0.6	0.0	—	—	—	—
0.1	0.5	0.8	0.1	0.1	0.0	0.0
7.6	2.5	3.7	3.3	3.0	2.5	3.7
9.0	11.0	25.0	7.0	8.0	8.0	12.0
31.1	29.4	52.6	23.1	24.4	23.0	34.4
15.6	13.4	15.4	4.6	3.9	3.6	3.8
567.1	436.8	413.2	—	—	—	—
23.2	18.6	25.3	15.2	15.8	13.0	18.2
613.8	479.7	481.2	27.7	28.3	26.6	38.2

TOTAL OOF NET

1984	1985	1986	1983	1984	1985	1986
—	—	—	—	—	—	—
—	—	—	—	—	—	—
—	—	—	—	—	—	—
0.6	0.6	—	—	0.6	0.3	—
—	—	—	—	—	—	—
—	—	—	—	—	—	—
—	—	—	8.4	-0.9	—	—
—	—	—	—	—	—	—
—	—	—	—	—	—	—
—	—	0.7	-0.3	-1.0	-1.0	-0.6
—	—	—	—	—	—	—
10.0	24.0	—	-32.0	-25.0	-19.0	-33.0
10.6	24.6	0.7	-23.9	-26.3	-19.7	-33.6
123.6	138.4	173.2	29.3	24.1	60.7	57.5
—	—	—	9.3	-3.3	-3.2	-3.1
4.4	5.6	4.4	13.8	2.6	4.2	2.3
134.2	162.9	173.9	14.7	-5.4	37.8	20.8

ODA COMMITMENTS : LOANS

DAC COUNTRIES	1983	1984	1985	1986
Australia	—	—	—	—
Austria	—	—	—	—
Belgium	—	—	—	—
Canada	—	—	—	—
Denmark	—	—	—	—
Finland	—	—	—	—
France	—	—	22.1	—
Germany, Fed. Rep.	7.6	46.1	—	4.6
Ireland	—	—	—	—
Italy	23.5	—	3.8	—
Japan	—	—	—	3.4
Netherlands	—	—	—	—
New Zealand	—	—	—	—
Norway	4.0	—	—	—
Sweden	—	—	—	—
Switzerland	—	—	—	—
United Kingdom	—	—	—	—
United States	17.0	—	5.0	—
TOTAL	52.1	46.1	30.8	8.0
MULTILATERAL	26.4	1.2	17.1	24.3
OPEC COUNTRIES	69.9	22.7	—	42.9
E.E.C.+ MEMBERS	36.0	47.3	25.8	4.6
TOTAL	148.4	70.0	47.9	75.2

GRANT ELEMENT OF ODA

DAC COUNTRIES	1983	1984	1985	1986
Australia	100.0	100.0	100.0	100.0
Austria	100.0	100.0	100.0	—
Belgium	—	—	—	100.0
Canada	—	100.0	100.0	100.0
Denmark	—	—	—	—
Finland	—	100.0	—	—
France	100.0	100.0	72.3	100.0
Germany, Fed. Rep.	75.1	63.2	100.0	84.4
Ireland	—	—	—	—
Italy	51.3	100.0	78.7	100.0
Japan	100.0	100.0	100.0	70.1
Netherlands	100.0	100.0	100.0	100.0
New Zealand	—	—	—	—
Norway	35.0	—	100.0	100.0
Sweden	—	—	100.0	100.0
Switzerland	100.0	100.0	88.8	100.0
United Kingdom	100.0	100.0	100.0	100.0
United States	66.2	100.0	97.0	100.0
TOTAL	63.6	76.9	91.8	96.1
MULTILATERAL	52.2	100.0	58.1	57.7
OPEC COUNTRIES	94.2	97.9	100.0	96.3
E.E.C.+ MEMBERS	66.0	72.8	81.9	91.8
TOTAL	88.8	95.4	95.9	94.1

OTHER AGGREGATES

COMMITMENTS: ALL SOURCES	1983	1984	1985	1986
TOTAL BILATERAL	800.4	843.3	587.6	729.2
of which				
OPEC	695.9	711.8	437.0	596.9
CMEA	—	—	—	—
TOTAL MULTILATERAL	190.2	242.9	195.6	231.1
TOTAL BIL.& MULTIL.	990.6	1086.3	783.2	960.3
of which				
ODA Grants	651.4	620.6	569.9	697.5
ODA Loans	148.4	70.0	47.9	75.2

DISBURSEMENTS:	1983	1984	1985	1986
DAC COUNTRIES COMBINED				
OFFICIAL & PRIVATE				
GROSS:				
Contractual Lending	286.1	316.6	176.6	183.5
Export Credits Total	222.3	269.7	120.2	107.3
Export Credits Private	210.9	259.7	96.2	106.6
NET:				
Contractual Lending	46.2	152.6	-231.7	53.0
Export Credits Total	-7.0	119.4	-273.0	-3.9
PRIVATE SECTOR NET	31.1	144.8	-252.7	35.8
Direct Investment	-2.8	-5.1	0.7	1.7
Portfolio Investment	17.0	3.7	-0.5	4.4
Export Credits	16.9	146.3	-253.0	29.6

MARKET BORROWING:	1983	1984	1985	1986
CHANGE IN CLAIMS				
Banks	—	119.0	80.0	261.0

MEMORANDUM ITEM:	1983	1984	1985	1986
CMEA Countr.(Gross)	0.7	0.8	5.4	1.0

DISBURSEMENTS, UNLESS OTHERWISE STATED

	1983	1984	1985	1986	1983	1984	1985	1986		1983
TOTAL RECEIPTS NET					**TOTAL ODA NET**				**TOTAL ODA GROSS**	
DAC COUNTRIES									Australia	2.3
Australia	2.3	1.7	2.3	1.2	2.3	1.7	2.3	1.2	Austria	0.0
Austria	0.0	0.0	0.1	0.0	0.0	0.0	0.1	0.0	Belgium	0.4
Belgium	0.4	0.3	0.1	0.7	0.4	0.3	0.1	0.3	Canada	–
Canada	–	–	–	–	–	–	–	–	Denmark	–
Denmark	–	-1.9	-0.1	–	–	0.2	-0.1	–	Finland	0.2
Finland	0.2	0.3	0.3	0.4	0.2	0.3	0.3	0.4	France	1.0
France	1.0	2.5	0.3	0.3	1.0	2.5	0.3	0.3	Germany, Fed. Rep.	0.2
Germany, Fed. Rep.	0.2	0.0	0.4	0.3	0.2	0.0	0.4	0.3	Ireland	–
Ireland	–	–	–	–	–	–	–	–	Italy	–
Italy	–	–	–	–	–	–	–	–	Japan	0.1
Japan	0.1	–	–	–	0.1	–	–	0.2	Netherlands	0.9
Netherlands	0.9	1.0	0.4	0.2	0.9	1.0	0.4	0.2	New Zealand	0.0
New Zealand	0.0	0.0	0.1	–	0.0	0.0	0.1	–	Norway	–
Norway	–	0.4	0.3	0.2	–	0.4	0.3	0.2	Sweden	2.0
Sweden	2.0	2.1	1.4	2.3	2.0	2.1	1.4	2.3	Switzerland	0.2
Switzerland	0.2	–	0.1	0.4	0.2	–	0.1	0.4	United Kingdom	1.1
United Kingdom	1.0	–	–	–	1.0	–	–	–	United States	–
United States	..	–	–	–	–	–	–	–		
TOTAL	8.3	6.4	5.6	6.0	8.3	8.4	5.6	5.7	TOTAL	8.3
MULTILATERAL										
AF.D.F.	–	–	–	–	–	–	–	–	AF.D.F.	–
AF.D.B.	–	–	–	–	–	–	–	–	AF.D.B.	–
AS.D.B	–	–	–	–	–	–	–	–	AS.D.B	–
CAR.D.B.	–	–	–	–	–	–	–	–	CAR.D.B.	–
E.E.C.	–	0.1	0.6	0.3	–	0.1	0.6	0.3	E.E.C.	–
IBRD	–	–	–	–	–	–	–	–	IBRD	–
IDA	–	–	–	–	–	–	–	–	IDA	–
I.D.B.	–	–	–	–	–	–	–	–	I.D.B.	–
IFAD	–	–	–	–	–	–	–	–	IFAD	–
I.F.C.	–	–	–	–	–	–	–	–	I.F.C.	–
IMF TRUST FUND	–	–	–	–	–	–	–	–	IMF TRUST FUND	–
U.N. AGENCIES	–	–	–	–	–	–	–	–	U.N. AGENCIES	–
UNDP	–	–	–	–	–	–	–	–	UNDP	–
UNTA	0.0	0.0	0.8	0.0	0.0	0.0	0.8	0.0	UNTA	0.0
UNICEF	7.4	4.3	4.2	5.8	7.4	4.3	4.2	5.8	UNICEF	7.4
UNRWA	–	–	–	–	–	–	–	–	UNRWA	–
WFP	17.3	1.7	0.0	–	17.3	1.7	0.0	–	WFP	17.3
UNHCR	1.0	2.3	0.7	1.2	1.0	2.3	0.7	1.2	UNHCR	1.0
Other Multilateral	2.7	0.1	1.0	0.0	2.7	0.1	1.0	0.0	Other Multilateral	2.7
Arab OPEC Agencies	–	–	–	–	–	–	–	–	Arab OPEC Agencies	–
TOTAL	28.4	8.5	7.3	7.5	28.4	8.5	7.3	7.5	TOTAL	28.4
OPEC COUNTRIES	–	–	–	–	–	–	–	–	OPEC COUNTRIES	–
E.E.C.+ MEMBERS	3.5	1.9	1.6	1.9	3.5	4.0	1.6	1.5	E.E.C.+ MEMBERS	3.5
TOTAL	36.7	14.8	12.9	13.5	36.7	16.9	12.9	13.2	TOTAL	36.7
ODA LOANS GROSS					**ODA LOANS NET**				**GRANTS**	
DAC COUNTRIES									Australia	2.3
Australia	–	–	–	–	–	–	–	–	Austria	0.0
Austria	–	–	–	–	–	–	–	–	Belgium	0.4
Belgium	–	–	–	–	–	–	–	–	Canada	–
Canada	–	–	–	–	–	–	–	–	Denmark	–
Denmark	–	–	–	–	–	–	-0.1	–	Finland	0.2
Finland	–	–	–	–	–	–	–	–	France	1.0
France	–	–	–	–	–	–	–	–	Germany, Fed. Rep.	0.2
Germany, Fed. Rep.	–	–	–	–	–	–	–	–	Ireland	–
Ireland	–	–	–	–	–	–	–	–	Italy	–
Italy	–	–	–	–	–	–	–	–	Japan	0.1
Japan	–	–	–	–	–	–	–	–	Netherlands	0.9
Netherlands	–	–	–	–	–	–	–	–	New Zealand	0.0
New Zealand	–	–	–	–	–	–	–	–	Norway	–
Norway	–	–	–	–	–	–	–	–	Sweden	2.0
Sweden	–	–	–	–	–	–	–	–	Switzerland	0.2
Switzerland	–	–	–	–	–	–	–	–	United Kingdom	1.1
United Kingdom	–	–	–	–	0.0	0.0	0.0	0.0	United States	–
United States	–	–	–	–	–	–	–	–		
TOTAL	–	–	–	–	0.0	0.0	-0.1	0.0	TOTAL	8.3
MULTILATERAL	–	–	–	–	–	–	–	–	MULTILATERAL	28.4
OPEC COUNTRIES	–	–	–	–	–	–	–	–	OPEC COUNTRIES	
E.E.C.+ MEMBERS	–	–	–	–	0.0	0.0	-0.1	0.0	E.E.C.+ MEMBERS	3.5
TOTAL	–	–	–	–	0.0	0.0	-0.1	0.0	TOTAL	36.7
TOTAL OFFICIAL GROSS					**TOTAL OFFICIAL NET**				**TOTAL OOF GROSS**	
DAC COUNTRIES									Australia	–
Australia	2.3	1.7	2.3	1.2	2.3	1.7	2.3	1.2	Austria	–
Austria	0.0	0.0	0.1	0.0	0.0	0.0	0.1	0.0	Belgium	–
Belgium	0.4	0.3	0.1	0.3	0.4	0.3	0.1	0.3	Canada	–
Canada	–	–	–	–	–	–	–	–	Denmark	–
Denmark	–	0.2	–	–	–	0.2	-0.1	–	Finland	–
Finland	0.2	0.3	0.3	0.4	0.2	0.3	0.3	0.4	France	–
France	1.0	2.5	0.3	0.3	1.0	2.5	0.3	0.3	Germany, Fed. Rep.	–
Germany, Fed. Rep.	0.2	0.0	0.4	0.3	0.2	0.0	0.4	0.3	Ireland	–
Ireland	–	–	–	–	–	–	–	–	Italy	–
Italy	–	–	–	–	–	–	–	–	Japan	–
Japan	0.1	–	–	–	0.1	–	–	–	Netherlands	–
Netherlands	0.9	1.0	0.4	0.2	0.9	1.0	0.4	0.2	New Zealand	–
New Zealand	0.0	0.0	0.1	–	0.0	0.0	0.1	–	Norway	–
Norway	–	0.4	0.3	0.2	–	0.4	0.3	0.2	Sweden	–
Sweden	2.0	2.1	1.4	2.3	2.0	2.1	1.4	2.3	Switzerland	–
Switzerland	0.2	–	0.1	0.4	0.2	–	0.1	0.4	United Kingdom	–
United Kingdom	1.1	0.0	0.0	0.0	1.0	–	–	–	United States	–
United States	–	–	–	–	–	–	–	–		
TOTAL	8.3	8.5	5.7	5.7	8.3	8.4	5.6	5.7	TOTAL	–
MULTILATERAL	28.4	8.5	7.3	7.5	28.4	8.5	7.3	7.5	MULTILATERAL	–
OPEC COUNTRIES	–	–	–	–	–	–	–	–	OPEC COUNTRIES	–
E.E.C.+ MEMBERS	3.5	4.0	1.7	1.5	3.5	4.0	1.6	1.5	E.E.C.+ MEMBERS	–
TOTAL	36.7	16.9	13.0	13.2	36.7	16.9	12.9	13.2	TOTAL	–

ODA COMMITMENTS

1984	1985	1986	1983	1984	1985	1986
1.7	2.3	1.2	3.7	1.7	0.3	—
0.0	0.1	0.0	0.0	0.0	0.1	—
0.3	0.1	0.3	—	—	—	0.3
—	—	—	—	—	—	—
0.2	—	—	—	—	—	—
0.3	0.3	0.4	0.2	0.3	0.3	—
2.5	0.3	0.3	1.1	2.5	0.3	0.3
0.0	0.4	0.3	0.6	0.2	0.3	—
—	—	—	—	—	—	—
—	—	—	0.9	—	—	—
1.0	0.4	0.2	1.8	0.2	0.6	0.2
0.0	0.1	—	0.0	0.0	0.1	—
0.4	0.3	0.2	—	0.0	—	—
2.1	1.4	2.3	2.1	3.3	1.2	2.3
—	0.1	0.4	0.2	—	0.1	0.4
0.0	0.0	0.0	1.1	0.0	0.0	0.0
—	—	—	0.1	0.1	0.0	0.2
8.5	5.7	5.7	11.7	8.4	3.2	3.8
—	—	—	—	—	—	—
—	—	—	—	—	—	—
—	—	—	—	—	—	—
0.1	0.6	0.3	0.1	0.3	0.3	0.4
—	—	—	—	—	—	—
—	—	—	—	—	—	—
—	—	—	—	—	—	—
—	—	—	—	—	—	—
—	—	—	28.4	8.4	6.8	7.1
0.0	0.8	0.0	—	—	—	—
4.3	4.2	5.8	—	—	—	—
1.7	0.0	—	—	—	—	—
2.3	0.7	1.2	—	—	—	—
0.1	1.0	0.0	—	—	—	—
—	—	—	—	—	—	—
8.5	7.3	7.5	28.5	8.7	7.1	7.6
—	—	—	—	—	—	—
4.0	1.7	1.5	4.6	3.2	1.4	1.3
16.9	13.0	13.2	40.2	17.1	10.3	11.3

TECH. COOP. GRANTS

1984	1985	1986	1983	1984	1985	1986
1.7	2.3	1.2	—	0.0	0.0	—
0.0	0.1	0.0	0.0	—	—	—
0.3	0.1	0.3	—	—	—	—
—	—	—	—	—	—	—
0.2	—	—	—	—	—	—
0.3	0.3	0.4	—	—	—	—
2.5	0.3	0.3	0.1	2.2	0.3	0.3
0.0	0.4	0.3	0.2	0.0	0.4	0.3
—	—	—	—	—	—	—
—	—	—	0.1	—	—	—
1.0	0.4	0.2	—	0.2	0.1	0.2
0.0	0.1	—	—	—	—	—
0.4	0.3	0.2	—	—	—	—
2.1	1.4	2.3	—	—	—	—
—	0.1	0.4	—	—	—	—
0.0	0.0	0.0	—	—	—	—
—	—	—	—	—	—	—
8.5	5.7	5.7	0.4	2.4	0.8	0.8
8.5	7.3	7.5	11.1	6.7	6.7	7.1
—	—	—	—	—	—	—
4.0	1.7	1.5	0.3	2.4	0.8	0.8
16.9	13.0	13.2	11.5	9.1	7.5	7.9

TOTAL OOF NET

1984	1985	1986	1983	1984	1985	1986
—	—	—	—	—	—	—
—	—	—	—	—	—	—
—	—	—	—	—	—	—
—	—	—	—	—	—	—
—	—	—	—	—	—	—
—	—	—	—	—	—	—
—	—	—	—	—	—	—
—	—	—	—	—	—	—
—	—	—	—	—	—	—
—	—	—	—	—	—	—
—	—	—	—	—	—	—
—	—	—	—	—	—	—
—	—	—	—	—	—	—
—	—	—	—	—	—	—
—	—	—	—	—	—	—
—	—	—	—	—	—	—

ODA COMMITMENTS : LOANS

DAC COUNTRIES	1983	1984	1985	1986
Australia	—	—	—	—
Austria	—	—	—	—
Belgium	—	—	—	—
Canada	—	—	—	—
Denmark	—	—	—	—
Finland	—	—	—	—
France	—	—	—	—
Germany, Fed. Rep.	—	—	—	—
Ireland	—	—	—	—
Italy	—	—	—	—
Japan	—	—	—	—
Netherlands	—	—	—	—
New Zealand	—	—	—	—
Norway	—	—	—	—
Sweden	—	—	—	—
Switzerland	—	—	—	—
United Kingdom	—	—	—	—
United States	0.1	0.1	0.0	0.2
TOTAL	0.1	0.1	0.0	0.2
MULTILATERAL	—	—	—	—
OPEC COUNTRIES	—	—	—	—
E.E.C.+ MEMBERS	—	—	—	—
TOTAL	0.1	0.1	0.0	0.2

GRANT ELEMENT OF ODA

DAC COUNTRIES	1983	1984	1985	1986
Australia	100.0	100.0	100.0	—
Austria	100.0	100.0	100.0	—
Belgium	—	—	—	100.0
Canada	—	—	—	—
Denmark	—	—	—	—
Finland	100.0	100.0	100.0	—
France	100.0	100.0	100.0	100.0
Germany, Fed. Rep.	100.0	100.0	100.0	—
Ireland	—	—	—	—
Italy	—	—	—	—
Japan	100.0	—	—	—
Netherlands	100.0	100.0	100.0	100.0
New Zealand	100.0	100.0	100.0	—
Norway	—	100.0	—	—
Sweden	100.0	100.0	100.0	100.0
Switzerland	100.0	—	100.0	100.0
United Kingdom	100.0	100.0	100.0	100.0
United States	67.1	67.1	67.1	67.1
TOTAL	99.7	99.5	99.7	97.9
MULTILATERAL	100.0	100.0	100.0	100.0
OPEC COUNTRIES	—	—	—	—
E.E.C.+ MEMBERS	100.0	100.0	100.0	100.0
TOTAL	99.9	99.7	99.9	99.3

OTHER AGGREGATES

COMMITMENTS: ALL SOURCES

	1983	1984	1985	1986
TOTAL BILATERAL	96.7	98.4	110.2	125.0
of which				
OPEC	—	—	—	—
CMEA	85.0	90.0	107.0	121.2
TOTAL MULTILATERAL	28.5	8.7	7.1	7.6
TOTAL BIL.& MULTIL.	125.2	107.1	117.3	132.5
of which				
ODA Grants	62.6	42.9	60.2	66.3
ODA Loans	62.6	64.1	57.0	66.2

DISBURSEMENTS:
DAC COUNTRIES COMBINED

	1983	1984	1985	1986
OFFICIAL & PRIVATE				
GROSS:				
Contractual Lending	—	—	—	—
Export Credits Total	—	—	—	—
Export Credits Private	—	—	—	—
NET:				
Contractual Lending	0.0	-2.1	-0.1	0.0
Export Credits Total	—	-2.1	—	—
PRIVATE SECTOR NET	—	-2.1	—	0.4
Direct Investment	—	—	—	—
Portfolio Investment	—	—	—	0.4
Export Credits	—	-2.1	—	—

MARKET BORROWING:
CHANGE IN CLAIMS

	1983	1984	1985	1986
Banks	—	-1.0	—	—

MEMORANDUM ITEM:

	1983	1984	1985	1986
CMEA Countr.(Gross)	85.0	90.0	109.5	135.5

	1983	1984	1985	1986		1983	1984	1985	1986		1983
TOTAL RECEIPTS NET					**TOTAL ODA NET**					**TOTAL ODA GROSS**	
DAC COUNTRIES											
Australia	6.1	2.5	4.7	2.9		6.2	2.6	4.8	2.9	Australia	6.2
Austria	0.4	-4.1	-1.9	0.4		0.4	0.3	2.3	0.4	Austria	0.4
Belgium	-8.8	4.3	2.0	1.7		1.1	3.2	2.9	2.1	Belgium	1.1
Canada	18.9	36.6	24.7	59.5		21.3	28.5	23.0	25.3	Canada	21.5
Denmark	16.3	19.8	24.2	25.5		16.5	19.6	24.6	25.9	Denmark	16.6
Finland	6.1	12.9	12.8	9.0		6.6	13.4	13.3	9.0	Finland	6.6
France	12.3	4.1	7.2	128.6		6.0	9.0	17.2	32.1	France	6.0
Germany, Fed. Rep.	33.1	33.0	22.7	108.6		43.4	37.6	34.5	43.0	Germany, Fed. Rep.	44.2
Ireland	0.2	0.2	0.2	0.4		0.2	0.2	0.2	0.4	Ireland	0.2
Italy	-1.4	4.9	7.8	30.8		1.3	2.3	6.4	31.7	Italy	1.5
Japan	43.2	16.7	22.3	43.2		52.1	30.0	29.6	49.8	Japan	54.8
Netherlands	29.3	22.5	18.1	45.5		30.2	25.2	19.6	44.4	Netherlands	31.5
New Zealand	–	0.0	0.0	0.0		–	0.0	0.0	0.0	New Zealand	–
Norway	22.2	20.6	21.2	31.8		22.2	20.6	21.1	31.7	Norway	22.2
Sweden	15.7	15.4	19.7	14.0		15.2	14.2	19.7	14.5	Sweden	15.2
Switzerland	19.4	6.5	4.9	5.9		2.5	6.8	4.2	5.9	Switzerland	2.5
United Kingdom	35.1	79.6	58.6	67.1		37.3	39.3	32.5	37.4	United Kingdom	46.0
United States	75.0	41.0	72.0	28.0		76.0	42.0	73.0	29.0	United States	78.0
TOTAL	323.2	316.4	321.2	602.9		338.6	294.4	328.9	385.3	TOTAL	354.6
MULTILATERAL											
AF.D.F.	0.9	1.2	5.1	9.4		0.9	1.2	5.1	9.4	AF.D.F.	0.9
AF.D.B.	3.2	4.4	4.5	4.5		–	–	–	–	AF.D.B.	–
AS.D.B	–	–	–	–		–	–	–	–	AS.D.B	–
CAR.D.B.	–	–	–	–		–	–	–	–	CAR.D.B.	–
E.E.C.	15.9	18.4	12.2	9.1		16.6	16.6	15.8	11.1	E.E.C.	16.6
IBRD	82.8	107.0	99.6	8.1		0.9	2.0	2.5	0.8	IBRD	0.9
IDA	18.9	34.4	33.4	28.2		18.9	34.4	33.4	28.2	IDA	19.8
I.D.B.	–	–	–	–		–	–	–	–	I.D.B.	–
IFAD	0.4	1.5	1.2	1.7		0.4	1.5	1.2	1.7	IFAD	0.4
I.F.C.	6.6	-1.1	2.3	-1.3		–	–	–	–	I.F.C.	–
IMF TRUST FUND	–	–	–	–		–	–	–	–	IMF TRUST FUND	–
U.N. AGENCIES										U.N. AGENCIES	
UNDP	5.9	5.2	5.6	6.3		5.9	5.2	5.6	6.3	UNDP	5.9
UNTA	1.0	0.9	1.1	0.9		1.0	0.9	1.1	0.9	UNTA	1.0
UNICEF	0.6	1.6	1.3	1.9		0.6	1.6	1.3	1.9	UNICEF	0.6
UNRWA	–	–	–	–		–	–	–	–	UNRWA	–
WFP	2.2	14.9	15.1	3.7		2.2	14.9	15.1	3.7	WFP	2.2
UNHCR	2.2	3.3	2.6	2.2		2.2	3.3	2.6	2.2	UNHCR	2.2
Other Multilateral	3.5	3.8	3.6	2.4		3.5	3.8	3.6	2.4	Other Multilateral	3.5
Arab OPEC Agencies	5.0	0.0	1.5	0.4		5.0	0.0	0.5	-0.6	Arab OPEC Agencies	5.7
TOTAL	149.0	195.5	189.0	77.5		58.0	85.5	87.8	68.0	TOTAL	59.7
OPEC COUNTRIES	3.9	31.2	21.4	4.7		3.9	31.2	21.4	4.7	OPEC COUNTRIES	5.7
E.E.C.+ MEMBERS	132.1	186.8	153.0	417.3		152.6	152.7	153.7	228.1	E.E.C.+ MEMBERS	163.8
TOTAL	476.2	543.1	531.6	685.1		400.5	411.1	438.1	458.0	TOTAL	420.0
ODA LOANS GROSS					**ODA LOANS NET**					**GRANTS**	
DAC COUNTRIES											
Australia	–	–	–	–		–	–	–	–	Australia	6.2
Austria	–	–	1.9	–		–	0.0	1.9	0.0	Austria	0.4
Belgium	–	–	–	–		–	–	–	–	Belgium	1.1
Canada	12.2	4.9	0.7	0.4		12.1	4.6	0.1	0.1	Canada	9.2
Denmark	2.7	5.6	2.4	5.1		2.6	4.9	1.9	4.4	Denmark	13.9
Finland	1.2	1.3	0.3	–		1.2	1.3	0.3	–	Finland	5.4
France	3.9	6.4	15.0	27.9		3.9	6.2	14.8	27.6	France	2.1
Germany, Fed. Rep.	21.3	22.7	17.5	18.5		20.4	21.3	15.6	15.2	Germany, Fed. Rep.	23.0
Ireland	–	–	–	–		–	–	–	–	Ireland	0.2
Italy	–	–	–	–		-0.2	-0.2	-0.2	-0.1	Italy	1.5
Japan	30.1	10.2	12.2	21.9		27.5	8.0	8.4	16.8	Japan	24.6
Netherlands	13.2	5.5	3.3	0.4		11.9	4.4	1.3	-3.0	Netherlands	18.3
New Zealand	–	–	–	–		–	–	–	–	New Zealand	–
Norway	–	–	0.2	–		–	–	0.2	–	Norway	22.2
Sweden	–	–	–	–		–	–	–	–	Sweden	15.2
Switzerland	0.2	1.4	0.5	0.6		0.2	1.4	0.5	0.6	Switzerland	2.3
United Kingdom	0.9	0.6	3.1	1.3		-7.8	-7.3	-4.9	-7.6	United Kingdom	45.1
United States	20.0	12.0	26.0	13.0		18.0	11.0	23.0	11.0	United States	58.0
TOTAL	105.7	70.5	83.0	88.9		89.7	55.6	62.8	64.8	TOTAL	248.8
MULTILATERAL	33.7	44.9	44.6	41.8		32.0	42.3	42.7	39.4	MULTILATERAL	25.8
OPEC COUNTRIES	3.5	32.8	23.3	7.3		1.8	31.2	21.1	4.6	OPEC COUNTRIES	2.1
E.E.C.+ MEMBERS	48.0	43.9	41.2	53.1		36.8	32.5	28.5	36.5	E.E.C.+ MEMBERS	115.8
TOTAL	143.0	148.1	150.9	138.0		123.5	129.0	126.6	108.8	TOTAL	277.0
TOTAL OFFICIAL GROSS					**TOTAL OFFICIAL NET**					**TOTAL OOF GROSS**	
DAC COUNTRIES											
Australia	6.2	2.6	4.8	2.9		6.1	2.5	4.7	2.9	Australia	
Austria	0.4	0.3	2.4	0.5		0.4	0.3	2.3	0.4	Austria	
Belgium	1.1	3.2	2.9	2.1		1.1	3.2	2.9	2.1	Belgium	
Canada	22.9	41.9	29.8	64.4		18.9	36.6	24.7	59.5	Canada	1.4
Denmark	16.6	20.2	25.1	26.7		16.5	19.6	24.6	25.9	Denmark	
Finland	6.6	13.4	13.3	9.0		6.6	13.4	13.3	9.0	Finland	
France	6.0	9.1	17.4	32.3		6.0	9.0	17.2	32.1	France	
Germany, Fed. Rep.	44.2	40.0	36.7	74.8		40.9	36.6	32.7	69.1	Germany, Fed. Rep.	
Ireland	0.2	0.2	0.2	0.4		0.2	0.2	0.2	0.4	Ireland	
Italy	1.5	2.5	6.6	31.8		1.2	2.3	6.4	31.7	Italy	
Japan	54.8	32.2	33.4	54.9		52.1	30.0	29.6	49.8	Japan	
Netherlands	33.0	26.3	23.0	48.1		31.7	24.9	20.8	44.3	Netherlands	1.5
New Zealand	–	0.0	0.0	0.0		–	0.0	0.0	0.0	New Zealand	
Norway	22.2	20.6	21.1	31.7		22.2	20.6	21.1	31.7	Norway	0.
Sweden	15.5	14.2	19.7	14.5		15.5	14.2	19.7	14.5	Sweden	
Switzerland	2.5	6.8	4.2	5.9		2.5	6.8	4.2	5.9	Switzerland	
United Kingdom	48.3	50.2	44.7	49.5		34.9	39.0	32.8	36.8	United Kingdom	2.
United States	78.0	44.0	78.0	31.0		75.0	41.0	72.0	28.0	United States	
TOTAL	360.2	327.7	363.1	480.3		332.0	300.1	329.2	444.0	TOTAL	5.
MULTILATERAL	176.6	232.2	239.7	138.5		149.0	195.5	189.0	77.5	MULTILATERAL	116.
OPEC COUNTRIES	5.7	32.8	23.6	7.5		3.9	31.2	21.4	4.7	OPEC COUNTRIES	
E.E.C.+ MEMBERS	171.5	175.5	175.0	281.1		148.5	153.0	149.7	251.6	E.E.C.+ MEMBERS	7.
TOTAL	542.4	592.7	626.4	626.2		484.9	526.7	539.6	526.3	TOTAL	122.

ODA COMMITMENTS

1984	1985	1986	1983	1984	1985	1986
2.6	4.8	2.9	2.6	5.5	2.9	0.7
0.3	2.4	0.5	0.2	0.0	2.4	–
3.2	2.9	2.1	0.6	2.0	1.4	2.1
28.8	23.6	25.6	6.7	105.5	16.2	1.4
20.2	25.1	26.6	17.6	7.5	23.6	36.4
13.4	13.3	9.0	15.6	14.3	5.2	32.7
9.1	17.4	32.3	14.3	13.3	26.5	32.3
39.0	36.4	46.2	13.6	83.4	15.9	42.8
0.2	0.2	0.4	0.2	0.2	0.2	0.4
2.5	6.6	31.8	11.6	8.8	8.4	65.0
32.2	33.4	54.9	57.4	30.3	38.2	90.6
26.3	21.6	47.8	25.6	28.4	14.4	35.8
0.0	0.0	0.0	–	0.0	0.1	–
20.6	21.1	31.7	15.4	32.2	47.0	12.9
14.2	19.7	14.5	17.1	29.2	15.4	14.5
6.8	4.2	5.9	3.6	6.8	3.9	0.8
47.2	40.5	46.3	33.0	33.1	26.8	26.6
43.0	76.0	31.0	82.8	79.1	67.1	57.5
309.4	*349.1*	*409.4*	*317.6*	*479.5*	*315.5*	*452.5*
1.2	5.1	9.4	6.3	–	24.5	23.8
–	–	–	–	–	–	–
16.6	15.8	11.2	14.1	21.8	13.7	10.1
2.0	2.5	0.8	–	–	–	–
35.6	34.9	30.0	37.0	64.5	6.0	121.0
1.5	1.2	1.7	5.9	–	–	8.6
–	–	–	–	–	–	–
–	–	–	15.4	29.7	29.3	17.4
5.2	5.6	6.3	–	–	–	–
0.9	1.1	0.9	–	–	–	–
1.6	1.3	1.9	–	–	–	–
–	–	–	–	–	–	–
14.9	15.1	3.7	–	–	–	–
3.3	2.6	2.2	–	–	–	–
3.8	3.6	2.4	–	–	–	–
1.4	0.9	–	–	3.0	3.2	10.6
88.1	*89.6*	*70.4*	*78.6*	*119.0*	*76.6*	*191.6*
32.8	*23.6*	*7.5*	*2.1*	*61.3*	*7.1*	–
164.1	*166.4*	*244.7*	*130.5*	*198.4*	*130.8*	*251.5*
430.3	**462.4**	**487.3**	**398.4**	**659.8**	**399.3**	**644.1**

TECH. COOP. GRANTS

1984	1985	1986	1983	1984	1985	1986
2.6	4.8	2.9	0.4	0.5	1.1	0.4
0.3	0.4	0.5	0.4	–	–	–
3.2	2.9	2.1	0.8	0.7	0.8	0.7
24.0	22.9	25.2	4.7	–	4.7	–
14.6	22.7	21.5	9.8	4.6	6.1	9.0
12.0	13.0	9.0	3.8	6.5	11.4	2.0
2.7	2.4	4.5	2.1	2.5	2.1	3.0
16.3	18.9	27.8	19.0	15.0	16.4	26.2
0.2	0.2	0.4	0.2	0.2	0.2	0.4
2.5	6.6	31.8	1.5	2.5	3.5	15.0
22.0	21.2	33.0	11.4	11.4	9.3	15.3
20.8	18.4	47.4	10.6	11.2	8.9	15.5
0.0	0.0	0.0	–	0.0	0.0	0.0
20.6	21.0	31.7	6.8	6.4	6.0	6.9
14.2	19.7	14.5	3.4	2.6	2.7	0.0
5.4	3.7	5.3	1.2	1.3	1.3	1.6
46.6	37.4	45.0	14.9	15.5	15.0	17.0
31.0	50.0	18.0	18.0	14.0	13.0	29.0
238.9	*266.1*	*320.5*	*108.9*	*94.7*	*102.7*	*141.9*
43.2	*45.0*	*28.6*	*13.2*	*14.8*	*14.2*	*14.4*
0.0	*0.3*	*0.2*	–	–	–	–
120.3	*125.2*	*191.6*	*58.8*	*52.1*	*53.0*	*87.3*
282.1	**311.5**	**349.2**	**122.1**	**109.5**	**116.9**	**156.3**

TOTAL OOF NET

1984	1985	1986	1983	1984	1985	1986
–	–	–	-0.1	-0.1	0.0	–
–	–	–	–	–	–	–
0.0	0.0	–	–	0.0	0.0	–
13.1	6.2	38.8	-2.4	8.1	1.7	34.2
0.0	–	0.0	–	0.0	–	–
–	–	–	–	–	–	–
1.1	0.3	28.5	-2.5	-1.0	-1.9	26.2
–	–	–	-0.1	–	–	–
–	–	–	–	–	–	–
–	1.4	0.3	1.5	-0.2	1.1	0.0
–	–	–	–	–	–	–
–	–	–	0.3	–	–	–
3.0	4.2	3.2	-2.4	-0.3	0.3	-0.6
1.0	2.0	–	-1.0	-1.0	-1.0	-1.0
18.3	14.0	70.9	-6.7	5.6	0.3	58.7
144.1	150.0	68.1	91.1	110.0	101.3	9.5
–	–	–	–	–	–	–
11.4	8.6	36.4	-4.1	0.3	-4.0	23.5
162.4	**164.0**	**139.0**	**84.4**	**115.6**	**101.5**	**68.3**

ODA COMMITMENTS : LOANS

DAC COUNTRIES

	1983	1984	1985	1986
Australia	–	–	–	–
Austria	–	–	1.9	–
Belgium	–	–	–	–
Canada	–	2.9	–	–
Denmark	–	–	–	16.7
Finland	–	–	–	–
France	12.2	10.6	23.1	27.9
Germany, Fed. Rep.	–	53.0	3.5	1.4
Ireland	–	–	–	–
Italy	9.0	4.7	–	–
Japan	30.5	5.9	23.2	46.5
Netherlands	–	0.1	0.3	1.2
New Zealand	–	–	–	–
Norway	–	–	0.2	–
Sweden	–	–	–	–
Switzerland	–	–	–	–
United Kingdom	–	–	–	–
United States	24.0	18.0	9.5	11.7
TOTAL	*75.6*	*95.2*	*61.7*	*105.4*
MULTILATERAL	*49.2*	*67.5*	*33.7*	*163.0*
OPEC COUNTRIES	–	*61.3*	*6.8*	–
E.E.C.+ MEMBERS	*21.2*	*68.4*	*26.9*	*47.2*
TOTAL	**124.8**	**224.0**	**102.2**	**268.4**

GRANT ELEMENT OF ODA

DAC COUNTRIES

	1983	1984	1985	1986
Australia	100.0	100.0	100.0	100.0
Austria	100.0	100.0	86.9	75.8
Belgium	100.0	100.0	100.0	100.0
Canada	100.0	99.5	100.0	100.0
Denmark	100.0	100.0	100.0	93.2
Finland	100.0	100.0	100.0	100.0
France	100.0	68.3	64.6	70.1
Germany, Fed. Rep.	100.0	82.7	96.2	99.5
Ireland	100.0	100.0	100.0	100.0
Italy	60.4	69.2	100.0	96.3
Japan	75.7	90.9	71.6	73.7
Netherlands	100.0	100.0	100.0	97.5
New Zealand	–	100.0	100.0	
Norway	100.0	100.0	99.8	100.0
Sweden	100.0	100.0	100.0	100.0
Switzerland	100.0	100.0	100.0	100.0
United Kingdom	100.0	100.0	100.0	100.0
United States	91.7	93.2	95.4	93.5
TOTAL	*91.7*	*93.8*	*92.3*	*89.3*
MULTILATERAL	*87.9*	*89.1*	*90.5*	*82.1*
OPEC COUNTRIES	*100.0*	*46.2*	*36.7*	–
E.E.C.+ MEMBERS	*96.1*	*89.2*	*92.4*	*91.9*
TOTAL	**90.8**	**88.5**	**90.9**	**87.3**

OTHER AGGREGATES

COMMITMENTS: ALL SOURCES

	1983	1984	1985	1986
TOTAL BILATERAL	360.1	550.6	352.4	500.0
of which				
OPEC	2.1	61.3	7.1	–
CMEA	4.8	4.5	–	–
TOTAL MULTILATERAL	248.5	190.0	180.0	198.4
TOTAL BIL.& MULTIL.	608.6	740.6	532.5	698.4
of which				
ODA Grants	273.5	435.8	297.1	375.7
ODA Loans	124.8	228.5	102.2	268.4

DISBURSEMENTS:

DAC COUNTRIES COMBINED

	1983	1984	1985	1986
OFFICIAL & PRIVATE				
GROSS:				
Contractual Lending	212.9	139.4	181.0	326.3
Export Credits Total	103.3	64.9	90.5	233.9
Export Credits Private	101.7	50.7	84.0	166.5
NET:				
Contractual Lending	78.5	50.0	38.2	204.9
Export Credits Total	-10.3	-6.0	-28.1	140.8
PRIVATE SECTOR NET	-8.7	16.4	-8.0	158.9
Direct Investment	-1.7	31.4	21.2	3.7
Portfolio Investment	-2.5	-3.9	-4.2	73.8
Export Credits	-4.5	-11.1	-24.9	81.4

MARKET BORROWING:

CHANGE IN CLAIMS

	1983	1984	1985	1986
Banks	–	23.0	-16.0	209.0

MEMORANDUM ITEM:

	1983	1984	1985	1986
CMEA Countr.(Gross)	–	–	–	–

DISBURSEMENTS, UNLESS OTHERWISE STATED

TOTAL RECEIPTS NET / TOTAL ODA NET / TOTAL ODA GROSS

	TOTAL RECEIPTS NET 1983	1984	1985	1986	TOTAL ODA NET 1983	1984	1985	1986		TOTAL ODA GROSS 1983
DAC COUNTRIES										
Australia	2.4	1.9	2.6	2.4	2.4	1.9	2.6	2.4	Australia	2.4
Austria	–	–	–	–	–	–	–	–	Austria	–
Belgium	–	–	–	–	–	–	–	–	Belgium	–
Canada	0.1	0.1	0.0	0.1	0.1	0.1	0.0	0.1	Canada	0.1
Denmark	–	–	–	–	–	–	–	–	Denmark	–
Finland	–	–	–	0.0	–	–	–	0.0	Finland	–
France	–	–	–	–	–	–	–	–	France	–
Germany, Fed. Rep.	-0.1	-0.5	-0.1	-0.1	0.0	0.0	0.0	0.0	Germany, Fed. Rep.	0.0
Ireland	–	–	–	–	–	–	–	–	Ireland	–
Italy	–	–	–	–	–	–	–	–	Italy	–
Japan	2.5	2.6	2.8	4.3	2.5	2.6	2.8	4.3	Japan	2.5
Netherlands	–	–	–	–	–	–	–	–	Netherlands	–
New Zealand	0.3	0.5	0.9	0.9	0.3	0.5	0.9	0.9	New Zealand	0.3
Norway	–	–	–	–	–	–	–	–	Norway	–
Sweden	–	–	–	–	–	–	–	–	Sweden	–
Switzerland	–	–	–	–	–	–	–	–	Switzerland	–
United Kingdom	9.0	5.3	4.6	4.6	9.0	5.3	4.6	4.2	United Kingdom	9.0
United States	..	–	–	–	–	–	–	–	United States	–
TOTAL	14.3	9.8	10.8	12.3	14.4	10.4	10.9	11.9	TOTAL	14.4
MULTILATERAL										
AF.D.F.	–	–	–	–	–	–	–	–	AF.D.F.	–
AF.D.B.	–	–	–	–	–	–	–	–	AF.D.B.	–
AS.D.B	0.4	0.4	0.2	0.2	0.4	0.4	0.2	0.2	AS.D.B	0.4
CAR.D.B.	–	–	–	–	–	–	–	–	CAR.D.B.	–
E.E.C.	1.5	0.9	0.5	1.1	1.5	0.9	0.5	1.1	E.E.C.	1.5
IBRD	–	–	–	–	–	–	–	–	IBRD	–
IDA	–	–	–	–	–	–	–	–	IDA	–
I.D.B.	–	–	–	–	–	–	–	–	I.D.B.	–
IFAD	–	–	–	–	–	–	–	–	IFAD	–
I.F.C.	–	–	–	–	–	–	–	–	I.F.C.	–
IMF TRUST FUND	–	–	–	–	–	–	–	–	IMF TRUST FUND	–
U.N. AGENCIES									U.N. AGENCIES	
UNDP	0.1	0.1	0.1	0.1	0.1	0.1	0.1	0.1	UNDP	0.1
UNTA	0.2	0.2	0.3	0.1	0.2	0.2	0.3	0.1	UNTA	0.2
UNICEF	–	–	–	–	–	–	–	–	UNICEF	–
UNRWA	–	–	–	–	–	–	–	–	UNRWA	–
WFP	–	–	–	–	–	–	–	–	WFP	–
UNHCR	–	–	–	–	–	–	–	–	UNHCR	–
Other Multilateral	0.2	0.1	0.1	0.1	0.2	0.1	0.1	0.1	Other Multilateral	0.2
Arab OPEC Agencies	–	–	–	–	–	–	–	–	Arab OPEC Agencies	–
TOTAL	2.4	1.6	1.2	1.5	2.4	1.6	1.2	1.5	TOTAL	2.4
OPEC COUNTRIES	–	–	–	–	–	–	–	–	OPEC COUNTRIES	
E.E.C.+ MEMBERS	10.4	5.6	5.0	5.7	10.5	6.2	5.1	5.3	E.E.C.+ MEMBERS	10.5
TOTAL	16.7	11.4	12.0	13.8	16.8	11.9	12.0	13.4	TOTAL	16.8

ODA LOANS GROSS / ODA LOANS NET / GRANTS

	ODA LOANS GROSS 1983	1984	1985	1986	ODA LOANS NET 1983	1984	1985	1986		GRANTS 1983
DAC COUNTRIES										
Australia	–	–	–	–	–	–	–	–	Australia	2.4
Austria	–	–	–	–	–	–	–	–	Austria	–
Belgium	–	–	–	–	–	–	–	–	Belgium	–
Canada	–	–	–	–	–	–	–	–	Canada	0.1
Denmark	–	–	–	–	–	–	–	–	Denmark	–
Finland	–	–	–	–	–	–	–	–	Finland	–
France	–	–	–	–	–	–	–	–	France	–
Germany, Fed. Rep.	–	–	–	–	–	–	–	–	Germany, Fed. Rep.	0.0
Ireland	–	–	–	–	–	–	–	–	Ireland	–
Italy	–	–	–	–	–	–	–	–	Italy	–
Japan	–	–	–	–	–	–	–	–	Japan	2.5
Netherlands	–	–	–	–	–	–	–	–	Netherlands	–
New Zealand	–	–	–	–	–	–	–	–	New Zealand	0.3
Norway	–	–	–	–	–	–	–	–	Norway	–
Sweden	–	–	–	–	–	–	–	–	Sweden	–
Switzerland	–	–	–	–	–	–	–	–	Switzerland	–
United Kingdom	–	–	–	–	–	–	–	–	United Kingdom	9.0
United States	–	–	–	–	–	–	–	–	United States	–
TOTAL	–	–	–	–	–	–	–	–	TOTAL	14.4
MULTILATERAL	0.1	0.1	0.1	0.1	0.1	-0.1	0.1	0.1	MULTILATERAL	2.4
OPEC COUNTRIES	–	–	–	–	–	–	–	–	OPEC COUNTRIES	–
E.E.C.+ MEMBERS	0.1	0.1	0.0	–	0.1	-0.1	0.0	–	E.E.C.+ MEMBERS	10.4
TOTAL	0.1	0.1	0.1	0.1	0.1	-0.1	0.1	0.1	TOTAL	16.7

TOTAL OFFICIAL GROSS / TOTAL OFFICIAL NET / TOTAL OOF GROSS

	TOTAL OFFICIAL GROSS 1983	1984	1985	1986	TOTAL OFFICIAL NET 1983	1984	1985	1986		TOTAL OOF GROSS 1983
DAC COUNTRIES										
Australia	2.4	1.9	2.6	2.4	2.4	1.9	2.6	2.4	Australia	–
Austria	–	–	–	–	–	–	–	–	Austria	–
Belgium	–	–	–	–	–	–	–	–	Belgium	–
Canada	0.1	0.1	0.0	0.1	0.1	0.1	0.0	0.1	Canada	–
Denmark	–	–	–	–	–	–	–	–	Denmark	–
Finland	–	–	–	0.0	–	–	–	0.0	Finland	–
France	–	–	–	–	–	–	–	–	France	–
Germany, Fed. Rep.	0.0	0.0	0.0	0.0	0.0	0.0	0.0	0.0	Germany, Fed. Rep.	–
Ireland	–	–	–	–	–	–	–	–	Ireland	–
Italy	–	–	–	–	–	–	–	–	Italy	–
Japan	2.5	2.6	2.8	4.3	2.5	2.6	2.8	4.3	Japan	–
Netherlands	–	–	–	–	–	–	–	–	Netherlands	–
New Zealand	0.3	0.5	0.9	0.9	0.3	0.5	0.9	0.9	New Zealand	–
Norway	–	–	–	–	–	–	–	–	Norway	–
Sweden	–	–	–	–	–	–	–	–	Sweden	–
Switzerland	–	–	–	–	–	–	–	–	Switzerland	–
United Kingdom	9.0	5.3	4.6	4.2	9.0	5.3	4.6	4.2	United Kingdom	–
United States	–	–	–	–	–	–	–	–	United States	–
TOTAL	14.4	10.4	10.9	11.9	14.4	10.4	10.9	11.9	TOTAL	–
MULTILATERAL	2.4	1.7	1.2	1.5	2.4	1.6	1.2	1.5	MULTILATERAL	–
OPEC COUNTRIES	–	–	–	–	–	–	–	–	OPEC COUNTRIES	–
E.E.C.+ MEMBERS	10.5	6.3	5.1	5.3	10.5	6.2	5.1	5.3	E.E.C.+ MEMBERS	–
TOTAL	16.8	12.1	12.0	13.4	16.8	11.9	12.0	13.4	TOTAL	–

ODA COMMITMENTS

DAC Countries	1984	1985	1986	1983	1984	1985	1986
Australia	1.9	2.6	2.4	4.1	1.4	1.5	1.2
Austria	–	–	–	–	–	–	–
Belgium	0.1	0.0	0.1	0.1	0.1	0.1	0.1
Canada	–	–	0.0	–	–	–	–
Denmark	–	–	–	–	–	–	–
Finland	–	–	–	–	–	–	–
France	0.0	0.0	0.0	0.0	0.0	0.0	0.0
Germany, Fed. Rep.	–	–	–	–	–	–	–
Ireland	–	–	–	–	–	–	–
Italy	–	–	–	–	–	–	–
Japan	2.6	2.8	4.3	3.7	3.0	4.3	1.8
Netherlands	–	–	–	–	–	–	–
New Zealand	0.5	0.9	0.9	0.4	0.6	1.1	0.4
Norway	–	–	–	–	–	–	–
Sweden	–	–	–	–	–	–	–
Switzerland	–	–	–	–	–	–	–
United Kingdom	5.3	4.6	4.2	5.8	3.4	3.7	2.7
United States	–	–	–	0.1	0.2	0.1	0.2
TOTAL	10.4	10.9	11.9	14.2	8.7	10.8	6.4
Multilateral agencies:							
	–	–	–	–	–	–	–
	0.4	0.2	0.2	–	0.6	0.1	0.7
	1.0	0.5	1.1	1.8	0.4	2.4	0.2
	–	–	–	0.5	0.3	0.5	0.3
	0.1	0.1	0.1	–	–	–	–
	0.2	0.3	0.1	–	–	–	–
	0.1	0.1	0.1	–	–	–	–
MULTILATERAL	1.7	1.2	1.5	2.3	1.3	2.9	1.1
	6.3	5.1	5.3	7.7	3.8	6.0	2.9
TOTAL	12.1	12.0	13.4	16.6	9.9	13.7	7.6

TECH. COOP. GRANTS

	1984	1985	1986	1983	1984	1985	1986
Australia	1.9	2.6	2.4	0.6	0.9	1.1	1.0
Belgium	0.1	0.0	0.1	–	–	0.0	–
Canada	–	–	0.0	–	–	–	0.0
France	0.0	0.0	0.0	0.0	0.0	0.0	0.0
Japan	2.6	2.8	4.3	0.4	0.5	0.4	0.4
New Zealand	0.5	0.9	0.9	0.2	0.2	0.4	0.4
United Kingdom	5.3	4.6	4.2	2.7	1.8	2.5	2.7
TOTAL	10.4	10.9	11.9	3.9	3.4	4.4	4.6
MULTILATERAL	1.6	1.1	1.4	0.5	0.3	0.5	0.5
	6.2	5.1	5.3	2.7	1.8	2.5	2.9
TOTAL	12.0	12.0	13.3	4.4	3.7	4.9	5.0

TOTAL OOF NET

	1984	1985	1986	1983	1984	1985	1986
(all entries)	–	–	–	–	–	–	–

ODA COMMITMENTS : LOANS

DAC COUNTRIES	1983	1984	1985	1986
Australia	–	–	–	–
Austria	–	–	–	–
Belgium	–	–	–	–
Canada	–	–	–	–
Denmark	–	–	–	–
Finland	–	–	–	–
France	–	–	–	–
Germany, Fed. Rep.	–	–	–	–
Ireland	–	–	–	–
Italy	–	–	–	–
Japan	–	–	–	–
Netherlands	–	–	–	–
New Zealand	–	–	–	–
Norway	–	–	–	–
Sweden	–	–	–	–
Switzerland	–	–	–	–
United Kingdom	–	–	–	–
United States	–	–	–	–
TOTAL	–	–	–	–
MULTILATERAL	0.2	0.6	0.1	0.7
OPEC COUNTRIES	–	–	–	–
E.E.C.+ MEMBERS	0.2	–	–	–
TOTAL	0.2	0.6	0.1	0.7

GRANT ELEMENT OF ODA

DAC COUNTRIES	1983	1984	1985	1986
Australia	100.0	100.0	100.0	100.0
Austria	–	–	–	–
Belgium	–	–	–	–
Canada	100.0	100.0	100.0	100.0
Denmark	–	–	–	–
Finland	–	–	–	–
France	–	–	–	–
Germany, Fed. Rep.	100.0	100.0	100.0	100.0
Ireland	–	–	–	–
Italy	–	–	–	–
Japan	100.0	100.0	100.0	100.0
Netherlands	–	–	–	–
New Zealand	100.0	100.0	100.0	100.0
Norway	–	–	–	–
Sweden	–	–	–	–
Switzerland	–	–	–	–
United Kingdom	100.0	100.0	100.0	100.0
United States	100.0	100.0	100.0	100.0
TOTAL	100.0	100.0	100.0	100.0
MULTILATERAL	100.0	90.4	100.0	86.5
OPEC COUNTRIES	–	–	–	–
E.E.C.+ MEMBERS	100.0	100.0	100.0	100.0
TOTAL	100.0	98.8	100.0	98.0

OTHER AGGREGATES

COMMITMENTS: ALL SOURCES	1983	1984	1985	1986
TOTAL BILATERAL	14.2	8.7	10.8	6.4
of which				
OPEC	–	–	–	–
CMEA	–	–	–	–
TOTAL MULTILATERAL	2.3	1.3	2.9	1.1
TOTAL BIL.& MULTIL.	16.6	9.9	13.7	7.6
of which				
ODA Grants	16.4	9.4	13.6	6.9
ODA Loans	0.2	0.6	0.1	0.7

DISBURSEMENTS: DAC COUNTRIES COMBINED	1983	1984	1985	1986
OFFICIAL & PRIVATE				
GROSS:				
Contractual Lending	–	–	–	1.0
Export Credits Total	–	–	–	1.0
Export Credits Private	–	–	–	1.0
NET:				
Contractual Lending	–	–	–	0.4
Export Credits Total	–	–	–	0.4
PRIVATE SECTOR NET	-0.1	-0.5	-0.1	0.3
Direct Investment	–	–	–	–
Portfolio Investment	-0.1	-0.5	-0.1	-0.1
Export Credits	–	–	–	0.4

MARKET BORROWING: CHANGE IN CLAIMS	1983	1984	1985	1986
Banks	–	–	–	–

MEMORANDUM ITEM:	1983	1984	1985	1986
CMEA Countr.(Gross)	–	–	–	–

TOTAL RECEIPTS NET / TOTAL ODA NET / TOTAL ODA GROSS

	1983	1984	1985	1986	1983	1984	1985	1986	1983
TOTAL RECEIPTS NET					**TOTAL ODA NET**				**TOTAL ODA GROSS**
DAC COUNTRIES									
Australia	0.5	0.5	0.6	0.7	0.2	0.5	0.8	0.7	0.2
Austria	0.9	-13.9	3.2	72.6	0.9	1.0	0.8	1.6	0.9
Belgium	-73.8	-157.7	24.3	-4.0	0.4	0.2	0.4	0.4	0.4
Canada	-1.9	-46.4	-46.9	-49.4	0.4	0.6	0.0	0.0	0.4
Denmark	-1.4	0.0	-0.3	-0.7	-0.1	-0.1	0.1	-0.1	0.0
Finland	-7.4	-7.4	0.0	0.0	0.0	0.0	0.0	0.0	0.0
France	32.1	223.5	226.4	186.9	2.2	7.0	2.5	3.6	2.2
Germany, Fed. Rep.	27.3	-7.6	22.7	136.6	24.9	18.7	9.9	6.5	29.8
Ireland	–	–	–	–	–	–	–	–	–
Italy	-0.7	-0.5	-1.5	-0.6	0.0	0.1	0.1	0.0	0.0
Japan	208.5	937.0	874.9	626.3	-6.6	-48.1	-4.4	-13.7	80.3
Netherlands	0.5	4.4	47.1	50.7	0.5	1.0	0.5	0.6	0.6
New Zealand	0.0	0.1	0.0	0.0	0.0	0.1	0.0	0.0	0.0
Norway	-0.8	25.9	24.1	21.0	–	0.0	–	–	–
Sweden	23.2	61.8	54.0	-3.9	–	–	–	–	–
Switzerland	-18.6	-41.8	0.0	–	0.0	0.0	0.0	–	0.0
United Kingdom	-9.6	-43.7	-60.9	-30.5	0.1	0.2	0.2	0.1	0.1
United States	664.0	603.0	289.0	-508.0	-13.0	-16.0	-19.0	-23.0	8.0
TOTAL	*842.8*	*1536.9*	*1456.8*	*497.6*	*9.9*	*-34.9*	*-8.1*	*-23.5*	*123.0*
MULTILATERAL									
AF.D.F.	–	–	–	–	–	–	–	–	–
AF.D.B.	–	–	–	–	–	–	–	–	–
AS.D.B	66.4	76.7	52.8	14.5	0.1	0.1	-0.1	0.0	0.3
CAR.D.B.	–	–	–	–	–	–	–	–	–
E.E.C.	–	–	0.5	–	–	–	0.5	–	–
IBRD	417.6	370.0	110.8	-102.4	–	–	–	–	–
IDA	-1.5	-1.5	-1.5	-1.5	-1.5	-1.5	-1.5	-1.5	–
I.D.B.	–	–	–	–	–	–	–	–	–
IFAD	–	–	–	–	–	–	–	–	–
I.F.C.	-8.0	-1.7	-1.9	4.4	–	–	–	–	–
IMF TRUST FUND	–	–	–	–	–	–	–	–	–
U.N. AGENCIES	–	–	–	–	–	–	–	–	
UNDP	1.6	2.0	2.4	3.3	1.6	2.0	2.4	3.3	1.6
UNTA	1.3	1.2	1.4	1.3	1.3	1.2	1.4	1.3	1.3
UNICEF	0.6	0.6	0.6	0.5	0.6	0.6	0.6	0.5	0.6
UNRWA	–	–	–	–	–	–	–	–	–
WFP	–	–	–	–	–	–	–	–	–
UNHCR	0.1	0.1	0.1	0.2	0.1	0.1	0.1	0.2	0.1
Other Multilateral	0.8	0.7	0.7	0.6	0.8	0.7	0.7	0.6	0.8
Arab OPEC Agencies	–	–	–	–	–	–	–	–	–
TOTAL	*478.7*	*447.9*	*165.9*	*-79.1*	*2.8*	*2.9*	*4.0*	*4.4*	*4.5*
OPEC COUNTRIES	*-14.5*	*-6.7*	*-6.5*	*1.4*	*-4.8*	*-4.7*	*-4.5*	*1.8*	*–*
E.E.C. + MEMBERS	*-25.6*	*18.2*	*258.3*	*338.4*	*28.0*	*27.0*	*14.1*	*11.1*	*33.1*
TOTAL	*1306.9*	*1978.1*	*1616.2*	*419.9*	*8.0*	*-36.6*	*-8.6*	*-17.3*	*127.6*

ODA LOANS GROSS / ODA LOANS NET / GRANTS

	1983	1984	1985	1986	1983	1984	1985	1986	1983
ODA LOANS GROSS					**ODA LOANS NET**				**GRANTS**
DAC COUNTRIES									
Australia	–	–	–	–	0.0	0.0	–	–	0.2
Austria	–	–	–	–	–	–	–	–	0.9
Belgium	–	–	–	–	–	–	–	–	0.4
Canada	–	–	–	–	0.0	0.0	–	0.0	0.4
Denmark	–	–	–	–	-0.1	-0.1	–	-0.1	0.0
Finland	–	–	–	–	–	–	–	–	0.0
France	–	4.6	–	–	–	4.6	–	–	2.2
Germany, Fed. Rep.	18.1	14.2	6.1	2.6	13.2	8.9	0.4	-5.4	11.7
Ireland	–	–	–	–	–	–	–	–	–
Italy	–	–	–	–	–	–	–	–	0.0
Japan	71.1	58.4	69.5	101.4	-15.9	-59.4	-19.6	-35.5	9.2
Netherlands	–	–	–	–	-0.1	-0.1	-0.1	-0.1	0.6
New Zealand	–	–	–	–	–	–	–	–	0.0
Norway	–	–	–	–	–	–	–	–	–
Sweden	–	–	–	–	–	–	–	–	–
Switzerland	–	–	–	–	–	–	–	–	–
United Kingdom	–	–	–	–	–	–	–	–	0.1
United States	8.0	8.0	7.0	5.0	-13.0	-16.0	-19.0	-23.0	–
TOTAL	*97.2*	*85.2*	*82.6*	*109.1*	*-15.9*	*-62.1*	*-38.3*	*-64.2*	*25.8*
MULTILATERAL	*–*	*–*	*–*	*–*	*-1.7*	*-1.7*	*-1.7*	*-1.7*	*4.5*
OPEC COUNTRIES	*–*	*–*	*–*	*6.2*	*-4.8*	*-4.7*	*-4.5*	*1.8*	*–*
E.E.C. + MEMBERS	*18.1*	*18.8*	*6.1*	*2.6*	*13.0*	*13.3*	*0.3*	*-5.6*	*15.0*
TOTAL	*97.2*	*85.2*	*82.6*	*115.3*	*-22.4*	*-68.5*	*-44.5*	*-64.1*	*30.4*

TOTAL OFFICIAL GROSS / TOTAL OFFICIAL NET / TOTAL OOF GROSS

	1983	1984	1985	1986	1983	1984	1985	1986	1983
TOTAL OFFICIAL GROSS					**TOTAL OFFICIAL NET**				**TOTAL OOF GROSS**
DAC COUNTRIES									
Australia	0.2	0.5	0.8	0.7	0.2	0.5	0.8	0.7	–
Austria	0.9	1.0	17.6	72.6	0.9	0.6	17.3	72.6	–
Belgium	0.4	5.9	6.3	0.4	0.4	5.9	6.3	0.4	–
Canada	34.6	0.7	0.0	0.0	-1.9	-46.4	-46.9	-49.4	34.2
Denmark	0.0	0.1	0.4	0.2	-0.1	0.0	0.4	-0.1	–
Finland	0.0	0.0	0.0	0.0	0.0	0.0	0.0	0.0	–
France	2.2	7.0	2.5	3.6	2.2	7.0	2.5	3.6	–
Germany, Fed. Rep.	31.8	42.3	24.8	102.0	11.2	22.5	1.9	72.6	1.9
Ireland	–	–	–	–	–	–	–	–	–
Italy	0.0	0.1	0.1	0.0	0.0	0.1	0.1	0.0	–
Japan	80.3	80.3	86.2	123.8	-6.6	-37.9	-4.2	-15.3	–
Netherlands	0.6	1.0	0.6	0.6	0.5	1.0	0.5	0.6	–
New Zealand	0.0	0.1	0.0	0.0	0.0	0.1	0.0	0.0	–
Norway	–	0.0	–	–	–	0.0	–	–	–
Sweden	29.7	69.4	66.0	17.8	27.5	65.8	58.0	–	29.7
Switzerland	0.0	0.0	0.0	–	0.0	0.0	0.0	–	–
United Kingdom	0.1	0.2	0.2	0.1	0.1	0.2	0.2	0.1	–
United States	511.0	291.0	140.0	35.0	432.0	152.0	-50.0	-200.0	503.0
TOTAL	*691.9*	*499.4*	*345.5*	*357.0*	*466.4*	*171.3*	*-13.1*	*-114.0*	*568.8*
MULTILATERAL	*722.2*	*723.7*	*500.0*	*428.5*	*478.7*	*447.9*	*165.9*	*-79.1*	*717.7*
OPEC COUNTRIES	*6.7*	*–*	*0.1*	*6.3*	*-14.5*	*-6.7*	*-6.5*	*1.4*	*6.7*
E.E.C. + MEMBERS	*35.1*	*56.6*	*35.3*	*107.1*	*14.3*	*36.6*	*12.3*	*77.4*	*1.9*
TOTAL	*1420.8*	*1223.2*	*845.5*	*791.7*	*930.6*	*612.5*	*146.2*	*-191.7*	*1293.2*

Left panel

ODA COMMITMENTS

1984	1985	1986	1983	1984	1985	1986
0.5	0.8	0.7	0.1	0.8	0.7	0.5
1.0	0.8	1.6	0.9	0.9	0.8	–
0.2	0.4	0.4	–	–	–	0.4
0.7	0.0	0.0	0.5	0.6	0.0	–
0.0	0.1	0.0	–	–	–	–
0.0	0.0	0.0	–	–	–	–
7.0	2.5	3.6	2.2	7.0	2.5	3.6
24.0	15.6	14.5	18.8	11.1	15.6	8.0
–	–	–	–	–	–	–
0.1	0.1	0.0	0.0	0.1	0.1	0.0
69.7	84.6	123.2	199.9	219.9	244.9	24.1
1.0	0.6	0.6	0.6	1.0	0.6	0.6
0.1	0.0	0.0	0.0	0.1	0.0	–
0.0	–	–	–	0.0	–	–
–	–	–	–	–	–	–
0.0	0.0	–	–	–	–	–
0.2	0.2	0.1	0.1	0.2	0.2	0.1
8.0	7.0	5.0	7.8	8.0	6.9	5.3
112.5	*112.7*	*149.8*	*231.0*	*249.7*	*272.3*	*42.7*
–	–	–	–	–	–	–
–	–	–	–	–	–	–
0.3	0.1	0.2	–	–	–	–
–	–	–	–	–	–	–
–	0.5	–	0.0	–	0.1	–
–	–	–	–	–	–	–
–	–	–	–	–	–	–
–	–	–	–	–	–	–
–	–	–	–	–	–	–
–	–	–	4.2	4.4	5.1	5.9
2.0	2.4	3.3	–	–	–	–
1.2	1.4	1.3	–	–	–	–
0.6	0.6	0.5	–	–	–	–
–	–	–	–	–	–	–
0.1	0.1	0.2	–	–	–	–
0.7	0.7	0.6	–	–	–	–
–	–	–	–	–	–	0.4
4.7	*5.7*	*6.1*	*4.3*	*4.4*	*5.2*	*6.3*
–	0.1	6.3	–	49.4	0.0	–
32.5	*19.9*	*19.3*	*21.7*	*19.4*	*19.1*	*12.8*
117.1	*118.5*	*162.1*	*235.3*	*303.4*	*277.6*	*49.0*

TECH. COOP. GRANTS

1984	1985	1986	1983	1984	1985	1986
0.5	0.8	0.7	0.2	0.5	0.8	0.6
1.0	0.8	1.6	0.9	–	–	–
0.2	0.4	0.4	0.3	0.1	0.1	–
0.7	0.0	0.0	0.3	–	0.0	–
0.0	0.1	0.0	0.0	0.0	0.1	0.0
0.0	0.0	0.0	0.0	0.0	0.0	0.0
2.4	2.5	3.6	2.2	2.4	2.5	3.6
9.8	9.5	11.8	11.6	9.8	9.5	11.8
–	–	–	–	–	–	–
0.1	0.1	0.0	0.0	0.1	0.1	0.0
11.3	15.1	21.8	9.2	11.2	15.1	21.8
1.0	0.6	0.6	0.6	1.0	0.6	0.6
0.1	0.0	0.0	0.0	0.0	0.0	0.0
0.0	–	–	–	0.0	–	–
–	–	–	–	–	–	–
0.0	0.0	–	0.0	0.0	–	–
0.2	0.2	0.1	0.1	0.2	0.2	0.1
–	–	–	–	–	–	–
27.2	*30.1*	*40.7*	*25.5*	*25.4*	*29.0*	*38.7*
4.7	5.7	6.1	4.2	4.4	5.1	5.9
–	0.1	0.0	–	–	–	–
13.7	13.8	16.7	14.8	13.7	13.0	16.3
31.9	*35.9*	*46.8*	*29.7*	*29.8*	*34.1*	*44.6*

TOTAL OOF NET

1984	1985	1986	1983	1984	1985	1986
–	–	–	–	–	–	–
–	16.8	71.1	0.0	-0.3	16.5	71.1
5.7	5.9	0.1	–	5.7	5.9	0.1
–	–	–	-2.2	-47.0	-46.9	-49.4
0.1	0.3	0.2	–	0.1	0.3	0.1
–	–	–	–	–	–	–
18.3	9.2	87.5	-13.7	3.9	-8.0	66.2
–	–	–	–	–	–	–
10.6	1.6	0.6	–	10.2	0.3	-1.5
–	–	–	–	–	–	–
–	–	–	–	–	–	–
69.4	66.0	17.8	27.5	65.8	58.0	–
–	–	–	–	–	–	–
283.0	*133.0*	*30.0*	*445.0*	*168.0*	*-31.0*	*-177.0*
387.0	*232.8*	*207.3*	*456.5*	*206.2*	*-4.9*	*-90.6*
719.0	*494.2*	*422.4*	*475.9*	*445.0*	*161.9*	*-83.5*
–	–	–	-9.8	-2.0	-2.0	-0.4
24.0	*15.4*	*87.8*	*-13.7*	*9.6*	*-1.8*	*66.3*
1106.0	*727.0*	*629.6*	*922.6*	*649.1*	*154.9*	*-174.5*

Right panel

ODA COMMITMENTS : LOANS

DAC COUNTRIES	1983	1984	1985	1986
Australia	–	–	–	–
Austria	–	–	–	–
Belgium	–	–	–	–
Canada	–	–	–	–
Denmark	–	–	–	–
Finland	–	–	–	–
France	–	4.6	–	–
Germany, Fed. Rep.	5.9	3.5	3.8	–
Ireland	–	–	–	–
Italy	–	–	–	–
Japan	189.9	208.4	228.5	0.1
Netherlands	–	–	–	–
New Zealand	–	–	–	–
Norway	–	–	–	–
Sweden	–	–	–	–
Switzerland	–	–	–	–
United Kingdom	–	–	–	–
United States	7.8	8.0	6.9	5.3
TOTAL	*203.6*	*224.5*	*239.3*	*5.3*
MULTILATERAL	–	–	–	–
OPEC COUNTRIES	–	49.4	–	–
E.E.C.+ MEMBERS	5.9	8.1	3.8	–
TOTAL	*203.6*	*273.8*	*239.3*	*5.3*

GRANT ELEMENT OF ODA

DAC COUNTRIES	1983	1984	1985	1986
Australia	100.0	100.0	100.0	100.0
Austria	100.0	100.0	100.0	–
Belgium	–	–	–	100.0
Canada	100.0	100.0	100.0	–
Denmark	–	–	–	–
Finland	–	–	–	–
France	100.0	78.4	100.0	80.8
Germany, Fed. Rep.	80.2	79.9	88.0	100.0
Ireland	–	–	–	–
Italy	100.0	100.0	100.0	100.0
Japan	43.6	41.9	41.0	99.8
Netherlands	100.0	100.0	100.0	100.0
New Zealand	100.0	100.0	100.0	–
Norway	–	100.0	–	–
Sweden	–	–	–	–
Switzerland	–	–	–	–
United Kingdom	100.0	100.0	100.0	100.0
United States	67.1	67.1	67.1	67.1
TOTAL	*48.4*	*46.3*	*45.4*	*92.7*
MULTILATERAL	*100.0*	*100.0*	*100.0*	*100.0*
OPEC COUNTRIES	–	28.6	100.0	–
E.E.C.+ MEMBERS	82.9	80.7	90.2	90.4
TOTAL	*49.4*	*44.2*	*46.4*	*93.5*

OTHER AGGREGATES

COMMITMENTS: ALL SOURCES

	1983	1984	1985	1986
TOTAL BILATERAL	341.3	449.5	459.1	105.1
of which				
OPEC	8.6	49.4	0.0	–
CMEA	–	–	–	–
TOTAL MULTILATERAL	955.0	638.4	783.2	591.6
TOTAL BIL.& MULTIL.	1296.3	1087.9	1242.3	696.6
of which				
ODA Grants	31.7	29.6	38.3	43.7
ODA Loans	203.6	273.8	239.3	5.3

DISBURSEMENTS:

DAC COUNTRIES COMBINED

OFFICIAL & PRIVATE	1983	1984	1985	1986
GROSS:				
Contractual Lending	1238.2	1158.0	1132.0	1262.7
Export Credits Total	1141.0	1072.7	1048.2	1153.5
Export Credits Private	572.1	691.4	822.6	946.5
NET:				
Contractual Lending	15.9	-40.8	6.9	-19.2
Export Credits Total	31.8	21.2	43.9	44.9
PRIVATE SECTOR NET	376.3	1365.6	1469.9	611.6
Direct Investment	-62.4	246.2	168.2	362.4
Portfolio Investment	863.5	1298.6	1245.7	113.7
Export Credits	-424.7	-179.2	56.1	135.6

MARKET BORROWING:

CHANGE IN CLAIMS

	1983	1984	1985	1986
Banks	–	1957.0	2414.0	-2458.0

MEMORANDUM ITEM:

	1983	1984	1985	1986
CMEA Countr.(Gross)	–	–	–	–

	1983	1984	1985	1986		1983	1984	1985	1986		1983
TOTAL RECEIPTS NET					**TOTAL ODA NET**					**TOTAL ODA GROSS**	
DAC COUNTRIES											
Australia	1.8	2.8	2.6	3.5		1.8	2.8	2.6	3.5	Australia	1.8
Austria	–	–	–	–		–	–	–	–	Austria	–
Belgium	0.0	0.0	–	0.0		0.0	0.0	–	–	Belgium	0.0
Canada	–	–	–	–		–	–	–	–	Canada	–
Denmark	–	–	–	–		–	–	–	–	Denmark	–
Finland	–	–	–	–		–	–	–	–	Finland	–
France	0.1	0.4	0.1	0.5		0.1	0.4	0.3	0.3	France	0.1
Germany, Fed. Rep.	-0.7	-0.5	-0.5	-0.8		-0.7	-0.5	-0.5	-0.8	Germany, Fed. Rep.	0.0
Ireland	–	–	–	–		–	–	–	–	Ireland	–
Italy	–	–	–	0.3		–	–	–	0.3	Italy	–
Japan	2.4	2.8	4.5	5.2		2.0	1.7	7.5	5.2	Japan	2.0
Netherlands	2.5	2.5	0.3	1.4		2.5	2.5	0.3	1.4	Netherlands	2.5
New Zealand	–	0.0	0.0	0.0		–	0.0	0.0	0.0	New Zealand	–
Norway	–	0.0	0.1	0.1		–	0.0	0.1	0.1	Norway	–
Sweden	6.8	6.8	5.2	9.1		6.8	6.8	5.2	9.1	Sweden	6.8
Switzerland	0.1	0.0	30.3	0.1		0.1	0.0	0.1	0.1	Switzerland	0.1
United Kingdom	0.0	–	–	0.0		0.0	–	–	0.0	United Kingdom	–
United States	..	–	–	–		–	–	–	–	United States	–
TOTAL	*12.9*	*14.8*	*42.6*	*19.4*		*12.6*	*13.8*	*15.5*	*19.2*	*TOTAL*	*13.3*
MULTILATERAL											
AF.D.F.	–	–	–	–		–	–	–	–	AF.D.F.	–
AF.D.B.	–	–	–	–		–	–	–	–	AF.D.B.	–
AS.D.B	4.0	2.5	3.9	6.1		4.0	2.5	3.9	6.1	AS.D.B	4.5
CAR.D.B.	–	–	–	–		–	–	–	–	CAR.D.B.	–
E.E.C.	0.4	0.3	–	0.6		0.4	0.3	–	0.6	E.E.C.	0.4
IBRD	–	–	–	–		–	–	–	–	IBRD	–
IDA	4.6	7.3	5.0	7.0		4.6	7.3	5.0	7.0	IDA	4.6
I.D.B.	–	–	–	–		–	–	–	–	I.D.B.	–
IFAD	-0.1	–	0.5	0.1		-0.1	–	0.5	0.1	IFAD	–
I.F.C.	–	–	–	–		–	–	–	–	I.F.C.	–
IMF TRUST FUND	–	–	–	–		–	–	–	–	IMF TRUST FUND	–
U.N. AGENCIES	–	–	–	–		–	–	–	–	U.N. AGENCIES	–
UNDP	4.0	5.1	7.4	10.3		4.0	5.1	7.4	10.3	UNDP	4.0
UNTA	0.9	1.3	1.2	0.7		0.9	1.3	1.2	0.7	UNTA	0.9
UNICEF	0.9	0.9	1.3	1.3		0.9	0.9	1.3	1.3	UNICEF	0.9
UNRWA	–	–	–	–		–	–	–	–	UNRWA	–
WFP	0.5	0.5	0.2	0.3		0.5	0.5	0.2	0.3	WFP	0.5
UNHCR	1.4	0.8	0.9	0.8		1.4	0.8	0.9	0.8	UNHCR	1.4
Other Multilateral	0.1	0.5	1.1	0.3		0.1	0.5	1.1	0.3	Other Multilateral	0.1
Arab OPEC Agencies	0.5	1.1	0.1	1.5		0.5	1.1	0.1	1.5	Arab OPEC Agencies	0.8
TOTAL	*17.2*	*20.4*	*21.5*	*29.0*		*17.2*	*20.4*	*21.5*	*29.0*	*TOTAL*	*18.0*
OPEC COUNTRIES	–	–	–	–		–	–	–	–	**OPEC COUNTRIES**	–
E.E.C.+ MEMBERS	*2.2*	*2.7*	*-0.1*	*2.0*		*2.2*	*2.7*	*0.0*	*1.8*	*E.E.C.+ MEMBERS*	*3.0*
TOTAL	**30.1**	**35.2**	**64.1**	**48.4**		**29.7**	**34.1**	**37.0**	**48.2**	**TOTAL**	**31.3**

	1983	1984	1985	1986		1983	1984	1985	1986		1983
ODA LOANS GROSS					**ODA LOANS NET**					**GRANTS**	
DAC COUNTRIES											
Australia	–	–	–	–		–	–	–	–	Australia	1.8
Austria	–	–	–	–		–	–	–	–	Austria	–
Belgium	–	–	–	–		–	–	–	–	Belgium	0.0
Canada	–	–	–	–		–	–	–	–	Canada	–
Denmark	–	–	–	–		–	–	–	–	Denmark	–
Finland	–	–	–	–		–	–	–	–	Finland	–
France	–	–	–	–		–	–	–	–	France	0.1
Germany, Fed. Rep.	–	–	0.1	–		-0.7	-0.6	-0.6	-0.9	Germany, Fed. Rep.	0.0
Ireland	–	–	–	–		–	–	–	–	Ireland	–
Italy	–	–	–	–		–	–	–	–	Italy	–
Japan	–	–	–	–		–	-0.6	-0.6	-1.5	Japan	2.0
Netherlands	–	–	–	–		–	–	–	–	Netherlands	2.5
New Zealand	–	–	–	–		–	–	–	–	New Zealand	–
Norway	–	–	–	–		–	–	–	–	Norway	–
Sweden	–	–	–	–		–	–	–	–	Sweden	6.8
Switzerland	–	–	–	–		–	–	–	–	Switzerland	0.1
United Kingdom	–	–	–	–		0.0	–	–	–	United Kingdom	–
United States	–	–	–	–		–	–	–	–	United States	–
TOTAL	*–*	*–*	*0.1*	*–*		*-0.7*	*-1.2*	*-1.2*	*-2.4*	*TOTAL*	*13.3*
MULTILATERAL	*9.8*	*10.3*	*9.9*	*14.3*		*8.9*	*10.2*	*9.5*	*13.9*	*MULTILATERAL*	*8.2*
OPEC COUNTRIES	–	–	–	–		–	–	–	–	**OPEC COUNTRIES**	–
E.E.C.+ MEMBERS	*–*	*–*	*0.1*	*–*		*-0.7*	*-0.6*	*-0.6*	*-0.9*	*E.E.C.+ MEMBERS*	*3.0*
TOTAL	**9.8**	**10.3**	**9.9**	**14.3**		**8.2**	**9.0**	**8.3**	**11.6**	**TOTAL**	**21.5**

	1983	1984	1985	1986		1983	1984	1985	1986		1983
TOTAL OFFICIAL GROSS					**TOTAL OFFICIAL NET**					**TOTAL OOF GROSS**	
DAC COUNTRIES											
Australia	1.8	2.8	2.6	3.5		1.8	2.8	2.6	3.5	Australia	–
Austria	–	–	–	–		–	–	–	–	Austria	–
Belgium	0.0	0.0	–	–		0.0	0.0	–	–	Belgium	–
Canada	–	–	–	–		–	–	–	–	Canada	–
Denmark	–	–	–	–		–	–	–	–	Denmark	–
Finland	–	–	–	–		–	–	–	–	Finland	–
France	0.1	0.4	0.3	0.3		0.1	0.4	0.3	0.3	France	–
Germany, Fed. Rep.	0.0	0.0	0.1	0.0		-0.7	-0.5	-0.5	-0.8	Germany, Fed. Rep.	–
Ireland	–	–	–	–		–	–	–	–	Ireland	–
Italy	–	–	–	0.3		–	–	–	0.3	Italy	–
Japan	2.0	2.4	8.2	6.7		2.0	1.7	7.5	5.2	Japan	–
Netherlands	2.5	2.5	0.3	1.4		2.5	2.5	0.3	1.4	Netherlands	–
New Zealand	–	0.0	0.0	0.0		–	0.0	0.0	0.0	New Zealand	–
Norway	–	0.0	0.1	0.1		–	0.0	0.1	0.1	Norway	–
Sweden	6.8	6.8	5.2	9.1		6.8	6.8	5.2	9.1	Sweden	–
Switzerland	0.1	0.0	0.1	0.1		0.1	0.0	0.1	0.1	Switzerland	–
United Kingdom	–	–	–	0.0		0.0	–	–	0.0	United Kingdom	–
United States	–	–	–	–		–	–	–	–	United States	–
TOTAL	*13.3*	*15.0*	*16.8*	*21.6*		*12.6*	*13.8*	*15.5*	*19.2*	*TOTAL*	*–*
MULTILATERAL	*18.0*	*20.5*	*21.9*	*29.4*		*17.2*	*20.4*	*21.5*	*29.0*	*MULTILATERAL*	*–*
OPEC COUNTRIES	–	–	–	–		–	–	–	–	**OPEC COUNTRIES**	–
E.E.C.+ MEMBERS	*3.0*	*3.2*	*0.7*	*2.7*		*2.2*	*2.7*	*0.0*	*1.8*	*E.E.C.+ MEMBERS*	*–*
TOTAL	**31.3**	**35.5**	**38.7**	**51.0**		**29.7**	**34.1**	**37.0**	**48.2**	**TOTAL**	

LAOS

ODA COMMITMENTS

1984	1985	1986	1983	1984	1985	1986
2.8	2.6	3.5	5.0	1.1	0.6	6.1
0.0	–	–	–	–	–	–
–	–	–	–	–	–	–
–	–	–	–	–	–	–
–	–	–	–	–	–	–
–	–	–	–	–	–	–
0.4	0.3	0.3	0.2	0.4	0.2	0.3
0.0	0.1	0.0	0.0	0.0	0.1	0.0
–	–	–	–	–	–	–
–	–	0.3	–	–	–	0.3
2.4	8.2	6.7	4.5	8.6	1.9	15.3
2.5	0.3	1.4	0.6	0.9	0.1	0.1
0.0	0.0	0.0	0.0	–	0.0	0.0
0.0	0.1	0.1	0.0	–	–	–
6.8	5.2	9.1	8.0	7.6	7.7	9.1
0.0	0.1	0.1	0.1	–	–	0.1
–	–	0.0	–	–	–	0.0
–	–	–	–	–	–	–
15.0	16.8	21.6	18.3	18.5	10.6	31.3
2.8	4.3	6.5	14.3	9.0	2.4	12.0
–	–	–	–	–	–	–
0.3	–	0.6	0.0	1.1	0.3	0.0
7.3	5.0	7.0	6.2	–	–	3.9
–	–	–	–	–	–	–
-0.1	0.5	0.1	7.3	–	–	0.2
–	–	–	–	–	–	–
–	–	–	7.8	9.1	12.0	13.7
5.1	7.4	10.3	–	–	–	–
1.3	1.2	0.7	–	–	–	–
0.9	1.3	1.3	–	–	–	–
–	–	–	–	–	–	–
0.5	0.2	0.3	–	–	–	–
0.8	0.9	0.8	–	–	–	–
0.5	1.1	0.3	–	–	–	–
1.1	0.1	1.5	–	3.1	–	–
20.5	21.9	29.4	35.6	22.3	14.8	29.7
–	–	–	–	–	–	–
3.2	0.7	2.7	0.8	2.4	0.7	0.7
35.5	38.7	51.0	53.9	40.8	25.4	61.0

TECH. COOP. GRANTS

1984	1985	1986	1983	1984	1985	1986
2.8	2.6	3.5	–	0.1	0.2	0.6
0.0	–	–	–	–	–	–
–	–	–	–	–	–	–
–	–	–	–	–	–	–
0.4	0.3	0.3	0.1	0.4	0.2	0.3
0.0	0.1	0.0	0.0	0.0	0.0	0.0
–	–	0.3	–	–	–	–
2.4	8.2	6.7	0.3	0.1	0.2	1.9
2.5	0.3	1.4	0.6	1.8	0.1	0.1
0.0	0.0	0.0	–	–	–	–
0.0	0.1	0.1	–	–	–	–
6.8	5.2	9.1	2.4	1.2	1.3	1.7
0.0	0.1	0.1	–	0.0	0.1	–
–	–	0.0	–	–	–	0.0
–	–	–	–	–	–	–
15.0	16.8	21.6	3.5	3.7	2.0	4.5
10.2	12.0	15.0	7.3	8.6	11.8	13.4
–	–	–	–	–	–	–
3.2	0.6	2.7	0.7	2.3	0.4	0.4
25.2	28.8	36.6	10.7	12.3	13.8	17.9

TOTAL OOF NET

1984	1985	1986	1983	1984	1985	1986
–	–	–	–	–	–	–
–	–	–	–	–	–	–
–	–	–	–	–	–	–
–	–	–	–	–	–	–
–	–	–	–	–	–	–
–	–	–	–	–	–	–
–	–	–	–	–	–	–
–	–	–	–	–	–	–
–	–	–	–	–	–	–
–	–	–	–	–	–	–
–	–	–	–	–	–	–
–	–	–	–	–	–	–
–	–	–	–	–	–	–
–	–	–	–	–	–	–
–	–	–	–	–	–	–
–	–	–	–	–	–	–
–	–	–	–	–	–	–
–	–	–	–	–	–	–

ODA COMMITMENTS : LOANS

DAC COUNTRIES	1983	1984	1985	1986
Australia	–	–	–	–
Austria	–	–	–	–
Belgium	–	–	–	–
Canada	–	–	–	–
Denmark	–	–	–	–
Finland	–	–	–	–
France	–	–	–	–
Germany, Fed. Rep.	–	–	–	–
Ireland	–	–	–	–
Italy	–	–	–	–
Japan	–	–	–	–
Netherlands	–	–	–	–
New Zealand	–	–	–	–
Norway	–	–	–	–
Sweden	–	–	–	–
Switzerland	–	–	–	–
United Kingdom	–	–	–	–
United States	–	–	–	–
TOTAL	–	–	–	–
MULTILATERAL	27.4	12.1	2.4	15.9
OPEC COUNTRIES	–	–	–	–
E.E.C.+ MEMBERS	–	–	–	–
TOTAL	27.4	12.1	2.4	15.9

GRANT ELEMENT OF ODA

DAC COUNTRIES	1983	1984	1985	1986
Australia	100.0	100.0	100.0	100.0
Austria	–	–	–	–
Belgium	–	–	–	–
Canada	–	–	–	–
Denmark	–	–	–	–
Finland	–	–	–	–
France	100.0	100.0	100.0	100.0
Germany, Fed. Rep.	100.0	100.0	100.0	100.0
Ireland	–	–	–	–
Italy	–	–	–	100.0
Japan	100.0	100.0	100.0	100.0
Netherlands	100.0	100.0	100.0	100.0
New Zealand	100.0	–	100.0	100.0
Norway	100.0	–	–	–
Sweden	100.0	100.0	100.0	100.0
Switzerland	100.0	–	–	100.0
United Kingdom	–	–	–	100.0
United States	–	–	–	–
TOTAL	100.0	100.0	100.0	100.0
MULTILATERAL	86.2	82.6	100.0	88.9
OPEC COUNTRIES	–	–	–	–
E.E.C.+ MEMBERS	100.0	100.0	100.0	100.0
TOTAL	92.4	88.7	100.0	94.6

OTHER AGGREGATES

COMMITMENTS: ALL SOURCES	1983	1984	1985	1986
TOTAL BILATERAL	113.3	87.5	105.9	139.5
of which				
OPEC	–	–	–	–
CMEA	95.0	69.0	95.3	108.2
TOTAL MULTILATERAL	35.6	22.3	14.8	29.7
TOTAL BIL.& MULTIL.	148.9	109.8	120.7	169.2
of which				
ODA Grants	69.5	53.7	74.1	103.3
ODA Loans	79.4	56.1	46.6	65.9

DISBURSEMENTS: DAC COUNTRIES COMBINED	1983	1984	1985	1986
OFFICIAL & PRIVATE				
GROSS:				
Contractual Lending	1.5	3.2	0.1	–
Export Credits Total	1.5	3.2	–	–
Export Credits Private	1.5	3.2	–	–
NET:				
Contractual Lending	-0.4	-0.1	27.6	-2.4
Export Credits Total	0.3	1.1	28.8	–
PRIVATE SECTOR NET	0.3	1.1	27.1	0.2
Direct Investment	–	–	-1.6	–
Portfolio Investment	–	–	-0.1	0.2
Export Credits	0.3	1.1	28.8	–

MARKET BORROWING: CHANGE IN CLAIMS	1983	1984	1985	1986
Banks	–	23.0	42.0	-71.0

MEMORANDUM ITEM:	1983	1984	1985	1986
CMEA Countr.(Gross)	95.0	69.0	91.5	85.0

DISBURSEMENTS, UNLESS OTHERWISE STATED

	TOTAL RECEIPTS NET				TOTAL ODA NET				TOTAL ODA GROSS
	1983	1984	1985	1986	1983	1984	1985	1986	1983
DAC COUNTRIES									
Australia	4.3	1.4	0.0	0.0	3.5	1.4	0.0	0.0	3.5
Austria	3.0	-2.2	4.8	0.9	3.0	-1.7	-0.6	-0.2	3.0
Belgium	-0.8	1.1	-1.7	0.3	0.7	0.9	0.2	0.2	0.7
Canada	1.8	1.0	1.6	0.8	1.8	1.0	1.6	0.9	1.8
Denmark	4.5	0.2	–	–	4.5	0.2	–	–	4.5
Finland	0.5	0.3	0.3	0.2	0.5	0.3	0.3	0.2	0.5
France	26.4	59.2	12.8	41.8	17.5	15.2	9.0	14.8	17.7
Germany, Fed. Rep.	-0.3	3.4	3.2	4.6	3.5	3.7	3.2	5.2	3.5
Ireland	–	–	–	–	–	–	–	–	–
Italy	1.5	4.4	-24.1	5.9	1.8	2.3	5.1	5.9	1.8
Japan	0.5	-0.1	0.0	0.1	0.5	0.0	0.0	0.1	0.5
Netherlands	1.2	0.9	0.8	2.1	1.6	1.2	0.8	0.5	1.6
New Zealand	–	0.0	0.0	0.0	–	0.0	0.0	0.0	–
Norway	–	15.8	15.0	0.5	–	0.7	0.7	0.5	–
Sweden	4.5	0.4	0.1	-0.1	3.4	0.7	1.1	0.2	3.4
Switzerland	-0.5	1.0	0.1	1.0	1.9	1.0	0.4	1.0	1.9
United Kingdom	-0.4	2.5	-0.1	-0.5	0.0	0.1	0.0	0.0	0.0
United States	6.0	1.0	21.0	68.0	27.0	28.0	23.0	9.0	28.0
TOTAL	*52.2*	*90.4*	*33.7*	*125.6*	*71.3*	*54.9*	*44.7*	*38.5*	*72.5*
MULTILATERAL									
AF.D.F.	–	–	–	–	–	–	–	–	–
AF.D.B.	–	–	–	–	–	–	–	–	–
AS.D.B	–	–	–	–	–	–	–	–	–
CAR.D.B.	–	–	–	–	–	–	–	–	–
E.E.C.	7.3	-1.9	6.2	0.8	5.3	0.7	6.2	5.8	5.3
IBRD	4.1	0.0	0.4	-2.6	–	–	–	–	–
IDA	–	–	–	–	–	–	–	–	–
I.D.B.	–	–	–	–	–	–	–	–	–
IFAD	–	–	–	–	–	–	–	–	–
I.F.C.	–	–	–	–	–	–	–	–	–
IMF TRUST FUND	–	–	–	–	–	–	–	–	–
U.N. AGENCIES	–	–	–	–	–	–	–	–	–
UNDP	1.3	0.8	0.7	0.2	1.3	0.8	0.7	0.2	1.3
UNTA	0.8	0.3	0.7	0.4	0.8	0.3	0.7	0.4	0.8
UNICEF	27.2	15.2	6.5	5.8	27.2	15.2	6.5	5.8	27.2
UNRWA	–	–	–	–	–	–	–	–	–
WFP	5.0	5.5	12.3	10.1	5.0	5.5	12.3	10.1	5.0
UNHCR	0.8	0.6	0.2	0.1	0.8	0.6	0.2	0.1	0.8
Other Multilateral	0.8	0.6	0.9	0.0	0.8	0.6	0.9	0.0	0.8
Arab OPEC Agencies	-1.7	-1.4	-1.2	-1.4	-1.7	-1.4	-1.2	-1.4	–
TOTAL	*45.5*	*19.8*	*26.7*	*13.4*	*39.5*	*22.4*	*26.3*	*21.1*	*41.2*
OPEC COUNTRIES	*15.9*	*0.1*	*23.2*	*2.7*	*15.9*	*0.1*	*23.2*	*2.7*	*17.4*
E.E.C.+ MEMBERS	*39.3*	*69.9*	*-2.9*	*55.0*	*35.0*	*24.3*	*24.4*	*32.5*	*35.2*
TOTAL	**113.6**	**110.3**	**83.6**	**141.7**	**126.7**	**77.4**	**94.2**	**62.2**	**131.1**

	ODA LOANS GROSS				ODA LOANS NET				GRANTS
	1983	1984	1985	1986	1983	1984	1985	1986	1983
DAC COUNTRIES									
Australia	–	–	–	–					3.5
Austria	2.7	–	–	–	2.7	-1.9	-0.9	-0.5	0.3
Belgium	–	–	–	–	–	–	–	–	0.7
Canada	–	–	–	–	–	–	–	–	1.8
Denmark	3.7	–	–	–	3.7	–	–	–	0.9
Finland	–	–	–	–	–	–	–	–	0.5
France	3.3	0.7	0.6	2.2	3.1	0.1	-0.3	1.6	14.4
Germany, Fed. Rep.	0.2	–	–	0.1	0.2	–	–	0.1	3.4
Ireland	–	–	–	–	–	–	–	–	–
Italy	–	–	–	–	–	–	–	–	1.8
Japan	–	–	–	–	–	–	–	–	0.5
Netherlands	–	–	–	–	–	–	–	–	1.6
New Zealand	–	–	–	–	–	–	–	–	–
Norway	–	–	–	–	–	–	–	–	–
Sweden	–	–	–	–	–	–	–	–	3.4
Switzerland	–	–	–	–	–	–	–	–	1.9
United Kingdom	–	–	–	–	–	–	–	–	0.0
United States	–	–	–	–	-1.0	-1.0	-1.0	-1.0	28.0
TOTAL	*9.8*	*0.7*	*0.6*	*2.2*	*8.6*	*-2.8*	*-2.2*	*0.2*	*62.7*
MULTILATERAL	–	*0.6*	*0.5*	–	*-1.7*	*-1.4*	*-1.2*	*-1.4*	*41.2*
OPEC COUNTRIES	*4.0*	*0.3*	*0.3*	–	*2.5*	*-0.9*	*-0.9*	*-1.2*	*13.3*
E.E.C.+ MEMBERS	*7.1*	*0.7*	*0.6*	*2.2*	*6.9*	*0.1*	*-0.3*	*1.6*	*28.1*
TOTAL	**13.8**	**1.6**	**1.4**	**2.2**	**9.4**	**-5.1**	**-4.4**	**-2.4**	**117.2**

	TOTAL OFFICIAL GROSS				TOTAL OFFICIAL NET				TOTAL OOF GROSS
	1983	1984	1985	1986	1983	1984	1985	1986	1983
DAC COUNTRIES									
Australia	3.5	1.4	0.0	0.0	3.5	1.4	0.0	0.0	–
Austria	3.0	0.2	0.3	1.6	3.0	-1.9	-0.8	0.9	0.9
Belgium	0.7	0.9	0.2	0.2	0.7	0.9	0.2	0.2	0.2
Canada	1.8	1.0	1.6	0.9	1.8	1.0	1.6	0.9	0.9
Denmark	4.5	0.2	–	–	4.5	0.2	–	–	–
Finland	0.5	0.3	0.3	0.2	0.5	0.3	0.3	0.2	0.2
France	17.7	15.7	9.8	15.4	17.5	15.2	9.0	14.8	14.8
Germany, Fed. Rep.	3.5	3.7	2.8	5.2	3.5	3.7	2.8	5.1	0.0
Ireland	–	–	–	–	–	–	–	–	–
Italy	1.8	2.3	5.1	5.9	1.8	2.3	5.1	5.9	5.9
Japan	0.5	0.0	0.0	0.1	0.5	0.0	0.0	0.1	0.1
Netherlands	1.6	1.2	0.8	0.5	1.6	1.2	0.8	0.5	0.5
New Zealand	–	0.0	0.0	0.0	–	0.0	0.0	0.0	0.0
Norway	–	0.7	0.7	0.5	–	0.7	0.7	0.5	0.5
Sweden	3.4	0.7	1.1	0.2	3.4	0.7	1.1	0.2	0.2
Switzerland	1.9	1.0	0.4	1.0	1.9	1.0	0.4	1.0	1.0
United Kingdom	0.0	0.1	0.0	0.0	0.0	0.1	0.0	0.0	0.0
United States	28.0	29.0	24.0	10.0	19.0	10.0	23.0	9.0	9.0
TOTAL	*72.5*	*58.4*	*47.1*	*41.8*	*63.3*	*36.7*	*44.2*	*39.5*	*0.0*
MULTILATERAL	*54.8*	*29.6*	*32.5*	*23.8*	*45.5*	*19.8*	*26.7*	*13.4*	*13.6*
OPEC COUNTRIES	*17.4*	*1.4*	*24.5*	*3.9*	*15.9*	*0.1*	*23.2*	*2.7*	*0.1*
E.E.C.+ MEMBERS	*39.7*	*24.9*	*24.9*	*33.1*	*37.0*	*21.7*	*24.1*	*27.4*	*4.5*
TOTAL	**144.7**	**89.4**	**104.0**	**69.5**	**124.7**	**56.7**	**94.1**	**55.6**	**13.7**

LEBANON

ODA COMMITMENTS

	1984	1985	1986	1983	1984	1985	1986
Australia	1.4	0.0	0.0	3.9	1.4	0.1	–
Austria	0.2	0.3	0.3	0.2	0.2	0.3	–
Belgium	0.9	0.2	0.2	–	–	–	0.2
Canada	1.0	1.6	0.9	1.8	1.1	1.4	1.1
Denmark	0.2	–	–	–	–	–	–
Finland	0.3	0.3	0.2	0.5	0.3	0.1	0.1
France	15.7	9.8	15.4	18.4	23.6	9.1	15.4
Germany, Fed. Rep.	3.7	3.2	5.2	4.9	5.0	4.2	4.2
Ireland	–	–	–	–	–	–	–
Italy	2.3	5.1	5.9	2.0	4.2	6.2	15.3
Japan	0.0	0.0	0.1	0.6	0.0	0.0	0.1
Netherlands	1.2	0.8	0.5	1.8	1.1	0.4	0.5
New Zealand	0.0	0.0	0.0	0.0	–	0.0	–
Norway	0.7	0.7	0.5	0.0	0.0	–	–
Sweden	0.7	1.1	0.2	1.0	0.5	1.1	0.2
Switzerland	1.0	0.4	1.0	1.9	0.9	0.4	1.0
United Kingdom	0.1	0.0	0.0	0.0	0.1	0.0	0.0
United States	29.0	24.0	10.0	40.4	22.8	15.0	16.0
TOTAL	*58.4*	*47.5*	*40.5*	*77.5*	*61.1*	*38.2*	*53.9*
	–	–	–	–	–	–	–
	–	–	–	–	–	–	–
	0.7	6.2	5.8	22.5	2.2	18.2	4.6
	–	–	–	–	–	–	–
	–	–	–	–	–	–	–
	–	–	–	–	–	–	–
	–	–	–	35.9	23.1	21.3	16.6
	0.8	0.7	0.2	–	–	–	–
	0.3	0.7	0.4	–	–	–	–
	15.2	6.5	5.8	–	–	–	–
	–	–	–	–	–	–	–
	5.5	12.3	10.1	–	–	–	–
	0.6	0.2	0.1	–	–	–	–
	0.6	0.9	0.0	–	–	–	–
	0.7	0.6	–	0.1	–	–	–
	24.5	28.1	22.5	58.5	25.2	39.5	21.2
	1.3	24.5	3.9	15.1	–	27.0	3.8
	24.9	25.3	33.1	49.6	36.1	38.1	40.2
	84.2	*100.0*	*66.8*	*151.1*	*86.3*	*104.7*	*79.0*

TECH. COOP. GRANTS

	1984	1985	1986	1983	1984	1985	1986
Australia	1.4	0.0	0.0		0.0	0.0	–
Austria	0.2	0.3	0.3	0.1	–	–	–
Belgium	0.9	0.2	0.2	0.1	0.0	0.0	0.0
Canada	1.0	1.6	0.9	0.1	–	0.0	–
Denmark	0.2	–	–	–	–	–	–
Finland	0.3	0.3	0.2	0.0	0.0	0.0	–
France	15.0	9.3	13.2	14.4	10.5	9.1	13.2
Germany, Fed. Rep.	3.7	3.2	5.2	2.1	2.9	2.2	4.4
Ireland	–	–	–	–	–	–	–
Italy	2.3	5.1	5.9	0.2	0.1	0.3	0.9
Japan	0.0	0.0	0.1	0.0	0.0	0.0	0.1
Netherlands	1.2	0.8	0.5	0.0	0.7	0.1	0.3
New Zealand	0.0	0.0	0.0	–	–	–	–
Norway	0.7	0.7	0.5	–	–	–	–
Sweden	0.7	1.1	0.2	–	–	0.0	–
Switzerland	1.0	0.4	1.0	0.0	0.0	0.0	0.0
United Kingdom	0.1	0.0	0.0	0.0	0.0	0.0	0.0
United States	29.0	24.0	10.0	6.0	23.0	13.0	10.0
TOTAL	*57.7*	*46.9*	*38.3*	*23.0*	*37.4*	*24.9*	*28.8*
	23.8	27.5	22.5	30.9	17.6	8.9	6.5
	1.0	24.2	3.9	–	–	–	–
	24.2	24.7	30.9	16.7	14.3	11.7	18.7
	82.5	*98.6*	*64.6*	*53.8*	*54.9*	*33.8*	*35.3*

TOTAL OOF NET

1984	1985	1986	1983	1984	1985	1986
–	–	–	–	–	–	–
–	–	1.3	–	-0.2	-0.1	1.1
–	–	–	–	–	–	–
–	–	–	–	–	–	–
–	–	–	–	–	–	–
–	–	–	–	–	–	–
–	-0.3	–	–	–	-0.3	-0.1
–	–	–	–	–	–	–
–	–	–	–	–	–	–
–	–	–	–	–	–	–
–	–	–	–	–	–	–
–	–	–	-8.0	-18.0	–	–
–	-0.3	1.3	-8.0	-18.2	-0.5	1.0
5.1	4.4	1.3	6.0	-2.6	0.4	-7.6
0.1	0.0	0.0	–	–	–	0.0
–	-0.3	–	1.9	-2.6	-0.3	-5.1
5.2	*4.1*	*2.7*	*-2.0*	*-20.7*	*-0.1*	*-6.6*

ODA COMMITMENTS : LOANS

	1983	1984	1985	1986
DAC COUNTRIES				
Australia	–	–	–	–
Austria	–	–	–	–
Belgium	–	–	–	–
Canada	–	–	–	–
Denmark	–	–	–	–
Finland	–	–	–	–
France	4.0	8.6	–	2.2
Germany, Fed. Rep.	–	–	–	–
Ireland	–	–	–	–
Italy	–	–	–	–
Japan	–	–	–	–
Netherlands	–	–	–	–
New Zealand	–	–	–	–
Norway	–	–	–	–
Sweden	–	–	–	–
Switzerland	–	–	–	–
United Kingdom	–	–	–	–
United States	–	–	0.1	–
TOTAL	*4.0*	*8.6*	*0.1*	*2.2*
MULTILATERAL	–	–	–	–
OPEC COUNTRIES	–	–	–	–
E.E.C.+ MEMBERS	4.0	8.6	–	2.2
TOTAL	*4.0*	*8.6*	*0.1*	*2.2*

GRANT ELEMENT OF ODA

	1983	1984	1985	1986
DAC COUNTRIES				
Australia	100.0	100.0	100.0	–
Austria	100.0	100.0	100.0	–
Belgium	–	–	–	100.0
Canada	100.0	100.0	100.0	100.0
Denmark	–	–	–	–
Finland	100.0	100.0	100.0	100.0
France	89.7	88.6	100.0	100.0
Germany, Fed. Rep.	100.0	100.0	100.0	100.0
Ireland	–	–	–	–
Italy	100.0	100.0	100.0	100.0
Japan	100.0	100.0	100.0	100.0
Netherlands	100.0	100.0	100.0	100.0
New Zealand	100.0	–	100.0	–
Norway	100.0	100.0	–	–
Sweden	100.0	100.0	100.0	100.0
Switzerland	100.0	100.0	100.0	100.0
United Kingdom	100.0	100.0	100.0	100.0
United States	100.0	100.0	99.8	100.0
TOTAL	*97.6*	*95.6*	*99.9*	*100.0*
MULTILATERAL	100.0	100.0	100.0	100.0
OPEC COUNTRIES	100.0	–	100.0	100.0
E.E.C.+ MEMBERS	96.2	92.5	100.0	100.0
TOTAL	*98.7*	*96.9*	*100.0*	*100.0*

OTHER AGGREGATES

COMMITMENTS: ALL SOURCES

	1983	1984	1985	1986
TOTAL BILATERAL	92.7	61.1	126.8	57.8
of which				
OPEC	15.1	–	27.0	3.8
CMEA	–	–	45.0	–
TOTAL MULTILATERAL	62.9	25.2	39.5	21.2
TOTAL BIL.& MULTIL.	155.6	86.3	166.3	79.0
of which				
ODA Grants	147.1	77.7	104.7	76.8
ODA Loans	4.0	8.6	45.1	2.2

DISBURSEMENTS:

DAC COUNTRIES COMBINED

	1983	1984	1985	1986
OFFICIAL & PRIVATE				
GROSS:				
Contractual Lending	29.4	122.6	69.0	25.3
Export Credits Total	19.6	121.9	68.8	23.1
Export Credits Private	19.6	121.9	68.8	21.7
NET:				
Contractual Lending	7.4	83.4	-2.1	5.1
Export Credits Total	-1.2	86.1	0.4	5.0
PRIVATE SECTOR NET	-11.1	53.7	-10.5	86.1
Direct Investment	0.6	5.1	6.9	10.5
Portfolio Investment	-18.5	-55.7	-17.9	71.7
Export Credits	6.8	104.3	0.5	3.9

MARKET BORROWING:

CHANGE IN CLAIMS

	1983	1984	1985	1986
Banks	–	–	–	–

MEMORANDUM ITEM:

	1983	1984	1985	1986
CMEA Countr.(Gross)	–	–	2.0	–

LESOTHO

TOTAL RECEIPTS NET / TOTAL ODA NET / TOTAL ODA GROSS

	TOTAL RECEIPTS NET 1983	1984	1985	1986	TOTAL ODA NET 1983	1984	1985	1986	TOTAL ODA GROSS 1983
DAC COUNTRIES									
Australia	0.4	0.3	0.3	0.2	0.4	0.3	0.3	0.2	0.4
Austria	0.0	0.0	—	0.0	0.0	0.0	0.1	0.1	0.0
Belgium	0.0	0.3	0.1	0.1	0.0	0.1	0.1	0.1	0.0
Canada	2.8	2.5	5.1	1.8	2.8	2.5	5.1	1.8	2.8
Denmark	2.0	1.5	1.7	1.8	2.0	1.4	1.7	1.8	2.0
Finland	1.0	1.5	0.5	0.4	1.0	1.5	0.5	0.4	1.0
France	-0.1	0.1	0.0	0.3	0.2	0.3	0.2	0.4	0.2
Germany, Fed. Rep.	15.0	11.6	8.2	14.6	14.8	11.7	8.2	12.0	14.8
Ireland	3.4	3.3	2.9	3.6	3.4	3.3	2.9	3.6	3.4
Italy	1.0	0.6	0.7	1.3	1.0	0.6	0.7	1.3	1.0
Japan	0.0	0.9	0.2	0.6	0.0	0.3	0.7	0.6	0.0
Netherlands	2.4	1.7	0.7	1.0	2.4	1.7	0.8	1.0	2.4
New Zealand	—	—	—	0.0	—	—	—	0.0	—
Norway	0.7	0.5	0.8	0.7	0.7	0.5	0.8	0.7	0.7
Sweden	3.5	3.8	9.9	7.3	3.4	2.6	6.9	6.7	3.4
Switzerland	0.7	0.4	0.7	0.9	0.7	0.4	0.7	0.9	0.7
United Kingdom	6.7	-4.0	15.2	7.5	7.1	7.0	3.1	5.5	7.1
United States	25.0	32.0	19.0	19.0	25.0	32.0	19.0	19.0	25.0
TOTAL	*64.4*	*56.9*	*66.0*	*60.9*	*64.7*	*66.0*	*51.5*	*56.0*	*64.8*
MULTILATERAL									
AF.D.F.	3.4	1.7	4.7	5.2	3.4	1.7	4.7	5.2	3.5
AF.D.B.	2.4	4.7	10.7	-0.6	—	—	—	—	—
AS.D.B	—	—	—	—	—	—	—	—	—
CAR.D.B.	—	—	—	—	—	—	—	—	—
E.E.C.	5.5	7.5	7.5	6.1	5.5	7.5	7.5	6.1	5.5
IBRD	—	—	—	—	—	—	—	—	—
IDA	8.4	5.9	7.8	5.7	8.4	5.9	7.8	5.7	8.5
I.D.B.	—	—	—	—	—	—	—	—	—
IFAD	0.4	0.3	0.7	0.8	0.4	0.3	0.7	0.8	0.4
I.F.C.	—	—	—	—	—	—	—	—	—
IMF TRUST FUND	—	—	—	—	—	—	—	—	—
U.N. AGENCIES	—	—	—	—	—	—	—	—	—
UNDP	3.7	2.6	3.3	4.3	3.7	2.6	3.3	4.3	3.7
UNTA	0.7	0.5	1.0	0.8	0.7	0.5	1.0	0.8	0.7
UNICEF	0.2	0.2	0.4	0.9	0.2	0.2	0.4	0.9	0.2
UNRWA	—	—	—	—	—	—	—	—	—
WFP	10.6	8.3	10.2	8.1	10.6	8.3	10.2	8.1	10.6
UNHCR	0.7	0.6	0.4	0.3	0.7	0.6	0.4	0.3	0.7
Other Multilateral	1.4	1.9	1.5	1.5	1.4	1.9	1.5	1.5	1.4
Arab OPEC Agencies	5.4	2.1	2.1	-1.5	5.4	2.1	2.1	-1.5	5.6
TOTAL	*42.8*	*36.2*	*50.3*	*31.6*	*40.4*	*31.5*	*39.6*	*32.2*	*40.8*
OPEC COUNTRIES	2.5	3.1	3.1	-0.5	2.6	3.1	3.1	-0.5	2.6
E.E.C. + MEMBERS	*35.9*	*22.6*	*37.1*	*36.2*	*36.4*	*33.5*	*25.1*	*31.8*	*36.5*
TOTAL	**109.7**	**96.2**	**119.3**	**92.1**	**107.7**	**100.7**	**94.2**	**87.8**	**108.3**

ODA LOANS GROSS / ODA LOANS NET / GRANTS

	ODA LOANS GROSS 1983	1984	1985	1986	ODA LOANS NET 1983	1984	1985	1986	GRANTS 1983
DAC COUNTRIES									
Australia	—	—	—	—	—	—	—	—	0.4
Austria	—	—	—	—	0.0	0.0	0.0	0.0	0.0
Belgium	—	—	—	—	—	—	—	—	0.0
Canada	—	—	—	—	—	—	—	—	2.8
Denmark	—	—	—	—	—	—	—	-2.1	2.0
Finland	—	—	—	—	—	—	—	—	1.0
France	—	0.1	0.1	0.1	—	0.1	0.1	0.1	0.2
Germany, Fed. Rep.	—	—	—	—	—	—	—	—	14.8
Ireland	—	—	—	—	—	—	—	—	3.4
Italy	—	—	—	—	—	—	—	—	1.0
Japan	—	—	—	—	—	—	—	—	0.0
Netherlands	—	—	—	—	—	—	0.0	—	2.4
New Zealand	—	—	—	—	—	—	—	—	—
Norway	—	—	—	—	—	—	—	—	0.7
Sweden	—	—	—	—	—	—	—	—	3.4
Switzerland	—	—	—	—	—	—	—	—	0.7
United Kingdom	—	—	—	—	0.0	0.0	0.0	0.0	7.1
United States	—	—	—	—	—	—	—	—	25.0
TOTAL	*—*	*0.1*	*0.1*	*0.1*	*-0.1*	*0.1*	*-0.1*	*-2.2*	*64.8*
MULTILATERAL	*17.5*	*11.5*	*16.3*	*12.6*	*17.2*	*11.2*	*15.3*	*10.4*	*23.3*
OPEC COUNTRIES	2.6	3.0	3.2	0.0	2.6	2.9	2.9	-0.5	—
E.E.C. + MEMBERS	*0.0*	*1.5*	*0.1*	*0.3*	*0.0*	*1.5*	*0.0*	*-1.9*	*36.4*
TOTAL	**20.2**	**14.6**	**19.5**	**12.7**	**19.6**	**14.2**	**18.1**	**7.7**	**88.1**

TOTAL OFFICIAL GROSS / TOTAL OFFICIAL NET / TOTAL OOF GROSS

	TOTAL OFFICIAL GROSS 1983	1984	1985	1986	TOTAL OFFICIAL NET 1983	1984	1985	1986	TOTAL OOF GROSS 1983
DAC COUNTRIES									
Australia	0.4	0.3	0.3	0.2	0.4	0.3	0.3	0.2	—
Austria	0.0	0.0	0.0	0.1	0.0	0.0	—	0.0	—
Belgium	0.0	0.1	0.1	0.1	0.0	0.1	0.1	0.1	—
Canada	2.8	2.5	5.1	1.8	2.8	2.5	5.1	1.8	—
Denmark	2.0	1.4	1.7	4.0	2.0	1.4	1.7	1.8	0.0
Finland	1.0	1.5	0.5	0.4	1.0	1.5	0.5	0.4	—
France	0.2	0.3	0.2	0.4	0.2	0.3	0.2	0.4	—
Germany, Fed. Rep.	14.8	11.7	8.2	14.9	14.8	11.7	8.2	14.7	—
Ireland	3.4	3.3	2.9	3.6	3.4	3.3	2.9	3.6	—
Italy	1.0	0.6	0.7	1.3	1.0	0.6	0.7	1.3	—
Japan	0.0	0.3	0.7	0.6	0.0	0.3	0.7	0.6	—
Netherlands	2.4	1.7	0.9	1.0	2.4	1.7	0.7	1.0	—
New Zealand	—	—	—	0.0	—	—	—	—	0.0
Norway	0.7	0.5	0.8	0.7	0.7	0.5	0.8	0.7	0.7
Sweden	3.5	3.8	9.9	7.8	3.5	3.8	9.9	7.3	0.1
Switzerland	0.7	0.4	0.7	0.9	0.7	0.4	0.7	0.9	—
United Kingdom	7.1	7.0	3.1	5.6	7.1	6.7	2.7	5.1	—
United States	25.0	32.0	19.0	19.0	25.0	32.0	19.0	19.0	—
TOTAL	*65.0*	*67.4*	*54.7*	*62.3*	*64.9*	*67.0*	*54.1*	*58.9*	*0.2*
MULTILATERAL	*43.2*	*37.0*	*52.7*	*35.4*	*42.8*	*36.2*	*50.3*	*31.6*	*2.4*
OPEC COUNTRIES	2.6	3.2	3.4	0.0	2.5	3.1	3.1	-0.5	—
E.E.C. + MEMBERS	*36.5*	*33.6*	*25.2*	*37.0*	*36.4*	*33.2*	*24.7*	*34.2*	*0.0*
TOTAL	**110.8**	**107.6**	**110.7**	**97.7**	**110.1**	**106.3**	**107.5**	**90.1**	**2.5**

ODA COMMITMENTS

1984	1985	1986	1983	1984	1985	1986
0.3	0.3	0.2	0.2	0.4	0.2	0.2
0.0	0.0	0.1	–	–	0.0	–
0.1	0.1	0.1	–	–	–	0.1
2.5	5.1	1.8	3.8	5.5	2.4	5.9
1.4	1.7	4.0	3.1	1.1	0.9	1.2
1.5	0.5	0.4	-0.3	-1.0	0.0	0.2
0.3	0.2	0.4	2.1	0.2	0.2	0.4
11.7	8.2	12.0	10.8	5.9	6.3	20.2
3.3	2.9	3.6	3.4	3.3	2.9	3.6
0.6	0.7	1.3	1.3	0.9	1.1	1.5
0.3	0.7	0.6	0.4	0.7	0.5	0.1
1.7	0.9	1.0	2.7	1.9	1.2	1.9
–	–	0.0	–	–	–	–
0.5	0.8	0.7	0.9	0.4	10.4	0.6
2.6	6.9	6.7	4.2	8.8	11.8	6.7
0.4	0.7	0.9	1.1	0.0	2.1	0.0
7.0	3.1	5.6	2.8	2.5	2.3	3.1
32.0	19.0	19.0	25.3	29.5	11.2	25.5
66.1	*51.7*	*58.2*	*61.8*	*60.2*	*53.3*	*71.0*
1.8	4.8	5.4	15.8	7.2	9.8	13.1
–	–	–	–	–	–	–
–	–	–	–	–	–	–
7.5	7.5	6.2	3.9	16.8	8.0	19.7
–	–	–	–	–	–	–
6.0	7.9	6.0	–	25.2	3.5	9.8
0.3	0.7	0.8	–	–	0.2	5.0
–	–	–	–	–	–	–
–	–	–	17.4	14.1	16.8	15.9
2.6	3.3	4.3	–	–	–	–
0.5	1.0	0.8	–	–	–	–
0.2	0.4	0.9	–	–	–	–
–	–	–	–	–	–	–
8.3	10.2	8.1	–	–	–	–
0.6	0.4	0.3	–	–	–	–
1.9	1.5	1.5	–	–	–	–
2.1	2.8	0.1	3.0	1.5	–	–
31.7	*40.6*	*34.4*	*40.1*	*64.8*	*38.4*	*63.3*
3.2	3.4	0.0	–	0.2	0.2	–
33.6	*25.2*	*34.0*	*30.2*	*32.5*	*22.8*	*51.5*
101.1	*95.6*	*92.7*	*101.8*	*125.2*	*91.9*	*134.4*

TECH. COOP. GRANTS

1984	1985	1986	1983	1984	1985	1986
0.3	0.3	0.2	0.4	0.3	0.2	0.1
0.0	0.0	0.1	0.0	–	–	–
0.1	0.1	0.1	–	–	–	–
2.5	5.1	1.8	1.8	–	1.8	–
1.4	1.7	4.0	0.2	0.5	1.1	1.4
1.5	0.5	0.4	0.0	0.3	0.3	0.3
0.2	0.2	0.4	0.2	0.2	0.2	0.4
11.7	8.2	12.0	4.5	3.4	3.3	4.9
3.3	2.9	3.6	1.7	2.3	2.2	2.5
0.6	0.7	1.3	1.0	0.6	0.3	1.3
0.3	0.7	0.6	0.0	0.0	0.0	0.1
1.7	0.9	1.0	1.1	0.9	0.6	0.8
–	–	0.0	–	–	–	0.0
0.5	0.8	0.7	0.2	0.2	0.3	0.1
2.6	6.9	6.7	1.6	0.8	1.8	3.0
0.4	0.7	0.9	0.5	0.4	0.4	0.2
7.0	3.1	5.6	2.8	2.4	2.2	3.0
32.0	19.0	19.0	12.0	16.0	10.0	12.0
66.0	*51.6*	*58.2*	*28.0*	*28.2*	*24.7*	*29.9*
20.3	*24.3*	*21.8*	*6.7*	*5.8*	*6.7*	*9.2*
0.2	0.2	–	–	–	–	–
32.1	*25.2*	*33.7*	*11.5*	*10.2*	*9.9*	*15.6*
86.5	*76.1*	*80.0*	*34.7*	*34.0*	*31.3*	*39.1*

TOTAL OOF NET

1984	1985	1986	1983	1984	1985	1986
–	–	–	–	–	–	–
–	–	–	–	–	–	–
–	–	–	–	–	–	–
0.1	0.0	–	0.0	0.0	–	–
–	–	–	–	–	–	–
–	–	3.0	–	–	–	2.7
–	–	–	–	–	–	–
–	–	–	–	–	–	–
–	–	–	–	–	-0.1	–
–	–	–	–	–	–	–
1.2	3.0	1.1	0.1	1.2	3.0	0.6
–	–	–	0.0	-0.3	-0.3	-0.4
1.3	*3.0*	*4.1*	*0.1*	*0.9*	*2.6*	*2.9*
5.2	*12.1*	*1.0*	*2.4*	*4.7*	*10.7*	*-0.6*
–	–	–	-0.1	–	–	–
0.1	*0.0*	*3.0*	*0.0*	*-0.3*	*-0.4*	*2.4*
6.5	*15.2*	*5.0*	*2.4*	*5.6*	*13.3*	*2.3*

ODA COMMITMENTS : LOANS

DAC COUNTRIES

	1983	1984	1985	1986
Australia	–	–	–	–
Austria	–	–	–	–
Belgium	–	–	–	–
Canada	–	–	–	–
Denmark	–	–	–	–
Finland	–	–	–	–
France	2.0	–	–	0.1
Germany, Fed. Rep.	–	–	–	–
Ireland	–	–	–	–
Italy	–	–	–	–
Japan	–	–	–	–
Netherlands	–	–	–	–
New Zealand	–	–	–	–
Norway	–	–	–	–
Sweden	–	–	–	–
Switzerland	–	–	–	–
United Kingdom	–	–	–	–
United States	–	–	–	–
TOTAL	*2.0*	*–*	*–*	*0.1*
MULTILATERAL	*18.8*	*43.2*	*15.6*	*31.2*
OPEC COUNTRIES	*–*	*–*	*–*	*–*
E.E.C.+ MEMBERS	*2.0*	*9.3*	*2.3*	*3.5*
TOTAL	*20.7*	*43.2*	*15.6*	*31.3*

GRANT ELEMENT OF ODA

DAC COUNTRIES

	1983	1984	1985	1986
Australia	100.0	100.0	100.0	100.0
Austria	–	–	100.0	–
Belgium	–	–	–	100.0
Canada	100.0	100.0	100.0	100.0
Denmark	100.0	100.0	100.0	100.0
Finland	100.0	100.0	100.0	100.0
France	55.1	100.0	100.0	100.0
Germany, Fed. Rep.	100.0	100.0	100.0	100.0
Ireland	100.0	100.0	100.0	100.0
Italy	100.0	100.0	100.0	100.0
Japan	100.0	100.0	100.0	100.0
Netherlands	100.0	100.0	100.0	100.0
New Zealand	–	–	–	–
Norway	100.0	100.0	100.0	100.0
Sweden	100.0	100.0	100.0	100.0
Switzerland	100.0	100.0	100.0	100.0
United Kingdom	100.0	100.0	100.0	100.0
United States	100.0	100.0	100.0	100.0
TOTAL	*98.5*	*100.0*	*100.0*	*100.0*
MULTILATERAL	*90.0*	*88.3*	*93.8*	*90.0*
OPEC COUNTRIES	*–*	*100.0*	*100.0*	*–*
E.E.C.+ MEMBERS	*96.8*	*100.0*	*100.0*	*100.0*
TOTAL	*95.1*	*94.4*	*97.5*	*95.4*

OTHER AGGREGATES

COMMITMENTS: ALL SOURCES

	1983	1984	1985	1986
TOTAL BILATERAL	67.0	61.6	56.5	74.6
of which				
OPEC	–	0.2	0.2	–
CMEA	5.0	–	–	–
TOTAL MULTILATERAL	40.1	79.7	45.7	63.3
TOTAL BIL.& MULTIL.	107.0	141.3	102.2	137.9
of which				
ODA Grants	81.1	82.0	76.4	103.1
ODA Loans	20.7	43.2	15.6	31.3

DISBURSEMENTS:

DAC COUNTRIES COMBINED

	1983	1984	1985	1986
OFFICIAL & PRIVATE				
GROSS:				
Contractual Lending	0.2	4.2	16.9	7.2
Export Credits Total	0.1	4.0	16.8	7.1
Export Credits Private	–	2.8	13.8	3.0
NET:				
Contractual Lending	-0.5	-9.2	14.4	2.8
Export Credits Total	-0.5	-8.9	14.9	5.4
PRIVATE SECTOR NET	-0.5	-10.0	11.9	2.0
Direct Investment	–	–	–	–
Portfolio Investment	0.1	0.1	–	-0.1
Export Credits	-0.6	-10.2	11.9	2.1

MARKET BORROWING:

CHANGE IN CLAIMS

	1983	1984	1985	1986
Banks	–	–	–	–

MEMORANDUM ITEM:

	1983	1984	1985	1986
CMEA Countr.(Gross)	0.5	0.4	0.2	0.2

	1983	1984	1985	1986		1983	1984	1985	1986		1983
TOTAL RECEIPTS NET					**TOTAL ODA NET**					**TOTAL ODA GROSS**	
DAC COUNTRIES											
Australia	..	—	0.0	—		—	—	0.0	—	Australia	—
Austria	—	0.0	—	0.0		—	0.0	—	0.0	Austria	—
Belgium	10.1	8.1	40.0	-93.7		—	1.5	—	—	Belgium	—
Canada	-3.4	-2.2	-0.8	-0.8		0.2	0.3	0.2	0.0	Canada	0.2
Denmark	-2.8	1.6	0.2	0.2		0.1	1.6	0.2	0.2	Denmark	0.1
Finland	-5.4	-3.5	-6.5	0.0		—	—	—	0.0	Finland	—
France	-22.9	-76.2	-32.8	-73.6		3.6	1.6	1.1	0.7	France	3.6
Germany, Fed. Rep.	23.0	23.1	-3.0	-17.5		18.9	11.9	6.8	11.0	Germany, Fed. Rep.	21.0
Ireland	0.0	0.0	0.0	0.1		0.0	0.0	0.0	0.1	Ireland	0.0
Italy	-1.4	0.3	0.9	0.9		—	0.3	0.3	0.2	Italy	—
Japan	-221.8	-170.8	-239.4	12.1		6.1	3.6	1.6	7.2	Japan	6.1
Netherlands	2.0	-7.6	-9.7	-0.2		0.9	0.6	0.5	0.3	Netherlands	1.3
New Zealand	—	—	—	—		—	—	—	—	New Zealand	—
Norway	35.9	69.7	174.2	163.7		0.2	0.1	0.1	0.1	Norway	0.2
Sweden	-2.7	0.3	0.2	-0.4		—	0.1	0.2	—	Sweden	—
Switzerland	-9.0	2.2	-0.4	—		—	—	—	—	Switzerland	—
United Kingdom	-16.5	-62.7	-40.0	-8.7		4.3	2.1	1.3	1.3	United Kingdom	4.3
United States	45.0	5.0	-41.0	-71.0		54.0	84.0	52.0	48.0	United States	57.0
TOTAL	*-169.7*	*-212.6*	*-158.1*	*-89.0*		*88.3*	*107.5*	*64.3*	*69.1*	*TOTAL*	*93.7*
MULTILATERAL											
AF.D.F.	2.9	3.7	3.7	3.7		2.9	3.7	3.7	3.7	AF.D.F.	2.9
AF.D.B.	7.5	13.7	19.0	5.6		—	—	—	—	AF.D.B.	—
AS.D.B	—	—	—	—		—	—	—	—	AS.D.B	—
CAR.D.B.	—	—	—	—		—	—	—	—	CAR.D.B.	—
E.E.C.	3.0	1.1	3.2	3.9		3.8	1.9	2.3	5.1	E.E.C.	3.8
IBRD	4.2	5.0	0.7	-4.6		0.0	—	—	—	IBRD	0.0
IDA	10.7	14.6	12.1	10.6		10.7	14.6	12.1	10.6	IDA	10.8
I.D.B.	—	—	—	—		—	—	—	—	I.D.B.	—
IFAD	1.3	1.6	3.7	3.5		1.3	1.6	3.7	3.5	IFAD	1.3
I.F.C.	—	0.2	0.2	—		—	—	—	—	I.F.C.	—
IMF TRUST FUND	—	—	—	—		—	—	—	—	IMF TRUST FUND	—
U.N. AGENCIES	—	—	—	—		—	—	—	—	U.N. AGENCIES	—
UNDP	2.4	1.6	1.8	2.2		2.4	1.6	1.8	2.2	UNDP	2.4
UNTA	0.6	0.6	0.8	0.9		0.6	0.6	0.8	0.9	UNTA	0.6
UNICEF	0.4	0.4	0.5	0.4		0.4	0.4	0.5	0.4	UNICEF	0.4
UNRWA	—	—	—	—		—	—	—	—	UNRWA	—
WFP	0.7	—	0.9	0.7		0.7	—	0.9	0.7	WFP	0.7
UNHCR	0.3	0.3	0.3	0.4		0.3	0.3	0.3	0.4	UNHCR	0.3
Other Multilateral	0.8	0.9	0.4	0.7		0.8	0.9	0.4	0.7	Other Multilateral	0.8
Arab OPEC Agencies	6.0	0.1	—	—		6.2	0.1	—	—	Arab OPEC Agencies	6.5
TOTAL	*40.7*	*43.7*	*47.1*	*27.9*		*30.0*	*25.6*	*26.3*	*28.1*	*TOTAL*	*30.4*
OPEC COUNTRIES	*0.2*	*0.1*	*0.1*	*0.0*		*0.2*	*0.1*	*0.1*	*0.0*	*OPEC COUNTRIES*	*0.5*
E.E.C.+ MEMBERS	*-5.3*	*-112.2*	*-41.3*	*-188.7*		*31.6*	*21.3*	*12.5*	*18.8*	*E.E.C.+ MEMBERS*	*34.0*
TOTAL	**-128.9**	**-168.8**	**-111.0**	**-61.1**		**118.5**	**133.2**	**90.6**	**97.3**	**TOTAL**	**124.6**
ODA LOANS GROSS					**ODA LOANS NET**					**GRANTS**	
DAC COUNTRIES											
Australia	—	—	—	—		—	—	—	—	Australia	—
Austria	—	—	—	—		—	—	—	—	Austria	—
Belgium	—	1.5	—	—		—	1.5	—	—	Belgium	—
Canada	—	—	—	—		—	—	—	—	Canada	0.2
Denmark	—	1.4	0.1	0.1		—	1.4	0.1	0.1	Denmark	0.1
Finland	—	—	—	—		—	—	—	—	Finland	—
France	2.7	1.0	0.7	—		2.7	1.0	0.7	—	France	0.9
Germany, Fed. Rep.	15.2	6.5	3.1	6.9		13.2	6.2	1.8	4.6	Germany, Fed. Rep.	5.7
Ireland	—	—	—	—		—	—	—	—	Ireland	0.0
Italy	—	—	—	—		—	—	—	—	Italy	—
Japan	0.5	1.3	—	1.8		0.5	1.2	—	1.2	Japan	5.6
Netherlands	0.8	0.2	0.2	—		0.4	0.2	0.2	0.0	Netherlands	0.5
New Zealand	—	—	—	—		—	—	—	—	New Zealand	—
Norway	—	—	—	—		—	—	—	—	Norway	0.2
Sweden	—	—	—	—		—	—	—	—	Sweden	—
Switzerland	—	—	—	—		—	—	—	—	Switzerland	—
United Kingdom	3.6	1.4	0.4	—		3.6	1.4	0.3	—	United Kingdom	0.7
United States	17.0	17.0	7.0	14.0		14.0	12.0	5.0	13.0	United States	40.0
TOTAL	*39.8*	*30.2*	*11.5*	*22.7*		*34.4*	*24.7*	*8.1*	*18.8*	*TOTAL*	*53.9*
MULTILATERAL	*21.4*	*20.1*	*19.6*	*17.9*		*21.0*	*20.0*	*19.5*	*17.8*	*MULTILATERAL*	*9.0*
OPEC COUNTRIES	*0.3*	*—*	*—*	*—*		*0.1*	*—*	*—*	*—*	*OPEC COUNTRIES*	*0.1*
E.E.C.+ MEMBERS	*22.3*	*12.0*	*4.5*	*6.9*		*19.9*	*11.6*	*3.1*	*4.6*	*E.E.C.+ MEMBERS*	*11.7*
TOTAL	**61.6**	**50.3**	**31.1**	**40.6**		**55.5**	**44.7**	**27.5**	**36.6**	**TOTAL**	**63.0**
TOTAL OFFICIAL GROSS					**TOTAL OFFICIAL NET**					**TOTAL OOF GROSS**	
DAC COUNTRIES											
Australia	—	—	0.0	—		—	—	0.0	—	Australia	—
Austria	—	0.0	—	0.0		—	0.0	—	0.0	Austria	—
Belgium	—	1.5	0.2	—		—	1.5	0.2	—	Belgium	—
Canada	0.2	0.3	0.2	0.0		-3.4	-2.2	-0.8	-0.8	Canada	—
Denmark	0.1	1.6	0.2	0.2		0.1	1.6	0.2	0.2	Denmark	—
Finland	—	—	—	0.0		—	—	—	0.0	Finland	—
France	3.6	2.0	1.1	0.7		3.6	2.0	1.1	0.7	France	0.1
Germany, Fed. Rep.	76.8	19.2	13.3	13.3		36.9	11.8	0.0	-0.4	Germany, Fed. Rep.	55.9
Ireland	0.0	0.0	0.0	0.1		0.0	0.0	0.0	0.1	Ireland	—
Italy	—	0.3	0.8	0.9		—	0.3	0.8	0.9	Italy	—
Japan	6.1	3.8	1.6	7.8		6.1	3.6	1.6	7.2	Japan	—
Netherlands	3.1	1.2	1.1	1.0		2.0	1.1	1.1	1.0	Netherlands	1.8
New Zealand	—	—	—	—		—	—	—	—	New Zealand	—
Norway	0.2	0.1	0.1	0.1		0.2	0.1	0.1	0.1	Norway	—
Sweden	—	0.1	0.2	—		-0.6	-0.6	0.2	-0.6	Sweden	—
Switzerland	—	—	—	—		—	—	—	—	Switzerland	—
United Kingdom	5.1	2.1	1.4	1.3		5.0	2.0	1.2	1.3	United Kingdom	0.8
United States	60.0	96.0	60.0	49.0		57.0	91.0	58.0	48.0	United States	3.0
TOTAL	*155.2*	*128.1*	*80.2*	*74.4*		*107.0*	*112.3*	*63.7*	*57.7*	*TOTAL*	*61.5*
MULTILATERAL	*47.1*	*51.9*	*55.3*	*37.6*		*40.7*	*43.7*	*47.1*	*27.9*	*MULTILATERAL*	*16.7*
OPEC COUNTRIES	*0.5*	*0.1*	*0.1*	*0.0*		*0.2*	*0.1*	*0.1*	*0.0*	*OPEC COUNTRIES*	*—*
E.E.C.+ MEMBERS	*92.5*	*29.8*	*22.2*	*22.5*		*50.8*	*21.4*	*7.7*	*7.6*	*E.E.C.+ MEMBERS*	*58.5*
TOTAL	**202.7**	**180.1**	**135.5**	**112.1**		**147.9**	**156.1**	**110.8**	**85.6**	**TOTAL**	**78.2**

ODA COMMITMENTS

1984	1985	1986	1983	1984	1985	1986
–	0.0	–	–	–	0.0	–
0.0	–	0.0	–	–	–	–
1.5	–	–	–	1.5	–	–
0.3	0.2	0.0	0.2	0.2	0.1	0.0
1.6	0.2	0.2	5.5	–	0.2	12.4
–	–	0.0	–	–	–	–
1.6	1.1	0.7	4.1	1.3	0.4	0.7
12.2	8.1	13.3	11.2	7.7	6.2	10.6
0.0	0.0	0.1	0.0	0.0	0.0	0.1
0.3	0.3	0.2	–	0.3	0.5	0.4
3.8	1.6	7.8	1.2	5.0	5.1	8.8
0.6	0.5	0.3	1.2	0.3	0.2	0.8
–	–	–	–	–	–	–
0.1	0.1	0.1	0.1	0.1	0.1	0.1
0.1	0.2	–	–	–	–	–
–	–	–	–	–	–	–
2.1	1.4	1.3	0.7	0.6	1.0	1.3
89.0	54.0	49.0	58.2	75.3	46.2	54.8
113.0	*67.7*	*73.0*	*82.3*	*92.4*	*60.1*	*90.0*
3.7	3.7	3.7	–	22.6	–	–
–	–	–	–	–	–	–
–	–	–	–	–	–	–
1.9	2.3	5.1	3.4	2.9	14.1	5.0
–	–	–	–	–	–	–
14.7	12.2	10.7	–	18.1	7.6	–
–	–	–	–	–	–	–
1.6	3.7	3.5	–	5.4	–	–
–	–	–	–	–	–	–
–	–	–	5.1	3.8	4.5	5.3
1.6	1.8	2.2	–	–	–	–
0.6	0.8	0.9	–	–	–	–
0.4	0.5	0.4	–	–	–	–
–	–	–	–	–	–	–
–	0.9	0.7	–	–	–	–
0.3	0.3	0.4	–	–	–	–
0.9	0.4	0.7	–	–	–	–
0.1	–	–	–	–	–	–
25.8	*26.5*	*28.3*	*8.5*	*52.8*	*26.2*	*10.2*
0.1	*0.1*	*0.0*	*0.1*	–	–	–
21.7	*13.9*	*21.1*	*26.0*	*14.7*	*22.6*	*31.2*
138.8	***94.2***	***101.3***	***91.0***	***145.2***	***86.3***	***100.3***

TECH. COOP. GRANTS

1984	1985	1986	1983	1984	1985	1986
–	0.0	–	–	–	0.0	–
0.0	–	0.0	–	–	–	–
–	–	–	–	–	–	–
0.3	0.2	0.0	0.2	–	0.1	–
0.2	0.1	0.1	0.1	0.3	0.1	0.3
–	–	0.0	–	–	–	0.0
0.6	0.4	0.7	0.7	0.6	0.4	0.7
5.7	5.0	6.4	5.2	5.4	5.0	6.4
0.0	0.0	0.1	0.0	0.0	0.0	0.1
0.3	0.3	0.2	–	0.3	0.3	0.2
2.5	1.6	6.0	1.4	1.3	1.4	1.7
0.4	0.3	0.3	0.2	0.3	0.2	0.2
–	–	–	–	–	–	–
0.1	0.1	0.1	–	0.0	0.0	0.0
0.1	0.2	–	–	–	–	–
–	–	–	–	–	–	–
0.6	1.0	1.3	0.7	0.6	1.0	1.3
72.0	47.0	35.0	13.0	16.0	17.0	16.0
82.8	*56.2*	*50.3*	*21.5*	*25.0*	*25.6*	*26.9*
5.7	6.9	10.4	4.4	3.8	3.7	5.0
0.1	0.1	0.0	–	–	–	–
9.7	9.5	14.2	6.9	7.6	7.1	9.6
88.5	***63.1***	***60.7***	***25.9***	***28.8***	***29.3***	***31.9***

TOTAL OOF NET

1984	1985	1986	1983	1984	1985	1986
–	–	–	–	–	–	–
–	–	–	–	–	–	–
0.1	0.2	–	–	0.1	0.2	–
–	–	–	-3.6	-2.4	-0.9	-0.8
–	–	–	–	–	–	–
–	–	–	–	–	–	–
0.4	0.0	–	0.1	0.4	0.0	–
7.1	5.2	0.1	18.0	-0.1	-6.8	-11.3
–	–	–	–	–	–	–
–	0.6	0.7	–	–	0.6	0.7
–	–	–	–	–	–	–
0.6	0.6	0.7	1.2	0.6	0.6	0.6
–	–	–	–	–	–	–
–	–	–	-0.6	-0.6	–	-0.6
–	–	–	–	–	–	–
–	–	–	0.7	0.0	-0.1	–
7.0	6.0	–	3.0	7.0	6.0	–
15.1	*12.5*	*1.4*	*18.7*	*4.8*	*-0.6*	*-11.4*
26.2	*28.8*	*9.4*	*10.7*	*18.0*	*20.8*	*-0.2*
–	–	–	–	–	–	–
8.1	*8.3*	*1.4*	*19.1*	*0.0*	*-4.8*	*-11.2*
41.3	***41.3***	***10.8***	***29.4***	***22.8***	***20.2***	***-11.6***

ODA COMMITMENTS : LOANS

DAC COUNTRIES	1983	1984	1985	1986
Australia	–	–	–	–
Austria	–	–	–	–
Belgium	–	1.5	–	–
Canada	–	–	–	–
Denmark	5.5	–	–	12.4
Finland	–	–	–	–
France	3.2	0.7	–	0.7
Germany, Fed. Rep.	5.7	2.8	2.2	3.6
Ireland	–	–	–	–
Italy	–	–	–	–
Japan	–	2.4	–	1.8
Netherlands	0.6	–	–	–
New Zealand	–	–	–	–
Norway	–	–	–	–
Sweden	–	–	–	–
Switzerland	–	–	–	–
United Kingdom	–	–	–	–
United States	16.7	–	6.0	11.0
TOTAL	*31.6*	*7.4*	*8.2*	*28.8*
MULTILATERAL	–	*47.3*	*7.6*	–
OPEC COUNTRIES	–	–	–	–
E.E.C.+ MEMBERS	*14.9*	*6.2*	*2.2*	*16.0*
TOTAL	*31.6*	*54.6*	*15.8*	*28.8*

GRANT ELEMENT OF ODA

DAC COUNTRIES	1983	1984	1985	1986
Australia	–	–	100.0	–
Austria	–	–	–	–
Belgium	–	84.8	–	–
Canada	100.0	100.0	100.0	100.0
Denmark	76.0	–	100.0	75.4
Finland	–	–	–	–
France	47.5	63.6	100.0	100.0
Germany, Fed. Rep.	71.9	87.6	73.7	73.4
Ireland	100.0	100.0	100.0	100.0
Italy	–	100.0	100.0	100.0
Japan	100.0	100.0	100.0	83.3
Netherlands	100.0	100.0	100.0	100.0
New Zealand	–	–	–	–
Norway	100.0	100.0	100.0	100.0
Sweden	–	–	–	–
Switzerland	–	–	–	–
United Kingdom	100.0	100.0	100.0	100.0
United States	87.7	100.0	95.8	93.5
TOTAL	*83.2*	*98.2*	*94.0*	*87.9*
MULTILATERAL	*97.1*	*84.7*	*95.0*	*100.0*
OPEC COUNTRIES	*100.0*	–	–	–
E.E.C.+ MEMBERS	*74.2*	*87.8*	*92.8*	*81.2*
TOTAL	*84.8*	*93.2*	*94.3*	*89.1*

OTHER AGGREGATES

COMMITMENTS: ALL SOURCES

	1983	1984	1985	1986
TOTAL BILATERAL	144.2	106.6	143.2	102.9
of which				
OPEC	0.1	–	–	–
CMEA	0.1	–	–	–
TOTAL MULTILATERAL	27.4	92.7	26.2	10.2
TOTAL BIL.& MULTIL.	171.6	199.4	169.4	113.2
of which				
ODA Grants	59.4	90.6	70.5	71.5
ODA Loans	31.6	54.6	15.8	28.8

DISBURSEMENTS:

DAC COUNTRIES COMBINED

OFFICIAL & PRIVATE	1983	1984	1985	1986
GROSS:				
Contractual Lending	220.4	137.8	72.0	0.4
Export Credits Total	124.0	92.5	48.1	-23.6
Export Credits Private	119.1	92.5	48.1	-23.6
NET:				
Contractual Lending	-363.7	-237.7	-202.6	-173.7
Export Credits Total	-416.2	-270.3	-212.3	-184.4
PRIVATE SECTOR NET	-276.7	-324.9	-221.8	-146.7
Direct Investment	249.7	-45.6	-55.0	68.3
Portfolio Investment	-109.7	-12.1	43.2	-33.8
Export Credits	-416.8	-267.2	-210.0	-181.2

MARKET BORROWING:
CHANGE IN CLAIMS

	1983	1984	1985	1986
Banks	–	–	–	–

MEMORANDUM ITEM:

	1983	1984	1985	1986
CMEA Countr.(Gross)	0.1	–	–	–

TOTAL RECEIPTS NET

DAC COUNTRIES	1983	1984	1985	1986
Australia	1.1	0.6	0.5	–
Austria	0.0	1.3	-0.5	-0.2
Belgium	0.5	-1.0	1.9	0.3
Canada	1.7	0.9	0.1	1.9
Denmark	0.0	0.2	0.1	0.0
Finland	–	0.0	–	0.0
France	38.4	152.1	49.1	88.2
Germany, Fed. Rep.	11.6	30.1	8.2	22.4
Ireland	–	–	–	–
Italy	7.4	25.2	21.9	-5.1
Japan	25.6	8.5	9.4	17.0
Netherlands	0.1	0.0	0.2	3.6
New Zealand	–	–	–	–
Norway	1.7	2.9	3.6	4.9
Sweden	–	0.1	–	–
Switzerland	10.6	4.9	4.8	11.8
United Kingdom	13.5	-1.2	-0.8	-1.9
United States	11.0	19.0	22.0	20.0
TOTAL	*123.1*	*243.5*	*120.4*	*162.8*
MULTILATERAL				
AF.D.F.	3.2	4.3	6.8	13.6
AF.D.B.	–	0.8	6.0	12.7
AS.D.B	–	–	–	–
CAR.D.B.	–	–	–	–
E.E.C.	20.6	20.1	17.6	22.7
IBRD	-1.0	-1.1	-1.4	-1.3
IDA	33.3	30.4	57.6	93.4
I.D.B.	–	–	–	–
IFAD	0.3	3.3	2.4	3.4
I.F.C.	-1.8	-1.2	-1.4	4.8
IMF TRUST FUND	–	–	–	–
U.N. AGENCIES	–	–	–	–
UNDP	4.0	3.4	5.0	7.0
UNTA	0.7	1.1	0.7	0.8
UNICEF	1.1	0.9	1.1	1.3
UNRWA	–	–	–	–
WFP	0.8	0.4	1.3	2.2
UNHCR	–	–	–	–
Other Multilateral	2.3	1.4	1.3	0.9
Arab OPEC Agencies	7.5	-0.1	-0.3	-2.2
TOTAL	*70.9*	*63.7*	*96.5*	*159.4*
OPEC COUNTRIES	*33.2*	*-23.5*	*-7.6*	*-1.5*
E.E.C.+ MEMBERS	*92.1*	*225.5*	*98.0*	*130.1*
TOTAL	**227.1**	**283.7**	**209.4**	**320.7**

TOTAL ODA NET

DAC COUNTRIES	1983	1984	1985	1986
Australia	1.1	0.6	0.5	–
Austria	0.0	1.8	0.0	0.0
Belgium	0.0	0.1	0.1	0.3
Canada	1.2	0.9	0.5	2.6
Denmark	0.0	0.2	0.1	0.0
Finland	–	0.0	–	0.0
France	51.5	56.5	46.8	95.5
Germany, Fed. Rep.	8.4	4.7	14.5	21.5
Ireland	–	–	–	–
Italy	2.6	2.3	2.6	4.2
Japan	27.9	6.9	9.0	15.8
Netherlands	0.8	0.3	0.2	2.0
New Zealand	–	–	–	–
Norway	1.7	2.9	3.6	4.9
Sweden	–	0.1	–	–
Switzerland	10.6	4.9	4.8	11.8
United Kingdom	0.3	0.5	0.6	0.8
United States	11.0	15.0	16.0	17.0
TOTAL	*117.0*	*97.5*	*99.4*	*176.2*
MULTILATERAL				
AF.D.F.	3.2	4.3	6.8	13.6
AF.D.B.	–	–	–	–
AS.D.B	–	–	–	–
CAR.D.B.	–	–	–	–
E.E.C.	20.6	20.1	17.6	22.7
IBRD	–	–	–	–
IDA	33.3	30.4	57.6	93.4
I.D.B.	–	–	–	–
IFAD	0.3	3.3	2.4	3.4
I.F.C.	–	–	–	–
IMF TRUST FUND	–	–	–	–
U.N. AGENCIES	–	–	–	–
UNDP	4.0	3.4	5.0	7.0
UNTA	0.7	1.1	0.7	0.8
UNICEF	1.1	0.9	1.1	1.3
UNRWA	–	–	–	–
WFP	0.8	0.4	1.3	2.2
UNHCR	–	–	–	–
Other Multilateral	2.3	1.4	1.3	0.9
Arab OPEC Agencies	7.2	-1.2	-0.6	-3.6
TOTAL	*73.4*	*64.1*	*93.1*	*141.7*
OPEC COUNTRIES	*-6.8*	*-8.2*	*-4.8*	*-1.5*
E.E.C.+ MEMBERS	*84.3*	*84.6*	*82.6*	*146.8*
TOTAL	**183.5**	**153.4**	**187.8**	**316.4**

TOTAL ODA GROSS

	1983
Australia	1.1
Austria	0.0
Belgium	0.0
Canada	1.2
Denmark	0.0
Finland	–
France	52.9
Germany, Fed. Rep.	10.6
Ireland	–
Italy	2.6
Japan	28.0
Netherlands	0.8
New Zealand	–
Norway	1.7
Sweden	–
Switzerland	10.6
United Kingdom	0.3
United States	11.0
TOTAL	*120.6*
AF.D.F.	3.2
AF.D.B.	–
AS.D.B	–
CAR.D.B.	–
E.E.C.	20.7
IBRD	–
IDA	35.8
I.D.B.	–
IFAD	0.3
I.F.C.	–
IMF TRUST FUND	–
U.N. AGENCIES	–
UNDP	4.0
UNTA	0.7
UNICEF	1.1
UNRWA	–
WFP	0.8
UNHCR	–
Other Multilateral	2.3
Arab OPEC Agencies	8.2
TOTAL	*77.1*
OPEC COUNTRIES	*0.0*
E.E.C.+ MEMBERS	*87.9*
TOTAL	**197.8**

ODA LOANS GROSS

DAC COUNTRIES	1983	1984	1985	1986
Australia	–	–	–	–
Austria	–	1.8	–	–
Belgium	–	–	–	–
Canada	0.6	0.3	0.1	–
Denmark	0.0	–	–	–
Finland	–	–	–	–
France	21.5	29.2	15.2	57.9
Germany, Fed. Rep.	6.9	0.7	11.5	15.1
Ireland	–	–	–	–
Italy	–	–	–	–
Japan	19.7	5.0	9.3	4.3
Netherlands	–	–	–	–
New Zealand	–	–	–	–
Norway	–	–	–	–
Sweden	–	–	–	–
Switzerland	–	–	–	–
United Kingdom	–	–	–	–
United States	8.0	8.0	14.0	7.0
TOTAL	*56.7*	*44.9*	*50.1*	*84.3*
MULTILATERAL	*52.8*	*43.8*	*70.2*	*119.6*
OPEC COUNTRIES	*0.0*	*–*	*–*	*–*
E.E.C.+ MEMBERS	*33.7*	*34.8*	*28.8*	*79.1*
TOTAL	**109.6**	**88.6**	**120.2**	**203.9**

ODA LOANS NET

DAC COUNTRIES	1983	1984	1985	1986
Australia	–	–	–	–
Austria	–	1.8	–	–
Belgium	–	–	–	–
Canada	0.6	0.3	0.1	–
Denmark	0.0	–	–	–
Finland	–	–	–	–
France	20.1	25.8	14.6	53.1
Germany, Fed. Rep.	4.8	0.7	9.7	13.3
Ireland	–	–	–	–
Italy	–	–	–	–
Japan	19.5	3.2	6.7	3.7
Netherlands	–	–	–	–
New Zealand	–	–	–	–
Norway	–	–	–	–
Sweden	–	–	–	–
Switzerland	–	–	–	–
United Kingdom	–	–	–	–
United States	8.0	7.0	13.0	7.0
TOTAL	*53.0*	*38.8*	*44.1*	*77.2*
MULTILATERAL	*49.2*	*41.5*	*68.1*	*112.2*
OPEC COUNTRIES	*-6.8*	*-8.4*	*-4.8*	*-1.5*
E.E.C.+ MEMBERS	*30.1*	*31.3*	*26.3*	*71.8*
TOTAL	**95.3**	**71.8**	**107.5**	**187.8**

GRANTS

	1983
Australia	1.1
Austria	0.0
Belgium	0.0
Canada	0.5
Denmark	0.0
Finland	–
France	31.4
Germany, Fed. Rep.	3.7
Ireland	–
Italy	2.6
Japan	8.3
Netherlands	0.8
New Zealand	–
Norway	1.7
Sweden	–
Switzerland	10.6
United Kingdom	0.3
United States	3.0
TOTAL	*64.0*
MULTILATERAL	*24.2*
OPEC COUNTRIES	*–*
E.E.C.+ MEMBERS	*54.2*
TOTAL	**88.2**

TOTAL OFFICIAL GROSS

DAC COUNTRIES	1983	1984	1985	1986
Australia	1.1	0.6	0.5	–
Austria	0.0	1.8	0.0	0.0
Belgium	2.5	2.3	3.2	3.0
Canada	1.9	0.9	0.5	2.6
Denmark	0.0	0.2	0.1	0.0
Finland	–	0.0	–	0.0
France	89.7	124.3	69.0	111.7
Germany, Fed. Rep.	20.0	17.1	32.8	37.4
Ireland	–	–	–	–
Italy	24.7	32.2	27.8	4.2
Japan	28.0	8.6	11.6	16.3
Netherlands	0.8	0.3	0.2	2.0
New Zealand	–	–	–	–
Norway	1.7	2.9	3.6	4.9
Sweden	–	0.1	–	–
Switzerland	10.6	4.9	4.8	11.8
United Kingdom	0.3	0.5	0.6	0.8
United States	11.0	20.0	23.0	20.0
TOTAL	*192.3*	*216.5*	*177.6*	*214.6*
MULTILATERAL	*77.4*	*70.0*	*101.6*	*169.9*
OPEC COUNTRIES	*55.3*	*1.4*	*–*	*–*
E.E.C.+ MEMBERS	*158.8*	*197.0*	*151.4*	*182.4*
TOTAL	**325.0**	**287.9**	**279.2**	**384.5**

TOTAL OFFICIAL NET

DAC COUNTRIES	1983	1984	1985	1986
Australia	1.1	0.6	0.5	–
Austria	0.0	1.5	-0.2	-0.2
Belgium	2.3	2.1	3.1	3.0
Canada	1.7	0.9	0.1	1.9
Denmark	0.0	0.2	0.1	0.0
Finland	–	0.0	–	0.0
France	87.6	114.5	68.3	106.2
Germany, Fed. Rep.	15.9	12.9	26.9	26.1
Ireland	–	–	–	–
Italy	24.7	32.2	27.8	4.2
Japan	27.9	6.9	9.0	15.8
Netherlands	0.8	0.3	0.2	2.0
New Zealand	–	–	–	–
Norway	1.7	2.9	3.6	4.9
Sweden	-0.9	0.1	–	–
Switzerland	10.6	4.9	4.8	11.8
United Kingdom	0.3	0.5	0.6	0.8
United States	11.0	19.0	22.0	20.0
TOTAL	*184.5*	*199.3*	*166.7*	*196.5*
MULTILATERAL	*70.9*	*63.7*	*96.5*	*159.4*
OPEC COUNTRIES	*33.2*	*-23.5*	*-7.6*	*-1.5*
E.E.C.+ MEMBERS	*152.2*	*182.8*	*144.5*	*164.9*
TOTAL	**288.6**	**239.5**	**255.7**	**354.3**

TOTAL OOF GROSS

	1983
Australia	–
Austria	–
Belgium	2.4
Canada	0.8
Denmark	–
Finland	–
France	36.9
Germany, Fed. Rep.	9.5
Ireland	–
Italy	22.1
Japan	–
Netherlands	–
New Zealand	–
Norway	–
Sweden	–
Switzerland	–
United Kingdom	–
United States	–
TOTAL	*71.6*
MULTILATERAL	*0.3*
OPEC COUNTRIES	*55.3*
E.E.C.+ MEMBERS	*70.9*
TOTAL	**127.2**

ODA COMMITMENTS

1984	1985	1986	1983	1984	1985	1986
0.6	0.5	–	0.7	0.6	–	–
1.8	0.0	0.0	0.0	1.8	0.0	–
0.1	0.1	0.3	–	–	–	0.3
0.9	0.5	2.6	0.7	0.8	0.3	4.3
0.2	0.1	0.0	–	–	–	–
0.0	–	0.0	–	0.0	–	–
59.9	47.4	100.3	74.4	56.0	74.7	100.3
4.7	16.3	23.2	3.6	22.1	10.7	18.7
–	–	–	–	–	–	–
2.3	2.6	4.2	4.1	1.2	2.8	4.4
8.6	11.6	16.3	22.0	9.6	16.8	9.9
0.3	0.2	2.0	0.8	0.3	0.2	2.0
–	–	–	–	–	–	–
2.9	3.6	4.9	1.5	6.9	4.2	4.2
0.1	–	–	–	0.1	–	–
4.9	4.8	11.8	5.5	7.7	15.9	11.1
0.5	0.6	0.8	0.2	0.3	0.6	0.8
16.0	17.0	17.0	6.8	28.6	14.8	18.0
103.6	*105.4*	*183.3*	*120.2*	*135.8*	*140.8*	*173.9*
4.3	7.2	14.1	15.4	40.0	0.7	26.8
–	–	–	–	–	–	–
–	–	–	–	–	–	–
20.2	17.8	23.4	28.3	21.9	40.4	22.3
–	–	–	–	–	–	–
31.3	58.4	95.1	50.9	27.8	72.0	95.3
–	–	–	–	–	–	–
3.3	2.4	4.3	13.5	–	–	0.2
–	–	–	–	–	–	–
–	–	–	8.8	7.2	9.3	12.2
3.4	5.0	7.0	–	–	–	–
1.1	0.7	0.8	–	–	–	–
0.9	1.1	1.3	–	–	–	–
–	–	–	–	–	–	–
0.4	1.3	2.2	–	–	–	–
–	–	–	–	–	–	–
1.4	1.3	0.9	–	–	–	–
–	–	–	11.0	2.2	–	–
66.3	*95.1*	*149.2*	*127.9*	*99.1*	*122.4*	*156.7*
0.2	–	–	–	–	–	–
88.1	85.1	154.1	111.3	101.8	129.4	148.7
170.1	**200.5**	**332.4**	**248.1**	**235.0**	**263.2**	**330.6**

TECH. COOP. GRANTS

1984	1985	1986	1983	1984	1985	1986
0.6	0.5	–	0.0	0.0	–	–
0.0	0.0	0.0	0.0	–	–	–
0.1	0.1	0.3	0.0	0.0	0.0	0.0
0.6	0.4	2.6	–	–	0.2	–
0.2	0.1	0.0	0.0	0.1	0.1	0.0
0.0	–	0.0	–	0.0	–	0.0
30.7	32.2	42.4	22.2	22.4	24.0	36.9
4.0	4.8	8.1	3.0	3.5	3.8	6.9
–	–	–	–	–	–	–
2.3	2.6	4.2	0.3	0.6	0.7	0.6
3.7	2.3	12.1	1.0	0.4	0.7	1.0
0.3	0.2	2.0	0.8	0.2	0.2	0.5
–	–	–	–	–	–	–
2.9	3.6	4.9	0.4	0.5	0.5	0.6
0.1	–	–	–	–	–	–
4.9	4.8	11.8	1.4	1.2	1.2	1.5
0.5	0.6	0.8	0.2	0.1	0.6	0.8
8.0	3.0	10.0	–	–	–	1.0
58.7	*55.3*	*99.0*	*29.3*	*29.1*	*32.0*	*49.8*
22.5	25.0	29.6	8.1	6.8	8.0	11.0
0.2	–	–	–	–	–	–
53.3	56.3	75.0	26.4	27.0	29.4	46.7
81.4	**80.3**	**128.6**	**37.3**	**35.9**	**40.0**	**60.8**

TOTAL OOF NET

1984	1985	1986	1983	1984	1985	1986
–	–	–	–	–	–	–
–	–	–	–	-0.3	-0.3	-0.2
2.2	3.0	2.7	2.2	2.0	3.0	2.7
–	–	–	0.5	–	-0.4	-0.7
–	–	–	–	–	–	–
–	–	–	–	–	–	–
64.4	21.6	11.4	36.1	58.0	21.5	10.8
12.4	16.5	14.2	7.5	8.2	12.3	4.7
–	–	–	–	–	–	–
29.9	25.1	–	22.1	29.9	25.1	–
–	–	–	–	–	–	–
–	–	–	–	–	–	–
–	–	–	-0.9	–	–	–
4.0	6.0	3.0	–	4.0	6.0	3.0
112.9	*72.3*	*31.3*	*67.6*	*101.8*	*67.3*	*20.3*
3.7	6.5	20.8	-2.5	-0.4	3.4	17.7
1.3	–	–	40.0	-15.3	-2.8	–
108.9	*66.3*	*28.3*	*68.0*	*98.1*	*61.9*	*18.1*
117.8	**78.7**	**52.1**	**105.1**	**86.1**	**67.9**	**38.0**

ODA COMMITMENTS : LOANS

DAC COUNTRIES

	1983	1984	1985	1986
Australia	–	–	–	–
Austria	–	1.8	–	–
Belgium	–	–	–	–
Canada	–	–	–	–
Denmark	–	–	–	–
Finland	–	–	–	–
France	42.0	24.3	40.4	57.9
Germany, Fed. Rep.	2.2	11.5	8.5	5.2
Ireland	–	–	–	–
Italy	–	–	–	–
Japan	19.2	5.0	9.3	4.3
Netherlands	–	–	–	–
New Zealand	–	–	–	–
Norway	–	–	–	–
Sweden	–	–	–	–
Switzerland	–	–	–	–
United Kingdom	–	–	–	–
United States	5.2	19.0	8.5	0.7
TOTAL	*68.7*	*61.5*	*66.6*	*68.1*
MULTILATERAL	*95.2*	*79.5*	*77.3*	*125.3*
OPEC COUNTRIES	–	–	–	–
E.E.C.+ MEMBERS	*48.7*	*45.3*	*53.5*	*66.3*
TOTAL	**163.9**	**141.0**	**143.9**	**193.4**

GRANT ELEMENT OF ODA

DAC COUNTRIES

	1983	1984	1985	1986
Australia	100.0	100.0	–	–
Austria	100.0	65.9	100.0	–
Belgium	–	–	–	100.0
Canada	100.0	100.0	100.0	100.0
Denmark	–	–	–	–
Finland	–	100.0	–	–
France	60.4	67.2	70.0	65.5
Germany, Fed. Rep.	54.2	91.4	71.5	90.2
Ireland	–	–	–	–
Italy	100.0	100.0	100.0	100.0
Japan	65.0	75.4	58.6	70.2
Netherlands	100.0	100.0	100.0	100.0
New Zealand	–	–	–	–
Norway	100.0	100.0	100.0	100.0
Sweden	–	100.0	–	–
Switzerland	100.0	100.0	100.0	100.0
United Kingdom	100.0	100.0	100.0	100.0
United States	64.9	70.6	74.9	98.1
TOTAL	*65.6*	*76.7*	*74.8*	*78.5*
MULTILATERAL	*84.0*	*85.7*	*89.5*	*86.3*
OPEC COUNTRIES	–	–	–	–
E.E.C.+ MEMBERS	*70.6*	*78.0*	*80.8*	*76.3*
TOTAL	**75.2**	**80.7**	**81.9**	**82.4**

OTHER AGGREGATES

COMMITMENTS: ALL SOURCES

	1983	1984	1985	1986
TOTAL BILATERAL	230.4	285.9	249.1	237.9
of which				
OPEC	53.1	–	–	–
CMEA	–	41.3	29.0	50.0
TOTAL MULTILATERAL	190.6	114.5	133.7	157.7
TOTAL BIL.& MULTIL.	421.0	400.4	382.8	395.6
of which				
ODA Grants	84.2	97.0	119.3	137.2
ODA Loans	163.9	179.3	173.0	243.4

DISBURSEMENTS:

DAC COUNTRIES COMBINED

OFFICIAL & PRIVATE

	1983	1984	1985	1986
GROSS:				
Contractual Lending	168.6	178.3	124.7	92.3
Export Credits Total	49.1	23.2	2.8	-23.2
Export Credits Private	40.3	21.1	2.8	-23.2
NET:				
Contractual Lending	106.4	115.3	70.7	52.3
Export Credits Total	-6.6	-22.9	-40.5	-46.0
PRIVATE SECTOR NET	-61.5	44.2	-46.3	-33.6
Direct Investment	3.7	8.6	-0.2	14.0
Portfolio Investment	-51.0	60.3	-5.9	-2.5
Export Credits	-14.2	-24.7	-40.3	-45.2

MARKET BORROWING:

CHANGE IN CLAIMS

	1983	1984	1985	1986
Banks	–	-29.0	-6.0	-63.0

MEMORANDUM ITEM:

	1983	1984	1985	1986
CMEA Countr.(Gross)	15.5	12.7	24.5	19.0

	1983	1984	1985	1986	1983	1984	1985	1986		1983
TOTAL RECEIPTS NET					**TOTAL ODA NET**				**TOTAL ODA GROSS**	
DAC COUNTRIES										
Australia	0.2	0.3	0.5	0.4	0.2	0.3	0.5	0.4	Australia	0.2
Austria	0.0	–	–	–	0.0	–	–	–	Austria	0.0
Belgium	0.0	-0.2	-0.5	-0.2	0.0	0.0	0.0	0.0	Belgium	0.0
Canada	7.8	3.3	4.3	1.4	7.8	3.3	4.3	1.4	Canada	7.8
Denmark	0.9	3.0	5.2	3.4	0.9	3.0	5.1	3.5	Denmark	0.9
Finland	0.1	0.2	0.0	0.2	0.1	0.2	0.0	0.2	Finland	0.1
France	3.6	3.7	5.8	6.4	3.3	3.0	3.2	3.8	France	3.3
Germany, Fed. Rep.	16.1	14.4	10.5	28.9	14.5	14.7	11.9	29.1	Germany, Fed. Rep.	14.5
Ireland	0.0	0.0	–	0.0	0.0	0.0	–	0.0	Ireland	0.0
Italy	0.0	0.1	0.1	2.3	0.0	0.1	0.1	2.3	Italy	0.0
Japan	0.0	4.1	3.2	14.5	5.1	6.4	4.9	16.1	Japan	5.1
Netherlands	-0.4	1.5	2.3	8.0	2.3	1.3	2.6	5.6	Netherlands	2.3
New Zealand	–	0.0	0.0	–	–	0.0	0.0	–	New Zealand	–
Norway	0.2	–	0.6	0.0	0.2	–	0.5	0.0	Norway	0.2
Sweden	0.4	1.2	–	-0.4	–	–	–	–	Sweden	–
Switzerland	0.6	0.2	0.0	0.0	0.6	0.2	0.0	0.0	Switzerland	0.6
United Kingdom	6.8	40.1	15.5	40.3	15.1	14.3	13.9	16.0	United Kingdom	18.1
United States	6.0	8.0	6.0	9.0	6.0	5.0	6.0	11.0	United States	6.0
TOTAL	*42.4*	*79.9*	*53.4*	*114.3*	*56.2*	*51.7*	*52.9*	*89.5*	*TOTAL*	*59.2*
MULTILATERAL										
AF.D.F.	5.7	3.3	2.0	3.2	5.7	3.3	2.0	3.2	AF.D.F.	5.7
AF.D.B.	2.7	5.6	6.9	0.6	–	–	–	–	AF.D.B.	–
AS.D.B	–	–	–	–	–	–	–	–	AS.D.B	–
CAR.D.B.	–	–	–	–	–	–	–	–	CAR.D.B.	–
E.E.C.	5.1	13.3	10.5	15.4	5.8	14.5	10.9	17.2	E.E.C.	5.8
IBRD	0.0	-1.7	-0.8	2.8	–	–	–	–	IBRD	–
IDA	29.2	76.0	32.7	78.0	29.2	76.0	32.7	78.0	IDA	30.4
I.D.B.	–	–	–	–	–	–	–	–	I.D.B.	–
IFAD	7.3	1.7	5.2	4.8	7.3	1.7	5.2	4.8	IFAD	7.3
I.F.C.	0.5	-1.3	-1.5	-0.3	–	–	–	–	I.F.C.	–
IMF TRUST FUND	–	–	–	–	–	–	–	–	IMF TRUST FUND	–
U.N. AGENCIES	–	–	–	–	–	–	–	–	U.N. AGENCIES	–
UNDP	7.2	7.9	4.8	4.7	7.2	7.9	4.8	4.7	UNDP	7.2
UNTA	0.6	0.3	0.7	0.9	0.6	0.3	0.7	0.9	UNTA	0.6
UNICEF	1.0	0.9	1.0	1.4	1.0	0.9	1.0	1.4	UNICEF	1.0
UNRWA	–	–	–	–	–	–	–	–	UNRWA	–
WFP	2.9	1.2	1.6	1.6	2.9	1.2	1.6	1.6	WFP	2.9
UNHCR	–	–	0.2	0.7	–	–	0.2	0.7	UNHCR	–
Other Multilateral	1.2	1.2	1.0	1.0	1.2	1.2	1.0	1.0	Other Multilateral	1.2
Arab OPEC Agencies	-0.1	-0.1	-0.1	-0.1	-0.1	-0.1	-0.1	-0.1	Arab OPEC Agencies	–
TOTAL	*63.0*	*108.2*	*64.3*	*114.6*	*60.6*	*106.8*	*60.1*	*113.2*	*TOTAL*	*62.0*
OPEC COUNTRIES	–	–	0.0	0.2	–	–	0.0	0.2	**OPEC COUNTRIES**	–
E.E.C.+ MEMBERS	*32.1*	*75.9*	*49.3*	*104.6*	*42.0*	*50.8*	*47.6*	*77.5*	*E.E.C.+ MEMBERS*	*45.0*
TOTAL	**105.4**	**188.1**	**117.7**	**229.0**	**116.8**	**158.5**	**113.0**	**202.9**	**TOTAL**	**121.2**
ODA LOANS GROSS					**ODA LOANS NET**				**GRANTS**	
DAC COUNTRIES										
Australia	–	–	–	–	–	–	–	–	Australia	0.2
Austria	–	–	–	–	–	–	–	–	Austria	0.0
Belgium	–	–	–	–	–	–	–	–	Belgium	0.0
Canada	–	–	–	–	–	–	–	–	Canada	7.8
Denmark	0.3	1.6	4.1	1.2	0.3	1.6	4.1	1.1	Denmark	0.7
Finland	–	–	–	–	–	–	–	–	Finland	0.1
France	1.2	1.7	2.1	2.3	1.2	1.7	2.1	2.3	France	2.1
Germany, Fed. Rep.	–	–	–	–	–	–	–	–	Germany, Fed. Rep.	14.5
Ireland	–	–	–	–	–	–	–	–	Ireland	0.0
Italy	–	–	–	–	–	–	–	–	Italy	0.0
Japan	–	1.3	–	10.4	–	1.1	0.0	10.4	Japan	5.1
Netherlands	0.7	0.1	0.2	0.0	0.7	0.1	-4.3	–	Netherlands	1.6
New Zealand	–	–	–	–	–	–	–	–	New Zealand	–
Norway	–	–	–	–	–	–	–	–	Norway	0.2
Sweden	–	–	–	–	–	–	–	–	Sweden	–
Switzerland	–	–	–	–	–	–	–	–	Switzerland	0.6
United Kingdom	0.5	0.7	–	–	-2.4	-2.0	-2.7	-3.1	United Kingdom	17.5
United States	–	–	–	–	–	-1.0	-1.0	-1.0	United States	6.0
TOTAL	*2.7*	*5.2*	*6.4*	*14.0*	*-0.3*	*1.4*	*-1.8*	*9.7*	*TOTAL*	*56.5*
MULTILATERAL	*44.5*	*85.2*	*43.8*	*90.1*	*43.0*	*82.3*	*42.1*	*88.3*	*MULTILATERAL*	*17.5*
OPEC COUNTRIES	–	–	–	–	–	–	–	–	**OPEC COUNTRIES**	–
E.E.C.+ MEMBERS	*3.7*	*5.4*	*8.7*	*6.3*	*0.7*	*2.7*	*1.6*	*2.8*	*E.E.C.+ MEMBERS*	*41.2*
TOTAL	**47.2**	**90.4**	**50.2**	**104.1**	**42.7**	**83.7**	**40.4**	**98.1**	**TOTAL**	**74.0**
TOTAL OFFICIAL GROSS					**TOTAL OFFICIAL NET**				**TOTAL OOF GROSS**	
DAC COUNTRIES										
Australia	0.2	0.3	0.5	0.4	0.2	0.3	0.5	0.4	Australia	–
Austria	0.0	–	–	–	0.0	–	–	–	Austria	–
Belgium	0.0	0.0	0.0	0.0	0.0	0.0	0.0	0.0	Belgium	–
Canada	7.8	3.3	4.3	1.4	7.8	3.3	4.3	1.4	Canada	–
Denmark	0.9	3.0	5.2	3.6	0.9	3.0	5.2	3.4	Denmark	–
Finland	0.1	0.2	0.0	0.2	0.1	0.2	0.0	0.2	Finland	–
France	3.3	3.0	3.9	3.8	3.3	3.0	3.8	-2.1	France	–
Germany, Fed. Rep.	16.0	16.6	13.3	30.0	15.3	15.2	11.5	29.4	Germany, Fed. Rep.	1.5
Ireland	0.0	0.0	–	0.0	0.0	0.0	–	0.0	Ireland	–
Italy	0.0	0.1	0.1	2.3	0.0	0.1	0.1	2.3	Italy	–
Japan	5.1	6.5	4.9	16.1	5.1	6.4	4.9	16.1	Japan	–
Netherlands	2.3	1.7	7.1	6.4	2.1	1.5	2.3	6.3	Netherlands	–
New Zealand	–	0.0	0.0	–	–	0.0	0.0	–	New Zealand	–
Norway	0.2	–	0.5	0.0	0.2	–	0.5	0.0	Norway	–
Sweden	0.8	1.6	–	–	–	1.2	–	-0.4	Sweden	0.8
Switzerland	0.6	0.2	0.0	0.0	0.6	0.2	0.0	0.0	Switzerland	–
United Kingdom	22.2	17.3	17.9	22.0	18.0	12.9	14.0	16.6	United Kingdom	4.1
United States	6.0	9.0	7.0	12.0	6.0	8.0	6.0	9.0	United States	–
TOTAL	*65.6*	*62.8*	*64.6*	*98.2*	*59.8*	*55.4*	*53.0*	*82.7*	*TOTAL*	*6.4*
MULTILATERAL	*70.4*	*117.8*	*71.2*	*128.3*	*63.0*	*108.2*	*64.3*	*114.6*	*MULTILATERAL*	*8.4*
OPEC COUNTRIES	–	–	0.0	0.2	–	–	0.0	0.2	**OPEC COUNTRIES**	–
E.E.C.+ MEMBERS	*51.2*	*56.2*	*59.5*	*86.4*	*44.9*	*49.1*	*47.4*	*71.4*	*E.E.C.+ MEMBERS*	*6.3*
TOTAL	**136.0**	**180.6**	**135.8**	**226.7**	**122.8**	**163.5**	**117.3**	**197.5**	**TOTAL**	**14.8**

ODA COMMITMENTS

1984	1985	1986	1983	1984	1985	1986
0.3	0.5	0.4	0.1	0.5	0.3	0.3
–	–	–	–	–	–	–
0.0	0.0	0.0	–	–	–	0.0
3.3	4.3	1.4	6.1	1.9	0.7	8.8
3.0	5.1	3.6	8.5	2.4	2.4	13.4
0.2	0.0	0.2	–	0.1	–	–
3.0	3.2	3.8	5.3	0.7	5.7	3.8
14.7	11.9	29.1	15.2	19.2	14.6	37.8
0.0	–	0.0	0.0	0.0	–	0.0
0.1	0.1	2.3	0.0	0.1	0.1	4.9
6.5	4.9	16.1	5.6	7.6	5.9	60.2
1.3	7.1	5.7	2.2	1.3	6.9	6.9
0.0	0.0	–	–	–	0.0	–
–	0.5	0.0	–	–	–	0.0
0.2	0.0	0.0	0.6	0.1	0.0	0.0
17.0	16.5	19.1	21.2	21.1	11.3	20.6
6.0	7.0	12.0	5.2	16.2	19.9	35.8
55.6	*61.1*	*93.7*	*69.9*	*71.3*	*67.8*	*192.6*
3.3	2.1	3.2	11.6	21.4	16.2	20.8
–	–	–	–	–	–	–
–	–	–	–	–	–	–
14.5	10.9	17.4	40.0	11.4	23.4	41.7
–	–	–	–	–	–	–
76.9	34.0	79.1	126.0	15.0	105.4	–
–	–	–	–	–	–	–
3.6	5.5	5.0	10.0	13.4	–	0.1
–	–	–	–	–	–	–
–	–	–	12.8	11.4	9.3	10.2
7.9	4.8	4.7	–	–	–	–
0.3	0.7	0.9	–	–	–	–
0.9	1.0	1.4	–	–	–	–
–	–	–	–	–	–	–
1.2	1.6	1.6	–	–	–	–
–	0.2	0.7	–	–	–	–
1.2	1.0	1.0	–	–	–	–
–	–	–	–	–	–	–
109.7	*61.7*	*115.0*	*200.4*	*72.5*	*154.3*	*72.8*
–	0.0	0.2	–	–	–	–
53.6	54.8	81.0	92.4	56.2	64.4	129.1
165.3	**122.8**	**208.9**	**270.3**	**143.9**	**222.0**	**265.4**

TECH. COOP. GRANTS

1984	1985	1986	1983	1984	1985	1986
0.3	0.5	0.4	0.2	0.3	0.5	0.3
–	–	–	0.0	–	–	–
0.0	0.0	0.0	–	–	–	–
3.3	4.3	1.4	1.0	–	1.4	–
1.5	1.0	2.4	0.5	0.9	0.6	0.7
0.2	0.0	0.2	0.1	0.2	0.0	0.8
1.3	1.1	1.5	0.7	0.6	0.6	1.0
14.7	11.9	29.1	3.9	8.3	7.1	7.0
0.0	–	0.0	0.0	0.0	–	0.0
0.1	0.1	2.3	0.0	0.1	0.0	2.3
5.3	4.9	5.7	2.3	2.5	2.0	2.9
1.2	6.9	5.6	1.5	1.2	1.5	0.5
0.0	0.0	–	–	0.0	0.0	–
–	0.5	0.0	–	–	–	0.0
0.2	0.0	0.0	0.0	0.0	–	0.0
16.3	16.5	19.1	10.6	9.3	8.4	10.5
6.0	7.0	12.0	4.0	6.0	5.0	8.0
50.3	*54.7*	*79.8*	*24.8*	*29.4*	*27.2*	*34.0*
24.5	17.9	24.9	9.9	10.2	7.7	10.8
–	0.0	0.2	–	–	–	–
48.2	46.1	74.7	17.3	20.4	18.3	24.2
74.8	**72.6**	**104.8**	**34.7**	**39.7**	**34.9**	**44.8**

TOTAL OOF NET

1984	1985	1986	1983	1984	1985	1986
–	–	–	–	–	–	–
–	–	–	–	–	–	–
–	–	–	–	–	–	–
–	0.0	–	–	–	0.0	0.0
–	0.7	–	–	–	0.6	-5.9
1.9	1.4	0.9	0.8	0.6	-0.4	0.3
–	–	–	–	–	–	–
–	–	–	–	–	–	–
0.4	–	0.7	-0.2	0.3	-0.3	0.7
–	–	–	–	–	–	–
1.6	–	–	–	1.2	–	-0.4
0.3	1.4	2.9	3.0	-1.4	0.1	0.6
3.0	–	–	–	3.0	–	-2.0
7.2	3.5	4.5	3.6	3.6	0.1	-6.8
8.1	9.6	13.3	2.5	1.4	4.2	1.4
–	–	–	–	–	–	–
2.6	4.7	5.3	2.9	-1.8	-0.3	-6.1
15.3	**13.1**	**17.8**	**6.1**	**5.0**	**4.3**	**-5.4**

ODA COMMITMENTS : LOANS

DAC COUNTRIES

	1983	1984	1985	1986
Australia	–	–	–	–
Austria	–	–	–	–
Belgium	–	–	–	0.0
Canada	–	–	–	–
Denmark	7.7	–	–	–
Finland	–	–	–	–
France	3.6	0.1	5.1	2.3
Germany, Fed. Rep.	–	–	–	–
Ireland	–	–	–	–
Italy	–	–	–	–
Japan	–	1.3	–	56.0
Netherlands	0.6	–	–	–
New Zealand	–	–	–	–
Norway	–	–	–	–
Sweden	–	–	–	–
Switzerland	–	–	–	–
United Kingdom	–	–	–	–
United States	–	0.0	0.0	0.0
TOTAL	*11.8*	*1.3*	*5.1*	*58.3*
MULTILATERAL	*158.4*	*52.5*	*123.1*	*26.2*
OPEC COUNTRIES	–	–	–	–
E.E.C.+ MEMBERS	*23.8*	*2.8*	*6.6*	*7.7*
TOTAL	**170.2**	**53.8**	**128.3**	**84.5**

GRANT ELEMENT OF ODA

DAC COUNTRIES

	1983	1984	1985	1986
Australia	100.0	100.0	100.0	100.0
Austria	–	–	–	–
Belgium	–	–	–	100.0
Canada	100.0	100.0	100.0	100.0
Denmark	91.0	100.0	100.0	100.0
Finland	–	100.0	–	–
France	74.5	94.5	66.3	100.0
Germany, Fed. Rep.	100.0	100.0	100.0	100.0
Ireland	100.0	100.0	–	100.0
Italy	100.0	100.0	100.0	100.0
Japan	100.0	100.0	100.0	73.2
Netherlands	94.9	100.0	100.0	100.0
New Zealand	–	–	100.0	–
Norway	–	–	–	100.0
Sweden	–	–	–	–
Switzerland	100.0	100.0	100.0	100.0
United Kingdom	100.0	100.0	100.0	100.0
United States	100.0	99.9	99.9	100.0
TOTAL	*96.8*	*99.9*	*97.2*	*91.5*
MULTILATERAL	*88.9*	*85.8*	*86.5*	*94.5*
OPEC COUNTRIES	–	–	–	–
E.E.C.+ MEMBERS	*97.2*	*99.9*	*97.0*	*100.0*
TOTAL	**91.8**	**90.9**	**89.9**	**92.3**

OTHER AGGREGATES

COMMITMENTS: ALL SOURCES

	1983	1984	1985	1986
TOTAL BILATERAL	74.0	84.6	70.3	202.1
of which				
OPEC	–	–	–	–
CMEA	–	–	–	–
TOTAL MULTILATERAL	228.0	87.2	174.6	97.9
TOTAL BIL.& MULTIL.	302.0	171.9	244.9	300.0
of which				
ODA Grants	100.1	90.0	93.8	180.9
ODA Loans	170.2	53.8	128.3	84.5

DISBURSEMENTS:
DAC COUNTRIES COMBINED
OFFICIAL & PRIVATE

	1983	1984	1985	1986
GROSS:				
Contractual Lending	21.0	18.3	15.4	55.8
Export Credits Total	13.1	8.1	6.9	38.2
Export Credits Private	11.9	5.9	5.4	37.3
NET:				
Contractual Lending	-11.5	3.1	-5.8	33.5
Export Credits Total	-14.8	-0.9	-3.8	30.9
PRIVATE SECTOR NET	-17.5	24.6	0.4	31.6
Direct Investment	-2.4	27.3	6.3	0.1
Portfolio Investment	-0.3	-0.8	-1.8	1.0
Export Credits	-14.8	-2.0	-4.1	30.5

MARKET BORROWING:
CHANGE IN CLAIMS

	1983	1984	1985	1986
Banks	–	-27.0	-21.0	2.0

MEMORANDUM ITEM:

	1983	1984	1985	1986
CMEA Countr.(Gross)	–	–	–	–

MALAYSIA

TOTAL RECEIPTS NET / TOTAL ODA NET

	TOTAL RECEIPTS NET 1983	1984	1985	1986	TOTAL ODA NET 1983	1984	1985	1986
DAC COUNTRIES								
Australia	31.4	47.4	40.7	42.3	7.1	29.0	46.1	40.8
Austria	18.1	1.5	-1.4	0.0	18.1	1.5	0.3	0.0
Belgium	3.2	67.5	55.5	-44.2	0.6	0.4	0.4	0.4
Canada	-0.2	0.3	78.4	18.6	0.6	1.0	3.0	2.5
Denmark	0.0	0.0	0.5	-0.5	0.2	0.0	-0.2	-0.2
Finland	-0.3	0.8	1.3	0.3	0.1	0.4	0.0	0.3
France	143.3	79.7	-6.8	-73.1	15.0	17.0	15.9	6.9
Germany, Fed. Rep.	232.0	2.0	48.0	35.8	5.9	4.2	7.2	6.4
Ireland	—	—	0.0	—	—	—	0.0	—
Italy	-0.8	-78.4	30.8	11.1	0.1	0.5	1.1	2.0
Japan	920.2	985.2	295.5	114.9	92.3	245.1	125.6	37.8
Netherlands	1.1	25.6	30.9	36.4	0.4	0.7	0.8	1.3
New Zealand	0.1	0.2	0.2	0.2	0.1	0.2	0.2	0.2
Norway	2.2	1.6	0.9	2.3	1.5	0.1	0.2	1.5
Sweden	4.7	13.7	36.0	5.0	—	0.0	—	0.2
Switzerland	-5.5	-0.9	-0.1	0.3	0.1	0.1	0.2	0.3
United Kingdom	9.7	136.7	49.9	72.2	1.3	0.2	1.9	76.2
United States	249.0	45.0	-473.0	-166.0	1.0	-1.0	—	-1.0
TOTAL	*1608.2*	*1327.8*	*187.2*	*55.3*	*144.3*	*299.3*	*202.6*	*175.3*
MULTILATERAL								
AF.D.F.	—	—	—	—	—	—	—	—
AF.D.B.	—	—	—	—	—	—	—	—
AS.D.B	48.6	29.4	15.3	19.1	0.5	0.9	1.9	1.0
CAR.D.B.	—	—	—	—	—	—	—	—
E.E.C.	—	—	—	0.0	—	—	—	0.0
IBRD	61.3	28.7	4.0	-42.8	—	—	—	—
IDA	—	—	—	—	—	—	—	—
I.D.B.	—	—	—	—	—	—	—	—
IFAD	—	—	—	—	—	—	—	—
I.F.C.	—	2.1	9.0	1.0	—	—	—	—
IMF TRUST FUND	—	—	—	—	—	—	—	—
U.N. AGENCIES								
UNDP	2.3	2.4	1.9	1.4	2.3	2.4	1.9	1.4
UNTA	0.9	0.8	1.3	1.2	0.9	0.8	1.3	1.2
UNICEF	0.5	0.3	0.3	0.2	0.5	0.3	0.3	0.2
UNRWA	—	—	—	—	—	—	—	—
WFP	—	—	—	—	—	—	—	—
UNHCR	6.8	6.6	5.4	4.8	6.8	6.6	5.4	4.8
Other Multilateral	1.8	1.6	1.4	1.3	1.8	1.6	1.4	1.3
Arab OPEC Agencies	3.1	6.4	-6.2	-1.2	3.1	0.7	-0.2	-1.1
TOTAL	*125.4*	*78.2*	*32.3*	*-15.1*	*15.9*	*13.3*	*11.9*	*8.8*
OPEC COUNTRIES	*16.4*	*14.0*	*14.7*	*8.7*	*16.4*	*14.0*	*14.7*	*8.7*
E.E.C.+ MEMBERS	*388.6*	*233.1*	*208.8*	*37.6*	*23.5*	*23.0*	*27.1*	*92.9*
TOTAL	*1750.0*	*1420.0*	*234.2*	*49.0*	*176.6*	*326.6*	*229.2*	*192.7*

TOTAL ODA GROSS

	1983
DAC COUNTRIES	
Australia	7.1
Austria	18.2
Belgium	0.6
Canada	1.1
Denmark	0.3
Finland	0.1
France	15.4
Germany, Fed. Rep.	7.1
Ireland	—
Italy	0.1
Japan	113.1
Netherlands	0.5
New Zealand	0.1
Norway	1.5
Sweden	—
Switzerland	0.1
United Kingdom	4.5
United States	1.0
TOTAL	*170.8*
AF.D.F.	—
AF.D.B.	—
AS.D.B	0.7
CAR.D.B.	—
E.E.C.	—
IBRD	—
IDA	—
I.D.B.	—
IFAD	—
I.F.C.	—
IMF TRUST FUND	—
U.N. AGENCIES	
UNDP	2.3
UNTA	0.9
UNICEF	0.5
UNRWA	—
WFP	—
UNHCR	6.8
Other Multilateral	1.8
Arab OPEC Agencies	3.4
TOTAL	*16.3*
OPEC COUNTRIES	*20.0*
E.E.C.+ MEMBERS	*28.6*
TOTAL	*207.1*

ODA LOANS GROSS / ODA LOANS NET

	ODA LOANS GROSS 1983	1984	1985	1986	ODA LOANS NET 1983	1984	1985	1986
DAC COUNTRIES								
Australia	—	—	—	—	—	—	—	—
Austria	18.1	1.6	0.3	—	18.0	1.5	0.3	-0.1
Belgium	—	—	—	—	—	—	—	—
Canada	—	—	0.4	0.9	-0.5	-0.5	-0.1	0.4
Denmark	—	—	—	—	-0.2	-0.2	-0.2	-0.2
Finland	—	—	—	—	—	—	—	—
France	14.6	15.8	15.0	5.6	14.2	15.5	14.6	5.1
Germany, Fed. Rep.	0.7	0.2	0.9	0.1	-0.5	-0.5	0.2	-0.9
Ireland	—	—	—	—	—	—	—	—
Italy	—	—	—	—	—	—	—	—
Japan	83.9	234.7	131.3	42.5	63.0	209.3	102.0	-5.7
Netherlands	—	—	0.1	0.7	0.0	0.0	0.1	0.7
New Zealand	—	—	—	—	—	—	—	—
Norway	1.3	—	—	—	1.3	—	0.0	-0.1
Sweden	—	—	—	—	—	—	—	—
Switzerland	—	—	—	—	—	—	—	—
United Kingdom	1.2	0.1	—	2.2	-2.1	-3.0	-3.5	-0.5
United States	—	—	—	—	—	-1.0	—	-1.0
TOTAL	*119.8*	*252.3*	*148.0*	*52.0*	*93.3*	*221.0*	*113.4*	*-2.4*
MULTILATERAL	*3.4*	*0.8*	*0.2*	*—*	*2.9*	*0.5*	*-0.4*	*-1.3*
OPEC COUNTRIES	*20.0*	*16.8*	*22.2*	*15.2*	*16.4*	*12.4*	*13.7*	*7.7*
E.E.C.+ MEMBERS	*16.5*	*16.1*	*16.0*	*8.6*	*11.4*	*11.8*	*11.2*	*4.1*
TOTAL	*143.1*	*269.9*	*170.5*	*67.1*	*112.6*	*233.9*	*126.6*	*3.9*

GRANTS

	1983
Australia	7.1
Austria	0.1
Belgium	0.6
Canada	1.1
Denmark	0.3
Finland	0.1
France	0.8
Germany, Fed. Rep.	6.4
Ireland	—
Italy	0.1
Japan	29.3
Netherlands	0.5
New Zealand	0.1
Norway	0.1
Sweden	—
Switzerland	0.1
United Kingdom	3.3
United States	1.0
TOTAL	*51.0*
MULTILATERAL	*13.0*
OPEC COUNTRIES	*0.0*
E.E.C.+ MEMBERS	*12.1*
TOTAL	*64.1*

TOTAL OFFICIAL GROSS / TOTAL OFFICIAL NET

	TOTAL OFFICIAL GROSS 1983	1984	1985	1986	TOTAL OFFICIAL NET 1983	1984	1985	1986
DAC COUNTRIES								
Australia	8.1	31.8	46.8	42.2	8.1	31.7	46.1	42.2
Austria	18.2	1.7	0.4	0.1	18.1	1.5	0.3	0.0
Belgium	0.6	0.5	0.5	0.4	0.6	0.5	0.5	0.4
Canada	1.1	1.5	82.9	25.3	0.1	0.3	78.4	18.6
Denmark	0.4	0.4	0.2	0.1	0.2	0.1	-0.1	-0.3
Finland	0.1	0.4	0.0	0.3	0.1	0.4	0.0	0.3
France	15.4	17.4	16.3	7.4	15.0	17.0	15.9	6.9
Germany, Fed. Rep.	7.1	4.9	19.4	32.2	-1.8	-2.7	13.2	26.0
Ireland	—	—	0.0	—	—	—	0.0	—
Italy	0.1	11.9	27.4	13.7	0.1	11.9	27.4	13.0
Japan	113.9	329.9	155.3	98.9	93.1	304.6	117.6	34.0
Netherlands	1.2	0.7	0.8	1.3	1.1	0.7	0.8	1.3
New Zealand	0.1	0.2	0.2	0.2	0.1	0.2	0.2	0.2
Norway	1.5	0.1	0.2	1.6	1.5	0.1	0.2	1.5
Sweden	11.6	12.7	44.0	17.2	11.3	10.8	39.0	5.7
Switzerland	0.1	0.1	0.2	0.3	0.1	0.1	0.2	0.3
United Kingdom	5.9	4.0	9.7	79.6	2.2	-3.4	4.8	76.5
United States	71.0	—	—	1.0	67.0	-12.0	-12.0	-11.0
TOTAL	*256.2*	*417.9*	*404.1*	*321.5*	*216.9*	*361.6*	*332.5*	*215.3*
MULTILATERAL	*191.6*	*155.0*	*128.4*	*117.9*	*125.4*	*78.2*	*32.3*	*-15.1*
OPEC COUNTRIES	*20.0*	*18.4*	*23.3*	*16.2*	*16.4*	*14.0*	*14.7*	*8.7*
E.E.C.+ MEMBERS	*30.6*	*39.7*	*74.3*	*134.6*	*17.5*	*24.1*	*62.6*	*123.7*
TOTAL	*467.8*	*591.2*	*555.8*	*455.7*	*358.6*	*453.8*	*379.6*	*209.0*

TOTAL OOF GROSS

	1983
Australia	1.0
Austria	—
Belgium	—
Canada	—
Denmark	0.0
Finland	—
France	—
Germany, Fed. Rep.	—
Ireland	—
Italy	—
Japan	0.8
Netherlands	0.7
New Zealand	—
Norway	—
Sweden	11.6
Switzerland	—
United Kingdom	1.3
United States	70.0
TOTAL	*85.4*
MULTILATERAL	*175.2*
OPEC COUNTRIES	*—*
E.E.C.+ MEMBERS	*2.1*
TOTAL	*260.7*

MALAYSIA

ODA COMMITMENTS

1984	1985	1986	1983	1984	1985	1986
29.0	46.1	40.8	1.9	48.5	43.1	34.5
1.7	0.4	0.1	0.0	0.0	0.1	—
0.4	0.4	0.4	—	—	—	0.4
1.5	3.6	3.0	1.4	9.7	7.9	4.3
0.2	—	—	0.2	0.2	—	—
0.4	0.0	0.3	0.2	0.2	—	—
17.4	16.3	7.4	19.0	30.3	20.8	7.4
4.9	7.8	7.4	2.6	7.2	4.0	10.7
—	0.0	—	—	—	0.0	—
0.5	1.1	2.0	0.1	0.5	3.0	3.0
270.5	154.9	86.0	107.1	229.5	107.3	155.0
0.7	0.8	1.3	0.5	0.8	0.7	1.2
0.2	0.2	0.2	0.1	0.3	0.2	0.5
0.1	0.2	1.6	0.6	0.1	0.2	3.9
0.0	—	0.2	—	—	—	0.3
0.1	0.2	0.3	0.1	—	0.1	0.3
3.3	5.5	78.9	4.6	6.3	3.3	92.2
—	—	—	0.4	—	0.0	—
330.6	*237.3*	*229.7*	*138.6*	*333.4*	*190.9*	*313.2*
—	—	—	—	—	—	—
—	—	—	—	—	—	—
1.1	2.1	1.2	—	—	—	—
—	—	—	—	—	—	—
—	—	0.0	0.0	—	—	0.0
—	—	—	—	—	—	—
—	—	—	—	—	—	—
—	—	—	—	—	—	—
—	—	—	—	—	—	—
—	—	—	—	—	—	—
—	—	—	12.3	11.7	10.3	8.8
2.4	1.9	1.4	—	—	—	—
0.8	1.3	1.2	—	—	—	—
0.3	0.3	0.2	—	—	—	—
—	—	—	—	—	—	—
6.6	5.4	4.8	—	—	—	—
1.6	1.4	1.3	—	—	—	—
0.9	0.2	—	—	8.3	8.3	2.6
13.6	*12.6*	*10.1*	*12.3*	*20.0*	*18.6*	*11.5*
18.4	*23.3*	*16.2*	*4.6*	*7.8*	*1.0*	*1.0*
27.3	*31.8*	*97.4*	*26.8*	*45.1*	*31.7*	*114.8*
362.6	*273.1*	*255.9*	*155.6*	*361.1*	*210.5*	*325.7*

TECH. COOP. GRANTS

1984	1985	1986	1983	1984	1985	1986
29.0	46.1	40.8	4.6	28.3	45.8	40.5
0.1	0.1	0.1	0.1	—	—	—
0.4	0.4	0.4	0.5	0.3	0.3	0.3
1.5	3.1	2.1	0.8	—	0.7	—
0.2	—	—	0.3	0.2	—	—
0.4	0.0	0.3	0.0	0.2	0.0	0.1
1.6	1.3	1.8	0.8	1.6	1.3	1.8
4.6	7.0	7.3	6.4	4.6	6.9	7.2
—	0.0	—	—	—	0.0	—
0.5	1.1	2.0	0.1	0.5	1.1	2.0
35.8	23.6	43.5	22.6	24.8	23.1	36.4
0.7	0.7	0.6	0.4	0.5	0.6	0.4
0.2	0.2	0.2	0.1	0.2	0.1	0.1
0.1	0.2	1.6	—	0.1	0.2	0.1
0.0	—	0.2	—	0.0	—	0.2
0.1	0.2	0.3	0.0	0.0	0.0	0.0
3.2	5.5	76.7	3.3	3.2	3.3	3.2
—	—	—	1.0	—	—	—
78.3	*89.2*	*177.7*	*41.1*	*64.4*	*83.3*	*92.3*
12.8	*12.3*	*10.1*	*12.3*	*11.7*	*10.3*	*8.8*
1.6	*1.1*	*1.0*	—	—	—	—
11.2	*15.9*	*88.8*	*11.9*	*11.0*	*13.5*	*14.9*
92.7	*102.6*	*188.8*	*53.4*	*76.1*	*93.6*	*101.2*

TOTAL OOF NET

1984	1985	1986	1983	1984	1985	1986
2.8	0.8	1.4	1.0	2.7	0.0	1.4
—	—	—	—	—	—	—
0.1	0.1	0.0	—	0.1	0.1	0.0
—	79.3	22.3	-0.5	-0.6	75.4	16.1
0.2	0.2	0.1	—	0.1	0.1	-0.1
—	—	—	—	—	—	—
—	—	—	—	—	—	—
—	11.6	24.8	-7.7	-6.9	6.1	19.7
—	—	—	—	—	—	—
11.4	26.4	11.7	—	11.4	26.4	11.0
59.5	0.4	13.0	0.8	59.5	-7.9	-3.8
—	—	—	0.7	—	—	—
—	—	—	—	—	—	—
12.7	44.0	17.0	11.3	10.8	39.0	5.5
—	—	—	—	—	—	—
0.7	4.2	0.7	0.9	-3.6	2.9	0.3
—	—	1.0	66.0	-11.0	-12.0	-10.0
87.3	*166.9*	*91.9*	*72.6*	*62.3*	*130.0*	*40.0*
141.3	*115.8*	*107.9*	*109.5*	*64.9*	*20.4*	*-23.8*
—	—	—	—	—	—	—
12.4	*42.4*	*37.2*	*-6.0*	*1.1*	*35.5*	*30.8*
228.6	*282.7*	*199.7*	*182.0*	*127.2*	*150.4*	*16.2*

ODA COMMITMENTS : LOANS

DAC COUNTRIES	1983	1984	1985	1986
Australia	—	—	—	—
Austria	—	—	—	—
Belgium	—	—	—	0.4
Canada	—	7.3	—	—
Denmark	—	—	—	—
Finland	—	—	—	—
France	18.2	28.7	19.5	5.6
Germany, Fed. Rep.	—	—	—	—
Ireland	—	—	—	—
Italy	—	—	—	—
Japan	71.8	204.1	76.7	109.3
Netherlands	—	—	0.1	0.7
New Zealand	—	—	—	—
Norway	0.5	—	—	—
Sweden	—	—	—	—
Switzerland	—	—	—	—
United Kingdom	1.3	—	—	—
United States	—	—	—	—
TOTAL	*91.8*	*240.1*	*96.3*	*115.6*
MULTILATERAL	—	*8.3*	*8.3*	—.
OPEC COUNTRIES	—	—	—	—
E.E.C.+ MEMBERS	*19.5*	*28.7*	*19.6*	*6.3*
TOTAL	*96.4*	*255.1*	*104.6*	*115.6*

GRANT ELEMENT OF ODA

DAC COUNTRIES	1983	1984	1985	1986
Australia	100.0	100.0	100.0	100.0
Austria	100.0	100.0	100.0	—
Belgium	—	—	—	100.0
Canada	100.0	92.2	100.0	100.0
Denmark	—	—	—	—
Finland	100.0	100.0	—	—
France	65.8	66.3	65.2	69.6
Germany, Fed. Rep.	100.0	100.0	100.0	100.0
Ireland	—	—	100.0	—
Italy	100.0	100.0	100.0	100.0
Japan	62.8	40.7	57.5	55.8
Netherlands	100.0	100.0	90.2	58.7
New Zealand	100.0	100.0	100.0	100.0
Norway	40.2	100.0	100.0	100.0
Sweden	—	—	100.0	—
Switzerland	100.0	—	100.0	100.0
United Kingdom	93.3	100.0	100.0	100.0
United States	100.0	—	100.0	—
TOTAL	*66.1*	*55.9*	*72.3*	*77.2*
MULTILATERAL	*100.0*	*77.8*	*75.9*	*100.0*
OPEC COUNTRIES	*53.5*	*41.4*	*100.0*	*100.0*
E.E.C.+ MEMBERS	*74.6*	*77.4*	*77.0*	*96.6*
TOTAL	*68.4*	*56.8*	*72.8*	*78.0*

OTHER AGGREGATES

COMMITMENTS: ALL SOURCES	1983	1984	1985	1986
TOTAL BILATERAL	352.1	372.7	279.8	352.9
of which				
OPEC	4.6	15.5	1.0	1.0
CMEA	—	—	—	—
TOTAL MULTILATERAL	187.1	314.5	312.0	556.2
TOTAL BIL.& MULTIL.	539.2	687.2	591.7	909.1
of which				
ODA Grants	59.2	106.0	105.9	210.2
ODA Loans	96.4	255.1	104.6	115.6

DISBURSEMENTS:	1983	1984	1985	1986
DAC COUNTRIES COMBINED				
OFFICIAL & PRIVATE				
GROSS:				
Contractual Lending	663.8	766.5	628.1	281.9
Export Credits Total	542.0	513.3	475.7	228.0
Export Credits Private	458.6	427.0	313.3	138.1
NET:				
Contractual Lending	395.2	396.1	220.0	-39.8
Export Credits Total	300.3	178.6	111.9	-26.8
PRIVATE SECTOR NET	1391.4	966.2	-145.3	-160.0
Direct Investment	234.4	228.7	141.4	-41.1
Portfolio Investment	927.7	624.7	-263.4	-41.4
Export Credits	229.3	112.9	-23.2	-77.4

MARKET BORROWING:	1983	1984	1985	1986
CHANGE IN CLAIMS				
Banks	—	31.0	-1317.0	-280.0

MEMORANDUM ITEM:	1983	1984	1985	1986
CMEA Countr.(Gross)	—	—	—	—

TOTAL RECEIPTS NET / TOTAL ODA NET / TOTAL ODA GROSS

	TOTAL RECEIPTS NET				TOTAL ODA NET				TOTAL ODA GROSS
	1983	1984	1985	1986	1983	1984	1985	1986	1983
DAC COUNTRIES									
Australia	–	0.3	–	0.0	–	0.3	–	0.0	–
Austria	0.3	0.1	0.0	0.0	0.3	0.1	0.0	0.0	0.3
Belgium	5.6	0.6	4.1	1.7	2.7	1.3	4.3	2.4	2.7
Canada	7.6	7.0	15.1	13.5	7.6	7.0	15.1	13.5	7.6
Denmark	0.0	3.1	1.5	0.6	0.0	3.1	1.0	0.6	0.0
Finland	0.0	0.5	–	0.3	0.0	0.5	–	0.3	0.0
France	26.9	127.1	124.8	63.8	27.9	129.9	120.9	66.6	27.9
Germany, Fed. Rep.	14.5	16.8	27.3	23.7	17.1	19.3	28.1	24.2	17.1
Ireland	–	–	–	–	–	–	–	–	–
Italy	1.8	10.3	9.5	26.4	2.0	10.4	9.5	26.4	2.0
Japan	8.6	1.5	3.7	5.3	8.6	1.5	3.7	5.3	8.6
Netherlands	8.4	15.6	15.5	20.0	8.0	15.6	15.5	20.0	8.0
New Zealand	–	–	–	–	–	–	–	–	–
Norway	0.3	2.8	2.7	4.5	0.3	2.8	2.7	4.5	0.3
Sweden	–	–	–	–	–	–	–	–	–
Switzerland	7.2	8.0	5.4	8.2	7.3	6.3	5.6	8.2	7.3
United Kingdom	0.6	-1.2	-0.3	-0.7	0.3	0.7	1.0	1.7	0.3
United States	15.0	25.0	44.0	30.0	15.0	25.0	44.0	30.0	15.0
TOTAL	*96.7*	*217.5*	*253.2*	*197.4*	*96.9*	*223.7*	*251.3*	*203.8*	*97.0*
MULTILATERAL									
AF.D.F.	13.4	3.2	11.3	19.6	13.4	3.2	11.3	19.6	13.5
AF.D.B.	-0.2	–	-0.9	-0.4	–	–	–	–	–
AS.D.B	–	–	–	–	–	–	–	–	–
CAR.D.B.	–	–	–	–	–	–	–	–	–
E.E.C.	10.9	29.4	24.7	20.9	10.9	29.4	24.7	20.9	10.9
IBRD	–	–	–	–	–	–	–	–	–
IDA	18.5	20.6	28.1	44.1	18.5	20.6	28.1	44.1	19.0
I.D.B.	–	–	–	–	–	–	–	–	–
IFAD	–	0.5	2.4	4.6	–	0.5	2.4	4.6	–
I.F.C.	1.0	–	–	-0.5	–	–	–	–	–
IMF TRUST FUND	–	–	–	–	–	–	–	–	–
U.N. AGENCIES	–	–	–	–	–	–	–	–	–
UNDP	11.4	11.0	10.9	12.9	11.4	11.0	10.9	12.9	11.4
UNTA	1.3	1.1	1.6	1.6	1.3	1.1	1.6	1.6	1.3
UNICEF	1.3	1.8	3.4	4.5	1.3	1.8	3.4	4.5	1.3
UNRWA	–	–	–	–	–	–	–	–	–
WFP	13.2	17.0	12.9	16.2	13.2	17.0	12.9	16.2	13.2
UNHCR	–	–	–	–	–	–	–	–	–
Other Multilateral	1.8	1.9	2.5	3.0	1.8	1.9	2.5	3.0	1.8
Arab OPEC Agencies	14.2	4.3	4.1	0.9	14.2	1.4	4.1	1.2	15.8
TOTAL	*86.8*	*90.7*	*101.0*	*127.2*	*85.9*	*87.9*	*101.9*	*128.5*	*88.0*
OPEC COUNTRIES	*36.7*	*13.7*	*26.8*	*39.9*	*31.7*	*8.7*	*26.8*	*39.9*	*33.3*
E.E.C.+ MEMBERS	*68.7*	*201.8*	*207.1*	*156.4*	*68.8*	*209.7*	*204.9*	*162.8*	*68.9*
TOTAL	*220.2*	*322.0*	*380.9*	*364.5*	*214.5*	*320.3*	*379.9*	*372.2*	*218.3*

ODA LOANS GROSS / ODA LOANS NET / GRANTS

	ODA LOANS GROSS				ODA LOANS NET				GRANTS
	1983	1984	1985	1986	1983	1984	1985	1986	1983
DAC COUNTRIES									
Australia	–	–	–	–	–	–	–	–	–
Austria	–	–	–	–	–	–	–	–	0.3
Belgium	–	–	–	–	–	–	–	–	2.7
Canada	–	–	–	–	–	–	–	–	7.6
Denmark	–	–	–	–	–	–	–	–	0.0
Finland	–	–	–	–	–	–	–	–	0.0
France	2.4	100.4	95.8	32.4	2.4	100.4	95.7	32.0	25.5
Germany, Fed. Rep.	–	–	–	–	–	–	–	–	17.1
Ireland	–	–	–	–	–	–	–	–	–
Italy	–	1.2	–	–	–	1.2	–	–	2.0
Japan	3.3	–	–	–	3.3	–	–	–	5.2
Netherlands	–	–	–	–	–	–	–	–	8.0
New Zealand	–	–	–	–	–	–	–	–	–
Norway	–	–	–	–	–	–	–	–	0.3
Sweden	–	–	–	–	–	–	–	–	–
Switzerland	–	–	–	–	–	–	–	–	7.3
United Kingdom	–	–	–	–	–	–	–	–	0.3
United States	–	–	–	–	–	–	–	–	15.0
TOTAL	*5.8*	*101.6*	*95.8*	*32.4*	*5.7*	*101.6*	*95.7*	*32.0*	*91.2*
MULTILATERAL	*48.4*	*28.8*	*46.7*	*72.2*	*46.3*	*25.9*	*43.4*	*68.3*	*39.6*
OPEC COUNTRIES	*32.1*	*9.9*	*29.4*	*32.9*	*30.5*	*8.2*	*22.6*	*28.2*	*1.1*
E.E.C.+ MEMBERS	*2.6*	*102.7*	*95.8*	*32.6*	*2.6*	*102.5*	*95.7*	*31.9*	*66.3*
TOTAL	*86.3*	*140.3*	*171.9*	*137.5*	*82.6*	*135.7*	*161.7*	*128.5*	*132.0*

TOTAL OFFICIAL GROSS / TOTAL OFFICIAL NET / TOTAL OOF GROSS

	TOTAL OFFICIAL GROSS				TOTAL OFFICIAL NET				TOTAL OOF GROSS
	1983	1984	1985	1986	1983	1984	1985	1986	1983
DAC COUNTRIES									
Australia	–	0.3	–	0.0	–	0.3	–	0.0	–
Austria	0.3	0.1	0.0	0.0	0.3	0.1	0.0	0.0	–
Belgium	2.7	1.4	4.4	2.4	2.7	1.4	4.4	2.4	–
Canada	7.6	7.0	15.1	13.5	7.6	7.0	15.1	13.5	–
Denmark	0.0	3.1	1.5	0.6	0.0	3.1	1.5	0.6	–
Finland	0.0	0.5	–	0.3	0.0	0.5	–	0.3	–
France	27.9	130.2	121.2	67.0	27.6	129.9	120.6	66.6	–
Germany, Fed. Rep.	17.1	19.3	28.1	24.2	17.1	18.5	27.6	23.7	–
Ireland	–	–	–	–	–	–	–	–	–
Italy	2.0	10.4	9.5	26.4	1.8	10.3	9.5	26.4	–
Japan	8.6	1.5	3.7	5.3	8.6	1.5	3.7	5.3	–
Netherlands	8.0	15.6	15.5	20.0	8.0	15.6	15.5	20.0	–
New Zealand	–	–	–	–	–	–	–	–	–
Norway	0.3	2.8	2.7	4.5	0.3	2.8	2.7	4.5	–
Sweden	–	–	–	–	–	–	–	–	–
Switzerland	7.3	6.3	5.6	8.2	7.3	6.3	5.6	8.2	–
United Kingdom	0.3	0.7	1.0	1.7	0.3	0.7	1.0	1.7	–
United States	15.0	25.0	44.0	30.0	15.0	25.0	44.0	30.0	–
TOTAL	*97.0*	*224.1*	*252.2*	*204.2*	*96.4*	*222.9*	*251.2*	*203.3*	*–*
MULTILATERAL	*89.1*	*93.6*	*105.2*	*132.4*	*86.8*	*90.7*	*101.0*	*127.2*	*1.1*
OPEC COUNTRIES	*38.3*	*15.4*	*33.5*	*44.7*	*36.7*	*13.7*	*26.8*	*39.9*	*5.0*
E.E.C.+ MEMBERS	*68.9*	*210.3*	*205.8*	*163.5*	*68.4*	*208.9*	*204.8*	*162.3*	*–*
TOTAL	*224.4*	*333.1*	*390.9*	*381.3*	*219.9*	*327.3*	*378.9*	*370.5*	*6.1*

ODA COMMITMENTS

	1984	1985	1986	1983	1984	1985	1986
Australia	0.3	–	0.0	–	0.0	–	–
Austria	0.1	0.0	0.0	0.6	0.0	0.0	–
Belgium	1.3	4.3	2.4	1.5	0.8	2.1	2.4
Canada	7.0	15.1	13.5	4.8	48.6	7.4	4.3
Denmark	3.1	1.0	0.6	5.5	4.8	–	–
Finland	0.5	–	0.3	–	0.0	–	–
France	129.9	121.0	67.0	55.4	139.7	116.9	67.0
Germany, Fed. Rep.	19.3	28.1	24.2	20.5	15.3	32.9	26.0
Ireland	–	–	–	–	–	–	–
Italy	10.4	9.5	26.4	22.8	5.9	8.6	45.9
Japan	1.5	3.7	5.3	5.9	3.0	6.2	4.5
Netherlands	15.6	15.5	20.0	9.0	23.3	11.7	14.5
New Zealand	–	–	–	–	–	–	–
Norway	2.8	2.7	4.5	–	1.6	–	3.7
Sweden	–	–	–	–	1.2	–	–
Switzerland	6.3	5.6	8.2	5.1	2.0	6.9	18.3
United Kingdom	0.7	1.0	1.7	0.3	0.7	1.0	1.7
United States	25.0	44.0	30.0	20.4	49.8	48.6	21.3
TOTAL	223.8	251.4	204.2	151.8	296.7	242.2	209.5

	1984	1985	1986	1983	1984	1985	1986
	3.3	11.4	19.7	1.4	10.5	46.1	7.4
	–	–	–	–	–	–	–
	–	–	–	–	–	–	–
	29.6	24.7	21.2	29.3	29.7	27.2	16.1
	–	–	–	–	–	–	–
	21.3	28.9	45.1	54.8	9.5	68.1	54.3
	–	–	–	–	–	–	–
	0.5	2.4	4.6	12.7	–	–	5.9
	–	–	–	–	–	–	–
	–	–	–	29.0	32.8	31.3	38.0
	11.0	10.9	12.9	–	–	–	–
	1.1	1.6	1.6	–	–	–	–
	1.8	3.4	4.5	–	–	–	–
	17.0	12.9	16.2	–	–	–	–
	1.9	2.5	3.0	–	–	–	–
	3.3	6.5	3.9	7.5	23.8	7.8	9.3
	90.7	105.2	132.4	134.6	106.2	180.4	131.0
	10.4	33.5	44.7	14.2	8.5	15.6	11.0
	210.0	205.0	163.4	144.2	220.1	200.2	173.5
	324.9	390.1	381.2	300.5	411.4	438.1	351.5

TECH. COOP. GRANTS

	1984	1985	1986	1983	1984	1985	1986
Australia	0.3	–	0.0	–	0.3	–	–
Austria	0.1	0.0	0.0	0.1	–	–	–
Belgium	1.3	4.3	2.4	0.1	0.1	0.4	1.0
Canada	7.0	15.1	13.5	1.2	–	1.9	–
Denmark	3.1	1.0	0.6	0.0	0.0	–	0.3
Finland	0.5	–	0.3	–	0.0	–	–
France	29.5	25.2	34.6	14.5	15.9	13.8	20.2
Germany, Fed. Rep.	19.3	28.1	24.2	9.2	9.9	7.9	11.4
Ireland	–	–	–	–	–	–	–
Italy	9.2	9.5	26.4	0.3	0.4	0.6	9.4
Japan	1.5	3.7	5.3	0.0	0.1	0.1	0.5
Netherlands	15.6	15.5	20.0	0.6	1.9	1.4	2.5
New Zealand	–	–	–	–	–	–	–
Norway	2.8	2.7	4.5	–	0.0	–	0.0
Sweden	–	–	–	–	–	–	–
Switzerland	6.3	5.6	8.2	1.0	1.5	1.4	1.5
United Kingdom	0.7	1.0	1.7	0.2	0.2	0.4	0.9
United States	25.0	44.0	30.0	10.0	14.0	15.0	19.0
TOTAL	122.1	155.5	171.8	37.1	44.1	42.8	66.6
	62.0	58.5	60.2	15.7	15.8	18.4	22.4
	0.5	4.1	11.8	–	–	–	–
	107.2	109.2	130.9	24.8	28.3	24.3	46.1
	184.6	218.2	243.7	52.8	59.9	61.1	89.0

TOTAL OOF NET

	1984	1985	1986	1983	1984	1985	1986
	–	–	–	–	–	–	–
	–	–	–	–	–	–	–
	0.1	0.1	0.1	–	0.1	0.1	0.1
	–	–	–	–	–	–	–
	–	0.6	–	–	–	0.6	–
	–	–	–	–	–	–	–
	0.3	0.1	–	-0.3	0.0	-0.4	0.0
	–	–	–	–	-0.8	-0.4	-0.5
	–	–	–	-0.2	-0.1	–	–
	–	–	–	–	–	–	–
	–	–	–	–	–	–	–
	–	–	–	–	–	–	–
	–	–	–	–	–	–	–
	–	–	–	–	–	–	–
	–	–	–	–	–	–	–
	0.3	0.8	0.1	-0.5	-0.8	-0.1	-0.5
	2.9	–	–	0.8	2.9	-0.9	-1.2
	5.0	–	–	5.0	5.0	–	–
	0.3	0.8	0.1	-0.5	-0.8	-0.1	-0.5
	8.2	0.8	0.1	5.4	7.0	-1.0	-1.7

ODA COMMITMENTS : LOANS

DAC COUNTRIES

	1983	1984	1985	1986
Australia	–	–	–	–
Austria	–	–	–	–
Belgium	–	–	–	–
Canada	–	–	–	–
Denmark	–	–	–	–
Finland	–	–	–	–
France	28.1	108.3	92.4	32.4
Germany, Fed. Rep.	–	–	–	–
Ireland	–	–	–	–
Italy	–	–	–	8.8
Japan	3.3	–	–	–
Netherlands	–	–	–	–
New Zealand	–	–	–	–
Norway	–	–	–	–
Sweden	–	–	–	–
Switzerland	–	–	–	–
United Kingdom	–	–	–	–
United States	–	–	–	–
TOTAL	31.4	108.3	92.4	41.2
MULTILATERAL	76.5	39.9	124.5	76.5
OPEC COUNTRIES	–	–	11.7	–
E.E.C.+ MEMBERS	28.2	108.3	95.0	41.2
TOTAL	107.9	148.2	228.6	117.7

GRANT ELEMENT OF ODA

DAC COUNTRIES

	1983	1984	1985	1986
Australia	–	100.0	–	–
Austria	100.0	100.0	100.0	–
Belgium	100.0	100.0	100.0	100.0
Canada	100.0	100.0	100.0	100.0
Denmark	100.0	100.0	–	–
Finland	–	100.0	–	–
France	79.3	79.3	89.0	78.8
Germany, Fed. Rep.	100.0	100.0	100.0	100.0
Ireland	–	–	–	–
Italy	100.0	100.0	100.0	93.7
Japan	80.0	100.0	100.0	100.0
Netherlands	100.0	100.0	100.0	100.0
New Zealand	–	–	–	–
Norway	–	100.0	–	100.0
Sweden	–	100.0	–	–
Switzerland	100.0	100.0	100.0	100.0
United Kingdom	100.0	100.0	100.0	100.0
United States	100.0	100.0	100.0	100.0
TOTAL	92.5	90.3	97.7	91.2
MULTILATERAL	89.9	87.6	87.2	87.0
OPEC COUNTRIES	100.0	100.0	61.7	100.0
E.E.C.+ MEMBERS	93.0	86.9	96.8	89.5
TOTAL	92.0	89.5	90.8	90.0

OTHER AGGREGATES

COMMITMENTS: ALL SOURCES

	1983	1984	1985	1986
TOTAL BILATERAL	176.0	320.7	261.0	220.5
of which				
OPEC	24.2	8.5	15.6	11.0
CMEA	–	14.8	3.3	0.0
TOTAL MULTILATERAL	137.6	106.2	180.4	131.0
TOTAL BIL.& MULTIL.	313.5	426.8	441.4	351.5
of which				
ODA Grants	192.6	263.2	209.5	233.8
ODA Loans	107.9	163.0	231.9	117.7

DISBURSEMENTS:

DAC COUNTRIES COMBINED

	1983	1984	1985	1986
OFFICIAL & PRIVATE				
GROSS:				
Contractual Lending	10.9	103.9	103.1	28.6
Export Credits Total	5.2	2.0	6.6	-3.7
Export Credits Private	5.2	2.0	6.6	-3.7
NET:				
Contractual Lending	3.0	97.5	97.8	24.5
Export Credits Total	-2.4	-3.4	2.3	-7.0
PRIVATE SECTOR NET	0.3	-5.3	2.1	-5.9
Direct Investment	0.4	0.1	0.0	1.0
Portfolio Investment	2.1	-2.2	-0.3	0.1
Export Credits	-2.2	-3.2	2.3	-7.0

MARKET BORROWING:

CHANGE IN CLAIMS

	1983	1984	1985	1986
Banks	–	-1.0	9.0	-4.0

MEMORANDUM ITEM:

	1983	1984	1985	1986
CMEA Countr.(Gross)	4.0	15.0	3.0	8.0

TOTAL RECEIPTS NET / TOTAL ODA NET / TOTAL ODA GROSS

	TOTAL RECEIPTS NET				TOTAL ODA NET				TOTAL ODA GROSS
	1983	1984	1985	1986	1983	1984	1985	1986	1983
DAC COUNTRIES									
Australia	–	–	0.0	–	–	–	0.0	–	–
Austria	0.1	-1.7	0.7	0.2	0.1	0.1	0.7	0.2	0.1
Belgium	1.2	0.2	1.0	-0.1	0.0	0.1	1.2	0.3	0.0
Canada	2.3	5.8	4.7	0.2	2.3	5.8	4.7	0.5	2.3
Denmark	1.2	0.4	0.4	0.4	1.2	0.4	0.4	0.5	1.2
Finland	0.1	–	–	–	0.1	–	–	–	0.1
France	29.7	24.6	43.1	30.9	22.2	20.6	32.7	35.6	22.8
Germany, Fed. Rep.	19.5	11.3	8.3	15.1	16.7	9.0	8.0	13.9	16.8
Ireland	–	–	–	–	–	–	–	–	–
Italy	0.5	2.2	10.2	20.0	0.5	2.2	10.2	20.0	0.5
Japan	3.8	1.4	3.9	11.0	3.6	1.5	3.9	11.0	3.6
Netherlands	2.8	2.7	2.5	8.4	2.8	2.7	2.5	3.9	2.8
New Zealand	–	–	–	–	–	–	–	–	–
Norway	0.5	1.6	0.1	0.3	0.5	1.6	0.1	0.3	0.5
Sweden	–	–	–	–	–	–	–	–	–
Switzerland	0.5	1.2	0.8	0.0	0.7	1.2	0.8	0.0	0.7
United Kingdom	7.8	3.7	0.7	-2.1	1.6	0.5	1.2	0.3	1.6
United States	20.0	23.0	37.0	18.0	20.0	23.0	34.0	19.0	20.0
TOTAL	*89.8*	*76.3*	*113.3*	*102.3*	*72.1*	*68.7*	*100.3*	*105.1*	*72.9*
MULTILATERAL									
AF.D.F.	5.8	2.6	1.9	0.3	5.8	2.6	1.9	0.3	5.9
AF.D.B.	1.4	-0.2	-0.6	-0.2	–	–	–	–	–
AS.D.B	–	–	–	–	–	–	–	–	–
CAR.D.B.	–	–	–	–	–	–	–	–	–
E.E.C.	17.6	16.2	14.8	13.5	11.3	14.9	14.1	15.5	11.5
IBRD	26.3	-2.2	-6.0	4.1	–	–	–	–	–
IDA	3.0	5.3	5.6	12.2	3.0	5.3	5.6	12.2	3.2
I.D.B.	–	–	–	–	–	–	–	–	–
IFAD	0.4	1.3	1.5	1.5	0.4	1.3	1.5	1.5	0.4
I.F.C.	–	–	–	–	–	–	–	–	–
IMF TRUST FUND	–	–	–	–	–	–	–	–	–
U.N. AGENCIES	–	–	–	–	–	–	–	–	–
UNDP	4.3	4.9	5.5	5.6	4.3	4.9	5.5	5.6	4.3
UNTA	1.0	0.9	1.2	0.8	1.0	0.9	1.2	0.8	1.0
UNICEF	0.7	0.5	1.6	1.0	0.7	0.5	1.6	1.0	0.7
UNRWA	–	–	–	–	–	–	–	–	–
WFP	7.3	8.4	8.8	2.8	7.3	8.4	8.8	2.8	7.3
UNHCR	–	–	–	–	–	–	–	–	–
Other Multilateral	1.3	2.1	2.5	1.4	1.3	2.1	2.5	1.4	1.3
Arab OPEC Agencies	14.8	16.0	16.0	5.4	22.7	16.0	6.0	15.7	25.8
TOTAL	*84.1*	*55.7*	*52.8*	*48.3*	*57.8*	*56.8*	*48.6*	*56.8*	*61.4*
OPEC COUNTRIES	*61.8*	*53.4*	*65.3*	*24.7*	*45.6*	*48.1*	*52.5*	*24.7*	*48.0*
E.E.C.+ MEMBERS	*80.3*	*61.3*	*81.0*	*86.1*	*56.2*	*50.5*	*70.3*	*89.9*	*57.1*
TOTAL	**235.7**	**185.3**	**231.4**	**175.3**	**175.6**	**173.6**	**201.4**	**186.6**	**182.2**

ODA LOANS GROSS / ODA LOANS NET / GRANTS

	ODA LOANS GROSS				ODA LOANS NET				GRANTS
	1983	1984	1985	1986	1983	1984	1985	1986	1983
DAC COUNTRIES									
Australia	–	–	–	–	–	–	–	–	–
Austria	–	–	–	–	–	–	–	–	0.1
Belgium	–	–	–	–	–	–	–	–	0.0
Canada	0.2	–	–	–	0.2	–	–	–	2.1
Denmark	–	–	–	0.5	–	–	–	0.5	1.2
Finland	–	–	–	–	–	–	–	–	0.1
France	3.7	4.1	8.4	10.4	3.0	3.5	7.9	9.8	19.1
Germany, Fed. Rep.	6.4	1.3	0.5	4.8	6.3	1.3	0.5	3.5	10.4
Ireland	–	–	–	–	–	–	–	–	–
Italy	–	0.6	–	–	–	0.6	–	–	0.5
Japan	2.2	0.3	2.7	7.6	2.2	0.3	2.7	7.6	1.5
Netherlands	–	–	–	–	–	–	–	–	2.8
New Zealand	–	–	–	–	–	–	–	–	–
Norway	–	–	–	–	–	–	–	–	0.5
Sweden	–	–	–	–	–	–	–	–	–
Switzerland	–	–	–	–	–	–	–	–	0.7
United Kingdom	–	–	–	–	–	–	–	–	1.6
United States	–	–	–	–	–	–	–	–	20.0
TOTAL	*12.4*	*6.3*	*11.5*	*23.3*	*11.6*	*5.7*	*11.1*	*21.4*	*60.5*
MULTILATERAL	*35.1*	*25.8*	*20.4*	*34.8*	*31.6*	*25.0*	*14.2*	*29.8*	*26.3*
OPEC COUNTRIES	*41.4*	*38.6*	*29.1*	*34.4*	*39.0*	*34.9*	*15.4*	*20.6*	*6.6*
E.E.C.+ MEMBERS	*10.0*	*6.2*	*8.8*	*16.5*	*9.1*	*5.5*	*8.4*	*14.5*	*47.1*
TOTAL	**88.9**	**70.7**	**61.1**	**92.5**	**82.2**	**65.6**	**40.7**	**71.7**	**93.3**

TOTAL OFFICIAL GROSS / TOTAL OFFICIAL NET / TOTAL OOF GROSS

	TOTAL OFFICIAL GROSS				TOTAL OFFICIAL NET				TOTAL OOF GROSS
	1983	1984	1985	1986	1983	1984	1985	1986	1983
DAC COUNTRIES									
Australia	–	–	0.0	–	–	–	0.0	–	–
Austria	0.1	0.1	0.7	0.2	0.1	0.1	0.7	0.2	–
Belgium	0.0	0.1	1.2	0.3	0.0	0.1	1.2	0.3	–
Canada	2.3	5.8	4.7	0.2	2.3	5.8	4.7	0.2	–
Denmark	1.2	0.4	0.4	0.5	1.2	0.4	0.4	0.4	–
Finland	0.1	–	–	–	0.1	–	–	–	–
France	24.7	21.3	39.0	38.7	23.9	20.7	38.1	36.5	2.0
Germany, Fed. Rep.	16.8	9.0	8.0	17.0	16.7	9.0	8.0	15.7	–
Ireland	–	–	–	–	–	–	–	–	–
Italy	0.5	2.2	10.2	20.0	0.5	2.2	10.2	20.0	–
Japan	3.6	1.5	3.9	11.0	3.6	1.5	3.9	11.0	–
Netherlands	2.8	2.7	2.5	3.9	2.8	2.7	2.5	3.9	–
New Zealand	–	–	–	–	–	–	–	–	–
Norway	0.5	1.6	0.1	0.3	0.5	1.6	0.1	0.3	–
Sweden	–	–	–	–	–	–	–	–	–
Switzerland	0.7	1.2	0.8	0.0	0.7	1.2	0.8	0.0	–
United Kingdom	1.6	0.5	1.2	0.3	1.6	0.5	1.2	0.3	–
United States	20.0	23.0	41.0	19.0	20.0	23.0	37.0	18.0	–
TOTAL	*74.9*	*69.4*	*113.7*	*111.4*	*73.9*	*68.8*	*108.7*	*106.8*	*2.0*
MULTILATERAL	*95.6*	*59.7*	*67.1*	*72.5*	*84.1*	*55.7*	*52.8*	*48.3*	*34.2*
OPEC COUNTRIES	*64.2*	*57.1*	*79.1*	*38.5*	*61.8*	*53.4*	*65.3*	*24.7*	*16.2*
E.E.C.+ MEMBERS	*65.5*	*52.7*	*78.8*	*96.3*	*64.3*	*51.9*	*76.4*	*90.6*	*8.3*
TOTAL	**234.6**	**186.2**	**259.8**	**222.4**	**219.7**	**177.8**	**226.8**	**179.9**	**52.4**

MILLION US DOLLARS, UNLESS OTHERWISE STATED

MAURITANIA

ODA COMMITMENTS

1984	1985	1986	1983	1984	1985	1986
–	0.0	–	–	–	0.0	–
0.1	0.7	0.2	0.1	0.0	0.7	–
0.1	1.2	0.3	–	–	0.6	0.3
5.8	4.7	0.2	1.9	5.7	4.2	0.3
0.4	0.4	0.5	0.6	0.2	8.6	5.2
–	–	–	0.1	–	–	–
21.1	33.2	36.2	20.2	50.3	25.8	36.2
9.0	8.0	15.2	15.9	9.9	3.6	17.7
–	–	–	–	–	–	–
2.2	10.2	20.0	2.4	3.3	11.7	25.7
1.5	3.9	11.0	1.2	1.3	2.5	2.8
2.7	2.5	3.9	2.0	2.6	1.7	8.5
–	–	–	–	–	–	–
1.6	0.1	0.3	0.7	1.1	0.0	0.5
–	–	–	–	–	0.0	–
1.2	0.8	0.0	0.7	1.2	0.8	0.0
0.5	1.2	0.3	1.6	0.5	1.2	0.3
23.0	34.0	19.0	13.5	30.5	29.5	14.2
69.2	*100.8*	*107.0*	*60.9*	*106.6*	*90.9*	*111.7*
2.6	2.1	0.3	–	–	9.0	13.6
–	–	–	–	–	–	–
–	–	–	–	–	–	–
15.1	14.1	15.6	14.3	17.3	18.8	15.3
–	–	–	–	–	–	–
5.5	6.0	12.9	8.1	–	29.2	7.6
–	–	–	–	–	–	–
1.3	1.5	1.5	–	–	3.9	4.9
–	–	–	–	–	–	–
–	–	–	–	–	–	–
–	–	–	14.6	16.7	19.5	11.5
4.9	5.5	5.6	–	–	–	–
0.9	1.2	0.8	–	–	–	–
0.5	1.6	1.0	–	–	–	–
–	–	–	–	–	–	–
8.4	8.8	2.8	–	–	–	–
2.1	2.5	1.4	–	–	–	–
16.5	11.5	20.0	56.2	28.0	22.4	14.3
57.6	*54.8*	*61.8*	*93.2*	*61.9*	*102.8*	*67.2*
51.9	*66.2*	*38.5*	*9.1*	*23.0*	*37.6*	*1.7*
51.2	*70.8*	*91.9*	*57.0*	*84.1*	*71.9*	*109.3*
178.6	*221.8*	*207.3*	*163.2*	*191.5*	*231.3*	*180.6*

TECH. COOP. GRANTS

1984	1985	1986	1983	1984	1985	1986
–	0.0	–	–	–	0.0	–
0.1	0.7	0.2	0.1	–	–	–
0.1	1.2	0.3	–	–	–	–
5.8	4.7	0.2	0.3	–	0.1	–
0.4	0.4	0.0	1.1	0.2	0.1	0.0
–	–	–	–	–	–	–
17.1	24.9	25.8	15.1	13.7	15.4	20.0
7.7	7.6	10.4	3.1	2.6	2.9	5.0
–	–	–	–	–	–	–
1.7	10.2	20.0	0.4	1.1	1.2	2.5
1.2	1.2	3.3	0.3	0.3	0.2	0.1
2.7	2.5	3.9	0.0	0.1	0.1	0.3
–	–	–	–	–	–	–
1.6	0.1	0.3	–	–	0.0	–
–	–	–	–	–	–	–
1.2	0.8	0.0	–	0.0	0.0	0.0
0.5	1.2	0.3	0.0	0.0	0.1	0.1
23.0	34.0	19.0	5.0	5.0	5.0	7.0
62.9	*89.3*	*83.7*	*25.3*	*23.0*	*25.1*	*35.0*
31.8	*34.4*	*27.0*	*7.3*	*8.3*	*10.8*	*8.8*
13.2	*37.1*	*4.1*	–	–	–	–
45.0	*62.0*	*75.4*	*19.6*	*17.7*	*19.8*	*28.0*
108.0	*160.7*	*114.8*	*32.6*	*31.3*	*35.9*	*43.8*

TOTAL OOF NET

1984	1985	1986	1983	1984	1985	1986
–	–	–	–	–	–	–
–	–	–	–	–	–	–
–	–	–	–	–	–	–
–	–	–	–	–	–	–
–	–	–	–	–	–	0.0
–	–	–	–	–	–	–
0.2	5.8	2.5	1.7	0.1	5.4	0.9
–	–	1.9	–	–	–	1.9
–	–	–	–	–	–	–
–	–	–	–	–	–	–
–	–	–	–	–	–	–
–	–	–	–	–	–	–
–	–	–	–	–	–	–
–	–	–	–	–	–	–
–	–	–	–	–	–	–
–	–	–	–	–	–	–
–	7.0	–	–	–	3.0	-1.0
0.2	*12.8*	*4.4*	*1.7*	*0.1*	*8.4*	*1.7*
2.1	*12.3*	*10.7*	*26.2*	*-1.1*	*4.2*	*-8.4*
5.2	*12.9*	–	*16.2*	*5.2*	*12.9*	–
1.5	*8.0*	*4.4*	*8.1*	*1.4*	*6.1*	*0.7*
7.6	*38.0*	*15.0*	*44.2*	*4.2*	*25.4*	*-6.7*

ODA COMMITMENTS : LOANS

DAC COUNTRIES

	1983	1984	1985	1986
Australia	–	–	–	–
Austria	–	–	–	–
Belgium	–	–	–	–
Canada	–	–	–	–
Denmark	–	–	7.6	–
Finland	–	–	–	–
France	2.1	32.1	2.2	10.4
Germany, Fed. Rep.	1.2	–	–	7.2
Ireland	–	–	–	–
Italy	–	–	–	–
Japan	–	–	–	–
Netherlands	–	–	–	–
New Zealand	–	–	–	–
Norway	–	–	–	–
Sweden	–	–	–	–
Switzerland	–	–	–	–
United Kingdom	–	–	–	–
United States	–	–	–	–
TOTAL	*3.2*	*32.1*	*9.8*	*17.6*
MULTILATERAL	*63.9*	*27.2*	*68.6*	*39.0*
OPEC COUNTRIES	–	*11.8*	*5.9*	–
E.E.C.+ MEMBERS	*3.2*	*34.0*	*15.1*	*17.6*
TOTAL	*67.1*	*71.2*	*84.3*	*56.6*

GRANT ELEMENT OF ODA

DAC COUNTRIES

	1983	1984	1985	1986
Australia	–	–	100.0	–
Austria	100.0	100.0	100.0	–
Belgium	–	–	100.0	100.0
Canada	100.0	100.0	100.0	100.0
Denmark	100.0	100.0	78.7	100.0
Finland	100.0	–	–	–
France	86.9	66.5	99.1	94.2
Germany, Fed. Rep.	98.8	100.0	100.0	84.6
Ireland	–	–	–	–
Italy	100.0	100.0	100.0	100.0
Japan	100.0	100.0	100.0	100.0
Netherlands	100.0	100.0	100.0	100.0
New Zealand	–	–	–	–
Norway	100.0	100.0	100.0	100.0
Sweden	–	–	100.0	–
Switzerland	100.0	100.0	100.0	100.0
United Kingdom	100.0	100.0	100.0	100.0
United States	100.0	100.0	100.0	100.0
TOTAL	*95.1*	*84.2*	*97.7*	*95.8*
MULTILATERAL	*63.7*	*75.3*	*81.1*	*79.8*
OPEC COUNTRIES	*100.0*	*80.2*	*89.8*	*100.0*
E.E.C.+ MEMBERS	*94.7*	*79.5*	*96.8*	*95.7*
TOTAL	*77.6*	*80.9*	*89.2*	*89.6*

OTHER AGGREGATES

COMMITMENTS: ALL SOURCES

	1983	1984	1985	1986
TOTAL BILATERAL	96.0	131.5	150.5	115.2
of which				
OPEC	34.8	24.9	37.6	1.7
CMEA	0.3	–	–	0.1
TOTAL MULTILATERAL	93.2	61.9	132.8	67.2
TOTAL BIL.& MULTIL.	189.2	193.4	283.2	182.4
of which				
ODA Grants	96.4	120.3	147.0	124.1
ODA Loans	67.1	71.2	84.3	56.6

DISBURSEMENTS:

DAC COUNTRIES COMBINED

	1983	1984	1985	1986
OFFICIAL & PRIVATE				
GROSS:				
Contractual Lending	42.4	24.4	35.9	32.0
Export Credits Total	28.0	17.9	11.5	4.3
Export Credits Private	28.0	17.9	11.5	4.3
NET:				
Contractual Lending	23.3	10.8	23.7	21.6
Export Credits Total	9.9	4.9	0.3	-2.5
PRIVATE SECTOR NET	15.9	7.5	4.6	-4.5
Direct Investment	0.1	0.2	0.1	-0.2
Portfolio Investment	5.9	2.4	0.2	-2.8
Export Credits	9.9	4.9	4.3	-1.5

MARKET BORROWING:

CHANGE IN CLAIMS

	1983	1984	1985	1986
Banks	–	-5.0	-13.0	17.0

MEMORANDUM ITEM:

	1983	1984	1985	1986
CMEA Countr.(Gross)	0.3	–	–	0.0

DISBURSEMENTS, UNLESS OTHERWISE STATED

TOTAL RECEIPTS NET / TOTAL ODA NET / TOTAL ODA GROSS

	TOTAL RECEIPTS NET 1983	1984	1985	1986	TOTAL ODA NET 1983	1984	1985	1986	TOTAL ODA GROSS 1983
DAC COUNTRIES									
Australia	3.2	1.8	1.8	2.0	3.3	1.8	1.8	2.0	3.3
Austria	0.0	0.0	-0.9	–	0.0	0.0	0.0	–	0.0
Belgium	-0.4	0.3	-1.2	0.5	0.1	0.1	0.1	0.1	0.1
Canada	0.1	0.1	0.2	0.3	0.1	0.1	0.2	0.3	0.1
Denmark	0.0	0.0	0.0	0.0	–	–	–	–	–
Finland	–	0.0	–	–	–	0.0	–	–	–
France	24.1	21.2	5.4	29.1	17.4	16.7	11.8	28.6	17.4
Germany, Fed. Rep.	1.1	0.7	1.5	1.2	0.7	1.0	1.5	1.4	0.7
Ireland	–	–	–	0.0	–	–	–	0.0	–
Italy	-9.2	0.2	-1.6	0.2	–	0.2	0.2	0.2	–
Japan	-0.2	2.3	0.5	11.5	0.2	3.7	0.7	5.2	0.4
Netherlands	-0.2	0.0	0.0	0.0	0.2	0.0	0.0	0.0	0.2
New Zealand	–	–	–	–	–	–	–	–	–
Norway	–	0.0	0.0	0.0	–	0.0	0.0	0.0	–
Sweden	–	–	–	0.1	–	–	–	0.1	–
Switzerland	0.0	0.0	0.0	0.0	0.0	0.0	0.0	0.0	0.0
United Kingdom	0.3	-1.1	-11.0	8.0	0.6	-0.3	0.9	6.0	2.0
United States	2.0	1.0	5.0	4.0	2.0	1.0	5.0	4.0	3.0
TOTAL	*20.9*	*26.5*	*-0.3*	*57.0*	*24.6*	*24.4*	*22.2*	*47.9*	*27.3*
MULTILATERAL									
AF.D.F.	1.0	–	–	–	1.0	–	–	–	1.0
AF.D.B.	-0.1	-1.0	-0.6	-0.8	–	–	–	–	–
AS.D.B	–	–	–	–	–	–	–	–	–
CAR.D.B.	–	–	–	–	–	–	–	–	–
E.E.C.	9.5	2.8	2.5	4.4	5.2	2.8	2.2	4.5	5.2
IBRD	1.3	23.9	24.9	4.0	0.1	0.1	–	–	0.1
IDA	-0.1	-0.2	-0.2	-0.2	-0.1	-0.2	-0.2	-0.2	–
I.D.B.	–	–	–	–	–	–	–	–	–
IFAD	–	0.1	0.2	0.2	–	0.1	0.2	0.2	–
I.F.C.	–	–	–	–	–	–	–	–	–
IMF TRUST FUND	–	–	–	–	–	–	–	–	–
U.N. AGENCIES									
UNDP	0.4	0.8	0.8	1.1	0.4	0.8	0.8	1.1	0.4
UNTA	0.3	0.4	0.4	0.7	0.3	0.4	0.4	0.7	0.3
UNICEF	0.1	0.1	0.1	0.1	0.1	0.1	0.1	0.1	0.1
UNRWA	–	–	–	–	–	–	–	–	–
WFP	2.5	2.8	0.9	1.1	2.5	2.8	0.9	1.1	2.5
UNHCR	–	–	–	–	–	–	–	–	–
Other Multilateral	0.5	0.5	0.3	0.2	0.5	0.5	0.3	0.2	0.5
Arab OPEC Agencies	5.3	0.6	-0.7	-1.7	3.7	0.8	-0.4	-0.9	3.7
TOTAL	*20.6*	*30.5*	*28.5*	*9.0*	*13.5*	*8.1*	*4.4*	*6.7*	*13.6*
OPEC COUNTRIES	*2.6*	*3.1*	*2.0*	*1.7*	*2.6*	*3.1*	*2.0*	*1.7*	*2.6*
E.E.C.+ MEMBERS	*25.1*	*24.0*	*-4.4*	*43.5*	*24.2*	*20.6*	*16.7*	*40.7*	*25.6*
TOTAL	**44.1**	**60.0**	**30.2**	**67.7**	**40.7**	**35.5**	**28.6**	**56.3**	**43.5**

ODA LOANS GROSS / ODA LOANS NET / GRANTS

	ODA LOANS GROSS 1983	1984	1985	1986	ODA LOANS NET 1983	1984	1985	1986	GRANTS 1983
DAC COUNTRIES									
Australia	–	–	–	–	–	–	–	–	3.3
Austria	–	–	–	–	–	–	–	–	0.0
Belgium	–	–	–	–	–	–	–	–	0.1
Canada	–	–	–	–	–	–	–	–	0.1
Denmark	–	–	–	–	–	–	–	–	–
Finland	–	–	–	–	–	–	–	–	–
France	9.2	10.7	5.3	19.5	9.2	10.7	5.1	18.7	8.2
Germany, Fed. Rep.	0.3	0.7	1.0	0.9	0.3	0.7	1.0	0.8	0.4
Ireland	–	–	–	–	–	–	–	–	–
Italy	–	–	–	–	–	–	–	–	–
Japan	–	–	–	2.4	-0.2	-0.2	-0.2	2.1	0.4
Netherlands	–	–	–	–	–	–	–	–	0.2
New Zealand	–	–	–	–	–	–	–	–	–
Norway	–	–	–	–	–	–	–	–	–
Sweden	–	–	–	–	–	–	–	–	–
Switzerland	–	–	–	–	–	–	–	–	0.0
United Kingdom	0.8	0.3	1.7	0.2	-0.7	-1.4	-0.2	-1.7	1.2
United States	3.0	–	–	–	2.0	-1.0	-1.0	–	–
TOTAL	*13.4*	*11.8*	*8.0*	*22.9*	*10.7*	*8.9*	*4.7*	*19.8*	*14.0*
MULTILATERAL	*5.9*	*2.0*	*0.3*	*0.2*	*5.8*	*1.8*	*-0.4*	*-1.1*	*7.7*
OPEC COUNTRIES	*1.5*	*3.1*	*2.7*	*3.1*	*1.5*	*2.9*	*1.9*	*1.6*	*1.1*
E.E.C.+ MEMBERS	*11.5*	*12.8*	*8.1*	*20.6*	*10.1*	*11.0*	*5.9*	*17.7*	*14.1*
TOTAL	**20.8**	**16.9**	**11.0**	**26.2**	**17.9**	**13.6**	**6.2**	**20.4**	**22.7**

TOTAL OFFICIAL GROSS / TOTAL OFFICIAL NET / TOTAL OOF GROSS

	TOTAL OFFICIAL GROSS 1983	1984	1985	1986	TOTAL OFFICIAL NET 1983	1984	1985	1986	TOTAL OOF GROSS 1983
DAC COUNTRIES									
Australia	3.3	1.8	1.8	2.0	3.3	1.8	1.8	2.0	–
Austria	0.0	0.0	0.0	–	0.0	0.0	0.0	–	–
Belgium	0.1	0.1	0.1	0.1	0.1	0.1	0.1	0.1	–
Canada	0.1	0.1	0.2	0.3	0.1	0.1	0.2	0.3	–
Denmark	–	–	–	–	–	–	–	–	–
Finland	–	0.0	–	–	–	0.0	–	–	–
France	17.4	21.3	12.0	32.1	16.4	19.9	10.4	31.3	–
Germany, Fed. Rep.	0.7	1.0	1.5	1.4	0.7	1.0	1.5	1.4	–
Ireland	–	–	–	0.0	–	–	–	0.0	–
Italy	–	0.2	0.2	0.2	–	0.2	0.2	0.2	–
Japan	0.4	3.9	0.9	5.5	0.2	3.7	0.7	5.2	–
Netherlands	0.2	0.0	0.0	0.0	0.2	0.0	0.0	0.0	–
New Zealand	–	–	–	–	–	–	–	–	–
Norway	–	0.0	0.0	0.0	–	0.0	0.0	0.0	–
Sweden	–	–	–	0.1	–	–	–	0.1	–
Switzerland	0.0	0.0	0.0	0.0	0.0	0.0	0.0	0.0	–
United Kingdom	2.0	1.9	2.8	8.5	0.4	0.1	0.8	6.4	–
United States	3.0	2.0	6.0	4.0	2.0	1.0	5.0	4.0	–
TOTAL	*27.3*	*32.4*	*25.5*	*54.3*	*23.4*	*28.0*	*20.8*	*51.0*	*–*
MULTILATERAL	*27.3*	*36.5*	*37.9*	*20.9*	*20.6*	*30.5*	*28.5*	*9.0*	*13.7*
OPEC COUNTRIES	*2.6*	*3.2*	*2.8*	*3.1*	*2.6*	*3.1*	*2.0*	*1.7*	*–*
E.E.C.+ MEMBERS	*30.5*	*28.1*	*19.9*	*47.9*	*27.3*	*24.1*	*15.5*	*43.8*	*4.9*
TOTAL	**57.1**	**72.1**	**66.3**	**78.3**	**46.6**	**61.5**	**51.4**	**61.7**	**13.7**

MAURITIUS

ODA COMMITMENTS

	1984	1985	1986	1983	1984	1985	1986
Australia	1.8	1.8	2.0	2.0	1.9	1.5	1.6
Austria	0.0	0.0	–	–	–	0.0	–
Belgium	0.1	0.1	0.1	–	–	–	0.1
Canada	0.1	0.2	0.3	0.2	0.2	0.2	0.2
Denmark	–	–	–	–	–	–	–
Finland	0.0			–	–	–	–
France	16.8	12.0	29.4	20.1	19.1	13.4	29.4
Germany, Fed. Rep.	1.0	1.5	1.4	0.6	1.0	0.3	4.8
Ireland	–		0.0	–	–	–	0.0
Italy	0.2	0.2	0.2	–	0.2	0.3	0.3
Japan	3.9	0.9	5.5	4.6	0.3	0.4	11.4
Netherlands	0.0	0.0	0.0	0.2	0.0	0.0	0.0
New Zealand	–	–	–	–	–	–	–
Norway	0.0	0.0	0.0	–	0.0	0.0	0.1
Sweden	–	–	0.1	–	–	–	0.1
Switzerland	0.0	0.0	0.0	0.0	0.0	0.0	0.0
United Kingdom	1.4	2.8	7.9	1.2	1.1	1.2	10.6
United States	2.0	6.0	4.0	2.2	4.2	7.2	2.1
TOTAL	27.4	25.5	51.0	30.9	28.0	24.5	60.8
	–	–	–	–	–	–	–
	–	–	–	–	–	–	–
	2.8	2.2	4.5	0.9	8.4	1.8	4.2
	0.1	–	–	–	–	–	–
	–	–	–	–	–	–	–
	0.1	0.2	0.2	–	–	–	–
	–	–	–	–	–	–	–
	–	–	–	3.7	4.5	2.6	3.1
	0.8	0.8	1.1	–	–	–	–
	0.4	0.4	0.7	–	–	–	–
	0.1	0.1	0.1	–	–	–	–
	–	–	–	–	–	–	–
	2.8	0.9	1.1	–	–	–	–
	0.5	0.3	0.2	–	–	–	–
	0.8	0.1	0.2	–	–	1.0	–
	8.3	5.1	8.0	4.6	12.9	5.4	7.3
	3.2	2.8	3.1	1.1	–	0.0	–
	22.3	18.8	43.5	22.9	29.8	17.0	49.4
	38.9	33.5	62.1	36.5	40.9	30.0	68.1

TECH. COOP. GRANTS

	1984	1985	1986	1983	1984	1985	1986
Australia	1.8	1.8	2.0	0.1	0.1	0.1	0.3
Austria	0.0	0.0	–	0.0	–	–	–
Belgium	0.1	0.1	0.1	0.0	0.0	0.0	0.0
Canada	0.1	0.2	0.3	0.0	–	0.0	–
Denmark	–	–	–	–	–	–	–
Finland	0.0	–	–	–	0.0	–	–
France	6.0	6.7	9.9	4.9	4.5	4.8	6.8
Germany, Fed. Rep.	0.3	0.5	0.6	0.4	0.3	0.5	0.6
Ireland	–	–	0.0	–	–	–	0.0
Italy	0.2	0.2	0.2	–	0.2	0.2	0.2
Japan	3.9	0.9	3.1	0.1	0.2	0.3	0.5
Netherlands	0.0	0.0	0.0	0.2	0.0	0.0	0.0
New Zealand	–	–	–	–	–	–	–
Norway	0.0	0.0	0.0	–	0.0	0.0	0.0
Sweden	–	–	0.1	–	–	–	0.1
Switzerland	0.0	0.0	0.0	–	–	–	0.0
United Kingdom	1.1	1.2	7.7	1.2	1.1	1.2	1.5
United States	2.0	6.0	4.0	–	–	–	–
	15.6	17.5	28.1	7.0	6.4	7.1	10.2
	6.3	4.8	7.8	1.2	1.7	1.7	1.4
	0.1	0.1	0.1	–	–	–	–
	9.5	10.7	23.0	6.7	6.1	6.6	9.2
	22.0	22.4	35.9	8.2	8.1	8.8	11.6

TOTAL OOF NET

	1984	1985	1986	1983	1984	1985	1986
	–	–	–	–	–	–	–
	0.0	0.0	–	–	0.0	0.0	–
	–	–	–	–	–	–	–
	–	–	–	–	–	–	–
	4.6	–	2.7	-1.1	3.2	-1.3	2.7
	–	–	–	–	–	–	–
	–	–	–	–	–	–	–
	–	–	–	–	–	–	–
	–	–	–	–	–	–	–
	–	–	–	–	–	–	–
	0.5	–	0.6	-0.1	0.4	-0.1	0.4
	–	–	–	–	–	–	–
	5.1	0.0	3.3	-1.2	3.6	-1.4	3.1
	28.2	32.8	12.9	7.2	22.4	24.1	2.3
	–	–	–	–	–	–	–
	5.7	1.2	4.3	3.1	3.6	-1.2	3.0
	33.2	32.8	16.2	6.0	26.0	22.7	5.4

ODA COMMITMENTS : LOANS

DAC COUNTRIES	1983	1984	1985	1986
Australia	–	–	–	–
Austria	–	–	–	–
Belgium	–	–	–	–
Canada	–	–	–	–
Denmark	–	–	–	–
Finland	–	–	–	–
France	11.2	10.7	7.2	19.5
Germany, Fed. Rep.	–	0.7	–	4.4
Ireland	–	–	–	0.0
Italy	–	–	–	–
Japan	–	–	–	5.2
Netherlands	–	–	–	–
New Zealand	–	–	–	–
Norway	–	–	–	–
Sweden	–	–	–	–
Switzerland	–	–	–	–
United Kingdom	–	–	–	–
United States	–	–	–	–
TOTAL	11.2	11.4	7.2	29.1
MULTILATERAL	0.8	6.7	–	3.5
OPEC COUNTRIES	–	–	–	–
E.E.C.+ MEMBERS	11.9	18.1	7.2	27.4
TOTAL	11.9	18.1	7.2	32.5

GRANT ELEMENT OF ODA

DAC COUNTRIES	1983	1984	1985	1986
Australia	100.0	100.0	100.0	100.0
Austria	–	–	100.0	–
Belgium	–	–	–	100.0
Canada	100.0	100.0	100.0	100.0
Denmark	–	–	–	–
Finland	–	–	–	–
France	90.6	61.2	50.1	63.9
Germany, Fed. Rep.	100.0	77.1	100.0	32.3
Ireland	–	–	–	100.0
Italy	–	100.0	100.0	100.0
Japan	100.0	100.0	100.0	71.0
Netherlands	100.0	100.0	100.0	100.0
New Zealand	–	–	–	–
Norway	–	100.0	100.0	100.0
Sweden	–	–	–	100.0
Switzerland	100.0	100.0	100.0	100.0
United Kingdom	100.0	100.0	100.0	100.0
United States	100.0	100.9	100.0	100.0
TOTAL	95.4	72.9	67.2	73.1
MULTILATERAL	100.0	100.0	100.0	100.0
OPEC COUNTRIES	100.0	–	100.0	–
E.E.C.+ MEMBERS	92.2	67.0	57.3	71.3
TOTAL	96.3	77.8	72.0	75.0

OTHER AGGREGATES

COMMITMENTS: ALL SOURCES

	1983	1984	1985	1986
TOTAL BILATERAL	37.2	35.3	25.3	64.1
of which				
OPEC	1.1	–	0.0	–
CMEA	–	–	–	–
TOTAL MULTILATERAL	66.8	17.0	5.4	58.1
TOTAL BIL.& MULTIL.	104.0	52.2	30.7	122.2
of which				
ODA Grants	24.6	22.8	22.8	35.6
ODA Loans	11.9	18.1	7.2	32.5

DISBURSEMENTS:

DAC COUNTRIES COMBINED

OFFICIAL & PRIVATE	1983	1984	1985	1986
GROSS:				
Contractual Lending	18.2	19.9	8.8	27.7
Export Credits Total	4.8	3.1	0.9	1.5
Export Credits Private	4.8	3.1	0.9	1.5
NET:				
Contractual Lending	0.8	12.8	-1.1	23.7
Export Credits Total	-8.7	0.3	-4.4	0.7
PRIVATE SECTOR NET	-2.6	-1.5	-21.1	6.0
Direct Investment	0.9	-0.6	-11.6	8.6
Portfolio Investment	5.2	-1.2	-5.1	-3.3
Export Credits	-8.7	0.3	-4.4	0.7

MARKET BORROWING:

CHANGE IN CLAIMS

	1983	1984	1985	1986
Banks	–	-3.0	-4.0	-1.0

MEMORANDUM ITEM:

	1983	1984	1985	1986
CMEA Countr.(Gross)	–	–	–	–

MEXICO

TOTAL RECEIPTS NET

DAC COUNTRIES	1983	1984	1985	1986
Australia	-1.4	-0.7	0.3	9.9
Austria	-0.2	-2.1	-1.9	0.3
Belgium	20.1	630.8	-339.5	-529.3
Canada	34.8	-30.1	-50.3	-19.0
Denmark	13.1	-13.1	-12.3	-11.3
Finland	-1.5	-0.6	1.8	0.7
France	527.4	924.9	688.9	373.0
Germany, Fed. Rep.	261.2	236.5	141.1	88.3
Ireland	–	–	–	–
Italy	-13.2	-14.8	2.8	-56.1
Japan	405.2	2176.2	-0.3	375.6
Netherlands	26.9	-2.7	6.0	15.5
New Zealand	–	–	0.1	0.0
Norway	10.3	41.5	36.4	38.1
Sweden	24.2	14.3	14.3	30.8
Switzerland	18.9	-14.4	17.3	1.0
United Kingdom	-32.6	-0.8	87.9	38.8
United States	2353.0	9147.0	-2887.0	42.0
TOTAL	3646.3	13091.9	-2294.4	398.3
MULTILATERAL				
AF.D.F.	–	–	–	–
AF.D.B.	–	–	–	–
AS.D.B	–	–	–	–
CAR.D.B.	–	–	0.2	0.3
E.E.C.	–	–	–	–
IBRD	177.9	418.9	505.1	591.7
IDA	–	–	–	–
I.D.B.	48.2	330.9	227.6	321.1
IFAD	6.7	-1.3	0.6	0.5
I.F.C.	-43.1	7.7	-71.8	-46.5
IMF TRUST FUND	–	–	–	–
U.N. AGENCIES				
UNDP	2.4	2.6	2.6	3.2
UNTA	0.6	0.6	1.0	0.9
UNICEF	0.9	1.1	1.1	2.9
UNRWA	–	–	–	–
WFP	1.5	2.7	8.1	4.4
UNHCR	–	9.7	11.7	8.8
Other Multilateral	2.1	3.3	3.5	1.6
Arab OPEC Agencies	–	–	–	–
TOTAL	197.1	776.3	689.8	888.9
OPEC COUNTRIES	-48.0	–	–	-0.1
E.E.C.+ MEMBERS	802.9	1760.7	575.2	-80.8
TOTAL	3795.4	13868.2	-1604.6	1287.1

TOTAL ODA NET

DAC COUNTRIES	1983	1984	1985	1986
Australia	0.1	0.1	0.9	0.1
Austria	-0.2	-0.2	-0.1	0.3
Belgium	0.3	0.4	0.4	0.8
Canada	1.1	1.5	1.7	2.8
Denmark	0.0	–	–	–
Finland	0.6	0.3	1.0	0.1
France	16.5	8.6	27.9	86.3
Germany, Fed. Rep.	28.1	6.7	7.1	9.5
Ireland	–	–	–	–
Italy	0.9	6.6	2.1	4.6
Japan	46.9	30.6	19.5	80.8
Netherlands	1.9	2.7	1.9	4.9
New Zealand	–	–	0.1	0.0
Norway	0.1	0.1	0.8	0.5
Sweden	0.1	0.0	0.3	2.4
Switzerland	0.5	0.2	1.0	1.0
United Kingdom	4.3	0.7	1.0	1.2
United States	35.0	17.0	57.0	52.0
TOTAL	135.9	75.3	122.6	247.2
MULTILATERAL				
AF.D.F.	–	–	–	–
AF.D.B.	–	–	–	–
AS.D.B	–	–	–	–
CAR.D.B.	–	–	0.2	0.3
E.E.C.	–	–	–	–
IBRD	–	–	–	–
IDA	–	–	–	–
I.D.B.	-18.4	-10.7	-6.8	-18.2
IFAD	6.7	-1.3	0.6	0.5
I.F.C.	–	–	–	–
IMF TRUST FUND	–	–	–	–
UNDP	2.4	2.6	2.6	3.2
UNTA	0.6	0.6	1.0	0.9
UNICEF	0.9	1.1	1.1	2.9
UNRWA	–	–	–	–
WFP	1.5	2.7	8.1	4.4
UNHCR	–	9.7	11.7	8.8
Other Multilateral	2.1	3.3	3.5	1.6
Arab OPEC Agencies	–	–	–	–
TOTAL	-4.2	8.1	22.0	4.4
OPEC COUNTRIES	–	–	–	–
E.E.C.+ MEMBERS	51.8	25.8	40.6	107.4
TOTAL	131.6	83.4	144.6	251.6

TOTAL ODA GROSS

	1983
Australia	0.1
Austria	0.5
Belgium	0.3
Canada	1.1
Denmark	0.0
Finland	0.6
France	19.0
Germany, Fed. Rep.	28.1
Ireland	–
Italy	0.9
Japan	48.2
Netherlands	1.9
New Zealand	–
Norway	0.1
Sweden	0.1
Switzerland	0.5
United Kingdom	4.3
United States	38.0
TOTAL	143.5
AF.D.F.	–
AF.D.B.	–
AS.D.B	–
CAR.D.B.	–
E.E.C.	–
IBRD	–
IDA	–
I.D.B.	5.3
IFAD	6.7
I.F.C.	–
IMF TRUST FUND	–
U.N. AGENCIES	
UNDP	2.4
UNTA	0.6
UNICEF	0.9
UNRWA	–
WFP	1.5
UNHCR	–
Other Multilateral	2.1
Arab OPEC Agencies	–
TOTAL	19.5
OPEC COUNTRIES	–
E.E.C.+ MEMBERS	54.4
TOTAL	163.0

ODA LOANS GROSS

DAC COUNTRIES	1983	1984	1985	1986
Australia	–	–	–	–
Austria	0.0	–	–	0.4
Belgium	–	–	–	–
Canada	–	–	–	–
Denmark	–	–	–	–
Finland	–	–	0.3	–
France	11.9	4.8	25.5	73.4
Germany, Fed. Rep.	17.8	0.4	0.4	–
Ireland	–	–	–	–
Italy	–	5.3	–	–
Japan	38.6	22.4	8.9	69.9
Netherlands	–	–	–	–
New Zealand	–	–	–	–
Norway	–	–	–	–
Sweden	–	–	–	–
Switzerland	–	–	–	–
United Kingdom	–	–	–	–
United States	–	–	–	–
TOTAL	68.3	32.9	35.1	143.8
MULTILATERAL	12.0	12.8	19.6	8.3
OPEC COUNTRIES	–	–	–	–
E.E.C.+ MEMBERS	29.7	10.6	25.9	73.4
TOTAL	80.4	45.8	54.8	152.1

ODA LOANS NET

DAC COUNTRIES	1983	1984	1985	1986
Australia	–	–	–	–
Austria	-0.7	-0.5	-0.5	0.0
Belgium	–	–	–	–
Canada	–	–	–	–
Denmark	–	–	–	–
Finland	–	–	0.3	–
France	9.5	1.5	21.3	70.7
Germany, Fed. Rep.	17.7	-0.7	-1.7	-2.8
Ireland	–	–	–	–
Italy	–	5.3	–	–
Japan	37.3	22.4	8.9	69.9
Netherlands	–	–	-0.2	–
New Zealand	–	–	–	–
Norway	–	–	–	–
Sweden	–	–	–	–
Switzerland	–	–	–	–
United Kingdom	–	–	–	–
United States	-3.0	-3.0	-3.0	-3.0
TOTAL	60.7	25.1	25.2	134.9
MULTILATERAL	-11.7	-12.0	-6.3	-17.8
OPEC COUNTRIES	–	–	–	–
E.E.C.+ MEMBERS	49.0	13.1	18.8	117.2

GRANTS

	1983
Australia	0.1
Austria	0.5
Belgium	0.3
Canada	1.1
Denmark	0.0
Finland	0.6
France	7.1
Germany, Fed. Rep.	10.3
Ireland	–
Italy	0.9
Japan	9.6
Netherlands	1.9
New Zealand	–
Norway	0.1
Sweden	0.1
Switzerland	0.5
United Kingdom	4.3
United States	38.0
TOTAL	75.1
MULTILATERAL	7.5
OPEC COUNTRIES	–
E.E.C.+ MEMBERS	24.7
TOTAL	82.6

TOTAL OFFICIAL GROSS

DAC COUNTRIES	1983	1984	1985	1986
Australia	0.1	0.1	0.9	0.1
Austria	0.5	0.2	0.3	0.7
Belgium	0.3	1.3	1.2	0.8
Canada	80.1	36.4	16.4	15.5
Denmark	0.1	–	0.2	0.1
Finland	0.6	0.3	1.0	0.1
France	19.0	11.9	32.1	89.0
Germany, Fed. Rep.	32.3	34.0	42.0	38.3
Ireland	–	–	–	–
Italy	4.9	6.6	9.9	7.2
Japan	265.5	245.3	264.9	238.3
Netherlands	1.9	2.7	2.1	4.9
New Zealand	–	–	0.1	0.0
Norway	0.1	0.1	0.8	0.5
Sweden	21.0	24.3	32.3	53.3
Switzerland	0.5	0.2	1.0	1.0
United Kingdom	4.3	0.7	1.0	1.2
United States	372.0	492.0	194.0	124.0
TOTAL	802.9	856.1	600.1	575.0
MULTILATERAL	497.0	1173.9	1192.9	1497.6
OPEC COUNTRIES	2.7	–	–	–
E.E.C.+ MEMBERS	62.6	57.2	88.6	141.7
TOTAL	1302.5	2030.0	1793.0	2072.6

TOTAL OFFICIAL NET

DAC COUNTRIES	1983	1984	1985	1986
Australia	-0.6	-0.6	0.4	-0.1
Austria	-0.2	-0.2	-0.1	0.3
Belgium	0.3	1.3	1.2	0.8
Canada	35.3	-29.7	-49.5	-35.9
Denmark	0.0	0.0	0.2	0.1
Finland	0.6	0.3	1.0	0.1
France	16.5	8.6	27.9	86.3
Germany, Fed. Rep.	24.7	24.8	28.9	23.2
Ireland	–	–	–	–
Italy	-3.2	-1.7	2.7	0.1
Japan	185.0	153.3	161.6	135.7
Netherlands	1.9	2.7	1.9	4.9
New Zealand	–	–	0.1	0.0
Norway	0.1	0.1	0.8	0.5
Sweden	16.8	15.4	24.3	39.4
Switzerland	0.5	0.2	1.0	1.0
United Kingdom	4.3	0.7	1.0	1.2
United States	-580.0	139.0	-43.0	-53.0
TOTAL	-298.2	314.1	160.3	204.5
MULTILATERAL	197.1	776.3	689.8	888.9
OPEC COUNTRIES	-48.0	–	–	-0.1
E.E.C.+ MEMBERS	44.4	36.3	64.0	116.7
TOTAL	-149.1	1090.4	850.0	1093.3

TOTAL OOF GROSS

	1983
Australia	–
Austria	–
Belgium	–
Canada	79.0
Denmark	0.0
Finland	–
France	–
Germany, Fed. Rep.	4.1
Ireland	–
Italy	4.1
Japan	217.3
Netherlands	–
New Zealand	–
Norway	–
Sweden	20.9
Switzerland	–
United Kingdom	–
United States	334.0
TOTAL	659.4
MULTILATERAL	477.4
OPEC COUNTRIES	2.7
E.E.C.+ MEMBERS	8.2
TOTAL	1139.5

ODA COMMITMENTS

1984	1985	1986	1983	1984	1985	1986
0.1	0.9	0.1	0.1	0.1	0.8	0.1
0.2	0.3	0.7	0.3	0.1	0.6	–
0.4	0.4	0.8	–	–	–	0.8
1.5	1.7	2.8	1.0	1.8	2.3	2.1
–	–	–	–	–	–	–
0.3	1.0	0.1	0.2	-0.1	0.6	0.6
11.9	32.1	89.0	12.0	61.8	74.3	89.0
7.8	9.2	12.3	10.4	7.3	9.7	22.6
–	–	–	–	–	–	–
6.6	2.1	4.6	1.3	1.7	4.8	7.0
30.6	19.5	80.8	12.5	41.3	61.7	12.2
2.7	2.1	4.9	2.0	2.6	2.4	4.7
–	0.1	0.0	–	–	0.2	–
0.1	0.8	0.5	–	0.1	0.1	0.1
0.0	0.3	2.4	–	0.5	2.0	2.4
0.2	1.0	1.0	0.5	0.1	0.9	0.8
0.7	1.0	1.2	1.3	0.7	1.0	1.2
20.0	60.0	55.0	37.2	12.6	57.5	49.7
83.2	*132.6*	*256.1*	*79.0*	*130.5*	*218.7*	*193.1*
–	–	–	–	–	–	–
–	–	–	–	–	–	–
–	–	–	–	–	–	–
–	0.2	0.3	0.2	0.2	0.6	6.1
–	–	–	–	–	–	–
12.7	17.4	5.7	16.2	–	10.0	11.3
0.1	2.3	2.6	–	–	–	–
–	–	–	–	–	–	–
–	–	–	7.5	20.1	28.0	21.9
2.6	2.6	3.2	–	–	–	–
0.6	1.0	0.9	–	–	–	–
1.1	1.1	2.9	–	–	–	–
–	–	–	–	–	–	–
2.7	8.1	4.4	–	–	–	–
9.7	11.7	8.8	–	–	–	–
3.3	3.5	1.6	–	–	–	–
–	–	–	–	–	–	–
32.9	*48.0*	*30.4*	*23.9*	*20.3*	*38.7*	*39.2*
–	–	–	–	–	–	–
30.1	*47.1*	*112.9*	*27.1*	*74.3*	*92.7*	*131.2*
116.0	*180.6*	*286.5*	*102.9*	*150.8*	*257.4*	*232.3*

TECH. COOP. GRANTS

1984	1985	1986	1983	1984	1985	1986
0.1	0.9	0.1	0.1	0.1	0.1	0.1
0.2	0.3	0.3	0.5	–	–	–
0.4	0.4	0.8	0.1	0.1	0.1	–
1.5	1.7	2.8	0.5	–	0.2	–
–	–	–	0.0	–	–	–
0.3	0.7	0.1	0.4	0.3	0.2	–
7.1	6.6	15.5	7.1	7.0	6.6	10.4
7.4	8.8	12.3	8.8	7.1	7.4	10.2
–	–	–	–	–	–	–
1.3	2.1	4.6	0.9	1.3	1.6	3.6
8.3	10.6	10.9	8.2	6.7	9.0	10.9
2.7	2.1	4.9	1.7	2.0	1.7	2.3
–	0.1	0.0	–	–	0.0	0.0
0.1	0.8	0.5	0.1	0.1	0.1	0.1
0.0	0.3	2.4	0.1	0.0	0.2	0.1
0.2	1.0	1.0	0.0	0.1	0.1	0.2
0.7	1.0	1.2	1.3	0.7	0.8	1.0
20.0	60.0	55.0	–	–	–	1.0
50.2	*97.5*	*112.3*	*29.6*	*25.5*	*27.9*	*39.8*
20.1	*28.4*	*22.1*	*6.0*	*17.3*	*19.9*	*17.6*
–	–	–	–	–	–	–
19.6	*21.2*	*39.5*	*19.7*	*18.2*	*18.0*	*27.6*
70.3	*125.8*	*134.4*	*35.6*	*42.8*	*47.8*	*57.4*

TOTAL OOF NET

1984	1985	1986	1983	1984	1985	1986
–	–	–	-0.7	-0.7	-0.5	-0.2
–	–	–	–	–	–	–
0.9	0.8	–	–	0.9	0.8	–
35.0	14.6	12.8	34.2	-31.1	-51.3	-38.6
–	0.2	0.1	0.0	0.0	0.2	0.1
–	–	–	–	–	–	–
26.2	32.8	26.1	-3.4	18.1	21.9	13.7
–	–	–	–	–	–	–
–	7.7	2.6	-4.1	-8.3	0.5	-4.5
214.7	245.4	157.5	138.1	122.7	142.1	55.0
–	–	–	–	–	–	–
–	–	–	–	–	–	–
24.3	32.0	50.8	16.7	15.4	24.0	36.9
–	–	–	–	–	–	–
472.0	134.0	69.0	-615.0	122.0	-100.0	-105.0
773.0	*467.5*	*318.9*	*-434.1*	*238.8*	*37.7*	*-42.7*
1141.0	*1144.9*	*1467.1*	*201.3*	*768.2*	*667.7*	*884.5*
–	–	–	-48.0	–	–	-0.1
27.0	*41.5*	*28.8*	*-7.5*	*10.6*	*23.4*	*9.3*
1914.0	*1612.4*	*1786.1*	*-280.7*	*1007.0*	*705.4*	*841.7*

ODA COMMITMENTS : LOANS

DAC COUNTRIES

	1983	1984	1985	1986
Australia	–	–	–	–
Austria	0.0	–	0.3	–
Belgium	–	–	–	0.8
Canada	–	–	–	–
Denmark	–	–	–	–
Finland	–	–	–	–
France	5.0	54.8	67.7	73.4
Germany, Fed. Rep.	–	–	–	7.3
Ireland	–	–	–	–
Italy	–	–	–	–
Japan	1.0	34.1	50.7	–
Netherlands	–	–	–	–
New Zealand	–	–	–	–
Norway	–	–	–	–
Sweden	–	–	–	–
Switzerland	–	–	–	–
United Kingdom	–	–	–	–
United States	–	–	–	–
TOTAL	*6.0*	*88.9*	*118.7*	*80.7*
MULTILATERAL	*16.2*	*–*	*10.0*	*11.3*
OPEC COUNTRIES				
E.E.C.+ MEMBERS	*5.0*	*54.8*	*67.7*	*80.7*
TOTAL	*22.2*	*88.9*	*128.7*	*92.0*

GRANT ELEMENT OF ODA

DAC COUNTRIES

	1983	1984	1985	1986
Australia	100.0	100.0	100.0	100.0
Austria	97.5	100.0	100.0	–
Belgium	–	–	–	100.0
Canada	100.0	100.0	100.0	100.0
Denmark	–	–	–	–
Finland	100.0	100.0	100.0	100.0
France	87.0	67.9	67.9	80.3
Germany, Fed. Rep.	100.0	100.0	100.0	76.4
Ireland	–	–	–	–
Italy	100.0	100.0	100.0	100.0
Japan	100.0	46.1	52.9	100.0
Netherlands	100.0	100.0	100.0	100.0
New Zealand	–	–	100.0	–
Norway	–	100.0	100.0	100.0
Sweden	–	100.0	100.0	100.0
Switzerland	100.0	100.0	100.0	100.0
United Kingdom	100.0	100.0	100.0	100.0
United States	100.0	100.0	100.0	100.0
TOTAL	*98.0*	*68.1*	*75.8*	*90.9*
MULTILATERAL	*56.9*	*100.0*	*88.8*	*91.6*
OPEC COUNTRIES	*–*	*–*	*–*	*–*
E.E.C.+ MEMBERS	*94.3*	*73.3*	*74.3*	*84.0*
TOTAL	*78.6*	*72.5*	*77.8*	*91.0*

OTHER AGGREGATES

COMMITMENTS: ALL SOURCES

	1983	1984	1985	1986
TOTAL BILATERAL	343.4	1090.7	383.9	498.2
of which				
OPEC	3.4	–	–	–
CMEA	–	–	–	–
TOTAL MULTILATERAL	1207.7	840.2	1354.0	1624.2
TOTAL BIL.& MULTIL.	1551.0	1930.8	1737.9	2122.5
of which				
ODA Grants	80.7	61.9	128.7	140.3
ODA Loans	22.2	88.9	128.7	92.1

DISBURSEMENTS:

DAC COUNTRIES COMBINED

	1983	1984	1985	1986
OFFICIAL & PRIVATE				
GROSS:				
Contractual Lending	2333.5	1745.0	1788.2	1373.0
Export Credits Total	2191.0	-1390.0	1695.1	1217.1
Export Credits Private	1605.7	940.0	1286.3	910.3
NET:				
Contractual Lending	479.5	106.4	160.8	77.7
Export Credits Total	1195.8	-240.6	77.7	-69.3
PRIVATE SECTOR NET	3944.5	12777.8	-2454.6	193.9
Direct Investment	-325.5	580.2	359.4	-49.5
Portfolio Investment	3417.1	12354.2	-2912.8	257.8
Export Credits	852.9	-156.6	98.7	-14.5

MARKET BORROWING:

CHANGE IN CLAIMS

	1983	1984	1985	1986
Banks	–	856.0	825.0	-2074.0

MEMORANDUM ITEM:

	1983	1984	1985	1986
CMEA Countr.(Gross)	–	–	–	–

	TOTAL RECEIPTS NET 1983	1984	1985	1986	TOTAL ODA NET 1983	1984	1985	1986	TOTAL ODA GROSS 1983
DAC COUNTRIES									
Australia	–	–	0.1	–	–	–	0.1	–	–
Austria	0.1	0.1	0.1	0.0	0.1	0.1	0.1	0.0	0.1
Belgium	37.6	-2.4	1.9	-6.5	8.1	3.9	5.4	3.9	8.1
Canada	3.9	8.1	1.9	4.6	3.7	6.3	3.3	5.2	3.8
Denmark	-0.2	0.1	0.0	15.8	-0.1	0.0	-0.1	15.8	–
Finland	–	–	–	–	–	–	–	–	–
France	176.9	477.8	468.6	229.6	98.9	100.2	158.0	131.7	116.2
Germany, Fed. Rep.	13.3	46.2	51.2	74.7	15.3	32.3	27.6	71.4	25.8
Ireland	–	–	–	–	–	–	–	–	–
Italy	-61.7	-23.6	35.0	76.4	5.7	3.9	1.8	2.8	6.0
Japan	81.2	41.4	-0.6	11.5	10.9	38.4	22.2	13.3	11.3
Netherlands	0.2	1.6	0.0	-0.3	0.2	1.6	0.9	0.1	0.2
New Zealand	–	–	–	–	–	–	–	–	–
Norway	0.0	0.1	0.0	0.1	–	0.1	0.0	0.0	–
Sweden	–	–	13.0	6.9	–	–	–	–	–
Switzerland	11.2	3.5	5.6	0.6	0.3	1.7	2.5	0.6	0.3
United Kingdom	40.8	13.4	6.1	11.0	0.2	0.3	0.1	0.2	0.2
United States	70.0	344.0	71.0	170.0	46.0	59.0	96.0	47.0	52.0
TOTAL	*373.2*	*910.4*	*653.9*	*594.5*	*189.5*	*247.7*	*317.8*	*292.1*	*224.0*
MULTILATERAL									
AF.D.F.	–	–	–	–	–	–	–	–	–
AF.D.B.	11.6	5.0	13.7	44.5	–	–	–	–	–
AS.D.B	–	–	–	–	–	–	–	–	–
CAR.D.B.	–	–	–	–	–	–	–	–	–
E.E.C.	64.3	14.2	52.7	29.2	40.9	3.9	29.4	11.2	40.9
IBRD	123.5	192.6	220.2	254.3	5.1	1.3	–	–	5.1
IDA	1.0	1.2	-0.3	-0.6	1.0	1.2	-0.3	-0.6	1.4
I.D.B.	–	–	–	–	–	–	–	–	–
IFAD	4.9	-1.3	0.9	1.1	4.9	-1.3	0.9	1.1	4.9
I.F.C.	48.0	0.7	-5.3	43.6	–	–	–	–	–
IMF TRUST FUND	–	–	–	–	–	–	–	–	–
U.N. AGENCIES	–	–	–	–	–	–	–	–	–
UNDP	3.7	3.2	2.9	3.4	3.7	3.2	2.9	3.4	3.7
UNTA	1.1	0.6	0.8	1.3	1.1	0.6	0.8	1.3	1.1
UNICEF	1.5	1.6	1.2	1.6	1.5	1.6	1.2	1.6	1.5
UNRWA	–	–	–	–	–	–	–	–	–
WFP	13.2	16.1	17.9	21.9	13.2	16.1	17.9	21.9	13.2
UNHCR	0.1	0.1	0.1	0.0	0.1	0.1	0.1	0.0	0.1
Other Multilateral	1.7	2.2	2.0	2.0	1.7	2.2	2.0	2.0	1.7
Arab OPEC Agencies	10.1	6.6	83.3	2.3	13.7	2.4	8.2	-0.8	15.7
TOTAL	*284.6*	*242.8*	*390.1*	*404.5*	*86.8*	*31.2*	*63.2*	*41.0*	*89.2*
OPEC COUNTRIES	*125.5*	*76.4*	*464.7*	*12.9*	*120.0*	*73.3*	*457.1*	*3.1*	*133.2*
E.E.C.+ MEMBERS	*271.0*	*527.4*	*615.6*	*429.9*	*169.3*	*146.0*	*223.2*	*237.1*	*197.4*
TOTAL	**783.3**	**1229.6**	**1508.7**	**1011.9**	**396.2**	**352.2**	**838.2**	**336.2**	**446.3**

	ODA LOANS GROSS 1983	1984	1985	1986	ODA LOANS NET 1983	1984	1985	1986	GRANTS 1983
DAC COUNTRIES									
Australia	–	–	–	–	–	–	–	–	–
Austria	–	–	–	–	–	–	–	–	0.1
Belgium	3.7	–	1.3	0.4	3.7	–	1.3	-0.1	4.4
Canada	1.4	0.0	0.4	–	1.3	-0.1	0.4	0.0	2.4
Denmark	–	–	–	15.9	-0.1	-0.1	-0.1	15.8	–
Finland	–	–	–	–	–	–	–	–	–
France	54.8	54.2	118.8	76.1	37.5	41.4	102.6	61.1	61.4
Germany, Fed. Rep.	19.7	26.8	35.6	93.4	9.3	26.6	20.7	62.3	6.1
Ireland	–	–	–	–	–	–	–	–	–
Italy	–	–	–	0.8	-0.3	-0.3	-0.3	0.5	6.0
Japan	9.1	35.9	18.0	6.0	8.8	35.8	18.0	4.0	2.1
Netherlands	0.1	1.3	0.5	–	0.1	1.3	0.5	–	0.1
New Zealand	–	–	–	–	–	–	–	–	–
Norway	–	–	–	–	–	–	–	–	–
Sweden	–	–	–	–	–	–	–	–	–
Switzerland	0.3	1.4	1.8	0.1	0.3	1.4	1.8	0.1	0.1
United Kingdom	–	–	–	–	–	–	–	–	0.2
United States	29.0	47.0	67.0	38.0	23.0	33.0	66.0	16.0	23.0
TOTAL	*118.1*	*166.5*	*243.4*	*230.5*	*83.6*	*139.0*	*210.9*	*159.7*	*105.8*
MULTILATERAL	*46.7*	*7.4*	*13.8*	*4.7*	*44.3*	*4.9*	*8.9*	*-0.3*	*42.5*
OPEC COUNTRIES	*133.1*	*93.2*	*122.1*	*10.2*	*120.0*	*73.3*	*107.1*	*3.1*	*0.0*
E.E.C.+ MEMBERS	*98.0*	*83.6*	*156.2*	*186.5*	*69.9*	*70.2*	*124.7*	*139.6*	*99.4*
TOTAL	**298.0**	**267.2**	**379.2**	**245.5**	**247.9**	**217.2**	**326.8**	**162.5**	**148.4**

	TOTAL OFFICIAL GROSS 1983	1984	1985	1986	TOTAL OFFICIAL NET 1983	1984	1985	1986	TOTAL OOF GROSS 1983
DAC COUNTRIES									
Australia	–	–	0.1	–	–	–	0.1	–	–
Austria	0.1	0.1	0.1	0.0	0.1	0.1	0.1	0.0	–
Belgium	8.1	5.0	7.1	6.9	8.1	4.9	7.0	5.8	–
Canada	4.2	8.4	3.8	5.2	3.9	8.1	1.9	4.6	0.5
Denmark	–	0.1	0.0	15.9	-0.1	0.0	0.0	15.8	–
Finland	–	–	–	–	–	–	–	–	–
France	116.2	427.3	530.8	391.6	98.9	401.3	436.2	302.9	–
Germany, Fed. Rep.	25.8	43.3	44.3	112.1	12.4	41.0	26.7	72.5	–
Ireland	–	–	–	–	–	–	–	–	–
Italy	6.2	4.3	43.0	97.1	5.3	3.9	42.7	96.7	0.2
Japan	41.5	95.8	22.3	20.7	41.1	95.7	22.1	18.6	30.2
Netherlands	0.2	1.6	0.9	0.1	0.2	1.6	0.9	0.1	–
New Zealand	–	–	–	–	–	–	–	–	–
Norway	–	0.1	0.0	0.0	–	0.1	0.0	0.0	–
Sweden	–	–	13.0	7.2	–	–	13.0	6.9	–
Switzerland	0.3	1.7	2.5	0.6	0.3	1.7	2.5	0.6	–
United Kingdom	0.2	0.3	0.1	0.2	0.2	0.3	0.1	0.2	–
United States	95.0	273.0	108.0	222.0	82.0	227.0	93.0	136.0	43.0
TOTAL	*297.9*	*860.8*	*776.0*	*879.6*	*252.5*	*785.6*	*646.2*	*660.8*	*73.9*
MULTILATERAL	*410.0*	*399.7*	*495.6*	*598.2*	*284.6*	*242.8*	*390.1*	*404.5*	*320.8*
OPEC COUNTRIES	*140.4*	*98.7*	*484.9*	*29.4*	*125.5*	*76.4*	*464.7*	*12.9*	*7.3*
E.E.C.+ MEMBERS	*221.3*	*497.1*	*680.8*	*656.0*	*189.3*	*467.2*	*566.3*	*523.3*	*23.9*
TOTAL	**848.3**	**1359.2**	**1756.5**	**1507.2**	**662.7**	**1104.8**	**1501.0**	**1078.3**	**401.9**

MOROCCO

ODA COMMITMENTS

1984	1985	1986	1983	1984	1985	1986
–	0.1	–	–	–	–	–
0.1	0.1	0.0	0.1	0.1	0.1	–
3.9	5.4	4.3	2.4	2.5	2.5	4.3
6.3	3.3	5.2	18.0	5.7	3.2	7.9
0.1	–	15.9	–	–	–	12.3
–	–	–	0.4	–	–	–
113.1	174.2	146.7	237.2	266.3	132.7	146.7
32.6	42.6	102.5	27.5	58.6	59.2	115.9
–	–	–	–	–	–	–
4.1	2.0	3.1	12.5	3.9	4.7	6.1
38.5	22.3	15.2	72.8	3.7	6.4	11.5
1.6	0.9	0.1	0.5	2.1	0.3	0.1
–	–	–	–	–	–	–
0.1	0.0	0.0	–	0.0	0.0	0.0
–	–	–	–	0.1	–	–
1.7	2.5	0.6	0.0	0.3	0.7	0.5
0.3	0.1	0.2	0.2	0.3	0.1	0.2
73.0	97.0	69.0	51.1	106.1	79.3	86.2
275.2	350.4	362.9	422.6	449.7	301.2	379.3
–	–	–	–	–	10.1	1.0
–	–	–	–	–	–	–
–	–	–	–	–	–	–
3.9	29.4	11.2	31.3	35.4	16.6	0.0
1.3	–	–	–	–	–	–
1.6	0.1	–	–	–	–	–
-1.3	2.4	2.8	16.4	0.1	–	8.3
–	–	–	–	–	–	–
–	–	–	21.2	23.8	24.9	30.2
3.2	2.9	3.4	–	–	–	–
0.6	0.8	1.3	–	–	–	–
1.6	1.2	1.6	–	–	–	–
16.1	17.9	21.9	–	–	–	–
0.1	0.1	0.0	–	–	–	–
2.2	2.0	2.0	–	–	–	–
4.5	11.3	1.9	–	0.5	7.3	69.0
33.7	68.1	46.1	69.0	59.9	58.9	108.5
93.3	472.1	10.2	50.0	30.0	500.0	128.0
159.4	254.6	284.0	311.6	369.1	228.2	273.2
402.2	890.6	419.2	541.6	539.6	860.1	615.8

TECH. COOP. GRANTS

1984	1985	1986	1983	1984	1985	1986
–	0.1	–	–	–	–	0.1
0.1	0.1	0.0	0.1	–	–	–
3.9	4.1	3.9	4.0	3.2	2.9	3.1
6.3	2.9	5.2	0.3	–	0.9	–
0.1	–	–	–	0.1	–	0.1
58.9	55.4	70.6	60.4	58.7	55.4	70.6
5.8	6.9	9.1	6.5	5.4	6.8	9.1
4.1	2.0	2.3	1.8	2.1	2.0	2.3
2.5	4.3	9.3	2.1	2.3	2.6	4.5
0.4	0.4	0.1	0.1	0.1	0.3	0.1
0.1	0.0	0.0	–	0.0	0.0	0.0
0.3	0.7	0.6	–	0.0	0.0	–
0.3	0.1	0.2	0.2	0.1	0.1	0.2
26.0	30.0	31.0	10.0	12.0	17.0	19.0
108.7	107.0	132.4	85.5	84.2	88.0	109.0
26.3	54.4	41.4	8.0	7.7	7.0	8.2
0.0	350.0	0.0	–	–	–	–
75.8	98.5	97.5	73.0	69.8	67.5	85.5
135.0	511.4	173.8	93.5	91.9	95.1	117.2

TOTAL OOF NET

1984	1985	1986	1983	1984	1985	1986
–	–	–	–	–	–	–
1.1	1.8	2.6	–	1.1	1.7	2.0
2.1	0.5	–	0.2	1.8	-1.4	-0.6
–	0.0	0.0	0.0	0.0	0.0	–
314.2	356.6	244.9	–	301.0	278.2	171.2
10.7	1.8	9.6	-2.9	8.7	-1.0	1.1
0.2	41.0	94.0	-0.4	0.0	40.9	93.9
57.3	–	5.5	30.2	57.3	-0.1	5.3
–	13.0	7.2	–	–	13.0	6.9
200.0	11.0	153.0	36.0	168.0	-3.0	89.0
585.6	425.6	516.8	63.0	537.9	328.3	368.8
366.0	427.5	552.1	197.8	211.5	326.9	363.5
5.5	12.8	19.1	5.6	3.1	7.6	9.8
337.6	426.1	372.0	20.0	321.2	343.1	286.1
957.0	865.9	1088.0	266.4	752.6	662.8	742.1

ODA COMMITMENTS : LOANS

DAC COUNTRIES

	1983	1984	1985	1986
Australia	–	–	–	–
Austria	–	–	–	–
Belgium	–	–	0.4	0.4
Canada	12.2	–	–	–
Denmark	–	–	12.3	–
Finland	0.3	–	–	–
France	175.8	207.4	77.3	76.1
Germany, Fed. Rep.	18.8	51.3	50.6	104.8
Ireland	–	–	–	–
Italy	–	–	–	0.9
Japan	70.2	–	–	4.5
Netherlands	0.4	1.9	–	–
New Zealand	–	–	–	–
Norway	–	–	–	–
Sweden	–	–	–	–
Switzerland	–	–	–	–
United Kingdom	–	–	–	–
United States	27.5	58.5	55.0	52.5
TOTAL	305.2	319.1	195.6	239.2
MULTILATERAL	28.9	22.1	17.4	77.8
OPEC COUNTRIES	50.0	30.0	150.0	111.4
E.E.C.+ MEMBERS	207.4	282.7	140.6	182.1
TOTAL	384.1	371.2	363.1	428.4

GRANT ELEMENT OF ODA

DAC COUNTRIES

	1983	1984	1985	1986
Australia	–	–	–	–
Austria	100.0	100.0	100.0	–
Belgium	100.0	100.0	91.5	97.3
Canada	93.1	100.0	100.0	100.0
Denmark	–	–	75.7	–
Finland	38.8	–	–	–
France	75.6	64.7	84.5	87.7
Germany, Fed. Rep.	76.9	70.3	53.9	55.9
Ireland	–	–	–	–
Italy	100.0	100.0	100.0	94.8
Japan	45.8	100.0	100.0	65.3
Netherlands	64.6	63.9	100.0	100.0
New Zealand	–	–	–	–
Norway	–	100.0	100.0	100.0
Sweden	–	100.0	–	–
Switzerland	100.0	100.0	100.0	100.0
United Kingdom	100.0	100.0	100.0	100.0
United States	71.3	74.1	70.1	76.1
TOTAL	70.8	68.9	73.9	73.9
MULTILATERAL	82.4	100.0	90.4	49.4
OPEC COUNTRIES	65.0	53.1	83.2	53.3
E.E.C.+ MEMBERS	79.3	67.6	76.3	72.6
TOTAL	71.6	70.3	80.7	64.8

OTHER AGGREGATES

COMMITMENTS: ALL SOURCES

	1983	1984	1985	1986
TOTAL BILATERAL	635.0	1314.1	1328.4	779.4
of which				
OPEC	95.9	52.7	522.3	128.0
CMEA	–	–	–	–
TOTAL MULTILATERAL	610.6	397.5	743.7	693.6
TOTAL BIL.& MULTIL.	1245.7	1711.6	2072.1	1473.0
of which				
ODA Grants	157.6	168.4	497.1	187.4
ODA Loans	384.1	371.2	363.1	428.4

DISBURSEMENTS:

DAC COUNTRIES COMBINED

	1983	1984	1985	1986
OFFICIAL & PRIVATE				
GROSS:				
Contractual Lending	782.2	1166.0	1163.4	752.3
Export Credits Total	662.1	516.1	508.5	21.8
Export Credits Private	590.2	414.4	495.0	5.0
NET:				
Contractual Lending	311.2	773.7	569.2	363.3
Export Credits Total	227.5	165.0	25.7	-221.3
PRIVATE SECTOR NET	120.7	124.8	7.7	-66.4
Direct Investment	5.1	4.6	27.0	27.9
Portfolio Investment	-49.0	23.0	-49.9	70.9
Export Credits	164.5	97.2	30.7	-165.2

MARKET BORROWING:

CHANGE IN CLAIMS

	1983	1984	1985	1986
Banks	–	169.0	108.0	40.0

MEMORANDUM ITEM:

	1983	1984	1985	1986
CMEA Countr.(Gross)	–	–	–	–

TOTAL RECEIPTS NET | TOTAL ODA NET | TOTAL ODA GROSS

	1983	1984	1985	1986	1983	1984	1985	1986		1983
DAC COUNTRIES										
Australia	3.6	2.2	1.2	3.2	3.7	2.2	1.4	3.3	Australia	3.7
Austria	0.2	3.0	2.9	1.1	0.2	3.0	2.9	1.1	Austria	0.2
Belgium	0.9	1.0	1.4	0.2	0.2	0.7	1.3	0.3	Belgium	0.2
Canada	3.1	11.4	4.8	5.3	3.1	11.4	4.8	5.3	Canada	3.1
Denmark	8.2	9.0	6.1	13.7	8.2	9.0	6.1	13.7	Denmark	8.2
Finland	2.9	6.5	3.0	5.3	3.6	4.8	3.2	5.3	Finland	3.6
France	23.7	-9.2	34.7	5.9	9.8	11.9	20.3	28.6	France	9.8
Germany, Fed. Rep.	-9.6	-5.8	-7.2	-7.5	1.7	6.5	4.8	11.4	Germany, Fed. Rep.	1.7
Ireland	–	–	–	0.0	–	–	–	0.0	Ireland	–
Italy	27.2	18.8	53.1	35.7	32.9	34.2	28.0	55.7	Italy	32.9
Japan	6.5	-0.9	1.8	14.3	7.5	6.3	4.4	15.5	Japan	7.5
Netherlands	16.8	29.2	24.8	43.0	16.8	29.2	24.8	36.1	Netherlands	16.8
New Zealand	–	–	–	–	–	–	–	–	New Zealand	–
Norway	18.0	14.9	21.2	31.8	18.0	14.9	21.2	31.8	Norway	18.0
Sweden	43.3	32.3	34.0	69.1	36.7	30.6	34.0	68.9	Sweden	36.7
Switzerland	2.9	4.3	5.1	3.2	2.7	4.4	3.5	3.2	Switzerland	2.7
United Kingdom	21.1	-3.5	5.4	-7.2	2.4	5.3	9.4	9.1	United Kingdom	2.7
United States	11.0	18.0	47.0	30.0	13.0	16.0	47.0	30.0	United States	13.0
TOTAL	*179.8*	*131.0*	*239.2*	*247.1*	*160.4*	*190.1*	*216.9*	*319.1*	*TOTAL*	*160.7*
MULTILATERAL										
AF.D.F.	1.7	3.2	8.7	4.4	1.7	3.2	8.7	4.4	AF.D.F.	1.8
AF.D.B.	4.9	2.2	7.9	6.4	–	–	–	–	AF.D.B.	–
AS.D.B	–	–	–	–	–	–	–	–	AS.D.B	–
CAR.D.B.	–	–	–	–	–	–	–	–	CAR.D.B.	–
E.E.C.	14.9	21.4	25.4	33.3	14.9	21.4	25.4	33.3	E.E.C.	14.9
IBRD	–	–	–	–	–	–	–	–	IBRD	–
IDA	–	–	5.0	23.7	–	–	5.0	23.7	IDA	–
I.D.B.	–	–	–	–	–	–	–	–	I.D.B.	–
IFAD	1.7	2.2	5.6	7.1	1.7	2.2	5.6	7.1	IFAD	1.7
I.F.C.	–	–	–	1.5	–	–	–	–	I.F.C.	–
IMF TRUST FUND	–	–	–	–	–	–	–	–	IMF TRUST FUND	–
U.N. AGENCIES	–	–	–	–	–	–	–	–	U.N. AGENCIES	–
UNDP	7.4	7.8	8.4	10.0	7.4	7.8	8.4	10.0	UNDP	7.4
UNTA	0.9	1.0	1.4	1.1	0.9	1.0	1.4	1.1	UNTA	0.9
UNICEF	1.9	3.0	4.2	6.6	1.9	3.0	4.2	6.6	UNICEF	1.9
UNRWA	–	–	–	–	–	–	–	–	UNRWA	–
WFP	12.5	19.6	12.1	9.5	12.5	19.6	12.1	9.5	WFP	12.5
UNHCR	0.0	0.7	1.1	0.1	0.0	0.7	1.1	0.1	UNHCR	0.0
Other Multilateral	4.7	5.7	5.3	2.4	4.7	5.7	5.3	2.4	Other Multilateral	4.7
Arab OPEC Agencies	3.6	1.5	0.2	-1.3	3.6	1.5	-0.3	-2.7	Arab OPEC Agencies	4.6
TOTAL	*54.1*	*68.3*	*85.3*	*104.7*	*49.2*	*66.1*	*76.9*	*95.4*	*TOTAL*	*50.2*
OPEC COUNTRIES	*1.2*	*2.9*	*6.3*	*6.8*	*1.2*	*2.9*	*6.3*	*6.8*	*OPEC COUNTRIES*	*1.2*
E.E.C.+ MEMBERS	*103.3*	*60.8*	*143.6*	*117.0*	*86.9*	*118.0*	*120.0*	*188.1*	*E.E.C.+ MEMBERS*	*87.2*
TOTAL	*235.1*	*202.2*	*330.7*	*358.6*	*210.8*	*259.1*	*300.1*	*421.3*	*TOTAL*	*212.1*

ODA LOANS GROSS | ODA LOANS NET | GRANTS

	1983	1984	1985	1986	1983	1984	1985	1986		1983
DAC COUNTRIES										
Australia	–	–	–	–	–	–	–	–	Australia	3.7
Austria	–	2.3	1.9	–	–	2.3	1.9	–	Austria	0.2
Belgium	–	–	–	0.2	–	–	–	0.2	Belgium	0.2
Canada	–	–	–	–	–	–	–	–	Canada	3.1
Denmark	2.2	1.4	0.1	0.5	2.2	1.4	0.1	0.5	Denmark	6.1
Finland	0.8	1.1	0.1	1.2	0.8	1.1	0.1	1.2	Finland	2.8
France	9.0	10.0	18.5	26.1	9.0	10.0	18.5	26.1	France	0.8
Germany, Fed. Rep.	–	1.7	0.8	6.0	–	1.7	0.8	6.0	Germany, Fed. Rep.	1.7
Ireland	–	–	–	–	–	–	–	–	Ireland	–
Italy	16.0	10.4	1.1	14.5	16.0	10.4	0.4	13.9	Italy	16.8
Japan	5.0	–	2.0	1.2	5.0	–	2.0	1.2	Japan	2.5
Netherlands	5.2	5.2	6.0	7.2	5.2	5.2	6.0	7.2	Netherlands	11.6
New Zealand	–	–	–	–	–	–	–	–	New Zealand	–
Norway	–	–	–	–	–	–	–	–	Norway	18.0
Sweden	–	–	–	–	–	–	–	–	Sweden	36.7
Switzerland	–	–	–	–	–	–	–	–	Switzerland	2.7
United Kingdom	0.9	2.5	1.5	0.4	0.6	2.1	0.1	-1.5	United Kingdom	1.9
United States	–	–	20.0	14.0	–	–	20.0	14.0	United States	13.0
TOTAL	*39.1*	*34.5*	*51.9*	*71.3*	*38.8*	*34.1*	*49.9*	*68.8*	*TOTAL*	*121.6*
MULTILATERAL	*8.0*	*10.1*	*20.4*	*35.6*	*6.9*	*6.9*	*19.1*	*32.5*	*MULTILATERAL*	*42.2*
OPEC COUNTRIES	*0.7*	*2.6*	*6.4*	*6.6*	*0.7*	*2.6*	*6.3*	*6.6*	*OPEC COUNTRIES*	*0.5*
E.E.C.+ MEMBERS	*33.3*	*31.1*	*28.0*	*54.8*	*33.0*	*30.7*	*25.9*	*52.4*	*E.E.C.+ MEMBERS*	*53.9*
TOTAL	*47.8*	*47.2*	*78.7*	*113.5*	*46.4*	*43.6*	*75.2*	*107.9*	*TOTAL*	*164.4*

TOTAL OFFICIAL GROSS | TOTAL OFFICIAL NET | TOTAL OOF GROSS

	1983	1984	1985	1986	1983	1984	1985	1986		1983
DAC COUNTRIES										
Australia	3.7	2.2	1.4	3.3	3.6	2.2	1.2	3.2	Australia	–
Austria	0.2	3.0	2.9	1.1	0.2	3.0	2.9	1.1	Austria	–
Belgium	0.2	0.9	1.6	0.3	0.2	0.9	1.6	0.3	Belgium	–
Canada	3.1	11.4	4.8	5.3	3.1	11.4	4.8	5.3	Canada	–
Denmark	8.2	9.0	6.1	13.7	8.2	9.0	6.1	13.7	Denmark	–
Finland	3.6	4.8	3.2	5.3	3.6	4.8	3.2	5.3	Finland	–
France	9.8	12.8	77.9	28.7	9.8	12.8	77.3	28.7	France	–
Germany, Fed. Rep.	1.7	6.8	5.7	11.5	-9.2	-5.8	-7.3	-7.3	Germany, Fed. Rep.	–
Ireland	–	–	–	0.0	–	–	–	0.0	Ireland	–
Italy	33.5	34.2	66.8	56.9	33.3	34.2	66.2	56.3	Italy	0.7
Japan	7.5	6.3	4.3	15.5	7.5	6.3	4.4	15.5	Japan	–
Netherlands	16.8	29.2	24.8	36.1	16.8	29.2	24.8	36.1	Netherlands	–
New Zealand	–	–	–	–	–	–	–	–	New Zealand	–
Norway	18.0	14.9	21.2	31.8	18.0	14.9	21.2	31.8	Norway	–
Sweden	45.7	30.6	34.0	69.1	43.3	30.6	34.0	65.5	Sweden	9.0
Switzerland	2.7	4.4	3.5	3.2	2.7	4.4	3.5	3.2	Switzerland	–
United Kingdom	2.7	5.6	10.9	10.9	2.4	5.3	9.4	9.1	United Kingdom	–
United States	13.0	18.0	47.0	30.0	11.0	18.0	47.0	30.0	United States	–
TOTAL	*170.4*	*193.8*	*315.9*	*322.7*	*154.4*	*180.8*	*300.1*	*297.8*	*TOTAL*	*9.7*
MULTILATERAL	*55.3*	*72.0*	*87.6*	*109.7*	*54.1*	*68.3*	*85.3*	*104.7*	*MULTILATERAL*	*5.1*
OPEC COUNTRIES	*1.2*	*2.9*	*6.4*	*6.8*	*1.2*	*2.9*	*6.3*	*6.8*	*OPEC COUNTRIES*	*–*
E.E.C.+ MEMBERS	*87.8*	*119.7*	*219.0*	*191.4*	*76.4*	*106.7*	*203.4*	*170.1*	*E.E.C.+ MEMBERS*	*0.7*
TOTAL	*226.9*	*268.8*	*409.8*	*439.2*	*209.6*	*252.0*	*391.7*	*409.2*	*TOTAL*	*14.8*

ODA COMMITMENTS

1984	1985	1986	1983	1984	1985	1986
2.2	1.4	3.3	2.2	3.9	3.8	3.1
3.0	2.9	1.1	–	3.0	3.6	–
0.7	1.3	0.3	–	–	0.7	0.3
11.4	4.8	5.3	3.0	11.5	4.6	5.0
9.0	6.1	13.7	11.4	2.2	7.9	11.1
4.8	3.2	5.3	8.4	8.1	1.9	8.5
11.9	20.3	28.6	19.1	28.5	19.0	28.6
6.5	4.8	11.4	4.6	8.6	12.8	18.9
–	–	0.0	–	–	–	0.0
34.2	28.6	56.3	62.8	35.2	39.7	153.7
6.3	4.3	15.5	10.1	4.6	9.1	18.5
29.2	24.8	36.1	18.1	30.5	25.3	27.6
–	–	–	–	–	–	–
14.9	21.2	31.8	21.2	8.4	13.8	43.5
30.6	34.0	68.9	35.8	36.9	35.4	68.9
4.4	3.5	3.2	3.9	3.8	3.4	3.9
5.6	10.9	10.9	1.4	2.7	13.7	16.3
16.0	47.0	30.0	12.8	37.0	44.5	36.5
190.5	*219.0*	*321.6*	*214.8*	*224.7*	*239.1*	*444.3*
3.3	8.8	4.5	–	9.6	–	3.7
–	–	–	–	–	–	–
–	–	–	–	–	–	–
21.4	25.4	33.3	20.1	31.4	30.9	39.9
–	5.0	23.7	–	–	45.0	–
–	–	–	–	–	–	–
4.5	6.7	7.5	–	–	–	–
–	–	–	–	–	–	–
–	–	–	27.4	37.8	32.5	29.7
7.8	8.4	10.0	–	–	–	–
1.0	1.4	1.1	–	–	–	–
3.0	4.2	6.6	–	–	–	–
–	–	–	–	–	–	–
19.6	12.1	9.5	–	–	–	–
0.7	1.1	0.1	–	–	–	–
5.7	5.3	2.4	–	–	–	–
2.3	–	–	–	–	–	8.0
69.3	*78.3*	*98.6*	*47.4*	*78.8*	*108.4*	*81.3*
2.9	*6.4*	*6.8*	–	*4.6*	*9.6*	–
118.4	*122.1*	*190.5*	*137.5*	*139.1*	*149.9*	*296.3*
262.7	*303.6*	*426.9*	*262.2*	*308.1*	*357.1*	*525.5*

TECH. COOP. GRANTS

1984	1985	1986	1983	1984	1985	1986
2.2	1.4	3.3	0.0	0.0	0.4	0.1
0.7	0.9	1.1	0.2	–	–	–
0.7	1.3	0.1	0.0	–	–	–
11.4	4.8	5.3	1.2	–	0.7	–
7.6	6.0	13.2	2.6	2.2	2.1	2.8
3.7	3.1	4.1	2.6	1.8	2.4	1.2
1.9	1.8	2.5	0.3	0.8	0.6	1.0
4.8	4.0	5.4	0.6	2.1	1.5	2.8
–	–	0.0	–	–	–	0.0
23.8	27.5	41.8	8.8	10.7	11.4	25.5
6.3	2.4	14.3	0.1	0.0	0.0	0.3
24.0	18.9	28.9	2.1	2.1	2.2	3.5
–	–	–	–	–	–	–
14.9	21.2	31.8	–	1.7	1.5	2.0
30.6	34.0	68.9	9.2	6.4	5.9	7.5
4.4	3.5	3.2	0.9	0.8	0.7	0.9
3.2	9.3	10.5	0.4	0.3	1.0	1.7
16.0	27.0	16.0	–	–	–	–
156.0	*167.0*	*250.3*	*28.9*	*28.9*	*30.3*	*49.2*
59.2	*57.9*	*62.9*	*14.9*	*18.2*	*20.4*	*20.6*
0.4	–	*0.1*	–	–	–	–
87.3	*94.1*	*135.7*	*14.8*	*18.2*	*18.8*	*37.6*
215.5	*224.9*	*313.4*	*43.8*	*47.1*	*50.7*	*69.9*

TOTAL OOF NET

1984	1985	1986	1983	1984	1985	1986
–	–	–	-0.1	–	-0.1	0.0
–	–	–	–	–	–	–
0.2	0.3	–	–	0.2	0.3	–
–	–	–	–	–	–	–
–	–	–	–	–	–	–
0.9	57.6	0.1	–	0.9	57.0	0.1
0.3	0.9	0.1	-10.9	-12.3	-12.1	-18.7
–	38.2	0.6	0.4	–	38.2	0.6
–	–	–	–	–	–	–
–	–	–	–	–	–	–
–	–	–	–	–	–	–
–	–	0.3	6.5	–	–	-3.4
–	–	–	–	–	–	–
2.0	–	–	-2.0	2.0	–	–
3.3	*96.9*	*1.2*	*-6.0*	*-9.3*	*83.2*	*-21.4*
2.7	*9.3*	*11.1*	*4.9*	*2.2*	*8.4*	*9.3*
–	–	–	–	–	–	–
1.3	*96.9*	*0.9*	*-10.5*	*-11.3*	*83.4*	*-18.0*
6.0	*106.2*	*12.3*	*-1.2*	*-7.1*	*91.6*	*-12.1*

ODA COMMITMENTS : LOANS

DAC COUNTRIES	1983	1984	1985	1986
Australia	–	–	–	–
Austria	–	2.3	1.9	–
Belgium	–	–	–	0.2
Canada	–	–	–	–
Denmark	4.4	–	–	–
Finland	–	4.2	–	–
France	18.4	26.6	17.5	26.1
Germany, Fed. Rep.	2.0	3.5	8.0	10.8
Ireland	–	–	–	–
Italy	35.1	1.1	1.0	67.6
Japan	5.0	–	2.0	1.2
Netherlands	–	7.9	–	–
New Zealand	–	–	–	–
Norway	–	–	–	–
Sweden	–	–	–	–
Switzerland	–	–	–	–
United Kingdom	–	–	–	–
United States	–	–	21.0	14.2
TOTAL	*64.8*	*45.6*	*51.4*	*120.0*
MULTILATERAL	–	*9.6*	*45.0*	*11.7*
OPEC COUNTRIES	–	*4.6*	*9.6*	–
E.E.C.+ MEMBERS	*59.8*	*39.2*	*26.5*	*104.6*
TOTAL	*64.8*	*59.8*	*106.0*	*131.7*

GRANT ELEMENT OF ODA

DAC COUNTRIES	1983	1984	1985	1986
Australia	100.0	100.0	100.0	100.0
Austria	–	89.5	100.0	86.9
Belgium	–	–	100.0	91.6
Canada	100.0	100.0	100.0	100.0
Denmark	94.4	100.0	100.0	100.0
Finland	100.0	84.1	100.0	100.0
France	37.5	36.4	36.6	36.8
Germany, Fed. Rep.	92.9	93.3	89.5	90.5
Ireland	–	–	–	100.0
Italy	70.6	98.1	99.8	85.1
Japan	82.4	100.0	84.7	95.1
Netherlands	100.0	95.5	100.0	100.0
New Zealand	–	–	–	–
Norway	100.0	100.0	100.0	100.0
Sweden	100.0	100.0	100.0	100.0
Switzerland	100.0	100.0	100.0	100.0
United Kingdom	100.0	100.0	100.0	100.0
United States	100.0	100.0	84.8	87.4
TOTAL	*83.5*	*90.1*	*90.9*	*87.7*
MULTILATERAL	*100.0*	*97.9*	*93.0*	*94.9*
OPEC COUNTRIES	–	*43.9*	*46.5*	–
E.E.C.+ MEMBERS	*75.8*	*85.1*	*91.0*	*83.7*
TOTAL	*86.4*	*91.4*	*90.3*	*88.8*

OTHER AGGREGATES

COMMITMENTS: ALL SOURCES

	1983	1984	1985	1986
TOTAL BILATERAL	250.0	340.7	340.6	485.3
of which				
OPEC	–	4.6	9.6	–
CMEA	26.2	51.9	53.0	43.8
TOTAL MULTILATERAL	47.4	123.6	108.4	91.8
TOTAL BIL.& MULTIL.	297.4	464.3	449.0	577.1
of which				
ODA Grants	223.6	255.9	270.1	425.6
ODA Loans	64.8	104.1	140.0	143.7

DISBURSEMENTS:
DAC COUNTRIES COMBINED

OFFICIAL & PRIVATE	1983	1984	1985	1986
GROSS:				
Contractual Lending	114.8	63.5	164.0	57.8
Export Credits Total	75.7	26.7	15.2	-14.3
Export Credits Private	66.0	25.7	15.2	-14.6
NET:				
Contractual Lending	51.3	-15.8	77.2	-7.3
Export Credits Total	12.5	-52.2	-69.0	-76.9
PRIVATE SECTOR NET	25.4	-49.8	-60.9	-50.7
Direct Investment	2.5	-2.9	0.3	-0.1
Portfolio Investment	4.4	-6.3	-5.4	4.2
Export Credits	18.6	-40.6	-55.9	-54.7

MARKET BORROWING:
CHANGE IN CLAIMS

	1983	1984	1985	1986
Banks	–	-17.0	-19.0	-9.0

MEMORANDUM ITEM:

	1983	1984	1985	1986
CMEA Countr.(Gross)	18.7	56.2	54.7	54.7

	1983	1984	1985	1986	1983	1984	1985	1986		1983
TOTAL RECEIPTS NET					**TOTAL ODA NET**				**TOTAL ODA GROSS**	
DAC COUNTRIES										
Australia	1.6	1.9	1.5	1.4	1.6	1.9	1.5	1.4	Australia	1.6
Austria	0.9	0.0	0.1	0.3	0.9	0.0	0.1	0.3	Austria	0.9
Belgium	0.0	0.0	0.1	25.7	0.0	0.0	0.1	5.7	Belgium	0.0
Canada	6.8	7.3	7.7	6.3	6.8	7.3	7.7	6.3	Canada	6.8
Denmark	0.5	0.3	0.9	5.8	0.5	0.3	0.9	5.8	Denmark	0.5
Finland	1.9	3.0	3.8	5.3	1.9	3.0	3.8	5.3	Finland	1.9
France	2.6	2.6	4.7	3.2	2.0	2.5	1.8	3.5	France	2.0
Germany, Fed. Rep.	16.5	11.0	10.9	23.8	17.2	10.3	10.6	21.3	Germany, Fed. Rep.	17.2
Ireland	0.0	0.0	0.0	0.0	0.0	0.0	0.0	0.0	Ireland	0.0
Italy	0.9	0.2	0.9	4.7	0.9	0.2	0.9	4.7	Italy	0.9
Japan	25.4	28.7	51.5	76.4	28.3	28.5	50.7	68.1	Japan	28.5
Netherlands	4.1	1.6	2.5	3.3	4.1	1.6	2.5	3.3	Netherlands	4.1
New Zealand	0.0	0.0	0.0	0.1	0.0	0.0	0.0	0.1	New Zealand	0.0
Norway	1.6	1.4	2.0	3.9	1.6	1.4	2.0	3.9	Norway	1.6
Sweden	–	0.1	1.0	-0.1	–	0.1	–	–	Sweden	–
Switzerland	10.7	8.0	10.4	9.1	10.7	8.0	7.6	9.1	Switzerland	10.7
United Kingdom	10.7	11.0	12.1	14.1	11.0	11.3	12.4	14.4	United Kingdom	11.2
United States	22.0	22.0	21.0	17.0	22.0	22.0	21.0	17.0	United States	22.0
TOTAL	*106.1*	*99.2*	*131.0*	*200.3*	*109.5*	*98.4*	*123.5*	*170.2*	*TOTAL*	*109.9*
MULTILATERAL										
AF.D.F.	–	–	–	–	–	–	–	–	AF.D.F.	–
AF.D.B.	–	–	–	–	–	–	–	–	AF.D.B.	–
AS.D.B	23.1	36.6	42.3	34.8	23.1	36.6	42.3	34.8	AS.D.B	24.7
CAR.D.B.	–	–	–	–	–	–	–	–	CAR.D.B.	–
E.E.C.	2.0	6.2	2.2	1.7	2.0	6.2	2.2	1.7	E.E.C.	2.0
IBRD	–	–	–	–	–	–	–	–	IBRD	–
IDA	30.4	29.3	32.5	54.0	30.4	29.3	32.5	54.0	IDA	30.6
I.D.B.	–	–	–	–	–	–	–	–	I.D.B.	–
IFAD	1.9	4.4	5.7	6.1	1.9	4.4	5.7	6.1	IFAD	1.9
I.F.C.	–	2.4	2.5	-0.2	–	–	–	–	I.F.C.	–
IMF TRUST FUND	–	–	–	–	–	–	–	–	IMF TRUST FUND	–
U.N. AGENCIES	–	–	–	–	–	–	–	–	U.N. AGENCIES	–
UNDP	10.8	11.0	12.1	12.0	10.8	11.0	12.1	12.0	UNDP	10.8
UNTA	2.7	1.2	2.5	1.2	2.7	1.2	2.5	1.2	UNTA	2.7
UNICEF	4.0	5.2	4.9	4.3	4.0	5.2	4.9	4.3	UNICEF	4.0
UNRWA	–	–	–	–	–	–	–	–	UNRWA	–
WFP	10.8	2.4	6.8	7.7	10.8	2.4	6.8	7.7	WFP	10.8
UNHCR	–	–	–	0.0	–	–	–	0.0	UNHCR	–
Other Multilateral	5.0	4.6	5.6	4.3	5.0	4.6	5.6	4.3	Other Multilateral	5.0
Arab OPEC Agencies	1.5	0.1	-0.1	0.6	1.5	0.1	-0.1	0.6	Arab OPEC Agencies	2.3
TOTAL	*92.2*	*103.2*	*116.8*	*126.5*	*92.2*	*100.8*	*114.3*	*126.7*	*TOTAL*	*94.7*
OPEC COUNTRIES	*-0.9*	*-0.9*	*-1.5*	*4.1*	*-0.9*	*-0.9*	*-1.5*	*4.1*	*OPEC COUNTRIES*	*0.0*
E.E.C.+ MEMBERS	*37.3*	*32.9*	*34.2*	*82.4*	*37.8*	*32.3*	*31.3*	*60.5*	*E.E.C.+ MEMBERS*	*38.0*
TOTAL	*197.4*	*201.5*	*246.3*	*330.8*	*200.7*	*198.3*	*236.3*	*300.9*	*TOTAL*	*204.6*
ODA LOANS GROSS					**ODA LOANS NET**				**GRANTS**	
DAC COUNTRIES										
Australia	–	–	–	–	–	–	–	–	Australia	1.6
Austria	–	–	–	–	–	–	–	–	Austria	0.9
Belgium	–	–	–	5.6	–	–	–	5.6	Belgium	0.0
Canada	–	–	–	–	–	–	–	–	Canada	6.8
Denmark	–	–	–	–	–	–	–	–	Denmark	0.5
Finland	–	–	–	–	–	–	–	–	Finland	1.9
France	1.0	1.2	1.2	0.5	1.0	1.2	1.2	0.5	France	1.0
Germany, Fed. Rep.	0.6	0.1	–	–	0.6	-0.4	–	–	Germany, Fed. Rep.	16.6
Ireland	–	–	–	–	–	–	–	–	Ireland	0.0
Italy	–	–	–	–	–	–	–	–	Italy	0.9
Japan	3.8	7.0	9.6	15.2	3.6	7.0	9.6	14.4	Japan	24.7
Netherlands	–	–	–	–	–	–	–	–	Netherlands	4.1
New Zealand	–	–	–	–	–	–	–	–	New Zealand	0.0
Norway	0.6	–	–	–	0.6	–	–	–	Norway	1.0
Sweden	–	–	–	–	–	–	–	–	Sweden	–
Switzerland	–	–	–	–	–	–	–	–	Switzerland	10.7
United Kingdom	–	–	–	–	-0.2	-0.2	-0.2	-0.2	United Kingdom	11.2
United States	–	–	–	–	–	–	–	–	United States	22.0
TOTAL	*6.0*	*8.3*	*10.8*	*21.3*	*5.6*	*7.7*	*10.7*	*20.2*	*TOTAL*	*103.9*
MULTILATERAL	*58.4*	*71.3*	*81.8*	*97.1*	*55.9*	*69.3*	*79.2*	*93.7*	*MULTILATERAL*	*36.3*
OPEC COUNTRIES	*–*	*–*	*–*	*5.0*	*-1.0*	*-0.9*	*-1.6*	*4.0*	*OPEC COUNTRIES*	*0.0*
E.E.C.+ MEMBERS	*1.7*	*1.3*	*1.2*	*6.1*	*1.4*	*0.7*	*1.0*	*5.9*	*E.E.C.+ MEMBERS*	*36.4*
TOTAL	*64.4*	*79.6*	*92.6*	*123.4*	*60.6*	*76.0*	*88.3*	*118.0*	*TOTAL*	*140.2*
TOTAL OFFICIAL GROSS					**TOTAL OFFICIAL NET**				**TOTAL OOF GROSS**	
DAC COUNTRIES										
Australia	1.6	1.9	1.5	1.4	1.6	1.9	1.5	1.4	Australia	–
Austria	0.9	0.0	0.1	0.3	0.9	0.0	0.1	0.3	Austria	–
Belgium	0.0	0.0	0.1	5.7	0.0	0.0	0.1	5.7	Belgium	–
Canada	6.8	7.3	7.7	6.3	6.8	7.3	7.7	6.3	Canada	–
Denmark	0.5	0.3	0.9	5.8	0.5	0.3	0.9	5.8	Denmark	–
Finland	1.9	3.0	3.8	5.3	1.9	3.0	3.8	5.3	Finland	–
France	2.0	2.5	1.8	3.5	2.0	2.5	1.8	3.5	France	–
Germany, Fed. Rep.	17.2	10.7	10.6	21.3	17.2	10.3	10.6	21.3	Germany, Fed. Rep.	–
Ireland	0.0	0.0	0.0	0.0	0.0	0.0	0.0	0.0	Ireland	–
Italy	0.9	0.2	0.9	4.7	0.9	0.2	0.9	4.7	Italy	–
Japan	28.5	28.6	50.7	68.9	28.3	28.5	50.7	68.1	Japan	–
Netherlands	4.1	1.6	2.5	3.3	4.1	1.6	2.5	3.3	Netherlands	–
New Zealand	0.0	0.0	0.0	0.1	0.0	0.0	0.0	0.1	New Zealand	–
Norway	1.6	1.4	2.0	3.9	1.6	1.4	2.0	3.9	Norway	–
Sweden	–	0.1	1.0	–	–	0.1	1.0	-0.1	Sweden	–
Switzerland	10.7	8.0	7.6	9.1	10.7	8.0	7.6	9.1	Switzerland	–
United Kingdom	11.2	11.5	12.5	14.6	11.0	11.3	12.4	14.4	United Kingdom	–
United States	22.0	22.0	21.0	17.0	22.0	22.0	21.0	17.0	United States	–
TOTAL	*109.9*	*99.1*	*124.6*	*171.2*	*109.5*	*98.4*	*124.5*	*170.0*	*TOTAL*	*–*
MULTILATERAL	*94.7*	*105.2*	*119.6*	*130.0*	*92.2*	*103.2*	*116.8*	*126.5*	*MULTILATERAL*	*–*
OPEC COUNTRIES	*0.0*	*0.0*	*0.0*	*5.0*	*-0.9*	*-0.9*	*-1.5*	*4.1*	*OPEC COUNTRIES*	*–*
E.E.C.+ MEMBERS	*38.0*	*32.9*	*31.5*	*60.7*	*37.8*	*32.3*	*31.3*	*60.5*	*E.E.C.+ MEMBERS*	*–*
TOTAL	*204.6*	*204.3*	*244.2*	*306.3*	*200.7*	*200.7*	*239.8*	*300.6*	*TOTAL*	*–*

MILLION US DOLLARS, UNLESS OTHERWISE STATED

ODA COMMITMENTS

1984	1985	1986	1983	1984	1985	1986
1.9	1.5	1.4	1.5	2.0	5.9	0.6
0.0	0.1	0.3	0.8	0.0	0.2	–
0.0	0.1	5.7	–	–	–	3.5
7.3	7.7	6.3	2.9	16.5	18.3	1.4
0.3	0.9	5.8	0.4	0.1	0.5	16.6
3.0	3.8	5.3	-0.1	4.0	14.0	-2.9
2.5	1.8	3.5	4.6	4.1	6.6	3.5
10.7	10.6	21.3	8.3	16.3	68.0	27.3
0.0	0.0	0.0	0.0	0.0	0.0	0.0
0.2	0.9	4.7	5.8	0.2	1.0	4.2
28.6	50.7	68.9	45.1	34.7	37.1	48.8
1.6	2.5	3.3	3.0	1.2	2.8	3.8
0.0	0.0	0.1	0.0	0.0	0.2	0.0
1.4	2.0	3.9	1.2	0.8	6.2	1.6
0.1	–	–	0.0	0.2	–	–
8.0	7.6	9.1	15.2	4.0	10.5	13.8
11.5	12.5	14.6	6.7	7.2	15.3	20.7
22.0	21.0	17.0	14.2	14.6	11.5	16.4
99.1	*123.6*	*171.2*	*109.7*	*106.0*	*198.1*	*159.2*
–	–	–	–	–	–	–
38.2	44.5	37.2	82.7	60.7	77.1	51.3
–	–	–	–	–	–	–
6.2	2.2	1.7	10.5	8.0	0.0	5.9
–	–	–	–	–	–	–
29.6	32.8	54.8	46.0	194.2	29.2	53.6
–	–	–	–	–	–	–
4.4	5.7	6.1	0.3	–	16.8	5.1
–	–	–	–	–	–	–
–	–	–	33.4	24.4	31.8	29.5
11.0	12.1	12.0	–	–	–	–
1.2	2.5	1.2	–	–	–	–
5.2	4.9	4.3	–	–	–	–
–	–	–	–	–	–	–
2.4	6.8	7.7	–	–	–	–
–	–	0.0	–	–	–	–
4.6	5.6	4.3	–	–	–	–
0.1	–	0.6	–	1.0	–	–
102.8	*117.0*	*130.0*	*172.8*	*288.3*	*154.8*	*145.4*
0.0	*0.0*	*5.0*	*0.0*	*24.4*	*20.0*	–
32.9	*31.5*	*60.7*	*39.3*	*37.1*	*94.3*	*85.5*
201.9	*240.6*	*306.2*	*282.5*	*418.7*	*372.8*	*304.6*

TECH. COOP. GRANTS

1984	1985	1986	1983	1984	1985	1986
1.9	1.5	1.4	0.7	0.8	0.5	0.2
0.0	0.1	0.3	0.1	–	–	–
0.0	0.1	0.1	–	–	–	–
7.3	7.7	6.3	0.7	–	2.1	–
0.3	0.9	5.8	0.5	0.2	0.5	0.5
3.0	3.8	5.3	0.2	0.3	0.9	3.4
1.2	0.6	3.0	0.2	0.4	0.2	0.3
10.6	10.6	21.3	9.8	9.0	7.7	11.8
0.0	0.0	0.0	0.0	0.0	0.0	0.0
0.2	0.9	4.7	0.0	0.2	0.1	0.2
21.6	41.1	53.7	5.4	6.4	4.8	9.1
1.6	2.5	3.3	1.1	1.0	1.6	1.8
0.0	0.0	0.1	0.0	0.0	0.0	0.0
1.4	2.0	3.9	–	0.2	0.2	0.3
0.1	–	–	–	–	–	–
8.0	7.6	9.1	2.5	3.0	2.3	2.7
11.5	12.5	14.6	5.2	5.0	6.5	7.7
22.0	21.0	17.0	19.0	20.0	18.0	15.0
90.8	*112.8*	*149.9*	*45.4*	*46.3*	*45.4*	*52.9*
31.5	*35.1*	*32.9*	*22.5*	*22.0*	*25.0*	*21.8*
0.0	*0.0*	*0.0*	–	–	–	–
31.6	*30.2*	*54.6*	*16.9*	*15.7*	*16.6*	*22.4*
122.3	*148.0*	*182.9*	*68.0*	*68.4*	*70.3*	*74.8*

TOTAL OOF NET

1984	1985	1986	1983	1984	1985	1986
–	–	–	–	–	–	–
–	–	–	–	–	–	–
–	–	–	–	–	–	–
–	–	–	–	–	–	–
–	–	–	–	–	–	–
–	–	–	–	–	–	–
–	–	–	–	–	–	–
–	–	–	–	–	–	–
–	–	–	–	–	–	–
–	–	–	–	–	–	–
–	–	–	–	–	–	–
–	–	–	–	–	–	–
–	1.0	–	–	–	1.0	-0.1
–	–	–	–	–	–	–
–	–	–	–	–	–	–
–	1.0	–	–	–	1.0	-0.1
2.4	*2.6*	–	–	*2.4*	*2.5*	*-0.2*
–	–	–	–	–	–	–
–	–	–	–	–	–	–
2.4	*3.6*	–	–	*2.4*	*3.5*	*-0.3*

ODA COMMITMENTS : LOANS

DAC COUNTRIES

	1983	1984	1985	1986
Australia	–	–	–	–
Austria	–	–	–	–
Belgium	–	–	–	3.4
Canada	–	–	–	–
Denmark	–	–	–	–
Finland	–	–	–	–
France	3.1	2.7	4.7	0.5
Germany, Fed. Rep.	–	–	–	–
Ireland	–	–	–	–
Italy	–	–	–	–
Japan	20.2	–	–	–
Netherlands	–	–	–	–
New Zealand	–	–	–	–
Norway	–	–	–	–
Sweden	–	–	–	–
Switzerland	–	–	–	–
United Kingdom	–	–	–	–
United States	–	–	–	–
TOTAL	*23.3*	*2.7*	*4.7*	*3.8*
MULTILATERAL	*128.7*	*254.9*	*122.9*	*110.0*
OPEC COUNTRIES	–	*24.4*	*20.0*	–
E.E.C.+ MEMBERS	*3.1*	*2.7*	*4.7*	*3.8*
TOTAL	*152.0*	*282.0*	*147.6*	*113.8*

GRANT ELEMENT OF ODA

DAC COUNTRIES

	1983	1984	1985	1986
Australia	100.0	100.0	100.0	100.0
Austria	100.0	100.0	100.0	–
Belgium	–	–	83.6	85.3
Canada	100.0	100.0	100.0	100.0
Denmark	100.0	100.0	100.0	100.0
Finland	100.0	100.0	100.0	100.0
France	79.1	76.9	74.3	100.0
Germany, Fed. Rep.	100.0	100.0	100.0	100.0
Ireland	100.0	100.0	100.0	100.0
Italy	100.0	100.0	100.0	100.0
Japan	87.5	100.0	100.0	100.0
Netherlands	100.0	100.0	100.0	100.0
New Zealand	100.0	100.0	100.0	100.0
Norway	100.0	100.0	100.0	100.0
Sweden	100.0	100.0	–	–
Switzerland	100.0	100.0	100.0	100.0
United Kingdom	100.0	100.0	100.0	100.0
United States	100.0	100.0	100.0	100.0
TOTAL	*94.2*	*99.1*	*99.0*	*99.7*
MULTILATERAL	*85.1*	*84.6*	*84.7*	*84.6*
OPEC COUNTRIES	*100.0*	*57.6*	*50.1*	–
E.E.C.+ MEMBERS	*98.5*	*97.5*	*98.0*	*99.4*
TOTAL	*88.6*	*87.6*	*90.9*	*92.5*

OTHER AGGREGATES

COMMITMENTS: ALL SOURCES

	1983	1984	1985	1986
TOTAL BILATERAL	109.7	130.4	219.0	159.1
of which				
OPEC	0.0	24.4	20.0	–
CMEA	–	–	–	–
TOTAL MULTILATERAL	172.8	288.3	154.9	145.4
TOTAL BIL.& MULTIL.	282.5	418.7	373.9	304.5
of which				
ODA Grants	130.6	136.7	225.3	190.8
ODA Loans	152.0	282.0	147.6	113.8

DISBURSEMENTS:

DAC COUNTRIES COMBINED

	1983	1984	1985	1986
OFFICIAL & PRIVATE				
GROSS:				
Contractual Lending	10.5	8.4	21.5	55.2
Export Credits Total	4.6	0.1	10.7	34.0
Export Credits Private	4.6	0.1	9.7	34.0
NET:				
Contractual Lending	3.9	7.5	17.4	49.0
Export Credits Total	-1.7	-0.2	6.7	28.8
PRIVATE SECTOR NET	-3.4	0.8	6.5	30.2
Direct Investment	-0.6	1.0	0.7	1.2
Portfolio Investment	-1.1	0.0	0.1	0.1
Export Credits	-1.7	-0.2	5.7	28.9

MARKET BORROWING:

CHANGE IN CLAIMS

	1983	1984	1985	1986
Banks	–	13.0	2.0	1.0

MEMORANDUM ITEM:

	1983	1984	1985	1986
CMEA Countr.(Gross)	0.7	–	–	–

TOTAL RECEIPTS NET | TOTAL ODA NET | TOTAL ODA GROSS

	TOTAL RECEIPTS NET 1983	1984	1985	1986	TOTAL ODA NET 1983	1984	1985	1986	TOTAL ODA GROSS 1983
DAC COUNTRIES									
Australia	–	0.1	0.1	0.1	–	0.1	0.1	0.1	–
Austria	8.1	0.5	4.4	1.3	8.1	0.5	4.4	1.3	8.1
Belgium	0.4	0.5	0.4	0.6	0.5	0.4	0.5	0.7	0.5
Canada	6.2	8.8	5.8	4.3	6.2	8.8	5.8	4.3	6.2
Denmark	1.6	0.8	0.9	3.2	1.6	0.8	0.9	3.2	1.6
Finland	1.6	3.0	3.2	7.1	1.6	3.0	3.2	7.1	1.6
France	20.4	12.3	5.5	22.9	8.7	8.5	7.0	14.1	8.7
Germany, Fed. Rep.	14.5	3.3	4.1	10.0	6.9	4.5	4.7	8.0	7.2
Ireland	–	–	–	–	–	–	–	–	–
Italy	4.7	2.3	9.5	14.2	3.2	2.3	4.3	13.7	3.2
Japan	-0.1	0.5	0.1	0.2	0.1	0.1	0.1	0.2	0.1
Netherlands	18.7	25.2	17.2	19.2	17.6	21.2	15.7	19.2	17.6
New Zealand	–	–	–	–	–	–	–	–	–
Norway	2.3	5.7	5.0	11.5	2.3	5.7	5.0	11.5	2.3
Sweden	12.1	16.3	17.6	12.9	10.6	13.7	12.6	17.5	10.6
Switzerland	2.5	2.1	2.9	3.6	2.5	2.1	2.9	3.6	2.5
United Kingdom	0.1	0.0	0.2	0.1	0.1	0.0	0.2	0.1	0.1
United States	4.0	–	–	–	3.0	–	–	–	3.0
TOTAL	*97.1*	*81.3*	*76.7*	*111.2*	*72.9*	*71.7*	*67.2*	*104.6*	*73.3*
MULTILATERAL									
AF.D.F.	–	–	–	–	–	–	–	–	–
AF.D.B.	–	–	–	–	–	–	–	–	–
AS.D.B	–	–	–	–	–	–	–	–	–
CAR.D.B.	–	–	–	–	–	–	–	–	–
E.E.C.	6.9	14.7	12.7	9.1	6.9	14.7	12.7	9.1	6.9
IBRD	16.7	13.0	0.1	0.0	–	–	–	–	–
IDA	1.7	1.9	0.1	–	1.7	1.9	0.1	–	1.9
I.D.B.	27.4	19.0	11.9	26.0	25.9	8.9	7.4	11.1	27.6
IFAD	-0.5	0.0	3.1	5.1	-0.5	0.0	3.1	5.1	-0.5
I.F.C.	–	–	–	–	–	–	–	–	–
IMF TRUST FUND	–	–	–	–	–	–	–	–	–
U.N. AGENCIES	–	–	–	–	–	–	–	–	–
UNDP	1.4	1.9	1.8	2.4	1.4	1.9	1.8	2.4	1.4
UNTA	0.8	0.5	1.3	0.7	0.8	0.5	1.3	0.7	0.8
UNICEF	0.5	2.8	1.9	1.2	0.5	2.8	1.9	1.2	0.5
UNRWA	–	–	–	–	–	–	–	–	–
WFP	7.9	7.5	2.4	13.0	7.9	7.5	2.4	13.0	7.9
UNHCR	2.1	1.7	1.4	0.9	2.1	1.7	1.4	0.9	2.1
Other Multilateral	0.9	2.0	3.2	2.3	0.9	2.0	3.2	2.3	0.9
Arab OPEC Agencies	9.2	-0.7	0.1	–	–	–	0.1	–	–
TOTAL	*74.8*	*64.4*	*39.8*	*60.7*	*47.5*	*42.0*	*35.2*	*45.8*	*49.3*
OPEC COUNTRIES	*-0.8*	*44.2*	*–*	*–*	*–*	*–*	*–*	*–*	*–*
E.E.C.+ MEMBERS	*67.2*	*59.0*	*50.3*	*79.3*	*45.5*	*52.5*	*45.9*	*68.1*	*45.9*
TOTAL	*171.0*	*189.9*	*116.5*	*171.9*	*120.4*	*113.7*	*102.4*	*150.3*	*122.6*

ODA LOANS GROSS | ODA LOANS NET | GRANTS

	ODA LOANS GROSS 1983	1984	1985	1986	ODA LOANS NET 1983	1984	1985	1986	GRANTS 1983
DAC COUNTRIES									
Australia	–	–	–	–	–	–	–	–	–
Austria	6.4	–	3.5	–	6.4	–	3.5	–	1.7
Belgium	–	–	–	–	–	–	–	–	0.5
Canada	–	5.4	3.3	3.5	–	5.4	3.3	3.5	6.2
Denmark	–	–	–	1.3	–	–	–	1.3	1.6
Finland	0.3	1.7	1.4	5.0	0.3	1.7	1.4	5.0	1.3
France	5.6	5.5	4.1	10.6	5.6	5.5	4.1	10.6	3.1
Germany, Fed. Rep.	0.4	0.1	–	6.0	0.1	0.1	–	2.4	6.8
Ireland	–	–	–	–	–	–	–	–	–
Italy	–	0.1	–	5.1	–	-0.1	-0.2	4.6	3.2
Japan	–	–	–	–	–	–	–	–	0.1
Netherlands	7.5	9.4	4.0	8.9	7.5	9.4	4.0	8.9	10.2
New Zealand	–	–	–	–	–	–	–	–	–
Norway	–	–	–	–	–	–	–	–	2.3
Sweden	–	–	–	–	–	–	–	–	10.6
Switzerland	–	–	–	–	–	–	–	–	2.5
United Kingdom	–	–	–	–	–	–	–	–	0.1
United States	–	–	–	–	–	–	–	–	3.0
TOTAL	*20.2*	*22.1*	*16.4*	*40.3*	*19.8*	*21.9*	*16.1*	*36.2*	*53.1*
MULTILATERAL	*28.5*	*13.8*	*12.6*	*20.0*	*26.6*	*10.8*	*10.6*	*16.2*	*20.8*
OPEC COUNTRIES	*–*	*–*	*–*	*–*	*–*	*–*	*–*	*–*	*–*
E.E.C.+ MEMBERS	*13.5*	*15.0*	*8.1*	*31.8*	*13.2*	*14.8*	*7.9*	*27.7*	*32.4*
TOTAL	*48.7*	*35.9*	*29.0*	*60.3*	*46.5*	*32.7*	*26.7*	*52.4*	*74.0*

TOTAL OFFICIAL GROSS | TOTAL OFFICIAL NET | TOTAL OOF GROSS

	TOTAL OFFICIAL GROSS 1983	1984	1985	1986	TOTAL OFFICIAL NET 1983	1984	1985	1986	TOTAL OOF GROSS 1983
DAC COUNTRIES									
Australia	–	0.1	0.1	0.1	–	0.1	0.1	0.1	–
Austria	8.1	0.5	4.4	1.3	8.1	0.5	4.4	1.3	–
Belgium	0.5	0.4	0.5	0.7	0.5	0.4	0.5	0.7	–
Canada	6.2	8.8	5.8	4.4	6.2	8.8	5.8	4.3	–
Denmark	1.6	0.8	0.9	3.2	1.6	0.8	0.9	3.2	–
Finland	1.6	3.0	3.2	7.1	1.6	3.0	3.2	7.1	–
France	8.7	8.5	7.0	14.1	8.7	8.5	7.0	14.1	–
Germany, Fed. Rep.	16.7	4.5	5.9	13.0	15.6	4.5	5.8	9.4	9.5
Ireland	–	–	–	–	–	–	–	–	–
Italy	3.2	2.6	4.5	14.2	3.2	2.3	4.3	13.7	–
Japan	0.1	0.1	0.1	0.2	0.1	0.1	0.1	0.2	–
Netherlands	17.6	21.2	15.7	19.2	17.6	21.2	15.7	19.2	–
New Zealand	–	–	–	–	–	–	–	–	–
Norway	2.3	5.7	5.0	11.5	2.3	5.7	5.0	11.5	–
Sweden	12.1	16.6	17.6	17.5	12.1	16.3	17.6	16.7	1.6
Switzerland	2.5	2.1	2.9	3.6	2.5	2.1	2.9	3.6	–
United Kingdom	0.1	0.0	0.2	0.1	0.1	0.0	0.2	0.1	–
United States	4.0	–	–	–	4.0	–	–	–	1.0
TOTAL	*85.4*	*74.8*	*73.7*	*110.2*	*84.2*	*74.3*	*73.3*	*105.2*	*12.0*
MULTILATERAL	*83.2*	*75.5*	*42.1*	*65.1*	*74.8*	*64.4*	*39.8*	*60.7*	*33.9*
OPEC COUNTRIES	*–*	*44.2*	*–*	*–*	*-0.8*	*44.2*	*–*	*–*	*–*
E.E.C.+ MEMBERS	*55.4*	*52.7*	*47.3*	*73.6*	*54.2*	*52.5*	*46.9*	*69.5*	*9.5*
TOTAL	*168.5*	*194.5*	*115.8*	*175.2*	*158.2*	*183.0*	*113.1*	*165.8*	*45.9*

ODA COMMITMENTS

1984	1985	1986	1983	1984	1985	1986
0.1	0.1	0.1	–	0.1	–	0.0
0.5	4.4	1.3	7.2	0.1	4.5	–
0.4	0.5	0.7	–	–	–	0.7
8.8	5.8	4.4	5.4	14.5	6.8	0.6
0.8	0.9	3.2	2.5	0.3	9.0	1.8
3.0	3.2	7.1	1.4	5.9	5.9	8.3
8.5	7.0	14.1	10.1	5.0	17.3	14.1
4.5	4.7	11.6	7.9	4.1	4.0	9.5
–	–	–	–	–	–	–
2.6	4.5	14.2	1.4	2.6	19.7	9.4
0.1	0.1	0.2	0.1	0.1	0.1	0.2
21.2	15.7	19.2	31.2	15.3	22.9	7.4
–	–	–	–	–	–	–
5.7	5.0	11.5	3.8	4.6	9.4	11.6
13.7	12.6	17.5	14.8	15.7	12.7	17.5
2.1	2.9	3.6	3.6	1.1	7.8	0.9
0.0	0.2	0.1	0.1	0.0	0.2	0.1
						–
71.9	67.5	108.7	89.5	69.4	120.2	82.0
–	–	–	–	–	–	–
–	–	–	–	–	–	–
–	–	–	–	–	–	–
14.7	12.7	9.1	11.4	6.6	9.6	14.1
–	–	–	–	–	–	–
2.1	0.1	–	–	–	–	–
11.8	9.4	14.9	–	–	–	–
0.0	3.1	5.1	–	–	–	–
–	–	–	–	–	–	–
–	–	–	13.5	16.5	11.9	20.5
1.9	1.8	2.4	–	–	–	–
0.5	1.3	0.7	–	–	–	–
2.8	1.9	1.2	–	–	–	–
–	–	–	–	–	–	–
7.5	2.4	13.0	–	–	–	–
1.7	1.4	0.9	–	–	–	–
2.0	3.2	2.3	–	–	–	–
–	0.1	–	–	–	–	–
45.0	37.2	49.6	24.9	23.1	21.5	34.6
–	–	–	–	–	–	–
52.7	46.2	72.2	64.6	33.9	82.6	57.1
116.9	104.7	158.3	114.4	92.5	141.7	116.6

TECH. COOP. GRANTS

1984	1985	1986	1983	1984	1985	1986
0.1	0.1	0.1	–	0.0	–	–
0.5	0.9	1.3	0.8	–	–	–
0.4	0.5	0.7	0.0	0.0	0.1	0.0
3.4	2.5	0.9	0.8	–	0.9	–
0.8	0.9	1.9	1.5	0.4	0.5	0.2
1.2	1.8	2.1	0.5	0.7	0.7	5.4
3.0	2.9	3.5	0.9	1.2	1.0	2.1
4.5	4.7	5.6	6.8	4.3	4.6	5.4
–	–	–	–	–	–	–
2.5	4.5	9.1	1.2	2.5	3.7	7.1
0.1	0.1	0.2	0.1	0.1	0.1	0.2
11.9	11.6	10.3	2.4	2.7	2.6	4.9
–	–	–	–	–	–	–
5.7	5.0	11.5	–	0.1	0.1	0.6
13.7	12.6	17.5	0.5	3.1	4.5	3.5
2.1	2.9	3.6	0.5	0.5	0.5	0.3
0.0	0.2	0.1	0.1	0.0	0.0	–
–	–	–	3.0	–	–	–
49.8	51.2	68.4	19.1	15.5	19.2	29.8
31.2	24.6	29.6	5.7	9.0	9.5	7.5
–	–	–	–	–	–	–
37.7	38.0	40.4	12.9	11.0	12.5	19.9
81.0	75.7	98.0	24.7	24.5	28.7	37.3

TOTAL OOF NET

1984	1985	1986	1983	1984	1985	1986
–	–	–	–	–	–	–
–	–	–	–	–	–	–
–	–	–	–	–	–	–
–	–	–	–	–	–	–
–	–	–	–	–	–	–
–	–	–	–	–	–	–
–	1.1	1.4	8.7	–	1.0	1.4
–	–	–	–	–	–	–
–	–	–	–	–	–	–
–	–	–	–	–	–	–
–	–	–	–	–	–	–
2.9	5.0	–	1.6	2.7	5.0	-0.8
–	–	–	–	–	–	–
–	–	–	1.0	–	–	–
2.9	6.1	1.4	11.3	2.7	6.0	0.6
30.4	4.9	15.5	27.3	22.4	4.6	14.9
44.2	–	–	-0.8	44.2	–	–
–	1.1	1.4	8.7	–	1.0	1.4
77.5	11.1	16.9	37.8	69.3	10.6	15.5

ODA COMMITMENTS : LOANS

	1983	1984	1985	1986
DAC COUNTRIES				
Australia	–	–	–	–
Austria	6.4	–	3.5	–
Belgium	–	–	–	–
Canada	–	10.0	5.1	–
Denmark	–	–	7.1	–
Finland	–	3.3	4.8	–
France	7.9	–	14.8	10.6
Germany, Fed. Rep.	–	–		6.0
Ireland	–	–	–	–
Italy	–	–	15.0	–
Japan	–	–	–	–
Netherlands	16.8	8.3	9.3	–
New Zealand	–	–	–	–
Norway	–	–	–	–
Sweden	–	–	–	–
Switzerland	–	–	–	–
United Kingdom	–	–	–	–
United States	–	–	–	–
TOTAL	31.0	21.7	59.6	16.6
MULTILATERAL	–	–	–	–
OPEC COUNTRIES				
E.E.C.+ MEMBERS	24.7	8.3	46.2	16.6
TOTAL	31.0	21.7	59.6	16.6

GRANT ELEMENT OF ODA

	1983	1984	1985	1986
DAC COUNTRIES				
Australia	–	100.0	–	100.0
Austria	71.3	100.0	80.2	–
Belgium	–	–	–	100.0
Canada	100.0	93.2	92.0	100.0
Denmark	100.0	100.0	81.1	100.0
Finland	100.0	82.2	75.4	100.0
France	68.2	100.0	65.0	100.0
Germany, Fed. Rep.	100.0	100.0	100.0	41.2
Ireland	–	–	–	–
Italy	100.0	100.0	56.5	100.0
Japan	100.0	100.0	100.0	100.0
Netherlands	78.5	78.3	83.7	100.0
New Zealand	–	–	–	–
Norway	100.0	100.0	100.0	100.0
Sweden	100.0	100.0	100.0	100.0
Switzerland	100.0	100.0	100.0	100.0
United Kingdom	100.0	100.0	100.0	100.0
United States	–	–	–	–
TOTAL	86.6	92.3	80.9	92.2
MULTILATERAL	100.0	100.0	100.0	100.0
OPEC COUNTRIES				
E.E.C.+ MEMBERS	84.6	90.2	75.7	88.0
TOTAL	89.5	94.2	83.8	94.8

OTHER AGGREGATES

COMMITMENTS: ALL SOURCES	1983	1984	1985	1986
TOTAL BILATERAL	248.4	374.3	497.2	201.5
of which				
OPEC	–	44.2	–	–
CMEA	146.0	257.8	372.0	120.3
TOTAL MULTILATERAL	55.6	23.1	21.5	34.6
TOTAL BIL.& MULTIL.	304.0	397.4	518.7	236.1
of which				
ODA Grants	99.0	112.7	84.1	195.4
ODA Loans	116.3	81.2	429.6	41.6

DISBURSEMENTS:	1983	1984	1985	1986
DAC COUNTRIES COMBINED				
OFFICIAL & PRIVATE				
GROSS:				
Contractual Lending	51.9	30.5	34.7	54.9
Export Credits Total	21.3	8.4	17.2	13.1
Export Credits Private	19.7	5.5	12.2	13.1
NET:				
Contractual Lending	42.5	27.4	26.1	40.3
Export Credits Total	13.0	5.5	9.0	2.7
PRIVATE SECTOR NET	12.9	7.0	3.4	6.0
Direct Investment	–	–	0.0	0.1
Portfolio Investment	1.5	4.1	-0.5	2.5
Export Credits	11.4	2.8	4.0	3.5

MARKET BORROWING:	1983	1984	1985	1986
CHANGE IN CLAIMS				
Banks	–	-105.0	220.0	-125.0

MEMORANDUM ITEM:	1983	1984	1985	1986
CMEA Countr.(Gross)	53.7	123.0	203.8	169.4

TOTAL RECEIPTS NET

DAC COUNTRIES	1983	1984	1985	1986
Australia	–	–	–	–
Austria	0.0	0.0	0.0	0.0
Belgium	10.1	1.9	5.9	4.9
Canada	6.4	7.6	16.2	17.2
Denmark	1.6	3.6	0.7	2.7
Finland	0.0	0.1	0.1	0.1
France	61.3	23.3	44.7	47.5
Germany, Fed. Rep.	28.2	13.5	21.6	20.5
Ireland	–	–	–	–
Italy	8.2	0.2	9.8	26.4
Japan	-4.2	4.7	-1.0	3.8
Netherlands	1.5	5.7	3.7	7.5
New Zealand	–	–	–	–
Norway	1.1	0.5	2.6	3.2
Sweden	-0.3	-1.8	–	-0.4
Switzerland	3.7	1.7	3.5	5.4
United Kingdom	-4.5	-1.5	-1.2	-1.7
United States	16.0	20.0	84.0	33.0
TOTAL	129.3	79.6	190.7	170.0
MULTILATERAL				
AF.D.F.	7.9	1.4	11.2	21.5
AF.D.B.	8.4	-1.3	-1.0	-2.0
AS.D.B	–	–	–	–
CAR.D.B.	–	–	–	–
E.E.C.	19.2	16.6	27.5	25.9
IBRD	–	–	–	–
IDA	12.6	17.2	21.3	38.6
I.D.B.	–	–	–	–
IFAD	0.9	0.8	1.0	1.5
I.F.C.	0.2	1.5	–	–
IMF TRUST FUND	–	–	–	–
U.N. AGENCIES	–	–	–	–
UNDP	9.8	9.0	10.2	9.3
UNTA	0.9	0.9	1.4	0.7
UNICEF	1.0	1.7	3.3	3.3
UNRWA	–	–	–	–
WFP	2.6	4.0	15.1	5.5
UNHCR	0.0	0.0	0.0	0.0
Other Multilateral	1.8	2.4	6.2	9.0
Arab OPEC Agencies	-7.8	-5.1	0.1	5.1
TOTAL	57.5	49.1	96.2	118.4
OPEC COUNTRIES	20.7	7.1	2.6	6.1
E.E.C.+ MEMBERS	125.7	63.2	112.7	133.6
TOTAL	207.5	135.7	289.6	294.6

TOTAL ODA NET

	1983	1984	1985	1986
Australia	–	–	–	–
Austria	0.0	0.0	0.0	0.0
Belgium	3.9	2.6	7.6	7.1
Canada	6.4	7.6	16.2	17.2
Denmark	1.6	3.6	0.7	2.7
Finland	0.0	0.1	0.1	0.1
France	28.5	40.5	46.4	54.6
Germany, Fed. Rep.	27.6	14.4	21.9	20.9
Ireland	–	–	–	–
Italy	7.9	0.5	9.8	26.4
Japan	8.5	3.5	9.3	5.7
Netherlands	1.5	5.7	3.7	7.5
New Zealand	–	–	–	–
Norway	1.1	0.5	2.6	3.2
Sweden	–	0.3	–	–
Switzerland	3.7	2.5	3.5	5.4
United Kingdom	0.1	0.1	0.4	0.1
United States	16.0	20.0	84.0	33.0
TOTAL	107.0	101.9	206.4	183.8
AF.D.F.	7.9	1.4	11.2	21.5
AF.D.B.	–	–	–	–
AS.D.B	–	–	–	–
CAR.D.B.	–	–	–	–
E.E.C.	13.3	16.1	27.5	27.0
IBRD	–	–	–	–
IDA	12.6	17.2	21.3	38.6
I.D.B.	–	–	–	–
IFAD	0.9	0.8	1.0	1.5
I.F.C.	–	–	–	–
IMF TRUST FUND	–	–	–	–
U.N. AGENCIES	–	–	–	–
UNDP	9.8	9.0	10.2	9.3
UNTA	0.9	0.9	1.4	0.7
UNICEF	1.0	1.7	3.3	3.3
UNRWA	–	–	–	–
WFP	2.6	4.0	15.1	5.5
UNHCR	0.0	0.0	0.0	0.0
Other Multilateral	1.8	2.4	6.2	9.0
Arab OPEC Agencies	-1.0	-1.6	-0.9	1.5
TOTAL	49.8	52.0	96.2	117.9
OPEC COUNTRIES	18.1	7.1	2.3	6.1
E.E.C.+ MEMBERS	84.5	83.5	118.1	146.1
TOTAL	174.8	161.0	304.9	307.8

TOTAL ODA GROSS

	1983
Australia	–
Austria	0.0
Belgium	3.9
Canada	6.4
Denmark	1.6
Finland	0.0
France	29.4
Germany, Fed. Rep.	27.6
Ireland	–
Italy	7.9
Japan	11.0
Netherlands	1.5
New Zealand	–
Norway	1.1
Sweden	–
Switzerland	3.7
United Kingdom	0.1
United States	16.0
TOTAL	110.3
AF.D.F.	7.9
AF.D.B.	–
AS.D.B	–
CAR.D.B.	–
E.E.C.	13.3
IBRD	–
IDA	14.0
I.D.B.	–
IFAD	0.9
I.F.C.	–
IMF TRUST FUND	–
U.N. AGENCIES	–
UNDP	9.8
UNTA	0.9
UNICEF	1.0
UNRWA	–
WFP	2.6
UNHCR	0.0
Other Multilateral	1.8
Arab OPEC Agencies	0.5
TOTAL	52.8
OPEC COUNTRIES	18.4
E.E.C.+ MEMBERS	85.4
TOTAL	181.5

ODA LOANS GROSS

DAC COUNTRIES	1983	1984	1985	1986
Australia	–	–	–	–
Austria	–	–	–	–
Belgium	2.0	–	–	–
Canada	–	–	–	–
Denmark	1.6	0.9	0.1	0.2
Finland	–	–	–	–
France	5.0	16.1	22.9	26.6
Germany, Fed. Rep.	–	–	–	–
Ireland	–	–	–	–
Italy	–	–	–	–
Japan	0.1	–	–	–
Netherlands	–	–	–	–
New Zealand	–	–	–	–
Norway	–	–	–	–
Sweden	–	–	–	–
Switzerland	–	–	–	–
United Kingdom	–	–	–	–
United States	–	–	–	–
TOTAL	8.7	17.0	23.0	26.7
MULTILATERAL	23.3	19.9	35.5	66.5
OPEC COUNTRIES	17.5	8.5	2.2	8.0
E.E.C.+ MEMBERS	8.6	17.0	23.0	26.7
TOTAL	49.6	45.3	60.7	101.2

ODA LOANS NET

	1983	1984	1985	1986
Australia	–	–	–	–
Austria	–	–	–	–
Belgium	2.0	–	–	–
Canada	–	–	–	-2.9
Denmark	1.6	0.9	0.0	-7.7
Finland	–	–	–	–
France	4.1	14.9	21.2	22.0
Germany, Fed. Rep.	–	–	–	–
Ireland	–	–	–	–
Italy	–	–	–	–
Japan	-2.4	-1.6	-1.9	-2.7
Netherlands	–	–	–	–
New Zealand	–	–	–	–
Norway	–	–	–	–
Sweden	–	–	–	–
Switzerland	–	–	–	–
United Kingdom	–	–	–	–
United States	–	–	–	–
TOTAL	5.3	14.1	19.3	8.6
MULTILATERAL	20.4	17.4	32.3	62.6
OPEC COUNTRIES	17.2	6.7	-0.6	6.1
E.E.C.+ MEMBERS	7.7	15.7	21.2	13.8
TOTAL	42.9	38.2	51.0	77.3

GRANTS

	1983
Australia	–
Austria	0.0
Belgium	1.9
Canada	6.4
Denmark	1.6
Finland	0.0
France	24.4
Germany, Fed. Rep.	27.6
Ireland	–
Italy	7.9
Japan	10.9
Netherlands	1.5
New Zealand	–
Norway	1.1
Sweden	–
Switzerland	3.7
United Kingdom	0.1
United States	16.0
TOTAL	101.6
MULTILATERAL	29.5
OPEC COUNTRIES	0.8
E.E.C.+ MEMBERS	76.8
TOTAL	131.9

TOTAL OFFICIAL GROSS

DAC COUNTRIES	1983	1984	1985	1986
Australia	–	–	–	–
Austria	0.0	0.0	0.0	0.0
Belgium	3.9	2.6	7.6	7.1
Canada	6.4	7.6	16.2	20.2
Denmark	1.6	3.6	0.8	10.6
Finland	0.0	0.1	0.1	0.1
France	45.7	76.7	77.3	81.6
Germany, Fed. Rep.	27.6	14.4	21.9	20.9
Ireland	–	–	–	–
Italy	7.9	0.5	9.8	26.4
Japan	11.0	5.1	11.2	8.3
Netherlands	1.5	5.7	3.7	7.5
New Zealand	–	–	–	–
Norway	1.1	0.5	2.6	3.2
Sweden	–	0.3	–	–
Switzerland	3.7	2.5	3.5	5.4
United Kingdom	0.1	0.1	0.4	0.1
United States	16.0	21.0	86.0	34.0
TOTAL	126.6	140.7	241.2	225.3
MULTILATERAL	72.3	57.2	100.8	129.8
OPEC COUNTRIES	21.0	8.8	5.5	8.0
E.E.C.+ MEMBERS	107.8	120.6	149.1	181.5
TOTAL	220.0	206.8	347.5	363.1

TOTAL OFFICIAL NET

	1983	1984	1985	1986
Australia	–	–	–	–
Austria	0.0	0.0	0.0	0.0
Belgium	3.9	2.6	7.6	7.1
Canada	6.4	7.6	16.2	17.2
Denmark	1.6	3.6	0.7	2.7
Finland	0.0	0.1	0.1	0.1
France	40.9	72.0	68.5	65.8
Germany, Fed. Rep.	27.0	13.6	21.9	20.9
Ireland	–	–	–	–
Italy	7.9	0.5	9.8	26.4
Japan	8.5	3.5	9.3	5.7
Netherlands	1.5	5.7	3.7	7.5
New Zealand	–	–	–	–
Norway	1.1	0.5	2.6	3.2
Sweden	-0.3	0.0	–	-0.4
Switzerland	3.7	2.5	3.5	5.4
United Kingdom	0.1	0.1	0.4	0.1
United States	16.0	20.0	84.0	33.0
TOTAL	118.4	132.4	228.5	194.6
MULTILATERAL	57.5	49.1	96.2	118.4
OPEC COUNTRIES	20.7	7.1	2.6	6.1
E.E.C.+ MEMBERS	102.1	114.6	140.2	156.3
TOTAL	196.7	188.5	327.4	319.1

TOTAL OOF GROSS

	1983
Australia	–
Austria	–
Belgium	–
Canada	–
Denmark	–
Finland	–
France	16.3
Germany, Fed. Rep.	–
Ireland	–
Italy	–
Japan	–
Netherlands	–
New Zealand	–
Norway	–
Sweden	–
Switzerland	–
United Kingdom	–
United States	–
TOTAL	16.3
MULTILATERAL	19.5
OPEC COUNTRIES	2.7
E.E.C.+ MEMBERS	22.4
TOTAL	38.5

ODA COMMITMENTS

1984	1985	1986	1983	1984	1985	1986
—	—	—	—	—	—	—
0.0	0.0	0.0	0.0	0.0	0.0	—
2.6	7.6	7.1	3.0	2.6	3.8	7.1
7.6	16.2	20.2	39.2	49.9	0.9	4.0
3.6	0.8	10.6	—	7.7	—	—
0.1	0.1	0.1	0.0	0.1	—	—
41.8	48.1	59.1	50.6	49.9	58.4	59.1
14.4	21.9	20.9	20.2	11.7	28.0	32.8
—	—	—	—	—	—	—
0.5	9.8	26.4	35.3	0.6	11.0	56.4
5.1	11.2	8.3	7.4	12.6	3.6	27.6
5.7	3.7	7.5	3.6	6.4	3.6	19.0
—	—	—	—	—	—	—
0.5	2.6	3.2	—	3.5	0.9	3.2
0.3	—	—	0.2	0.3	0.1	—
2.5	3.5	5.4	1.8	3.0	7.3	1.2
0.1	0.4	0.1	0.1	0.1	0.4	0.1
20.0	84.0	33.0	27.5	48.3	51.3	38.2
104.8	*210.1*	*201.9*	*188.9*	*196.6*	*169.4*	*248.8*
1.4	11.2	21.6	2.4	30.7	—	5.6
—	—	—	—	—	—	—
—	—	—	—	—	—	—
16.1	27.5	27.4	8.6	43.5	21.3	18.6
—	—	—	—	—	—	—
17.4	21.5	39.6	23.6	19.2	9.3	136.2
0.8	1.0	1.5	—	—	—	—
—	—	—	—	—	—	—
—	—	—	16.2	18.1	36.2	27.8
9.0	10.2	9.3	—	—	—	—
0.9	1.4	0.7	—	—	—	—
1.7	3.3	3.3	—	—	—	—
—	—	—	—	—	—	—
4.0	15.1	5.5	—	—	—	—
0.0	0.0	0.0	—	—	—	—
2.4	6.2	9.0	—	—	—	—
0.8	2.0	4.1	5.0	20.0	13.2	—
54.5	*99.4*	*121.9*	*55.8*	*131.5*	*80.0*	*188.3*
8.8	*5.1*	*8.0*	*9.6*	*18.0*	*11.6*	*5.9*
84.7	*119.9*	*159.0*	*121.4*	*122.5*	*126.5*	*193.2*
168.2	*314.6*	*331.8*	*254.3*	*346.0*	*261.0*	*443.0*

TECH. COOP. GRANTS

1984	1985	1986	1983	1984	1985	1986
—	—	—	—	—	—	—
0.0	0.0	0.0	0.0	—	—	—
2.6	7.6	7.1	1.8	2.1	3.0	3.4
7.6	16.2	20.2	1.4	—	2.7	—
2.7	0.7	10.5	—	2.8	0.0	—
0.1	0.1	0.1	0.0	0.1	—	—
25.6	25.3	32.6	18.5	18.6	16.7	21.3
14.4	21.9	20.9	9.4	7.7	8.6	11.4
—	—	—	—	—	—	—
0.5	9.8	26.4	0.1	0.5	2.7	5.2
5.1	11.2	8.3	0.8	0.3	0.6	1.7
5.7	3.7	7.5	0.8	1.0	1.2	2.2
—	—	—	—	—	—	—
0.5	2.6	3.2	—	0.1	—	—
0.3	—	—	—	—	—	—
2.5	3.5	5.4	1.3	0.8	0.9	1.9
0.1	0.4	0.1	0.1	0.1	0.2	0.1
20.0	84.0	33.0	13.0	13.0	18.0	22.0
87.8	*187.1*	*175.1*	*47.2*	*47.1*	*54.5*	*69.2*
34.7	*63.9*	*55.4*	*13.6*	*14.1*	*21.1*	*22.8*
0.4	*2.9*	*0.0*	—	—	—	—
67.7	*97.0*	*132.3*	*30.7*	*32.8*	*32.3*	*44.1*
122.8	*253.9*	*230.6*	*60.8*	*61.1*	*75.6*	*92.0*

TOTAL OOF NET

1984	1985	1986	1983	1984	1985	1986
—	—	—	—	—	—	—
—	—	—	—	—	—	—
0.0	—	0.0	—	0.0	—	0.0
—	—	—	—	—	—	—
—	—	—	—	—	—	—
34.9	29.2	22.5	12.3	31.5	22.1	11.2
—	—	—	-0.6	-0.8	—	—
—	—	—	—	—	—	—
—	—	—	—	—	—	—
—	—	—	—	—	—	—
—	—	—	—	—	—	—
—	—	—	—	—	—	—
—	—	—	-0.3	-0.2	—	-0.4
—	—	—	—	—	—	—
1.0	2.0	1.0	—	—	—	—
35.9	*31.2*	*23.5*	*11.5*	*30.4*	*22.1*	*10.8*
2.7	*1.4*	*7.9*	*7.7*	*-3.0*	*0.0*	*0.5*
—	*0.4*	—	*2.7*	—	*0.4*	—
35.8	*29.2*	*22.5*	*17.7*	*31.1*	*22.1*	*10.2*
38.6	*33.0*	*31.4*	*21.8*	*27.5*	*22.4*	*11.3*

ODA COMMITMENTS : LOANS

DAC COUNTRIES

	1983	1984	1985	1986
Australia	—	—	—	—
Austria	—	—	—	—
Belgium	2.0	—	—	—
Canada	—	—	—	—
Denmark	—	—	—	—
Finland	—	—	—	—
France	24.3	22.9	33.2	26.6
Germany, Fed. Rep.	—	—	—	—
Ireland	—	—	—	—
Italy	—	—	—	—
Japan	—	—	—	—
Netherlands	—	—	—	—
New Zealand	—	—	—	—
Norway	—	—	—	—
Sweden	—	—	—	—
Switzerland	—	—	—	—
United Kingdom	—	—	—	—
United States	—	—	—	—
TOTAL	*26.3*	*22.9*	*33.2*	*26.6*
MULTILATERAL	*31.0*	*74.5*	*22.1*	*141.8*
OPEC COUNTRIES	—	*17.9*	*8.3*	*5.9*
E.E.C.+ MEMBERS	*26.3*	*29.2*	*33.2*	*26.6*
TOTAL	*57.3*	*115.2*	*63.5*	*174.3*

GRANT ELEMENT OF ODA

DAC COUNTRIES

	1983	1984	1985	1986
Australia	—	—	—	—
Austria	100.0	100.0	100.0	—
Belgium	89.2	100.0	100.0	100.0
Canada	100.0	100.0	100.0	100.0
Denmark	—	100.0	—	—
Finland	100.0	100.0	—	—
France	80.4	74.1	79.9	84.4
Germany, Fed. Rep.	100.0	100.0	100.0	100.0
Ireland	—	—	—	—
Italy	100.0	100.0	100.0	100.0
Japan	100.0	100.0	100.0	100.0
Netherlands	100.0	100.0	100.0	100.0
New Zealand	—	—	—	—
Norway	—	100.0	100.0	100.0
Sweden	100.0	100.0	100.0	—
Switzerland	100.0	100.0	100.0	100.0
United Kingdom	100.0	100.0	100.0	100.0
United States	100.0	100.0	100.0	100.0
TOTAL	*95.5*	*93.4*	*94.4*	*96.6*
MULTILATERAL	*85.4*	*87.4*	*88.9*	*87.2*
OPEC COUNTRIES	*100.0*	*60.9*	*66.4*	*81.0*
E.E.C.+ MEMBERS	*92.7*	*88.9*	*92.3*	*95.6*
TOTAL	*93.1*	*89.5*	*91.2*	*92.3*

OTHER AGGREGATES

COMMITMENTS: ALL SOURCES

	1983	1984	1985	1986
TOTAL BILATERAL	212.6	256.5	210.0	255.6
of which				
OPEC	9.6	22.6	11.6	5.9
CMEA	—	—	—	—
TOTAL MULTILATERAL	67.9	139.5	88.3	193.4
TOTAL BIL.& MULTIL.	280.6	396.0	298.3	449.0
of which				
ODA Grants	197.0	230.8	197.5	268.7
ODA Loans	57.3	115.2	63.5	174.3

DISBURSEMENTS:

DAC COUNTRIES COMBINED

	1983	1984	1985	1986
OFFICIAL & PRIVATE				
GROSS:				
Contractual Lending	59.5	64.1	56.8	32.0
Export Credits Total	34.5	11.2	2.7	-18.2
Export Credits Private	34.5	11.2	2.7	-18.2
NET:				
Contractual Lending	17.0	13.6	11.3	-2.3
Export Credits Total	0.0	-32.2	-32.1	-23.1
PRIVATE SECTOR NET	10.9	-52.8	-37.8	-24.6
Direct Investment	5.9	1.5	-11.1	-2.3
Portfolio Investment	4.7	-23.4	3.4	-0.6
Export Credits	0.2	-31.0	-30.1	-21.7

MARKET BORROWING:

CHANGE IN CLAIMS

	1983	1984	1985	1986
Banks	—	8.0	-60.0	—

MEMORANDUM ITEM:

	1983	1984	1985	1986
CMEA Countr.(Gross)	—	—	—	—

	1983	1984	1985	1986	1983	1984	1985	1986		1983
TOTAL RECEIPTS NET					**TOTAL ODA NET**				**TOTAL ODA GROSS**	
DAC COUNTRIES										
Australia	0.5	0.5	0.4	0.3	0.5	0.5	0.4	0.3	Australia	0.5
Austria	101.6	-12.0	-12.8	0.6	0.4	0.6	0.3	0.6	Austria	0.4
Belgium	9.1	45.6	-20.1	-18.7	0.2	0.2	0.3	0.5	Belgium	0.2
Canada	0.6	1.5	1.4	0.6	0.6	1.5	1.4	1.1	Canada	1.4
Denmark	58.4	22.4	11.3	-8.9	0.0	0.2	-0.1	–	Denmark	0.1
Finland	0.4	0.0	0.0	0.1	0.0	0.0	0.0	0.1	Finland	0.0
France	643.7	143.7	119.6	-81.3	4.5	4.3	3.9	5.8	France	4.5
Germany, Fed. Rep.	507.7	306.3	-60.5	-84.6	0.7	1.8	3.1	7.5	Germany, Fed. Rep.	7.8
Ireland	0.1	0.1	0.0	0.1	0.1	0.1	0.0	0.1	Ireland	0.1
Italy	-22.0	-17.2	-29.6	-22.6	0.6	1.6	0.7	2.9	Italy	0.6
Japan	69.3	-1.0	35.2	129.0	17.8	0.7	1.7	13.0	Japan	23.0
Netherlands	140.1	-2.2	-39.8	-28.4	0.0	0.6	0.6	2.3	Netherlands	1.2
New Zealand	–	0.0	0.0	–	–	0.0	0.0	–	New Zealand	–
Norway	-2.3	11.8	7.5	4.5	–	0.0	0.1	0.1	Norway	–
Sweden	0.0	0.0	0.0	0.0	0.1	0.1	0.0	0.0	Sweden	0.1
Switzerland	12.0	6.9	0.0	0.0	0.1	0.1	0.2	0.0	Switzerland	0.1
United Kingdom	310.3	-6.2	11.9	-4.0	5.7	3.5	4.4	6.4	United Kingdom	8.3
United States	78.0	-198.0	-116.0	552.0	-2.0	-1.0	-1.0	-1.0	United States	–
TOTAL	*1907.2*	*302.2*	*-91.5*	*438.8*	*29.2*	*14.7*	*15.9*	*39.7*	*TOTAL*	*48.2*
MULTILATERAL										
AF.D.F.	–	–	–	–	–	–	–	–	AF.D.F.	–
AF.D.B.	-0.4	-0.4	-0.3	-1.3	–	–	–	–	AF.D.B.	–
AS.D.B	–	–	–	–	–	–	–	–	AS.D.B	–
CAR.D.B.	–	–	–	–	–	–	–	–	CAR.D.B.	–
E.E.C.	4.8	6.1	6.4	13.2	1.1	1.7	1.4	3.8	E.E.C.	1.1
IBRD	150.1	219.9	229.8	446.3	–	–	–	–	IBRD	–
IDA	-0.4	-0.4	-1.2	-1.2	-0.4	-0.4	-1.2	-1.2	IDA	–
I.D.B.	–	–	–	–	–	–	–	–	I.D.B.	–
IFAD	–	–	–	–	–	–	–	–	IFAD	–
I.F.C.	-0.1	7.8	4.9	-0.2	–	–	–	–	I.F.C.	–
IMF TRUST FUND	–	–	–	–	–	–	–	–	IMF TRUST FUND	–
U.N. AGENCIES									U.N. AGENCIES	
UNDP	8.7	7.3	5.7	6.4	8.7	7.3	5.7	6.4	UNDP	8.7
UNTA	1.6	1.7	1.6	1.5	1.6	1.7	1.6	1.5	UNTA	1.6
UNICEF	4.7	5.3	6.3	7.1	4.7	5.3	6.3	7.1	UNICEF	4.7
UNRWA	–	–	–	–	–	–	–	–	UNRWA	–
WFP	–	–	–	–	–	–	–	–	WFP	–
UNHCR	1.3	1.0	0.8	0.6	1.3	1.0	0.8	0.6	UNHCR	1.3
Other Multilateral	1.5	1.7	1.8	1.9	1.5	1.7	1.8	1.9	Other Multilateral	1.5
Arab OPEC Agencies	–	–	–	–	–	–	–	–	Arab OPEC Agencies	–
TOTAL	*171.8*	*249.9*	*255.6*	*474.3*	*18.4*	*18.3*	*16.3*	*20.0*	*TOTAL*	*18.8*
OPEC COUNTRIES	*0.0*	*0.1*	*0.1*	*0.1*	*0.0*	*0.1*	*0.1*	*0.1*	*OPEC COUNTRIES*	*0.0*
E.E.C.+ MEMBERS	*1652.1*	*498.6*	*-0.8*	*-235.1*	*12.7*	*13.8*	*14.2*	*29.3*	*E.E.C.+ MEMBERS*	*23.8*
TOTAL	*2079.0*	*552.2*	*164.2*	*913.2*	*47.6*	*33.0*	*32.3*	*59.8*	*TOTAL*	*67.1*
ODA LOANS GROSS					**ODA LOANS NET**				**GRANTS**	
DAC COUNTRIES										
Australia	–	0.3	–	–	0.0	0.2	–	-0.1	Australia	0.5
Austria	–	0.3	–	–	0.0	0.2	-0.1	-0.1	Austria	0.4
Belgium	–	–	–	–	–	–	–	–	Belgium	0.2
Canada	–	–	–	–	-0.8	-0.5	–	–	Canada	1.4
Denmark	–	–	–	–	-0.1	0.0	-0.2	–	Denmark	0.1
Finland	–	–	–	–	–	–	–	–	Finland	0.0
France	–	–	–	–	–	–	–	–	France	4.5
Germany, Fed. Rep.	0.5	–	0.8	0.6	-6.5	-3.3	-2.8	-2.3	Germany, Fed. Rep.	7.2
Ireland	–	–	–	–	–	–	–	–	Ireland	0.1
Italy	–	–	–	–	–	-0.2	-0.6	–	Italy	0.6
Japan	21.1	4.4	5.8	15.2	16.0	-1.8	-0.6	10.2	Japan	1.8
Netherlands	–	–	0.4	–	-1.3	-0.8	-0.5	-0.4	Netherlands	1.2
New Zealand	–	–	–	–	–	–	–	–	New Zealand	–
Norway	–	–	–	–	–	–	–	–	Norway	–
Sweden	–	–	–	–	–	–	–	–	Sweden	0.1
Switzerland	–	–	–	–	–	–	–	–	Switzerland	0.1
United Kingdom	–	–	–	–	-2.6	-4.0	-3.6	-1.7	United Kingdom	8.3
United States	–	–	–	–	-2.0	-2.0	-2.0	-1.0	United States	–
TOTAL	*21.7*	*4.7*	*6.9*	*15.8*	*2.6*	*-12.4*	*-10.5*	*4.7*	*TOTAL*	*26.6*
MULTILATERAL	–	–	–	–	*-0.4*	*-0.4*	*-1.2*	*-1.2*	*MULTILATERAL*	*18.8*
OPEC COUNTRIES									*OPEC COUNTRIES*	*0.0*
E.E.C.+ MEMBERS	*0.5*	–	*1.1*	*0.6*	*-10.6*	*-8.3*	*-7.8*	*-4.4*	*E.E.C.+ MEMBERS*	*23.3*
TOTAL	*21.7*	*4.7*	*6.9*	*15.8*	*2.2*	*-12.8*	*-11.7*	*3.5*	*TOTAL*	*45.4*
TOTAL OFFICIAL GROSS					**TOTAL OFFICIAL NET**				**TOTAL OOF GROSS**	
DAC COUNTRIES										
Australia	0.5	0.5	0.4	0.3	0.5	0.5	0.4	0.3	Australia	–
Austria	0.4	0.7	0.4	0.7	0.4	0.6	0.3	0.6	Austria	–
Belgium	0.2	2.9	1.9	0.8	0.2	2.9	1.9	0.8	Belgium	–
Canada	1.4	2.0	1.4	1.1	0.6	1.5	1.4	1.1	Canada	–
Denmark	14.8	28.6	16.7	0.8	11.2	25.6	13.7	-7.8	Denmark	14.7
Finland	0.0	0.0	0.0	0.1	0.0	0.0	0.0	0.1	Finland	–
France	110.5	4.3	3.9	5.8	78.2	4.3	3.9	5.8	France	106.0
Germany, Fed. Rep.	223.9	150.6	62.0	117.9	186.3	131.9	42.0	100.0	Germany, Fed. Rep.	216.1
Ireland	0.1	0.1	0.0	0.1	0.1	0.1	0.0	0.1	Ireland	–
Italy	0.6	1.8	1.3	2.9	0.6	1.6	0.7	2.9	Italy	–
Japan	23.0	6.9	8.1	18.0	17.8	0.7	1.7	13.0	Japan	–
Netherlands	1.2	1.4	1.5	2.7	0.0	0.6	0.0	2.3	Netherlands	–
New Zealand	–	0.0	0.0	–	–	0.0	0.0	–	New Zealand	–
Norway	–	0.0	0.1	0.1	–	0.0	0.1	0.1	Norway	–
Sweden	0.1	0.1	0.0	0.0	0.0	0.0	0.0	-0.1	Sweden	–
Switzerland	0.1	0.1	0.2	0.0	0.1	0.1	0.2	0.0	Switzerland	–
United Kingdom	8.3	7.5	8.1	8.2	5.7	2.4	4.2	6.1	United Kingdom	–
United States	85.0	55.0	159.0	2.0	80.0	50.0	152.0	1.0	United States	85.0
TOTAL	*470.0*	*262.5*	*265.0*	*161.5*	*381.5*	*222.7*	*222.5*	*126.2*	*TOTAL*	*421.8*
MULTILATERAL	*213.2*	*294.0*	*301.5*	*558.3*	*171.8*	*249.9*	*255.6*	*474.3*	*MULTILATERAL*	*194.3*
OPEC COUNTRIES	*0.0*	*0.1*	*0.1*	*0.1*	*0.0*	*0.1*	*0.1*	*0.1*	*OPEC COUNTRIES*	–
E.E.C.+ MEMBERS	*366.6*	*205.5*	*104.9*	*156.5*	*286.9*	*175.4*	*72.8*	*123.4*	*E.E.C.+ MEMBERS*	*342.8*
TOTAL	*683.2*	*556.5*	*566.6*	*719.9*	*553.3*	*472.7*	*478.2*	*600.6*	*TOTAL*	*616.1*

ODA COMMITMENTS

1984	1985	1986	1983	1984	1985	1986
0.5	0.4	0.3	0.5	0.5	0.2	0.1
0.7	0.4	0.7	2.2	0.3	0.4	—
0.2	0.3	0.5	—	—	—	0.5
2.0	1.4	1.1	1.6	2.9	4.6	4.7
0.2	0.0	—	—	—	—	—
0.0	0.0	0.1	0.0	0.0	—	0.0
4.3	3.9	5.8	4.5	4.3	3.9	5.8
5.1	6.6	10.4	8.0	4.8	5.3	8.5
0.1	0.0	0.1	0.1	0.1	0.0	0.1
1.8	1.3	2.9	1.8	4.2	3.1	4.8
6.9	8.1	18.0	2.0	3.4	1.8	9.0
1.4	1.5	2.7	0.9	1.2	1.5	2.9
0.0	0.0	—	—	—	—	—
0.0	0.1	0.1	—	0.0	0.1	0.1
0.1	0.0	0.0	—	—	—	0.0
0.1	0.2	0.0	—	—	—	—
7.5	8.1	8.2	8.3	7.5	8.1	8.2
1.0	1.0	—	0.0	1.6	—	2.1
31.7	*33.2*	*50.8*	*29.8*	*30.9*	*28.8*	*46.8*
—	—	—	—	—	—	—
—	—	—	—	—	—	—
1.7	1.4	3.8	15.6	7.4	1.9	1.3
—	—	—	—	—	—	—
—	—	—	—	—	—	—
—	—	—	—	—	12.6	—
—	—	—	—	—	—	—
—	—	—	17.7	17.0	16.1	17.5
7.3	5.7	6.4	—	—	—	—
1.7	1.6	1.5	—	—	—	—
5.3	6.3	7.1	—	—	—	—
—	—	—	—	—	—	—
—	—	—	—	—	—	—
1.0	0.8	0.6	—	—	—	—
1.7	1.8	1.9	—	—	—	—
—	—	—	—	—	—	—
18.7	*17.5*	*21.2*	*33.3*	*24.4*	*30.5*	*18.8*
0.1	*0.1*	*0.1*	*0.0*	—	*0.0*	—
22.2	*23.1*	*34.3*	*39.1*	*29.5*	*23.8*	*32.1*
50.5	**50.8**	**72.2**	**63.1**	**55.3**	**59.4**	**65.5**

TECH. COOP. GRANTS

1984	1985	1986	1983	1984	1985	1986
0.5	0.4	0.3	0.4	0.5	0.4	0.3
0.4	0.4	0.7	0.4	—	—	—
0.2	0.3	0.5	0.0	0.1	0.1	0.1
2.0	1.4	1.1	4.9	—	2.7	—
0.2	0.0	—	0.1	0.2	0.0	—
0.0	0.0	0.1	0.0	0.0	0.0	0.0
4.3	3.9	5.8	4.5	4.3	3.9	5.8
5.1	5.9	9.8	4.8	4.5	4.8	7.2
0.1	0.0	0.1	0.1	0.1	0.0	0.1
1.8	1.3	2.9	0.6	1.8	1.3	2.5
2.5	2.3	2.8	1.7	1.4	1.6	2.8
1.4	1.1	2.7	1.2	1.4	0.9	2.7
0.0	0.0	—	—	—	—	—
0.0	0.1	0.1	—	0.0	0.1	0.1
0.1	0.0	0.0	0.1	—	0.0	0.0
0.1	0.2	0.0	0.1	0.1	0.2	0.0
7.5	8.1	8.2	8.3	7.5	8.1	8.2
1.0	1.0	—	—	—	—	—
27.0	*26.3*	*35.0*	*27.3*	*21.8*	*24.1*	*29.7*
18.7	*17.5*	*21.2*	*17.7*	*17.0*	*16.1*	*17.9*
0.1	*0.1*	*0.1*	—	—	—	—
22.2	*22.0*	*33.6*	*19.6*	*19.8*	*19.1*	*26.9*
45.8	**43.9**	**56.3**	**45.0**	**38.8**	**40.2**	**47.6**

TOTAL OOF NET

1984	1985	1986	1983	1984	1985	1986
—	—	—	—	—	—	—
2.7	1.7	0.3	—	2.7	1.7	0.3
—	—	—	—	—	—	—
28.4	16.7	0.8	11.3	25.4	13.8	-7.8
—	—	—	73.7	—	—	—
145.6	55.4	107.5	185.5	130.1	39.0	92.5
—	—	—	—	—	—	—
—	—	—	—	—	—	—
—	—	—	—	—	-0.5	0.0
—	—	—	—	—	—	—
—	—	—	-0.1	-0.1	—	-0.1
—	—	—	—	-1.0	-0.3	-0.3
54.0	158.0	2.0	82.0	51.0	153.0	2.0
230.7	*231.8*	*110.6*	*352.4*	*208.1*	*206.6*	*86.5*
275.3	*284.0*	*537.1*	*153.3*	*231.7*	*239.3*	*454.2*
—	—	—	—	—	—	—
183.3	*81.9*	*122.2*	*274.2*	*161.6*	*58.6*	*94.1*
506.0	**515.8**	**647.7**	**505.7**	**439.7**	**446.0**	**540.8**

ODA COMMITMENTS : LOANS

DAC COUNTRIES

	1983	1984	1985	1986
Australia	—	—	—	—
Austria	0.3	—	—	—
Belgium	—	—	—	—
Canada	—	—	—	—
Denmark	—	—	—	—
Finland	—	—	—	—
France	—	—	—	—
Germany, Fed. Rep.	—	—	—	—
Ireland	—	—	—	—
Italy	—	—	—	—
Japan	—	—	—	—
Netherlands	—	—	0.4	—
New Zealand	—	—	—	—
Norway	—	—	—	—
Sweden	—	—	—	—
Switzerland	—	—	—	—
United Kingdom	—	—	—	—
United States	—	—	—	—
TOTAL	*0.3*	—	*0.4*	—
MULTILATERAL	—	—	*12.6*	—
OPEC COUNTRIES	—	—	—	—
E.E.C.+ MEMBERS	—	—	*0.4*	—
TOTAL	*0.3*	—	*13.0*	—

GRANT ELEMENT OF ODA

DAC COUNTRIES

	1983	1984	1985	1986
Australia	100.0	100.0	100.0	100.0
Austria	90.4	100.0	100.0	—
Belgium	—	—	—	100.0
Canada	100.0	100.0	100.0	100.0
Denmark	—	—	—	—
Finland	100.0	100.0	—	100.0
France	100.0	100.0	100.0	100.0
Germany, Fed. Rep.	100.0	100.0	100.0	100.0
Ireland	100.0	100.0	100.0	100.0
Italy	100.0	100.0	100.0	100.0
Japan	100.0	100.0	100.0	100.0
Netherlands	100.0	100.0	100.0	100.0
New Zealand	—	—	—	—
Norway	—	100.0	100.0	100.0
Sweden	—	—	—	100.0
Switzerland	—	—	—	—
United Kingdom	100.0	100.0	100.0	100.0
United States	100.0	100.0	—	100.0
TOTAL	*99.3*	*100.0*	*100.0*	*100.0*
MULTILATERAL	*100.0*	*100.0*	*100.0*	*100.0*
OPEC COUNTRIES	*100.0*	—	*100.0*	—
E.E.C.+ MEMBERS	*100.0*	*100.0*	*100.0*	*100.0*
TOTAL	**99.7**	**100.0**	**100.0**	**100.0**

OTHER AGGREGATES

COMMITMENTS: ALL SOURCES

	1983	1984	1985	1986
TOTAL BILATERAL	197.8	109.3	372.4	50.7
of which				
OPEC	0.0	—	0.0	—
CMEA	76.0	45.8	340.0	3.0
TOTAL MULTILATERAL	438.9	232.2	267.0	996.9
TOTAL BIL.& MULTIL.	636.7	341.5	639.4	1047.6
of which				
ODA Grants	62.8	55.3	46.5	65.5
ODA Loans	76.3	—	13.0	—

DISBURSEMENTS:

DAC COUNTRIES COMBINED

	1983	1984	1985	1986
OFFICIAL & PRIVATE				
GROSS:				
Contractual Lending	1813.0	988.9	1057.2	749.0
Export Credits Total	1546.2	868.9	994.7	624.0
Export Credits Private	1369.6	756.2	820.1	622.9
NET:				
Contractual Lending	1209.5	702.2	514.9	300.4
Export Credits Total	1019.5	603.8	473.2	191.5
PRIVATE SECTOR NET	1525.8	79.4	-314.0	312.6
Direct Investment	70.9	-491.9	-392.3	521.5
Portfolio Investment	600.3	62.1	-242.1	-418.3
Export Credits	854.5	509.3	320.4	209.4

MARKET BORROWING:

CHANGE IN CLAIMS

	1983	1984	1985	1986
Banks	—	-566.0	83.0	159.0

MEMORANDUM ITEM:

	1983	1984	1985	1986
CMEA Countr.(Gross)	—	—	—	—

TOTAL RECEIPTS NET

DAC COUNTRIES	1983	1984	1985	1986
Australia	5.4	-0.5	3.0	-0.8
Austria	0.1	0.1	0.1	0.2
Belgium	-1.5	5.3	-0.2	-1.7
Canada	52.8	49.7	53.5	39.4
Denmark	-0.3	-0.9	-1.0	-4.3
Finland	0.1	0.2	0.4	0.3
France	-21.3	-61.4	-44.2	-66.4
Germany, Fed. Rep.	17.1	31.1	69.4	100.9
Ireland	—	—	—	—
Italy	6.8	24.7	-7.9	49.7
Japan	63.4	57.7	92.8	166.8
Netherlands	9.5	12.7	13.8	27.6
New Zealand	0.0	0.0	0.0	0.0
Norway	13.3	12.0	10.5	16.1
Sweden	1.0	0.7	1.4	1.0
Switzerland	-18.8	5.0	0.6	5.3
United Kingdom	25.9	31.0	45.6	14.8
United States	66.0	13.0	162.0	253.0
TOTAL	*219.4*	*180.4*	*399.7*	*601.9*
MULTILATERAL				
AF.D.F.	—	—	—	—
AF.D.B.	—	—	—	—
AS.D.B	100.0	139.2	137.6	139.3
CAR.D.B.	—	—	—	—
E.E.C.	8.5	11.3	1.0	8.3
IBRD	10.8	6.6	29.3	75.0
IDA	100.3	125.6	100.2	124.2
I.D.B.	—	—	—	—
IFAD	6.5	13.8	13.9	14.0
I.F.C.	11.8	12.8	23.2	-9.4
IMF TRUST FUND	—	—	—	—
U.N. AGENCIES	—	—	—	—
UNDP	11.4	11.3	12.2	10.7
UNTA	2.2	1.9	2.0	1.9
UNICEF	11.5	10.0	7.9	5.9
UNRWA	—	—	—	—
WFP	98.9	65.5	81.8	64.0
UNHCR	82.7	81.1	64.7	75.0
Other Multilateral	4.8	3.7	4.0	5.0
Arab OPEC Agencies	30.3	52.1	34.0	-70.4
TOTAL	*479.7*	*534.9*	*512.0*	*443.4*
OPEC COUNTRIES	*-2.7*	*-50.7*	*-51.0*	*-71.6*
E.E.C.+ MEMBERS	*44.5*	*53.8*	*76.5*	*128.8*
TOTAL	**696.4**	**664.6**	**860.7**	**973.7**

TOTAL ODA NET

DAC COUNTRIES	1983	1984	1985	1986
Australia	6.7	0.8	3.6	0.5
Austria	0.1	0.1	0.1	0.2
Belgium	-0.4	6.4	-0.2	-1.0
Canada	55.0	53.7	58.4	44.4
Denmark	0.1	—	-0.2	-0.3
Finland	0.1	0.2	0.4	0.3
France	10.1	8.2	5.4	15.1
Germany, Fed. Rep.	9.1	34.6	74.0	74.9
Ireland	—	—	—	—
Italy	-0.4	-0.3	4.6	62.7
Japan	72.8	67.0	93.3	151.6
Netherlands	9.0	10.2	14.1	23.0
New Zealand	0.0	0.0	0.0	0.0
Norway	12.0	11.1	9.8	15.2
Sweden	1.0	0.7	1.4	1.0
Switzerland	1.9	5.2	3.8	5.3
United Kingdom	18.1	17.8	15.4	23.5
United States	59.0	87.0	144.0	194.0
TOTAL	*254.1*	*302.7*	*427.9*	*610.4*
MULTILATERAL				
AF.D.F.	—	—	—	—
AF.D.B.	—	—	—	—
AS.D.B	63.2	102.8	99.4	105.0
CAR.D.B.	—	—	—	—
E.E.C.	8.5	11.3	1.0	8.3
IBRD	4.6	1.2	1.0	1.0
IDA	100.3	125.6	100.2	124.2
I.D.B.	—	—	—	—
IFAD	6.5	13.8	13.9	14.0
I.F.C.	—	—	—	—
IMF TRUST FUND	—	—	—	—
U.N. AGENCIES	—	—	—	—
UNDP	11.4	11.3	12.2	10.7
UNTA	2.2	1.9	2.0	1.9
UNICEF	11.5	10.0	7.9	5.9
UNRWA	—	—	—	—
WFP	98.9	65.5	81.8	64.0
UNHCR	82.7	81.1	64.7	75.0
Other Multilateral	4.8	3.7	4.0	5.0
Arab OPEC Agencies	20.1	6.4	1.7	-1.8
TOTAL	*414.6*	*434.7*	*389.8*	*413.2*
OPEC COUNTRIES	*-0.1*	*-54.4*	*-82.5*	*-71.6*
E.E.C.+ MEMBERS	*54.0*	*88.1*	*114.1*	*206.2*
TOTAL	**668.6**	**683.0**	**735.2**	**951.9**

TOTAL ODA GROSS

	1983
Australia	6.7
Austria	0.1
Belgium	0.1
Canada	57.1
Denmark	0.1
Finland	0.1
France	11.2
Germany, Fed. Rep.	28.2
Ireland	—
Italy	1.3
Japan	92.7
Netherlands	12.8
New Zealand	0.0
Norway	12.0
Sweden	1.0
Switzerland	1.9
United Kingdom	25.2
United States	104.0
TOTAL	*354.4*
AF.D.F.	—
AF.D.B.	—
AS.D.B	64.3
CAR.D.B.	—
E.E.C.	8.5
IBRD	4.6
IDA	105.3
I.D.B.	—
IFAD	6.5
I.F.C.	—
IMF TRUST FUND	—
U.N. AGENCIES	—
UNDP	11.4
UNTA	2.2
UNICEF	11.5
UNRWA	—
WFP	98.9
UNHCR	82.7
Other Multilateral	4.8
Arab OPEC Agencies	20.5
TOTAL	*421.2*
OPEC COUNTRIES	*89.6*
E.E.C.+ MEMBERS	*87.3*
TOTAL	**865.2**

ODA LOANS GROSS

DAC COUNTRIES	1983	1984	1985	1986
Australia	—	—	—	—
Austria	—	—	—	—
Belgium	—	6.9	—	—
Canada	22.7	23.3	24.8	16.8
Denmark	—	—	—	—
Finland	—	—	—	—
France	7.5	7.2	6.1	17.7
Germany, Fed. Rep.	17.9	40.3	59.5	79.8
Ireland	—	—	—	—
Italy	—	—	—	52.6
Japan	47.3	41.3	67.4	136.0
Netherlands	5.1	2.9	10.4	5.7
New Zealand	—	—	—	—
Norway	0.0	0.7	—	1.0
Sweden	—	—	—	—
Switzerland	—	—	—	—
United Kingdom	0.6	0.3	0.2	0.7
United States	63.0	80.0	118.0	98.0
TOTAL	*164.2*	*202.9*	*286.5*	*408.2*
MULTILATERAL	*200.9*	*256.5*	*226.2*	*264.2*
OPEC COUNTRIES	*78.5*	*34.8*	*12.7*	*10.2*
E.E.C.+ MEMBERS	*31.1*	*57.6*	*76.2*	*156.4*
TOTAL	**443.7**	**494.1**	**525.4**	**682.6**

ODA LOANS NET

DAC COUNTRIES	1983	1984	1985	1986
Australia	—	—	—	—
Austria	—	—	—	—
Belgium	-0.5	6.3	-0.7	-1.1
Canada	20.6	19.7	20.6	11.8
Denmark	—	-0.1	-0.3	-0.4
Finland	—	—	—	—
France	6.4	5.9	4.1	13.7
Germany, Fed. Rep.	-1.2	23.3	50.7	38.4
Ireland	—	—	—	—
Italy	-1.7	-2.2	-1.3	51.8
Japan	27.4	21.3	50.0	112.7
Netherlands	1.4	-0.3	6.7	0.8
New Zealand	—	—	—	—
Norway	0.0	0.7	0.0	1.0
Sweden	—	—	—	—
Switzerland	—	—	—	—
United Kingdom	-6.5	-6.0	-5.9	-6.2
United States	18.0	34.0	57.0	28.0
TOTAL	*63.9*	*102.6*	*180.9*	*250.5*
MULTILATERAL	*194.4*	*248.5*	*214.5*	*239.7*
OPEC COUNTRIES	*-11.2*	*-63.3*	*-89.1*	*-73.4*
E.E.C.+ MEMBERS	*-2.2*	*26.9*	*53.3*	*97.0*
TOTAL	**247.2**	**287.7**	**306.4**	**416.7**

GRANTS

	1983
Australia	6.7
Austria	0.1
Belgium	0.1
Canada	34.4
Denmark	0.1
Finland	0.1
France	3.7
Germany, Fed. Rep.	10.3
Ireland	—
Italy	1.3
Japan	45.4
Netherlands	7.6
New Zealand	0.0
Norway	11.9
Sweden	1.0
Switzerland	1.9
United Kingdom	24.6
United States	41.0
TOTAL	*190.2*
MULTILATERAL	*220.2*
OPEC COUNTRIES	*11.1*
E.E.C.+ MEMBERS	*56.2*
TOTAL	**421.5**

TOTAL OFFICIAL GROSS

DAC COUNTRIES	1983	1984	1985	1986
Australia	6.7	0.8	3.6	0.5
Austria	0.1	0.1	0.1	0.2
Belgium	0.1	7.0	0.6	0.1
Canada	57.1	57.3	62.6	49.4
Denmark	0.1	0.2	0.2	0.1
Finland	0.1	0.2	0.4	0.3
France	11.2	9.5	7.5	19.0
Germany, Fed. Rep.	34.6	51.8	84.3	129.7
Ireland	—	—	—	—
Italy	1.3	1.9	5.9	63.5
Japan	92.7	87.0	110.7	174.9
Netherlands	12.9	15.8	18.4	28.7
New Zealand	0.0	0.0	0.0	0.0
Norway	12.0	11.1	9.8	15.2
Sweden	1.0	0.7	1.4	1.0
Switzerland	1.9	5.2	3.8	5.3
United Kingdom	25.2	24.1	21.5	30.4
United States	107.0	133.0	245.0	273.0
TOTAL	*364.0*	*405.7*	*575.7*	*791.2*
MULTILATERAL	*618.3*	*680.4*	*657.6*	*707.8*
OPEC COUNTRIES	*89.6*	*50.9*	*54.4*	*12.0*
E.E.C.+ MEMBERS	*93.9*	*121.6*	*139.3*	*279.7*
TOTAL	**1071.9**	**1137.0**	**1287.7**	**1511.1**

TOTAL OFFICIAL NET

DAC COUNTRIES	1983	1984	1985	1986
Australia	5.4	-0.5	2.6	-0.5
Austria	0.1	0.1	0.1	0.2
Belgium	-0.4	6.4	-0.2	-1.0
Canada	52.8	49.7	53.5	39.4
Denmark	-0.3	-0.9	-1.0	-4.3
Finland	0.1	0.2	0.4	0.3
France	10.1	8.2	5.4	14.7
Germany, Fed. Rep.	13.7	33.0	73.1	85.1
Ireland	—	—	—	—
Italy	-1.2	-0.6	3.6	62.3
Japan	72.8	67.0	93.3	151.6
Netherlands	9.2	12.7	14.7	23.2
New Zealand	0.0	0.0	0.0	0.0
Norway	12.0	11.1	9.8	15.2
Sweden	1.0	0.7	1.4	1.0
Switzerland	1.9	5.2	3.8	5.3
United Kingdom	18.1	17.8	15.4	23.5
United States	59.0	82.0	171.0	140.0
TOTAL	*254.2*	*292.1*	*446.8*	*556.0*
MULTILATERAL	*479.7*	*534.9*	*512.0*	*443.4*
OPEC COUNTRIES	*-2.7*	*-50.7*	*-51.0*	*-71.6*
E.E.C.+ MEMBERS	*57.7*	*87.8*	*112.0*	*211.8*
TOTAL	**731.2**	**776.2**	**907.8**	**927.9**

TOTAL OOF GROSS

	1983
Australia	—
Austria	—
Belgium	—
Canada	—
Denmark	—
Finland	—
France	—
Germany, Fed. Rep.	6.4
Ireland	—
Italy	—
Japan	—
Netherlands	0.2
New Zealand	—
Norway	—
Sweden	—
Switzerland	—
United Kingdom	—
United States	3.0
TOTAL	*9.5*
MULTILATERAL	*197.2*
OPEC COUNTRIES	*—*
E.E.C.+ MEMBERS	*6.5*
TOTAL	**206.7**

ODA COMMITMENTS

1984	1985	1986	1983	1984	1985	1986
0.8	3.6	0.5	7.2	1.0	0.7	3.2
0.1	0.1	0.2	0.1	0.1	0.4	—
7.0	0.5	0.1	—	6.9	—	0.1
57.3	62.6	49.4	34.3	53.4	101.1	57.4
0.2	0.1	0.1	—	0.1	0.2	0.2
0.2	0.4	0.3	0.1	0.2	0.2	—
9.5	7.5	19.0	16.4	13.2	14.7	19.0
51.6	82.8	116.3	135.5	86.5	74.2	95.9
—	—	—	—	—	—	—
1.9	5.9	63.5	4.9	22.2	61.3	14.8
87.0	110.7	174.9	102.9	209.5	149.7	23.2
13.4	17.7	27.9	17.4	18.1	13.2	29.0
0.0	0.0	0.0	0.0	0.0	0.0	—
11.1	9.8	15.2	7.9	24.8	13.8	16.3
0.7	1.4	1.0	0.9	1.2	1.3	1.0
5.2	3.8	5.3	2.2	4.3	11.1	5.4
24.1	21.5	30.4	42.4	12.5	45.1	14.0
133.0	205.0	264.0	329.2	205.2	320.7	314.4
403.0	*533.4*	*768.1*	*701.4*	*659.2*	*807.4*	*594.0*
—	—	—	—	—	—	—
—	—	—	—	—	—	—
104.6	101.8	108.4	185.3	209.8	302.9	258.9
—	—	—	—	—	—	—
11.3	1.0	8.3	13.0	5.0	2.5	28.1
1.2	1.0	1.0	—	—	—	—
131.9	109.4	138.8	178.8	332.8	87.0	177.2
—	—	—	—	—	—	—
13.8	13.9	18.5	24.3	8.5	0.2	—
—	—	—	—	—	—	—
—	—	—	211.4	173.5	172.7	162.5
11.3	12.2	10.7	—	—	—	—
1.9	2.0	1.9	—	—	—	—
10.0	7.9	5.9	—	—	—	—
—	—	—	—	—	—	—
65.5	81.8	64.0	—	—	—	—
81.1	64.7	75.0	—	—	—	—
3.7	4.0	5.0	—	—	—	—
6.5	1.7	0.3	32.0	11.3	—	20.1
442.8	*401.5*	*437.7*	*644.8*	*740.9*	*565.2*	*646.8*
43.7	*19.3*	*12.0*	*3.6*	*3.0*	*21.1*	*51.0*
118.8	*137.0*	*265.6*	*229.6*	*164.4*	*211.1*	*201.1*
889.4	*954.2*	*1217.8*	*1349.9*	*1403.0*	*1393.7*	*1291.7*

TECH. COOP. GRANTS

1984	1985	1986	1983	1984	1985	1986
0.8	3.6	0.5	0.5	0.5	0.6	0.5
0.1	0.1	0.2	0.1	—	—	—
0.1	0.5	0.1	—	0.0	—	0.0
34.0	37.9	32.6	1.0	—	4.9	—
0.2	0.1	0.1	0.1	0.2	0.1	0.1
0.2	0.4	0.3	0.0	0.1	0.2	0.0
2.3	1.4	1.4	0.8	0.8	0.6	0.9
11.3	23.3	36.5	6.8	8.5	11.3	17.5
—	—	—	—	—	—	—
1.9	5.9	10.9	0.9	0.8	4.8	9.2
45.7	43.3	38.8	3.5	3.0	4.7	6.9
10.5	7.4	22.2	2.1	2.5	3.6	6.6
0.0	0.0	0.0	0.0	0.0	0.0	0.0
10.4	9.8	14.2	0.2	0.3	0.3	0.3
0.7	1.4	1.0	—	0.6	0.5	0.6
5.2	3.8	5.3	0.4	0.5	0.6	0.7
23.8	21.3	29.7	3.1	3.9	4.5	6.8
53.0	87.0	166.0	12.0	20.0	44.0	72.0
200.1	*246.9*	*359.9*	*31.6*	*41.6*	*80.6*	*122.2*
186.3	*175.3*	*173.5*	*112.6*	*108.1*	*90.8*	*98.4*
8.9	*6.6*	*1.8*	—	—	—	—
61.2	*60.7*	*109.2*	*13.8*	*16.6*	*24.7*	*41.2*
395.3	*428.8*	*535.2*	*144.2*	*149.7*	*171.4*	*220.6*

TOTAL OOF NET

1984	1985	1986	1983	1984	1985	1986
—	—	—	-1.3	-1.3	-1.0	-1.0
—	—	—	—	—	—	—
—	0.0	0.0	—	—	0.0	0.0
—	—	—	-2.2	-4.0	-5.0	-4.9
—	0.2	—	-0.5	-0.9	-0.8	-4.1
—	—	—	—	—	—	—
—	—	—	—	—	—	-0.4
0.3	1.5	13.4	4.7	-1.6	-0.9	10.2
—	—	—	—	—	—	—
—	—	—	-0.7	-0.3	-1.0	-0.4
—	—	—	—	—	—	—
2.5	0.7	0.8	0.2	2.5	0.7	0.2
—	—	—	—	—	—	—
—	—	—	—	—	—	—
—	—	—	—	—	—	—
—	40.0	9.0	—	-5.0	27.0	-54.0
2.7	*42.3*	*23.1*	*0.1*	*-10.6*	*19.0*	*-54.4*
237.7	*256.1*	*270.1*	*65.1*	*100.2*	*122.2*	*30.3*
7.2	*35.0*	—	*-2.6*	*3.7*	*31.5*	—
2.7	*2.3*	*14.1*	*3.6*	*-0.3*	*-2.0*	*5.6*
247.6	*333.5*	*293.3*	*62.6*	*93.3*	*172.7*	*-24.1*

ODA COMMITMENTS : LOANS

DAC COUNTRIES

	1983	1984	1985	1986
Australia	—	—	0.3	—
Austria	—	—	—	—
Belgium	—	6.9	—	—
Canada	2.6	—	35.2	—
Denmark	—	—	—	—
Finland	—	—	—	—
France	12.8	10.9	13.4	17.7
Germany, Fed. Rep.	120.8	73.6	46.2	64.1
Ireland	—	—	—	—
Italy	—	20.0	49.6	2.1
Japan	76.8	167.6	97.7	—
Netherlands	9.5	6.0	—	7.4
New Zealand	—	—	—	—
Norway	1.2	0.7	—	1.0
Sweden	—	—	—	—
Switzerland	—	—	—	—
United Kingdom	—	—	—	—
United States	139.5	97.5	139.1	118.5
TOTAL	*363.1*	*383.1*	*381.3*	*210.7*
MULTILATERAL	*420.4*	*562.4*	*389.9*	*456.2*
OPEC COUNTRIES	—	—	*20.0*	*50.0*
E.E.C.+ MEMBERS	*143.0*	*117.4*	*109.2*	*91.2*
TOTAL	*783.4*	*945.5*	*791.2*	*716.9*

GRANT ELEMENT OF ODA

DAC COUNTRIES

	1983	1984	1985	1986
Australia	100.0	100.0	100.0	100.0
Austria	100.0	100.0	100.0	—
Belgium	—	83.3	—	100.0
Canada	99.3	100.0	96.5	100.0
Denmark	—	100.0	100.0	100.0
Finland	100.0	100.0	100.0	—
France	63.9	63.2	60.1	58.0
Germany, Fed. Rep.	81.8	75.6	76.6	78.5
Ireland	—	—	—	—
Italy	100.0	49.2	54.9	92.8
Japan	70.0	63.9	69.5	100.0
Netherlands	78.3	85.5	100.0	89.9
New Zealand	100.0	100.0	100.0	—
Norway	89.3	99.5	100.0	95.6
Sweden	100.0	100.0	100.0	100.0
Switzerland	100.0	100.0	100.0	100.0
United Kingdom	100.0	100.0	100.0	100.0
United States	87.3	85.5	86.9	88.6
TOTAL	*84.6*	*77.8*	*82.4*	*87.8*
MULTILATERAL	*86.6*	*85.8*	*85.2*	*85.1*
OPEC COUNTRIES	*100.0*	*100.0*	*35.3*	*50.4*
E.E.C.+ MEMBERS	*85.1*	*75.1*	*75.9*	*82.4*
TOTAL	*85.6*	*81.6*	*83.1*	*85.0*

OTHER AGGREGATES

COMMITMENTS: ALL SOURCES

	1983	1984	1985	1986
TOTAL BILATERAL	992.4	810.5	886.7	814.8
of which				
OPEC	8.6	71.9	28.6	77.0
CMEA	277.0	—	—	32.3
TOTAL MULTILATERAL	999.8	1056.9	1352.4	1612.7
TOTAL BIL.& MULTIL.	1992.2	1867.4	2239.1	2427.5
of which				
ODA Grants	566.4	457.5	602.6	574.8
ODA Loans	1060.4	945.5	791.2	749.2

DISBURSEMENTS:

DAC COUNTRIES COMBINED

	1983	1984	1985	1986
OFFICIAL & PRIVATE				
GROSS:				
Contractual Lending	257.9	309.2	410.5	388.3
Export Credits Total	93.4	103.9	123.2	-20.7
Export Credits Private	84.1	103.6	81.8	-43.1
NET:				
Contractual Lending	-9.5	33.9	141.8	110.7
Export Credits Total	-73.5	-71.1	-40.0	-136.5
PRIVATE SECTOR NET	-34.8	-111.6	-47.2	45.9
Direct Investment	-0.6	16.3	16.0	3.3
Portfolio Investment	39.2	-69.9	-5.0	128.0
Export Credits	-73.5	-58.1	-58.2	-85.4

MARKET BORROWING:

CHANGE IN CLAIMS

	1983	1984	1985	1986
Banks	—	76.0	691.0	38.0

MEMORANDUM ITEM:

	1983	1984	1985	1986
CMEA Countr.(Gross)	30.5	36.0	25.4	49.1

TOTAL RECEIPTS NET | TOTAL ODA NET | TOTAL ODA GROSS

	1983	1984	1985	1986	1983	1984	1985	1986		1983
TOTAL RECEIPTS NET					**TOTAL ODA NET**				**TOTAL ODA GROSS**	
DAC COUNTRIES										
Australia	0.0	–	–	–	–	–	–	–	Australia	–
Austria	0.0	–	–	–	0.0	–	–	–	Austria	0.0
Belgium	40.7	21.1	-53.9	-10.8	0.0	0.1	0.0	0.0	Belgium	0.0
Canada	-7.9	-6.7	-5.6	-0.8	0.7	0.5	0.5	0.3	Canada	0.7
Denmark	-25.7	-9.4	-23.1	-3.9	–	–	–	–	Denmark	–
Finland	-0.2	-1.3	–	–	–	–	–	–	Finland	–
France	-72.0	-10.6	-19.7	14.2	0.4	0.5	0.5	0.7	France	0.4
Germany, Fed. Rep.	-5.1	-12.7	21.8	141.5	0.8	4.1	0.9	1.2	Germany, Fed. Rep.	0.8
Ireland	–	–	–	–	–	–	–	–	Ireland	–
Italy	48.3	3.7	-2.5	-7.4	0.1	0.1	0.1	0.6	Italy	0.1
Japan	537.3	1428.0	1778.8	1565.5	4.2	4.9	4.1	5.7	Japan	4.2
Netherlands	-53.1	-6.4	20.6	1.2	0.6	0.4	0.4	0.4	Netherlands	0.6
New Zealand	–	–	–	–	–	–	–	–	New Zealand	–
Norway	-0.1	51.7	59.8	74.5	–	0.1	–	0.1	Norway	–
Sweden	6.4	6.8	-6.0	-6.3	–	0.1	–	–	Sweden	–
Switzerland	–	0.3	0.1	–	–	–	0.0	–	Switzerland	–
United Kingdom	-25.4	8.8	1.2	-26.9	0.1	0.1	0.1	0.1	United Kingdom	0.1
United States	243.0	-309.0	-123.0	15.0	16.0	46.0	38.0	19.0	United States	18.0
TOTAL	*686.2*	*1164.3*	*1648.6*	*1755.7*	*22.9*	*56.8*	*44.5*	*28.2*	*TOTAL*	*24.9*
MULTILATERAL										
AF.D.F.	–	–	–	–	–	–	–	–	AF.D.F.	–
AF.D.B.	–	–	–	–	–	–	–	–	AF.D.B.	–
AS.D.B	–	–	–	–	–	–	–	–	AS.D.B	–
CAR.D.B.	–	–	–	–	–	–	–	–	CAR.D.B.	–
E.E.C.	–	–	–	0.0	–	–	–	0.0	E.E.C.	–
IBRD	62.7	34.0	5.7	52.1	–	–	–	–	IBRD	–
IDA	–	–	–	–	–	–	–	–	IDA	–
I.D.B.	38.9	78.5	52.5	27.1	14.8	9.5	19.9	16.5	I.D.B.	17.6
IFAD	4.7	2.0	1.4	3.2	4.7	2.0	1.4	3.2	IFAD	4.7
I.F.C.	-0.1	–	16.8	13.8	–	–	–	–	I.F.C.	–
IMF TRUST FUND	–	–	–	–	–	–	–	–	IMF TRUST FUND	–
U.N. AGENCIES	–	–	–	–	–	–	–	–	U.N. AGENCIES	–
UNDP	2.2	2.3	2.1	2.6	2.2	2.3	2.1	2.6	UNDP	2.2
UNTA	0.8	0.6	0.5	0.9	0.8	0.6	0.5	0.9	UNTA	0.8
UNICEF	0.1	0.1	0.0	0.0	0.1	0.1	0.0	0.0	UNICEF	0.1
UNRWA	–	–	–	–	–	–	–	–	UNRWA	–
WFP	0.8	0.3	0.3	0.2	0.8	0.3	0.3	0.2	WFP	0.8
UNHCR	–	–	–	–	–	–	–	–	UNHCR	–
Other Multilateral	0.6	0.6	0.6	0.5	0.6	0.6	0.6	0.5	Other Multilateral	0.6
Arab OPEC Agencies	–	–	–	–	–	–	–	–	Arab OPEC Agencies	–
TOTAL	*110.7*	*118.2*	*79.9*	*100.5*	*24.0*	*15.2*	*24.7*	*24.0*	*TOTAL*	*26.8*
OPEC COUNTRIES	*31.3*	*11.4*	*-10.3*	*-12.0*	–	–	–	–	*OPEC COUNTRIES*	–
E.E.C.+ MEMBERS	*-92.3*	*-5.6*	*-55.5*	*107.9*	*2.0*	*5.3*	*1.9*	*3.1*	*E.E.C.+ MEMBERS*	*2.0*
TOTAL	*828.2*	*1293.9*	*1718.1*	*1844.2*	*46.9*	*72.1*	*69.2*	*52.2*	*TOTAL*	*51.7*

ODA LOANS GROSS | ODA LOANS NET | GRANTS

	1983	1984	1985	1986	1983	1984	1985	1986		1983
ODA LOANS GROSS					**ODA LOANS NET**				**GRANTS**	
DAC COUNTRIES										
Australia	–	–	–	–	–	–	–	–	Australia	0.0
Austria	–	–	–	–	–	–	–	–	Austria	0.0
Belgium	–	–	–	–	–	–	–	–	Belgium	–
Canada	–	–	–	–	–	–	–	–	Canada	0.7
Denmark	–	–	–	–	–	–	–	–	Denmark	–
Finland	–	–	–	–	–	–	–	–	Finland	–
France	–	–	–	–	–	–	–	–	France	0.4
Germany, Fed. Rep.	–	2.5	–	–	–	2.3	-0.2	-0.3	Germany, Fed. Rep.	0.8
Ireland	–	–	–	–	–	–	–	–	Ireland	–
Italy	–	–	–	–	–	–	–	–	Italy	0.1
Japan	–	–	–	–	–	–	–	–	Japan	4.2
Netherlands	–	–	–	–	–	–	–	–	Netherlands	0.6
New Zealand	–	–	–	–	–	–	–	–	New Zealand	–
Norway	–	–	–	–	–	–	–	–	Norway	–
Sweden	–	–	–	–	–	–	–	–	Sweden	–
Switzerland	–	–	–	–	–	–	–	–	Switzerland	–
United Kingdom	–	–	–	–	–	–	–	–	United Kingdom	0.1
United States	10.0	10.0	10.0	8.0	8.0	7.0	8.0	3.0	United States	8.0
TOTAL	*10.0*	*12.5*	*10.0*	*8.0*	*8.0*	*9.4*	*7.8*	*2.7*	*TOTAL*	*14.9*
MULTILATERAL	*18.2*	*17.3*	*27.1*	*26.5*	*15.4*	*11.5*	*20.2*	*19.7*	*MULTILATERAL*	*8.6*
OPEC COUNTRIES	–	–	–	–	–	–	–	–	*OPEC COUNTRIES*	–
E.E.C.+ MEMBERS	–	*2.5*	–	–	–	*2.3*	*-0.2*	*-0.3*	*E.E.C.+ MEMBERS*	*2.0*
TOTAL	*28.2*	*29.7*	*37.1*	*34.5*	*23.4*	*20.8*	*28.0*	*22.5*	*TOTAL*	*23.5*

TOTAL OFFICIAL GROSS | TOTAL OFFICIAL NET | TOTAL OOF GROSS

	1983	1984	1985	1986	1983	1984	1985	1986		1983
TOTAL OFFICIAL GROSS					**TOTAL OFFICIAL NET**				**TOTAL OOF GROSS**	
DAC COUNTRIES										
Australia	–	–	–	–	–	–	–	–	Australia	–
Austria	0.0	–	–	–	0.0	–	–	–	Austria	–
Belgium	0.0	0.1	0.1	0.1	0.0	0.1	0.1	0.1	Belgium	–
Canada	0.7	0.5	0.5	0.3	-7.9	-6.7	-5.6	-0.8	Canada	–
Denmark	–	–	–	–	–	–	–	–	Denmark	–
Finland	–	–	–	–	–	–	–	–	Finland	–
France	0.4	0.5	0.5	0.7	0.4	0.5	0.5	0.7	France	–
Germany, Fed. Rep.	12.3	4.2	1.1	1.5	11.6	2.9	-0.3	-8.3	Germany, Fed. Rep.	11.5
Ireland	–	–	–	–	–	–	–	–	Ireland	–
Italy	0.1	0.1	0.1	3.4	0.1	0.1	0.1	3.4	Italy	–
Japan	4.2	4.9	4.1	5.7	4.2	4.9	4.1	5.7	Japan	–
Netherlands	0.6	0.4	0.4	0.4	0.6	0.4	0.4	0.4	Netherlands	–
New Zealand	–	–	–	–	–	–	–	–	New Zealand	–
Norway	–	0.1	–	0.1	–	0.1	–	0.1	Norway	–
Sweden	11.3	8.9	1.0	–	9.8	6.8	1.0	-1.7	Sweden	11.3
Switzerland	–	–	0.0	–	–	–	0.0	–	Switzerland	–
United Kingdom	0.1	0.1	0.1	0.1	0.1	0.1	0.1	0.1	United Kingdom	–
United States	439.0	442.0	466.0	463.0	40.0	18.0	33.0	15.0	United States	421.0
TOTAL	*468.8*	*461.8*	*473.8*	*475.3*	*58.9*	*27.2*	*33.3*	*14.7*	*TOTAL*	*443.9*
MULTILATERAL	*160.2*	*145.3*	*112.7*	*157.3*	*110.7*	*118.2*	*79.9*	*100.5*	*MULTILATERAL*	*133.4*
OPEC COUNTRIES	*39.8*	*21.7*	*10.2*	*9.5*	*31.3*	*11.4*	*-10.3*	*-12.0*	*OPEC COUNTRIES*	*39.8*
E.E.C.+ MEMBERS	*13.5*	*5.4*	*2.2*	*6.2*	*12.8*	*4.1*	*0.8*	*-3.6*	*E.E.C.+ MEMBERS*	*11.5*
TOTAL	*668.8*	*628.8*	*596.7*	*642.1*	*201.0*	*156.7*	*102.8*	*103.2*	*TOTAL*	*617.1*

MILLION US DOLLARS, UNLESS OTHERWISE STATED

ODA COMMITMENTS

1984	1985	1986	1983	1984	1985	1986
—	—	—	—	—	—	—
0.1	0.0	0.0	—	—	—	0.0
0.5	0.5	0.3	0.7	0.4	0.7	0.2
—	—	—	—	—	—	—
—	—	—	—	—	—	—
—	—	—	—	—	—	—
0.5	0.5	0.7	0.4	0.5	0.5	0.7
4.2	1.1	1.5	1.2	3.7	0.6	5.2
—	—	—	—	—	—	—
0.1	0.1	0.6	0.2	0.1	0.2	0.7
4.9	4.1	5.7	4.7	4.8	4.5	6.1
0.4	0.4	0.4	0.7	0.4	0.3	0.4
—	—	—	—	—	—	—
0.1	—	0.1	—	0.1	—	0.1
0.1	—	—	—	0.1	—	—
—	0.0	—	—	—	—	—
0.1	0.1	0.1	0.1	0.1	0.1	0.1
49.0	40.0	24.0	8.6	42.5	47.0	30.9
59.9	*46.7*	*33.5*	*16.5*	*52.6*	*53.8*	*44.3*
—	—	—	—	—	—	—
—	—	—	—	—	—	—
—	—	—	—	—	—	—
—	—	0.0	0.0	—	—	0.1
—	—	—	—	—	—	—
—	—	—	—	—	—	—
15.3	26.1	22.6	7.0	8.4	19.7	1.0
2.0	2.0	3.9	8.9	—	6.2	—
—	—	—	—	—	—	—
—	—	—	4.6	3.8	3.4	4.2
2.3	2.1	2.6	—	—	—	—
0.6	0.5	0.9	—	—	—	—
0.1	0.0	0.0	—	—	—	—
—	—	—	—	—	—	—
0.3	0.3	0.2	—	—	—	—
—	—	—	—	—	—	—
0.6	0.6	0.5	—	—	—	—
—	—	—	—	—	—	—
21.1	*31.5*	*30.8*	*20.5*	*12.2*	*29.3*	*5.3*
—	—	—	—	—	—	—
5.4	*2.1*	*3.4*	*2.6*	*4.8*	*1.6*	*7.1*
81.0	*78.2*	*64.2*	*37.0*	*64.8*	*83.1*	*49.6*

TECH. COOP. GRANTS

1984	1985	1986	1983	1984	1985	1986
—	—	—	0.0	—	—	—
0.1	0.0	0.0	—	—	—	—
0.5	0.5	0.3	0.3	—	0.1	—
—	—	—	—	—	—	—
0.5	0.5	0.7	0.4	0.5	0.5	0.7
1.8	1.1	1.5	0.7	1.3	1.1	1.5
—	—	—	—	—	—	—
0.1	0.1	0.6	0.1	0.1	—	0.6
4.9	4.1	5.7	4.2	4.7	4.0	5.5
0.4	0.4	0.4	0.5	0.4	0.3	0.4
0.1	—	0.1	—	—	—	0.0
0.1	—	—	—	0.1	—	—
—	0.0	—	—	—	0.0	—
0.1	0.1	0.1	0.1	0.1	0.1	0.1
39.0	30.0	16.0	2.0	4.0	6.0	8.0
47.5	*36.7*	*25.5*	*8.4*	*11.2*	*12.1*	*16.8*
3.8	4.4	4.3	3.7	3.5	3.1	4.0
—	—	—	—	—	—	—
3.0	*2.1*	*3.4*	*1.8*	*2.4*	*1.9*	*3.3*
51.3	*41.2*	*29.7*	*12.1*	*14.7*	*15.2*	*20.7*

TOTAL OOF NET

1984	1985	1986	1983	1984	1985	1986
—	—	—	—	—	—	—
—	0.0	0.1	—	—	0.0	0.1
—	—	—	-8.6	-7.2	-6.1	-1.1
—	—	—	—	—	—	—
—	—	—	—	—	—	—
—	—	—	—	—	—	—
—	—	2.8	10.8	-1.2	-1.2	-9.6
—	—	—	—	—	—	2.8
—	—	—	—	—	—	—
—	—	—	—	—	—	—
8.8	1.0	—	9.8	6.8	1.0	-1.7
—	—	—	—	—	—	—
393.0	426.0	439.0	24.0	-28.0	-5.0	-4.0
401.8	*427.0*	*441.9*	*36.0*	*-29.7*	*-11.2*	*-13.5*
124.3	*81.3*	*126.6*	*86.7*	*103.0*	*55.2*	*76.5*
21.7	*10.2*	*9.5*	*31.3*	*11.4*	*-10.3*	*-12.0*
—	0.0	2.9	10.8	-1.2	-1.1	-6.7
547.8	*518.5*	*577.9*	*154.0*	*84.7*	*33.6*	*51.0*

ODA COMMITMENTS : LOANS

DAC COUNTRIES

	1983	1984	1985	1986
Australia	—	—	—	—
Austria	—	—	—	—
Belgium	—	—	—	—
Canada	—	—	—	—
Denmark	—	—	—	—
Finland	—	—	—	—
France	—	—	—	—
Germany, Fed. Rep.	—	2.5	—	—
Ireland	—	—	—	—
Italy	—	—	—	—
Japan	—	—	—	—
Netherlands	—	—	—	—
New Zealand	—	—	—	—
Norway	—	—	—	—
Sweden	—	—	—	—
Switzerland	—	—	—	—
United Kingdom	—	—	—	—
United States	3.8	5.0	8.2	7.2
TOTAL	*3.8*	*7.5*	*8.2*	*7.2*
MULTILATERAL	*15.9*	*8.4*	*25.9*	*1.0*
OPEC COUNTRIES	—	—	—	—
E.E.C.+ MEMBERS	—	*2.5*	—	—
TOTAL	*19.7*	*15.9*	*34.0*	*8.2*

GRANT ELEMENT OF ODA

DAC COUNTRIES

	1983	1984	1985	1986
Australia	—	—	—	—
Austria	—	—	—	—
Belgium	—	—	—	100.0
Canada	100.0	100.0	100.0	100.0
Denmark	—	—	—	—
Finland	—	—	—	—
France	100.0	100.0	100.0	100.0
Germany, Fed. Rep.	100.0	49.8	100.0	100.0
Ireland	—	—	—	—
Italy	100.0	100.0	100.0	100.0
Japan	100.0	100.0	100.0	100.0
Netherlands	100.0	100.0	100.0	100.0
New Zealand	—	—	—	—
Norway	—	100.0	—	100.0
Sweden	—	100.0	—	—
Switzerland	—	—	—	—
United Kingdom	100.0	100.0	100.0	100.0
United States	84.8	95.6	93.5	89.0
TOTAL	*92.1*	*93.0*	*94.3*	*92.3*
MULTILATERAL	*100.0*	*71.4*	*74.0*	*94.5*
OPEC COUNTRIES	—	—	—	—
E.E.C.+ MEMBERS	*100.0*	*61.4*	*100.0*	*100.0*
TOTAL	*93.8*	*87.2*	*89.0*	*92.5*

OTHER AGGREGATES

COMMITMENTS: ALL SOURCES

	1983	1984	1985	1986
TOTAL BILATERAL	84.9	97.6	89.9	80.0
of which				
OPEC	21.0	10.2	9.8	—
CMEA	—	—	—	—
TOTAL MULTILATERAL	233.1	12.2	134.7	222.7
TOTAL BIL.& MULTIL.	318.0	109.8	224.6	302.7
of which				
ODA Grants	17.3	49.0	49.1	41.4
ODA Loans	19.7	15.9	34.0	8.2

DISBURSEMENTS:

DAC COUNTRIES COMBINED

OFFICIAL & PRIVATE

	1983	1984	1985	1986
GROSS:				
Contractual Lending	748.5	587.3	471.7	478.2
Export Credits Total	317.5	181.9	35.7	28.4
Export Credits Private	294.7	173.0	34.7	28.4
NET:				
Contractual Lending	-47.9	-34.0	-199.1	-137.1
Export Credits Total	-86.9	-20.4	-203.9	-142.7
PRIVATE SECTOR NET	627.3	1137.1	1615.3	1741.0
Direct Investment	869.7	734.1	1294.8	1884.9
Portfolio Investment	-150.4	416.7	516.1	-17.6
Export Credits	-92.0	-13.7	-195.6	-126.3

MARKET BORROWING:

CHANGE IN CLAIMS

	1983	1984	1985	1986
Banks	—	—	—	—

MEMORANDUM ITEM:

	1983	1984	1985	1986
CMEA Countr.(Gross)	—	—	—	—

DISBURSEMENTS, UNLESS OTHERWISE STATED

	TOTAL RECEIPTS NET 1983	1984	1985	1986	TOTAL ODA NET 1983	1984	1985	1986	TOTAL ODA GROSS 1983
DAC COUNTRIES									
Australia	359.2	396.9	253.6	228.8	264.2	275.2	226.9	222.3	267.2
Austria	0.3	0.3	0.3	0.4	0.3	0.3	0.3	0.4	0.3
Belgium	0.6	1.2	0.1	-0.1	0.1	0.2	0.1	0.0	0.1
Canada	0.8	-0.7	-4.9	-10.4	0.4	0.7	0.5	0.2	0.4
Denmark	—	—	—	0.0	—	—	—	—	—
Finland	0.0	—	—	4.4	0.0	—	—	0.0	0.0
France	1.0	0.1	8.5	3.3	0.1	0.1	1.1	0.2	0.1
Germany, Fed. Rep.	58.0	39.0	12.8	3.7	2.1	8.9	3.4	5.9	2.1
Ireland	—	—	—	0.0	—	—	—	0.0	—
Italy	—	—	—	—	—	—	—	—	—
Japan	0.3	-5.9	26.8	-1.1	3.5	6.2	4.0	10.4	8.0
Netherlands	1.0	0.2	0.4	0.3	0.2	0.2	0.4	0.3	0.2
New Zealand	1.6	2.4	2.9	1.7	1.6	2.1	2.9	1.7	1.6
Norway	0.8	0.0	—	0.1	0.8	0.0	—	0.1	0.8
Sweden	—	—	—	—	—	—	—	—	—
Switzerland	0.1	0.1	—	0.1	0.1	0.1	—	0.1	0.1
United Kingdom	83.6	49.1	-1.5	-69.8	0.1	0.1	0.1	0.2	0.1
United States	1.0	1.0	1.0	1.0	1.0	1.0	1.0	1.0	1.0
TOTAL	*508.2*	*483.6*	*299.8*	*162.4*	*274.4*	*294.9*	*240.6*	*243.0*	*281.9*
MULTILATERAL									
AF.D.F.	—	—	—	—	—	—	—	—	—
AF.D.B.	—	—	—	—	—	—	—	—	—
AS.D.B	9.2	5.5	7.8	9.8	8.7	4.2	4.4	2.4	9.5
CAR.D.B.	—	—	—	—	—	—	—	—	—
E.E.C.	31.6	3.7	4.2	31.9	30.1	4.3	4.2	11.7	30.1
IBRD	6.1	9.9	9.1	9.2	—	—	—	—	—
IDA	16.6	13.5	3.5	—	16.6	13.5	3.5	—	16.9
I.D.B.	—	—	—	—	—	—	—	—	—
IFAD	—	0.1	0.5	0.8	—	0.1	0.5	0.8	—
I.F.C.	—	—	—	—	—	—	—	—	—
IMF TRUST FUND	—	—	—	—	—	—	—	—	—
U.N. AGENCIES	—	—	—	—	—	—	—	—	—
UNDP	1.6	1.3	1.3	1.1	1.6	1.3	1.3	1.1	1.6
UNTA	1.1	1.0	1.5	1.1	1.1	1.0	1.5	1.1	1.1
UNICEF	0.2	0.1	0.1	0.1	0.2	0.1	0.1	0.1	0.2
UNRWA	—	—	—	—	—	—	—	—	—
WFP	—	—	—	—	—	—	—	—	—
UNHCR	0.1	1.1	2.2	2.9	0.1	1.1	2.2	2.9	0.1
Other Multilateral	0.4	0.2	0.3	0.4	0.4	0.2	0.3	0.4	0.4
Arab OPEC Agencies	0.0	1.3	1.9	0.6	0.0	1.3	0.7	0.5	0.0
TOTAL	*66.9*	*37.6*	*32.3*	*57.8*	*58.7*	*27.1*	*18.6*	*20.8*	*59.8*
OPEC COUNTRIES	*-0.3*	*-0.2*	*-0.3*	*-0.2*	*-0.3*	*-0.2*	*-0.3*	*-0.2*	*—*
E.E.C.+ MEMBERS	*175.9*	*93.2*	*24.4*	*-30.8*	*32.6*	*13.7*	*9.3*	*18.3*	*32.6*
TOTAL	*574.8*	*521.0*	*331.8*	*220.0*	*332.8*	*321.8*	*258.9*	*263.6*	*341.7*

	ODA LOANS GROSS 1983	1984	1985	1986	ODA LOANS NET 1983	1984	1985	1986	GRANTS 1983
DAC COUNTRIES									
Australia	—	—	—	—	-3.0	-1.6	-0.2	-0.2	267.2
Austria	—	—	—	—	—	—	—	—	0.3
Belgium	—	—	—	—	—	—	—	—	0.1
Canada	—	—	—	—	—	—	—	—	0.4
Denmark	—	—	—	—	—	—	—	—	—
Finland	—	—	—	—	—	—	—	—	0.0
France	—	—	1.1	—	—	—	1.1	—	0.1
Germany, Fed. Rep.	0.1	6.3	0.0	1.7	0.1	6.3	0.0	1.7	2.0
Ireland	—	—	—	—	—	—	—	—	—
Italy	—	—	—	—	—	—	—	—	—
Japan	6.9	6.2	9.3	7.4	2.4	4.6	1.7	6.6	1.1
Netherlands	—	—	—	—	—	—	—	—	0.2
New Zealand	—	—	—	—	—	—	—	—	1.6
Norway	—	—	—	—	—	—	—	—	0.8
Sweden	—	—	—	—	—	—	—	—	—
Switzerland	—	—	—	—	—	—	—	—	0.1
United Kingdom	—	—	—	—	—	—	—	—	0.1
United States	—	—	—	—	—	—	—	—	1.0
TOTAL	*7.0*	*12.5*	*10.4*	*9.1*	*-0.6*	*9.3*	*2.6*	*8.2*	*275.0*
MULTILATERAL	*54.1*	*22.0*	*10.0*	*3.4*	*53.0*	*20.8*	*8.9*	*2.1*	*5.7*
OPEC COUNTRIES	*—*	*—*	*—*	*—*	*-0.3*	*-0.2*	*-0.3*	*-0.2*	*—*
E.E.C.+ MEMBERS	*28.0*	*9.4*	*2.2*	*1.7*	*28.0*	*9.4*	*2.2*	*1.6*	*4.6*
TOTAL	*61.1*	*34.4*	*20.4*	*12.6*	*52.2*	*29.9*	*11.2*	*10.0*	*280.6*

	TOTAL OFFICIAL GROSS 1983	1984	1985	1986	TOTAL OFFICIAL NET 1983	1984	1985	1986	TOTAL OOF GROSS 1983
DAC COUNTRIES									
Australia	361.7	319.0	227.0	222.6	357.8	316.6	215.2	149.9	94.5
Austria	0.3	0.3	0.3	0.4	0.3	0.3	0.3	0.4	—
Belgium	0.1	0.2	0.1	0.0	0.1	0.2	0.1	0.0	—
Canada	4.2	3.3	0.5	0.2	0.8	-0.7	-4.9	-10.4	3.8
Denmark	—	—	—	0.0	—	—	—	0.0	—
Finland	0.0	—	—	0.0	0.0	—	—	0.0	—
France	0.1	0.1	1.1	0.2	0.1	0.1	1.1	0.2	—
Germany, Fed. Rep.	33.6	29.6	3.4	5.9	33.6	29.6	3.4	5.9	31.5
Ireland	—	—	—	0.0	—	—	—	0.0	—
Italy	—	—	—	—	—	—	—	—	—
Japan	8.0	7.8	11.6	11.2	3.5	6.2	4.0	10.4	—
Netherlands	0.2	0.2	0.4	0.3	0.2	0.2	0.4	0.3	—
New Zealand	1.6	2.1	2.9	1.7	1.6	2.1	2.9	1.7	—
Norway	0.8	0.0	—	0.1	0.8	0.0	—	0.1	—
Sweden	—	—	—	—	—	—	—	—	—
Switzerland	0.1	0.1	—	0.1	0.1	0.1	—	0.1	—
United Kingdom	0.2	0.1	3.0	14.5	0.2	-0.2	2.4	13.9	0.2
United States	1.0	1.0	1.0	1.0	1.0	1.0	1.0	1.0	—
TOTAL	*411.8*	*363.8*	*251.3*	*258.3*	*400.0*	*355.4*	*225.8*	*173.7*	*129.9*
MULTILATERAL	*72.2*	*43.7*	*38.3*	*66.7*	*66.9*	*37.6*	*32.3*	*57.8*	*12.4*
OPEC COUNTRIES	*—*	*—*	*—*	*—*	*-0.3*	*-0.2*	*-0.3*	*-0.2*	*—*
E.E.C.+ MEMBERS	*66.3*	*34.4*	*12.2*	*53.8*	*65.8*	*33.5*	*11.6*	*52.3*	*33.7*
TOTAL	*484.0*	*407.5*	*289.6*	*325.0*	*466.6*	*392.8*	*257.8*	*231.2*	*142.3*

ODA COMMITMENTS

1984	1985	1986		1983	1984	1985	1986
276.7	227.0	222.5		275.0	282.3	229.2	221.3
0.3	0.3	0.4		–	–	0.3	–
0.2	0.1	0.0		–	–	–	0.0
0.7	0.5	0.2		0.6	0.8	0.5	0.5
–	–	0.0		0.0	–	–	–
0.1	1.1	0.2		0.1	0.1	0.1	0.2
8.9	3.4	5.9		8.0	9.4	5.1	2.4
–	–	0.0		–	–	–	0.0
7.8	11.6	11.2		24.5	4.0	4.6	4.5
0.2	0.4	0.3		0.2	0.3	0.3	0.3
2.1	2.9	1.7		1.4	3.0	6.1	1.1
0.0	–	0.1		–	0.0	–	0.1
–	–	–		–	–	–	–
0.1	–	0.1		–	0.0	–	–
0.1	0.1	0.2		0.1	0.1	0.1	0.2
1.0	1.0	1.0		0.5	0.6	0.6	0.7
298.1	*248.4*	*243.9*		*310.3*	*300.5*	*246.7*	*231.3*
–	–	–		–	–	–	–
5.1	5.3	3.3		15.0	15.0	12.6	15.9
–	–	–		–	–	–	–
4.3	4.2	11.8		28.6	1.7	4.7	18.5
–	–	–		–	–	–	–
13.7	3.8	0.3		–	–	–	–
–	–	–		–	–	–	–
0.1	0.5	0.8		0.2	–	–	3.7
–	–	–		–	–	–	–
–	–	–		3.3	3.7	5.4	5.5
1.3	1.3	1.1		–	–	–	–
1.0	1.5	1.1		–	–	–	–
0.1	0.1	0.1		–	–	–	–
–	–	–		–	–	–	–
–	–	–		–	–	–	–
1.1	2.2	2.9		–	–	–	–
0.2	0.3	0.4		–	–	–	–
1.3	0.7	0.5		–	–	–	–
28.2	*19.7*	*22.2*		*47.1*	*20.4*	*22.7*	*43.6*
–	–	–		–	–	–	–
13.7	9.3	18.5		37.0	11.5	10.2	21.7
326.3	*268.1*	*266.1*		*357.4*	*320.9*	*269.4*	*274.9*

TECH. COOP. GRANTS

1984	1985	1986		1983	1984	1985	1986
276.7	227.0	222.5		2.6	5.4	6.0	5.2
0.3	0.3	0.4		0.3	–	–	–
0.2	0.1	0.0		–	0.0	0.0	0.0
0.7	0.5	0.2		2.0	–	1.7	–
–	–	0.0		0.0	–	–	0.0
0.1	0.1	0.2		0.1	0.1	0.1	0.2
2.6	3.4	4.1		2.0	2.3	3.2	3.9
–	–	0.0		–	–	–	0.0
1.6	2.3	3.9		1.1	1.6	2.2	3.4
0.2	0.4	0.3		0.1	0.1	0.2	0.1
2.1	2.9	1.7		0.6	0.5	0.7	0.6
0.0	–	0.1		–	0.0	–	0.1
–	–	–		–	–	–	–
0.1	–	0.1		0.1	0.1	–	0.1
0.1	0.1	0.2		0.1	0.1	0.1	0.2
1.0	1.0	1.0		1.0	1.0	1.0	1.0
285.6	*238.0*	*234.8*		*10.1*	*11.2*	*15.2*	*14.8*
6.2	9.7	18.7		3.3	3.7	5.4	5.8
–	–	–		–	–	–	–
4.3	7.1	16.8		2.3	2.6	3.6	4.8
291.9	*247.7*	*253.6*		*13.4*	*14.9*	*20.5*	*20.6*

TOTAL OOF NET

1984	1985	1986		1983	1984	1985	1986
42.3	–	0.1		93.6	41.4	-11.7	-72.4
–	–	–		–	–	–	–
2.7	–	–		0.4	-1.4	-5.5	-10.6
–	–	0.0		–	–	–	0.0
–	–	–		–	–	–	–
20.7	–	–		31.5	20.7	–	–
–	–	–		–	–	–	–
–	–	–		–	–	–	–
–	–	–		–	–	–	–
–	–	–		–	–	–	–
–	–	–		–	–	–	–
–	2.9	14.2		0.2	-0.3	2.4	13.7
–	–	–		–	–	–	–
65.7	2.9	14.3		125.6	60.5	-14.8	-69.3
15.6	18.5	44.6		8.2	10.6	13.7	37.0
–	–	–		–	–	–	–
20.7	2.9	35.3		33.2	19.8	2.4	33.9
81.2	*21.5*	*58.9*		*133.8*	*71.0*	*-1.1*	*-32.3*

ODA COMMITMENTS : LOANS

DAC COUNTRIES

	1983	1984	1985	1986
Australia	–	–	–	–
Austria	–	–	–	–
Belgium	–	–	–	–
Canada	–	–	–	–
Denmark	–	–	–	–
Finland	–	–	–	–
France	–	–	–	–
Germany, Fed. Rep.	3.6	7.0	–	–
Ireland	–	–	–	–
Italy	–	–	–	–
Japan	23.2	2.3	2.0	0.5
Netherlands	–	–	–	–
New Zealand	–	–	–	–
Norway	–	–	–	–
Sweden	–	–	–	–
Switzerland	–	–	–	–
United Kingdom	–	–	–	–
United States	–	–	–	–
TOTAL	*26.8*	*9.4*	*2.0*	*0.5*
MULTILATERAL	*42.0*	*15.0*	*12.6*	*19.6*
OPEC COUNTRIES				
E.E.C.+ MEMBERS	*30.6*	*7.0*	*–*	*–*
TOTAL	*68.9*	*24.4*	*14.6*	*20.0*

GRANT ELEMENT OF ODA

DAC COUNTRIES

	1983	1984	1985	1986
Australia	100.0	100.0	100.0	100.0
Austria	–	–	100.0	–
Belgium	–	–	–	100.0
Canada	100.0	100.0	100.0	100.0
Denmark	–	–	–	–
Finland	100.0	–	–	–
France	100.0	100.0	100.0	100.0
Germany, Fed. Rep.	84.9	74.5	100.0	100.0
Ireland	–	–	–	100.0
Italy	–	–	–	–
Japan	56.9	66.0	78.0	95.5
Netherlands	100.0	100.0	100.0	100.0
New Zealand	100.0	100.0	100.0	100.0
Norway	–	100.0	–	100.0
Sweden	–	–	–	–
Switzerland	–	100.0	–	–
United Kingdom	100.0	100.0	100.0	100.0
United States	100.0	100.0	100.0	100.0
TOTAL	*96.2*	*98.8*	*99.6*	*99.9*
MULTILATERAL	*69.5*	*84.0*	*90.1*	*88.6*
OPEC COUNTRIES				
E.E.C.+ MEMBERS	*87.8*	*79.3*	*100.0*	*100.0*
TOTAL	*93.9*	*97.8*	*98.9*	*98.1*

OTHER AGGREGATES

COMMITMENTS: ALL SOURCES

	1983	1984	1985	1986
TOTAL BILATERAL	331.3	305.1	266.9	248.3
of which				
OPEC	–	–	–	–
CMEA				
TOTAL MULTILATERAL	106.9	97.7	85.5	168.0
TOTAL BIL.& MULTIL.	438.2	402.7	352.4	416.3
of which				
ODA Grants	288.5	296.6	254.9	254.9
ODA Loans	68.9	24.4	14.6	20.0

DISBURSEMENTS:

DAC COUNTRIES COMBINED

OFFICIAL & PRIVATE

	1983	1984	1985	1986
GROSS:				
Contractual Lending	238.1	118.1	25.2	28.1
Export Credits Total	199.5	85.0	11.9	4.8
Export Credits Private	101.2	40.0	11.9	4.7
NET:				
Contractual Lending	203.5	101.4	-19.3	-146.5
Export Credits Total	172.4	71.6	-24.3	-168.4
PRIVATE SECTOR NET	108.2	128.2	74.0	-11.2
Direct Investment	11.7	81.7	40.8	74.8
Portfolio Investment	18.0	14.9	40.4	-0.7
Export Credits	78.5	31.6	-7.1	-85.4

MARKET BORROWING:

CHANGE IN CLAIMS

	1983	1984	1985	1986
Banks	–	17.0	64.0	-78.0

MEMORANDUM ITEM:

	1983	1984	1985	1986
CMEA Countr.(Gross)	–	–	–	–

DISBURSEMENTS, UNLESS OTHERWISE STATED

TOTAL RECEIPTS NET / TOTAL ODA NET / TOTAL ODA GROSS

	TOTAL RECEIPTS NET				TOTAL ODA NET				TOTAL ODA GROSS
	1983	1984	1985	1986	1983	1984	1985	1986	1983
DAC COUNTRIES									
Australia	—	—	—	—	—	—	—	—	—
Austria	0.0	—	—	0.0	0.0	—	—	0.0	0.0
Belgium	2.6	2.4	9.0	-1.3	0.2	0.3	0.1	0.2	0.2
Canada	0.4	0.3	0.2	0.1	0.4	0.3	0.2	0.1	0.4
Denmark	0.0	0.0	-0.1	-0.2	—	—	—	—	—
Finland	—	—	—	—	—	—	—	—	—
France	38.2	34.2	20.6	24.0	0.3	2.4	0.3	0.5	0.3
Germany, Fed. Rep.	18.1	3.4	2.4	12.6	6.2	5.6	6.7	10.0	7.2
Ireland	—	—	—	—	—	—	—	—	—
Italy	0.1	0.0	0.2	-0.5	0.2	0.2	0.3	0.4	0.2
Japan	45.9	31.6	13.2	28.8	21.8	23.0	18.9	34.1	26.0
Netherlands	6.9	4.9	-1.8	-7.8	0.9	0.2	0.3	0.4	0.9
New Zealand	—	—	—	—	—	—	—	—	—
Norway	—	—	—	—	—	—	—	—	—
Sweden	0.5	-0.6	—	-0.1	—	—	—	—	—
Switzerland	0.1	0.7	0.4	0.7	0.8	0.8	0.6	0.7	0.8
United Kingdom	12.4	2.8	-13.4	6.9	2.0	0.3	0.1	0.3	2.0
United States	3.0	-1.0	1.0	-1.0	3.0	—	1.0	-1.0	4.0
TOTAL	*128.2*	*78.6*	*31.7*	*62.1*	*35.7*	*33.1*	*28.3*	*45.6*	*42.0*
MULTILATERAL									
AF.D.F.	—	—	—	—	—	—	—	—	—
AF.D.B.	—	—	—	—	—	—	—	—	—
AS.D.B	—	—	—	—	—	—	—	—	—
CAR.D.B.	—	—	—	—	—	—	—	—	—
E.E.C.	0.1	1.4	0.1	2.6	0.1	1.4	0.1	2.6	0.1
IBRD	21.1	44.4	23.9	6.2	—	—	—	—	—
IDA	-0.1	-0.5	-0.7	-0.9	-0.1	-0.5	-0.7	-0.9	0.4
I.D.B.	14.0	19.7	21.4	37.0	7.0	9.5	16.5	13.3	13.6
IFAD	1.5	0.1	1.1	2.4	1.5	0.1	1.1	2.4	1.5
I.F.C.	3.1	—	0.8	-0.4	—	—	—	—	—
IMF TRUST FUND	—	—	—	—	—	—	—	—	—
U.N. AGENCIES	—	—	—	—	—	—	—	—	—
UNDP	1.7	1.1	1.4	1.6	1.7	1.1	1.4	1.6	1.7
UNTA	0.5	0.4	0.4	0.4	0.5	0.4	0.4	0.4	0.5
UNICEF	0.3	0.3	0.3	0.3	0.3	0.3	0.3	0.3	0.3
UNRWA	—	—	—	—	—	—	—	—	—
WFP	0.9	3.7	2.0	1.1	0.9	3.7	2.0	1.1	0.9
UNHCR	—	—	—	—	—	—	—	—	—
Other Multilateral	0.6	0.5	0.5	0.5	0.6	0.5	0.5	0.5	0.6
Arab OPEC Agencies	3.1	0.8	0.2	-0.4	3.1	0.8	0.2	-0.4	3.2
TOTAL	*46.9*	*71.7*	*51.4*	*50.2*	*15.7*	*17.3*	*21.8*	*20.8*	*22.9*
OPEC COUNTRIES	—	—	—	—	—	—	—	—	—
E.E.C.+ MEMBERS	*78.4*	*49.1*	*17.1*	*36.2*	*9.8*	*10.4*	*7.8*	*14.3*	*10.8*
TOTAL	*175.1*	*150.3*	*83.2*	*112.3*	*51.3*	*50.4*	*50.1*	*66.4*	*64.9*

ODA LOANS GROSS / ODA LOANS NET / GRANTS

	ODA LOANS GROSS				ODA LOANS NET				GRANTS
	1983	1984	1985	1986	1983	1984	1985	1986	1983
DAC COUNTRIES									
Australia	—	—	—	—	—	—	—	—	—
Austria	—	—	—	—	—	—	—	—	0.0
Belgium	—	—	—	—	—	—	—	—	0.2
Canada	—	—	—	—	0.0	—	0.0	0.0	0.4
Denmark	—	—	—	—	—	—	—	—	—
Finland	—	—	—	—	—	—	—	—	—
France	—	1.8	—	—	—	1.8	—	—	0.3
Germany, Fed. Rep.	3.4	2.8	3.1	6.1	2.4	1.8	2.4	4.4	3.8
Ireland	—	—	—	—	—	—	—	—	—
Italy	—	—	—	—	—	—	—	—	0.2
Japan	15.7	9.5	4.7	10.7	11.5	9.0	2.2	6.6	10.3
Netherlands	—	—	—	—	—	—	—	—	0.9
New Zealand	—	—	—	—	—	—	—	—	—
Norway	—	—	—	—	—	—	—	—	—
Sweden	—	—	—	—	—	—	—	—	—
Switzerland	—	—	—	—	—	—	—	—	0.8
United Kingdom	1.6	0.2	—	—	1.6	0.2	—	—	0.3
United States	1.0	—	1.0	—	—	-2.0	-1.0	-2.0	3.0
TOTAL	*21.7*	*14.3*	*8.9*	*16.8*	*15.4*	*10.8*	*3.6*	*9.0*	*20.2*
MULTILATERAL	*18.6*	*14.3*	*25.4*	*23.6*	*11.4*	*7.1*	*17.1*	*14.1*	*4.3*
OPEC COUNTRIES	—	—	—	—	—	—	—	—	—
E.E.C.+ MEMBERS	*5.0*	*4.8*	*3.1*	*6.1*	*4.0*	*3.8*	*2.4*	*4.4*	*5.8*
TOTAL	*40.4*	*28.6*	*34.2*	*40.4*	*26.8*	*18.0*	*20.7*	*23.1*	*24.5*

TOTAL OFFICIAL GROSS / TOTAL OFFICIAL NET / TOTAL OOF GROSS

	TOTAL OFFICIAL GROSS				TOTAL OFFICIAL NET				TOTAL OOF GROSS
	1983	1984	1985	1986	1983	1984	1985	1986	1983
DAC COUNTRIES									
Australia	—	—	—	—	—	—	—	—	—
Austria	0.0	—	—	0.0	0.0	—	—	0.0	—
Belgium	0.2	0.3	0.1	0.2	0.2	0.3	0.1	0.2	—
Canada	0.4	0.3	0.2	0.1	0.4	0.3	0.2	0.1	—
Denmark	—	—	—	—	—	—	—	—	—
Finland	—	—	—	—	—	—	—	—	—
France	0.3	2.4	0.3	0.5	0.3	2.4	0.3	0.5	—
Germany, Fed. Rep.	12.4	7.1	8.1	13.5	3.3	3.1	4.1	9.0	5.2
Ireland	—	—	—	—	—	—	—	—	—
Italy	0.2	0.2	0.3	0.4	0.1	0.0	0.3	0.2	—
Japan	52.1	33.6	21.4	38.1	47.9	32.2	14.5	31.0	26.1
Netherlands	0.9	0.2	0.3	0.4	0.9	0.2	0.3	0.4	—
New Zealand	—	—	—	—	—	—	—	—	—
Norway	—	—	—	—	—	—	—	—	—
Sweden	0.8	—	—	—	0.8	-0.2	—	—	0.8
Switzerland	0.8	0.8	0.6	0.7	0.8	0.8	0.6	0.7	—
United Kingdom	2.0	0.3	0.1	0.3	2.0	0.3	0.1	0.3	—
United States	5.0	2.0	3.0	1.0	3.0	-1.0	1.0	-1.0	1.0
TOTAL	*75.0*	*47.2*	*34.3*	*55.1*	*59.6*	*38.3*	*21.3*	*41.3*	*33.1*
MULTILATERAL	*62.8*	*94.4*	*76.2*	*83.0*	*46.9*	*71.7*	*51.4*	*50.2*	*39.9*
OPEC COUNTRIES	—	—	—	—	—	—	—	—	—
E.E.C.+ MEMBERS	*16.0*	*11.9*	*9.2*	*17.8*	*6.8*	*7.7*	*5.2*	*13.1*	*5.2*
TOTAL	*137.8*	*141.5*	*110.5*	*138.1*	*106.5*	*110.0*	*72.8*	*91.5*	*72.9*

PARAGUAY

ODA COMMITMENTS

1984	1985	1986	1983	1984	1985	1986
–	–	–	0.0	–	–	–
–	–	0.0	0.0	–	–	–
0.3	0.1	0.2	–	–	–	0.2
0.3	0.2	0.1	0.4	0.4	0.1	0.2
–	–	–	–	–	–	–
–	–	–	–	–	–	–
2.4	0.3	0.5	3.5	4.9	0.3	0.5
6.6	7.4	11.8	7.7	4.5	5.9	12.5
–	–	–	–	–	–	–
0.2	0.3	0.4	0.2	0.2	0.4	0.5
23.6	21.4	38.1	13.9	21.3	67.4	33.7
0.2	0.3	0.4	1.1	0.2	0.3	0.3
–	–	–	–	–	–	–
–	–	–	–	–	–	–
–	–	–	–	0.3	0.7	–
0.8	0.6	0.7	0.5	0.8	0.3	1.0
0.3	0.1	0.3	0.3	0.1	0.1	0.3
2.0	3.0	1.0	1.3	1.3	1.7	2.0
36.6	*33.5*	*53.4*	*29.0*	*33.9*	*77.1*	*51.0*
–	–	–	–	–	–	–
–	–	–	–	–	–	–
–	–	–	–	–	–	–
1.4	0.1	2.6	1.7	0.2	0.0	0.0
–	–	–	–	–	–	–
16.0	23.6	21.0	48.6	–	–	–
0.3	1.6	2.9	–	7.0	–	–
–	–	–	–	–	–	–
–	–	–	4.1	6.0	4.6	3.9
1.1	1.4	1.6	–	–	–	–
0.4	0.4	0.4	–	–	–	–
0.3	0.3	0.3	–	–	–	–
–	–	–	–	–	–	–
3.7	2.0	1.1	–	–	–	–
–	–	–	–	–	–	–
0.5	0.5	0.5	–	–	–	–
0.8	0.2	–	–	–	–	–
24.5	*30.1*	*30.3*	*54.3*	*13.2*	*4.6*	*3.9*
–	–	–	–	–	–	–
11.4	*8.5*	*16.1*	*14.5*	*10.0*	*6.9*	*14.3*
61.0	**63.6**	**83.8**	**83.3**	**47.1**	**81.7**	**54.9**

TECH. COOP. GRANTS

1984	1985	1986	1983	1984	1985	1986
–	–	0.0	0.0	–	–	–
0.3	0.1	0.2	–	–	–	0.0
0.3	0.2	0.1	0.2	–	0.1	–
–	–	–	–	–	–	–
0.6	0.3	0.5	0.3	0.6	0.3	0.5
3.8	4.3	5.6	3.5	3.7	4.3	5.5
–	–	–	–	–	–	–
0.2	0.3	0.4	0.1	0.2	0.3	0.4
14.0	16.7	27.4	9.5	13.0	13.1	18.4
0.2	0.3	0.4	0.7	0.1	0.3	0.3
–	–	–	–	–	–	–
–	–	–	–	–	–	–
0.8	0.6	0.7	0.4	0.3	0.1	0.1
0.1	0.1	0.3	0.3	0.1	0.1	0.3
2.0	2.0	1.0	2.0	1.0	2.0	1.0
22.3	*24.7*	*36.6*	*16.9*	*19.0*	*20.3*	*26.5*
10.1	*4.7*	*6.7*	*3.1*	*2.3*	*2.6*	*2.8*
–	–	–	–	–	–	–
6.6	*5.4*	*10.0*	*4.8*	*4.7*	*5.1*	*7.1*
32.4	**29.4**	**43.3**	**20.0**	**21.3**	**22.9**	**29.3**

TOTAL OOF NET

1984	1985	1986	1983	1984	1985	1986
–	–	–	–	–	–	–
–	–	–	–	–	–	–
–	–	–	–	–	–	–
–	–	–	–	–	–	–
–	–	–	–	–	–	–
–	–	–	–	–	–	–
0.6	0.8	1.7	-2.9	-2.5	-2.5	-1.1
–	–	–	-0.1	-0.2	–	-0.2
10.1	–	–	26.1	9.1	-4.4	-3.1
–	–	–	–	–	–	–
–	–	–	0.8	-0.2	–	–
–	–	–	–	–	–	–
–	–	–	–	-1.0	–	–
10.6	*0.8*	*1.7*	*24.0*	*5.2*	*-6.9*	*-4.3*
69.9	*46.1*	*52.7*	*31.2*	*54.5*	*29.6*	*29.4*
–	–	–	–	–	–	–
0.6	*0.8*	*1.7*	*-2.9*	*-2.7*	*-2.5*	*-1.2*
80.5	**46.9**	**54.4**	**55.2**	**59.7**	**22.7**	**25.1**

ODA COMMITMENTS : LOANS

DAC COUNTRIES

	1983	1984	1985	1986
Australia	–	–	–	–
Austria	–	–	–	–
Belgium	–	–	–	–
Canada	–	–	–	–
Denmark	–	–	–	–
Finland	–	–	–	–
France	3.2	4.3	–	–
Germany, Fed. Rep.	3.9	–	–	–
Ireland	–	–	–	–
Italy	–	–	–	–
Japan	3.3	3.7	46.2	4.7
Netherlands	–	–	–	–
New Zealand	–	–	–	–
Norway	–	–	–	–
Sweden	–	–	–	–
Switzerland	–	–	–	–
United Kingdom	–	–	–	–
United States	–	–	–	–
TOTAL	*10.4*	*8.0*	*46.2*	*4.7*
MULTILATERAL	*48.6*	*7.0*	–	–
OPEC COUNTRIES	–	–	–	–
E.E.C.+ MEMBERS	*7.1*	*4.3*	–	–
TOTAL	**59.0**	**15.0**	**46.2**	**4.7**

GRANT ELEMENT OF ODA

DAC COUNTRIES

	1983	1984	1985	1986
Australia	100.0	–	–	–
Austria	100.0	–	–	–
Belgium	–	–	–	100.0
Canada	100.0	100.0	100.0	100.0
Denmark	–	–	–	–
Finland	–	–	–	–
France	71.0	72.4	100.0	100.0
Germany, Fed. Rep.	66.4	100.0	100.0	100.0
Ireland	–	–	–	–
Italy	100.0	100.0	100.0	100.0
Japan	82.5	87.1	57.7	88.9
Netherlands	100.0	100.0	100.0	100.0
New Zealand	–	–	–	–
Norway	–	–	–	–
Sweden	–	100.0	100.0	–
Switzerland	100.0	100.0	100.0	100.0
United Kingdom	100.0	100.0	100.0	100.0
United States	100.0	100.0	100.0	100.0
TOTAL	*79.2*	*88.0*	*63.0*	*92.6*
MULTILATERAL	*78.0*	*83.3*	*87.4*	*100.0*
OPEC COUNTRIES	–	–	–	–
E.E.C.+ MEMBERS	*75.2*	*86.7*	*100.0*	*100.0*
TOTAL	**78.3**	**86.2**	**66.4**	**93.2**

OTHER AGGREGATES

COMMITMENTS: ALL SOURCES

	1983	1984	1985	1986
TOTAL BILATERAL	72.4	33.9	77.8	51.0
of which				
OPEC	–	–	–	–
CMEA	–	–	–	–
TOTAL MULTILATERAL	94.3	87.8	5.4	4.2
TOTAL BIL.& MULTIL.	166.7	121.7	83.2	55.2
of which				
ODA Grants	24.3	32.1	35.5	50.2
ODA Loans	59.0	15.0	46.2	4.7

DISBURSEMENTS:

DAC COUNTRIES COMBINED

	1983	1984	1985	1986
OFFICIAL & PRIVATE				
GROSS:				
Contractual Lending	125.6	60.4	37.6	49.6
Export Credits Total	102.9	45.7	28.2	32.7
Export Credits Private	70.8	35.5	28.0	31.1
NET:				
Contractual Lending	83.3	37.0	10.2	22.0
Export Credits Total	66.8	25.9	6.1	13.1
PRIVATE SECTOR NET	68.6	40.3	10.4	20.8
Direct Investment	2.6	4.0	-13.6	-1.0
Portfolio Investment	22.2	15.3	10.5	4.5
Export Credits	43.9	21.0	13.6	17.3

MARKET BORROWING:

CHANGE IN CLAIMS

	1983	1984	1985	1986
Banks	–	228.0	-106.0	15.0

MEMORANDUM ITEM:

	1983	1984	1985	1986
CMEA Countr.(Gross)	–	–	–	–

TOTAL RECEIPTS NET | TOTAL ODA NET | TOTAL ODA GROSS

	1983	1984	1985	1986	1983	1984	1985	1986	1983
DAC COUNTRIES									
Australia	-0.1	-0.2	-0.1	0.0	0.0	0.0	0.0	0.0	0.0
Austria	0.2	-0.3	-0.1	0.6	0.2	0.2	0.4	0.6	0.2
Belgium	-1.5	8.1	0.1	11.1	3.4	1.7	1.8	3.0	3.4
Canada	69.6	33.2	31.2	24.5	6.8	14.5	13.1	17.1	6.9
Denmark	-1.2	-0.8	-1.9	-1.2	0.1	0.4	0.0	0.1	0.2
Finland	1.8	1.9	3.2	1.4	3.1	2.3	3.2	1.4	3.1
France	102.9	77.9	33.5	-18.1	7.0	9.0	3.5	3.9	7.2
Germany, Fed. Rep.	53.0	44.8	44.9	56.8	41.3	35.3	35.6	62.8	43.3
Ireland	0.0	0.0	—	0.1	0.0	0.0	—	0.1	0.0
Italy	-60.9	37.6	-15.6	-32.2	6.6	4.2	8.9	8.5	6.6
Japan	145.0	20.9	-122.3	-4.2	45.1	24.9	21.5	32.3	49.8
Netherlands	37.5	40.0	94.9	61.9	21.1	29.4	15.2	18.2	21.1
New Zealand	0.0	0.1	0.1	0.1	0.0	0.1	0.1	0.1	0.0
Norway	-1.7	37.3	34.2	35.2	0.3	0.6	0.6	1.2	0.3
Sweden	36.0	0.4	13.1	0.3	0.6	0.5	0.1	0.7	0.6
Switzerland	4.1	2.3	-3.2	3.8	4.5	4.1	3.8	3.8	4.5
United Kingdom	-4.0	3.0	1.7	-5.1	6.6	0.6	1.2	1.8	6.7
United States	478.0	156.0	-296.0	-185.0	89.0	114.0	177.0	95.0	93.0
TOTAL	*858.7*	*462.3*	*-182.2*	*-49.9*	*235.6*	*241.6*	*285.7*	*250.5*	*246.9*
MULTILATERAL									
AF.D.F.	—	—	—	—	—	—	—	—	—
AF.D.B.	—	—	—	—	—	—	—	—	—
AS.D.B	—	—	—	—	—	—	—	—	—
CAR.D.B.	—	—	—	—	—	—	—	—	—
E.E.C.	7.8	3.1	4.7	4.2	7.8	3.1	4.7	4.2	7.8
IBRD	48.8	87.4	91.2	53.1	—	—	—	—	—
IDA	—	—	—	—	—	—	—	—	—
I.D.B.	113.4	104.7	32.6	40.7	40.7	39.5	4.9	-2.1	48.3
IFAD	0.0	4.7	5.1	4.9	0.0	4.7	5.1	4.9	0.0
I.F.C.	0.1	1.2	2.5	3.4	—	—	—	—	—
IMF TRUST FUND	—	—	—	—	—	—	—	—	—
U.N. AGENCIES									
UNDP	3.5	5.2	3.5	5.0	3.5	5.2	3.5	5.0	3.5
UNTA	1.1	0.8	0.9	0.6	1.1	0.8	0.9	0.6	1.1
UNICEF	1.5	1.4	1.6	1.8	1.5	1.4	1.6	1.8	1.5
UNRWA	—	—	—	—	—	—	—	—	—
WFP	3.3	9.9	5.2	3.2	3.3	9.9	5.2	3.2	3.3
UNHCR	0.4	0.5	0.1	0.1	0.4	0.5	0.1	0.1	0.4
Other Multilateral	3.3	3.4	4.7	3.3	3.3	3.4	4.7	3.3	3.3
Arab OPEC Agencies	—				—				—
TOTAL	*183.1*	*222.4*	*152.1*	*120.3*	*61.5*	*68.5*	*30.7*	*21.1*	*69.1*
OPEC COUNTRIES	-26.0	-2.7	—	—	—	—	—	—	—
E.E.C.+ MEMBERS	*133.6*	*213.8*	*162.5*	*77.6*	*93.8*	*83.6*	*70.8*	*102.5*	*96.3*
TOTAL	**1015.8**	**681.9**	**-30.1**	**70.5**	**297.1**	**310.1**	**316.4**	**271.5**	**316.0**

ODA LOANS GROSS | ODA LOANS NET | GRANTS

	1983	1984	1985	1986	1983	1984	1985	1986	1983
DAC COUNTRIES									
Australia	—	—	—	—	—	—	—	—	0.0
Austria	—	—	—	—	—	—	—	—	0.2
Belgium	2.0	—	—	—	2.0	—	—	—	1.4
Canada	—	0.2	0.0	8.5	-0.1	0.1	0.0	8.3	6.9
Denmark	—	—	—	—	-0.2	—	—	—	0.2
Finland	2.5	1.7	1.8	0.5	2.5	1.7	1.8	0.5	0.6
France	4.3	6.1	1.8	0.0	4.1	5.7	1.2	0.0	2.9
Germany, Fed. Rep.	19.5	16.5	16.4	33.4	17.6	15.6	14.7	29.0	23.8
Ireland	—	—	—	—	—	—	—	—	0.0
Italy	—	—	—	—	—	—	—	—	6.6
Japan	23.0	12.3	8.4	17.0	18.3	10.1	8.2	10.2	26.8
Netherlands	6.3	6.2	3.6	0.8	6.3	3.5	3.5	0.8	14.8
New Zealand	—	—	—	—	—	—	—	—	0.0
Norway	—	—	—	—	—	—	—	—	0.3
Sweden	—	—	—	—	—	—	—	—	0.6
Switzerland	—	1.2	—	1.1	—	1.2	—	0.0	4.5
United Kingdom	—	—	—	—	-0.2	0.0	—	—	6.7
United States	44.0	68.0	111.0	49.0	40.0	61.0	108.0	35.0	49.0
TOTAL	*101.6*	*112.1*	*143.0*	*110.3*	*90.3*	*99.0*	*137.4*	*83.7*	*145.3*
MULTILATERAL	*48.2*	*53.0*	*20.2*	*14.1*	*40.6*	*43.3*	*10.0*	*2.9*	*20.9*
OPEC COUNTRIES	—	—	—	—	—	—	—	—	—
E.E.C.+ MEMBERS	*32.1*	*28.7*	*21.8*	*34.2*	*29.5*	*24.8*	*19.4*	*29.8*	*64.2*
TOTAL	**149.8**	**165.2**	**163.2**	**124.4**	**130.9**	**142.3**	**147.5**	**86.6**	**166.2**

TOTAL OFFICIAL GROSS | TOTAL OFFICIAL NET | TOTAL OOF GROSS

	1983	1984	1985	1986	1983	1984	1985	1986	1983
DAC COUNTRIES									
Australia	0.0	0.0	0.0	0.0	-0.1	-0.2	-0.1	0.0	—
Austria	0.2	0.2	0.4	0.6	0.2	0.2	0.4	0.6	—
Belgium	3.8	10.9	2.9	3.0	3.2	10.2	2.9	3.0	0.4
Canada	75.7	35.0	31.9	25.3	69.6	33.2	31.3	24.5	68.8
Denmark	0.2	0.4	0.0	0.1	0.1	0.4	0.0	0.1	—
Finland	3.1	2.3	3.2	1.4	3.1	2.3	3.2	1.4	—
France	7.2	39.7	30.3	3.9	4.3	38.1	29.6	3.9	—
Germany, Fed. Rep.	43.7	41.3	42.0	70.8	40.0	39.3	38.8	65.2	0.4
Ireland	0.0	0.0	—	0.1	0.0	0.0	—	0.1	—
Italy	6.6	52.7	8.9	8.5	-1.4	52.3	8.9	8.5	—
Japan	52.1	28.5	22.1	39.1	47.4	26.2	21.9	32.3	2.3
Netherlands	21.1	32.2	15.2	18.2	20.7	28.1	15.1	18.2	—
New Zealand	0.0	0.1	0.1	0.1	0.0	0.1	0.1	0.1	—
Norway	0.3	0.6	0.6	1.2	0.3	0.6	0.6	1.2	—
Sweden	0.6	0.6	0.1	0.7	0.5	0.5	0.1	0.5	—
Switzerland	4.5	4.1	3.8	4.9	3.7	4.1	3.8	3.8	—
United Kingdom	6.7	0.6	1.2	1.8	6.6	0.6	1.2	1.8	—
United States	112.0	224.0	180.0	115.0	72.0	204.0	177.0	96.0	19.0
TOTAL	*337.9*	*473.1*	*342.6*	*294.6*	*270.1*	*440.0*	*334.8*	*261.2*	*91.0*
MULTILATERAL	*230.5*	*284.7*	*224.3*	*228.0*	*183.1*	*222.4*	*152.1*	*120.3*	*161.4*
OPEC COUNTRIES	-19.3	—	—	—	-26.0	-2.7	—	—	-19.3
E.E.C.+ MEMBERS	*97.2*	*180.9*	*105.3*	*110.6*	*81.2*	*172.1*	*101.3*	*104.9*	*0.9*
TOTAL	**549.1**	**757.8**	**566.9**	**522.6**	**427.2**	**659.7**	**486.9**	**381.5**	**233.1**

ODA COMMITMENTS

1984	1985	1986		1983	1984	1985	1986
0.0	0.0	0.0		—	0.0	0.0	—
0.2	0.4	0.6		0.1	0.1	0.4	—
1.7	1.8	3.0		2.8	1.1	0.9	3.0
14.5	13.1	17.2		20.5	14.6	20.6	11.9
0.4	0.0	0.1		—	—	—	—
2.3	3.2	1.4		0.5	2.0	3.3	-8.2
9.3	4.1	3.9		2.9	4.8	2.3	3.9
36.1	37.2	67.2		34.1	19.6	72.0	44.0
0.0	—	0.1		0.0	0.0	—	0.1
4.2	8.9	8.5		16.5	12.7	15.3	10.7
27.1	21.6	39.1		59.5	16.2	21.5	32.0
32.0	15.2	18.2		13.2	28.7	8.9	18.5
0.1	0.1	0.1		0.0	0.1	0.1	0.1
0.6	0.6	1.2		0.4	0.2	0.6	1.2
0.5	0.1	0.7		0.4	0.5	0.9	0.7
4.1	3.8	4.9		8.6	2.9	5.5	1.9
0.6	1.2	1.8		1.2	0.6	1.0	1.4
121.0	180.0	109.0		132.9	165.3	54.2	69.7
254.8	*291.2*	*277.0*		*293.5*	*269.2*	*207.3*	*190.8*
—	—	—		—	—	—	—
—	—	—		—	—	—	—
—	—	—		—	—	—	—
3.1	4.7	4.2		14.6	2.9	3.3	22.5
—	—	—		—	—	—	—
49.1	15.1	8.4		5.1	—	—	—
4.7	5.1	5.7		—	—	—	7.5
—	—	—		—	—	—	—
—	—	—		13.1	21.2	16.0	14.0
5.2	3.5	5.0		—	—	—	—
0.8	0.9	0.6		—	—	—	—
1.4	1.6	1.8		—	—	—	—
—	—	—		—	—	—	—
9.9	5.2	3.2		—	—	—	—
0.5	0.1	0.1		—	—	—	—
3.4	4.7	3.3		—	—	—	—
—	—	—		—	—	—	—
78.2	40.9	32.3		32.7	24.0	19.2	44.0
—	—	—		—	—	—	—
87.5	73.2	107.0		85.2	70.3	103.5	104.1
332.9	*332.2*	*309.3*		*326.2*	*293.3*	*226.5*	*234.8*

TECH. COOP. GRANTS

1984	1985	1986		1983	1984	1985	1986
0.0	0.0	0.0		0.0	—	—	—
0.2	0.4	0.6		0.2	—	—	—
1.7	1.8	3.0		0.9	0.9	1.1	1.4
14.4	13.1	8.8		2.9	—	3.4	—
0.4	0.0	0.1		0.1	0.3	0.0	—
0.6	1.4	1.0		0.4	0.2	0.2	0.5
3.2	2.3	3.9		2.9	2.8	2.3	3.9
19.6	20.8	33.8		20.5	19.4	19.2	29.3
0.0	—	0.1		0.0	0.0	—	0.1
4.2	8.9	8.5		2.8	2.8	6.8	3.5
14.8	13.3	22.1		10.7	12.3	11.8	14.5
25.8	11.6	17.5		11.3	7.4	7.5	7.9
0.1	0.1	0.1		0.0	0.0	0.0	0.0
0.6	0.6	1.2		—	0.1	0.2	0.2
0.5	0.1	0.7		—	—	—	0.1
2.9	3.8	3.8		1.3	1.0	0.9	1.2
0.6	1.2	1.8		1.0	0.6	1.0	1.2
53.0	69.0	60.0		6.0	9.0	14.0	15.0
142.6	*148.3*	*166.8*		*61.1*	*57.0*	*68.3*	*78.8*
25.1	*20.7*	*18.2*		*9.8*	*11.3*	*10.8*	*11.0*
—	—	—		—	—	—	—
58.8	51.3	72.8		39.6	34.4	37.8	47.6
167.8	*168.9*	*184.9*		*71.0*	*68.3*	*79.1*	*89.9*

TOTAL OOF NET

1984	1985	1986		1983	1984	1985	1986
—	—	—		-0.1	-0.2	-0.1	—
—	—	—		—	—	—	—
9.2	1.2	—		-0.2	8.5	1.2	—
20.5	18.8	8.0		62.7	18.8	18.2	7.5
—	—	—		—	—	—	—
—	—	—		—	—	—	—
30.4	26.2	—		-2.6	29.1	26.2	—
5.1	4.8	3.6		-1.3	4.1	3.3	2.4
—	—	—		—	—	—	—
48.4	—	—		-8.0	48.1	—	—
1.4	0.5	—		2.3	1.4	0.5	—
0.2	—	—		-0.4	-1.3	-0.1	0.0
—	—	—		—	—	—	—
0.1	—	—		-0.1	—	—	-0.1
—	—	—		-0.7	—	—	—
103.0	—	6.0		-17.0	90.0	—	1.0
218.3	*51.4*	*17.6*		*34.5*	*198.4*	*49.1*	*10.7*
206.5	*183.4*	*195.7*		*121.6*	*153.9*	*121.4*	*99.2*
—	—	—		-26.0	-2.7	—	—
93.4	32.1	3.6		-12.5	88.5	30.5	2.4
424.8	*234.8*	*213.3*		*130.2*	*349.6*	*170.5*	*110.0*

ODA COMMITMENTS : LOANS

DAC COUNTRIES

	1983	1984	1985	1986
Australia	—	—	—	—
Austria	—	—	—	—
Belgium	2.0	—	—	—
Canada	7.4	—	5.1	3.5
Denmark	—	—	—	—
Finland	—	—	3.2	—
France	—	1.6	—	0.0
Germany, Fed. Rep.	7.8	0.9	51.0	13.9
Ireland	—	—	—	—
Italy	3.0	3.0	—	—
Japan	41.6	3.4	1.2	9.5
Netherlands	—	2.2	—	—
New Zealand	—	—	—	—
Norway	—	—	—	—
Sweden	—	—	—	—
Switzerland	4.0	—	—	—
United Kingdom	—	—	—	—
United States	67.4	103.2	25.0	21.2
TOTAL	*133.1*	*114.2*	*85.6*	*48.1*
MULTILATERAL	*5.1*	*—*	*—*	*7.5*
OPEC COUNTRIES	*—*	*—*	*—*	*—*
E.E.C.+ MEMBERS	*12.8*	*7.6*	*51.0*	*13.9*
TOTAL	*138.2*	*114.2*	*85.6*	*55.6*

GRANT ELEMENT OF ODA

DAC COUNTRIES

	1983	1984	1985	1986
Australia	—	100.0	100.0	—
Austria	100.0	100.0	100.0	—
Belgium	84.7	100.0	100.0	100.0
Canada	96.4	100.0	97.6	97.0
Denmark	—	—	—	—
Finland	100.0	100.0	69.3	100.0
France	100.0	74.8	100.0	100.0
Germany, Fed. Rep.	92.3	96.8	75.9	81.9
Ireland	100.0	100.0	—	100.0
Italy	90.3	86.6	100.0	100.0
Japan	59.8	100.0	97.6	72.6
Netherlands	100.0	97.0	100.0	100.0
New Zealand	100.0	100.0	100.0	100.0
Norway	100.0	100.0	100.0	100.0
Sweden	100.0	100.0	100.0	100.0
Switzerland	82.4	100.0	100.0	100.0
United Kingdom	100.0	100.0	100.0	100.0
United States	77.5	76.4	76.0	83.9
TOTAL	*79.3*	*83.7*	*84.4*	*85.2*
MULTILATERAL	*70.8*	*100.0*	*100.0*	*93.2*
OPEC COUNTRIES	*—*	*—*	*—*	*—*
E.E.C.+ MEMBERS	*94.5*	*93.7*	*83.3*	*92.4*
TOTAL	*77.6*	*85.0*	*85.8*	*86.7*

OTHER AGGREGATES

COMMITMENTS: ALL SOURCES

	1983	1984	1985	1986
TOTAL BILATERAL	335.1	528.1	243.1	196.6
of which				
OPEC	—	—	—	—
CMEA	—	25.0	12.0	—
TOTAL MULTILATERAL	407.4	362.7	40.0	53.2
TOTAL BIL.& MULTIL.	742.5	890.8	283.1	249.7
of which				
ODA Grants	188.1	179.0	140.9	179.2
ODA Loans	138.2	114.2	85.6	55.6

DISBURSEMENTS:

DAC COUNTRIES COMBINED

OFFICIAL & PRIVATE	1983	1984	1985	1986
GROSS:				
Contractual Lending	492.6	610.6	393.4	230.1
Export Credits Total	371.1	305.2	218.8	110.2
Export Credits Private	300.1	280.8	199.5	102.2
NET:				
Contractual Lending	132.9	341.2	187.4	51.2
Export Credits Total	28.0	53.1	20.0	-39.2
PRIVATE SECTOR NET	588.6	22.2	-516.9	-311.0
Direct Investment	113.7	-121.4	-313.6	-56.9
Portfolio Investment	466.8	99.2	-204.7	-210.8
Export Credits	8.1	44.5	1.4	-43.3

MARKET BORROWING:

CHANGE IN CLAIMS

	1983	1984	1985	1986
Banks	—	-702.0	-245.0	-543.0

MEMORANDUM ITEM:

	1983	1984	1985	1986
CMEA Countr.(Gross)	15.0	5.7	14.0	10.0

	1983	1984	1985	1986	1983	1984	1985	1986		1983

TOTAL RECEIPTS NET / TOTAL ODA NET / TOTAL ODA GROSS

	1983	1984	1985	1986	1983	1984	1985	1986		1983
TOTAL RECEIPTS NET					**TOTAL ODA NET**				**TOTAL ODA GROSS**	
DAC COUNTRIES										
Australia	15.2	14.3	12.4	9.5	14.9	15.7	13.8	11.6	Australia	14.9
Austria	1.8	16.5	8.5	2.3	1.4	10.2	8.6	2.3	Austria	1.4
Belgium	23.5	91.1	76.8	-36.0	2.7	3.2	1.3	0.8	Belgium	2.9
Canada	4.9	0.3	3.2	2.7	5.1	8.1	4.9	6.1	Canada	5.1
Denmark	50.9	-1.0	0.8	2.2	-0.1	0.0	1.4	2.5	Denmark	0.3
Finland	-2.2	-3.0	0.0	3.3	0.2	0.1	0.0	0.6	Finland	0.2
France	17.8	-16.4	27.5	51.6	0.7	0.9	0.9	1.4	France	0.7
Germany, Fed. Rep.	87.5	3.7	45.9	42.0	35.4	17.7	17.9	37.6	Germany, Fed. Rep.	36.0
Ireland	0.0	0.0	0.0	0.1	0.0	0.0	0.0	0.1	Ireland	0.0
Italy	3.1	-6.4	20.9	-7.6	0.4	0.9	0.2	0.2	Italy	0.4
Japan	341.2	201.0	113.7	462.4	147.0	160.1	240.0	438.0	Japan	174.0
Netherlands	4.3	-6.6	6.8	21.3	4.3	4.3	6.8	13.9	Netherlands	4.3
New Zealand	1.0	1.3	0.9	0.8	1.0	1.3	0.9	0.8	New Zealand	1.0
Norway	5.7	2.8	3.9	2.9	5.8	2.8	3.9	2.8	Norway	5.8
Sweden	-0.2	-0.1	0.1	-0.1	–	0.2	0.1	0.4	Sweden	–
Switzerland	-1.3	-3.3	1.0	0.6	0.5	1.0	1.0	0.6	Switzerland	0.5
United Kingdom	0.2	16.1	26.7	-35.6	1.2	0.3	0.6	0.3	United Kingdom	1.2
United States	232.0	266.0	37.0	438.0	138.0	129.0	135.0	367.0	United States	146.0
TOTAL	**785.1**	**576.2**	**386.2**	**960.3**	**358.5**	**355.8**	**437.6**	**886.8**	**TOTAL**	**394.6**
MULTILATERAL										
AF.D.F.	–	–	–	–	–	–	–	–	AF.D.F.	–
AF.D.B.	–	–	–	–	–	–	–	–	AF.D.B.	–
AS.D.B	166.4	147.2	82.0	103.0	7.7	4.0	3.8	29.9	AS.D.B	8.1
CAR.D.B.	–	–	–	–	–	–	–	–	CAR.D.B.	–
E.E.C.	3.7	1.9	3.5	3.6	3.7	1.9	3.5	3.6	E.E.C.	3.7
IBRD	527.6	185.5	123.2	19.5	2.9	0.6	–	–	IBRD	2.9
IDA	12.5	10.0	13.0	7.7	12.5	10.0	13.0	7.7	IDA	12.8
I.D.B.	–	–	–	–	–	–	–	–	I.D.B.	–
IFAD	5.0	1.6	0.9	1.3	5.0	1.6	0.9	1.3	IFAD	5.0
I.F.C.	3.6	0.4	-1.1	-3.5	–	–	–	–	I.F.C.	–
IMF TRUST FUND	–	–	–	–	–	–	–	–	IMF TRUST FUND	–
U.N. AGENCIES	–	–	–	–	–	–	–	–	U.N. AGENCIES	–
UNDP	4.7	4.3	4.9	5.6	4.7	4.3	4.9	5.6	UNDP	4.7
UNTA	1.6	1.0	2.2	1.6	1.6	1.0	2.2	1.6	UNTA	1.6
UNICEF	3.3	3.6	3.3	4.4	3.3	3.6	3.3	4.4	UNICEF	3.3
UNRWA	–	–	–	–	–	–	–	–	UNRWA	–
WFP	6.2	1.8	2.7	4.5	6.2	1.8	2.7	4.5	WFP	6.2
UNHCR	8.0	9.0	8.1	7.5	8.0	9.0	8.1	7.5	UNHCR	8.0
Other Multilateral	2.4	2.9	4.1	2.4	2.4	2.9	4.1	2.4	Other Multilateral	2.4
Arab OPEC Agencies	13.1	1.1	2.6	0.8	13.1	1.1	2.6	0.8	Arab OPEC Agencies	13.6
TOTAL	**758.0**	**370.1**	**249.6**	**158.4**	**71.0**	**41.5**	**49.3**	**69.3**	**TOTAL**	**72.1**
OPEC COUNTRIES	**-0.5**	**-0.4**	**-0.6**	**-0.2**	**-0.5**	**-0.4**	**-0.6**	**-0.2**	**OPEC COUNTRIES**	**0.3**
E.E.C. + MEMBERS	**190.9**	**82.3**	**208.9**	**41.5**	**48.4**	**29.2**	**32.7**	**60.4**	**E.E.C. + MEMBERS**	**49.5**
TOTAL	**1542.6**	**945.9**	**635.2**	**1118.4**	**429.0**	**396.9**	**486.2**	**955.8**	**TOTAL**	**467.0**

ODA LOANS GROSS / ODA LOANS NET / GRANTS

	1983	1984	1985	1986	1983	1984	1985	1986		1983
ODA LOANS GROSS					**ODA LOANS NET**				**GRANTS**	
DAC COUNTRIES										
Australia	–	–	–	–	–	–	–	–	Australia	14.9
Austria	1.4	10.1	8.6	2.2	1.4	10.1	8.6	2.2	Austria	0.0
Belgium	2.0	1.7	0.2	–	1.8	1.7	0.0	-0.1	Belgium	0.9
Canada	–	–	–	0.1	–	–	–	0.0	Canada	5.1
Denmark	–	–	1.4	2.9	-0.4	-0.2	1.3	2.4	Denmark	0.3
Finland	–	–	–	–	–	–	–	–	Finland	0.2
France	0.1	0.1	0.6	0.6	0.1	0.1	0.4	-0.1	France	0.6
Germany, Fed. Rep.	24.0	7.2	12.7	19.3	23.4	5.1	3.8	16.7	Germany, Fed. Rep.	12.0
Ireland	–	–	–	–	–	–	–	–	Ireland	0.0
Italy	–	–	–	–	–	–	–	–	Italy	0.4
Japan	112.1	132.4	173.4	479.7	85.1	102.4	170.3	357.6	Japan	62.0
Netherlands	–	–	0.7	–	–	–	0.7	–	Netherlands	4.3
New Zealand	–	–	–	–	–	–	–	–	New Zealand	1.0
Norway	–	–	–	–	–	–	–	–	Norway	5.8
Sweden	–	–	–	–	–	–	–	–	Sweden	–
Switzerland	–	–	–	–	–	–	–	–	Switzerland	0.5
United Kingdom	0.9	0.0	0.1	–	0.9	0.0	0.1	–	United Kingdom	0.3
United States	27.0	15.0	48.0	38.0	19.0	7.0	39.0	24.0	United States	119.0
TOTAL	**167.4**	**166.6**	**245.8**	**542.7**	**131.3**	**126.4**	**224.2**	**402.7**	**TOTAL**	**227.2**
MULTILATERAL	**40.8**	**16.1**	**19.7**	**39.2**	**39.7**	**15.1**	**18.2**	**37.7**	**MULTILATERAL**	**31.3**
OPEC COUNTRIES	**0.1**	**0.2**	**–**	**–**	**-0.6**	**-0.6**	**-0.9**	**-0.5**	**OPEC COUNTRIES**	**0.1**
E.E.C. + MEMBERS	**27.0**	**9.1**	**15.8**	**22.7**	**25.9**	**6.8**	**6.4**	**18.9**	**E.E.C. + MEMBERS**	**22.5**
TOTAL	**208.4**	**182.8**	**265.4**	**581.9**	**170.4**	**140.8**	**241.5**	**439.9**	**TOTAL**	**258.6**

TOTAL OFFICIAL GROSS / TOTAL OFFICIAL NET / TOTAL OOF GROSS

	1983	1984	1985	1986	1983	1984	1985	1986		1983
TOTAL OFFICIAL GROSS					**TOTAL OFFICIAL NET**				**TOTAL OOF GROSS**	
DAC COUNTRIES										
Australia	15.3	15.7	13.8	11.6	14.3	14.4	13.3	10.8	Australia	0.4
Austria	1.8	16.6	8.7	2.3	1.8	16.6	8.6	2.3	Austria	0.4
Belgium	2.9	7.5	13.8	5.7	2.7	7.5	11.2	2.3	Belgium	–
Canada	7.5	8.1	5.7	7.0	4.1	1.1	3.2	2.7	Canada	2.4
Denmark	0.3	0.8	1.5	3.1	-0.1	0.6	1.3	2.6	Denmark	0.0
Finland	0.2	0.1	0.0	0.6	0.2	0.1	0.0	0.6	Finland	–
France	0.7	0.9	18.5	26.7	0.7	0.9	18.3	24.2	France	–
Germany, Fed. Rep.	47.4	22.1	55.5	62.5	43.8	19.8	40.1	37.7	Germany, Fed. Rep.	11.4
Ireland	0.0	0.0	0.0	0.1	0.0	0.0	0.0	0.1	Ireland	–
Italy	10.0	2.7	27.0	0.2	7.8	0.9	27.0	-0.3	Italy	9.6
Japan	314.0	252.0	246.7	594.6	286.9	220.7	243.6	453.3	Japan	140.0
Netherlands	4.3	4.3	6.8	13.9	4.3	4.3	6.8	13.9	Netherlands	–
New Zealand	1.0	1.3	0.9	0.8	1.0	1.3	0.9	0.8	New Zealand	–
Norway	5.8	2.8	3.9	2.8	5.8	2.8	3.9	2.8	Norway	–
Sweden	0.1	0.2	0.1	0.4	-0.2	-0.1	0.1	-0.1	Sweden	0.1
Switzerland	0.5	1.0	1.0	0.6	0.5	1.0	1.0	0.6	Switzerland	–
United Kingdom	5.6	5.1	2.4	0.3	5.6	4.9	1.7	-0.4	United Kingdom	4.4
United States	168.0	145.0	280.0	458.0	146.0	118.0	252.0	420.0	United States	22.0
TOTAL	**585.3**	**486.1**	**686.4**	**1190.9**	**525.1**	**414.7**	**633.1**	**973.8**	**TOTAL**	**190.7**
MULTILATERAL	**859.3**	**508.1**	**394.6**	**370.6**	**758.0**	**370.1**	**249.6**	**158.4**	**MULTILATERAL**	**787.1**
OPEC COUNTRIES	**0.3**	**0.4**	**0.3**	**0.3**	**-0.5**	**-0.4**	**-0.6**	**-0.2**	**OPEC COUNTRIES**	**–**
E.E.C. + MEMBERS	**74.9**	**45.3**	**129.0**	**116.0**	**68.6**	**40.7**	**109.9**	**83.6**	**E.E.C. + MEMBERS**	**25.4**
TOTAL	**1444.8**	**994.5**	**1081.2**	**1561.9**	**1282.6**	**784.4**	**882.1**	**1131.9**	**TOTAL**	**977.8**

ODA COMMITMENTS

1984	1985	1986	1983	1984	1985	1986
15.7	13.8	11.6	8.1	7.4	6.8	12.6
10.2	8.7	2.3	0.0	0.1	0.1	–
3.2	1.6	0.9	2.0	1.0	0.7	0.9
8.1	4.9	6.3	8.9	5.6	6.9	26.7
0.2	1.5	3.0	–	0.1	11.9	0.1
0.1	0.0	0.6	–	–	–	–
0.9	1.1	2.1	0.6	0.8	1.5	2.1
19.8	26.7	40.2	11.6	25.4	31.5	22.2
0.0	0.0	0.1	0.0	0.0	0.0	0.1
0.9	0.2	0.2	1.0	1.0	0.3	0.3
190.1	243.1	560.1	309.8	257.4	75.8	531.1
4.3	6.8	13.9	4.4	4.5	6.8	13.6
1.3	0.9	0.8	1.0	0.5	0.9	0.9
2.8	3.9	2.8	–	3.4	1.5	2.0
0.2	0.1	0.4	–	0.2	0.1	0.4
1.0	1.0	0.6	0.5	0.9	1.0	0.8
0.3	0.6	0.3	0.3	0.3	0.5	0.3
137.0	144.0	381.0	159.7	114.7	192.5	395.2
396.0	*459.1*	*1026.8*	*507.9*	*423.3*	*338.7*	*1008.9*
–	–	–	–	–	–	–
–	–	–	–	–	–	–
4.4	4.3	30.4	–	–	–	50.0
–	–	–	–	–	–	–
1.9	3.5	3.6	0.5	1.3	1.5	13.9
0.6	–	–	–	–	–	–
10.2	13.3	8.1	–	–	–	–
–	–	–	–	–	–	–
1.9	1.6	2.0	0.2	–	–	4.8
–	–	–	–	–	–	–
–	–	–	26.1	22.5	25.5	26.0
4.3	4.9	5.6	–	–	–	–
1.0	2.2	1.6	–	–	–	–
3.6	3.3	4.4	–	–	–	–
–	–	–	–	–	–	–
1.8	2.7	4.5	–	–	–	–
9.0	8.1	7.5	–	–	–	–
2.9	4.1	2.4	–	–	–	–
1.1	2.6	0.8	–	1.7	–	–
42.5	*50.7*	*70.8*	*26.8*	*25.5*	*27.0*	*94.6*
0.4	*0.3*	*0.3*	*0.1*	*10.1*	*0.2*	–
31.5	*42.1*	*64.1*	*20.3*	*34.5*	*54.7*	*53.3*
438.9	*510.2*	*1097.9*	*534.9*	*458.9*	*365.9*	*1103.5*

TECH. COOP. GRANTS

1984	1985	1986	1983	1984	1985	1986
15.7	13.8	11.6	4.5	5.6	4.5	4.3
0.1	0.1	0.1	0.0	–	–	–
1.5	1.4	0.9	0.1	0.2	0.1	0.1
8.1	4.9	6.1	1.5	–	0.4	–
0.2	0.1	0.1	0.3	0.2	1.5	0.1
0.1	0.0	0.6	0.2	0.1	0.0	0.0
0.8	0.6	1.6	0.6	0.8	0.6	1.2
12.6	14.0	20.9	10.0	11.0	12.2	19.4
0.0	0.0	0.1	0.0	0.0	0.0	0.1
0.9	0.2	0.2	0.4	0.9	0.2	0.2
57.7	69.7	80.4	26.1	31.3	29.8	39.3
4.3	6.0	13.9	4.0	3.9	5.3	6.9
1.3	0.9	0.8	0.9	1.1	0.9	0.6
2.8	3.9	2.8	0.7	0.3	0.4	0.3
0.2	0.1	0.4	–	–	–	–
1.0	1.0	0.6	0.0	0.0	0.0	0.1
0.3	0.5	0.3	0.3	0.3	0.4	0.3
122.0	96.0	343.0	106.0	41.0	32.0	21.0
229.4	*213.4*	*484.1*	*155.5*	*96.6*	*88.2*	*93.9*
26.5	*31.1*	*31.6*	*20.0*	*20.7*	*17.8*	*21.5*
0.2	*0.3*	*0.3*	–	–	–	–
22.4	*26.4*	*41.4*	*15.6*	*17.2*	*20.3*	*28.3*
256.1	*244.7*	*516.0*	*175.5*	*117.3*	*106.1*	*115.3*

TOTAL OOF NET

1984	1985	1986	1983	1984	1985	1986
–	–	–	-0.6	-1.3	-0.5	-0.7
6.4	–	–	0.4	6.4	–	–
4.3	12.2	4.8	–	4.3	9.9	1.5
–	0.8	0.7	-1.0	-7.0	-1.7	-3.4
0.6	–	0.1	0.0	0.6	-0.1	0.1
–	–	–	–	–	–	–
–	17.4	24.6	–	–	17.4	22.8
2.3	28.8	22.3	8.4	2.0	22.2	0.1
–	–	–	–	–	–	–
1.9	26.8	–	7.4	0.0	26.8	-0.5
61.9	3.6	34.6	139.8	60.7	3.6	15.3
–	–	–	–	–	–	–
–	–	–	–	–	–	–
–	–	–	-0.2	-0.2	–	-0.4
4.7	1.8	–	4.4	4.6	1.0	-0.7
8.0	136.0	77.0	8.0	-11.0	117.0	53.0
90.0	*227.3*	*164.1*	*166.6*	*58.9*	*195.5*	*87.0*
465.6	*343.8*	*299.9*	*687.0*	*328.5*	*200.3*	*89.1*
–	–	–	–	–	–	–
13.8	*86.9*	*51.9*	*20.2*	*11.4*	*77.2*	*23.2*
555.6	*571.0*	*464.0*	*853.6*	*387.5*	*395.9*	*176.1*

ODA COMMITMENTS : LOANS

DAC COUNTRIES

	1983	1984	1985	1986
Australia	–	–	–	–
Austria	–	–	–	–
Belgium	2.0	–	–	–
Canada	–	–	–	0.1
Denmark	–	–	11.8	–
Finland	–	–	–	–
France	–	–	0.9	0.6
Germany, Fed. Rep.	–	10.5	14.5	0.9
Ireland	–	–	–	–
Italy	–	–	–	–
Japan	244.8	179.2	6.8	433.5
Netherlands	–	–	0.7	–
New Zealand	–	–	–	–
Norway	–	–	–	–
Sweden	–	–	–	–
Switzerland	–	–	–	–
United Kingdom	–	–	–	–
United States	24.3	23.1	58.8	35.0
TOTAL	*271.0*	*212.9*	*93.6*	*470.1*
MULTILATERAL	–	–	–	*54.8*
OPEC COUNTRIES	–	*10.1*	–	–
E.E.C.+ MEMBERS	*2.0*	*10.5*	*28.0*	*1.5*
TOTAL	*271.0*	*223.0*	*93.6*	*524.9*

GRANT ELEMENT OF ODA

DAC COUNTRIES

	1983	1984	1985	1986
Australia	100.0	100.0	100.0	100.0
Austria	100.0	100.0	100.0	–
Belgium	83.6	100.0	95.8	100.0
Canada	100.0	100.0	100.0	99.9
Denmark	–	100.0	75.5	100.0
Finland	–	–	–	–
France	100.0	100.0	100.0	100.0
Germany, Fed. Rep.	100.0	88.8	71.3	98.6
Ireland	100.0	100.0	100.0	100.0
Italy	100.0	100.0	100.0	100.0
Japan	64.5	61.4	94.7	49.8
Netherlands	100.0	100.0	95.9	100.0
New Zealand	100.0	100.0	100.0	100.0
Norway	–	100.0	100.0	100.0
Sweden	–	100.0	100.0	100.0
Switzerland	100.0	100.0	100.0	100.0
United Kingdom	100.0	100.0	100.0	100.0
United States	95.6	94.2	88.4	96.2
TOTAL	*76.3*	*74.3*	*88.6*	*72.1*
MULTILATERAL	*100.0*	*100.0*	*100.0*	*86.4*
OPEC COUNTRIES	*100.0*	*31.6*	*100.0*	–
E.E.C.+ MEMBERS	*98.4*	*91.8*	*77.3*	*99.4*
TOTAL	*77.4*	*74.8*	*89.4*	*73.3*

OTHER AGGREGATES

COMMITMENTS: ALL SOURCES

	1983	1984	1985	1986
TOTAL BILATERAL	522.8	512.7	614.9	1151.3
of which				
OPEC	0.1	10.1	0.2	–
CMEA	–	–	–	–
TOTAL MULTILATERAL	656.2	609.0	131.0	544.4
TOTAL BIL.& MULTIL.	1179.0	1121.7	745.8	1695.7
of which				
ODA Grants	263.8	235.9	272.3	578.7
ODA Loans	271.0	223.0	93.6	524.9

DISBURSEMENTS:

DAC COUNTRIES COMBINED

	1983	1984	1985	1986
OFFICIAL & PRIVATE				
GROSS:				
Contractual Lending	816.4	753.5	732.4	753.2
Export Credits Total	644.5	579.3	309.0	104.8
Export Credits Private	458.3	501.2	264.1	46.4
NET:				
Contractual Lending	392.6	317.7	263.1	206.4
Export Credits Total	256.9	183.9	-129.1	-286.1
PRIVATE SECTOR NET	260.0	161.5	-246.9	-13.5
Direct Investment	-168.2	167.1	-248.9	81.3
Portfolio Investment	333.6	-142.3	153.9	188.5
Export Credits	94.7	136.7	-151.8	-283.2

MARKET BORROWING:

CHANGE IN CLAIMS

	1983	1984	1985	1986
Banks	–	211.0	-655.0	346.0

MEMORANDUM ITEM:

	1983	1984	1985	1986
CMEA Countr.(Gross)	0.2	–	–	–

TOTAL RECEIPTS NET / TOTAL ODA NET / TOTAL ODA GROSS

	TOTAL RECEIPTS NET 1983	1984	1985	1986	TOTAL ODA NET 1983	1984	1985	1986	TOTAL ODA GROSS 1983
DAC COUNTRIES									
Australia	0.4	–	–	–	–	–	–	–	–
Austria	0.1	0.1	0.2	0.2	0.1	0.1	0.2	0.2	0.1
Belgium	-18.0	92.8	-14.1	17.4	–	–	0.0	–	–
Canada	-1.9	-1.7	-1.7	-1.8	–	–	–	–	–
Denmark	2.8	-3.2	-3.9	-4.1	–	–	–	–	–
Finland	-0.3	-0.5	-0.6	–	–	–	–	–	–
France	166.7	-56.7	55.6	-536.1	5.8	5.5	5.5	5.3	5.8
Germany, Fed. Rep.	-0.9	20.7	62.3	1.7	20.7	30.0	21.7	28.8	22.2
Ireland	–	–	–	–	–	–	–	–	–
Italy	4.3	10.6	-4.3	10.7	0.1	0.2	0.0	0.1	0.1
Japan	75.1	402.7	184.3	201.0	0.1	0.0	0.2	0.4	0.1
Netherlands	-12.3	-11.3	16.8	-61.6	0.5	1.0	0.1	1.7	0.5
New Zealand	–	–	–	–	–	–	–	–	–
Norway	1.0	11.7	15.3	8.3	4.6	2.4	0.6	0.1	4.6
Sweden	-2.6	-8.5	-5.6	-5.1	-0.6	-0.5	-0.6	-0.9	0.2
Switzerland	84.8	-13.7	14.8	0.3	0.1	0.4	0.2	0.3	0.1
United Kingdom	33.7	3.1	179.8	-23.3	-4.2	-4.2	0.1	0.0	0.8
United States	60.0	57.0	-146.0	-158.0	8.0	46.0	71.0	85.0	26.0
TOTAL	393.0	503.2	352.6	-550.4	35.3	80.8	98.9	120.9	60.6
MULTILATERAL									
AF.D.F.	–	–	–	–	–	–	–	–	–
AF.D.B.	–	–	–	–	–	–	–	–	–
AS.D.B	–	–	–	–	–	–	–	–	–
CAR.D.B.	–	–	–	–	–	–	–	–	–
E.E.C.	69.4	-4.3	0.3	17.0	6.4	14.3	0.3	17.0	6.4
IBRD	62.3	30.7	63.4	26.9	–	–	–	–	–
IDA	–	–	–	–	–	–	–	–	–
I.D.B.	–	–	–	–	–	–	–	–	–
IFAD	–	–	–	–	–	–	–	–	–
I.F.C.	4.6	7.9	-0.3	11.4	–	–	–	–	–
IMF TRUST FUND	–	–	–	–	–	–	–	–	–
U.N. AGENCIES	–	–	–	–	–	–	–	–	–
UNDP	0.5	0.6	0.5	0.4	0.5	0.6	0.5	0.4	0.5
UNTA	0.4	0.3	0.8	0.7	0.4	0.3	0.8	0.7	0.4
UNICEF	–	–	–	–	–	–	–	–	–
UNRWA	–	–	–	–	–	–	–	–	–
WFP	–	–	–	–	–	–	–	–	–
UNHCR	0.7	0.5	0.3	0.4	0.7	0.5	0.3	0.4	0.7
Other Multilateral	2.1	1.1	60.5	-22.8	2.1	1.1	1.5	-0.3	2.2
Arab OPEC Agencies	–	–	–	–	–	–	–	–	–
TOTAL	140.0	36.8	125.5	34.0	10.0	16.8	3.4	18.2	10.1
OPEC COUNTRIES	–	–	–	–	–	–	–	–	–
E.E.C.+ MEMBERS	245.8	51.8	292.4	-578.4	29.4	46.6	27.8	52.9	35.9
TOTAL	533.0	540.0	478.1	-516.5	45.4	97.5	102.4	139.1	70.7

ODA LOANS GROSS / ODA LOANS NET / GRANTS

	ODA LOANS GROSS 1983	1984	1985	1986	ODA LOANS NET 1983	1984	1985	1986	GRANTS 1983
DAC COUNTRIES									
Australia	–	–	–	–	–	–	–	–	–
Austria	–	0.1	0.1	0.1	–	0.1	0.1	0.1	0.1
Belgium	–	–	–	–	–	–	–	–	–
Canada	–	–	–	–	–	–	–	–	–
Denmark	–	–	–	–	–	–	–	–	–
Finland	–	–	–	–	–	–	–	–	–
France	0.7	0.3	1.5	–	0.7	0.3	1.5	-0.3	5.1
Germany, Fed. Rep.	11.2	21.8	16.8	24.3	9.7	19.8	12.5	16.3	11.1
Ireland	–	–	–	–	–	–	–	–	–
Italy	–	–	–	–	–	–	–	–	0.1
Japan	–	–	–	–	–	–	–	–	0.1
Netherlands	0.3	0.9	0.1	1.1	0.3	0.9	0.0	1.0	0.2
New Zealand	–	–	–	–	–	–	–	–	–
Norway	–	–	0.5	–	–	–	-0.4	-0.9	4.6
Sweden	–	–	–	–	-0.8	-0.8	-0.7	-0.9	0.2
Switzerland	–	–	–	–	–	–	–	–	0.1
United Kingdom	–	–	–	–	-5.0	-4.9	–	–	0.8
United States	2.0	–	–	–	-16.0	-18.0	-13.0	-18.0	24.0
TOTAL	14.2	23.0	18.9	25.6	-11.1	-2.7	-0.1	-2.7	46.4
MULTILATERAL	2.0	1.2	1.6	–	1.9	0.9	1.3	-0.4	8.1
OPEC COUNTRIES	–	–	–	–	–	–	–	–	–
E.E.C.+ MEMBERS	12.2	22.9	18.4	25.5	5.7	16.1	14.0	17.0	23.7
TOTAL	16.2	24.1	20.6	25.6	-9.2	-1.7	1.2	-3.1	54.6

TOTAL OFFICIAL GROSS / TOTAL OFFICIAL NET / TOTAL OOF GROSS

	TOTAL OFFICIAL GROSS 1983	1984	1985	1986	TOTAL OFFICIAL NET 1983	1984	1985	1986	TOTAL OOF GROSS 1983
DAC COUNTRIES									
Australia	–	–	–	–	–	–	–	–	–
Austria	0.1	0.1	0.2	0.2	0.1	0.1	0.2	0.2	–
Belgium	–	0.6	0.3	–	–	0.6	0.3	–	–
Canada	–	0.4	0.2	–	-1.9	-1.7	-1.7	-1.8	–
Denmark	–	–	–	–	-0.6	–	–	–	–
Finland	–	–	–	–	–	–	–	–	–
France	5.8	5.5	5.5	5.6	5.8	5.5	5.5	5.3	–
Germany, Fed. Rep.	22.2	31.9	26.0	36.8	19.1	28.8	21.5	28.8	–
Ireland	–	–	–	–	–	–	–	–	–
Italy	0.1	0.2	0.0	0.1	-0.1	-0.1	-0.1	-0.2	–
Japan	0.1	0.0	0.2	0.4	-16.6	-16.6	-16.4	-11.4	–
Netherlands	0.5	1.0	0.2	1.9	-1.7	-1.0	-1.8	-0.8	–
New Zealand	–	–	–	–	–	–	–	–	–
Norway	4.6	2.4	1.4	1.0	2.6	0.4	-1.4	-1.9	–
Sweden	4.7	1.1	1.1	–	-0.2	-4.8	-4.6	-4.2	4.6
Switzerland	0.1	0.4	0.2	0.3	0.1	0.4	0.2	0.3	–
United Kingdom	0.8	0.8	0.1	0.0	-4.2	-4.2	0.1	0.0	–
United States	82.0	78.0	84.0	103.0	14.0	8.0	10.0	27.0	56.0
TOTAL	121.2	122.3	119.4	149.2	16.5	15.3	11.6	41.1	60.6
MULTILATERAL	198.3	129.1	192.0	128.8	140.0	36.8	125.5	34.0	188.2
OPEC COUNTRIES	–	–	–	–	–	–	–	–	–
E.E.C.+ MEMBERS	120.6	80.4	32.5	61.3	87.7	25.3	25.8	50.0	84.8
TOTAL	319.5	251.4	311.4	278.0	156.5	52.1	137.1	75.1	248.8

ODA COMMITMENTS

1984	1985	1986	1983	1984	1985	1986
0.1	0.2	0.2	0.1	0.4	0.1	–
–	0.0	–	–	–	–	–
–	–	–	–	–	–	–
–	–	–	–	–	–	–
5.5	5.5	5.6	5.1	5.2	4.0	5.6
31.9	26.0	36.8	24.7	72.7	10.2	24.2
–	–	–	–	–	–	–
0.2	0.0	0.1	0.1	0.2	0.0	0.1
0.0	0.2	0.4	0.1	0.0	0.2	0.4
1.0	0.2	1.9	0.2	0.1	0.2	0.3
–	–	–	–	–	–	–
2.4	1.4	1.0	1.3	0.8	0.6	0.1
0.3	0.1	–	0.1	0.1	–	–
0.4	0.2	0.3	0.0	0.2	0.0	0.0
0.8	0.1	0.0	0.8	0.8	0.1	0.0
64.0	84.0	103.0	20.0	60.1	81.0	103.4
106.4	*117.9*	*149.2*	*52.6*	*140.5*	*96.5*	*134.1*
–	–	–	–	–	–	–
–	–	–	–	–	–	–
14.3	0.3	17.0	8.9	8.5	7.6	42.9
–	–	–	–	–	–	–
–	–	–	–	–	–	–
–	–	–	–	–	–	–
–	–	–	1.8	1.6	1.8	1.6
0.6	0.5	0.4	–	–	–	–
0.3	0.8	0.7	–	–	–	–
–	–	–	–	–	–	–
0.5	0.3	0.4	–	–	–	–
1.4	1.8	0.1	–	–	1.6	–
–	–	–	–	–	–	–
17.0	3.8	18.6	10.6	10.1	11.0	44.5
–	–	–	–	–	–	–
53.5	32.2	61.3	39.9	87.4	22.1	73.1
123.4	*121.7*	*167.8*	*63.3*	*150.6*	*107.5*	*178.6*

TECH. COOP. GRANTS

1984	1985	1986	1983	1984	1985	1986
–	–	–	–	–	–	–
0.1	0.1	0.1	0.1	–	–	–
–	0.0	–	–	–	0.0	–
–	–	–	–	–	–	–
–	–	–	–	–	–	–
5.2	4.0	5.6	5.1	5.2	4.0	5.6
10.1	9.3	12.4	11.0	10.0	9.2	12.3
–	–	–	–	–	–	–
0.2	0.0	0.1	0.1	0.2	0.0	0.1
0.0	0.2	0.4	0.1	0.0	0.2	0.4
0.1	0.1	0.8	0.1	0.1	0.1	0.3
–	–	–	–	–	–	–
2.4	1.0	1.0	0.5	0.2	0.2	0.1
0.3	0.1	–	0.2	0.2	0.1	–
0.4	0.2	0.3	0.1	0.1	0.2	0.3
0.8	0.1	0.0	0.8	0.7	0.1	0.0
64.0	84.0	103.0	3.0	4.0	4.0	2.0
83.4	*99.0*	*123.6*	*21.1*	*20.7*	*18.0*	*20.6*
15.8	*2.1*	*18.6*	*1.8*	*1.6*	*1.8*	*1.6*
–	–	–	–	–	–	–
30.6	13.8	35.8	17.1	16.2	13.4	18.3
99.3	*101.1*	*142.2*	*22.9*	*22.2*	*19.8*	*22.2*

TOTAL OOF NET

1984	1985	1986	1983	1984	1985	1986
–	–	–	–	–	–	–
0.6	0.2	–	–	0.6	0.2	–
0.4	0.2	–	-1.9	-1.7	-1.7	-1.8
–	–	–	-0.6	–	–	–
–	–	–	–	–	–	–
–	–	–	-1.6	-1.2	-0.2	–
–	–	–	–	–	–	–
–	–	–	-0.2	-0.2	-0.1	-0.4
–	–	–	-16.7	-16.7	-16.6	-11.7
–	–	–	-2.2	-1.9	-1.9	-2.5
–	–	–	–	–	–	–
–	–	–	-2.0	-2.0	-2.0	-2.0
0.9	1.0	–	0.4	-4.4	-4.0	-3.4
–	–	–	–	–	–	–
14.0	–	–	6.0	-38.0	-61.0	-58.0
15.8	*1.5*	–	*-18.8*	*-65.5*	*-87.3*	*-79.8*
112.1	*188.3*	*110.2*	*129.9*	*20.0*	*122.1*	*15.8*
–	–	–	–	–	–	–
26.9	*0.2*	–	*58.4*	*-21.3*	*-2.0*	*-2.9*
128.0	*189.7*	*110.2*	*111.1*	*-45.5*	*34.8*	*-64.0*

ODA COMMITMENTS : LOANS

DAC COUNTRIES	1983	1984	1985	1986
Australia	–	–	–	–
Austria	–	0.3	–	–
Belgium	–	–	–	–
Canada	–	–	–	–
Denmark	–	–	–	–
Finland	–	–	–	–
France	–	–	–	–
Germany, Fed. Rep.	12.5	60.5	–	17.0
Ireland	–	–	–	–
Italy	–	–	–	–
Japan	–	–	–	–
Netherlands	–	–	–	–
New Zealand	–	–	–	–
Norway	–	–	0.5	–
Sweden	–	–	–	–
Switzerland	–	–	–	–
United Kingdom	–	–	–	–
United States	–	–	–	–
TOTAL	12.5	60.8	0.5	17.0
MULTILATERAL	–	–	1.6	–
OPEC COUNTRIES	–	–	–	–
E.E.C.+ MEMBERS	12.5	60.5	–	17.0
TOTAL	12.5	60.8	2.1	17.0

GRANT ELEMENT OF ODA

DAC COUNTRIES	1983	1984	1985	1986
Australia	–	–	–	–
Austria	100.0	48.6	100.0	–
Belgium	–	–	–	–
Canada	–	–	–	–
Denmark	–	–	–	–
Finland	–	–	–	–
France	100.0	100.0	100.0	100.0
Germany, Fed. Rep.	67.9	47.4	100.0	55.2
Ireland	–	–	–	–
Italy	100.0	100.0	100.0	100.0
Japan	100.0	100.0	100.0	100.0
Netherlands	100.0	100.0	100.0	100.0
New Zealand	–	–	–	–
Norway	100.0	100.0	45.7	100.0
Sweden	100.0	100.0	–	–
Switzerland	100.0	100.0	100.0	100.0
United Kingdom	100.0	100.0	100.0	100.0
United States	100.0	100.0	100.0	100.0
TOTAL	84.9	72.6	99.6	91.9
MULTILATERAL	100.0	100.0	100.0	100.0
OPEC COUNTRIES	–	–	–	–
E.E.C.+ MEMBERS	80.1	56.2	100.0	85.2
TOTAL	87.4	74.5	99.7	93.9

OTHER AGGREGATES

COMMITMENTS: ALL SOURCES

	1983	1984	1985	1986
TOTAL BILATERAL	69.7	148.8	156.1	134.3
of which				
OPEC	–	7.5	48.4	–
CMEA	–	–	–	–
TOTAL MULTILATERAL	253.0	158.4	174.4	54.5
TOTAL BIL.& MULTIL.	322.7	307.3	330.5	188.8
of which				
ODA Grants	50.7	89.8	105.4	161.6
ODA Loans	12.5	60.8	2.1	17.0

DISBURSEMENTS:

DAC COUNTRIES COMBINED

OFFICIAL & PRIVATE	1983	1984	1985	1986
GROSS:				
Contractual Lending	704.4	678.2	424.2	31.5
Export Credits Total	690.2	655.2	405.3	6.0
Export Credits Private	629.6	639.9	404.1	6.0
NET:				
Contractual Lending	226.3	58.2	-237.5	-482.5
Export Credits Total	277.6	103.8	-174.9	-418.5
PRIVATE SECTOR NET	376.5	487.9	341.0	-591.6
Direct Investment	-0.5	46.4	152.4	82.1
Portfolio Investment	120.8	314.6	338.5	-273.7
Export Credits	256.3	126.9	-149.8	-400.0

MARKET BORROWING:

CHANGE IN CLAIMS

	1983	1984	1985	1986
Banks	–	-96.0	-33.0	-1905.0

MEMORANDUM ITEM:

	1983	1984	1985	1986
CMEA Countr.(Gross)	–	–	–	–

RWANDA

	1983	1984	1985	1986	1983	1984	1985	1986		1983

TOTAL RECEIPTS NET / TOTAL ODA NET / TOTAL ODA GROSS

DAC COUNTRIES

	1983	1984	1985	1986	1983	1984	1985	1986		1983
Australia	0.0	–	–	–	0.0	–	–	–	Australia	0.0
Austria	0.2	0.3	0.6	1.8	0.2	0.3	0.6	1.8	Austria	0.2
Belgium	20.6	20.6	21.0	27.6	20.2	20.6	20.2	24.6	Belgium	20.2
Canada	10.9	11.9	10.7	4.7	10.9	11.9	10.7	4.7	Canada	10.9
Denmark	0.0	0.0	0.1	0.3	0.0	0.0	0.1	0.1	Denmark	0.0
Finland	0.0	0.0	0.0	0.0	0.0	0.0	0.0	0.0	Finland	0.0
France	9.2	8.8	15.4	19.0	9.2	9.4	15.4	20.0	France	9.2
Germany, Fed. Rep.	23.6	20.3	24.8	18.8	23.8	20.1	23.6	19.3	Germany, Fed. Rep.	23.8
Ireland	0.2	0.1	0.7	0.2	0.2	0.1	0.7	0.2	Ireland	0.2
Italy	10.1	0.0	6.2	5.8	0.7	0.8	3.7	6.2	Italy	0.7
Japan	5.6	3.1	1.6	9.3	5.9	3.1	1.6	9.3	Japan	5.9
Netherlands	5.5	4.2	3.0	9.3	5.5	4.2	3.0	6.0	Netherlands	5.5
New Zealand	–	–	–	–	–	–	–	–	New Zealand	–
Norway	0.8	0.3	–	–	0.8	0.3	–	–	Norway	0.8
Sweden	–	–	–	–	–	–	–	–	Sweden	–
Switzerland	7.4	7.3	8.4	10.3	7.4	7.3	8.4	10.3	Switzerland	7.4
United Kingdom	0.2	-1.1	0.7	2.3	0.1	0.0	0.1	0.2	United Kingdom	0.1
United States	10.0	18.0	15.0	21.0	10.0	18.0	15.0	21.0	United States	10.0
TOTAL	*104.3*	*93.8*	*108.1*	*130.4*	*94.7*	*96.0*	*103.2*	*123.7*	*TOTAL*	*94.7*

MULTILATERAL

	1983	1984	1985	1986	1983	1984	1985	1986		1983
AF.D.F.	9.2	7.2	5.4	7.7	9.2	7.2	5.4	7.7	AF.D.F.	9.3
AF.D.B.	0.7	-0.2	-0.3	-0.3	–	–	–	–	AF.D.B.	–
AS.D.B	–	–	–	–	–	–	–	–	AS.D.B	–
CAR.D.B.	–	–	–	–	–	–	–	–	CAR.D.B.	–
E.E.C.	8.8	15.4	11.7	19.4	8.8	15.4	11.7	19.4	E.E.C.	8.8
IBRD	–	–	–	–	–	–	–	–	IBRD	–
IDA	17.9	23.3	29.2	36.3	17.9	23.3	29.2	36.3	IDA	18.1
I.D.B.	–	–	–	–	–	–	–	–	I.D.B.	–
IFAD	0.7	0.6	1.4	1.5	0.7	0.6	1.4	1.5	IFAD	0.7
I.F.C.	-0.1	-0.1	-0.1	0.2	–	–	–	–	I.F.C.	–
IMF TRUST FUND	–	–	–	–	–	–	–	–	IMF TRUST FUND	–
U.N. AGENCIES	–	–	–	–	–	–	–	–	U.N. AGENCIES	–
UNDP	6.3	5.1	8.4	5.3	6.3	5.1	8.4	5.3	UNDP	6.3
UNTA	1.0	1.0	1.1	1.7	1.0	1.0	1.1	1.7	UNTA	1.0
UNICEF	1.3	0.9	1.0	1.3	1.3	0.9	1.0	1.3	UNICEF	1.3
UNRWA	–	–	–	–	–	–	–	–	UNRWA	–
WFP	3.7	2.7	5.9	1.5	3.7	2.7	5.9	1.5	WFP	3.7
UNHCR	3.8	4.2	5.1	1.1	3.8	4.2	5.1	1.1	UNHCR	3.8
Other Multilateral	1.1	2.4	3.6	3.8	1.1	2.4	3.6	3.8	Other Multilateral	1.1
Arab OPEC Agencies	-0.6	0.1	0.0	1.2	-0.6	0.1	0.0	1.2	Arab OPEC Agencies	0.4
TOTAL	*53.7*	*62.5*	*72.5*	*80.8*	*53.1*	*62.8*	*72.8*	*80.9*	*TOTAL*	*54.4*
OPEC COUNTRIES	*1.6*	*5.8*	*5.2*	*6.1*	*1.6*	*5.8*	*5.2*	*6.1*	*OPEC COUNTRIES*	*2.2*
E.E.C.+ MEMBERS	*78.2*	*68.3*	*83.5*	*102.8*	*68.4*	*70.6*	*78.6*	*96.0*	*E.E.C.+ MEMBERS*	*68.4*
TOTAL	*159.5*	*162.1*	*185.8*	*217.4*	*149.4*	*164.7*	*181.2*	*210.7*	*TOTAL*	*151.3*

ODA LOANS GROSS / ODA LOANS NET / GRANTS

DAC COUNTRIES

	1983	1984	1985	1986	1983	1984	1985	1986		1983
Australia	–	–	–	–	–	–	–	–	Australia	0.0
Austria	–	–	–	–	–	–	–	–	Austria	0.2
Belgium	–	–	0.1	–	–	–	0.1	–	Belgium	20.2
Canada	–	–	–	–	–	–	–	–	Canada	10.9
Denmark	–	–	–	–	–	–	–	–	Denmark	0.0
Finland	–	–	–	–	–	–	–	–	Finland	0.0
France	1.4	2.3	8.1	10.9	1.4	2.1	7.5	10.0	France	7.8
Germany, Fed. Rep.	–	–	–	–	–	–	–	–	Germany, Fed. Rep.	23.8
Ireland	–	–	–	–	–	–	–	–	Ireland	0.2
Italy	–	–	–	–	–	–	–	–	Italy	0.7
Japan	–	–	0.2	–	–	–	-0.1	-0.3	Japan	5.9
Netherlands	1.0	–	–	3.1	1.0	–	–	3.1	Netherlands	4.5
New Zealand	–	–	–	–	–	–	–	–	New Zealand	–
Norway	–	–	–	–	–	–	–	–	Norway	0.8
Sweden	–	–	–	–	–	–	–	–	Sweden	–
Switzerland	–	–	–	–	–	–	–	0.0	Switzerland	7.4
United Kingdom	–	–	–	–	–	–	–	–	United Kingdom	0.1
United States	–	–	–	–	–	–	–	–	United States	10.0
TOTAL	*2.4*	*2.3*	*8.3*	*14.0*	*2.4*	*2.1*	*7.5*	*12.7*	*TOTAL*	*92.3*
MULTILATERAL	*28.5*	*37.2*	*38.5*	*50.9*	*27.2*	*34.2*	*36.3*	*47.1*	*MULTILATERAL*	*25.9*
OPEC COUNTRIES	*2.0*	*6.5*	*6.4*	*7.4*	*1.4*	*5.8*	*5.2*	*6.1*	*OPEC COUNTRIES*	*0.2*
E.E.C.+ MEMBERS	*2.4*	*5.3*	*8.3*	*14.4*	*2.4*	*5.2*	*7.8*	*13.5*	*E.E.C.+ MEMBERS*	*66.0*
TOTAL	*32.9*	*45.9*	*53.1*	*72.3*	*31.0*	*42.1*	*48.9*	*66.0*	*TOTAL*	*118.4*

TOTAL OFFICIAL GROSS / TOTAL OFFICIAL NET / TOTAL OOF GROSS

DAC COUNTRIES

	1983	1984	1985	1986	1983	1984	1985	1986		1983
Australia	0.0	–	–	–	0.0	0.3	0.6	1.8	Australia	–
Austria	0.2	0.3	0.6	1.8	0.2	0.3	0.6	1.8	Austria	–
Belgium	20.2	20.6	20.2	24.6	20.2	20.6	20.2	24.6	Belgium	–
Canada	10.9	11.9	10.7	4.7	10.9	11.9	10.7	4.7	Canada	–
Denmark	0.0	0.0	0.1	0.3	0.0	0.0	0.1	0.3	Denmark	–
Finland	0.0	0.0	0.0	0.0	0.0	0.0	0.0	0.0	Finland	–
France	9.2	9.5	16.0	20.9	9.2	9.4	15.4	20.0	France	–
Germany, Fed. Rep.	23.8	20.1	23.6	19.3	23.8	20.1	23.6	19.3	Germany, Fed. Rep.	–
Ireland	0.2	0.1	0.7	0.2	0.2	0.1	0.7	0.2	Ireland	–
Italy	0.7	0.8	3.7	6.2	0.7	0.8	3.7	6.2	Italy	–
Japan	5.9	3.1	1.9	9.6	5.9	3.1	1.6	9.3	Japan	–
Netherlands	5.5	4.2	3.0	6.0	5.5	4.2	3.0	6.0	Netherlands	–
New Zealand	–	–	–	–	–	–	–	–	New Zealand	–
Norway	0.8	0.3	–	–	0.8	0.3	–	–	Norway	–
Sweden	–	–	–	–	–	–	–	–	Sweden	–
Switzerland	7.4	7.3	8.4	10.3	7.4	7.3	8.4	10.3	Switzerland	–
United Kingdom	0.1	0.0	0.1	0.2	0.1	0.0	0.1	0.2	United Kingdom	–
United States	10.0	18.0	15.0	21.0	10.0	18.0	15.0	21.0	United States	–
TOTAL	*94.7*	*96.2*	*104.0*	*125.2*	*94.7*	*96.0*	*103.2*	*123.9*	*TOTAL*	*–*
MULTILATERAL	*55.3*	*65.8*	*75.1*	*85.2*	*53.7*	*62.5*	*72.5*	*80.8*	*MULTILATERAL*	*0.9*
OPEC COUNTRIES	*2.2*	*6.5*	*6.4*	*7.4*	*1.6*	*5.8*	*5.2*	*6.1*	*OPEC COUNTRIES*	*–*
E.E.C.+ MEMBERS	*68.4*	*70.7*	*79.1*	*97.2*	*68.4*	*70.6*	*78.6*	*96.2*	*E.E.C.+ MEMBERS*	*–*
TOTAL	*152.2*	*168.5*	*185.4*	*217.9*	*150.0*	*164.4*	*180.9*	*210.9*	*TOTAL*	*0.9*

ODA COMMITMENTS

1984	1985	1986	1983	1984	1985	1986
–	–	–	0.0	–	–	–
0.3	0.6	1.8	0.1	0.2	0.6	–
20.6	20.2	24.6	11.1	13.1	9.9	24.6
11.9	10.7	4.7	3.3	8.8	18.1	3.2
0.0	0.1	0.1	0.0	–	0.1	0.1
0.0	0.0	0.0	0.0	0.0	–	0.0
9.5	16.0	20.9	13.9	22.4	19.3	20.9
20.1	23.6	19.3	15.8	22.5	17.9	19.0
0.1	0.7	0.2	0.2	0.1	0.7	0.2
0.8	3.7	6.2	4.2	1.8	0.5	9.2
3.1	1.9	9.6	2.7	4.0	4.0	10.0
4.2	3.0	6.0	7.2	4.4	4.9	7.0
–	–	–	–	–	–	–
0.3	–	–	–	–	–	–
–	–	–	–	–	–	–
7.3	8.4	10.3	8.6	5.3	13.5	1.5
0.0	0.1	0.2	0.1	0.0	0.1	0.2
18.0	15.0	21.0	12.2	27.7	20.5	14.4
96.2	*103.9*	*125.0*	*79.6*	*110.2*	*110.0*	*110.3*
7.3	5.6	7.8	22.8	8.5	6.2	14.7
–	–	–	–	–	–	–
–	–	–	–	–	–	–
15.4	11.7	19.4	23.7	8.3	3.1	11.5
–	–	–	–	–	–	–
24.9	29.6	37.6	35.0	9.0	42.3	48.1
–	–	–	–	–	–	–
0.6	1.4	2.9	–	3.7	–	–
–	–	–	–	–	–	–
–	–	–	17.1	16.3	25.1	14.8
5.1	8.4	5.3	–	–	–	–
1.0	1.1	1.7	–	–	–	–
0.9	1.0	1.3	–	–	–	–
–	–	–	–	–	–	–
2.7	5.9	1.5	–	–	–	–
4.2	5.1	1.1	–	–	–	–
2.4	3.6	3.8	–	–	–	–
1.4	1.7	2.2	–	5.0	–	7.6
65.7	*75.1*	*84.6*	*98.6*	*50.8*	*76.6*	*96.6*
6.5	*6.4*	*7.4*	*18.9*	–	*12.5*	*10.4*
70.7	*79.1*	*96.9*	*76.3*	*72.6*	*56.4*	*92.6*
168.4	*185.4*	*217.0*	*197.0*	*161.0*	*199.1*	*217.3*

TECH. COOP. GRANTS

1984	1985	1986	1983	1984	1985	1986
–	–	–	–	–	–	–
0.3	0.6	1.8	0.2	–	–	–
20.6	20.2	24.6	13.6	13.8	13.9	17.0
11.9	10.7	4.7	3.1	–	2.5	–
0.0	0.1	0.1	0.0	0.0	0.0	–
0.0	0.0	0.0	0.0	0.0	0.0	0.0
7.3	7.9	10.0	6.1	5.4	5.0	7.0
20.1	23.6	19.3	9.3	8.2	9.5	12.6
0.1	0.7	0.2	0.0	–	0.6	0.1
0.8	3.7	6.2	0.0	0.0	0.1	1.4
3.1	1.7	9.6	0.3	0.9	0.5	1.3
4.2	3.0	3.0	1.5	1.2	2.2	1.9
–	–	–	–	–	–	–
0.3	–	–	–	–	–	–
7.3	8.4	10.3	2.2	3.0	2.3	3.6
0.0	0.1	0.2	0.1	0.0	0.1	0.2
18.0	15.0	21.0	4.0	4.0	5.0	7.0
93.9	*95.7*	*111.0*	*40.4*	*36.5*	*41.7*	*52.1*
28.6	*36.6*	*33.7*	*13.4*	*13.6*	*19.2*	*14.3*
0.0	*0.0*	*0.0*	–	–	–	–
65.4	*70.8*	*82.5*	*30.7*	*28.7*	*31.4*	*41.2*
122.5	*132.3*	*144.7*	*53.8*	*50.1*	*60.9*	*66.4*

TOTAL OOF NET

1984	1985	1986	1983	1984	1985	1986
–	–	–	–	–	–	–
–	–	–	–	–	–	–
–	–	–	–	–	–	–
–	–	–	–	–	–	–
–	0.0	0.2	–	–	0.0	0.2
–	–	–	–	–	–	–
–	–	–	–	–	–	–
–	–	–	–	–	–	–
–	–	–	–	–	–	–
–	–	–	–	–	–	–
–	–	–	–	–	–	–
–	–	–	–	–	–	–
–	–	–	–	–	–	–
–	0.0	0.2	–	–	0.0	0.2
0.1	–	*0.6*	*0.6*	*-0.3*	*-0.4*	*-0.1*
–	–	–	–	–	–	–
–	0.0	0.2	–	–	0.0	0.2
0.1	*0.0*	*0.9*	*0.6*	*-0.3*	*-0.4*	*0.2*

ODA COMMITMENTS : LOANS

DAC COUNTRIES

	1983	1984	1985	1986
Australia	–	–	–	–
Austria	–	–	–	–
Belgium	–	–	–	–
Canada	–	–	–	–
Denmark	–	–	–	–
Finland	–	–	–	–
France	5.3	13.2	13.4	10.9
Germany, Fed. Rep.	–	–	–	–
Ireland	–	–	–	–
Italy	–	–	–	–
Japan	–	–	–	–
Netherlands	1.0	–	2.3	–
New Zealand	–	–	–	–
Norway	–	–	–	–
Sweden	–	–	–	–
Switzerland	–	–	–	–
United Kingdom	–	–	–	–
United States	–	–	–	–
TOTAL	*6.3*	*13.2*	*15.7*	*10.9*
MULTILATERAL	*69.0*	*27.8*	*48.5*	*70.4*
OPEC COUNTRIES	*18.9*	–	*12.5*	*10.4*
E.E.C.+ MEMBERS	*17.5*	*14.7*	*15.7*	*10.9*
TOTAL	*94.1*	*41.0*	*76.7*	*91.7*

GRANT ELEMENT OF ODA

DAC COUNTRIES

	1983	1984	1985	1986
Australia	100.0	–	–	–
Austria	100.0	100.0	100.0	–
Belgium	100.0	100.0	100.0	100.0
Canada	100.0	100.0	100.0	100.0
Denmark	100.0	–	100.0	100.0
Finland	100.0	100.0	–	100.0
France	73.4	76.0	55.1	83.8
Germany, Fed. Rep.	100.0	100.0	100.0	100.0
Ireland	100.0	100.0	100.0	100.0
Italy	100.0	100.0	100.0	100.0
Japan	100.0	100.0	100.0	100.0
Netherlands	100.0	100.0	81.5	100.0
New Zealand	–	–	–	–
Norway	–	–	–	–
Sweden	–	–	–	–
Switzerland	100.0	100.0	100.0	100.0
United Kingdom	100.0	100.0	100.0	100.0
United States	100.0	100.0	100.0	100.0
TOTAL	*94.8*	*95.1*	*91.3*	*96.9*
MULTILATERAL	*90.0*	*86.9*	*90.3*	*83.0*
OPEC COUNTRIES	*54.1*	–	*53.7*	*46.3*
E.E.C.+ MEMBERS	*93.7*	*92.4*	*83.0*	*96.3*
TOTAL	*88.3*	*92.1*	*88.3*	*88.3*

OTHER AGGREGATES

COMMITMENTS: ALL SOURCES

	1983	1984	1985	1986
TOTAL BILATERAL	98.5	110.2	122.9	121.2
of which				
OPEC	18.9	–	12.5	10.4
CMEA	–	–	–	–
TOTAL MULTILATERAL	107.8	50.8	76.8	96.6
TOTAL BIL.& MULTIL.	206.3	161.0	199.7	217.7
of which				
ODA Grants	102.9	120.1	122.5	125.6
ODA Loans	94.1	41.0	76.7	91.7

DISBURSEMENTS:

DAC COUNTRIES COMBINED

	1983	1984	1985	1986
OFFICIAL & PRIVATE				
GROSS:				
Contractual Lending	13.8	4.2	14.0	15.9
Export Credits Total	11.4	1.9	5.7	1.7
Export Credits Private	11.4	1.9	5.7	1.7
NET:				
Contractual Lending	11.5	-0.3	11.3	13.4
Export Credits Total	9.1	-2.4	3.8	0.4
PRIVATE SECTOR NET	9.6	-2.2	4.9	6.6
Direct Investment	0.6	-0.2	1.2	1.6
Portfolio Investment	-0.1	0.4	-0.1	4.5
Export Credits	9.1	-2.4	3.8	0.4

MARKET BORROWING:

CHANGE IN CLAIMS

	1983	1984	1985	1986
Banks	–	1.0	3.0	5.0

MEMORANDUM ITEM:

	1983	1984	1985	1986
CMEA Countr.(Gross)	–	–	–	–

DISBURSEMENTS, UNLESS OTHERWISE STATED

TOTAL RECEIPTS NET / TOTAL ODA NET / TOTAL ODA GROSS

	TOTAL RECEIPTS NET				TOTAL ODA NET				TOTAL ODA GROSS
	1983	1984	1985	1986	1983	1984	1985	1986	1983
DAC COUNTRIES									
Australia	0.0	–	–	–	0.0	–	–	–	0.0
Austria	0.6	0.3	0.3	0.6	0.6	0.3	0.3	0.6	0.6
Belgium	3.9	8.8	8.1	3.4	4.8	4.6	5.1	5.0	4.8
Canada	21.5	24.2	13.8	17.1	20.1	24.5	13.9	18.0	20.3
Denmark	-2.5	8.5	0.1	12.7	0.4	9.1	0.6	13.3	0.4
Finland	0.6	0.3	0.1	0.2	0.6	0.3	0.1	0.2	0.6
France	191.6	151.2	82.4	229.4	87.3	87.6	80.1	141.2	87.9
Germany, Fed. Rep.	19.4	24.3	14.3	19.5	19.3	20.7	14.6	19.7	19.7
Ireland	–	–	–	–	–	–	–	–	–
Italy	8.8	7.6	18.6	31.2	7.0	8.1	15.7	31.0	7.0
Japan	15.0	11.4	9.9	12.7	14.9	12.7	11.4	12.8	15.3
Netherlands	5.3	4.5	3.3	14.7	4.9	4.0	3.6	14.8	4.9
New Zealand	–	–	–	–	–	–	–	–	–
Norway	1.3	30.8	30.5	22.5	1.3	0.8	1.9	0.5	1.3
Sweden	–	0.0	–	–	–	0.0	–	–	–
Switzerland	5.4	5.5	3.8	11.5	3.6	3.7	3.8	11.5	3.6
United Kingdom	-4.1	4.3	1.1	4.9	0.6	0.5	1.3	7.2	0.6
United States	48.0	70.0	44.0	39.0	47.0	69.0	44.0	40.0	47.0
TOTAL	*314.7*	*351.6*	*230.2*	*419.2*	*212.4*	*245.7*	*196.5*	*315.7*	*214.0*
MULTILATERAL									
AF.D.F.	0.2	0.5	2.3	9.5	0.2	0.5	2.3	9.5	0.2
AF.D.B.	4.5	2.3	4.8	2.0	–	–	–	–	–
AS.D.B	–	–	–	–	–	–	–	–	–
CAR.D.B.	–	–	–	–	–	–	–	–	–
E.E.C.	36.4	22.4	6.6	62.7	16.2	20.7	6.0	64.8	16.2
IBRD	7.7	4.6	-0.1	2.8	0.8	0.8	0.3	0.3	0.8
IDA	18.6	18.3	27.0	110.0	18.6	18.3	27.0	110.0	20.1
I.D.B.	–	–	–	–	–	–	–	–	–
IFAD	0.0	–	0.5	1.2	0.0	–	0.5	1.2	0.0
I.F.C.	1.3	1.7	0.1	-0.1	–	–	–	–	–
IMF TRUST FUND	–	–	–	–	–	–	–	–	–
U.N. AGENCIES	–	–	–	–	–	–	–	–	–
UNDP	5.7	8.0	5.4	8.8	5.7	8.0	5.4	8.8	5.7
UNTA	0.5	0.9	1.1	1.4	0.5	0.9	1.1	1.4	0.5
UNICEF	1.0	1.6	1.8	2.1	1.0	1.6	1.8	2.1	1.0
UNRWA	–	–	–	–	–	–	–	–	–
WFP	5.6	5.2	3.2	4.6	5.6	5.2	3.2	4.6	5.6
UNHCR	0.8	1.0	0.8	0.8	0.8	1.0	0.8	0.8	0.8
Other Multilateral	3.6	4.8	4.5	4.1	3.6	4.8	4.5	4.1	3.6
Arab OPEC Agencies	13.7	-1.4	5.9	12.8	9.1	2.0	7.4	10.7	10.6
TOTAL	*99.5*	*69.7*	*63.9*	*222.7*	*62.0*	*63.6*	*60.2*	*218.2*	*65.1*
OPEC COUNTRIES	*46.0*	*70.3*	*46.4*	*34.1*	*47.9*	*58.6*	*37.4*	*33.5*	*48.4*
E.E.C.+ MEMBERS	*258.7*	*231.7*	*134.4*	*378.5*	*140.6*	*155.2*	*127.1*	*297.0*	*141.1*
TOTAL	*460.2*	*491.6*	*340.4*	*676.0*	*322.3*	*367.9*	*294.1*	*567.4*	*327.5*

ODA LOANS GROSS / ODA LOANS NET / GRANTS

	ODA LOANS GROSS				ODA LOANS NET				GRANTS
	1983	1984	1985	1986	1983	1984	1985	1986	1983
DAC COUNTRIES									
Australia	–	–	–	–	–	–	–	–	0.0
Austria	–	–	–	–	–	–	–	–	0.6
Belgium	–	–	–	–	–	–	–	–	4.8
Canada	0.3	0.4	0.2	–	0.1	0.4	0.2	–	20.0
Denmark	0.1	8.1	–	13.2	0.1	8.1	-0.5	13.2	0.3
Finland	–	–	–	–	–	–	–	–	0.6
France	19.6	25.6	16.7	90.6	19.0	19.7	14.4	78.1	68.3
Germany, Fed. Rep.	11.7	15.1	9.3	16.8	11.3	12.9	8.0	9.6	8.0
Ireland	–	–	–	–	–	–	–	–	–
Italy	–	1.5	11.9	9.0	–	1.5	11.9	9.0	7.0
Japan	1.7	0.9	–	–	1.3	0.6	-0.3	–	13.6
Netherlands	0.4	–	0.1	–	0.4	–	0.1	-0.1	4.6
New Zealand	–	–	–	–	–	–	–	–	–
Norway	–	–	–	–	–	–	–	–	1.3
Sweden	–	–	–	–	–	–	–	–	–
Switzerland	1.1	1.5	0.8	0.4	1.1	1.5	0.8	0.4	2.4
United Kingdom	–	–	–	–	–	–	–	–	0.6
United States	–	–	–	9.0	–	–	–	9.0	47.0
TOTAL	*34.9*	*53.1*	*39.0*	*139.0*	*33.3*	*44.7*	*34.5*	*119.2*	*179.1*
MULTILATERAL	*37.7*	*26.9*	*37.4*	*138.1*	*34.6*	*24.3*	*34.6*	*131.4*	*27.4*
OPEC COUNTRIES	*47.4*	*58.8*	*38.6*	*35.8*	*46.9*	*57.5*	*36.6*	*33.3*	*1.0*
E.E.C.+ MEMBERS	*37.8*	*53.2*	*38.6*	*130.5*	*36.7*	*45.1*	*34.3*	*110.7*	*103.9*
TOTAL	*119.9*	*138.8*	*114.9*	*312.9*	*114.7*	*126.5*	*105.7*	*283.9*	*207.6*

TOTAL OFFICIAL GROSS / TOTAL OFFICIAL NET / TOTAL OOF GROSS

	TOTAL OFFICIAL GROSS				TOTAL OFFICIAL NET				TOTAL OOF GROSS
	1983	1984	1985	1986	1983	1984	1985	1986	1983
DAC COUNTRIES									
Australia	0.0	–	–	–	0.0	–	–	–	–
Austria	0.6	0.3	0.3	0.6	0.6	0.3	0.3	0.6	–
Belgium	6.0	5.6	5.6	5.0	5.9	5.5	5.5	4.5	1.2
Canada	21.9	24.6	13.9	18.1	21.5	24.2	13.8	17.1	1.6
Denmark	0.6	9.1	1.3	13.3	0.6	9.1	0.6	13.3	0.2
Finland	0.6	0.3	0.1	0.2	0.6	0.3	0.1	0.2	–
France	133.4	161.9	106.1	219.9	130.7	146.1	101.4	195.7	45.6
Germany, Fed. Rep.	19.7	22.9	15.9	26.9	19.3	20.7	14.6	19.6	–
Ireland	–	–	–	–	–	–	–	–	–
Italy	9.7	9.5	19.0	31.5	9.4	8.8	19.0	31.5	2.7
Japan	15.3	13.0	11.7	12.8	14.9	12.7	11.4	12.8	–
Netherlands	5.3	4.5	3.7	14.9	5.3	4.5	3.7	14.7	0.4
New Zealand	–	–	–	–	–	–	–	–	–
Norway	1.3	0.8	1.9	0.5	1.3	0.8	1.9	0.5	–
Sweden	–	0.0	–	–	–	0.0	–	–	–
Switzerland	3.6	3.7	3.8	11.5	3.6	3.7	3.8	11.5	–
United Kingdom	0.6	0.5	1.3	7.2	0.6	0.5	1.3	7.2	–
United States	49.0	70.0	44.0	40.0	48.0	70.0	44.0	39.0	2.0
TOTAL	*267.7*	*326.6*	*228.7*	*402.3*	*262.2*	*307.1*	*221.3*	*368.2*	*53.7*
MULTILATERAL	*118.0*	*85.8*	*74.8*	*247.2*	*99.5*	*69.7*	*63.9*	*222.7*	*52.9*
OPEC COUNTRIES	*48.9*	*72.0*	*48.9*	*36.6*	*46.0*	*70.3*	*46.4*	*34.1*	*0.5*
E.E.C.+ MEMBERS	*212.3*	*237.0*	*160.7*	*383.6*	*208.2*	*217.6*	*152.6*	*349.3*	*70.5*
TOTAL	*434.6*	*484.5*	*352.4*	*686.1*	*407.7*	*447.1*	*331.5*	*624.9*	*107.2*

ODA COMMITMENTS

1984	1985	1986	1983	1984	1985	1986
–	–	–	0.1	0.1	0.3	–
0.3	0.3	0.6	2.6	2.9	2.5	5.0
4.6	5.1	5.0	23.2	21.4	11.2	20.4
24.6	13.9	18.0	17.5	0.9	2.2	11.1
9.1	1.1	13.3	0.3	0.2	–	0.7
0.3	0.1	0.2				
93.4	82.4	153.7	101.3	120.9	141.9	153.7
22.9	15.9	26.9	21.9	15.2	12.7	23.4
–	–	–	–	–	–	–
8.1	15.7	31.0	33.2	9.1	5.2	86.4
13.0	11.7	12.8	12.9	14.0	6.9	15.8
4.0	3.6	14.9	5.9	3.0	2.8	17.2
–	–	–	–	–	–	–
0.8	1.9	0.5	–	1.0	0.5	0.7
0.0	–	–	0.6	–	0.6	–
3.7	3.8	11.5	3.9	1.5	7.3	8.0
0.5	1.3	7.2	0.6	0.5	5.8	1.8
69.0	44.0	40.0	56.1	68.2	46.5	52.4
254.2	*200.9*	*335.5*	*280.1*	*258.8*	*246.4*	*396.4*
0.5	2.3	9.8	5.4	7.5	6.8	16.3
–	–	–	–	–	–	–
–	–	–	–	–	–	–
20.8	6.2	64.8	15.9	17.6	3.1	70.3
0.8	0.3	0.3	–	–	–	–
20.0	29.1	113.3	44.3	35.0	34.4	118.0
–	0.5	1.2	–	–	–	–
–	–	–	–	–	–	–
–	–	–	17.1	21.3	16.8	21.7
8.0	5.4	8.8	–	–	–	–
0.9	1.1	1.4	–	–	–	–
1.6	1.8	2.1	–	–	–	–
–	–	–	–	–	–	–
5.2	3.2	4.6	–	–	–	–
1.0	0.8	0.8	–	–	–	–
4.8	4.5	4.1	–	–	–	–
2.7	7.8	13.8	9.3	17.3	1.4	2.5
66.1	*62.9*	*224.8*	*92.0*	*98.7*	*62.6*	*228.8*
59.9	*39.5*	*36.0*	*56.1*	*88.2*	*4.0*	*16.0*
163.4	*131.4*	*316.8*	*199.0*	*170.0*	*176.2*	*368.8*
380.2	*303.3*	*596.4*	*428.2*	*445.8*	*312.9*	*641.2*

TECH. COOP. GRANTS

1984	1985	1986	1983	1984	1985	1986
–	–	–	0.0	–	–	–
0.3	0.3	0.6	0.2	–	–	–
4.6	5.1	5.0	2.1	1.7	1.7	2.7
24.2	13.7	18.0	2.1	–	3.0	–
1.0	1.1	0.1	0.3	0.7	0.1	0.4
0.3	0.1	0.2	0.6	0.3	0.1	0.0
67.8	65.7	63.1	52.5	55.9	42.6	58.3
7.8	6.6	10.1	6.2	5.1	4.5	6.7
–	–	–	–	–	–	–
6.6	3.8	22.0	1.1	3.5	2.5	9.8
12.1	11.7	12.8	1.2	2.0	2.5	5.5
4.0	3.6	14.9	0.8	1.6	0.6	1.5
–	–	–	–	–	–	–
0.8	1.9	0.5	0.1	0.0	0.1	0.0
0.0	–	–	–	–	–	–
2.2	2.9	11.0	1.0	1.6	1.0	1.3
0.5	1.3	7.2	0.6	0.4	0.8	1.8
69.0	44.0	31.0	19.0	26.0	19.0	16.0
201.0	*162.0*	*196.6*	*88.0*	*98.8*	*78.5*	*104.0*
39.2	*25.6*	*86.8*	*11.5*	*16.1*	*13.6*	*17.8*
1.1	*0.9*	*0.2*	–	–	–	–
110.1	*92.8*	*186.3*	*63.7*	*68.8*	*52.9*	*81.9*
241.4	*188.4*	*283.5*	*99.5*	*114.9*	*92.2*	*121.7*

TOTAL OOF NET

1984	1985	1986	1983	1984	1985	1986
–	–	–	–	–	–	–
1.1	0.5	–	1.1	1.0	0.3	-0.5
–	0.1	0.1	1.4	-0.3	-0.1	-0.9
–	0.2	0.0	0.2	–	0.0	0.0
–	–	–	–	–	–	–
68.5	23.7	66.2	43.4	58.5	21.3	54.5
–	–	–	0.0	0.0	–	-0.1
1.4	3.3	0.5	2.3	0.7	3.3	0.5
0.6	0.0	–	0.4	0.6	0.0	-0.1
–	–	–	–	–	–	–
–	–	–	–	–	–	–
1.0	–	–	1.0	1.0	–	-1.0
72.5	*27.8*	*66.8*	*49.8*	*61.3*	*24.8*	*52.4*
19.7	*11.9*	*22.4*	*37.5*	*6.2*	*3.7*	*4.5*
12.1	*9.4*	*0.6*	*-1.9*	*11.7*	*9.0*	*0.6*
73.6	*29.3*	*66.8*	*67.6*	*62.4*	*25.5*	*52.3*
104.3	*49.1*	*89.8*	*85.4*	*79.2*	*37.5*	*57.5*

ODA COMMITMENTS : LOANS

DAC COUNTRIES

	1983	1984	1985	1986
Australia	–	–	–	–
Austria	–	–	–	–
Belgium	–	–	–	–
Canada	0.1	–	–	–
Denmark	17.5	–	–	11.1
Finland	–	–	–	–
France	35.0	52.8	77.1	90.6
Germany, Fed. Rep.	9.4	10.2	1.6	13.7
Ireland	–	–	–	–
Italy	19.6	–	–	29.9
Japan	–	–	–	–
Netherlands	0.4	–	0.1	0.5
New Zealand	–	–	–	–
Norway	–	–	–	–
Sweden	–	–	–	–
Switzerland	–	–	–	–
United Kingdom	–	–	–	–
United States	–	–	5.5	4.0
TOTAL	*81.9*	*62.9*	*84.3*	*149.7*
MULTILATERAL	*59.4*	*61.0*	*42.5*	*150.0*
OPEC COUNTRIES	*41.7*	*88.1*	*2.8*	*16.0*
E.E.C.+ MEMBERS	*82.3*	*68.4*	*78.8*	*159.0*
TOTAL	**183.1**	**212.0**	**129.5**	**315.7**

GRANT ELEMENT OF ODA

DAC COUNTRIES

	1983	1984	1985	1986
Australia	–	–	–	–
Austria	100.0	100.0	100.0	–
Belgium	100.0	100.0	100.0	100.0
Canada	100.0	100.0	100.0	100.0
Denmark	75.9	100.0	100.0	85.8
Finland	100.0	100.0	–	100.0
France	91.2	68.6	80.6	59.2
Germany, Fed. Rep.	92.7	77.2	90.6	77.2
Ireland	–	–	–	–
Italy	73.0	100.0	100.0	88.1
Japan	100.0	100.0	100.0	100.0
Netherlands	100.0	100.0	100.0	98.9
New Zealand	–	–	–	–
Norway	–	100.0	100.0	100.0
Sweden	100.0	–	100.0	–
Switzerland	100.0	100.0	100.0	100.0
United Kingdom	100.0	100.0	100.0	100.0
United States	100.0	100.0	96.2	97.5
TOTAL	*91.6*	*84.0*	*89.4*	*79.7*
MULTILATERAL	*84.0*	*87.1*	*88.5*	*88.6*
OPEC COUNTRIES	*58.8*	*45.7*	*63.0*	*55.4*
E.E.C.+ MEMBERS	*87.6*	*74.9*	*84.9*	*77.7*
TOTAL	**85.2**	**77.0**	**88.8**	**82.1**

OTHER AGGREGATES

COMMITMENTS: ALL SOURCES

	1983	1984	1985	1986
TOTAL BILATERAL	394.3	402.3	451.4	415.4
of which				
OPEC	56.1	108.6	4.4	16.0
CMEA	0.1	–	150.0	–
TOTAL MULTILATERAL	101.0	106.5	70.0	262.3
TOTAL BIL.& MULTIL.	495.3	508.8	521.4	677.7
of which				
ODA Grants	245.1	233.8	183.4	325.5
ODA Loans	183.1	212.0	129.5	315.7

DISBURSEMENTS:

DAC COUNTRIES COMBINED

	1983	1984	1985	1986
OFFICIAL & PRIVATE				
GROSS:				
Contractual Lending	178.6	202.4	117.6	239.2
Export Credits Total	91.1	76.9	51.2	34.0
Export Credits Private	90.1	76.9	50.8	33.5
NET:				
Contractual Lending	131.5	128.8	75.0	188.4
Export Credits Total	47.8	22.1	16.1	16.4
PRIVATE SECTOR NET	52.5	44.6	8.9	51.0
Direct Investment	2.4	4.2	0.4	0.3
Portfolio Investment	1.6	17.5	-7.3	34.0
Export Credits	48.4	22.8	15.8	16.8

MARKET BORROWING:

CHANGE IN CLAIMS

	1983	1984	1985	1986
Banks	–	18.0	-22.0	36.0

MEMORANDUM ITEM:

	1983	1984	1985	1986
CMEA Countr.(Gross)	0.1	–	–	–

TOTAL RECEIPTS NET / TOTAL ODA NET / TOTAL ODA GROSS

	TOTAL RECEIPTS NET 1983	1984	1985	1986	TOTAL ODA NET 1983	1984	1985	1986	TOTAL ODA GROSS 1983
DAC COUNTRIES									
Australia	0.1	0.7	0.5	0.7	0.1	0.7	0.5	0.7	0.1
Austria	0.0	–	0.2	0.1	0.0	–	0.2	0.1	0.0
Belgium	-0.1	8.4	-0.3	7.7	0.1	0.8	0.2	2.5	0.1
Canada	0.2	0.2	0.2	0.1	0.2	0.2	0.2	0.1	0.2
Denmark	–	–	–	–	–	–	–	–	–
Finland	–	–	–	–	–	–	–	–	–
France	6.4	4.4	7.9	7.5	5.1	4.2	5.6	7.6	5.1
Germany, Fed. Rep.	0.2	0.1	0.6	0.6	0.2	0.1	0.6	0.5	0.2
Ireland	–	–	–	–	–	–	–	–	–
Italy	0.1	0.2	0.1	0.3	0.1	0.2	0.1	0.3	0.1
Japan	0.1	1.4	0.1	0.4	0.1	1.4	0.1	0.4	0.1
Netherlands	0.0	0.1	0.1	0.9	0.0	0.1	0.1	0.1	0.0
New Zealand	–	0.0	0.0	0.0	–	0.0	0.0	0.0	–
Norway	0.7	0.9	1.0	0.6	0.7	0.9	1.0	0.6	0.7
Sweden	–	0.0	0.3	0.3	–	0.0	0.3	0.3	–
Switzerland	0.0	0.0	-0.1	0.4	0.0	0.0	0.0	0.4	0.0
United Kingdom	4.3	3.4	1.8	0.0	4.1	2.0	1.2	3.1	4.2
United States	3.0	3.0	2.0	4.0	3.0	3.0	2.0	4.0	3.0
TOTAL	15.0	22.7	14.4	23.5	13.7	13.6	12.2	20.7	13.7
MULTILATERAL									
AF.D.F.	–	0.3	0.1	3.1	–	0.3	0.1	3.1	–
AF.D.B.	0.7	0.4	2.3	1.6	–	–	–	–	–
AS.D.B	–	–	–	–	–	–	–	–	–
CAR.D.B.	–	–	–	–	–	–	–	–	–
E.E.C.	0.5	0.5	7.6	2.6	0.5	0.5	7.6	2.6	0.5
IBRD	–	–	2.0	1.2	–	–	–	–	–
IDA	–	–	–	–	–	–	–	–	–
I.D.B.	–	–	–	–	–	–	–	–	–
IFAD	–	–	–	–	–	–	–	–	–
I.F.C.	–	–	–	–	–	–	–	–	–
IMF TRUST FUND	–	–	–	–	–	–	–	–	–
U.N. AGENCIES	–	–	–	–	–	–	–	–	–
UNDP	0.4	0.2	0.2	0.3	0.4	0.2	0.2	0.3	0.4
UNTA	0.3	0.3	0.3	0.3	0.3	0.3	0.3	0.3	0.3
UNICEF	0.0	0.1	0.1	0.0	0.0	0.1	0.1	0.0	0.0
UNRWA	–	–	–	–	–	–	–	–	–
WFP	0.3	0.2	0.2	0.1	0.3	0.2	0.2	0.1	0.3
UNHCR	–	–	–	–	–	–	–	–	–
Other Multilateral	0.4	0.2	0.2	0.1	0.4	0.2	0.2	0.1	0.4
Arab OPEC Agencies	0.5	0.2	0.1	0.8	0.0	-0.1	-0.1	-0.1	–
TOTAL	3.0	2.2	13.0	10.2	1.9	1.5	8.5	6.5	1.9
OPEC COUNTRIES	3.8	-0.2	0.6	1.3	0.1	–	1.5	1.4	0.1
E.E.C.+ MEMBERS	11.4	16.9	17.9	19.4	10.1	7.8	15.5	16.7	10.1
TOTAL	21.8	24.6	28.0	35.0	15.6	15.2	22.2	28.6	15.7

ODA LOANS GROSS / ODA LOANS NET / GRANTS

	ODA LOANS GROSS 1983	1984	1985	1986	ODA LOANS NET 1983	1984	1985	1986	GRANTS 1983
DAC COUNTRIES									
Australia	–	–	–	–	–	–	–	–	0.1
Austria	–	–	–	–	–	–	–	–	0.0
Belgium	–	0.7	–	2.2	–	0.7	–	2.2	0.1
Canada	–	–	–	–	–	–	–	–	0.2
Denmark	–	–	–	–	–	–	–	–	–
Finland	–	–	–	–	–	–	–	–	–
France	1.0	0.5	2.2	3.8	1.0	0.5	2.2	3.8	4.1
Germany, Fed. Rep.	–	–	0.5	0.3	–	–	0.5	0.3	0.2
Ireland	–	–	–	–	–	–	–	–	–
Italy	–	–	–	–	–	–	–	–	0.1
Japan	–	–	–	–	–	–	–	–	0.1
Netherlands	–	–	–	–	–	–	–	–	0.0
New Zealand	–	–	–	–	–	–	–	–	–
Norway	–	–	–	–	–	–	–	–	0.7
Sweden	–	–	–	–	–	–	–	–	–
Switzerland	–	–	–	–	–	–	–	–	0.0
United Kingdom	0.5	0.3	0.3	1.4	0.5	0.3	0.0	0.8	3.6
United States	–	–	–	–	–	–	–	–	3.0
TOTAL	1.5	1.5	2.9	7.7	1.5	1.4	2.6	7.1	12.2
MULTILATERAL	0.2	0.4	0.1	4.8	0.1	0.3	0.0	4.8	1.7
OPEC COUNTRIES	–	–	1.4	1.1	–	–	1.4	1.1	0.1
E.E.C.+ MEMBERS	1.7	1.6	2.9	9.4	1.6	1.5	2.6	8.8	8.5
TOTAL	1.7	1.9	4.4	13.7	1.6	1.7	4.0	13.0	14.1

TOTAL OFFICIAL GROSS / TOTAL OFFICIAL NET / TOTAL OOF GROSS

	TOTAL OFFICIAL GROSS 1983	1984	1985	1986	TOTAL OFFICIAL NET 1983	1984	1985	1986	TOTAL OOF GROSS 1983
DAC COUNTRIES									
Australia	0.1	0.7	0.5	0.7	0.1	0.7	0.5	0.7	–
Austria	0.0	–	0.2	0.1	0.0	–	0.2	0.1	–
Belgium	0.1	0.8	0.3	2.5	0.1	0.8	0.3	2.5	–
Canada	0.2	0.2	0.2	0.1	0.2	0.2	0.2	0.1	–
Denmark	–	–	–	–	–	–	–	–	–
Finland	–	–	–	–	–	–	–	–	–
France	5.1	4.2	5.7	7.6	4.9	4.0	5.1	7.6	–
Germany, Fed. Rep.	0.2	0.1	0.6	0.5	0.2	0.1	0.6	0.5	–
Ireland	–	–	–	–	–	–	–	–	–
Italy	0.1	0.2	0.1	0.3	0.1	0.2	0.1	0.3	–
Japan	0.1	1.4	0.1	0.4	0.1	1.4	0.1	0.4	–
Netherlands	0.0	0.1	0.1	0.1	0.0	0.1	0.1	0.0	–
New Zealand	–	0.0	0.0	0.0	–	0.0	0.0	0.0	–
Norway	0.7	0.9	1.0	0.6	0.7	0.9	1.0	0.6	–
Sweden	–	0.0	0.3	0.3	–	0.0	0.3	0.3	–
Switzerland	0.0	0.0	0.0	0.4	0.0	0.0	0.0	0.4	–
United Kingdom	4.8	2.2	1.5	3.7	4.6	1.9	0.9	3.0	0.7
United States	3.0	3.0	2.0	4.0	3.0	3.0	2.0	4.0	–
TOTAL	14.3	13.8	12.5	21.3	13.9	13.3	11.4	20.5	0.7
MULTILATERAL	3.5	2.7	14.0	11.3	3.0	2.2	13.0	10.2	1.6
OPEC COUNTRIES	3.9	0.2	1.8	1.5	3.8	-0.2	0.6	1.3	3.8
E.E.C.+ MEMBERS	10.8	8.0	15.8	17.3	10.3	7.5	14.6	16.6	0.7
TOTAL	21.8	16.6	28.3	34.1	20.8	15.2	24.9	32.0	6.1

1984	1985	1986	1983	1984	1985	1986

ODA COMMITMENTS

1984	1985	1986	1983	1984	1985	1986
0.7	0.5	0.7	0.1	1.1	0.8	0.7
–	0.2	0.1	0.0	0.0	0.2	–
0.8	0.2	2.5	–	0.7	–	2.6
0.2	0.2	0.1	0.2	0.2	0.2	0.1
–	–	–	–	–	–	–
4.2	5.6	7.6	7.4	4.4	6.2	7.6
0.1	0.6	0.5	0.1	0.8	0.1	0.2
–	–	–	–	–	–	–
0.2	0.1	0.3	0.1	0.2	0.3	0.7
1.4	0.1	0.4	1.3	0.2	0.1	0.4
0.1	0.1	0.1	0.0	0.1	0.1	0.1
0.0	0.0	0.0	–	0.0	0.0	–
0.9	1.0	0.6	3.5	0.4	0.0	0.6
0.0	0.3	0.3	–	0.3	–	0.3
0.0	0.0	0.4	0.3	0.0	0.0	0.2
2.1	1.5	3.7	3.0	1.7	1.2	2.1
3.0	2.0	4.0	2.6	2.8	2.3	2.6
13.7	12.5	21.3	18.6	12.7	11.4	18.1
0.3	0.1	3.1	–	–	–	–
–	–	–	–	–	–	–
–	–	–	–	–	–	–
0.5	7.6	2.6	2.6	0.4	4.9	0.4
–	–	–	–	–	–	–
–	–	–	–	–	–	–
–	–	–	–	–	–	–
–	–	–	1.4	0.9	1.0	0.9
0.2	0.2	0.3	–	–	–	–
0.3	0.3	0.3	–	–	–	–
0.1	0.1	0.0	–	–	–	–
0.2	0.2	0.1	–	–	–	–
–	–	–	–	–	–	–
0.2	0.2	0.1	–	–	–	–
–	–	–	–	–	–	–
1.6	8.6	6.6	3.9	1.3	5.8	1.2
–	1.5	1.4	–	–	5.9	–
7.9	15.8	17.3	13.1	8.3	12.7	13.6
15.3	22.6	29.3	22.5	14.0	23.1	19.3

TECH. COOP. GRANTS

1984	1985	1986	1983	1984	1985	1986
0.7	0.5	0.7	0.1	0.3	0.3	0.4
–	0.2	0.1	0.0	–	–	–
0.1	0.2	0.3	0.0	0.1	0.2	0.2
0.2	0.2	0.1	0.3	–	0.0	–
–	–	–	–	–	–	–
3.7	3.5	3.8	1.7	2.1	1.9	2.9
0.1	0.1	0.2	0.2	0.1	0.1	0.2
–	–	–	–	–	–	–
0.2	0.1	0.3	0.1	0.2	0.1	0.3
1.4	0.1	0.4	0.1	0.1	0.1	0.2
0.1	0.1	0.1	0.0	0.1	0.1	0.1
0.0	0.0	0.0	–	0.0	0.0	0.0
0.9	1.0	0.6	–	0.1	–	–
0.0	0.3	0.3	–	0.0	–	–
0.0	0.0	0.4	0.0	0.0	0.0	0.3
1.8	1.2	2.3	3.0	1.7	1.2	2.1
3.0	2.0	4.0	1.0	1.0	–	–
12.2	9.6	13.6	6.5	5.7	4.1	6.8
1.2	8.6	1.7	1.1	0.7	0.8	0.9
–	0.0	0.3	–	–	–	–
6.3	12.9	7.9	5.0	4.2	3.6	6.0
13.4	18.2	15.6	7.6	6.4	4.8	7.7

TOTAL OOF NET

1984	1985	1986	1983	1984	1985	1986
–	–	–	–	–	–	–
–	0.0	–	–	–	0.0	–
–	–	–	–	–	–	–
–	–	–	–	–	–	–
0.0	0.0	–	-0.2	-0.2	-0.5	–
–	–	–	–	–	–	–
–	–	–	–	–	–	–
–	–	–	–	–	–	–
–	–	–	–	–	–	–
–	–	–	–	–	–	–
0.1	–	–	0.5	-0.1	-0.3	-0.2
–	–	–	–	–	–	–
0.1	0.1	–	0.3	-0.3	-0.8	-0.2
1.1	5.4	4.8	1.2	0.6	4.5	3.7
0.2	0.3	0.0	3.7	-0.2	-0.9	-0.2
0.1	0.1	–	0.3	-0.3	-0.8	-0.2
1.4	5.8	4.8	5.1	0.1	2.8	3.4

ODA COMMITMENTS : LOANS

DAC COUNTRIES

	1983	1984	1985	1986
Australia	–	–	–	–
Austria	–	–	–	–
Belgium	–	0.7	–	2.2
Canada	–	–	–	–
Denmark	–	–	–	–
Finland	–	–	–	–
France	2.9	1.1	3.6	3.8
Germany, Fed. Rep.	–	0.7	–	–
Ireland	–	–	–	–
Italy	–	–	–	–
Japan	–	–	–	–
Netherlands	–	–	–	–
New Zealand	–	–	–	–
Norway	–	–	–	–
Sweden	–	–	–	–
Switzerland	–	–	–	–
United Kingdom	–	–	–	–
United States	–	–	–	–
TOTAL	2.9	2.5	3.6	6.0
MULTILATERAL	–	–	2.3	–
OPEC COUNTRIES	–	–	5.4	–
E.E.C.+ MEMBERS	2.9	2.5	5.9	6.0
TOTAL	2.9	2.5	11.3	6.0

GRANT ELEMENT OF ODA

DAC COUNTRIES

	1983	1984	1985	1986
Australia	100.0	100.0	100.0	100.0
Austria	100.0	100.0	100.0	–
Belgium	–	80.4	–	82.6
Canada	100.0	100.0	100.0	100.0
Denmark	–	–	–	–
Finland	–	–	–	–
France	82.5	82.3	56.0	60.4
Germany, Fed. Rep.	100.0	68.7	100.0	100.0
Ireland	–	–	–	–
Italy	100.0	100.0	100.0	100.0
Japan	100.0	100.0	100.0	100.0
Netherlands	100.0	100.0	100.0	100.0
New Zealand	–	100.0	100.0	–
Norway	100.0	100.0	100.0	100.0
Sweden	–	100.0	–	100.0
Switzerland	100.0	100.0	100.0	100.0
United Kingdom	100.0	100.0	100.0	100.0
United States	100.0	100.0	100.0	100.0
TOTAL	93.8	90.9	74.4	79.4
MULTILATERAL	100.0	100.0	100.0	100.0
OPEC COUNTRIES	–	–	34.1	–
E.E.C.+ MEMBERS	91.0	86.0	72.2	73.3
TOTAL	95.0	91.8	67.7	80.6

OTHER AGGREGATES

COMMITMENTS: ALL SOURCES

	1983	1984	1985	1986
TOTAL BILATERAL	22.3	14.7	22.3	18.1
of which				
OPEC	–	–	5.9	–
CMEA	3.0	2.0	5.0	–
TOTAL MULTILATERAL	9.6	14.1	18.3	1.2
TOTAL BIL.& MULTIL.	31.9	28.9	40.6	19.3
of which				
ODA Grants	22.6	13.5	16.9	13.3
ODA Loans	2.9	2.5	11.3	6.0

DISBURSEMENTS:

DAC COUNTRIES COMBINED

	1983	1984	1985	1986
OFFICIAL & PRIVATE				
GROSS:				
Contractual Lending	3.9	4.8	10.0	15.0
Export Credits Total	1.7	3.2	7.1	7.3
Export Credits Private	1.7	3.2	7.1	7.3
NET:				
Contractual Lending	2.7	3.2	6.5	7.7
Export Credits Total	1.0	2.1	4.8	0.8
PRIVATE SECTOR NET	1.1	9.3	3.1	3.0
Direct Investment	0.0	1.4	0.8	0.1
Portfolio Investment	0.1	5.9	-2.5	2.1
Export Credits	1.0	2.1	4.8	0.8

MARKET BORROWING:

CHANGE IN CLAIMS

	1983	1984	1985	1986
Banks	–	12.0	12.0	-5.0

MEMORANDUM ITEM:

	1983	1984	1985	1986
CMEA Countr.(Gross)	3.0	2.0	1.0	5.0

TOTAL RECEIPTS NET / TOTAL ODA NET / TOTAL ODA GROSS

	1983	1984	1985	1986		1983	1984	1985	1986		1983
TOTAL RECEIPTS NET					**TOTAL ODA NET**					**TOTAL ODA GROSS**	
DAC COUNTRIES											
Australia	0.1	0.1	0.0	4.1	Australia	0.1	0.1	0.0	0.1	Australia	0.1
Austria	0.0	0.0	0.0	0.0	Austria	0.0	0.0	0.0	0.0	Austria	0.0
Belgium	0.1	2.4	—	0.1	Belgium	—	0.1	0.0	0.1	Belgium	—
Canada	0.9	0.8	0.9	0.5	Canada	0.9	0.8	0.9	0.5	Canada	0.9
Denmark	0.2	0.1	0.1	6.2	Denmark	0.2	0.1	0.1	6.2	Denmark	0.2
Finland	0.0	0.1	—	0.0	Finland	0.0	0.1	—	0.0	Finland	0.0
France	2.5	0.9	0.5	1.3	France	0.9	1.3	0.9	1.7	France	0.9
Germany, Fed. Rep.	12.0	16.1	8.5	8.2	Germany, Fed. Rep.	10.4	7.1	10.5	8.4	Germany, Fed. Rep.	10.4
Ireland	0.0	0.1	0.1	0.1	Ireland	0.0	0.1	0.1	0.1	Ireland	0.0
Italy	5.1	0.0	0.1	11.0	Italy	6.0	0.4	0.3	11.3	Italy	6.0
Japan	1.6	0.1	2.2	3.9	Japan	1.6	0.1	2.3	3.9	Japan	1.6
Netherlands	0.9	0.8	1.4	2.1	Netherlands	1.5	0.5	1.4	2.1	Netherlands	1.5
New Zealand	—	—	—	—	New Zealand	—	—	—	—	New Zealand	—
Norway	0.3	4.7	4.4	4.5	Norway	0.3	0.2	0.1	0.3	Norway	0.3
Sweden	—	—	—	—	Sweden	—	—	—	—	Sweden	—
Switzerland	-1.3	0.0	0.1	0.0	Switzerland	0.0	0.0	0.1	0.0	Switzerland	0.0
United Kingdom	3.7	7.9	-1.9	5.0	United Kingdom	3.7	2.8	3.7	4.7	United Kingdom	4.9
United States	11.0	9.0	10.0	12.0	United States	10.0	9.0	10.0	12.0	United States	10.0
TOTAL	*36.9*	*43.0*	*26.4*	*59.0*	*TOTAL*	*35.6*	*22.6*	*30.3*	*51.3*	*TOTAL*	*36.7*
MULTILATERAL											
AF.D.F.	1.6	3.0	1.6	1.3	AF.D.F.	1.6	3.0	1.6	1.3	AF.D.F.	1.6
AF.D.B.	-0.1	-2.4	—	-1.4	AF.D.B.	—	—	—	—	AF.D.B.	—
AS.D.B	—	—	—	—	AS.D.B	—	—	—	—	AS.D.B	—
CAR.D.B.	—	—	—	—	CAR.D.B.	—	—	—	—	CAR.D.B.	—
E.E.C.	13.2	5.7	8.2	5.8	E.E.C.	13.2	5.7	8.2	5.8	E.E.C.	13.2
IBRD	-0.8	-1.2	-0.6	-1.4	IBRD	—	—	—	—	IBRD	—
IDA	6.5	5.2	9.1	8.8	IDA	6.5	5.2	9.1	8.8	IDA	6.6
I.D.B.	—	—	—	—	I.D.B.	—	—	—	—	I.D.B.	—
IFAD	2.4	1.0	3.6	3.2	IFAD	2.4	1.0	3.6	3.2	IFAD	2.4
I.F.C.	—	—	—	—	I.F.C.	—	—	—	—	I.F.C.	—
IMF TRUST FUND	—	—	—	—	IMF TRUST FUND	—	—	—	—	IMF TRUST FUND	—
U.N. AGENCIES	—	—	—	—	U.N. AGENCIES	—	—	—	—	U.N. AGENCIES	—
UNDP	3.0	4.0	4.7	6.0	UNDP	3.0	4.0	4.7	6.0	UNDP	3.0
UNTA	0.7	0.7	0.8	0.7	UNTA	0.7	0.7	0.8	0.7	UNTA	0.7
UNICEF	0.3	0.6	0.5	0.8	UNICEF	0.3	0.6	0.5	0.8	UNICEF	0.3
UNRWA	—	—	—	—	UNRWA	—	—	—	—	UNRWA	—
WFP	—	—	0.4	0.1	WFP	—	—	0.4	0.1	WFP	—
UNHCR	0.4	0.5	0.3	0.3	UNHCR	0.4	0.5	0.3	0.3	UNHCR	0.4
Other Multilateral	0.9	1.2	1.6	1.3	Other Multilateral	0.9	1.2	1.6	1.3	Other Multilateral	0.9
Arab OPEC Agencies	1.5	2.8	4.7	1.6	Arab OPEC Agencies	1.5	2.8	4.7	1.6	Arab OPEC Agencies	1.8
TOTAL	*29.5*	*21.1*	*34.8*	*27.1*	*TOTAL*	*30.4*	*24.7*	*35.4*	*30.0*	*TOTAL*	*30.9*
OPEC COUNTRIES	*0.1*	*13.6*	*0.2*	*5.8*	*OPEC COUNTRIES*	*0.1*	*13.6*	*0.2*	*5.8*	*OPEC COUNTRIES*	*0.1*
E.E.C.+ MEMBERS	*37.6*	*34.0*	*17.0*	*39.8*	*E.E.C.+ MEMBERS*	*36.0*	*18.1*	*25.1*	*40.3*	*E.E.C.+ MEMBERS*	*37.1*
TOTAL	*66.4*	*77.7*	*61.4*	*91.9*	*TOTAL*	*66.0*	*60.8*	*65.9*	*87.1*	*TOTAL*	*67.7*

ODA LOANS GROSS / ODA LOANS NET / GRANTS

	1983	1984	1985	1986		1983	1984	1985	1986		1983
ODA LOANS GROSS					**ODA LOANS NET**					**GRANTS**	
DAC COUNTRIES											
Australia	—	—	—	—	Australia	—	—	—	—	Australia	0.1
Austria	—	—	—	—	Austria	—	—	—	—	Austria	0.0
Belgium	—	—	—	—	Belgium	—	—	—	—	Belgium	—
Canada	—	—	—	—	Canada	—	—	—	—	Canada	0.9
Denmark	—	—	—	—	Denmark	—	—	—	—	Denmark	0.2
Finland	—	—	—	—	Finland	—	—	—	—	Finland	0.0
France	0.4	0.6	—	—	France	0.4	0.6	—	—	France	0.5
Germany, Fed. Rep.	4.2	2.0	1.5	1.2	Germany, Fed. Rep.	4.2	2.0	-46.5	0.2	Germany, Fed. Rep.	6.2
Ireland	—	—	—	—	Ireland	—	—	—	—	Ireland	0.0
Italy	6.0	—	—	—	Italy	6.0	—	—	—	Italy	0.1
Japan	—	—	—	1.5	Japan	—	—	—	1.5	Japan	1.6
Netherlands	—	—	—	—	Netherlands	—	—	-3.0	—	Netherlands	1.5
New Zealand	—	—	—	—	New Zealand	—	—	—	—	New Zealand	—
Norway	—	—	—	—	Norway	—	—	—	—	Norway	0.3
Sweden	—	—	—	—	Sweden	—	—	—	—	Sweden	—
Switzerland	—	—	—	—	Switzerland	—	—	—	—	Switzerland	0.0
United Kingdom	—	—	—	—	United Kingdom	-1.1	-1.0	-1.0	-1.0	United Kingdom	4.9
United States	4.0	3.0	4.0	8.0	United States	4.0	3.0	4.0	8.0	United States	6.0
TOTAL	*14.5*	*5.6*	*5.5*	*10.7*	*TOTAL*	*13.4*	*4.6*	*-46.5*	*8.7*	*TOTAL*	*22.2*
MULTILATERAL	*12.6*	*12.8*	*18.5*	*15.3*	*MULTILATERAL*	*12.1*	*12.3*	*18.5*	*14.9*	*MULTILATERAL*	*18.3*
OPEC COUNTRIES	*—*	*—*	*0.2*	*0.3*	*OPEC COUNTRIES*	*—*	*—*	*0.2*	*0.3*	*OPEC COUNTRIES*	*0.1*
E.E.C.+ MEMBERS	*10.7*	*2.9*	*1.5*	*1.5*	*E.E.C.+ MEMBERS*	*9.6*	*1.9*	*-50.5*	*-0.4*	*E.E.C.+ MEMBERS*	*26.4*
TOTAL	*27.1*	*18.4*	*24.2*	*26.3*	*TOTAL*	*25.5*	*16.9*	*-27.9*	*24.0*	*TOTAL*	*40.5*

TOTAL OFFICIAL GROSS / TOTAL OFFICIAL NET / TOTAL OOF GROSS

	1983	1984	1985	1986		1983	1984	1985	1986		1983
TOTAL OFFICIAL GROSS					**TOTAL OFFICIAL NET**					**TOTAL OOF GROSS**	
DAC COUNTRIES											
Australia	0.1	0.1	0.0	4.1	Australia	0.1	0.1	0.0	4.1	Australia	—
Austria	0.0	0.0	0.0	0.0	Austria	0.0	0.0	0.0	0.0	Austria	—
Belgium	—	3.1	0.0	0.1	Belgium	—	3.1	0.0	0.1	Belgium	—
Canada	0.9	0.8	0.9	0.5	Canada	0.9	0.8	0.9	0.5	Canada	—
Denmark	0.2	0.1	0.1	6.2	Denmark	0.2	0.1	0.1	6.2	Denmark	—
Finland	0.0	0.1	—	0.0	Finland	0.0	0.1	—	0.0	Finland	—
France	0.9	1.3	0.9	1.7	France	0.9	1.3	0.9	1.7	France	—
Germany, Fed. Rep.	12.9	7.7	62.7	11.2	Germany, Fed. Rep.	12.9	7.1	14.7	10.2	Germany, Fed. Rep.	2.6
Ireland	0.0	0.1	0.1	0.1	Ireland	0.0	0.1	0.1	0.1	Ireland	—
Italy	6.0	0.4	0.3	11.3	Italy	6.0	0.4	0.3	11.3	Italy	—
Japan	1.6	0.1	2.3	3.9	Japan	1.6	0.1	2.3	3.9	Japan	—
Netherlands	1.5	0.5	4.4	2.1	Netherlands	0.9	0.5	1.4	2.1	Netherlands	—
New Zealand	—	—	—	—	New Zealand	—	—	—	—	New Zealand	—
Norway	0.3	0.2	0.1	0.3	Norway	0.3	0.2	0.1	0.3	Norway	—
Sweden	—	—	—	—	Sweden	—	—	—	—	Sweden	—
Switzerland	0.0	0.0	0.1	0.0	Switzerland	0.0	0.0	0.1	0.0	Switzerland	—
United Kingdom	4.9	3.8	4.7	5.6	United Kingdom	3.7	2.8	3.7	4.7	United Kingdom	—
United States	11.0	9.0	11.0	12.0	United States	11.0	9.0	10.0	12.0	United States	1.0
TOTAL	*40.3*	*27.2*	*87.6*	*59.0*	*TOTAL*	*38.5*	*25.6*	*34.6*	*57.1*	*TOTAL*	*3.6*
MULTILATERAL	*30.9*	*25.4*	*35.5*	*30.3*	*MULTILATERAL*	*29.5*	*21.1*	*34.8*	*27.1*	*MULTILATERAL*	*—*
OPEC COUNTRIES	*0.1*	*13.6*	*0.2*	*5.8*	*OPEC COUNTRIES*	*0.1*	*13.6*	*0.2*	*5.8*	*OPEC COUNTRIES*	*—*
E.E.C.+ MEMBERS	*39.7*	*22.7*	*81.3*	*44.0*	*E.E.C.+ MEMBERS*	*37.9*	*21.1*	*29.3*	*42.1*	*E.E.C.+ MEMBERS*	*2.6*
TOTAL	*71.2*	*66.1*	*123.2*	*95.2*	*TOTAL*	*68.0*	*60.2*	*69.6*	*90.0*	*TOTAL*	*3.6*

ODA COMMITMENTS

1984	1985	1986	1983	1984	1985	1986
0.1	0.0	0.1	0.0	0.1	0.0	0.0
0.0	0.0	0.0	–	0.0	0.0	–
0.1	0.0	0.1	–	–	–	0.1
0.8	0.9	0.5	1.0	1.3	1.3	0.2
0.1	0.1	6.2	–	–	9.5	–
0.1	–	0.0	–	–	–	–
1.3	0.9	1.7	0.5	0.7	0.8	1.7
7.1	58.4	9.4	5.0	9.2	63.2	12.7
0.1	0.1	0.1	0.0	0.1	0.1	0.1
0.4	0.3	11.3	0.1	0.7	0.3	23.5
0.1	2.3	3.9	0.6	2.3	1.0	3.4
0.5	4.4	2.1	1.3	0.5	4.0	0.9
–	–	–	–	–	–	–
0.2	0.1	0.3	1.3	0.0	0.1	0.1
–	–	–	–	–	–	–
0.0	0.1	0.0	–	–	0.1	–
3.8	4.7	5.6	5.9	3.4	4.0	4.8
9.0	10.0	12.0	9.1	9.4	6.5	11.4
23.6	82.3	53.3	24.7	27.6	90.9	58.9
3.1	1.6	1.3	–	–	1.2	–
–	–	–	–	–	–	–
–	–	–	–	–	–	–
5.7	8.2	5.8	8.4	5.2	3.0	11.5
–	–	–	–	–	–	–
5.3	9.2	9.2	20.0	21.5	–	5.3
–	–	–	–	–	–	–
1.0	3.6	3.2	–	5.0	–	0.2
–	–	–	–	–	–	–
–	–	–	5.2	7.0	8.3	9.2
4.0	4.7	6.0	–	–	–	–
0.7	0.8	0.7	–	–	–	–
0.6	0.5	0.8	–	–	–	–
–	–	–	–	–	–	–
–	0.4	0.1	–	–	–	–
0.5	0.3	0.3	–	–	–	–
1.2	1.6	1.3	–	–	–	–
3.2	4.7	1.6	1.1	5.1	6.1	0.4
25.3	35.5	30.3	34.7	43.8	18.6	26.5
13.6	0.2	5.8	0.0	13.5	1.5	5.3
19.1	77.1	42.3	21.2	19.8	84.8	55.2
62.4	118.0	89.4	59.5	84.9	110.9	90.7

TECH. COOP. GRANTS

1984	1985	1986	1983	1984	1985	1986
0.1	0.0	0.1	0.1	0.0	0.0	0.1
0.0	0.0	0.0	0.0	–	–	–
0.1	0.0	0.1	–	–	–	–
0.8	0.9	0.5	0.9	–	0.6	–
0.1	0.1	6.2	0.2	0.1	0.1	0.1
0.1	–	0.0	0.0	0.1	–	0.0
0.7	0.9	1.7	0.5	0.7	0.8	1.0
5.1	56.9	8.3	5.9	4.8	5.5	6.7
0.1	0.1	0.1	0.0	0.1	0.1	0.1
0.4	0.3	11.3	0.1	0.2	0.3	5.2
0.1	2.3	2.4	0.5	0.1	0.2	0.4
0.5	4.4	2.1	0.7	0.5	0.9	0.9
–	–	–	–	–	–	–
0.2	0.1	0.3	–	0.0	0.0	–
–	–	–	–	–	–	–
0.0	0.1	0.0	0.0	0.0	–	0.0
3.8	4.7	5.6	2.2	1.8	2.8	3.7
6.0	6.0	4.0	3.0	4.0	3.0	2.0
18.0	76.8	42.6	14.0	12.5	14.3	20.1
12.4	17.0	15.0	5.2	7.0	7.9	9.5
13.6	0.0	5.5	–	–	–	–
16.2	75.6	40.8	9.5	8.2	10.5	18.0
44.0	93.8	63.1	19.2	19.4	22.2	29.6

TOTAL OOF NET

1984	1985	1986	1983	1984	1985	1986
–	–	4.0	–	–	–	4.0
–	–	–	–	–	–	–
3.0	–	–	–	3.0	–	–
–	–	–	–	–	–	–
–	–	–	–	–	–	–
0.6	4.3	1.8	2.6	0.0	4.3	1.8
–	–	–	–	–	–	–
–	–	–	-0.7	–	–	–
–	–	–	–	–	–	–
–	–	–	–	–	–	–
–	1.0	–	1.0	–	–	–
3.6	5.3	5.8	2.9	3.0	4.3	5.8
0.1	–	–	-0.9	-3.6	-0.6	-2.8
–	–	–	–	–	–	–
3.6	4.3	1.8	1.9	3.0	4.3	1.8
3.7	5.3	5.8	2.0	-0.6	3.6	2.9

ODA COMMITMENTS : LOANS

DAC COUNTRIES

	1983	1984	1985	1986
Australia	–	–	–	–
Austria	–	–	–	–
Belgium	–	–	–	–
Canada	–	–	–	–
Denmark	–	–	–	–
Finland	–	–	–	–
France	–	–	–	–
Germany, Fed. Rep.	–	0.4	2.4	–
Ireland	–	–	–	–
Italy	–	–	–	–
Japan	–	–	–	1.5
Netherlands	–	–	–	–
New Zealand	–	–	–	–
Norway	–	–	–	–
Sweden	–	–	–	–
Switzerland	–	–	–	–
United Kingdom	–	–	–	–
United States	3.7	3.0	4.0	8.0
TOTAL	3.7	3.4	6.4	9.5
MULTILATERAL	20.8	31.5	7.3	5.6
OPEC COUNTRIES	–	–	1.0	–
E.E.C.+ MEMBERS	–	0.4	2.4	–
TOTAL	24.5	34.9	14.6	15.1

GRANT ELEMENT OF ODA

DAC COUNTRIES

	1983	1984	1985	1986
Australia	100.0	100.0	100.0	100.0
Austria	–	100.0	100.0	–
Belgium	–	–	–	100.0
Canada	100.0	100.0	100.0	100.0
Denmark	–	–	100.0	–
Finland	–	–	–	–
France	100.0	100.0	100.0	100.0
Germany, Fed. Rep.	100.0	99.2	96.8	100.0
Ireland	100.0	100.0	100.0	100.0
Italy	100.0	100.0	100.0	100.0
Japan	100.0	100.0	100.0	65.6
Netherlands	100.0	100.0	100.0	100.0
New Zealand	–	–	–	–
Norway	100.0	100.0	100.0	100.0
Sweden	–	–	–	–
Switzerland	–	–	100.0	–
United Kingdom	100.0	100.0	100.0	100.0
United States	86.8	89.6	80.0	77.2
TOTAL	95.1	96.2	96.3	93.6
MULTILATERAL	88.8	84.7	85.3	96.1
OPEC COUNTRIES	100.0	100.0	68.9	100.0
E.E.C.+ MEMBERS	100.0	99.6	97.6	100.0
TOTAL	91.5	90.9	94.1	94.7

OTHER AGGREGATES

COMMITMENTS: ALL SOURCES

	1983	1984	1985	1986
TOTAL BILATERAL	24.8	47.7	95.2	73.3
of which				
OPEC	0.0	13.5	1.5	5.3
CMEA	–	–	2.2	–
TOTAL MULTILATERAL	34.7	43.8	18.6	26.5
TOTAL BIL.& MULTIL.	59.5	91.5	113.8	99.8
of which				
ODA Grants	34.9	49.9	96.3	75.6
ODA Loans	24.5	34.9	16.8	15.1

DISBURSEMENTS:

DAC COUNTRIES COMBINED

	1983	1984	1985	1986
OFFICIAL & PRIVATE				
GROSS:				
Contractual Lending	20.2	21.1	15.3	21.1
Export Credits Total	2.1	11.9	4.5	8.7
Export Credits Private	2.1	11.9	4.5	4.7
NET:				
Contractual Lending	15.5	17.7	-44.6	16.5
Export Credits Total	-0.8	10.2	-3.3	6.0
PRIVATE SECTOR NET	-1.6	17.5	-8.1	1.9
Direct Investment	-0.1	5.1	-5.7	–
Portfolio Investment	-0.7	2.2	-0.1	-0.1
Export Credits	-0.8	10.2	-2.3	2.0

MARKET BORROWING:

CHANGE IN CLAIMS

	1983	1984	1985	1986
Banks	–	-2.0	15.0	13.0

MEMORANDUM ITEM:

	1983	1984	1985	1986
CMEA Countr.(Gross)	–	1.5	0.1	0.1

	1983	1984	1985	1986	1983	1984	1985	1986		1983

TOTAL RECEIPTS NET / TOTAL ODA NET / TOTAL ODA GROSS

DAC COUNTRIES

	1983	1984	1985	1986	1983	1984	1985	1986		1983
Australia	26.3	83.3	4.0	5.0	2.4	4.1	5.8	5.0	Australia	2.4
Austria	–	0.0	1.0	0.0	–	0.0	0.3	0.0	Austria	–
Belgium	8.0	128.2	56.2	-43.2	0.0	0.0	–	–	Belgium	0.0
Canada	-0.1	-0.2	-0.1	-4.0	0.7	0.9	1.0	0.4	Canada	0.7
Denmark	-0.8	–	–	0.0	–	–	–	–	Denmark	–
Finland	0.0	-0.1	–		0.0	0.0	–	0.0	Finland	0.0
France	-6.9	7.7	17.6	-148.3	2.2	2.5	1.8	2.6	France	2.2
Germany, Fed. Rep.	58.0	95.9	29.3	381.3	4.6	4.5	6.6	5.4	Germany, Fed. Rep.	4.6
Ireland	–	–	–	–	–	–	–	–	Ireland	–
Italy	11.2	22.1	12.4	-0.7	–	–	0.0	–	Italy	–
Japan	176.0	245.6	154.2	176.0	3.9	28.4	7.9	15.3	Japan	8.0
Netherlands	-1.3	1.3	8.1	118.4	0.1	0.0	0.0	0.0	Netherlands	0.1
New Zealand	0.1	0.1	0.1	0.1	0.1	0.1	0.1	0.1	New Zealand	0.1
Norway	3.4	28.9	75.4	65.8	–	0.0	0.0	–	Norway	–
Sweden	-1.0	-6.9	-1.0	-44.8	–	–	–	–	Sweden	–
Switzerland	-9.3	-2.3	–	–	–	–	–	–	Switzerland	–
United Kingdom	-25.0	264.3	2.7	-1.9	-1.7	-1.8	-1.8	-1.1	United Kingdom	0.6
United States	-46.0	479.0	-536.0	-603.0	–	–	–	–	United States	–
TOTAL	192.5	1347.1	-176.2	-99.1	12.3	38.7	21.8	27.8	TOTAL	18.7

MULTILATERAL

	1983	1984	1985	1986	1983	1984	1985	1986		1983
AF.D.F.	–	–	–	–	–	–	–	–	AF.D.F.	–
AF.D.B.	–	–	–	–	–	–	–	–	AF.D.B.	–
AS.D.B	7.3	-0.7	-6.4	-8.6	-0.2	-0.2	-0.2	-0.2	AS.D.B	–
CAR.D.B.	–	–	–	–	–	–	–	–	CAR.D.B.	–
E.E.C.	–	–	0.0	0.1	–	–	0.0	0.1	E.E.C.	–
IBRD	-10.4	-10.4	-12.0	-16.2	–	–	–	–	IBRD	–
IDA	–	–	–	–	–	–	–	–	IDA	–
I.D.B.	–	–	–	–	–	–	–	–	I.D.B.	–
IFAD	–	–	–	–	–	–	–	–	IFAD	–
I.F.C.	–	–	–	–	–	–	–	–	I.F.C.	–
IMF TRUST FUND	–	–	–	–	–	–	–	–	IMF TRUST FUND	–
U.N. AGENCIES									U.N. AGENCIES	
UNDP	1.3	0.6	0.9	1.0	1.3	0.6	0.9	1.0	UNDP	1.3
UNTA	0.3	0.4	0.3	0.2	0.3	0.4	0.3	0.2	UNTA	0.3
UNICEF	–	–	–	–	–	–	–	–	UNICEF	–
UNRWA	–	–	–	–	–	–	–	–	UNRWA	–
WFP	–	–	–	–	–	–	–	–	WFP	–
UNHCR	0.7	0.6	0.4	0.4	0.7	0.6	0.4	0.4	UNHCR	0.7
Other Multilateral	0.3	0.9	0.7	0.1	0.3	0.9	0.7	0.1	Other Multilateral	0.3
Arab OPEC Agencies	–	–	–	0.4	–	–	–	0.4	Arab OPEC Agencies	–
TOTAL	-0.6	-8.7	-16.0	-22.7	2.4	2.2	2.1	1.9	TOTAL	2.6
OPEC COUNTRIES	0.0	0.1	0.0	0.1	0.0	0.1	0.0	0.1	OPEC COUNTRIES	0.0
E.E.C.+ MEMBERS	43.2	519.6	126.3	305.8	5.2	5.2	6.7	7.0	E.E.C.+ MEMBERS	7.4
TOTAL	191.9	1338.5	-192.2	-121.8	14.6	41.0	23.9	29.7	TOTAL	21.2

ODA LOANS GROSS / ODA LOANS NET / GRANTS

DAC COUNTRIES

	1983	1984	1985	1986	1983	1984	1985	1986		1983
Australia	–	–	0.3	–	–	–	0.3	–	Australia	2.4
Austria	–	–	–	–	–	–	–	–	Austria	–
Belgium	–	–	–	–	–	–	–	–	Belgium	0.0
Canada	–	–	–	–	–	–	–	–	Canada	0.7
Denmark	–	–	–	–	–	–	–	–	Denmark	–
Finland	–	–	–	–	–	–	–	–	Finland	0.0
France	–	–	–	–	–	–	–	–	France	2.2
Germany, Fed. Rep.	0.0	0.4	2.4	1.5	0.0	0.4	2.3	1.2	Germany, Fed. Rep.	4.6
Ireland	–	–	–	–	–	–	–	–	Ireland	–
Italy	–	–	–	–	–	–	–	–	Italy	–
Japan	–	19.3	–	–	-4.1	15.2	-4.1	-5.9	Japan	8.0
Netherlands	–	–	–	–	–	–	–	–	Netherlands	0.1
New Zealand	–	–	–	–	–	–	–	–	New Zealand	0.1
Norway	–	–	–	–	–	–	–	–	Norway	–
Sweden	–	–	–	–	–	–	–	–	Sweden	–
Switzerland	–	–	–	–	–	–	–	–	Switzerland	–
United Kingdom	–	–	–	–	-2.2	-2.3	-2.2	-1.9	United Kingdom	0.6
United States	–	–	–	–	–	–	–	–	United States	–
TOTAL	0.0	19.7	2.7	1.5	-6.4	13.2	-3.7	-6.6	TOTAL	18.7
MULTILATERAL	–	–	–	–	-0.2	-0.2	-0.2	-0.2	MULTILATERAL	2.6
OPEC COUNTRIES	–	–	–	–	–	–	–	–	OPEC COUNTRIES	0.0
E.E.C.+ MEMBERS	0.0	0.4	2.4	1.5	-2.3	-1.9	0.1	-0.7	E.E.C.+ MEMBERS	7.4
TOTAL	0.0	19.7	2.7	1.5	-6.6	13.0	-3.9	-6.7	TOTAL	21.2

TOTAL OFFICIAL GROSS / TOTAL OFFICIAL NET / TOTAL OOF GROSS

DAC COUNTRIES

	1983	1984	1985	1986	1983	1984	1985	1986		1983
Australia	2.4	4.1	5.8	5.0	2.4	4.1	5.8	5.0	Australia	–
Austria	–	0.0	0.3	0.0	–	0.0	0.3	0.0	Austria	–
Belgium	0.0	0.1	0.1	–	0.0	0.1	0.1	–	Belgium	–
Canada	1.5	0.9	1.0	0.4	-0.1	-0.2	-0.1	-4.0	Canada	0.8
Denmark	–	–	–	–	–	–	–	–	Denmark	–
Finland	0.0	0.0	–	0.0	0.0	0.0	–	0.0	Finland	–
France	2.2	2.5	1.8	2.6	2.2	2.5	1.8	2.6	France	–
Germany, Fed. Rep.	4.6	15.1	18.0	5.7	1.5	12.8	0.3	2.5	Germany, Fed. Rep.	–
Ireland	–	–	–	–	–	–	–	–	Ireland	–
Italy	1.6	–	0.0	–	1.3	-0.2	0.0	–	Italy	1.6
Japan	8.0	32.5	12.1	21.2	3.9	28.4	7.9	15.3	Japan	–
Netherlands	0.1	0.0	0.0	0.0	0.1	0.0	0.0	0.0	Netherlands	–
New Zealand	0.1	0.1	0.1	0.1	0.1	0.1	0.1	0.1	New Zealand	–
Norway	–	0.0	0.0	–	–	0.0	0.0	–	Norway	–
Sweden	3.3	1.2	5.0	–	-5.2	-5.9	-1.0	-1.7	Sweden	3.3
Switzerland	–	–	–	–	–	–	–	–	Switzerland	–
United Kingdom	0.6	0.5	0.4	0.8	-2.0	-2.1	-2.1	-1.5	United Kingdom	–
United States	–	112.0	–	–	-34.0	56.0	-53.0	-184.0	United States	–
TOTAL	24.4	169.1	44.5	35.8	-29.9	95.5	-39.9	-165.7	TOTAL	5.7
MULTILATERAL	17.6	11.4	6.3	4.5	-0.6	-8.7	-16.0	-22.7	MULTILATERAL	15.1
OPEC COUNTRIES	0.0	0.1	0.0	0.1	0.0	0.1	0.0	0.1	OPEC COUNTRIES	–
E.E.C.+ MEMBERS	9.1	18.2	20.3	9.2	3.1	13.0	0.1	3.7	E.E.C.+ MEMBERS	1.6
TOTAL	42.0	180.5	50.8	40.4	-30.4	86.9	-55.9	-188.3	TOTAL	20.8

ODA COMMITMENTS

1984	1985	1986	1983	1984	1985	1986
4.1	5.8	5.0	0.5	6.3	4.9	3.3
0.0	0.3	0.0	–	0.3	0.0	–
0.0	–	–	–	–	–	–
0.9	1.0	0.4	0.9	0.9	1.1	0.6
–	–	–	–	–	–	–
0.0	–	0.0	0.0	–	–	–
2.5	1.8	2.6	2.2	2.5	1.8	2.6
4.5	6.7	5.7	2.4	3.7	4.0	3.5
–	–	–	–	–	–	–
–	0.0	–	–	–	0.0	–
32.5	12.1	21.2	12.5	31.8	16.1	14.5
0.0	0.0	0.0	0.1	0.0	0.0	0.0
0.1	0.1	0.1	0.2	0.1	0.1	–
0.0	0.0	–	–	0.0	0.0	–
–	–	–	–	–	–	–
0.5	0.4	0.8	0.6	0.5	0.4	0.8
45.2	28.2	35.8	19.1	46.1	28.4	25.3
–	–	–	–	–	–	–
–	–	–	–	–	–	–
–	–	–	–	–	–	–
–	0.0	0.1	–	–	1.6	–
–	–	–	–	–	–	–
–	–	–	–	–	–	–
–	–	–	2.6	2.4	2.3	1.6
0.6	0.9	1.0	–	–	–	–
0.4	0.3	0.2	–	–	–	–
–	–	–	–	–	–	–
0.6	0.4	0.4	–	–	–	–
0.9	0.7	0.1	–	–	–	–
–	–	0.4	–	–	1.0	0.3
2.4	2.3	2.1	2.6	2.4	4.9	1.9
0.1	0.0	0.1	0.0	–	0.0	–
7.6	9.0	9.2	5.2	6.8	7.8	6.9
47.7	30.5	38.0	21.7	48.6	33.4	27.3

TECH. COOP. GRANTS

1984	1985	1986	1983	1984	1985	1986
4.1	5.8	5.0	1.5	4.1	5.0	5.0
0.0	0.0	0.0	–	–	–	–
0.0	–	–	–	–	–	–
0.9	1.0	0.4	0.5	–	0.1	–
–	–	–	–	–	–	–
0.0	–	0.0	0.0	0.0	–	0.0
2.5	1.8	2.6	2.2	2.5	1.8	2.6
4.1	4.3	4.2	4.6	4.0	4.2	4.1
–	–	–	–	–	–	–
–	0.0	–	–	–	0.0	–
13.2	12.1	21.2	7.8	10.5	9.5	12.9
0.0	0.0	0.0	0.1	0.0	0.0	0.0
0.1	0.1	0.1	0.1	0.1	0.1	0.1
0.0	0.0	–	–	0.0	0.0	–
–	–	–	–	–	–	–
0.5	0.4	0.8	0.6	0.5	0.4	0.8
–	–	–	–	–	–	–
25.5	25.5	34.3	17.4	21.7	21.1	25.4
2.4	2.3	2.1	2.6	2.4	2.3	1.6
0.1	0.0	0.1	–	–	–	–
7.2	6.6	7.7	7.4	7.1	6.5	7.5
28.0	27.8	36.5	20.0	24.1	23.4	27.1

TOTAL OOF NET

1984	1985	1986	1983	1984	1985	1986
–	–	–	–	–	–	–
0.1	0.1	–	–	0.1	0.1	–
–	–	–	-0.8	-1.1	-1.1	-4.5
–	–	–	–	–	–	–
–	–	–	–	–	–	–
10.6	11.3	–	-3.0	8.4	-6.3	-2.9
–	–	–	1.3	-0.2	–	–
–	–	–	–	–	–	–
–	–	–	–	–	–	–
1.2	5.0	–	-5.2	-5.9	-1.0	-1.7
–	–	–	-0.4	-0.3	-0.3	-0.4
112.0	–	–	-34.0	56.0	-53.0	-184.0
123.9	16.3	–	-42.1	56.8	-61.6	-193.4
9.0	4.0	2.4	-2.9	-10.9	-18.2	-24.6
–	–	–	–	–	–	–
10.7	11.3	–	-2.1	7.8	-6.5	-3.3
132.9	20.3	2.4	-45.1	45.9	-79.8	-218.0

ODA COMMITMENTS : LOANS

DAC COUNTRIES	1983	1984	1985	1986
Australia	–	–	–	–
Austria	–	0.3	–	–
Belgium	–	–	–	–
Canada	–	–	–	–
Denmark	–	–	–	–
Finland	–	–	–	–
France	–	–	–	–
Germany, Fed. Rep.	–	–	–	–
Ireland	–	–	–	–
Italy	–	–	–	–
Japan	–	19.3	–	–
Netherlands	–	–	–	–
New Zealand	–	–	–	–
Norway	–	–	–	–
Sweden	–	–	–	–
Switzerland	–	–	–	–
United Kingdom	–	–	–	–
United States	–	–	–	–
TOTAL	–	19.6	–	–
MULTILATERAL	–	–	–	–
OPEC COUNTRIES	–	–	–	–
E.E.C.+ MEMBERS	–	–	–	–
TOTAL	–	19.6	–	–

GRANT ELEMENT OF ODA

DAC COUNTRIES	1983	1984	1985	1986
Australia	100.0	100.0	100.0	100.0
Austria	–	49.2	100.0	–
Belgium	–	–	–	–
Canada	100.0	100.0	100.0	100.0
Denmark	–	–	–	–
Finland	100.0	–	–	–
France	100.0	100.0	100.0	100.0
Germany, Fed. Rep.	100.0	100.0	100.0	100.0
Ireland	–	–	–	–
Italy	–	–	100.0	–
Japan	100.0	100.0	100.0	100.0
Netherlands	100.0	100.0	100.0	100.0
New Zealand	100.0	100.0	100.0	–
Norway	–	100.0	100.0	–
Sweden	–	–	–	–
Switzerland	–	–	–	–
United Kingdom	100.0	100.0	100.0	100.0
United States	–	–	–	–
TOTAL	100.0	99.4	100.0	100.0
MULTILATERAL	100.0	100.0	100.0	100.0
OPEC COUNTRIES	100.0	–	100.0	–
E.E.C.+ MEMBERS	100.0	100.0	100.0	100.0
TOTAL	100.0	99.4	100.0	100.0

OTHER AGGREGATES

COMMITMENTS: ALL SOURCES

	1983	1984	1985	1986
TOTAL BILATERAL	295.4	66.5	33.4	23.6
of which				
OPEC	0.0	–	0.0	–
CMEA	–	–	–	–
TOTAL MULTILATERAL	2.6	2.4	4.9	1.9
TOTAL BIL.& MULTIL.	297.9	68.9	38.4	25.6
of which				
ODA Grants	21.7	29.0	33.4	27.3
ODA Loans	–	19.6	–	–

DISBURSEMENTS:

DAC COUNTRIES COMBINED

OFFICIAL & PRIVATE	1983	1984	1985	1986
GROSS:				
Contractual Lending	148.2	429.9	201.8	277.8
Export Credits Total	148.2	410.2	199.1	276.3
Export Credits Private	142.5	286.4	182.9	276.3
NET:				
Contractual Lending	-145.1	92.5	-127.5	-211.7
Export Credits Total	-138.3	79.6	-123.5	-204.8
PRIVATE SECTOR NET	222.3	1251.6	-136.3	66.5
Direct Investment	417.8	889.6	327.3	589.6
Portfolio Investment	-98.9	339.4	-401.5	-511.3
Export Credits	-96.6	22.5	-62.1	-11.7

MARKET BORROWING:

CHANGE IN CLAIMS

	1983	1984	1985	1986
Banks	–	–	–	–

MEMORANDUM ITEM:

	1983	1984	1985	1986
CMEA Countr.(Gross)	–	–	–	–

TOTAL RECEIPTS NET / TOTAL ODA NET / TOTAL ODA GROSS

	TOTAL RECEIPTS NET 1983	1984	1985	1986	TOTAL ODA NET 1983	1984	1985	1986	TOTAL ODA GROSS 1983
DAC COUNTRIES									
Australia	2.0	0.8	0.8	0.4	2.0	0.8	0.8	0.4	2.0
Austria	0.1	0.0	–	0.3	0.1	0.0	–	0.3	0.1
Belgium	0.2	-0.3	0.8	1.1	0.1	0.2	2.2	1.0	0.1
Canada	0.8	1.0	0.9	0.6	0.8	1.0	0.9	0.6	0.8
Denmark	1.9	1.7	1.9	2.4	1.3	1.5	2.3	2.4	1.3
Finland	1.3	2.2	2.1	10.4	1.3	2.2	2.1	10.4	1.3
France	15.3	2.7	-0.4	14.8	8.1	2.1	1.7	9.8	8.1
Germany, Fed. Rep.	28.2	35.9	43.9	46.4	25.1	17.7	20.7	43.6	25.1
Ireland	–	–	–	0.0	–	–	–	0.0	–
Italy	24.0	97.0	53.1	249.1	51.5	104.6	55.9	159.3	51.8
Japan	2.8	3.2	17.5	27.5	2.8	3.2	12.8	30.3	2.8
Netherlands	2.9	2.9	2.6	1.7	2.9	2.9	2.6	1.7	2.9
New Zealand	–	–	–	–	–	–	–	–	–
Norway	2.7	1.3	3.4	1.9	2.7	0.3	2.7	1.4	2.7
Sweden	1.9	1.2	1.0	1.0	1.9	1.2	1.0	1.0	1.9
Switzerland	1.2	1.7	1.9	4.0	1.2	1.7	1.2	4.0	1.2
United Kingdom	3.8	2.8	2.3	5.8	3.8	2.8	2.3	5.8	3.8
United States	46.0	51.0	57.0	82.0	46.0	51.0	54.0	82.0	48.0
TOTAL	*134.7*	*205.0*	*188.6*	*449.3*	*151.4*	*193.1*	*163.2*	*353.9*	*153.8*
MULTILATERAL									
AF.D.F.	7.1	6.1	5.7	9.1	7.1	6.1	5.7	9.1	7.3
AF.D.B.	-0.4	0.6	2.4	1.8	–	–	–	–	–
AS.D.B	–	–	–	–	–	–	–	–	–
CAR.D.B.	–	–	–	–	–	–	–	–	–
E.E.C.	19.6	19.3	10.5	10.7	19.6	19.3	10.5	10.7	19.6
IBRD	–	–	–	–	–	–	–	–	–
IDA	16.9	20.2	38.2	46.0	16.9	20.2	38.2	46.0	21.4
I.D.B.	–	–	–	–	–	–	–	–	–
IFAD	2.4	2.6	3.8	4.3	2.4	2.6	3.8	4.3	2.4
I.F.C.	–	–	-0.1	0.6	–	–	–	–	–
IMF TRUST FUND	–	–	–	–	–	–	–	–	–
U.N. AGENCIES									–
UNDP	6.6	7.2	6.4	7.9	6.6	7.2	6.4	7.9	6.6
UNTA	2.4	1.8	2.1	1.9	2.4	1.8	2.1	1.9	2.4
UNICEF	4.0	3.2	3.0	2.9	4.0	3.2	3.0	2.9	4.0
UNRWA	–	–	–	–	–	–	–	–	–
WFP	24.6	34.8	38.1	26.4	24.6	34.8	38.1	26.4	24.6
UNHCR	45.2	42.4	40.9	52.1	45.2	42.4	40.9	52.1	45.2
Other Multilateral	3.0	3.2	3.3	3.5	3.0	3.2	3.3	3.5	3.0
Arab OPEC Agencies	15.9	9.4	-8.0	-5.5	20.5	9.4	1.9	2.0	22.6
TOTAL	*147.4*	*150.8*	*146.2*	*161.6*	*152.4*	*150.1*	*153.8*	*166.8*	*159.2*
OPEC COUNTRIES	*63.8*	*6.8*	*36.3*	*2.6*	*39.2*	*6.8*	*36.3*	*2.6*	*40.0*
E.E.C.+ MEMBERS	*95.7*	*162.0*	*114.5*	*332.0*	*112.4*	*151.0*	*98.1*	*234.3*	*112.7*
TOTAL	**346.0**	**362.6**	**371.0**	**613.5**	**343.0**	**350.1**	**353.3**	**523.3**	**352.9**

ODA LOANS GROSS / ODA LOANS NET / GRANTS

	ODA LOANS GROSS 1983	1984	1985	1986	ODA LOANS NET 1983	1984	1985	1986	GRANTS 1983
DAC COUNTRIES									
Australia	–	–	–	–	–	–	–	–	2.0
Austria	–	–	–	–	–	–	–	–	0.1
Belgium	–	–	–	–	–	–	–	–	0.1
Canada	–	–	–	–	–	–	–	–	0.8
Denmark	0.3	0.0	2.1	0.1	0.3	0.0	2.1	0.1	1.1
Finland	–	–	–	–	–	–	–	–	1.3
France	6.4	0.8	0.5	8.3	6.4	0.8	0.5	8.3	1.7
Germany, Fed. Rep.	–	0.0	–	–	–	0.0	–	–	25.1
Ireland	–	–	–	–	–	–	–	–	–
Italy	21.9	70.8	–	–	21.5	67.9	-4.7	–	30.0
Japan	–	0.4	5.3	17.9	–	0.4	5.3	17.9	2.8
Netherlands	–	–	–	–	–	–	–	–	2.9
New Zealand	–	–	–	–	–	–	–	–	–
Norway	–	–	–	–	–	–	–	–	2.7
Sweden	–	–	–	–	–	–	–	–	1.9
Switzerland	–	–	–	–	–	–	–	–	1.2
United Kingdom	–	–	–	–	–	–	–	–	3.8
United States	16.0	17.0	24.0	20.0	14.0	16.0	22.0	20.0	32.0
TOTAL	*44.6*	*89.0*	*31.8*	*46.3*	*42.2*	*85.1*	*25.1*	*46.3*	*109.2*
MULTILATERAL	*54.2*	*41.2*	*50.6*	*63.3*	*47.4*	*40.8*	*49.5*	*60.5*	*105.0*
OPEC COUNTRIES	*36.1*	*20.3*	*40.9*	*2.7*	*35.3*	*6.4*	*33.9*	*0.8*	*3.9*
E.E.C.+ MEMBERS	*29.1*	*74.4*	*2.5*	*8.4*	*28.7*	*71.5*	*-2.2*	*8.4*	*83.6*
TOTAL	**134.8**	**150.5**	**123.2**	**112.3**	**124.9**	**132.4**	**108.5**	**107.6**	**218.1**

TOTAL OFFICIAL GROSS / TOTAL OFFICIAL NET / TOTAL OOF GROSS

	TOTAL OFFICIAL GROSS 1983	1984	1985	1986	TOTAL OFFICIAL NET 1983	1984	1985	1986	TOTAL OOF GROSS 1983
DAC COUNTRIES									
Australia	2.0	0.8	0.8	0.4	2.0	0.8	0.8	0.4	–
Austria	0.1	0.0	–	0.3	0.1	0.0	–	0.3	–
Belgium	0.1	0.2	2.2	1.0	0.1	0.2	2.2	1.0	–
Canada	0.8	1.0	0.9	0.6	0.8	1.0	0.9	0.6	–
Denmark	1.3	1.5	2.3	2.4	1.3	1.5	2.3	2.4	–
Finland	1.3	2.2	2.1	10.4	1.3	2.2	2.1	10.4	–
France	10.1	3.3	2.6	10.0	10.1	3.3	2.6	10.0	2.0
Germany, Fed. Rep.	25.1	17.7	20.7	43.6	25.1	16.7	20.7	43.6	–
Ireland	–	–	–	0.0	–	–	–	0.0	–
Italy	51.8	107.5	60.6	244.7	51.5	104.6	55.9	244.7	–
Japan	2.8	3.2	12.8	30.3	2.8	3.2	12.8	30.3	–
Netherlands	2.9	2.9	2.6	1.7	2.9	2.9	2.6	1.7	–
New Zealand	–	–	–	–	–	–	–	–	–
Norway	2.7	0.3	2.7	1.4	2.7	0.3	2.7	1.4	–
Sweden	1.9	1.2	1.0	1.0	1.9	1.2	1.0	1.0	–
Switzerland	1.2	1.7	1.2	4.0	1.2	1.7	1.2	4.0	–
United Kingdom	3.8	2.8	2.3	5.8	3.8	2.8	2.3	5.8	–
United States	48.0	52.0	59.0	82.0	46.0	51.0	57.0	82.0	–
TOTAL	*155.8*	*198.2*	*173.7*	*439.5*	*153.4*	*193.3*	*167.1*	*439.5*	*2.0*
MULTILATERAL	*159.2*	*151.2*	*157.4*	*172.2*	*147.4*	*150.8*	*146.2*	*161.6*	*–*
OPEC COUNTRIES	*64.6*	*20.7*	*43.3*	*4.5*	*63.8*	*6.8*	*36.3*	*2.6*	*24.6*
E.E.C.+ MEMBERS	*114.7*	*155.1*	*103.7*	*319.9*	*114.4*	*151.2*	*99.0*	*319.9*	*2.0*
TOTAL	**379.5**	**370.1**	**374.5**	**616.3**	**364.6**	**350.9**	**349.5**	**603.7**	**26.6**

ODA COMMITMENTS

	1984	1985	1986	1983	1984	1985	1986
Australia	0.8	0.8	0.4	3.6	0.7	0.1	1.9
Austria	0.0	–	0.3	–	0.0	–	–
Belgium	0.2	2.2	1.0	–	–	1.1	1.0
Canada	1.0	0.9	0.6	1.2	0.8	0.8	0.6
Denmark	1.5	2.3	2.4	1.3	3.5	0.2	24.2
Finland	2.2	2.1	10.4	0.2	1.7	21.0	13.4
France	2.1	1.7	9.8	16.1	1.7	2.4	9.8
Germany, Fed. Rep.	17.7	20.7	43.6	7.9	30.8	18.8	55.0
Ireland	–	–	0.0	–	–	–	0.0
Italy	107.5	60.6	159.3	65.4	52.6	75.1	368.8
Japan	3.2	12.8	30.3	24.7	7.4	7.9	9.2
Netherlands	2.9	2.6	1.7	3.0	2.7	2.1	1.2
New Zealand	–	–	–	–	–	–	–
Norway	0.3	2.7	1.4	0.7	–	0.3	0.3
Sweden	1.2	1.0	1.0	0.7	1.0	0.8	1.0
Switzerland	1.7	1.2	4.0	1.2	1.7	1.2	4.0
United Kingdom	2.8	2.3	5.8	2.5	2.0	3.1	5.8
United States	52.0	56.0	82.0	69.3	79.3	73.1	68.5
TOTAL	197.0	169.9	353.9	197.7	185.9	207.9	564.6

1984	1985	1986	1983	1984	1985	1986
6.1	5.8	9.1	–	–	29.0	–
–	–	–	–	–	–	–
–	–	–	–	–	–	–
19.3	10.5	10.7	7.1	23.9	14.7	22.4
–	–	–	–	–	–	–
20.5	39.1	47.8	23.0	31.5	20.6	89.5
–	–	–	–	–	–	–
2.6	3.8	4.3	–	7.0	6.5	–
–	–	–	–	–	–	–
–	–	–	85.9	92.6	93.7	94.7
7.2	6.4	7.9	–	–	–	–
1.8	2.1	1.9	–	–	–	–
3.2	3.0	2.9	–	–	–	–
–	–	–	–	–	–	–
34.8	38.1	26.4	–	–	–	–
42.4	40.9	52.1	–	–	–	–
3.2	3.3	3.5	–	–	–	–
9.4	1.9	3.0	21.3	16.2	5.0	4.9
150.5	154.8	169.7	137.2	171.2	169.4	211.5
20.7	43.3	4.5	17.5	60.1	12.1	2.0
153.9	102.8	234.3	103.3	117.2	117.5	488.2
368.2	368.0	528.0	352.4	417.2	389.5	778.1

TECH. COOP. GRANTS

1984	1985	1986	1983	1984	1985	1986
0.8	0.8	0.4	0.0	0.4	0.4	0.0
0.0	–	0.3	0.0	0.0	–	–
0.2	2.2	1.0	–	0.0	–	–
1.0	0.9	0.6	0.3	–	0.3	–
1.5	0.3	2.3	1.1	0.6	0.3	0.5
2.2	2.1	10.4	0.6	1.6	1.4	6.3
1.3	1.3	1.5	0.8	1.3	0.8	1.2
17.7	20.7	43.6	11.9	7.7	10.5	13.2
–	–	0.0	–	–	–	0.0
36.7	60.6	159.3	21.8	24.0	48.7	39.6
2.8	7.5	12.3	0.2	0.2	0.7	0.5
2.9	2.6	1.7	0.4	0.0	0.5	0.1
–	–	–	–	–	–	–
0.3	2.7	1.4	–	–	–	0.0
1.2	1.0	1.0	1.2	0.8	0.7	–
1.7	1.2	4.0	–	–	–	0.0
2.8	2.3	5.8	1.9	2.0	1.8	2.5
35.0	32.0	62.0	12.0	11.0	10.0	26.0
108.0	138.1	307.6	52.2	49.5	76.0	89.9
109.3	104.2	106.3	61.3	57.8	55.6	69.9
0.4	2.5	1.8	–	–	–	–
79.5	100.3	225.9	37.9	35.6	62.5	58.5
217.7	244.7	415.7	113.5	107.4	131.6	159.7

TOTAL OOF NET

1984	1985	1986	1983	1984	1985	1986
–	–	–	–	–	–	–
–	–	–	–	–	–	–
–	–	–	–	–	–	–
–	–	–	–	–	–	–
0.0	–	–	–	0.0	–	–
1.3	0.9	0.2	2.0	1.3	0.9	0.2
–	–	–	–	-1.0	0.0	–
–	–	85.4	–	–	–	85.4
–	–	–	–	–	–	–
–	–	–	–	–	–	–
–	–	–	–	–	–	–
–	–	–	–	–	–	–
–	3.0	–	–	–	3.0	–
1.3	3.9	85.6	2.0	0.2	3.8	85.6
0.7	2.6	2.7	-5.0	0.6	-7.6	-5.2
–	–	–	24.6	–	–	–
1.3	0.9	85.6	2.0	0.2	0.9	85.6
2.0	6.5	88.4	21.6	0.8	-3.8	80.4

ODA COMMITMENTS : LOANS

DAC COUNTRIES

	1983	1984	1985	1986
Australia	–	–	–	–
Austria	–	–	–	–
Belgium	–	–	–	–
Canada	–	–	–	–
Denmark	–	–	–	–
Finland	–	–	–	–
France	14.9	0.4	1.3	8.3
Germany, Fed. Rep.	–	–	–	–
Ireland	–	–	–	–
Italy	2.3	–	–	–
Japan	22.2	–	–	–
Netherlands	–	–	–	–
New Zealand	–	–	–	–
Norway	–	–	–	–
Sweden	–	–	–	–
Switzerland	–	–	–	–
United Kingdom	–	–	–	–
United States	15.6	16.9	25.7	20.8
TOTAL	54.9	17.3	27.0	29.0
MULTILATERAL	44.3	60.1	61.0	94.1
OPEC COUNTRIES	16.4	60.0	–	–
E.E.C.+ MEMBERS	17.2	5.9	1.3	8.3
TOTAL	115.6	137.4	88.1	123.1

GRANT ELEMENT OF ODA

DAC COUNTRIES

	1983	1984	1985	1986
Australia	100.0	100.0	100.0	100.0
Austria	–	100.0	–	–
Belgium	–	–	100.0	100.0
Canada	100.0	100.0	100.0	100.0
Denmark	100.0	100.0	100.0	100.0
Finland	100.0	100.0	100.0	100.0
France	50.4	81.5	100.0	100.0
Germany, Fed. Rep.	100.0	100.0	100.0	100.0
Ireland	–	–	–	100.0
Italy	98.0	100.0	100.0	100.0
Japan	73.0	100.0	100.0	100.0
Netherlands	100.0	100.0	100.0	100.0
New Zealand	–	–	–	–
Norway	100.0	–	100.0	100.0
Sweden	100.0	100.0	100.0	100.0
Switzerland	100.0	100.0	100.0	100.0
United Kingdom	100.0	100.0	100.0	100.0
United States	92.8	93.1	88.6	90.2
TOTAL	91.8	96.9	96.0	98.8
MULTILATERAL	87.5	90.0	90.9	91.7
OPEC COUNTRIES	34.2	53.3	100.0	100.0
E.E.C.+ MEMBERS	96.1	99.7	100.0	100.0
TOTAL	87.1	87.7	93.9	96.9

OTHER AGGREGATES

COMMITMENTS: ALL SOURCES

	1983	1984	1985	1986
TOTAL BILATERAL	227.5	245.9	226.0	652.0
of which				
OPEC	29.8	60.1	12.1	2.0
CMEA	–	–	–	–
TOTAL MULTILATERAL	142.5	171.2	170.4	211.7
TOTAL BIL.& MULTIL.	369.9	417.2	396.4	863.7
of which				
ODA Grants	236.8	279.7	301.4	655.0
ODA Loans	115.6	137.4	88.1	123.1

DISBURSEMENTS:

DAC COUNTRIES COMBINED

	1983	1984	1985	1986
OFFICIAL & PRIVATE				
GROSS:				
Contractual Lending	52.3	99.2	45.4	148.9
Export Credits Total	5.7	9.0	9.7	17.0
Export Credits Private	5.7	9.0	9.7	17.0
NET:				
Contractual Lending	22.0	82.0	33.3	143.9
Export Credits Total	-22.2	-3.3	4.3	12.0
PRIVATE SECTOR NET	-18.7	11.7	21.5	9.8
Direct Investment	4.4	20.3	23.8	3.1
Portfolio Investment	-0.8	-5.3	-6.7	-5.2
Export Credits	-22.2	-3.3	4.3	12.0

MARKET BORROWING:

CHANGE IN CLAIMS

	1983	1984	1985	1986
Banks	–	16.0	-23.0	-22.0

MEMORANDUM ITEM:

	1983	1984	1985	1986
CMEA Countr.(Gross)	–	–	–	–

TOTAL RECEIPTS NET

DAC COUNTRIES	1983	1984	1985	1986
Australia	9.2	8.6	2.2	2.0
Austria	0.1	0.1	0.1	0.1
Belgium	-0.3	0.6	2.0	-0.9
Canada	39.4	33.9	20.4	19.9
Denmark	2.4	1.8	3.1	3.4
Finland	4.7	5.3	6.0	10.3
France	10.0	25.9	16.6	-17.9
Germany, Fed. Rep.	49.5	38.3	60.6	74.9
Ireland	0.0	—	0.0	—
Italy	-3.3	-2.5	0.2	-1.0
Japan	84.0	137.0	123.4	139.4
Netherlands	27.0	19.4	16.5	16.7
New Zealand	0.0	0.0	0.0	0.0
Norway	11.7	12.0	11.3	12.3
Sweden	40.5	43.3	41.3	2.1
Switzerland	7.2	0.3	3.0	3.8
United Kingdom	49.1	75.7	40.9	37.8
United States	62.0	84.0	86.0	65.0
TOTAL	*393.3*	*483.8*	*433.4*	*368.0*
MULTILATERAL				
AF.D.F.	—	—	—	—
AF.D.B.	—	—	—	—
AS.D.B	27.3	24.9	28.3	38.7
CAR.D.B.	—	—	—	—
E.E.C.	13.5	16.7	15.0	12.8
IBRD	12.5	10.8	1.0	-2.2
IDA	59.3	79.3	73.3	84.3
I.D.B.	—	—	—	—
IFAD	1.8	3.6	6.1	5.9
I.F.C.	6.3	4.9	1.1	-0.1
IMF TRUST FUND	—	—	—	—
U.N. AGENCIES				
UNDP	7.8	6.6	7.3	7.7
UNTA	2.0	1.5	2.5	1.6
UNICEF	2.6	2.6	3.2	4.0
UNRWA	—	—	—	—
WFP	4.1	1.3	7.0	3.9
UNHCR	—	—	—	—
Other Multilateral	2.9	3.8	0.8	1.7
Arab OPEC Agencies	1.9	2.9	0.7	-0.6
TOTAL	*141.8*	*158.9*	*146.1*	*157.7*
OPEC COUNTRIES	*-4.7*	*-0.2*	*5.5*	*21.9*
E.E.C.+ MEMBERS	*147.9*	*176.0*	*154.8*	*125.9*
TOTAL	*530.4*	*642.4*	*585.0*	*547.6*

TOTAL ODA NET

DAC COUNTRIES	1983	1984	1985	1986
Australia	7.9	8.7	2.5	2.2
Austria	0.1	0.1	0.1	0.1
Belgium	0.3	0.7	1.1	1.0
Canada	36.1	30.4	21.9	21.6
Denmark	2.4	1.8	3.0	3.4
Finland	4.7	5.3	6.0	10.3
France	5.1	2.9	3.4	8.8
Germany, Fed. Rep.	42.6	33.7	53.6	73.2
Ireland	0.0	—	0.0	—
Italy	0.7	0.2	0.2	0.1
Japan	73.1	63.8	83.7	126.9
Netherlands	25.4	20.7	14.5	17.2
New Zealand	0.0	0.0	0.0	0.0
Norway	11.7	11.9	10.3	12.2
Sweden	28.3	32.3	33.3	24.0
Switzerland	4.5	1.9	3.3	3.8
United Kingdom	42.3	28.4	12.3	17.3
United States	62.0	76.0	85.0	66.0
TOTAL	*347.0*	*318.7*	*334.1*	*388.2*
MULTILATERAL				
AF.D.F.	—	—	—	—
AF.D.B.	—	—	—	—
AS.D.B	28.7	26.2	29.3	39.3
CAR.D.B.	—	—	—	—
E.E.C.	13.5	16.7	15.0	12.8
IBRD	—	—	—	—
IDA	59.3	79.3	73.3	84.3
I.D.B.	—	—	—	—
IFAD	1.8	3.6	6.1	5.9
I.F.C.	—	—	—	—
IMF TRUST FUND	—	—	—	—
U.N. AGENCIES				
UNDP	7.8	6.6	7.3	7.7
UNTA	2.0	1.5	2.5	1.6
UNICEF	2.6	2.6	3.2	4.0
UNRWA	—	—	—	—
WFP	4.1	1.3	7.0	3.9
UNHCR	—	—	—	—
Other Multilateral	2.9	3.8	0.8	1.7
Arab OPEC Agencies	1.9	2.9	0.7	-0.6
TOTAL	*124.4*	*144.4*	*145.0*	*160.6*
OPEC COUNTRIES	*1.2*	*3.4*	*5.5*	*21.9*
E.E.C.+ MEMBERS	*132.2*	*105.0*	*103.0*	*133.9*
TOTAL	*472.6*	*466.6*	*484.6*	*570.7*

TOTAL ODA GROSS

	1983
Australia	7.9
Austria	0.1
Belgium	0.3
Canada	36.5
Denmark	2.7
Finland	4.7
France	5.5
Germany, Fed. Rep.	45.9
Ireland	0.0
Italy	0.8
Japan	79.1
Netherlands	25.6
New Zealand	0.0
Norway	11.7
Sweden	28.3
Switzerland	4.5
United Kingdom	44.7
United States	66.0
TOTAL	*364.2*
AF.D.F.	—
AF.D.B.	—
AS.D.B	29.9
CAR.D.B.	—
E.E.C.	13.5
IBRD	—
IDA	61.0
I.D.B.	—
IFAD	1.8
I.F.C.	—
IMF TRUST FUND	—
UNDP	7.8
UNTA	2.0
UNICEF	2.6
UNRWA	—
WFP	4.1
UNHCR	—
Other Multilateral	2.9
Arab OPEC Agencies	2.5
TOTAL	*128.0*
OPEC COUNTRIES	*5.0*
E.E.C.+ MEMBERS	*138.8*
TOTAL	*497.2*

ODA LOANS GROSS

DAC COUNTRIES	1983	1984	1985	1986
Australia	—	—	—	—
Austria	—	—	—	—
Belgium	—	—	—	—
Canada	12.1	3.9	0.3	—
Denmark	0.2	—	0.0	0.3
Finland	—	—	—	—
France	5.0	2.8	3.3	8.8
Germany, Fed. Rep.	37.2	29.7	50.1	65.6
Ireland	—	—	—	—
Italy	—	—	—	—
Japan	43.9	34.6	48.7	68.2
Netherlands	6.4	0.4	1.8	2.5
New Zealand	—	—	—	—
Norway	—	0.2	0.2	0.4
Sweden	—	—	—	—
Switzerland	3.1	1.1	1.1	0.4
United Kingdom	—	—	—	—
United States	50.0	69.0	80.0	58.0
TOTAL	*157.8*	*141.6*	*185.5*	*204.0*
MULTILATERAL	*94.7*	*113.9*	*110.4*	*131.3*
OPEC COUNTRIES	*5.0*	*7.2*	*10.0*	*27.3*
E.E.C.+ MEMBERS	*48.8*	*32.9*	*55.2*	*77.1*
TOTAL	*257.5*	*262.7*	*305.9*	*362.6*

ODA LOANS NET

DAC COUNTRIES	1983	1984	1985	1986
Australia	—	—	—	—
Austria	—	—	—	—
Belgium	—	—	—	—
Canada	11.6	3.4	-0.3	-0.6
Denmark	0.0	-0.2	-0.3	-0.1
Finland	—	—	—	—
France	4.6	2.4	2.9	8.2
Germany, Fed. Rep.	33.9	26.3	46.6	59.7
Ireland	—	—	—	—
Italy	-0.1	0.0	—	—
Japan	37.8	28.5	42.7	59.2
Netherlands	6.2	-0.1	1.0	0.1
New Zealand	—	—	—	—
Norway	—	0.2	0.2	0.4
Sweden	—	—	—	—
Switzerland	3.1	1.1	1.1	0.4
United Kingdom	-2.4	-2.1	-2.1	-2.3
United States	46.0	65.0	73.0	50.0
TOTAL	*140.6*	*124.4*	*164.8*	*174.9*
MULTILATERAL	*91.1*	*111.0*	*108.6*	*127.6*
OPEC COUNTRIES	*1.1*	*3.3*	*5.5*	*21.9*
E.E.C.+ MEMBERS	*42.1*	*26.3*	*48.1*	*65.6*
TOTAL	*232.9*	*238.7*	*278.9*	*324.3*

GRANTS

	1983
Australia	7.9
Austria	0.1
Belgium	0.3
Canada	24.5
Denmark	2.4
Finland	4.7
France	0.5
Germany, Fed. Rep.	8.7
Ireland	0.0
Italy	0.8
Japan	35.3
Netherlands	19.2
New Zealand	0.0
Norway	11.7
Sweden	28.3
Switzerland	1.4
United Kingdom	44.7
United States	16.0
TOTAL	*206.4*
MULTILATERAL	*33.3*
OPEC COUNTRIES	*0.0*
E.E.C.+ MEMBERS	*90.1*
TOTAL	*239.7*

TOTAL OFFICIAL GROSS

DAC COUNTRIES	1983	1984	1985	1986
Australia	9.2	8.7	2.5	2.2
Austria	0.1	0.1	0.1	0.1
Belgium	0.3	0.7	1.1	1.0
Canada	39.9	34.5	22.7	22.2
Denmark	2.7	2.1	3.4	3.9
Finland	4.7	5.3	6.0	10.3
France	5.5	3.3	3.8	9.4
Germany, Fed. Rep.	45.9	37.1	57.1	79.1
Ireland	0.0	—	0.0	—
Italy	0.8	0.2	0.2	0.1
Japan	79.1	69.8	89.8	139.7
Netherlands	27.1	21.2	17.3	19.9
New Zealand	0.0	0.0	0.0	0.0
Norway	11.7	11.9	10.3	12.2
Sweden	40.5	43.3	41.3	31.4
Switzerland	4.5	1.9	3.3	3.9
United Kingdom	44.7	35.0	22.5	22.5
United States	66.0	88.0	93.0	74.0
TOTAL	*382.7*	*363.1*	*374.3*	*431.9*
MULTILATERAL	*149.0*	*165.6*	*153.8*	*167.7*
OPEC COUNTRIES	*5.0*	*7.3*	*10.1*	*27.3*
E.E.C.+ MEMBERS	*140.5*	*116.3*	*120.4*	*148.6*
TOTAL	*536.7*	*536.1*	*538.2*	*626.9*

TOTAL OFFICIAL NET

DAC COUNTRIES	1983	1984	1985	1986
Australia	9.2	8.6	2.2	2.0
Austria	0.1	0.1	0.1	0.1
Belgium	0.3	0.7	1.1	1.0
Canada	39.4	33.9	20.4	19.9
Denmark	2.4	1.8	3.1	3.4
Finland	4.7	5.3	6.0	10.3
France	5.1	2.9	3.4	8.8
Germany, Fed. Rep.	42.1	33.3	53.2	72.9
Ireland	0.0	—	0.0	—
Italy	0.7	0.2	0.2	0.1
Japan	73.1	63.8	83.7	130.8
Netherlands	27.0	20.7	16.5	17.5
New Zealand	0.0	0.0	0.0	0.0
Norway	11.7	11.9	10.3	12.2
Sweden	40.5	43.3	41.3	23.1
Switzerland	4.5	1.9	3.3	3.8
United Kingdom	42.3	32.9	20.4	20.2
United States	62.0	84.0	86.0	65.0
TOTAL	*365.0*	*345.3*	*351.2*	*391.2*
MULTILATERAL	*141.8*	*158.9*	*146.1*	*157.7*
OPEC COUNTRIES	*-4.7*	*-0.2*	*5.5*	*21.9*
E.E.C.+ MEMBERS	*133.3*	*109.2*	*112.9*	*136.8*
TOTAL	*502.1*	*504.0*	*502.8*	*570.8*

TOTAL OOF GROSS

	1983
Australia	1.3
Austria	—
Belgium	—
Canada	3.4
Denmark	0.1
Finland	—
France	—
Germany, Fed. Rep.	—
Ireland	—
Italy	—
Japan	—
Netherlands	1.6
New Zealand	—
Norway	—
Sweden	12.3
Switzerland	—
United Kingdom	—
United States	—
TOTAL	*18.5*
MULTILATERAL	*21.0*
OPEC COUNTRIES	—
E.E.C.+ MEMBERS	*1.6*
TOTAL	*39.5*

MILLION US DOLLARS, UNLESS OTHERWISE STATED

SRI LANKA

1984	1985	1986	1983	1984	1985	1986
			ODA COMMITMENTS			
8.7	2.5	2.2	4.6	6.7	2.7	1.2
0.1	0.1	0.1	0.0	0.0	0.1	–
0.7	1.1	1.0	–	–	0.6	1.0
31.0	22.5	22.2	39.3	62.8	14.8	41.2
2.0	3.3	3.8	7.6	0.1	0.1	11.3
5.3	6.0	10.3	14.9	3.1	12.0	28.3
3.3	3.8	9.4	9.0	5.1	5.5	9.4
37.1	57.1	79.1	21.7	12.2	10.5	114.9
–	0.0	–	0.0	–	0.0	–
0.2	0.2	0.1	0.8	0.2	0.4	0.3
69.8	89.8	135.9	85.2	78.4	121.5	161.6
21.1	15.3	19.6	18.7	14.2	27.7	38.7
0.0	0.0	0.0	0.0	0.1	0.0	–
11.9	10.3	12.2	6.2	18.8	15.0	6.6
32.3	33.3	24.0	40.6	32.9	32.9	24.0
1.9	3.3	3.9	1.5	2.5	7.2	1.2
30.5	14.3	19.6	6.1	26.0	5.8	32.4
80.0	92.0	74.0	90.7	111.8	37.6	52.8
335.9	*354.8*	*417.3*	*346.8*	*374.8*	*294.3*	*524.7*
–	–	–	–	–	–	–
–	–	–	–	–	–	–
27.4	30.6	41.6	35.4	56.0	66.0	102.3
–	–	–	–	–	–	–
16.7	15.0	12.8	8.7	23.8	8.3	11.4
–	–	–	–	–	–	–
80.9	73.8	85.0	57.0	47.0	55.0	137.0
–	–	–	–	–	–	–
3.6	6.1	5.9	–	–	8.2	–
–	–	–	–	–	–	–
–	–	–	19.4	15.9	20.8	18.9
6.6	7.3	7.7	–	–	–	–
1.5	2.5	1.6	–	–	–	–
2.6	3.2	4.0	–	–	–	–
1.3	7.0	3.9	–	–	–	–
3.8	0.8	1.7	–	–	–	–
2.9	0.7	–	–	–	–	–
147.3	*146.8*	*164.3*	*120.5*	*142.6*	*158.3*	*269.6*
7.3	*10.1*	*27.3*	*0.0*	*24.1*	*0.0*	*–*
111.6	*110.1*	*145.4*	*72.5*	*81.5*	*58.7*	*219.2*
490.5	*511.7*	*608.9*	*467.4*	*541.5*	*452.5*	*794.3*
			TECH. COOP. GRANTS			
8.7	2.5	2.2	0.8	1.2	1.8	1.3
0.1	0.1	0.1	0.0	–	–	–
0.7	1.1	1.0	0.2	0.5	0.9	0.5
27.0	22.2	22.2	1.5	–	1.9	–
2.0	3.3	3.5	2.4	0.7	2.4	1.1
5.3	6.0	10.3	2.1	2.6	2.7	4.9
0.5	0.5	0.6	0.5	0.5	0.4	0.6
7.5	7.0	13.5	8.4	7.4	6.8	13.4
–	0.0	–	0.0	–	0.0	–
0.2	0.2	0.1	0.0	0.2	0.2	0.1
35.2	41.1	67.7	5.8	5.8	7.7	11.1
20.7	13.5	17.1	5.3	3.3	4.1	7.8
0.0	0.0	0.0	0.0	0.0	0.0	0.0
11.7	10.2	11.9	0.7	1.0	0.8	0.9
32.3	33.3	24.0	5.1	1.3	1.2	–
0.9	2.2	3.5	0.3	0.4	0.5	0.6
30.5	14.3	19.6	3.6	3.1	3.7	5.4
11.0	12.0	16.0	4.0	5.0	6.0	9.0
194.3	*169.3*	*213.3*	*40.5*	*33.0*	*41.1*	*56.8*
33.4	*36.4*	*33.0*	*15.3*	*14.5*	*13.8*	*15.0*
0.1	*0.0*	*0.0*	*–*	*–*	*–*	*–*
78.8	*54.9*	*68.3*	*20.3*	*15.7*	*18.5*	*29.0*
227.8	*205.8*	*246.3*	*55.7*	*47.5*	*54.9*	*71.8*
			TOTAL OOF NET			
0.1	–	–	1.3	-0.1	-0.2	-0.2
–	–	–	–	–	–	–
0.0	0.0	–	–	0.0	0.0	–
3.5	0.3	–	3.3	3.5	-1.5	-1.7
0.1	0.1	0.1	0.0	0.1	0.1	–
–	–	–	–	–	–	–
–	–	–	-0.5	-0.4	-0.4	-0.3
–	–	–	–	–	–	–
–	–	3.9	–	–	–	3.9
0.1	2.0	0.3	1.6	0.1	2.0	0.3
–	–	–	–	–	–	–
11.0	8.0	7.4	12.3	11.0	8.0	-0.8
–	–	–	–	–	–	–
4.5	8.1	2.9	–	4.5	8.1	2.9
8.0	1.0	–	–	8.0	1.0	-1.0
27.2	*19.5*	*14.6*	*18.0*	*26.7*	*17.1*	*3.0*
18.3	*7.0*	*3.4*	*17.4*	*14.4*	*1.1*	*-2.9*
–	*–*	*–*	*-5.9*	*-3.6*	*–*	*–*
4.7	*10.3*	*3.2*	*1.1*	*4.2*	*9.8*	*2.9*
45.6	*26.5*	*18.0*	*29.5*	*37.5*	*18.2*	*0.1*

ODA COMMITMENTS : LOANS

DAC COUNTRIES	1983	1984	1985	1986
Australia	–	–	–	–
Austria	–	–	–	–
Belgium	–	–	–	–
Canada	9.7	–	–	–
Denmark	–	–	–	8.7
Finland	–	–	–	–
France	8.5	4.6	5.0	8.8
Germany, Fed. Rep.	10.4	4.2	3.4	106.0
Ireland	–	–	–	–
Italy	–	–	–	–
Japan	43.1	51.5	64.4	100.9
Netherlands	1.1	0.1	0.5	–
New Zealand	–	–	–	–
Norway	–	0.2	0.2	–
Sweden	–	–	–	–
Switzerland	–	–	–	–
United Kingdom	–	–	–	–
United States	76.4	82.2	26.0	32.7
TOTAL	149.2	142.7	99.5	257.0
MULTILATERAL	92.4	103.0	129.2	239.3
OPEC COUNTRIES	–	24.1	–	–
E.E.C.+ MEMBERS	20.0	8.9	8.9	123.4
TOTAL	241.7	269.9	228.7	496.3

GRANT ELEMENT OF ODA

DAC COUNTRIES	1983	1984	1985	1986
Australia	100.0	100.0	100.0	100.0
Austria	100.0	100.0	100.0	–
Belgium	–	–	100.0	100.0
Canada	97.4	100.0	100.0	100.0
Denmark	100.0	100.0	100.0	88.5
Finland	100.0	100.0	100.0	100.0
France	60.1	63.1	62.6	60.6
Germany, Fed. Rep.	92.1	94.2	94.6	59.1
Ireland	100.0	–	100.0	–
Italy	100.0	100.0	100.0	100.0
Japan	79.4	69.0	75.8	71.5
Netherlands	97.1	100.0	100.0	100.0
New Zealand	100.0	100.0	100.0	–
Norway	100.0	99.4	99.3	100.0
Sweden	100.0	100.0	100.0	100.0
Switzerland	100.0	100.0	100.0	100.0
United Kingdom	100.0	100.0	100.0	100.0
United States	74.6	78.2	78.1	81.0
TOTAL	86.3	86.3	86.3	79.3
MULTILATERAL	85.1	86.3	84.6	83.0
OPEC COUNTRIES	100.0	46.2	100.0	–
E.E.C.+ MEMBERS	91.9	96.8	95.5	76.1
TOTAL	86.0	84.4	85.7	80.6

OTHER AGGREGATES

COMMITMENTS: ALL SOURCES	1983	1984	1985	1986
TOTAL BILATERAL	370.3	429.4	303.7	574.4
of which				
OPEC	0.0	24.1	0.0	–
CMEA	–	–	–	–
TOTAL MULTILATERAL	120.8	154.8	223.3	269.6
TOTAL BIL.& MULTIL.	491.1	584.2	527.0	844.0
of which				
ODA Grants	225.7	271.7	223.8	298.0
ODA Loans	241.7	269.9	228.7	496.3

DISBURSEMENTS: DAC COUNTRIES COMBINED	1983	1984	1985	1986
OFFICIAL & PRIVATE				
GROSS:				
Contractual Lending	220.3	258.2	307.4	242.1
Export Credits Total	60.9	112.0	111.7	34.9
Export Credits Private	44.0	89.5	102.4	23.5
NET:				
Contractual Lending	171.2	200.7	245.0	151.0
Export Credits Total	29.4	72.2	70.4	-26.8
PRIVATE SECTOR NET	28.2	138.4	82.2	-23.2
Direct Investment	12.1	70.6	5.3	-1.0
Portfolio Investment	3.6	18.1	13.8	4.7
Export Credits	12.5	49.7	63.1	-27.0

MARKET BORROWING: CHANGE IN CLAIMS	1983	1984	1985	1986
Banks	–	9.0	-65.0	68.0

MEMORANDUM ITEM:	1983	1984	1985	1986
CMEA Countr.(Gross)	–	0.1	–	–

	1983	1984	1985	1986		1983	1984	1985	1986			1983
TOTAL RECEIPTS NET						**TOTAL ODA NET**					**TOTAL ODA GROSS**	
DAC COUNTRIES												
Australia	3.1	0.2	1.5	0.1		3.2	0.2	1.5	0.1		Australia	3.2
Austria	-1.2	-10.9	-6.7	-2.1		0.4	0.2	1.0	0.4		Austria	0.4
Belgium	0.8	18.1	-35.4	-1.0		1.2	0.9	4.0	1.3		Belgium	1.2
Canada	13.2	13.2	22.5	15.8		13.2	13.2	22.5	15.8		Canada	13.2
Denmark	12.1	-3.2	-2.4	-6.9		16.3	0.8	0.5	2.4		Denmark	16.3
Finland	4.6	2.3	4.0	7.2		4.6	2.3	4.0	7.2		Finland	4.6
France	53.5	41.4	-17.0	-29.6		19.6	7.5	5.5	8.5		France	19.6
Germany, Fed. Rep.	115.2	49.1	77.3	90.9		67.5	47.7	70.8	56.9		Germany, Fed. Rep.	67.8
Ireland	0.6	0.4	1.0	2.1		0.6	0.4	1.0	2.1		Ireland	0.6
Italy	111.9	8.1	96.8	93.4		26.9	11.3	65.3	90.8		Italy	26.9
Japan	17.1	24.9	23.7	39.9		25.5	28.8	25.8	32.7		Japan	25.5
Netherlands	63.5	33.6	23.3	16.1		34.4	28.0	27.8	52.5		Netherlands	34.4
New Zealand	–	–	–	–		–	–	–	–		New Zealand	–
Norway	10.0	24.5	29.7	25.1		10.1	3.1	9.5	7.4		Norway	10.1
Sweden	3.2	1.8	2.3	1.5		3.2	1.8	2.3	1.5		Sweden	3.2
Switzerland	6.6	6.0	5.5	3.7		6.1	6.0	5.5	3.7		Switzerland	6.1
United Kingdom	42.2	48.4	60.1	27.9		47.8	35.8	54.2	32.8		United Kingdom	48.8
United States	158.0	138.0	374.0	146.0		158.0	121.0	346.0	148.0		United States	158.0
TOTAL	*614.2*	*395.9*	*660.3*	*430.1*		*438.6*	*309.0*	*647.2*	*464.1*		*TOTAL*	*439.8*
MULTILATERAL												
AF.D.F.	2.4	–	2.6	1.0		2.4	–	2.6	1.0		AF.D.F.	2.4
AF.D.B.	-1.1	-3.7	-0.1	0.3		–	–	–	–		AF.D.B.	–
AS.D.B	–	–	–	–		–	–	–	–		AS.D.B	–
CAR.D.B.	–	–	–	–		–	–	–	–		CAR.D.B.	–
E.E.C.	36.7	28.0	62.1	86.2		36.7	28.0	62.1	86.2		E.E.C.	37.5
IBRD	-2.2	-4.8	-4.8	-4.3		2.3	–	–	–		IBRD	2.3
IDA	55.0	79.3	36.1	64.3		55.0	79.3	36.1	64.3		IDA	56.0
I.D.B.	–	–	–	–		–	–	–	–		I.D.B.	–
IFAD	2.7	2.6	4.0	6.9		2.7	2.6	4.0	6.9		IFAD	2.7
I.F.C.	0.2	–	–	–		–	–	–	–		I.F.C.	–
IMF TRUST FUND	–	–	–	–		–	–	–	–		IMF TRUST FUND	–
U.N. AGENCIES	–	–	–	–		–	–	–	–		U.N. AGENCIES	–
UNDP	7.3	4.0	5.2	6.1		7.3	4.0	5.2	6.1		UNDP	7.3
UNTA	2.4	1.7	4.1	2.5		2.4	1.7	4.1	2.5		UNTA	2.4
UNICEF	6.6	6.2	7.6	12.9		6.6	6.2	7.6	12.9		UNICEF	6.6
UNRWA	–	–	–	–		–	–	–	–		UNRWA	–
WFP	10.5	17.1	40.3	19.9		10.5	17.1	40.3	19.9		WFP	10.5
UNHCR	29.9	47.3	99.1	58.1		29.9	47.3	99.1	58.1		UNHCR	29.9
Other Multilateral	4.9	5.2	5.2	10.7		4.9	5.2	5.2	10.7		Other Multilateral	4.9
Arab OPEC Agencies	-2.0	-3.4	1.0	-7.0		5.2	4.3	1.0	17.1		Arab OPEC Agencies	6.5
TOTAL	*153.4*	*179.5*	*262.4*	*257.5*		*166.0*	*195.6*	*267.2*	*285.5*		*TOTAL*	*169.1*
OPEC COUNTRIES	*441.5*	*122.5*	*217.1*	*196.8*		*357.3*	*117.2*	*214.2*	*190.6*		**OPEC COUNTRIES**	*366.0*
E.E.C.+ MEMBERS	*436.4*	*224.0*	*265.7*	*279.1*		*251.0*	*160.4*	*291.1*	*333.4*		*E.E.C.+ MEMBERS*	*253.1*
TOTAL	**1209.1**	**697.8**	**1139.8**	**884.3**		**961.9**	**621.8**	**1128.6**	**940.2**		**TOTAL**	**975.0**
ODA LOANS GROSS						**ODA LOANS NET**					**GRANTS**	
DAC COUNTRIES												
Australia	–	–	–	–		–	–	–	–		Australia	3.2
Austria	–	–	–	–		–	–	-0.1	–		Austria	0.4
Belgium	–	–	–	–		–	–	–	–		Belgium	1.2
Canada	–	–	–	–		–	–	–	–		Canada	13.2
Denmark	0.7	0.0	0.0	–		0.7	0.0	0.0	–		Denmark	15.6
Finland	0.3	–	–	–		0.3	–	0.0	–		Finland	4.2
France	13.6	3.5	1.7	1.4		13.6	3.4	1.6	1.4		France	6.0
Germany, Fed. Rep.	3.7	1.1	0.1	1.0		3.4	-2.3	-0.6	-1.1		Germany, Fed. Rep.	64.2
Ireland	–	–	–	–		–	–	–	–		Ireland	0.6
Italy	22.4	–	3.1	5.9		22.4	–	1.6	3.3		Italy	4.5
Japan	–	10.2	0.3	–		–	10.2	0.3	–		Japan	25.5
Netherlands	–	0.0	–	–		–	–	–	–		Netherlands	34.4
New Zealand	–	–	–	–		–	–	–	–		New Zealand	–
Norway	–	–	0.7	–		–	–	0.7	–		Norway	10.1
Sweden	–	–	–	–		–	–	–	–		Sweden	3.2
Switzerland	–	–	–	–		–	–	–	–		Switzerland	6.1
United Kingdom	0.1	0.1	–	0.1		-0.9	-0.5	-0.6	-0.6		United Kingdom	48.7
United States	30.0	30.0	77.0	52.0		30.0	29.0	76.0	51.0		United States	128.0
TOTAL	*70.8*	*45.0*	*82.8*	*60.2*		*69.5*	*39.9*	*79.0*	*54.0*		*TOTAL*	*369.0*
MULTILATERAL	*71.2*	*90.6*	*45.5*	*125.3*		*68.1*	*87.2*	*43.1*	*84.8*		*MULTILATERAL*	*97.9*
OPEC COUNTRIES	*259.6*	*15.0*	*28.7*	*9.1*		*251.0*	*9.5*	*27.6*	*-27.5*		**OPEC COUNTRIES**	*106.4*
E.E.C.+ MEMBERS	*43.6*	*6.7*	*4.8*	*8.2*		*41.5*	*2.0*	*2.1*	*2.1*		*E.E.C.+ MEMBERS*	*209.6*
TOTAL	**401.6**	**150.6**	**157.0**	**194.6**		**388.6**	**136.6**	**149.7**	**111.3**		**TOTAL**	**573.3**
TOTAL OFFICIAL GROSS						**TOTAL OFFICIAL NET**					**TOTAL OOF GROSS**	
DAC COUNTRIES												
Australia	3.2	0.2	1.5	0.1		3.2	0.2	1.5	0.1		Australia	–
Austria	0.4	0.2	1.1	0.4		-1.2	-3.0	-0.2	-2.1		Austria	–
Belgium	1.2	31.5	5.9	9.6		1.2	31.5	5.9	9.6		Belgium	–
Canada	13.2	13.2	22.5	15.8		13.2	13.2	22.5	15.8		Canada	–
Denmark	21.0	1.1	0.5	2.5		21.0	0.9	-1.2	-6.3		Denmark	4.7
Finland	4.6	2.3	4.0	7.2		4.6	2.3	4.0	7.2		Finland	–
France	20.8	54.5	14.7	9.5		20.8	54.4	9.8	9.5		France	1.2
Germany, Fed. Rep.	110.7	53.2	79.0	60.9		110.4	48.9	78.4	58.8		Germany, Fed. Rep.	42.9
Ireland	0.6	0.4	1.0	2.1		0.6	0.4	1.0	2.1		Ireland	–
Italy	96.7	11.3	99.3	93.3		96.0	10.8	97.8	90.8		Italy	69.8
Japan	25.5	28.8	25.8	32.7		25.5	28.8	25.8	32.7		Japan	–
Netherlands	34.4	28.0	27.8	52.5		34.4	28.0	27.8	52.5		Netherlands	–
New Zealand	–	–	–	–		–	–	–	–		New Zealand	–
Norway	10.1	3.1	9.5	7.4		10.1	3.1	9.5	7.4		Norway	–
Sweden	3.2	1.8	2.3	1.5		3.2	1.8	2.3	1.5		Sweden	–
Switzerland	7.4	6.4	5.5	3.7		7.3	6.4	5.5	3.7		Switzerland	1.4
United Kingdom	48.8	36.7	54.8	33.5		47.9	36.1	54.3	32.9		United Kingdom	0.1
United States	158.0	145.0	379.0	149.0		158.0	138.0	374.0	146.0		United States	–
TOTAL	*559.9*	*417.7*	*734.2*	*481.6*		*556.1*	*401.7*	*718.8*	*462.1*		*TOTAL*	*120.1*
MULTILATERAL	*169.8*	*199.0*	*270.7*	*328.4*		*153.4*	*179.4*	*262.4*	*257.5*		*MULTILATERAL*	*0.7*
OPEC COUNTRIES	*450.2*	*128.0*	*218.2*	*233.4*		*441.5*	*122.5*	*217.1*	*196.8*		**OPEC COUNTRIES**	*84.2*
E.E.C.+ MEMBERS	*371.8*	*245.4*	*345.0*	*350.9*		*369.0*	*238.9*	*335.9*	*335.9*		*E.E.C.+ MEMBERS*	*118.7*
TOTAL	**1179.8**	**744.7**	**1223.0**	**1043.4**		**1151.1**	**703.6**	**1198.2**	**916.4**		**TOTAL**	**204.9**

ODA COMMITMENTS

1984	1985	1986	1983	1984	1985	1986
0.2	1.5	0.1	4.2	1.6	0.1	1.8
0.2	1.1	0.4	0.1	0.0	1.1	–
0.9	4.0	1.3	0.7	–	2.0	1.3
13.2	22.5	15.8	14.5	9.0	22.6	11.5
0.8	0.5	2.4	15.9	1.4	–	13.2
2.3	4.0	7.2	3.6	4.9	13.2	0.3
7.6	5.5	8.5	16.9	3.4	3.7	8.5
51.0	71.4	59.0	63.9	22.1	98.3	41.3
0.4	1.0	2.1	0.6	0.4	1.0	2.1
11.3	66.8	93.3	11.0	27.6	97.6	149.2
28.8	25.8	32.7	26.7	19.1	15.3	65.2
28.0	27.8	52.5	40.9	20.9	28.1	54.5
–	–	–	–	–	–	–
3.1	9.5	7.4	5.3	0.7	4.4	1.6
1.8	2.3	1.5	1.9	1.8	2.4	1.5
6.0	5.5	3.7	5.6	2.9	5.1	3.7
36.4	54.8	33.5	22.9	43.2	39.5	47.1
122.0	347.0	149.0	195.9	237.4	302.5	131.6
314.1	*651.0*	*470.4*	*430.3*	*396.3*	*636.9*	*534.3*
–	2.7	1.0	–	–	21.3	63.7
–	–	–	–	–	–	–
–	–	–	–	–	–	–
28.6	62.1	87.1	29.2	26.1	32.8	107.4
–	–	–	–	–	–	–
80.8	38.1	67.2	130.0	108.9	82.6	–
3.4	4.3	7.0	10.0	6.1	10.4	9.9
–	–	–	–	–	–	–
–	–	–	61.6	81.4	161.5	110.2
4.0	5.2	6.1	–	–	–	–
1.7	4.1	2.5	–	–	–	–
6.2	7.6	12.9	–	–	–	–
–	–	–	–	–	–	–
17.1	40.3	19.9	–	–	–	–
47.3	99.1	58.1	–	–	–	–
5.2	5.2	10.7	–	–	–	–
4.8	1.0	53.6	66.8	50.1	13.7	69.3
198.9	*269.7*	*326.1*	*297.5*	*272.6*	*322.2*	*360.4*
122.7	*215.3*	*227.2*	*517.4*	*51.5*	*342.8*	*409.8*
165.2	*293.9*	*339.6*	*201.7*	*145.0*	*303.0*	*424.5*
635.7	*1135.9*	*1023.6*	*1245.2*	*720.4*	*1301.9*	*1304.5*

TECH. COOP. GRANTS

1984	1985	1986	1983	1984	1985	1986
0.2	1.5	0.1	0.2	0.1	0.2	0.0
0.2	1.1	0.4	0.3	–	–	–
0.9	4.0	1.3	0.8	0.8	0.6	0.9
13.2	22.5	15.8	0.8	–	0.8	–
0.8	0.5	2.4	15.6	0.2	0.1	0.6
2.3	4.0	7.2	0.8	0.9	1.3	2.0
4.1	3.9	7.1	1.7	2.0	1.4	2.3
49.9	71.3	58.0	22.1	17.3	12.0	14.8
0.4	1.0	2.1	0.3	0.2	0.5	1.2
11.3	63.7	87.5	1.1	5.8	34.2	11.1
18.6	25.5	32.7	0.9	1.3	1.0	1.7
28.0	27.8	52.5	8.8	5.8	6.2	12.1
–	–	–	–	–	–	–
3.1	8.8	7.4	0.2	0.3	0.3	0.8
1.8	2.3	1.5	0.1	0.6	0.1	0.3
6.0	5.5	3.7	0.1	0.0	0.0	–
36.3	54.8	33.4	7.2	7.3	10.1	12.7
92.0	270.0	97.0	16.0	15.0	14.0	9.0
269.1	*568.2*	*410.1*	*76.8*	*57.4*	*82.6*	*69.7*
108.3	*224.1*	*200.7*	*51.1*	*64.3*	*121.2*	*91.4*
107.7	*186.6*	*218.1*	–	–	–	–
158.5	*289.0*	*331.4*	*57.4*	*39.2*	*64.9*	*57.0*
485.2	*978.9*	*829.0*	*127.9*	*121.8*	*203.8*	*161.1*

TOTAL OOF NET

1984	1985	1986	1983	1984	1985	1986
–	–	–	-1.7	-3.2	-1.2	-2.4
30.6	2.0	8.2	–	30.6	2.0	8.2
–	–	–	–	–	–	–
0.3	–	0.1	4.7	0.1	-1.6	-8.7
–	–	–	–	–	–	–
46.9	9.1	1.0	1.2	46.9	4.3	1.0
2.2	7.6	1.9	42.9	1.2	7.6	1.9
–	32.5	–	69.2	-0.6	32.5	–
–	–	–	–	–	–	–
–	–	–	–	–	–	–
–	–	–	–	–	–	–
0.4	0.0	–	1.3	0.4	0.0	–
0.2	0.0	0.0	0.1	0.2	0.0	0.0
23.0	32.0	–	–	17.0	28.0	-2.0
103.6	*83.2*	*11.3*	*117.6*	*92.7*	*71.6*	*-2.0*
0.1	*1.0*	*2.3*	*-12.6*	*-16.1*	*-4.9*	*-28.1*
5.3	*2.9*	*6.2*	*84.2*	*5.3*	*2.9*	*6.2*
80.2	*51.2*	*11.3*	*118.0*	*78.4*	*44.7*	*2.5*
109.0	*87.1*	*19.8*	*189.1*	*81.9*	*69.6*	*-23.8*

ODA COMMITMENTS : LOANS

DAC COUNTRIES

	1983	1984	1985	1986
Australia	–	–	–	–
Austria	–	–	–	–
Belgium	–	–	–	–
Canada	–	–	–	–
Denmark	–	–	–	–
Finland	–	–	–	–
France	10.4	–	–	1.4
Germany, Fed. Rep.	–	0.6	–	0.9
Ireland	–	–	–	–
Italy	0.5	–	3.1	28.4
Japan	–	–	–	–
Netherlands	–	–	–	–
New Zealand	–	–	–	–
Norway	–	–	0.7	–
Sweden	–	–	–	–
Switzerland	–	–	–	–
United Kingdom	–	–	–	–
United States	60.0	25.0	52.7	54.0
TOTAL	*70.9*	*25.6*	*56.5*	*84.6*
MULTILATERAL	*205.7*	*164.8*	*121.9*	*151.1*
OPEC COUNTRIES	*285.0*	*16.1*	*72.0*	*83.2*
E.E.C.+ MEMBERS	*11.1*	*0.6*	*10.8*	*39.5*
TOTAL	*561.6*	*206.5*	*250.3*	*319.0*

GRANT ELEMENT OF ODA

DAC COUNTRIES

	1983	1984	1985	1986
Australia	100.0	100.0	100.0	100.0
Austria	100.0	100.0	100.0	–
Belgium	100.0	–	100.0	100.0
Canada	100.0	100.0	100.0	100.0
Denmark	100.0	100.0	–	100.0
Finland	100.0	100.0	100.0	100.0
France	78.8	100.0	100.0	100.0
Germany, Fed. Rep.	100.0	98.1	100.0	98.8
Ireland	100.0	100.0	100.0	100.0
Italy	100.0	100.0	100.0	90.9
Japan	100.0	100.0	100.0	100.0
Netherlands	100.0	100.0	100.0	100.0
New Zealand	–	–	–	–
Norway	100.0	100.0	88.7	100.0
Sweden	100.0	100.0	100.0	100.0
Switzerland	100.0	100.0	100.0	100.0
United Kingdom	100.0	100.0	100.0	100.0
United States	90.2	96.6	94.3	86.7
TOTAL	*94.8*	*97.9*	*97.2*	*94.1*
MULTILATERAL	*78.6*	*82.3*	*95.0*	*83.7*
OPEC COUNTRIES	*71.1*	*81.9*	*87.8*	*93.5*
E.E.C.+ MEMBERS	*98.4*	*99.7*	*100.0*	*96.6*
TOTAL	*81.1*	*90.8*	*94.2*	*91.1*

OTHER AGGREGATES

COMMITMENTS: ALL SOURCES

	1983	1984	1985	1986
TOTAL BILATERAL	1155.2	504.1	1076.1	944.1
of which				
OPEC	529.0	81.5	355.3	409.8
CMEA	–	–	9.0	0.0
TOTAL MULTILATERAL	297.5	272.6	340.7	360.4
TOTAL BIL.& MULTIL.	1452.8	776.7	1416.8	1304.5
of which				
ODA Grants	683.7	513.9	1051.6	985.5
ODA Loans	561.6	206.5	250.3	319.0

DISBURSEMENTS:

DAC COUNTRIES COMBINED

	1983	1984	1985	1986
OFFICIAL & PRIVATE				
GROSS:				
Contractual Lending	272.7	205.7	206.8	91.6
Export Credits Total	86.6	58.3	42.8	22.1
Export Credits Private	81.9	58.1	42.8	22.1
NET:				
Contractual Lending	195.8	100.3	109.5	-1.5
Export Credits Total	11.0	-41.0	-44.9	-62.8
PRIVATE SECTOR NET	58.0	-5.8	-58.4	-32.1
Direct Investment	6.3	-0.6	6.7	4.8
Portfolio Investment	43.1	26.1	-25.9	14.6
Export Credits	8.7	-31.3	-39.1	-51.5

MARKET BORROWING:

CHANGE IN CLAIMS

	1983	1984	1985	1986
Banks	–	-88.0	161.0	-126.0

MEMORANDUM ITEM:

	1983	1984	1985	1986
CMEA Countr.(Gross)	2.1	8.0	7.0	5.0

TOTAL RECEIPTS NET

DAC COUNTRIES	1983	1984	1985	1986
Australia	–	–	–	–
Austria	–	–	–	–
Belgium	0.8	0.8	0.9	1.9
Canada	0.0	0.0	0.0	-0.3
Denmark	-0.1	-0.2	–	–
Finland	–	–	–	–
France	0.1	0.1	1.6	0.1
Germany, Fed. Rep.	0.0	0.0	0.2	0.8
Ireland	–	–	–	–
Italy	–	–	3.2	–
Japan	-2.6	-1.3	-0.1	-1.0
Netherlands	1.3	-1.1	0.5	72.0
New Zealand	–	–	–	–
Norway	–	0.0	0.0	–
Sweden	–	–	–	–
Switzerland	–	–	0.0	0.0
United Kingdom	0.0	–	–	–
United States	..	–	–	–
TOTAL	-0.5	-1.7	6.4	73.5
MULTILATERAL				
AF.D.F.	–	–	–	–
AF.D.B.	–	–	–	–
AS.D.B	–	–	–	–
CAR.D.B.	–	–	–	–
E.E.C.	0.7	3.1	1.0	1.4
IBRD	–	–	–	–
IDA	–	–	–	–
I.D.B.	–	–	1.1	0.2
IFAD	–	–	–	–
I.F.C.	–	–	–	–
IMF TRUST FUND	–	–	–	–
U.N. AGENCIES				
UNDP	0.6	0.3	0.4	0.4
UNTA	0.2	0.2	0.1	0.2
UNICEF	–	–	0.0	–
UNRWA	–	–	–	–
WFP	–	–	–	–
UNHCR	–	–	–	–
Other Multilateral	0.1	0.0	0.4	0.1
Arab OPEC Agencies	–	–	–	–
TOTAL	1.6	3.6	3.1	2.3
OPEC COUNTRIES	–	–	–	–
E.E.C.+ MEMBERS	2.8	2.6	7.5	76.2
TOTAL	1.1	1.9	9.4	75.8

TOTAL ODA NET

DAC COUNTRIES	1983	1984	1985	1986
Australia	–	–	–	–
Austria	–	–	–	–
Belgium	0.8	0.8	0.9	1.8
Canada	0.0	0.0	0.0	–
Denmark	–	–	–	–
Finland	–	–	–	–
France	0.1	0.1	0.1	0.1
Germany, Fed. Rep.	0.0	0.0	0.0	0.1
Ireland	–	–	–	–
Italy	–	–	–	–
Japan	-1.7	-0.1	-0.1	-0.4
Netherlands	3.1	0.7	2.0	1.8
New Zealand	–	–	–	–
Norway	–	0.0	0.0	–
Sweden	–	–	–	–
Switzerland	–	–	0.0	0.0
United Kingdom	–	–	–	–
United States	–	–	–	–
TOTAL	2.3	1.5	3.0	3.3
MULTILATERAL				
AF.D.F.	–	–	–	–
AF.D.B.	–	–	–	–
AS.D.B	–	–	–	–
CAR.D.B.	–	–	–	–
E.E.C.	0.7	3.1	1.0	1.4
IBRD	–	–	–	–
IDA	–	–	–	–
I.D.B.	–	–	1.1	0.2
IFAD	–	–	–	–
I.F.C.	–	–	–	–
IMF TRUST FUND	–	–	–	–
U.N. AGENCIES				
UNDP	0.6	0.3	0.4	0.4
UNTA	0.2	0.2	0.1	0.2
UNICEF	–	–	0.0	–
UNRWA	–	–	–	–
WFP	–	–	–	–
UNHCR	–	–	–	–
Other Multilateral	0.1	0.0	0.4	0.1
Arab OPEC Agencies	–	–	–	–
TOTAL	1.6	3.6	3.1	2.3
OPEC COUNTRIES	–	–	–	–
E.E.C.+ MEMBERS	4.7	4.6	4.0	5.1
TOTAL	3.9	5.1	6.0	5.6

TOTAL ODA GROSS

	1983
Australia	–
Austria	–
Belgium	0.8
Canada	0.0
Denmark	–
Finland	–
France	0.1
Germany, Fed. Rep.	0.0
Ireland	–
Italy	–
Japan	0.0
Netherlands	3.1
New Zealand	–
Norway	–
Sweden	–
Switzerland	–
United Kingdom	–
United States	–
TOTAL	4.0
AF.D.F.	–
AF.D.B.	–
AS.D.B	–
CAR.D.B.	–
E.E.C.	0.9
IBRD	–
IDA	–
I.D.B.	–
IFAD	–
I.F.C.	–
IMF TRUST FUND	–
U.N. AGENCIES	
UNDP	0.6
UNTA	0.2
UNICEF	–
UNRWA	–
WFP	–
UNHCR	–
Other Multilateral	0.1
Arab OPEC Agencies	–
TOTAL	1.7
OPEC COUNTRIES	–
E.E.C.+ MEMBERS	4.8
TOTAL	5.7

ODA LOANS GROSS

DAC COUNTRIES	1983	1984	1985	1986
Australia	–	–	–	–
Austria	–	–	–	–
Belgium	–	–	–	–
Canada	–	–	–	–
Denmark	–	–	–	–
Finland	–	–	–	–
France	–	–	–	–
Germany, Fed. Rep.	–	–	–	–
Ireland	–	–	–	–
Italy	–	–	–	–
Japan	–	–	–	–
Netherlands	–	–	–	–
New Zealand	–	–	–	–
Norway	–	–	–	–
Sweden	–	–	–	–
Switzerland	–	–	–	–
United Kingdom	–	–	–	–
United States	–	–	–	–
TOTAL	–	–	–	–
MULTILATERAL	0.5	2.0	0.0	0.9
OPEC COUNTRIES	–	–	–	–
E.E.C.+ MEMBERS	0.5	2.0	0.0	0.9
TOTAL	0.5	2.0	0.0	0.9

ODA LOANS NET

DAC COUNTRIES	1983	1984	1985	1986
Australia	–	–	–	–
Austria	–	–	–	–
Belgium	–	–	–	–
Canada	–	–	–	–
Denmark	–	–	–	–
Finland	–	–	–	–
France	–	–	–	–
Germany, Fed. Rep.	–	–	–	–
Ireland	–	–	–	–
Italy	–	–	–	–
Japan	-1.7	-0.1	-0.1	-0.4
Netherlands	–	–	–	–
New Zealand	–	–	–	–
Norway	–	–	–	–
Sweden	–	–	–	–
Switzerland	–	–	–	–
United Kingdom	–	–	–	–
United States	–	–	–	–
TOTAL	-1.7	-0.1	-0.1	-0.4
MULTILATERAL	0.4	1.9	-0.1	0.8
OPEC COUNTRIES	–	–	–	–
E.E.C.+ MEMBERS	0.4	1.9	-0.1	0.8
TOTAL	-1.3	1.8	-0.2	0.4

GRANTS

	1983
Australia	–
Austria	–
Belgium	0.8
Canada	0.0
Denmark	–
Finland	–
France	0.1
Germany, Fed. Rep.	0.0
Ireland	–
Italy	–
Japan	0.0
Netherlands	3.1
New Zealand	–
Norway	–
Sweden	–
Switzerland	–
United Kingdom	–
United States	–
TOTAL	4.0
MULTILATERAL	1.2
OPEC COUNTRIES	–
E.E.C.+ MEMBERS	4.3
TOTAL	5.2

TOTAL OFFICIAL GROSS

DAC COUNTRIES	1983	1984	1985	1986
Australia	–	–	–	–
Austria	–	–	–	–
Belgium	0.8	0.8	0.9	1.8
Canada	0.0	0.0	0.0	–
Denmark	–	–	–	–
Finland	–	–	–	–
France	0.1	0.1	0.1	0.1
Germany, Fed. Rep.	0.0	0.0	0.3	0.8
Ireland	–	–	–	–
Italy	–	–	–	–
Japan	0.0	0.0	0.0	0.0
Netherlands	3.1	0.7	2.0	1.8
New Zealand	–	–	–	–
Norway	–	0.0	0.0	–
Sweden	–	–	–	–
Switzerland	–	–	0.0	0.0
United Kingdom	–	–	–	–
United States	–	–	–	–
TOTAL	4.0	1.6	3.2	4.5
MULTILATERAL	1.7	3.7	3.2	2.4
OPEC COUNTRIES	–	–	–	–
E.E.C.+ MEMBERS	4.8	4.7	4.3	6.0
TOTAL	5.7	5.3	6.4	6.9

TOTAL OFFICIAL NET

DAC COUNTRIES	1983	1984	1985	1986
Australia	–	–	–	–
Austria	–	–	–	–
Belgium	0.8	0.8	0.9	1.8
Canada	0.0	0.0	0.0	-0.3
Denmark	–	–	–	–
Finland	–	–	–	–
France	0.1	0.1	0.1	0.1
Germany, Fed. Rep.	0.0	0.0	0.2	0.7
Ireland	–	–	–	–
Italy	–	–	–	–
Japan	-1.7	-0.1	-0.1	-0.4
Netherlands	3.1	0.7	2.0	1.8
New Zealand	–	–	–	–
Norway	–	0.0	0.0	–
Sweden	–	–	–	–
Switzerland	–	–	0.0	0.0
United Kingdom	–	–	–	–
United States	–	–	–	–
TOTAL	2.3	1.5	3.1	3.7
MULTILATERAL	1.6	3.6	3.1	2.3
OPEC COUNTRIES	–	–	–	–
E.E.C.+ MEMBERS	4.7	4.6	4.2	5.8
TOTAL	3.9	5.1	6.2	6.0

TOTAL OOF GROSS

	1983
Australia	–
Austria	–
Belgium	–
Canada	–
Denmark	–
Finland	–
France	–
Germany, Fed. Rep.	–
Ireland	–
Italy	–
Japan	–
Netherlands	–
New Zealand	–
Norway	–
Sweden	–
Switzerland	0.0
United Kingdom	–
United States	–
TOTAL	–
MULTILATERAL	–
OPEC COUNTRIES	–
E.E.C.+ MEMBERS	–
TOTAL	–

ODA COMMITMENTS

	1984	1985	1986	1983	1984	1985	1986
Australia	–	–	–	–	–	–	–
Austria	–	–	–	–	–	–	–
Belgium	0.8	0.9	1.8	–	–	–	1.8
Canada	0.0	0.0	–	–	0.0	0.0	–
Denmark	–	–	–	–	–	–	–
Finland	–	–	–	–	–	–	–
France	0.1	0.1	0.1	0.1	0.1	0.1	0.1
Germany, Fed. Rep.	0.0	0.0	0.1	0.0	0.1	0.0	0.1
Ireland	–	–	–	–	–	–	–
Italy	–	–	–	–	–	–	–
Japan	0.0	0.0	0.0	0.0	0.0	0.0	0.0
Netherlands	0.7	2.0	1.8	3.1	0.7	2.0	2.6
New Zealand	–	–	–	–	–	–	–
Norway	0.0	0.0	–	–	0.0	0.0	–
Sweden	–	0.0	0.0	–	–	–	–
Switzerland	–	–	–	–	–	–	–
United Kingdom	–	–	–	–	–	–	–
United States	–	–	–	–	–	–	–
TOTAL	1.6	3.0	3.8	3.2	0.8	2.2	4.5
	3.2	1.1	1.6	9.2	5.9	6.6	0.3
	–	1.1	0.2	–	–	1.5	–
	–	–	–	0.9	0.5	1.0	0.6
	0.3	0.4	0.4	–	–	–	–
	0.2	0.1	0.2	–	–	–	–
	0.0	0.4	0.1	–	–	–	–
MULTILATERAL	3.7	3.2	2.4	10.1	6.5	9.0	0.9
OPEC COUNTRIES	–	–	–	–	–	–	–
E.E.C.+ MEMBERS	4.7	4.1	5.3	12.4	6.7	8.7	4.7
TOTAL	5.3	6.2	6.2	13.3	7.3	11.2	5.4

TECH. COOP. GRANTS

	1984	1985	1986	1983	1984	1985	1986
Australia	–	–	–	–	–	–	–
Austria	–	–	–	–	–	–	–
Belgium	0.8	0.9	1.8	0.5	0.5	0.5	0.9
Canada	0.0	0.0	–	0.0	–	0.0	–
Denmark	–	–	–	–	–	–	–
Finland	0.1	0.1	0.1	0.1	0.1	0.1	0.0
France	0.0	0.0	0.1	0.0	0.0	0.0	0.1
Germany, Fed. Rep.	–	–	–	–	–	–	–
Ireland	0.0	0.0	0.0	0.0	0.0	0.0	0.0
Italy	0.7	2.0	1.8	3.1	0.7	2.0	0.1
Japan	–	–	–	–	–	–	–
Netherlands	0.0	0.0	–	–	0.0	0.0	–
New Zealand	–	–	–	–	–	–	–
Norway	–	0.0	0.0	–	–	0.0	0.0
Sweden	–	–	–	–	–	–	–
Switzerland	–	–	–	–	–	–	–
United Kingdom	–	–	–	–	–	–	–
United States	–	–	–	–	–	–	–
TOTAL	1.6	3.0	3.8	3.7	1.3	2.6	1.1
MULTILATERAL	1.7	3.1	1.5	0.9	0.5	1.0	0.7
OPEC COUNTRIES	–	–	–	–	–	–	–
E.E.C.+ MEMBERS	2.7	4.1	4.4	3.6	1.3	2.6	1.1
TOTAL	3.3	6.2	5.3	4.5	1.9	3.6	1.8

TOTAL OOF NET

	1984	1985	1986	1983	1984	1985	1986
Australia	–	–	–	–	–	–	–
Austria	–	–	–	–	–	–	–
Belgium	–	–	–	–	–	–	–
Canada	–	–	–	–	–	–	–
Denmark	–	–	–	–	–	–	–
Finland	–	0.2	0.7	–	–	0.2	0.7
France	–	–	–	–	–	–	–
Germany, Fed. Rep.	–	–	–	–	–	–	–
Ireland	–	–	–	–	–	–	–
Italy	–	–	–	–	–	–	–
Japan	–	–	–	–	–	–	–
Netherlands	–	–	–	–	–	–	–
New Zealand	–	–	–	–	–	–	–
Norway	–	–	–	–	–	–	–
Sweden	–	–	–	–	–	–	–
Switzerland	–	–	–	–	–	–	–
United Kingdom	–	–	–	–	–	–	–
United States	–	–	–	–	–	–	–
TOTAL	–	0.2	0.7	–	–	0.2	0.7
MULTILATERAL	–	–	–	–	–	–	-0.3
OPEC COUNTRIES	–	–	–	–	–	–	–
E.E.C.+ MEMBERS	–	0.2	0.7	–	–	0.2	0.7
TOTAL	–	0.2	0.7	–	–	0.2	0.4

ODA COMMITMENTS : LOANS

	1983	1984	1985	1986
DAC COUNTRIES				
Australia	–	–	–	–
Austria	–	–	–	–
Belgium	–	–	–	–
Canada	–	–	–	–
Denmark	–	–	–	–
Finland	–	–	–	–
France	–	–	–	–
Germany, Fed. Rep.	–	–	–	–
Ireland	–	–	–	–
Italy	–	–	–	–
Japan	–	–	–	–
Netherlands	–	–	–	–
New Zealand	–	–	–	–
Norway	–	–	–	–
Sweden	–	–	–	–
Switzerland	–	–	–	–
United Kingdom	–	–	–	–
United States	–	–	–	–
TOTAL	–	–	–	–
MULTILATERAL	2.4	5.9	4.7	–
OPEC COUNTRIES	–	–	–	–
E.E.C.+ MEMBERS	2.4	5.9	3.2	–
TOTAL	2.4	5.9	4.7	–

GRANT ELEMENT OF ODA

	1983	1984	1985	1986
DAC COUNTRIES				
Australia	–	–	–	–
Austria	–	–	–	–
Belgium	–	–	–	100.0
Canada	–	100.0	100.0	–
Denmark	–	–	–	–
Finland	–	–	–	–
France	100.0	100.0	100.0	100.0
Germany, Fed. Rep.	100.0	100.0	100.0	100.0
Ireland	–	–	–	–
Italy	–	–	–	–
Japan	100.0	100.0	100.0	100.0
Netherlands	100.0	100.0	100.0	100.0
New Zealand	–	–	–	–
Norway	–	100.0	100.0	–
Sweden	–	–	–	–
Switzerland	–	–	–	–
United Kingdom	–	–	–	–
United States	–	–	–	–
TOTAL	100.0	100.0	100.0	100.0
MULTILATERAL	100.0	100.0	100.0	100.0
OPEC COUNTRIES	–	–	–	–
E.E.C.+ MEMBERS	100.0	100.0	100.0	100.0
TOTAL	100.0	100.0	100.0	100.0

OTHER AGGREGATES

	1983	1984	1985	1986
COMMITMENTS: ALL SOURCES				
TOTAL BILATERAL	3.2	0.8	2.2	4.5
of which				
OPEC	–	–	–	–
CMEA	–	–	–	–
TOTAL MULTILATERAL	10.1	6.5	15.5	6.9
TOTAL BIL.& MULTIL.	13.3	7.3	17.7	11.4
of which				
ODA Grants	10.9	1.4	6.5	5.4
ODA Loans	2.4	5.9	4.7	–
DISBURSEMENTS:				
DAC COUNTRIES COMBINED				
OFFICIAL & PRIVATE				
GROSS:				
Contractual Lending	3.0	–	3.5	0.8
Export Credits Total	3.0	–	3.3	0.1
Export Credits Private	3.0	–	3.3	0.1
NET:				
Contractual Lending	-2.8	-0.3	3.4	0.0
Export Credits Total	-1.1	-0.2	3.3	-0.2
PRIVATE SECTOR NET	-2.8	-3.2	3.2	69.8
Direct Investment	-1.3	-1.2	1.2	71.6
Portfolio Investment	-0.4	-1.8	-1.2	-1.9
Export Credits	-1.1	-0.2	3.3	0.1
MARKET BORROWING:				
CHANGE IN CLAIMS				
Banks	–	-26.0	8.0	-6.0
MEMORANDUM ITEM:				
CMEA Countr.(Gross)	–	–	–	–

TOTAL RECEIPTS NET

DAC COUNTRIES	1983	1984	1985	1986
Australia	0.1	0.3	0.3	0.2
Austria	0.0	–	–	0.0
Belgium	-0.2	0.1	0.0	0.5
Canada	3.0	0.6	3.8	1.0
Denmark	0.0	–	0.0	2.2
Finland	–	0.0	1.6	0.0
France	0.1	0.1	1.1	2.3
Germany, Fed. Rep.	3.7	1.9	1.9	2.5
Ireland	0.1	0.0	–	0.0
Italy	–	0.1	0.3	0.7
Japan	0.8	-0.1	1.8	0.5
Netherlands	0.5	0.5	0.4	0.8
New Zealand	–	–	–	–
Norway	–	6.2	0.2	–
Sweden	0.8	3.4	0.6	2.5
Switzerland	0.1	0.1	-1.8	–
United Kingdom	6.5	22.3	9.8	5.9
United States	10.0	7.0	8.0	8.0
TOTAL	25.5	42.5	28.0	27.0
MULTILATERAL				
AF.D.F.	1.8	1.6	1.2	3.5
AF.D.B.	6.4	-1.2	-0.2	5.9
AS.D.B	–	–	–	–
CAR.D.B.	–	–	–	–
E.E.C.	6.4	5.7	0.6	0.1
IBRD	7.3	2.3	-1.9	2.0
IDA	-0.1	-0.1	-0.1	-0.1
I.D.B.	–	–	–	–
IFAD	–	–	0.2	0.3
I.F.C.	-1.0	-1.0	0.2	1.3
IMF TRUST FUND	–	–	–	–
U.N. AGENCIES	–	–	–	–
UNDP	1.3	1.0	1.2	1.0
UNTA	0.4	0.4	0.5	0.4
UNICEF	0.1	0.3	0.2	0.2
UNRWA	–	–	–	–
WFP	2.7	1.1	–	0.8
UNHCR	1.0	0.6	0.9	0.9
Other Multilateral	1.3	1.1	1.3	0.9
Arab OPEC Agencies	–	–	-0.1	-0.1
TOTAL	27.5	11.8	3.9	16.8
OPEC COUNTRIES	–	–	–	–
E.E.C.+ MEMBERS	17.1	30.8	14.1	15.0
TOTAL	53.0	54.3	31.8	43.8

TOTAL ODA NET

DAC COUNTRIES	1983	1984	1985	1986
Australia	0.1	0.3	0.3	0.2
Austria	0.0	–	–	0.0
Belgium	–	0.2	0.1	0.6
Canada	2.1	1.2	4.4	1.5
Denmark	0.0	–	0.0	2.7
Finland	–	0.0	–	0.0
France	0.1	0.1	0.7	1.0
Germany, Fed. Rep.	3.7	1.8	1.7	2.9
Ireland	0.1	0.0	–	0.0
Italy	–	0.1	0.3	0.7
Japan	0.5	0.9	0.8	0.5
Netherlands	0.5	0.5	0.4	0.8
New Zealand	–	–	–	–
Norway	–	0.1	0.2	–
Sweden	0.8	3.4	0.6	2.5
Switzerland	0.1	0.1	0.0	–
United Kingdom	2.6	1.8	0.8	3.4
United States	10.0	7.0	8.0	8.0
TOTAL	20.6	17.6	18.2	24.8
MULTILATERAL				
AF.D.F.	1.8	1.6	1.2	3.5
AF.D.B.	–	–	–	–
AS.D.B	–	–	–	–
CAR.D.B.	–	–	–	–
E.E.C.	4.6	6.2	2.0	2.4
IBRD	–	–	–	–
IDA	-0.1	-0.1	-0.1	-0.1
I.D.B.	–	–	–	–
IFAD	–	–	0.2	0.3
I.F.C.	–	–	–	–
IMF TRUST FUND	–	–	–	–
U.N. AGENCIES	–	–	–	–
UNDP	1.3	1.0	1.2	1.0
UNTA	0.4	0.4	0.5	0.4
UNICEF	0.1	0.3	0.2	0.2
UNRWA	–	–	–	–
WFP	2.7	1.1	–	0.8
UNHCR	1.0	0.6	0.9	0.9
Other Multilateral	1.3	1.1	1.3	0.9
Arab OPEC Agencies	–	–	-0.1	-0.1
TOTAL	13.0	12.1	7.1	9.8
OPEC COUNTRIES	–	–	–	–
E.E.C.+ MEMBERS	11.5	10.8	6.0	14.5
TOTAL	33.5	29.7	25.4	34.6

TOTAL ODA GROSS

	1983
Australia	0.1
Austria	0.0
Belgium	–
Canada	2.1
Denmark	0.2
Finland	0.0
France	0.1
Germany, Fed. Rep.	3.7
Ireland	0.1
Italy	–
Japan	0.5
Netherlands	0.5
New Zealand	–
Norway	–
Sweden	0.8
Switzerland	0.1
United Kingdom	4.5
United States	10.0
TOTAL	22.7
AF.D.F.	1.9
AF.D.B.	–
AS.D.B	–
CAR.D.B.	–
E.E.C.	4.6
IBRD	–
IDA	–
I.D.B.	–
IFAD	–
I.F.C.	–
IMF TRUST FUND	–
U.N. AGENCIES	–
UNDP	1.3
UNTA	0.4
UNICEF	0.1
UNRWA	–
WFP	2.7
UNHCR	1.0
Other Multilateral	1.3
Arab OPEC Agencies	–
TOTAL	13.1
OPEC COUNTRIES	–
E.E.C.+ MEMBERS	13.7
TOTAL	35.8

ODA LOANS GROSS

DAC COUNTRIES	1983	1984	1985	1986
Australia	–	–	–	–
Austria	–	–	–	–
Belgium	–	–	–	–
Canada	0.0	–	–	–
Denmark	–	–	0.1	2.8
Finland	–	–	–	–
France	–	–	0.6	0.8
Germany, Fed. Rep.	3.0	1.2	0.5	1.6
Ireland	–	–	–	–
Italy	–	–	–	–
Japan	–	–	–	–
Netherlands	–	–	–	0.3
New Zealand	–	–	–	–
Norway	–	–	–	–
Sweden	–	–	–	–
Switzerland	–	–	–	–
United Kingdom	0.3	0.7	0.2	0.3
United States	3.0	1.0	–	–
TOTAL	6.3	2.9	1.4	5.7
MULTILATERAL	2.1	1.6	1.9	3.8
OPEC COUNTRIES	–	–	–	–
E.E.C.+ MEMBERS	3.5	1.9	1.9	5.8
TOTAL	8.3	4.6	3.3	9.5

ODA LOANS NET

DAC COUNTRIES	1983	1984	1985	1986
Australia	–	–	–	–
Austria	–	–	–	–
Belgium	–	–	–	–
Canada	0.0	–	–	0.0
Denmark	-0.2	-0.1	-0.1	2.6
Finland	–	–	–	–
France	–	–	0.6	0.8
Germany, Fed. Rep.	3.0	1.2	0.5	1.5
Ireland	–	–	–	–
Italy	–	–	–	–
Japan	–	–	–	–
Netherlands	–	–	–	0.3
New Zealand	–	–	–	–
Norway	–	–	–	–
Sweden	–	–	–	–
Switzerland	–	–	–	–
United Kingdom	-1.6	-1.1	-1.7	-2.0
United States	3.0	1.0	–	–
TOTAL	4.2	0.9	-0.7	3.3
MULTILATERAL	1.9	1.5	1.5	3.3
OPEC COUNTRIES	–	–	–	–
E.E.C.+ MEMBERS	1.3	-0.1	-0.2	3.3
TOTAL	6.1	2.4	0.7	6.6

GRANTS

	1983
Australia	0.1
Austria	0.0
Belgium	–
Canada	2.1
Denmark	0.2
Finland	–
France	0.1
Germany, Fed. Rep.	0.7
Ireland	0.1
Italy	–
Japan	0.5
Netherlands	0.5
New Zealand	–
Norway	–
Sweden	0.8
Switzerland	0.1
United Kingdom	4.2
United States	7.0
TOTAL	16.4
MULTILATERAL	11.0
OPEC COUNTRIES	–
E.E.C.+ MEMBERS	10.2
TOTAL	27.4

TOTAL OFFICIAL GROSS

DAC COUNTRIES	1983	1984	1985	1986
Australia	0.1	0.3	0.3	0.2
Austria	0.0	–	–	0.0
Belgium	–	0.2	0.1	0.6
Canada	3.5	1.2	4.4	1.6
Denmark	0.2	0.1	0.1	2.9
Finland	–	0.0	–	0.0
France	0.1	0.1	0.7	1.0
Germany, Fed. Rep.	3.7	1.8	1.8	2.9
Ireland	0.1	0.0	–	0.0
Italy	–	0.1	0.3	0.7
Japan	0.5	0.9	0.8	0.5
Netherlands	0.5	0.5	0.4	0.8
New Zealand	–	–	–	–
Norway	–	0.1	0.2	–
Sweden	0.8	3.4	0.6	2.5
Switzerland	0.1	0.1	0.0	–
United Kingdom	8.6	7.5	4.4	11.3
United States	10.0	7.0	8.0	8.0
TOTAL	28.1	23.4	22.0	32.9
MULTILATERAL	32.6	19.0	12.1	26.4
OPEC COUNTRIES	–	–	–	–
E.E.C.+ MEMBERS	20.9	17.4	10.1	22.7
TOTAL	60.7	42.4	34.1	59.3

TOTAL OFFICIAL NET

DAC COUNTRIES	1983	1984	1985	1986
Australia	0.1	0.3	0.3	0.2
Austria	0.0	–	–	0.0
Belgium	–	0.2	0.1	0.6
Canada	3.0	0.6	3.8	1.0
Denmark	0.0	–	0.0	2.7
Finland	–	0.0	–	0.0
France	0.1	0.1	0.7	1.0
Germany, Fed. Rep.	3.7	1.8	1.7	2.9
Ireland	0.1	0.0	–	0.0
Italy	–	0.1	0.3	0.7
Japan	0.5	0.9	0.8	0.5
Netherlands	0.5	0.5	0.4	0.8
New Zealand	–	–	–	–
Norway	–	0.1	0.2	–
Sweden	0.8	3.4	0.6	2.5
Switzerland	0.1	0.1	0.0	–
United Kingdom	6.7	5.7	2.1	8.4
United States	10.0	7.0	8.0	8.0
TOTAL	25.5	20.9	19.0	29.3
MULTILATERAL	27.5	11.8	3.9	16.8
OPEC COUNTRIES	–	–	–	–
E.E.C.+ MEMBERS	17.4	14.2	6.0	17.2
TOTAL	53.0	32.6	22.8	46.1

TOTAL OOF GROSS

	1983
Australia	–
Austria	–
Belgium	–
Canada	1.4
Denmark	–
Finland	–
France	–
Germany, Fed. Rep.	–
Ireland	–
Italy	–
Japan	–
Netherlands	–
New Zealand	–
Norway	–
Sweden	–
Switzerland	–
United Kingdom	4.1
United States	–
TOTAL	5.4
MULTILATERAL	19.5
OPEC COUNTRIES	–
E.E.C.+ MEMBERS	7.2
TOTAL	24.9

ODA COMMITMENTS

1984	1985	1986	1983	1984	1985	1986
0.3	0.3	0.2	0.1	0.4	0.2	0.1
–	–	0.0	–	–	–	–
0.2	0.1	0.6	–	–	–	0.6
1.2	4.4	1.6	7.9	1.3	6.7	0.5
0.1	0.1	2.9	–	0.5	4.8	10.0
0.0	–	0.0	–	–	–	–
0.1	0.7	1.0	0.1	1.6	0.1	1.0
1.8	1.8	2.9	1.8	0.3	1.9	6.2
0.0	–	0.0	0.1	0.0	–	0.0
0.1	0.3	0.7	6.0	0.1	0.4	1.4
0.9	0.8	0.5	0.5	1.0	0.8	0.6
0.5	0.4	0.8	0.5	1.1	0.4	1.0
–	–	–	–	–	–	–
0.1	0.2	–	–	0.0	0.2	–
3.4	0.6	2.5	2.4	1.2	0.4	2.5
0.1	0.0	–	0.1	0.1	–	–
3.7	2.7	5.6	3.2	3.0	4.7	3.1
7.0	8.0	8.0	7.2	12.2	3.6	18.1
19.6	*20.3*	*27.2*	*29.8*	*22.7*	*24.2*	*45.1*
1.6	1.2	3.5	–	4.5	–	3.8
–	–	–	–	–	–	–
–	–	–	–	–	–	–
6.2	2.0	2.5	12.2	7.2	-0.3	1.7
–	–	–	–	–	–	–
–	–	–	–	–	–	–
–	0.2	0.3	6.0	–	–	–
–	–	–	–	–	–	–
–	–	–	6.7	4.4	4.0	4.0
1.0	1.2	1.0	–	–	–	–
0.4	0.5	0.4	–	–	–	–
0.3	0.2	0.2	–	–	–	–
–	–	–	–	–	–	–
1.1	–	0.8	–	–	–	–
0.6	0.9	0.9	–	–	–	–
1.1	1.3	0.9	–	–	–	–
–	0.2	0.2	–	0.3	–	–
12.3	*7.6*	*10.4*	*24.9*	*16.5*	*3.7*	*9.5*
–	–	–	–	–	–	–
12.8	*8.2*	*17.0*	*23.8*	*13.9*	*12.1*	*25.1*
31.8	**27.9**	**37.6**	**54.7**	**39.3**	**28.0**	**54.6**

TECH. COOP. GRANTS

1984	1985	1986	1983	1984	1985	1986
0.3	0.3	0.2	0.1	0.3	0.3	0.2
–	–	0.0	0.0	–	–	–
0.2	0.1	0.6	–	0.1	0.0	0.5
1.2	4.4	1.6	1.3	–	2.0	1.6
0.1	0.1	0.1	0.2	0.1	0.1	0.1
0.0	–	0.0	–	0.0	–	0.0
0.1	0.1	0.1	0.1	0.1	0.1	0.1
0.7	1.3	1.3	0.7	0.6	1.3	1.3
0.0	–	0.0	0.1	0.0	–	0.0
0.1	0.3	0.7	–	0.0	0.0	0.5
0.9	0.8	0.5	0.5	0.9	0.8	0.5
0.5	0.4	0.5	0.5	0.3	0.4	0.4
–	–	–	–	–	–	–
0.1	0.2	–	–	0.0	0.0	–
3.4	0.6	2.5	0.6	0.8	0.1	–
0.1	0.0	–	–	–	–	3.7
3.0	2.5	5.4	3.2	2.8	2.1	3.1
6.0	8.0	8.0	7.0	6.0	6.0	7.0
16.7	*19.0*	*21.5*	*14.2*	*12.1*	*13.1*	*17.4*
10.6	5.7	6.6	4.0	3.4	4.0	4.1
–	–	–	–	–	–	–
10.9	6.2	11.2	4.7	4.1	4.0	7.0
27.3	**24.7**	**28.1**	**18.2**	**15.4**	**17.1**	**21.6**

TOTAL OOF NET

1984	1985	1986	1983	1984	1985	1986
–	–	–	–	–	–	–
–	–	–	–	–	–	–
–	–	0.0	–	–	–	0.0
–	–	–	0.9	-0.6	-0.6	-0.5
–	–	–	–	–	–	–
–	–	–	–	–	–	–
–	–	–	–	–	–	–
–	–	–	–	–	–	–
–	–	–	–	–	–	–
–	–	–	–	–	–	–
–	–	–	–	–	–	–
–	–	–	–	–	–	–
–	–	–	–	–	–	–
3.8	1.6	5.7	4.1	3.8	1.3	5.0
–	–	–	–	–	–	–
3.8	*1.6*	*5.7*	*5.0*	*3.3*	*0.7*	*4.5*
6.7	4.5	16.0	14.5	-0.3	-3.3	7.0
–	–	–	–	–	–	–
4.6	*2.0*	*5.7*	*5.9*	*3.4*	*-0.1*	*2.7*
10.6	**6.1**	**21.7**	**19.5**	**3.0**	**-2.5**	**11.4**

ODA COMMITMENTS : LOANS

DAC COUNTRIES	1983	1984	1985	1986
Australia	–	–	–	–
Austria	–	–	–	–
Belgium	–	–	–	–
Canada	–	–	–	–
Denmark	–	–	4.7	9.9
Finland	–	–	–	–
France	–	1.5	–	0.8
Germany, Fed. Rep.	–	–	–	4.4
Ireland	–	–	–	–
Italy	6.0	–	–	–
Japan	–	–	–	–
Netherlands	–	–	–	0.6
New Zealand	–	–	–	–
Norway	–	–	–	–
Sweden	–	–	–	–
Switzerland	–	–	–	–
United Kingdom	–	–	–	–
United States	–	–	–	–
TOTAL	*6.0*	*1.5*	*4.7*	*15.7*
MULTILATERAL	*8.8*	*5.7*	*0.0*	*3.8*
OPEC COUNTRIES	–	–	–	–
E.E.C.+ MEMBERS	*8.8*	*2.6*	*4.8*	*15.7*
TOTAL	**14.8**	**7.2**	**4.8**	**19.5**

GRANT ELEMENT OF ODA

DAC COUNTRIES	1983	1984	1985	1986
Australia	100.0	100.0	100.0	100.0
Austria	–	–	–	–
Belgium	–	–	–	100.0
Canada	100.0	100.0	100.0	100.0
Denmark	–	100.0	75.6	76.2
Finland	–	–	–	–
France	100.0	62.9	100.0	100.0
Germany, Fed. Rep.	100.0	100.0	100.0	77.3
Ireland	100.0	100.0	–	100.0
Italy	46.9	100.0	100.0	100.0
Japan	100.0	100.0	100.0	100.0
Netherlands	100.0	100.0	100.0	100.0
New Zealand	–	–	–	–
Norway	–	100.0	100.0	–
Sweden	100.0	100.0	100.0	100.0
Switzerland	100.0	100.0	–	–
United Kingdom	100.0	100.0	100.0	100.0
United States	100.0	100.0	100.0	100.0
TOTAL	*89.3*	*97.4*	*95.1*	*91.3*
MULTILATERAL	*100.0*	*79.5*	*100.0*	*92.8*
OPEC COUNTRIES	–	–	–	–
E.E.C.+ MEMBERS	*84.8*	*95.4*	*90.2*	*83.9*
TOTAL	**93.1**	**88.8**	**95.8**	**91.6**

OTHER AGGREGATES

COMMITMENTS: ALL SOURCES

	1983	1984	1985	1986
TOTAL BILATERAL	39.8	26.9	27.8	47.8
of which				
OPEC	–	–	–	–
CMEA	–	–	–	–
TOTAL MULTILATERAL	30.2	22.1	22.1	19.8
TOTAL BIL.& MULTIL.	70.0	49.0	49.9	67.6
of which				
ODA Grants	39.8	32.1	23.2	35.1
ODA Loans	14.8	7.2	4.8	19.5

DISBURSEMENTS:
DAC COUNTRIES COMBINED

OFFICIAL & PRIVATE	1983	1984	1985	1986
GROSS:				
Contractual Lending	13.2	13.1	11.8	14.9
Export Credits Total	2.8	6.3	8.8	3.5
Export Credits Private	1.5	6.3	8.8	3.5
NET:				
Contractual Lending	9.2	9.2	5.1	5.7
Export Credits Total	0.9	4.4	4.5	-2.6
PRIVATE SECTOR NET	–	21.7	9.0	-2.2
Direct Investment	-0.1	17.3	3.8	0.0
Portfolio Investment	0.1	-0.6	0.1	-0.2
Export Credits	0.0	5.0	5.1	-2.0

MARKET BORROWING:
CHANGE IN CLAIMS

	1983	1984	1985	1986
Banks	–	24.0	7.0	-33.0

MEMORANDUM ITEM:

	1983	1984	1985	1986
CMEA Countr.(Gross)	–	–	–	–

TOTAL RECEIPTS NET / TOTAL ODA NET / TOTAL ODA GROSS

	1983	1984	1985	1986	1983	1984	1985	1986		1983
TOTAL RECEIPTS NET					**TOTAL ODA NET**				**TOTAL ODA GROSS**	
DAC COUNTRIES										
Australia	0.0	0.0	0.1	—	0.0	0.0	0.1	—	Australia	0.0
Austria	0.3	0.2	0.2	0.4	0.3	0.2	0.2	0.4	Austria	0.3
Belgium	-0.7	0.0	-0.1	0.1	0.2	0.1	0.1	0.1	Belgium	0.2
Canada	0.6	0.1	—	0.3	0.6	0.1	—	0.3	Canada	0.6
Denmark	—	—	—	—	—	—	—	—	Denmark	—
Finland	-0.1	0.0	—	—	—	—	—	—	Finland	—
France	10.1	4.5	10.1	28.8	6.2	7.1	7.0	12.5	France	6.6
Germany, Fed. Rep.	19.4	2.1	39.7	85.9	18.6	3.5	2.1	18.8	Germany, Fed. Rep.	18.6
Ireland	—	—	—	—	—	—	—	—	Ireland	—
Italy	10.5	-1.6	-4.3	0.9	0.0	0.3	0.2	0.2	Italy	0.0
Japan	1.7	22.0	-16.8	6.2	16.2	1.6	-1.0	7.7	Japan	16.4
Netherlands	0.4	0.3	0.9	0.3	0.4	0.3	0.3	0.3	Netherlands	0.4
New Zealand	—	—	—	—	—	—	—	—	New Zealand	—
Norway	—	—	—	—	—	—	—	—	Norway	—
Sweden	-0.1	0.0	2.0	-0.4	—	0.0	—	—	Sweden	—
Switzerland	0.3	0.3	0.5	0.7	0.3	0.3	0.5	0.7	Switzerland	0.3
United Kingdom	1.7	31.7	5.6	-4.4	2.7	0.8	3.6	0.5	United Kingdom	2.7
United States	24.0	11.0	—	-10.0	24.0	1.0	—	—	United States	28.0
TOTAL	68.0	70.6	38.0	108.7	69.5	15.2	13.1	41.4	TOTAL	74.0
MULTILATERAL										
AF.D.F.	—	—	—	—	—	—	—	—	AF.D.F.	—
AF.D.B.	—	—	—	—	—	—	—	—	AF.D.B.	—
AS.D.B	—	—	—	—	—	—	—	—	AS.D.B	—
CAR.D.B.	—	—	—	—	—	—	—	—	CAR.D.B.	—
E.E.C.	13.0	5.4	15.4	8.2	5.1	1.9	2.0	4.8	E.E.C.	5.1
IBRD	30.9	26.7	4.1	2.8	1.5	1.9	—	—	IBRD	1.5
IDA	0.6	-0.6	-0.7	-0.3	0.6	-0.6	-0.7	-0.3	IDA	1.0
I.D.B.	—	—	—	—	—	—	—	—	I.D.B.	—
IFAD	—	0.2	2.1	6.4	—	0.2	2.1	6.4	IFAD	—
I.F.C.	—	—	—	—	—	—	—	—	I.F.C.	—
IMF TRUST FUND	—	—	—	—	—	—	—	—	IMF TRUST FUND	—
U.N. AGENCIES									U.N. AGENCIES	
UNDP	1.8	2.2	0.9	1.0	1.8	2.2	0.9	1.0	UNDP	1.8
UNTA	1.2	1.0	1.4	1.6	1.2	1.0	1.4	1.6	UNTA	1.2
UNICEF	0.5	0.5	0.5	0.5	0.5	0.5	0.5	0.5	UNICEF	0.5
UNRWA	—	—	—	—	—	—	—	—	UNRWA	—
WFP	17.8	13.5	22.3	30.1	17.8	13.5	22.3	30.1	WFP	17.8
UNHCR	0.3	0.2	0.2	0.1	0.3	0.2	0.2	0.1	UNHCR	0.3
Other Multilateral	1.2	1.1	1.1	0.5	1.2	1.1	1.1	0.5	Other Multilateral	1.2
Arab OPEC Agencies	10.4	13.8	43.9	20.6	10.4	2.4	7.1	10.6	Arab OPEC Agencies	13.9
TOTAL	77.6	63.9	91.1	71.4	40.3	24.1	36.9	55.2	TOTAL	44.1
OPEC COUNTRIES	890.4	813.5	573.0	745.9	880.1	813.5	573.0	745.9	**OPEC COUNTRIES**	910.4
E.E.C.+ MEMBERS	54.3	42.4	67.3	119.7	33.1	13.9	15.3	37.1	**E.E.C.+ MEMBERS**	33.4
TOTAL	1036.0	948.0	702.1	926.0	989.8	852.9	623.0	842.6	**TOTAL**	1028.5

ODA LOANS GROSS / ODA LOANS NET / GRANTS

	1983	1984	1985	1986	1983	1984	1985	1986		1983
ODA LOANS GROSS					**ODA LOANS NET**				**GRANTS**	
DAC COUNTRIES										
Australia	—	—	—	—	—	—	—	—	Australia	0.0
Austria	—	—	—	—	—	—	—	—	Austria	0.3
Belgium	—	—	—	—	—	—	—	—	Belgium	0.2
Canada	—	—	—	—	—	—	—	—	Canada	0.6
Denmark	—	—	—	—	—	—	—	—	Denmark	—
Finland	—	—	—	—	—	—	—	—	Finland	—
France	0.7	1.0	—	2.4	0.3	0.6	—	1.8	France	5.9
Germany, Fed. Rep.	15.0	1.3	0.7	16.8	15.0	1.3	0.5	16.6	Germany, Fed. Rep.	3.6
Ireland	—	—	—	—	—	—	—	—	Ireland	—
Italy	—	—	—	—	—	—	—	—	Italy	0.0
Japan	15.4	1.8	0.0	9.3	15.2	0.5	-2.4	5.8	Japan	1.0
Netherlands	—	—	—	—	—	—	—	—	Netherlands	0.4
New Zealand	—	—	—	—	—	—	—	—	New Zealand	—
Norway	—	—	—	—	—	—	—	—	Norway	—
Sweden	—	—	—	—	—	—	—	—	Sweden	—
Switzerland	—	—	—	—	—	—	—	—	Switzerland	0.3
United Kingdom	—	—	—	—	—	—	—	—	United Kingdom	2.7
United States	26.0	1.0	—	—	22.0	1.0	—	—	United States	2.0
TOTAL	57.1	5.1	0.7	28.5	52.6	3.4	-1.9	24.2	TOTAL	16.9
MULTILATERAL	18.0	8.4	13.7	21.4	14.1	3.8	8.5	16.3	MULTILATERAL	26.1
OPEC COUNTRIES	27.0	22.0	19.0	34.0	-3.3	-10.8	-14.5	16.9	**OPEC COUNTRIES**	883.4
E.E.C.+ MEMBERS	17.3	2.3	0.7	19.2	17.0	1.9	0.5	18.4	**E.E.C.+ MEMBERS**	16.1
TOTAL	102.0	35.5	33.3	83.9	63.4	-3.6	-7.9	57.4	**TOTAL**	926.4

TOTAL OFFICIAL GROSS / TOTAL OFFICIAL NET / TOTAL OOF GROSS

	1983	1984	1985	1986	1983	1984	1985	1986		1983
TOTAL OFFICIAL GROSS					**TOTAL OFFICIAL NET**				**TOTAL OOF GROSS**	
DAC COUNTRIES										
Australia	0.0	0.0	0.1	—	0.0	0.0	0.1	—	Australia	—
Austria	0.3	0.2	0.2	0.4	0.3	0.2	0.2	0.4	Austria	—
Belgium	0.2	0.1	0.1	0.1	0.2	0.1	0.1	0.1	Belgium	—
Canada	0.6	0.1	—	0.3	0.6	0.1	—	0.3	Canada	—
Denmark	—	—	—	—	—	—	—	—	Denmark	—
Finland	—	—	—	—	—	—	—	—	Finland	—
France	6.6	7.5	7.0	13.1	6.2	7.1	7.0	12.5	France	—
Germany, Fed. Rep.	19.5	3.7	2.3	19.1	19.4	2.5	2.1	18.8	Germany, Fed. Rep.	0.9
Ireland	—	—	—	—	—	—	—	—	Ireland	—
Italy	0.0	0.3	0.2	0.2	-0.4	0.2	0.2	0.2	Italy	—
Japan	16.4	2.9	1.4	11.2	16.2	1.6	-1.0	7.7	Japan	—
Netherlands	0.4	0.3	0.3	0.3	0.4	0.3	0.3	0.3	Netherlands	—
New Zealand	—	—	—	—	—	—	—	—	New Zealand	—
Norway	—	—	—	—	—	—	—	—	Norway	—
Sweden	—	0.0	—	—	-0.1	0.0	—	—	Sweden	—
Switzerland	0.3	0.3	0.5	0.7	0.3	0.3	0.5	0.7	Switzerland	—
United Kingdom	2.7	0.8	3.6	0.5	2.7	0.8	3.6	0.5	United Kingdom	—
United States	28.0	1.0	—	—	24.0	1.0	—	—	United States	—
TOTAL	74.9	17.2	15.7	45.7	69.7	14.1	13.1	41.4	TOTAL	0.9
MULTILATERAL	102.7	89.2	114.7	106.6	77.6	63.9	91.1	71.4	MULTILATERAL	58.6
OPEC COUNTRIES	921.9	846.3	606.5	763.1	890.4	813.5	573.0	745.9	**OPEC COUNTRIES**	11.5
E.E.C.+ MEMBERS	42.3	18.6	29.3	42.0	41.4	16.4	28.6	40.5	**E.E.C.+ MEMBERS**	8.9
TOTAL	1099.5	952.7	736.9	915.4	1037.7	891.6	677.2	858.7	**TOTAL**	71.0

MILLION US DOLLARS, UNLESS OTHERWISE STATED

ODA COMMITMENTS

1984	1985	1986	1983	1984	1985	1986
0.0	0.1	–	0.0	–	–	–
0.2	0.2	0.4	0.3	0.2	0.2	–
0.1	0.1	0.1	–	–	–	0.1
0.1	–	0.3	0.1	0.0	–	0.3
–	–	–	–	–	–	–
7.5	7.0	13.1	13.8	13.4	7.0	13.1
3.5	2.3	19.1	2.3	1.1	1.1	13.2
–	–	–	–	–	–	–
0.3	0.2	0.2	0.0	0.3	0.3	0.3
2.9	1.4	11.2	1.1	1.1	1.8	1.7
0.3	0.3	0.3	0.1	0.2	0.4	0.2
–	–	–	–	–	–	–
0.0	–	–	–	0.0	–	–
0.3	0.5	0.7	0.2	0.2	0.4	0.5
0.8	3.6	0.5	2.7	0.8	3.6	0.5
1.0	–	–	–	–	–	–
16.9	*15.7*	*45.7*	*20.5*	*17.2*	*14.9*	*29.7*
–	–	–	–	–	–	–
–	–	–	–	–	–	–
1.9	2.0	4.8	0.4	10.4	6.9	17.3
1.9	–	–	–	–	–	–
0.2	2.1	6.4	–	–	8.3	–
–	–	–	–	–	–	–
–	–	–	22.7	18.3	26.3	33.7
2.2	0.9	1.0	–	–	–	–
1.0	1.4	1.6	–	–	–	–
0.5	0.5	0.5	–	–	–	–
13.5	22.3	30.1	–	–	–	–
0.2	0.2	0.1	–	–	–	–
1.1	1.1	0.5	–	–	–	–
6.4	11.6	15.4	–	30.4	–	–
28.7	*42.1*	*60.3*	*23.1*	*59.2*	*41.6*	*51.0*
846.3	*606.5*	*763.1*	*1076.9*	*824.4*	*829.5*	*919.3*
14.3	*15.5*	*37.9*	*19.3*	*26.2*	*19.3*	*44.5*
892.0	*664.3*	*869.1*	*1120.5*	*900.7*	*885.9*	*1000.0*

TECH. COOP. GRANTS

1984	1985	1986	1983	1984	1985	1986
0.0	0.1	–	0.0	0.0	0.1	–
0.2	0.2	0.4	0.3	–	–	–
0.1	0.1	0.1	0.0	0.0	0.0	0.0
0.1	–	0.3	0.6	–	–	–
–	–	–	–	–	–	–
6.5	7.0	10.7	5.9	6.4	7.0	10.7
2.2	1.6	2.2	3.6	2.2	1.6	2.2
–	–	–	–	–	–	–
0.3	0.2	0.2	0.0	0.3	0.2	0.2
1.1	1.4	1.9	1.0	0.9	1.4	1.5
0.3	0.3	0.3	0.2	0.2	0.1	0.2
–	–	–	–	–	–	–
0.0	–	–	–	0.0	–	–
0.3	0.5	0.7	0.1	0.1	0.1	0.2
0.8	3.6	0.5	0.6	0.8	0.6	0.5
–	–	–	2.0	–	–	–
11.8	*15.0*	*17.2*	*14.2*	*10.8*	*11.1*	*15.4*
20.3	*28.4*	*38.9*	*4.9*	*4.9*	*4.1*	*3.7*
824.4	*587.5*	*729.1*	–	–	–	–
12.0	*14.8*	*18.7*	*10.2*	*9.8*	*9.6*	*13.7*
856.5	*630.9*	*785.2*	*19.1*	*15.7*	*15.2*	*19.1*

TOTAL OOF NET

1984	1985	1986	1983	1984	1985	1986
–	–	–	–	–	–	–
0.0	0.0	–	–	0.0	0.0	–
–	–	–	–	–	–	–
–	–	–	–	–	–	–
–	–	–	–	–	–	–
0.2	–	–	0.8	-1.0	–	–
–	–	–	-0.5	-0.1	–	–
–	–	–	–	–	–	–
–	–	–	–	–	–	–
–	–	–	–	–	–	–
–	–	–	-0.1	–	–	–
–	–	–	–	–	–	–
–	–	–	–	–	–	–
0.2	0.0	–	0.2	-1.1	0.0	–
60.4	72.6	46.3	37.3	39.8	54.2	16.2
–	–	–	10.3	–	–	–
4.3	13.9	4.1	8.3	2.5	13.4	3.4
60.7	*72.6*	*46.3*	*47.9*	*38.7*	*54.2*	*16.2*

ODA COMMITMENTS : LOANS

	1983	1984	1985	1986
DAC COUNTRIES				
Australia	–	–	–	–
Austria	–	–	–	–
Belgium	–	–	–	–
Canada	–	–	–	–
Denmark	–	–	–	–
Finland	–	–	–	–
France	7.9	6.9	–	2.4
Germany, Fed. Rep.	–	–	–	11.8
Ireland	–	–	–	–
Italy	–	–	–	–
Japan	–	–	–	–
Netherlands	–	–	–	–
New Zealand	–	–	–	–
Norway	–	–	–	–
Sweden	–	–	–	–
Switzerland	–	–	–	–
United Kingdom	–	–	–	–
United States	–	–	–	–
TOTAL	*7.9*	*6.9*	–	*14.1*
MULTILATERAL	–	*40.3*	*8.3*	–
OPEC COUNTRIES	–	–	*64.7*	–
E.E.C.+ MEMBERS	*7.9*	*16.7*	–	*14.1*
TOTAL	*7.9*	*47.1*	*73.0*	*14.1*

GRANT ELEMENT OF ODA

	1983	1984	1985	1986
DAC COUNTRIES				
Australia	100.0	–	–	–
Austria	100.0	100.0	100.0	–
Belgium	–	–	–	100.0
Canada	100.0	100.0	–	100.0
Denmark	–	–	–	–
Finland	–	–	–	–
France	100.0	83.9	100.0	100.0
Germany, Fed. Rep.	100.0	100.0	100.0	69.8
Ireland	–	–	–	–
Italy	100.0	100.0	100.0	100.0
Japan	100.0	100.0	100.0	100.0
Netherlands	100.0	100.0	100.0	100.0
New Zealand	–	–	–	–
Norway	–	–	–	–
Sweden	–	100.0	–	–
Switzerland	100.0	100.0	100.0	100.0
United Kingdom	100.0	100.0	100.0	100.0
United States	–	–	–	–
TOTAL	*100.0*	*87.5*	*100.0*	*85.4*
MULTILATERAL	*100.0*	*54.4*	*96.0*	*100.0*
OPEC COUNTRIES	*100.0*	*100.0*	*95.2*	*100.0*
E.E.C.+ MEMBERS	*100.0*	*86.8*	*100.0*	*90.5*
TOTAL	*100.0*	*97.2*	*95.3*	*99.6*

OTHER AGGREGATES

COMMITMENTS: ALL SOURCES	1983	1984	1985	1986
TOTAL BILATERAL	1166.7	1001.6	1229.9	949.0
of which				
OPEC	1076.9	824.4	878.0	919.3
CMEA	69.3	160.0	337.0	–
TOTAL MULTILATERAL	23.1	182.9	116.8	182.5
TOTAL BIL.& MULTIL.	1189.8	1184.4	1346.7	1131.5
of which				
ODA Grants	1112.6	853.6	813.0	985.9
ODA Loans	77.2	107.1	410.0	14.1

DISBURSEMENTS:

DAC COUNTRIES COMBINED

OFFICIAL & PRIVATE	1983	1984	1985	1986
GROSS:				
Contractual Lending	101.7	70.1	19.7	32.4
Export Credits Total	43.7	64.7	19.0	3.9
Export Credits Private	43.7	64.7	19.0	3.9
NET:				
Contractual Lending	47.0	47.5	-14.5	16.1
Export Credits Total	-6.4	45.1	-12.6	-8.1
PRIVATE SECTOR NET	-1.8	56.5	24.9	67.2
Direct Investment	0.0	0.1	36.9	64.5
Portfolio Investment	4.1	11.3	0.6	10.8
Export Credits	-5.9	45.2	-12.6	-8.1

MARKET BORROWING:

CHANGE IN CLAIMS

	1983	1984	1985	1986
Banks	–	155.0	182.0	-23.0

MEMORANDUM ITEM:

	1983	1984	1985	1986
CMEA Countr.(Gross)	29.0	92.7	81.6	71.0

TOTAL RECEIPTS NET / TOTAL ODA NET / TOTAL ODA GROSS

	TOTAL RECEIPTS NET 1983	1984	1985	1986	TOTAL ODA NET 1983	1984	1985	1986	TOTAL ODA GROSS 1983
DAC COUNTRIES									
Australia	0.1	0.1	0.1	0.1	–	0.1	0.2	0.1	–
Austria	0.9	0.4	0.8	1.2	0.9	0.4	0.8	1.2	0.9
Belgium	-9.5	14.1	-6.5	-32.7	0.1	0.1	0.1	0.1	0.1
Canada	–	0.1	–	0.1	–	0.1	–	0.1	–
Denmark	-0.1	-0.1	0.0	-0.1	–	–	–	–	–
Finland	-0.1	-0.1	-0.1	–	–	–	–	–	–
France	-9.9	-6.0	4.3	-29.5	0.2	0.2	0.3	0.3	0.2
Germany, Fed. Rep.	-1.2	-2.3	-0.8	-32.0	2.5	4.7	1.5	2.7	2.5
Ireland	–	–	–	–	–	–	–	–	–
Italy	6.4	-1.3	-0.5	-1.0	0.1	–	–	–	0.1
Japan	-73.7	160.5	14.8	-19.6	–	–	–	–	–
Netherlands	–	-93.2	20.2	-35.9	–	–	–	–	–
New Zealand	–	–	–	–	–	–	–	–	–
Norway	–	–	–	–	–	–	–	–	–
Sweden	-2.0	-0.4	-1.0	-1.4	–	–	–	–	–
Switzerland	4.7	-15.6	-0.1	0.0	–	–	0.0	0.0	–
United Kingdom	-8.0	-14.6	-0.6	-20.6	–	–	–	–	–
United States	48.0	-105.0	-524.0	-281.0	-9.0	-7.0	-5.0	-5.0	-4.0
TOTAL	*-44.5*	*-63.3*	*-493.4*	*-452.6*	*-5.3*	*-1.4*	*-2.1*	*-0.6*	*-0.3*
MULTILATERAL									
AF.D.F.	–	–	–	–	–	–	–	–	–
AF.D.B.	–	–	–	–	–	–	–	–	–
AS.D.B	–	–	–	–	–	–	–	–	–
CAR.D.B.	–	–	–	–	–	–	–	–	–
E.E.C.	–	–	–	–	–	–	–	–	–
IBRD	-17.1	-17.2	-16.9	-20.9	–	–	–	–	–
IDA	-0.5	-0.5	-0.5	-0.5	-0.5	-0.5	-0.5	-0.5	–
I.D.B.	–	–	–	–	–	–	–	–	–
IFAD	–	–	–	–	–	–	–	–	–
I.F.C.	–	–	–	–	–	–	–	–	–
IMF TRUST FUND	–	–	–	–	–	–	–	–	–
U.N. AGENCIES	–	–	–	–	–	–	–	–	–
UNDP	–	–	–	–	–	–	–	–	–
UNTA	–	–	–	–	–	–	–	–	–
UNICEF	–	–	–	–	–	–	–	–	–
UNRWA	–	–	–	–	–	–	–	–	–
WFP	–	–	–	–	–	–	–	–	–
UNHCR	–	–	–	–	–	–	–	–	–
Other Multilateral	–	–	–	–	–	–	–	–	–
Arab OPEC Agencies	–	–	–	–	–	–	–	–	–
TOTAL	*-17.6*	*-17.6*	*-17.4*	*-21.3*	*-0.5*	*-0.5*	*-0.5*	*-0.5*	–
OPEC COUNTRIES	*14.0*	*7.3*	*-7.2*	*-9.1*	*14.0*	*7.3*	*-7.2*	*-9.1*	*21.4*
E.E.C.+ MEMBERS	*-22.4*	*-103.4*	*16.0*	*-151.9*	*2.8*	*5.0*	*1.9*	*3.1*	*2.8*
TOTAL	**-48.1**	**-73.7**	**-518.0**	**-483.0**	**8.2**	**5.4**	**-9.7**	**-10.1**	**21.1**

ODA LOANS GROSS / ODA LOANS NET / GRANTS

	ODA LOANS GROSS 1983	1984	1985	1986	ODA LOANS NET 1983	1984	1985	1986	GRANTS 1983
DAC COUNTRIES									
Australia	–	–	–	–	–	–	–	–	–
Austria	–	–	–	–	–	-0.5	–	–	0.9
Belgium	–	–	–	–	–	–	–	–	0.1
Canada	–	–	–	–	–	–	–	–	–
Denmark	–	–	–	–	–	–	–	–	–
Finland	–	–	–	–	–	–	–	–	–
France	–	–	–	–	–	–	–	–	0.2
Germany, Fed. Rep.	1.1	–	0.2	0.6	1.1	-1.0	0.2	0.6	1.4
Ireland	–	–	–	–	–	–	–	–	–
Italy	–	–	–	–	–	–	–	–	0.1
Japan	–	–	–	–	–	–	–	–	–
Netherlands	–	–	–	–	–	–	–	–	–
New Zealand	–	–	–	–	–	–	–	–	–
Norway	–	–	–	–	–	–	–	–	–
Sweden	–	–	–	–	–	–	–	–	–
Switzerland	–	–	–	–	–	–	–	–	–
United Kingdom	–	–	–	–	–	–	–	–	–
United States	–	–	–	–	-5.0	-3.0	-2.0	-1.0	-4.0
TOTAL	*1.1*	–	*0.2*	*0.6*	*-3.9*	*-4.5*	*-1.8*	*-0.4*	*-1.4*
MULTILATERAL	–	–	–	–	*-0.5*	*-0.5*	*-0.5*	*-0.5*	–
OPEC COUNTRIES	*21.4*	*20.5*	*0.9*	*0.4*	*14.0*	*7.3*	*-7.2*	*-9.1*	–
E.E.C.+ MEMBERS	*1.1*	–	*0.2*	*0.6*	*1.1*	*-1.0*	*0.2*	*0.6*	*1.7*
TOTAL	**22.5**	**20.5**	**1.1**	**1.0**	**9.6**	**2.3**	**-9.5**	**-9.9**	**-1.4**

TOTAL OFFICIAL GROSS / TOTAL OFFICIAL NET / TOTAL OOF GROSS

	TOTAL OFFICIAL GROSS 1983	1984	1985	1986	TOTAL OFFICIAL NET 1983	1984	1985	1986	TOTAL OOF GROSS 1983
DAC COUNTRIES									
Australia	–	0.1	0.2	0.1	–	0.1	0.2	0.1	–
Austria	0.9	0.9	0.8	1.2	0.9	0.4	0.8	1.2	–
Belgium	0.1	1.0	0.8	0.2	0.1	1.0	0.8	0.2	–
Canada	–	0.1	–	0.1	–	0.1	–	0.1	–
Denmark	–	–	–	–	–	–	–	–	–
Finland	–	–	–	–	–	–	–	–	–
France	0.2	0.2	0.3	0.3	0.2	0.2	0.3	0.3	–
Germany, Fed. Rep.	16.1	5.8	1.5	2.7	7.7	-8.1	-13.3	-32.4	13.5
Ireland	–	–	–	–	–	–	–	–	–
Italy	3.9	–	–	–	2.2	-0.8	–	–	3.8
Japan	–	–	–	–	–	–	–	–	–
Netherlands	–	–	–	–	–	–	–	–	–
New Zealand	–	–	–	–	–	–	–	–	–
Norway	–	–	–	–	–	–	–	–	–
Sweden	–	1.2	–	–	–	1.1	–	-0.3	–
Switzerland	–	–	0.0	0.0	–	–	0.0	0.0	–
United Kingdom	–	–	–	–	–	–	–	–	–
United States	96.0	36.0	1.0	-4.0	-11.0	-129.0	-246.0	-255.0	100.0
TOTAL	*117.0*	*45.3*	*4.6*	*0.5*	*0.0*	*-135.0*	*-257.2*	*-286.0*	*117.4*
MULTILATERAL	–	–	–	–	*-17.6*	*-17.6*	*-17.4*	*-21.3*	–
OPEC COUNTRIES	*21.4*	*20.5*	*0.9*	*0.4*	*14.0*	*7.3*	*-7.2*	*-9.1*	–
E.E.C.+ MEMBERS	*20.2*	*7.0*	*2.6*	*3.1*	*10.1*	*-7.7*	*-12.2*	*-32.0*	*17.4*
TOTAL	**138.4**	**65.7**	**5.6**	**0.9**	**-3.7**	**-145.4**	**-281.7**	**-316.4**	**117.4**

ODA COMMITMENTS

	1984	1985	1986	1983	1984	1985	1986
Australia	0.1	0.2	0.1	–	0.2	0.1	0.1
Austria	0.9	0.8	1.2	0.9	0.9	0.8	–
Belgium	0.1	0.1	0.1	–	–	–	0.1
Canada	0.1	–	0.1	–	0.4	–	–
Denmark	–	–	–	–	–	–	–
Finland	0.2	0.3	0.3	0.2	0.2	0.3	0.3
France	5.8	1.5	2.7	1.6	6.0	1.2	2.1
Germany, Fed. Rep.	–	–	–	0.1	–	–	–
Ireland	–	–	–	–	–	–	–
Italy	–	–	–	–	–	–	–
Japan	–	–	–	–	–	–	–
Netherlands	–	–	–	–	–	–	–
New Zealand	–	–	–	–	–	–	–
Norway	–	0.0	0.0	–	–	–	–
Sweden	–	–	–	–	–	–	–
Switzerland	-4.0	-3.0	-4.0	–	–	–	–
United Kingdom	3.2	-0.1	0.5	2.7	7.6	2.4	2.5
United States	–	–	–	–	–	–	–
(multilateral / nil rows)	–	–	–	–	–	–	–
OPEC COUNTRIES	20.5	0.9	0.4	–	77.9	–	–
E.E.C.+ MEMBERS	6.0	1.9	3.1	1.9	6.2	1.4	2.5
TOTAL	23.6	0.9	0.8	2.7	85.5	2.4	2.5

TECH. COOP. GRANTS

	1984	1985	1986	1983	1984	1985	1986
Australia	0.1	0.2	0.1	–	0.1	0.2	0.1
Austria	0.9	0.8	1.2	0.9	–	–	–
Belgium	0.1	0.1	0.1	–	–	–	–
Canada	0.1	–	0.1	–	–	–	–
Denmark	–	–	–	–	–	–	–
Finland	0.2	0.3	0.3	0.2	0.2	0.3	0.3
France	5.8	1.3	2.1	1.2	1.3	1.2	1.5
Germany, Fed. Rep.	–	–	–	0.1	–	–	–
Ireland	–	–	–	–	–	–	–
Italy	–	–	–	–	–	–	–
Japan	–	–	–	–	–	–	–
Netherlands	–	0.0	0.0	–	–	0.0	0.0
New Zealand	–	–	–	–	–	–	–
Norway	-4.0	-3.0	-4.0	–	–	–	–
Sweden	3.2	-0.3	-0.2	2.3	1.6	1.6	1.9
MULTILATERAL	–	–	–	–	–	–	–
OPEC COUNTRIES	–	–	–	–	–	–	–
E.E.C.+ MEMBERS	6.0	1.7	2.5	1.4	1.5	1.4	1.8
TOTAL	3.2	-0.3	-0.2	2.3	1.6	1.6	1.9

TOTAL OOF NET

	1984	1985	1986	1983	1984	1985	1986
Australia	–	–	–	–	–	–	–
Austria	0.9	0.7	0.0	–	0.9	0.7	0.0
Belgium	–	–	–	–	–	–	–
Canada	–	–	–	–	–	–	–
Denmark	–	–	–	5.1	-12.9	-14.8	-35.2
France	–	–	–	2.1	-0.8	–	–
Italy	1.2	–	–	–	1.1	–	-0.3
(sub-total rows)	40.0	4.0	–	-2.0	-122.0	-241.0	-250.0
	42.1	4.7	0.0	5.3	-133.6	-255.1	-285.4
	–	–	–	-17.1	-17.2	-16.9	-20.9
E.E.C.+ MEMBERS	0.9	0.7	0.0	7.3	-12.7	-14.1	-35.1
TOTAL	42.1	4.7	0.0	-11.8	-150.8	-272.0	-306.3

ODA COMMITMENTS : LOANS

DAC COUNTRIES

	1983	1984	1985	1986
Australia	–	–	–	–
Austria	–	–	–	–
Belgium	–	–	–	–
Canada	–	–	–	–
Denmark	–	–	–	–
Finland	–	–	–	–
France	–	–	–	–
Germany, Fed. Rep.	–	–	–	–
Ireland	–	–	–	–
Italy	–	–	–	–
Japan	–	–	–	–
Netherlands	–	–	–	–
New Zealand	–	–	–	–
Norway	–	–	–	–
Sweden	–	–	–	–
Switzerland	–	–	–	–
United Kingdom	–	–	–	–
United States	–	–	–	–
TOTAL	–	–	–	–
MULTILATERAL	–	–	–	–
OPEC COUNTRIES	–	77.9	–	–
E.E.C.+ MEMBERS	–	–	–	–
TOTAL	–	77.9	–	–

GRANT ELEMENT OF ODA

DAC COUNTRIES

	1983	1984	1985	1986
Australia	–	100.0	100.0	100.0
Austria	100.0	100.0	100.0	–
Belgium	–	–	–	100.0
Canada	–	100.0	–	–
Denmark	–	–	–	–
Finland	–	–	–	–
France	100.0	100.0	100.0	100.0
Germany, Fed. Rep.	100.0	100.0	100.0	100.0
Ireland	–	–	–	–
Italy	100.0	–	–	–
Japan	–	–	–	37.4
Netherlands	–	–	–	–
New Zealand	–	–	–	–
Norway	–	–	–	–
Sweden	–	–	–	–
Switzerland	–	–	–	–
United Kingdom	–	–	–	–
United States	–	–	–	–
TOTAL	100.0	100.0	100.0	87.6
MULTILATERAL	–	–	–	–
OPEC COUNTRIES	–	32.4	–	–
E.E.C.+ MEMBERS	100.0	100.0	100.0	100.0
TOTAL	100.0	38.4	100.0	87.6

OTHER AGGREGATES

COMMITMENTS: ALL SOURCES

	1983	1984	1985	1986
TOTAL BILATERAL	2.9	86.7	2.4	2.3
of which OPEC	–	77.9	–	–
CMEA	–	–	–	–
TOTAL MULTILATERAL	–	–	–	–
TOTAL BIL.& MULTIL.	2.9	86.7	2.4	2.3
of which ODA Grants	2.7	7.6	2.4	2.5
ODA Loans	–	77.9	–	–

DISBURSEMENTS:

DAC COUNTRIES COMBINED

OFFICIAL & PRIVATE	1983	1984	1985	1986
GROSS: Contractual Lending	338.0	350.1	172.3	104.6
Export Credits Total	336.9	350.1	172.1	103.9
Export Credits Private	219.6	308.9	168.1	103.9
NET: Contractual Lending	-198.4	-186.4	-344.7	-572.7
Export Credits Total	-194.6	-181.9	-342.9	-572.3
PRIVATE SECTOR NET	-44.4	71.7	-236.2	-166.6
Direct Investment	120.1	208.1	109.7	271.5
Portfolio Investment	35.3	-89.1	-258.9	-151.2
Export Credits	-199.8	-47.3	-87.1	-286.9

MARKET BORROWING:

CHANGE IN CLAIMS

	1983	1984	1985	1986
Banks	–	-814.0	-555.0	3965.0

MEMORANDUM ITEM:

	1983	1984	1985	1986
CMEA Countr.(Gross)	–	–	–	–

	1983	1984	1985	1986	1983	1984	1985	1986		1983
TOTAL RECEIPTS NET					**TOTAL ODA NET**				**TOTAL ODA GROSS**	
DAC COUNTRIES										
Australia	10.5	7.0	4.1	3.0	10.5	7.0	4.1	3.0	Australia	10.5
Austria	1.2	0.5	-0.3	0.7	1.2	1.2	0.4	0.7	Austria	1.2
Belgium	-9.8	13.7	2.8	1.3	4.5	4.7	3.6	3.2	Belgium	4.5
Canada	33.9	24.7	30.4	27.2	33.9	24.7	30.4	27.2	Canada	33.9
Denmark	39.5	30.7	36.4	55.0	40.4	31.6	37.0	54.9	Denmark	40.4
Finland	16.8	21.1	14.8	28.9	18.8	21.1	16.6	28.9	Finland	18.8
France	21.9	2.8	-6.2	-8.5	5.0	5.6	1.5	2.0	France	5.0
Germany, Fed. Rep.	38.4	51.1	33.8	45.4	36.3	49.9	32.9	45.0	Germany, Fed. Rep.	36.3
Ireland	2.1	2.2	2.8	2.8	2.1	2.2	2.8	2.8	Ireland	2.1
Italy	9.4	82.3	57.3	29.1	18.7	36.4	34.8	28.1	Italy	19.4
Japan	15.7	19.5	22.6	30.9	30.0	26.1	28.5	35.0	Japan	30.0
Netherlands	37.5	39.0	38.5	63.4	34.5	40.6	36.9	60.7	Netherlands	35.0
New Zealand	0.0	0.1	0.1	0.1	0.0	0.1	0.1	0.1	New Zealand	0.0
Norway	54.8	46.4	51.0	78.8	54.9	46.4	45.4	71.8	Norway	54.9
Sweden	69.2	55.1	49.0	106.3	69.3	55.1	49.0	106.4	Sweden	69.3
Switzerland	5.8	6.1	5.6	19.2	5.8	6.1	6.1	19.2	Switzerland	5.8
United Kingdom	24.3	21.0	33.3	12.1	43.5	29.2	22.6	17.1	United Kingdom	43.9
United States	20.0	22.0	20.0	8.0	20.0	22.0	20.0	8.0	United States	20.0
TOTAL	*391.4*	*445.2*	*395.8*	*503.7*	*429.4*	*409.8*	*372.6*	*514.2*	*TOTAL*	*431.0*
MULTILATERAL										
AF.D.F.	10.1	6.9	10.7	2.3	10.1	6.9	10.7	2.3	AF.D.F.	10.1
AF.D.B.	5.6	0.3	4.5	-2.0	–	–	–	–	AF.D.B.	–
AS.D.B	–	–	–	–	–	–	–	–	AS.D.B	–
CAR.D.B.	–	–	–	–	–	–	–	–	CAR.D.B.	–
E.E.C.	27.0	31.8	29.9	37.2	27.1	31.9	29.9	37.4	E.E.C.	27.1
IBRD	12.0	7.9	27.6	-19.3	0.2	0.5	0.4	–	IBRD	0.2
IDA	63.6	55.2	28.1	83.5	63.6	55.2	28.1	83.5	IDA	64.9
I.D.B.	–	–	–	–	–	–	–	–	I.D.B.	–
IFAD	1.5	1.0	0.8	–	1.5	1.0	0.8	–	IFAD	1.5
I.F.C.	–	-0.1	2.3	0.6	–	–	–	–	I.F.C.	–
IMF TRUST FUND	–	–	–	–	–	–	–	–	IMF TRUST FUND	–
U.N. AGENCIES	–	–	–	–	–	–	–	–	U.N. AGENCIES	–
UNDP	9.4	9.9	7.7	6.3	9.4	9.9	7.7	6.3	UNDP	9.4
UNTA	1.5	1.4	2.1	2.0	1.5	1.4	2.1	2.0	UNTA	1.5
UNICEF	6.5	8.6	9.2	13.5	6.5	8.6	9.2	13.5	UNICEF	6.5
UNRWA	–	–	–	–	–	–	–	–	UNRWA	–
WFP	4.3	4.7	4.3	5.0	4.3	4.7	4.3	5.0	WFP	4.3
UNHCR	5.8	5.4	3.7	5.1	5.8	5.4	3.7	5.1	UNHCR	5.8
Other Multilateral	5.6	7.7	8.1	6.6	5.6	7.7	8.1	6.6	Other Multilateral	5.6
Arab OPEC Agencies	13.9	7.0	-0.7	–	13.9	7.0	-0.7	–	Arab OPEC Agencies	14.4
TOTAL	*166.9*	*147.9*	*138.3*	*140.6*	*149.6*	*140.4*	*104.3*	*161.5*	*TOTAL*	*151.3*
OPEC COUNTRIES	*106.3*	*61.7*	*30.6*	*5.2*	*14.9*	*7.6*	*10.0*	*5.2*	*OPEC COUNTRIES*	*19.1*
E.E.C.+ MEMBERS	*190.3*	*274.6*	*228.6*	*237.8*	*212.1*	*232.1*	*202.1*	*251.2*	*E.E.C.+ MEMBERS*	*213.7*
TOTAL	*664.6*	*654.8*	*564.7*	*649.4*	*593.9*	*557.9*	*486.9*	*680.9*	*TOTAL*	*601.4*

	1983	1984	1985	1986	1983	1984	1985	1986		1983
ODA LOANS GROSS					**ODA LOANS NET**				**GRANTS**	
DAC COUNTRIES										
Australia	–	–	–	–	–	–	–	–	Australia	10.5
Austria	0.1	–	–	–	0.0	0.0	–	0.0	Austria	1.2
Belgium	3.4	2.3	2.2	–	3.4	2.3	2.2	–	Belgium	1.1
Canada	–	–	–	–	–	–	–	–	Canada	33.9
Denmark	10.2	2.5	0.7	5.2	10.2	2.5	-3.1	-77.6	Denmark	30.2
Finland	1.9	–	–	3.9	1.9	–	–	3.9	Finland	16.9
France	2.1	4.1	0.2	–	2.1	4.1	0.2	–	France	2.9
Germany, Fed. Rep.	–	0.0	0.5	0.1	–	0.0	0.5	0.1	Germany, Fed. Rep.	36.3
Ireland	–	–	–	–	–	–	–	–	Ireland	2.1
Italy	11.8	27.2	21.4	11.4	11.1	27.0	21.1	10.5	Italy	7.6
Japan	17.5	7.8	5.6	4.7	17.5	7.8	5.6	4.7	Japan	12.6
Netherlands	0.3	0.4	0.6	1.1	-0.1	0.2	0.6	0.3	Netherlands	34.7
New Zealand	–	–	–	–	–	–	–	–	New Zealand	0.0
Norway	0.1	0.8	–	–	0.1	0.8	–	0.0	Norway	54.8
Sweden	–	–	–	–	–	–	–	–	Sweden	69.3
Switzerland	–	–	–	–	–	–	–	–	Switzerland	5.8
United Kingdom	–	–	–	–	-0.4	-0.5	-0.4	-0.3	United Kingdom	43.9
United States	6.0	2.0	1.0	1.0	6.0	2.0	1.0	1.0	United States	14.0
TOTAL	*53.4*	*47.0*	*32.1*	*27.3*	*51.8*	*46.2*	*27.7*	*-57.5*	*TOTAL*	*377.6*
MULTILATERAL	*99.0*	*76.8*	*44.6*	*89.8*	*97.3*	*74.6*	*41.2*	*86.5*	*MULTILATERAL*	*52.3*
OPEC COUNTRIES	*19.1*	*12.3*	*10.0*	*8.3*	*14.9*	*7.5*	*10.0*	*5.1*	*OPEC COUNTRIES*	*0.0*
E.E.C.+ MEMBERS	*35.9*	*40.4*	*27.5*	*18.8*	*34.3*	*39.6*	*23.0*	*-66.4*	*E.E.C.+ MEMBERS*	*177.8*
TOTAL	*171.5*	*136.2*	*86.7*	*125.4*	*164.0*	*128.3*	*78.9*	*34.0*	*TOTAL*	*429.9*

	1983	1984	1985	1986	1983	1984	1985	1986		1983
TOTAL OFFICIAL GROSS					**TOTAL OFFICIAL NET**				**TOTAL OOF GROSS**	
DAC COUNTRIES										
Australia	10.5	7.0	4.1	3.0	10.5	7.0	4.1	3.0	Australia	–
Austria	1.2	1.2	0.4	0.7	1.2	1.2	0.4	0.7	Austria	–
Belgium	4.5	5.6	4.6	3.2	4.5	5.6	4.6	3.2	Belgium	–
Canada	33.9	24.7	30.4	27.2	33.9	24.7	30.4	27.2	Canada	–
Denmark	40.4	31.6	40.8	138.3	39.9	31.1	36.6	55.0	Denmark	–
Finland	18.8	21.1	16.6	28.9	18.8	21.1	16.6	28.9	Finland	–
France	5.0	5.6	1.5	2.0	5.0	5.6	1.5	2.0	France	–
Germany, Fed. Rep.	41.9	52.1	34.4	46.4	41.4	52.0	34.4	46.4	Germany, Fed. Rep.	5.6
Ireland	2.1	2.2	2.8	2.8	2.1	2.2	2.8	2.8	Ireland	–
Italy	21.3	57.4	42.5	32.8	20.2	56.7	42.3	31.9	Italy	1.9
Japan	30.0	26.1	28.5	35.0	30.0	26.1	28.5	35.0	Japan	–
Netherlands	35.9	42.0	37.0	61.5	35.4	41.2	37.0	60.6	Netherlands	0.9
New Zealand	0.0	0.1	0.1	0.1	0.0	0.1	0.1	0.1	New Zealand	–
Norway	54.9	46.4	45.4	71.8	54.9	46.4	45.4	71.8	Norway	–
Sweden	69.3	55.1	49.0	106.4	65.7	53.3	48.0	105.0	Sweden	–
Switzerland	5.8	6.1	6.1	19.2	5.8	6.1	5.6	19.2	Switzerland	–
United Kingdom	46.1	40.4	23.3	18.6	45.7	38.9	22.5	17.3	United Kingdom	2.2
United States	20.0	22.0	20.0	8.0	20.0	22.0	20.0	8.0	United States	–
TOTAL	*441.6*	*446.5*	*387.3*	*606.0*	*435.1*	*441.1*	*380.6*	*518.1*	*TOTAL*	*10.6*
MULTILATERAL	*181.5*	*169.2*	*167.1*	*173.5*	*166.9*	*147.9*	*138.3*	*140.6*	*MULTILATERAL*	*30.2*
OPEC COUNTRIES	*111.2*	*67.2*	*32.1*	*8.4*	*106.3*	*61.7*	*30.6*	*5.2*	*OPEC COUNTRIES*	*92.1*
E.E.C.+ MEMBERS	*224.3*	*268.8*	*216.9*	*343.5*	*221.2*	*265.1*	*211.5*	*256.5*	*E.E.C.+ MEMBERS*	*10.6*
TOTAL	*734.3*	*683.0*	*586.5*	*787.9*	*708.2*	*650.7*	*549.4*	*663.9*	*TOTAL*	*133.0*

ODA COMMITMENTS

1984	1985	1986	1983	1984	1985	1986
7.0	4.1	3.0	10.2	8.3	2.7	0.6
1.2	0.4	0.7	0.9	1.1	0.5	–
4.7	3.6	3.2	4.0	3.8	1.5	3.2
24.7	30.4	27.2	25.9	15.6	32.5	60.5
31.6	40.8	137.7	10.1	35.0	44.2	76.5
21.1	16.6	28.9	12.8	23.5	42.2	49.6
5.6	1.5	2.0	12.7	1.4	1.2	2.0
49.9	32.9	45.0	27.0	46.6	15.3	36.2
2.2	2.8	2.8	2.1	2.2	2.8	2.8
36.6	35.1	29.0	60.3	32.3	22.5	48.5
26.1	28.5	35.0	24.0	22.9	24.5	35.8
40.8	36.9	61.5	33.5	31.1	21.3	62.9
0.1	0.1	0.1	0.0	0.1	0.1	0.0
46.4	45.4	71.8	45.5	67.6	53.6	105.8
55.1	49.0	106.4	60.8	55.5	58.6	106.4
6.1	6.1	19.2	10.0	4.0	16.9	14.8
29.7	23.0	17.5	36.9	21.7	18.9	27.9
22.0	20.0	8.0	8.6	11.7	8.9	4.3
410.6	*377.0*	*599.0*	*385.2*	*384.3*	*367.9*	*637.7*
6.9	10.7	2.4	21.9	–	0.6	1.5
–	–	–	–	–	–	–
–	–	–	–	–	–	–
31.9	30.0	37.8	11.7	42.4	37.4	19.2
0.5	0.4	–	–	–	–	–
57.3	30.8	86.3	59.3	37.0	8.0	186.2
1.0	0.8	–	–	0.2	15.9	–
–	–	–	–	–	–	–
–	–	–	33.1	37.8	35.1	38.3
9.9	7.7	6.3	–	–	–	–
1.4	2.1	2.0	–	–	–	–
8.6	9.2	13.5	–	–	–	–
4.7	4.3	5.0	–	–	–	–
5.4	3.7	5.1	–	–	–	–
7.7	8.1	6.6	–	–	–	–
7.2	–	–	5.0	–	–	1.4
142.6	*107.7*	*164.9*	*131.0*	*117.3*	*97.0*	*246.5*
12.4	*10.0*	*8.4*	*0.0*	*15.0*	–	–
232.9	*206.5*	*336.4*	*198.2*	*216.5*	*164.9*	*279.1*
565.7	**494.7**	**772.2**	**516.3**	**516.7**	**464.9**	**884.3**

TECH. COOP. GRANTS

1984	1985	1986	1983	1984	1985	1986
7.0	4.1	3.0	0.8	0.7	0.7	0.7
1.2	0.4	0.7	0.3	–	–	–
2.4	1.4	3.2	0.3	0.1	0.2	0.4
24.7	30.4	27.2	3.4	–	5.8	–
29.1	40.1	132.5	26.4	6.1	8.3	12.2
21.1	16.6	25.0	10.2	8.0	9.0	1.4
1.5	1.3	2.0	0.6	0.9	0.7	0.8
49.8	32.4	44.9	24.5	21.2	18.7	23.8
2.2	2.8	2.8	0.6	0.8	1.2	1.4
9.4	13.7	17.6	3.1	2.8	3.1	10.5
18.3	22.9	30.4	5.4	5.4	5.5	8.7
40.4	36.3	60.5	15.6	10.5	12.2	15.7
0.1	0.1	0.1	0.0	0.0	0.0	0.1
45.7	45.4	71.8	10.4	11.3	10.7	11.1
55.1	49.0	106.4	19.9	17.2	16.4	17.4
6.1	6.1	19.2	2.4	3.3	2.4	0.2
29.7	23.0	17.5	10.2	8.4	9.0	10.4
20.0	19.0	7.0	11.0	9.0	7.0	4.0
363.6	*344.9*	*571.7*	*145.1*	*105.7*	*110.6*	*118.6*
65.8	*63.1*	*75.1*	*28.8*	*33.0*	*30.8*	*33.6*
0.2	–	*0.1*	–	–	–	–
192.5	*179.0*	*317.6*	*81.4*	*50.7*	*53.3*	*75.3*
429.5	**408.0**	**646.8**	**173.9**	**138.7**	**141.4**	**152.2**

TOTAL OOF NET

1984	1985	1986	1983	1984	1985	1986
–	–	–	–	–	–	–
0.9	0.9	0.0	–	0.9	0.9	0.0
–	0.0	0.6	-0.5	-0.5	-0.4	0.1
–	–	–	–	–	–	–
2.3	1.5	1.4	5.1	2.2	1.5	1.4
–	–	–	–	–	–	–
20.8	7.4	3.8	1.5	20.4	7.4	3.8
1.2	0.1	–	0.9	0.6	0.1	-0.1
–	–	–	–	–	–	–
–	–	–	-3.5	-1.8	-1.0	-1.4
–	–	–	–	–	-0.5	–
10.7	0.3	1.2	2.2	9.7	0.0	0.1
–	–	–	–	–	–	–
35.9	*10.3*	*7.0*	*5.7*	*31.3*	*8.0*	*4.0*
26.6	*59.4*	*8.7*	*17.3*	*7.5*	*34.0*	*-20.9*
54.8	*22.1*	–	*91.4*	*54.0*	*20.5*	–
35.9	*10.3*	*7.0*	*9.1*	*33.0*	*9.5*	*5.2*
117.3	**91.8**	**15.7**	**114.3**	**92.8**	**62.6**	**-16.9**

ODA COMMITMENTS : LOANS

DAC COUNTRIES

	1983	1984	1985	1986
Australia	–	–	–	–
Austria	0.1	–	–	–
Belgium	3.4	2.3	0.8	–
Canada	–	–	–	–
Denmark	–	–	–	–
Finland	–	–	3.0	5.9
France	8.4	–	–	–
Germany, Fed. Rep.	–	–	–	–
Ireland	–	–	–	–
Italy	50.2	21.4	5.1	15.7
Japan	10.0	–	–	–
Netherlands	0.4	–	0.5	0.2
New Zealand	–	–	–	–
Norway	0.1	0.8	–	–
Sweden	–	–	–	–
Switzerland	–	–	–	–
United Kingdom	–	–	–	–
United States	5.2	0.5	0.2	0.2
TOTAL	*77.8*	*24.9*	*9.7*	*22.0*
MULTILATERAL	*86.2*	*39.8*	*24.5*	*187.7*
OPEC COUNTRIES	–	*15.0*	–	–
E.E.C.+ MEMBERS	*62.5*	*26.4*	*6.4*	*15.8*
TOTAL	**164.0**	**79.7**	**34.2**	**209.7**

GRANT ELEMENT OF ODA

DAC COUNTRIES

	1983	1984	1985	1986
Australia	100.0	100.0	100.0	100.0
Austria	96.2	100.0	100.0	–
Belgium	87.1	90.7	88.5	100.0
Canada	100.0	100.0	100.0	100.0
Denmark	100.0	100.0	100.0	100.0
Finland	100.0	100.0	100.0	96.2
France	73.4	100.0	100.0	100.0
Germany, Fed. Rep.	100.0	100.0	100.0	100.0
Ireland	100.0	100.0	100.0	100.0
Italy	59.0	65.8	89.2	88.2
Japan	85.2	100.0	100.0	100.0
Netherlands	100.0	100.0	99.8	100.0
New Zealand	100.0	100.0	100.0	100.0
Norway	99.9	99.2	100.0	100.0
Sweden	100.0	100.0	100.0	100.0
Switzerland	100.0	100.0	100.0	100.0
United Kingdom	100.0	100.0	100.0	100.0
United States	80.0	98.6	99.1	98.2
TOTAL	*91.2*	*96.9*	*99.2*	*98.8*
MULTILATERAL	*87.1*	*100.0*	*93.4*	*87.1*
OPEC COUNTRIES	*100.0*	*42.4*	–	–
E.E.C.+ MEMBERS	*85.5*	*94.7*	*98.3*	*97.9*
TOTAL	**90.0**	**95.6**	**97.8**	**95.5**

OTHER AGGREGATES

COMMITMENTS: ALL SOURCES

	1983	1984	1985	1986
TOTAL BILATERAL	532.6	439.1	368.2	660.3
of which				
OPEC	137.8	39.0	–	–
CMEA	8.7	14.7	–	22.8
TOTAL MULTILATERAL	131.0	120.5	97.2	251.6
TOTAL BIL.& MULTIL.	663.7	559.6	465.4	911.9
of which				
ODA Grants	352.2	437.6	430.7	676.1
ODA Loans	164.0	79.7	34.2	231.0

DISBURSEMENTS:

DAC COUNTRIES COMBINED

	1983	1984	1985	1986
OFFICIAL & PRIVATE				
GROSS:				
Contractual Lending	100.7	139.7	67.5	36.3
Export Credits Total	38.5	78.5	33.4	5.8
Export Credits Private	36.6	57.6	26.0	1.9
NET:				
Contractual Lending	11.8	89.1	36.3	-70.5
Export Credits Total	-48.3	30.5	7.5	-14.8
PRIVATE SECTOR NET	-43.6	4.1	15.2	-14.5
Direct Investment	1.5	-8.4	14.5	3.3
Portfolio Investment	0.6	0.0	-0.8	-0.9
Export Credits	-45.7	12.5	1.5	-16.9

MARKET BORROWING:

CHANGE IN CLAIMS

	1983	1984	1985	1986
Banks	–	-39.0	15.0	-14.0

MEMORANDUM ITEM:

	1983	1984	1985	1986
CMEA Countr.(Gross)	10.2	1.4	1.0	4.5

	1983	1984	1985	1986	1983	1984	1985	1986		1983
TOTAL RECEIPTS NET					**TOTAL ODA NET**				**TOTAL ODA GROSS**	
DAC COUNTRIES										
Australia	15.5	33.5	16.6	16.0	15.9	22.6	21.8	18.7	Australia	15.9
Austria	0.1	-1.6	-2.7	-0.6	0.1	0.1	-1.0	-0.6	Austria	0.1
Belgium	2.5	26.5	43.1	-7.9	1.3	2.9	5.0	3.8	Belgium	1.3
Canada	36.7	17.9	9.3	17.9	9.9	17.1	14.1	17.2	Canada	9.9
Denmark	9.0	2.5	3.0	-15.6	3.9	0.7	5.7	8.2	Denmark	4.0
Finland	0.2	0.2	0.0	0.4	0.3	0.1	0.2	0.4	Finland	0.3
France	2.6	28.6	34.8	-20.8	2.8	8.5	7.6	5.1	France	2.9
Germany, Fed. Rep.	35.5	20.9	94.4	6.7	23.7	26.1	32.2	27.7	Germany, Fed. Rep.	28.9
Ireland	0.1	0.1	0.1	–	0.1	0.1	0.1	–	Ireland	0.1
Italy	1.0	2.6	1.8	7.7	0.9	1.2	1.8	2.5	Italy	0.9
Japan	429.5	583.1	409.1	360.8	248.1	232.0	264.1	260.4	Japan	272.6
Netherlands	4.5	21.6	17.0	-42.3	3.5	4.2	4.7	7.9	Netherlands	3.5
New Zealand	0.8	0.8	0.7	0.9	0.8	0.8	0.7	0.9	New Zealand	0.8
Norway	1.8	0.8	0.8	1.7	2.4	0.7	0.8	0.9	Norway	2.4
Sweden	-2.2	-3.4	-4.0	-1.3	–	0.1	–	0.1	Sweden	–
Switzerland	8.9	2.8	0.1	3.8	1.4	2.6	2.2	3.8	Switzerland	1.4
United Kingdom	10.6	45.8	-16.5	-55.6	1.7	2.3	1.6	2.2	United Kingdom	1.9
United States	166.0	241.0	-119.0	23.0	23.0	35.0	24.0	32.0	United States	24.0
TOTAL	722.9	1023.6	488.7	294.8	339.7	357.1	385.5	391.1	TOTAL	370.8
MULTILATERAL										
AF.D.F.	–	–	–	–	–	–	–	–	AF.D.F.	–
AF.D.B.	–	–	–	–	–	–	–	–	AF.D.B.	–
AS.D.B	93.6	102.0	105.9	79.3	7.9	9.7	10.5	12.4	AS.D.B	7.9
CAR.D.B.	–	–	–	–	–	–	–	–	CAR.D.B.	–
E.E.C.	6.2	13.3	12.7	31.2	6.2	13.3	12.7	31.2	E.E.C.	6.2
IBRD	380.4	244.2	196.8	72.8	0.6	0.1	–	–	IBRD	0.6
IDA	17.4	10.5	7.6	3.7	17.4	10.5	7.6	3.7	IDA	17.5
I.D.B.	–	–	–	–	–	–	–	–	I.D.B.	–
IFAD	2.4	19.9	7.3	2.6	2.4	19.9	7.3	2.6	IFAD	2.4
I.F.C.	-3.4	-4.9	3.4	8.1	–	–	–	–	I.F.C.	–
IMF TRUST FUND	–	–	–	–	–	–	–	–	IMF TRUST FUND	–
U.N. AGENCIES	–	–	–	–	–	–	–	–	U.N. AGENCIES	–
UNDP	4.9	4.7	4.1	4.1	4.9	4.7	4.1	4.1	UNDP	4.9
UNTA	2.4	2.1	3.4	2.2	2.4	2.1	3.4	2.2	UNTA	2.4
UNICEF	2.7	3.3	4.7	4.2	2.7	3.3	4.7	4.2	UNICEF	2.7
UNRWA	–	–	–	–	–	–	–	–	UNRWA	–
WFP	–	–	–	–	–	–	–	–	WFP	–
UNHCR	28.6	28.5	24.3	23.3	28.6	28.5	24.3	23.3	UNHCR	28.6
Other Multilateral	3.0	2.8	3.1	2.0	3.0	2.8	3.1	2.0	Other Multilateral	3.0
Arab OPEC Agencies	5.6	4.0	6.9	15.2	5.6	4.0	6.5	11.5	Arab OPEC Agencies	6.0
TOTAL	543.8	430.5	380.1	248.7	81.6	99.0	84.2	97.1	TOTAL	82.1
OPEC COUNTRIES	10.4	17.9	11.2	8.1	10.4	17.9	11.2	8.1	OPEC COUNTRIES	11.6
E.E.C. + MEMBERS	71.8	161.9	190.4	-96.6	44.0	59.3	71.4	88.5	E.E.C. + MEMBERS	49.6
TOTAL	1277.0	1472.1	880.0	551.6	431.7	474.1	480.9	496.3	TOTAL	464.6

	1983	1984	1985	1986	1983	1984	1985	1986		1983
ODA LOANS GROSS					**ODA LOANS NET**				**GRANTS**	
DAC COUNTRIES										
Australia	–	–	–	–	–	–	–	–	Australia	15.9
Austria	–	–	–	–	–	–	-1.2	-1.1	Austria	0.1
Belgium	–	–	1.2	–	–	–	1.2	–	Belgium	1.3
Canada	4.1	3.2	–	–	4.0	3.1	0.0	0.0	Canada	5.9
Denmark	3.0	0.1	5.4	7.5	2.8	0.0	5.3	7.1	Denmark	1.1
Finland	–	–	–	–	–	–	–	–	Finland	0.3
France	–	5.2	4.4	0.0	-0.1	4.9	3.9	-0.6	France	2.9
Germany, Fed. Rep.	12.7	11.3	15.3	9.4	7.5	7.7	11.0	2.8	Germany, Fed. Rep.	16.2
Ireland	–	–	–	–	–	–	–	–	Ireland	0.1
Italy	–	–	–	–	–	–	–	–	Italy	0.9
Japan	183.3	169.6	181.8	192.5	158.8	141.6	146.9	134.7	Japan	89.4
Netherlands	–	–	–	0.6	–	–	–	0.6	Netherlands	3.5
New Zealand	–	–	–	–	–	–	–	–	New Zealand	0.8
Norway	0.9	–	–	0.2	0.9	–	0.0	0.2	Norway	1.4
Sweden	–	–	–	–	–	–	–	–	Sweden	–
Switzerland	0.7	1.5	0.5	2.4	0.7	1.4	0.4	1.9	Switzerland	0.7
United Kingdom	0.1	–	–	–	0.0	-0.5	-0.7	-0.5	United Kingdom	1.7
United States	5.0	8.0	10.0	7.0	4.0	7.0	9.0	6.0	United States	19.0
TOTAL	209.8	198.9	218.6	219.5	178.7	165.2	175.6	151.0	TOTAL	161.0
MULTILATERAL	33.7	45.4	32.4	32.4	33.2	43.4	30.5	29.3	MULTILATERAL	48.4
OPEC COUNTRIES	11.6	20.1	15.1	13.4	10.4	17.9	11.1	8.0	OPEC COUNTRIES	0.0
E.E.C. + MEMBERS	15.8	16.6	26.3	17.5	10.2	12.1	20.6	9.4	E.E.C. + MEMBERS	33.7
TOTAL	255.1	264.4	266.0	265.3	222.2	226.4	217.2	188.4	TOTAL	209.5

	1983	1984	1985	1986	1983	1984	1985	1986		1983
TOTAL OFFICIAL GROSS					**TOTAL OFFICIAL NET**				**TOTAL OOF GROSS**	
DAC COUNTRIES										
Australia	26.9	35.0	21.8	18.7	26.3	33.4	19.2	16.0	Australia	11.0
Austria	0.1	0.1	0.2	0.5	0.1	0.1	-1.0	-0.6	Austria	–
Belgium	1.3	5.4	7.8	3.8	1.3	5.4	7.8	3.8	Belgium	–
Canada	38.9	21.1	17.3	27.0	36.8	18.0	9.4	17.9	Canada	28.9
Denmark	24.8	12.0*	17.7	9.1	24.4	11.9	15.3	1.5	Denmark	20.8
Finland	0.3	0.4	0.2	0.4	0.3	0.4	0.2	0.4	Finland	–
France	2.9	8.8	8.1	5.7	2.8	8.5	7.6	5.1	France	–
Germany, Fed. Rep.	45.8	35.3	90.4	38.4	34.2	23.7	77.9	16.9	Germany, Fed. Rep.	16.9
Ireland	0.1	0.1	0.1	–	0.1	0.1	0.1	–	Ireland	–
Italy	0.9	1.2	1.8	2.5	0.9	1.2	1.8	2.5	Italy	–
Japan	354.2	305.7	315.9	337.3	317.9	265.2	264.8	242.5	Japan	81.6
Netherlands	3.5	4.2	7.1	9.1	3.5	4.2	7.1	9.1	Netherlands	–
New Zealand	0.8	0.8	0.7	0.9	0.8	0.8	0.7	0.9	New Zealand	–
Norway	2.4	0.7	0.8	0.9	2.4	0.7	0.8	0.9	Norway	–
Sweden	1.0	0.1	–	0.1	-0.4	-1.6	-1.0	-2.1	Sweden	1.0
Switzerland	1.4	2.7	2.4	4.3	1.4	2.6	2.2	3.8	Switzerland	–
United Kingdom	8.4	26.8	9.6	6.2	8.0	25.1	7.0	2.0	United Kingdom	6.6
United States	33.0	54.0	25.0	34.0	16.0	22.0	-5.0	6.0	United States	9.0
TOTAL	546.7	514.4	526.9	498.8	476.9	421.6	414.9	326.4	TOTAL	175.8
MULTILATERAL	614.0	519.0	496.3	428.1	543.8	430.5	380.1	248.7	MULTILATERAL	531.9
OPEC COUNTRIES	11.6	20.1	15.2	13.5	10.4	17.9	11.2	8.1	OPEC COUNTRIES	–
E.E.C. + MEMBERS	93.8	107.0	155.4	105.9	81.4	93.4	137.3	72.0	E.E.C. + MEMBERS	44.2
TOTAL	1172.3	1053.5	1038.4	940.4	1031.0	870.1	806.3	583.3	TOTAL	707.7

ODA COMMITMENTS

1984	1985	1986	1983	1984	1985	1986
22.6	21.8	18.7	17.3	29.2	9.8	13.8
0.1	0.2	0.5	0.1	0.1	0.3	–
2.9	5.0	3.8	0.7	1.8	2.3	3.8
17.1	14.1	17.2	27.7	30.0	27.7	19.5
0.9	5.8	8.6	0.1	0.2	15.3	0.2
0.1	0.2	0.4	0.2	0.2	0.0	0.2
8.8	8.1	5.7	32.1	8.8	8.3	5.7
29.8	36.6	34.3	39.9	37.2	31.1	44.1
0.1	0.1	–	0.1	0.1	0.1	–
1.2	1.8	2.5	1.4	1.4	3.2	8.0
260.0	299.0	318.2	370.3	307.8	347.4	311.2
4.2	4.7	7.9	6.2	4.4	3.4	9.8
0.8	0.7	0.9	0.4	0.7	1.3	0.3
0.7	0.8	0.9	0.7	0.7	0.2	0.5
0.1	–	0.1	–	0.3	–	0.0
2.7	2.4	4.3	0.4	9.7	1.8	1.9
2.8	2.3	2.7	1.7	4.5	2.0	3.6
36.0	25.0	33.0	31.8	31.9	37.3	36.5
390.8	*428.5*	*459.6*	*530.9*	*468.8*	*491.2*	*459.1*
–	–	–	–	–	–	–
9.8	10.6	12.6	–	–	–	–
–	–	–				
13.3	12.7	31.2	23.2	9.0	31.2	1.5
0.1	–	–				
10.8	8.2	4.0				
–	–	–				
20.5	8.5	5.1	19.6	–	–	–
–	–	–				
–	–	–	41.6	41.4	39.6	35.8
4.7	4.1	4.1				
2.1	3.4	2.2				
3.3	4.7	4.2				
–	–	–				
–	–	–				
28.5	24.3	23.3				
2.8	3.1	2.0				
5.1	6.5	11.5	–	–	–	1.2
101.1	*86.1*	*100.1*	*84.5*	*50.4*	*70.7*	*38.6*
20.1	*15.2*	*13.5*	*0.0*	–	*0.0*	–
63.9	*77.1*	*96.6*	*105.5*	*67.4*	*96.7*	*76.7*
512.0	*529.7*	*573.2*	*615.4*	*519.3*	*562.0*	*497.7*

TECH. COOP. GRANTS

1984	1985	1986	1983	1984	1985	1986
22.6	21.8	18.7	12.7	17.9	19.1	16.3
0.1	0.2	0.5	0.1	–	–	–
2.9	3.8	3.8	0.1	0.2	1.0	1.5
13.9	14.1	17.2	2.1	–	3.3	–
0.7	0.4	1.2	1.1	0.8	3.8	1.2
0.1	0.2	0.4	0.2	0.1	0.2	0.2
3.6	3.7	5.7	2.9	3.6	3.1	5.7
18.4	21.2	24.9	11.6	13.4	12.2	16.4
0.1	0.1	–	0.1	0.1	0.1	–
1.2	1.8	2.5	0.3	0.7	0.7	2.5
90.4	117.2	125.8	37.2	40.2	40.7	54.2
4.2	4.7	7.3	2.2	2.7	2.6	4.2
0.8	0.7	0.9	0.5	0.5	0.5	0.7
0.7	0.8	0.6	0.4	0.2	0.2	0.2
0.1	–	0.1	–	–	–	0.0
1.2	1.9	1.9	0.2	0.2	0.2	0.2
2.8	2.3	2.7	1.7	2.5	2.0	2.1
28.0	15.0	26.0	12.0	16.0	14.0	15.0
191.9	*209.9*	*240.1*	*85.2*	*99.2*	*103.7*	*120.3*
55.7	*53.7*	*67.8*	*41.6*	*41.4*	*39.6*	*35.8*
0.1	*0.1*	*0.1*	–	–	–	–
47.3	*50.8*	*79.1*	*19.9*	*24.0*	*25.5*	*33.6*
247.7	*263.7*	*307.9*	*126.8*	*140.6*	*143.3*	*156.1*

TOTAL OOF NET

1984	1985	1986	1983	1984	1985	1986
12.4	–	–	10.5	10.8	-2.5	-2.7
–	–	–				
2.5	2.9	–	–	2.5	2.9	–
4.0	3.2	9.9	26.9	0.9	-4.7	0.7
11.2	11.9	0.5	20.5	11.1	9.6	-6.7
0.3	–	–	–	0.3	–	–
–	–	–				
5.5	53.8	4.2	10.6	-2.4	45.7	-10.8
–	–	–				
45.6	17.0	19.1	69.8	33.1	0.7	-17.9
–	2.4	1.2	–	–	2.4	1.2
–	–	–				
–	–	–	-0.4	-1.7	-1.0	-2.2
23.9	7.3	3.5	6.3	22.8	5.4	-0.2
18.0	–	1.0	-7.0	-13.0	-29.0	-26.0
123.5	*98.4*	*39.2*	*137.2*	*64.5*	*29.4*	*-64.7*
417.9	*410.3*	*327.9*	*462.1*	*331.5*	*296.0*	*151.6*
–	–	–				
43.2	*78.3*	*9.3*	*37.4*	*34.0*	*66.0*	*-16.5*
541.5	*508.7*	*367.1*	*599.3*	*396.0*	*325.4*	*87.0*

ODA COMMITMENTS : LOANS

DAC COUNTRIES

	1983	1984	1985	1986
Australia	–	–	–	–
Austria	–	–	–	–
Belgium	–	–	0.4	–
Canada	–	–	–	–
Denmark	–	–	15.1	–
Finland	–	–	–	–
France	29.2	5.2	4.6	0.0
Germany, Fed. Rep.	21.4	19.8	6.2	22.6
Ireland	–	–	–	–
Italy	–	–	–	–
Japan	285.8	208.5	237.1	218.4
Netherlands	–	–	–	0.7
New Zealand	–	–	–	–
Norway	–	–	–	0.2
Sweden	–	–	–	–
Switzerland	–	8.5	–	–
United Kingdom	–	–	–	–
United States	7.0	18.1	10.1	3.5
TOTAL	*343.4*	*260.0*	*273.5*	*245.5*
MULTILATERAL	*19.6*	–	–	–
OPEC COUNTRIES	–	–	–	–
E.E.C.+ MEMBERS	*50.6*	*24.9*	*26.3*	*23.3*
TOTAL	*363.0*	*260.0*	*273.5*	*245.5*

GRANT ELEMENT OF ODA

DAC COUNTRIES

	1983	1984	1985	1986
Australia	100.0	100.0	100.0	100.0
Austria	100.0	100.0	100.0	
Belgium	100.0	100.0	93.2	100.0
Canada	100.0	100.0	100.0	100.0
Denmark	100.0	100.0	75.3	100.0
Finland	100.0	100.0	100.0	100.0
France	100.0	77.9	78.6	100.0
Germany, Fed. Rep.	78.8	75.8	86.3	74.4
Ireland	100.0	100.0	100.0	–
Italy	100.0	100.0	100.0	100.0
Japan	66.8	68.2	67.7	65.9
Netherlands	100.0	100.0	100.0	100.0
New Zealand	100.0	100.0	100.0	100.0
Norway	100.0	100.0	100.0	63.8
Sweden	–	100.0	–	100.0
Switzerland	100.0	85.6	100.0	100.0
United Kingdom	100.0	100.0	100.0	100.0
United States	93.7	83.5	92.2	97.1
TOTAL	*73.4*	*75.4*	*74.6*	*74.1*
MULTILATERAL	*85.9*	*100.0*	*100.0*	*100.0*
OPEC COUNTRIES	*100.0*	–	*100.0*	
E.E.C.+ MEMBERS	*88.9*	*83.7*	*89.8*	*85.2*
TOTAL	*75.1*	*77.7*	*77.8*	*76.1*

OTHER AGGREGATES

COMMITMENTS: ALL SOURCES

	1983	1984	1985	1986
TOTAL BILATERAL	618.7	574.3	531.8	527.8
of which				
OPEC	0.0	12.5	0.0	–
CMEA	–	–	–	–
TOTAL MULTILATERAL	648.9	439.6	386.3	153.5
TOTAL BIL.& MULTIL.	1267.6	1013.9	918.1	681.3
of which				
ODA Grants	252.4	259.3	288.5	252.2
ODA Loans	363.0	260.0	273.5	245.5

DISBURSEMENTS:

DAC COUNTRIES COMBINED

	1983	1984	1985	1986
OFFICIAL & PRIVATE				
GROSS:				
Contractual Lending	580.9	484.2	473.9	327.5
Export Credits Total	363.6	260.0	245.2	102.0
Export Credits Private	195.3	164.2	159.7	68.8
NET:				
Contractual Lending	249.4	174.9	132.7	-47.1
Export Credits Total	64.7	-14.4	-50.0	-199.3
PRIVATE SECTOR NET	246.0	602.0	73.7	-31.6
Direct Investment	200.1	348.3	-96.9	-31.0
Portfolio Investment	112.3	306.0	240.1	132.8
Export Credits	-66.4	-52.4	-69.5	-133.5

MARKET BORROWING:

CHANGE IN CLAIMS

	1983	1984	1985	1986
Banks	–	812.0	-254.0	-786.0

MEMORANDUM ITEM:

	1983	1984	1985	1986
CMEA Countr.(Gross)	–	–	–	–

TOTAL RECEIPTS NET

DAC COUNTRIES	1983	1984	1985	1986
Australia	—	—	—	—
Austria	0.0	-1.1	-1.1	0.0
Belgium	6.0	-1.0	1.8	-9.4
Canada	0.5	1.7	8.6	5.2
Denmark	0.0	-0.1	0.9	1.6
Finland	—	—	—	—
France	24.1	37.0	4.6	9.9
Germany, Fed. Rep.	11.0	18.6	11.7	13.7
Ireland	—	—	—	—
Italy	-0.4	0.5	0.9	2.3
Japan	2.2	2.6	1.7	19.2
Netherlands	0.5	-0.9	0.8	1.3
New Zealand	—	—	—	—
Norway	0.2	0.2	0.2	1.4
Sweden	—	—	—	-0.3
Switzerland	1.5	0.0	0.3	-0.3
United Kingdom	-4.6	-3.6	0.1	0.2
United States	8.0	7.0	8.0	10.0
TOTAL	49.0	61.0	38.6	54.8
MULTILATERAL				
AF.D.F.	2.2	1.0	3.8	0.3
AF.D.B.	-0.1	0.8	-0.5	-1.3
AS.D.B	—	—	—	—
CAR.D.B.	—	—	—	—
E.E.C.	16.0	18.8	7.4	13.2
IBRD	-0.3	-0.3	-0.2	-0.3
IDA	32.3	24.9	30.5	50.3
I.D.B.	—	—	—	—
IFAD	—	—	0.3	0.6
I.F.C.	—	—	—	—
IMF TRUST FUND	—	—	—	—
U.N. AGENCIES	—	—	—	—
UNDP	2.0	3.1	3.3	4.4
UNTA	0.5	0.5	0.5	0.7
UNICEF	0.3	0.2	0.4	0.6
UNRWA	—	—	—	—
WFP	2.5	2.2	1.7	1.6
UNHCR	0.2	0.4	0.3	0.2
Other Multilateral	0.9	0.8	1.0	0.8
Arab OPEC Agencies	2.8	1.5	2.0	1.5
TOTAL	59.3	53.9	50.6	72.3
OPEC COUNTRIES	2.8	2.0	9.1	7.9
E.E.C.+ MEMBERS	52.7	69.4	28.2	32.7
TOTAL	111.1	116.9	98.2	135.0

TOTAL ODA NET

DAC COUNTRIES	1983	1984	1985	1986
Australia	—	—	—	—
Austria	0.0	0.0	0.0	0.0
Belgium	0.2	0.3	0.4	2.7
Canada	0.5	1.7	8.6	5.2
Denmark	0.0	-0.1	0.7	0.9
Finland	—	—	—	—
France	23.8	28.3	18.1	31.7
Germany, Fed. Rep.	13.0	11.4	14.1	16.0
Ireland	—	—	—	—
Italy	0.1	0.4	0.3	3.1
Japan	2.2	2.6	1.7	19.2
Netherlands	0.5	0.7	0.8	0.9
New Zealand	—	—	—	—
Norway	0.2	0.2	0.2	1.4
Sweden	—	—	—	—
Switzerland	0.2	0.3	0.3	0.4
United Kingdom	0.1	0.1	0.2	0.2
United States	8.0	7.0	8.0	10.0
TOTAL	48.8	53.1	53.3	91.7
MULTILATERAL				
AF.D.F.	2.2	1.0	3.8	0.3
AF.D.B.	—	—	—	—
AS.D.B	—	—	—	—
CAR.D.B.	—	—	—	—
E.E.C.	16.8	20.4	9.4	15.4
IBRD	—	—	—	—
IDA	32.3	24.9	30.5	50.3
I.D.B.	—	—	—	—
IFAD	—	—	0.3	0.6
I.F.C.	—	—	—	—
IMF TRUST FUND	—	—	—	—
U.N. AGENCIES	—	—	—	—
UNDP	2.0	3.1	3.3	4.4
UNTA	0.5	0.5	0.5	0.7
UNICEF	0.3	0.2	0.4	0.6
UNRWA	—	—	—	—
WFP	2.5	2.2	1.7	1.6
UNHCR	0.2	0.4	0.3	0.2
Other Multilateral	0.9	0.8	1.0	0.8
Arab OPEC Agencies	2.8	1.5	2.0	—
TOTAL	60.4	54.9	51.7	74.7
OPEC COUNTRIES	2.8	2.0	9.1	7.9
E.E.C.+ MEMBERS	54.5	61.6	43.8	70.8
TOTAL	112.0	110.0	114.0	174.3

TOTAL ODA GROSS

	1983
Australia	—
Austria	0.0
Belgium	0.2
Canada	0.6
Denmark	0.0
Finland	—
France	23.9
Germany, Fed. Rep.	25.7
Ireland	—
Italy	0.1
Japan	2.2
Netherlands	0.5
New Zealand	—
Norway	0.2
Sweden	—
Switzerland	0.2
United Kingdom	0.1
United States	8.0
TOTAL	61.8
AF.D.F.	2.2
AF.D.B.	—
AS.D.B	—
CAR.D.B.	—
E.E.C.	16.8
IBRD	—
IDA	32.4
I.D.B.	—
IFAD	—
I.F.C.	—
IMF TRUST FUND	—
U.N. AGENCIES	—
UNDP	2.0
UNTA	0.5
UNICEF	0.3
UNRWA	—
WFP	2.5
UNHCR	0.2
Other Multilateral	0.9
Arab OPEC Agencies	2.8
TOTAL	60.5
OPEC COUNTRIES	2.8
E.E.C.+ MEMBERS	67.4
TOTAL	125.0

ODA LOANS GROSS

DAC COUNTRIES	1983	1984	1985	1986
Australia	—	—	—	—
Austria	—	—	—	—
Belgium	—	—	—	—
Canada	—	—	—	—
Denmark	—	—	—	—
Finland	—	—	—	—
France	7.5	12.6	7.8	10.6
Germany, Fed. Rep.	18.2	9.1	1.3	—
Ireland	—	—	—	—
Italy	—	—	—	—
Japan	—	—	—	14.8
Netherlands	—	—	—	0.4
New Zealand	—	—	—	—
Norway	—	—	—	1.2
Sweden	—	—	—	—
Switzerland	—	—	—	—
United Kingdom	—	—	—	—
United States	—	—	—	—
TOTAL	25.7	21.7	9.1	27.0
MULTILATERAL	37.6	28.8	35.4	52.3
OPEC COUNTRIES	2.4	2.0	9.1	9.4
E.E.C.+ MEMBERS	25.9	22.9	9.1	11.0
TOTAL	65.6	52.5	53.5	88.8

ODA LOANS NET

DAC COUNTRIES	1983	1984	1985	1986
Australia	—	—	—	—
Austria	—	—	0.0	—
Belgium	—	—	—	—
Canada	-0.1	—	—	—
Denmark	—	-0.1	-9.3	—
Finland	—	—	—	—
France	7.4	10.6	-2.1	9.2
Germany, Fed. Rep.	5.4	4.0	-95.7	-2.2
Ireland	—	—	—	—
Italy	—	—	-0.1	—
Japan	—	—	—	14.8
Netherlands	—	—	—	0.4
New Zealand	—	—	—	—
Norway	—	—	—	1.2
Sweden	—	—	—	—
Switzerland	—	—	—	—
United Kingdom	—	—	—	—
United States	—	—	—	—
TOTAL	12.7	14.5	-107.3	23.4
MULTILATERAL	37.5	28.6	35.1	50.9
OPEC COUNTRIES	2.4	2.0	8.9	7.9
E.E.C.+ MEMBERS	13.1	15.6	-107.3	7.1
TOTAL	52.6	45.0	-63.3	82.2

GRANTS

	1983
Australia	—
Austria	0.0
Belgium	0.2
Canada	0.6
Denmark	0.0
Finland	—
France	16.4
Germany, Fed. Rep.	7.5
Ireland	—
Italy	0.1
Japan	2.2
Netherlands	0.5
New Zealand	—
Norway	0.2
Sweden	—
Switzerland	0.2
United Kingdom	0.1
United States	8.0
TOTAL	36.1
MULTILATERAL	23.0
OPEC COUNTRIES	0.4
E.E.C.+ MEMBERS	41.5
TOTAL	59.4

TOTAL OFFICIAL GROSS

DAC COUNTRIES	1983	1984	1985	1986
Australia	—	—	—	—
Austria	0.0	0.0	0.0	0.0
Belgium	8.0	5.2	2.6	4.2
Canada	0.6	1.7	8.6	5.2
Denmark	0.0	0.0	10.5	1.7
Finland	—	—	—	—
France	48.9	76.5	38.2	36.9
Germany, Fed. Rep.	27.0	26.7	111.1	18.2
Ireland	—	—	—	—
Italy	0.1	1.0	1.2	3.1
Japan	2.2	2.6	1.7	19.2
Netherlands	0.5	0.7	0.8	0.9
New Zealand	—	—	—	—
Norway	0.2	0.2	0.2	1.4
Sweden	—	—	—	—
Switzerland	2.2	0.3	0.3	0.4
United Kingdom	0.1	0.1	0.2	0.2
United States	8.0	7.0	8.0	10.0
TOTAL	97.9	122.1	183.4	101.3
MULTILATERAL	63.1	57.2	54.9	78.2
OPEC COUNTRIES	2.8	2.0	9.2	9.5
E.E.C.+ MEMBERS	102.6	131.0	174.0	81.3
TOTAL	163.8	181.3	247.4	188.9

TOTAL OFFICIAL NET

DAC COUNTRIES	1983	1984	1985	1986
Australia	—	—	—	—
Austria	0.0	0.0	0.0	0.0
Belgium	7.9	4.4	0.6	0.9
Canada	0.5	1.7	8.6	5.2
Denmark	0.0	-0.1	0.9	1.6
Finland	—	—	—	—
France	47.9	57.2	19.2	25.1
Germany, Fed. Rep.	13.9	17.5	12.6	13.1
Ireland	—	—	—	—
Italy	0.1	1.0	1.2	2.9
Japan	2.2	2.6	1.7	19.2
Netherlands	0.5	0.7	0.8	0.9
New Zealand	—	—	—	—
Norway	0.2	0.2	0.2	1.4
Sweden	-0.5	—	—	—
Switzerland	0.3	0.1	0.3	-0.3
United Kingdom	0.1	0.1	0.2	0.2
United States	8.0	7.0	8.0	10.0
TOTAL	81.2	92.3	54.3	80.2
MULTILATERAL	59.3	53.9	50.6	72.3
OPEC COUNTRIES	2.8	2.0	9.1	7.9
E.E.C.+ MEMBERS	86.5	99.5	42.8	57.8
TOTAL	143.3	148.2	113.9	160.4

TOTAL OOF GROSS

	1983
Australia	—
Austria	—
Belgium	7.9
Canada	—
Denmark	—
Finland	—
France	24.9
Germany, Fed. Rep.	1.3
Ireland	—
Italy	—
Japan	—
Netherlands	—
New Zealand	—
Norway	—
Sweden	—
Switzerland	2.0
United Kingdom	—
United States	—
TOTAL	36.1
MULTILATERAL	2.6
OPEC COUNTRIES	—
E.E.C.+ MEMBERS	35.3
TOTAL	38.7

ODA COMMITMENTS

1984	1985	1986		1983	1984	1985	1986
–	–	–		–	–	–	–
0.0	0.0	0.0		0.0	0.0	0.0	–
0.3	0.4	2.7		–	–	–	2.7
1.7	8.6	5.2		0.7	15.4	2.2	0.4
0.0	10.0	0.9		–	–	9.4	0.1
–	–	–		–	–	–	–
30.3	28.0	33.2		32.3	23.4	21.2	33.2
16.5	111.1	18.2		35.6	24.3	116.3	30.6
–	–	–		–	–	–	–
0.4	0.4	3.1		0.8	0.7	0.4	4.6
2.6	1.7	19.2		2.8	1.5	3.1	18.4
0.7	0.8	0.9		0.5	0.7	0.8	0.9
–	–	–		–	–	–	–
0.2	0.2	1.4		–	–	0.0	1.2
–	–	–		–	–	–	–
0.3	0.3	0.4		0.2	0.1	0.1	0.5
0.1	0.2	0.2		0.1	0.1	0.2	0.2
7.0	8.0	10.0		8.4	9.4	5.2	15.9
60.3	169.6	95.4		81.5	75.7	159.0	108.7
1.1	3.9	0.3		–	–	–	16.5
–	–	–		–	–	–	–
–	–	–		–	–	–	–
20.4	9.4	15.6		15.1	16.5	11.3	13.3
–	–	–		–	–	–	–
25.0	30.7	50.5		37.7	15.0	56.4	24.8
–	0.3	0.6		7.8	–	–	–
–	–	–		–	–	–	–
–	–	–		6.3	7.1	7.2	8.2
3.1	3.3	4.4		–	–	–	–
0.5	0.5	0.7		–	–	–	–
0.2	0.4	0.6		–	–	–	–
–	–	–		–	–	–	–
2.2	1.7	1.6		–	–	–	–
0.4	0.3	0.2		–	–	–	–
0.8	1.0	0.8		–	–	–	–
1.5	0.4	0.9		4.0	1.3	0.3	2.4
55.2	52.0	76.1		70.9	40.0	75.2	65.2
2.0	9.2	9.5		17.2	10.1	–	1.0
68.8	160.1	74.7		84.4	65.7	159.6	85.6
117.4	230.8	180.9		169.5	125.8	234.2	174.9

TECH. COOP. GRANTS

1984	1985	1986		1983	1984	1985	1986
–	–	–		–	–	–	–
0.0	0.0	0.0		0.0	–	–	–
0.3	0.4	2.7		–	–	–	0.1
1.7	8.6	5.2		0.3	–	1.1	–
0.0	10.0	0.9		0.0	0.0	0.3	0.6
–	–	–		–	–	–	–
17.7	20.2	22.6		10.4	12.2	9.3	15.4
7.4	109.8	18.2		7.0	7.2	7.1	10.8
–	–	–		–	–	–	–
0.4	0.4	3.1		0.1	0.4	0.4	1.1
2.6	1.7	4.4		0.1	0.0	0.2	0.3
0.7	0.8	0.6		0.5	0.7	0.8	0.6
–	–	–		–	–	–	–
0.2	0.2	0.2		–	–	0.0	–
–	–	–		–	–	–	–
0.3	0.3	0.4		0.1	0.2	0.1	0.1
0.1	0.2	0.2		0.1	0.1	0.2	0.2
7.0	8.0	10.0		5.0	4.0	5.0	6.0
38.6	160.6	68.3		23.6	24.9	24.6	35.1
26.4	16.6	23.8		3.9	5.0	5.5	7.2
0.0	0.1	0.0		–	–	–	–
46.0	151.1	63.8		18.2	20.7	18.0	29.4
65.0	177.3	92.1		27.5	29.9	30.0	42.3

TOTAL OOF NET

1984	1985	1986		1983	1984	1985	1986
–	–	–		–	–	–	–
–	–	–		–	–	–	–
4.9	2.2	1.4		7.7	4.2	0.3	-1.9
–	–	–		–	–	–	–
–	0.5	0.8		–	-0.1	0.2	0.8
–	–	–		–	–	–	–
46.2	10.2	3.7		24.0	28.8	1.1	-6.6
10.2	–	–		1.0	6.0	-1.4	-2.9
–	–	–		–	–	–	–
0.6	0.8	–		–	0.6	0.8	-0.2
–	–	–		–	–	–	–
–	–	–		–	–	–	–
–	–	–		–	–	–	–
–	–	–		-0.5	–	–	–
–	–	–		0.2	-0.3	–	-0.7
–	–	–		–	–	–	–
61.8	13.8	5.9		32.4	39.2	1.0	-11.5
2.0	2.9	2.1		-1.1	-1.0	-1.1	-2.4
–	–	–		–	–	–	–
62.2	13.9	6.6		32.0	37.9	-1.1	-13.1
63.9	16.7	8.0		31.3	38.2	-0.2	-13.9

ODA COMMITMENTS : LOANS

DAC COUNTRIES

	1983	1984	1985	1986
Australia	–	–	–	–
Austria	–	–	–	–
Belgium	–	–	–	2.7
Canada	–	–	–	0.4
Denmark	–	–	–	0.1
Finland	–	–	–	–
France	15.5	4.9	5.4	10.6
Germany, Fed. Rep.	30.4	4.2	0.3	–
Ireland	–	–	–	–
Italy	–	–	–	–
Japan	–	–	–	14.8
Netherlands	–	–	–	0.4
New Zealand	–	–	–	–
Norway	–	–	–	1.2
Sweden	–	–	–	–
Switzerland	–	–	–	–
United Kingdom	–	–	–	–
United States	–	–	–	–
TOTAL	*45.9*	*9.1*	*5.7*	*27.0*
MULTILATERAL	*52.6*	*16.9*	*56.4*	*43.7*
OPEC COUNTRIES	*17.2*	*10.1*	–	–
E.E.C.+ MEMBERS	*49.0*	*11.0*	*5.7*	*11.0*
TOTAL	**115.6**	**36.1**	**62.1**	**70.7**

GRANT ELEMENT OF ODA

DAC COUNTRIES

	1983	1984	1985	1986
Australia	–	–	–	–
Austria	100.0	100.0	100.0	–
Belgium	–	–	–	100.0
Canada	100.0	100.0	100.0	100.0
Denmark	–	–	100.0	100.0
Finland	–	–	–	–
France	60.8	83.8	95.9	74.1
Germany, Fed. Rep.	47.4	90.3	99.8	100.0
Ireland	–	–	–	–
Italy	100.0	100.0	100.0	100.0
Japan	100.0	100.0	100.0	77.5
Netherlands	100.0	100.0	100.0	100.0
New Zealand	–	–	–	–
Norway	–	–	100.0	28.9
Sweden	–	–	–	–
Switzerland	100.0	100.0	100.0	100.0
United Kingdom	100.0	100.0	100.0	100.0
United States	100.0	100.0	100.0	100.0
TOTAL	*61.4*	*91.9*	*99.4*	*87.2*
MULTILATERAL	*84.7*	*93.3*	*87.4*	*86.9*
OPEC COUNTRIES	*42.9*	*42.1*	–	*100.0*
E.E.C.+ MEMBERS	*61.3*	*90.4*	*99.4*	*89.5*
TOTAL	**71.9**	**88.3**	**95.5**	**87.1**

OTHER AGGREGATES

COMMITMENTS: ALL SOURCES

	1983	1984	1985	1986
TOTAL BILATERAL	145.1	129.3	163.4	111.2
of which				
OPEC	17.2	10.1	–	1.0
CMEA	–	–	–	–
TOTAL MULTILATERAL	70.9	45.0	75.5	65.2
TOTAL BIL.& MULTIL.	216.0	174.3	238.9	176.4
of which				
ODA Grants	53.9	89.7	172.1	104.1
ODA Loans	115.6	36.1	62.1	70.7

DISBURSEMENTS:

DAC COUNTRIES COMBINED

	1983	1984	1985	1986
OFFICIAL & PRIVATE				
GROSS:				
Contractual Lending	68.2	86.7	25.7	22.1
Export Credits Total	6.4	3.1	2.9	-10.8
Export Credits Private	6.4	3.1	2.9	-10.8
NET:				
Contractual Lending	-1.5	21.4	-118.8	-4.2
Export Credits Total	-47.1	-32.3	-12.5	-16.2
PRIVATE SECTOR NET	-32.1	-31.3	-15.7	-25.3
Direct Investment	-1.2	1.3	-0.8	0.6
Portfolio Investment	15.7	-0.3	-2.4	-9.9
Export Credits	-46.6	-32.3	-12.5	-16.1

MARKET BORROWING:

CHANGE IN CLAIMS

	1983	1984	1985	1986
Banks	–	-44.0	9.0	-12.0

MEMORANDUM ITEM:

	1983	1984	1985	1986
CMEA Countr.(Gross)	–	–	–	–

DISBURSEMENTS, UNLESS OTHERWISE STATED

	TOTAL RECEIPTS NET 1983	1984	1985	1986	TOTAL ODA NET 1983	1984	1985	1986	TOTAL ODA GROSS 1983
DAC COUNTRIES									
Australia	—	—	—	—	—	—	—	—	—
Austria	0.0	-1.2	-1.1	0.0	0.0	—	—	0.0	0.0
Belgium	0.3	-0.5	-5.1	0.3	—	—	—	—	—
Canada	7.2	22.0	11.6	-7.7	0.7	0.5	-0.1	0.0	1.4
Denmark	—	—	-0.1	—	—	—	—	—	—
Finland	—	—	—	—	—	—	—	—	—
France	38.3	8.0	13.8	-1.4	0.4	0.3	0.2	0.3	0.4
Germany, Fed. Rep.	-10.9	-0.3	8.7	27.4	0.4	0.1	0.1	15.8	0.4
Ireland	—	—	—	—	—	—	—	—	—
Italy	1.7	-11.1	-5.7	—	—	—	—	—	—
Japan	65.3	117.6	65.2	-18.3	0.0	0.0	0.1	0.1	0.0
Netherlands	1.3	2.2	0.4	3.5	0.2	0.6	0.4	0.2	0.2
New Zealand	—	—	—	—	—	—	—	—	—
Norway	—	—	0.0	0.0	—	—	0.0	0.0	—
Sweden	—	—	—	—	—	—	—	—	—
Switzerland	0.1	0.1	0.7	0.1	0.1	0.1	0.1	0.1	0.1
United Kingdom	1.7	-7.3	-23.3	-10.6	0.0	-0.1	0.1	—	0.1
United States	-37.0	17.0	-384.0	-89.0	—	—	—	—	—
TOTAL	*68.0*	*146.4*	*-318.9*	*-95.8*	*1.7*	*1.5*	*0.8*	*16.4*	*2.5*
MULTILATERAL									
AF.D.F.	—	—	—	—	—	—	—	—	—
AF.D.B.	—	—	—	—	—	—	—	—	—
AS.D.B	—	—	—	—	—	—	—	—	—
CAR.D.B.	—	—	—	0.3	—	—	—	—	—
E.E.C.	1.2	2.9	3.6	8.7	1.0	0.5	3.6	0.6	1.0
IBRD	-5.1	-5.1	-4.3	-6.0	—	—	—	—	—
IDA	—	—	—	—	—	—	—	—	—
I.D.B.	-0.7	-0.8	-0.8	-0.7	-0.7	-0.8	-0.8	-0.7	—
IFAD	—	—	—	—	—	—	—	—	—
I.F.C.	-0.4	-0.4	-0.4	96.7	—	—	—	—	—
IMF TRUST FUND	—	—	—	—	—	—	—	—	—
U.N. AGENCIES	—	—	—	—	—	—	—	—	—
UNDP	2.7	2.7	2.2	2.1	2.7	2.7	2.2	2.1	2.7
UNTA	0.5	0.4	0.5	0.5	0.5	0.4	0.5	0.5	0.5
UNICEF	—	—	—	—	—	—	—	—	—
UNRWA	—	—	—	—	—	—	—	—	—
WFP	—	—	—	—	—	—	—	—	—
UNHCR	—	—	—	—	—	—	—	—	—
Other Multilateral	0.3	0.2	0.2	0.2	0.3	0.2	0.2	0.2	0.3
Arab OPEC Agencies	—	—	—	—	—	—	—	—	—
TOTAL	*-1.5*	*-0.1*	*1.1*	*101.8*	*3.8*	*3.1*	*5.8*	*2.7*	*4.5*
OPEC COUNTRIES	—	—	—	—	—	—	—	—	—
E.E.C.+ MEMBERS	*33.7*	*-6.2*	*-7.7*	*27.7*	*2.0*	*1.4*	*4.3*	*16.8*	*2.1*
TOTAL	**66.5**	**146.3**	**-317.8**	**6.0**	**5.6**	**4.6**	**6.6**	**19.1**	**7.1**

	ODA LOANS GROSS 1983	1984	1985	1986	ODA LOANS NET 1983	1984	1985	1986	GRANTS 1983
DAC COUNTRIES									
Australia	—	—	—	—	—	—	—	—	—
Austria	—	—	—	—	—	—	—	—	0.0
Belgium	—	—	—	—	—	—	—	—	—
Canada	0.6	0.4	0.2	0.3	-0.1	-0.3	-0.7	-0.3	0.8
Denmark	—	—	—	—	—	—	—	—	—
Finland	—	—	—	—	—	—	—	—	—
France	—	—	—	—	—	—	—	—	0.4
Germany, Fed. Rep.	—	—	—	15.7	—	—	—	15.7	0.4
Ireland	—	—	—	—	—	—	—	—	—
Italy	—	—	—	—	—	—	—	—	—
Japan	—	—	—	—	—	—	—	—	0.0
Netherlands	0.1	0.6	0.3	—	0.1	0.6	0.3	—	0.0
New Zealand	—	—	—	—	—	—	—	—	—
Norway	—	—	—	—	—	—	—	—	—
Sweden	—	—	—	—	—	—	—	—	—
Switzerland	—	—	—	—	—	—	—	—	0.1
United Kingdom	—	—	—	—	-0.1	-0.2	-0.1	-0.1	0.1
United States	—	—	—	—	—	—	—	—	—
TOTAL	*0.7*	*0.9*	*0.5*	*16.0*	*-0.1*	*0.1*	*-0.5*	*15.3*	*1.8*
MULTILATERAL	*0.4*	—	—	—	*-0.4*	*-0.8*	*-0.8*	*-0.8*	*4.2*
OPEC COUNTRIES	—	—	—	—	—	—	—	—	—
E.E.C.+ MEMBERS	*0.5*	*0.6*	*0.3*	*15.7*	*0.4*	*0.4*	*0.2*	*15.6*	*1.6*
TOTAL	**1.1**	**0.9**	**0.5**	**16.0**	**-0.4**	**-0.7**	**-1.2**	**14.5**	**6.0**

	TOTAL OFFICIAL GROSS 1983	1984	1985	1986	TOTAL OFFICIAL NET 1983	1984	1985	1986	TOTAL OOF GROSS 1983
DAC COUNTRIES									
Australia	—	—	—	—	—	—	—	—	—
Austria	0.0	—	—	0.0	0.0	—	—	0.0	—
Belgium	—	—	—	—	—	—	—	—	—
Canada	19.8	36.1	36.0	11.7	7.2	22.0	11.6	-7.7	18.4
Denmark	—	—	—	—	—	—	—	—	—
Finland	—	—	—	—	—	—	—	—	—
France	0.4	0.3	0.2	0.3	0.4	0.3	0.2	0.3	—
Germany, Fed. Rep.	0.4	0.1	0.1	15.8	0.4	0.1	0.1	15.8	—
Ireland	—	—	—	—	—	—	—	—	—
Italy	—	—	—	—	—	—	—	—	—
Japan	0.0	2.3	0.1	0.1	-1.5	0.9	-1.2	-1.7	—
Netherlands	0.2	0.6	0.4	0.2	0.2	0.6	0.4	0.2	—
New Zealand	—	—	—	—	—	—	—	—	—
Norway	—	—	0.0	0.0	—	—	0.0	0.0	—
Sweden	—	—	—	—	—	—	—	—	—
Switzerland	0.1	0.1	0.1	0.1	0.1	0.1	0.1	0.1	—
United Kingdom	0.1	0.0	0.2	0.1	0.0	-0.1	0.1	—	—
United States	—	33.0	2.0	—	-19.0	19.0	-21.0	-32.0	—
TOTAL	*20.9*	*72.5*	*39.0*	*28.3*	*-12.3*	*42.8*	*-9.7*	*-25.0*	*18.4*
MULTILATERAL	*6.0*	*7.2*	*6.5*	*110.3*	*-1.5*	*-0.1*	*1.1*	*101.8*	*1.4*
OPEC COUNTRIES	—	—	—	—	—	—	—	—	—
E.E.C.+ MEMBERS	*2.9*	*4.8*	*4.4*	*26.4*	*2.1*	*3.8*	*4.3*	*24.9*	*0.8*
TOTAL	**26.9**	**79.6**	**45.5**	**138.5**	**-13.8**	**42.7**	**-8.7**	**76.7**	**19.8**

ODA COMMITMENTS

1984	1985	1986	1983	1984	1985	1986
–	–	0.0	0.0	–	–	–
–	–	–	–	–	–	–
1.2	0.8	0.6	0.8	0.7	0.7	0.3
–	–	–	–	–	–	–
–	–	–	–	–	–	–
0.3	0.2	0.3	0.4	0.3	0.2	0.3
0.1	0.1	15.8	0.0	0.1	11.7	26.0
–	–	–	–	–	–	–
–	–	–	–	–	–	–
0.0	0.1	0.1	0.0	0.0	0.1	0.1
0.6	0.4	0.2	1.0	0.5	0.2	0.2
–	0.0	0.0	–	–	–	–
–	–	–	–	–	0.0	0.0
0.1	0.1	0.1	0.1	–	0.0	0.2
0.0	0.2	0.1	0.1	0.0	0.2	0.1
–	–	–	–	–	–	–
2.3	*1.8*	*17.1*	*2.5*	*1.7*	*13.1*	*27.1*
–	–	–	–	–	–	–
–	–	–	–	–	–	–
–	–	–	–	–	–	–
–	–	–	–	–	0.0	2.0
0.5	3.6	0.6	3.2	1.4	2.9	–
–	–	–	–	–	–	–
–	–	0.1	–	–	–	6.9
–	–	–	–	–	–	–
–	–	–	3.5	3.3	2.9	2.8
2.7	2.2	2.1	–	–	–	–
0.4	0.5	0.5	–	–	–	–
–	–	–	–	–	–	–
–	–	–	–	–	–	–
0.2	0.2	0.2	–	–	–	–
–	–	–	–	–	–	–
3.9	*6.5*	*3.4*	*6.7*	*4.8*	*5.8*	*11.7*
–	–	–	–	–	–	–
1.6	*4.4*	*16.9*	*4.7*	*2.4*	*15.1*	*26.5*
6.2	*8.3*	*20.5*	*9.2*	*6.5*	*18.9*	*38.8*

TECH. COOP. GRANTS

1984	1985	1986	1983	1984	1985	1986
–	–	0.0	0.0	–	–	–
–	–	–	–	–	–	–
0.8	0.6	0.3	0.4	–	0.3	–
–	–	–	–	–	–	–
–	–	–	–	–	–	–
0.3	0.2	0.3	0.4	0.3	0.2	0.3
0.1	0.1	0.1	0.4	0.0	0.1	0.1
–	–	–	–	–	–	–
0.0	0.1	0.1	0.0	0.0	0.1	0.1
0.0	0.1	0.2	0.0	0.0	0.1	0.2
–	0.0	0.0	–	–	0.0	0.0
–	–	–	–	–	–	–
0.1	0.1	0.1	–	–	0.0	–
0.0	0.2	0.1	0.1	0.0	0.2	0.1
–	–	–	–	–	–	–
1.4	*1.3*	*1.2*	*1.3*	*0.5*	*0.9*	*0.7*
3.9	*6.5*	*3.4*	*3.5*	*3.3*	*2.9*	*2.8*
–	–	–	–	–	–	–
1.0	*4.1*	*1.2*	*0.9*	*0.4*	*0.5*	*0.7*
5.3	*7.8*	*4.6*	*4.8*	*3.8*	*3.8*	*3.6*

TOTAL OOF NET

1984	1985	1986	1983	1984	1985	1986
–	–	–	–	–	–	–
–	–	–	–	–	–	–
34.9	35.1	11.2	6.5	21.5	11.7	-7.7
–	–	–	–	–	–	–
–	–	–	–	–	–	–
–	–	–	–	–	–	–
2.2	–	–	-1.5	0.8	-1.3	-1.8
–	–	–	–	–	–	–
–	–	–	–	–	–	–
–	–	–	–	–	–	–
33.0	2.0	–	-19.0	19.0	-21.0	-32.0
70.1	*37.1*	*11.2*	*-14.1*	*41.3*	*-10.6*	*-41.4*
3.3	–	*106.8*	*-5.3*	*-3.2*	*-4.7*	*99.1*
–	–	–	–	–	–	–
3.2	–	*9.5*	*0.2*	*2.3*	–	*8.1*
73.4	*37.1*	*118.0*	*-19.4*	*38.2*	*-15.3*	*57.7*

ODA COMMITMENTS : LOANS

DAC COUNTRIES

	1983	1984	1985	1986
Australia	–	–	–	–
Austria	–	–	–	–
Belgium	–	–	–	–
Canada	–	–	–	–
Denmark	–	–	–	–
Finland	–	–	–	–
France	–	–	–	–
Germany, Fed. Rep.	–	–	11.6	25.9
Ireland	–	–	–	–
Italy	–	–	–	–
Japan	–	–	–	–
Netherlands	1.0	0.5	0.1	–
New Zealand	–	–	–	–
Norway	–	–	–	–
Sweden	–	–	–	–
Switzerland	–	–	–	–
United Kingdom	–	–	–	–
United States	–	–	–	–
TOTAL	*1.0*	*0.5*	*11.7*	*25.9*
MULTILATERAL	–	–	–	*8.9*
OPEC COUNTRIES	–	–	–	–
E.E.C.+ MEMBERS	*1.0*	*0.5*	*11.7*	*25.9*
TOTAL	*1.0*	*0.5*	*11.7*	*34.8*

GRANT ELEMENT OF ODA

DAC COUNTRIES

	1983	1984	1985	1986
Australia	–	–	–	–
Austria	100.0	–	–	–
Belgium	–	–	–	–
Canada	100.0	100.0	100.0	100.0
Denmark	–	–	–	–
Finland	–	–	–	–
France	100.0	100.0	100.0	100.0
Germany, Fed. Rep.	100.0	100.0	27.2	29.6
Ireland	–	–	–	–
Italy	–	–	–	–
Japan	100.0	100.0	100.0	100.0
Netherlands	61.7	63.2	87.4	100.0
New Zealand	–	–	–	–
Norway	–	–	100.0	100.0
Sweden	–	–	–	–
Switzerland	100.0	–	100.0	100.0
United Kingdom	100.0	100.0	100.0	100.0
United States	–	–	–	–
TOTAL	*84.4*	*88.4*	*34.9*	*32.6*
MULTILATERAL	*100.0*	*100.0*	*100.0*	*79.3*
OPEC COUNTRIES	–	–	–	–
E.E.C.+ MEMBERS	*91.8*	*92.1*	*43.5*	*31.1*
TOTAL	*95.7*	*97.0*	*54.9*	*44.9*

OTHER AGGREGATES

COMMITMENTS: ALL SOURCES

	1983	1984	1985	1986
TOTAL BILATERAL	105.5	176.1	31.3	27.1
of which				
OPEC	9.0	–	–	–
CMEA	–	–	–	–
TOTAL MULTILATERAL	6.7	5.9	48.7	244.5
TOTAL BIL.& MULTIL.	112.2	182.0	80.0	271.7
of which				
ODA Grants	8.2	6.0	7.2	4.0
ODA Loans	1.0	0.5	11.7	34.8

DISBURSEMENTS:

DAC COUNTRIES COMBINED

	1983	1984	1985	1986
OFFICIAL & PRIVATE				
GROSS:				
Contractual Lending	169.2	128.3	67.2	29.8
Export Credits Total	168.4	127.4	66.7	13.8
Export Credits Private	150.1	57.2	29.6	2.6
NET:				
Contractual Lending	87.1	57.0	-38.7	-49.7
Export Credits Total	87.2	56.9	-38.2	-64.9
PRIVATE SECTOR NET	80.4	103.6	-309.1	-70.8
Direct Investment	-45.2	-6.8	-388.6	-111.6
Portfolio Investment	24.3	94.9	107.2	64.4
Export Credits	101.2	15.6	-27.7	-23.5

MARKET BORROWING:

CHANGE IN CLAIMS

	1983	1984	1985	1986
Banks	–	-130.0	76.0	-37.0

MEMORANDUM ITEM:

	1983	1984	1985	1986
CMEA Countr.(Gross)	–	–	–	–

DISBURSEMENTS, UNLESS OTHERWISE STATED

TOTAL RECEIPTS NET

DAC COUNTRIES	1983	1984	1985	1986
Australia	0.0	—	0.1	—
Austria	9.3	-4.8	-5.3	-2.2
Belgium	32.0	37.6	-5.5	-6.4
Canada	10.5	17.5	-3.3	-1.6
Denmark	-0.6	0.0	-0.6	-0.9
Finland	-0.2	—	0.8	0.0
France	174.5	80.6	80.0	134.3
Germany, Fed. Rep.	51.3	23.9	22.5	10.9
Ireland	—	—	—	—
Italy	44.4	48.4	22.3	29.8
Japan	48.4	32.6	45.1	-4.1
Netherlands	0.2	4.7	3.5	13.8
New Zealand	—	—	—	—
Norway	0.1	0.0	—	—
Sweden	5.1	4.6	-6.0	7.2
Switzerland	-0.2	-4.2	-1.1	0.2
United Kingdom	-2.8	5.1	2.2	-1.4
United States	18.0	26.0	-4.0	—
TOTAL	390.0	271.9	150.7	179.9
MULTILATERAL				
AF.D.F.	—	—	—	—
AF.D.B.	5.1	1.1	16.9	20.2
AS.D.B	—	—	—	—
CAR.D.B.	—	—	—	—
E.E.C.	16.2	14.0	13.4	26.6
IBRD	58.6	46.7	61.9	94.4
IDA	-0.8	-0.8	-0.8	-1.0
I.D.B.	—	—	—	—
IFAD	1.5	2.4	5.8	5.8
I.F.C.	-1.4	-1.2	-0.7	2.8
IMF TRUST FUND	—	—	—	—
U.N. AGENCIES	—	—	—	—
UNDP	2.0	1.6	1.3	2.2
UNTA	1.0	0.5	1.5	0.9
UNICEF	0.2	0.4	0.7	0.9
UNRWA	—	—	—	—
WFP	14.9	9.9	12.9	9.4
UNHCR	0.2	0.2	0.1	0.1
Other Multilateral	1.6	0.9	0.9	1.1
Arab OPEC Agencies	10.6	31.4	31.1	-27.9
TOTAL	109.7	107.1	144.9	135.3
OPEC COUNTRIES	8.2	48.4	11.7	10.8
E.E.C.+ MEMBERS	315.1	214.4	137.7	206.9
TOTAL	507.8	427.3	307.4	326.0

TOTAL ODA NET

DAC COUNTRIES	1983	1984	1985	1986
Australia	0.0	—	0.1	—
Austria	8.5	0.4	2.1	-0.1
Belgium	7.6	2.9	3.8	5.0
Canada	6.1	6.1	0.0	0.9
Denmark	-0.3	-0.3	-0.3	-0.3
Finland	—	—	0.8	0.0
France	37.3	50.9	49.5	57.6
Germany, Fed. Rep.	50.7	23.7	18.1	8.4
Ireland	—	—	—	—
Italy	11.5	8.9	22.8	35.3
Japan	13.9	19.5	10.5	5.2
Netherlands	2.1	6.2	3.2	7.7
New Zealand	—	—	—	—
Norway	—	0.0	—	—
Sweden	1.6	1.1	0.0	4.4
Switzerland	1.5	0.6	0.3	0.2
United Kingdom	0.1	2.8	1.7	0.7
United States	16.0	18.0	9.0	22.0
TOTAL	156.7	140.7	121.7	147.1
MULTILATERAL				
AF.D.F.	—	—	—	—
AF.D.B.	—	—	—	—
AS.D.B	—	—	—	—
CAR.D.B.	—	—	—	—
E.E.C.	14.2	12.5	8.9	16.0
IBRD	—	—	—	—
IDA	-0.8	-0.8	-0.8	-1.0
I.D.B.	—	—	—	—
IFAD	1.5	2.4	5.8	5.8
I.F.C.	—	—	—	—
IMF TRUST FUND	—	—	—	—
U.N. AGENCIES	—	—	—	—
UNDP	2.0	1.6	1.3	2.2
UNTA	1.0	0.5	1.5	0.9
UNICEF	0.2	0.4	0.7	0.9
UNRWA	—	—	—	—
WFP	14.9	9.9	12.9	9.4
UNHCR	0.2	0.2	0.1	0.1
Other Multilateral	1.6	0.9	0.9	1.1
Arab OPEC Agencies	2.5	1.5	4.4	1.2
TOTAL	37.2	29.0	35.7	36.5
OPEC COUNTRIES	11.5	8.5	5.2	15.9
E.E.C.+ MEMBERS	123.3	107.6	107.9	130.4
TOTAL	205.4	178.2	162.6	199.5

TOTAL ODA GROSS

	1983
Australia	0.0
Austria	8.5
Belgium	7.7
Canada	7.2
Denmark	0.0
Finland	—
France	44.0
Germany, Fed. Rep.	57.7
Ireland	—
Italy	13.7
Japan	13.9
Netherlands	3.1
New Zealand	—
Norway	—
Sweden	2.1
Switzerland	1.5
United Kingdom	0.2
United States	26.0
TOTAL	185.6
AF.D.F.	—
AF.D.B.	—
AS.D.B	—
CAR.D.B.	—
E.E.C.	14.2
IBRD	—
IDA	—
I.D.B.	—
IFAD	1.5
I.F.C.	—
IMF TRUST FUND	—
U.N. AGENCIES	—
UNDP	2.0
UNTA	1.0
UNICEF	0.2
UNRWA	—
WFP	14.9
UNHCR	0.2
Other Multilateral	1.6
Arab OPEC Agencies	4.0
TOTAL	39.5
OPEC COUNTRIES	31.3
E.E.C.+ MEMBERS	140.6
TOTAL	256.3

ODA LOANS GROSS

DAC COUNTRIES	1983	1984	1985	1986
Australia	—	—	—	—
Austria	8.2	0.1	2.6	0.2
Belgium	3.9	—	1.3	2.4
Canada	4.9	1.3	0.1	1.1
Denmark	0.0	—	—	—
Finland	—	—	0.8	—
France	15.4	26.4	29.6	32.9
Germany, Fed. Rep.	50.4	29.0	21.1	17.6
Ireland	—	—	—	—
Italy	9.7	4.2	19.3	14.4
Japan	12.8	19.1	10.1	5.2
Netherlands	2.5	6.1	4.4	0.8
New Zealand	—	—	—	—
Norway	—	—	—	—
Sweden	—	—	—	—
Switzerland	1.2	0.3	—	—
United Kingdom	—	—	—	—
United States	20.0	20.0	8.0	17.0
TOTAL	128.9	106.4	97.4	91.7
MULTILATERAL	17.8	10.2	13.4	14.4
OPEC COUNTRIES	30.2	30.3	30.0	38.6
E.E.C.+ MEMBERS	94.2	70.1	77.0	71.3
TOTAL	176.9	146.9	140.7	144.7

ODA LOANS NET

DAC COUNTRIES	1983	1984	1985	1986
Australia	—	—	—	—
Austria	8.2	0.1	2.0	-0.7
Belgium	3.8	-0.1	1.1	2.2
Canada	3.8	0.7	-2.1	-1.1
Denmark	-0.3	-0.3	-0.3	-0.3
Finland	—	—	0.8	—
France	8.7	21.0	24.0	25.7
Germany, Fed. Rep.	43.4	16.4	11.3	-3.0
Ireland	—	—	—	—
Italy	7.5	2.1	17.3	11.2
Japan	12.8	18.7	9.2	2.6
Netherlands	1.5	4.8	2.9	-1.4
New Zealand	—	—	—	—
Norway	—	—	—	—
Sweden	-0.5	-0.5	-0.5	—
Switzerland	1.2	0.3	—	—
United Kingdom	-0.1	-0.1	0.0	-0.1
United States	10.0	9.0	-3.0	4.0
TOTAL	100.0	72.1	62.7	38.9
MULTILATERAL	15.6	7.5	10.7	9.2
OPEC COUNTRIES	10.4	8.4	5.1	15.6
E.E.C.+ MEMBERS	76.9	48.3	57.6	37.3
TOTAL	126.0	87.9	78.5	63.7

GRANTS

	1983
Australia	0.0
Austria	0.4
Belgium	3.8
Canada	2.3
Denmark	—
Finland	—
France	28.6
Germany, Fed. Rep.	7.3
Ireland	—
Italy	4.0
Japan	1.1
Netherlands	0.7
New Zealand	—
Norway	—
Sweden	2.1
Switzerland	0.3
United Kingdom	0.2
United States	6.0
TOTAL	56.6
MULTILATERAL	21.6
OPEC COUNTRIES	1.1
E.E.C.+ MEMBERS	46.3
TOTAL	79.4

TOTAL OFFICIAL GROSS

DAC COUNTRIES	1983	1984	1985	1986
Australia	0.0	—	0.1	—
Austria	8.5	0.4	2.7	0.9
Belgium	7.7	3.4	4.4	5.3
Canada	11.8	18.2	2.6	4.0
Denmark	0.0	—	0.0	0.1
Finland	—	—	0.8	0.0
France	44.0	56.3	55.1	64.8
Germany, Fed. Rep.	57.8	36.3	29.1	29.3
Ireland	—	—	—	—
Italy	39.5	56.1	40.3	45.0
Japan	15.4	77.3	13.6	30.6
Netherlands	3.1	7.5	4.7	10.0
New Zealand	—	—	—	—
Norway	—	0.0	—	—
Sweden	12.4	12.6	2.6	14.3
Switzerland	1.5	0.6	0.3	0.2
United Kingdom	0.2	2.9	1.8	0.7
United States	36.0	48.0	28.0	35.0
TOTAL	237.8	319.5	186.0	240.0
MULTILATERAL	162.7	172.8	225.6	282.1
OPEC COUNTRIES	40.7	78.5	41.3	39.2
E.E.C.+ MEMBERS	170.0	178.0	150.7	184.5
TOTAL	441.2	570.8	452.8	561.3

TOTAL OFFICIAL NET

DAC COUNTRIES	1983	1984	1985	1986
Australia	0.0	—	0.1	—
Austria	8.5	0.4	-0.2	-2.2
Belgium	7.6	3.3	4.3	5.0
Canada	10.5	17.5	-3.3	-1.6
Denmark	-0.3	-0.3	-0.2	-0.3
Finland	—	—	0.8	0.0
France	37.3	50.9	49.5	57.6
Germany, Fed. Rep.	50.2	23.2	18.7	7.9
Ireland	—	—	—	—
Italy	36.2	36.6	10.4	12.7
Japan	11.1	72.6	8.5	18.5
Netherlands	2.1	5.9	3.2	7.7
New Zealand	—	—	—	—
Norway	—	0.0	—	—
Sweden	6.0	5.6	-6.0	7.8
Switzerland	1.5	0.6	0.3	0.2
United Kingdom	0.1	2.8	1.7	0.7
United States	18.0	26.0	-4.0	—
TOTAL	188.8	245.1	83.8	114.1
MULTILATERAL	109.7	107.1	144.9	135.3
OPEC COUNTRIES	8.2	48.4	11.7	10.8
E.E.C.+ MEMBERS	149.5	136.5	101.0	117.9
TOTAL	306.7	400.5	240.5	260.2

TOTAL OOF GROSS

	1983
Australia	—
Austria	—
Belgium	—
Canada	4.7
Denmark	—
Finland	—
France	—
Germany, Fed. Rep.	0.1
Ireland	—
Italy	25.8
Japan	1.5
Netherlands	—
New Zealand	—
Norway	—
Sweden	10.3
Switzerland	—
United Kingdom	—
United States	10.0
TOTAL	52.3
MULTILATERAL	123.3
OPEC COUNTRIES	9.4
E.E.C.+ MEMBERS	29.4
TOTAL	184.9

ODA COMMITMENTS

1984	1985	1986	1983	1984	1985	1986
–	0.1	–	0.0	–	–	–
0.4	2.7	0.9	0.4	0.1	0.0	–
3.1	4.0	5.3	4.5	2.0	1.8	5.3
6.7	2.2	3.1	3.2	5.4	2.0	5.0
–	–	–	–	–	–	–
–	0.8	0.0	–	0.2	–	–
56.3	55.1	64.8	52.5	59.7	103.1	64.8
36.3	28.0	29.1	7.2	17.5	33.1	61.9
–	–	–	–	–	–	–
10.9	24.8	38.5	19.8	39.8	29.2	120.4
19.9	11.4	7.9	1.1	0.8	1.4	2.9
7.5	4.7	10.0	0.3	7.5	4.4	9.3
–	–	–	–	–	–	–
0.0	–	–	–	0.0	–	–
1.6	0.6	4.4	0.5	2.5	0.5	4.2
0.6	0.3	0.2	0.1	0.1	0.2	11.8
2.9	1.8	0.7	0.2	2.9	1.8	0.7
29.0	20.0	35.0	18.7	22.6	25.0	40.0
175.0	*156.4*	*199.9*	*108.5*	*160.9*	*202.5*	*326.4*
–	–	–	–	–	–	–
–	–	–	–	–	–	–
–	–	–	–	–	–	–
12.5	8.9	16.0	6.3	8.3	15.5	62.8
–	–	–	–	–	–	–
–	–	–	–	–	–	–
2.4	5.8	6.4	7.2	–	6.7	–
–	–	–	–	–	–	–
–	–	–	19.8	13.5	17.3	14.5
1.6	1.3	2.2	–	–	–	–
0.5	1.5	0.9	–	–	–	–
0.4	0.7	0.9	–	–	–	–
–	–	–	–	–	–	–
9.9	12.9	9.4	–	–	–	–
0.2	0.1	0.1	–	–	–	–
0.9	0.9	1.1	–	–	–	–
3.4	6.3	4.8	6.0	20.3	7.2	63.0
31.8	*38.4*	*41.7*	*39.3*	*42.0*	*46.7*	*140.2*
30.4	*30.0*	*39.0*	*67.0*	*87.2*	*47.0*	*84.8*
129.4	*127.3*	*164.4*	*90.8*	*137.6*	*188.9*	*325.2*
237.1	***224.8***	***280.6***	***214.9***	***290.2***	***296.1***	***551.4***

TECH. COOP. GRANTS

1984	1985	1986	1983	1984	1985	1986
–	0.1	–	0.0	0.0	0.1	–
0.3	0.1	0.6	0.2	–	–	–
3.1	2.7	2.9	2.7	2.3	2.3	1.9
5.4	2.1	2.0	0.3	–	0.8	–
–	–	0.0	–	–	–	0.0
29.9	25.5	31.9	25.8	26.9	22.2	29.7
7.3	6.9	11.5	6.9	6.7	5.6	9.0
–	–	–	–	–	–	–
6.7	5.5	24.1	1.6	3.5	4.7	7.9
0.8	1.3	2.7	1.1	0.8	1.3	2.4
1.4	0.3	9.2	0.3	0.7	0.2	0.3
–	–	–	–	–	–	–
0.0	–	–	–	–	–	–
1.6	0.6	4.4	1.1	0.6	0.3	–
0.3	0.3	0.2	0.1	0.1	0.1	0.1
2.9	1.8	0.7	0.1	0.2	0.2	0.2
9.0	12.0	18.0	6.0	10.0	12.0	10.0
68.6	*59.1*	*108.1*	*46.3*	*51.8*	*49.8*	*61.3*
21.5	*25.0*	*27.4*	*4.9*	*3.6*	*4.5*	*5.1*
0.1	*0.1*	*0.4*	–	–	–	–
59.3	*50.3*	*93.1*	*37.4*	*40.2*	*35.2*	*48.9*
90.2	***84.1***	***135.9***	***51.2***	***55.3***	***54.3***	***66.4***

TOTAL OOF NET

1984	1985	1986	1983	1984	1985	1986
–	–	–	–	–	–	–
–	–	–	–	–	-2.3	-2.1
0.3	0.5	–	–	0.3	0.5	–
11.5	0.3	0.9	4.5	11.4	-3.3	-2.4
–	0.0	0.1	–	–	0.0	0.1
–	–	–	–	–	–	–
–	1.1	0.2	-0.5	-0.5	0.6	-0.6
–	–	–	–	–	–	–
45.2	15.5	6.5	24.7	27.8	-12.4	-22.6
57.4	2.2	22.7	-2.8	53.1	-2.0	13.3
–	–	–	-0.1	-0.3	0.0	–
–	–	–	–	–	–	–
11.0	2.0	9.8	4.4	4.6	-6.0	3.4
–	–	–	–	–	–	–
19.0	8.0	–	2.0	8.0	-13.0	-22.0
144.5	*29.6*	*40.2*	*32.2*	*104.4*	*-38.0*	*-33.0*
141.0	*187.2*	*240.4*	*72.4*	*78.0*	*109.3*	*98.8*
48.2	*11.2*	*0.2*	*-3.4*	*39.9*	*6.5*	*-5.1*
48.7	*23.4*	*20.1*	*26.2*	*28.9*	*-6.9*	*-12.5*
333.6	***228.0***	***280.7***	***101.3***	***222.3***	***77.8***	***60.7***

ODA COMMITMENTS : LOANS

DAC COUNTRIES

	1983	1984	1985	1986
Australia	–	–	–	–
Austria	–	–	–	–
Belgium	2.4	–	0.5	2.4
Canada	–	–	–	–
Denmark	–	–	–	–
Finland	–	–	–	–
France	26.3	29.8	77.8	32.9
Germany, Fed. Rep.	2.7	8.0	28.2	48.2
Ireland	–	–	–	–
Italy	–	27.9	16.7	56.8
Japan	–	–	–	–
Netherlands	–	6.1	4.2	–
New Zealand	–	–	–	–
Norway	–	–	–	–
Sweden	–	–	–	–
Switzerland	–	–	–	11.7
United Kingdom	–	–	–	–
United States	11.1	13.5	4.5	13.0
TOTAL	*42.4*	*85.2*	*131.8*	*164.9*
MULTILATERAL	*13.2*	*21.5*	*17.7*	*75.8*
OPEC COUNTRIES	*65.0*	*87.2*	*43.8*	*84.8*
E.E.C.+ MEMBERS	*31.4*	*72.9*	*131.1*	*153.1*
TOTAL	*120.6*	*193.9*	*193.3*	*325.5*

GRANT ELEMENT OF ODA

DAC COUNTRIES

	1983	1984	1985	1986
Australia	100.0	–	–	–
Austria	100.0	100.0	100.0	36.1
Belgium	89.4	100.0	90.3	90.9
Canada	100.0	100.0	100.0	100.0
Denmark	–	–	–	–
Finland	–	100.0	–	–
France	93.2	77.7	70.2	73.1
Germany, Fed. Rep.	87.3	74.6	52.4	64.4
Ireland	–	–	–	–
Italy	100.0	60.7	67.5	80.0
Japan	100.0	100.0	100.0	100.0
Netherlands	100.0	60.1	62.3	100.0
New Zealand	–	–	–	–
Norway	–	100.0	–	–
Sweden	100.0	100.0	100.0	100.0
Switzerland	100.0	100.0	100.0	87.6
United Kingdom	100.0	100.0	100.0	100.0
United States	63.9	65.8	89.7	81.3
TOTAL	*88.2*	*72.6*	*70.8*	*77.2*
MULTILATERAL	*90.0*	*62.9*	*87.9*	*65.1*
OPEC COUNTRIES	*46.8*	*41.9*	*38.7*	*50.2*
E.E.C.+ MEMBERS	*95.0*	*73.3*	*69.4*	*78.9*
TOTAL	*73.6*	*61.9*	*68.1*	*70.5*

OTHER AGGREGATES

COMMITMENTS: ALL SOURCES

	1983	1984	1985	1986
TOTAL BILATERAL	368.9	432.2	251.5	422.9
of which				
OPEC	82.7	192.5	47.0	86.0
CMEA	50.0	–	–	7.3
TOTAL MULTILATERAL	306.3	262.1	302.0	497.9
TOTAL BIL.& MULTIL.	675.2	694.3	553.5	920.7
of which				
ODA Grants	94.2	96.3	102.9	225.9
ODA Loans	120.6	193.9	193.3	325.5

DISBURSEMENTS:

DAC COUNTRIES COMBINED

	1983	1984	1985	1986
OFFICIAL & PRIVATE				
GROSS:				
Contractual Lending	494.1	471.4	308.1	182.5
Export Credits Total	363.7	363.6	210.7	90.8
Export Credits Private	313.0	220.9	181.6	50.6
NET:				
Contractual Lending	311.7	154.1	26.2	-23.6
Export Credits Total	210.2	80.9	-36.5	-62.6
PRIVATE SECTOR NET	201.2	26.9	66.9	65.8
Direct Investment	20.3	13.3	8.0	45.3
Portfolio Investment	1.4	35.6	57.0	50.0
Export Credits	179.5	-22.0	2.0	-29.6

MARKET BORROWING:

CHANGE IN CLAIMS

	1983	1984	1985	1986
Banks	–	115.0	159.0	105.0

MEMORANDUM ITEM:

	1983	1984	1985	1986
CMEA Countr.(Gross)	4.2	1.6	2.1	–

TURKEY

	1983	1984	1985	1986	1983	1984	1985	1986		1983
TOTAL RECEIPTS NET					**TOTAL ODA NET**				**TOTAL ODA GROSS**	
DAC COUNTRIES										
Australia	0.2	—	5.2	2.1	0.1	—	—	—	Australia	0.1
Austria	5.9	-1.6	-1.2	7.2	5.9	4.5	5.3	7.2	Austria	6.2
Belgium	-8.4	34.4	94.1	48.5	10.2	3.7	3.7	6.1	Belgium	11.8
Canada	0.5	12.6	-3.3	11.8	0.1	0.2	-1.5	-1.3	Canada	0.6
Denmark	0.2	0.3	-0.2	1.2	0.1	-0.2	-0.2	-0.3	Denmark	0.1
Finland	-7.3	-5.7	2.7	10.9	-0.2	-0.2	-0.2	-0.1	Finland	—
France	47.7	-49.0	105.6	0.5	16.4	4.6	0.8	8.0	France	18.5
Germany, Fed. Rep.	-20.0	-15.1	108.7	212.8	42.9	17.7	38.1	89.1	Germany, Fed. Rep.	67.2
Ireland	—	—	—	—	—	—	—	—	Ireland	—
Italy	70.5	76.3	213.4	-13.2	2.0	17.9	22.2	19.3	Italy	2.9
Japan	-15.2	17.2	82.2	618.2	25.5	36.9	26.0	71.2	Japan	32.1
Netherlands	3.9	0.6	18.7	32.2	0.3	-0.4	-2.2	-1.6	Netherlands	0.4
New Zealand	—	—	—	—	—	—	—	—	New Zealand	—
Norway	-6.0	29.7	53.1	16.0	0.5	0.1	0.1	0.1	Norway	0.5
Sweden	-0.4	6.4	4.6	75.7	-0.2	0.0	-0.4	-0.6	Sweden	—
Switzerland	-38.2	229.9	-20.3	-7.4	4.1	-1.6	-0.2	-1.1	Switzerland	5.8
United Kingdom	-28.6	-54.0	-1.7	97.3	4.2	-3.4	7.4	-1.0	United Kingdom	8.2
United States	245.0	272.0	-234.0	25.0	182.0	109.0	38.0	40.0	United States	223.0
TOTAL	*249.7*	*554.0*	*427.6*	*1138.7*	*293.9*	*188.7*	*136.7*	*234.7*	**TOTAL**	*377.3*
MULTILATERAL										
AF.D.F.	—	—	—	—	—	—	—	—	AF.D.F.	—
AF.D.B.	—	—	—	—	—	—	—	—	AF.D.B.	—
AS.D.B	—	—	—	—	—	—	—	—	AS.D.B	—
CAR.D.B.	—	—	—	—	—	—	—	—	CAR.D.B.	—
E.E.C.	30.8	16.5	52.1	64.0	27.8	17.4	4.3	72.7	E.E.C.	38.9
IBRD	373.9	487.3	480.6	402.0	—	—	—	—	IBRD	—
IDA	-2.6	-2.9	-3.5	-3.9	-2.6	-2.9	-3.5	-3.9	IDA	—
I.D.B.	—	—	—	—	—	—	—	—	I.D.B.	—
IFAD	2.0	2.3	2.5	3.7	2.0	2.3	2.5	3.7	IFAD	2.0
I.F.C.	-10.0	-4.1	-4.3	18.0	—	—	—	—	I.F.C.	—
IMF TRUST FUND	—	—	—	—	—	—	—	—	IMF TRUST FUND	—
U.N. AGENCIES									U.N. AGENCIES	
UNDP	2.5	2.3	2.2	3.0	2.5	2.3	2.2	3.0	UNDP	2.5
UNTA	0.9	0.8	0.9	1.2	0.9	0.8	0.9	1.2	UNTA	0.9
UNICEF	0.2	0.2	0.3	0.4	0.2	0.2	0.3	0.4	UNICEF	0.2
UNRWA	—	—	—	—	—	—	—	—	UNRWA	—
WFP	0.9	0.6	3.3	0.5	0.9	0.6	3.3	0.5	WFP	0.9
UNHCR	0.5	0.7	0.6	0.6	0.5	0.7	0.6	0.6	UNHCR	0.5
Other Multilateral	2.2	0.5	119.4	188.5	2.2	0.5	2.7	2.5	Other Multilateral	2.4
Arab OPEC Agencies	5.0	1.3	-17.8	-9.7	0.1	0.0	-0.8	-0.2	Arab OPEC Agencies	0.4
TOTAL	*406.2*	*505.4*	*636.2*	*668.1*	*34.3*	*21.7*	*12.4*	*80.2*	**TOTAL**	*48.6*
OPEC COUNTRIES	*47.9*	*209.1*	*123.4*	*62.3*	*24.2*	*30.1*	*27.4*	*32.3*	**OPEC COUNTRIES**	*32.3*
E.E.C.+ MEMBERS	*96.1*	*10.0*	*590.7*	*443.3*	*103.9*	*57.2*	*73.9*	*192.1*	**E.E.C.+ MEMBERS**	*148.1*
TOTAL	**703.8**	**1268.4**	**1187.2**	**1869.1**	**352.4**	**240.5**	**176.5**	**347.2**	**TOTAL**	**458.3**
ODA LOANS GROSS					**ODA LOANS NET**				**GRANTS**	
DAC COUNTRIES										
Australia	—	—	—	—	—	—	—	—	Australia	0.1
Austria	1.6	1.7	1.8	2.2	1.4	0.5	1.1	1.5	Austria	4.5
Belgium	11.7	4.3	4.2	5.6	10.2	3.7	3.5	5.6	Belgium	0.0
Canada	—	—	—	—	-0.5	—	-1.7	-2.1	Canada	0.6
Denmark	—	—	—	—	-0.2	-0.2	-0.2	-0.3	Denmark	0.1
Finland	—	—	—	—	-0.2	-0.2	-0.2	-0.1	Finland	—
France	14.2	3.5	0.6	3.9	12.1	0.5	-3.2	1.5	France	4.3
Germany, Fed. Rep.	52.1	53.4	56.3	145.6	27.8	1.9	25.5	71.2	Germany, Fed. Rep.	15.1
Ireland	—	—	—	—	—	—	—	—	Ireland	—
Italy	1.2	19.3	22.0	20.2	0.3	16.4	19.0	16.3	Italy	1.7
Japan	30.3	41.9	30.9	73.5	23.7	35.2	23.0	66.4	Japan	1.8
Netherlands	—	—	—	—	-0.1	-0.7	-2.4	-1.8	Netherlands	0.4
New Zealand	—	—	—	—	—	—	—	—	New Zealand	—
Norway	—	—	—	—	—	—	—	—	Norway	0.5
Sweden	—	—	—	—	-0.2	-0.4	-0.4	-0.6	Sweden	—
Switzerland	4.8	—	—	—	3.1	-2.2	-1.4	-1.9	Switzerland	1.0
United Kingdom	7.5	0.1	12.9	6.3	3.5	-3.9	6.9	-1.6	United Kingdom	0.7
United States	149.0	85.0	1.0	1.0	108.0	19.0	-62.0	-59.0	United States	74.0
TOTAL	*272.5*	*209.2*	*129.6*	*258.2*	*189.1*	*69.7*	*7.5*	*95.1*	**TOTAL**	*104.9*
MULTILATERAL	*34.2*	*25.8*	*17.7*	*54.3*	*19.9*	*11.4*	*0.9*	*32.4*	**MULTILATERAL**	*14.5*
OPEC COUNTRIES	*22.0*	*33.6*	*42.0*	*40.6*	*13.8*	*29.6*	*27.3*	*32.1*	**OPEC COUNTRIES**	*10.3*
E.E.C.+ MEMBERS	*116.9*	*103.7*	*107.9*	*227.9*	*72.7*	*29.9*	*49.8*	*122.3*	**E.E.C.+ MEMBERS**	*31.2*
TOTAL	**328.6**	**268.5**	**189.3**	**353.0**	**222.8**	**110.6**	**35.6**	**159.6**	**TOTAL**	**129.6**
TOTAL OFFICIAL GROSS					**TOTAL OFFICIAL NET**				**TOTAL OOF GROSS**	
DAC COUNTRIES										
Australia	0.1	—	0.2	—	0.1	—	0.2	0.0	Australia	—
Austria	6.2	6.0	6.0	7.9	5.9	4.8	5.3	7.2	Austria	—
Belgium	13.6	7.5	5.6	6.1	7.6	2.3	0.0	1.0	Belgium	1.8
Canada	32.8	65.9	65.9	72.0	0.5	12.6	-3.3	11.8	Canada	32.2
Denmark	0.2	0.5	1.6	1.5	0.2	0.3	-0.2	1.2	Denmark	0.0
Finland	—	—	—	—	-0.2	-0.2	-0.2	-0.1	Finland	—
France	98.5	12.0	11.3	10.3	86.0	-4.5	-8.8	-16.4	France	80.0
Germany, Fed. Rep.	113.5	105.3	79.1	206.3	31.0	-1.7	-9.6	64.3	Germany, Fed. Rep.	46.3
Ireland	—	—	—	—	—	—	—	—	Ireland	—
Italy	5.6	20.7	39.2	50.5	4.1	17.0	32.7	≤0.4	Italy	2.7
Japan	93.8	60.1	49.1	95.0	80.4	28.5	17.0	44.5	Japan	61.7
Netherlands	4.0	1.2	0.8	1.6	3.9	0.2	-3.3	-5.3	Netherlands	3.6
New Zealand	—	—	—	—	—	—	—	—	New Zealand	—
Norway	0.5	0.1	0.1	0.1	0.5	0.1	0.1	0.1	Norway	—
Sweden	—	0.4	2.0	3.7	-0.5	0.0	1.6	1.6	Sweden	—
Switzerland	35.4	1.1	1.2	0.8	19.8	-6.4	-4.8	-7.4	Switzerland	29.6
United Kingdom	8.2	0.5	13.3	6.8	3.8	-5.8	5.8	-1.5	United Kingdom	—
United States	275.0	246.0	112.0	100.0	181.0	118.0	-22.0	-27.0	United States	52.0
TOTAL	*687.4*	*527.2*	*387.2*	*562.4*	*424.2*	*165.1*	*10.6*	*114.3*	**TOTAL**	*310.1*
MULTILATERAL	*646.1*	*754.8*	*945.3*	*1049.0*	*406.2*	*505.4*	*636.2*	*668.1*	**MULTILATERAL**	*597.4*
OPEC COUNTRIES	*56.1*	*228.1*	*153.2*	*70.7*	*47.9*	*209.1*	*123.4*	*62.3*	**OPEC COUNTRIES**	*23.8*
E.E.C.+ MEMBERS	*290.3*	*183.7*	*218.4*	*370.8*	*167.4*	*24.3*	*68.8*	*147.7*	**E.E.C.+ MEMBERS**	*142.2*
TOTAL	**1389.5**	**1510.0**	**1485.7**	**1682.1**	**878.3**	**879.5**	**770.2**	**844.6**	**TOTAL**	**931.2**

ODA COMMITMENTS

1984	1985	1986	1983	1984	1985	1986
–	–	–	0.1	–	–	–
5.7	6.0	7.9	4.5	3.9	4.2	–
4.3	4.3	6.1	5.9	4.3	1.5	6.1
0.2	0.2	0.8	0.5	0.2	0.1	1.2
0.0	–	–	–	–	–	–
–	–	–	–	–	–	–
7.5	4.6	10.3	15.3	13.6	4.1	10.3
69.2	68.8	163.5	24.3	257.7	73.2	167.4
–	–	–	–	–	–	–
20.7	25.2	23.1	41.8	2.2	3.6	23.1
43.6	33.9	78.2	7.1	66.6	105.1	5.5
0.4	0.2	0.2	0.5	0.3	0.2	0.2
–	–	–	–	–	–	–
0.1	0.1	0.1	–	0.1	0.1	0.1
0.4	–	–	0.4	–	–	–
0.6	1.2	0.8	0.5	0.1	2.0	–
0.5	13.3	6.8	23.4	3.4	0.5	0.6
175.0	101.0	100.0	225.0	176.5	101.4	100.2
328.2	*258.8*	*397.7*	*349.2*	*529.0*	*295.7*	*314.5*
–	–	–	–	–	–	–
–	–	–	–	–	–	–
–	–	–	–	–	–	–
28.3	15.5	87.7	0.5	–	–	18.4
–	–	–	–	–	–	–
–	–	–	–	–	–	–
2.3	2.5	4.4	–	9.5	–	–
–	–	–	–	–	–	–
–	–	–	5.7	5.2	8.1	6.6
2.3	2.2	3.0	–	–	–	–
0.8	0.9	1.2	–	–	–	–
0.2	0.3	0.4	–	–	–	–
–	–	–	–	–	–	–
0.6	3.3	0.5	–	–	–	–
0.7	0.6	0.6	–	–	–	–
0.7	3.0	2.8	–	–	2.2	1.7
0.3	1.0	1.7	–	7.3	–	–
36.1	*29.2*	*102.1*	*6.1*	*22.0*	*10.2*	*26.7*
34.1	*42.1*	*40.7*	*111.8*	*16.9*	*58.2*	*32.3*
131.0	*132.0*	*297.7*	*111.7*	*281.6*	*82.9*	*226.0*
398.4	***330.1***	***540.6***	***467.0***	***567.9***	***364.2***	***373.5***

TECH. COOP. GRANTS

1984	1985	1986	1983	1984	1985	1986
–	–	–	–	–	–	–
4.0	4.2	5.7	4.3	–	–	–
–	0.1	0.5	–	–	–	–
0.2	0.2	0.8	0.1	–	–	–
0.0	–	–	0.0	0.0	–	–
–	–	–	–	–	–	–
4.0	4.1	6.4	4.3	4.0	4.1	6.4
15.8	12.5	17.9	14.7	13.8	12.5	16.7
–	–	–	–	–	–	–
1.5	3.3	2.9	1.4	1.3	1.3	1.8
1.7	3.0	4.7	1.4	1.7	2.9	4.7
0.4	0.2	0.2	0.4	0.3	0.2	0.2
–	–	–	–	–	–	–
0.1	0.1	0.1	0.1	0.1	0.1	0.1
0.4	–	–	–	–	–	–
0.6	1.2	0.8	0.1	0.1	0.1	0.3
0.4	0.5	0.6	0.6	0.4	0.5	0.6
90.0	100.0	99.0	–	–	–	–
119.0	*129.2*	*139.6*	*27.2*	*21.7*	*21.5*	*30.7*
10.3	*11.5*	*47.9*	*4.8*	*4.6*	*4.8*	*6.1*
0.6	*0.1*	*0.2*	–	–	–	–
27.3	*24.1*	*69.8*	*21.3*	*19.8*	*18.5*	*25.6*
129.9	***140.8***	***187.6***	***32.0***	***26.3***	***26.2***	***36.8***

TOTAL OOF NET

1984	1985	1986	1983	1984	1985	1986
–	0.2	–	–	–	0.2	0.0
0.3	–	–	–	0.3	–	–
3.2	1.2	–	-2.5	-1.4	-3.6	-5.0
65.7	65.7	71.2	0.4	12.4	-1.7	13.1
0.4	1.6	1.5	0.0	0.4	0.1	1.5
–	–	–	–	–	–	–
4.5	6.6	–	69.6	-9.0	-9.6	-24.4
36.1	10.3	42.8	-11.9	-19.4	-47.7	-24.8
–	14.0	27.4	2.1	-0.9	10.5	21.1
16.5	15.2	16.8	54.9	-8.4	-9.0	-26.7
0.8	0.6	1.4	3.6	0.6	-1.1	-3.7
–	–	–	–	–	–	–
–	2.0	3.7	-0.3	–	2.0	2.3
0.6	–	–	15.7	-4.8	-4.6	-6.4
–	–	–	-0.5	-2.4	-1.5	-0.4
71.0	11.0	–	-1.0	9.0	-60.0	-67.0
199.0	*128.4*	*164.7*	*130.3*	*-23.6*	*-126.2*	*-120.4*
718.7	*916.1*	*946.8*	*371.8*	*483.7*	*623.8*	*587.9*
193.9	*111.1*	*30.0*	*23.8*	*178.9*	*96.1*	*30.0*
52.7	*86.4*	*73.1*	*63.6*	*-32.9*	*-5.1*	*-44.4*
1111.6	***1155.6***	***1141.5***	***525.9***	***639.0***	***593.7***	***497.5***

ODA COMMITMENTS : LOANS

DAC COUNTRIES

	1983	1984	1985	1986
Australia	–	–	–	–
Austria	–	–	–	–
Belgium	5.9	4.3	1.5	5.6
Canada	–	–	–	–
Denmark				
Finland				
France	11.0	9.6	–	3.9
Germany, Fed. Rep.	5.7	239.7	56.4	142.9
Ireland	–	–	–	–
Italy	40.0	–	–	20.0
Japan	5.2	64.8	101.9	–
Netherlands	–	–	–	–
New Zealand	–	–	–	¬
Norway	–	–	–	–
Sweden	–	–	–	–
Switzerland	–	–	–	–
United Kingdom	22.8	3.0	–	–
United States	149.0	85.5	0.5	0.5
TOTAL	*239.5*	*406.9*	*160.3*	*172.9*
MULTILATERAL	–	*16.8*	*2.2*	*20.1*
OPEC COUNTRIES	*101.2*	*16.9*	*58.1*	*22.3*
E.E.C.+ MEMBERS	*85.3*	*256.6*	*57.9*	*190.8*
TOTAL	***340.7***	***440.7***	***220.6***	***215.3***

GRANT ELEMENT OF ODA

DAC COUNTRIES

	1983	1984	1985	1986
Australia	100.0	–	–	–
Austria	100.0	100.0	100.0	28.7
Belgium	80.1	84.0	80.0	81.4
Canada	100.0	100.0	100.0	100.0
Denmark	–	–	–	–
Finland	–	–	–	–
France	100.0	73.1	100.0	100.0
Germany, Fed. Rep.	92.1	52.5	50.3	49.2
Ireland	–	–	–	–
Italy	48.1	100.0	100.0	65.0
Japan	40.0	44.0	38.7	100.0
Netherlands	100.0	100.0	100.0	100.0
New Zealand	–	–	–	–
Norway	–	100.0	100.0	100.0
Sweden	100.0	–	–	–
Switzerland	100.0	100.0	100.0	–
United Kingdom	29.9	35.4	100.0	100.0
United States	59.2	71.0	99.8	99.8
TOTAL	*59.4*	*58.9*	*65.9*	*65.8*
MULTILATERAL	*100.0*	*68.6*	*100.0*	*100.0*
OPEC COUNTRIES	*47.2*	*35.2*	*45.3*	*49.9*
E.E.C.+ MEMBERS	*59.1*	*54.2*	*56.5*	*53.7*
TOTAL	***56.9***	***58.4***	***63.4***	***65.1***

OTHER AGGREGATES

COMMITMENTS: ALL SOURCES

	1983	1984	1985	1986
TOTAL BILATERAL	742.1	1049.7	969.7	678.3
of which				
OPEC	125.8	239.1	240.3	95.8
CMEA	38.7	–	255.5	160.0
TOTAL MULTILATERAL	721.9	928.7	1074.2	1669.3
TOTAL BIL.& MULTIL.	1464.0	1978.4	2043.9	2347.6
of which				
ODA Grants	126.4	127.2	143.6	158.2
ODA Loans	340.7	440.7	220.6	215.3

DISBURSEMENTS:

DAC COUNTRIES COMBINED

	1983	1984	1985	1986
OFFICIAL & PRIVATE				
GROSS:				
Contractual Lending	701.3	1024.3	1138.2	1188.0
Export Credits Total	249.6	784.4	999.9	927.0
Export Credits Private	118.8	617.6	881.5	765.2
NET:				
Contractual Lending	73.1	270.8	437.8	449.7
Export Credits Total	-206.5	253.6	512.0	454.8
PRIVATE SECTOR NET	-174.5	388.9	417.1	1024.5
Direct Investment	9.1	98.2	36.6	33.4
Portfolio Investment	62.7	64.4	-177.2	516.0
Export Credits	-246.3	226.3	557.7	475.0

MARKET BORROWING:

CHANGE IN CLAIMS

	1983	1984	1985	1986
Banks	–	700.0	1454.0	1398.0

MEMORANDUM ITEM:

	1983	1984	1985	1986
CMEA Countr.(Gross)	–	–	–	13.0

	1983	1984	1985	1986		1983	1984	1985	1986		1983
TOTAL RECEIPTS NET					**TOTAL ODA NET**					**TOTAL ODA GROSS**	
DAC COUNTRIES											
Australia	4.2	3.5	0.3	0.2		4.2	3.5	0.3	0.2	Australia	4.2
Austria	0.0	0.1	0.0	0.1		0.0	0.1	0.0	0.1	Austria	0.0
Belgium	0.4	0.4	2.0	-0.1		0.4	0.3	1.7	0.2	Belgium	0.4
Canada	2.0	6.5	2.6	1.7		2.0	6.5	2.6	1.7	Canada	2.0
Denmark	2.3	2.6	0.8	2.8		2.3	2.6	0.8	2.8	Denmark	2.3
Finland	0.9	0.1	0.4	1.6		0.9	0.1	0.4	1.6	Finland	0.9
France	9.5	7.2	0.1	-2.9		1.7	1.9	1.7	1.1	France	1.7
Germany, Fed. Rep.	7.0	3.6	4.4	13.0		6.0	3.5	4.4	12.9	Germany, Fed. Rep.	29.4
Ireland	0.0	0.1	0.0	0.1		1.9	0.1	0.0	0.1	Ireland	0.0
Italy	1.9	1.8	10.8	30.0		1.9	6.7	10.8	30.0	Italy	1.9
Japan	3.6	5.3	3.1	2.6		3.6	5.3	3.1	2.6	Japan	4.1
Netherlands	8.1	4.6	1.9	8.2		7.3	4.6	1.9	6.3	Netherlands	7.3
New Zealand	0.0	0.0	0.0	0.0		0.0	0.0	0.0	0.0	New Zealand	0.0
Norway	1.2	1.1	1.2	2.2		1.2	1.1	1.2	2.2	Norway	1.2
Sweden	0.7	0.2	–	1.9		0.7	0.2	–	1.9	Sweden	0.7
Switzerland	0.5	0.3	0.3	1.6		0.5	0.3	0.3	1.6	Switzerland	0.5
United Kingdom	2.1	3.5	-1.3	8.7		7.1	7.5	8.4	9.2	United Kingdom	9.3
United States	5.0	3.0	5.0	3.0		4.0	3.0	5.0	3.0	United States	4.0
TOTAL	**49.3**	**43.9**	**31.5**	**74.5**		**43.7**	**47.2**	**42.3**	**77.3**	**TOTAL**	**69.9**
MULTILATERAL											
AF.D.F.	3.6	–	0.7	0.2		3.6	–	0.7	0.2	AF.D.F.	3.6
AF.D.B.	6.6	5.4	11.7	4.1		–	–	–	–	AF.D.B.	–
AS.D.B	–	–	–	–		–	–	–	–	AS.D.B	–
CAR.D.B.	–	–	–	–		–	–	–	–	CAR.D.B.	–
E.E.C.	16.6	22.6	16.1	16.8		16.6	22.6	16.1	16.8	E.E.C.	16.6
IBRD	–	–	33.3	-1.9		–	–	–	–	IBRD	–
IDA	27.6	57.7	91.3	61.2		27.6	57.7	91.3	61.2	IDA	32.5
I.D.B.	–	–	–	–		–	–	–	–	I.D.B.	–
IFAD	4.1	4.6	2.8	3.6		4.1	4.6	2.8	3.6	IFAD	5.4
I.F.C.	–	–	4.0	1.3		–	–	–	–	I.F.C.	–
IMF TRUST FUND	–	–	–	–		–	–	–	–	IMF TRUST FUND	–
U.N. AGENCIES	–	–	–	–		–	–	–	–	U.N. AGENCIES	–
UNDP	6.6	7.0	8.3	7.0		6.6	7.0	8.3	7.0	UNDP	6.6
UNTA	1.3	1.1	1.2	1.1		1.3	1.1	1.2	1.1	UNTA	1.3
UNICEF	6.1	5.4	7.6	6.2		6.1	5.4	7.6	6.2	UNICEF	6.1
UNRWA	–	–	–	–		–	–	–	–	UNRWA	–
WFP	9.9	13.5	7.7	9.2		9.9	13.5	7.7	9.2	WFP	9.9
UNHCR	4.4	5.4	3.6	10.5		4.4	5.4	3.6	10.5	UNHCR	4.4
Other Multilateral	0.4	0.7	0.8	0.9		0.4	0.7	0.8	0.9	Other Multilateral	0.4
Arab OPEC Agencies	10.8	0.1	1.0	0.9		8.4	0.2	-0.4	0.3	Arab OPEC Agencies	8.7
TOTAL	**98.1**	**123.3**	**190.0**	**121.2**		**89.1**	**118.1**	**139.6**	**117.1**	**TOTAL**	**95.5**
OPEC COUNTRIES	**4.3**	**-2.6**	**0.7**	**3.4**		**4.3**	**-2.6**	**0.7**	**3.4**	**OPEC COUNTRIES**	**4.8**
E.E.C.+ MEMBERS	**47.9**	**46.4**	**34.8**	**76.4**		**43.3**	**49.7**	**45.6**	**79.2**	**E.E.C.+ MEMBERS**	**69.0**
TOTAL	**151.7**	**164.6**	**222.2**	**199.1**		**137.1**	**162.6**	**182.7**	**197.8**	**TOTAL**	**170.2**
ODA LOANS GROSS					**ODA LOANS NET**					**GRANTS**	
DAC COUNTRIES											
Australia	–	–	–	–		–	–	–	–	Australia	4.2
Austria	–	–	–	–		–	–	–	–	Austria	0.0
Belgium	–	–	–	–		–	–	–	–	Belgium	0.4
Canada	–	–	–	–		–	–	–	–	Canada	2.0
Denmark	–	–	–	–		–	–	–	–	Denmark	2.3
Finland	–	–	–	–		–	–	–	–	Finland	0.9
France	0.8	0.8	1.2	0.2		0.8	0.8	1.2	0.2	France	0.9
Germany, Fed. Rep.	–	–	–	–		-23.5	–	–	–	Germany, Fed. Rep.	29.4
Ireland	–	–	–	–		–	–	–	–	Ireland	0.0
Italy	–	1.9	3.7	–		–	1.9	3.7	–	Italy	1.9
Japan	–	–	–	–		-0.5	-0.3	-0.2	-0.5	Japan	4.1
Netherlands	–	–	–	–		–	–	–	–	Netherlands	7.3
New Zealand	–	–	–	–		–	–	–	–	New Zealand	0.0
Norway	–	–	–	–		–	–	–	–	Norway	1.2
Sweden	–	–	–	–		–	–	–	–	Sweden	0.7
Switzerland	–	–	–	–		–	–	–	–	Switzerland	0.5
United Kingdom	–	–	–	–		-2.2	-2.0	-2.0	-1.6	United Kingdom	9.3
United States	–	–	–	–		–	–	–	-1.0	United States	4.0
TOTAL	**0.8**	**2.7**	**4.8**	**0.2**		**-25.4**	**0.3**	**2.7**	**-2.9**	**TOTAL**	**69.1**
MULTILATERAL	**54.4**	**67.8**	**98.3**	**68.1**		**47.9**	**66.6**	**95.4**	**65.8**	**MULTILATERAL**	**41.1**
OPEC COUNTRIES	**4.6**	**0.4**	**1.0**	**6.0**		**4.1**	**-2.8**	**0.6**	**3.4**	**OPEC COUNTRIES**	**0.2**
E.E.C.+ MEMBERS	**5.0**	**6.8**	**5.9**	**0.7**		**-20.6**	**4.8**	**3.8**	**-1.0**	**E.E.C.+ MEMBERS**	**63.9**
TOTAL	**59.8**	**70.8**	**104.1**	**74.2**		**26.6**	**64.2**	**98.6**	**66.3**	**TOTAL**	**110.4**
TOTAL OFFICIAL GROSS					**TOTAL OFFICIAL NET**					**TOTAL OOF GROSS**	
DAC COUNTRIES											
Australia	4.2	3.5	0.3	0.2		4.2	3.5	0.3	0.2	Australia	–
Austria	0.0	0.1	0.0	0.1		0.0	0.1	0.0	0.1	Austria	–
Belgium	0.4	0.3	1.7	0.2		0.4	0.3	1.7	0.2	Belgium	–
Canada	2.0	6.5	2.6	1.7		2.0	6.5	2.6	1.7	Canada	–
Denmark	2.3	2.6	0.8	2.8		2.3	2.6	0.8	2.8	Denmark	–
Finland	0.9	0.1	0.4	1.6		0.9	0.1	0.4	1.6	Finland	–
France	8.6	4.7	1.8	1.1		8.3	4.4	1.6	1.0	France	6.9
Germany, Fed. Rep.	30.5	3.7	4.4	12.9		7.0	3.5	4.2	12.8	Germany, Fed. Rep.	1.0
Ireland	0.0	0.1	0.0	0.1		0.0	0.1	0.0	0.1	Ireland	–
Italy	1.9	13.9	10.8	30.0		1.9	13.9	10.8	30.0	Italy	–
Japan	4.1	5.6	3.2	3.1		3.6	5.3	3.1	2.6	Japan	–
Netherlands	8.1	4.6	1.9	8.2		8.1	4.6	1.9	8.2	Netherlands	0.8
New Zealand	0.0	0.0	0.0	0.0		0.0	0.0	0.0	0.0	New Zealand	–
Norway	1.2	1.1	1.2	2.2		1.2	1.1	1.2	2.2	Norway	–
Sweden	0.7	0.2	–	1.9		0.7	0.2	–	1.9	Sweden	–
Switzerland	0.5	0.3	0.3	1.6		0.5	0.3	0.3	1.6	Switzerland	–
United Kingdom	9.3	9.5	11.9	12.6		7.1	7.4	9.6	10.6	United Kingdom	–
United States	5.0	3.0	5.0	4.0		5.0	3.0	5.0	3.0	United States	1.0
TOTAL	**79.6**	**59.7**	**46.2**	**84.0**		**53.1**	**56.7**	**43.3**	**80.4**	**TOTAL**	**9.7**
MULTILATERAL	**106.5**	**127.3**	**200.3**	**130.9**		**98.1**	**123.3**	**190.0**	**121.2**	**MULTILATERAL**	**11.0**
OPEC COUNTRIES	**4.8**	**0.6**	**1.0**	**6.0**		**4.3**	**-2.6**	**0.7**	**3.4**	**OPEC COUNTRIES**	**–**
E.E.C.+ MEMBERS	**77.7**	**61.9**	**49.4**	**84.6**		**51.7**	**59.3**	**46.6**	**82.4**	**E.E.C.+ MEMBERS**	**8.7**
TOTAL	**190.9**	**187.5**	**247.5**	**220.9**		**155.4**	**177.4**	**234.0**	**205.1**	**TOTAL**	**20.7**

ODA COMMITMENTS

1984	1985	1986	1983	1984	1985	1986
3.5	0.3	0.2	4.3	0.5	0.2	0.1
0.1	0.0	0.1	0.0	0.0	0.0	–
0.3	1.7	0.2	–	–	0.8	0.2
6.5	2.6	1.7	6.8	5.5	1.9	1.1
2.6	0.8	2.8	2.3	6.2	–	–
0.1	0.4	1.6	0.1	0.1	1.3	-0.1
1.9	1.7	1.1	3.8	3.2	0.5	1.1
3.5	4.4	12.9	30.1	2.2	13.2	22.8
0.1	0.0	0.1	0.0	0.1	0.0	0.1
6.7	10.8	30.0	6.9	32.1	8.5	45.3
5.6	3.2	3.1	4.6	7.2	2.8	0.1
4.6	1.9	6.3	7.9	7.0	1.8	2.2
0.0	0.0	0.0	0.0	0.0	0.0	–
1.1	1.2	2.2	0.4	1.2	0.9	0.8
0.2	–	1.9	–	0.5	–	1.9
0.3	0.3	1.6	0.4	0.3	0.3	1.5
9.5	10.4	10.8	17.5	12.9	7.4	30.4
3.0	5.0	4.0	8.1	9.5	9.0	14.8
49.5	*44.5*	*80.4*	*93.2*	*88.4*	*48.6*	*122.2*
–	0.7	0.2	14.5	1.1	17.1	36.8
–	–	–	–	–	–	–
–	–	–	–	–	–	–
–	–	–	–	–	–	–
22.6	16.2	16.8	20.0	21.7	1.5	22.1
–	–	–	–	–	–	–
58.2	91.7	61.7	139.0	136.0	43.9	–
–	–	–	–	–	–	–
5.0	4.2	4.3	–	14.3	–	–
–	–	–	–	–	–	–
–	–	–	–	–	–	–
–	–	–	28.7	33.0	29.2	35.0
7.0	8.3	7.0	–	–	–	–
1.1	1.2	1.1	–	–	–	–
5.4	7.6	6.2	–	–	–	–
–	–	–	–	–	–	–
13.5	7.7	9.2	–	–	–	–
5.4	3.6	10.5	–	–	–	–
0.7	0.8	0.9	–	–	–	–
0.5	0.7	1.3	0.1	4.6	–	–
119.3	*142.6*	*119.3*	*202.2*	*210.6*	*91.7*	*93.9*
0.6	*1.0*	*6.0*	*0.0*	*9.8*	*10.0*	–
51.7	*47.7*	*80.9*	*88.3*	*85.2*	*33.7*	*124.1*
169.3	*188.2*	*205.7*	*295.5*	*308.8*	*150.3*	*216.1*

TECH. COOP. GRANTS

1984	1985	1986	1983	1984	1985	1986
3.5	0.3	0.2	0.4	0.3	0.3	0.1
0.1	0.0	0.1	0.0	–	–	–
0.3	1.7	0.2	0.1	0.1	0.1	0.1
6.5	2.6	1.7	0.3	–	0.4	–
2.6	0.8	2.8	2.3	0.2	0.1	0.1
0.1	0.4	1.6	0.1	0.1	0.1	0.9
1.1	0.6	0.9	0.6	0.6	0.5	0.7
3.5	4.4	12.9	1.8	1.3	1.6	4.2
0.1	0.0	0.1	0.0	0.1	0.0	0.1
4.9	7.1	30.0	1.8	2.9	3.2	8.1
5.6	3.2	3.1	0.1	0.1	0.3	0.1
4.6	1.9	6.3	0.8	0.2	0.8	0.6
0.0	0.0	0.0	0.0	0.0	0.0	0.0
1.1	1.2	2.2	–	0.0	0.1	0.1
0.2	–	1.9	–	–	–	–
0.3	0.3	1.6	0.0	0.0	0.0	0.3
9.5	10.4	10.8	3.7	4.9	4.9	5.3
3.0	5.0	4.0	3.0	2.0	3.0	3.0
46.8	*39.7*	*80.2*	*15.2*	*12.7*	*15.3*	*23.5*
51.5	*44.3*	*51.3*	*18.8*	*19.5*	*21.5*	*26.4*
0.2	*0.1*	*0.0*	–	–	–	–
44.9	*41.8*	*80.2*	*11.2*	*10.2*	*11.1*	*19.6*
98.5	*84.0*	*131.5*	*34.0*	*32.2*	*36.7*	*49.9*

TOTAL OOF NET

1984	1985	1986	1983	1984	1985	1986
–	–	–	–	–	–	–
–	–	–	–	–	–	–
–	–	–	–	–	–	–
–	–	–	–	–	–	–
–	–	–	–	–	–	–
2.8	0.1	–	6.6	2.5	-0.1	0.0
0.2	0.0	–	1.0	0.0	-0.1	0.0
–	–	–	–	–	–	–
7.2	–	–	–	7.2	–	–
–	–	1.9	0.8	–	–	1.9
–	–	–	–	–	–	–
–	–	–	–	–	–	–
–	–	–	–	–	–	–
–	1.5	1.7	–	-0.1	1.2	1.4
–	–	–	1.0	–	–	–
10.2	*1.7*	*3.7*	*9.4*	*9.6*	*0.9*	*3.2*
8.0	*57.6*	*11.6*	*9.0*	*5.2*	*50.4*	*4.1*
–	–	–	–	–	–	–
10.2	*1.7*	*3.7*	*8.4*	*9.6*	*0.9*	*3.2*
18.2	*59.3*	*15.2*	*18.4*	*14.8*	*51.3*	*7.3*

ODA COMMITMENTS : LOANS

DAC COUNTRIES	1983	1984	1985	1986
Australia	–	–	–	–
Austria	–	–	–	–
Belgium	–	–	–	–
Canada	–	–	–	–
Denmark	–	–	–	–
Finland	–	–	–	–
France	2.5	2.0	–	0.2
Germany, Fed. Rep.	–	–	–	–
Ireland	–	–	–	–
Italy	–	22.1	–	–
Japan	–	–	–	–
Netherlands	–	–	–	–
New Zealand	–	–	–	–
Norway	–	–	–	–
Sweden	–	–	–	–
Switzerland	–	–	–	–
United Kingdom	–	–	–	–
United States	–	–	–	–
TOTAL	*2.5*	*24.1*	–	*0.2*
MULTILATERAL	*153.5*	*157.9*	*61.0*	*36.8*
OPEC COUNTRIES	–	*9.8*	*10.0*	–
E.E.C.+ MEMBERS	*2.5*	*26.1*	–	*0.2*
TOTAL	*155.9*	*191.8*	*71.0*	*37.0*

GRANT ELEMENT OF ODA

DAC COUNTRIES	1983	1984	1985	1986
Australia	100.0	100.0	100.0	100.0
Austria	100.0	100.0	100.0	–
Belgium	–	–	100.0	100.0
Canada	100.0	100.0	100.0	100.0
Denmark	100.0	100.0	–	–
Finland	100.0	100.0	100.0	100.0
France	100.0	72.9	100.0	100.0
Germany, Fed. Rep.	100.0	100.0	100.0	100.0
Ireland	100.0	100.0	100.0	100.0
Italy	100.0	66.5	100.0	100.0
Japan	100.0	100.0	100.0	100.0
Netherlands	100.0	100.0	100.0	100.0
New Zealand	100.0	100.0	100.0	–
Norway	100.0	100.0	100.0	100.0
Sweden	–	100.0	–	100.0
Switzerland	100.0	100.0	100.0	100.0
United Kingdom	100.0	100.0	100.0	100.0
United States	100.0	100.0	100.0	100.0
TOTAL	*100.0*	*86.9*	*100.0*	*100.0*
MULTILATERAL	*87.5*	*86.8*	*87.4*	*92.9*
OPEC COUNTRIES	*100.0*	*51.3*	*54.9*	–
E.E.C.+ MEMBERS	*100.0*	*86.1*	*100.0*	*100.0*
TOTAL	*91.6*	*85.7*	*89.1*	*96.9*

OTHER AGGREGATES

COMMITMENTS: ALL SOURCES

	1983	1984	1985	1986
TOTAL BILATERAL	108.3	123.9	71.1	122.6
of which				
OPEC	0.0	9.8	10.0	–
CMEA	6.7	12.3	–	–
TOTAL MULTILATERAL	243.6	210.8	100.7	94.0
TOTAL BIL.& MULTIL.	351.9	334.7	171.8	216.5
of which				
ODA Grants	139.6	117.0	79.3	179.1
ODA Loans	162.6	191.8	71.0	37.0

DISBURSEMENTS:
DAC COUNTRIES COMBINED

	1983	1984	1985	1986
OFFICIAL & PRIVATE				
GROSS:				
Contractual Lending	16.0	24.4	9.6	0.1
Export Credits Total	5.5	11.6	3.1	-3.7
Export Credits Private	5.5	11.6	3.1	-3.7
NET:				
Contractual Lending	-17.9	-3.1	-4.4	-5.4
Export Credits Total	-1.9	-13.0	-8.0	-5.7
PRIVATE SECTOR NET	-3.8	-12.9	-11.8	-5.9
Direct Investment	–	–	-4.0	–
Portfolio Investment	-1.8	0.2	0.3	-0.3
Export Credits	-1.9	-13.0	-8.0	-5.7

MARKET BORROWING:
CHANGE IN CLAIMS

	1983	1984	1985	1986
Banks	–	26.0	-27.0	25.0

MEMORANDUM ITEM:

	1983	1984	1985	1986
CMEA Countr.(Gross)	0.1	0.1	0.5	1.0

DISBURSEMENTS, UNLESS OTHERWISE STATED

	1983	1984	1985	1986	1983	1984	1985	1986	1983
	TOTAL RECEIPTS NET				**TOTAL ODA NET**				**TOTAL ODA GROSS**
DAC COUNTRIES									
Australia	—	—	—	—	—	—	—	—	—
Austria	0.0	0.0	0.0	0.0	0.0	0.0	0.0	0.0	0.0
Belgium	-0.6	15.1	-2.8	0.0	0.2	0.1	0.1	0.3	0.2
Canada	0.1	—	-0.3	-12.1	0.2	0.3	0.3	0.3	0.2
Denmark	0.2	-0.8	-2.4	-0.1	—	—	—	—	—
Finland	2.8	-0.5	-0.4	0.0	—	—	0.0	0.0	0.0
France	15.9	-6.8	-3.4	-4.5	1.5	1.2	1.7	6.1	1.5
Germany, Fed. Rep.	11.3	2.5	6.0	19.8	3.1	2.4	3.0	3.9	3.1
Ireland	—	—	—	—	—	—	—	—	—
Italy	4.3	11.3	-0.2	-0.3	0.2	0.4	0.5	0.7	0.2
Japan	4.0	1.1	0.6	4.6	1.4	1.8	1.7	1.5	1.4
Netherlands	13.2	0.7	4.0	0.3	0.3	0.7	1.0	0.8	0.6
New Zealand	—	—	—	—	—	—	—	—	—
Norway	-0.1	0.2	0.1	0.3	—	0.0	0.0	0.2	—
Sweden	-0.5	-0.1	4.0	6.3	—	0.2	—	0.4	—
Switzerland	-0.1	0.9	-0.2	0.0	0.1	0.1	0.5	0.0	0.1
United Kingdom	1.2	-1.3	-0.6	0.8	0.0	0.0	0.0	0.0	0.0
United States	332.0	195.0	-155.0	1.0	-3.0	-3.0	-3.0	11.0	—
TOTAL	*383.7*	*217.3*	*-150.7*	*15.9*	*4.0*	*4.2*	*5.8*	*25.3*	*7.3*
MULTILATERAL									
AF.D.F.	—	—	—	—	—	—	—	—	—
AF.D.B.	—	—	—	—	—	—	—	—	—
AS.D.B	—	—	—	—	—	—	—	—	—
CAR.D.B.	—	—	—	—	—	—	—	—	—
E.E.C.	—	—	0.1	0.5	—	—	0.1	0.5	—
IBRD	6.8	39.7	11.0	20.5	—	—	—	—	—
IDA	—	—	—	—	—	—	—	—	—
I.D.B.	8.4	14.6	15.2	20.7	-3.0	-2.0	-2.9	-1.4	0.1
IFAD	—	—	—	—	—	—	—	—	—
I.F.C.	4.9	-0.1	-1.3	1.0	—	—	—	—	—
IMF TRUST FUND	—	—	—	—	—	—	—	—	—
U.N. AGENCIES	—	—	—	—	—	—	—	—	—
UNDP	1.2	0.9	1.2	1.5	1.2	0.9	1.2	1.5	1.2
UNTA	0.3	0.5	0.5	0.4	0.3	0.5	0.5	0.4	0.3
UNICEF	—	—	—	—	—	—	—	—	—
UNRWA	—	—	—	—	—	—	—	—	—
WFP	—	—	—	—	—	—	—	—	—
UNHCR	—	—	—	0.1	—	—	—	0.1	—
Other Multilateral	0.2	0.3	0.3	0.3	0.2	0.3	0.3	0.3	0.2
Arab OPEC Agencies	—	—	—	—	—	—	—	—	—
TOTAL	*21.9*	*55.9*	*26.9*	*45.1*	*-1.3*	*-0.3*	*-0.9*	*1.4*	*1.9*
OPEC COUNTRIES	—	—	—	—	—	—	—	—	—
E.E.C.+ MEMBERS	*45.5*	*20.6*	*0.6*	*16.3*	*5.3*	*4.8*	*6.3*	*12.3*	*5.6*
TOTAL	**405.6**	**273.3**	**-123.7**	**61.0**	**2.7**	**3.9**	**4.9**	**26.7**	**9.2**

	1983	1984	1985	1986	1983	1984	1985	1986	1983
	ODA LOANS GROSS				**ODA LOANS NET**				**GRANTS**
DAC COUNTRIES									
Australia	—	—	—	—	—	—	—	—	—
Austria	—	—	—	—	—	—	—	—	0.0
Belgium	—	—	—	—	—	—	—	—	0.2
Canada	—	—	—	—	—	—	—	—	0.2
Denmark	—	—	—	—	—	—	—	—	—
Finland	—	—	—	—	—	—	—	—	—
France	—	—	0.6	4.5	—	—	0.6	4.5	1.5
Germany, Fed. Rep.	0.4	0.1	0.0	0.1	0.4	0.1	0.0	0.0	2.6
Ireland	—	—	—	—	—	—	—	—	—
Italy	—	—	—	—	—	—	—	—	0.2
Japan	0.3	0.1	0.1	0.0	0.3	0.1	0.1	0.0	1.0
Netherlands	—	—	—	—	-0.3	—	—	—	0.6
New Zealand	—	—	—	—	—	—	—	—	—
Norway	—	—	—	—	—	—	—	—	—
Sweden	—	—	—	—	—	—	—	—	—
Switzerland	—	—	—	—	—	—	—	—	0.1
United Kingdom	—	—	—	—	—	—	—	—	0.0
United States	—	—	—	—	-3.0	-3.0	-3.0	-3.0	—
TOTAL	*0.7*	*0.2*	*0.7*	*4.6*	*-2.6*	*-2.8*	*-2.3*	*1.5*	*6.5*
MULTILATERAL	—	—	*0.3*	*0.7*	*-3.1*	*-3.1*	*-2.9*	*-2.2*	*1.9*
OPEC COUNTRIES	—	—	—	—	—	—	—	—	—
E.E.C.+ MEMBERS	*0.4*	*0.1*	*0.6*	*4.6*	*0.1*	*0.1*	*0.5*	*4.5*	*5.2*
TOTAL	**0.7**	**0.2**	**1.0**	**5.3**	**-5.7**	**-5.9**	**-5.3**	**-0.6**	**8.4**

	1983	1984	1985	1986	1983	1984	1985	1986	1983
	TOTAL OFFICIAL GROSS				**TOTAL OFFICIAL NET**				**TOTAL OOF GROSS**
DAC COUNTRIES									
Australia	—	—	—	—	—	—	—	—	—
Austria	0.0	0.0	0.0	0.0	0.0	0.0	0.0	0.0	—
Belgium	0.2	0.2	0.2	0.3	0.2	0.2	0.2	0.3	—
Canada	0.2	0.3	0.3	0.3	0.1	—	-0.3	-12.1	—
Denmark	1.0	—	—	1.6	1.0	—	—	1.6	1.0
Finland	—	—	0.0	0.0	—	—	0.0	0.0	—
France	1.5	1.2	1.7	6.1	1.5	1.2	1.7	6.1	—
Germany, Fed. Rep.	3.1	2.4	3.0	4.0	3.1	2.4	3.0	3.9	—
Ireland	—	—	—	—	—	—	—	—	—
Italy	7.5	14.9	3.4	3.2	7.3	13.6	0.9	0.4	7.2
Japan	1.4	1.8	1.7	1.5	1.4	1.8	1.7	1.5	—
Netherlands	0.6	0.7	1.0	0.8	0.3	0.7	1.0	0.8	—
New Zealand	—	—	—	—	—	—	—	—	—
Norway	—	0.0	0.0	0.2	—	0.0	0.0	0.2	—
Sweden	—	0.2	2.0	6.6	-0.3	-0.1	2.0	6.3	—
Switzerland	0.1	0.1	0.5	0.0	0.1	0.1	0.5	0.0	—
United Kingdom	0.0	0.0	0.0	0.0	0.0	0.0	0.0	0.0	—
United States	—	—	—	14.0	-3.0	-3.0	-3.0	11.0	—
TOTAL	*15.5*	*21.7*	*13.8*	*38.6*	*11.5*	*16.9*	*7.6*	*20.1*	*8.2*
MULTILATERAL	*41.4*	*80.6*	*56.1*	*78.5*	*21.9*	*55.9*	*26.9*	*45.1*	*39.5*
OPEC COUNTRIES	—	—	—	—	—	—	—	—	—
E.E.C.+ MEMBERS	*13.8*	*19.3*	*9.3*	*16.5*	*13.3*	*18.1*	*6.8*	*13.6*	*8.2*
TOTAL	**56.9**	**102.4**	**69.9**	**117.1**	**33.5**	**72.8**	**34.6**	**65.1**	**47.7**

URUGUAY

ODA COMMITMENTS

1984	1985	1986	1983	1984	1985	1986
–	–	–	–	–	–	–
0.0	0.0	0.0	0.0	0.0	0.0	–
0.1	0.1	0.3	–	–	–	0.3
0.3	0.3	0.3	0.3	0.5	0.1	0.4
–	–	–	–	–	–	–
–	0.0	0.0	–	–	–	0.0
1.2	1.7	6.1	1.5	8.9	1.1	6.1
2.4	3.0	4.0	3.3	3.2	2.8	9.8
–	–	–	–	–	–	–
0.4	0.5	0.7	0.2	0.4	0.6	0.8
1.8	1.7	1.5	1.1	2.4	1.7	1.7
0.7	1.0	0.8	0.5	0.7	1.1	0.6
–	–	–	–	–	–	–
0.0	0.0	0.2	–	–	0.0	0.2
0.2	–	0.4	–	0.4	1.5	0.4
0.1	0.5	0.0	0.1	0.1	0.5	0.0
0.0	0.0	0.0	0.0	0.0	0.0	0.0
–	–	14.0	–	–	–	14.4
7.2	8.9	28.3	7.2	16.5	9.3	34.8
–	–	–	–	–	–	–
–	–	–	–	–	–	–
–	–	–	–	–	–	–
–	0.1	0.5	0.0	0.1	0.5	0.5
–	–	–	–	–	–	–
1.2	0.3	1.5	–	37.3	7.0	–
–	–	–	–	–	–	–
–	–	–	–	–	–	–
–	–	–	1.8	1.7	1.9	2.4
0.9	1.2	1.5	–	–	–	–
0.5	0.5	0.4	–	–	–	–
–	–	–	–	–	–	–
–	–	0.1	–	–	–	–
0.3	0.3	0.3	–	–	–	–
–	–	–	–	–	–	–
2.8	2.3	4.3	1.8	39.1	9.4	2.9
–	–	–	–	–	–	–
4.8	6.4	12.4	5.6	13.3	6.0	18.2
10.1	11.1	32.6	9.0	55.5	18.7	37.6

TECH. COOP. GRANTS

1984	1985	1986	1983	1984	1985	1986
–	–	–	–	–	–	–
0.0	0.0	0.0	0.0	–	–	–
0.1	0.1	0.3	0.1	0.0	0.0	0.0
0.3	0.3	0.3	0.2	–	0.0	–
–	0.0	0.0	–	–	0.0	–
1.2	1.1	1.6	1.5	1.2	1.1	1.6
2.3	3.0	3.9	2.6	2.3	2.8	3.9
–	–	–	–	–	–	–
0.4	0.5	0.7	0.2	0.4	0.5	0.7
1.7	1.6	1.5	1.0	1.7	1.4	1.2
0.7	1.0	0.8	0.4	0.6	0.7	0.6
–	–	–	–	–	–	–
0.0	0.0	0.2	–	–	–	–
0.2	–	0.4	–	–	–	0.0
0.1	0.5	0.0	–	–	0.0	0.0
0.0	0.0	0.0	0.0	0.0	0.0	0.0
–	–	14.0	–	–	–	–
7.0	8.1	23.7	6.0	6.2	6.6	8.2
2.8	2.0	3.6	1.8	1.7	1.9	2.4
–	–	–	–	–	–	–
4.7	5.8	7.8	4.8	4.5	5.1	6.9
9.9	10.1	27.3	7.8	7.9	8.5	10.5

TOTAL OOF NET

1984	1985	1986	1983	1984	1985	1986
–	–	–	–	–	–	–
–	–	–	–	–	–	–
0.0	0.0	–	–	0.0	0.0	–
–	–	–	-0.1	-0.3	-0.6	-12.4
–	–	1.6	1.0	–	–	1.6
–	–	–	–	–	–	–
–	–	–	–	–	–	–
–	–	–	–	–	–	–
14.5	2.9	2.5	7.0	13.2	0.4	-0.3
–	–	–	–	–	–	–
–	–	–	–	–	–	–
–	2.0	6.2	-0.3	-0.2	2.0	5.9
–	–	–	–	–	–	–
–	–	–	–	–	–	–
14.5	4.9	10.3	7.6	12.7	1.8	-5.2
77.8	53.8	74.2	23.2	56.2	27.9	43.6
–	–	–	–	–	–	–
14.5	2.9	4.1	8.0	13.2	0.5	1.3
92.3	58.7	84.5	30.8	68.9	29.7	38.5

ODA COMMITMENTS : LOANS

DAC COUNTRIES

	1983	1984	1985	1986
Australia	–	–	–	–
Austria	–	–	–	–
Belgium	–	–	–	–
Canada	–	–	–	–
Denmark	–	–	–	–
Finland	–	–	–	–
France	–	7.7	–	4.5
Germany, Fed. Rep.	–	–	–	–
Ireland	–	–	–	–
Italy	–	–	–	–
Japan	–	0.4	–	–
Netherlands	–	–	–	–
New Zealand	–	–	–	–
Norway	–	–	–	–
Sweden	–	–	–	–
Switzerland	–	–	–	–
United Kingdom	–	–	–	–
United States	–	–	–	–
TOTAL	–	8.1	–	4.5
MULTILATERAL	–	37.3	7.0	–
OPEC COUNTRIES	–	–	–	–
E.E.C.+ MEMBERS	–	7.7	–	4.5
TOTAL	–	45.4	7.0	4.5

GRANT ELEMENT OF ODA

DAC COUNTRIES

	1983	1984	1985	1986
Australia	–	–	–	–
Austria	100.0	100.0	100.0	–
Belgium	–	–	–	100.0
Canada	100.0	100.0	100.0	100.0
Denmark	–	–	–	–
Finland	–	–	–	100.0
France	100.0	73.0	100.0	100.0
Germany, Fed. Rep.	100.0	100.0	100.0	100.0
Ireland	–	–	–	–
Italy	100.0	100.0	100.0	100.0
Japan	100.0	88.3	100.0	100.0
Netherlands	100.0	100.0	100.0	100.0
New Zealand	–	–	–	–
Norway	–	–	100.0	100.0
Sweden	–	100.0	100.0	100.0
Switzerland	100.0	100.0	100.0	100.0
United Kingdom	100.0	100.0	100.0	100.0
United States	–	–	–	100.0
TOTAL	100.0	83.7	100.0	100.0
MULTILATERAL	100.0	66.3	100.0	100.0
OPEC COUNTRIES	–	–	–	–
E.E.C.+ MEMBERS	100.0	81.9	100.0	100.0
TOTAL	100.0	71.5	100.0	100.0

OTHER AGGREGATES

COMMITMENTS: ALL SOURCES

	1983	1984	1985	1986
TOTAL BILATERAL	7.2	16.5	12.9	40.7
of which				
OPEC	–	–	–	–
CMEA	–	–	–	–
TOTAL MULTILATERAL	98.2	180.9	76.8	96.4
TOTAL BIL.& MULTIL.	105.4	197.3	89.7	137.0
of which				
ODA Grants	9.0	10.1	11.7	33.1
ODA Loans	–	45.4	7.0	4.5

DISBURSEMENTS:

DAC COUNTRIES COMBINED

	1983	1984	1985	1986
OFFICIAL & PRIVATE				
GROSS:				
Contractual Lending	21.1	22.2	19.1	8.0
Export Credits Total	19.4	22.0	18.4	1.8
Export Credits Private	12.2	7.6	13.5	-6.9
NET:				
Contractual Lending	-6.1	-1.6	-7.4	-16.6
Export Credits Total	-4.5	1.2	-5.0	-19.8
PRIVATE SECTOR NET	372.1	200.4	-158.3	-4.1
Direct Investment	17.4	0.1	0.5	-2.2
Portfolio Investment	365.9	211.9	-152.0	11.0
Export Credits	-11.1	-11.5	-6.8	-13.0

MARKET BORROWING:

CHANGE IN CLAIMS

	1983	1984	1985	1986
Banks	–	108.0	-96.0	84.0

MEMORANDUM ITEM:

	1983	1984	1985	1986
CMEA Countr.(Gross)	–	–	–	–

DISBURSEMENTS, UNLESS OTHERWISE STATED

TOTAL RECEIPTS NET

DAC COUNTRIES	1983	1984	1985	1986
Australia	4.5	5.2	4.2	5.3
Austria	–	–	–	–
Belgium	–	–	–	0.3
Canada	0.3	0.1	0.1	0.1
Denmark	–	–	1.1	–
Finland	–	–	–	–
France	16.4	25.7	20.6	-42.2
Germany, Fed. Rep.	0.0	0.1	0.2	-0.2
Ireland	–	–	–	–
Italy	–	–	–	–
Japan	0.6	0.5	0.3	-4.0
Netherlands	–	0.1	–	–
New Zealand	0.8	0.9	1.0	1.0
Norway	–	–	–	–
Sweden	–	–	–	–
Switzerland	–	–	–	–
United Kingdom	9.6	10.6	8.0	7.4
United States	..			
TOTAL	32.1	43.0	35.6	-32.3
MULTILATERAL				
AF.D.F.	–	–	–	–
AF.D.B.	–	–	–	–
AS.D.B	0.4	0.5	0.6	0.7
CAR.D.B.	–	–	–	–
E.E.C.	1.0	0.7	1.1	1.6
IBRD	–	–	–	–
IDA	–	0.1	0.1	0.3
I.D.B.	–	–	–	–
IFAD	–	–	–	–
I.F.C.	–	–	–	–
IMF TRUST FUND	–	–	–	–
U.N. AGENCIES	–	–	–	–
UNDP	0.5	0.3	0.2	0.3
UNTA	0.4	0.5	0.6	0.5
UNICEF	–	–	–	–
UNRWA	–	–	–	–
WFP	–	–	–	–
UNHCR	–	–	–	–
Other Multilateral	0.3	0.2	0.2	0.3
Arab OPEC Agencies	–	–	–	–
TOTAL	2.5	2.3	2.9	3.6
OPEC COUNTRIES	1.0	–	–	–
E.E.C.+ MEMBERS	27.0	37.1	30.0	-33.2
TOTAL	35.6	45.3	38.5	-28.7

TOTAL ODA NET

DAC COUNTRIES	1983	1984	1985	1986
Australia	5.9	3.6	4.4	5.3
Austria	–	–	–	–
Belgium	–	–	–	–
Canada	0.3	0.1	0.1	0.1
Denmark	–	–	–	–
Finland	–	–	0.1	–
France	8.2	7.9	5.9	6.9
Germany, Fed. Rep.	0.0	0.0	0.0	–
Ireland	–	–	–	–
Italy	–	–	–	–
Japan	0.3	0.1	0.8	1.1
Netherlands	–	0.1	–	–
New Zealand	0.8	0.9	1.0	1.0
Norway	–	–	–	–
Sweden	–	–	–	–
Switzerland	–	–	–	–
United Kingdom	8.9	9.5	6.6	6.3
United States	–	–	–	–
TOTAL	24.4	22.2	18.9	20.8
MULTILATERAL				
AF.D.F.	–	–	–	–
AF.D.B.	–	–	–	–
AS.D.B	0.4	0.5	0.6	0.7
CAR.D.B.	–	–	–	–
E.E.C.	1.0	0.7	1.1	1.6
IBRD	–	–	–	–
IDA	–	0.1	0.1	0.3
I.D.B.	–	–	–	–
IFAD	–	–	–	–
I.F.C.	–	–	–	–
IMF TRUST FUND	–	–	–	–
U.N. AGENCIES	–	–	–	–
UNDP	0.5	0.3	0.2	0.3
UNTA	0.4	0.5	0.6	0.5
UNICEF	–	–	–	–
UNRWA	–	–	–	–
WFP	–	–	–	–
UNHCR	–	–	–	–
Other Multilateral	0.3	0.2	0.2	0.3
Arab OPEC Agencies	–	–	–	–
TOTAL	2.5	2.3	2.9	3.6
OPEC COUNTRIES	–	–	–	–
E.E.C.+ MEMBERS	18.1	18.3	13.6	14.8
TOTAL	26.9	24.5	21.8	24.4

TOTAL ODA GROSS

	1983
Australia	5.9
Austria	–
Belgium	–
Canada	0.3
Denmark	–
Finland	–
France	8.6
Germany, Fed. Rep.	0.0
Ireland	–
Italy	–
Japan	0.3
Netherlands	–
New Zealand	0.8
Norway	–
Sweden	–
Switzerland	–
United Kingdom	8.9
United States	–
TOTAL	24.8
AF.D.F.	–
AF.D.B.	–
AS.D.B	0.4
CAR.D.B.	–
E.E.C.	1.0
IBRD	–
IDA	–
I.D.B.	–
IFAD	–
I.F.C.	–
IMF TRUST FUND	–
U.N. AGENCIES	–
UNDP	0.5
UNTA	0.4
UNICEF	–
UNRWA	–
WFP	–
UNHCR	–
Other Multilateral	0.3
Arab OPEC Agencies	–
TOTAL	2.5
OPEC COUNTRIES	–
E.E.C.+ MEMBERS	18.5
TOTAL	27.4

ODA LOANS GROSS

DAC COUNTRIES	1983	1984	1985	1986
Australia	–	–	–	–
Austria	–	–	–	–
Belgium	–	–	–	–
Canada	–	–	–	–
Denmark	–	–	–	–
Finland	–	–	–	–
France	0.0	0.5	0.5	0.5
Germany, Fed. Rep.	–	–	–	–
Ireland	–	–	–	–
Italy	–	–	–	–
Japan	–	–	–	–
Netherlands	–	–	–	–
New Zealand	–	–	–	–
Norway	–	–	–	–
Sweden	–	–	–	–
Switzerland	–	–	–	–
United Kingdom	–	–	–	–
United States	–	–	–	–
TOTAL	0.0	0.5	0.5	0.5
MULTILATERAL	0.2	0.6	0.6	0.6
OPEC COUNTRIES	–	–	–	–
E.E.C.+ MEMBERS	0.2	0.7	0.6	0.6
TOTAL	0.2	1.1	1.1	1.1

ODA LOANS NET

DAC COUNTRIES	1983	1984	1985	1986
Australia	–	–	–	–
Austria	–	–	–	–
Belgium	–	–	–	–
Canada	–	–	–	–
Denmark	–	–	–	–
Finland	–	–	–	–
France	-0.5	0.3	0.1	–
Germany, Fed. Rep.	–	–	–	–
Ireland	–	–	–	–
Italy	–	–	–	–
Japan	–	–	–	–
Netherlands	–	–	–	–
New Zealand	–	–	–	–
Norway	–	–	–	–
Sweden	–	–	–	–
Switzerland	–	–	–	–
United Kingdom	0.0	0.0	0.0	0.0
United States	–	–	–	–
TOTAL	-0.5	0.3	0.1	0.0
MULTILATERAL	0.2	0.6	0.6	0.6
OPEC COUNTRIES	–	–	–	–
E.E.C.+ MEMBERS	-0.3	0.5	0.2	0.1
TOTAL	-0.3	0.9	0.7	0.6

GRANTS

	1983
Australia	5.9
Austria	–
Belgium	–
Canada	0.3
Denmark	–
Finland	–
France	8.6
Germany, Fed. Rep.	0.0
Ireland	–
Italy	–
Japan	0.3
Netherlands	–
New Zealand	0.8
Norway	–
Sweden	–
Switzerland	–
United Kingdom	8.9
United States	–
TOTAL	24.8
MULTILATERAL	2.4
OPEC COUNTRIES	–
E.E.C.+ MEMBERS	18.4
TOTAL	27.2

TOTAL OFFICIAL GROSS

DAC COUNTRIES	1983	1984	1985	1986
Australia	5.9	3.6	4.4	5.3
Austria	–	–	–	–
Belgium	–	–	–	–
Canada	0.3	0.1	0.1	0.1
Denmark	–	–	–	–
Finland	–	–	0.1	–
France	8.6	8.1	6.2	7.4
Germany, Fed. Rep.	0.0	0.0	0.0	–
Ireland	–	–	–	–
Italy	–	–	–	–
Japan	0.3	0.1	0.8	1.1
Netherlands	–	0.1	–	–
New Zealand	0.8	0.9	1.0	1.0
Norway	–	–	–	–
Sweden	–	–	–	–
Switzerland	–	–	–	–
United Kingdom	8.9	10.8	7.8	8.0
United States	–	–	–	–
TOTAL	24.8	23.6	20.4	23.0
MULTILATERAL	2.5	2.3	2.9	3.6
OPEC COUNTRIES	1.0	–	–	–
E.E.C.+ MEMBERS	18.5	19.7	15.1	17.0
TOTAL	28.4	25.9	23.3	26.6

TOTAL OFFICIAL NET

DAC COUNTRIES	1983	1984	1985	1986
Australia	5.9	3.6	4.4	5.3
Austria	–	–	–	–
Belgium	–	–	–	–
Canada	0.3	0.1	0.1	0.1
Denmark	–	–	–	–
Finland	–	–	0.1	–
France	8.2	7.8	5.7	-30.5
Germany, Fed. Rep.	0.0	0.0	0.0	–
Ireland	–	–	–	–
Italy	–	–	–	–
Japan	0.3	0.1	0.8	1.1
Netherlands	–	0.1	–	–
New Zealand	0.8	0.9	1.0	1.0
Norway	–	–	–	–
Sweden	–	–	–	–
Switzerland	–	–	–	–
United Kingdom	8.9	10.8	7.7	7.6
United States	–	–	–	–
TOTAL	24.4	23.3	19.9	-15.4
MULTILATERAL	2.5	2.3	2.9	3.6
OPEC COUNTRIES	1.0	–	–	–
E.E.C.+ MEMBERS	18.1	19.4	14.6	-21.3
TOTAL	27.9	25.6	22.8	-11.7

TOTAL OOF GROSS

	1983
Australia	–
Austria	–
Belgium	–
Canada	–
Denmark	–
Finland	–
France	–
Germany, Fed. Rep.	–
Ireland	–
Italy	–
Japan	–
Netherlands	–
New Zealand	–
Norway	–
Sweden	–
Switzerland	–
United Kingdom	–
United States	–
TOTAL	–
MULTILATERAL	–
OPEC COUNTRIES	1.0
E.E.C.+ MEMBERS	–
TOTAL	1.0

ODA COMMITMENTS

1984	1985	1986	1983	1984	1985	1986
3.6	4.4	5.3	5.6	5.9	5.3	3.3
–	–	–	–	–	–	–
0.1	0.1	0.1	0.2	0.2	0.3	0.1
–	0.1	–	–	–	0.0	–
8.1	6.2	7.4	11.5	7.7	8.8	7.4
0.0	0.0	0.0	0.0	0.0	0.0	–
–	–	–	–	–	–	–
0.1	0.8	1.1	0.1	0.1	1.4	2.6
0.1	–	–	–	0.1	–	–
0.9	1.0	1.0	0.7	0.7	1.2	0.6
–	–	–	–	–	–	–
–	–	–	–	–	–	–
9.6	6.6	6.3	7.0	7.1	4.3	5.0
22.4	19.2	21.3	25.0	21.7	21.2	19.0
–	–	–	–	–	–	–
0.5	0.6	0.7	1.1	–	3.2	–
–	–	–	–	–	–	–
0.7	1.1	1.6	1.5	0.1	3.6	–
0.1	0.1	0.3	2.0	–	–	2.0
–	–	–	–	–	–	–
–	–	–	–	–	–	–
–	–	–	1.1	1.0	1.0	1.1
0.3	0.2	0.3	–	–	–	–
0.5	0.6	0.5	–	–	–	–
–	–	–	–	–	–	–
0.2	0.2	0.3	–	–	–	–
–	–	–	–	–	–	–
2.3	2.9	3.6	5.7	1.0	7.8	3.1
18.5	13.9	15.3	20.0	14.9	16.6	12.4
24.7	22.1	24.9	30.7	22.7	29.0	22.1

TECH. COOP. GRANTS

1984	1985	1986	1983	1984	1985	1986
3.6	4.4	5.3	1.2	2.0	1.9	2.2
–	–	–	–	–	–	–
0.1	0.1	0.1	0.7	–	0.6	–
–	0.1	–	–	–	0.0	–
7.7	5.8	6.9	8.6	6.4	5.0	6.9
0.0	0.0	–	0.0	0.0	0.0	–
–	–	–	–	–	–	–
0.1	0.8	1.1	0.1	0.1	0.2	0.2
0.1	–	–	–	0.1	–	–
0.9	1.0	1.0	0.4	0.5	0.4	0.5
–	–	–	–	–	–	–
9.6	6.6	6.3	4.0	3.1	3.2	4.7
21.9	18.8	20.8	14.9	12.1	11.3	14.5
1.7	2.3	3.0	1.1	1.0	1.0	1.1
–	–	–	–	–	–	–
17.7	13.3	14.7	12.6	9.6	8.2	11.6
23.6	21.0	23.8	16.0	13.1	12.3	15.6

TOTAL OOF NET

1984	1985	1986	1983	1984	1985	1986
–	–	–	–	–	–	–
–	–	–	–	–	–	–
–	–	–	–	–	–	–
–	–	–	–	–	–	–
–	–	–	–	-0.1	-0.1	-37.4
–	–	–	–	–	–	–
–	–	–	–	–	–	–
–	–	–	–	–	–	–
–	–	–	–	–	–	–
–	–	–	–	–	–	–
1.2	1.2	1.7	–	1.2	1.2	1.3
–	–	–	–	–	–	–
1.2	1.2	1.7	–	1.1	1.0	-36.1
–	–	–	–	–	–	–
–	–	–	1.0	–	–	–
1.2	1.2	1.7	–	1.1	1.0	-36.1
1.2	1.2	1.7	1.0	1.1	1.0	-36.1

ODA COMMITMENTS : LOANS

	1983	1984	1985	1986
DAC COUNTRIES				
Australia	–	–	–	–
Austria	–	–	–	–
Belgium	–	–	–	–
Canada	–	–	–	–
Denmark	–	–	–	–
Finland	–	–	–	–
France	2.9	–	3.1	0.5
Germany, Fed. Rep.	–	–	–	–
Ireland	–	–	–	–
Italy	–	–	–	–
Japan	–	–	–	–
Netherlands	–	–	–	–
New Zealand	–	–	–	–
Norway	–	–	–	–
Sweden	–	–	–	–
Switzerland	–	–	–	–
United Kingdom	–	–	–	–
United States	–	–	–	–
TOTAL	*2.9*	*–*	*3.1*	*0.5*
MULTILATERAL	*3.1*	*–*	*4.7*	*2.0*
OPEC COUNTRIES	*–*	*–*	*–*	*–*
E.E.C.+ MEMBERS	*2.9*	*–*	*4.6*	*0.5*
TOTAL	*6.0*	*–*	*7.8*	*2.5*

GRANT ELEMENT OF ODA

	1983	1984	1985	1986
DAC COUNTRIES				
Australia	100.0	100.0	100.0	100.0
Austria	–	–	–	–
Belgium	–	–	–	–
Canada	100.0	100.0	100.0	100.0
Denmark	–	–	–	–
Finland	–	–	100.0	–
France	84.1	100.0	77.1	89.2
Germany, Fed. Rep.	100.0	100.0	100.0	–
Ireland	–	–	–	–
Italy	–	–	–	–
Japan	100.0	100.0	100.0	100.0
Netherlands	–	100.0	–	–
New Zealand	100.0	100.0	100.0	100.0
Norway	–	–	–	–
Sweden	–	–	–	–
Switzerland	–	–	–	–
United Kingdom	100.0	100.0	100.0	100.0
United States	–	–	–	–
TOTAL	*92.7*	*100.0*	*90.6*	*95.5*
MULTILATERAL	*89.8*	*100.0*	*89.2*	*89.1*
OPEC COUNTRIES	*–*	*–*	*–*	*–*
E.E.C.+ MEMBERS	*90.8*	*100.0*	*86.7*	*93.2*
TOTAL	*92.2*	*100.0*	*90.3*	*94.6*

OTHER AGGREGATES

COMMITMENTS: ALL SOURCES

	1983	1984	1985	1986
TOTAL BILATERAL	30.2	22.7	23.4	20.1
of which				
OPEC	–	–	–	–
CMEA	–	–	–	–
TOTAL MULTILATERAL	5.7	1.0	7.8	3.1
TOTAL BIL.& MULTIL.	35.8	23.7	31.2	23.2
of which				
ODA Grants	24.7	22.7	21.2	19.6
ODA Loans	6.0	–	7.8	2.5

DISBURSEMENTS:

DAC COUNTRIES COMBINED

	1983	1984	1985	1986
OFFICIAL & PRIVATE				
GROSS:				
Contractual Lending	10.0	25.6	33.8	-12.3
Export Credits Total	10.0	23.9	32.2	-14.4
Export Credits Private	10.0	23.9	32.2	-14.4
NET:				
Contractual Lending	9.0	19.5	19.2	-50.8
Export Credits Total	9.5	18.2	18.1	-14.7
PRIVATE SECTOR NET	7.7	19.7	15.8	-16.9
Direct Investment	-1.6	2.0	-1.1	-4.2
Portfolio Investment	-0.2	-0.4	-1.2	2.0
Export Credits	9.5	18.2	18.1	-14.7

MARKET BORROWING:

CHANGE IN CLAIMS

	1983	1984	1985	1986
Banks	–	–	–	–

MEMORANDUM ITEM:

	1983	1984	1985	1986
CMEA Countr.(Gross)	–	–	–	–

TOTAL RECEIPTS NET

DAC COUNTRIES	1983	1984	1985	1986
Australia	—	0.0	0.4	0.3
Austria	0.5	-3.3	-3.3	0.1
Belgium	1.4	18.7	9.8	-0.2
Canada	—	—	0.0	—
Denmark	-3.2	-1.5	-0.4	—
Finland	7.8	4.1	5.8	9.9
France	1.6	-6.7	-5.9	4.5
Germany, Fed. Rep.	-3.5	-0.1	2.2	7.3
Ireland	—	—	—	—
Italy	0.1	0.0	-3.2	-3.7
Japan	4.3	-4.2	-7.3	1.5
Netherlands	4.5	4.4	2.4	2.9
New Zealand	—	—	—	—
Norway	1.6	6.3	5.5	5.6
Sweden	30.5	63.0	37.5	64.0
Switzerland	0.4	0.3	-5.8	0.0
United Kingdom	-4.2	—	-0.1	-2.2
United States	..	—	1.0	1.0
TOTAL	*41.8*	*81.1*	*38.7*	*90.8*
MULTILATERAL				
AF.D.F.	—	—	—	—
AF.D.B.	—	—	—	—
AS.D.B	0.4	0.2	1.6	0.6
CAR.D.B.	—	—	—	—
E.E.C.	—	—	0.3	0.8
IBRD	—	—	—	—
IDA	3.0	6.2	7.3	5.2
I.D.B.	—	—	—	—
IFAD	—	—	—	—
I.F.C.	—	—	—	—
IMF TRUST FUND	—	—	—	—
U.N. AGENCIES	—	—	—	—
UNDP	10.8	10.0	11.9	15.2
UNTA	2.9	1.1	3.4	3.3
UNICEF	3.7	5.3	5.4	8.0
UNRWA	—	—	—	—
WFP	2.2	0.4	5.1	10.0
UNHCR	3.8	3.2	3.0	2.7
Other Multilateral	4.0	2.8	7.0	6.7
Arab OPEC Agencies	1.4	—	-0.6	—
TOTAL	*32.3*	*29.1*	*44.3*	*52.4*
OPEC COUNTRIES	*2.6*	*0.0*	*15.4*	*4.0*
E.E.C.+ MEMBERS	*-3.3*	*14.9*	*5.1*	*9.2*
TOTAL	**76.7**	**110.2**	**98.4**	**147.2**

TOTAL ODA NET

DAC COUNTRIES	1983	1984	1985	1986
Australia	—	0.0	0.4	0.3
Austria	0.5	0.3	0.2	0.1
Belgium	0.7	0.8	0.5	1.8
Canada	—	—	0.0	—
Denmark	0.3	1.4	1.0	—
Finland	7.8	4.1	5.8	9.9
France	4.0	4.0	2.8	3.9
Germany, Fed. Rep.	0.6	0.5	0.8	0.9
Ireland	—	—	—	—
Italy	0.1	0.0	0.0	0.0
Japan	0.7	1.1	0.6	5.7
Netherlands	4.5	4.4	2.4	1.7
New Zealand	—	—	—	—
Norway	1.6	0.9	0.4	0.8
Sweden	49.8	63.0	37.5	64.0
Switzerland	0.4	0.3	0.9	0.0
United Kingdom	0.0	—	—	—
United States	—	—	1.0	1.0
TOTAL	*70.9*	*80.7*	*54.2*	*90.0*
MULTILATERAL				
AF.D.F.	—	—	—	—
AF.D.B.	—	—	—	—
AS.D.B	0.5	0.3	1.7	0.6
CAR.D.B.	—	—	—	—
E.E.C.	—	—	0.3	0.8
IBRD	—	—	—	—
IDA	3.0	6.2	7.3	5.2
I.D.B.	—	—	—	—
IFAD	—	—	—	—
I.F.C.	—	—	—	—
IMF TRUST FUND	—	—	—	—
U.N. AGENCIES	—	—	—	—
UNDP	10.8	10.0	11.9	15.2
UNTA	2.9	1.1	3.4	3.3
UNICEF	3.7	5.3	5.4	8.0
UNRWA	—	—	—	—
WFP	2.2	0.4	5.1	10.0
UNHCR	3.8	3.2	3.0	2.7
Other Multilateral	4.0	2.8	7.0	6.7
Arab OPEC Agencies	1.4	—	-0.6	—
TOTAL	*32.4*	*29.2*	*44.4*	*52.5*
OPEC COUNTRIES	*2.6*	*0.0*	*15.4*	*4.0*
E.E.C.+ MEMBERS	*10.1*	*11.1*	*7.7*	*9.0*
TOTAL	**105.9**	**109.9**	**114.0**	**146.5**

TOTAL ODA GROSS

	1983
Australia	—
Austria	0.5
Belgium	0.7
Canada	—
Denmark	0.3
Finland	7.8
France	4.0
Germany, Fed. Rep.	0.6
Ireland	—
Italy	0.1
Japan	0.7
Netherlands	4.5
New Zealand	—
Norway	1.6
Sweden	49.8
Switzerland	0.4
United Kingdom	0.0
United States	—
TOTAL	*70.9*
AF.D.F.	—
AF.D.B.	—
AS.D.B	0.9
CAR.D.B.	—
E.E.C.	—
IBRD	—
IDA	3.0
I.D.B.	—
IFAD	—
I.F.C.	—
IMF TRUST FUND	—
U.N. AGENCIES	—
UNDP	10.8
UNTA	2.9
UNICEF	3.7
UNRWA	—
WFP	2.2
UNHCR	3.8
Other Multilateral	4.0
Arab OPEC Agencies	2.2
TOTAL	*33.6*
OPEC COUNTRIES	*2.6*
E.E.C.+ MEMBERS	*10.1*
TOTAL	**107.1**

ODA LOANS GROSS

DAC COUNTRIES	1983	1984	1985	1986
Australia	—	—	—	—
Austria	—	—	—	—
Belgium	—	—	—	—
Canada	—	—	—	—
Denmark	—	1.2	1.0	—
Finland	—	—	—	—
France	0.0	—	—	—
Germany, Fed. Rep.	—	—	—	—
Ireland	—	—	—	—
Italy	0.0	—	—	—
Japan	—	—	—	—
Netherlands	0.0	0.9	—	—
New Zealand	—	—	—	—
Norway	—	—	—	—
Sweden	—	—	—	—
Switzerland	—	—	—	—
United Kingdom	—	—	—	—
United States	—	—	1.0	1.0
TOTAL	*0.1*	*2.1*	*2.0*	*1.0*
MULTILATERAL	*6.1*	*7.0*	*9.7*	*6.0*
OPEC COUNTRIES	*2.6*	*0.0*	*15.8*	*4.0*
E.E.C.+ MEMBERS	*0.1*	*2.1*	*1.0*	*—*
TOTAL	**8.8**	**9.1**	**27.4**	**11.1**

ODA LOANS NET

DAC COUNTRIES	1983	1984	1985	1986
Australia	—	—	—	—
Austria	—	—	—	—
Belgium	—	—	—	—
Canada	—	—	—	—
Denmark	—	1.2	1.0	—
Finland	—	—	—	—
France	0.0	—	—	—
Germany, Fed. Rep.	—	—	—	—
Ireland	—	—	—	—
Italy	0.0	—	—	—
Japan	—	—	—	—
Netherlands	0.0	0.9	—	—
New Zealand	—	—	—	—
Norway	—	—	—	—
Sweden	—	—	—	—
Switzerland	—	—	—	—
United Kingdom	—	—	—	—
United States	—	—	1.0	1.0
TOTAL	*0.1*	*2.1*	*2.0*	*1.0*
MULTILATERAL	*4.9*	*6.5*	*8.4*	*5.9*
OPEC COUNTRIES	*2.6*	*0.0*	*15.4*	*4.0*
E.E.C.+ MEMBERS	*0.1*	*2.1*	*1.0*	*—*
TOTAL	**7.6**	**8.6**	**25.8**	**10.9**

GRANTS

	1983
Australia	—
Austria	0.5
Belgium	0.7
Canada	—
Denmark	0.3
Finland	7.8
France	4.0
Germany, Fed. Rep.	0.6
Ireland	—
Italy	0.0
Japan	0.7
Netherlands	4.5
New Zealand	—
Norway	1.6
Sweden	49.8
Switzerland	0.4
United Kingdom	0.0
United States	—
TOTAL	*70.9*
MULTILATERAL	*27.5*
OPEC COUNTRIES	*—*
E.E.C.+ MEMBERS	*10.1*
TOTAL	**98.3**

TOTAL OFFICIAL GROSS

DAC COUNTRIES	1983	1984	1985	1986
Australia	—	0.0	0.4	0.3
Austria	0.5	0.3	0.2	0.1
Belgium	0.7	0.9	1.3	1.8
Canada	—	—	0.0	—
Denmark	0.3	1.4	1.0	—
Finland	7.8	4.1	5.8	9.9
France	4.0	4.0	2.8	3.9
Germany, Fed. Rep.	1.0	0.8	1.2	1.4
Ireland	—	—	—	—
Italy	0.1	0.0	0.0	0.0
Japan	0.7	1.1	0.6	5.7
Netherlands	4.5	4.4	2.4	1.7
New Zealand	—	—	—	—
Norway	1.6	0.9	0.4	0.8
Sweden	49.8	63.0	37.5	64.0
Switzerland	0.4	0.3	0.9	0.0
United Kingdom	0.0	—	—	—
United States	—	—	1.0	1.0
TOTAL	*71.4*	*81.1*	*55.3*	*90.5*
MULTILATERAL	*33.6*	*29.8*	*45.7*	*52.7*
OPEC COUNTRIES	*2.6*	*0.0*	*15.8*	*4.0*
E.E.C.+ MEMBERS	*10.6*	*11.5*	*8.9*	*9.5*
TOTAL	**107.6**	**110.9**	**116.8**	**147.2**

TOTAL OFFICIAL NET

DAC COUNTRIES	1983	1984	1985	1986
Australia	—	0.0	0.4	0.3
Austria	0.5	0.3	0.2	0.1
Belgium	0.7	0.9	1.3	1.8
Canada	—	—	0.0	—
Denmark	0.3	1.4	1.0	—
Finland	7.8	4.1	5.8	9.9
France	4.0	4.0	2.8	3.9
Germany, Fed. Rep.	1.0	0.8	1.2	1.4
Ireland	—	—	—	—
Italy	0.1	0.0	0.0	0.0
Japan	0.7	1.1	0.6	5.7
Netherlands	4.5	4.4	2.4	1.7
New Zealand	—	—	—	—
Norway	1.6	0.9	0.4	0.8
Sweden	49.8	63.0	37.5	64.0
Switzerland	0.4	0.3	0.9	0.0
United Kingdom	0.0	—	—	—
United States	—	—	1.0	1.0
TOTAL	*71.4*	*81.1*	*55.3*	*90.5*
MULTILATERAL	*32.3*	*29.1*	*44.3*	*52.4*
OPEC COUNTRIES	*2.6*	*0.0*	*15.4*	*4.0*
E.E.C.+ MEMBERS	*10.6*	*11.5*	*8.9*	*9.5*
TOTAL	**106.3**	**110.2**	**115.0**	**146.9**

TOTAL OOF GROSS

	1983
Australia	—
Austria	—
Belgium	—
Canada	—
Denmark	—
Finland	—
France	—
Germany, Fed. Rep.	0.5
Ireland	—
Italy	—
Japan	—
Netherlands	—
New Zealand	—
Norway	—
Sweden	—
Switzerland	—
United Kingdom	—
United States	—
TOTAL	*0.5*
MULTILATERAL	*—*
OPEC COUNTRIES	*—*
E.E.C.+ MEMBERS	*0.5*
TOTAL	**0.5**

ODA COMMITMENTS

1984	1985	1986	1983	1984	1985	1986
0.0	0.4	0.3	0.6	0.0	0.4	0.1
0.3	0.2	0.1	0.5	0.3	0.2	–
0.8	0.5	1.8	–	–	–	1.8
–	0.0	–	–	–	0.0	–
1.4	1.0	–	–	–	–	–
4.1	5.8	9.9	7.1	1.2	20.8	5.2
4.0	2.8	3.9	3.8	4.0	3.0	3.9
0.5	0.8	0.9	0.6	0.5	0.8	0.9
–	–	–	–	–	–	–
0.0	0.0	0.0	0.0	0.0	0.0	0.1
1.1	0.6	5.7	13.2	1.2	0.5	7.8
4.4	2.4	1.7	1.4	2.0	1.5	1.3
–	–	–	–	–	–	–
0.9	0.4	0.8	–	1.3	0.1	0.1
63.0	37.5	64.0	50.7	44.5	35.8	64.0
0.3	0.9	0.0	0.4	0.3	0.9	–
–	–	–	0.0	–	–	–
–	1.0	1.0	0.5	0.5	0.7	0.7
80.7	*54.2*	*90.0*	*78.7*	*55.6*	*64.6*	*85.7*
–	–	–	–	–	–	–
0.8	2.4	0.8	–	–	–	–
–	–	–	–	–	–	–
–	0.3	0.8	–	–	0.9	0.9
–	–	–	–	–	–	–
6.2	7.3	5.2	–	–	–	–
–	–	–	–	–	–	–
–	–	–	–	–	–	–
–	–	–	27.5	22.8	35.7	45.9
10.0	11.9	15.2	–	–	–	–
1.1	3.4	3.3	–	–	–	–
5.3	5.4	8.0	–	–	–	–
–	–	–	–	–	–	–
0.4	5.1	10.0	–	–	–	–
3.2	3.0	2.7	–	–	–	–
2.8	7.0	6.7	–	–	–	–
–	–	–	–	–	–	–
29.8	*45.7*	*52.7*	*27.5*	*22.8*	*36.6*	*46.7*
0.0	*15.8*	*4.0*	–	*20.3*	–	–
11.1	*7.7*	*9.0*	*5.8*	*6.5*	*6.1*	*8.7*
110.5	**115.6**	**146.7**	**106.1**	**98.7**	**101.2**	**132.4**

TECH. COOP. GRANTS

1984	1985	1986	1983	1984	1985	1986
0.0	0.4	0.3	–	0.0	0.0	0.0
0.3	0.2	0.1	0.0	–	–	0.0
0.8	0.5	1.8	0.1	0.2	0.2	0.0
–	0.0	–	–	–	–	–
0.2	0.0	–	0.0	0.1	0.0	–
4.1	5.8	9.9	4.9	2.8	2.3	5.9
4.0	2.8	3.9	2.9	2.9	2.6	3.2
0.5	0.8	0.9	0.1	0.2	0.1	0.2
–	–	–	–	–	–	–
0.0	0.0	0.0	–	0.0	0.0	0.0
1.1	0.6	5.7	0.6	1.1	0.3	4.8
3.6	2.4	1.7	0.8	0.6	1.3	1.3
–	–	–	–	–	–	–
0.9	0.4	0.8	–	0.1	0.1	0.1
63.0	37.5	64.0	19.2	8.8	12.7	19.4
0.3	0.9	0.0	0.0	0.0	0.0	0.0
–	–	–	0.0	–	–	–
–	–	–	–	–	–	–
78.6	*52.2*	*89.0*	*28.7*	*16.7*	*19.5*	*34.9*
22.8	*36.0*	*46.6*	*25.3*	*22.4*	*30.7*	*35.9*
–	–	–	–	–	–	–
9.0	*6.7*	*9.0*	*4.0*	*3.9*	*4.2*	*4.6*
101.4	**88.2**	**135.6**	**54.0**	**39.0**	**50.2**	**70.7**

TOTAL OOF NET

1984	1985	1986	1983	1984	1985	1986
–	–	–	–	–	–	–
–	–	–	–	–	–	–
0.1	0.8	–	–	0.1	0.8	–
–	–	–	–	–	–	–
–	–	–	–	–	–	–
–	–	–	–	–	–	–
0.3	0.4	0.5	0.5	0.3	0.4	0.5
–	–	–	–	–	–	–
–	–	–	–	–	–	–
–	–	–	–	–	–	–
–	–	–	–	–	–	–
–	–	–	–	–	–	–
–	–	–	–	–	–	–
0.4	*1.2*	*0.5*	*0.5*	*0.4*	*1.2*	*0.5*
–	–	–	*-0.1*	*-0.1*	*-0.1*	*0.0*
–	–	–	–	–	–	–
0.4	*1.2*	*0.5*	*0.5*	*0.4*	*1.2*	*0.5*
0.4	**1.2**	**0.5**	**0.4**	**0.3**	**1.1**	**0.5**

ODA COMMITMENTS : LOANS

DAC COUNTRIES

	1983	1984	1985	1986
Australia	–	–	–	–
Austria	–	–	–	–
Belgium	–	–	–	–
Canada	–	–	–	–
Denmark	–	–	–	–
Finland	–	–	–	–
France	–	–	–	–
Germany, Fed. Rep.	–	–	–	–
Ireland	–	–	–	–
Italy	–	–	–	–
Japan	–	–	–	–
Netherlands	–	–	–	–
New Zealand	–	–	–	–
Norway	–	–	–	–
Sweden	–	–	–	–
Switzerland	–	–	–	–
United Kingdom	–	–	–	–
United States	0.5	0.5	0.7	0.7
TOTAL	*0.5*	*0.5*	*0.7*	*0.7*
MULTILATERAL	–	–	–	–
OPEC COUNTRIES	–	20.3	–	–
E.E.C.+ MEMBERS	–	–	–	–
TOTAL	**0.5**	**20.7**	**0.7**	**0.7**

GRANT ELEMENT OF ODA

DAC COUNTRIES

	1983	1984	1985	1986
Australia	100.0	100.0	100.0	100.0
Austria	100.0	100.0	100.0	–
Belgium	–	–	–	100.0
Canada	–	–	100.0	–
Denmark	–	–	–	–
Finland	100.0	100.0	100.0	100.0
France	100.0	100.0	100.0	100.0
Germany, Fed. Rep.	100.0	100.0	100.0	100.0
Ireland	–	–	–	–
Italy	100.0	100.0	100.0	100.0
Japan	100.0	100.0	100.0	100.0
Netherlands	100.0	100.0	100.0	100.0
New Zealand	–	–	–	–
Norway	–	100.0	100.0	100.0
Sweden	100.0	100.0	100.0	100.0
Switzerland	100.0	100.0	100.0	–
United Kingdom	100.0	–	–	–
United States	67.1	67.1	67.1	67.1
TOTAL	*99.8*	*99.7*	*99.6*	*99.7*
MULTILATERAL	*100.0*	*100.0*	*100.0*	*100.0*
OPEC COUNTRIES	–	43.5	–	–
E.E.C.+ MEMBERS	*100.0*	*100.0*	*100.0*	*100.0*
TOTAL	**99.9**	**88.2**	**99.8**	**99.8**

OTHER AGGREGATES

COMMITMENTS: ALL SOURCES

	1983	1984	1985	1986
TOTAL BILATERAL	1258.7	1253.9	1341.8	2200.1
of which				
OPEC	–	20.3	–	–
CMEA	1180.1	1178.0	1277.2	2114.4
TOTAL MULTILATERAL	27.5	22.8	36.6	46.7
TOTAL BIL.& MULTIL.	1286.2	1276.7	1378.4	2246.9
of which				
ODA Grants	155.8	128.9	250.7	283.1
ODA Loans	1130.5	1147.7	1127.7	1838.7

DISBURSEMENTS:

DAC COUNTRIES COMBINED

	1983	1984	1985	1986
OFFICIAL & PRIVATE				
GROSS:				
Contractual Lending	12.9	7.9	8.8	7.4
Export Credits Total	12.3	5.6	6.4	5.9
Export Credits Private	12.3	5.6	6.4	5.9
NET:				
Contractual Lending	-35.4	-14.8	-20.4	-4.8
Export Credits Total	-35.9	-17.2	-22.8	-6.4
PRIVATE SECTOR NET	-29.6	0.0	-16.6	0.3
Direct Investment	–	–	-0.1	0.0
Portfolio Investment	6.4	17.1	6.3	6.6
Export Credits	-35.9	-17.2	-22.8	-6.4

MARKET BORROWING:

CHANGE IN CLAIMS

	1983	1984	1985	1986
Banks	–	3.0	41.0	-21.0

MEMORANDUM ITEM:

	1983	1984	1985	1986
CMEA Countr.(Gross)	1180.1	1178.0	1277.2	1990.0

	1983	1984	1985	1986	1983	1984	1985	1986		1983
TOTAL RECEIPTS NET					**TOTAL ODA NET**				**TOTAL ODA GROSS**	
DAC COUNTRIES										
Australia	7.3	2.8	5.3	3.4	7.3	2.8	5.3	3.4	Australia	7.3
Austria	–	–	–	–	–	–	–	–	Austria	–
Belgium	0.2	–	0.7	-0.1	–	–	–	–	Belgium	–
Canada	0.2	–	0.7	-0.1	0.2	–	0.1	0.1	Canada	0.2
Denmark	0.1	0.1	–	–	0.1	0.1	–	–	Denmark	0.1
Finland	–	–	0.0	0.0	–	–	0.0	0.0	Finland	–
France	0.1	0.1	0.1	0.1	0.1	0.1	0.1	0.1	France	0.1
Germany, Fed. Rep.	5.3	0.8	0.8	1.8	0.9	1.1	0.8	1.9	Germany, Fed. Rep.	0.9
Ireland	–	–	–	–	–	–	–	–	Ireland	–
Italy	–	–	–	–	–	–	–	–	Italy	–
Japan	3.0	2.0	2.2	9.2	3.0	2.0	1.8	9.2	Japan	3.0
Netherlands	0.2	0.3	0.3	0.0	0.2	0.3	0.3	0.0	Netherlands	0.2
New Zealand	3.9	3.8	3.8	3.4	3.9	3.8	3.8	3.4	New Zealand	3.9
Norway	–	–	–	–	–	–	–	–	Norway	–
Sweden	–	–	–	–	–	–	–	–	Sweden	–
Switzerland	–	–	–	–	–	–	–	–	Switzerland	–
United Kingdom	0.0	-6.4	0.0	0.0	0.0	0.0	0.1	–	United Kingdom	0.0
United States	1.0	1.0	1.0	–	1.0	1.0	1.0	–	United States	1.0
TOTAL	*20.9*	*4.3*	*14.2*	*17.7*	*16.6*	*11.0*	*13.2*	*18.0*	*TOTAL*	*16.6*
MULTILATERAL										
AF.D.F.	–	–	–	–	–	–	–	–	AF.D.F.	–
AF.D.B.	–	–	–	–	–	–	–	–	AF.D.B.	–
AS.D.B	3.5	3.8	1.4	0.7	3.5	3.8	1.4	0.7	AS.D.B	3.9
CAR.D.B.	–	–	–	–	–	–	–	–	CAR.D.B.	–
E.E.C.	4.5	3.6	1.7	1.5	4.5	3.6	1.7	1.5	E.E.C.	4.5
IBRD	–	–	–	–	–	–	–	–	IBRD	–
IDA	0.6	0.5	0.6	0.8	0.6	0.5	0.6	0.8	IDA	0.6
I.D.B.	–	–	–	–	–	–	–	–	I.D.B.	–
IFAD	0.1	0.2	0.3	0.1	0.1	0.2	0.3	0.1	IFAD	0.1
I.F.C.	–	–	–	–	–	–	–	–	I.F.C.	–
IMF TRUST FUND	–	–	–	–	–	–	–	–	IMF TRUST FUND	–
U.N. AGENCIES	–	–	–	–	–	–	–	–	U.N. AGENCIES	–
UNDP	1.0	0.7	1.3	1.0	1.0	0.7	1.3	1.0	UNDP	1.0
UNTA	0.4	0.2	0.5	0.7	0.4	0.2	0.5	0.7	UNTA	0.4
UNICEF	–	–	–	–	–	–	–	–	UNICEF	–
UNRWA	–	–	–	–	–	–	–	–	UNRWA	–
WFP	–	–	0.0	–	–	–	0.0	–	WFP	–
UNHCR	–	–	–	–	–	–	–	–	UNHCR	–
Other Multilateral	0.3	0.2	0.2	0.1	0.3	0.2	0.2	0.1	Other Multilateral	0.3
Arab OPEC Agencies	-0.3	0.1	-0.1	-0.6	-0.3	0.1	-0.1	-0.6	Arab OPEC Agencies	–
TOTAL	*10.1*	*9.3*	*5.9*	*4.5*	*10.1*	*9.3*	*5.9*	*4.5*	*TOTAL*	*10.8*
OPEC COUNTRIES	–	–	*0.3*	*0.7*	–	–	*0.3*	*0.7*	*OPEC COUNTRIES*	–
E.E.C.+ MEMBERS	*10.0*	*-1.7*	*2.9*	*3.4*	*5.7*	*5.0*	*2.9*	*3.6*	*E.E.C.+ MEMBERS*	*5.7*
TOTAL	*31.1*	*13.6*	*20.4*	*22.9*	*26.7*	*20.2*	*19.4*	*23.3*	*TOTAL*	*27.4*
ODA LOANS GROSS					**ODA LOANS NET**				**GRANTS**	
DAC COUNTRIES										
Australia	–	–	–	–	–	–	–	–	Australia	7.3
Austria	–	–	–	–	–	–	–	–	Austria	–
Belgium	–	–	–	–	–	–	–	–	Belgium	–
Canada	–	–	–	–	–	–	–	–	Canada	0.2
Denmark	–	–	–	–	–	–	–	–	Denmark	0.1
Finland	–	–	–	–	–	–	–	–	Finland	–
France	–	–	–	–	–	–	–	–	France	0.1
Germany, Fed. Rep.	–	–	–	0.3	–	–	–	0.3	Germany, Fed. Rep.	0.9
Ireland	–	–	–	–	–	–	–	–	Ireland	–
Italy	–	–	–	–	–	–	–	–	Italy	–
Japan	–	–	–	–	–	–	–	–	Japan	3.0
Netherlands	–	–	–	–	–	–	–	–	Netherlands	0.2
New Zealand	–	–	–	–	–	–	–	–	New Zealand	3.9
Norway	–	–	–	–	–	–	–	–	Norway	–
Sweden	–	–	–	–	–	–	–	–	Sweden	–
Switzerland	–	–	–	–	–	–	–	–	Switzerland	–
United Kingdom	–	–	–	–	0.0	0.0	0.0	0.0	United Kingdom	0.0
United States	–	–	–	–	–	–	–	–	United States	1.0
TOTAL	–	–	–	*0.3*	*0.0*	*0.0*	*0.0*	*0.2*	*TOTAL*	*16.6*
MULTILATERAL	*5.6*	*5.7*	*2.2*	*1.6*	*4.9*	*5.3*	*1.7*	*0.5*	*MULTILATERAL*	*5.2*
OPEC COUNTRIES	–	–	–	*0.6*	–	–	–	*0.6*	*OPEC COUNTRIES*	–
E.E.C.+ MEMBERS	*1.2*	*1.6*	*0.1*	*0.3*	*1.1*	*1.6*	*0.1*	*0.2*	*E.E.C.+ MEMBERS*	*4.6*
TOTAL	*5.6*	*5.7*	*2.2*	*2.5*	*4.9*	*5.3*	*1.7*	*1.4*	*TOTAL*	*21.9*
TOTAL OFFICIAL GROSS					**TOTAL OFFICIAL NET**				**TOTAL OOF GROSS**	
DAC COUNTRIES										
Australia	7.3	2.8	5.3	3.4	7.3	2.8	5.3	3.4	Australia	–
Austria	–	–	–	–	–	–	–	–	Austria	–
Belgium	–	–	–	–	–	–	–	–	Belgium	–
Canada	0.2	–	0.7	0.1	0.2	–	0.7	-0.1	Canada	–
Denmark	0.1	0.1	–	–	0.1	0.1	–	–	Denmark	–
Finland	–	–	0.0	0.0	–	–	0.0	0.0	Finland	–
France	0.1	0.1	0.1	0.1	0.1	0.1	0.1	0.1	France	–
Germany, Fed. Rep.	0.9	1.2	1.0	2.0	0.7	0.9	0.8	1.7	Germany, Fed. Rep.	–
Ireland	–	–	–	–	–	–	–	–	Ireland	–
Italy	–	–	–	–	–	–	–	–	Italy	–
Japan	3.0	2.0	1.8	9.2	3.0	2.0	1.8	9.2	Japan	–
Netherlands	0.2	0.3	0.3	0.0	0.2	0.3	0.3	0.0	Netherlands	–
New Zealand	3.9	3.8	3.8	3.4	3.9	3.8	3.8	3.4	New Zealand	–
Norway	–	–	–	–	–	–	–	–	Norway	–
Sweden	–	–	–	–	–	–	–	–	Sweden	–
Switzerland	–	–	–	–	–	–	–	–	Switzerland	–
United Kingdom	0.0	0.0	0.1	0.0	0.0	0.0	0.1	–	United Kingdom	–
United States	1.0	1.0	1.0	–	1.0	1.0	1.0	–	United States	–
TOTAL	*16.6*	*11.1*	*14.1*	*18.2*	*16.4*	*10.8*	*13.8*	*17.6*	*TOTAL*	–
MULTILATERAL	*10.8*	*9.6*	*6.4*	*5.5*	*10.1*	*9.3*	*5.9*	*4.5*	*MULTILATERAL*	–
OPEC COUNTRIES	–	–	*0.3*	*0.7*	–	–	*0.3*	*0.7*	*OPEC COUNTRIES*	–
E.E.C.+ MEMBERS	*5.7*	*5.1*	*3.1*	*3.7*	*5.5*	*4.8*	*2.9*	*3.4*	*E.E.C.+ MEMBERS*	–
TOTAL	*27.4*	*20.7*	*20.8*	*24.5*	*26.5*	*20.0*	*20.0*	*22.9*	*TOTAL*	–

ODA COMMITMENTS

1984	1985	1986	1983	1984	1985	1986
2.8	5.3	3.4	3.3	6.0	3.8	2.8
–	–	–	–	–	–	–
–	0.1	0.1	0.2	0.1	0.1	0.1
0.1	–	–	–	–	–	–
–	0.0	0.0	–	–	–	–
0.1	0.1	0.1	0.1	0.1	0.1	0.1
1.1	0.8	1.9	1.7	3.7	0.1	1.3
–	–	–	–	–	–	–
–	–	–	–	–	–	–
2.0	1.8	9.2	4.2	0.9	7.3	5.4
0.3	0.3	0.0	0.2	0.2	0.1	0.0
3.8	3.8	3.4	2.2	3.5	7.9	2.1
–	–	–	–	–	–	–
–	–	–	–	–	–	–
–	–	–	–	–	–	–
0.0	0.1	0.0	0.0	0.0	0.1	0.0
1.0	1.0	–	0.6	0.6	2.1	0.6
11.0	*13.2*	*18.1*	*12.3*	*15.2*	*21.6*	*12.4*
–	–	–	–	–	–	–
4.1	1.8	1.1	1.6	4.0	5.0	5.4
–	–	–	–	–	–	–
3.5	1.7	1.5	2.1	0.8	0.2	2.9
–	–	–	–	–	–	–
0.5	0.6	0.8	–	–	2.0	2.5
–	–	–	–	–	–	–
0.2	0.3	0.1	–	–	–	–
–	–	–	–	–	–	–
–	–	–	1.7	1.1	2.0	1.9
0.7	1.3	1.0	–	–	–	–
0.2	0.5	0.7	–	–	–	–
–	–	–	–	–	–	–
–	0.0	–	–	–	–	–
–	–	–	–	–	–	–
0.2	0.2	0.1	–	–	–	–
0.1	–	–	–	1.0	–	–
9.6	*6.4*	*5.5*	*5.3*	*6.9*	*9.3*	*12.6*
–	0.3	0.7	0.5	4.1	–	4.3
5.0	*2.9*	*3.6*	*3.9*	*4.7*	*0.6*	*4.3*
20.6	*19.9*	*24.3*	*18.2*	*26.1*	*30.9*	*29.4*

TECH. COOP. GRANTS

1984	1985	1986	1983	1984	1985	1986
2.8	5.3	3.4	1.1	1.6	1.4	2.2
–	–	–	–	–	–	–
–	0.1	0.1	0.1	–	0.1	–
0.1	–	–	0.1	0.1	–	–
–	0.0	0.0	–	–	0.0	0.0
0.1	0.1	0.1	0.1	0.1	0.1	0.1
1.1	0.8	1.6	0.9	0.7	0.5	0.9
–	–	–	–	–	–	–
2.0	1.8	9.2	0.8	0.9	1.0	1.2
0.3	0.3	0.0	0.2	0.2	0.2	0.0
3.8	3.8	3.4	1.4	1.3	1.4	1.9
–	–	–	–	–	–	–
–	–	–	–	–	–	–
0.0	0.1	0.0	0.0	–	0.1	0.0
1.0	1.0	–	1.0	1.0	1.0	–
11.0	*13.2*	*17.8*	*5.6*	*5.7*	*5.6*	*6.3*
4.0	4.2	3.9	1.7	1.1	2.0	1.9
–	0.3	0.1	–	–	–	–
3.4	*2.8*	*3.3*	*1.2*	*0.9*	*0.8*	*1.0*
14.9	*17.8*	*21.9*	*7.3*	*6.9*	*7.6*	*8.2*

TOTAL OOF NET

1984	1985	1986	1983	1984	1985	1986
–	–	–	–	–	–	–
–	–	–	–	–	–	–
–	0.7	–	–	–	0.6	-0.2
–	–	–	–	–	–	–
0.1	0.2	0.2	-0.2	-0.2	–	-0.2
–	–	–	–	–	–	–
–	–	–	–	–	–	–
–	–	–	–	–	–	–
–	–	–	–	–	–	–
–	–	–	–	–	–	–
0.1	0.9	0.2	-0.2	-0.2	0.6	-0.4
–	–	–	–	–	–	–
–	–	–	–	–	–	–
0.1	0.2	0.2	-0.2	-0.2	–	-0.2
0.1	*0.9*	*0.2*	*-0.2*	*-0.2*	*0.6*	*-0.4*

ODA COMMITMENTS : LOANS

DAC COUNTRIES

	1983	1984	1985	1986
Australia	–	–	–	–
Austria	–	–	–	–
Belgium	–	–	–	–
Canada	–	–	–	–
Denmark	–	–	–	–
Finland	–	–	–	–
France	–	–	–	–
Germany, Fed. Rep.	–	–	–	–
Ireland	–	–	–	–
Italy	–	–	–	–
Japan	–	–	–	–
Netherlands	–	–	–	–
New Zealand	–	–	–	–
Norway	–	–	–	–
Sweden	–	–	–	–
Switzerland	–	–	–	–
United Kingdom	–	–	–	–
United States	–	–	–	–
TOTAL	–	–	–	–
MULTILATERAL	*1.6*	*5.0*	*7.0*	*7.9*
OPEC COUNTRIES	–	*4.1*	–	*4.3*
E.E.C.+ MEMBERS	–	–	–	–
TOTAL	*1.6*	*9.1*	*7.0*	*12.2*

GRANT ELEMENT OF ODA

DAC COUNTRIES

	1983	1984	1985	1986
Australia	100.0	100.0	100.0	100.0
Austria	–	–	–	–
Belgium	–	–	–	–
Canada	100.0	100.0	100.0	100.0
Denmark	–	–	–	–
Finland	–	–	–	–
France	100.0	100.0	100.0	100.0
Germany, Fed. Rep.	100.0	100.0	100.0	100.0
Ireland	–	–	–	–
Italy	–	–	–	–
Japan	100.0	100.0	100.0	100.0
Netherlands	100.0	100.0	100.0	100.0
New Zealand	100.0	100.0	100.0	100.0
Norway	–	–	–	–
Sweden	–	–	–	–
Switzerland	–	–	–	–
United Kingdom	100.0	100.0	100.0	100.0
United States	100.0	100.0	100.0	100.0
TOTAL	*100.0*	*100.0*	*100.0*	*100.0*
MULTILATERAL	*93.7*	*78.0*	*85.0*	*87.2*
OPEC COUNTRIES	*100.0*	*48.3*	–	*53.0*
E.E.C.+ MEMBERS	*100.0*	*100.0*	*100.0*	*100.0*
TOTAL	*98.1*	*86.2*	*95.7*	*87.6*

OTHER AGGREGATES

COMMITMENTS: ALL SOURCES

	1983	1984	1985	1986
TOTAL BILATERAL	12.9	20.4	21.6	16.7
of which				
OPEC	0.5	4.1	–	4.3
CMEA	–	–	–	–
TOTAL MULTILATERAL	5.3	6.9	9.3	12.6
TOTAL BIL.& MULTIL.	18.2	27.3	30.9	29.4
of which				
ODA Grants	16.6	17.1	23.8	17.2
ODA Loans	1.6	9.1	7.0	12.2

DISBURSEMENTS:

DAC COUNTRIES COMBINED

OFFICIAL & PRIVATE

	1983	1984	1985	1986
GROSS:				
Contractual Lending	0.4	0.5	0.9	0.4
Export Credits Total	0.4	0.5	0.9	0.2
Export Credits Private	0.4	0.4	–	–
NET:				
Contractual Lending	-0.5	-6.7	0.6	-0.2
Export Credits Total	-0.4	-6.6	0.6	-0.5
PRIVATE SECTOR NET	4.6	-6.4	0.4	0.1
Direct Investment	-0.1	0.0	0.4	-0.2
Portfolio Investment	4.9	0.0	0.0	0.3
Export Credits	-0.2	-6.4	-0.1	0.0

MARKET BORROWING:

CHANGE IN CLAIMS

	1983	1984	1985	1986
Banks	–	–	–	–

MEMORANDUM ITEM:

	1983	1984	1985	1986
CMEA Countr.(Gross)	–	–	–	–

TOTAL RECEIPTS NET

DAC COUNTRIES	1983	1984	1985	1986
Australia	0.1	–	0.0	22.8
Austria	0.0	0.0	0.0	0.0
Belgium	-2.7	-0.1	8.5	0.2
Canada	0.1	-1.5	-1.1	0.2
Denmark	0.9	2.8	-0.4	2.7
Finland	–	–	–	–
France	-3.3	-4.0	-1.9	9.3
Germany, Fed. Rep.	11.0	13.4	7.6	14.2
Ireland	0.0	–	–	–
Italy	143.8	8.0	-0.4	-17.1
Japan	2.5	4.9	5.9	8.0
Netherlands	11.0	13.4	12.2	23.9
New Zealand	–	–	–	–
Norway	0.2	0.0	–	–
Sweden	0.9	-0.1	0.2	-0.1
Switzerland	1.6	0.4	-0.4	–
United Kingdom	8.0	1.3	11.0	1.8
United States	34.0	27.0	35.0	35.0
TOTAL	208.1	65.4	76.0	100.8
MULTILATERAL				
AF.D.F.	–	–	–	–
AF.D.B.	–	–	–	–
AS.D.B	–	–	–	–
CAR.D.B.	–	–	–	–
E.E.C.	1.4	3.3	1.5	–
IBRD	–	–	–	–
IDA	27.9	25.7	30.0	26.6
I.D.B.	–	–	–	–
IFAD	3.8	6.5	7.0	5.6
I.F.C.	-0.9	-0.5	11.1	5.8
IMF TRUST FUND	–	–	–	–
U.N. AGENCIES	–	–	–	–
UNDP	7.4	5.1	4.5	4.1
UNTA	2.1	1.6	2.2	1.3
UNICEF	3.9	2.0	1.3	1.5
UNRWA	–	–	–	–
WFP	1.1	4.7	2.1	4.5
UNHCR	–	–	–	–
Other Multilateral	4.6	4.3	3.5	3.0
Arab OPEC Agencies	28.1	12.6	2.6	20.1
TOTAL	79.4	65.3	65.7	72.5
OPEC COUNTRIES	192.3	186.7	130.7	60.5
E.E.C.+ MEMBERS	170.2	38.0	38.0	35.0
TOTAL	479.7	317.4	272.4	233.7

TOTAL ODA NET

DAC COUNTRIES	1983	1984	1985	1986
Australia	0.1	–	0.0	–
Austria	0.0	0.0	0.0	0.0
Belgium	0.1	0.0	0.0	0.0
Canada	0.1	0.3	0.4	0.2
Denmark	1.1	0.2	0.1	3.0
Finland	–	–	–	–
France	1.8	1.4	2.1	4.0
Germany, Fed. Rep.	9.4	12.4	9.7	15.5
Ireland	0.0	–	–	–
Italy	7.5	8.0	4.4	9.5
Japan	8.7	9.9	10.5	15.8
Netherlands	11.0	13.4	12.8	22.7
New Zealand	–	–	–	–
Norway	0.2	0.0	–	–
Sweden	0.9	–	0.2	–
Switzerland	2.6	2.5	1.2	–
United Kingdom	5.7	4.2	4.0	5.5
United States	23.0	30.0	39.0	39.0
TOTAL	72.1	82.2	84.3	115.2
MULTILATERAL				
AF.D.F.	–	–	–	–
AF.D.B.	–	–	–	–
AS.D.B	–	–	–	–
CAR.D.B.	–	–	–	–
E.E.C.	1.4	3.3	1.5	–
IBRD	–	–	–	–
IDA	27.9	25.7	30.0	26.6
I.D.B.	–	–	–	–
IFAD	3.8	6.5	7.0	5.6
I.F.C.	–	–	–	–
IMF TRUST FUND	–	–	–	–
U.N. AGENCIES	–	–	–	–
UNDP	7.4	5.1	4.5	4.1
UNTA	2.1	1.6	2.2	1.3
UNICEF	3.9	2.0	1.3	1.5
UNRWA	–	–	–	–
WFP	1.1	4.7	2.1	4.5
UNHCR	–	–	–	–
Other Multilateral	4.6	4.3	3.5	3.0
Arab OPEC Agencies	11.4	3.1	8.3	11.2
TOTAL	63.5	56.3	60.3	57.8
OPEC COUNTRIES	192.3	186.7	130.7	60.5
E.E.C.+ MEMBERS	38.0	42.7	34.5	60.2
TOTAL	327.9	325.2	275.3	233.5

TOTAL ODA GROSS

	1983
Australia	0.1
Austria	0.0
Belgium	0.1
Canada	0.1
Denmark	1.1
Finland	–
France	1.9
Germany, Fed. Rep.	9.4
Ireland	0.0
Italy	7.5
Japan	8.7
Netherlands	29.0
New Zealand	–
Norway	0.2
Sweden	0.9
Switzerland	2.6
United Kingdom	5.7
United States	23.0
TOTAL	90.2
AF.D.F.	–
AF.D.B.	–
AS.D.B	–
CAR.D.B.	–
E.E.C.	1.4
IBRD	–
IDA	28.1
I.D.B.	–
IFAD	3.8
I.F.C.	–
IMF TRUST FUND	–
U.N. AGENCIES	–
UNDP	7.4
UNTA	2.1
UNICEF	3.9
UNRWA	–
WFP	1.1
UNHCR	–
Other Multilateral	4.6
Arab OPEC Agencies	16.4
TOTAL	68.8
OPEC COUNTRIES	198.6
E.E.C.+ MEMBERS	56.1
TOTAL	357.6

ODA LOANS GROSS

DAC COUNTRIES	1983	1984	1985	1986
Australia	–	–	–	–
Austria	–	–	–	–
Belgium	–	–	–	–
Canada	–	–	–	–
Denmark	1.1	0.2	0.0	–
Finland	–	–	–	–
France	–	–	–	0.6
Germany, Fed. Rep.	–	–	0.0	–
Ireland	–	–	–	–
Italy	7.4	5.9	4.4	6.0
Japan	3.2	2.2	1.8	3.1
Netherlands	0.9	0.6	–	1.3
New Zealand	–	–	–	–
Norway	–	–	–	–
Sweden	–	–	–	–
Switzerland	–	–	–	–
United Kingdom	–	–	–	–
United States	–	4.0	12.0	10.0
TOTAL	12.5	12.8	18.3	21.0
MULTILATERAL	48.3	41.1	53.4	49.9
OPEC COUNTRIES	33.7	18.5	45.0	33.2
E.E.C.+ MEMBERS	9.3	6.7	4.5	7.9
TOTAL	94.5	72.5	116.7	104.1

ODA LOANS NET

DAC COUNTRIES	1983	1984	1985	1986
Australia	–	–	–	–
Austria	–	–	–	–
Belgium	–	–	–	–
Canada	–	–	–	–
Denmark	1.1	0.2	0.0	–
Finland	–	–	–	–
France	-0.1	-0.2	–	0.5
Germany, Fed. Rep.	–	–	0.0	–
Ireland	–	–	–	–
Italy	7.4	5.9	4.1	4.8
Japan	3.2	2.2	1.8	3.1
Netherlands	-17.1	–	–	1.3
New Zealand	–	–	–	–
Norway	–	–	–	–
Sweden	–	–	–	–
Switzerland	–	–	–	–
United Kingdom	–	–	–	–
United States	–	4.0	12.0	9.0
TOTAL	-5.6	12.1	17.9	18.6
MULTILATERAL	43.1	35.2	45.0	42.5
OPEC COUNTRIES	27.3	0.2	22.2	11.4
E.E.C.+ MEMBERS	-8.8	5.9	4.2	6.5
TOTAL	64.8	47.5	85.1	72.5

GRANTS

	1983
Australia	0.1
Austria	0.0
Belgium	0.1
Canada	0.1
Denmark	–
Finland	–
France	1.9
Germany, Fed. Rep.	9.4
Ireland	0.0
Italy	0.2
Japan	5.5
Netherlands	28.2
New Zealand	–
Norway	0.2
Sweden	0.9
Switzerland	2.6
United Kingdom	5.7
United States	23.0
TOTAL	77.7
MULTILATERAL	20.4
OPEC COUNTRIES	164.9
E.E.C.+ MEMBERS	46.8
TOTAL	263.1

TOTAL OFFICIAL GROSS

DAC COUNTRIES	1983	1984	1985	1986
Australia	0.1	–	0.0	–
Austria	0.0	0.0	0.0	0.0
Belgium	0.1	0.0	0.1	0.2
Canada	0.1	0.3	0.4	0.2
Denmark	1.1	0.2	0.1	3.0
Finland	–	–	–	–
France	1.9	1.6	2.1	4.1
Germany, Fed. Rep.	9.4	12.4	9.7	15.5
Ireland	0.0	–	–	–
Italy	7.5	8.0	4.7	10.7
Japan	8.7	9.9	10.5	15.8
Netherlands	29.0	13.9	12.8	22.7
New Zealand	–	–	–	–
Norway	0.2	0.0	–	–
Sweden	0.9	–	0.2	–
Switzerland	2.6	2.5	1.2	–
United Kingdom	5.7	4.2	4.0	5.5
United States	34.0	31.0	39.0	40.0
TOTAL	101.2	84.0	84.7	117.7
MULTILATERAL	91.9	104.1	107.3	82.8
OPEC COUNTRIES	198.6	205.0	153.5	82.2
E.E.C.+ MEMBERS	56.1	43.5	34.9	61.7
TOTAL	391.7	393.0	345.5	282.7

TOTAL OFFICIAL NET

DAC COUNTRIES	1983	1984	1985	1986
Australia	0.1	–	0.0	–
Austria	0.0	0.0	0.0	0.0
Belgium	0.1	0.0	0.1	0.2
Canada	0.1	-1.5	-1.1	0.2
Denmark	1.1	0.2	0.1	3.0
Finland	–	–	–	–
France	1.8	1.4	2.1	4.0
Germany, Fed. Rep.	9.4	12.4	9.7	15.5
Ireland	0.0	–	–	–
Italy	7.5	8.0	4.4	9.5
Japan	8.7	9.9	10.5	15.8
Netherlands	11.0	13.4	12.8	22.7
New Zealand	–	–	–	–
Norway	0.2	0.0	–	–
Sweden	0.9	-0.1	0.2	-0.1
Switzerland	2.6	2.5	1.2	–
United Kingdom	5.7	4.2	4.0	5.5
United States	34.0	27.0	35.0	35.0
TOTAL	83.1	77.3	78.8	111.2
MULTILATERAL	79.4	65.3	65.7	72.5
OPEC COUNTRIES	192.3	186.7	130.7	60.5
E.E.C.+ MEMBERS	38.0	42.7	34.6	60.3
TOTAL	354.7	329.3	275.2	244.1

TOTAL OOF GROSS

	1983
Australia	–
Austria	–
Belgium	–
Canada	–
Denmark	–
Finland	–
France	–
Germany, Fed. Rep.	–
Ireland	–
Italy	–
Japan	–
Netherlands	–
New Zealand	–
Norway	–
Sweden	–
Switzerland	–
United Kingdom	–
United States	11.0
TOTAL	11.0
MULTILATERAL	23.1
OPEC COUNTRIES	–
E.E.C.+ MEMBERS	–
TOTAL	34.1

YEMEN

ODA COMMITMENTS

1984	1985	1986	1983	1984	1985	1986
–	0.0	–	0.1	–	–	–
0.0	0.0	0.0	0.0	0.0	0.0	–
0.0	0.0	0.0	–	–	–	0.0
0.3	0.4	0.2	0.2	0.3	0.4	0.4
0.2	0.1	3.0	–	–	–	–
–	–	–	–	–	–	0.1
1.6	2.1	4.1	1.4	1.6	1.4	4.1
12.4	9.7	15.5	12.6	12.0	9.0	29.7
–	–	–	0.0	–	–	–
8.0	4.7	10.7	8.2	4.6	0.3	7.6
9.9	10.5	15.8	5.4	0.7	10.0	5.5
13.9	12.8	22.7	35.2	10.6	14.1	22.1
0.0	–	–	–	0.0	0.9	–
–	0.2	–	0.8	–	–	–
2.5	1.2	–	1.3	2.7	1.2	–
4.2	4.0	5.5	5.7	4.2	4.0	5.5
30.0	39.0	40.0	22.3	39.7	38.8	42.1
83.0	*84.6*	*117.5*	*93.0*	*76.4*	*80.0*	*117.1*
–	–	–	–	–	–	–
–	–	–	–	–	–	–
3.3	1.5	–	5.0	–	4.6	0.2
–	–	–	–	–	–	–
26.2	30.6	27.5	42.0	43.0	35.4	43.7
–	–	–	–	–	–	–
6.5	8.2	5.7	–	3.8	0.2	–
–	–	–	–	–	–	–
–	–	–	19.0	17.7	13.5	14.4
5.1	4.5	4.1	–	–	–	–
1.6	2.2	1.3	–	–	–	–
2.0	1.3	1.5	–	–	–	–
–	–	–	–	–	–	–
4.7	2.1	4.5	–	–	–	–
–	–	–	–	–	–	–
4.3	3.5	3.0	–	–	–	–
8.6	15.0	17.6	39.8	33.6	40.3	25.6
62.2	*68.7*	*65.2*	*105.8*	*98.1*	*94.0*	*83.9*
205.0	*153.5*	*82.2*	*205.8*	*323.8*	*78.6*	*121.7*
43.5	*34.8*	*61.5*	*67.9*	*32.9*	*33.3*	*69.2*
350.2	*306.9*	*265.0*	*404.5*	*498.3*	*252.5*	*322.7*

TECH. COOP. GRANTS

1984	1985	1986	1983	1984	1985	1986
–	0.0	–	0.0	–	0.0	–
0.0	0.0	0.0	0.0	–	–	–
0.0	0.0	0.0	0.0	–	0.0	–
0.3	0.4	0.2	–	–	–	–
–	0.1	3.0	–	–	0.1	0.0
–	–	–	–	–	–	–
1.6	2.1	3.5	1.1	1.3	1.1	3.0
12.4	9.6	15.5	8.9	8.7	8.1	8.6
–	–	–	0.0	–	–	–
2.1	0.3	4.7	–	2.1	0.3	4.7
7.7	8.7	12.7	0.4	1.0	1.4	1.5
13.4	12.8	21.5	5.6	8.0	7.9	16.5
0.0	–	–	–	–	–	–
–	0.2	–	–	–	–	–
2.5	1.2	–	0.4	0.2	0.1	–
4.2	4.0	5.5	5.5	4.2	4.0	5.5
26.0	27.0	30.0	20.0	23.5	22.0	26.0
70.1	*66.4*	*96.6*	*41.9*	*48.5*	*44.9*	*65.8*
21.1	*15.3*	*15.3*	*18.0*	*13.0*	*11.5*	*9.9*
186.5	*108.5*	*49.1*	–	–	–	–
36.8	*30.4*	*53.6*	*21.1*	*24.3*	*21.4*	*38.3*
277.7	*190.2*	*160.9*	*59.9*	*61.5*	*56.4*	*75.7*

TOTAL OOF NET

1984	1985	1986	1983	1984	1985	1986
–	–	–	–	–	–	–
–	0.1	0.2	–	–	0.1	0.2
–	–	–	–	-1.8	-1.6	–
–	–	–	–	–	–	–
–	–	–	–	–	–	–
–	–	–	–	–	–	–
–	–	–	–	–	–	–
–	–	–	–	–	–	–
–	–	–	–	–	–	–
–	–	–	–	–	–	–
–	–	–	–	–	–	–
–	–	–	–	-0.1	–	-0.1
–	–	–	–	–	–	–
1.0	–	–	11.0	-3.0	-4.0	-4.0
1.0	*0.1*	*0.2*	*11.0*	*-4.9*	*-5.5*	*-4.0*
41.8	*38.5*	*17.5*	*15.9*	*9.0*	*5.4*	*14.6*
–	–	–	–	–	–	–
–	0.1	0.2	–	–	0.1	0.2
42.8	*38.6*	*17.7*	*26.9*	*4.1*	*-0.1*	*10.6*

ODA COMMITMENTS : LOANS

DAC COUNTRIES

	1983	1984	1985	1986
Australia	–	–	–	–
Austria	–	–	–	–
Belgium	–	–	–	–
Canada	–	–	–	–
Denmark	–	–	–	–
Finland	–	–	–	–
France	–	–	–	0.6
Germany, Fed. Rep.	–	–	–	–
Ireland	–	–	–	–
Italy	8.0	–	–	–
Japan	–	–	–	–
Netherlands	–	–	2.1	–
New Zealand	–	–	–	–
Norway	–	–	–	–
Sweden	–	–	–	–
Switzerland	–	–	–	–
United Kingdom	–	–	–	–
United States	–	3.0	12.0	10.0
TOTAL	*8.0*	*3.0*	*14.1*	*10.6*
MULTILATERAL	*79.8*	*80.3*	*74.8*	*68.7*
OPEC COUNTRIES	*22.3*	–	–	*44.6*
E.E.C.+ MEMBERS	*8.0*	–	*2.1*	*0.6*
TOTAL	*110.0*	*83.3*	*88.9*	*123.9*

GRANT ELEMENT OF ODA

DAC COUNTRIES

	1983	1984	1985	1986
Australia	100.0	–	–	–
Austria	100.0	100.0	100.0	–
Belgium	–	–	–	100.0
Canada	100.0	100.0	100.0	100.0
Denmark	–	–	–	–
Finland	–	–	–	100.0
France	100.0	100.0	100.0	100.0
Germany, Fed. Rep.	100.0	100.0	100.0	100.0
Ireland	100.0	–	–	–
Italy	56.2	100.0	100.0	100.0
Japan	100.0	100.0	100.0	100.0
Netherlands	100.0	100.0	94.1	100.0
New Zealand	–	–	–	–
Norway	–	100.0	100.0	–
Sweden	100.0	–	–	–
Switzerland	100.0	100.0	100.0	–
United Kingdom	100.0	100.0	100.0	100.0
United States	100.0	96.8	87.0	90.0
TOTAL	*96.1*	*98.3*	*92.7*	*96.4*
MULTILATERAL	*73.2*	*71.5*	*68.3*	*72.6*
OPEC COUNTRIES	*94.4*	*100.0*	*100.0*	*81.8*
E.E.C.+ MEMBERS	*94.7*	*100.0*	*97.5*	*100.0*
TOTAL	*88.9*	*94.3*	*86.8*	*84.7*

OTHER AGGREGATES

COMMITMENTS: ALL SOURCES

	1983	1984	1985	1986
TOTAL BILATERAL	311.0	400.2	179.5	238.6
of which				
OPEC	205.8	323.8	78.6	121.7
CMEA	–	–	21.0	–
TOTAL MULTILATERAL	147.3	147.6	145.2	86.6
TOTAL BIL.& MULTIL.	458.3	547.8	324.7	325.3
of which				
ODA Grants	294.5	415.0	163.7	198.8
ODA Loans	110.0	83.3	104.9	123.9

DISBURSEMENTS:

DAC COUNTRIES COMBINED

	1983	1984	1985	1986
OFFICIAL & PRIVATE				
GROSS:				
Contractual Lending	205.4	44.8	41.6	44.5
Export Credits Total	192.9	32.0	23.4	23.5
Export Credits Private	181.9	31.0	23.4	23.5
NET:				
Contractual Lending	147.5	-5.8	-7.0	-19.9
Export Credits Total	153.1	-17.9	-24.9	-38.5
PRIVATE SECTOR NET	125.0	-11.8	-2.8	-10.4
Direct Investment	15.8	0.1	2.1	4.2
Portfolio Investment	-32.8	1.0	14.5	19.9
Export Credits	142.1	-13.0	-19.4	-34.4

MARKET BORROWING:
CHANGE IN CLAIMS

	1983	1984	1985	1986
Banks	–	77.0	-57.0	155.0

MEMORANDUM ITEM:

	1983	1984	1985	1986
CMEA Countr.(Gross)	10.0	10.0	10.0	3.0

DISBURSEMENTS, UNLESS OTHERWISE STATED

	1983	1984	1985	1986	1983	1984	1985	1986		1983
TOTAL RECEIPTS NET					**TOTAL ODA NET**				**TOTAL ODA GROSS**	
DAC COUNTRIES										
Australia	0.2	-0.1	0.0	—	0.0	0.0	0.0	—	Australia	0.0
Austria	—	0.0	0.0	0.0	—	0.0	0.0	0.0	Austria	—
Belgium	—	0.1	0.0	-1.0	—	0.1	0.0	—	Belgium	—
Canada	-1.2	0.0	0.1	-1.4	0.4	0.0	0.1	0.0	Canada	0.4
Denmark	-0.7	0.1	3.9	0.0	0.1	0.1	3.9	0.0	Denmark	0.1
Finland	0.0	0.1	0.0	0.0	0.0	0.1	0.0	0.0	Finland	0.0
France	2.7	4.5	5.3	0.9	2.6	3.5	3.3	1.2	France	2.6
Germany, Fed. Rep.	0.1	0.2	-0.1	0.1	0.1	0.1	0.1	0.1	Germany, Fed. Rep.	0.1
Ireland	—	—	—	—	—	—	—	—	Ireland	—
Italy	1.7	-1.2	1.5	-4.0	1.7	0.0	1.5	0.0	Italy	1.7
Japan	-3.8	-4.3	0.7	-7.3	0.1	-0.1	-0.9	-1.5	Japan	0.7
Netherlands	0.4	—	0.3	0.0	0.4	—	0.3	0.0	Netherlands	0.4
New Zealand	—	—	—	—	—	—	—	—	New Zealand	—
Norway	—	—	0.9	—	—	—	0.9	—	Norway	—
Sweden	1.6	0.6	-1.0	-1.1	—	0.2	—	—	Sweden	—
Switzerland	0.9	0.1	0.0	0.3	0.0	0.1	0.0	0.3	Switzerland	0.0
United Kingdom	1.2	1.3	1.2	1.0	1.2	1.3	1.3	1.4	United Kingdom	1.2
United States	..				—	—	—	—	United States	—
TOTAL	*3.1*	*1.4*	*12.9*	*-12.4*	*6.6*	*5.3*	*10.5*	*1.6*	*TOTAL*	*7.2*
MULTILATERAL										
AF.D.F.	—	—	—	—	—	—	—	—	AF.D.F.	—
AF.D.B.	—	—	—	—	—	—	—	—	AF.D.B.	—
AS.D.B	—	—	—	—	—	—	—	—	AS.D.B	—
CAR.D.B.	—	—	—	—	—	—	—	—	CAR.D.B.	—
E.E.C.	—	—	—	—	—	—	—	—	E.E.C.	—
IBRD	—	—	—	—	—	—	—	—	IBRD	—
IDA	21.9	19.0	14.2	18.7	21.9	19.0	14.2	18.7	IDA	21.9
I.D.B.	—	—	—	—	—	—	—	—	I.D.B.	—
IFAD	4.8	2.5	3.4	2.8	4.8	2.5	3.4	2.8	IFAD	4.8
I.F.C.	—	—	—	—	—	—	—	—	I.F.C.	—
IMF TRUST FUND	—	—	—	—	—	—	—	—	IMF TRUST FUND	—
U.N. AGENCIES									U.N. AGENCIES	—
UNDP	5.6	3.6	3.6	2.0	5.6	3.6	3.6	2.0	UNDP	5.6
UNTA	2.1	1.3	2.4	1.1	2.1	1.3	2.4	1.1	UNTA	2.1
UNICEF	0.5	0.6	0.7	1.2	0.5	0.6	0.7	1.2	UNICEF	0.5
UNRWA	—	—	—	—	—	—	—	—	UNRWA	—
WFP	13.9	11.9	11.4	10.2	13.9	11.9	11.4	10.2	WFP	13.9
UNHCR	—	—	—	0.4	—	—	—	0.4	UNHCR	—
Other Multilateral	1.9	2.0	2.0	1.6	1.9	2.0	2.0	1.6	Other Multilateral	1.9
Arab OPEC Agencies	-3.8	12.1	24.6	7.2	16.7	12.1	19.0	9.0	Arab OPEC Agencies	19.8
TOTAL	*47.0*	*53.0*	*62.4*	*45.3*	*67.4*	*53.0*	*56.8*	*47.0*	*TOTAL*	*70.6*
OPEC COUNTRIES	*32.6*	*43.8*	*45.3*	*9.4*	*31.8*	*43.8*	*45.3*	*9.4*	*OPEC COUNTRIES*	*36.0*
E.E.C. + MEMBERS	*5.4*	*5.0*	*12.2*	*-3.0*	*6.0*	*5.1*	*10.4*	*2.7*	*E.E.C. + MEMBERS*	*6.0*
TOTAL	*82.6*	*98.2*	*120.5*	*42.3*	*105.7*	*102.1*	*112.5*	*58.0*	*TOTAL*	*113.7*
ODA LOANS GROSS					**ODA LOANS NET**				**GRANTS**	
DAC COUNTRIES										
Australia	—	—	—	—	—	—	—	—	Australia	0.0
Austria	—	—	—	—	—	—	—	—	Austria	—
Belgium	—	—	—	—	—	—	—	—	Belgium	—
Canada	—	—	—	—	—	—	—	—	Canada	0.4
Denmark	0.1	0.1	0.0	0.0	0.1	0.1	0.0	0.0	Denmark	0.0
Finland	—	—	—	—	—	—	—	—	Finland	0.0
France	1.4	2.5	2.6	—	1.4	2.5	2.6	—	France	1.2
Germany, Fed. Rep.	—	—	—	—	—	—	—	—	Germany, Fed. Rep.	0.1
Ireland	—	—	—	—	—	—	—	—	Ireland	—
Italy	—	—	—	—	—	—	—	—	Italy	1.7
Japan	0.5	—	—	—	-0.1	-0.9	-1.2	-1.6	Japan	0.2
Netherlands	—	—	—	—	—	—	—	—	Netherlands	0.4
New Zealand	—	—	—	—	—	—	—	—	New Zealand	—
Norway	—	—	—	—	—	—	—	—	Norway	—
Sweden	—	—	—	—	—	—	—	—	Sweden	—
Switzerland	—	—	—	—	—	—	—	—	Switzerland	0.0
United Kingdom	—	—	—	—	—	—	—	—	United Kingdom	1.2
United States	—	—	—	—	—	—	—	—	United States	—
TOTAL	*2.0*	*2.6*	*2.6*	*0.0*	*1.4*	*1.7*	*1.4*	*-1.6*	*TOTAL*	*5.2*
MULTILATERAL	*46.6*	*36.7*	*39.2*	*36.4*	*43.4*	*33.4*	*34.7*	*28.8*	*MULTILATERAL*	*24.0*
OPEC COUNTRIES	*22.7*	*29.7*	*4.4*	*2.8*	*18.5*	*22.6*	*-1.8*	*-3.5*	*OPEC COUNTRIES*	*13.3*
E.E.C. + MEMBERS	*1.4*	*2.6*	*2.6*	*0.0*	*1.4*	*2.6*	*2.6*	*0.0*	*E.E.C. + MEMBERS*	*4.5*
TOTAL	*71.2*	*68.9*	*46.3*	*39.2*	*63.2*	*57.7*	*34.3*	*23.7*	*TOTAL*	*42.5*
TOTAL OFFICIAL GROSS					**TOTAL OFFICIAL NET**				**TOTAL OOF GROSS**	
DAC COUNTRIES										
Australia	0.0	0.0	0.0	—	0.0	0.0	0.0	—	Australia	—
Austria	—	0.0	0.0	0.0	—	0.0	0.0	0.0	Austria	—
Belgium	—	0.1	0.0	—	—	0.1	0.0	—	Belgium	—
Canada	0.4	0.0	0.1	0.0	-1.2	0.0	0.1	-1.4	Canada	—
Denmark	0.1	0.1	3.9	0.0	0.1	0.1	3.9	0.0	Denmark	—
Finland	0.0	0.1	0.0	0.0	0.0	0.1	0.0	0.0	Finland	—
France	2.6	3.5	3.3	1.2	2.6	3.5	3.3	1.2	France	—
Germany, Fed. Rep.	0.1	0.1	0.1	0.1	0.1	0.1	0.1	0.1	Germany, Fed. Rep.	—
Ireland	—	—	—	—	—	—	—	—	Ireland	—
Italy	1.7	0.0	1.5	0.0	1.7	0.0	1.5	0.0	Italy	—
Japan	0.7	0.7	0.3	0.1	0.1	-0.1	-0.9	-1.5	Japan	—
Netherlands	0.4	—	0.3	0.0	0.4	—	0.3	0.0	Netherlands	—
New Zealand	—	—	—	—	—	—	—	—	New Zealand	—
Norway	—	—	0.9	—	—	—	0.9	—	Norway	—
Sweden	0.8	1.3	—	0.3	0.7	0.7	—	-0.6	Sweden	0.8
Switzerland	0.0	0.1	0.0	0.3	0.0	0.1	0.0	0.3	Switzerland	—
United Kingdom	1.2	1.3	1.3	1.4	1.2	1.3	1.3	1.4	United Kingdom	—
United States	—	—	—	—	—	—	—	—	United States	—
TOTAL	*8.0*	*7.3*	*11.7*	*3.2*	*5.6*	*5.8*	*10.5*	*-0.4*	*TOTAL*	*0.8*
MULTILATERAL	*78.1*	*56.3*	*66.9*	*60.4*	*47.0*	*53.0*	*62.4*	*45.3*	*MULTILATERAL*	*7.5*
OPEC COUNTRIES	*36.8*	*50.9*	*51.5*	*15.7*	*32.6*	*43.8*	*45.3*	*9.4*	*OPEC COUNTRIES*	*0.8*
E.E.C. + MEMBERS	*6.0*	*5.1*	*10.4*	*2.7*	*6.0*	*5.1*	*10.4*	*2.7*	*E.E.C. + MEMBERS*	*—*
TOTAL	*122.8*	*114.4*	*130.1*	*79.3*	*85.1*	*102.6*	*118.2*	*54.2*	*TOTAL*	*9.1*

YEMEN, DEM.

ODA COMMITMENTS

1984	1985	1986	1983	1984	1985	1986
0.0	0.0	–	0.0	0.0	–	–
0.0	0.0	0.0	–	–	0.0	–
0.1	0.0	–	–	–	–	–
0.0	0.1	0.0	0.4	0.2	0.1	0.1
0.1	3.9	0.0	–	–	16.5	–
0.1	0.0	0.0	–	0.2	–	–
3.5	3.3	1.2	1.2	9.0	0.6	1.2
0.1	0.1	0.1	0.1	0.1	0.1	0.1
–	–	–	–	–	–	–
0.0	1.5	0.0	4.1	3.7	4.0	0.0
0.7	0.3	0.1	0.2	8.6	4.3	0.1
–	0.3	0.0	0.6	–	0.2	0.0
–	–	–	–	–	–	–
–	0.9	–	–	–	–	–
0.2	–	–	0.2	0.2	–	–
0.1	0.0	0.3	0.0	0.1	0.0	0.3
1.3	1.3	1.4	1.2	1.3	1.3	1.4
–	–	–	–	–	–	–
6.2	*11.7*	*3.2*	*8.0*	*23.3*	*26.9*	*3.2*
–	–	–	–	–	–	–
–	–	–	–	–	–	–
–	–	–	–	–	–	–
–	–	–	–	–	–	0.4
–	–	–	–	–	–	–
19.1	14.5	19.1	23.6	10.4	19.4	5.6
2.5	3.4	2.8	–	–	–	–
–	–	–	–	–	–	–
–	–	–	24.0	19.4	20.1	16.5
3.6	3.6	2.0	–	–	–	–
1.3	2.4	1.1	–	–	–	–
0.6	0.7	1.2	–	–	–	–
–	–	–	–	–	–	–
11.9	11.4	10.2	–	–	–	–
–	–	0.4	–	–	–	–
2.0	2.0	1.6	–	–	–	–
15.2	23.3	16.2	20.2	30.6	37.3	21.2
56.3	*61.3*	*54.6*	*67.9*	*60.4*	*76.8*	*43.8*
50.9	*51.5*	*15.7*	*20.7*	*48.2*	*109.6*	*13.3*
5.1	*10.4*	*2.7*	*7.1*	*14.1*	*22.6*	*3.1*
113.3	*124.5*	*73.5*	*96.5*	*131.9*	*213.3*	*60.3*

TECH. COOP. GRANTS

1984	1985	1986	1983	1984	1985	1986
0.0	0.0	–	0.0	–	0.0	–
0.0	0.0	0.0	–	–	–	–
0.1	0.0	–	–	–	–	–
0.0	0.1	0.0	–	–	–	–
–	3.9	–	–	–	0.0	–
0.1	0.0	0.0	0.0	0.1	0.0	–
1.0	0.7	1.2	1.0	0.8	0.4	0.9
0.1	0.1	0.1	0.1	0.1	0.0	0.1
–	–	–	–	–	–	–
0.0	1.5	0.0	1.7	0.0	1.5	0.0
0.7	0.3	0.1	0.2	0.1	0.3	0.1
–	0.3	0.0	0.0	–	0.2	0.0
–	–	–	–	–	–	–
–	0.9	–	–	–	–	–
0.2	–	–	–	–	–	–
0.1	0.0	0.3	–	–	–	–
1.3	1.3	1.4	1.2	1.3	1.3	1.2
–	–	–	–	–	–	–
3.6	*9.1*	*3.2*	*4.2*	*2.4*	*3.8*	*2.2*
19.6	*22.1*	*18.2*	*10.1*	*7.5*	*8.7*	*6.3*
21.2	*47.1*	*12.9*	–	–	–	–
2.5	*7.7*	*2.7*	*4.0*	*2.2*	*3.5*	*2.1*
44.4	*78.2*	*34.3*	*14.3*	*9.9*	*12.5*	*8.6*

TOTAL OOF NET

1984	1985	1986	1983	1984	1985	1986
–	–	–	–	–	–	–
–	–	–	–	–	–	–
–	–	–	-1.6	–	–	-1.4
–	–	–	–	–	–	–
–	–	–	–	–	–	–
–	–	–	–	–	–	–
–	–	–	–	–	–	–
–	–	–	–	–	–	–
–	–	–	–	–	–	–
1.1	–	–	0.7	0.5	–	-0.6
–	–	–	–	–	–	–
–	–	–	–	–	–	–
1.1	–	–	-1.0	0.5	–	-2.0
–	5.7	5.8	-20.4	–	5.7	-1.8
–	–	–	0.8	–	–	–
–	–	–	–	–	–	–
1.1	*5.7*	*5.8*	*-20.6*	*0.5*	*5.7*	*-3.7*

ODA COMMITMENTS : LOANS

DAC COUNTRIES

	1983	1984	1985	1986
Australia	–	–	–	–
Austria	–	–	–	–
Belgium	–	–	–	–
Canada	–	–	–	–
Denmark	–	–	–	–
Finland	–	–	–	–
France	–	8.0	–	–
Germany, Fed. Rep.	–	–	–	–
Ireland	–	–	–	–
Italy	–	–	–	–
Japan	–	–	–	–
Netherlands	–	–	–	–
New Zealand	–	–	–	–
Norway	–	–	–	–
Sweden	–	–	–	–
Switzerland	–	–	–	–
United Kingdom	–	–	–	–
United States	–	–	–	–
TOTAL	–	*8.0*	–	–
MULTILATERAL	*42.5*	*40.5*	*56.7*	*26.8*
OPEC COUNTRIES	*11.7*	*37.9*	*64.2*	–
E.E.C.+ MEMBERS	–	*8.0*	–	–
TOTAL	*54.1*	*86.4*	*120.9*	*26.8*

GRANT ELEMENT OF ODA

DAC COUNTRIES

	1983	1984	1985	1986
Australia	100.0	100.0	–	–
Austria	–	–	100.0	–
Belgium	–	–	–	–
Canada	100.0	100.0	100.0	100.0
Denmark	–	–	100.0	–
Finland	–	100.0	–	–
France	100.0	63.6	100.0	100.0
Germany, Fed. Rep.	100.0	100.0	100.0	100.0
Ireland	–	–	–	–
Italy	100.0	100.0	100.0	100.0
Japan	100.0	100.0	100.0	100.0
Netherlands	100.0	–	100.0	100.0
New Zealand	–	–	–	–
Norway	–	–	–	–
Sweden	100.0	100.0	–	–
Switzerland	100.0	100.0	100.0	100.0
United Kingdom	100.0	100.0	100.0	100.0
United States	–	–	–	–
TOTAL	*100.0*	*85.9*	*100.0*	*100.0*
MULTILATERAL	*76.1*	*70.4*	*66.4*	*68.4*
OPEC COUNTRIES	*83.8*	*55.4*	*70.6*	*100.0*
E.E.C.+ MEMBERS	*100.0*	*76.7*	*100.0*	*100.0*
TOTAL	*80.0*	*67.9*	*72.8*	*77.0*

OTHER AGGREGATES

COMMITMENTS: ALL SOURCES

	1983	1984	1985	1986
TOTAL BILATERAL	54.4	565.6	185.2	222.8
of which				
OPEC	20.7	48.2	109.6	13.3
CMEA	24.9	493.0	48.7	206.9
TOTAL MULTILATERAL	67.9	91.8	76.8	58.8
TOTAL BIL.& MULTIL.	122.2	657.4	262.0	281.6
of which				
ODA Grants	42.4	65.5	107.4	55.6
ODA Loans	79.0	559.4	154.6	211.5

DISBURSEMENTS:

DAC COUNTRIES COMBINED

	1983	1984	1985	1986
OFFICIAL & PRIVATE				
GROSS:				
Contractual Lending	13.3	7.9	14.8	6.6
Export Credits Total	11.3	5.3	12.2	6.6
Export Credits Private	10.6	4.2	12.2	6.6
NET:				
Contractual Lending	-0.6	-2.3	4.1	-15.4
Export Credits Total	-2.0	-4.0	2.6	-13.8
PRIVATE SECTOR NET	-2.5	-4.4	2.3	-12.0
Direct Investment	–	–	–	–
Portfolio Investment	-1.5	0.1	-0.3	-0.2
Export Credits	-1.0	-4.5	2.6	-11.8

MARKET BORROWING:

CHANGE IN CLAIMS

	1983	1984	1985	1986
Banks	–	4.0	–	2.0

MEMORANDUM ITEM:

	1983	1984	1985	1986
CMEA Countr.(Gross)	117.2	101.3	127.8	116.4

TOTAL RECEIPTS NET / TOTAL ODA NET / TOTAL ODA GROSS

	TOTAL RECEIPTS NET 1983	1984	1985	1986	TOTAL ODA NET 1983	1984	1985	1986	TOTAL ODA GROSS 1983
DAC COUNTRIES									
Australia	1.1	-1.1	-1.0	-1.0	–	–	–	–	–
Austria	2.0	-15.9	-13.5	1.8	2.0	1.5	1.9	1.8	2.1
Belgium	-1.0	43.0	33.4	-1.0	–	–	–	0.1	–
Canada	-15.5	17.2	-8.0	-5.0	–	0.0	–	–	–
Denmark	-8.7	-6.7	-5.4	4.3	–	–	–	–	–
Finland	-0.3	0.9	-1.1	8.9	–	–	–	–	–
France	12.7	-15.7	39.8	-66.1	2.4	1.9	2.2	3.1	2.4
Germany, Fed. Rep.	63.6	109.1	14.8	34.1	-0.6	-5.0	1.9	-3.3	2.1
Ireland	–	–	–	–	–	–	–	–	–
Italy	72.9	26.6	102.1	-8.2	0.3	1.6	2.4	10.8	1.6
Japan	-30.8	-12.9	-13.7	52.1	-3.0	0.4	0.3	0.9	0.2
Netherlands	45.6	15.7	-13.7	-36.9	0.1	0.1	0.2	0.9	0.1
New Zealand	–	–	–	–	–	–	–	–	–
Norway	2.7	0.9	0.8	65.4	5.5	–	–	–	5.5
Sweden	-2.5	-1.6	–	-3.6	–	–	–	–	–
Switzerland	-23.6	6.7	-17.7	-5.0	–	0.0	–	–	–
United Kingdom	11.2	28.5	-9.8	-93.4	–	–	–	–	–
United States	195.0	117.0	-70.0	1.0	-7.0	-2.0	-2.0	–	-2.0
TOTAL	*324.3*	*311.8*	*36.8*	*-47.5*	*-0.4*	*-1.4*	*6.8*	*14.4*	*12.0*
MULTILATERAL									
AF.D.F.	–	–	–	–	–	–	–	–	–
AF.D.B.	–	–	–	–	–	–	–	–	–
AS.D.B	–	–	–	–	–	–	–	–	–
CAR.D.B.	–	–	–	–	–	–	–	–	–
E.E.C.	-3.6	18.4	–	54.3	–	–	–	–	–
IBRD	132.3	233.6	134.4	-14.1	–	–	–	–	–
IDA	–	–	–	–	–	–	–	–	–
I.D.B.	–	–	–	–	–	–	–	–	–
IFAD	–	–	–	–	–	–	–	–	–
I.F.C.	33.7	19.8	78.1	46.1	–	–	–	–	–
IMF TRUST FUND	–	–	–	–	–	–	–	–	–
U.N. AGENCIES									
UNDP	1.3	1.1	1.0	0.7	1.3	1.1	1.0	0.7	1.3
UNTA	0.5	0.4	0.4	0.6	0.5	0.4	0.4	0.6	0.5
UNICEF	–	–	–	–	–	–	–	–	–
UNRWA	–	–	–	–	–	–	–	–	–
WFP	–	–	–	–	–	–	–	–	–
UNHCR	1.0	1.7	1.8	2.4	1.0	1.7	1.8	2.4	1.0
Other Multilateral	0.2	0.3	0.4	0.5	0.2	0.3	0.4	0.5	0.2
Arab OPEC Agencies	–	0.9	0.2	–	–	0.9	0.2	–	–
TOTAL	*165.4*	*276.1*	*216.3*	*90.4*	*3.0*	*4.3*	*3.8*	*4.2*	*3.0*
OPEC COUNTRIES	*-82.8*	*-1.1*	*-10.0*	*-2.3*	–	–	*0.0*	*0.0*	–
E.E.C.+ MEMBERS	*192.7*	*218.8*	*161.0*	*-112.9*	*2.1*	*-1.4*	*6.6*	*11.7*	*6.2*
TOTAL	**406.9**	**586.7**	**243.1**	**40.6**	**2.6**	**2.9**	**10.6**	**18.6**	**15.0**

ODA LOANS GROSS / ODA LOANS NET / GRANTS

	ODA LOANS GROSS 1983	1984	1985	1986	ODA LOANS NET 1983	1984	1985	1986	GRANTS 1983
DAC COUNTRIES									
Australia	–	–	–	–	–	–	–	–	–
Austria	–	–	–	–	-0.1	-0.1	-0.1	-0.1	2.1
Belgium	–	–	–	–	–	–	–	–	–
Canada	–	–	–	–	–	–	–	–	–
Denmark	–	–	–	–	–	–	–	–	–
Finland	–	–	–	–	–	–	–	–	–
France	–	–	–	–	0.0	–	–	–	2.4
Germany, Fed. Rep.	–	–	–	66.9	-2.7	-7.1	0.0	-5.5	2.1
Ireland	–	–	–	–	–	–	–	–	–
Italy	1.3	1.3	2.3	10.2	0.0	1.3	2.2	10.1	0.3
Japan	–	–	–	6.2	-3.2	–	-0.3	-0.6	0.2
Netherlands	–	–	–	–	–	–	–	–	0.1
New Zealand	–	–	–	–	–	–	–	–	–
Norway	5.5	–	–	–	5.5	–	–	–	–
Sweden	–	–	–	–	–	–	–	–	–
Switzerland	–	–	–	–	–	–	–	–	–
United Kingdom	–	–	–	–	–	–	–	–	–
United States	–	–	–	–	-5.0	-1.0	-1.0	–	-2.0
TOTAL	*6.8*	*1.3*	*2.3*	*83.3*	*-5.6*	*-6.9*	*0.8*	*3.8*	*5.2*
MULTILATERAL	–	–	–	–	–	–	–	–	*3.0*
OPEC COUNTRIES	–	–	–	–	–	–	–	–	–
E.E.C.+ MEMBERS	*1.3*	*1.3*	*2.3*	*77.1*	*-2.7*	*-5.8*	*2.2*	*4.5*	*4.9*
TOTAL	**6.8**	**1.3**	**2.3**	**83.3**	**-5.6**	**-6.9**	**0.8**	**3.8**	**8.2**

TOTAL OFFICIAL GROSS / TOTAL OFFICIAL NET / TOTAL OOF GROSS

	TOTAL OFFICIAL GROSS 1983	1984	1985	1986	TOTAL OFFICIAL NET 1983	1984	1985	1986	TOTAL OOF GROSS 1983
DAC COUNTRIES									
Australia	1.6	0.0	–	–	0.8	-1.1	-1.0	-1.0	1.6
Austria	2.1	1.6	2.0	1.9	2.0	1.5	1.9	1.8	–
Belgium	–	1.4	1.4	0.1	–	1.4	1.4	0.1	–
Canada	–	20.4	1.5	2.8	-13.7	17.8	-7.7	-4.8	–
Denmark	–	–	–	–	-0.5	–	–	–	–
Finland	–	–	–	–	–	–	–	–	–
France	2.4	45.4	68.6	49.6	2.4	45.2	68.2	49.6	–
Germany, Fed. Rep.	46.4	111.3	88.9	183.2	39.5	94.9	55.7	78.5	44.4
Ireland	–	–	–	–	–	–	–	–	–
Italy	94.0	28.7	125.6	33.1	89.5	28.7	117.5	7.7	92.4
Japan	0.2	1.4	0.6	9.7	-3.0	1.4	0.3	2.5	–
Netherlands	22.8	1.2	0.2	0.9	22.8	1.2	0.2	-7.9	22.7
New Zealand	–	–	–	–	–	–	–	–	–
Norway	5.5	–	–	–	5.5	–	–	–	–
Sweden	10.6	3.5	6.0	4.4	3.5	0.5	-1.0	-4.2	10.6
Switzerland	–	0.0	–	–	–	0.0	–	–	–
United Kingdom	–	–	–	–	–	–	–	–	–
United States	32.0	21.0	107.0	99.0	19.0	17.0	18.0	-20.0	34.0
TOTAL	*217.6*	*235.8*	*401.7*	*384.7*	*167.7*	*208.4*	*253.3*	*102.2*	*205.6*
MULTILATERAL	*346.2*	*473.6*	*401.8*	*341.1*	*165.4*	*276.1*	*216.3*	*90.4*	*343.2*
OPEC COUNTRIES	–	–	*0.0*	*0.0*	*-82.8*	*-1.1*	*-10.0*	*-2.3*	–
E.E.C.+ MEMBERS	*165.6*	*210.2*	*284.6*	*325.9*	*150.1*	*189.7*	*242.9*	*182.3*	*159.4*
TOTAL	**563.8**	**709.5**	**803.5**	**725.8**	**250.3**	**483.3**	**459.6**	**190.3**	**548.8**

ODA COMMITMENTS

1984	1985	1986	1983	1984	1985	1986
1.6	2.0	1.9	2.1	1.6	2.0	–
–	–	0.1	–	–	–	0.1
0.0	–	–	0.0	0.1	–	–
–	–	–	–	–	–	–
1.9	2.2	3.1	2.4	1.9	2.2	3.1
2.1	1.9	69.1	2.1	2.1	1.9	69.1
–	–	–	–	–	–	–
1.6	2.5	11.0	0.3	32.2	0.2	0.5
0.4	0.6	7.6	0.3	0.4	3.9	8.1
0.1	0.2	0.9	0.1	0.1	0.2	0.8
–	–	–	5.5	–	–	–
–	–	–	–	–	–	–
0.0	–	–	–	–	0.0	–
–	–	–	–	–	–	–
-1.0	-1.0	–	–	–	–	–
6.7	8.3	93.9	12.7	38.3	10.3	81.6
1.1	1.0	0.7	3.0	3.4	3.6	4.2
0.4	0.4	0.6	–	–	–	–
–	–	–	–	–	–	–
1.7	1.8	2.4	–	–	–	–
0.3	0.4	0.5	–	–	–	–
0.9	0.2	–	–	2.0	–	–
4.3	3.8	4.2	3.0	5.5	3.6	4.2
–	0.0	0.0	–	–	–	–
5.7	6.7	84.3	4.9	36.2	4.4	73.5
11.0	12.1	98.1	15.7	43.8	13.9	85.8

TECH. COOP. GRANTS

1984	1985	1986	1983	1984	1985	1986
1.6	2.0	1.9	1.4	–	–	–
0.0	–	0.1	–	–	–	–
–	–	–	–	–	–	–
1.9	2.2	3.1	2.4	1.9	2.2	3.1
2.1	1.9	2.3	2.1	2.1	1.9	2.2
0.4	0.2	0.8	0.3	0.4	0.2	0.5
0.4	0.6	1.5	0.2	0.4	0.6	1.5
0.1	0.2	0.9	0.1	0.1	0.2	0.8
–	–	–	–	–	–	–
0.0	–	–	–	0.0	–	–
–	–	–	–	–	–	–
-1.0	-1.0	–	–	–	–	–
5.5	6.0	10.6	6.5	4.9	5.0	8.0
4.3	3.8	4.2	3.0	3.4	3.6	4.2
–	0.0	0.0	–	–	–	–
4.4	4.4	7.2	4.9	4.4	4.4	6.6
9.8	9.8	14.8	9.5	8.3	8.6	12.2

TOTAL OOF NET

1984	1985	1986	1983	1984	1985	1986
0.0	–	–	0.8	-1.1	-1.0	-1.0
–	–	–	–	–	–	–
1.4	1.4	–	–	1.4	1.4	–
20.3	1.5	2.8	-13.7	17.7	-7.7	-4.8
–	–	–	-0.5	–	–	–
43.4	66.4	46.5	–	43.2	66.0	46.5
109.3	87.0	114.1	40.1	99.9	53.9	81.8
–	–	–	–	–	–	–
27.1	123.1	22.1	89.2	27.1	115.1	-3.1
1.0	–	2.1	–	1.0	–	1.6
1.1	–	–	22.7	1.1	–	-8.8
–	–	–	–	–	–	–
3.5	6.0	4.4	3.5	0.5	-1.0	-4.2
–	–	–	–	–	–	–
22.0	108.0	99.0	26.0	19.0	20.0	-20.0
229.1	393.4	290.9	168.1	209.8	246.5	87.8
469.3	398.0	336.9	162.4	271.8	212.4	86.2
–	–	–	-82.8	-1.1	-10.0	-2.3
204.5	277.9	241.6	148.0	191.1	236.3	170.6
698.4	791.4	627.8	247.8	480.4	449.0	171.8

ODA COMMITMENTS : LOANS

DAC COUNTRIES

	1983	1984	1985	1986
Australia	–	–	–	–
Austria	–	–	–	–
Belgium	–	–	–	–
Canada	–	–	–	–
Denmark	–	–	–	–
Finland	–	–	–	–
France	–	–	–	–
Germany, Fed. Rep.	–	–	–	66.8
Ireland	–	–	–	–
Italy	–	30.0	–	–
Japan	–	–	3.2	6.2
Netherlands	–	–	–	–
New Zealand	–	–	–	–
Norway	5.5	–	–	–
Sweden	–	–	–	–
Switzerland	–	–	–	–
United Kingdom	–	–	–	–
United States	–	–	–	–
TOTAL	5.5	30.0	3.2	73.0
MULTILATERAL	–	–	–	–
OPEC COUNTRIES				
E.E.C.+ MEMBERS	–	30.0	–	66.8
TOTAL	5.5	30.0	3.2	73.0

GRANT ELEMENT OF ODA

DAC COUNTRIES

	1983	1984	1985	1986
Australia	–	–	–	–
Austria	100.0	100.0	100.0	34.8
Belgium	–	–	–	100.0
Canada	100.0	100.0	–	–
Denmark	–	–	–	–
Finland	–	–	–	–
France	100.0	100.0	100.0	100.0
Germany, Fed. Rep.	100.0	100.0	100.0	31.5
Ireland	–	–	–	–
Italy	100.0	34.8	100.0	100.0
Japan	100.0	100.0	100.0	36.2
Netherlands	100.0	100.0	100.0	100.0
New Zealand	–	–	–	–
Norway	25.0	–	–	–
Sweden	–	–	–	–
Switzerland	–	–	100.0	–
United Kingdom	–	–	–	–
United States	–	–	–	–
TOTAL	67.6	45.3	100.0	35.7
MULTILATERAL	100.0	100.0	100.0	100.0
OPEC COUNTRIES	–	–	–	–
E.E.C.+ MEMBERS	100.0	42.2	100.0	35.6
TOTAL	73.8	52.1	100.0	38.9

OTHER AGGREGATES

COMMITMENTS: ALL SOURCES

	1983	1984	1985	1986
TOTAL BILATERAL	202.0	562.9	348.3	370.3
of which				
OPEC	–	2.6	–	–
CMEA	–	180.0	–	–
TOTAL MULTILATERAL	976.1	294.2	370.9	192.8
TOTAL BIL.& MULTIL.	1178.1	857.1	719.2	563.1
of which				
ODA Grants	10.2	13.8	10.7	12.8
ODA Loans	5.5	30.0	3.2	73.0

DISBURSEMENTS:

DAC COUNTRIES COMBINED

	1983	1984	1985	1986
OFFICIAL & PRIVATE				
GROSS:				
Contractual Lending	632.8	596.6	684.6	561.3
Export Credits Total	566.1	471.2	407.2	252.4
Export Credits Private	420.3	367.6	290.3	187.1
NET:				
Contractual Lending	139.9	186.6	152.2	-92.9
Export Credits Total	85.8	69.6	-117.0	-305.0
PRIVATE SECTOR NET	156.6	103.4	-216.5	-149.7
Direct Investment	18.3	-6.6	15.3	-27.6
Portfolio Investment	161.0	124.9	-138.0	62.4
Export Credits	-22.7	-14.9	-93.7	-184.5

MARKET BORROWING:

CHANGE IN CLAIMS

	1983	1984	1985	1986
Banks	–	209.0	145.0	-867.0

MEMORANDUM ITEM:

	1983	1984	1985	1986
CMEA Countr.(Gross)	–	–	–	–

DISBURSEMENTS, UNLESS OTHERWISE STATED

TOTAL RECEIPTS NET

DAC COUNTRIES	1983	1984	1985	1986
Australia	—	0.0	—	—
Austria	-0.1	-0.5	-0.5	0.0
Belgium	16.6	132.0	221.5	173.5
Canada	16.9	24.1	17.8	10.7
Denmark	0.0	—	—	—
Finland	—	—	—	—
France	-12.2	155.3	42.2	80.5
Germany, Fed. Rep.	47.4	114.0	35.4	31.2
Ireland	—	—	—	—
Italy	-8.9	64.0	5.8	49.6
Japan	-106.8	25.2	-40.6	8.1
Netherlands	1.5	3.6	1.7	-7.4
New Zealand	—	—	—	—
Norway	0.5	1.6	1.9	1.6
Sweden	1.1	—	—	—
Switzerland	0.9	1.1	1.4	1.0
United Kingdom	3.6	-2.9	11.2	1.0
United States	30.0	151.0	54.0	88.0
TOTAL	-9.5	668.6	351.8	437.7
MULTILATERAL				
AF.D.F.	3.4	3.8	11.3	22.7
AF.D.B.	7.5	5.9	24.4	41.7
AS.D.B	—	—	—	—
CAR.D.B.	—	—	—	—
E.E.C.	49.6	33.1	20.5	21.4
IBRD	-8.1	-8.8	-8.1	-11.3
IDA	42.2	49.7	57.4	81.1
I.D.B.	—	—	—	—
IFAD	1.1	2.4	3.4	4.8
I.F.C.	-0.6	-0.1	7.7	16.2
IMF TRUST FUND	—	—	—	—
U.N. AGENCIES	—	—	—	—
UNDP	5.3	0.8	7.6	9.5
UNTA	1.4	0.9	1.0	0.9
UNICEF	2.0	1.5	2.4	3.3
UNRWA	—	—	—	—
WFP	0.8	0.1	2.4	0.2
UNHCR	12.7	9.1	10.2	7.3
Other Multilateral	1.3	2.7	0.8	1.1
Arab OPEC Agencies	0.0	-2.5	-1.8	-1.8
TOTAL	118.2	98.7	139.2	196.9
OPEC COUNTRIES	-7.8	-8.9	—	—
E.E.C.+ MEMBERS	97.6	499.2	338.3	349.7
TOTAL	100.9	758.3	491.0	634.7

TOTAL ODA NET

	1983	1984	1985	1986
Australia	—	0.0	—	—
Austria	-0.1	0.0	0.0	0.0
Belgium	90.0	75.6	79.7	142.3
Canada	12.7	14.7	17.7	12.3
Denmark	0.0	—	—	—
Finland	—	—	—	—
France	23.1	25.1	28.5	38.0
Germany, Fed. Rep.	30.9	26.1	20.0	39.7
Ireland	—	—	—	—
Italy	3.0	29.1	11.5	27.6
Japan	3.0	26.0	9.2	10.0
Netherlands	1.9	1.4	1.7	1.2
New Zealand	—	—	—	—
Norway	0.5	0.6	1.0	0.5
Sweden	1.1	—	—	—
Switzerland	0.9	1.1	1.4	1.0
United Kingdom	3.3	1.7	1.0	0.4
United States	23.0	8.0	38.0	23.0
TOTAL	193.5	209.4	209.6	296.1
AF.D.F.	3.4	3.8	11.3	22.7
AF.D.B.	—	—	—	—
AS.D.B	—	—	—	—
CAR.D.B.	—	—	—	—
E.E.C.	50.7	34.2	20.5	23.0
IBRD	—	—	—	—
IDA	42.2	49.7	57.4	81.1
I.D.B.	—	—	—	—
IFAD	1.1	2.4	3.4	4.8
I.F.C.	—	—	—	—
IMF TRUST FUND	—	—	—	—
U.N. AGENCIES	—	—	—	—
UNDP	5.3	0.8	7.6	9.5
UNTA	1.4	0.9	1.0	0.9
UNICEF	2.0	1.5	2.4	3.3
UNRWA	—	—	—	—
WFP	0.8	0.1	2.4	0.2
UNHCR	12.7	9.1	10.2	7.3
Other Multilateral	1.3	2.7	0.8	1.1
Arab OPEC Agencies	0.0	-2.5	-1.8	-1.8
TOTAL	120.6	102.8	115.2	152.0
OPEC COUNTRIES	0.5	0.0	—	—
E.E.C.+ MEMBERS	202.9	193.2	162.8	272.2
TOTAL	314.5	312.2	324.8	448.1

TOTAL ODA GROSS

	1983
Australia	—
Austria	0.1
Belgium	90.3
Canada	12.8
Denmark	0.0
Finland	—
France	23.1
Germany, Fed. Rep.	32.0
Ireland	—
Italy	3.0
Japan	13.8
Netherlands	1.9
New Zealand	—
Norway	0.5
Sweden	1.1
Switzerland	0.9
United Kingdom	3.3
United States	29.0
TOTAL	212.0
AF.D.F.	3.4
AF.D.B.	—
AS.D.B	—
CAR.D.B.	—
E.E.C.	51.3
IBRD	—
IDA	42.8
I.D.B.	—
IFAD	1.1
I.F.C.	—
IMF TRUST FUND	—
U.N. AGENCIES	—
UNDP	5.3
UNTA	1.4
UNICEF	2.0
UNRWA	—
WFP	0.8
UNHCR	12.7
Other Multilateral	1.3
Arab OPEC Agencies	0.2
TOTAL	122.0
OPEC COUNTRIES	0.5
E.E.C.+ MEMBERS	204.9
TOTAL	334.4

ODA LOANS GROSS

DAC COUNTRIES	1983	1984	1985	1986
Australia	—	—	—	—
Austria	—	—	—	—
Belgium	9.3	6.9	10.1	51.2
Canada	1.9	0.5	0.4	1.3
Denmark	—	—	—	—
Finland	—	—	—	—
France	6.6	10.1	13.4	15.9
Germany, Fed. Rep.	19.8	15.4	9.1	25.9
Ireland	—	—	—	—
Italy	—	26.2	0.9	19.2
Japan	11.4	8.4	0.1	—
Netherlands	—	—	—	—
New Zealand	—	—	—	—
Norway	—	—	—	—
Sweden	—	—	—	—
Switzerland	—	—	—	—
United Kingdom	—	—	—	—
United States	16.0	21.0	22.0	15.0
TOTAL	65.0	88.5	56.1	128.5
MULTILATERAL	77.2	71.3	73.5	111.3
OPEC COUNTRIES	0.5	—	—	—
E.E.C.+ MEMBERS	65.4	72.9	33.7	113.7
TOTAL	142.6	159.7	129.6	239.8

ODA LOANS NET

	1983	1984	1985	1986
Australia	—	—	—	—
Austria	-0.2	-0.1	-0.1	-0.1
Belgium	9.0	6.6	9.8	50.5
Canada	1.8	0.5	—	1.3
Denmark	—	—	—	—
Finland	—	—	—	—
France	6.6	7.9	12.0	14.5
Germany, Fed. Rep.	18.7	15.3	9.0	21.3
Ireland	—	—	—	—
Italy	—	26.2	0.9	18.3
Japan	0.6	8.0	0.0	-0.5
Netherlands	—	—	—	—
New Zealand	—	—	—	—
Norway	—	—	—	—
Sweden	—	—	—	—
Switzerland	—	—	—	—
United Kingdom	—	—	—	—
United States	10.0	-8.0	21.0	-3.0
TOTAL	46.5	56.4	52.7	102.3
MULTILATERAL	75.7	67.0	69.7	107.3
OPEC COUNTRIES	0.5	—	—	—
E.E.C.+ MEMBERS	63.4	69.5	31.2	105.1
TOTAL	122.7	123.3	122.3	209.6

GRANTS

	1983
Australia	—
Austria	0.1
Belgium	81.0
Canada	10.9
Denmark	0.0
Finland	—
France	16.5
Germany, Fed. Rep.	12.2
Ireland	—
Italy	3.0
Japan	2.4
Netherlands	1.9
New Zealand	—
Norway	0.5
Sweden	1.1
Switzerland	0.9
United Kingdom	3.3
United States	13.0
TOTAL	147.0
MULTILATERAL	44.9
OPEC COUNTRIES	
E.E.C.+ MEMBERS	139.5
TOTAL	191.8

TOTAL OFFICIAL GROSS

DAC COUNTRIES	1983	1984	1985	1986
Australia	—	0.0	—	—
Austria	0.1	0.1	0.1	0.2
Belgium	90.3	169.0	95.8	165.4
Canada	17.0	24.8	19.2	12.3
Denmark	0.0	—	—	—
Finland	—	—	—	—
France	23.1	214.1	73.6	111.2
Germany, Fed. Rep.	61.0	188.1	41.6	73.8
Ireland	—	—	—	—
Italy	3.0	112.6	11.5	66.3
Japan	13.8	26.4	9.3	10.5
Netherlands	1.9	1.4	1.7	1.2
New Zealand	—	—	—	—
Norway	0.5	0.6	1.0	0.5
Sweden	1.1	—	—	—
Switzerland	0.9	1.1	1.4	1.0
United Kingdom	3.3	1.7	1.0	0.4
United States	52.0	366.0	61.0	169.0
TOTAL	268.1	1105.8	317.0	611.8
MULTILATERAL	133.1	116.2	155.3	220.1
OPEC COUNTRIES	0.5	0.0	—	—
E.E.C.+ MEMBERS	233.9	721.8	246.3	442.3
TOTAL	401.7	1222.0	472.3	831.9

TOTAL OFFICIAL NET

	1983	1984	1985	1986
Australia	—	0.0	0.0	—
Austria	-0.1	0.0	0.0	0.0
Belgium	88.9	166.9	87.9	162.4
Canada	16.9	24.1	17.8	10.7
Denmark	0.0	—	—	—
Finland	—	—	—	—
France	23.1	210.7	64.9	100.1
Germany, Fed. Rep.	52.9	120.8	32.9	29.6
Ireland	—	—	—	—
Italy	1.2	110.8	9.6	63.5
Japan	3.0	26.0	9.2	10.0
Netherlands	1.9	1.4	1.7	1.2
New Zealand	—	—	—	—
Norway	0.5	0.6	1.0	0.5
Sweden	1.1	—	—	—
Switzerland	0.9	1.1	1.4	1.0
United Kingdom	3.3	1.7	1.0	0.4
United States	46.0	172.0	50.0	91.0
TOTAL	239.7	836.1	277.2	470.5
MULTILATERAL	118.2	98.7	139.2	196.9
OPEC COUNTRIES	-7.8	-8.9	—	—
E.E.C.+ MEMBERS	220.9	645.4	218.4	378.6
TOTAL	350.1	925.8	416.4	667.4

TOTAL OOF GROSS

	1983
Australia	—
Austria	—
Belgium	—
Canada	4.2
Denmark	—
Finland	—
France	—
Germany, Fed. Rep.	29.0
Ireland	—
Italy	—
Japan	—
Netherlands	—
New Zealand	—
Norway	—
Sweden	—
Switzerland	—
United Kingdom	—
United States	23.0
TOTAL	56.2
MULTILATERAL	11.1
OPEC COUNTRIES	
E.E.C.+ MEMBERS	29.0
TOTAL	67.3

ODA COMMITMENTS

1984	1985	1986	1983	1984	1985	1986
0.0	—	—	—	0.0	—	—
0.1	0.1	0.2	0.1	0.1	0.1	—
75.9	80.0	143.1	61.5	54.1	37.9	116.5
14.7	18.1	12.3	23.4	42.4	18.9	6.4
—	—	—	—	—	—	—
—	—	—	—	—	—	—
27.3	29.9	39.4	16.6	49.5	28.6	39.4
26.1	20.1	44.3	41.7	13.9	25.8	36.6
—	—	—	—	—	—	—
29.1	11.5	28.5	35.8	6.8	10.4	40.4
26.4	9.3	10.5	8.8	7.0	6.5	3.0
1.4	1.7	1.2	1.9	2.0	1.2	1.1
—	—	—	—	—	—	—
0.6	1.0	0.5	0.8	0.4	1.0	0.4
—	—	—	—	—	—	—
1.1	1.4	1.0	0.7	1.0	1.0	0.7
1.7	1.0	0.4	0.4	0.9	0.3	0.4
37.0	39.0	41.0	31.0	58.0	57.5	60.0
241.4	*213.0*	*322.2*	*222.5*	*236.0*	*189.1*	*304.8*
3.9	11.5	22.9	16.9	22.6	51.2	38.2
—	—	—	—	—	—	—
—	—	—	—	—	—	—
35.0	21.3	24.0	51.2	24.8	9.5	48.2
—	—	—	—	—	—	—
50.8	58.5	82.2	64.5	71.0	112.4	167.0
2.4	3.4	4.8	—	6.5	—	—
—	—	—	—	—	—	—
—	—	—	23.3	15.2	24.5	22.2
0.8	7.6	9.5	—	—	—	—
0.9	1.0	0.9	—	—	—	—
1.5	2.4	3.3	—	—	—	—
—	—	—	—	—	—	—
0.1	2.4	0.2	—	—	—	—
9.1	10.2	7.3	—	—	—	—
2.7	0.8	1.1	—	—	—	—
—	—	—	—	—	—	—
107.1	*119.1*	*156.1*	*155.9*	*140.1*	*197.5*	*275.6*
0.0	—	—	—	—	—	—
196.5	*165.4*	*280.8*	*209.0*	*151.9*	*113.5*	*282.6*
348.6	*332.0*	*478.3*	*378.4*	*376.1*	*386.6*	*580.4*

TECH. COOP. GRANTS

1984	1985	1986	1983	1984	1985	1986
0.0	—	—	—	0.0	—	—
0.1	0.1	0.2	0.1	—	—	—
68.9	69.9	91.9	51.1	42.0	43.2	57.0
14.3	17.7	11.0	1.7	—	3.7	—
—	—	—	0.0	—	—	—
17.2	16.5	23.5	11.6	12.4	12.1	17.6
10.8	11.0	18.4	10.3	9.8	9.9	17.2
—	—	—	—	—	—	—
2.9	10.5	9.3	3.0	2.1	4.6	5.4
18.0	9.2	10.5	1.9	3.1	2.0	2.7
1.4	1.7	1.2	1.7	0.9	1.2	1.1
—	—	—	—	—	—	—
0.6	1.0	0.5	—	0.1	0.1	0.2
—	—	—	—	—	—	—
1.1	1.4	1.0	0.3	0.2	0.3	0.1
1.7	1.0	0.4	0.4	0.2	0.3	0.4
16.0	17.0	26.0	10.0	11.0	12.0	15.0
153.0	*156.9*	*193.8*	*92.1*	*81.9*	*89.2*	*116.6*
35.9	*45.6*	*44.7*	*22.5*	*15.1*	*22.0*	*23.4*
0.0	—	—	—	—	—	—
123.6	*131.7*	*167.1*	*78.2*	*67.4*	*71.2*	*100.0*
188.9	*202.5*	*238.5*	*114.7*	*97.0*	*111.3*	*140.0*

TOTAL OOF NET

1984	1985	1986	1983	1984	1985	1986
—	—	—	—	—	—	—
—	—	—	—	—	—	—
93.1	15.8	22.4	-1.1	91.3	8.2	20.1
10.0	1.1	0.0	4.2	9.3	0.1	-1.6
—	—	—	—	—	—	—
186.8	43.7	71.9	—	185.7	36.4	62.1
161.9	21.5	29.5	22.0	94.7	12.9	-10.1
—	—	—	—	—	—	—
83.5	—	37.8	-1.8	81.6	-1.9	35.9
—	—	—	—	—	—	—
—	—	—	—	—	—	—
—	—	—	—	—	—	—
—	—	—	—	—	—	—
329.0	*22.0*	*128.0*	*23.0*	*164.0*	*12.0*	*68.0*
864.4	*104.0*	*289.6*	*46.3*	*626.7*	*67.6*	*174.4*
9.0	*36.2*	*64.1*	*-2.4*	*-4.1*	*24.0*	*45.0*
—	—	—	*-8.3*	*-8.9*	—	—
525.4	*81.0*	*161.5*	*18.0*	*452.2*	*55.5*	*106.4*
873.4	*140.2*	*353.6*	*35.6*	*613.6*	*91.6*	*219.4*

ODA COMMITMENTS : LOANS

DAC COUNTRIES

	1983	1984	1985	1986
Australia	—	—	—	—
Austria	—	—	—	—
Belgium	17.1	10.4	3.5	24.6
Canada	—	—	0.4	—
Denmark	—	—	—	—
Finland	—	—	—	—
France	—	32.0	15.7	15.9
Germany, Fed. Rep.	28.3	—	11.6	16.8
Ireland	—	—	—	—
Italy	26.0	0.9	1.1	28.0
Japan	—	—	—	—
Netherlands	—	—	—	—
New Zealand	—	—	—	—
Norway	—	—	—	—
Sweden	—	—	—	—
Switzerland	—	—	—	—
United Kingdom	—	—	—	—
United States	12.4	21.9	26.4	1.0
TOTAL	*83.8*	*65.2*	*58.7*	*86.2*
MULTILATERAL	*90.6*	*111.2*	*163.6*	*205.2*
OPEC COUNTRIES	—	—	—	—
E.E.C.+ MEMBERS	*80.6*	*54.5*	*31.9*	*85.3*
TOTAL	*174.5*	*176.4*	*222.3*	*291.4*

GRANT ELEMENT OF ODA

DAC COUNTRIES

	1983	1984	1985	1986
Australia	—	100.0	—	—
Austria	100.0	100.0	100.0	—
Belgium	95.4	96.9	100.0	96.7
Canada	100.0	100.0	98.8	100.0
Denmark	—	—	—	—
Finland	—	—	—	—
France	100.0	54.4	69.7	66.5
Germany, Fed. Rep.	76.9	100.0	84.7	71.5
Ireland	—	—	—	—
Italy	56.5	92.7	94.0	76.7
Japan	100.0	100.0	100.0	100.0
Netherlands	100.0	100.0	100.0	100.0
New Zealand	—	—	—	—
Norway	100.0	100.0	100.0	100.0
Sweden	—	—	—	—
Switzerland	100.0	100.0	100.0	100.0
United Kingdom	100.0	100.0	100.0	100.0
United States	86.4	87.6	85.1	99.4
TOTAL	*85.5*	*86.5*	*88.8*	*87.3*
MULTILATERAL	*91.5*	*86.7*	*84.2*	*87.2*
OPEC COUNTRIES	—	—	—	—
E.E.C.+ MEMBERS	*86.0*	*82.5*	*89.0*	*86.4*
TOTAL	*87.7*	*86.6*	*86.3*	*87.3*

OTHER AGGREGATES

COMMITMENTS: ALL SOURCES

	1983	1984	1985	1986
TOTAL BILATERAL	266.7	1024.8	308.4	500.4
of which				
OPEC	—	—	—	—
CMEA	—	—	—	—
TOTAL MULTILATERAL	211.4	154.1	251.8	546.7
TOTAL BIL.& MULTIL.	478.2	1178.9	560.1	1047.1
of which				
ODA Grants	204.0	199.7	164.3	289.0
ODA Loans	174.5	176.4	222.3	291.4

DISBURSEMENTS:

DAC COUNTRIES COMBINED

	1983	1984	1985	1986
OFFICIAL & PRIVATE				
GROSS:				
Contractual Lending	127.6	940.0	169.1	416.8
Export Credits Total	9.9	0.1	9.7	-1.1
Export Credits Private	6.4	-12.9	9.0	-1.2
NET:				
Contractual Lending	29.9	507.6	86.2	232.3
Export Credits Total	-64.4	-335.3	-46.5	-127.9
PRIVATE SECTOR NET	-249.2	-167.5	74.6	-32.7
Direct Investment	-192.8	-32.4	69.2	4.6
Portfolio Investment	6.4	40.4	39.5	7.2
Export Credits	-62.8	-175.5	-34.1	-44.5

MARKET BORROWING:

CHANGE IN CLAIMS

	1983	1984	1985	1986
Banks	—	-66.0	49.0	100.0

MEMORANDUM ITEM:

	1983	1984	1985	1986
CMEA Countr.(Gross)	—	—	—	—

TOTAL RECEIPTS NET / TOTAL ODA NET / TOTAL ODA GROSS

	TOTAL RECEIPTS NET 1983	1984	1985	1986	**TOTAL ODA NET** 1983	1984	1985	1986	**TOTAL ODA GROSS** 1983
DAC COUNTRIES									
Australia	2.8	3.1	2.2	0.4	2.8	3.1	2.2	0.4	2.8
Austria	0.4	0.3	0.2	0.4	0.4	0.3	0.2	0.4	0.4
Belgium	5.9	1.0	1.8	2.5	1.1	1.5	1.3	1.5	1.1
Canada	10.8	18.5	10.9	17.7	10.8	18.8	10.9	13.4	10.8
Denmark	6.4	2.2	6.2	9.7	6.4	2.2	6.2	9.7	6.4
Finland	10.2	9.4	11.8	16.6	10.2	9.4	11.8	16.6	10.2
France	-2.3	11.5	-1.7	37.8	0.8	1.7	0.7	3.3	0.8
Germany, Fed. Rep.	44.9	89.8	64.9	118.1	25.0	19.2	18.7	32.5	25.0
Ireland	1.4	1.3	2.4	2.8	1.4	1.3	2.4	2.8	1.4
Italy	-1.9	18.2	7.5	44.8	0.7	3.5	1.3	13.6	0.7
Japan	10.4	-1.9	60.9	30.8	19.1	4.9	41.3	52.2	19.3
Netherlands	12.1	19.8	16.9	48.7	12.1	19.6	15.7	47.5	12.1
New Zealand	0.0	0.0	0.0	–	0.0	0.0	0.0	–	0.0
Norway	16.1	16.0	16.7	29.0	16.1	16.0	16.7	28.7	16.1
Sweden	29.4	21.9	23.9	43.9	29.4	20.4	22.9	44.4	29.4
Switzerland	0.4	-0.3	4.5	0.2	0.3	0.5	4.4	0.2	0.3
United Kingdom	3.2	57.8	42.1	47.6	20.4	19.5	22.8	43.9	21.1
United States	25.0	53.0	61.0	77.0	23.0	40.0	36.0	38.0	23.0
TOTAL	*175.3*	*321.5*	*332.2*	*528.0*	*180.2*	*181.8*	*215.4*	*349.0*	*181.0*
MULTILATERAL									
AF.D.F.	4.5	2.4	5.9	8.8	4.5	2.4	5.9	8.8	4.5
AF.D.B.	7.8	-0.5	25.2	14.3	–	–	–	–	–
AS.D.B	–	–	–	–	–	–	–	–	–
CAR.D.B.	–	–	–	–	–	–	–	–	–
E.E.C.	10.8	22.8	46.1	13.0	8.4	23.9	29.1	16.3	8.4
IBRD	-2.3	-5.8	26.6	13.8	–	–	–	–	–
IDA	8.2	15.5	66.0	74.0	8.2	15.5	66.0	74.0	8.2
I.D.B.	–	–	–	–	–	–	–	–	–
IFAD	1.0	1.3	2.2	3.4	1.0	1.3	2.2	3.4	1.0
I.F.C.	-5.6	22.0	-4.0	0.6	–	–	–	–	–
IMF TRUST FUND	–	–	–	–	–	–	–	–	–
U.N. AGENCIES	–	–	–	–	–	–	–	–	–
UNDP	2.3	2.4	2.0	1.9	2.3	2.4	2.0	1.9	2.3
UNTA	1.4	1.3	1.7	1.8	1.4	1.3	1.7	1.8	1.4
UNICEF	0.4	0.4	0.5	0.6	0.4	0.4	0.5	0.6	0.4
UNRWA	–	–	–	–	–	–	–	–	–
WFP	2.1	3.2	0.7	2.0	2.1	3.2	0.7	2.0	2.1
UNHCR	2.6	3.2	1.9	2.8	2.6	3.2	1.9	2.8	2.6
Other Multilateral	2.4	3.3	3.8	3.8	2.4	3.3	3.8	3.8	2.4
Arab OPEC Agencies	0.7	5.3	0.1	1.8	0.1	0.9	-0.7	–	0.3
TOTAL	*36.1*	*76.7*	*178.7*	*142.6*	*33.3*	*57.7*	*113.1*	*115.4*	*33.4*
OPEC COUNTRIES	*3.4*	*–*	*–*	*–*	*3.4*	*–*	*–*	*–*	*3.4*
E.E.C.+ MEMBERS	*80.4*	*224.4*	*186.2*	*325.0*	*76.4*	*92.4*	*98.1*	*171.0*	*77.0*
TOTAL	**214.8**	**398.2**	**510.9**	**670.6**	**216.9**	**239.5**	**328.5**	**464.5**	**217.9**

ODA LOANS GROSS / ODA LOANS NET / GRANTS

	ODA LOANS GROSS 1983	1984	1985	1986	**ODA LOANS NET** 1983	1984	1985	1986	**GRANTS** 1983
DAC COUNTRIES									
Australia	–	–	–	–	–	–	–	–	2.8
Austria	–	–	–	–	–	–	–	–	0.4
Belgium	–	–	–	–	–	–	–	–	1.1
Canada	7.1	9.2	2.5	0.7	7.1	8.8	2.5	0.7	3.7
Denmark	4.7	0.4	3.1	6.0	4.7	0.4	3.1	5.2	1.8
Finland	–	–	–	–	–	–	–	–	10.2
France	–	0.7	0.0	2.3	–	0.7	0.0	2.3	0.8
Germany, Fed. Rep.	14.8	9.3	7.2	23.2	14.8	9.3	6.6	20.8	10.2
Ireland	–	–	–	–	–	–	–	–	1.4
Italy	–	–	–	9.3	–	–	–	9.3	0.7
Japan	8.0	0.3	26.0	32.7	7.7	0.1	25.1	29.0	11.4
Netherlands	0.3	–	–	0.1	0.3	-0.2	–	-1.0	11.8
New Zealand	–	–	–	–	–	–	–	–	0.0
Norway	–	–	–	–	–	–	–	–	16.1
Sweden	–	–	–	8.3	–	–	–	8.3	29.4
Switzerland	–	–	–	–	–	–	–	–	0.3
United Kingdom	4.2	5.2	8.4	6.2	3.6	4.6	7.3	2.8	16.9
United States	12.0	29.0	13.0	11.0	12.0	29.0	13.0	8.0	11.0
TOTAL	*51.0*	*54.1*	*60.2*	*99.7*	*50.2*	*52.8*	*57.6*	*85.3*	*130.0*
MULTILATERAL	*14.2*	*27.6*	*74.3*	*87.0*	*14.0*	*27.4*	*73.6*	*87.0*	*19.3*
OPEC COUNTRIES	*3.4*	*–*	*–*	*–*	*3.4*	*–*	*–*	*–*	*–*
E.E.C.+ MEMBERS	*24.2*	*23.1*	*19.0*	*47.8*	*23.5*	*22.3*	*17.3*	*40.0*	*52.8*
TOTAL	**68.6**	**81.6**	**134.5**	**186.7**	**67.6**	**80.3**	**131.3**	**172.3**	**149.3**

TOTAL OFFICIAL GROSS / TOTAL OFFICIAL NET / TOTAL OOF GROSS

	TOTAL OFFICIAL GROSS 1983	1984	1985	1986	**TOTAL OFFICIAL NET** 1983	1984	1985	1986	**TOTAL OOF GROSS** 1983
DAC COUNTRIES									
Australia	2.8	3.1	2.2	0.4	2.8	3.1	2.2	0.4	–
Austria	0.4	0.3	0.2	0.4	0.4	0.3	0.2	0.4	–
Belgium	6.1	1.5	1.8	2.7	6.1	1.1	1.8	2.7	5.0
Canada	10.8	19.6	10.9	17.9	10.8	18.5	10.9	17.7	–
Denmark	6.4	2.2	6.2	10.5	6.4	2.2	6.2	9.7	–
Finland	10.2	9.4	11.8	16.6	10.2	9.4	11.8	16.6	–
France	0.8	22.5	5.2	5.9	0.8	21.4	2.7	5.9	–
Germany, Fed. Rep.	44.5	108.8	82.0	160.3	44.4	106.6	73.6	122.1	19.5
Ireland	1.4	1.3	2.4	2.8	1.4	1.3	2.4	2.8	–
Italy	0.7	19.7	1.3	44.1	0.7	19.7	1.3	44.1	–
Japan	19.3	5.0	42.1	55.9	19.1	4.9	41.3	52.2	–
Netherlands	12.1	19.9	16.9	49.0	12.1	19.8	16.9	47.9	–
New Zealand	0.0	0.0	0.0	–	0.0	0.0	0.0	–	–
Norway	16.1	16.0	16.7	28.7	16.1	16.0	16.7	28.7	–
Sweden	29.4	21.8	22.9	44.4	29.4	21.8	22.9	44.3	–
Switzerland	0.3	0.5	4.4	0.2	0.3	0.5	4.4	0.2	–
United Kingdom	22.0	42.8	33.2	51.9	19.6	39.0	27.2	45.3	0.9
United States	26.0	68.0	73.0	98.0	25.0	53.0	61.0	77.0	3.0
TOTAL	*209.4*	*362.3*	*333.2*	*589.7*	*205.6*	*338.4*	*303.5*	*518.0*	*28.4*
MULTILATERAL	*65.2*	*107.6*	*211.0*	*180.2*	*36.1*	*76.7*	*178.7*	*142.6*	*31.8*
OPEC COUNTRIES	*3.4*	*–*	*–*	*–*	*3.4*	*–*	*–*	*–*	*–*
E.E.C.+ MEMBERS	*105.4*	*242.8*	*197.1*	*343.8*	*102.2*	*233.9*	*178.2*	*293.4*	*28.4*
TOTAL	**278.0**	**469.9**	**544.2**	**769.9**	**245.1**	**415.1**	**482.2**	**660.6**	**60.2**

ODA COMMITMENTS

1984	1985	1986	1983	1984	1985	1986
3.1	2.2	0.4	3.8	1.8	0.7	0.4
0.3	0.2	0.4	0.0	0.4	0.2	–
1.5	1.3	1.5	0.6	0.9	0.7	9.8
19.2	10.9	13.4	12.9	13.8	13.8	5.8
2.2	6.2	10.5	2.0	4.6	10.2	2.3
9.4	11.8	16.6	6.5	21.4	16.6	23.9
1.7	0.7	3.3	0.6	4.1	0.7	3.3
19.2	19.3	34.9	18.9	16.5	52.4	28.2
1.3	2.4	2.8	1.4	1.3	2.4	2.8
3.5	1.3	13.6	1.8	5.8	3.1	14.4
5.0	42.1	55.9	57.1	43.7	17.0	23.0
19.8	15.7	48.6	13.8	19.6	16.4	51.2
0.0	0.0	–	–	–	0.0	–
16.0	16.7	28.7	23.2	34.1	18.9	31.8
20.4	22.9	44.4	22.8	22.8	23.5	44.4
0.5	4.4	0.2	0.1	0.4	4.3	0.2
20.1	23.9	47.3	23.7	22.3	15.5	48.4
40.0	36.0	41.0	30.0	39.4	69.4	17.5
183.1	*218.0*	*363.4*	*219.2*	*252.7*	*265.8*	*307.3*
2.4	5.9	8.8	–	37.1	–	22.7
–	–	–	–	–	–	–
–	–	–	–	–	–	–
23.9	29.1	16.3	12.3	10.3	53.7	7.8
–	–	–	–	–	–	–
15.5	66.0	74.0	14.3	29.5	120.1	101.4
–	–	–	–	–	–	–
1.3	2.2	3.4	–	–	0.1	–
–	–	–	–	–	–	–
–	–	–	11.1	13.7	10.7	12.9
2.4	2.0	1.9	–	–	–	–
1.3	1.7	1.8	–	–	–	–
0.4	0.5	0.6	–	–	–	–
–	–	–	–	–	–	–
3.2	0.7	2.0	–	–	–	–
3.2	1.9	2.8	–	–	–	–
3.3	3.8	3.8	–	–	–	–
1.0	–	–	–	–	–	–
57.8	*113.7*	*115.4*	*37.7*	*90.6*	*184.6*	*144.7*
–	–	–	–	–	–	–
93.2	*99.8*	*178.7*	*75.1*	*85.3*	*155.0*	*168.1*
240.9	*331.7*	*478.9*	*256.9*	*343.3*	*450.4*	*452.0*

TECH. COOP. GRANTS

1984	1985	1986	1983	1984	1985	1986
3.1	2.2	0.4	0.4	0.5	0.4	0.3
0.3	0.2	0.4	0.3	–	–	–
1.5	1.3	1.5	0.9	1.2	1.2	1.3
10.0	8.4	12.7	1.8	–	4.0	–
1.8	3.1	4.5	1.6	1.9	2.8	3.9
9.4	11.8	16.6	4.3	2.4	2.8	10.1
1.0	0.7	1.0	0.6	1.0	0.7	1.0
9.9	12.1	11.7	9.9	11.3	11.0	11.1
1.3	2.4	2.8	0.9	0.9	1.3	2.0
3.5	1.3	4.3	0.5	0.2	0.3	0.3
4.8	16.2	23.2	2.1	1.5	5.1	8.0
19.8	15.7	48.5	5.4	7.3	6.7	7.6
0.0	0.0	–	0.0	0.0	0.0	–
16.0	16.7	28.7	4.2	4.8	4.9	6.2
20.4	22.9	36.1	11.9	6.4	7.2	7.5
0.5	4.4	0.2	0.1	0.1	0.1	0.8
14.9	15.5	41.2	16.8	14.9	12.7	24.2
11.0	23.0	30.0	3.0	3.0	4.0	5.0
129.0	*157.8*	*263.7*	*64.7*	*57.2*	*64.9*	*89.2*
30.3	*39.4*	*28.5*	*9.0*	*10.5*	*9.9*	*11.6*
–	–	–	–	–	–	–
70.2	*80.8*	*131.0*	*36.6*	*38.6*	*36.6*	*52.0*
159.2	*197.3*	*292.2*	*73.8*	*67.7*	*74.8*	*100.8*

TOTAL OOF NET

1984	1985	1986	1983	1984	1985	1986
–	–	–	–	–	–	–
0.1	0.5	1.3	5.0	-0.3	0.5	1.3
0.4	–	4.6	–	-0.3	–	4.4
–	–	–	–	–	–	–
20.7	4.5	2.6	–	19.7	2.1	2.6
89.6	62.7	125.4	19.4	87.4	54.9	89.6
16.2	–	30.5	–	16.2	–	30.5
–	–	–	–	–	–	–
0.1	1.2	0.4	–	0.1	1.2	0.4
–	–	–	–	–	–	–
1.5	–	–	–	1.5	–	-0.1
–	–	–	–	–	–	–
22.7	9.3	4.5	-0.8	19.5	4.4	1.4
28.0	37.0	57.0	2.0	13.0	25.0	39.0
179.2	*115.2*	*226.3*	*25.5*	*156.6*	*88.0*	*169.0*
49.8	*97.3*	*64.7*	*2.8*	*19.0*	*65.6*	*27.2*
–	–	–	–	–	–	–
149.6	*97.3*	*165.1*	*25.8*	*141.5*	*80.1*	*122.5*
229.0	*212.4*	*291.1*	*28.3*	*175.7*	*153.7*	*196.2*

ODA COMMITMENTS : LOANS
DAC COUNTRIES

	1983	1984	1985	1986
Australia	–	–	–	–
Austria	–	–	–	–
Belgium	–	–	–	8.3
Canada	–	0.4	–	–
Denmark	–	–	8.0	–
Finland	–	–	–	–
France	–	3.1	–	2.3
Germany, Fed. Rep.	2.3	6.7	36.2	20.3
Ireland	–	–	–	–
Italy	–	–	–	11.8
Japan	40.5	26.7	3.0	6.8
Netherlands	–	–	–	0.0
New Zealand	–	–	–	–
Norway	–	–	–	–
Sweden	–	–	–	8.3
Switzerland	–	–	–	–
United Kingdom	6.8	7.4	–	3.7
United States	22.0	10.0	10.3	10.1
TOTAL	*71.6*	*54.1*	*57.6*	*71.5*
MULTILATERAL	*14.3*	*66.6*	*120.5*	*124.1*
OPEC COUNTRIES				
E.E.C.+ MEMBERS	*9.1*	*17.1*	*44.6*	*46.4*
TOTAL	**85.9**	**120.7**	**178.0**	**195.6**

GRANT ELEMENT OF ODA
DAC COUNTRIES

	1983	1984	1985	1986
Australia	100.0	100.0	100.0	100.0
Austria	100.0	100.0	100.0	–
Belgium	100.0	100.0	100.0	100.0
Canada	100.0	100.0	100.0	100.0
Denmark	100.0	100.0	80.1	100.0
Finland	100.0	100.0	100.0	100.0
France	100.0	67.4	100.0	100.0
Germany, Fed. Rep.	95.9	86.3	75.3	67.9
Ireland	100.0	100.0	100.0	100.0
Italy	100.0	100.0	100.0	73.2
Japan	65.6	71.3	86.9	75.4
Netherlands	100.0	100.0	100.0	100.0
New Zealand	–	–	100.0	–
Norway	100.0	100.0	100.0	100.0
Sweden	100.0	100.0	100.0	100.0
Switzerland	100.0	100.0	100.0	100.0
United Kingdom	88.6	86.9	100.0	95.4
United States	78.1	91.7	95.2	81.4
TOTAL	*87.1*	*91.2*	*92.3*	*91.7*
MULTILATERAL	*92.1*	*87.9*	*90.3*	*85.3*
OPEC COUNTRIES	–	–	–	–
E.E.C.+ MEMBERS	*95.4*	*92.4*	*90.3*	*90.4*
TOTAL	**88.0**	**90.3**	**91.6**	**89.5**

OTHER AGGREGATES
COMMITMENTS: ALL SOURCES

	1983	1984	1985	1986
TOTAL BILATERAL	271.1	399.2	361.9	513.5
of which				
OPEC	–	–	–	–
CMEA	16.0	–	–	–
TOTAL MULTILATERAL	65.0	215.4	260.7	177.8
TOTAL BIL.& MULTIL.	336.0	614.5	622.6	691.3
of which				
ODA Grants	170.9	222.6	272.4	256.5
ODA Loans	85.9	120.7	178.0	195.6

DISBURSEMENTS:
DAC COUNTRIES COMBINED

	1983	1984	1985	1986
OFFICIAL & PRIVATE				
GROSS:				
Contractual Lending	96.0	236.0	210.5	341.0
Export Credits Total	16.6	4.1	44.1	25.9
Export Credits Private	16.6	2.7	35.1	15.0
NET:				
Contractual Lending	44.4	163.1	151.2	228.7
Export Credits Total	-32.2	-59.9	2.5	-33.1
PRIVATE SECTOR NET	-30.4	-17.0	28.7	10.0
Direct Investment	-2.5	28.8	22.0	-10.7
Portfolio Investment	3.4	0.6	1.3	46.3
Export Credits	-31.2	-46.3	5.5	-25.6

MARKET BORROWING:
CHANGE IN CLAIMS

	1983	1984	1985	1986
Banks	–	21.0	131.0	-75.0

MEMORANDUM ITEM:

	1983	1984	1985	1986
CMEA Countr.(Gross)	7.8	3.4	–	–

TOTAL RECEIPTS NET / TOTAL ODA NET / TOTAL ODA GROSS

	1983	1984	1985	1986	1983	1984	1985	1986	1983
DAC COUNTRIES									
Australia	2.6	4.2	4.1	1.8	2.6	4.2	4.1	1.8	2.6
Austria	0.5	0.6	0.5	0.5	0.5	0.6	0.5	0.5	0.5
Belgium	1.8	2.6	-1.2	-2.1	0.6	0.3	0.5	0.8	0.6
Canada	4.0	8.5	16.2	10.1	4.9	9.6	17.3	11.2	4.9
Denmark	4.2	11.0	6.0	9.5	4.2	11.0	6.0	9.5	4.2
Finland	1.4	2.9	4.3	4.3	1.4	1.9	4.5	4.3	1.4
France	33.9	13.5	-1.4	-12.2	8.8	6.7	5.3	5.1	8.8
Germany, Fed. Rep.	49.8	37.6	24.9	37.4	34.1	26.6	27.3	40.8	34.1
Ireland	0.2	0.3	0.4	0.7	0.2	0.3	0.4	0.7	0.2
Italy	28.6	12.7	2.4	3.6	3.7	17.0	7.5	5.2	3.7
Japan	10.7	17.8	8.4	4.5	10.7	17.7	8.5	4.3	10.7
Netherlands	11.4	22.6	17.4	28.3	9.6	22.6	17.7	24.2	9.6
New Zealand	0.0	0.0	0.0	0.0	0.0	0.0	0.0	0.0	0.0
Norway	8.6	13.7	8.3	16.8	8.6	13.7	8.3	16.4	8.6
Sweden	14.7	19.0	23.5	19.0	15.3	19.4	23.5	20.9	15.3
Switzerland	-2.2	-2.5	1.3	3.5	2.9	2.4	2.2	3.5	2.9
United Kingdom	53.8	88.7	69.1	-2.4	21.6	16.7	24.6	15.3	22.1
United States	62.0	72.0	54.0	22.0	56.0	73.0	56.0	27.0	56.0
TOTAL	*286.1*	*325.2*	*238.1*	*145.1*	*185.6*	*243.6*	*214.2*	*191.3*	*186.2*
MULTILATERAL									
AF.D.F.	–	0.6	3.2	3.1	–	0.6	3.2	3.1	–
AF.D.B.	–	0.5	3.2	4.9	–	–	–	–	–
AS.D.B	–	–	–	–	–	–	–	–	–
CAR.D.B.	–	–	–	–	–	–	–	–	–
E.E.C.	10.4	25.9	12.8	12.0	10.4	25.9	3.9	3.9	10.4
IBRD	40.8	51.0	41.6	26.4	–	–	–	–	–
IDA	4.1	7.5	4.2	12.7	4.1	7.5	4.2	12.7	4.1
I.D.B.	–	–	–	–	–	–	–	–	–
IFAD	0.1	0.9	1.3	0.6	0.1	0.9	1.3	0.6	0.1
I.F.C.	3.8	1.3	-3.1	-1.1	–	–	–	–	–
IMF TRUST FUND	–	–	–	–	–	–	–	–	–
U.N. AGENCIES	–	–	–	–	–	–	–	–	–
UNDP	2.1	2.5	4.1	4.7	2.1	2.5	4.1	4.7	2.1
UNTA	1.0	0.8	1.2	1.0	1.0	0.8	1.2	1.0	1.0
UNICEF	1.5	1.3	1.3	2.3	1.5	1.3	1.3	2.3	1.5
UNRWA	–	–	–	–	–	–	–	–	–
WFP	1.9	5.3	–	0.7	1.9	5.3	–	0.7	1.9
UNHCR	0.3	2.7	0.5	0.8	0.3	2.7	0.5	0.8	0.3
Other Multilateral	1.4	1.6	2.5	2.4	1.4	1.6	2.5	2.4	1.4
Arab OPEC Agencies	–	4.3	3.3	3.5	–	4.3	3.3	3.5	–
TOTAL	*67.4*	*106.2*	*76.0*	*73.9*	*22.8*	*53.3*	*25.5*	*35.6*	*22.8*
OPEC COUNTRIES	*0.2*	*0.8*	*-2.6*	*-2.1*	*0.2*	*0.8*	*-2.6*	*-2.1*	*0.2*
E.E.C.+ MEMBERS	*194.1*	*214.8*	*130.3*	*74.7*	*93.1*	*126.9*	*93.2*	*105.4*	*93.7*
TOTAL	*353.6*	*432.3*	*311.6*	*217.0*	*208.5*	*297.8*	*237.1*	*224.8*	*209.1*

ODA LOANS GROSS / ODA LOANS NET / GRANTS

	1983	1984	1985	1986	1983	1984	1985	1986	1983
DAC COUNTRIES									
Australia	–	–	–	–	–	–	–	–	2.6
Austria	–	–	–	–	–	–	0.0	–	0.5
Belgium	–	–	–	–	–	–	–	-0.8	0.6
Canada	–	2.8	5.1	4.7	–	2.8	5.1	4.7	4.9
Denmark	0.2	4.3	3.2	5.4	0.2	4.3	3.2	5.4	4.0
Finland	1.2	1.0	4.3	3.6	1.2	1.0	4.3	3.6	0.2
France	8.0	5.7	4.6	3.6	8.0	5.7	4.6	3.6	0.8
Germany, Fed. Rep.	20.8	13.5	16.0	22.8	20.8	13.5	15.6	21.8	13.3
Ireland	–	–	–	–	–	–	–	–	0.2
Italy	–	13.4	3.6	0.2	–	13.4	3.6	0.2	3.7
Japan	7.6	9.3	2.6	1.4	7.6	9.3	2.6	1.4	3.1
Netherlands	4.2	7.5	8.1	4.2	4.2	7.5	8.1	4.2	5.5
New Zealand	–	–	–	–	–	–	–	–	0.0
Norway	–	–	–	–	–	–	–	–	8.6
Sweden	–	–	–	–	–	–	–	–	15.3
Switzerland	1.9	1.1	1.9	2.0	1.9	1.1	1.9	2.0	1.0
United Kingdom	6.6	3.9	2.8	0.6	6.0	3.6	2.5	0.6	15.5
United States	–	3.0	9.0	–	–	3.0	9.0	–	56.0
TOTAL	*50.5*	*65.5*	*61.0*	*48.4*	*49.9*	*65.3*	*60.3*	*46.6*	*135.7*
MULTILATERAL	*4.5*	*14.4*	*11.9*	*21.1*	*4.5*	*14.4*	*11.9*	*20.5*	*18.3*
OPEC COUNTRIES	*0.0*	*0.8*	*0.6*	*–*	*0.0*	*0.8*	*-2.6*	*-2.3*	*0.1*
E.E.C.+ MEMBERS	*40.0*	*49.4*	*38.3*	*37.6*	*39.4*	*49.1*	*37.6*	*35.7*	*53.7*
TOTAL	*55.0*	*80.8*	*73.6*	*69.5*	*54.4*	*80.5*	*69.6*	*64.8*	*154.1*

TOTAL OFFICIAL GROSS / TOTAL OFFICIAL NET / TOTAL OOF GROSS

	1983	1984	1985	1986	1983	1984	1985	1986	1983
DAC COUNTRIES									
Australia	2.6	4.2	4.1	1.8	2.6	4.2	4.1	1.8	–
Austria	0.5	0.6	0.5	0.5	0.5	0.6	0.5	0.5	–
Belgium	0.6	0.5	0.8	1.9	0.6	0.5	0.8	1.2	–
Canada	4.9	9.6	17.3	11.2	4.0	8.5	16.2	10.1	–
Denmark	4.2	11.0	6.0	9.5	4.2	11.0	6.0	9.5	–
Finland	1.4	1.9	4.5	4.3	1.4	1.9	4.5	4.3	–
France	8.8	6.7	5.3	5.1	8.8	6.7	5.3	5.1	–
Germany, Fed. Rep.	39.0	27.0	27.8	41.8	38.7	26.5	26.8	40.1	4.9
Ireland	0.2	0.3	0.4	0.7	0.2	0.3	0.4	0.7	–
Italy	3.7	17.0	7.5	5.2	3.7	17.0	7.5	5.2	–
Japan	10.7	17.7	8.5	4.3	10.7	17.7	8.5	4.3	–
Netherlands	9.6	22.6	17.7	24.2	9.6	22.6	17.7	24.2	–
New Zealand	0.0	0.0	0.0	0.0	0.0	0.0	0.0	0.0	–
Norway	8.6	13.7	8.3	16.4	8.6	13.7	8.3	16.4	–
Sweden	15.3	19.4	23.5	20.9	14.7	19.0	23.5	19.0	–
Switzerland	2.9	2.4	2.2	3.5	2.9	2.4	2.2	3.5	–
United Kingdom	29.7	20.1	30.6	18.0	22.4	13.9	24.6	11.5	7.6
United States	62.0	73.0	56.0	27.0	62.0	72.0	54.0	22.0	6.0
TOTAL	*204.6*	*247.6*	*221.0*	*196.1*	*195.5*	*238.3*	*210.8*	*179.2*	*18.5*
MULTILATERAL	*67.4*	*108.9*	*80.2*	*80.7*	*67.4*	*106.2*	*76.0*	*73.9*	*44.6*
OPEC COUNTRIES	*0.2*	*0.8*	*0.6*	*0.3*	*0.2*	*0.8*	*-2.6*	*-2.1*	*–*
E.E.C.+ MEMBERS	*106.2*	*130.9*	*108.8*	*118.4*	*98.5*	*124.2*	*101.8*	*109.4*	*12.5*
TOTAL	*272.2*	*357.4*	*301.9*	*277.0*	*263.1*	*345.3*	*284.3*	*251.1*	*63.1*

ODA COMMITMENTS

1984	1985	1986	1983	1984	1985	1986
4.2	4.1	1.8	2.3	7.1	2.2	0.2
0.6	0.5	0.5	0.3	0.4	0.4	–
0.3	0.5	1.6	–	–	–	1.6
9.6	17.3	11.2	12.3	19.5	17.5	0.8
11.0	6.0	9.5	10.1	6.2	9.0	12.4
1.9	4.5	4.3	2.0	0.2	4.0	11.1
6.7	5.3	5.1	0.4	1.0	0.6	5.1
26.6	27.7	41.8	36.5	57.9	13.0	47.5
0.3	0.4	0.7	0.2	0.3	0.4	0.7
17.0	7.5	5.2	17.4	6.5	9.9	26.9
17.7	8.5	4.3	9.8	16.5	1.4	1.3
22.6	17.7	24.2	11.3	21.0	12.1	28.3
0.0	0.0	0.0	–	0.1	–	0.0
13.7	8.3	16.4	10.1	7.7	10.8	44.7
19.4	23.5	20.9	20.2	21.6	14.7	20.9
2.4	2.2	3.5	1.9	0.5	0.3	1.8
17.0	24.9	15.3	15.4	21.7	14.0	7.5
73.0	56.0	27.0	71.4	81.0	35.6	15.7
243.9	*214.9*	*193.1*	*221.6*	*269.0*	*145.8*	*226.3*
0.6	3.2	3.1	–	9.7	–	10.9
–	–	–	–	–	–	–
–	–	–	–	–	–	–
25.9	3.9	3.9	30.4	22.2	6.0	11.1
–	–	–	–	–	–	–
7.5	4.2	12.7	7.3	–	–	–
–	–	–	–	–	–	–
0.9	1.3	0.6	17.5	–	–	0.1
–	–	–	–	–	–	–
–	–	–	–	–	–	–
–	–	–	8.2	14.1	9.7	11.9
2.5	4.1	4.7	–	–	–	–
0.8	1.2	1.0	–	–	–	–
1.3	1.3	2.3	–	–	–	–
–	–	–	–	–	–	–
5.3	–	0.7	–	–	–	–
2.7	0.5	0.8	–	–	–	–
1.6	2.5	2.4	–	–	–	–
4.3	3.3	4.0	10.0	–	0.1	–
53.3	*25.5*	*36.2*	*73.3*	*46.0*	*15.8*	*34.0*
0.8	*0.6*	*0.3*	–	–	–	*0.2*
127.2	*93.8*	*107.2*	*121.7*	*136.7*	*65.0*	*141.0*
298.1	*241.0*	*229.5*	*294.9*	*315.0*	*161.5*	*260.5*

TECH. COOP. GRANTS

1984	1985	1986	1983	1984	1985	1986
4.2	4.1	1.8	1.8	1.3	1.6	0.4
0.6	0.5	0.5	0.5	–	–	–
0.3	0.5	1.6	0.3	0.1	0.1	0.1
6.9	12.3	6.5	3.7	–	3.7	–
6.7	2.8	4.1	4.0	1.1	1.0	2.2
0.8	0.2	0.7	0.2	0.4	0.2	1.5
1.0	0.7	1.5	0.4	1.0	0.6	1.5
13.1	11.7	19.0	13.2	10.1	11.1	18.5
0.3	0.4	0.7	0.2	0.3	0.4	0.7
3.7	3.9	5.0	3.7	3.5	3.8	3.8
8.3	6.0	3.0	0.9	0.5	0.5	1.2
15.1	9.6	20.0	1.1	2.2	2.3	3.5
0.0	0.0	0.0	0.0	0.0	0.0	0.0
13.7	8.3	16.4	–	0.6	0.8	0.8
19.4	23.5	20.9	1.7	5.6	5.0	4.4
1.3	0.3	1.5	0.1	0.1	0.2	–
13.1	22.1	14.7	10.1	7.3	5.7	5.6
70.0	47.0	27.0	3.0	4.0	7.0	9.0
178.4	*153.9*	*144.6*	*44.9*	*38.1*	*43.8*	*53.0*
38.9	*13.6*	*15.1*	*6.3*	*8.8*	*9.7*	*11.5*
–	–	*0.3*	–	–	–	–
77.9	*55.6*	*69.7*	*33.0*	*25.5*	*24.9*	*36.1*
217.3	*167.4*	*160.0*	*51.2*	*46.9*	*53.4*	*64.5*

TOTAL OOF NET

1984	1985	1986	1983	1984	1985	1986
–	–	–	–	–	–	–
–	–	–	–	–	–	–
0.2	0.3	0.4	–	0.2	0.3	0.4
–	–	–	-0.9	-1.1	-1.1	-1.1
–	–	–	–	–	–	–
–	–	–	–	–	–	–
0.4	0.1	–	4.6	-0.2	-0.5	-0.7
–	–	–	–	–	–	–
–	–	–	–	–	–	–
–	–	–	–	–	–	–
–	–	–	–	–	–	–
–	–	–	–	–	–	–
–	–	–	-0.5	-0.5	–	-1.8
3.2	5.8	2.7	0.8	-2.8	0.0	-3.8
–	–	–	6.0	-1.0	-2.0	-5.0
3.7	*6.1*	*3.0*	*10.0*	*-5.4*	*-3.3*	*-12.1*
55.6	*54.8*	*44.5*	*44.6*	*52.9*	*50.6*	*38.3*
–	–	–	–	–	–	–
3.7	*15.0*	*11.2*	*5.4*	*-2.8*	*8.7*	*4.0*
59.3	*60.9*	*47.5*	*54.6*	*47.5*	*47.2*	*26.2*

ODA COMMITMENTS : LOANS

DAC COUNTRIES	1983	1984	1985	1986
Australia	–	–	–	–
Austria	–	–	–	–
Belgium	–	–	–	1.6
Canada	–	–	10.8	0.8
Denmark	5.5	–	8.5	6.8
Finland	–	–	4.0	5.9
France	–	–	–	3.6
Germany, Fed. Rep.	19.7	40.9	–	21.7
Ireland	–	–	–	–
Italy	9.8	–	–	15.3
Japan	–	10.7	–	–
Netherlands	–	8.4	6.0	2.5
New Zealand	–	–	–	0.0
Norway	–	–	–	–
Sweden	–	–	–	–
Switzerland	–	–	–	–
United Kingdom	4.6	–	-0.2	–
United States	–	–	8.0	0.2
TOTAL	*39.5*	*60.0*	*37.1*	*56.0*
MULTILATERAL	*39.2*	*13.0*	–	*10.9*
OPEC COUNTRIES	–	–	–	–
E.E.C.+ MEMBERS	*44.0*	*52.6*	*14.3*	*49.9*
TOTAL	*78.7*	*72.9*	*37.1*	*66.8*

GRANT ELEMENT OF ODA

DAC COUNTRIES	1983	1984	1985	1986
Australia	100.0	100.0	100.0	100.0
Austria	100.0	100.0	100.0	–
Belgium	–	–	–	100.0
Canada	100.0	100.0	93.5	100.0
Denmark	86.5	100.0	76.6	86.8
Finland	100.0	100.0	70.0	83.5
France	100.0	100.0	100.0	60.1
Germany, Fed. Rep.	74.7	69.3	100.0	84.6
Ireland	100.0	100.0	100.0	100.0
Italy	69.5	100.0	100.0	79.0
Japan	100.0	60.3	100.0	100.0
Netherlands	100.0	85.6	80.2	96.6
New Zealand	–	100.0	–	100.0
Norway	100.0	100.0	100.0	100.0
Sweden	100.0	100.0	100.0	100.0
Switzerland	83.1	100.0	100.0	100.0
United Kingdom	88.0	100.0	100.0	100.0
United States	100.0	100.0	90.6	99.6
TOTAL	*91.7*	*89.8*	*93.0*	*89.1*
MULTILATERAL	*72.5*	*96.2*	*100.0*	*94.2*
OPEC COUNTRIES	–	–	–	*100.0*
E.E.C.+ MEMBERS	*84.9*	*84.4*	*93.1*	*84.4*
TOTAL	*87.2*	*90.7*	*93.7*	*89.7*

OTHER AGGREGATES

COMMITMENTS: ALL SOURCES

	1983	1984	1985	1986
TOTAL BILATERAL	245.4	285.8	168.9	225.4
of which				
OPEC	–	–	–	0.2
CMEA	–	4.0	5.0	–
TOTAL MULTILATERAL	252.1	89.0	80.9	50.0
TOTAL BIL.& MULTIL.	497.5	374.8	249.8	275.4
of which				
ODA Grants	216.2	242.0	124.5	193.7
ODA Loans	78.7	76.9	42.1	66.8

DISBURSEMENTS:
DAC COUNTRIES COMBINED

OFFICIAL & PRIVATE	1983	1984	1985	1986
GROSS:				
Contractual Lending	169.1	142.7	117.8	71.9
Export Credits Total	111.0	74.0	51.0	20.8
Export Credits Private	100.1	73.7	51.0	20.8
NET:				
Contractual Lending	126.8	103.7	62.3	13.1
Export Credits Total	76.0	41.2	2.1	-29.8
PRIVATE SECTOR NET	90.5	87.0	27.2	-34.1
Direct Investment	0.1	38.7	39.4	1.4
Portfolio Investment	23.6	4.3	-17.8	-14.3
Export Credits	66.9	44.0	5.7	-21.1

MARKET BORROWING:
CHANGE IN CLAIMS

	1983	1984	1985	1986
Banks	–	-84.0	-127.0	-16.0

MEMORANDUM ITEM:

	1983	1984	1985	1986
CMEA Countr.(Gross)	1.2	3.2	3.7	–

	1983	1984	1985	1986	1983	1984	1985	1986	1983

TOTAL RECEIPTS NET | TOTAL ODA NET | TOTAL ODA GROSS

DAC COUNTRIES

	1983	1984	1985	1986	1983	1984	1985	1986	1983
Australia	55.2	113.8	29.2	73.9	56.6	72.0	39.0	40.5	56.6
Austria	5.1	-11.0	-3.3	5.2	7.1	5.5	7.2	7.6	7.2
Belgium	55.3	104.7	65.6	91.5	56.0	55.3	91.4	84.4	56.0
Canada	225.7	233.5	292.2	227.4	230.4	236.6	282.5	216.8	230.5
Denmark	92.7	76.2	107.0	133.3	98.4	78.3	109.6	138.6	98.5
Finland	30.8	37.8	42.7	68.1	32.8	37.8	43.6	68.1	32.8
France	557.4	587.3	539.9	429.0	412.1	526.3	538.3	614.8	415.9
Germany, Fed. Rep.	524.9	481.7	488.5	639.8	458.5	420.4	450.7	570.4	502.1
Ireland	6.8	6.8	8.0	10.0	6.8	6.8	8.0	10.0	6.8
Italy	368.2	304.4	436.4	831.8	165.5	250.8	344.6	736.6	167.6
Japan	215.1	263.9	311.3	584.4	271.6	282.6	331.4	577.7	277.7
Netherlands	234.9	241.5	204.1	270.5	205.7	238.6	202.1	298.6	224.3
New Zealand	5.5	5.8	6.3	6.9	5.5	5.8	6.3	6.9	5.5
Norway	120.0	231.5	244.9	301.7	120.7	100.0	121.8	182.9	120.7
Sweden	150.5	126.1	134.0	225.1	147.7	124.8	131.0	220.0	147.7
Switzerland	72.4	60.4	92.4	108.1	66.8	69.8	68.3	108.7	66.8
United Kingdom	203.8	273.1	281.5	224.7	228.5	208.0	244.8	225.9	239.8
United States	731.0	784.0	1190.0	844.0	713.0	759.0	1189.0	862.0	726.0
TOTAL	*3655.2*	*3921.6*	*4470.6*	*5075.3*	*3283.6*	*3478.4*	*4209.6*	*4970.4*	*3382.3*

MULTILATERAL

	1983	1984	1985	1986	1983	1984	1985	1986	1983
AF.D.F.	119.5	77.8	137.1	165.7	119.5	77.8	137.1	165.7	120.3
AF.D.B.	52.2	37.6	71.6	30.5	–	–	–	–	—
AS.D.B	81.0	121.4	194.6	183.9	81.7	122.1	195.2	184.6	84.6
CAR.D.B.	–	–	–	–	–	–	–	–	—
E.E.C.	401.1	477.4	451.1	503.8	383.9	472.2	445.4	509.5	385.4
IBRD	42.0	6.2	52.6	-37.1	2.5	0.5	0.4	–	2.5
IDA	742.3	884.9	909.1	1234.6	742.3	884.9	909.1	1234.6	764.2
I.D.B.	14.9	16.2	10.7	3.1	14.9	16.2	10.7	3.1	15.6
IFAD	50.7	51.6	91.0	101.4	50.7	51.6	91.0	101.4	52.2
I.F.C.	7.5	17.1	17.9	8.5	–	–	–	–	—
IMF TRUST FUND	–	–	–	–	–	–	–	–	—
U.N. AGENCIES									
UNDP	202.2	207.0	231.3	256.6	202.2	207.0	231.3	256.6	202.2
UNTA	42.4	32.6	50.9	42.0	42.4	32.6	50.9	42.0	42.4
UNICEF	78.6	80.7	99.4	105.5	78.6	80.7	99.4	105.5	78.6
UNRWA	–	–	–	–	–	–	–	–	—
WFP	236.8	298.9	340.7	239.9	236.8	298.9	340.7	239.9	236.8
UNHCR	111.1	133.2	183.1	160.2	111.1	133.2	183.1	160.2	111.1
Other Multilateral	73.7	78.6	91.3	97.7	73.7	78.6	91.3	97.7	73.7
Arab OPEC Agencies	154.3	74.2	78.3	38.8	154.7	93.7	76.4	87.6	184.1
TOTAL	*2410.3*	*2595.3*	*3010.7*	*3135.2*	*2295.0*	*2549.9*	*2862.0*	*3188.4*	*2353.8*
OPEC COUNTRIES	*1182.7*	*648.2*	*632.4*	*526.1*	*952.0*	*568.9*	*594.9*	*517.9*	*1002.5*
E.E.C.+ MEMBERS	*2445.0*	*2553.1*	*2582.1*	*3134.5*	*2015.4*	*2256.7*	*2434.9*	*3188.7*	*2096.4*
TOTAL	**7248.3**	**7165.1**	**8113.7**	**8736.7**	**6530.6**	**6597.2**	**7666.4**	**8676.7**	**6738.6**

ODA LOANS GROSS | ODA LOANS NET | GRANTS

DAC COUNTRIES

	1983	1984	1985	1986	1983	1984	1985	1986	1983
Australia	–	–	–	–	–	–	–	–	56.6
Austria	0.1	–	–	–	–	0.0	-0.1	-0.1	7.1
Belgium	7.3	4.0	13.2	6.6	7.3	3.9	13.2	5.9	48.7
Canada	0.2	–	–	–	0.0	–	–	-2.9	230.3
Denmark	18.4	14.2	11.9	6.4	18.3	14.0	-1.3	-114.7	80.1
Finland	2.6	–	–	3.9	2.6	–	0.0	3.9	30.2
France	111.8	220.6	248.7	237.1	107.9	210.2	220.3	220.7	304.2
Germany, Fed. Rep.	36.3	15.4	4.5	10.8	-7.3	-13.2	-144.6	-20.3	465.8
Ireland	–	–	–	–	–	–	–	–	6.8
Italy	71.9	141.8	52.8	44.2	69.9	137.5	44.6	38.3	95.6
Japan	92.4	108.9	92.8	281.3	86.4	98.8	79.6	256.2	185.2
Netherlands	9.0	3.9	2.8	9.4	-9.5	1.9	-12.7	7.9	215.3
New Zealand	–	–	–	–	–	–	–	–	5.5
Norway	0.6	0.8	0.7	3.7	0.6	0.8	0.7	3.6	120.0
Sweden	–	–	–	–	–	–	–	–	147.7
Switzerland	–	–	–	–	–	–	0.0	0.0	66.8
United Kingdom	0.8	0.9	0.1	0.1	-10.5	-10.3	-10.3	-10.8	239.0
United States	113.0	99.0	137.0	120.0	100.0	80.0	125.0	89.0	613.0
TOTAL	*464.4*	*609.4*	*564.3*	*723.4*	*365.7*	*523.4*	*314.3*	*476.9*	*2917.9*
MULTILATERAL	*1245.1*	*1314.8*	*1483.9*	*1897.7*	*1186.3*	*1265.9*	*1413.0*	*1764.7*	*1108.7*
OPEC COUNTRIES	*609.5*	*247.9*	*280.0*	*304.8*	*559.0*	*161.7*	*186.0*	*181.3*	*393.0*
E.E.C.+ MEMBERS	*284.0*	*433.1*	*344.3*	*324.9*	*203.0*	*374.5*	*119.4*	*132.3*	*1812.4*
TOTAL	**2319.0**	**2172.1**	**2328.2**	**2925.9**	**2111.0**	**1951.0**	**1913.3**	**2422.8**	**4419.6**

TOTAL OFFICIAL GROSS | TOTAL OFFICIAL NET | TOTAL OOF GROSS

DAC COUNTRIES

	1983	1984	1985	1986	1983	1984	1985	1986	1983
Australia	56.6	72.0	39.1	44.5	56.6	72.0	39.1	44.5	–
Austria	7.2	5.6	7.3	7.7	5.1	2.0	6.0	5.2	–
Belgium	63.9	96.5	98.3	103.3	63.7	95.7	96.4	99.3	7.9
Canada	230.5	237.7	296.6	236.4	225.7	233.5	292.2	227.4	–
Denmark	103.2	78.9	125.1	262.5	102.5	77.9	109.6	132.0	4.7
Finland	32.8	37.8	43.6	68.1	32.8	37.8	43.6	68.1	–
France	482.3	670.6	630.2	669.0	471.2	637.5	577.5	584.9	66.4
Germany, Fed. Rep.	560.4	500.2	637.7	645.3	511.7	458.5	475.8	607.4	58.3
Ireland	6.8	6.8	8.0	10.0	6.8	6.8	8.0	10.0	–
Italy	242.7	294.9	406.5	847.0	239.1	288.7	398.3	840.9	75.1
Japan	277.7	292.7	344.5	602.7	271.6	282.6	331.4	577.7	–
Netherlands	226.1	242.8	218.8	304.8	206.6	240.0	202.9	303.2	1.8
New Zealand	5.5	5.8	6.3	6.9	5.5	5.8	6.3	6.9	–
Norway	120.7	100.0	121.8	182.9	120.7	100.0	121.8	182.9	–
Sweden	150.7	129.0	135.0	229.5	145.1	125.6	134.0	225.1	3.0
Switzerland	70.1	70.3	68.3	108.8	68.2	70.0	67.8	108.1	3.4
United Kingdom	251.3	240.4	263.2	253.1	237.5	224.8	248.8	236.7	11.5
United States	750.0	823.0	1250.0	896.0	731.0	784.0	1190.0	844.0	24.0
TOTAL	*3638.3*	*3905.2*	*4700.4*	*5478.5*	*3501.4*	*3743.1*	*4349.5*	*5104.1*	*256.0*
MULTILATERAL	*2638.9*	*2842.4*	*3293.9*	*3525.7*	*2410.3*	*2595.3*	*3010.7*	*3135.2*	*285.1*
OPEC COUNTRIES	*1234.1*	*735.1*	*727.9*	*649.7*	*1182.7*	*648.2*	*632.4*	*526.1*	*231.6*
E.E.C.+ MEMBERS	*2343.3*	*2615.0*	*2845.6*	*3614.4*	*2240.3*	*2507.2*	*2568.5*	*3318.3*	*246.9*
TOTAL	**7511.2**	**7482.7**	**8722.2**	**9653.9**	**7094.4**	**6986.6**	**7992.7**	**8765.5**	**772.7**

ODA COMMITMENTS

1984	1985	1986	1983	1984	1985	1986
72.0	39.0	40.5	58.9	51.8	47.5	37.7
5.6	7.3	7.7	5.7	4.9	7.4	–
55.4	91.4	85.1	32.2	34.4	41.8	84.5
236.6	282.5	219.7	306.9	342.5	305.5	283.1
78.5	122.8	259.7	88.7	153.8	135.4	191.5
37.8	43.6	68.1	21.2	42.6	108.5	78.1
536.6	566.7	631.1	574.7	648.9	609.9	631.1
449.0	599.8	601.5	504.6	494.1	709.1	662.2
6.8	8.0	10.0	6.8	6.8	8.0	10.0
255.1	352.9	742.4	284.5	296.3	418.0	1205.7
292.7	344.5	602.7	324.8	397.7	367.1	682.3
240.6	217.6	300.1	253.8	203.7	204.6	350.9
5.8	6.3	6.9	3.7	5.4	11.4	9.3
100.0	121.8	182.9	86.0	108.1	128.0	201.4
124.8	131.0	220.0	145.2	145.5	146.7	220.0
69.8	68.3	108.8	80.9	51.2	103.6	101.3
219.2	255.1	236.8	192.5	235.6	197.5	317.2
778.0	1201.0	893.0	789.1	1061.0	1074.8	909.6
3564.4	**4459.5**	**5216.9**	**3760.2**	**4284.1**	**4624.8**	**5975.8**
78.6	139.5	167.6	243.6	173.5	293.3	385.4
–	–	–	–	–	–	–
125.1	200.3	191.0	378.1	390.8	372.8	163.9
–	–	–	–	–	–	–
474.1	445.7	514.8	479.2	536.0	421.8	562.6
0.5	0.4	–	–	–	–	–
901.4	932.1	1266.9	1295.5	1362.5	1158.6	1449.7
17.5	12.1	5.5	17.4	–	24.7	56.0
57.9	96.2	105.0	82.8	89.6	83.1	57.6
–	–	–	–	–	–	–
–	–	–	744.8	830.9	996.7	902.0
207.0	231.3	256.6	–	–	–	–
32.6	50.9	42.0	–	–	–	–
80.7	99.4	105.5	–	–	–	–
–	–	–	–	–	–	–
298.9	340.7	239.9	–	–	–	–
133.2	183.1	160.2	–	–	–	–
78.6	91.3	97.7	–	–	–	–
112.8	110.0	168.7	294.7	297.7	190.2	203.3
2598.8	2932.9	3321.4	3536.1	3681.1	3541.2	3780.5
655.1	688.9	641.5	1367.0	782.3	741.6	632.5
2315.3	2659.9	3381.4	2416.3	2609.6	2746.1	4015.7
6818.2	**8081.3**	**9179.8**	**8663.3**	**8747.5**	**8907.6**	**10388.8**

TECH. COOP. GRANTS

1984	1985	1986	1983	1984	1985	1986
72.0	39.0	40.5	8.7	12.1	10.7	10.2
5.6	7.3	7.7	2.8	–	–	–
51.3	78.2	78.5	27.5	28.4	30.5	38.5
236.6	282.5	219.7	25.1	–	37.7	–
64.2	110.9	253.3	59.9	18.5	19.9	28.7
37.8	43.6	64.1	13.8	13.8	17.5	18.9
316.1	318.0	394.0	172.8	178.1	162.2	234.4
433.6	595.3	590.7	201.8	192.9	183.1	239.5
6.8	8.0	10.0	3.2	3.9	5.0	6.3
113.4	300.1	698.2	39.7	61.1	133.3	174.7
183.8	251.8	321.4	27.3	29.3	31.2	48.3
236.7	214.8	290.7	63.4	59.6	62.3	90.4
5.8	6.3	6.9	2.2	2.2	2.5	3.4
99.3	121.2	179.3	14.5	16.7	16.0	17.8
124.8	131.0	220.0	39.7	31.8	33.1	32.8
69.8	68.3	108.8	14.8	16.7	14.4	16.3
218.3	255.1	236.7	77.8	74.7	82.0	102.1
679.0	1064.0	773.0	275.0	271.0	286.0	290.0
2955.0	3895.3	4493.5	1069.9	1010.6	1127.6	1352.2
1284.0	1448.9	1423.8	508.0	532.0	643.4	678.8
407.2	408.9	336.6	–	–	–	–
1882.2	2315.6	3056.5	646.1	617.1	678.4	931.3
4646.2	**5753.1**	**6253.9**	**1577.9**	**1542.6**	**1770.9**	**2031.1**

TOTAL OOF NET

1984	1985	1986	1983	1984	1985	1986
–	0.1	4.0	–	–	0.1	4.0
–	–	–	-2.0	-3.6	-1.2	-2.4
41.2	6.9	18.2	7.7	40.4	5.0	14.9
1.1	14.1	16.8	-4.6	-3.1	9.7	10.6
0.4	2.3	2.8	4.2	-0.4	0.0	-6.6
–	–	–	–	–	–	–
134.0	63.5	37.9	59.1	111.2	39.2	-29.8
51.2	37.9	43.9	53.2	38.1	25.2	37.0
–	–	–	–	–	–	–
39.8	53.6	104.6	73.6	37.9	53.6	104.4
–	–	–	–	–	–	–
2.2	1.2	4.7	0.9	1.4	0.8	4.6
–	–	–	–	–	–	–
–	–	–	–	–	–	–
4.2	4.0	9.5	-2.6	0.8	3.0	5.1
0.4	0.0	–	1.4	0.2	-0.5	-0.7
21.3	8.1	16.4	9.0	16.8	4.0	10.8
45.0	49.0	3.0	18.0	25.0	1.0	-18.0
340.8	240.8	261.6	217.8	264.7	140.0	133.7
243.6	361.0	204.3	115.4	45.5	148.7	-53.2
80.1	39.1	8.2	230.7	79.3	37.6	8.2
299.7	185.7	233.0	224.9	250.6	133.6	129.6
664.5	**640.9**	**474.1**	**563.9**	**389.5**	**326.3**	**88.8**

ODA COMMITMENTS : LOANS

DAC COUNTRIES

	1983	1984	1985	1986
Australia	–	–	–	–
Austria	0.1	–	–	–
Belgium	7.3	4.1	4.6	6.0
Canada	–	–	–	–
Denmark	7.7	–	7.6	–
Finland	–	–	3.0	5.9
France	259.9	318.2	319.6	237.1
Germany, Fed. Rep.	31.6	5.2	6.0	8.3
Ireland	–	–	–	–
Italy	61.0	117.7	33.2	54.6
Japan	127.4	157.0	113.2	277.7
Netherlands	7.4	0.3	15.5	0.8
New Zealand	–	–	–	–
Norway	0.1	0.8	0.7	3.7
Sweden	–	–	–	–
Switzerland	–	–	–	–
United Kingdom	–	–	–	–
United States	115.4	89.7	109.8	119.7
TOTAL	*617.6*	*692.9*	*613.2*	*713.7*
MULTILATERAL	*2365.8*	*2351.9*	*2133.6*	*2331.1*
OPEC COUNTRIES	*593.4*	*324.0*	*278.3*	*172.5*
E.E.C.+ MEMBERS	*442.4*	*506.4*	*417.5*	*331.9*
TOTAL	*3576.8*	*3368.8*	*3025.1*	*3217.3*

GRANT ELEMENT OF ODA

DAC COUNTRIES

	1983	1984	1985	1986
Australia	100.0	100.0	100.0	100.0
Austria	99.4	100.0	100.0	–
Belgium	96.4	98.2	95.4	98.4
Canada	100.0	100.0	100.0	100.0
Denmark	99.1	100.0	98.7	100.0
Finland	100.0	100.0	100.0	97.6
France	79.9	77.1	76.8	82.9
Germany, Fed. Rep.	96.2	99.4	99.6	99.5
Ireland	100.0	100.0	100.0	100.0
Italy	89.6	80.3	96.5	98.1
Japan	88.1	89.1	91.4	88.2
Netherlands	99.1	100.0	97.5	100.0
New Zealand	100.0	100.0	100.0	100.0
Norway	99.9	99.5	99.6	98.7
Sweden	100.0	100.0	100.0	100.0
Switzerland	100.0	100.0	100.0	100.0
United Kingdom	100.0	100.0	100.0	100.0
United States	95.2	97.2	96.5	95.6
TOTAL	*93.8*	*93.4*	*95.3*	*95.7*
MULTILATERAL	*84.7*	*85.9*	*87.6*	*86.6*
OPEC COUNTRIES	*76.7*	*79.8*	*80.8*	*88.8*
E.E.C.+ MEMBERS	*93.2*	*91.7*	*94.6*	*96.7*
TOTAL	*87.3*	*89.0*	*91.0*	*92.0*

OTHER AGGREGATES

COMMITMENTS: ALL SOURCES

	1983	1984	1985	1986
TOTAL BILATERAL	6511.2	6496.1	6396.0	7507.9
of which				
OPEC	1601.9	844.6	759.7	640.0
CMEA	803.3	1114.4	792.5	725.2
TOTAL MULTILATERAL	3852.1	4004.1	3872.6	3921.2
TOTAL BIL.& MULTIL.	10363.3	10500.1	10268.6	11429.2
of which				
ODA Grants	5464.0	5586.9	5989.7	7379.0
ODA Loans	3988.9	4248.6	3696.4	3734.6

DISBURSEMENTS:

DAC COUNTRIES COMBINED

	1983	1984	1985	1986
OFFICIAL & PRIVATE				
GROSS:				
Contractual Lending	1313.7	1533.2	1302.8	1253.6
Export Credits Total	618.9	630.5	533.5	310.4
Export Credits Private	593.3	586.7	502.4	271.3
NET:				
Contractual Lending	687.8	876.3	571.1	533.4
Export Credits Total	109.5	100.8	95.4	-76.0
PRIVATE SECTOR NET	153.8	178.5	121.0	-28.8
Direct Investment	30.0	65.1	30.7	26.4
Portfolio Investment	19.5	21.6	-31.2	19.2
Export Credits	104.4	91.8	121.6	-74.4

MARKET BORROWING:

CHANGE IN CLAIMS

	1983	1984	1985	1986
Banks	–	84.0	172.0	-156.0

MEMORANDUM ITEM:

	1983	1984	1985	1986
CMEA Countr.(Gross)	765.4	639.0	641.0	622.8

TOTAL RECEIPTS NET

DAC COUNTRIES	1983	1984	1985	1986
Australia	6.1	10.9	34.8	25.4
Austria	5.5	-3.6	-3.8	1.5
Belgium	6.5	60.0	61.1	20.0
Canada	38.8	72.3	76.7	103.5
Denmark	51.5	41.9	55.1	52.8
Finland	4.7	0.7	9.9	0.9
France	147.5	186.7	465.6	899.1
Germany, Fed. Rep.	261.5	135.3	176.4	330.7
Ireland	0.1	0.1	0.1	0.2
Italy	-16.5	85.9	76.9	124.6
Japan	583.0	719.7	1250.1	2543.6
Netherlands	81.9	64.2	67.1	112.0
New Zealand	0.0	0.0	0.0	0.1
Norway	55.2	64.0	64.2	66.8
Sweden	56.1	60.4	88.5	257.4
Switzerland	29.9	11.7	59.3	10.4
United Kingdom	4.1	151.3	67.4	295.0
United States	145.0	-149.0	299.0	182.0
TOTAL	1460.7	1512.3	2848.4	5025.9
MULTILATERAL				
AF.D.F.	—	—	—	—
AF.D.B.	—	—	—	—
AS.D.B	-4.1	-4.2	-4.6	-4.8
CAR.D.B.	—	—	—	—
E.E.C.	80.2	91.6	73.0	66.2
IBRD	312.3	337.3	523.4	721.8
IDA	966.6	905.9	1033.7	1170.2
I.D.B.	—	—	—	—
IFAD	17.7	23.4	54.6	49.2
I.F.C.	13.4	3.1	29.9	-10.0
IMF TRUST FUND	—	—	—	—
U.N. AGENCIES				
UNDP	40.2	41.4	38.1	49.7
UNTA	7.7	3.3	10.1	5.4
UNICEF	39.3	36.2	38.5	63.1
UNRWA	—	—	—	—
WFP	53.5	97.3	91.3	101.7
UNHCR	9.5	8.1	7.1	8.8
Other Multilateral	30.7	33.9	29.1	25.5
Arab OPEC Agencies	8.9	0.2	2.8	-2.1
TOTAL	1575.8	1577.4	1927.0	2244.5
OPEC COUNTRIES	-40.5	9.0	-6.9	-20.4
E.E.C.+ MEMBERS	616.6	816.9	1042.8	1900.5
TOTAL	2996.0	3098.7	4768.5	7250.0

TOTAL ODA NET

DAC COUNTRIES	1983	1984	1985	1986
Australia	8.2	13.0	19.9	16.1
Austria	5.5	-0.9	-0.5	5.5
Belgium	12.3	11.6	6.1	0.1
Canada	45.6	71.6	57.8	64.5
Denmark	49.3	33.2	32.5	57.9
Finland	0.2	0.7	2.6	0.9
France	25.5	49.6	71.5	82.2
Germany, Fed. Rep.	236.8	152.6	184.1	217.7
Ireland	0.1	0.1	0.1	0.2
Italy	9.2	20.2	27.7	62.2
Japan	479.7	411.0	409.8	723.7
Netherlands	70.3	60.8	60.5	103.5
New Zealand	0.0	0.0	0.0	0.1
Norway	26.2	31.3	27.0	29.3
Sweden	48.4	51.1	52.5	87.1
Switzerland	21.9	20.6	14.2	10.4
United Kingdom	145.1	144.8	94.9	165.3
United States	58.0	65.0	29.0	49.0
TOTAL	1242.3	1136.1	1089.6	1675.6
MULTILATERAL				
AF.D.F.	—	—	—	—
AF.D.B.	—	—	—	—
AS.D.B	—	—	—	0.1
CAR.D.B.	—	—	—	—
E.E.C.	80.2	91.6	73.0	66.2
IBRD	14.7	21.2	14.0	0.2
IDA	966.6	905.9	1033.7	1170.2
I.D.B.	—	—	—	—
IFAD	17.7	23.4	54.6	49.2
I.F.C.	—	—	—	—
IMF TRUST FUND	—	—	—	—
U.N. AGENCIES				
UNDP	40.2	41.4	38.1	49.7
UNTA	7.7	3.3	10.1	5.4
UNICEF	39.3	36.2	38.5	63.1
UNRWA	—	—	—	—
WFP	53.5	97.3	91.3	101.7
UNHCR	9.5	8.1	7.1	8.8
Other Multilateral	30.7	33.9	29.1	25.5
Arab OPEC Agencies	8.9	0.2	2.8	-2.1
TOTAL	1268.9	1262.4	1392.3	1537.9
OPEC COUNTRIES	-100.9	9.0	-15.2	-20.4
E.E.C.+ MEMBERS	628.7	564.4	550.4	755.3
TOTAL	2410.3	2407.5	2466.8	3193.0

TOTAL ODA GROSS

DAC COUNTRIES	1983
Australia	8.2
Austria	7.4
Belgium	13.6
Canada	53.7
Denmark	50.3
Finland	0.2
France	31.7
Germany, Fed. Rep.	291.0
Ireland	0.1
Italy	11.3
Japan	529.1
Netherlands	80.3
New Zealand	0.0
Norway	26.2
Sweden	48.4
Switzerland	21.9
United Kingdom	193.9
United States	159.0
TOTAL	1526.3
AF.D.F.	—
AF.D.B.	—
AS.D.B	—
CAR.D.B.	—
E.E.C.	80.2
IBRD	14.7
IDA	998.2
I.D.B.	—
IFAD	17.7
I.F.C.	—
IMF TRUST FUND	—
U.N. AGENCIES	
UNDP	40.2
UNTA	7.7
UNICEF	39.3
UNRWA	—
WFP	53.5
UNHCR	9.5
Other Multilateral	30.7
Arab OPEC Agencies	10.9
TOTAL	1302.5
OPEC COUNTRIES	52.1
E.E.C.+ MEMBERS	752.4
TOTAL	2880.9

ODA LOANS GROSS

DAC COUNTRIES	1983	1984	1985	1986
Australia	—	—	—	—
Austria	6.8	0.0	0.2	6.6
Belgium	12.7	11.8	6.1	0.4
Canada	30.8	47.2	33.1	23.4
Denmark	32.1	15.3	17.9	31.8
Finland	—	—	2.3	0.3
France	21.3	43.0	64.1	71.9
Germany, Fed. Rep.	248.0	165.9	200.2	255.8
Ireland	—	—	—	—
Italy	1.0	11.6	11.7	43.8
Japan	464.6	402.1	404.5	678.7
Netherlands	39.8	14.2	33.6	38.9
New Zealand	—	—	—	—
Norway	—	—	—	—
Sweden	—	—	—	—
Switzerland	—	—	1.1	1.2
United Kingdom	—	—	—	—
United States	33.0	62.0	29.0	70.0
TOTAL	890.1	773.2	803.8	1222.7
MULTILATERAL	1041.5	988.8	1154.2	1277.7
OPEC COUNTRIES	51.9	101.6	77.2	65.2
E.E.C.+ MEMBERS	354.9	261.9	333.6	442.5
TOTAL	1983.5	1863.5	2035.2	2565.6

ODA LOANS NET

DAC COUNTRIES	1983	1984	1985	1986
Australia	—	—	—	—
Austria	4.9	-1.3	-1.1	4.7
Belgium	11.4	10.4	4.4	-2.3
Canada	22.7	43.2	21.6	15.5
Denmark	31.2	14.5	17.0	30.8
Finland	—	—	2.3	0.3
France	15.1	37.7	58.7	64.5
Germany, Fed. Rep.	193.8	110.3	136.0	149.7
Ireland	—	—	—	—
Italy	-1.1	9.9	10.6	42.2
Japan	415.2	351.9	352.9	607.3
Netherlands	29.7	2.2	20.4	18.7
New Zealand	—	—	—	—
Norway	—	—	—	—
Sweden	—	—	—	—
Switzerland	—	—	1.1	1.2
United Kingdom	-48.7	-51.7	-44.7	-48.3
United States	-68.0	-48.0	-74.0	-51.0
TOTAL	606.1	479.1	505.1	833.3
MULTILATERAL	1007.9	950.6	1105.0	1217.4
OPEC COUNTRIES	-101.0	8.7	-17.7	-20.7
E.E.C.+ MEMBERS	231.3	133.3	202.4	255.3
TOTAL	1513.0	1438.4	1592.4	2030.0

GRANTS

	1983
Australia	8.2
Austria	0.7
Belgium	0.9
Canada	22.2
Denmark	18.1
Finland	0.2
France	10.4
Germany, Fed. Rep.	43.0
Ireland	0.1
Italy	10.3
Japan	64.5
Netherlands	40.6
New Zealand	0.0
Norway	26.2
Sweden	48.4
Switzerland	21.9
United Kingdom	193.9
United States	126.0
TOTAL	636.3
MULTILATERAL	261.0
OPEC COUNTRIES	0.1
E.E.C.+ MEMBERS	397.4
TOTAL	897.3

TOTAL OFFICIAL GROSS

DAC COUNTRIES	1983	1984	1985	1986
Australia	9.4	14.4	23.8	37.8
Austria	7.4	0.4	0.8	7.4
Belgium	13.6	16.7	10.5	2.8
Canada	53.7	83.6	92.1	118.3
Denmark	53.8	55.1	38.0	65.0
Finland	0.2	0.7	2.6	0.9
France	31.7	54.9	76.9	89.7
Germany, Fed. Rep.	302.1	228.4	326.0	408.4
Ireland	0.1	0.1	0.1	0.2
Italy	22.0	51.9	41.9	64.3
Japan	745.3	604.6	516.0	1187.5
Netherlands	80.3	72.8	77.3	126.8
New Zealand	0.0	0.0	0.0	0.1
Norway	26.2	31.3	27.0	29.3
Sweden	57.3	67.0	93.5	265.4
Switzerland	21.9	20.6	14.2	10.4
United Kingdom	193.9	196.6	139.6	213.6
United States	172.0	203.0	140.0	172.0
TOTAL	1790.9	1702.3	1620.3	2799.6
MULTILATERAL	1696.0	1728.8	2078.3	2488.0
OPEC COUNTRIES	129.6	101.9	88.0	65.5
E.E.C.+ MEMBERS	777.7	768.2	783.3	1036.9
TOTAL	3616.5	3533.0	3786.6	5353.1

TOTAL OFFICIAL NET

DAC COUNTRIES	1983	1984	1985	1986
Australia	5.9	11.0	23.6	36.5
Austria	5.5	-3.6	-3.6	1.5
Belgium	12.3	15.3	8.9	0.1
Canada	36.3	72.3	76.7	103.5
Denmark	52.9	54.3	37.1	59.0
Finland	0.2	0.7	2.6	0.9
France	25.5	49.6	71.5	82.2
Germany, Fed. Rep.	243.0	162.5	246.2	270.8
Ireland	0.1	0.1	0.1	0.2
Italy	18.2	47.5	33.5	54.0
Japan	591.6	543.8	461.4	876.2
Netherlands	70.3	60.8	64.1	106.6
New Zealand	0.0	0.0	0.0	0.1
Norway	26.2	31.3	27.0	29.3
Sweden	52.9	61.1	87.5	257.8
Switzerland	21.9	20.6	14.2	10.4
United Kingdom	145.1	144.8	94.9	165.3
United States	59.0	83.0	29.0	14.0
TOTAL	1366.8	1354.9	1274.7	2068.2
MULTILATERAL	1575.8	1577.4	1927.0	2244.5
OPEC COUNTRIES	-40.5	9.0	-6.9	-20.4
E.E.C.+ MEMBERS	647.5	626.5	629.3	804.4
TOTAL	2902.1	2941.3	3194.7	4292.3

TOTAL OOF GROSS

	1983
Australia	1.2
Austria	—
Belgium	—
Canada	—
Denmark	3.6
Finland	—
France	—
Germany, Fed. Rep.	11.1
Ireland	—
Italy	10.7
Japan	216.2
Netherlands	—
New Zealand	—
Norway	—
Sweden	8.9
Switzerland	—
United Kingdom	—
United States	13.0
TOTAL	264.6
MULTILATERAL	393.5
OPEC COUNTRIES	77.5
E.E.C.+ MEMBERS	25.3
TOTAL	735.6

ODA COMMITMENTS

1984	1985	1986	1983	1984	1985	1986
13.0	19.9	16.1	13.8	21.0	19.4	17.4
0.4	0.8	7.4	6.1	0.4	0.6	–
13.0	7.8	2.7	19.6	5.2	2.1	12.0
75.5	69.3	72.3	77.9	262.7	33.2	89.2
34.0	33.4	58.9	24.0	50.6	52.6	77.7
0.7	2.6	0.9	1.3	2.3	0.2	10.3
54.9	76.9	89.7	48.1	80.9	50.7	89.7
208.2	248.3	323.8	345.7	284.9	118.4	282.2
0.1	0.1	0.2	0.1	0.1	0.1	0.2
21.9	28.8	63.8	34.4	70.6	113.9	84.7
461.1	461.4	795.1	399.6	755.8	541.6	933.4
72.8	73.7	123.7	103.9	69.5	36.0	157.7
0.0	0.0	0.1	0.0	0.0	0.1	0.1
31.3	27.0	29.3	28.8	39.1	23.6	6.7
51.1	52.5	87.1	49.8	44.2	68.6	87.2
20.6	14.2	10.4	38.5	22.4	29.6	9.9
196.6	139.6	213.6	224.3	285.5	23.3	119.2
175.0	132.0	170.0	227.4	280.8	156.4	201.7
1430.2	*1388.3*	*2065.0*	*1643.1*	*2275.9*	*1270.5*	*2179.0*
–	–	–	–	–	–	–
–	–	–	–	–	–	–
–	–	0.1	–	–	–	–
–	–	–	–	–	–	–
91.6	73.0	66.2	103.7	109.3	42.0	126.7
21.2	14.0	0.2	–	–	–	–
944.1	1082.8	1228.2	1013.0	1079.2	1607.6	753.0
23.4	54.6	49.2	33.5	24.0	–	12.6
–	–	–	–	–	–	–
–	–	–	180.8	220.1	214.3	254.2
41.4	38.1	49.7	–	–	–	–
3.3	10.1	5.4	–	–	–	–
36.2	38.5	63.1	–	–	–	–
–	–	–	–	–	–	–
97.3	91.3	101.7	–	–	–	–
8.1	7.1	8.8	–	–	–	–
33.9	29.1	25.5	–	–	–	–
0.2	2.8	–	22.5	–	–	–
1300.6	*1441.4*	*1598.1*	*1353.5*	*1432.6*	*1863.8*	*1146.4*
101.9	*79.8*	*65.5*	*125.7*	–	*93.2*	*37.7*
693.1	*681.6*	*942.6*	*903.7*	*956.5*	*439.1*	*949.9*
2832.7	**2909.5**	**3728.5**	**3122.3**	**3708.5**	**3227.5**	**3363.1**

TECH. COOP. GRANTS

1984	1985	1986	1983	1984	1985	1986
13.0	19.9	16.1	6.6	12.3	11.2	13.3
0.4	0.6	0.8	0.6	–	–	–
1.2	1.7	2.4	0.1	0.3	0.5	1.0
28.4	36.2	49.0	2.3	–	9.6	–
18.6	15.5	27.2	13.7	8.2	6.2	13.1
0.7	0.3	0.6	0.2	0.4	0.2	0.1
11.9	12.8	17.7	10.4	11.9	12.8	17.7
42.3	48.1	68.0	42.6	42.0	45.7	63.7
0.1	0.1	0.2	0.1	0.1	0.1	0.2
10.3	17.1	20.0	3.2	6.6	6.7	11.8
59.1	56.9	116.3	23.4	30.5	35.6	68.1
58.6	40.2	84.9	8.9	10.2	11.5	23.5
0.0	0.0	0.1	0.0	0.0	–	0.0
31.3	27.0	29.3	1.8	1.6	1.3	3.2
51.1	52.5	87.1	18.0	2.9	3.9	3.7
20.6	13.1	9.2	2.4	1.2	0.8	1.3
196.6	139.6	213.6	16.0	18.7	23.1	23.7
113.0	103.0	100.0	2.0	5.0	13.0	16.0
657.0	*584.5*	*842.3*	*152.1*	*151.7*	*182.2*	*260.3*
311.9	*287.3*	*320.4*	*127.3*	*122.8*	*123.0*	*152.5*
0.3	*2.5*	*0.2*	–	–	–	–
431.2	*348.0*	*500.0*	*94.9*	*98.0*	*106.6*	*154.7*
969.2	**874.3**	**1163.0**	**279.4**	**274.6**	**305.2**	**412.8**

TOTAL OOF NET

1984	1985	1986	1983	1984	1985	1986
1.4	3.9	21.6	-2.3	-2.1	3.7	20.4
–	–	–	-0.1	-2.8	-3.0	-4.1
3.7	2.8	0.0	–	3.7	2.8	0.0
8.1	22.8	45.9	-9.3	0.7	18.9	39.0
21.2	4.6	6.1	3.6	21.2	4.6	1.1
–	–	–	–	–	–	–
20.2	77.7	84.6	6.2	9.9	62.1	53.1
–	–	–	–	–	–	–
30.1	13.1	0.5	9.0	27.3	5.8	-8.2
143.5	54.6	392.4	111.9	132.8	51.6	152.5
–	3.6	3.1	–	–	3.6	3.1
–	–	–	–	–	–	–
–	–	–	–	–	–	–
16.0	41.0	178.3	4.4	10.1	35.0	170.7
–	–	–	–	–	–	–
28.0	8.0	2.0	1.0	18.0	–	-35.0
272.1	*232.0*	*734.6*	*124.5*	*218.8*	*185.0*	*392.6*
428.2	*636.8*	*889.9*	*306.9*	*315.0*	*534.7*	*706.7*
–	*8.3*	–	*60.4*	–	*8.3*	–
75.1	*101.7*	*94.3*	*18.8*	*62.0*	*78.9*	*49.0*
700.3	**877.1**	**1624.5**	**491.8**	**533.8**	**728.0**	**1099.3**

ODA COMMITMENTS : LOANS

DAC COUNTRIES

	1983	1984	1985	1986
Australia	–	–	–	–
Austria	5.5	–	–	–
Belgium	19.6	5.2	2.1	9.6
Canada	–	205.4	–	–
Denmark	21.9	37.7	22.7	55.0
Finland	0.4	1.2	–	9.9
France	37.7	68.7	37.9	71.9
Germany, Fed. Rep.	295.6	225.1	58.9	193.2
Ireland	–	–	–	–
Italy	13.4	40.0	100.4	64.2
Japan	328.0	689.4	483.2	770.7
Netherlands	64.8	17.8	3.6	26.9
New Zealand	–	–	–	–
Norway	–	–	–	–
Sweden	–	–	–	–
Switzerland	19.1	–	16.3	–
United Kingdom	–	–	–	–
United States	64.4	100.6	20.2	45.0
TOTAL	*870.2*	*1391.0*	*745.2*	*1246.4*
MULTILATERAL	*1069.0*	*1103.0*	*1607.6*	*765.4*
OPEC COUNTRIES	*125.6*	–	*90.7*	*37.7*
E.E.C.+ MEMBERS	*452.9*	*394.3*	*225.5*	*420.9*
TOTAL	**2064.8**	**2493.9**	**2443.6**	**2049.5**

GRANT ELEMENT OF ODA

DAC COUNTRIES

	1983	1984	1985	1986
Australia	100.0	100.0	100.0	100.0
Austria	63.5	100.0	100.0	65.7
Belgium	84.3	84.7	84.6	86.9
Canada	100.0	92.1	100.0	100.0
Denmark	86.9	89.1	93.9	89.6
Finland	80.0	66.1	100.0	70.9
France	67.2	66.3	70.5	54.7
Germany, Fed. Rep.	57.7	68.1	91.1	73.3
Ireland	100.0	100.0	100.0	100.0
Italy	78.3	67.6	58.2	64.2
Japan	65.1	59.9	58.6	61.9
Netherlands	75.2	89.8	96.0	93.2
New Zealand	100.0	100.0	100.0	100.0
Norway	100.0	100.0	100.0	100.0
Sweden	100.0	100.0	100.0	100.0
Switzerland	90.1	100.0	100.0	100.0
United Kingdom	100.0	100.0	100.0	100.0
United States	91.8	89.7	96.3	93.6
TOTAL	*77.7*	*77.7*	*75.4*	*74.3*
MULTILATERAL	*86.1*	*86.7*	*85.9*	*88.4*
OPEC COUNTRIES	*39.1*	–	*42.9*	*30.9*
E.E.C.+ MEMBERS	*77.7*	*83.9*	*82.2*	*79.6*
TOTAL	**79.5**	**81.3**	**79.9**	**78.5**

OTHER AGGREGATES

COMMITMENTS: ALL SOURCES

	1983	1984	1985	1986
TOTAL BILATERAL	2414.5	2681.9	3280.8	5398.4
of which				
OPEC	145.7	–	109.7	37.7
CMEA	211.9	–	1203.0	2119.9
TOTAL MULTILATERAL	2374.4	3772.2	4494.1	3707.2
TOTAL BIL.& MULTIL.	4788.9	6454.1	7774.9	9105.6
of which				
ODA Grants	1057.5	1214.6	783.9	1313.6
ODA Loans	2253.8	2493.9	3646.6	3754.4

DISBURSEMENTS:

DAC COUNTRIES COMBINED

	1983	1984	1985	1986
OFFICIAL & PRIVATE				
GROSS:				
Contractual Lending	2350.1	1786.0	2166.4	3781.0
Export Credits Total	1252.0	874.7	1304.1	2163.3
Export Credits Private	1195.4	744.5	1133.4	1823.7
NET:				
Contractual Lending	523.9	398.1	777.4	2086.8
Export Credits Total	-186.8	-210.7	213.8	1094.4
PRIVATE SECTOR NET	94.0	157.4	1573.8	2957.7
Direct Investment	2.5	84.9	328.7	287.5
Portfolio Investment	298.1	368.5	1155.1	1809.3
Export Credits	-206.7	-296.0	90.1	860.9

MARKET BORROWING:

CHANGE IN CLAIMS

	1983	1984	1985	1986
Banks	–	2557.0	6629.0	1566.0

MEMORANDUM ITEM:

	1983	1984	1985	1986
CMEA Countr.(Gross)	72.6	91.0	132.0	224.0

TOTAL RECEIPTS NET

DAC COUNTRIES	1983	1984	1985	1986
Australia	-93.3	115.7	167.5	155.8
Austria	40.9	17.5	20.5	23.6
Belgium	49.1	314.3	414.8	97.8
Canada	165.5	342.2	132.3	198.4
Denmark	45.7	35.5	38.5	37.7
Finland	34.0	47.9	41.8	70.8
France	1016.3	1372.2	736.1	1243.9
Germany, Fed. Rep.	810.6	923.6	529.4	758.3
Ireland	1.7	1.5	2.7	3.3
Italy	714.4	258.5	200.6	247.6
Japan	560.3	903.4	812.0	1116.4
Netherlands	319.2	256.1	145.5	522.1
New Zealand	6.5	5.9	3.7	5.7
Norway	117.1	354.3	444.0	477.2
Sweden	190.8	218.0	171.7	234.7
Switzerland	98.5	60.0	59.0	75.2
United Kingdom	463.8	428.5	315.6	337.1
United States	2936.0	2754.0	2585.0	1913.0
TOTAL	7476.9	8408.9	6820.8	7518.4
MULTILATERAL				
AF.D.F.	32.2	28.2	63.6	92.3
AF.D.B.	44.8	38.0	102.3	115.3
AS.D.B	294.5	330.7	344.0	381.7
CAR.D.B.	0.8	2.7	2.2	0.9
E.E.C.	276.4	306.7	233.5	343.6
IBRD	675.3	982.2	936.1	718.2
IDA	556.7	652.5	631.3	903.7
I.D.B.	98.3	195.3	141.1	148.3
IFAD	21.8	38.1	65.3	73.6
I.F.C.	31.8	54.1	35.1	26.2
IMF TRUST FUND	–	–	–	–
U.N. AGENCIES	–	–	–	–
UNDP	109.2	97.6	117.0	134.1
UNTA	25.0	19.2	30.0	24.3
UNICEF	58.7	56.6	59.8	66.7
UNRWA	–	–	–	–
WFP	220.0	157.3	174.5	146.1
UNHCR	125.1	122.2	101.3	110.2
Other Multilateral	47.0	48.2	49.8	44.6
Arab OPEC Agencies	73.1	58.7	35.9	-65.0
TOTAL	2690.8	3188.4	3122.8	3264.6
OPEC COUNTRIES	-71.1	-49.3	-26.5	47.5
E.E.C.+ MEMBERS	3697.2	3896.9	2616.8	3591.3
TOTAL	10096.7	11548.0	9917.1	10830.5

TOTAL ODA NET

DAC COUNTRIES	1983	1984	1985	1986
Australia	97.7	98.6	78.5	77.9
Austria	21.3	27.3	26.1	19.3
Belgium	113.3	103.6	97.6	168.4
Canada	197.8	280.0	226.8	223.9
Denmark	38.9	53.5	52.1	69.2
Finland	39.8	47.0	48.9	65.4
France	313.7	315.7	298.3	537.7
Germany, Fed. Rep.	491.8	481.7	559.7	622.7
Ireland	1.7	1.5	2.7	3.3
Italy	69.4	125.3	87.2	284.1
Japan	737.2	626.0	742.3	1071.9
Netherlands	202.2	231.6	177.7	330.7
New Zealand	6.5	5.9	3.7	5.7
Norway	92.0	86.4	91.4	134.4
Sweden	166.8	165.6	153.7	220.0
Switzerland	41.8	50.0	54.7	75.2
United Kingdom	200.4	177.7	197.6	233.1
United States	1579.0	1936.0	2180.0	1979.0
TOTAL	4411.3	4813.2	5079.0	6121.9
MULTILATERAL				
AF.D.F.	32.2	28.2	63.6	92.3
AF.D.B.	–	–	–	–
AS.D.B	114.0	157.7	170.8	178.5
CAR.D.B.	0.3	1.3	1.6	0.7
E.E.C.	230.1	284.9	212.9	321.0
IBRD	13.8	13.8	16.9	3.7
IDA	556.7	652.5	631.3	903.7
I.D.B.	79.3	121.3	85.1	100.2
IFAD	21.8	38.1	65.3	73.6
I.F.C.	–	–	–	–
IMF TRUST FUND	–	–	–	–
U.N. AGENCIES	–	–	–	–
UNDP	109.2	97.6	117.0	134.1
UNTA	25.0	19.2	30.0	24.3
UNICEF	58.7	56.6	59.8	66.7
UNRWA	–	–	–	–
WFP	220.0	157.3	174.5	146.1
UNHCR	125.1	122.2	101.3	110.2
Other Multilateral	47.0	48.2	49.8	44.6
Arab OPEC Agencies	58.4	11.9	3.0	-3.6
TOTAL	1691.7	1810.8	1782.9	2196.0
OPEC COUNTRIES	1.0	-0.6	-49.3	33.2
E.E.C.+ MEMBERS	1661.4	1775.3	1685.8	2570.3
TOTAL	6103.9	6623.4	6812.6	8351.1

TOTAL ODA GROSS

	1983
Australia	97.7
Austria	24.0
Belgium	115.0
Canada	201.4
Denmark	40.9
Finland	39.8
France	323.6
Germany, Fed. Rep.	554.2
Ireland	1.7
Italy	73.3
Japan	913.9
Netherlands	217.9
New Zealand	6.5
Norway	92.0
Sweden	166.8
Switzerland	41.8
United Kingdom	226.4
United States	1748.0
TOTAL	4884.9
AF.D.F.	32.3
AF.D.B.	–
AS.D.B	120.1
CAR.D.B.	0.3
E.E.C.	231.0
IBRD	13.8
IDA	576.2
I.D.B.	85.8
IFAD	21.8
I.F.C.	–
IMF TRUST FUND	–
U.N. AGENCIES	–
UNDP	109.2
UNTA	25.0
UNICEF	58.7
UNRWA	–
WFP	220.0
UNHCR	125.1
Other Multilateral	47.0
Arab OPEC Agencies	74.9
TOTAL	1741.3
OPEC COUNTRIES	177.1
E.E.C.+ MEMBERS	1784.1
TOTAL	6803.3

ODA LOANS GROSS

DAC COUNTRIES	1983	1984	1985	1986
Australia	–	–	–	–
Austria	19.7	28.6	24.0	14.7
Belgium	17.6	18.3	10.1	59.6
Canada	69.2	71.6	62.7	65.2
Denmark	13.3	26.9	18.2	28.9
Finland	3.6	6.6	1.5	5.4
France	161.5	159.1	149.1	354.3
Germany, Fed. Rep.	393.1	392.7	461.8	523.9
Ireland	–	–	–	–
Italy	21.4	64.1	15.2	121.8
Japan	607.9	479.3	584.5	845.4
Netherlands	73.6	92.1	67.4	78.8
New Zealand	–	–	–	–
Norway	0.9	2.2	1.6	3.1
Sweden	–	–	–	8.3
Switzerland	6.4	7.3	4.2	2.6
United Kingdom	22.3	17.8	22.5	12.6
United States	659.0	648.0	729.0	618.0
TOTAL	2069.4	2014.6	2151.7	2742.6
MULTILATERAL	970.9	1133.0	1093.3	1445.8
OPEC COUNTRIES	160.8	170.5	128.1	138.7
E.E.C.+ MEMBERS	757.9	834.1	748.4	1194.1
TOTAL	3201.2	3318.1	3373.1	4327.1

ODA LOANS NET

DAC COUNTRIES	1983	1984	1985	1986
Australia	–	–	–	–
Austria	17.0	23.5	21.7	13.1
Belgium	15.9	16.3	7.7	55.6
Canada	65.7	65.7	54.3	55.2
Denmark	11.3	24.6	14.9	19.4
Finland	3.6	6.6	1.5	5.4
France	151.6	142.3	131.4	321.9
Germany, Fed. Rep.	330.7	327.4	388.6	359.0
Ireland	–	–	–	–
Italy	17.5	60.1	11.3	116.8
Japan	431.2	291.0	393.4	571.7
Netherlands	57.9	74.7	44.5	45.7
New Zealand	–	–	–	–
Norway	0.9	2.2	1.4	3.1
Sweden	–	–	–	8.3
Switzerland	6.4	7.3	4.0	2.6
United Kingdom	-3.7	-5.2	-4.0	-19.4
United States	490.0	454.0	534.0	399.0
TOTAL	1595.9	1490.4	1604.7	1957.3
MULTILATERAL	921.3	1076.3	1030.2	1350.4
OPEC COUNTRIES	-15.4	-11.7	-58.8	-26.2
E.E.C.+ MEMBERS	635.3	702.1	597.5	911.0
TOTAL	2501.7	2555.0	2576.0	3281.5

GRANTS

	1983
Australia	97.7
Austria	4.3
Belgium	97.4
Canada	132.1
Denmark	27.6
Finland	36.2
France	162.2
Germany, Fed. Rep.	161.1
Ireland	1.7
Italy	51.9
Japan	306.0
Netherlands	144.3
New Zealand	6.5
Norway	91.1
Sweden	166.8
Switzerland	35.4
United Kingdom	204.1
United States	1089.0
TOTAL	2815.4
MULTILATERAL	770.4
OPEC COUNTRIES	16.4
E.E.C.+ MEMBERS	1026.2
TOTAL	3602.2

TOTAL OFFICIAL GROSS

DAC COUNTRIES	1983	1984	1985	1986
Australia	102.6	109.6	91.6	87.6
Austria	25.6	32.4	28.5	26.0
Belgium	123.6	210.3	129.8	198.7
Canada	229.7	434.7	262.0	302.4
Denmark	68.6	61.7	61.5	81.1
Finland	39.8	47.0	48.9	65.4
France	406.1	674.2	467.1	722.4
Germany, Fed. Rep.	795.5	955.2	847.8	1095.4
Ireland	1.7	1.5	2.7	3.3
Italy	98.8	292.4	180.3	360.3
Japan	925.3	819.7	933.4	1373.0
Netherlands	225.2	255.1	214.2	376.0
New Zealand	6.5	5.9	3.7	5.7
Norway	92.0	86.4	91.6	134.4
Sweden	230.5	219.8	208.7	278.5
Switzerland	41.8	50.0	55.0	75.2
United Kingdom	244.1	260.1	252.0	280.1
United States	2077.0	2798.0	2662.0	2445.0
TOTAL	5734.5	7314.0	6541.0	7910.5
MULTILATERAL	3149.4	3723.1	3716.2	4206.5
OPEC COUNTRIES	257.3	222.5	200.6	220.2
E.E.C.+ MEMBERS	2251.3	3031.4	2405.5	3486.2
TOTAL	9141.2	11259.5	10457.8	12337.2

TOTAL OFFICIAL NET

DAC COUNTRIES	1983	1984	1985	1986
Australia	92.2	103.2	81.4	79.5
Austria	23.0	26.7	25.5	23.6
Belgium	120.5	205.9	119.7	192.0
Canada	165.8	342.4	132.4	198.5
Denmark	60.4	49.5	48.4	51.2
Finland	39.8	47.0	48.9	65.4
France	393.2	638.5	436.5	667.2
Germany, Fed. Rep.	637.1	745.6	663.9	722.0
Ireland	1.7	1.5	2.7	3.3
Italy	86.8	280.7	165.3	339.9
Japan	748.6	627.1	733.9	1087.3
Netherlands	206.5	236.8	189.0	341.0
New Zealand	6.5	5.9	3.7	5.7
Norway	92.0	86.4	91.4	134.4
Sweden	213.2	209.5	171.7	252.3
Switzerland	41.8	50.0	54.7	75.2
United Kingdom	209.7	230.2	216.0	239.3
United States	1805.0	2322.0	2343.0	1975.0
TOTAL	4943.9	6208.6	5528.1	6452.5
MULTILATERAL	2690.8	3188.4	3122.8	3264.6
OPEC COUNTRIES	-71.1	-49.3	-26.5	47.5
E.E.C.+ MEMBERS	1992.4	2695.3	2074.9	2899.4
TOTAL	7563.6	9347.7	8624.4	9764.6

TOTAL OOF GROSS

	1983
Australia	4.9
Austria	1.6
Belgium	8.6
Canada	28.3
Denmark	27.8
Finland	–
France	82.5
Germany, Fed. Rep.	241.3
Ireland	–
Italy	25.5
Japan	11.4
Netherlands	7.3
New Zealand	–
Norway	–
Sweden	63.8
Switzerland	–
United Kingdom	17.7
United States	329.0
TOTAL	849.6
MULTILATERAL	1408.1
OPEC COUNTRIES	80.2
E.E.C.+ MEMBERS	467.2
TOTAL	2337.9

MILLION US DOLLARS, UNLESS OTHERWISE STATED

ODA COMMITMENTS

1984	1985	1986	1983	1984	1985	1986
98.6	78.5	77.9	101.1	102.0	84.8	79.3
32.4	28.3	20.9	37.6	41.3	9.7	—
105.6	100.0	172.4	81.2	72.2	46.8	145.9
285.9	235.2	234.0	269.1	391.7	262.4	228.9
55.9	55.4	78.8	79.7	22.1	55.9	112.7
47.0	48.9	65.4	56.5	90.5	70.0	116.2
332.5	316.0	570.2	412.1	378.7	486.8	570.2
547.0	632.9	787.6	551.1	657.0	548.5	674.3
1.5	2.7	3.3	1.7	1.5	2.7	3.3
129.3	91.1	289.1	182.6	129.3	190.4	462.1
814.3	933.4	1345.6	1210.5	1265.6	1483.0	948.7
249.0	200.6	363.8	189.6	277.2	163.7	366.4
5.9	3.7	5.7	3.4	4.2	3.6	4.1
86.4	91.6	134.4	85.9	133.9	119.6	131.6
165.6	153.7	220.0	174.4	172.5	148.6	220.0
50.0	55.0	75.2	34.9	57.9	83.9	82.3
200.7	224.1	265.1	173.0	191.5	207.9	242.9
2130.0	2375.0	2198.0	1984.7	2291.2	2565.3	2153.6
5337.5	5626.0	6907.3	5629.0	6280.2	6533.4	6542.3
28.3	64.3	93.6	75.0	180.9	132.5	131.5
—	—	—	—	—	—	—
165.5	179.9	189.9	308.1	277.8	379.7	400.4
1.3	1.6	0.7	3.2	0.2	1.7	2.5
286.0	214.0	323.1	301.9	303.4	244.1	386.6
13.8	16.9	3.7	—	—	—	—
674.4	658.2	938.7	626.3	775.7	769.6	1170.4
127.2	93.7	110.6	68.1	34.2	54.0	107.6
42.7	67.8	84.0	43.8	43.1	21.6	27.6
—	—	—	—	—	—	—
—	—	—	585.1	501.2	532.4	526.0
97.6	117.0	134.1	—	—	—	—
19.2	30.0	24.3	—	—	—	—
56.6	59.8	66.7	—	—	—	—
—	—	—	—	—	—	—
157.3	174.5	146.1	—	—	—	—
122.2	101.3	110.2	—	—	—	—
48.2	49.8	44.6	—	—	—	—
26.8	17.1	21.2	73.6	40.3	24.0	44.4
1867.3	1846.0	2291.4	2085.1	2156.8	2159.6	2797.0
181.6	137.7	198.1	129.2	206.7	101.1	159.6
1907.4	1836.7	2853.3	1972.9	2032.7	1946.6	2964.2
7386.3	7609.7	9396.7	7843.3	8643.7	8794.1	9498.9

TECH. COOP. GRANTS

1984	1985	1986	1983	1984	1985	1986
98.6	78.5	77.9	30.1	35.3	35.5	36.8
3.9	4.3	6.2	3.1	—	—	—
87.3	89.9	112.8	57.4	48.6	51.2	66.1
214.3	172.6	168.8	20.2	—	35.5	—
29.0	37.2	49.9	18.7	12.0	14.6	18.4
40.4	47.4	60.0	21.2	19.1	25.2	30.4
173.4	166.9	215.8	117.4	127.1	108.6	162.3
154.2	171.2	263.7	140.5	137.7	142.3	198.6
1.5	2.7	3.3	1.2	1.1	1.6	2.5
65.2	75.9	167.3	25.4	33.2	38.7	94.7
335.0	348.9	500.2	94.6	102.6	108.4	158.7
156.9	133.1	285.0	61.2	56.6	59.7	96.2
5.9	3.7	5.7	1.8	1.9	1.3	2.0
84.1	90.0	131.3	12.4	15.4	14.8	18.3
165.6	153.7	211.7	48.8	26.1	30.9	35.8
42.7	50.7	72.6	8.4	9.0	8.5	12.6
182.9	201.7	252.6	70.9	63.8	65.1	91.7
1482.0	1646.0	1580.0	552.0	721.0	684.0	649.0
3322.8	3474.4	4164.6	1285.2	1410.4	1425.9	1674.0
734.3	752.7	845.6	365.1	343.8	357.9	386.8
11.1	9.6	59.4	—	—	—	—
1073.3	1088.3	1659.3	492.7	480.0	481.7	737.3
4068.2	4236.6	5069.6	1650.3	1754.2	1783.8	2060.8

TOTAL OOF NET

1984	1985	1986	1983	1984	1985	1986
11.0	13.2	9.8	-5.5	4.6	2.9	1.6
—	0.2	5.1	1.6	-0.6	-0.5	4.3
104.8	29.9	26.4	7.2	102.3	22.0	23.6
148.8	26.8	68.4	-32.0	62.4	-94.4	-25.4
5.7	6.1	2.3	21.5	-4.0	-3.7	-18.0
—	—	—	—	—	—	—
341.7	151.1	152.3	79.5	322.8	138.2	129.4
408.2	215.0	307.8	145.4	263.9	104.2	99.3
—	—	—	—	—	—	—
163.2	89.2	71.3	17.4	155.4	78.1	55.9
5.4	—	27.3	11.4	1.1	-8.5	15.4
6.1	13.7	12.2	4.2	5.2	11.4	10.2
—	—	—	—	—	—	—
54.2	55.0	58.5	46.4	43.9	18.0	32.3
—	—	—	—	—	—	—
59.5	27.9	15.0	9.3	52.5	18.3	6.1
668.0	287.0	247.0	226.0	386.0	163.0	-4.0
1976.5	914.9	1003.3	532.6	1395.5	449.1	330.6
1855.8	1870.2	1915.1	999.1	1377.6	1340.0	1068.6
40.9	63.0	22.1	-72.1	-48.7	22.7	14.3
1124.0	568.8	632.8	331.0	920.0	389.2	329.1
3873.2	2848.1	2940.5	1459.6	2724.4	1811.7	1413.6

ODA COMMITMENTS : LOANS

DAC COUNTRIES

	1983	1984	1985	1986
Australia	—	—	—	—
Austria	32.9	38.5	4.6	—
Belgium	28.9	18.8	3.5	33.1
Canada	67.2	25.4	37.6	21.6
Denmark	43.7	6.3	19.3	76.6
Finland	—	33.3	—	—
France	245.2	207.6	322.3	354.3
Germany, Fed. Rep.	376.6	478.5	361.9	381.7
Ireland	—	—	—	—
Italy	89.7	26.8	72.2	161.0
Japan	867.2	942.5	1092.1	462.1
Netherlands	29.7	116.7	13.3	43.8
New Zealand	—	—	—	—
Norway	3.7	2.2	1.6	2.8
Sweden	—	—	—	8.3
Switzerland	—	12.8	—	—
United Kingdom	6.8	7.4	—	3.7
United States	479.9	840.3	604.4	509.0
TOTAL	2271.6	2756.9	2532.8	2058.0
MULTILATERAL	1246.7	1393.4	1390.2	1899.3
OPEC COUNTRIES	107.1	203.6	89.1	103.6
E.E.C. + MEMBERS	869.6	907.9	800.6	1070.7
TOTAL	3625.3	4354.0	4012.0	4060.9

GRANT ELEMENT OF ODA

DAC COUNTRIES

	1983	1984	1985	1986
Australia	100.0	100.0	100.0	100.0
Austria	38.8	40.0	92.3	47.3
Belgium	94.2	95.7	97.5	97.2
Canada	97.4	99.3	98.5	99.1
Denmark	87.3	93.2	91.2	86.4
Finland	100.0	88.6	100.0	100.0
France	72.7	67.6	71.2	66.2
Germany, Fed. Rep.	79.1	68.5	71.7	76.3
Ireland	100.0	100.0	100.0	100.0
Italy	73.9	88.3	78.9	87.1
Japan	69.4	66.6	65.3	77.7
Netherlands	93.7	82.9	97.4	95.1
New Zealand	100.0	100.0	100.0	100.0
Norway	96.8	99.1	99.0	98.5
Sweden	100.0	100.0	100.0	100.0
Switzerland	100.0	95.9	98.1	100.0
United Kingdom	98.4	98.5	100.0	99.1
United States	92.2	88.4	92.4	92.4
TOTAL	85.0	82.1	83.9	86.9
MULTILATERAL	87.2	87.9	87.6	86.5
OPEC COUNTRIES	55.4	46.4	47.9	66.3
E.E.C. + MEMBERS	84.3	79.9	82.6	84.3
TOTAL	85.1	82.6	84.4	86.4

OTHER AGGREGATES

COMMITMENTS: ALL SOURCES

	1983	1984	1985	1986
TOTAL BILATERAL	8300.2	10131.0	9145.9	10782.3
of which				
OPEC	203.9	308.3	113.5	185.6
CMEA	1702.9	1694.9	1733.2	3145.1
TOTAL MULTILATERAL	5102.0	5118.7	5343.5	6007.5
TOTAL BIL.& MULTIL.	13402.2	15249.7	14489.4	16789.9
of which				
ODA Grants	4317.6	4377.5	5001.3	5676.5
ODA Loans	5094.8	5782.1	5359.0	6742.6

DISBURSEMENTS:

DAC COUNTRIES COMBINED

	1983	1984	1985	1986
OFFICIAL & PRIVATE				
GROSS:				
Contractual Lending	6879.1	7999.9	6145.0	6547.0
Export Credits Total	4530.6	4712.0	3545.4	3165.7
Export Credits Private	3960.1	4017.6	3095.4	2801.1
NET:				
Contractual Lending	3181.0	4118.0	2723.7	2997.9
Export Credits Total	1379.9	1477.5	750.0	540.4
PRIVATE SECTOR NET	2533.1	2200.3	1292.7	1065.9
Direct Investment	753.7	793.6	251.0	-497.4
Portfolio Investment	726.8	165.6	354.8	853.3
Export Credits	1052.5	1241.0	686.9	710.0

MARKET BORROWING:

CHANGE IN CLAIMS

	1983	1984	1985	1986
Banks	—	1652.0	1034.0	352.0

MEMORANDUM ITEM:

	1983	1984	1985	1986
CMEA Countr.(Gross)	1938.0	1955.3	2090.5	2940.3

TOTAL RECEIPTS NET / TOTAL ODA NET / TOTAL ODA GROSS

	1983	1984	1985	1986	1983	1984	1985	1986		1983
DAC COUNTRIES									**TOTAL ODA GROSS**	
Australia	402.0	461.3	305.8	264.2	307.8	325.6	275.5	262.4	Australia	310.8
Austria	127.0	-4.0	-13.0	12.4	27.3	22.5	23.5	15.3	Austria	27.6
Belgium	139.9	378.4	234.4	8.9	48.0	36.5	29.3	39.9	Belgium	49.8
Canada	222.4	186.4	138.8	129.2	100.9	147.9	131.2	148.4	Canada	104.5
Denmark	132.8	50.8	17.6	21.4	12.0	26.1	14.3	64.0	Denmark	13.5
Finland	-3.5	1.7	8.9	36.0	6.5	7.4	12.0	15.5	Finland	6.9
France	2076.6	1236.1	1340.6	892.9	412.3	411.6	419.7	520.8	France	451.1
Germany, Fed. Rep.	898.1	620.1	435.3	548.3	314.7	254.5	269.2	464.4	Germany, Fed. Rep.	376.4
Ireland	0.5	0.5	0.5	1.0	0.5	0.5	0.5	1.0	Ireland	0.5
Italy	21.1	202.6	337.9	207.5	57.3	93.1	130.5	161.4	Italy	60.7
Japan	1026.0	937.2	641.5	1639.8	537.8	571.6	637.8	908.3	Japan	612.0
Netherlands	276.7	136.8	165.8	143.4	87.9	123.6	92.8	128.6	Netherlands	91.0
New Zealand	14.9	14.5	15.3	29.3	13.7	14.2	14.2	28.3	New Zealand	13.7
Norway	14.7	169.4	169.8	145.4	25.0	28.1	23.0	38.3	Norway	25.0
Sweden	78.6	64.3	81.7	154.1	43.2	55.9	57.7	64.5	Sweden	44.0
Switzerland	-59.6	175.9	10.8	21.0	22.0	19.8	23.0	27.4	Switzerland	23.7
United Kingdom	544.8	280.0	134.1	20.1	67.7	45.5	66.2	55.7	United Kingdom	82.4
United States	2213.0	2040.0	283.0	1925.0	1292.0	1283.0	1399.0	1502.0	United States	1373.0
TOTAL	*8125.9*	*6952.1*	*4308.7*	*6199.9*	*3376.6*	*3467.3*	*3619.4*	*4446.2*	*TOTAL*	*3666.6*
MULTILATERAL										
AF.D.F.	3.3	3.1	6.3	8.0	3.3	3.1	6.3	8.0	AF.D.F.	3.3
AF.D.B.	37.1	28.0	51.3	114.2	–	–	–	–	AF.D.B.	27.1
AS.D.B	270.8	255.8	196.7	193.1	25.8	19.1	19.7	45.8	AS.D.B	17.4
CAR.D.B.	23.4	14.0	21.9	20.3	17.4	8.1	11.2	15.6	CAR.D.B.	17.4
E.E.C.	233.5	174.8	242.6	346.0	195.9	155.8	147.0	272.3	E.E.C.	210.0
IBRD	2012.7	1837.7	1711.2	1513.9	14.2	3.5	2.5	–	IBRD	14.2
IDA	70.8	52.9	29.9	24.3	70.8	52.9	29.9	24.3	IDA	77.5
I.D.B.	345.6	294.7	252.0	203.7	161.6	110.6	68.7	44.3	I.D.B.	179.6
IFAD	20.6	36.1	34.8	43.3	20.6	36.1	34.8	43.3	IFAD	20.6
I.F.C.	39.5	-3.0	-6.1	77.6	–	–	–	–	I.F.C.	–
IMF TRUST FUND	–	–	–	–	–	–	–	–	IMF TRUST FUND	–
U.N. AGENCIES	–	–	–	–	–	–	–	–	U.N. AGENCIES	–
UNDP	66.5	56.5	63.0	76.2	66.5	56.5	63.0	76.2	UNDP	66.5
UNTA	20.8	16.9	25.3	22.7	20.8	16.9	25.3	22.7	UNTA	20.8
UNICEF	22.4	26.0	28.7	32.3	22.4	26.0	28.7	32.3	UNICEF	22.4
UNRWA	–	–	–	–	–	–	–	–	UNRWA	–
WFP	75.3	80.0	97.4	92.1	75.3	80.0	97.4	92.1	WFP	75.3
UNHCR	52.9	60.9	53.6	50.7	52.9	60.9	53.6	50.7	UNHCR	52.9
Other Multilateral	30.3	29.5	152.9	216.4	30.3	29.5	36.2	30.4	Other Multilateral	30.5
Arab OPEC Agencies	62.3	55.3	108.3	-17.1	42.8	20.6	21.1	17.6	Arab OPEC Agencies	50.9
TOTAL	*3387.9*	*3019.1*	*3069.5*	*3017.4*	*820.8*	*679.5*	*645.3*	*775.4*	*TOTAL*	*869.3*
OPEC COUNTRIES	*271.3*	*429.9*	*642.4*	*77.8*	*194.2*	*154.1*	*501.9*	*77.5*	*OPEC COUNTRIES*	*244.2*
E.E.C. + MEMBERS	*4323.9*	*3080.0*	*2908.7*	*2189.4*	*1196.4*	*1147.2*	*1169.4*	*1708.1*	*E.E.C. + MEMBERS*	*1335.4*
TOTAL	**11785.0**	**10401.2**	**8020.6**	**9295.1**	**4391.7**	**4300.9**	**4766.6**	**5299.1**	**TOTAL**	**4780.6**

ODA LOANS GROSS / ODA LOANS NET / GRANTS

	1983	1984	1985	1986	1983	1984	1985	1986		1983
DAC COUNTRIES									**GRANTS**	
Australia	–	–	–	–	-3.0	-1.6	-0.2	-0.2	Australia	310.8
Austria	17.5	15.9	17.7	5.3	17.2	14.5	15.0	2.3	Austria	10.1
Belgium	24.2	12.2	8.3	14.0	22.5	11.4	7.2	12.4	Belgium	25.5
Canada	40.6	48.9	35.9	34.0	36.9	47.3	29.1	28.4	Canada	63.9
Denmark	3.2	16.4	10.2	57.9	1.7	15.3	8.9	56.0	Denmark	10.3
Finland	4.0	4.5	8.3	9.1	3.7	4.2	8.0	8.7	Finland	2.8
France	185.2	191.3	258.5	274.8	146.5	158.6	219.0	227.7	France	265.9
Germany, Fed. Rep.	232.4	192.8	206.1	420.4	170.7	114.4	123.6	243.7	Germany, Fed. Rep.	143.9
Ireland	–	–	–	–	–	–	–	–	Ireland	0.5
Italy	23.1	55.3	80.2	67.6	19.7	49.6	74.1	59.5	Italy	37.7
Japan	413.0	445.2	470.8	819.1	338.8	368.5	404.6	611.5	Japan	199.0
Netherlands	34.9	48.2	39.4	31.2	31.7	42.3	33.4	24.6	Netherlands	56.2
New Zealand	–	–	–	–	–	–	–	–	New Zealand	13.7
Norway	0.9	–	–	0.2	0.9	0.9	0.0	0.2	Norway	24.1
Sweden	–	–	–	–	-0.8	-0.9	-0.9	-0.7	Sweden	44.0
Switzerland	9.4	7.8	7.4	10.9	7.7	5.4	5.8	7.4	Switzerland	14.3
United Kingdom	28.4	20.2	36.7	17.7	13.7	1.6	17.1	0.2	United Kingdom	54.0
United States	644.0	486.0	476.0	356.0	563.0	357.0	370.0	215.0	United States	729.0
TOTAL	*1660.9*	*1544.6*	*1655.4*	*2118.1*	*1370.8*	*1187.7*	*1314.7*	*1496.9*	*TOTAL*	*2005.8*
MULTILATERAL	*487.7*	*337.1*	*261.4*	*317.0*	*439.3*	*279.0*	*191.5*	*227.1*	*MULTILATERAL*	*381.6*
OPEC COUNTRIES	*231.5*	*208.0*	*221.4*	*128.9*	*181.0*	*151.7*	*151.0*	*76.1*	*OPEC COUNTRIES*	*13.2*
E.E.C. + MEMBERS	*634.2*	*583.4*	*655.0*	*935.6*	*495.1*	*426.3*	*485.9*	*656.4*	*E.E.C. + MEMBERS*	*701.2*
TOTAL	**2380.0**	**2089.7**	**2138.2**	**2564.0**	**1991.1**	**1618.4**	**1657.2**	**1800.1**	**TOTAL**	**2400.5**

TOTAL OFFICIAL GROSS / TOTAL OFFICIAL NET / TOTAL OOF GROSS

	1983	1984	1985	1986	1983	1984	1985	1986		1983
DAC COUNTRIES									**TOTAL OOF GROSS**	
Australia	416.7	387.0	282.0	262.8	410.9	381.1	265.9	184.4	Australia	105.9
Austria	28.6	30.5	26.2	18.3	25.1	27.2	19.4	12.4	Austria	1.0
Belgium	59.3	78.2	78.3	66.3	52.6	71.9	69.8	55.7	Belgium	9.6
Canada	294.9	277.9	271.6	263.6	221.8	187.3	139.0	129.7	Canada	190.4
Denmark	57.0	73.3	50.0	71.4	51.6	66.7	39.9	48.3	Denmark	43.5
Finland	6.9	8.1	12.4	15.8	6.5	7.7	12.0	15.5	Finland	–
France	724.6	953.8	975.1	1108.5	624.6	876.9	817.2	939.0	France	273.5
Germany, Fed. Rep.	736.2	606.8	530.8	884.1	566.8	435.7	346.6	557.4	Germany, Fed. Rep.	360.2
Ireland	0.5	0.5	0.5	1.0	0.5	0.5	0.5	1.0	Ireland	–
Italy	107.8	239.8	258.0	318.1	82.6	204.0	214.0	268.4	Italy	47.1
Japan	929.3	888.3	742.4	1214.5	831.5	768.7	631.4	897.6	Japan	317.3
Netherlands	94.8	131.1	102.5	139.5	89.8	123.0	93.3	127.2	Netherlands	3.8
New Zealand	14.9	14.2	15.3	29.3	14.9	14.2	15.3	29.3	New Zealand	1.3
Norway	25.0	28.1	23.1	38.3	25.0	28.1	23.0	38.3	Norway	–
Sweden	70.9	70.8	80.6	98.6	44.2	59.5	69.7	75.1	Sweden	26.9
Switzerland	53.4	22.7	24.6	30.9	37.0	15.0	18.4	21.0	Switzerland	29.6
United Kingdom	121.2	119.7	133.2	128.3	97.6	88.6	97.7	93.3	United Kingdom	38.8
United States	1636.0	1984.0	1958.0	2113.0	1381.0	1629.0	1632.0	1705.0	United States	263.0
TOTAL	*5378.3*	*5914.6*	*5564.7*	*6802.1*	*4564.0*	*4985.1*	*4505.2*	*5198.9*	*TOTAL*	*1711.7*
MULTILATERAL	*4216.4*	*4004.8*	*4167.1*	*4619.9*	*3387.9*	*3019.1*	*3069.5*	*3017.4*	*MULTILATERAL*	*3347.2*
OPEC COUNTRIES	*370.9*	*548.6*	*787.9*	*226.8*	*271.3*	*429.9*	*642.4*	*77.8*	*OPEC COUNTRIES*	*126.3*
E.E.C. + MEMBERS	*2172.9*	*2419.4*	*2409.9*	*3121.3*	*1799.7*	*2042.0*	*1921.6*	*2436.4*	*E.E.C. + MEMBERS*	*837.6*
TOTAL	**9965.7**	**10468.0**	**10519.6**	**11648.8**	**8223.1**	**8434.1**	**8217.1**	**8294.1**	**TOTAL**	**5185.1**

ODA COMMITMENTS

1984	1985	1986	1983	1984	1985	1986
327.2	275.7	262.6	309.3	334.4	254.1	255.0
23.9	26.2	18.3	20.0	9.3	12.0	–
37.3	30.4	41.5	25.5	25.0	12.5	41.5
149.6	137.9	154.0	188.0	249.0	210.4	176.3
27.1	15.6	66.0	12.8	21.4	62.6	55.8
7.7	12.4	15.8	4.6	8.8	13.4	11.8
444.2	459.2	567.9	638.2	656.5	491.9	567.9
332.9	351.7	641.1	296.5	565.8	387.4	689.0
0.5	0.5	1.0	0.5	0.5	0.5	1.0
98.7	136.6	169.5	153.5	167.0	199.8	289.3
648.3	704.0	1115.9	946.0	731.7	656.3	955.6
129.5	98.8	135.2	94.6	124.9	73.5	130.6
14.2	14.2	28.3	12.2	13.0	15.8	11.2
28.1	23.1	38.3	17.3	20.0	28.3	63.7
56.8	58.6	65.2	53.1	68.3	50.6	64.9
22.1	24.6	30.9	19.3	18.9	33.5	26.2
64.0	85.8	73.2	85.0	63.6	63.8	48.1
1412.0	1505.0	1643.0	1421.1	1701.8	1427.4	1694.6
3824.1	3960.1	5067.4	4297.5	4780.0	3993.6	5082.4
3.1	6.3	8.0	14.5	14.9	12.9	54.6
–	–	–	–	–	–	–
20.5	21.3	47.4	17.2	15.0	12.7	68.9
8.1	11.2	15.6	11.9	30.0	23.0	26.7
170.0	160.1	292.0	266.6	162.1	140.8	284.2
3.5	2.5	–	–	–	–	–
60.5	39.1	34.4	7.3	5.0	5.0	–
135.8	97.5	80.0	78.7	28.3	35.6	37.5
37.0	38.0	50.9	89.5	22.1	21.5	43.2
–	–	–	–	–	–	–
–	–	–	266.8	270.0	302.2	302.7
56.5	63.0	76.2	–	–	–	–
16.9	25.3	22.7	–	–	–	–
26.0	28.7	32.3	–	–	–	–
–	–	–	–	–	–	–
80.0	97.4	92.1	–	–	–	–
60.9	53.6	50.7	–	–	–	–
29.7	36.5	30.6	–	–	2.2	1.7
29.3	34.8	32.6	17.1	36.2	15.8	137.1
737.7	715.2	865.4	769.6	583.6	571.6	956.6
210.4	572.2	130.3	239.5	183.2	644.0	256.3
1304.3	1338.5	1987.3	1573.2	1786.8	1432.7	2107.4
4772.2	5247.6	6063.0	5306.7	5546.8	5209.3	6295.3

TECH. COOP. GRANTS

1984	1985	1986	1983	1984	1985	1986
327.2	275.7	262.6	25.8	33.2	34.5	29.9
8.0	8.5	13.0	8.7	–	–	–
25.1	22.1	27.5	11.3	10.4	10.4	11.9
100.7	102.1	119.9	25.5	–	33.1	–
10.8	5.3	8.0	9.3	4.3	7.7	7.2
3.2	4.1	6.8	1.7	1.9	1.5	7.7
253.0	200.7	293.1	233.4	215.5	176.2	275.5
140.1	145.5	220.7	127.0	122.3	125.7	192.2
0.5	0.5	1.0	0.5	0.5	0.5	1.0
43.5	56.5	101.9	17.5	27.0	34.0	50.7
203.1	233.2	296.8	87.9	101.1	101.7	142.2
81.2	59.4	104.0	30.4	28.5	30.4	45.1
14.2	14.2	28.3	3.4	3.7	3.8	3.6
28.1	23.1	38.0	1.3	1.7	1.9	2.8
56.8	58.6	65.2	10.2	15.8	17.1	14.9
14.4	17.2	20.0	3.5	3.4	3.3	7.7
43.9	49.1	55.5	34.1	28.1	27.4	31.9
926.0	1029.0	1287.0	188.0	169.0	194.0	221.0
2279.5	2304.8	2949.3	820.1	766.3	803.2	1045.2
400.6	453.8	548.3	191.5	190.0	199.9	214.5
2.4	350.9	1.4	–	–	–	–
720.9	683.5	1051.7	464.1	436.5	412.4	619.9
2682.5	3109.4	3499.0	1011.6	956.2	1003.1	1259.7

TOTAL OOF NET

1984	1985	1986	1983	1984	1985	1986
59.8	6.4	0.2	103.1	55.6	-9.6	-78.0
6.6	–	–	-2.2	4.7	-4.1	-2.8
40.8	48.0	24.8	4.6	35.3	40.5	15.8
128.3	133.6	109.6	120.9	39.4	7.8	-18.7
46.1	34.4	5.5	39.6	40.6	25.7	-15.7
0.3	–	–	–	0.3	–	–
509.6	515.9	540.6	212.3	465.3	397.5	418.2
273.9	179.1	243.0	252.2	181.2	77.5	93.1
–	–	–	–	–	–	–
141.1	121.4	148.7	25.3	111.0	83.5	107.1
240.0	38.5	98.6	293.7	197.1	-6.4	-10.7
1.6	3.8	4.3	1.9	-0.6	0.5	-1.4
–	1.1	1.0	1.3	–	1.1	1.0
–	–	–	–	–	–	–
14.0	22.0	33.4	0.9	3.6	12.0	10.7
0.6	–	–	15.0	-4.8	-4.6	-6.4
55.7	47.4	55.1	29.9	43.1	31.5	37.6
572.0	453.0	470.0	89.0	346.0	233.0	203.0
2090.5	1604.5	1734.7	1187.4	1517.8	885.8	752.7
3267.1	3451.9	3754.6	2567.1	2339.6	2424.2	2242.0
338.2	215.6	96.5	77.1	275.8	140.5	0.3
1115.1	1071.3	1134.0	603.3	894.8	752.2	728.3
5695.8	5272.1	5585.8	3831.5	4133.2	3450.5	2995.0

ODA COMMITMENTS : LOANS

DAC COUNTRIES

	1983	1984	1985	1986
Australia	–	–	–	–
Austria	10.3	2.8	3.5	–
Belgium	13.2	10.5	2.8	14.0
Canada	61.1	86.2	34.5	3.6
Denmark	5.5	13.0	59.5	47.6
Finland	0.3	3.3	12.1	5.9
France	366.8	390.9	284.8	274.8
Germany, Fed. Rep.	139.4	403.2	223.5	437.8
Ireland	–	–	–	–
Italy	81.0	91.6	100.0	121.4
Japan	741.6	509.6	414.0	673.5
Netherlands	29.1	50.2	20.9	21.4
New Zealand	–	–	–	–
Norway	–	–	–	0.2
Sweden	–	–	–	–
Switzerland	4.0	8.5	9.8	11.7
United Kingdom	40.0	15.7	23.2	–
United States	603.6	704.6	313.8	239.7
TOTAL	2095.9	2290.3	1502.1	1851.6
MULTILATERAL	326.0	191.6	125.4	409.7
OPEC COUNTRIES	225.6	183.2	290.5	229.5
E.E.C.+ MEMBERS	766.3	1018.3	718.4	963.5
TOTAL	2647.4	2665.1	1918.0	2490.8

GRANT ELEMENT OF ODA

DAC COUNTRIES

	1983	1984	1985	1986
Australia	100.0	100.0	100.0	100.0
Austria	77.1	89.7	92.7	28.7
Belgium	89.8	93.0	90.9	93.5
Canada	96.8	96.4	97.5	99.8
Denmark	89.3	85.4	76.6	78.8
Finland	95.0	88.1	72.7	84.5
France	76.4	68.1	76.6	71.8
Germany, Fed. Rep.	84.4	67.3	70.2	67.4
Ireland	100.0	100.0	100.0	100.0
Italy	71.0	69.3	71.8	82.7
Japan	62.5	63.7	66.5	59.2
Netherlands	87.8	83.7	88.9	94.1
New Zealand	100.0	100.0	100.0	100.0
Norway	100.0	100.0	100.0	99.7
Sweden	100.0	100.0	100.0	100.0
Switzerland	89.0	92.6	95.6	94.4
United Kingdom	71.9	77.9	84.0	100.0
United States	81.2	83.0	91.1	93.8
TOTAL	78.7	78.0	83.2	80.8
MULTILATERAL	85.2	89.1	94.2	83.0
OPEC COUNTRIES	51.2	43.9	74.3	51.2
E.E.C.+ MEMBERS	81.6	72.2	77.7	77.7
TOTAL	78.3	77.9	83.3	79.9

OTHER AGGREGATES

COMMITMENTS: ALL SOURCES

	1983	1984	1985	1986
TOTAL BILATERAL	6913.4	8803.2	8037.4	7791.7
of which				
OPEC	384.0	648.3	891.9	321.0
CMEA	1031.9	1127.0	1765.6	1408.6
TOTAL MULTILATERAL	5516.3	4092.8	4267.8	6275.1
TOTAL BIL.& MULTIL.	12429.6	12896.0	12305.2	14066.8
of which				
ODA Grants	2675.0	2925.0	3298.4	4006.7
ODA Loans	3529.7	3496.6	3069.0	3498.5

DISBURSEMENTS:

DAC COUNTRIES COMBINED

OFFICIAL & PRIVATE	1983	1984	1985	1986
GROSS:				
Contractual Lending	7927.5	7694.2	7220.4	5619.9
Export Credits Total	5629.0	4945.0	4587.2	2327.2
Export Credits Private	4556.2	4074.5	3977.0	1918.8
NET:				
Contractual Lending	3805.4	3862.5	2938.6	1882.3
Export Credits	1978.9	1605.1	877.0	-536.4
PRIVATE SECTOR NET	3561.9	1967.0	-196.5	1001.0
Direct Investment	486.0	234.2	-799.5	854.7
Portfolio Investment	1827.4	560.4	-151.8	361.8
Export Credits	1248.5	1172.4	754.7	-215.5

MARKET BORROWING:

CHANGE IN CLAIMS

	1983	1984	1985	1986
Banks	–	-152.0	1665.0	764.0

MEMORANDUM ITEM:

	1983	1984	1985	1986
CMEA Countr.(Gross)	804.6	859.7	1014.6	1220.9

TOTAL RECEIPTS NET / TOTAL ODA NET / TOTAL ODA GROSS

	TOTAL RECEIPTS NET 1983	1984	1985	1986	TOTAL ODA NET 1983	1984	1985	1986	TOTAL ODA GROSS 1983
DAC COUNTRIES									
Australia	254.9	425.7	138.1	96.8	24.7	51.7	77.1	70.9	24.7
Austria	58.0	-12.5	52.4	149.9	56.0	73.4	109.2	79.8	58.4
Belgium	139.3	2391.9	99.0	-1428.0	13.1	17.6	12.6	18.0	13.1
Canada	201.6	109.4	-60.1	-152.0	48.0	50.2	40.4	33.3	52.0
Denmark	513.1	49.2	23.7	-112.5	4.7	-0.2	-0.7	4.8	5.5
Finland	-45.2	-20.4	1.1	23.3	2.5	1.8	3.3	4.8	2.5
France	4142.5	4101.1	3999.6	3321.1	1501.8	1310.7	1397.5	1833.2	1556.8
Germany, Fed. Rep.	2106.1	2289.7	2400.9	3001.3	352.9	251.3	236.2	353.3	423.0
Ireland	0.0	0.0	0.0	0.0	0.0	0.0	0.0	0.0	0.0
Italy	937.7	485.0	416.0	-325.9	63.0	49.0	65.8	88.0	64.5
Japan	2376.6	8874.7	4387.8	5685.5	287.3	404.1	299.7	332.6	432.1
Netherlands	-243.1	-299.2	457.5	139.7	99.0	93.1	107.5	142.6	105.9
New Zealand	9.1	6.7	7.3	6.4	9.1	6.7	7.3	6.4	9.1
Norway	46.5	319.0	374.8	375.7	17.8	4.9	7.1	6.1	17.8
Sweden	268.2	288.1	140.0	127.0	9.0	2.7	5.0	15.1	9.8
Switzerland	123.1	-225.2	-181.6	11.3	7.9	6.9	9.3	11.3	7.9
United Kingdom	604.4	2418.3	771.8	154.3	45.0	36.7	63.8	134.5	63.2
United States	10013.0	16404.0	-6282.0	2652.0	1392.0	1464.0	2272.0	2154.0	1565.0
TOTAL	*21505.8*	*37605.5*	*6746.3*	*13725.9*	*3933.6*	*3824.6*	*4713.0*	*5288.6*	*4411.3*
MULTILATERAL									
AF.D.F.	–	0.3	0.1	3.1	–	0.3	0.1	3.1	–
AF.D.B.	5.1	4.2	2.7	13.2	–	–	–	–	1.8
AS.D.B	130.3	109.4	56.3	20.3	1.2	1.3	1.7	1.2	6.6
CAR.D.B.	9.7	8.3	2.6	11.0	6.6	1.8	1.2	2.8	6.6
E.E.C.	242.2	141.1	174.1	360.8	142.4	103.3	144.7	263.6	143.0
IBRD	2160.0	2541.3	1991.6	2515.8	1.5	1.9	–	–	1.5
IDA	-1.6	-6.0	-6.0	-6.6	-1.6	-6.0	-6.0	-6.6	3.8
I.D.B.	804.7	1419.0	1285.0	1134.6	84.7	163.1	154.9	125.3	215.5
IFAD	17.5	4.9	12.6	19.1	17.5	4.9	12.6	19.1	17.5
I.F.C.	77.1	54.6	14.8	45.2	–	–	–	–	–
IMF TRUST FUND	–	–	–	–	–	–	–	–	–
U.N. AGENCIES	–	–	–	–	–	–	–	–	–
UNDP	79.2	73.9	75.1	100.4	79.2	73.9	75.1	100.4	79.2
UNTA	20.1	17.3	23.5	23.1	20.1	17.3	23.5	23.1	20.1
UNICEF	35.6	23.2	15.3	16.8	35.6	23.2	15.3	16.8	35.6
UNRWA	–	–	–	–	–	–	–	–	–
WFP	40.4	45.1	73.7	66.1	40.4	45.1	73.7	66.1	40.4
UNHCR	29.8	48.4	48.4	39.1	29.8	48.4	48.4	39.1	29.8
Other Multilateral	25.3	22.2	208.8	109.3	25.3	22.2	32.0	21.8	25.6
Arab OPEC Agencies	68.3	137.6	176.5	27.2	22.8	12.8	12.6	19.7	34.0
TOTAL	*3743.6*	*4644.7*	*4154.9*	*4498.3*	*505.5*	*513.5*	*589.9*	*695.4*	*654.5*
OPEC COUNTRIES	*1988.2*	*1640.5*	*1267.3*	*1405.4*	*1893.2*	*1699.1*	*1224.5*	*1367.9*	*1997.0*
E.E.C.+ MEMBERS	*8442.3*	*11577.2*	*8342.6*	*5110.8*	*2221.8*	*1861.5*	*2027.3*	*2838.0*	*2375.1*
TOTAL	*27237.6*	*43890.7*	*12168.6*	*19629.6*	*6332.3*	*6037.2*	*6527.4*	*7351.9*	*7062.8*

ODA LOANS GROSS / ODA LOANS NET / GRANTS

	ODA LOANS GROSS 1983	1984	1985	1986	ODA LOANS NET 1983	1984	1985	1986	GRANTS 1983
DAC COUNTRIES									
Australia	–	–	–	–	–	–	–	–	24.7
Austria	41.9	64.6	97.8	63.9	39.4	59.6	94.9	61.0	16.5
Belgium	1.0	5.3	1.4	2.2	0.9	5.1	1.4	2.0	12.1
Canada	22.9	13.1	8.8	5.8	18.9	8.8	4.6	0.5	29.1
Denmark	3.7	–	–	5.6	2.8	-0.8	-0.9	4.3	1.9
Finland	0.9	–	0.6	0.9	0.9	–	0.6	0.9	1.6
France	138.8	133.3	104.4	153.1	83.8	82.0	61.3	101.1	1418.0
Germany, Fed. Rep.	186.4	144.9	127.4	345.1	116.3	65.8	45.7	94.5	236.6
Ireland	–	–	–	–	–	–	–	–	0.0
Italy	26.0	7.5	20.0	20.7	24.5	7.4	19.9	18.5	38.5
Japan	309.7	435.0	317.4	355.9	164.9	258.4	146.5	104.2	122.4
Netherlands	23.5	33.6	31.6	52.1	16.5	27.0	24.3	39.4	82.4
New Zealand	–	–	–	–	–	–	–	–	9.1
Norway	10.8	–	0.5	–	10.8	–	-0.9	-1.6	7.0
Sweden	–	–	–	–	-0.8	-0.8	-0.7	-0.9	9.8
Switzerland	–	–	–	–	–	–	–	-0.2	7.9
United Kingdom	4.4	1.1	1.0	8.2	-13.9	-16.9	-11.1	-4.0	58.9
United States	109.0	114.0	108.0	107.0	-64.0	-34.0	-85.0	-83.0	1456.0
TOTAL	*878.8*	*952.4*	*818.7*	*1120.3*	*401.0*	*461.8*	*300.5*	*336.7*	*3532.5*
MULTILATERAL	*289.2*	*336.0*	*348.3*	*349.1*	*140.2*	*181.1*	*178.8*	*167.7*	*365.3*
OPEC COUNTRIES	*209.3*	*224.4*	*198.7*	*174.9*	*105.6*	*75.8*	*47.9*	*64.6*	*1787.6*
E.E.C.+ MEMBERS	*398.3*	*337.8*	*290.1*	*594.8*	*245.0*	*181.5*	*144.6*	*262.7*	*1976.8*
TOTAL	*1377.3*	*1512.7*	*1365.8*	*1644.3*	*646.9*	*718.7*	*527.1*	*569.1*	*5685.4*

TOTAL OFFICIAL GROSS / TOTAL OFFICIAL NET / TOTAL OOF GROSS

	TOTAL OFFICIAL GROSS 1983	1984	1985	1986	TOTAL OFFICIAL NET 1983	1984	1985	1986	TOTAL OOF GROSS 1983
DAC COUNTRIES									
Australia	28.6	54.5	78.5	75.8	25.4	47.9	72.4	70.8	3.9
Austria	58.4	78.4	128.9	155.0	53.9	70.6	123.9	149.9	–
Belgium	13.1	50.8	40.5	19.4	12.1	49.3	39.4	18.3	–
Canada	500.6	417.4	355.7	220.9	228.5	128.9	-47.1	-170.0	448.7
Denmark	101.1	117.9	102.4	40.5	86.9	96.4	65.5	-8.5	95.6
Finland	2.5	1.8	3.3	4.8	2.5	1.8	3.3	4.8	–
France	1738.3	1822.4	2195.9	2634.3	1608.6	1658.3	2055.3	2267.5	181.5
Germany, Fed. Rep.	790.2	958.6	1288.7	1832.8	519.6	727.4	927.1	1192.9	367.2
Ireland	0.0	0.0	0.0	0.0	0.0	0.0	0.0	0.0	–
Italy	253.1	172.8	521.7	431.3	175.9	113.8	461.5	343.6	188.6
Japan	951.5	1090.4	903.5	1063.8	539.2	609.9	388.5	386.5	519.4
Netherlands	129.5	101.8	116.1	157.5	119.9	92.6	106.5	131.8	23.6
New Zealand	9.1	6.7	7.3	6.4	9.1	6.7	7.3	6.4	–
Norway	17.8	4.9	8.5	7.8	15.8	2.9	5.1	4.1	–
Sweden	299.4	282.1	322.8	304.9	240.7	123.0	147.0	183.2	289.6
Switzerland	7.9	6.9	9.3	11.5	7.3	6.9	9.3	11.3	–
United Kingdom	67.1	60.7	83.6	157.4	46.8	37.1	67.7	141.7	3.9
United States	3591.0	3388.0	4201.0	3737.0	1273.0	1722.0	2096.0	1503.0	2026.0
TOTAL	*8559.4*	*8616.1*	*10367.6*	*10861.1*	*4965.2*	*5495.3*	*6528.8*	*6237.5*	*4148.1*
MULTILATERAL	*5777.8*	*7198.6*	*7026.8*	*8550.6*	*3743.6*	*4644.7*	*4154.9*	*4498.3*	*5123.4*
OPEC COUNTRIES	*2413.2*	*1955.6*	*1565.2*	*1571.1*	*1988.2*	*1640.5*	*1267.3*	*1405.4*	*416.2*
E.E.C.+ MEMBERS	*3383.4*	*3505.3*	*4529.3*	*5663.9*	*2812.2*	*2916.0*	*3897.1*	*4448.2*	*1008.3*
TOTAL	*16750.4*	*17770.2*	*18959.6*	*20982.7*	*10697.1*	*11780.5*	*11951.1*	*12141.2*	*9687.7*

Left tables

1984	1985	1986	1983	1984	1985	1986

ODA COMMITMENTS

1984	1985	1986	1983	1984	1985	1986
51.7	77.1	70.9	14.6	82.6	71.2	70.8
78.4	112.1	82.6	100.4	14.1	27.4	–
17.7	12.6	18.2	9.5	4.4	3.8	18.2
54.5	44.5	38.5	39.1	65.1	66.7	30.3
0.6	0.2	6.1	–	–	0.2	5.4
1.8	3.3	4.8	1.1	0.9	4.6	5.4
1361.9	1440.6	1885.1	2140.1	1818.5	1532.0	1885.1
330.4	317.8	603.9	323.9	468.1	379.9	600.9
0.0	0.0	0.0	0.0	0.0	0.0	0.0
49.1	65.9	90.2	95.7	121.6	83.2	108.1
580.7	470.6	584.2	494.5	676.9	881.2	569.8
99.7	114.8	155.2	117.0	94.7	131.4	126.4
6.7	7.3	6.4	8.6	7.3	7.7	3.9
4.9	8.5	7.8	16.2	2.1	2.1	6.5
3.5	5.8	16.0	4.3	8.2	12.8	15.8
6.9	9.3	11.5	6.6	7.8	6.9	14.0
54.7	76.0	146.7	78.9	41.4	44.2	148.5
1612.0	2465.0	2344.0	1609.1	1642.1	2572.0	2427.0
4315.3	5231.3	6072.1	5059.7	5055.8	5827.3	6030.8
0.3	0.1	3.1	–	–	–	–
1.9	2.3	1.8	–	–	–	–
1.8	1.2	2.8	1.4	1.9	2.0	7.7
103.6	145.0	264.7	196.1	141.2	173.1	215.6
1.9	–	–	–	–	–	–
295.2	298.3	275.6	247.8	224.2	131.1	94.6
8.0	17.1	24.3	14.3	11.7	14.5	10.3
–	–	–	–	–	–	–
–	–	–	227.4	229.4	261.5	264.4
73.9	75.1	100.4	–	–	–	–
17.3	23.5	23.1	–	–	–	–
23.2	15.3	16.8	–	–	–	–
45.1	73.7	66.1	–	–	–	–
48.4	48.4	39.1	–	–	–	–
22.6	32.7	22.8	–	–	7.3	3.9
25.1	26.8	36.2	46.9	52.6	31.4	32.2
668.3	759.5	876.9	733.9	660.9	620.7	628.8
1847.7	1375.0	1478.2	2158.5	1943.1	1508.4	1677.2
2017.8	2172.9	3170.1	2961.2	2689.9	2347.7	3102.9
6831.2	7366.0	8427.1	7952.1	7659.8	7956.3	8336.8

TECH. COOP. GRANTS

1984	1985	1986	1983	1984	1985	1986
51.7	77.1	70.9	10.6	45.0	69.7	63.7
13.8	14.3	18.7	14.7	–	–	–
12.5	11.2	16.0	4.6	4.4	4.3	5.0
41.4	35.7	32.7	12.0	–	11.4	–
0.6	0.2	0.5	0.7	0.5	0.2	0.5
1.8	2.7	3.9	0.6	1.0	1.7	0.3
1228.7	1336.2	1732.1	771.2	656.4	703.6	974.2
185.5	190.4	258.8	192.0	170.0	179.6	246.3
0.0	0.0	0.0	0.0	0.0	0.0	0.0
41.6	45.9	69.5	18.9	36.3	32.9	50.1
145.8	153.2	228.3	109.2	120.2	131.6	192.0
66.1	83.2	103.2	34.4	30.9	32.3	40.9
6.7	7.3	6.4	1.4	1.3	1.5	2.4
4.9	8.0	7.8	0.6	0.6	1.3	0.9
3.5	5.8	16.0	1.7	1.0	2.0	1.0
6.9	9.3	11.5	1.8	1.6	1.6	2.3
53.6	75.0	138.5	27.8	22.6	22.0	26.3
1498.0	2357.0	2237.0	35.0	59.0	54.0	61.0
3362.9	4412.5	4951.8	1237.3	1150.8	1249.6	1666.9
332.3	411.2	527.7	187.1	184.2	187.8	199.8
1623.3	1176.6	1303.3	–	–	–	–
1680.0	1882.8	2575.3	1049.7	921.1	974.8	1344.9
5318.5	6000.3	6782.8	1424.4	1335.0	1437.3	1866.7

TOTAL OOF NET

1984	1985	1986	1983	1984	1985	1986
2.8	1.4	4.8	0.7	-3.8	-4.7	-0.1
–	16.8	72.4	-2.1	-2.9	14.7	70.2
33.1	27.9	1.2	-0.9	31.6	26.9	0.3
362.9	311.1	182.4	180.5	78.7	-87.4	-203.3
117.3	102.2	34.4	82.3	96.5	66.3	-13.3
–	–	–	–	–	–	–
460.4	755.3	749.1	106.9	347.6	657.8	434.4
628.2	970.9	1228.9	166.7	476.2	690.9	839.6
–	–	–	–	–	–	–
123.7	455.8	341.1	112.8	64.8	395.7	255.6
509.7	433.0	479.6	252.0	205.7	88.9	54.0
2.1	1.4	2.3	21.0	-0.4	-1.0	-10.8
–	–	–	-2.0	-2.0	-2.0	-2.0
278.6	317.0	288.9	231.7	120.3	142.0	168.1
–	–	–	-0.6	–	–	–
6.0	7.6	10.8	1.9	0.4	3.9	7.3
1776.0	1736.0	1393.0	-119.0	258.0	-176.0	-651.0
4300.8	5136.4	4789.0	1031.7	1670.7	1815.8	949.0
6530.3	6267.3	7673.7	3238.1	4131.2	3565.0	3802.8
107.9	189.9	92.9	95.0	-58.6	42.9	37.5
1487.5	2356.5	2493.8	590.4	1054.5	1869.8	1610.2
10939.0	11593.6	12555.6	4364.8	5743.3	5423.7	4789.3

Right tables

ODA COMMITMENTS : LOANS

DAC COUNTRIES	1983	1984	1985	1986
Australia	–	–	–	–
Austria	85.1	0.9	13.1	–
Belgium	5.9	1.0	0.5	2.2
Canada	4.0	19.6	9.1	–
Denmark	–	–	–	–
Finland	–	–	2.0	–
France	73.7	211.9	187.0	153.1
Germany, Fed. Rep.	85.7	271.9	165.4	302.9
Ireland	–	–	–	–
Italy	38.5	50.4	5.4	–
Japan	348.3	533.2	710.9	328.8
Netherlands	23.1	30.8	48.0	26.1
New Zealand	–	–	–	–
Norway	9.9	–	0.5	–
Sweden	–	–	–	–
Switzerland	–	–	–	4.1
United Kingdom	1.3	0.2	–	–
United States	109.1	120.7	105.4	82.1
TOTAL	784.5	1240.5	1247.0	899.3
MULTILATERAL	322.1	310.1	196.0	144.8
OPEC COUNTRIES	208.5	261.3	184.4	56.6
E.E.C.+ MEMBERS	241.2	589.1	418.4	486.7
TOTAL	1315.1	1812.0	1627.4	1100.7

GRANT ELEMENT OF ODA

DAC COUNTRIES	1983	1984	1985	1986
Australia	100.0	100.0	100.0	100.0
Austria	40.8	96.1	66.4	34.8
Belgium	88.0	95.8	94.1	97.6
Canada	99.0	97.0	98.6	100.0
Denmark	–	–	100.0	–
Finland	100.0	100.0	100.0	100.0
France	97.7	93.6	94.7	98.2
Germany, Fed. Rep.	84.8	65.5	70.2	66.2
Ireland	100.0	100.0	100.0	100.0
Italy	77.1	73.3	96.4	100.0
Japan	60.2	50.9	49.9	64.4
Netherlands	92.4	86.7	80.8	91.5
New Zealand	100.0	100.0	100.0	100.0
Norway	54.2	100.0	84.1	100.0
Sweden	100.0	100.0	100.0	100.0
Switzerland	100.0	100.0	93.6	95.9
United Kingdom	99.6	97.3	100.0	100.0
United States	97.0	97.2	98.0	98.4
TOTAL	91.5	86.5	87.6	91.9
MULTILATERAL	80.1	75.5	89.5	91.7
OPEC COUNTRIES	94.2	91.1	92.4	98.1
E.E.C.+ MEMBERS	95.6	87.9	90.3	91.8
TOTAL	91.0	86.5	88.6	93.1

OTHER AGGREGATES

COMMITMENTS: ALL SOURCES

	1983	1984	1985	1986
TOTAL BILATERAL	11179.0	13364.8	11605.1	11073.3
of which				
OPEC	3004.3	2289.9	1788.0	1705.1
CMEA	784.9	2358.0	617.6	525.0
TOTAL MULTILATERAL	9189.3	7685.0	10190.8	10161.6
TOTAL BIL.& MULTIL.	20368.3	21049.8	21796.0	21234.8
of which				
ODA Grants	6639.9	5849.8	6334.6	7236.1
ODA Loans	1634.4	3872.0	2009.4	1125.7

DISBURSEMENTS:

DAC COUNTRIES COMBINED

OFFICIAL & PRIVATE

	1983	1984	1985	1986
GROSS:				
Contractual Lending	22160.8	19556.2	18853.8	14205.2
Export Credits Total	20489.0	16960.5	15090.5	10259.8
Export Credits Private	17133.8	14327.2	12924.3	8284.5
NET:				
Contractual Lending	3919.6	4128.4	1563.7	-1226.6
Export Credits Total	4148.3	2624.7	-1026.1	-3409.5
PRIVATE SECTOR NET	16540.6	32110.2	217.5	7488.4
Direct Investment	3925.5	7716.7	4871.2	7389.8
Portfolio Investment	10128.1	22373.3	-4126.6	2613.9
Export Credits	2486.9	2020.2	-527.1	-2515.4

MARKET BORROWING:

CHANGE IN CLAIMS

	1983	1984	1985	1986
Banks	–	6950.0	4991.0	-3556.0

MEMORANDUM ITEM:

	1983	1984	1985	1986
CMEA Countr.(Gross)	67.5	114.3	105.7	96.4

	1983	1984	1985	1986		1983	1984	1985	1986		1983
TOTAL RECEIPTS NET					**TOTAL ODA NET**					**TOTAL ODA GROSS**	
DAC COUNTRIES											
Australia	57.0	96.5	264.9	599.8		39.0	47.1	45.0	45.1	Australia	39.0
Austria	-149.8	13.2	15.5	-133.9		9.3	9.0	8.9	14.1	Austria	9.3
Belgium	195.7	33.8	52.9	59.5		55.9	38.4	38.2	51.0	Belgium	55.9
Canada	1010.2	928.4	95.5	237.5		226.2	252.4	258.5	367.5	Canada	226.2
Denmark	64.7	87.6	63.3	10.6		33.3	31.8	20.7	27.6	Denmark	33.4
Finland	105.6	33.2	42.1	71.9		10.9	13.4	17.3	33.0	Finland	10.9
France	487.5	552.0	449.2	573.4		479.7	556.2	536.6	573.6	France	481.3
Germany, Fed. Rep.	539.7	432.9	-36.5	410.7		246.3	307.6	280.2	414.0	Germany, Fed. Rep.	256.8
Ireland	4.8	9.0	43.3	42.6		4.8	5.8	5.9	10.8	Ireland	4.8
Italy	269.2	162.8	210.0	254.6		84.4	86.4	125.6	154.5	Italy	84.4
Japan	155.0	-3963.5	190.8	241.2		111.6	132.2	135.9	232.1	Japan	117.6
Netherlands	206.4	314.0	361.1	291.8		147.2	131.0	121.6	176.4	Netherlands	147.2
New Zealand	67.0	30.4	35.6	39.7		12.8	11.2	11.3	13.4	New Zealand	12.8
Norway	70.1	107.2	73.2	191.2		50.5	53.8	57.9	88.1	Norway	50.5
Sweden	269.1	225.9	456.8	308.3		110.5	125.9	179.8	170.3	Sweden	110.6
Switzerland	2176.0	2024.0	721.9	358.6		57.9	51.3	58.1	90.3	Switzerland	57.9
United Kingdom	3446.3	493.5	13.8	5404.0		172.1	170.7	192.4	207.6	United Kingdom	173.6
United States	2095.0	2586.0	693.0	700.0		529.0	950.0	1113.0	1056.0	United States	531.0
TOTAL	*11069.4*	*4166.8*	*3746.4*	*9661.4*		*2381.1*	*2974.2*	*3206.9*	*3725.3*	*TOTAL*	*2403.0*
MULTILATERAL											
AF.D.F.	2.8	1.9	3.1	2.7		2.8	1.9	3.1	2.7	AF.D.F.	2.8
AF.D.B.	6.1	2.4	7.1	8.6		–	–	–	–	AF.D.B.	–
AS.D.B	–	3.7	5.5	6.3		–	3.7	5.5	6.3	AS.D.B	–
CAR.D.B.	6.4	4.8	6.4	8.9		6.4	4.8	6.4	5.8	CAR.D.B.	6.4
E.E.C.	183.4	179.9	384.6	228.9		182.6	179.4	384.4	226.7	E.E.C.	182.7
IBRD	-38.0	-35.5	-139.7	-10.9		0.7	–	–	–	IBRD	0.7
IDA	0.7	1.4	0.8	0.6		0.7	1.4	0.8	0.6	IDA	0.7
I.D.B.	58.0	63.1	60.8	17.0		24.0	27.1	31.5	10.2	I.D.B.	27.2
IFAD	15.5	16.3	11.8	–		15.5	16.3	11.8	–	IFAD	15.5
I.F.C.	-3.3	0.7	2.2	8.7		–	–	–	–	I.F.C.	–
IMF TRUST FUND	–	–	–	–		–	–	–	–	IMF TRUST FUND	–
U.N. AGENCIES	–	–	–	–		–	–	–	–	U.N. AGENCIES	–
UNDP	119.9	119.9	110.1	152.1		119.9	119.9	110.1	152.1	UNDP	119.9
UNTA	137.4	128.1	155.6	136.3		137.4	128.1	155.6	136.3	UNTA	137.4
UNICEF	11.5	21.7	36.9	41.6		11.5	21.7	36.9	41.6	UNICEF	11.5
UNRWA	210.9	191.3	187.4	186.5		210.9	191.3	187.4	186.5	UNRWA	210.9
WFP	3.7	0.6	1.7	2.7		3.7	0.6	1.7	2.7	WFP	3.7
UNHCR	27.1	23.9	24.5	17.5		27.1	23.9	24.5	17.5	UNHCR	27.1
Other Multilateral	223.5	226.3	224.7	265.2		223.5	226.3	224.7	265.2	Other Multilateral	223.5
Arab OPEC Agencies	26.8	7.4	11.8	24.3		26.5	7.4	11.8	24.3	Arab OPEC Agencies	27.1
TOTAL	*992.4*	*957.7*	*1095.3*	*1097.0*		*993.3*	*953.5*	*1196.2*	*1078.4*	*TOTAL*	*997.1*
OPEC COUNTRIES	*936.6*	*1296.9*	*669.4*	*1784.1*		*934.3*	*1291.5*	*659.2*	*1775.6*	*OPEC COUNTRIES*	*934.3*
E.E.C.+ MEMBERS	*5397.6*	*2265.5*	*1541.7*	*7276.0*		*1406.1*	*1507.3*	*1705.7*	*1842.0*	*E.E.C.+ MEMBERS*	*1420.0*
TOTAL	*12998.4*	*6421.5*	*5511.1*	*12542.5*		*4308.7*	*5219.2*	*5062.3*	*6579.3*	*TOTAL*	*4334.4*

	1983	1984	1985	1986		1983	1984	1985	1986		1983
ODA LOANS GROSS					**ODA LOANS NET**					**GRANTS**	
DAC COUNTRIES											
Australia	–	–	–	–		–	–	–	–	Australia	39.0
Austria	–	–	–	–		–	–	–	–	Austria	9.3
Belgium	0.8	0.1	1.0	–		0.8	0.0	1.0	–	Belgium	55.1
Canada	–	–	–	–		–	0.0	0.0	0.0	Canada	226.2
Denmark	–	–	–	–		-0.1	–	–	–	Denmark	33.4
Finland	–	–	–	0.3		–	–	–	0.3	Finland	10.9
France	39.5	38.0	38.9	61.3		37.9	34.5	35.5	49.3	France	441.8
Germany, Fed. Rep.	34.4	19.1	16.5	34.9		23.8	9.0	4.1	17.0	Germany, Fed. Rep.	222.5
Ireland	–	–	–	–		–	–	–	–	Ireland	4.8
Italy	–	–	–	–		–	–	–	–	Italy	84.4
Japan	1.3	1.0	0.8	0.9		-4.7	-4.9	-4.9	-7.9	Japan	116.3
Netherlands	–	–	–	–		–	–	–	–	Netherlands	147.2
New Zealand	–	–	–	–		–	–	–	–	New Zealand	12.8
Norway	–	–	–	–		–	–	0.0	–	Norway	50.5
Sweden	4.1	–	–	4.2		3.9	-0.1	-0.1	3.0	Sweden	106.6
Switzerland	1.6	–	0.0	1.8		1.6	–	0.0	1.4	Switzerland	56.3
United Kingdom	0.2	11.3	–	4.7		-1.3	7.0	-1.6	2.7	United Kingdom	173.3
United States	4.0	6.0	4.0	3.0		2.0	4.0	2.0	–	United States	527.0
TOTAL	*85.8*	*75.4*	*61.3*	*111.1*		*63.9*	*49.5*	*36.1*	*65.8*	*TOTAL*	*2317.2*
MULTILATERAL	*53.9*	*25.7*	*27.7*	*35.1*		*50.0*	*20.4*	*21.8*	*31.2*	*MULTILATERAL*	*943.3*
OPEC COUNTRIES	*400.0*	–	–	–		*400.0*	–	–	–	*OPEC COUNTRIES*	*534.3*
E.E.C.+ MEMBERS	*98.5*	*73.0*	*56.5*	*103.4*		*84.7*	*55.1*	*39.0*	*71.6*	*E.E.C.+ MEMBERS*	*1321.5*
TOTAL	*539.7*	*101.1*	*89.0*	*146.2*		*513.9*	*69.9*	*57.8*	*97.0*	*TOTAL*	*3794.7*

	1983	1984	1985	1986		1983	1984	1985	1986		1983
TOTAL OFFICIAL GROSS					**TOTAL OFFICIAL NET**					**TOTAL OOF GROSS**	
DAC COUNTRIES											
Australia	39.0	47.1	45.0	45.1		39.0	47.1	45.0	45.1	Australia	–
Austria	9.3	9.0	8.9	14.1		9.3	8.2	8.9	14.1	Austria	–
Belgium	117.0	44.0	39.5	51.2		116.9	44.0	39.5	51.2	Belgium	61.0
Canada	226.2	252.4	258.5	367.5		226.2	252.4	258.5	367.5	Canada	–
Denmark	33.4	31.9	20.8	28.0		33.3	31.9	20.8	28.0	Denmark	0.0
Finland	10.9	13.4	17.3	33.0		10.9	13.4	17.3	33.0	Finland	–
France	490.6	559.7	540.0	585.7		488.5	555.6	447.0	573.6	France	9.3
Germany, Fed. Rep.	290.4	339.9	314.2	467.3		273.9	321.8	293.6	434.0	Germany, Fed. Rep.	33.5
Ireland	4.8	5.8	5.9	10.8		4.8	5.8	5.9	10.8	Ireland	–
Italy	85.8	86.4	126.2	154.6		85.1	86.4	126.2	154.6	Italy	1.5
Japan	117.6	138.1	201.2	240.9		111.6	132.2	192.9	230.2	Japan	–
Netherlands	147.2	131.0	121.6	176.4		147.2	131.0	121.6	176.4	Netherlands	–
New Zealand	12.8	12.2	11.3	13.4		11.6	11.5	11.3	13.4	New Zealand	–
Norway	70.1	53.8	73.2	88.1		70.1	53.8	73.2	88.1	Norway	19.6
Sweden	110.6	126.0	179.9	171.6		110.5	125.9	179.8	168.4	Sweden	–
Switzerland	57.9	51.3	58.1	90.7		57.9	51.3	58.1	90.3	Switzerland	–
United Kingdom	574.1	535.1	575.1	493.9		572.6	530.8	573.5	492.0	United Kingdom	400.5
United States	547.0	959.0	1116.0	1060.0		542.0	954.0	1087.0	1037.0	United States	16.0
TOTAL	*2944.4*	*3396.1*	*3712.7*	*4092.2*		*2911.2*	*3357.1*	*3560.1*	*4007.6*	*TOTAL*	*541.4*
MULTILATERAL	*1056.4*	*1027.3*	*1133.5*	*1133.6*		*992.4*	*957.7*	*1095.3*	*1097.0*	*MULTILATERAL*	*59.2*
OPEC COUNTRIES	*936.6*	*1296.9*	*669.4*	*1785.8*		*936.6*	*1296.9*	*669.4*	*1784.1*	*OPEC COUNTRIES*	*2.4*
E.E.C.+ MEMBERS	*1926.8*	*1914.5*	*2128.0*	*2197.5*		*1905.7*	*1887.3*	*2012.7*	*2149.5*	*E.E.C.+ MEMBERS*	*506.9*
TOTAL	*4937.4*	*5720.3*	*5515.7*	*7011.7*		*4840.3*	*5611.7*	*5324.8*	*6888.6*	*TOTAL*	*603.0*

ODA COMMITMENTS

1984	1985	1986	1983	1984	1985	1986
47.1	45.0	45.1	37.9	101.9	54.8	72.2
9.0	8.9	14.1	13.0	8.5	2.5	126.0
38.5	38.2	51.0	19.6	39.2	25.0	54.6
252.4	258.5	367.5	258.4	264.0	293.7	371.2
31.8	20.7	27.6	55.2	40.5	33.5	42.0
13.4	17.3	33.0	11.3	25.5	35.8	54.7
559.7	540.0	585.7	566.6	819.3	585.3	585.7
317.7	292.7	431.9	248.8	330.1	284.0	428.6
5.8	5.9	10.8	4.8	4.1	5.9	10.8
86.4	125.6	154.5	131.3	118.2	173.0	177.2
138.1	141.6	240.9	107.8	140.3	146.4	252.1
131.0	121.6	176.4	142.3	131.6	121.8	166.7
11.2	11.3	13.4	12.1	11.2	8.9	5.2
53.8	57.9	88.1	53.7	47.1	44.4	137.7
126.0	179.9	171.6	98.5	137.7	139.1	171.2
51.3	58.1	90.7	59.3	60.2	49.9	95.7
174.9	194.0	209.5	173.4	191.3	194.3	204.7
952.0	1115.0	1059.0	958.0	1167.2	1361.4	1359.7
3000.2	*3232.2*	*3770.6*	*2952.0*	*3637.9*	*3559.8*	*4315.9*
2.0	3.4	3.0	10.9	–	–	14.6
–	–	–	–	–	–	–
3.7	5.5	6.3	–	–	–	–
4.8	6.4	5.8	0.5	15.5	0.2	0.3
179.4	384.4	226.7	210.7	282.7	227.0	301.9
–	–	–	–	–	–	–
1.4	0.8	0.6	21.0	–	–	–
31.1	35.8	13.8	–	20.0	5.3	–
16.3	11.8	–	15.3	12.8	8.4	4.3
–	–	–	–	–	–	–
–	–	–	734.0	711.6	740.9	802.0
119.9	110.1	152.1	–	–	–	–
128.1	155.6	136.3	–	–	–	–
21.7	36.9	41.6	–	–	–	–
191.3	187.4	186.5	–	–	–	–
0.6	1.7	2.7	–	–	–	–
23.9	24.5	17.5	–	–	–	–
226.3	224.7	265.2	–	–	–	–
8.5	13.2	24.3	15.6	12.0	16.8	10.1
958.8	*1202.2*	*1082.3*	*1007.9*	*1054.6*	*998.5*	*1133.1*
1291.5	*659.2*	*1775.6*	*942.7*	*1517.1*	*540.1*	*1973.1*
1525.2	*1723.1*	*1873.9*	*1552.7*	*1956.9*	*1649.8*	*1972.1*
5250.4	**5093.5**	**6628.5**	**4902.6**	**6209.6**	**5098.4**	**7422.1**

TECH. COOP. GRANTS

1984	1985	1986	1983	1984	1985	1986
47.1	45.0	45.1	17.3	26.2	27.7	22.4
9.0	8.9	14.1	2.4	–	–	–
38.4	37.2	51.0	28.4	5.9	8.6	15.0
252.4	258.5	367.5	32.6	102.1	123.8	–
31.8	20.7	27.6	13.1	12.4	5.1	7.7
13.4	17.3	32.7	4.6	5.1	8.4	0.5
521.7	501.1	524.4	302.6	321.8	357.2	310.8
298.6	276.1	396.9	129.7	212.6	199.1	290.0
5.8	5.9	10.8	0.6	0.7	–	2.6
86.4	125.6	154.5	47.4	17.1	60.4	29.7
137.1	140.8	240.1	42.6	54.7	140.1	239.0
131.0	121.6	176.4	95.8	82.4	69.6	90.2
11.2	11.3	13.4	2.1	1.0	0.8	2.3
53.8	57.9	88.1	9.0	5.3	7.6	14.4
126.0	179.9	167.4	22.8	30.8	34.2	14.6
51.3	58.1	89.0	3.3	3.9	2.7	17.8
163.7	194.0	204.8	118.8	103.5	113.2	127.5
946.0	1111.0	1056.0	394.0	392.0	233.0	286.0
2924.7	*3170.9*	*3659.6*	*1267.0*	*1377.6*	*1391.6*	*1470.5*
933.1	*1174.5*	*1047.2*	*730.4*	*711.1*	*739.2*	*818.2*
1291.5	*659.2*	*1775.6*	–	–	–	–
1452.3	*1666.6*	*1770.4*	*736.3*	*756.5*	*813.2*	*892.4*
5149.3	**5004.5**	**6482.3**	**1997.4**	**2088.6**	**2130.8**	**2288.7**

TOTAL OOF NET

1984	1985	1986	1983	1984	1985	1986
–	–	–	–	–	–	–
–	–	–	–	-0.8	–	–
5.5	1.3	0.2	61.0	5.5	1.3	0.2
–	–	–	–	–	–	–
0.1	0.1	0.4	0.0	0.1	0.1	0.4
–	–	–	–	–	–	–
–	–	–	8.8	-0.6	-89.6	–
22.2	21.6	35.4	27.6	14.3	13.4	20.0
–	–	–	–	–	–	–
–	0.6	0.1	0.7	–	0.6	0.1
–	59.5	–	–	–	57.0	-2.0
–	–	–	–	–	–	–
1.0	–	–	-1.2	0.3	–	–
–	15.3	–	19.6	–	15.3	-2.0
360.1	381.1	284.5	400.5	360.0	381.1	284.5
7.0	1.0	1.0	13.0	4.0	-26.0	-19.0
395.9	*480.5*	*321.6*	*530.1*	*382.9*	*353.1*	*282.3*
68.5	-68.7	51.3	-0.9	4.2	-100.9	18.6
5.4	10.2	10.2	2.4	5.4	10.2	8.5
389.3	*404.9*	*323.6*	*499.5*	*379.9*	*307.1*	*307.5*
469.9	**422.1**	**383.2**	**531.6**	**392.5**	**262.5**	**309.3**

ODA COMMITMENTS : LOANS

	1983	1984	1985	1986
DAC COUNTRIES				
Australia	–	–	–	–
Austria	–	–	–	66.3
Belgium	-18.8	4.0	0.5	3.6
Canada	–	–	–	–
Denmark	–	–	–	–
Finland	–	–	–	–
France	98.9	66.4	46.0	61.3
Germany, Fed. Rep.	–	–	–	–
Ireland	–	–	–	–
Italy	–	–	–	–
Japan	1.3	1.0	0.8	1.4
Netherlands	–	–	–	–
New Zealand	–	–	–	–
Norway	–	–	–	–
Sweden	3.3	–	–	3.6
Switzerland	–	4.3	–	–
United Kingdom	–	16.2	–	–
United States	4.0	4.0	6.5	8.4
TOTAL	*88.6*	*95.8*	*53.8*	*144.6*
MULTILATERAL	*71.3*	*52.0*	*15.7*	*14.6*
OPEC COUNTRIES	*400.0*	*–*	*–*	*–*
E.E.C.+ MEMBERS	*119.6*	*106.3*	*46.8*	*64.9*
TOTAL	**560.0**	**147.8**	**69.4**	**159.2**

GRANT ELEMENT OF ODA

	1983	1984	1985	1986
DAC COUNTRIES				
Australia	100.0	100.0	100.0	100.0
Austria	100.0	100.0	100.0	100.0
Belgium	100.0	100.0	100.0	100.0
Canada	100.0	100.0	100.0	100.0
Denmark	100.0	100.0	100.0	100.0
Finland	100.0	100.0	100.0	100.0
France	93.9	97.6	95.0	100.0
Germany, Fed. Rep.	100.0	100.0	100.0	100.0
Ireland	100.0	100.0	100.0	100.0
Italy	100.0	100.0	100.0	100.0
Japan	99.4	99.6	100.0	100.0
Netherlands	100.0	100.0	100.0	100.0
New Zealand	100.0	100.0	100.0	100.0
Norway	100.0	100.0	100.0	100.0
Sweden	98.8	100.0	100.0	98.9
Switzerland	100.0	98.3	100.0	100.0
United Kingdom	100.0	100.0	100.0	100.0
United States	100.0	100.0	100.0	99.8
TOTAL	*98.8*	*99.4*	*99.2*	*99.9*
MULTILATERAL	*99.4*	*99.6*	*99.2*	*99.8*
OPEC COUNTRIES	*80.1*	*100.0*	*100.0*	*100.0*
E.E.C.+ MEMBERS	*97.8*	*99.0*	*98.2*	*100.0*
TOTAL	**95.3**	**99.6**	**99.3**	**99.9**

OTHER AGGREGATES

COMMITMENTS: ALL SOURCES

	1983	1984	1985	1986
TOTAL BILATERAL	4654.6	5887.5	4838.8	6986.5
of which				
OPEC	950.5	1517.9	540.1	2044.3
CMEA	270.0	289.0	320.0	335.0
TOTAL MULTILATERAL	1031.0	1081.7	1046.0	1142.3
TOTAL BIL.& MULTIL.	5685.6	6969.1	5884.8	8128.9
of which				
ODA Grants	4612.6	6350.7	5349.0	7597.9
ODA Loans	560.0	147.8	69.4	159.2

DISBURSEMENTS:
DAC COUNTRIES COMBINED

	1983	1984	1985	1986
OFFICIAL & PRIVATE				
GROSS:				
Contractual Lending	747.8	484.3	434.7	831.1
Export Credits Total	583.5	377.9	334.8	683.1
Export Credits Private	582.0	377.9	275.3	683.1
NET:				
Contractual Lending	137.3	130.1	16.7	-463.8
Export Credits Total	1.2	58.2	40.9	-533.1
PRIVATE SECTOR NET	8158.2	809.7	186.3	5653.8
Direct Investment	3929.7	2437.4	1845.1	3983.5
Portfolio Investment	4223.7	-1690.4	-1668.7	2197.5
Export Credits	4.8	62.7	9.9	-527.2

MARKET BORROWING:
CHANGE IN CLAIMS

	1983	1984	1985	1986
Banks	–	–	–	–

MEMORANDUM ITEM:

	1983	1984	1985	1986
CMEA Countr.(Gross)	270.0	290.0	320.0	340.0

TOTAL RECEIPTS NET

DAC COUNTRIES	1983	1984	1985	1986
Australia	681.8	1223.9	940.2	1215.9
Austria	86.6	-0.5	68.4	58.7
Belgium	585.8	3283.0	927.8	-1150.3
Canada	1864.2	1872.2	675.4	744.0
Denmark	900.5	341.3	305.2	143.3
Finland	126.5	100.8	146.5	270.9
France	8427.7	8035.3	7531.0	7359.4
Germany, Fed. Rep.	5140.8	4883.5	3994.0	5689.0
Ireland	14.0	17.8	54.6	57.1
Italy	2293.9	1499.2	1677.8	1340.1
Japan	4916.0	7735.5	7593.5	11810.9
Netherlands	875.9	713.3	1401.2	1479.4
New Zealand	102.9	63.3	68.2	88.0
Norway	423.6	1245.5	1370.9	1557.9
Sweden	1013.2	982.8	1072.8	1306.5
Switzerland	2440.3	2106.8	761.7	584.7
United Kingdom	5267.2	4044.7	1584.1	6435.2
United States	18133.0	24419.0	-1232.0	8216.0
TOTAL	*53293.9*	*62567.2*	*28941.3*	*47206.8*
MULTILATERAL				
AF.D.F.	157.8	111.3	210.1	271.7
AF.D.B.	145.2	110.2	235.0	281.7
AS.D.B	772.5	816.7	792.4	780.5
CAR.D.B.	40.3	29.7	33.1	41.1
E.E.C.	1416.8	1371.7	1559.0	1849.3
IBRD	5164.3	5669.2	5075.0	5421.7
IDA	2335.6	2491.6	2598.9	3326.7
I.D.B.	1321.5	1988.2	1749.5	1506.7
IFAD	143.9	170.3	270.1	286.6
I.F.C.	166.0	126.6	93.8	156.2
IMF TRUST FUND	—	—	—	—
U.N. AGENCIES	—	—	—	—
UNDP	617.1	596.3	634.7	769.1
UNTA	253.4	217.3	295.4	253.8
UNICEF	246.1	244.3	278.6	326.0
UNRWA	210.9	191.3	187.4	186.5
WFP	629.7	679.2	779.3	648.6
UNHCR	355.6	396.6	418.0	386.5
Other Multilateral	430.5	438.8	756.5	758.7
Arab OPEC Agencies	393.7	333.5	413.5	6.0
TOTAL	*14800.9*	*15982.6*	*16380.2*	*17257.1*
OPEC COUNTRIES	*4267.2*	*3975.3*	*3178.1*	*3820.5*
E.E.C.+ MEMBERS	*24922.6*	*24189.7*	*19034.7*	*23202.5*
TOTAL	*72362.0*	*82525.1*	*48499.6*	*68284.3*

TOTAL ODA NET

DAC COUNTRIES	1983	1984	1985	1986
Australia	534.0	608.0	534.9	513.0
Austria	126.5	137.0	174.3	141.5
Belgium	298.5	263.0	275.2	361.7
Canada	848.9	1038.7	997.1	1054.3
Denmark	236.5	222.7	228.4	362.2
Finland	92.7	108.0	127.7	187.6
France	3145.1	3170.0	3262.0	4162.3
Germany, Fed. Rep.	2101.0	1868.0	1980.0	2642.5
Ireland	14.0	14.6	17.2	25.3
Italy	448.8	624.8	781.4	1486.8
Japan	2425.2	2427.4	2556.9	3846.3
Netherlands	812.2	878.6	762.2	1180.4
New Zealand	47.5	43.8	42.8	60.7
Norway	332.2	304.4	328.3	479.1
Sweden	525.6	525.9	579.8	777.0
Switzerland	218.2	218.4	227.6	323.4
United Kingdom	858.7	783.5	859.6	1022.1
United States	5563.0	6457.0	8182.0	7602.0
TOTAL	*18628.5*	*19693.8*	*21917.6*	*26227.9*
MULTILATERAL				
AF.D.F.	157.8	111.3	210.1	271.7
AF.D.B.	—	—	—	—
AS.D.B	222.7	303.7	392.9	416.4
CAR.D.B.	30.8	16.0	20.4	24.9
E.E.C.	1215.1	1287.2	1407.4	1659.2
IBRD	47.5	41.0	33.8	3.9
IDA	2335.6	2491.6	2598.9	3326.7
I.D.B.	364.5	438.1	351.0	283.1
IFAD	143.9	170.3	270.1	286.6
I.F.C.	—	—	—	—
IMF TRUST FUND	—	—	—	—
U.N. AGENCIES	—	—	—	—
UNDP	617.1	596.3	634.7	769.1
UNTA	253.4	217.3	295.4	253.8
UNICEF	246.1	244.3	278.6	326.0
UNRWA	210.9	191.3	187.4	186.5
WFP	629.7	679.2	779.3	648.6
UNHCR	355.6	396.6	418.0	386.5
Other Multilateral	430.5	438.8	463.1	485.2
Arab OPEC Agencies	314.0	146.6	127.7	143.5
TOTAL	*7575.2*	*7769.5*	*8468.6*	*9471.6*
OPEC COUNTRIES	*3873.8*	*3722.0*	*2916.0*	*3751.7*
E.E.C.+ MEMBERS	*9129.9*	*9112.4*	*9573.5*	*12902.4*
TOTAL	*30077.5*	*31185.3*	*33302.1*	*39451.1*

TOTAL ODA GROSS

	1983
Australia	537.0
Austria	133.9
Belgium	303.4
Canada	868.3
Denmark	242.0
Finland	93.0
France	3260.4
Germany, Fed. Rep.	2403.6
Ireland	14.0
Italy	461.7
Japan	2882.3
Netherlands	866.6
New Zealand	47.5
Norway	332.2
Sweden	527.4
Switzerland	219.9
United Kingdom	979.2
United States	6102.0
TOTAL	*20274.5*
AF.D.F.	158.8
AF.D.B.	—
AS.D.B	233.5
CAR.D.B.	30.8
E.E.C.	1232.3
IBRD	47.5
IDA	2420.7
I.D.B.	523.8
IFAD	145.4
I.F.C.	—
IMF TRUST FUND	—
U.N. AGENCIES	—
UNDP	617.1
UNTA	253.4
UNICEF	246.1
UNRWA	210.9
WFP	629.7
UNHCR	355.6
Other Multilateral	431.0
Arab OPEC Agencies	381.9
TOTAL	*7918.5*
OPEC COUNTRIES	*4407.6*
E.E.C.+ MEMBERS	*9763.3*
TOTAL	*32600.5*

ODA LOANS GROSS

DAC COUNTRIES	1983	1984	1985	1986
Australia	—	—	—	—
Austria	85.9	109.0	139.7	90.5
Belgium	63.6	51.8	40.0	82.8
Canada	163.7	180.8	140.4	128.4
Denmark	70.7	72.9	58.2	130.6
Finland	11.1	11.1	12.6	19.9
France	658.1	785.2	863.7	1152.5
Germany, Fed. Rep.	1130.7	930.8	1016.5	1590.8
Ireland	—	—	—	—
Italy	143.3	280.2	179.9	298.0
Japan	1888.9	1871.4	1870.8	2981.2
Netherlands	180.7	192.1	174.8	210.3
New Zealand	—	—	—	—
Norway	13.2	3.0	2.7	7.0
Sweden	4.1	—	—	12.5
Switzerland	17.4	15.0	12.7	16.5
United Kingdom	56.1	51.2	60.3	43.1
United States	1562.0	1415.0	1483.0	1274.0
TOTAL	*6049.4*	*5969.5*	*6055.2*	*8038.1*
MULTILATERAL	*4088.3*	*4135.3*	*4368.9*	*5322.4*
OPEC COUNTRIES	*1663.0*	*952.4*	*905.4*	*812.6*
E.E.C.+ MEMBERS	*2527.8*	*2523.3*	*2428.0*	*3595.4*
TOTAL	*11800.7*	*11057.3*	*11329.4*	*14173.1*

ODA LOANS NET

DAC COUNTRIES	1983	1984	1985	1986
Australia	-3.0	-1.6	-0.2	-0.2
Austria	78.5	96.3	130.4	81.1
Belgium	58.7	47.3	34.9	73.6
Canada	144.3	165.0	109.6	96.7
Denmark	65.1	67.7	38.6	-4.2
Finland	10.8	10.8	12.3	19.6
France	542.9	665.3	726.2	985.2
Germany, Fed. Rep.	828.0	613.7	553.4	843.6
Ireland	—	—	—	—
Italy	130.4	264.5	160.4	275.3
Japan	1431.8	1363.5	1372.1	2143.1
Netherlands	126.3	148.0	109.9	136.3
New Zealand	—	—	—	—
Norway	13.2	3.0	1.1	5.4
Sweden	2.3	-1.9	-1.7	9.7
Switzerland	15.7	12.7	10.9	12.3
United Kingdom	-64.4	-75.5	-54.6	-79.6
United States	1023.0	813.0	872.0	569.0
TOTAL	*4403.5*	*4191.8*	*4075.3*	*5166.8*
MULTILATERAL	*3744.9*	*3773.3*	*3940.3*	*4758.5*
OPEC COUNTRIES	*1129.2*	*386.2*	*308.3*	*275.2*
E.E.C.+ MEMBERS	*1894.4*	*1872.6*	*1588.8*	*2289.3*
TOTAL	*9277.7*	*8351.3*	*8323.9*	*10200.5*

GRANTS

	1983
Australia	537.0
Austria	48.0
Belgium	239.8
Canada	704.6
Denmark	171.4
Finland	81.9
France	2602.3
Germany, Fed. Rep.	1272.9
Ireland	14.0
Italy	318.4
Japan	993.4
Netherlands	685.9
New Zealand	47.5
Norway	319.0
Sweden	523.3
Switzerland	202.5
United Kingdom	923.1
United States	4540.0
TOTAL	*14225.0*
MULTILATERAL	*3830.2*
OPEC COUNTRIES	*2744.6*
E.E.C.+ MEMBERS	*7235.4*
TOTAL	*20799.8*

TOTAL OFFICIAL GROSS

DAC COUNTRIES	1983	1984	1985	1986
Australia	652.9	684.6	560.0	553.5
Austria	136.5	156.3	200.7	228.4
Belgium	390.5	496.5	397.0	441.6
Canada	1535.6	1703.8	1536.4	1509.0
Denmark	417.2	418.8	397.9	548.6
Finland	93.0	108.7	128.0	187.9
France	3873.6	4735.6	4885.2	5809.5
Germany, Fed. Rep.	3475.2	3589.2	3945.2	5333.3
Ireland	14.0	14.6	17.2	25.3
Italy	810.1	1138.3	1534.6	2175.6
Japan	3946.6	3833.8	3641.1	5682.4
Netherlands	903.1	934.6	850.7	1280.9
New Zealand	48.8	44.8	44.0	61.7
Norway	351.8	304.4	345.2	480.7
Sweden	919.5	894.8	1020.5	1348.5
Switzerland	252.9	221.7	229.4	327.6
United Kingdom	1451.7	1412.6	1446.6	1526.5
United States	8773.0	10155.0	11327.0	10423.0
TOTAL	*28045.9*	*30848.2*	*32506.7*	*37944.1*
MULTILATERAL	*18534.9*	*20525.0*	*21415.7*	*24524.3*
OPEC COUNTRIES	*5341.7*	*4860.6*	*4039.1*	*4519.1*
E.E.C.+ MEMBERS	*12855.4*	*14253.8*	*15101.7*	*19120.1*
TOTAL	*51922.5*	*56233.8*	*57961.5*	*66987.4*

TOTAL OFFICIAL NET

DAC COUNTRIES	1983	1984	1985	1986
Australia	629.9	662.3	527.4	460.8
Austria	121.7	131.0	180.2	206.6
Belgium	378.1	481.9	373.6	416.6
Canada	1104.3	1216.8	851.7	856.5
Denmark	387.7	376.7	321.4	310.0
Finland	92.7	108.3	127.7	187.6
France	3611.8	4416.3	4405.0	5114.4
Germany, Fed. Rep.	2752.2	2851.5	2953.2	3784.6
Ireland	14.0	14.6	17.2	25.3
Italy	687.7	1021.2	1398.9	2001.5
Japan	3094.2	2964.2	2739.5	4055.4
Netherlands	840.2	884.1	777.5	1186.1
New Zealand	47.6	44.1	44.0	61.7
Norway	349.8	302.4	341.6	477.1
Sweden	806.5	704.6	789.8	1161.8
Switzerland	233.9	213.8	222.5	316.4
United Kingdom	1309.3	1256.3	1298.5	1368.4
United States	5791.0	7494.0	8377.0	7078.0
TOTAL	*22252.5*	*25144.0*	*25746.4*	*29068.8*
MULTILATERAL	*14800.9*	*15982.6*	*16380.2*	*17257.1*
OPEC COUNTRIES	*4267.2*	*3975.3*	*3178.1*	*3820.5*
E.E.C.+ MEMBERS	*11397.7*	*12674.2*	*13104.2*	*16056.2*
TOTAL	*41320.6*	*45102.0*	*45304.8*	*50146.4*

TOTAL OOF GROSS

	1983
Australia	115.9
Austria	2.6
Belgium	87.1
Canada	667.3
Denmark	175.2
Finland	—
France	613.2
Germany, Fed. Rep.	1071.6
Ireland	—
Italy	348.4
Japan	1064.2
Netherlands	36.5
New Zealand	1.3
Norway	19.6
Sweden	392.2
Switzerland	33.0
United Kingdom	472.4
United States	2671.0
TOTAL	*7771.4*
MULTILATERAL	*10616.4*
OPEC COUNTRIES	*934.1*
E.E.C.+ MEMBERS	*3092.1*
TOTAL	*19322.0*

ODA COMMITMENTS

1984	1985	1986	1983	1984	1985	1986
609.6	535.1	513.1	535.6	693.7	531.7	532.4
149.7	183.6	150.9	182.8	78.6	59.6	126.0
267.5	280.3	370.8	187.5	180.3	132.0	356.6
1054.6	1028.0	1086.0	1139.3	1574.9	1171.8	1179.0
227.9	248.0	497.0	260.4	288.5	340.1	479.6
108.3	128.0	187.9	96.1	170.5	232.6	276.4
3290.0	3399.5	4329.6	4379.9	4402.8	3756.4	4329.6
2185.1	2443.1	3389.7	2270.6	2799.9	2427.3	3337.0
14.6	17.2	25.3	14.0	12.9	17.2	25.3
640.5	800.9	1509.4	882.0	902.9	1178.3	2327.1
2935.3	3055.5	4684.4	3483.2	3968.0	4075.6	4341.9
922.7	827.1	1254.4	901.0	901.5	731.0	1298.7
43.8	42.8	60.7	40.1	41.2	47.5	33.8
304.4	329.9	480.7	288.0	350.4	346.0	547.6
527.8	581.5	779.8	525.3	576.4	566.4	779.0
220.7	229.4	327.6	239.5	218.4	307.4	329.3
910.1	974.6	1144.8	926.9	1008.8	731.0	1080.7
7059.0	8793.0	8307.0	6989.4	8144.1	9157.3	8746.2
21471.5	*23897.5*	*29099.3*	*23341.5*	*26313.9*	*25809.3*	*30126.2*
112.3	213.5	275.2	343.9	369.3	438.8	586.1
—	—	—	—	—	—	—
316.6	409.3	436.5	703.4	683.6	765.2	633.2
16.0	20.4	24.9	17.0	47.6	26.8	37.2
1304.7	1422.2	1687.4	1558.3	1534.7	1248.6	1877.6
41.0	33.8	3.9	—	—	—	—
2581.8	2712.9	3468.8	2963.1	3222.4	3540.8	3373.1
606.8	537.5	485.5	412.0	306.7	250.7	295.7
185.2	285.5	313.4	279.1	203.2	149.0	155.6
—	—	—	—	—	—	—
—	—	—	2739.0	2763.1	3047.9	3051.2
596.3	634.7	769.1	—	—	—	—
217.3	295.4	253.8	—	—	—	—
244.3	278.6	326.0	—	—	—	—
191.3	187.4	186.5	—	—	—	—
679.2	779.3	648.6	—	—	—	—
396.6	418.0	386.5	—	—	—	—
439.4	464.0	486.4	—	—	9.4	5.7
202.7	204.8	282.9	470.3	438.8	278.1	427.1
8131.4	*8897.2*	*10035.4*	*9486.1*	*9569.5*	*9755.3*	*10442.4*
4288.2	*3513.0*	*4289.1*	*4962.7*	*4632.4*	*3628.5*	*4736.4*
9763.1	*10412.7*	*14208.6*	*11380.6*	*12032.4*	*10562.0*	*15112.2*
33891.1	*36307.7*	*43423.7*	*37790.2*	*40515.8*	*39193.2*	*45305.1*

TECH. COOP. GRANTS

1984	1985	1986	1983	1984	1985	1986
609.6	535.1	513.1	99.0	164.0	189.3	176.3
40.7	43.9	60.5	32.2	—	—	—
215.8	240.3	288.1	129.4	98.0	105.4	137.4
873.8	887.6	957.6	117.7	102.1	251.2	—
155.0	189.8	366.4	115.5	55.9	53.7	75.5
97.2	115.4	168.0	42.1	41.3	54.4	57.8
2504.7	2535.8	3177.1	1607.7	1510.9	1520.6	1974.8
1254.3	1426.6	1798.9	833.6	877.4	875.6	1230.3
14.6	17.2	25.3	5.7	6.2	7.2	12.7
360.3	621.0	1211.4	152.1	181.4	305.9	411.7
1063.9	1184.8	1703.2	385.1	438.3	548.7	848.3
730.6	652.3	1044.1	294.5	268.0	265.8	386.3
43.8	42.8	60.7	10.9	10.2	10.0	13.8
301.4	327.2	473.7	39.6	41.2	42.9	57.4
527.8	581.5	767.3	141.1	108.4	121.3	102.8
205.7	216.7	311.1	34.2	35.8	31.2	57.9
858.9	914.3	1101.7	345.4	311.3	332.9	403.2
5644.0	7310.0	7033.0	1446.0	1617.0	1464.0	1523.0
15502.0	*17842.3*	*21061.1*	*5831.6*	*5867.4*	*6180.0*	*7469.1*
3996.1	*4528.3*	*4713.0*	*2109.3*	*2084.0*	*2251.1*	*2450.6*
3335.8	*2607.7*	*3476.5*	—	—	—	—
7239.8	*7984.8*	*10613.1*	*3483.8*	*3309.1*	*3467.0*	*4680.5*
22833.9	*24978.2*	*29250.6*	*7940.9*	*7951.3*	*8431.1*	*9919.7*

TOTAL OOF NET

1984	1985	1986	1983	1984	1985	1986
75.1	24.9	40.4	95.9	54.2	-7.5	-52.2
6.6	17.1	77.5	-4.8	-5.9	5.9	65.1
229.0	116.7	70.7	79.6	218.8	98.4	54.9
649.2	508.4	423.1	255.4	178.0	-145.5	-197.7
190.9	149.9	51.6	151.2	154.0	92.9	-52.2
0.3	—	—	—	0.3	—	—
1445.2	1485.8	1479.9	466.7	1246.3	1143.0	952.2
1404.1	1502.1	1943.6	651.3	983.5	973.2	1142.1
—	—	—	—	—	—	—
497.8	733.8	666.2	238.9	396.4	617.5	514.8
898.6	585.5	998.0	669.0	536.8	182.6	209.2
11.9	23.6	26.5	28.0	5.5	15.2	5.7
1.0	1.1	1.0	0.0	0.3	1.1	1.0
—	15.3	—	17.6	-2.0	13.3	-2.0
367.0	439.0	568.7	280.9	178.7	210.0	384.8
1.0	0.0	—	15.7	-4.6	-5.1	-7.0
502.5	472.0	381.7	450.5	472.9	438.9	346.3
3096.0	2534.0	2116.0	228.0	1037.0	195.0	-524.0
9376.7	*8609.2*	*8844.8*	*3623.9*	*5450.2*	*3828.8*	*2840.9*
12393.6	*12518.5*	*14488.9*	*7225.7*	*8213.1*	*7911.7*	*7785.5*
572.5	*526.1*	*230.0*	*393.4*	*253.3*	*262.2*	*68.8*
4490.7	*4689.0*	*4911.6*	*2267.9*	*3561.8*	*3530.7*	*3153.8*
22342.7	*21653.8*	*23563.7*	*11243.1*	*13916.7*	*12002.6*	*10695.3*

ODA COMMITMENTS : LOANS

DAC COUNTRIES

	1983	1984	1985	1986
Australia	—	—	—	—
Austria	133.8	42.2	21.1	66.3
Belgium	56.0	43.5	14.0	68.6
Canada	132.3	336.5	81.2	25.2
Denmark	78.7	57.0	109.0	179.2
Finland	0.7	37.8	17.1	21.7
France	1082.1	1263.7	1197.5	1152.5
Germany, Fed. Rep.	928.8	1383.8	815.7	1323.8
Ireland	—	—	—	—
Italy	283.6	326.4	311.1	401.2
Japan	2413.8	2832.8	2814.3	2514.2
Netherlands	154.1	215.7	101.3	119.1
New Zealand	—	—	—	—
Norway	13.7	3.0	2.7	6.6
Sweden	3.3	—	—	11.9
Switzerland	23.1	25.5	26.1	15.8
United Kingdom	48.2	39.4	23.2	3.7
United States	1376.4	1860.0	1160.0	1003.8
TOTAL	*6728.4*	*8467.5*	*6694.1*	*6913.7*
MULTILATERAL	*5400.9*	*5401.9*	*5468.4*	*5564.9*
OPEC COUNTRIES	*1660.1*	*972.2*	*932.9*	*599.8*
E.E.C.+ MEMBERS	*2891.9*	*3522.4*	*2627.3*	*3338.6*
TOTAL	*13789.4*	*14841.6*	*13095.4*	*13078.5*

GRANT ELEMENT OF ODA

DAC COUNTRIES

	1983	1984	1985	1986
Australia	100.0	100.0	100.0	100.0
Austria	51.1	66.6	81.6	68.6
Belgium	93.8	96.3	95.9	97.1
Canada	98.8	97.8	99.1	99.8
Denmark	94.1	96.5	92.8	92.7
Finland	99.5	92.9	98.4	97.6
France	89.8	85.3	86.9	86.1
Germany, Fed. Rep.	83.4	76.9	83.7	80.0
Ireland	100.0	100.0	100.0	100.0
Italy	82.9	80.1	86.3	93.0
Japan	68.3	65.7	64.9	71.4
Netherlands	93.3	90.3	93.4	96.4
New Zealand	100.0	100.0	100.0	100.0
Norway	96.4	99.5	99.4	99.1
Sweden	99.8	100.0	100.0	99.7
Switzerland	97.3	97.8	98.6	99.4
United Kingdom	97.1	98.0	98.6	99.8
United States	92.5	91.9	95.4	95.9
TOTAL	*87.9*	*86.0*	*88.4*	*89.4*
MULTILATERAL	*86.6*	*87.2*	*89.1*	*88.2*
OPEC COUNTRIES	*82.2*	*88.2*	*85.4*	*93.5*
E.E.C.+ MEMBERS	*90.2*	*86.5*	*89.3*	*89.8*
TOTAL	*86.8*	*86.6*	*88.3*	*89.6*

OTHER AGGREGATES

COMMITMENTS: ALL SOURCES

	1983	1984	1985	1986
TOTAL BILATERAL	39972.8	47364.5	43304.1	49540.1
of which				
OPEC	6290.2	5609.1	4202.9	4933.8
CMEA	4804.7	6583.3	6431.9	8258.8
TOTAL MULTILATERAL	27065.0	25754.4	29214.8	31215.0
TOTAL BIL.& MULTIL.	67037.8	73119.0	72518.9	80755.1
of which				
ODA Grants	24766.6	26304.6	26756.8	33209.8
ODA Loans	17061.7	20041.0	17849.7	19015.0

DISBURSEMENTS:

DAC COUNTRIES COMBINED

	1983	1984	1985	1986
OFFICIAL & PRIVATE				
GROSS:				
Contractual Lending	41378.9	39053.7	36123.2	32237.7
Export Credits Total	33103.0	28500.5	25395.4	18909.5
Export Credits Private	28020.9	24128.3	21907.7	15782.5
NET:				
Contractual Lending	12255.0	13513.3	8591.2	5810.0
Export Credits Total	7431.2	5655.6	951.0	-2920.2
PRIVATE SECTOR NET	31041.5	37423.1	3194.9	18138.0
Direct Investment	9127.4	11332.1	6527.3	12044.6
Portfolio Investment	17223.7	21799.0	-4468.5	7854.9
Export Credits	4690.4	4292.0	1136.0	-1761.6

MARKET BORROWING:

CHANGE IN CLAIMS

	1983	1984	1985	1986
Banks	—	11091.0	14491.0	-1030.0

MEMORANDUM ITEM:

	1983	1984	1985	1986
CMEA Countr.(Gross)	3918.1	3949.3	4303.8	5444.5

Left margin

PRINCIPAUX AGRÉGATS

ENGAGEMENTS EN PROVENANCE DE TOUTES ORIGINES

TOTAL BILATÉRAL
dont :
    OPEP
    Pays du CAEM
TOTAL MULTILATÉRAL
TOTAL BILATÉRAL + MULTILATÉRAL
dont :
    Dons APD
    Prêts APD

VERSEMENTS :

ENSEMBLE DES PAYS DU CAD

SECTEURS PUBLICS + PRIVÉS
  MONTANTS BRUTS :
    Prêts contractuels
    Crédits à l'exportation, total
    Crédits à l'exportation, privés
  MONTANTS NETS :
    Prêts contractuels
    Crédits à l'exportation, total
SECTEUR PRIVÉ NET
    Investissements directs
    Investissements de portefeuille
    Crédits à l'exportation garantis

EMPRUNTS AUX CONDITIONS DU MARCHÉ

VARIATION DE CRÉANCES

  Banques

Pour mémoire :

  Pays du CAEM (Brut)

Table

1983	1984	1985	1986		1983
TOTAL ODA NET				**TOTAL ODA GROSS**	
162.5	183.6	137.4	134.5	Australia	162.5
34.0	32.0	32.7	32.4	Austria	38.6
181.5	170.4	195.1	252.8	Belgium	184.6
473.8	588.2	567.1	505.2	Canada	485.6
186.6	165.0	194.2	265.8	Denmark	189.6
72.7	85.4	95.0	134.3	Finland	72.7
751.4	891.5	908.1	1234.7	France	771.3
1187.1	1054.7	1194.5	1410.8	Germany, Fed. Rep.	1347.4
8.6	8.3	10.8	13.5	Ireland	8.6
244.0	396.3	459.5	1082.8	Italy	252.1
1488.5	1319.5	1483.5	2373.2	Japan	1720.6
478.2	531.0	440.3	732.9	Netherlands	522.5
12.0	11.8	10.1	12.7	New Zealand	12.0
238.9	217.6	240.2	346.6	Norway	238.9
362.9	341.5	337.2	527.1	Sweden	362.9
130.4	140.4	137.2	194.3	Switzerland	130.4
574.0	530.5	537.3	624.4	United Kingdom	660.0
2350.0	2760.0	3398.0	2890.0	United States	2633.0
8937.3	*9427.7*	*10378.2*	*12767.9*	*TOTAL*	*9793.5*
151.7	106.0	200.7	257.9	AF.D.F.	152.7
—	—	—	—	AF.D.B.	—
195.6	279.8	366.0	363.1	AS.D.B	204.7
0.3	1.3	1.6	0.7	CAR.D.B.	0.3
694.1	848.7	731.2	896.7	E.E.C.	696.6
31.0	35.5	31.3	3.9	IBRD	31.0
2265.6	2443.3	2574.1	3308.4	IDA	2338.6
94.1	137.4	95.8	103.3	I.D.B.	101.4
90.2	113.0	210.9	224.2	IFAD	91.7
—	—	—	—	I.F.C.	—
—	—	—	—	IMF TRUST FUND	—
—	—	—	—	U.N. AGENCIES	—
351.5	346.0	386.5	440.5	UNDP	351.5
75.1	55.1	91.0	71.6	UNTA	75.1
176.7	173.4	197.7	235.2	UNICEF	176.7
—	—	—	—	UNRWA	—
510.4	553.5	606.5	487.7	WFP	510.4
245.7	263.4	291.6	279.2	UNHCR	245.7
151.3	160.7	170.2	167.8	Other Multilateral	151.3
222.0	105.8	82.2	81.9	Arab OPEC Agencies	269.9
5255.5	*5623.1*	*6037.1*	*6922.3*	*TOTAL*	*5397.6*
852.1	*577.3*	*530.4*	*530.6*	*OPEC COUNTRIES*	*1231.5*
4305.6	*4596.5*	*4671.1*	*6514.3*	*E.E.C.+ MEMBERS*	*4632.8*
15044.8	*15628.1*	*16945.8*	*20220.8*	*TOTAL*	*16422.8*
ODA LOANS NET				**GRANTS**	
—	—	—	—	Australia	162.5
21.9	22.2	20.5	17.7	Austria	12.2
34.5	30.7	25.4	59.2	Belgium	147.0
88.5	108.9	75.8	67.7	Canada	385.4
60.8	53.1	30.6	-64.5	Denmark	125.8
6.2	6.6	3.7	9.6	Finland	66.6
274.6	390.1	410.4	607.1	France	476.7
517.2	424.5	380.0	488.4	Germany, Fed. Rep.	669.9
—	—	—	—	Ireland	8.6
86.2	207.5	66.5	197.3	Italy	157.8
932.8	741.6	825.9	1435.3	Japan	555.7
78.1	78.8	52.2	72.3	Netherlands	400.2
—	—	—	—	New Zealand	12.0
1.5	3.0	2.1	6.8	Norway	237.4
—	—	—	8.3	Sweden	362.9
6.4	7.3	5.1	3.8	Switzerland	124.0
-62.9	-67.3	-59.0	-78.5	United Kingdom	636.9
522.0	486.0	585.0	437.0	United States	1828.0
2567.6	*2492.8*	*2424.1*	*3267.4*	*TOTAL*	*6369.6*
3115.4	*3292.8*	*3548.3*	*4332.5*	*MULTILATERAL*	*2140.1*
442.6	*158.8*	*109.4*	*134.4*	*OPEC COUNTRIES*	*409.4*
1069.6	*1209.8*	*919.2*	*1298.6*	*E.E.C.+ MEMBERS*	*3236.0*
6125.7	*5944.4*	*6081.8*	*7734.3*	*TOTAL*	*8919.1*
TOTAL OFFICIAL NET				**TOTAL OOF GROSS**	
154.7	186.1	144.1	160.4	Australia	6.1
33.5	25.0	28.0	30.2	Austria	1.6
196.5	316.8	224.9	291.4	Belgium	16.5
427.8	648.2	501.3	529.3	Canada	28.3
215.9	181.7	195.1	242.2	Denmark	36.0
72.7	85.4	95.0	134.3	Finland	—
890.0	1325.9	1085.5	1334.3	France	148.9
1391.8	1366.6	1385.9	1600.3	Germany, Fed. Rep.	310.7
8.6	8.3	10.8	13.5	Ireland	—
344.1	616.9	597.1	1234.9	Italy	111.3
1611.9	1453.4	1526.6	2541.1	Japan	227.6
483.4	537.5	456.1	750.7	Netherlands	9.1
12.0	11.8	10.1	12.7	New Zealand	—
238.9	217.6	240.2	346.6	Norway	—
411.2	396.2	393.2	735.1	Sweden	75.7
131.8	140.6	136.8	193.7	Switzerland	3.4
592.3	599.9	559.6	641.3	United Kingdom	29.2
2595.0	3189.0	3562.0	2833.0	United States	366.0
9812.1	*11306.6*	*11152.3*	*13624.9*	*TOTAL*	*1370.2*
6676.9	*7361.1*	*8060.5*	*8644.4*	*MULTILATERAL*	*2086.6*
1071.1	*608.0*	*599.0*	*553.2*	*OPEC COUNTRIES*	*389.3*
4880.2	*5829.0*	*5272.7*	*7022.1*	*E.E.C.+ MEMBERS*	*739.4*
17560.1	*19275.6*	*19811.8*	*22822.4*	*TOTAL*	*3846.2*

ODA COMMITMENTS

1984	1985	1986	1983	1984	1985	1986
183.6	137.4	134.5	173.9	174.8	151.6	134.3
38.5	36.4	36.0	49.4	46.6	17.7	–
174.0	199.1	260.2	133.0	111.8	90.7	242.3
598.1	587.0	526.0	653.8	996.8	601.0	601.2
168.3	211.5	397.4	192.5	226.6	243.8	381.8
85.4	95.0	134.3	79.0	135.4	178.8	204.6
924.1	959.7	1290.9	1034.9	1108.5	1147.3	1290.9
1204.2	1480.9	1712.9	1401.4	1435.9	1376.0	1618.6
8.3	10.8	13.5	8.6	8.3	10.8	13.5
406.2	472.8	1095.0	501.5	496.1	722.3	1752.5
1568.2	1739.3	2743.4	1934.9	2419.0	2391.7	2564.4
562.5	491.9	787.6	547.2	550.3	404.3	875.0
11.8	10.1	12.7	7.2	9.7	15.1	13.5
217.7	240.4	346.6	200.7	281.1	271.2	339.6
341.5	337.2	527.1	369.3	362.2	363.9	527.2
140.4	137.5	194.4	154.2	131.6	217.2	193.5
616.4	618.8	715.5	589.7	712.5	428.6	679.4
3083.0	3708.0	3261.0	3001.2	3633.0	3796.5	3265.0
10332.0	*11473.9*	*14189.2*	*11032.3*	*12840.2*	*12428.7*	*14697.1*

(continued)

1984	1985	1986
106.9	203.8	261.1
–	–	–
290.7	380.2	381.0
1.3	1.6	0.7
851.7	732.7	904.0
35.5	31.3	3.9
2520.0	2673.1	3433.8
144.7	105.8	116.1
124.0	218.6	238.2
–	–	–
–	–	–
346.0	386.5	440.5
55.1	91.0	71.6
173.4	197.7	235.2
553.5	606.5	487.7
263.4	291.6	279.2
160.7	170.2	167.8
139.8	129.9	189.9
5766.7	*6220.3*	*7210.9*
938.5	*906.3*	*905.0*
4915.8	*5178.2*	*7177.3*
17037.3	*18600.5*	*22305.0*

1983	1984	1985	1986
318.6	354.4	425.8	516.9
–	–	–	–
686.2	668.6	752.5	564.3
3.2	0.2	1.7	2.5
884.8	948.7	707.8	1075.9
85.5	34.2	78.7	163.6
2934.8	3217.4	3535.8	3373.1
160.1	156.7	104.7	97.9
–	–	–	–
1510.7	1552.2	1743.4	1682.1
–	–	–	–
–	–	–	–
–	–	–	–
–	–	–	–
–	–	–	–
390.8	338.1	214.2	247.7
6974.7	*7270.5*	*7564.5*	*7723.9*
1621.9	*989.0*	*936.0*	*829.8*
5293.5	*5598.7*	*5131.8*	*7929.8*
19628.9	*21099.7*	*20929.2*	*23250.8*

TECH. COOP. GRANTS

1984	1985	1986	1983	1984	1985	1986
183.6	137.4	134.5	45.4	59.6	57.4	60.3
9.9	12.2	14.7	6.4	–	–	–
139.8	169.7	193.6	85.1	77.3	82.1	105.5
479.3	491.3	437.4	47.6	–	82.9	–
111.8	163.6	330.3	92.3	38.7	40.8	60.1
78.8	91.3	124.7	35.2	33.3	42.8	49.4
501.4	497.7	627.6	300.6	317.2	283.6	414.4
630.2	814.5	922.4	384.9	372.5	371.1	501.8
8.3	10.8	13.5	4.5	5.0	6.7	9.0
188.8	393.0	885.5	68.3	101.0	178.6	281.2
577.9	657.5	938.0	145.4	162.3	175.3	275.2
452.2	388.1	660.6	133.4	126.3	133.6	210.2
11.8	10.1	12.7	4.0	4.2	3.8	5.5
214.7	238.1	339.8	28.7	33.6	32.1	39.3
341.5	337.2	518.7	106.4	60.8	67.9	72.2
133.1	132.1	190.6	25.5	26.8	23.7	30.2
597.8	596.3	702.9	164.7	157.2	170.2	217.5
2274.0	2813.0	2453.0	829.0	997.0	983.0	955.0
6934.8	*7954.1*	*9500.5*	*2507.2*	*2572.7*	*2735.7*	*3286.6*
2330.1	*2488.9*	*2589.8*	*1000.4*	*998.7*	*1124.2*	*1218.1*
418.6	*421.0*	*396.2*	–	–	–	–
3386.6	*3751.9*	*5215.8*	*1233.7*	*1195.1*	*1266.6*	*1823.3*
9683.5	*10864.0*	*12486.5*	*3507.6*	*3571.4*	*3859.9*	*4504.7*

TOTAL OOF NET

1984	1985	1986	1983	1984	1985	1986
12.5	17.2	35.4	-7.8	2.5	6.7	25.9
–	0.2	5.1	-0.5	-7.0	-4.7	-2.2
149.6	39.5	44.6	15.0	146.4	29.8	38.5
158.0	63.7	131.1	-46.0	60.0	-65.8	24.2
27.4	13.1	11.2	29.3	16.8	0.9	-23.6
–	–	–	–	–	–	–
475.6	214.5	190.2	138.7	434.0	177.4	99.6
479.7	330.6	436.3	204.8	311.8	191.4	189.4
–	–	–	–	–	–	–
233.0	155.9	176.3	100.0	220.6	137.6	152.0
148.9	54.6	419.8	123.3	133.9	43.1	167.9
8.3	18.5	19.9	5.1	6.5	15.8	17.9
–	–	–	–	–	–	–
–	–	–	–	–	–	–
74.4	100.0	246.4	48.3	54.8	56.0	208.1
0.4	0.0	–	1.4	0.2	-0.5	-0.7
80.7	35.9	31.3	18.3	69.4	22.4	17.0
741.0	344.0	252.0	245.0	429.0	164.0	-57.0
2589.4	*1387.7*	*1999.5*	*874.8*	*1878.9*	*774.1*	*857.0*
2527.6	*2868.0*	*3009.3*	*1421.4*	*1738.0*	*2023.4*	*1722.1*
121.0	*110.3*	*30.3*	*219.1*	*30.6*	*68.6*	*22.5*
1498.8	*856.3*	*960.2*	*574.6*	*1232.6*	*601.6*	*507.7*
5238.0	*4366.1*	*5039.2*	*2515.3*	*3647.6*	*2866.0*	*2601.6*

ODA COMMITMENTS : LOANS

DAC COUNTRIES

	1983	1984	1985	1986
Australia	–	–	–	–
Austria	38.4	38.5	4.6	–
Belgium	55.8	28.0	10.3	48.7
Canada	67.2	230.8	37.6	21.6
Denmark	73.3	43.9	49.5	131.6
Finland	0.4	34.5	3.0	15.8
France	542.8	594.5	679.8	663.3
Germany, Fed. Rep.	703.8	708.8	426.8	583.2
Ireland	–	–	–	–
Italy	164.0	184.4	205.8	279.8
Japan	1322.6	1789.0	1688.5	1510.5
Netherlands	101.9	134.8	32.5	71.6
New Zealand	–	–	–	–
Norway	3.8	3.0	2.3	6.4
Sweden	–	–	–	8.3
Switzerland	19.1	12.8	16.3	–
United Kingdom	6.8	7.4	–	3.7
United States	659.7	1030.7	734.4	673.7
TOTAL	*3759.4*	*4840.8*	*3891.2*	*4018.1*
MULTILATERAL	*4681.5*	*4848.3*	*5131.4*	*4995.8*
OPEC COUNTRIES	*826.0*	*527.7*	*458.0*	*313.7*
E.E.C.+ MEMBERS	*1764.9*	*1808.7*	*1443.6*	*1823.5*
TOTAL	**9266.9**	**10216.7**	**9480.6**	**9327.7**

GRANT ELEMENT OF ODA

DAC COUNTRIES

	1983	1984	1985	1986
Australia	100.0	100.0	100.0	100.0
Austria	48.9	46.9	96.2	50.8
Belgium	93.3	96.0	95.9	97.1
Canada	98.9	97.6	99.3	99.7
Denmark	92.7	96.9	95.9	93.9
Finland	99.7	91.8	100.0	97.6
France	76.3	73.1	74.1	71.7
Germany, Fed. Rep.	80.0	79.1	87.8	85.3
Ireland	100.0	100.0	100.0	100.0
Italy	83.1	80.5	85.8	93.5
Japan	71.6	68.1	67.8	74.7
Netherlands	92.7	90.1	97.3	96.7
New Zealand	100.0	100.0	100.0	100.0
Norway	98.6	99.4	99.4	98.7
Sweden	100.0	100.0	100.0	100.0
Switzerland	97.5	98.2	99.1	100.0
United Kingdom	99.5	99.6	100.0	99.7
United States	93.0	91.1	93.8	93.4
TOTAL	*86.9*	*85.1*	*87.3*	*88.5*
MULTILATERAL	*85.7*	*86.6*	*87.2*	*86.8*
OPEC COUNTRIES	*72.1*	*72.8*	*73.5*	*81.9*
E.E.C.+ MEMBERS	*87.2*	*86.1*	*88.9*	*89.8*
TOTAL	**85.2**	**85.0**	**86.6**	**87.7**

OTHER AGGREGATES

COMMITMENTS: ALL SOURCES

	1983	1984	1985	1986
TOTAL BILATERAL	17225.8	19309.0	18822.8	23688.7
of which				
OPEC	1951.5	1152.9	982.9	863.3
CMEA	2718.1	2809.3	3728.7	5990.2
TOTAL MULTILATERAL	11328.5	12895.0	13710.1	13636.0
TOTAL BIL.& MULTIL.	28554.3	32204.0	32532.9	37324.6
of which				
ODA Grants	10839.1	11179.1	11774.9	14369.0
ODA Loans	11337.5	12524.6	12701.9	14231.6

DISBURSEMENTS:

DAC COUNTRIES COMBINED

	1983	1984	1985	1986
OFFICIAL & PRIVATE				
GROSS:				
Contractual Lending	10542.9	11319.2	9614.2	11581.5
Export Credits Total	6401.5	6217.2	5382.9	5639.4
Export Credits Private	5748.8	5348.7	4731.1	4896.1
NET:				
Contractual Lending	4392.7	5392.4	4072.2	5618.1
Export Credits Total	1302.6	1367.6	1059.2	1558.8
PRIVATE SECTOR NET	2780.8	2536.2	2987.6	3994.8
Direct Investment	786.2	943.7	610.4	-183.4
Portfolio Investment	1044.4	555.7	1478.6	2681.8
Export Credits	950.2	1036.8	898.5	1496.5

MARKET BORROWING:

CHANGE IN CLAIMS

	1983	1984	1985	1986
Banks	–	4293.0	7835.0	1762.0

MEMORANDUM ITEM:

	1983	1984	1985	1986
CMEA Countr.(Gross)	2776.0	2685.3	2863.5	3787.2

ECONOMIC INDICATORS

INDICATEURS ECONOMIQUES

	1980	1981	1982	1983	1984	1985	1986
EUROPE							
Cyprus	2120	2050	2100	2080	2220	2310	–
Gibraltar	140	130	120	120	110	120	–
Greece	41490	38010	39070	35000	33770	33160	39260
Malta	1220	1240	1250	1150	1100	1110	1370
Portugal	24020	22940	22060	19590	18090	19780	–
Turkey	55800	56240	51540	49680	48230	51450	56330
Yugoslavia	72280	70450	63110	46780	44270	46200	64660
Europe Unallocated							
TOTAL	*197070*	*191060*	*179250*	*154400*	*147790*	*154130*	
NORTH OF SAHARA							
Algeria	41130	43060	43880	47570	50800	58160	58890
Egypt	21740	23060	24650	26930	30290	34740	38440
Libya	35470	31680	28790	28060	26210	25850	–
Morocco	17230	14110	14290	12680	11310	11090	14070
Tunisia	8510	8130	7840	7830	7780	7920	8540
North of Sahara Unall.							
TOTAL	*124080*	*120030*	*119450*	*123080*	*126380*	*137750*	
SOUTH OF SAHARA							
Angola	6310	7010	7450	7670	8440	9450	–
Benin	1140	1040	1020	960	940	1020	1380
Botswana	840	800	690	820	870	890	980
Burkina Faso	1440	1330	1220	1100	1000	1070	1470
Burundi	950	970	1000	1050	970	1050	1200
Cameroon	6580	7370	7010	6990	7670	7720	–
Cape Verde	130	120	130	130	130	130	160
Central African Rep.	800	700	670	620	650	720	990
Chad	730	620	570	550	510	660	810
Comoros	120	110	110	110	110	110	160
Congo	1580	1840	2000	1930	2070	2040	1990
Cote d'Ivoire	8960	8070	7100	6300	6070	6440	8850
Djibouti	310	340	350	390	430	460	–
Equatorial Guinea							
Ethiopia	4110	4270	4430	4730	4810	4750	5680
Gabon	3800	3530	3340	3240	3290	3420	2930
Gambia	240	230	200	200	200	150	170
Ghana	4430	4210	4030	4020	4350	4440	5630
Guinea	1630	1610	1570	1760	1840	1840	1540
Guinea-Bissau	100	150	160	160	130	150	160
Kenya	6870	6470	5990	5560	5650	5630	6660
Lesotho	690	730	720	810	690	570	620
Liberia	1090	1070	1050	970	980	1030	1010
Madagascar	3220	2810	2750	2720	2240	2220	2490
Malawi	1150	1150	1110	1160	1140	1130	1160
Mali	1680	1400	1250	1100	1070	1090	
Mauritania	670	720	700	740	680	650	750
Mauritius	1120	1100	1030	1050	1000	1030	1340
Mayotte							
Mozambique	2380	2240	2360	2160	2460	3280	4300
Namibia	2010	1930	1650	1700	1660	1700	–
Niger	2500	2140	1870	1700	1340	1440	2010
Nigeria	86260	78450	76240	77920	77820	75530	–
Reunion	2000	1860	1870	1800	1710	1800	–
Rwanda	1160	1330	1420	1500	1530	1680	1640
St. Helena							
Sao Tome & Principe	50	30	30	40	30	40	40
Senegal	2870	2360	2450	2340	2190	2420	–
Seychelles	140	150	150	150	160	170	200
Sierra Leone	1070	1160	1300	1460	1070	1200	1140
Somalia	1450	2020	2290	2170	3240	2440	–
Sudan	6690	7820	7290	6860	6760	6950	7280
Swaziland	590	650	540	580	510	410	460
Tanzania	5120	5910	6250	6120	5450	6150	–
Togo	1110	910	770	680	830	860	940
Uganda	2970	2840	4350	4700	5000	5500	–
Zaire	10020	8880	8700	7130	4420	4310	5610
Zambia	3590	3900	3640	3150	2540	2130	–
Zimbabwe	5280	6260	6540	5810	5230	4890	5290
East African Community							
DOM/TOM Unallocated							
EAMA Unallocated							
South of Sahara Unall.							
TOTAL	*198050*	*190690*	*187470*	*184900*	*181910*	*182840*	
Africa Unspecified	–	–	–	–	–	–	–
AFRICA TOTAL	*322130*	*310720*	*306920*	*307970*	*308290*	*320590*	
N.& C. AMERICA							
Aruba							
Bahamas	1050	1110	1290	1410	1540	1570	–
Barbados	840	950	990	1040	1130	1200	1300

	1980	1981
Belize	170	180
Bermuda	640	780
Costa Rica	4600	2330
Cuba		
Dominican Republic	5960	6490
El Salvador	3520	3370
Guadeloupe	1430	1270
Guatemala	7810	8500
Haiti	1450	1460
Honduras	2330	2490
Jamaica	2400	2580
Martinique	1440	1360
Mexico	180320	230120
Netherlands Antilles	790	980
Nicaragua	2040	2290
Panama	3330	3660
St. Pierre & Miquelon		
Trinidad & Tobago	6340	6870
Anguilla		
Antigua and Barbuda	100	120
Cayman Islands		
Dominica	60	70
Grenada	60	70
Montserrat		
St. Kitts-Nevis	50	60
St. Lucia	110	130
St. Vincent and Gr.	60	70
Turks & Caicos Isl.		
Virgin Islands		
West Indies Unall.		
DOM/TOM Unallocated		
N.& C. America Unall.		
TOTAL	*235200*	*287010*
SOUTH AMERICA		
Argentina	55460	55660
Bolivia	2710	3040
Brazil	242070	264350
Chile	26640	31180
Colombia	33190	35960
Ecuador	11150	13210
Falkland Islands		
Guiana	210	190
Guyana	550	510
Paraguay	4390	4960
Peru	19850	24220
Suriname	880	1020
Uruguay	10030	11240
Venezuela	58940	65930
South America Unall.		
TOTAL	*466080*	*511500*
America Unspecified	–	–
AMERICA TOTAL	*701280*	*798510*
MIDDLE EAST		
Bahrain	3090	3510
Iran	96860	104410
Iraq	39500	22230
Israel	18570	19680
Jordan	3280	3560
Kuwait	32400	31830
Lebanon		
Oman	5340	6570
Qatar	6490	7040
Saudi Arabia	116660	159780
Syria	13210	14170
United Arab Emirates	27430	31200
Yemen	3040	3300
Yemen, Dem.	810	910
Middle East Unall.		
TOTAL	*371460*	*413190*
SOUTH ASIA		
Afghanistan	3970	4000
Bangladesh	12810	14250
Bhutan	100	120
Burma	5760	5740
India	162460	165180
Maldives	20	30
Nepal	1960	2290
Pakistan	25620	30610
Sri Lanka	4000	4320

1982	1983	1984	1985	1986
160	170	180	180	190
810	920	1020	1090	1180
2180	2810	3240	3490	3750
6610	6150	4750	4150	4960
3370	3570	3920	3680	3840
1160	1110	1200	1300	–
8600	8940	9260	8370	7280
1470	1610	1800	1920	2130
2590	2790	2970	3170	3410
2770	3070	2020	1690	1970
1360	1310	1350	1400	–
155050	133130	161310	169050	121370
1180	1220	1190	1180	–
2270	2360	2590	2660	2700
3960	4120	4290	4540	4810
7950	7590	7600	7190	–
130	130	160	180	190
70	80	90	90	100
70	80	100	110	130
60	60	70	70	80
130	140	150	170	190
80	90	100	110	110
214650	*194860*	*223620*	*230780*	
54530	57950	64420	64650	72920
2830	2850	2850	3120	3540
268650	196570	198090	214910	270070
22460	18060	17240	14100	14940
38180	37810	36740	32910	31250
11520	9800	9240	11690	10720
180	190	200	210	–
430	420	380	380	410
4280	3220	3070	2930	3850
24700	18850	19250		
1050	1020	980	990	980
9070	5070	4890	4770	5950
66320	64500	48080	47140	47900
504210	*416330*	*405430*	*413650*	
–	–	–	–	–
718860	*611190*	*629050*	*644420*	
3620	3880	3990	3720	–
127360	157550	160000	165000	–
31600	34710	38220	41800	–
20060	21770	24970	23310	28290
3770	3870	3680	3800	4330
26770	27020	26660	23730	–
6900	7040	7810	8850	8540
6250	5010	5650	4930	–
154120	115510	102910	91930	–
15020	15850	15940	15940	17310
29410	26790	26150	24490	–
4090	4390	4050	4100	4990
950	1070	1140	1070	1020
435240	*430110*	*427170*	*419000*	
4340	4540	4760	4960	–
13130	12030	13960	16040	15550
150	170	180	190	210
5900	6080	6260	7000	8340
170400	187230	179520	198250	214960
40	40	40	50	60
2410	2460	2510	2350	2570
32660	31280	33810	33150	34920
4670	5030	5910	5920	6400

	1980	1981	1982	1983	1984	1985	1986
South Asia Unall.							
TOTAL	*216690*	*226530*	*233710*	*248850*	*246940*	*267900*	
FAR EAST ASIA							
Brunei	4910	4330	4250	3820	3840	3730	–
China	286510	268410	261240	277980	282800	265980	258690
Hong Kong	27570	29580	30790	28680	31820	33830	37410
Indonesia	74810	89430	90130	77360	81260	81540	71920
Kampuchea							
Korea	60370	66260	69380	76040	82390	83740	95110
Korea, Dem.							
Laos	400	450	480	500	530	600	–
Macao	640	850	810	780	1070	1140	
Malaysia	23710	24220	25610	28220	31710	28950	25780
Mongolia							
Philippines	35210	38430	39270	34090	31580	31800	30110
Singapore	11080	13320	14820	16940	19130	18140	18000
Taiwan	39970	45830	50600	54060	57840	60080	–
Thailand	32840	35030	35640	39080	40490	36840	40160
Viet Nam							
Far East Asia Unall.							
TOTAL	*624480*	*645240*	*654180*	*670310*	*698990*	*682590*	
Asia Unspecified	–	–	–	–	–	–	–
ASIA TOTAL	*1212630*	*1284960*	*1323120*	*1349270*	*1373100*	*1369490*	
OCEANIA							
Cook Islands							
Fiji	1190	1230	1160	1100	1150	1130	1280
Kiribati	20	30	30	30	30	30	–
Nauru							
New Caledonia	1180	980	910	830	790	830	–
Niue							
Pacif. Isl.(Trust Tr.)	120	140	150	150	160	160	–
Papua New Guinea	2460	2410	2280	2240	2310	2180	2410
Polynesia, French	1140	1100	1150	1190	1210	1380	–
Solomon Islands	100	120	130	120	150	130	120
Tokelau							
Tonga	50	60	70	80	70	60	60
Tuvalu							
Vanuatu	100	110	130	140	140	150	–
Wallis & Futuna							
Western Samoa							
TOM Unallocated							
Oceania Unallocated							
TOTAL	*6510*	*6350*	*6190*	*6080*	*6240*	*6280*	
LDCs Unspecified	–	–	–	–	–	–	–
TOTAL,ALL LDCS	*2439620*	*2591590*	*2534340*	*2428910*	*2464480*	*2494920*	
INCOME GROUPS							
LLDCS	63690	67550	68870	68760	70720	74330	
CHINA AND INDIA	448970	433590	431640	465210	462320	464230	
OTHER LOW-INCOME	183720	204090	208770	195600	204350	211170	
LOW MIDDLE-INCOME	332410	334700	330640	322790	321630	316810	
UPPER MIDDLE-INCOME	1410840	1551670	1494420	1376540	1405470	1428390	
UNALLOCATED	–	–	–	–	–	–	–

Billion US Dollars

Chart (y-axis: 0, 200, 400, 600, 800, 1000, 1200, 1400, 1600; x-axis: 80, 81, 82, 83, 84, 85)

Legend:
- ○○○○○ LLDCS
- - - - - - CHINA AND INDIA
- —·—·— OTHER LICS
- ——— LMICS
- – – – UMICS

	1980	1981	1982	1983	1984	1985	1986
EUROPE							
Cyprus	3150	3500	3620	3430	3620	3940	4200
Gibraltar	4300	4880	4830	4810	4420	4370	–
Greece	4370	4460	4290	3940	3810	3610	3680
Malta	3150	3590	3800	3480	3370	3280	3480
Portugal	2340	2460	2480	2230	1970	1960	2230
Turkey	1400	1450	1300	1180	1100	1080	1110
Yugoslavia	3250	3450	3230	2640	2270	2060	2300
Europe Unallocated							
TOTAL	*2330*	*2430*	*2270*	*1980*	*1800*	*1710*	
NORTH OF SAHARA							
Algeria	1980	2280	2400	2410	2430	2570	2560
Egypt	490	560	580	590	620	670	730
Libya	9550	9160	9200	8570	7710	7170	–
Morocco	880	840	820	710	620	560	590
Tunisia	1290	1390	1320	1250	1220	1190	1140
North of Sahara Unall.							
TOTAL	*1250*	*1340*	*1370*	*1330*	*1300*	*1320*	
SOUTH OF SAHARA							
Angola	730	820	940	950	980	1050	–
Benin	320	350	330	280	260	260	270
Botswana	790	910	880	920	950	810	840
Burkina Faso	200	210	200	170	150	150	150
Burundi	210	250	240	240	230	230	240
Cameroon	750	910	910	850	830	820	910
Cape Verde	500	460	450	430	430	430	500
Central African Rep.	320	330	320	270	350	280	300
Chad	160	160	150	130	110	140	140
Comoros	300	330	310	280	270	260	280
Congo	880	1190	1310	1210	1210	1110	1040
Cote d'Ivoire	1130	1160	940	750	660	650	720
Djibouti	970	1080	1050	1160	1210	1260	–
Equatorial Guinea							
Ethiopia	120	120	120	120	120	110	130
Gabon	4760	4780	4390	3930	3800	3670	3100
Gambia	360	360	360	350	280	230	230
Ghana	400	400	370	340	360	370	390
Guinea	300	310	300	290	300	320	290
Guinea-Bissau	140	170	190	190	180	180	170
Kenya	410	430	390	340	310	290	310
Lesotho	460	550	610	560	510	470	410
Liberia	590	590	550	500	470	470	450
Madagascar	350	330	320	300	260	240	230
Malawi	180	180	190	190	180	170	160
Mali	240	240	220	180	160	150	170
Mauritania	440	490	460	480	450	420	420
Mauritius	1200	1250	1230	1140	1080	1100	1200
Mayotte							
Mozambique	200	210	190	160	150	160	210
Namibia	1670	1930	1940	1710	1520	1510	–
Niger	430	440	380	320	240	240	260
Nigeria	890	920	910	830	790	800	620
Reunion	3800	4100	4120	3820	3580	3580	–
Rwanda	240	270	260	260	250	310	290
St. Helena							
Sao Tome & Principe	380	350	390	340	330	320	340
Senegal	490	470	490	430	370	370	420
Seychelles	2050	2210	2390	2430	2480	2630	2800
Sierra Leone	320	360	390	390	360	350	310
Somalia	280	360	430	460	490	510	–
Sudan	430	430	400	390	330	290	320
Swaziland	800	990	960	890	790	670	610
Tanzania	270	290	310	310	290	280	230
Togo	430	400	340	270	240	230	250
Uganda	230	240	290	310	360	370	–
Zaire	430	400	340	290	210	170	160
Zambia	600	720	660	570	480	410	300
Zimbabwe	690	860	880	850	740	680	620
East African Community							
DOM/TOM Unallocated							
EAMA Unallocated							
South of Sahara Unall.							
TOTAL	*510*	*540*	*520*	*480*	*450*	*450*	
Africa Unspecified	–	–	–	–	–	–	–
AFRICA TOTAL	**660**	**700**	**690**	**650**	**620**	**620**	
N.& C. AMERICA							
Aruba							
Bahamas	4980	4920	5850	6330	6790	7070	–
Barbados	3130	3510	3760	4020	4400	4660	4980

	1980	1981
Belize	1200	1270
Bermuda	9600	10930
Costa Rica	1900	1480
Cuba		
Dominican Republic	1010	1120
El Salvador	750	750
Guadeloupe	4100	4370
Guatemala	1120	1200
Haiti	250	270
Honduras	630	670
Jamaica	1180	1290
Martinique	4220	4680
Mexico	2240	2880
Netherlands Antilles	4020	4940
Nicaragua	690	760
Panama	1680	1880
St. Pierre & Miquelon		
Trinidad & Tobago	5050	6040
Anguilla		
Antigua and Barbuda	1310	1530
Cayman Islands		
Dominica	740	920
Grenada	700	780
Montserrat		
St. Kitts-Nevis	1090	1260
St. Lucia	840	960
St. Vincent and Gr.	530	610
Turks & Caicos Isl.		
Virgin Islands		
West Indies Unall.		
DOM/TOM Unallocated		
N.& C. America Unall.		
TOTAL	*1770*	*2190*
SOUTH AMERICA		
Argentina	1960	1940
Bolivia	490	530
Brazil	2140	2170
Chile	2100	2600
Colombia	1220	1370
Ecuador	1260	1490
Falkland Islands		
Guiana	3040	3040
Guyana	720	730
Paraguay	1290	1550
Peru	1030	1290
Suriname	2420	2950
Uruguay	2810	3610
Venezuela	3470	4060
South America Unall.		
TOTAL	*1950*	*2080*
America Unspecified	–	–
AMERICA TOTAL	**1890**	**2110**
MIDDLE EAST		
Bahrain	7710	9070
Iran	2040	2460
Iraq	2970	1610
Israel	4710	5190
Jordan	1050	1220
Kuwait	20640	25060
Lebanon		
Oman	4280	5700
Qatar	24650	29020
Saudi Arabia	10460	13500
Syria	1470	1650
United Arab Emirates	26820	28980
Yemen	420	470
Yemen, Dem.	420	490
Middle East Unall.		
TOTAL	*3520*	*4000*
SOUTH ASIA		
Afghanistan	250	250
Bangladesh	140	160
Bhutan	90	110
Burma	180	190
India	220	250
Maldives	150	180
Nepal	130	150
Pakistan	310	350
Sri Lanka	260	300

1982	1983	1984	1985	1986
1190	1110	1140	1170	1190
10220	10280	11900	13060	
1100	1020	1190	1300	1380
1170	1130	950	760	710
740	760	800	820	820
4140	3760	3900	4190	–
1190	1170	1060	1020	930
270	270	290	310	330
660	670	700	720	740
1330	1390	1140	910	860
4830	4410	4550	4710	–
2680	2190	2040	2100	1850
6060	6340	6230	6110	–
800	820	800	770	790
2000	1980	1990	2100	2170
6780	6510	6240	6020	5140
1670	1700	1960	2190	2440
990	1010	1090	1150	1220
820	830	1070	1170	1240
1320	1370	1480	1550	1520
1040	1080	1160	1250	1320
680	780	830	900	940
2080	*1790*	*1700*	*1730*	
1870	1960	2140	2120	2360
480	470	460	490	540
2170	1870	1700	1660	1840
2210	1920	1700	1440	1320
1440	1440	1420	1320	1230
1490	1310	1150	1160	1160
2800	2730	2780	2800	–
620	530	520	500	500
1480	1180	1000	890	880
1430	1190	1150	1010	1130
2880	2750	2640	2550	2510
3420	2450	1930	1670	1870
4240	3980	3520	3080	2820
2080	*1870*	*1740*	*1650*	
–	–	–	–	–
2080	***1840***	***1730***	***1680***	
9970	10600	10570	9420	–
3140	3610	3730	3850	–
2210	2350	2490	2630	–
5280	5320	6350	6220	6220
1300	1270	1170	1170	1150
20870	18170	16900	14470	–
6320	6240	6740	7380	6550
24790	18340	19560	16430	–
15320	12410	10930	8840	–
1670	1640	1570	1560	1750
26510	23570	22000	19290	–
540	560	570	550	550
480	510	560	530	480
4510	*4350*	*4290*	*4110*	
270	280	290	300	–
160	150	140	150	160
130	140	150	160	160
190	180	180	190	200
260	260	260	270	270
220	230	250	290	300
160	160	160	160	160
380	390	380	370	380
320	330	360	380	400

	1980	1981	1982	1983	1984	1985	1986
South Asia Unall.							
TOTAL	*220*	*250*	*260*	*260*	*260*	*260*	
FAR EAST ASIA							
Brunei	17320	18030	22830	20880	19060	17570	–
China	290	310	310	300	310	310	280
Hong Kong	5220	6050	6300	6130	6350	6190	6800
Indonesia	480	560	620	590	560	530	500
Kampuchea							
Korea	1620	1830	1880	2020	2120	2160	2370
Korea, Dem.							
Laos	120	130	140	150	150	170	–
Macao	1980	2520	2320	2150	2840	2920	
Malaysia	1690	1900	1910	1910	2050	1990	1860
Mongolia							
Philippines	700	790	810	750	640	580	570
Singapore	4510	5440	6100	6790	7730	7590	7410
Taiwan	2250	2530	2750	2880	3030	3100	–
Thailand	670	760	790	810	830	800	810
Viet Nam							
Far East Asia Unall.							
TOTAL	*440*	*490*	*510*	*500*	*510*	*500*	
Asia Unspecified	–	–	–	–	–	–	–
ASIA TOTAL	***480***	***530***	***570***	***560***	***570***	***560***	
OCEANIA							
Cook Islands							
Fiji	1750	2000	1880	1720	1850	1710	1800
Kiribati	410	440	480	500	480	500	–
Nauru							
New Caledonia	8190	7700	7270	6270	5880	5750	–
Niue							
Pacif. Isl.(Trust Tr.)	880	970	1020	1040	1050	1040	–
Papua New Guinea	760	810	780	720	700	680	690
Polynesia, French	7270	8020	8250	7770	7620	7830	–
Solomon Islands	420	510	540	530	560	520	540
Tokelau							
Tonga	520	640	770	820	780	730	690
Tuvalu							
Vanuatu	820	890	1020	1060	1090	1120	–
Wallis & Futuna							
Western Samoa							
TOM Unallocated							
Oceania Unallocated							
TOTAL	*1290*	*1370*	*1340*	*1250*	*1230*	*1210*	
LDCs Unspecified	–	–	–	–	–	–	–
TOTAL,ALL LDCS	***700***	***780***	***790***	***750***	***730***	***720***	
INCOME GROUPS							
LLDCS	220	230	240	230	220	220	
CHINA AND INDIA	260	290	290	290	290	290	
OTHER LOW-INCOME	370	420	440	420	410	400	
LOW MIDDLE-INCOME	910	980	970	900	860	840	
UPPER MIDDLE-INCOME	2530	2820	2900	2690	2610	2530	
UNALLOCATED	–	–	–	–	–	–	

Legend:
- ○─○─○ LLDCS
- --------- CHINA AND INDIA
- —·—·— OTHER LICS
- ——— LMICS
- ----- UMICS

	1980	1981	1982	1983	1984	1985	1986
EUROPE							
Cyprus	629	637	645	655	657	665	671
Gibraltar	29	29	29	29	29	29	–
Greece	9643	9729	9792	9840	9896	9935	9975
Malta	364	364	360	360	359	358	357
Portugal	9909	9957	9997	10099	10164	10229	10283
Turkey	44438	45544	46677	47838	49028	50248	51323
Yugoslavia	22304	22471	22646	22800	22963	23123	23256
Europe Unallocated							
TOTAL	*87316*	*88731*	*90146*	*91621*	*93096*	*94587*	*95865*
NORTH OF SAHARA							
Algeria	18666	19246	19857	20529	21221	21905	22582
Egypt	42289	43465	44673	45915	47191	48503	49697
Libya	3103	3225	3352	3484	3621	3764	3914
Morocco	19382	19866	20361	20869	21390	21925	22474
Tunisia	6369	6517	6668	6823	6981	7143	7308
North of Sahara Unall.							
TOTAL	*89809*	*92319*	*94911*	*97620*	*100404*	*103240*	*105975*
SOUTH OF SAHARA							
Angola	7723	7919	8120	8326	8537	8754	8993
Benin	3464	3573	3685	3801	3920	4043	4177
Botswana	902	933	966	999	1034	1070	1105
Burkina Faso	6947	7125	7308	7495	7688	7885	8106
Burundi	4114	4224	4338	4454	4573	4696	4835
Cameroon	8701	8980	9269	9567	9874	10191	10555
Cape Verde	296	303	310	315	320	327	330
Central African Rep.	2286	2343	2400	2460	2521	2583	2655
Chad	4477	4577	4681	4789	4902	5018	5143
Comoros	383	396	410	424	439	452	460
Congo	1605	1655	1707	1760	1815	1872	1940
Cote d'Ivoire	8358	8676	9006	9348	9703	10072	10431
Djibouti	310	320	331	341	351	362	370
Equatorial Guinea	341	347	353	360	366	373	381
Ethiopia	37717	38784	39881	41009	42169	42271	43557
Gabon	797	834	872	912	953	997	1023
Gambia	634	655	677	700	723	748	772
Ghana	10828	11181	11545	11921	12309	12710	13125
Guinea	5488	5617	5750	5885	6024	6166	6331
Guinea-Bissau	809	824	839	854	870	886	904
Kenya	16642	17330	18046	18791	19567	20375	21217
Lesotho	1355	1391	1428	1466	1505	1545	1587
Liberia	1864	1927	1993	2061	2131	2204	2279
Madagascar	8714	8995	9285	9584	9893	10212	10545
Malawi	6046	6234	6427	6626	6832	7044	7271
Mali	6699	6854	7013	7175	7341	7511	7701
Mauritania	1529	1560	1593	1625	1659	1693	1737
Mauritius	957	972	983	993	1011	1020	1032
Mayotte	48	49	50	51	52	53	–
Mozambique	12103	12423	12752	13089	13436	13791	14185
Namibia	980	1008	1036	1066	1096	1127	1162
Niger	5515	5680	5850	6025	6205	6391	6589
Nigeria	84732	87529	90418	93402	96485	99669	103136
Reunion	510	514	518	523	527	531	539
Rwanda	5139	5305	5477	5654	5837	6026	6236
St. Helena	5	5	5	5	5	5	–
Sao Tome & Principe	94	97	99	102	105	108	111
Senegal	5706	5869	6036	6208	6385	6567	6768
Seychelles	63	64	64	64	65	65	65
Sierra Leone	3279	3352	3425	3501	3578	3657	3749
Somalia	4674	4808	4946	5088	5234	5384	5545
Sudan	19152	19678	20219	20774	21345	21931	22563
Swaziland	633	656	680	705	730	757	784
Tanzania	18757	19407	20080	20776	21497	22242	23048
Togo	2578	2664	2753	2845	2940	3038	3139
Uganda	12637	13021	13418	13826	14247	14680	15159
Zaire	26379	27166	27977	28811	29671	30557	31511
Zambia	5647	5844	6048	6259	6478	6704	6945
Zimbabwe	7009	7268	7538	7817	8106	8406	8694
East African Community							
DOM/TOM Unallocated							
EAMA Unallocated							
South of Sahara Unall.							
TOTAL	*365626*	*376936*	*388605*	*400632*	*413054*	*424769*	*438490*
Africa Unspecified	–	–	–	–	–	–	–
AFRICA TOTAL	*455435*	*469255*	*483516*	*498252*	*513458*	*528009*	*544465*
N.& C. AMERICA							
Aruba							
Bahamas	210	214	218	222	226	231	236
Barbados	249	250	251	252	253	252	255

	1980	1981
Belize	145	148
Bermuda	71	73
Costa Rica	2279	2343
Cuba	9718	9717
Dominican Republic	5697	5834
El Salvador	4525	4573
Guadeloupe	327	328
Guatemala	6917	7113
Haiti	5413	5511
Honduras	3691	3822
Jamaica	2065	2081
Martinique	326	326
Mexico	69393	71184
Netherlands Antilles	188	190
Nicaragua	2771	2860
Panama	1956	2000
St. Pierre & Miquelon	7	7
Trinidad & Tobago	1095	1112
Anguilla	8	8
Antigua and Barbuda	75	76
Cayman Islands	18	18
Dominica	73	74
Grenada	87	88
Montserrat	12	12
St. Kitts-Nevis	44	44
St. Lucia	124	126
St. Vincent and Gr.	108	110
Turks & Caicos Isl.	7	7
Virgin Islands	13	13
West Indies Unall.		
DOM/TOM Unallocated		
N.& C. America Unall.		
TOTAL	*117676*	*120326*
SOUTH AMERICA		
Argentina	28237	28694
Bolivia	5570	5720
Brazil	121286	124015
Chile	11104	11294
Colombia	25892	26379
Ecuador	8123	8361
Falkland Islands	2	2
Guiana	69	71
Guyana	760	766
Paraguay	3147	3249
Peru	16609	16992
Suriname	356	355
Uruguay	2908	2927
Venezuela	15024	15487
South America Unall.		
TOTAL	*239087*	*244312*
America Unspecified	–	–
AMERICA TOTAL	*356763*	*364638*
MIDDLE EAST		
Bahrain	347	360
Iran	38635	39775
Iraq	13291	13776
Israel	3878	3948
Jordan	2923	3031
Kuwait	1372	1434
Lebanon	3272	3337
Oman	984	1035
Qatar	224	240
Saudi Arabia	9372	9804
Syria	8800	9110
United Arab Emirates	1016	1079
Yemen	7039	7213
Yemen, Dem.	1838	1885
Middle East Unall.		
TOTAL	*92991*	*96027*
SOUTH ASIA		
Afghanistan	15950	16084
Bangladesh	88513	90660
Bhutan	1112	1137
Burma	33511	34171
India	687332	702235
Maldives	158	162
Nepal	14640	15029
Pakistan	82581	85118
Sri Lanka	14738	14962

1982	1983	1984	1985	1986
150	153	156	159	159
74	76	77	79	–
2406	2470	2534	2600	2660
9782	9897	9992	10090	10205
5974	6118	6265	6416	6561
4621	4669	4718	4768	4861
330	331	333	334	–
7315	7524	7740	7963	8177
5611	5713	5817	5922	6034
3957	4094	4232	4383	4528
2120	2165	2196	2227	2261
327	327	328	328	–
73020	74905	76837	78820	80745
192	194	196	198	–
2955	3056	3162	3272	3373
2044	2089	2134	2180	2222
7	7	7	7	–
1129	1149	1166	1185	1205
8	8	8	8	–
77	78	78	79	79
19	19	20	20	–
75	76	77	78	79
91	92	94	96	98
12	13	12	12	–
45	45	44	43	48
129	131	134	136	140
112	114	117	119	121
7	7	7	7	–
13	13	13	14	–
123136	*126072*	*129039*	*132092*	*134047*
29157	29625	30094	30531	30944
5874	6034	6211	6383	6548
126806	129662	132580	135564	138370
11487	11682	11878	12074	12246
26874	27379	27894	28418	28948
8605	8857	9114	9378	9639
2	2	2	2	–
74	77	79	82	–
772	779	785	790	798
3355	3464	3577	3693	3803
17383	17784	18193	18612	19017
364	374	383	393	402
2947	2968	2990	3012	3034
15944	16397	16853	17339	17818
249644	*255084*	*260633*	*266271*	*271567*
–	–	–	–	–
372780	*381156*	*389672*	*398363*	*405614*
373	387	402	417	430
40945	42146	43376	44632	46026
14278	14799	15339	15898	16490
4023	4097	4194	4233	4300
3143	3259	3380	3505	3624
1498	1566	1636	1710	1771
3403	3470	3539	2668	2665
1088	1142	1193	1242	1288
257	276	295	311	333
10231	10658	11093	11542	12007
9434	9774	10130	10505	10856
1146	1218	1294	1371	1424
7392	7575	7763	7955	8187
1933	1983	2034	2086	2136
99144	*102350*	*105668*	*108075*	*111537*
16219	16355	16493	16631	17480
93046	95495	98009	100592	103086
1162	1187	1213	1240	1268
34844	35530	36230	36943	37660
717460	733016	748909	765147	780184
167	172	177	182	187
15390	15760	16139	16527	16960
87758	90480	93286	96180	98858
15189	15416	15606	15837	16108

	1980	1981	1982	1983	1984	1985	1986
South Asia Unall.							
TOTAL	*938535*	*959558*	*981235*	*1003411*	*1026062*	*1049279*	*1071791*
FAR EAST ASIA							
Brunei	185	193	201	209	216	224	232
China	978334	991635	1008173	1018664	1029156	1040338	1053401
Hong Kong	5039	5154	5233	5313	5364	5423	5496
Indonesia	146345	149389	152497	155669	158915	162212	165419
Kampuchea	6400	6473	6668	6866	7070	7282	7452
Korea	38124	38723	39331	39951	40578	41056	41585
Korea, Dem.	18025	18482	18946	19417	19896	20385	20845
Laos	3272	3337	3403	3470	3539	3609	3695
Macao	323	336	349	363	377	392	–
Malaysia	13763	14107	14460	14821	15191	15571	15918
Mongolia	1663	1706	1750	1796	1843	1891	1941
Philippines	48300	49522	50774	52058	53375	54725	56017
Singapore	2415	2443	2472	2502	2529	2558	2585
Taiwan	17786	18099	18418	18742	19072	19408	19670
Thailand	46700	47659	48639	49639	50660	51700	52631
Viet Nam	54175	55601	57064	58566	60107	61689	63307
Far East Asia Unall.							
TOTAL	*1380849*	*1402859*	*1428378*	*1448046*	*1467888*	*1488463*	*1510194*
Asia Unspecified	–	–	–	–	–	–	–
ASIA TOTAL	*2412375*	*2458444*	*2508757*	*2553807*	*2599618*	*2645817*	*2693522*
OCEANIA							
Cook Islands	22	22	22	22	22	22	–
Fiji	634	646	658	672	686	696	710
Kiribati	58	59	60	62	63	64	65
Nauru	8	8	8	8	8	8	–
New Caledonia	139	141	143	145	147	149	–
Niue	3	3	3	3	3	3	–
Pacif. Isl.(Trust Tr.)	136	139	143	147	150	154	–
Papua New Guinea	3086	3167	3249	3334	3422	3511	3593
Polynesia, French	151	156	160	165	170	175	–
Solomon Islands	228	235	243	251	259	267	275
Tokelau	2	2	2	2	2	2	–
Tonga	90	92	94	95	96	97	98
Tuvalu	8	8	8	8	8	9	–
Vanuatu	117	120	124	127	130	134	137
Wallis & Futuna	11	11	11	11	11	12	–
Western Samoa	156	157	158	160	161	163	165
TOM Unallocated							
Oceania Unallocated							
TOTAL	*4849*	*4966*	*5086*	*5212*	*5338*	*5466*	
LDCs Unspecified	–	–	–	–	–	–	–
TOTAL,ALL LDCS	*3316738*	*3386034*	*3460285*	*3530048*	*3601182*	*3672242*	*3744509*
INCOME GROUPS							
LLDCS	293896	301434	309330	317436	325771	333244	342961
CHINA AND INDIA	1665666	1693870	1725633	1751680	1778065	1805485	1833585
OTHER LOW-INCOME	479904	492234	505043	518193	531679	545555	559166
LOW MIDDLE-INCOME	351742	360945	370489	380347	390449	400826	411053
UPPER MIDDLE-INCOME	525530	537551	549790	562392	575218	587132	597744
UNALLOCATED	–	–	–	–	–	–	–

Legend: LLDCS, CHINA AND INDIA, OTHER LICS, LMICS, UMICS

	1980	1981	1982	1983	1984	1985	1986		1980	1981
EUROPE								Belize	108.4	107.8
Cyprus	104.0	106.0	110.3	111.8	122.8	125.8	—	Bermuda	115.4	124.0
Gibraltar	92.1	92.1	92.1	101.3	102.0	105.3	—	Costa Rica	96.5	89.8
Greece	100.9	99.5	98.2	97.2	99.5	101.2	101.6	Cuba		
Malta	104.8	109.2	114.0	111.2	113.6	115.5	118.4	Dominican Republic	95.8	96.3
Portugal	103.1	101.9	103.1	102.4	98.3	101.7	106.0	El Salvador	88.8	79.8
Turkey	96.7	98.1	100.2	101.4	104.5	107.5	113.4	Guadeloupe	100.2	101.1
Yugoslavia	101.1	101.2	100.2	98.2	99.1	98.9	102.6	Guatemala	100.3	97.8
Europe Unallocated								Haiti	105.7	101.1
TOTAL	*99.8*	*99.4*	*99.3*	*98.3*	*99.3*	*100.5*		Honduras	98.3	96.5
								Jamaica	92.7	95.8
NORTH OF SAHARA								Martinique	98.4	103.0
Algeria	100.9	102.5	103.4	106.2	107.3	110.5	106.9	Mexico	104.0	108.5
Egypt	109.4	113.8	115.2	117.8	117.9	118.6	117.7	Netherlands Antilles	110.8	120.5
Libya	99.3	78.0	71.1	67.0	62.5	59.0	—	Nicaragua	107.8	105.3
Morocco	100.8	95.7	100.2	99.6	99.1	99.4	104.4	Panama	107.9	110.8
Tunisia	105.8	108.0	105.0	107.8	111.6	114.0	109.8	St. Pierre & Miquelon		
North of Sahara Unall.								Trinidad & Tobago	109.5	109.7
TOTAL	*102.6*	*97.4*	*96.5*	*97.0*	*96.5*	*97.1*		Anguilla		
								Antigua and Barbuda	107.5	111.2
SOUTH OF SAHARA								Cayman Islands		
Angola	102.1	97.5	100.3	99.3	99.2	101.8	—	Dominica	111.0	123.1
Benin	103.4	110.1	113.8	107.1	105.8	110.0	106.0	Grenada	94.2	97.2
Botswana	111.0	109.1	109.2	127.5	147.9	147.5	160.5	Montserrat		
Burkina Faso	100.9	103.0	100.1	96.0	93.0	98.9	98.3	St. Kitts-Nevis	110.3	116.2
Burundi	101.7	108.2	101.4	99.9	99.9	101.1	102.8	St. Lucia	95.5	94.8
Cameroon	110.2	121.3	124.8	128.4	134.3	140.0	146.7	St. Vincent and Gr.	102.9	106.1
Cape Verde	128.8	119.7	120.4	118.3	122.4	123.1	134.3	Turks & Caicos Isl.		
Central African Rep.	94.1	90.1	89.9	82.3	87.3	87.5	87.5	Virgin Islands		
Chad	91.7	90.6	93.4	94.4	87.4	113.6	105.2	West Indies Unall.		
Comoros	113.4	121.5	122.6	121.2	122.0	120.8	121.9	DOM/TOM Unallocated		
Congo	115.1	137.9	150.4	151.1	158.2	148.1	138.1	N.& C. America Unall.		
Cote d'Ivoire	106.6	114.8	104.4	94.3	87.3	88.0	89.6	*TOTAL*	*103.1*	*106.6*
Djibouti	102.2	102.8	97.0	97.7	98.3	99.0	—			
Equatorial Guinea								**SOUTH AMERICA**		
Ethiopia	101.8	101.1	99.8	101.6	96.9	89.6	99.0	Argentina	99.8	88.7
Gabon	100.8	92.7	91.4	88.7	92.0	93.3	83.0	Bolivia	95.2	92.0
Gambia	98.3	87.0	91.2	99.5	89.1	78.1	80.7	Brazil	104.2	99.4
Ghana	97.6	91.4	82.4	76.3	79.9	81.8	82.5	Chile	105.6	108.2
Guinea	99.8	96.6	94.6	92.7	91.5	93.9	96.0	Colombia	102.3	102.2
Guinea-Bissau	81.5	94.1	95.9	90.6	92.8	94.6	91.9	Ecuador	101.2	101.9
Kenya	101.5	103.5	99.1	98.3	93.4	93.0	95.0	Falkland Islands		
Lesotho	102.6	109.6	124.5	121.1	108.4	114.4	111.1	Guiana	115.2	112.3
Liberia	92.0	87.3	79.2	73.0	67.9	68.3	64.3	Guyana	99.6	97.6
Madagascar	97.2	84.1	78.8	75.3	71.3	69.9	69.0	Paraguay	107.1	113.3
Malawi	93.6	85.9	86.1	87.4	88.9	87.4	84.4	Peru	104.4	106.6
Mali	96.1	90.6	93.9	87.7	85.0	81.7	87.4	Suriname	98.6	108.6
Mauritania	104.3	107.9	100.1	105.4	102.8	101.5	102.0	Uruguay	105.1	107.0
Mauritius	88.4	89.0	92.9	92.6	94.7	100.9	108.2	Venezuela	95.5	92.8
Mayotte								South America Unall.		
Mozambique	97.7	95.5	89.1	72.4	57.7	49.1	46.5	*TOTAL*	*102.4*	*98.6*
Namibia	102.2	101.8	100.7	96.4	93.8	91.2	—	America Unspecified	–	–
Niger	104.3	102.5	95.9	90.8	74.8	76.7	79.5	*AMERICA TOTAL*	*102.6*	*101.3*
Nigeria	99.1	90.0	84.1	77.2	71.3	71.5	66.5			
Reunion	101.8	103.4	108.7	110.9	111.3	111.7	—	**MIDDLE EAST**		
Rwanda	107.4	115.2	111.8	109.5	98.4	102.3	103.6	Bahrain	101.6	100.7
St. Helena								Iran	76.8	76.2
Sao Tome & Principe	112.7	78.9	91.6	82.8	78.7	73.3	72.9	Iraq	102.0	50.7
Senegal	93.5	89.3	99.9	99.4	91.2	92.2	94.3	Israel	99.7	102.9
Seychelles	101.3	91.8	91.3	90.9	92.6	98.2	99.6	Jordan	107.8	113.0
Sierra Leone	101.4	105.7	108.5	105.5	103.8	101.6	100.2	Kuwait	94.5	101.4
Somalia	93.1	96.5	99.0	98.3	94.2	98.6	—	Lebanon		
Sudan	97.7	95.1	98.8	99.3	89.8	75.1	79.9	Oman	110.6	113.9
Swaziland	105.6	111.7	107.9	107.0	104.7	102.0	100.4	Qatar	101.4	97.5
Tanzania	101.0	96.1	93.7	89.7	88.0	85.8	84.1	Saudi Arabia	103.1	107.6
Togo	110.1	100.7	93.2	84.0	82.9	84.2	85.5	Syria	104.4	109.1
Uganda	92.7	94.9	100.5	102.2	104.3	101.8	—	United Arab Emirates	118.7	117.5
Zaire	98.7	98.9	92.1	89.6	83.4	83.9	84.9	Yemen	103.2	104.7
Zambia	102.0	110.2	100.7	95.2	89.8	87.1	83.2	Yemen, Dem.	93.4	97.3
Zimbabwe	103.4	114.6	107.0	109.7	102.8	109.5	105.1	Middle East Unall.		
East African Community								*TOTAL*	*95.5*	*92.9*
DOM/TOM Unallocated										
EAMA Unallocated								**SOUTH ASIA**		
South of Sahara Unall.								Afghanistan	94.5	96.3
TOTAL	*100.1*	*96.6*	*92.9*	*88.7*	*84.2*	*84.4*		Bangladesh	99.3	103.2
Africa Unspecified	–	–	–	–	–	–	–	Bhutan	103.3	111.1
AFRICA TOTAL	*101.1*	*96.8*	*94.1*	*91.7*	*88.7*	*89.0*		Burma	106.0	110.6
								India	104.5	107.4
N.& C. AMERICA								Maldives	106.9	116.1
Aruba								Nepal	95.3	100.4
Bahamas	107.0	93.7	102.7	104.3	108.1	110.6	—	Pakistan	105.7	110.0
Barbados	104.4	100.4	94.8	93.7	96.6	96.9	98.6	Sri Lanka	103.7	106.3

1982	1983	1984	1985	1986
101.4	95.2	98.7	98.0	99.2
108.6	96.1	95.5	91.8	
77.8	79.7	84.1	82.8	83.3
96.4	98.3	94.6	88.2	86.7
73.9	73.7	74.0	74.4	74.5
100.6	102.2	103.6	105.3	—
91.6	86.8	84.0	80.8	78.8
95.8	94.4	93.4	93.0	90.1
90.1	88.4	87.5	87.0	86.7
95.0	96.1	86.9	78.3	81.0
111.0	111.8	112.3	113.2	—
101.5	94.3	96.3	97.8	91.3
135.0	135.2	129.8	125.7	—
100.8	102.8	98.1	90.1	87.1
113.2	110.4	107.0	109.3	110.3
109.5	100.3	88.8	81.9	79.8
114.8	113.9	122.7	130.2	136.2
126.4	127.2	128.2	130.1	128.5
94.3	91.3	116.3	122.3	125.3
112.2	112.5	117.4	119.2	110.8
95.6	95.7	100.9	105.8	109.3
109.2	117.0	120.4	126.6	129.4
100.7	*94.9*	*95.9*	*96.6*	
82.1	82.4	83.2	78.7	83.2
77.1	74.7	72.1	66.2	63.5
97.1	91.2	89.6	95.2	102.5
87.9	86.3	88.3	90.5	91.7
100.3	99.6	100.0	100.1	102.5
97.8	92.3	91.3	92.3	93.3
107.9	103.8	101.4	97.8	—
83.3	73.8	73.3	71.1	70.2
109.0	101.7	101.2	101.9	100.4
104.5	88.1	89.6	88.7	96.7
99.8	92.7	96.3	93.2	92.2
94.9	85.8	81.7	81.6	88.7
87.3	79.0	77.0	73.7	74.9
94.0	*88.7*	*87.7*	*89.7*	
—	—	—	—	—
96.2	*90.7*	*90.5*	*92.0*	
98.5	104.3	106.1	97.2	—
84.6	93.2	102.8	113.3	—
65.5	66.9	68.3	69.8	—
101.3	101.6	114.9	117.3	117.8
117.4	118.7	113.4	118.9	116.1
88.0	82.8	79.0	67.7	—
108.3	102.6	109.1	118.9	79.3
76.6	55.7	58.0	48.4	—
102.7	83.9	82.6	74.0	—
107.4	105.8	98.6	95.7	93.3
102.3	91.8	88.8	81.8	—
110.6	109.5	109.0	107.6	105.0
88.7	89.9	92.4	84.2	76.9
93.6	*89.8*	*92.9*	*93.3*	
96.3	96.3	96.2	96.2	—
100.9	101.7	103.7	105.2	106.6
128.5	135.4	140.1	138.0	—
114.1	116.5	120.7	125.7	127.8
109.1	115.1	117.2	122.0	125.4
123.7	118.4	122.3	136.5	140.4
101.9	96.5	101.0	101.5	103.1
111.3	115.9	121.8	125.0	130.1
109.2	113.1	118.7	120.2	122.8

	1980	1981	1982	1983	1984	1985	1986
South Asia Unall.							
TOTAL	*104.1*	*107.3*	*108.8*	*113.9*	*116.6*	*120.8*	
FAR EAST ASIA							
Brunei	90.0	69.2	69.0	66.7	64.8	62.7	—
China	105.3	108.6	115.7	125.9	142.2	157.4	167.8
Hong Kong	109.7	117.3	118.9	124.8	135.2	134.6	144.3
Indonesia	106.9	114.5	115.0	115.9	120.3	120.7	121.9
Kampuchea							
Korea	93.3	97.9	101.7	112.0	119.6	124.5	138.3
Korea, Dem.							
Laos	99.9	99.2	98.5	97.7	97.0	104.3	—
Macao	98.0	114.1	112.4	112.0	111.8	111.4	—
Malaysia	106.8	112.0	113.9	115.4	120.1	115.4	114.9
Mongolia							
Philippines	102.1	102.9	102.3	100.9	91.4	85.4	84.7
Singapore	105.3	114.7	121.3	130.7	147.9	145.9	147.3
Taiwan	103.7	107.1	109.3	110.6	111.9	110.5	—
Thailand	102.7	105.5	107.1	111.7	114.7	116.1	122.0
Viet Nam							
Far East Asia Unall.							
TOTAL	*103.8*	*107.7*	*111.8*	*118.4*	*127.7*	*134.5*	
Asia Unspecified	—	—	—	—	—	—	—
ASIA TOTAL	*101.5*	*103.5*	*106.3*	*109.5*	*115.9*	*120.2*	
OCEANIA							
Cook Islands							
Fiji	96.4	101.2	91.5	86.5	96.6	92.3	98.8
Kiribati	102.5	100.8	103.3	103.9	94.4	96.8	—
Nauru							
New Caledonia	99.6	88.7	86.3	81.0	81.2	81.4	—
Niue							
Pacif. Isl.(Trust Tr.)	100.1	98.1	95.5	93.6	91.4	88.4	—
Papua New Guinea	94.3	91.8	89.1	87.2	86.9	89.1	91.0
Polynesia, French	97.8	102.7	110.2	112.6	115.2	118.0	—
Solomon Islands	82.9	90.3	87.3	87.4	113.1	110.4	127.0
Tokelau							
Tonga	114.6	128.8	144.8	150.2	137.2	124.5	—
Tuvalu							
Vanuatu	99.5	99.0	107.6	107.0	106.4	105.0	—
Wallis & Futuna							
Western Samoa							
TOM Unallocated							
Oceania Unallocated							
TOTAL	*96.1*	*95.1*	*93.2*	*91.1*	*93.6*	*93.9*	
LDCs Unspecified	—	—	—	—	—	—	—
TOTAL,ALL LDCS	*101.7*	*101.7*	*101.2*	*100.9*	*103.7*	*106.4*	
INCOME GROUPS							
LLDCS	99.5	99.9	99.7	98.9	97.0	95.8	
CHINA AND INDIA	105.0	108.1	113.2	121.7	132.6	143.7	
OTHER LOW-INCOME	104.5	108.3	107.5	108.0	109.6	110.2	
LOW MIDDLE-INCOME	100.1	98.6	96.8	94.2	92.3	92.5	
UPPER MIDDLE-INCOME	100.4	99.1	97.2	94.2	95.8	96.9	
UNALLOCATED	—	—	—	—	—	—	

LLDCS
CHINA AND INDIA
OTHER LICS
LMICS
UMICS

CURRENT ACCOUNT DEFICIT (MINUS), MILLION US DOLLARS

	1980	1981	1982	1983	1984	1985	1986
EUROPE							
Cyprus	-281	-183	-203	-237	-229	-172	-35
Gibraltar	–	–	–	–	–	–	–
Greece	-2209	-2582	-2452	-2714	-2847	-4145	-3068
Malta	20	33	-21	-35	-22	-42	-23
Portugal	-1071	-2605	-3250	-1005	-551	305	951
Turkey	-3427	-1932	-1040	-2134	-1636	-1266	-1774
Yugoslavia	-2315	-960	-475	278	–	–	–
Europe Unallocated							
TOTAL	*-9283*	*-8229*	*-7441*	*-5848*			
NORTH OF SAHARA							
Algeria	225	80	-166	-86	79	1004	-2229
Egypt	-438	-2136	-1852	-411	-2081	-2244	-1871
Libya	8258	-3887	-1483	-1586	-1443	1890	–
Morocco	-2275	-2640	-2776	-1762	-1842	-1904	-1376
Tunisia	-455	-501	-702	-614	-812	-636	-664
North of Sahara Unall.							
TOTAL	*5315*	*-9084*	*-6979*	*-4459*	*-6099*	*-1890*	
SOUTH OF SAHARA							
Angola	–	–	–	–	–	–	–
Benin	-111	-154	-449	-201	–	–	68
Botswana	-207	-346	-164	-124	-99	39	68
Burkina Faso	-259	-223	-281	-226	–	–	–
Burundi	–	–	–	–	–	–	–
Cameroon	-521	-542	-453	-493	-237	-670	–
Cape Verde	–	–	–	–	–	–	–
Central African Rep.	-140	-78	-113	-105	-97	-114	-189
Chad	-16	-21	-43	-76	-78	-221	–
Comoros	–	–	–	–	–	–	–
Congo	-230	-505	-361	-438	168	-202	–
Cote d'Ivoire	-1836	-1427	-1046	-955	-83	-50	-352
Djibouti	–	–	–	–	–	–	–
Equatorial Guinea	–	–	–	–	–	–	–
Ethiopia	-280	-295	-298	-329	-318	–	–
Gabon	350	375	285	66	87	-176	-983
Gambia	-188	-154	-78	-86	97	70	–
Ghana	-54	-508	-192	-248	-180	-244	-165
Guinea	–	–	–	–	–	–	–
Guinea-Bissau	–	–	–	–	–	–	–
Kenya	453	598	811	989	982	972	1111
Lesotho	-117	-129	-82	-77	-68	-50	-63
Liberia	97	53	97	-139	1	23	199
Madagascar	-634	-491	-387	-303	-264	31	–
Malawi	-256	-134	-108	–	–	–	–
Mali	-87	-127	-214	-201	-104	-176	-168
Mauritania	-251	-264	-370	-299	-217	-240	-23
Mauritius	-129	-158	-62	-32	-64	-43	81
Mayotte	–	–	–	–	–	–	–
Mozambique	–	–	–	–	–	–	–
Namibia	–	–	–	–	–	–	–
Niger	-429	-342	-383	-198	-159	-220	-154
Nigeria	5270	-6103	-7200	-4316	139	1264	372
Reunion	–	–	–	–	–	–	–
Rwanda	-155	-173	-192	-161	-141	-176	-186
St. Helena	–	–	–	–	–	–	–
Sao Tome & Principe	–	–	–	–	–	–	–
Senegal	-526	-639	-448	-445	-411	17	–
Seychelles	-30	-32	-50	-40	-28	-33	-48
Sierra Leone	-209	-164	-206	-51	-48	-9	–
Somalia	-279	-210	-341	-290	-326	-301	-307
Sudan	-337	-661	-248	-220	5	43	-262
Swaziland	-196	-152	-150	-167	-128	-82	-36
Tanzania	-662	-839	–	–	-841	-590	-522
Togo	-181	-114	-155	-111	-49	-79	-179
Uganda	-121	-124	10	25	121	110	85
Zaire	-2562	-2289	-2192	-2035	-2244	-2072	-2241
Zambia	-544	-766	-593	-310	-162	-209	-324
Zimbabwe	-301	-727	-754	-501	-188	-140	-4
East African Community							
DOM/TOM Unallocated							
EAMA Unallocated							
South of Sahara Unall.							
TOTAL	*-5683*	*-17865*	*-16411*	*-12096*	*-4935*		
Africa Unspecified	–	–	–	–	–	–	–
AFRICA TOTAL	**-368**	**-26949**	**-23390**	**-16555**	**-11034**		
N.& C. AMERICA							
Aruba							
Bahamas	-34	-93	-85	-52	-60	-53	-39
Barbados	-26	-113	-42	-46	21	49	–

	1980	1981
Belize	–	–
Bermuda	–	–
Costa Rica	-659	-409
Cuba		
Dominican Republic	-725	-400
El Salvador	-1	-272
Guadeloupe	–	–
Guatemala	-164	-574
Haiti	-140	-242
Honduras	-331	-321
Jamaica	-175	-338
Martinique	–	–
Mexico	-8173	-13960
Netherlands Antilles	-127	-23
Nicaragua	-534	-649
Panama	-377	-23
St. Pierre & Miquelon	–	–
Trinidad & Tobago	357	398
Anguilla	–	–
Antigua and Barbuda	-22	-35
Cayman Islands	–	–
Dominica	-32	-22
Grenada	-11	-25
Montserrat	–	–
St. Kitts-Nevis	–	–
St. Lucia	-37	-45
St. Vincent and Gr.	-13	-6
Turks & Caicos Isl.	–	–
Virgin Islands	–	–
West Indies Unall.		
DOM/TOM Unallocated		
N.& C. America Unall.		
TOTAL	*-11225*	*-17151*
SOUTH AMERICA		
Argentina	-4774	-4712
Bolivia	-40	-478
Brazil	-12848	-11761
Chile	2129	-456
Colombia	-207	-1962
Ecuador	-700	-1037
Falkland Islands	–	–
Guiana	–	–
Guyana	-127	-179
Paraguay	-278	-377
Peru	-248	-1889
Suriname	-58	-122
Uruguay	-716	-468
Venezuela	4749	4026
South America Unall.		
TOTAL	*-13118*	*-19416*
America Unspecified	–	–
AMERICA TOTAL	**-24343**	**-36567**
MIDDLE EAST		
Bahrain	75	235
Iran	-2436	-3446
Iraq		
Israel	-2710	-3126
Jordan	-939	-1299
Kuwait	16189	14750
Lebanon		
Oman	840	1216
Qatar	8863	9048
Saudi Arabia	48653	46829
Syria	-1269	-2093
United Arab Emirates		
Yemen	-831	-987
Yemen, Dem.	-239	-242
Middle East Unall.		
TOTAL	*66197*	*60885*
SOUTH ASIA		
Afghanistan	–	–
Bangladesh	-1522	-1550
Bhutan	–	–
Burma	-354	-300
India	-2376	-3424
Maldives	-25	-23
Nepal	-113	-107
Pakistan	-1155	-1268
Sri Lanka	-793	-605

1982	1983	1984	1985	1986
–	–	-17	-8	4
–	–	–	–	–
-273	-329	-264	-306	-198
–	–	–	–	–
-458	-438	-223	-222	-148
-271	-211	-243	-243	–
–	–	–	–	–
-400	-225	-378	-247	-42
-192	-206	-203	-191	-168
-249	-254	-386	-322	-271
-419	-362	-372	-370	–
-6318	5361	4289	859	-1180
72	-85	-29	172	–
-557	-638	-753	-802	–
-151	311	-44	132	320
–	–	–	–	–
-586	-993	-511	-86	-422
–	–	–	–	–
-42	-9	-8	-25	-79
–	–	–	–	–
-14	-9	-18	-20	-9
-33	-29	-21	-27	-35
–	–	–	–	–
-36	-13	-24	-19	–
-11	-6	–	–	–
–	–	–	–	–
–	–	–	–	–
-10066	*1767*	*756*	*-1728*	
-2353	-2436	-2495	-954	–
-185	-164	-219	-322	–
-16314	-6839	32	-289	–
-1205	-515	-1213	-627	-311
-3057	-3022	-1411	-1815	413
-1246	-28	-168	69	-658
–	–	–	–	–
–	–	–	–	–
-139	-161	-98	-93	–
-378	-253	-325	-231	-369
-1776	-1091	-379	-9	-1125
-153	-163	-45	-25	-3
-245	-71	-139	-119	66
-4222	4451	5447	3112	-1990
-31274	*-10291*	*-1013*	*-1304*	
–	–	–	–	–
-41340	***-8524***	***-257***	***-3032***	
381	36	80	145	-85
5733	358	-414	–	–
–	–	–	–	–
-3732	-4112	-3993	-3216	-2939
-1366	-1186	-952	-1000	-674
5520	5973	6788	5344	6343
–	–	–	–	–
459	358	107	110	-969
5620	–	–	–	–
11974	-12953	-14803	-9170	-10480
-1630	-2093	-2052	-2013	–
–	5612	7355	–	–
-1046	-719	-442	-534	-560
-265	-276	-397	–	–
21647	*-9002*	*-8723*	*-10334*	
–	–	–	–	–
-1405	-828	-1273	-1190	-1249
–	–	–	–	–
-462	-350	-212	-211	–
-2841	-2327	-2835	-4497	–
-24	-29	-24	-12	–
-194	-239	-178	-207	-182
-1162	-234	-1580	-1434	-1176
-711	-636	-202	-596	-589

	1980	1981	1982	1983	1984	1985	1986
South Asia Unall.							
TOTAL	*-6338*	*-7278*	*-6799*	*-4643*	*-6304*	*-8147*	
FAR EAST ASIA							
Brunei	–	–	–	–	–	–	–
China	–	–	5867	4412	2372	-11489	-7158
Hong Kong	–	–	–	–	–	–	–
Indonesia	2810	-816	-5458	-6442	-1970	-1950	-4099
Kampuchea	–	–	–	–	–	–	–
Korea	-5371	-4725	-2702	-1632	-1397	-910	4606
Korea, Dem.	–	–	–	–	–	–	–
Laos	–	–	–	–	–	–	–
Macao	–	–	–	–	–	–	–
Malaysia	-307	-2507	-3622	-3523	-1696	-753	-311
Mongolia	–	–	–	–	–	–	–
Philippines	-2052	-2243	-3364	-2986	-1536	-225	790
Singapore	-1501	-1366	-1192	-566	-356	-3	493
Taiwan	–	–	–	–	–	–	–
Thailand	-2212	-2689	-1111	-2998	-2225	-1655	149
Viet Nam	–	–	–	–	–	–	–
Far East Asia Unall.							
TOTAL	*-8633*	*-14346*	*-11582*	*-13735*	*-6808*	*-16985*	*-5530*
Asia Unspecified	–	–	–	–	–	–	–
ASIA TOTAL			*3266*	*-27380*	*-21836*		
OCEANIA							
Cook Islands	–	–	–	–	–	–	–
Fiji	-60	-201	-113	-91	-46	-46	-10
Kiribati	–	–	–	–	–	–	–
Nauru	–	–	–	–	–	–	–
New Caledonia	–	–	–	–	–	–	–
Niue	–	–	–	–	–	–	–
Pacif. Isl.(Trust Tr.)	–	–	–	–	–	–	–
Papua New Guinea	-1118	-1353	-1277	-1142	-1141	341	412
Polynesia, French	–	–	–	–	–	–	–
Solomon Islands	-31	-44	-22	-21	-9	-31	–
Tokelau	–	–	–	–	–	–	–
Tonga	–	–	–	–	–	–	–
Tuvalu	–	–	–	–	–	–	–
Vanuatu	–	–	-23	-18	-9	-22	-24
Wallis & Futuna	–	–	–	–	–	–	–
Western Samoa	-30	-29	-20	-12	-12	-9	-5
TOM Unallocated							
Oceania Unallocated							
TOTAL	*-1239*	*-1627*	*-1455*	*-1284*	*-1218*	*233*	
LDCs Unspecified	–	–	–	–	–	–	–
TOTAL, ALL LDCS							

	1980	1981	1982	1983	1984	1985	1986
EUROPE							
Cyprus	341	263	263	242	278	270	345
Gibraltar	13	11	11	27	17	21	20
Greece	3919	3701	3301	3482	3871	3966	4947
Malta	395	345	329	306	322	353	418
Portugal	3909	3407	3597	3929	4650	5225	6877
Turkey	1895	2263	2422	2635	3097	3875	4587
Yugoslavia	4071	3391	3541	4083	4519	4890	6227
Europe Unallocated							
TOTAL	*14545*	*13382*	*13465*	*14704*	*16754*	*18600*	*23420*
NORTH OF SAHARA							
Algeria	13695	13996	13031	12747	12517	12235	8992
Egypt	4427	4784	4055	3732	3960	4052	2591
Libya	19794	16477	12481	10789	9712	10407	6072
Morocco	2165	1856	1857	1826	1851	1938	2283
Tunisia	2042	1541	1428	1394	1293	1366	1507
North of Sahara Unall.							
TOTAL	*42122*	*38654*	*32853*	*30489*	*29332*	*29997*	*21445*
SOUTH OF SAHARA							
Angola	798	1284	1274	1438	1781	1930	1313
Benin	66	31	28	76	114	161	122
Botswana	15	47	68	58	50	66	106
Burkina Faso	62	54	48	39	54	31	36
Burundi	106	89	137	93	92	94	131
Cameroon	1764	1922	1849	1795	2316	2382	1733
Cape Verde	3	4	2	2	2	3	3
Central African Rep.	104	116	96	106	123	104	121
Chad	60	57	32	120	86	47	49
Comoros	11	22	23	18	11	16	18
Congo	692	997	1254	1127	1359	1123	833
Cote d'Ivoire	2631	2183	2031	1946	2306	2582	2753
Djibouti	10	2	2	9	6	3	4
Equatorial Guinea	20	29	27	24	33	30	41
Ethiopia	310	264	300	303	341	267	393
Gabon	1677	1491	1571	1583	1761	1668	1059
Gambia	26	19	25	40	38	23	30
Ghana	1024	749	859	466	385	488	680
Guinea	341	385	393	377	448	453	429
Guinea-Bissau	11	19	7	9	11	8	8
Kenya	793	602	595	608	761	748	933
Lesotho	7	6	6	3	5	5	4
Liberia	1205	1153	854	692	734	659	763
Madagascar	365	253	252	291	323	256	324
Malawi	210	217	199	178	220	257	225
Mali	117	79	51	62	82	69	78
Mauritania	249	352	273	263	278	311	347
Mauritius	505	360	388	360	395	419	642
Mayotte	–	–	–	–	–	–	–
Mozambique	262	210	178	124	85	67	61
Namibia	–	–	–	–	–	–	–
Niger	485	334	252	262	202	203	251
Nigeria	23884	17321	14872	11730	11762	12771	7786
Reunion	147	107	77	66	80	61	134
Rwanda	130	92	78	81	128	122	170
St. Helena	–	–	–	–	–	–	–
Sao Tome & Principe	22	15	10	7	9	6	7
Senegal	325	238	324	366	349	279	341
Seychelles	3	5	3	5	7	25	31
Sierra Leone	175	196	113	146	172	140	147
Somalia	28	15	27	29	14	31	25
Sudan	361	338	247	256	295	212	203
Swaziland	125	88	116	70	95	99	139
Tanzania	372	298	299	301	316	256	340
Togo	258	200	153	142	180	164	217
Uganda	425	260	359	333	392	370	434
Zaire	2258	1907	1440	1305	1591	1606	1590
Zambia	1331	895	729	637	650	562	573
Zimbabwe	372	595	579	608	577	598	718
East African Community							
DOM/TOM Unallocated							
EAMA Unallocated							
South of Sahara Unall.							
TOTAL	*44150*	*35914*	*32514*	*28606*	*31038*	*31799*	*26370*
Africa Unspecified	–	–	–	–	–	–	–
AFRICA TOTAL	**86269**	**74555**	**65357**	**59041**	**60351**	**61771**	**47786**
N.& C. AMERICA							
Aruba							
Bahamas	2484	1648	1518	1972	1502	986	624
Barbados	147	120	148	235	298	233	151

	1980	1981
Belize	99	83
Bermuda	37	39
Costa Rica	831	825
Cuba	848	713
Dominican Republic	931	1042
El Salvador	888	665
Guadeloupe	166	124
Guatemala	1057	801
Haiti	367	355
Honduras	819	783
Jamaica	878	871
Martinique	74	103
Mexico	16908	20569
Netherlands Antilles	3483	3577
Nicaragua	415	349
Panama	844	948
St. Pierre & Miquelon	7	15
Trinidad & Tobago	2944	2913
Anguilla	–	–
Antigua and Barbuda	2	5
Cayman Islands	–	–
Dominica	12	30
Grenada	19	24
Montserrat	–	–
St. Kitts-Nevis	–	–
St. Lucia	22	28
St. Vincent and Gr.	17	21
Turks & Caicos Isl.	–	–
Virgin Islands	–	–
West Indies Unall.		
DOM/TOM Unallocated		
N.& C. America Unall.		
TOTAL	*34299*	*36650*
SOUTH AMERICA		
Argentina	4105	4065
Bolivia	472	417
Brazil	13469	14126
Chile	3271	2749
Colombia	3673	2685
Ecuador	1570	1779
Falkland Islands	–	–
Guiana	31	39
Guyana	357	309
Paraguay	401	253
Peru	2812	2506
Suriname	516	482
Uruguay	494	544
Venezuela	11777	12904
South America Unall.		
TOTAL	*43036*	*42942*
America Unspecified	–	–
AMERICA TOTAL	**77246**	**79507**
MIDDLE EAST		
Bahrain	770	875
Iran	10780	7124
Iraq	20611	6931
Israel	4005	4008
Jordan	86	96
Kuwait	9870	7800
Lebanon	164	99
Oman	2788	3704
Qatar	4546	5153
Saudi Arabia	77531	88412
Syria	1439	1492
United Arab Emirates	18361	17791
Yemen	11	22
Yemen, Dem.	160	98
Middle East Unall.		
TOTAL	*151124*	*143605*
SOUTH ASIA		
Afghanistan	171	150
Bangladesh	384	312
Bhutan	0	0
Burma	157	133
India	5170	4978
Maldives	5	8
Nepal	34	27
Pakistan	1115	1116
Sri Lanka	571	562

1982	1983	1984	1985	1986		1980	1981	1982	1983	1984	1985	1986
74	58	78	75	86	South Asia Unall.							
40	48	38	106	53	*TOTAL*	*7606*	*7286*	*8087*	*8333*	*9520*	*9670*	*10465*
783	822	905	936	1237	**FAR EAST ASIA**							
610	512	435	463	498	Brunei	3560	3291	2892	2447	2250	1926	1481
731	882	1072	1059	1183	China	8923	10879	11072	10766	12873	14673	16261
591	688	673	661	718	Hong Kong	12378	12948	12590	13406	16266	15752	18324
108	101	106	90	134	Indonesia	21022	21851	18787	17901	19002	16916	13033
746	711	785	740	1032	Kampuchea	1	2	2	1	1	2	1
405	442	475	484	494	Korea	11285	12817	13189	15134	18534	19640	25756
710	680	730	768	881	Korea, Dem.	355	177	203	178	180	180	208
692	615	696	575	653	Laos	8	5	4	7	5	5	4
113	101	99	102	156	Macao	517	532	606	626	774	790	1024
22455	24376	26194	26618	22356	Malaysia	9358	7811	7263	7821	10242	9608	9297
3060	2875	2745	1165	737	Mongolia	14	24	21	11	25	27	30
277	317	340	242	239	Philippines	5366	5322	4794	4706	5398	4770	4691
824	942	1051	984	940	Singapore	6514	6912	6791	6987	8841	8880	9391
13	18	10	16	17	Taiwan	13674	15778	16261	19289	24631	26435	33525
2232	1677	1758	1630	1158	Thailand	4064	4044	4086	3909	4426	4615	5915
–	–	–	–	–	Viet Nam	65	56	50	65	79	99	141
11	3	1	3	4	Far East Asia Unall.							
–	–	–	–	–	*TOTAL*	*97696*	*102524*	*98675*	*103321*	*123612*	*124409*	*139220*
21	19	24	26	43	Asia Unspecified	–	–	–	–	–	–	–
12	14	13	14	19	*ASIA TOTAL*	*255833*	*253340*	*217794*	*195637*	*211322*	*201722*	*201570*
–	–	–	–	–	**OCEANIA**							
–	–	–	–	–	Cook Islands	–	–	–	–	–	–	–
27	33	39	57	89	Fiji	241	213	150	149	157	109	149
19	19	20	29	33	Kiribati	–	–	–	–	–	–	–
–	–	–	–	–	Nauru	121	101	85	117	73	60	56
–	–	–	–	–	New Caledonia	526	426	289	207	245	316	214
					Niue	–	–	–	–	–	–	–
					Pacif. Isl.(Trust Tr.)	20	26	19	20	30	21	11
36218	*38161*	*40088*	*38061*	*33531*	Papua New Guinea	1024	828	695	724	806	712	772
					Polynesia, French	21	18	14	13	25	22	21
3976	3822	4353	4458	4068	Solomon Islands	75	89	67	61	73	86	66
273	331	261	164	174	Tokelau	–	–	–	–	–	–	–
13998	15160	19354	19634	18074	Tonga	8	8	5	5	8	6	5
2851	2986	2823	2858	3183	Tuvalu	–	–	–	–	–	–	–
2608	2758	3013	3210	4849	Vanuatu	19	27	14	15	34	23	14
1501	1775	2059	2324	2041	Wallis & Futuna	–	–	–	–	–	–	–
–	–	–	–	–	Western Samoa	20	14	11	9	12	10	10
44	37	30	24	34	TOM Unallocated							
252	205	232	203	230	Oceania Unallocated							
265	363	330	292	219	*TOTAL*	*2077*	*1751*	*1348*	*1319*	*1462*	*1364*	*1318*
2442	2402	2567	2281	1988	LDCs Unspecified	–	–	–	–	–	–	–
361	363	319	286	286	*TOTAL,ALL LDCS*	*435970*	*422535*	*373524*	*349460*	*376912*	*368905*	*350923*
471	439	484	427	534	**INCOME GROUPS**							
10298	9955	11111	11224	7618	LLDCS	5164	4558	4562	4605	5195	5065	5354
					CHINA AND INDIA	14092	15857	16824	16672	19534	21080	22917
39420	*40692*	*47038*	*47552*	*43460*	OTHER LOW-INCOME	36659	36134	31266	29338	31372	29418	25395
–	–	–	–	–	LOW MIDDLE-INCOME	55610	47730	44166	40683	44254	45486	42526
75560	*78759*	*87022*	*85449*	*76830*	UPPER MIDDLE-INCOME	324446	318256	276704	258162	276557	267857	254731
					UNALLOCATED	–	–	–	–	–	–	–
528	621	585	596	559								
12735	15614	12740	10104	5618								
6046	4915	5486	7323	5308								
3813	3906	4504	5053	5939								
94	148	157	268	215								
3792	4686	5547	5357	4063								
123	103	98	114	158								
3000	3132	2796	3297	1831								
3665	2677	4038	2867	1647								
60676	34718	28898	20256	18849								
947	802	932	908	521								
15325	12495	12255	11327	7247								
12	14	25	37	15								
340	216	215	229	53								
111097	*84048*	*78275*	*67736*	*52023*								
124	111	107	129	91								
356	404	562	592	630								
0	0	0	0	0								
142	142	137	123	125								
5753	5906	6661	6407	6656								
10	8	12	11	13								
29	44	47	94	91								
1090	1123	1224	1527	1965								
583	596	770	787	894								

Billion US Dollars

Legend:
- LLDCS
- CHINA AND INDIA
- OTHER LICS
- LMICS
- UMICS

	1980	1981	1982	1983	1984	1985	1986		1980	1981
EUROPE								Belize	99	108
Cyprus	980	966	1000	1020	1231	1182	1262	Bermuda	291	393
Gibraltar	132	187	165	125	110	183	211	Costa Rica	838	599
Greece	8122	8405	8035	7390	7274	7304	8493	Cuba	1509	1351
Malta	770	701	654	609	614	632	775	Dominican Republic	1171	1055
Portugal	6517	6889	6252	5593	5019	5017	7072	El Salvador	423	476
Turkey	3724	3978	4132	4267	5363	6460	7226	Guadeloupe	635	556
Yugoslavia	8160	6946	5784	5565	5343	6086	7504	Guatemala	910	940
Europe Unallocated								Haiti	426	426
TOTAL	28404	28072	26022	24570	24954	26865	32543	Honduras	591	516
								Jamaica	512	747
NORTH OF SAHARA								Martinique	499	432
Algeria	8756	8657	8141	8114	7905	7273	6596	Mexico	20301	24417
Egypt	8056	8963	9119	9073	9792	8933	7735	Netherlands Antilles	857	1271
Libya	7802	12238	6248	5655	4852	3725	3175	Nicaragua	346	295
Morocco	2956	2826	2905	2481	2591	2580	2947	Panama	3023	4391
Tunisia	2791	2766	2724	2397	2441	2041	2271	St. Pierre & Miquelon	34	31
North of Sahara Unall.								Trinidad & Tobago	1407	1339
TOTAL	30360	35451	29138	27721	27581	24552	22725	Anguilla	–	–
								Antigua and Barbuda	26	35
SOUTH OF SAHARA								Cayman Islands	–	–
Angola	969	1194	733	584	748	934	688	Dominica	28	22
Benin	460	561	592	303	210	304	284	Grenada	11	12
Botswana	17	15	24	35	47	42	60	Montserrat	–	–
Burkina Faso	192	187	158	143	122	158	226	St. Kitts-Nevis	–	–
Burundi	73	75	100	85	101	88	108	St. Lucia	21	19
Cameroon	1279	1294	1206	1086	1065	1190	1358	St. Vincent and Gr.	9	10
Cape Verde	79	58	55	68	64	88	85	Turks & Caicos Isl.	–	–
Central African Rep.	75	60	60	54	57	83	88	Virgin Islands	–	–
Chad	20	28	37	49	78	104	79	West Indies Unall.		
Comoros	27	41	26	27	28	29	38	DOM/TOM Unallocated		
Congo	413	555	721	492	386	447	424	N.& C. America Unall.		
Cote d'Ivoire	2029	1439	1169	1033	927	988	1274	TOTAL	34908	40753
Djibouti	141	154	148	149	160	154	138			
Equatorial Guinea	61	51	48	15	24	19	24	**SOUTH AMERICA**		
Ethiopia	438	456	412	475	655	820	794	Argentina	7574	6281
Gabon	643	714	636	578	619	739	714	Bolivia	398	553
Gambia	90	67	64	62	65	75	102	Brazil	10547	9255
Ghana	642	641	396	428	350	423	560	Chile	2989	3520
Guinea	245	245	187	176	228	264	270	Colombia	3506	3409
Guinea-Bissau	77	63	81	60	64	65	60	Ecuador	1761	1716
Kenya	1290	1070	830	696	859	814	1158	Falkland Islands	–	–
Lesotho	13	12	18	14	19	14	16	Guiana	155	204
Liberia	2372	2627	2212	1562	1747	1636	1464	Guyana	212	218
Madagascar	497	268	255	259	220	223	242	Paraguay	352	337
Malawi	149	110	101	76	82	88	107	Peru	2339	3171
Mali	205	167	165	189	186	244	254	Suriname	265	282
Mauritania	236	300	297	251	247	250	308	Uruguay	671	579
Mauritius	243	196	177	177	178	211	310	Venezuela	8718	9742
Mayotte	–	–	–	–	–	–	–	South America Unall.		
Mozambique	378	378	366	338	250	236	249	TOTAL	39857	39806
Namibia	–	–	–	–	–	–	–	America Unspecified	–	–
Niger	339	334	277	178	155	203	182	AMERICA TOTAL	74397	80018
Nigeria	12161	13843	10050	6190	4563	4780	3779			
Reunion	579	526	551	552	538	555	781	**MIDDLE EAST**		
Rwanda	119	100	107	107	100	112	138	Bahrain	886	1016
St. Helena	–	–	–	–	–	–	–	Iran	7811	8208
Sao Tome & Principe	27	22	21	8	10	10	11	Iraq	9915	14252
Senegal	740	656	700	641	615	574	660	Israel	4593	4558
Seychelles	43	37	41	35	28	45	55	Jordan	1673	2556
Sierra Leone	249	181	147	82	110	101	123	Kuwait	4662	5463
Somalia	371	279	293	264	244	215	270	Lebanon	2405	2280
Sudan	964	1023	1054	900	737	875	688	Oman	985	1297
Swaziland	13	25	18	16	11	14	16	Qatar	970	1132
Tanzania	854	644	640	467	523	540	551	Saudi Arabia	22587	26811
Togo	413	359	368	405	260	273	360	Syria	2698	2474
Uganda	180	138	147	136	134	141	146	United Arab Emirates	5613	5956
Zaire	982	864	721	648	760	822	978	Yemen	877	831
Zambia	636	448	443	265	340	350	347	Yemen, Dem.	373	395
Zimbabwe	164	420	516	433	394	345	430	Middle East Unall.		
East African Community								TOTAL	66050	77230
DOM/TOM Unallocated										
EAMA Unallocated								**SOUTH ASIA**		
South of Sahara Unall.								Afghanistan	203	163
TOTAL	32198	32946	27383	20810	19321	20701	21015	Bangladesh	1112	935
Africa Unspecified	–	–	–	–	–	–	–	Bhutan	1	2
AFRICA TOTAL	62548	68379	56501	48510	46888	45238	43722	Burma	447	512
								India	6545	7681
N.& C. AMERICA								Maldives	12	13
Aruba								Nepal	76	71
Bahamas	656	1001	886	602	1104	1080	1290	Pakistan	2735	2561
Barbados	285	309	294	332	359	302	317	Sri Lanka	779	765

1982	1983	1984	1985	1986
91	55	81	82	82
314	364	536	460	433
455	560	652	694	766
908	883	1189	1357	1323
934	920	887	1023	1277
403	494	535	564	587
537	532	500	491	725
696	504	603	631	611
398	465	511	525	498
381	439	497	469	512
746	781	738	616	674
441	450	430	442	662
15735	11712	14714	16693	15703
1212	1089	1019	712	725
246	260	286	239	215
4961	3923	5116	5174	5039
39	33	44	35	41
1749	1426	1177	938	977
–	–	–	–	–
26	22	45	56	96
–	–	–	–	–
19	19	18	23	23
12	17	17	19	23
–	–	–	–	–
–	–	–	–	–
18	15	19	26	36
9	11	15	20	19
–	–	–	–	–
–	–	–	–	–
31509	*25909*	*31094*	*32671*	*32657*
3380	3500	3054	2374	3243
229	180	231	255	226
8024	6189	6536	6707	9508
2000	1531	2022	1620	2015
3618	3055	2879	2892	2819
1601	1111	1189	1249	1435
–	–	–	–	–
231	296	439	591	307
113	71	86	92	105
230	181	230	224	375
2458	1761	1555	1149	1738
274	223	187	167	169
381	230	273	253	381
9944	4899	5636	5635	6018
32869	*23716*	*24794*	*23754*	*29170*
–	–	–	–	–
63991	*49135*	*55412*	*55878*	*60994*
1104	1189	1105	962	804
6855	12375	9916	7627	6354
14861	6532	6376	6728	5629
4799	5680	5569	5765	7114
2665	2035	1762	1688	1630
5940	5491	5101	4385	4113
2351	2317	1822	1328	1361
1675	1809	1763	2048	1670
1550	1117	829	849	752
29655	28906	24161	18302	15891
1785	1793	1594	1695	1313
6306	5301	4659	4700	4404
858	859	839	890	772
395	350	408	303	228
80800	*75757*	*65905*	*57271*	*52084*
181	206	189	166	201
936	815	1127	1014	1078
3	7	4	4	19
552	463	346	360	380
8095	7502	7367	8649	10514
9	12	20	20	21
93	85	93	116	119
2733	2831	3065	3308	3692
795	817	748	770	781

	1980	1981	1982	1983	1984	1985	1986
South Asia Unall.							
TOTAL	*11909*	*12704*	*13397*	*12737*	*12959*	*14406*	*16804*

FAR EAST ASIA

	1980	1981	1982	1983	1984	1985	1986
Brunei	227	221	341	353	326	285	579
China	13405	12770	10791	11814	15506	24480	22379
Hong Kong	11438	11935	11146	11605	13755	13794	15830
Indonesia	7367	8533	10048	7934	6911	5367	6240
Kampuchea	70	28	13	11	12	8	7
Korea	12233	13401	12905	14727	16697	16814	21393
Korea, Dem.	499	446	456	454	350	339	305
Laos	34	24	24	29	11	17	21
Macao	35	30	51	44	33	39	54
Malaysia	5617	6292	6239	6819	7112	5647	5347
Mongolia	11	10	12	10	6	9	15
Philippines	4934	4919	4923	4874	3677	3052	3347
Singapore	10447	10866	11074	11599	12130	11145	11752
Taiwan	10945	11625	10643	11831	13347	12333	16764
Thailand	4528	4757	4072	5071	5005	4439	4794
Viet Nam	456	316	228	217	228	242	316
Far East Asia Unall.							
TOTAL	*82685*	*86242*	*83037*	*87488*	*95201*	*98087*	*109456*
Asia Unspecified	–	–	–	–	–	–	–
ASIA TOTAL	*160203*	*176106*	*177160*	*175886*	*173970*	*169686*	*177978*

OCEANIA

	1980	1981	1982	1983	1984	1985	1986
Cook Islands	–	–	–	–	–	–	–
Fiji	371	420	313	321	298	275	250
Kiribati	–	–	–	–	–	–	–
Nauru	25	23	16	16	14	13	13
New Caledonia	321	320	322	250	285	275	387
Niue	–	–	–	–	–	–	–
Pacif. Isl.(Trust Tr.)	113	124	137	134	178	160	212
Papua New Guinea	723	797	723	733	658	607	642
Polynesia, French	238	207	206	225	255	260	412
Solomon Islands	52	51	44	61	58	56	62
Tokelau	–	–	–	–	–	–	–
Tonga	21	29	22	21	22	24	24
Tuvalu	–	–	–	–	–	–	–
Vanuatu	30	28	26	33	42	42	48
Wallis & Futuna	–	–	–	–	–	–	–
Western Samoa	36	28	19	24	20	23	20
TOM Unallocated							
Oceania Unallocated							
TOTAL	*1930*	*2027*	*1828*	*1818*	*1831*	*1735*	*2070*
LDCs Unspecified	–	–	–	–	–	–	–
TOTAL,ALL LDCS	*327482*	*354601*	*325503*	*299918*	*303054*	*299402*	*317308*

INCOME GROUPS

	1980	1981	1982	1983	1984	1985	1986
LLDCS	9295	8648	8568	7662	7973	8479	8535
CHINA AND INDIA	19950	20452	18885	19315	22873	33129	32892
OTHER LOW-INCOME	28707	29979	30188	26943	27122	24948	25728
LOW MIDDLE-INCOME	44607	47358	40742	35805	34266	34029	36146
UPPER MIDDLE-INCOME	224923	248164	227118	210192	210819	198817	214008
UNALLOCATED	–	–	–	–	–	–	–

Billion US Dollars

○—○—○ **LLDCS**
------ **CHINA AND INDIA**
—·—·— **OTHER LICS**
——— **LMICS**
- - - - **UMICS**

DEFINITION OF CONCEPTS USED IN THIS REPORT

A1.   Disbursements represent the actual international transfer of financial resources. They may be recorded at one of several stages: provision of goods and services, placing of funds at the disposal of the recipient in an earmarked fund or account, withdrawal of funds by the recipient from an earmarked fund or account, payment by the donor of invoices on behalf of the recipient, etc. The disbursement mechanism used tends to vary as a function of the type of financial (or technical) co-operation flow involved. Disbursements may be recorded gross (the actual amounts disbursed) or net (i.e., less repayments of principal in respect of earlier loans).

A2.   A commitment is a firm obligation expressed in an agreement or equivalent contract and supported by the availability of public funds, undertaken by the government, an official agency of the reporting country or an international organisation, to furnish assistance of a specified amount under agreed financial terms and conditions and for specific purposes, for the benefit of a recipient country.

A3.   *Grant Element:*   Reflects the financial terms of a transaction: interest rate, maturity (interval to final repayment) and grace period (interval to first repayment of capital). It is a measure of the concessionality (i.e., softness) of a loan. The extent of the benefit depends on the difference between the interest rate and the market rate of interest, and the length of time the funds are available to the borrower. To calculate this benefit, the present value at the market rate of interest of each repayment is ascertained. The excess of the loan's face value over the sum of these present values, expressed as a percentage of the face value, is the "grant element" of the loan. For operating purposes, the market rate is taken as 10 per cent. Thus, the grant element is nil for a loan carrying an interest rate of 10 per cent; it is 100 per cent for a grant; and it lies between these two limits for a soft loan. Generally speaking, a loan will not convey a grant element of over 25 per cent if its maturity is less than 10 years, unless its interest rate is well below 5 per cent. If the face value of a loan is multiplied by its grant element, the result is referred to as the grant equivalent of that loan.

Aggregates and Resource Flow Categories

A4.   Official Development Assistance is defined as those flows to developing countries and multilateral institutions provided by official agencies, including state and local governments, or by their executive agencies, each transaction of which meets the following tests:

   a)   It is administered with the promotion of the economic development and welfare of developing countries as its main objective, and

   b)   It is concessional in character and contains a grant element (see paragraph A3) of at least 25 per cent.

A5.   *Grants:*   This heading covers transfers, in money or in kind, for which no repayment is required. It includes grants for technical co-operation, grant-like flows, i.e., loans repayable in recipients' currencies, extended by governments or official agencies in currencies of the donor countries, for which repayment is required in the currencies of the recipient countries, and transfer of resources through sales of commodities for recipients' currencies, less local currency balances used by the donor for other than development purposes (for example, to defray the local costs of embassy operations). In the case of overseas territories, grants are shown after deduction of tax receipts. The following are excluded: reparations and indemnification payments to private individuals, insurance and similar payments to residents of less-developed countries, and loans extended in and repayable in recipients' currencies.

A6.   Technical Co-operation Grants: This heading covers practically all disbursements for technical co-operation, but small amounts are occasionally financed in loan form. Technical Co-operation is the provision of resources with the primary purpose of:

   a)   Augmenting the level of knowledge, skills, technical knowhow or productive aptitudes of the population of developing countries, i.e., increasing their stock of human intellectual capital, or

   b)   Augmenting developing countries' capacity for more effective use of their existing endowment (as distinct from transfers intended to increase the stock of physical capital).

A7.   *ODA Loans:*   Loans with maturities of over one year and meeting the criteria set out in paragraph A4, extended by governments or official agencies, and for which repayment is required in convertible currencies or in kind. Reschedulings (maturity extension of loans originally made by a government or official agency) and loans made by a government or an official agency to refinance indebtedness due to the private or official sector, are included if reported as Official Development Assistance, otherwise as "Other Official Flows". The net data are reported after deduction of amortization payments.

A8.   *Other Official Flows:*   Transactions by the official sector whose main objective is other than development motived, or, if development-motivated, whose grant element is below the 25 per cent threshold which would make them eligible to be recorded as ODA. The main classes of transactions included here are official export credits, official sector equity and portfolio investment, and debt reorganisation undertaken by the official sector at non-concessional terms (irrespective of the nature or the identity of the original creditor).

A9.   *Total Official Flows:*   The sum of Official Development Assistance (ODA) and Other Official Flows (OOF) represents the total (gross or net) disbursements by the official sector at large to the recipient country shown.

A10. Funds provided by the official sector to support export credits or direct investment by the private sector are recorded in this report as an indistinguishable part of the relevant private sector transactions. This treatment differs from that in the aggregate statistics presented in other DAC reviews, where these amounts are included as part of the official sector total, and the aggregate amounts for the private sector reduced correspondingly. For purposes of geographical allocation, the pertinent concept is the transactor dealing with a developing country; this latter is not concerned with the sources of the transactor's funds, as its indebtedness is towards the transactor, not his sources of finance. By contrast, the aggregate statistics place emphasis on the source of funds, which governs the extent to which official policy can determine the amount, terms and distribution of transactions in which official sector resources form part of the total financing package.

A11. *Total Contractual Lending:* Bilateral ODA and OOF loans plus guaranteed private export credits i.e., all borrowing at fixed terms other than financial credits extended by the banking sector.

A12. *Multilateral Agencies:* The list of multilateral agencies for which data are shown separately in this report is given in the Introduction. To the extent possible, a distinction has been made between concessional and non-concessional flows from multilateral agencies. Loan disbursements for which it was not possible to make this distinction on a transaction by transaction basis have been treated as non-concessional if made from "ordinary capital" resources and as concessional if made from a "soft window". Thus, for some agencies "total loans" are significantly larger than loans on concessional terms, and the volume of loans on concessional terms actually received by the borrowing country is correspondingly understated. The "net" multilateral disbursements concept used in this report, like the net bilateral concept, is defined as gross disbursements of grants and loans to developing countries minus repayments on earlier loans. Capital subscription payments to multilateral agencies by their developing country Members are not subtracted out.

A13. *Total Receipts, Net:* In addition to Official Development Assistance, this heading includes in particular: other official bilateral transactions which are not concessional or which, even though they have concessional elements, are primarily trade facilitating in character (i.e., "Other Official Flows"); changes in bilateral long-term assets of the private non-monetary and monetary sectors, in particular guaranteed export credits, private direct investment, portfolio investment and, to the extent they are not covered in the preceding headings, loans by private banks. Flows from the multilateral sector which are not classified as concessional are also included here.

Relationships Between the Categories Shown in the Report

A14. The total net resource flow data presented for a recipient country ("total net receipts") is the sum of items (1 + 2 + 3 = 4) in the table below.

CATEGORIES	DAC DONORS	MULTILATERAL DONORS	OPEC DONORS	CMEA DONORS
1. Official Development Assistance (ODA), Net	By country	By agency	As a group	Not available
2. Other Official Flows (OOF), Net	By country	As a group	As a group	Not available
3. Private Sector Flows, Net	By group	Not applicable	Not available	Not available
4. Total Resource Flows, Net	By country	By agency	Incomplete	Not available
Memo:				
ODA Gross	By country	By agency	As a group	As a group
ODA Commitments	By country	By agency	As a group	As a group

A15. For any given recipient country, the DAC total for "private sector net" can be broken down by country of origin, by subtracting (ODA + OOF net) for the donor country concerned, from the total receipts figure against its name.

A16. "Private sector, net" is broken down, for DAC Members combined, into direct investment, portfolio investment and export credits (net). The transactions covered are those undertaken by residents of DAC Member countries. Portfolio investment corresponds largely, but not wholly, to transactions by the private monetary sector, adjusted where necessary and possible to transfer export credit claims to the corresponding heading. Accordingly, the coverage of portfolio investment differs in these regards from the coverage of (bank sector loans), which includes indistinguishably export credit lending by banks. The (bank sector loan) data represent the net change in banks' claims after adjustment to eliminate the effect of changes in exchange rates. They are therefore a proxy for net flow data, but are not themselves a net flow figure. They differ in three further regards from the other data in the report. First, they relate to loans by banks resident in countries which report quarterly to the Bank for International Settlements (BIS) i.e., DAC Members other than Australia and New Zealand, a number of offshore financial centres, and Spain (see the BIS quarterly survey *International Banking and Financial Market Developments*). Second, for offshore centres viewed as debtor countries, the standard OECD/BIS approach is not to take account of borrowing by their resident banks, most of which operate as intermediaries relending internationally. As it has not been possible to make a valuation adjustment for borrowing by non-banks, the (bank sector loans) line for the countries concerned has been left blank. Finally, no adjustment has been made to exclude short-term claims. Recent statistical developments make it possible in principle to reconcile valuation-adjusted data derived from banking system statistics of outstanding claims with valuation-adjusted data on guaranteed trade credits extended by banks. It is hoped to expand the data in the OECD/BIS semi-annual survey *Statistics on External Indebtedness: Bank and Trade-Related Non-Bank External Claims on Individual Borrowing Countries and Territories* to show the results, starting in 1988.

NOTES ON THE INTERPRETATION OF CERTAIN DATA

A17. In establishing the statistical data in the present report, the aim is to present the fullest possible record of the resources put at the disposal of each country covered. However, there are some inconsistencies in Members' reporting. Although they are of marginal impact on the aggregate data, it was nevertheless necessary to make estimates which in some instances affect the data shown, and in others were intended to fill gaps in the data originally submitted.

A18. The following list sets out the main areas in which particularities of the data stemming from these causes could have some influence on their understanding or use by the reader.

Data for Country Groups

a) Contents of the Groups

A19. Low-Income Countries are those whose per capita GNP in 1983, as shown in the World Bank Atlas, was below approximately $700. Three sub-groups of Low-Income Countries are shown separately: those on the UN list of Least-developed Countries[1], India and China as a single group and all other Low-Income Countries. A further table located at the end of Section B gives the figures for Low-Income countries combined. The remaining countries are subdivided into Lower Middle-Income Countries (LMIC's) i.e., those with a per capita GNP in 1983 between $700 and $1 300, and Upper Middle-Income Countries (UMIC's), with a per capita GNP exceeding $1 300. These groups have been defined purely for analytical purposes and, except for the Least-developed Countries, are not internationally agreed lists.

b) Treatment of Unallocated Amounts

A20. Some reporting countries are unable to supply a full geographical distribution down to country level. One element here is that some commitments or disbursements in fact relate to expenditures in a given region (e.g., West Africa) or group of countries (e.g., the Least-developed Countries). The data shown for countries and for groups are restricted to those which are available, broken down by recipient. Amounts reported as provided to a region or group are included as "unallocated". The problem of the very large proportion of unallocated amounts of OPEC aid has already been referred to in the Introduction. Unallocated amounts also include commitments and disbursements concerning expenditures on the territory of the donor country for research specific to some developing countries' problems (e.g., tropical diseases) or in the form of subsidies to nationals of developing countries, e.g., for apprenticeships, or school or university tuition; there are obvious statistical difficulties in assigning these amounts to the countries of origin of these trainees and students.

A21. In computing the share of a given country or group in a total for developing countries, the usual practice is to use as denominator the total excluding unallocated amounts. Implicit in this approach is the assumption that the percentage geographical distribution of allocated and unallocated amounts is the same.

A22. *Negative Grants:* In describing the recording methodology for grants, it was noted that the total of new grants is reduced by the amounts of a donor's local currency balances used by the donor for its own purposes. If the latter exceeds the volume of new grants, a "negative grant" is shown.

A23. *Cancellations of Commitments:* The data on commitments concern new commitments entered into during the calendar year. They exclude commitments that were cancelled in the year they were made, but are not adjusted to allow for cancellations during the year of commitments made in earlier years.

A24. *ODA Commitments of International Financial Institutions:* As a general rule, international financial institutions report their commitments on an "approval basis" and these are the data shown in the "ODA commitments" panel. However, in order to calculate their "grant element" (shown under "All Source Commitments") the terms of each individual transaction must be ascertained. To do this, the "signature date" of each commitment is used. This normally postdates the approval date. This explains why an entry may be found under the heading loan commitments accompanied by a nil entry under grant element (or vice versa). Discrepancies in either direction in any one year due to this cause are balanced by a counterpart entry in an adjacent year.

A25. A figure for grant element may also appear in the absence of an amount under commitments if the amount concerned is less than $50 000 i.e., too small to be shown separately.

A26. *Partial Components of a Total:* In the "All Sources Commitments" block, certain components only are shown. The presentation of full detail would have lengthened processing time so greatly as to delay the appearance of the report. The total of the missing components can be established by direct subtraction from the grand total of which they are part.

A27. *Commitments and Disbursements of the UN Agencies:* Disbursement data are shown separately for each UN agency. Comparable commitment data are not available for the UN family. In the commitments table, gross disbursement data are shown as a proxy for the UN family as a group, with no entries against the individual agencies. This procedure was necessary to provide an order of magnitude of the commitments of multilateral organisations combined.

A28. *Effect of Changes in Exchange Rates:* The currency unit used throughout this report is the US dollar. Loans are often denominated in another currency. If that currency strengthens vis-à-vis the dollar, repayments on the loan are reflected in the statistics by an increased number of dollars. This accounts for a number of cases in which cumulative repayments appear to exceed the original amount of a loan. Similarly, the weakening of a currency produces cases in which repayments, expressed in dollars, appear to be less than the original amount lent. In comparing data on changes in debt (e.g., in *The Financing and External Debt of Developing Countries* or the semi-annual OECD/BIS survey) with the figures shown for net resource flows in this report, it should be borne in mind that the debt data are converted to dollars at the end-of-period rate, whereas the flow data are converted at the annual average rate. (See Annex, paragraph A16.)

A29. *Unusually High Amortization Entries:* These relate in practically all cases to the continued implementation of Retroactive Terms Adjustment in the form of forgiveness of the outstanding principal on loans. The effect of cancellation is to extend a grant, which is applied to pay off the loans concerned. Exceptionally large negative net loans on ODA account for the Least-Developed Countries will thus be found to be accompanied

by exceptionally high entries for the same donor, in the same year, for disbursements of grants.

A30. *ODA from IBRD:* Most IBRD lending is recorded as "Other Official Flows"; the principal agency of the World Bank group for ODA is the International Development Association (IDA). Some small amounts listed against IBRD correspond in the main to "Third Window" lending.

A31. *Belgium's Data for Commitments:* By reason of the institutional procedures used, there is no stage at which it is possible for the Belgian authorities to identify the commitment of a grant (no problem arises with respect to loan reporting). In order not to leave blank entries in the commitments data for Belgium, the Secretariat has made estimates, by distributing the total budget allocation for grants among recipient countries in proportion to each country's receipts of gross disbursements of grants in the same year. The errors involved are too small in any way to distort the figure for a recipient country's total receipts from DAC Members combined or from all sources. If analysing Belgium's commitment figures in isolation, a still closer approximation to the order of magnitude is obtained by taking an average over several years of the commitments data shown for Belgian grants.

A32. *Resource Flows from the European Economic Community:* The figures shown pertain to outflows from the EEC, including outflows from the European Investment Bank at market terms. The latter can be ascertained from the data in the present volume as the difference between a country's Total Net Receipts from the EEC and its receipts of Total Net ODA from the EEC.

---

1. In the table headings, space limitations made it necessary to use the abbreviation LLDC's for the Least-developed countries.

DÉFINITION DES CONCEPTS UTILISÉS DANS LE PRÉSENT RAPPORT

A1. Les versements, tels que définis dans le présent rapport, représentent le transfert effectif de ressources financières au niveau international. Ils peuvent être saisis à l'un des stades suivants : fourniture de biens et services, dépôt de sommes mises à la disposition du bénéficiaire dans un fonds ou un compte réservé, retrait de fonds par le bénéficiaire sur un compte ou un fonds réservé, paiement de factures par le donneur pour le compte du bénéficiaire, etc. Les modalités de versement tendent à varier en fonction du type d'apport de coopération financière (ou technique) en cause. Les versements sont comptabilisés soit bruts (c'est-à-dire les montants effectivement versés), soit nets (c'est-à-dire moins le remboursement du capital au titre de prêts antérieurs).

A2. Un engagement s'entend d'une obligation ferme, stipulée dans un contrat ou un accord similaire et étayée par la mise à disposition de fonds publics ; par cette obligation, le gouvernement, un organisme public du pays déclarant ou un organisme multilatéral s'engage à fournir, au profit du pays bénéficiaire, une aide d'un montant spécifié, assortie de conditions financières déterminées et destinées à des fins données.

A3. *Elément de libéralité :* résume les conditions financières d'une opération : taux d'intérêt, durée de remboursement (délai jusqu'au remboursement final) et différé d'amortissement (délai jusqu'au premier remboursement du capital). Il s'agit d'une mesure de la libéralité d'un prêt. Le bénéfice qu'en retire l'emprunteur dépend de la différence entre le taux d'intérêt octroyé et le taux du marché, ainsi que de la durée pendant laquelle les fonds sont à sa disposition. Pour calculer cet avantage, on détermine la valeur actualisée, au taux d'intérêt du marché, de chaque remboursement. La différence, par excès, entre le montant nominal du prêt et le total de ces valeurs actualisées, exprimée en pourcentage de ce montant nominal, est « l'élément de libéralité » du prêt. Le taux du marché est conventionnellement fixé à 10 pour cent. Par conséquent, l'élément de libéralité d'un prêt de 10 pour cent est nul ; il est de 100 pour cent dans le cas d'un don ; et il se situe entre ces deux extrêmes pour un prêt libéral. En général, l'élément de libéralité d'un prêt remboursable en moins de 10 ans ne dépassera pas 25 pour cent, sauf si son taux d'intérêt est très inférieur à 5 pour cent. En multipliant la valeur nominale d'un prêt par son élément de libéralité, on obtient « l'équivalent-don » de ce prêt.

Agrégats et apports de ressource par catégories

A4. Par aide publique au développement, on entend l'ensemble des apports de ressources qui sont fournis aux pays en développement et aux institutions multilatérales par des organismes officiels, y compris les collectivités locales, ou par leurs agents d'exécution et qui, considérés au niveau de chaque opération, répondent aux critères suivants :

a) Etre dispensés dans le but essentiel de favoriser le développement économique et l'amélioration du niveau de vie dans les pays en développement, et

b) Revêtir un caractère favorable et comporter un élément de libéralité (voir paragraphe A3) d'au moins 25 pour cent.

A5. *Dons :* cette rubrique couvre les transferts, en espèces ou en nature, qui n'impliquent aucun remboursement. Elle inclut les dons au titre de la coopération technique, les apports assimilables à des dons, c'est-à-dire les prêts remboursables dans la monnaie du bénéficiaire, consentis par les pouvoirs publics ou des organismes publics dans la monnaie du pays donneur, ainsi que le transfert de ressources opéré par le biais de la vente de biens payables dans la monnaie du bénéficiaire, déduction faite du montant de ses avoirs en monnaie locale que le pays donneur a utilisés à des fins autres que le développement du pays bénéficiaire (par exemple pour le financement des dépenses locales afférentes au fonctionnement des ambassades). Dans le cas des Territoires d'Outre-Mer les dons sont présentés nets des recettes d'impôts. Sont également exclus les paiements de réparation et d'indemnisation à des particuliers, les paiements d'assurances et autres paiements similaires à des résidents de pays en développement, et les prêts accordés et remboursables dans les monnaies des bénéficiaires.

A6. *Dons de coopération technique :* sont couverts par cette rubrique la quasi-totalité des versements au titre de la coopération technique, encore qu'il puisse arriver que de petits financements soient consentis sous la forme d'un prêt. La coopération technique se définit comme tout apport de ressources ayant pour but essentiel :

a) D'augmenter le niveau des connaissances, des qualifications, du savoir-faire technique ou des aptitudes productives de la population des pays en développement, c'est-à-dire d'accroître leur capital intellectuel, ou

b) D'augmenter l'aptitude des pays en développement à utiliser plus efficacement les facteurs de production dont ils disposent (par opposition aux transferts destinés à accroître leur stock de capital physique).

A7. *Prêts d'APD :* ce sont les prêts à plus d'un an accordés par des gouvernements et des organismes publics, remboursables en monnaies convertibles ou en nature, qui satisfont aux critères énoncés dans le paragraphe A4 ci-dessus. Les opérations de rééchelonnement des échéances (allongement de la durée de prêts initialement accordés par un gouvernement ou un organisme public) et les prêts octroyés par un gouvernement ou un organisme public pour refinancer une dette contractée auprès du secteur privé ou du secteur public sont inclus dans cette catégorie s'ils sont notifiés comme aide publique au développement ; sinon, ils sont classés dans les « autres apports du secteur public ». Les montants nets sont indiqués après déduction des remboursements.

293

A8. *Autres apports du secteur public (AASP) :* il s'agit des opérations du secteur public dont le but essentiel est autre que le développement ou qui, tout en visant à favoriser le développement, sont assorties d'un élément de libéralité inférieur au seuil de 25 pour cent à partir duquel elles auraient pu être notifiées comme de l'APD. Les principales catégories d'opérations couvertes dans les AASP sont les crédits publics à l'exportation, les prises de participation et les investissements de portefeuille du secteur public et le réaménagement de la dette effectué par le secteur public aux conditions du marché (et ce, quelle que soit la nature ou l'identité du créancier initial).

A9. *Apports totaux du secteur public :* il s'agit du total de l'aide publique au développement (APD) et des autres apports du secteur public (AASP). Cet agrégat correspond aux versements (bruts ou nets) effectués par le secteur public dans son ensemble aux pays bénéficiaires considérés.

A10. Les ressources fournies par le secteur public pour soutenir les crédits à l'exportation ou les investissements directs du secteur privé sont comptabilisées dans le présent rapport avec les opérations correspondantes du secteur privé. Cette approche diffère de celle utilisée dans les données statistiques agrégées présentées dans certains autres documents établis par le CAD, où les montants en cause sont inclus dans les totaux afférents au secteur public et où les montants relatifs au secteur privé sont réduits proportionnellement. Dans l'optique de la répartition géographique, il convient de retenir comme unité statistique l'opérateur qui est en relation avec un pays en développement ; l'emprunteur ne s'intéresse pas à l'origine des capitaux que cet opérateur lui fournit, son endettement étant envers cet opérateur et non envers ses sources de financement. Dans les statistiques agrégées, en revanche, l'accent est mis sur les sources des fonds, car ce sont elles qui déterminent la mesure dans laquelle les politiques mises en œuvre par le secteur public peuvent déterminer sur les montants totaux, les conditions financières et la répartition géographique des apports, dès lors que ceux-ci englobent des ressources en provenance du secteur public.

A11. *Total des prêts contractuels :* il s'agit du total des prêts bilatéraux au titre de l'APD ou des AASP, et des crédits privés garantis à l'exportation, c'est-à-dire la totalité des emprunts effectués à conditions fixes, à l'exception des crédits financiers accordés par le secteur bancaire.

A12. *Organismes multilatéraux :* la liste des organismes multilatéraux auxquels se réfèrent les données dans le présent rapport a été présentée dans l'introduction. Dans la mesure du possible, on a distingué, dans les apports fournis par ces organismes, ceux qui sont assortis de conditions libérales de ceux qui sont assortis des conditions du marché. Les versements de prêts pour lesquels il n'a pas été possible d'opérer cette distinction sur la base des différentes opérations ont été considérés comme non libéraux lorsqu'ils étaient effectués à l'aide de ressources en capital ordinaire et comme libéraux lorsqu'ils venaient de « guichets spéciaux ». Ainsi, pour certains organismes, les « prêts totaux » sont beaucoup plus élevés que les prêts à des conditions libérales, et le volume des prêts à des conditions libérales effectivement reçu par le pays emprunteur est proportionnellement sous-évalué. Dans le cas des apports des organismes multilatéraux comme dans celui des apports bilatéraux, on entend par « versements nets » le montant brut des dons et prêts versés aux pays en développement, diminué des remboursements de prêts antérieurs. Les paiements effectués par les pays en développement à titre de souscription au capital des organismes multilatéraux dont ils sont membres ne sont pas déduits.

A13. *Recettes totales nettes :* outre l'aide publique au développement, cette rubrique comprend en particulier : les autres transactions publiques bilatérales qui ne sont pas assorties de conditions libérales ou qui, dans le cas contraire, restent néanmoins de nature essentiellement commerciale (« autres apports du secteur public ») ; les variations des actifs bilatéraux à long terme du secteur privé monétaire et non monétaire, en particulier les crédits à l'exportation garantis, les investissements privés directs et, dans la mesure où ils ne sont pas repris dans les rubriques précédentes, les prêts des banques privées. Les apports en provenance des organismes multilatéraux qui ne sont pas considérés comme assortis de conditions libérales sont aussi inclus dans cette rubrique.

Liens entre les catégories d'apports présentées dans le rapport

A14. Pour un pays bénéficiaire donné, le total net des apports de ressources (« recettes totales nettes ») est la somme des rubriques (1 + 2 + 3 = 4) figurant dans le tableau ci-après.

	CATÉGORIES	DONNEURS DU CAD	DONNEURS MULTILATÉRAUX	DONNEURS DE L'OPEP	DONNEURS DU CAEM
1.	Aide publique au développement (APD), montants nets	Par pays	Par organisme	En tant que groupe	Non disponible
2.	Autres apports du secteur public (AASP), montants nets	Par pays	En tant que groupe	En tant que groupe	Non disponible
3.	Apports nets du secteur privé	En tant que groupe	Sans objet	Non disponible	Non disponible
4.	Total net des apports de ressources	Par pays	Par organisme	Incomplet	Non disponible
	Pour mémoire :				
	APD, montants bruts	Par pays	Par organisme	En tant que groupe	En tant que groupe
	APD, engagements	Par pays	Par organisme	En tant que groupe	En tant que groupe

A15. Le total, pour l'ensemble des pays du CAD, des « apports nets du secteur privé » peut être ventilé par pays d'origine en soustrayant du total net des apports en provenance du pays concerné le total (APD + AASP) que l'on lira en regard de son nom dans le tableau se rapportant au pays bénéficiaire.

A16. La rubrique « apports nets du secteur privé » est ventilée, pour l'ensemble des Membres du CAD, en investissements directs, investissements de portefeuille et crédits à l'exportation

(nets). Les opérations recensées dans chaque catégorie sont celles qui sont entreprises par des opérateurs résidents des pays Membres du CAD. Les investissements de portefeuille correspondent, dans une grande mesure mais pas dans leur totalité, aux opérations du secteur monétaire privé, ajustées si nécessaire et dans la mesure du possible de façon à transférer les créances au titre de crédits à l'exportation à la rubrique correspondante. Le champ de couverture des investissements de portefeuille

différe donc à ces deux égards de celui de la rubrique « prêts du secteur bancaire » laquelle englobe les crédits à l'exportation consentis par les banques. Les données sur les « prêts du secteur bancaire » correspondent à la variation des créances des banques après correction pour l'effet des variations des taux de change. Il s'agit donc d'un indicateur des apports nets, et non d'une mesure des apports nets. Il existe trois autres différences par rapport aux autres données dans le rapport. En premier lieu, sont compris les prêts octroyés par des succursales établies dans des centres financiers de banques mères résidant dans des pays qui effectuent tous les trimestres des déclarations statistiques auprès de la BRI, c'est-à-dire les Membres du CAD autres que l'Australie, et la Nouvelle-Zélande, y compris un certain nombre de centres financiers, et l'Espagne (voir l'enquête trimestrielle de la BRI *Evolution de l'activité bancaire internationale et des marchés financiers internationaux*). En second lieu, pour les centres financiers en tant que débiteurs, sont omis des

données établies conjointement par l'OCDE et la BRI, et les emprunts des banques qui y résident, dont la plupart agissent comme des intermédiaires qui prêtent sur le plan international. Comme il s'est avéré impossible d'ajuster les prêts aux emprunteurs non bancaires pour les corriger des effets des variations des taux de change, la ligne « prêts du secteur bancaire » a été laissée en blanc. Enfin, aucun ajustement n'a été opéré en vue d'exclure les créances à court terme. Les derniers développements statistiques permettent en principe de réconcilier les données corrigées tirées des statistiques bancaires sur l'encours des créances avec les données corrigées sur les crédits commerciaux garantis consentis par les banques. A ce propos, on espère développer le contenu de l'étude semestrielle de l'OCDE/BRI *Statistiques sur l'endettement extérieur : créances extérieures bancaires et créances extérieures non bancaires liées au commerce, ventilées par pays et territoire emprunteur*, en y présentant, à partir de 1988, les résultats obtenus.

NOTE SUR L'INTERPRÉTATION DE CERTAINES DONNÉES

A17. L'élaboration des données statistiques présentées dans ce rapport a pour but de dresser un tableau aussi complet que possible des ressources mises à la disposition de chaque pays visé. Les déclarations des pays Membres comportent néanmoins certaines incohérences ou lacunes qui, bien que n'ayant qu'une incidence marginale sur les données agrégées, ont obligé à recourir à des estimations influant, dans certains cas, sur le contenu des données ou permettant, dans d'autres, de combler les lacunes constatées.

A18. On trouvera ci-après la liste des principaux domaines où certaines particularités des données dues à ces facteurs pourraient gêner leur compréhension ou utilisation par le lecteur.

Données par groupes de pays

a) Groupes retenus

A19. Les pays à faible revenu sont ceux dont le PNB par habitant en 1983, tel qu'il figure dans l'Atlas de la Banque mondiale, était inférieur à environ 700 dollars. Trois sous-catégories de pays à faible revenu sont présentées séparément : les pays figurant sur la liste des pays les moins avancés établie par l'ONU[1], l'Inde et la Chine en tant que groupe et les autres pays à faible revenu. Un autre tableau, figurant à la fin de la section B, donne les chiffres pour tous les pays à faible revenu combinés. Les pays restants sont subdivisés en deux catégories : les pays à revenu intermédiaire de la tranche inférieure (PRITI), soit les pays dont le PNB moyen par habitant en 1983 était compris entre 700 et 1 300 dollars, et les pays à revenu intermédiaire de la tranche supérieure (PRITS), dont le PNB par habitant dépassait 1 300 dollars. Ces groupes ont été définis uniquement à des fins analytiques et, à l'exception des « pays les moins avancés », ils ne correspondent pas à des classifications agréées sur le plan international.

b) Traitement des montants non ventilés

A20. Certains pays déclarants ne sont pas en mesure de ventiler la totalité de leurs apports par pays de destination, dans la mesure où les engagements ou les versements concernent des dépenses à entreprendre soit dans une région donnée (par exemple, l'Afrique de l'Ouest), soit dans un groupe de pays

donnés (par exemple, les pays les moins avancés). Dans ce rapport, les données présentées pour les pays et pour les groupes sont limitées à celles pouvant être ventilées par bénéficiaires. Les montants notifiés comme ayant été versés à une région ou à un groupe sont inscrits à la rubrique des montants « non ventilés ». Le problème des montants importants non ventilés de l'aide de l'OPEP a déjà été abordé dans l'introduction. A la rubrique des montants non ventilés sont inscrites par ailleurs les ressources engagées ou versées sur le territoire du pays donneur soit pour des recherches consacrées à certains problèmes propres aux pays en développement (maladies tropicales, par exemple), soit sous la forme de subventions à des ressortissants de pays en développement, par exemple pour des stages d'apprentissage ou des cours dans des établissements scolaires ou universitaires ; pour des raisons statistiques évidentes, ces sommes ne peuvent être réparties entre les pays bénéficiaires.

A21. S'agissant du calcul de la part d'un pays ou d'un groupe donné dans le total des pays en développement, il est d'usage d'utiliser comme dénominateur le total hors montants non ventilés. On suppose, ce faisant, que la répartition géographique en pourcentage des montants non ventilés est la même que celles des montants ventilés.

A22. *Dons négatifs :* en décrivant la méthode de comptabilisation des dons, il a été noté que les montants inscrits dans les statistiques ont été minorés pour tenir compte des dépenses engagées pour son propre compte par un pays donneur en utilisant les avoirs en monnaie locale dont il dispose. Il peut arriver que ces montants dépassent celui des nouveaux dons accordés, d'où inscription de « dons négatifs ».

A23. *Annulation des engagements :* les données relatives aux engagements concernent les nouveaux engagements souscrits dans l'année. Elles excluent les engagements annulés dans l'année où ils ont été souscrits, mais aucune défalcation n'est faite pour tenir compte des annulations au cours de l'année d'engagements souscrits pendant des années antérieures.

A24. *Engagements d'APD des institutions financières internationales :* en règle générale, ces institutions notifient les « autorisations d'engagement », qui sont reprises en tant qu'engagements dans le pavé « engagements d'APD ». Toutefois, aux fins du calcul de l'élément de libéralité (présenté sous la rubrique

« engagements de toutes provenances »), il convient de déterminer les conditions dont sont assortis les différents engagements, et la date retenue est alors celle de la signature, laquelle est normalement postérieure à celle de l'autorisation. C'est pourquoi, il peut arriver qu'une écriture sous la rubrique « engagements de prêts » ne soit pas assortie d'une écriture pour l'élément de libéralité correspondant (ou vice versa). Des déséquilibres dans un sens ou dans l'autre dus à cette cause sont compensés par un déséquilibre dans le sens inverse pour une année voisine.

A25. Au cas où un chiffre d'élément de libéralité est présenté sans être accompagné d'un montant d'engagement, cela est dû au fait que le montant en cause est inférieur à 50 000 dollars, c'est-à-dire trop petit pour être repris dans le tableau.

A26. *Composantes manquantes :* il convient de mentionner que dans le sous-pavé « engagements de toutes provenances », seules certaines composantes des totaux apparaissent, pour éviter certains traitements complexes qui auraient retardé la parution du rapport. Le total des composantes manquantes peut être établi par la soustraction des composantes qui sont présentées du total dont elles font partie.

A27. *Engagements et versements des organismes des Nations Unies :* les données sur les versements sont indiquées séparément pour chaque organisme des Nations Unies. Des données comparables sur les engagements n'étant pas disponibles pour l'ensemble de ces organismes, on a inscrit dans les tableaux des engagements les données relatives aux versements bruts des organismes des Nations Unies, avec inscription d'un montant nul en regard des différents organismes. Ce procédé répond à la nécessité de fournir un ordre de grandeur des engagements souscrits par l'ensemble du secteur multilatéral.

A28. *Effet des variations des taux de change :* l'unité monétaire utilisée dans le présent rapport est le dollar des Etats-Unis. Or, les prêts sont souvent libellés dans une autre monnaie. Si celle-ci se raffermit par rapport au dollar, le montant des remboursements apparaissant dans les statistiques représente un chiffre en dollars plus important. Il est ainsi des cas où le total des remboursements paraît dépasser le montant primitif du prêt. De même, l'affaiblissement d'une monnaie se traduit dans les statistiques par des remboursements dont le total, estimé en dollars, paraît être inférieur au principal. Si on effectue une comparaison des variations de la dette (par exemple à partir du rapport *Financement et dette extérieure des pays en développement* ou l'étude semestrielle OCDE/BRI) avec les chiffres présentés pour les apports totaux nets de ressources dans le présent rapport, il faut garder à l'esprit que les données relatives à la dette sont converties en dollars au taux s'appliquant en fin de période, tandis que les données relatives aux apports sont

converties au taux annuel moyen. (Voir l'Annexe paragraphe A16).

A29. Les montants exceptionnellement élevés d'amortissement tiennent, dans la quasi-totalité des cas, à la mise en œuvre de « l'ajustement rétroactif des conditions » sous la forme de l'annulation de l'endettement au titre des prêts antérieurs. L'annulation correspond à l'octroi d'un don, dont l'objet est de permettre le remboursement du principal des prêts en cours. La comptabilisation d'un montant exceptionnellement élevé d'amortissement (soit des prêts nets négatifs) dans les statistiques de l'aide publique au développement consentie aux pays les moins avancés s'accompagne, dans tous les cas, de la comptabilisation d'un montant exceptionnellement élevé de dons versés par le même donneur, la même année.

A30. *APD en provenance de la BIRD :* la plupart des prêts de la BIRD sont classés sous la rubrique « autres apports du secteur public » ; en effet, l'APD est en règle générale dispensée par l'Association internationale du développement (IDA). Certains montants inscrits en regard de la BIRD correspondent aux prêts consentis par le biais du mécanisme du « troisième guichet ».

A31. *Données concernant les engagements de la Belgique :* en raison des procédures administratives utilisées, les autorités belges ne peuvent déterminer les engagements de dons (ce problème n'existe pas pour la notification des prêts). Afin d'éviter de laisser en blanc les lignes relatives aux engagements de la Belgique, le Secrétariat a fait des estimations, en répartissant l'enveloppe budgétaire affectée aux dons au prorata de la part de chaque bénéficiaire dans les versements bruts des années en question. Les petites erreurs ainsi induites ne sauraient fausser le chiffre des données pour le total des engagements de toutes provenances, ou en provenance de l'ensemble des Membres du CAD. Cependant, s'il s'agit d'analyser les seuls chiffres de la Belgique, une meilleure estimation consisterait à faire une moyenne pluriannuelle des engagements de dons de la Belgique.

A32. *Apports de ressources en provenance de la Communauté économique européenne :* les chiffres présentés englobent les dons et les prêts de la CEE ainsi que les fonds mis à disposition par la Banque européenne d'investissement aux conditions du marché. Ces derniers montants peuvent être déterminés à partir des données figurant dans le présent volume en calculant la différence entre le total des apports de la CEE reçus par un pays et le montant de ses recettes d'APD en provenance de la CEE.

---

1. Dans les rubriques des tableaux, le sigle LLDCs (PMA—pays les moins avancés) est utilisé par souci de brièveté.

WHERE TO OBTAIN OECD PUBLICATIONS
OÙ OBTENIR LES PUBLICATIONS DE L'OCDE

ARGENTINA - ARGENTINE
Carlos Hirsch S.R.L.,
Florida 165, 4° Piso,
(Galeria Guemes) 1333 Buenos Aires
Tel. 33.1787.2391 y 30.7122

AUSTRALIA - AUSTRALIE
D.A. Book (Aust.) Pty. Ltd.
11-13 Station Street (P.O. Box 163)
Mitcham, Vic. 3132   Tel. (03) 873 4411

AUSTRIA - AUTRICHE
OECD Publications and Information Centre,
4 Simrockstrasse,
5300 Bonn (Germany)   Tel. (0228) 21.60.45
Gerold & Co., Graben 31, Wien 1 Tel. 52.22.35

BELGIUM - BELGIQUE
Jean de Lannoy,
avenue du Roi 202
B-1060 Bruxelles   Tel. (02) 538.51.69

CANADA
Renouf Publishing Company Ltd/
Éditions Renouf Ltée,
1294 Algoma Road, Ottawa, Ont. K1B 3W8
Tel: (613) 741-4333
Toll Free/Sans Frais:
Ontario, Quebec, Maritimes:
1-800-267-1805
Western Canada, Newfoundland:
1-800-267-1826
Stores/Magasins:
61 rue Sparks St., Ottawa, Ont. K1P 5A6
Tel: (613) 238-8985
211 rue Yonge St., Toronto, Ont. M5B 1M4
Tel: (416) 363-3171

DENMARK - DANEMARK
Munksgaard Export and Subscription Service
35, Nørre Søgade, DK-1370 København K
Tel. +45.1.12.85.70

FINLAND - FINLANDE
Akateeminen Kirjakauppa,
Keskuskatu 1, 00100 Helsinki 10   Tel. 0.12141

FRANCE
OCDE/OECD
Mail Orders/Commandes par correspondance :
2, rue André-Pascal,
75775 Paris Cedex 16
Tel. (1) 45.24.82.00
Bookshop/Librairie : 33, rue Octave-Feuillet
75016 Paris
Tel. (1) 45.24.81.67 or/ou (1) 45.24.81.81
Librairie de l'Université,
12a, rue Nazareth,
13602 Aix-en-Provence   Tel. 42.26.18.08

GERMANY - ALLEMAGNE
OECD Publications and Information Centre,
4 Simrockstrasse,
5300 Bonn   Tel. (0228) 21.60.45

GREECE - GRÈCE
Librairie Kauffmann,
28, rue du Stade, 105 64 Athens   Tel. 322.21.60

HONG KONG
Government Information Services,
Publications (Sales) Office,
Information Services Department
No. 1, Battery Path, Central

ICELAND - ISLANDE
Snæbjörn Jónsson & Co., h.f.,
Hafnarstræti 4 & 9,
P.O.B. 1131 – Reykjavik
Tel. 13133/14281/11936

INDIA - INDE
Oxford Book and Stationery Co.,
Scindia House, New Delhi 1 Tel. 331.5896/5308
17 Park St., Calcutta 700016   Tel. 240832
INDONESIA - INDONÉSIE
Pdii-Lipi, P.O. Box 3065/JKT.Jakarta
Tel. 583467

IRELAND - IRLANDE
TDC Publishers - Library Suppliers,
12 North Frederick Street, Dublin 1
Tel. 744835-749677

ITALY - ITALIE
Libreria Commissionaria Sansoni,
Via Lamarmora 45, 50121 Firenze
Tel. 579751/584468
Via Bartolini 29, 20155 Milano   Tel. 365083
Editrice e Libreria Herder,
Piazza Montecitorio 120, 00186 Roma
Tel. 6794628
Libreria Hœpli,
Via Hœpli 5, 20121 Milano   Tel. 865446
Libreria Scientifica
Dott. Lucio de Biasio "Aeiou"
Via Meravigli 16, 20123 Milano   Tel. 807679
Libreria Lattes,
Via Garibaldi 3, 10122 Torino   Tel. 519274
La diffusione delle edizioni OCSE è inoltre
assicurata dalle migliori librerie nelle città più
importanti.

JAPAN - JAPON
OECD Publications and Information Centre,
Landic Akasaka Bldg., 2-3-4 Akasaka,
Minato-ku, Tokyo 107   Tel. 586.2016

KOREA - CORÉE
Kyobo Book Centre Co. Ltd.
P.O.Box: Kwang Hwa Moon 1658,
Seoul   Tel. (REP) 730.78.91

LEBANON - LIBAN
Documenta Scientifica/Redico,
Edison Building, Bliss St.,
P.O.B. 5641, Beirut   Tel. 354429-344425

MALAYSIA - MALAISIE
University of Malaya Co-operative Bookshop
Ltd.,
P.O.Box 1127, Jalan Pantai Baru,
Kuala Lumpur   Tel. 577701/577072

NETHERLANDS - PAYS-BAS
Staatsuitgeverij
Chr. Plantijnstraat, 2 Postbus 20014
2500 EA S-Gravenhage   Tel. 070-789911
Voor bestellingen: Tel. 070-789880

NEW ZEALAND - NOUVELLE-ZÉLANDE
Government Printing Office Bookshops:
Auckland: Retail Bookshop, 25 Rutland Stseet,
Mail Orders, 85 Beach Road
Private Bag C.P.O.
Hamilton: Retail: Ward Street,
Mail Orders, P.O. Box 857
Wellington: Retail, Mulgrave Street, (Head
Office)
Cubacade World Trade Centre,
Mail Orders, Private Bag
Christchurch: Retail, 159 Hereford Street,
Mail Orders, Private Bag
Dunedin: Retail, Princes Street,
Mail Orders, P.O. Box 1104

NORWAY - NORVÈGE
Tanum-Karl Johan
Karl Johans gate 43, Oslo 1
PB 1177 Sentrum, 0107 Oslo 1Tel. (02) 42.93.10

PAKISTAN
Mirza Book Agency
65 Shahrah Quaid-E-Azam, Lahore 3 Tel. 66839

PORTUGAL
Livraria Portugal,
Rua do Carmo 70-74, 1117 Lisboa Codex
Tel. 360582/3

SINGAPORE - SINGAPOUR
Information Publications Pte Ltd
Pei-Fu Industrial Building,
24 New Industrial Road No. 02-06
Singapore 1953   Tel. 2831786, 2831798

SPAIN - ESPAGNE
Mundi-Prensa Libros, S.A.,
Castelló 37, Apartado 1223, Madrid-28001
Tel. 431.33.99
Libreria Bosch, Ronda Universidad 11,
Barcelona 7   Tel. 317.53.08/317.53.58

SWEDEN - SUÈDE
AB CE Fritzes Kungl. Hovbokhandel,
Box 16356, S 103 27 STH,
Regeringsgatan 12,
DS Stockholm   Tel. (08) 23.89.00
Subscription Agency/Abonnements:
Wennergren-Williams AB,
Box 30004, S104 25 Stockholm Tel. (08)54.12.00

SWITZERLAND - SUISSE
OECD Publications and Information Centre,
4 Simrockstrasse,
5300 Bonn (Germany)   Tel. (0228) 21.60.45
Librairie Payot,
6 rue Grenus, 1211 Genève 11
Tel. (022) 31.89.50

United Nations Bookshop/
Librairie des Nations-Unies
Palais des Nations,
1211 – Geneva 10
Tel. 022-34-60-11 (ext. 48 72)

TAIWAN - FORMOSE
Good Faith Worldwide Int'l Co., Ltd.
9th floor, No. 118, Sec.2
Chung Hsiao E. Road
Taipei   Tel. 391.7396/391.7397

THAILAND - THAILANDE
Suksit Siam Co., Ltd.,
1715 Rama IV Rd.,
Samyam Bangkok 5   Tel. 2511630

TURKEY - TURQUIE
Kültur Yayinlari Is-Türk Ltd. Sti.
Atatürk Bulvari No: 191/Kat. 21
Kavaklidere/Ankara   Tel. 25.07.60
Dolmabahce Cad. No: 29
Besiktas/Istanbul   Tel. 160.71.88

UNITED KINGDOM - ROYAUME-UNI
H.M. Stationery Office,
Postal orders only: (01)211-5656
P.O.B. 276, London SW8 5DT
Telephone orders: (01) 622.3316, or
Personal callers:
49 High Holborn, London WC1V 6HB
Branches at: Belfast, Birmingham,
Bristol, Edinburgh, Manchester

UNITED STATES - ÉTATS-UNIS
OECD Publications and Information Centre,
2001 L Street, N.W., Suite 700,
Washington, D.C. 20036 - 4095
Tel. (202) 785.6323

VENEZUELA
Libreria del Este,
Avda F. Miranda 52, Aptdo. 60337,
Edificio Galipan, Caracas 106
Tel. 32.23.01/33.26.04/31.58.38

YUGOSLAVIA - YOUGOSLAVIE
Jugoslovenska Knjiga, Knez Mihajlova 2,
P.O.B. 36, Beograd   Tel. 621.992

Orders and inquiries from countries where
Distributors have not yet been appointed should be
sent to:
OECD, Publications Service, Sales and
Distribution Division, 2, rue André-Pascal, 75775
PARIS CEDEX 16.

Les commandes provenant de pays où l'OCDE n'a
pas encore désigné de distributeur peuvent être
adressées à :
OCDE, Service des Publications. Division des
Ventes et Distribution. 2. rue André-Pascal. 75775
PARIS CEDEX 16.

71055-09-1987

PUBLICATIONS DE L'OCDE, 2, rue André-Pascal, 75775 PARIS CEDEX 16 - N° 44202 1987
IMPRIMÉ EN FRANCE
(43 87 04 3) ISBN 92-64-03013-1

ENQUIRY FORM
FORMULAIRE D'INFORMATION

This publication is drawn from the OECD/DAC computerised data base and is available both on magnetic tape and in the form of microfiches. The full data base, which likewise is available on magnetic tape, contains annual financial flow data going back to 1969. For the period 1960 to 1968 the data are available in published form only and with no distinction between Official Development Assistance (ODA) and Other Official Flows (OOF).

Aggregate annual data by donor country and type of resource flow are discussed in the DAC Chairman's Annual Report, *Development Co-operation - Efforts and Policies of Members of the Development Assistance Committee,* and presented in detail in the statistical Annex to that report. These publications are also available from OECD Publications Distributors.

Detailed data of external debt and debt service, by debtor country are contained in successive OECD surveys of the *Financing and External Debt of Developing Countries.*

Cette publication est tirée de la base de données informatisée OCDE/CAD, et est disponible soit sur bande magnétique, soit sous forme de microfiches. La base, qui est également disponible sur bande magnétique, contient des données annuelles sur les flux financiers remontant jusqu'en 1969. Pour la période allant de 1960 à 1968 les données ne sont disponibles que sous forme de publication, et ce, sans distinction entre l'Aide Publique au Développement (APD) et les Autres Apports du Secteur Public (AASP).

Les données agrégées par pays donneur et par type de flux sont présentées et analysées dans le rapport annuel du Président du CAD, *Coopération pour le développement — Efforts et politiques poursuivis par les membres du Comité d'Aide au Développement,* qui comporte une annexe statistique ; ces publications sont également en vente chez les distributeurs des publications de l'OCDE.

Des données détaillées de la dette et du service de la dette extérieure par pays débiteurs sont inclues dans la série de publications de l'OCDE *Financement et Dette Extérieure des Pays en Développement*.

Please send me more information about and prices for:
Veuillez me faire parvenir des informations complémentaires
et des indications sur les prix des :

_____

PUBLICATIONS

☐ DAC CHAIRMAN'S REPORT
RAPPORT DU PRÉSIDENT DU CAD

☐ FINANCING AND EXTERNAL DEBT OF DEVELOPING COUNTRIES
FINANCEMENT ET DETTE EXTÉRIEURE DES PAYS EN DÉVELOPPEMENT

☐ EXTERNAL DEBT STATISTICS AT END DECEMBER 1983-86
(DISKETTE)
STATISTIQUES DE LA DETTE EXTÉRIEURE A FIN DÉCEMBRE 1983-86
(DISQUETTE)

GEOGRAPHICAL DATA - DONNÉES GÉOGRAPHIQUES

☐ MICROFICHES

☐ MAGNETIC TAPES
BANDES MAGNÉTIQUES

☐ MICRO COMPUTER DISKETTE
(contains Section A)
(contient la Section A)

_____

Name/Nom _____

Title/Fonction _____

Organisation _____

Address/Adresse _____

_____ **Tél.** _____

DIVISION DES SYSTÈMES STATISTIQUES

DIRECTION DE LA COOPÉRATION POUR LE DÉVELOPPEMENT

2, rue André-Pascal

75775 Paris Cedex 16 - France